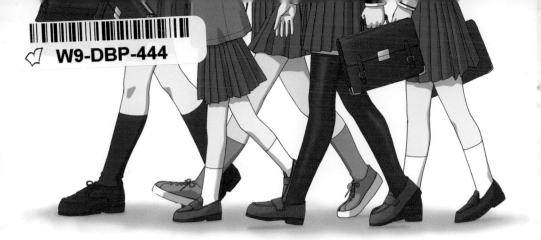

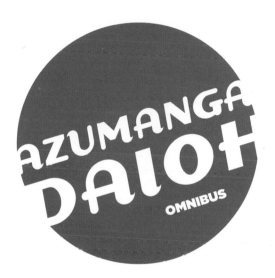

AZUMANGA DAIOH

OMNIBUS

KIYOHIKO AZUMA

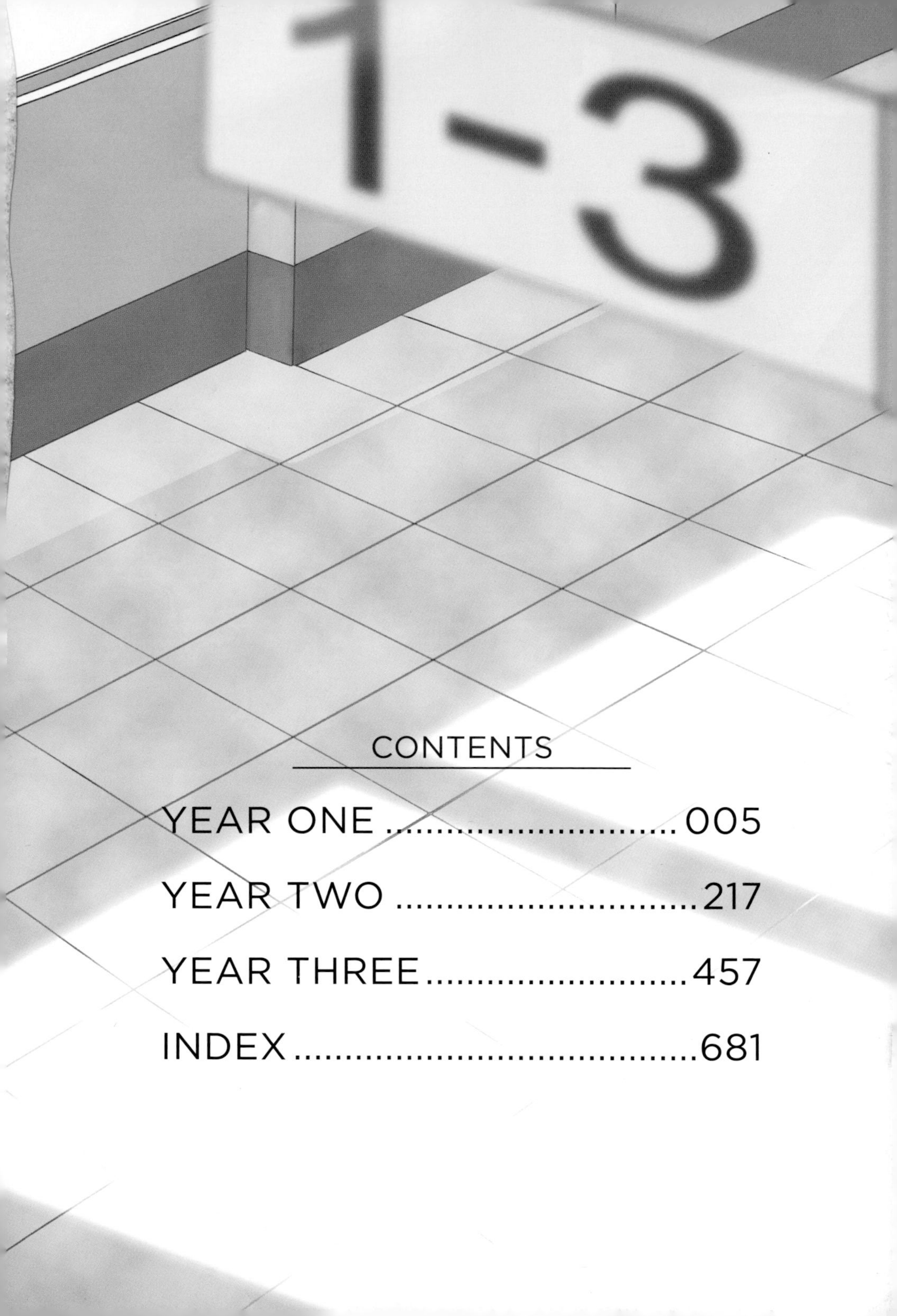
1-3

CONTENTS

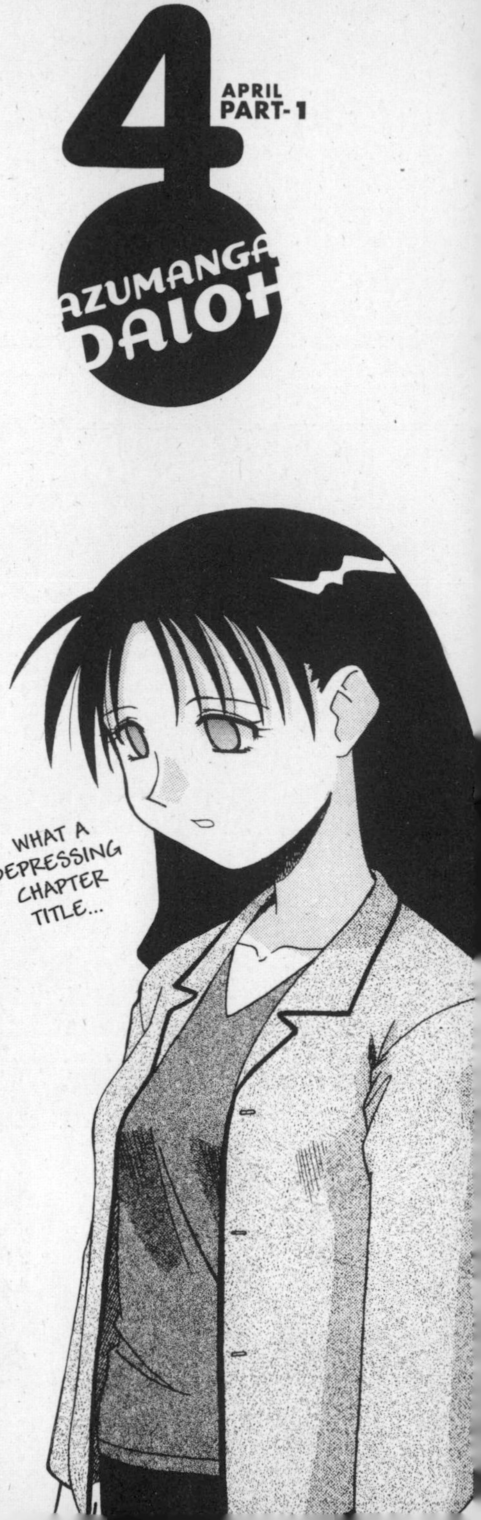
4
APRIL
PART-1
AZUMANGA DAIOH
WHAT A DEPRESSING CHAPTER TITLE...

YUKARI-SENSEI

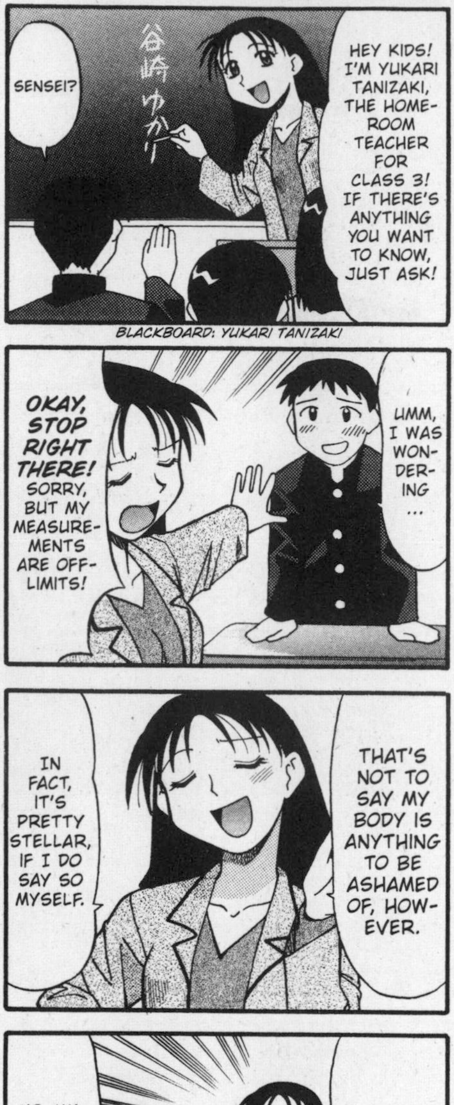
谷崎ゆかり
HEY KIDS! I'M YUKARI TANIZAKI, THE HOME-ROOM TEACHER FOR CLASS 3! IF THERE'S ANYTHING YOU WANT TO KNOW, JUST ASK!
SENSEI?
BLACKBOARD: YUKARI TANIZAKI
UMM, I WAS WON-DER-ING...
OKAY, STOP RIGHT THERE! SORRY, BUT MY MEASURE-MENTS ARE OFF-LIMITS!
THAT'S NOT TO SAY MY BODY IS ANYTHING TO BE ASHAMED OF, HOW-EVER.
IN FACT, IT'S PRETTY STELLAR, IF I DO SAY SO MYSELF.
OH, BUT LISTEN TO ME GO ON AND ON! YOU SHAMELESS SUCK-UP, YOU!
NO, UM, ACTUALLY, I WAS WON-DERING WHY YOU AREN'T NEXT DOOR...
THIS IS CLASS 4...

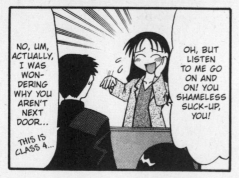

POP QUIZ ①

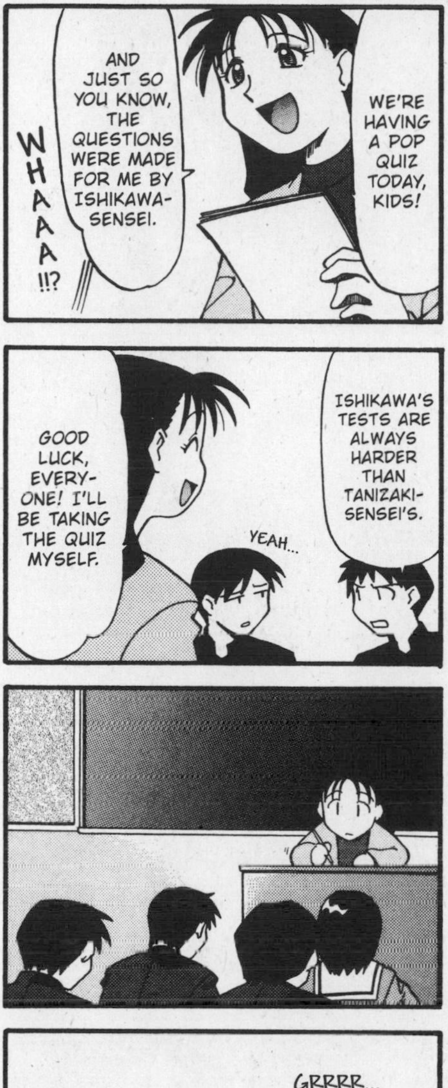
WE'RE HAVING A POP QUIZ TODAY, KIDS!
AND JUST SO YOU KNOW, THE QUESTIONS WERE MADE FOR ME BY ISHIKAWA-SENSEI.
WHAAA!!?
ISHIKAWA'S TESTS ARE ALWAYS HARDER THAN TANIZAKI-SENSEI'S.
YEAH...
GOOD LUCK, EVERYONE! I'LL BE TAKING THE QUIZ MYSELF.
GRRRR...
HEY! SHE'S HAVING TROUBLE!
YIKES...

POP QUIZ ②

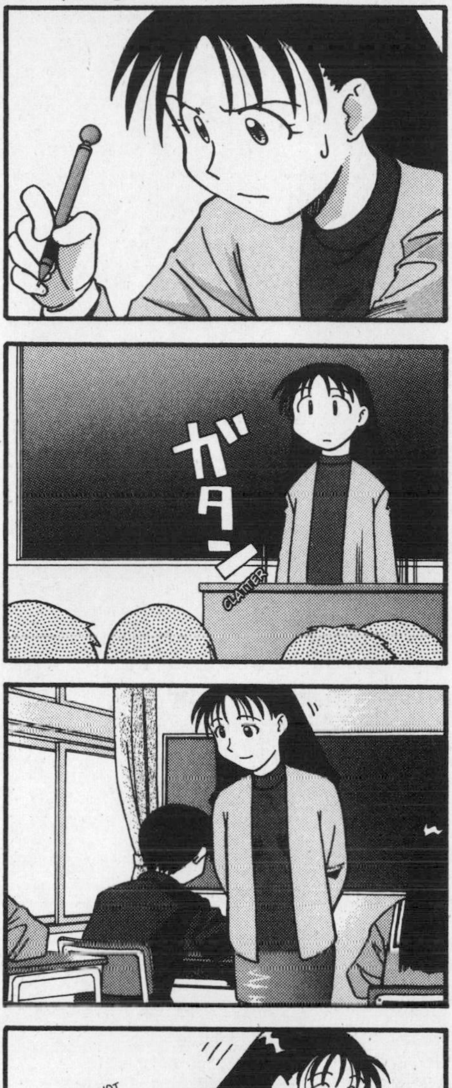
ガタン
CLATTER
CHECKING US, SHE'S JUST CHEATING.

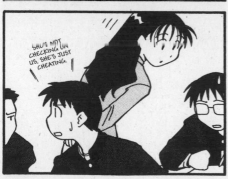

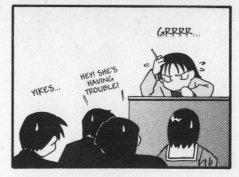

I GOT A 93

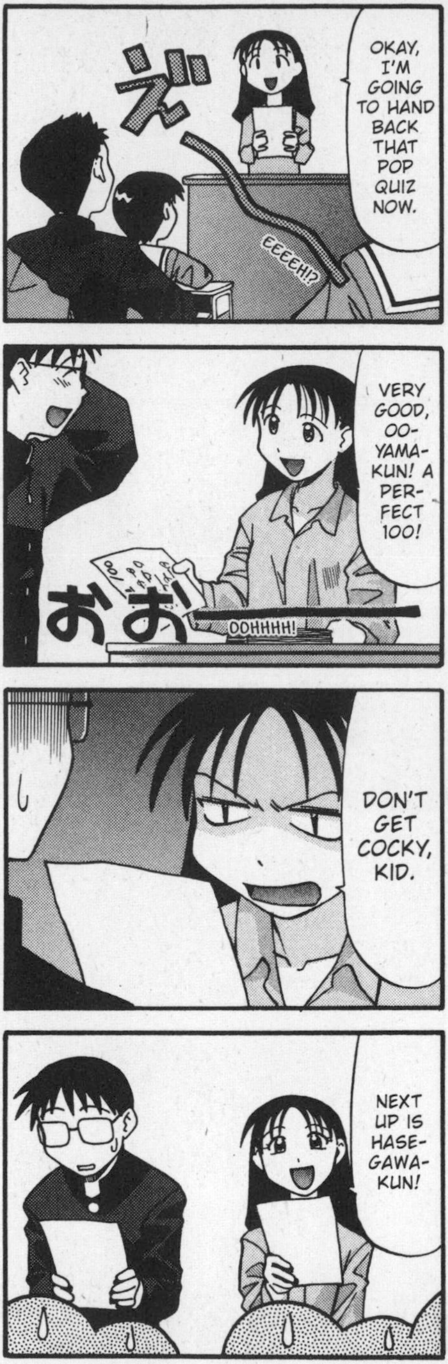

OKAY, I'M GOING TO HAND BACK THAT POP QUIZ NOW.
EEEEH!?
VERY GOOD, OO-YAMA-KUN! A PER-FECT 100!
おお
OOHHHH!
DON'T GET COCKY, KID.
NEXT UP IS HASE-GAWA-KUN!

A KID IN HIGH SCHOOL

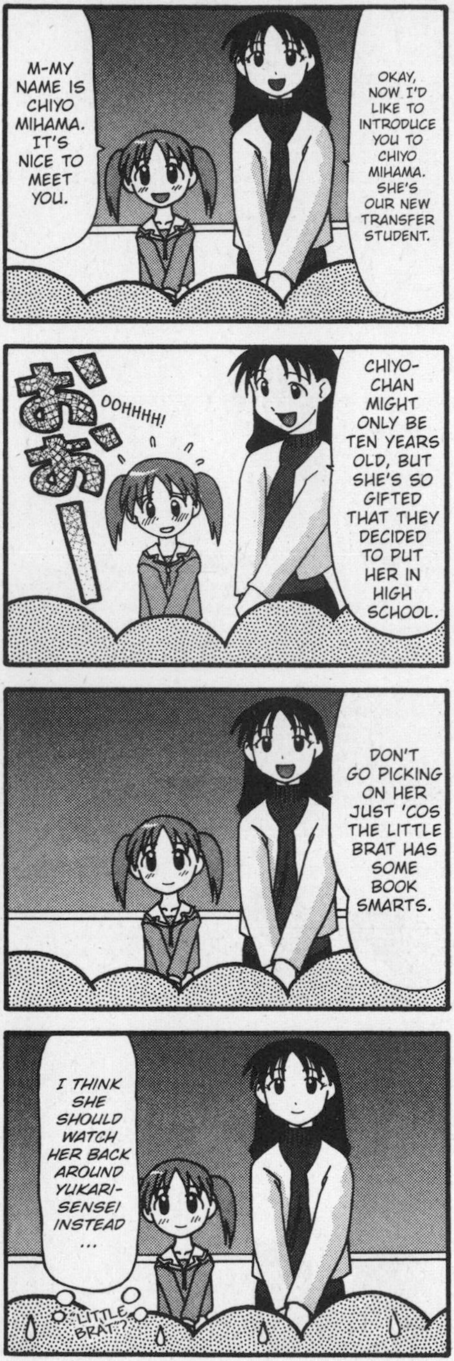

OKAY, NOW I'D LIKE TO INTRODUCE YOU TO CHIYO MIHAMA. SHE'S OUR NEW TRANSFER STUDENT.
M-MY NAME IS CHIYO MIHAMA. IT'S NICE TO MEET YOU.
CHIYO-CHAN MIGHT ONLY BE TEN YEARS OLD, BUT SHE'S SO GIFTED THAT THEY DECIDED TO PUT HER IN HIGH SCHOOL.
おおー
OOHHHH!
DON'T GO PICKING ON HER JUST 'COS THE LITTLE BRAT HAS SOME BOOK SMARTS.
I THINK SHE SHOULD WATCH HER BACK AROUND YUKARI-SENSEI INSTEAD ...
"LITTLE BRAT"?

SHE'S A GENIUS

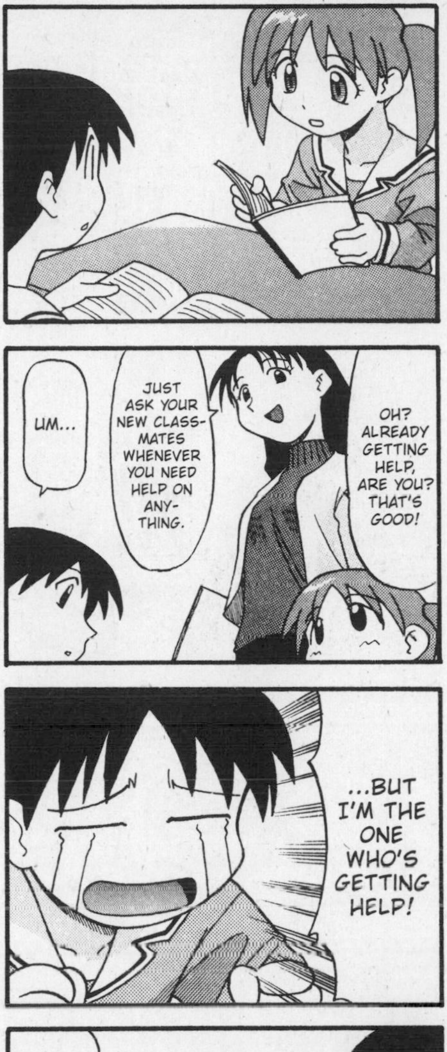
OH? ALREADY GETTING HELP, ARE YOU? THAT'S GOOD!
JUST ASK YOUR NEW CLASSMATES WHENEVER YOU NEED HELP ON ANYTHING.
UM...
...BUT I'M THE ONE WHO'S GETTING HELP!
BOO-HOO!
DOES THIS MEAN I'M AN IDIOT...?
B-BUT, WE'RE IN THE SAME GRADE ...

PERFECT CHILD

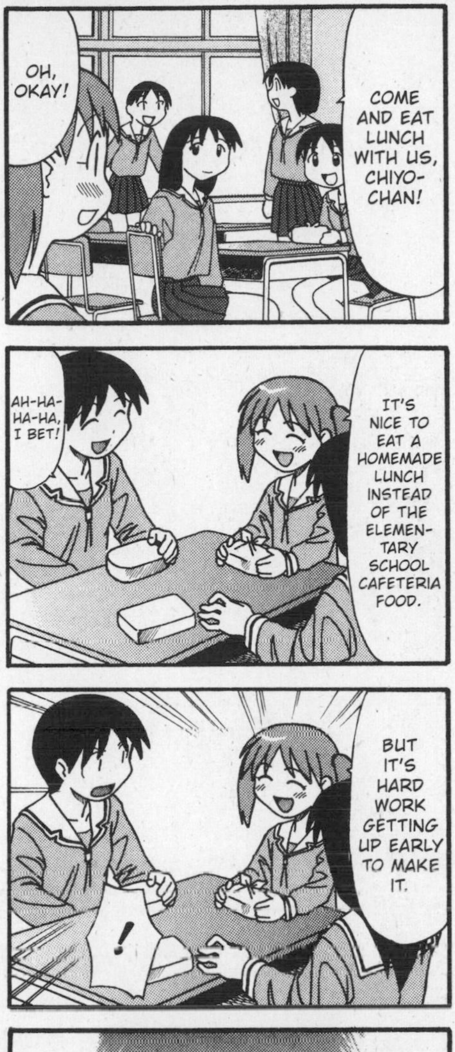
COME AND EAT LUNCH WITH US, CHIYO-CHAN!
OH, OKAY!
IT'S NICE TO EAT A HOMEMADE LUNCH INSTEAD OF THE ELEMENTARY SCHOOL CAFETERIA FOOD.
AH-HA-HA-HA, I BET!
BUT IT'S HARD WORK GETTING UP EARLY TO MAKE IT.
!
YOU MEAN THIS LITTLE RUNT COOKS HER OWN LUNCH !?
IS SHE SOME KIND OF WUNDERKIND!?

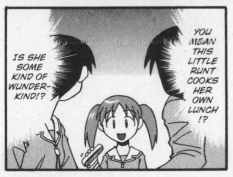

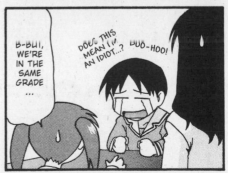

IS SHE SCARY?

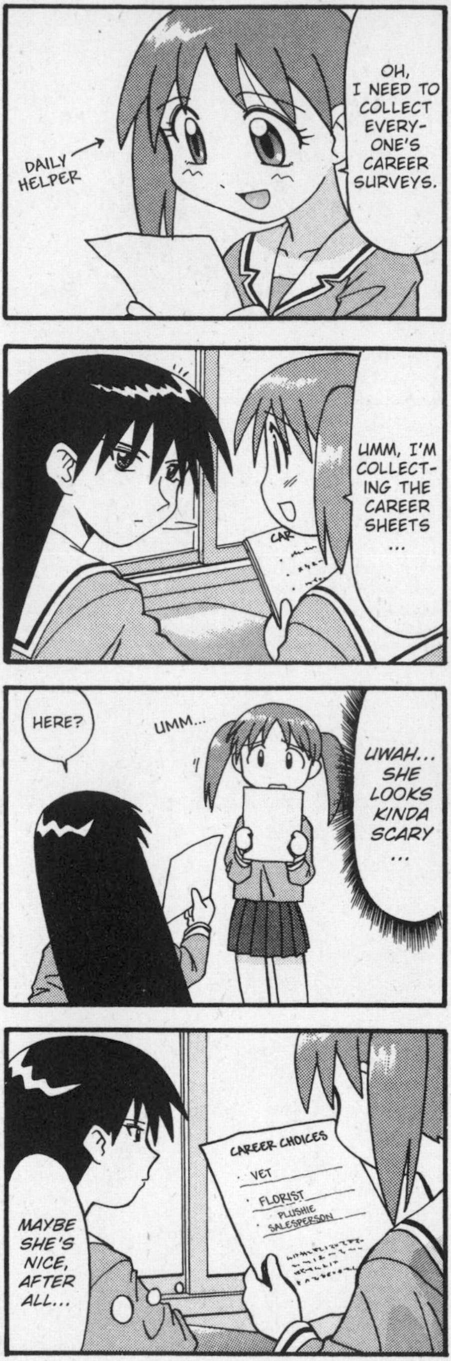

OH, I NEED TO COLLECT EVERYONE'S CAREER SURVEYS.
DAILY HELPER
UMM, I'M COLLECTING THE CAREER SHEETS...
UWAH... SHE LOOKS KINDA SCARY...
UMM...
HERE?
CAREER CHOICES
VET
FLORIST
PLUSHIE SALESPERSON
MAYBE SHE'S NICE, AFTER ALL...

SAKAKI-SAN IS COOL

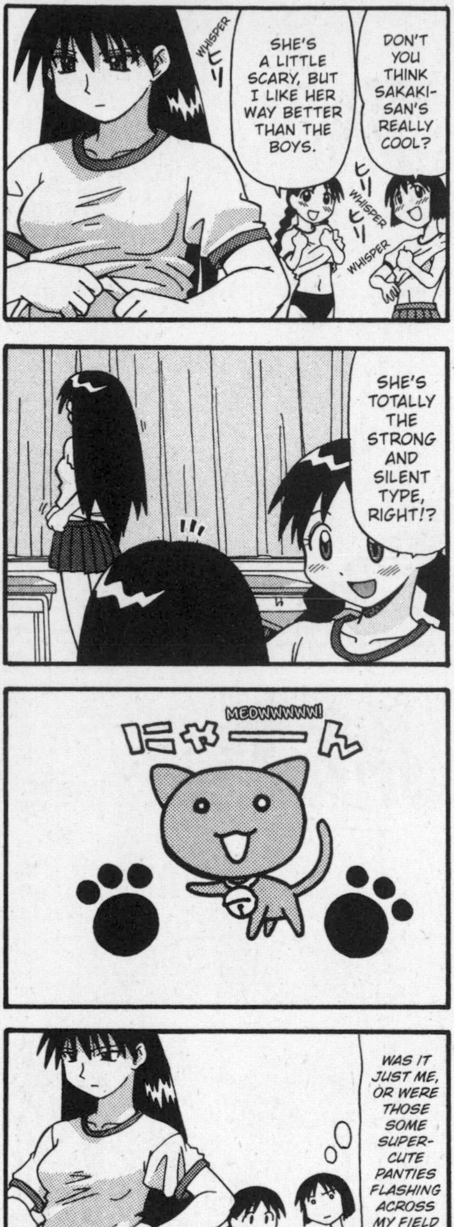

DON'T YOU THINK SAKAKI-SAN'S REALLY COOL?
SHE'S A LITTLE SCARY, BUT I LIKE HER WAY BETTER THAN THE BOYS.
WHISPER ヒソ
WHISPER ヒソ
WHISPER ヒソ
SHE'S TOTALLY THE STRONG AND SILENT TYPE, RIGHT!?
MEOWWWWWW!
にゃーーん
WAS IT JUST ME, OR WERE THOSE SOME SUPER-CUTE PANTIES FLASHING ACROSS MY FIELD OF VISION JUST NOW...?

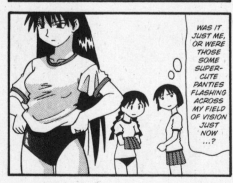

KITTY CAT...

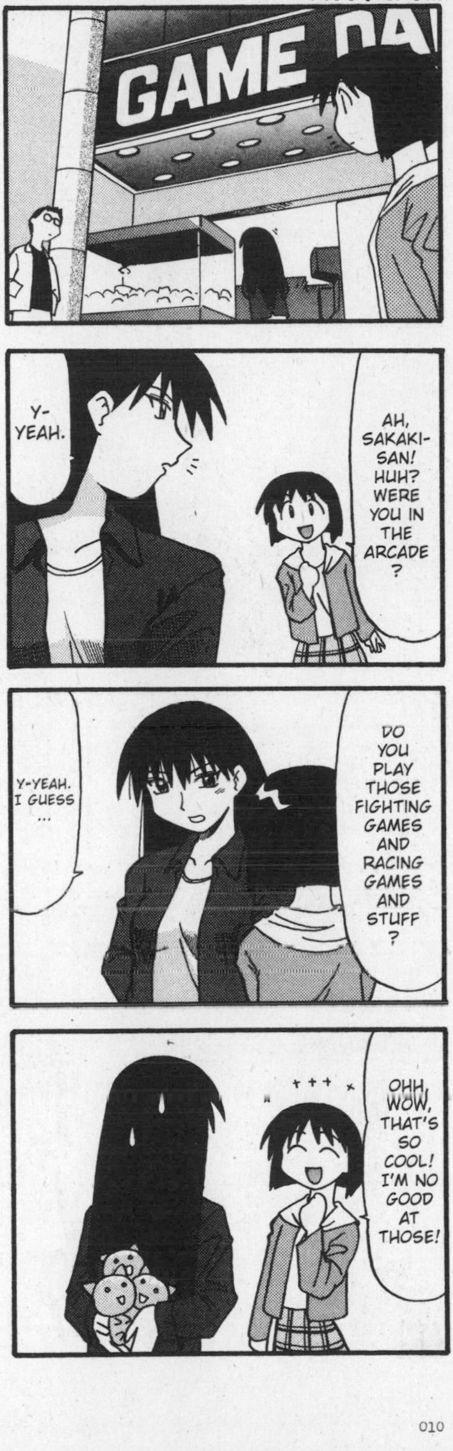
GAME
AH, SAKAKI-SAN! HUH? WERE YOU IN THE ARCADE?
Y-YEAH.
DO YOU PLAY THOSE FIGHTING GAMES AND RACING GAMES AND STUFF?
Y-YEAH. I GUESS...
OHH, WOW, THAT'S SO COOL! I'M NO GOOD AT THOSE!

ALONE

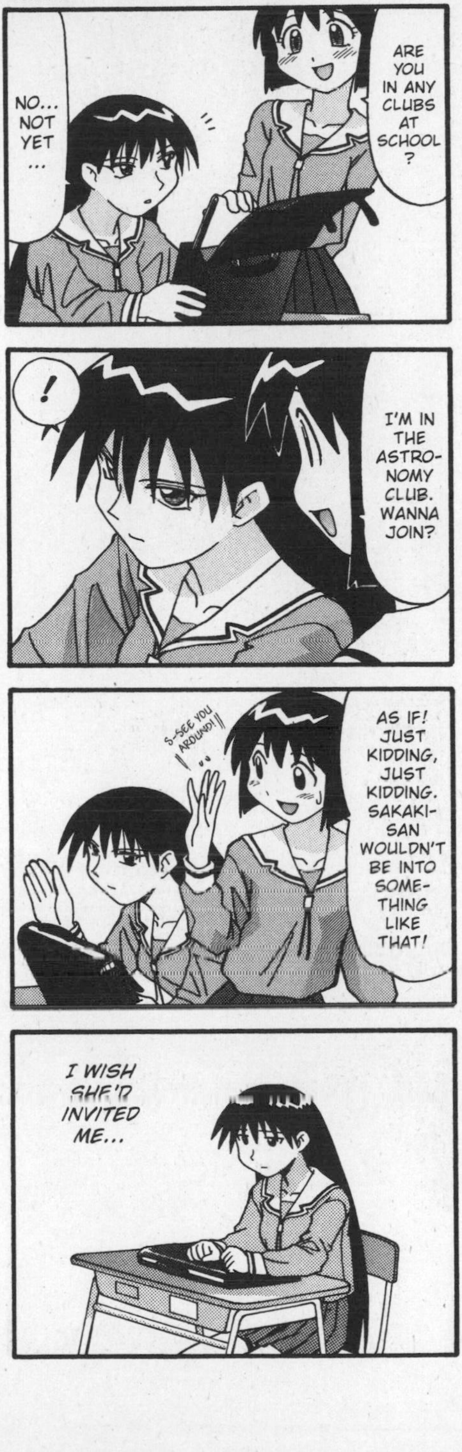
ARE YOU IN ANY CLUBS AT SCHOOL?
NO... NOT YET...
!
I'M IN THE ASTRONOMY CLUB. WANNA JOIN?
AS IF! JUST KIDDING, JUST KIDDING. SAKAKI-SAN WOULDN'T BE INTO SOMETHING LIKE THAT!
S-SEE YOU AROUND!
I WISH SHE'D INVITED ME...

TOMO-CHAN GONE WILD!

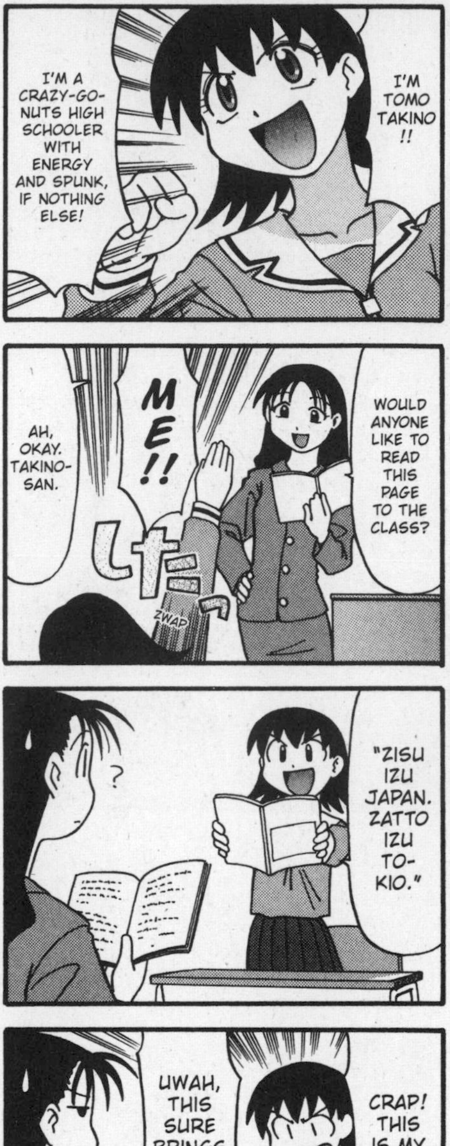
I'M TOMO TAKINO!!
I'M A CRAZY-GO-NUTS HIGH SCHOOLER WITH ENERGY AND SPUNK, IF NOTHING ELSE!
WOULD ANYONE LIKE TO READ THIS PAGE TO THE CLASS?
ME!!
ZWAP
AH, OKAY. TAKINO-SAN.
"ZISU IZU JAPAN. ZATTO IZU TO-KIO."
?
CRAP! THIS IS MY SEVENTH GRADE TEXTBOOK!
UWAH, THIS SURE BRINGS ME BACK!
......

STAND UP, TOMO-CHAN!

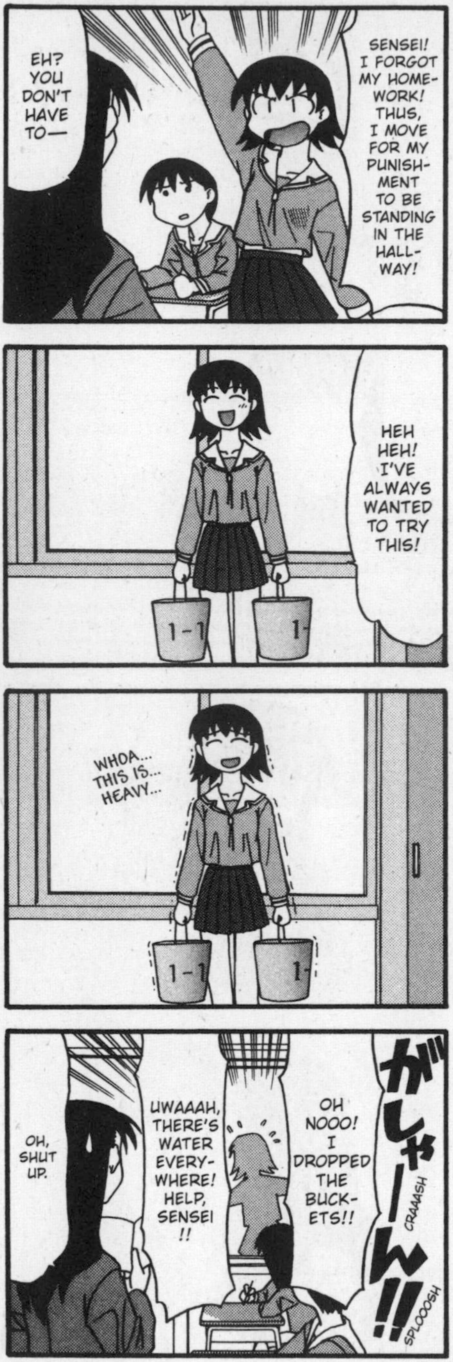
SENSEI! I FORGOT MY HOMEWORK! THUS, I MOVE FOR MY PUNISHMENT TO BE STANDING IN THE HALLWAY!
EH? YOU DON'T HAVE TO—
HEH HEH! I'VE ALWAYS WANTED TO TRY THIS!
1-1
WHOA... THIS IS... HEAVY...
がしゃーん!!
CRAAASH
SPLOOOSH
OH NOOO! I DROPPED THE BUCKETS!!
UWAAAH, THERE'S WATER EVERYWHERE! HELP, SENSEI!!
OH, SHUT UP.

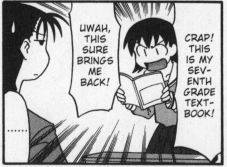

RUN, TOMO-CHAN!

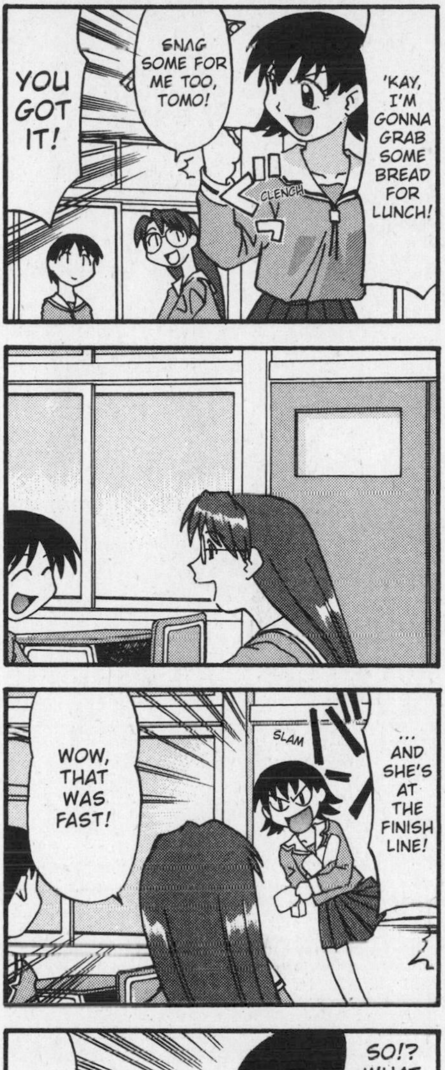
'KAY, I'M GONNA GRAB SOME BREAD FOR LUNCH!
CLENCH
SNAG SOME FOR ME TOO, TOMO!
YOU GOT IT!
... AND SHE'S AT THE FINISH LINE!
SLAM
WOW, THAT WAS FAST!
SO!? WHAT WAS IT!? WHAT WAS MY TIME !?
WHY WOULD I BE TIMING YOU?

WAY TO GO, TOMO-CHAN!

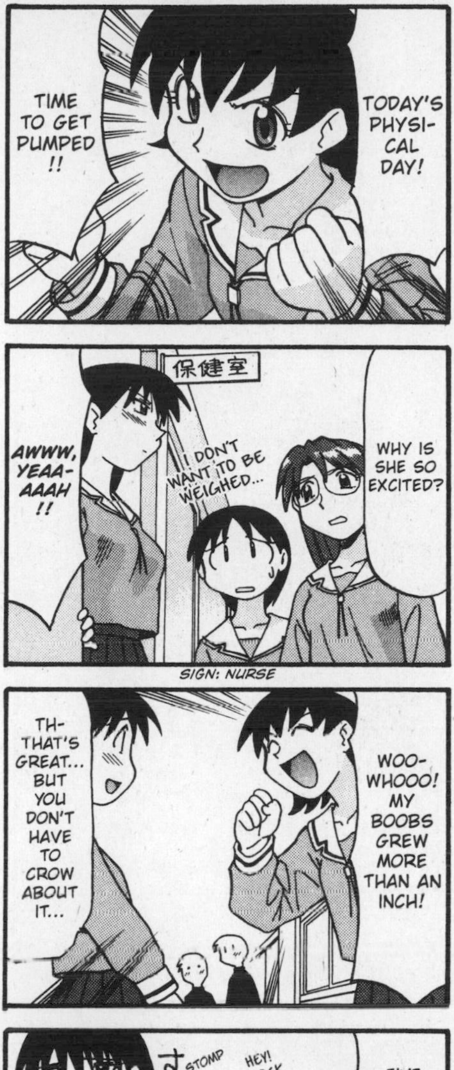
TODAY'S PHYSICAL DAY!
TIME TO GET PUMPED !!
WHY IS SHE SO EXCITED?
I DON'T WANT TO BE WEIGHED...
保健室
AWWW, YEAAAAAH !!
SIGN: NURSE
WOO-WHOOO! MY BOOBS GREW MORE THAN AN INCH!
TH-THAT'S GREAT... BUT YOU DON'T HAVE TO CROW ABOUT IT...
I'VE GOT A WAYS TO GO BEFORE I CATCH UP WITH SAKAKI-SAN, THOUGH! EYES ON THE PRIZE!!
HEY! KNOCK IT OFF!
すたすた
STOMP
STOMP
HEAR THAT? SAKAKI'S STACKED.
I KNEW IT.

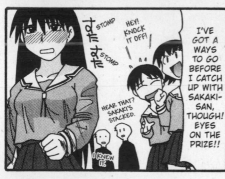

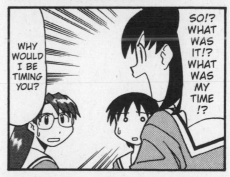

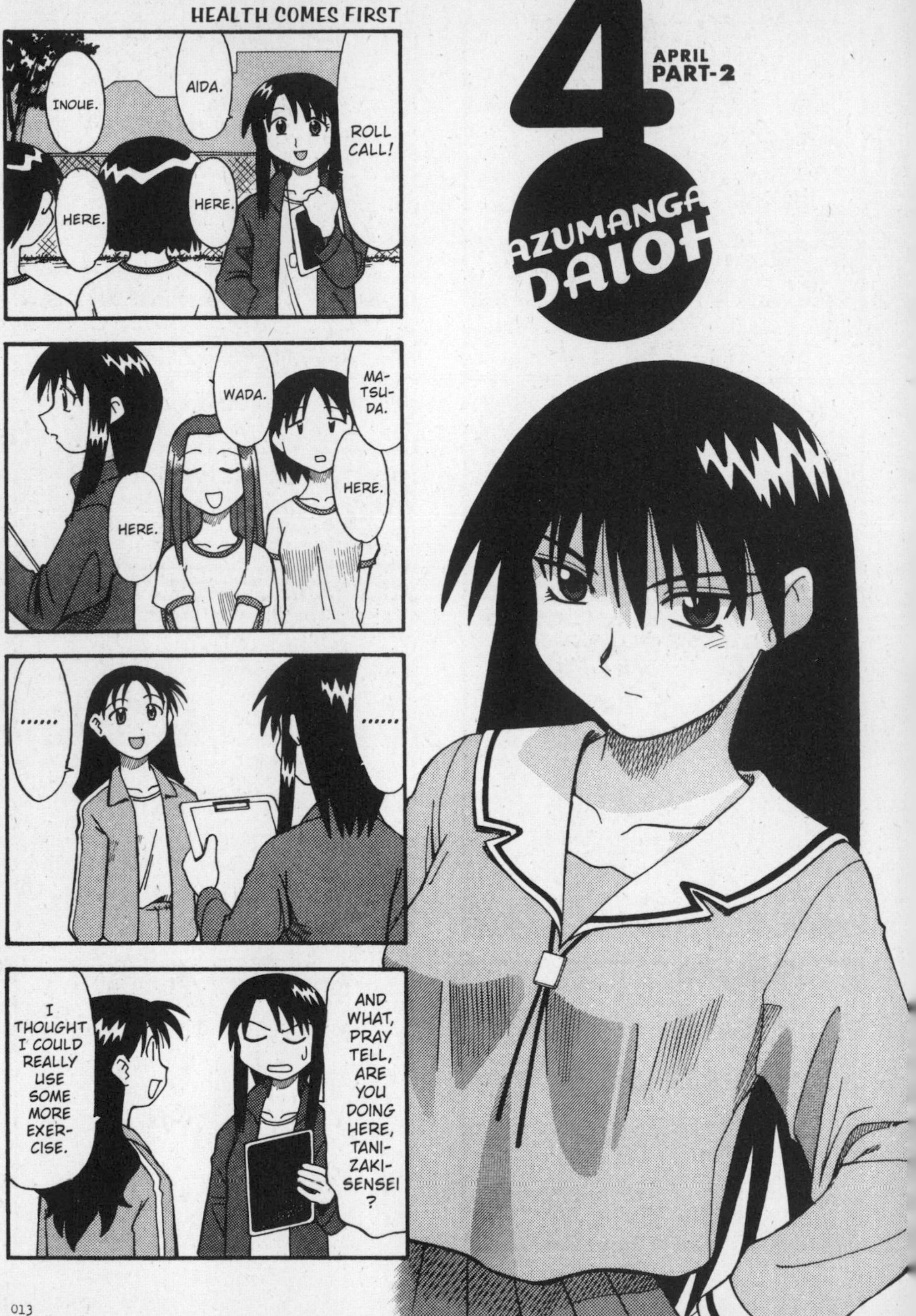
4
APRIL PART-2
AZUMANGA DAIOH
HEALTH COMES FIRST
ROLL CALL!
AIDA.
HERE.
INOUE.
HERE.
MA-TSU-DA.
WADA.
HERE.
HERE.
......
......
AND WHAT, PRAY TELL, ARE YOU DOING HERE, TANI-ZAKI-SENSEI?
I THOUGHT I COULD REALLY USE SOME MORE EXER-CISE.

RIVAL FACTIONS

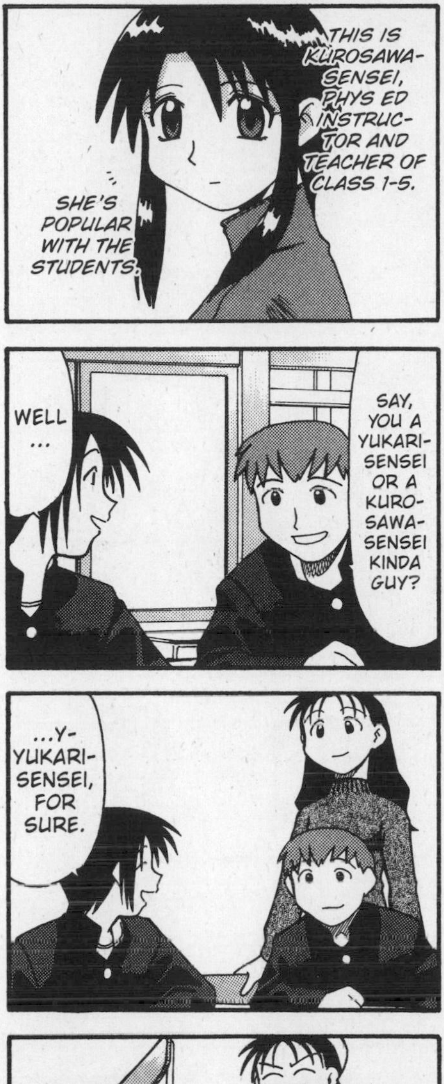
THIS IS KUROSAWA-SENSEI, PHYS ED INSTRUCTOR AND TEACHER OF CLASS 1-5.
SHE'S POPULAR WITH THE STUDENTS.
SAY, YOU A YUKARI-SENSEI OR A KUROSAWA-SENSEI KINDA GUY?
WELL ...
...Y-YUKARI-SENSEI, FOR SURE.
UWAH-HA-HA-HA! YOU LIKE 'EM WEIRD, HUH?

POOR CLEANER

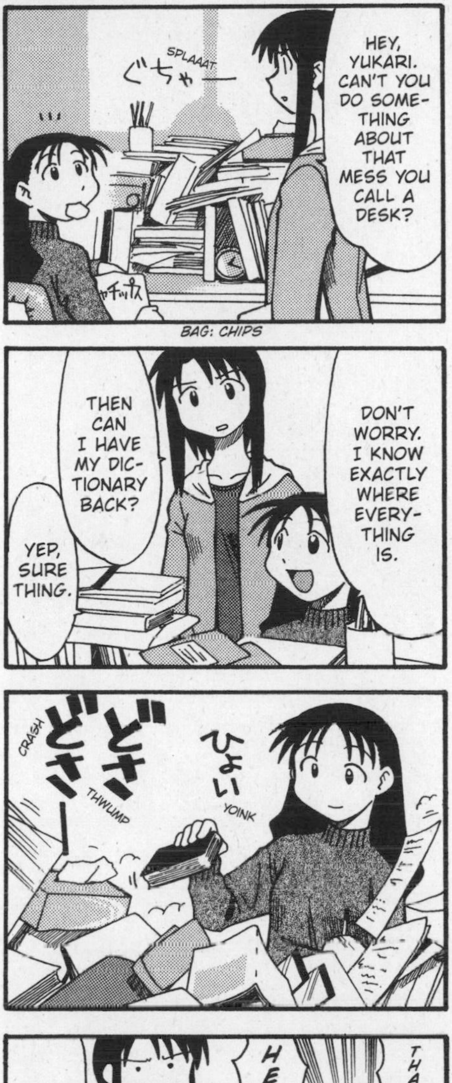
HEY, YUKARI. CAN'T YOU DO SOMETHING ABOUT THAT MESS YOU CALL A DESK?
ぐちゃー
SPLAAAT
BAG: CHIPS
DON'T WORRY. I KNOW EXACTLY WHERE EVERYTHING IS.
THEN CAN I HAVE MY DICTIONARY BACK?
YEP, SURE THING.
どさどさー
CRASH
THWUMP
ひょい
YOINK
THANKS A LOT!
HERE!!
WHAT'S YOUR PROBLEM...?

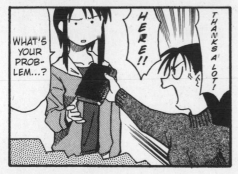

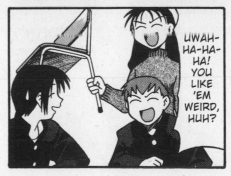

SECRET

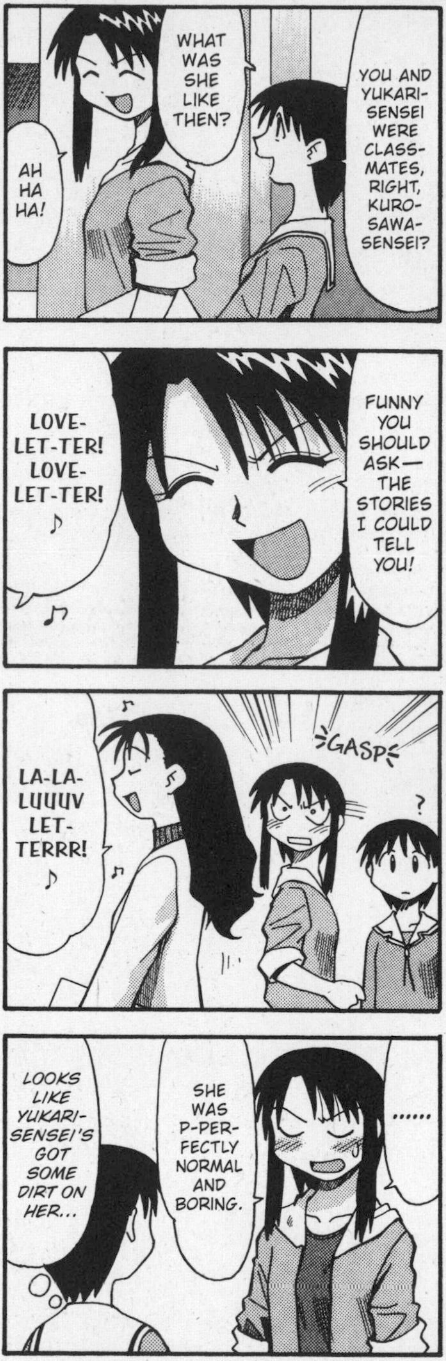
YOU AND YUKARI-SENSEI WERE CLASSMATES, RIGHT, KURO-SAWA-SENSEI?
WHAT WAS SHE LIKE THEN?
AH HA HA!
FUNNY YOU SHOULD ASK—THE STORIES I COULD TELL YOU!
LOVE-LET-TER! LOVE-LET-TER! ♪
♪
GASP
?
LA-LA-LUUUV LET-TERRR! ♪
♪
♪
......
SHE WAS P-PERFECTLY NORMAL AND BORING.
LOOKS LIKE YUKARI-SENSEI'S GOT SOME DIRT ON HER...

TEENY-WEENY CHIYO-CHAN

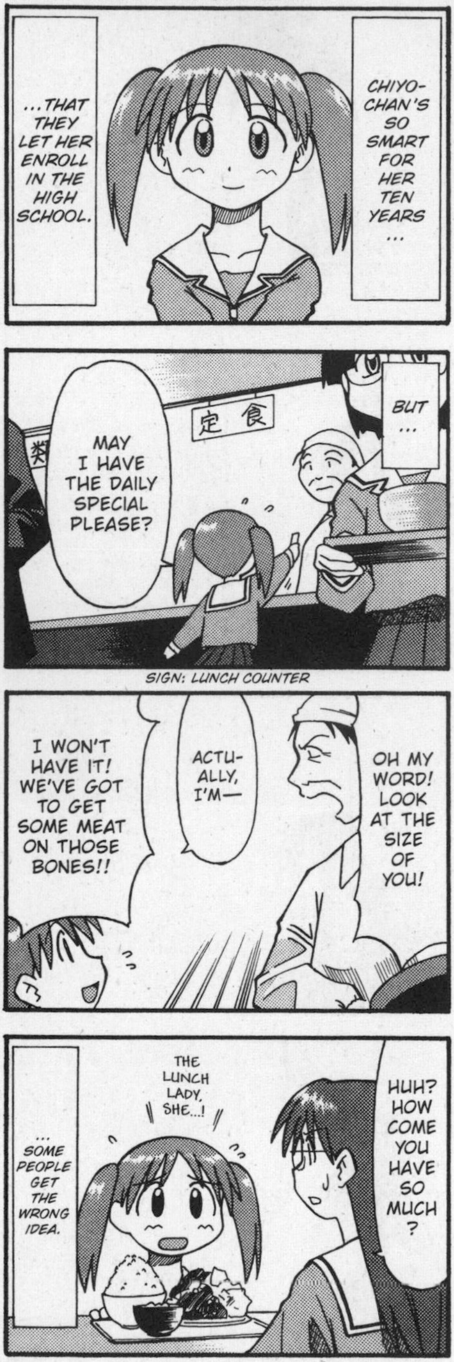
CHIYO-CHAN'S SO SMART FOR HER TEN YEARS ...
...THAT THEY LET HER ENROLL IN THE HIGH SCHOOL.
BUT ...
定食
MAY I HAVE THE DAILY SPECIAL PLEASE?
OH MY WORD! LOOK AT THE SIZE OF YOU!
ACTU-ALLY, I'M—
I WON'T HAVE IT! WE'VE GOT TO GET SOME MEAT ON THOSE BONES!!
HUH? HOW COME YOU HAVE SO MUCH?
THE LUNCH LADY, SHE...!
...SOME PEOPLE GET THE WRONG IDEA.

SIGN: LUNCH COUNTER

SEESAW

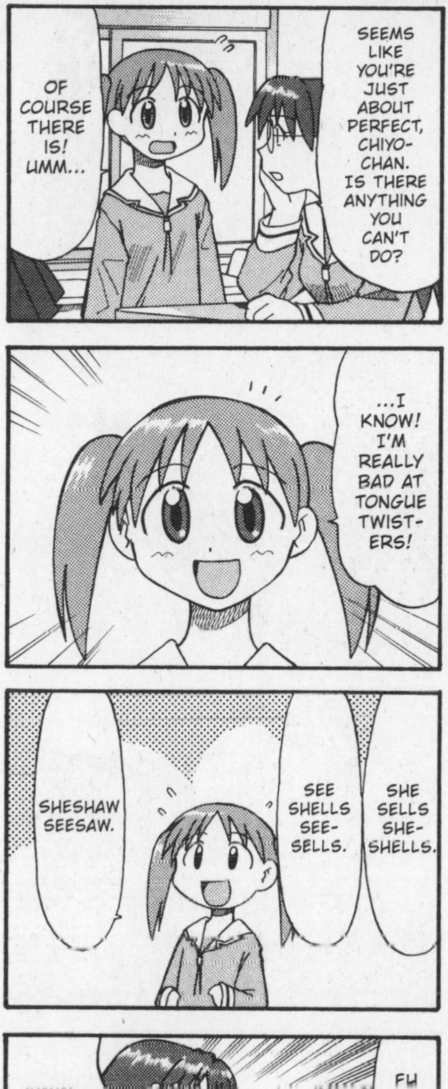
SEEMS LIKE YOU'RE JUST ABOUT PERFECT, CHIYO-CHAN. IS THERE ANYTHING YOU CAN'T DO?
OF COURSE THERE IS! UMM...
...I KNOW! I'M REALLY BAD AT TONGUE TWIST-ERS!
SHE SELLS SHE-SHELLS.
SEE SHELLS SEE-SELLS.
SHESHAW SEESAW.
FU HEH HEH!
AWW, MAN! AND YOU'RE STILL CUTE DOING IT!

I'M SCARED

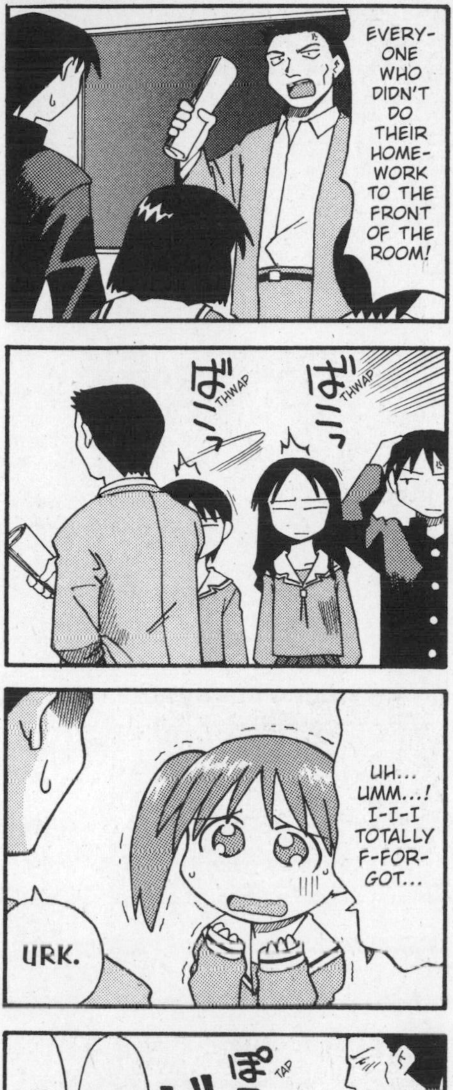
EVERY-ONE WHO DIDN'T DO THEIR HOME-WORK TO THE FRONT OF THE ROOM!
ばこっ
THWAP
ばこっ
THWAP
UH... UMM...! I-I-I TOTALLY F-FOR-GOT...
URK.
ぽこ…
TAP
ビクッ
FLINCH
HE LIKES 'EM YOUNG.
LIKES 'EM YOUNG.

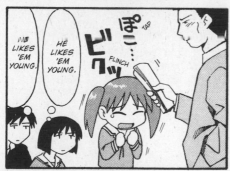

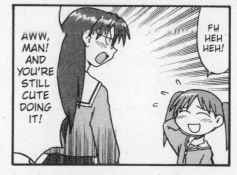

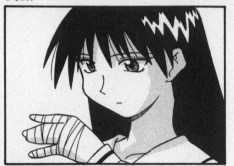

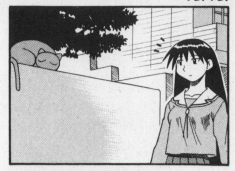

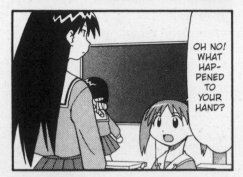

OH NO! WHAT HAP-PENED TO YOUR HAND?

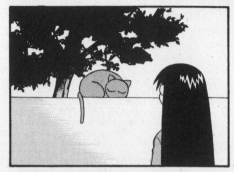

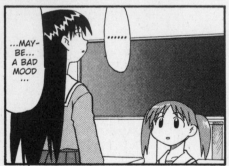

...MAY-BE... A BAD MOOD...

......

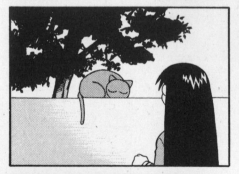

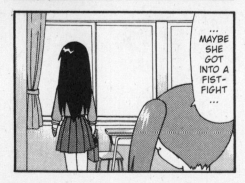

...MAYBE SHE GOT INTO A FIST-FIGHT...

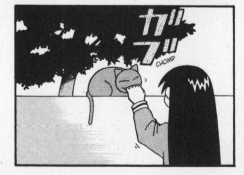

CHOMP

WHY?

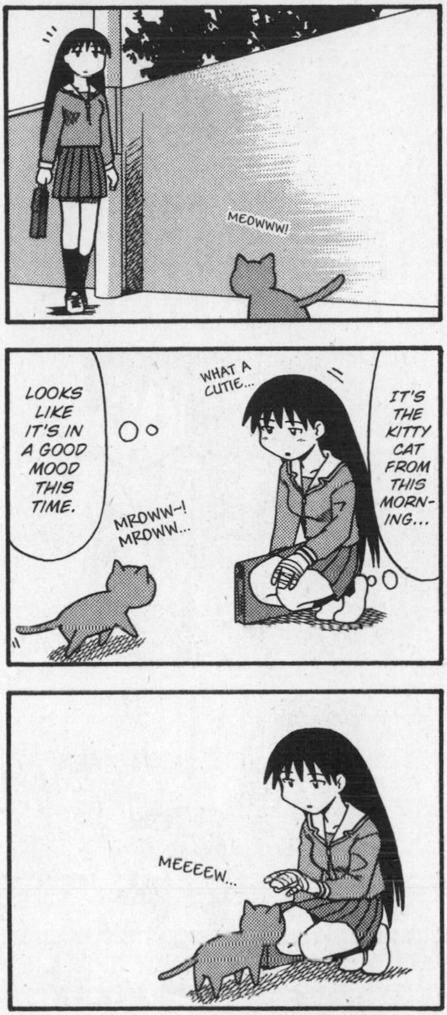
MEOWWW!
IT'S THE KITTY CAT FROM THIS MORNING...
WHAT A CUTIE...
LOOKS LIKE IT'S IN A GOOD MOOD THIS TIME.
MROWW-! MROWW...
MEEEEW...
がぶ
CHOMP

I WON'T GIVE UP ON MY DREAMS

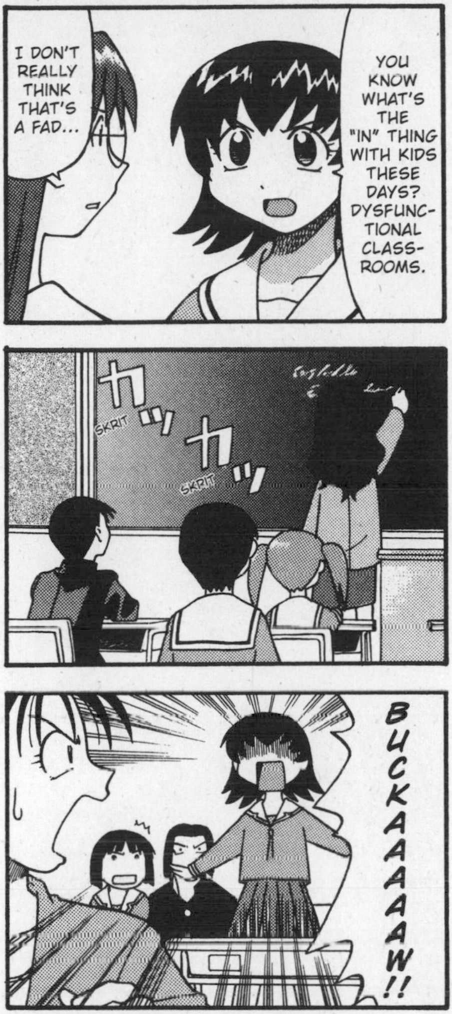
YOU KNOW WHAT'S THE "IN" THING WITH KIDS THESE DAYS? DYSFUNCTIONAL CLASSROOMS.
I DON'T REALLY THINK THAT'S A FAD...
カッ
SKRIT
カッ
SKRIT
BUCKAAAAAAAW!!
I COULD FULFILL ALL MY DREAMS OF MAKING WEIRD NOISES IN CLASS!
GIVE UP ON THAT KINDA DREAM, WILL YA?

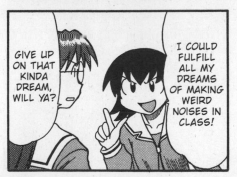

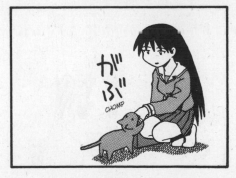

OVER-ENTHUSIASTIC

WHY DON'T YOU BURN OFF SOME OF THAT EXCESS ENERGY BY JOINING A SCHOOL CLUB?
ALTHOUGH BEING ENERGETIC DOESN'T MEAN YOU'RE GOOD AT SPORTS...
GOOD POINT. IF THERE'S ONE CLUB FOR ME, IT'D HAVE TO BE ...
THAT'S IT! THE PEP SQUAD!
OH, COME ON, I'M JUST JOKING! SAY SOME-THING!
AH. THAT WAS A JOKE? I THOUGHT IT WAS PERFECT.

BUNNY CLUB

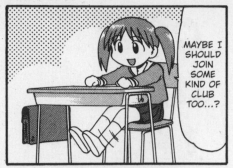

MAYBE I SHOULD JOIN SOME KIND OF CLUB TOO...?
WHAT SORT OF CLUB WOULD YOU JOIN, CHIYO-CHAN?
UMM, UMM...
...THE ANIMAL CLUB! I'D LIKE TO HELP RAISE PETS!
!
SORRY, I DON'T THINK WE HAVE ONE OF THOSE.
AWW...

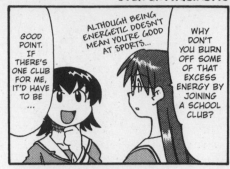

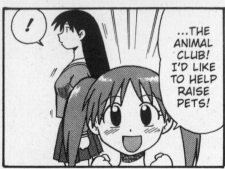

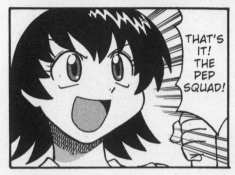

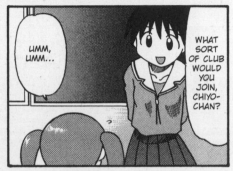

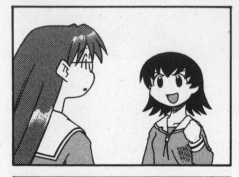

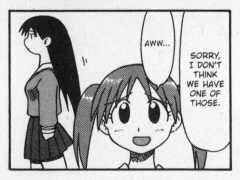

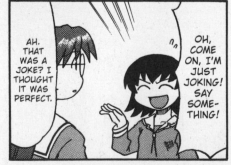

100-METER SCRAMBLE

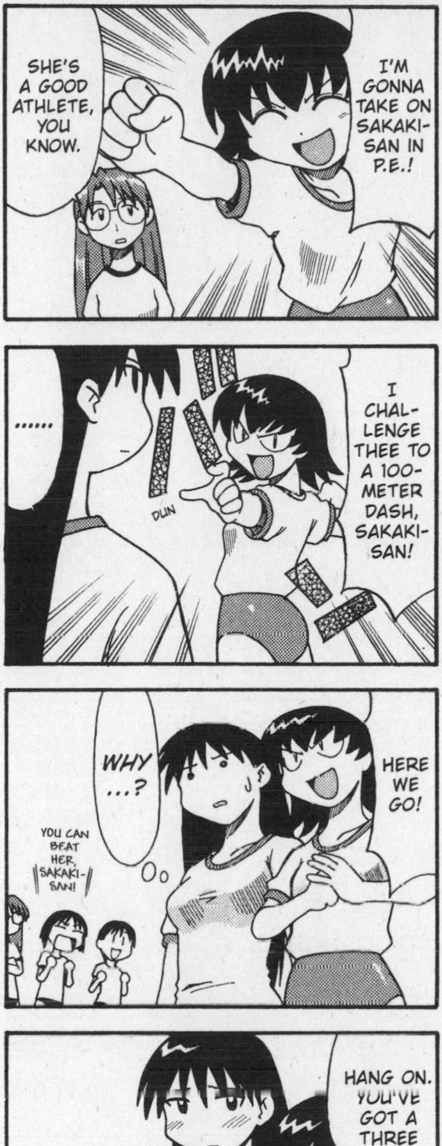
I'M GONNA TAKE ON SAKAKI-SAN IN P.E.!
SHE'S A GOOD ATHLETE, YOU KNOW.
I CHALLENGE THEE TO A 100-METER DASH, SAKAKI-SAN!
DUN
......
HERE WE GO!
WHY ...?
YOU CAN BEAT HER, SAKAKI-SAN!
HANG ON. YOU'VE GOT A THREE INCH BUST ADVANTAGE, SO I GET A THREE INCH LEAD.
NO FAIR, TOMO, YOU WEIRDO!!
REALLY? THREE INCHES?

A HARD-FOUGHT BATTLE

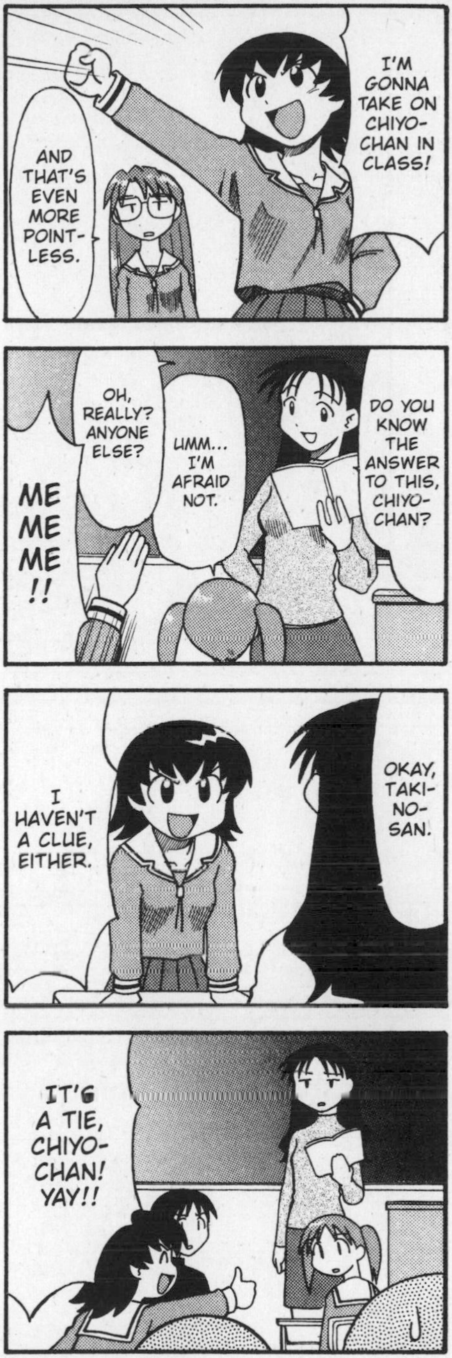
I'M GONNA TAKE ON CHIYO-CHAN IN CLASS!
AND THAT'S EVEN MORE POINTLESS.
DO YOU KNOW THE ANSWER TO THIS, CHIYO-CHAN?
UMM... I'M AFRAID NOT.
OH, REALLY? ANYONE ELSE?
ME ME ME!!
OKAY, TAKINO-SAN.
I HAVEN'T A CLUE, EITHER.
IT'S A TIE, CHIYO-CHAN! YAY!!

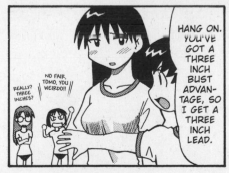

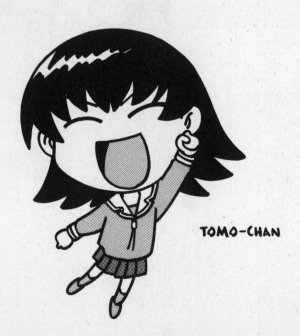

TOMO-CHAN

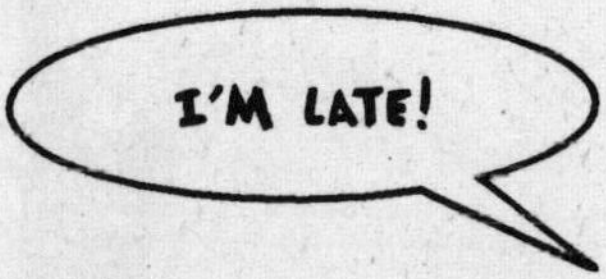
I'M LATE!

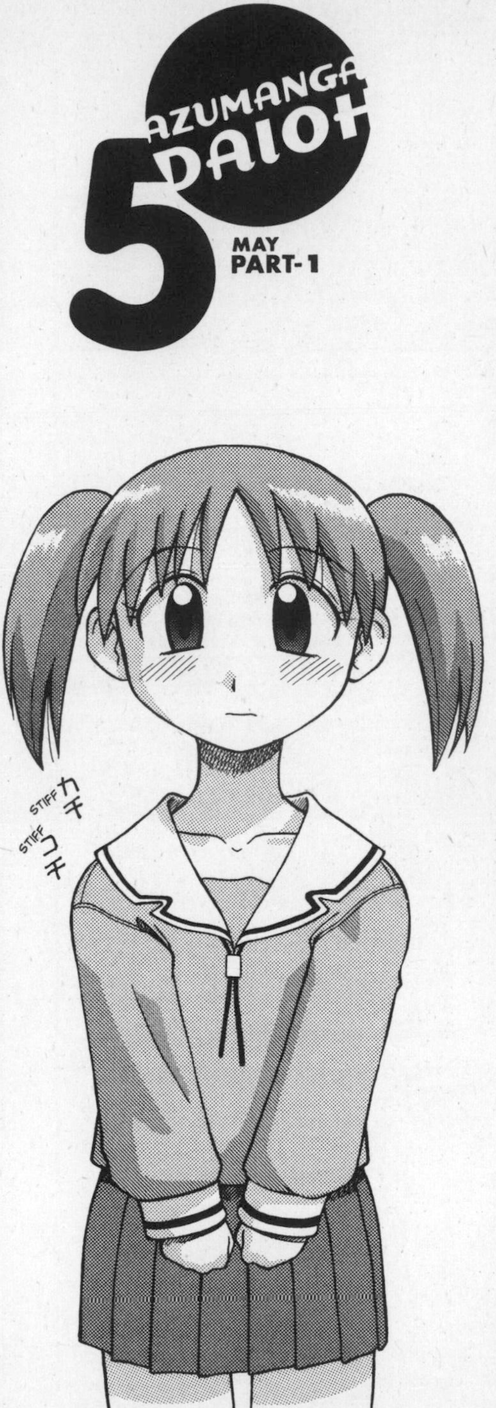

AZUMANGA DAIOH
5
MAY
PART-1
STIFF
STIFF

YUKARI-SENSEI COMMUTES BY BICYCLE

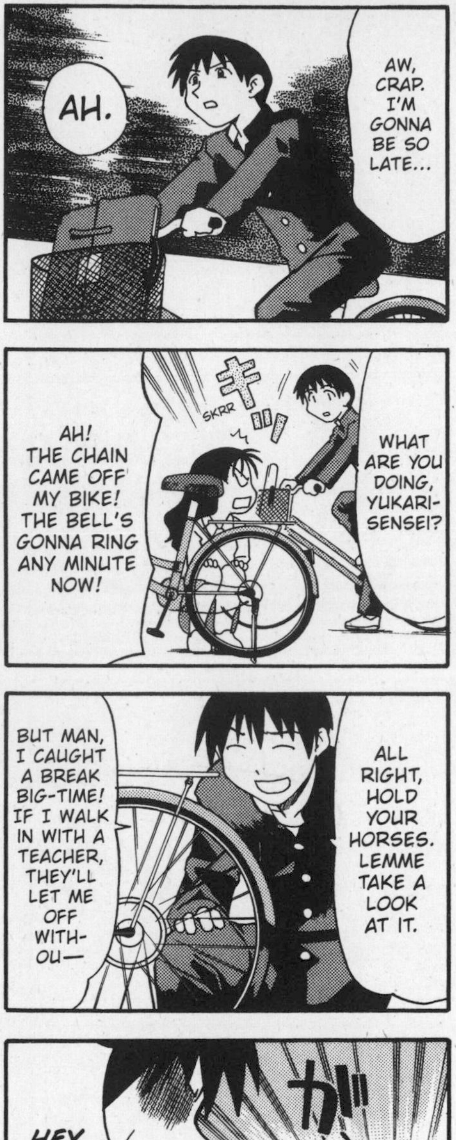

AW, CRAP. I'M GONNA BE SO LATE...
AH.
WHAT ARE YOU DOING, YUKARI-SENSEI?
SKRR
AH! THE CHAIN CAME OFF MY BIKE! THE BELL'S GONNA RING ANY MINUTE NOW!
ALL RIGHT, HOLD YOUR HORSES. LEMME TAKE A LOOK AT IT.
BUT MAN, I CAUGHT A BREAK BIG-TIME! IF I WALK IN WITH A TEACHER, THEY'LL LET ME OFF WITHOU—
ZOOOOM
HEY, THAT'S MY BIKE!!

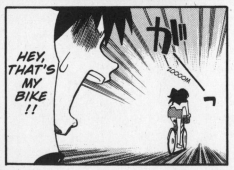

<GO> BY CAR!

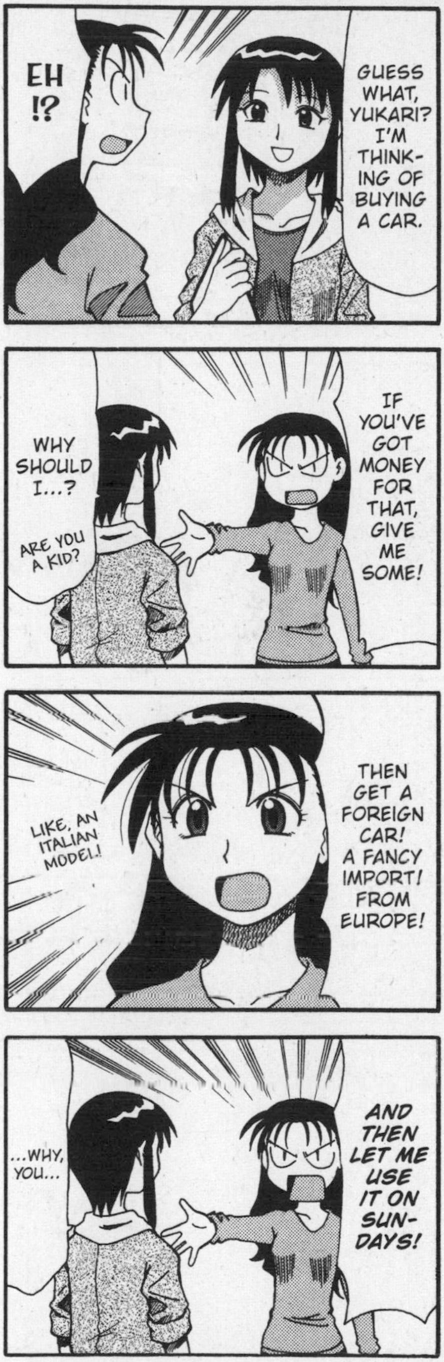
GUESS WHAT, YUKARI? I'M THINKING OF BUYING A CAR.
EH !?
IF YOU'VE GOT MONEY FOR THAT, GIVE ME SOME!
WHY SHOULD I...?
ARE YOU A KID?
THEN GET A FOREIGN CAR! A FANCY IMPORT! FROM EUROPE!
LIKE, AN ITALIAN MODEL!
AND THEN LET ME USE IT ON SUNDAYS!
...WHY, YOU...

YOU LITTLE BRAT

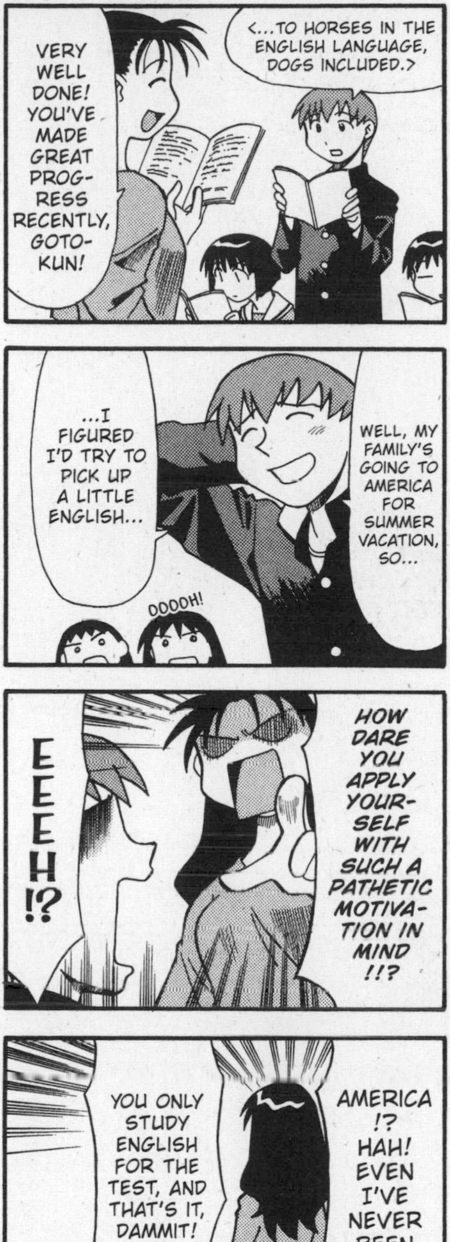
<...TO HORSES IN THE ENGLISH LANGUAGE, DOGS INCLUDED.>
VERY WELL DONE! YOU'VE MADE GREAT PROGRESS RECENTLY, GOTO-KUN!
WELL, MY FAMILY'S GOING TO AMERICA FOR SUMMER VACATION, SO...
...I FIGURED I'D TRY TO PICK UP A LITTLE ENGLISH...
OOOOH!
HOW DARE YOU APPLY YOURSELF WITH SUCH A PATHETIC MOTIVATION IN MIND !!?
EEEEH !?
AMERICA !? HAH! EVEN I'VE NEVER BEEN THERE!
YOU ONLY STUDY ENGLISH FOR THE TEST, AND THAT'S IT, DAMMIT!

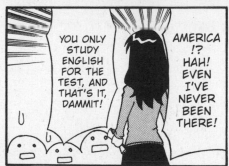

SUNDAY WITH CHIYO-CHAN

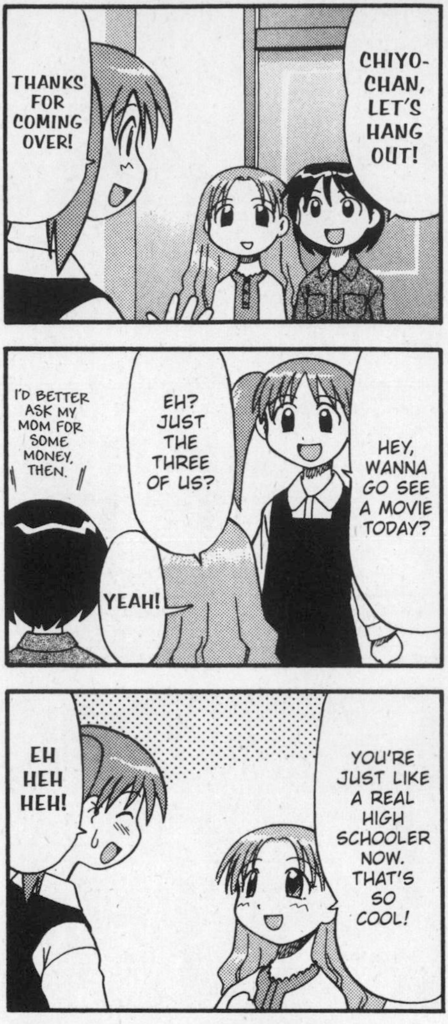
CHIYO-CHAN, LET'S HANG OUT!
THANKS FOR COMING OVER!
HEY, WANNA GO SEE A MOVIE TODAY?
EH? JUST THE THREE OF US?
YEAH!
I'D BETTER ASK MY MOM FOR SOME MONEY, THEN.
YOU'RE JUST LIKE A REAL HIGH SCHOOLER NOW. THAT'S SO COOL!
EH HEH HEH!
I EVEN WENT TO Mc-DONALD'S WITH MY FRIENDS AFTER SCHOOL.
WHOA!!
YOU BOUGHT YOUR OWN FOOD!

HUH?

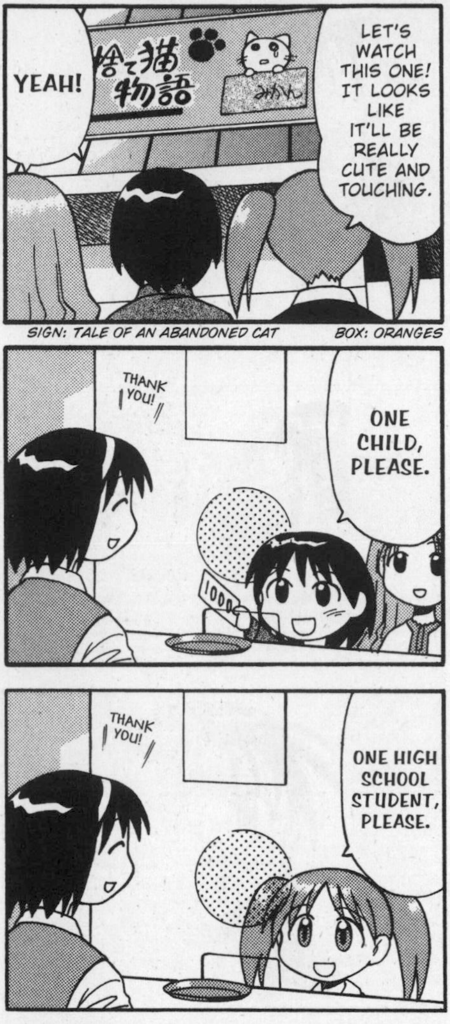
LET'S WATCH THIS ONE! IT LOOKS LIKE IT'LL BE REALLY CUTE AND TOUCHING.
捨て猫物語
みかん
YEAH!
ONE CHILD, PLEASE.
THANK YOU!
1000
ONE HIGH SCHOOL STUDENT, PLEASE.
THANK YOU!
...?

SIGN: TALE OF AN ABANDONED CAT BOX: ORANGES

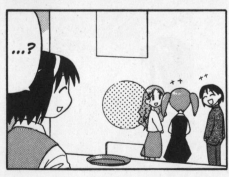

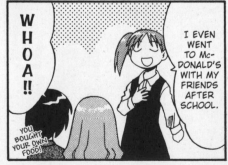

A MOVING MOVIE

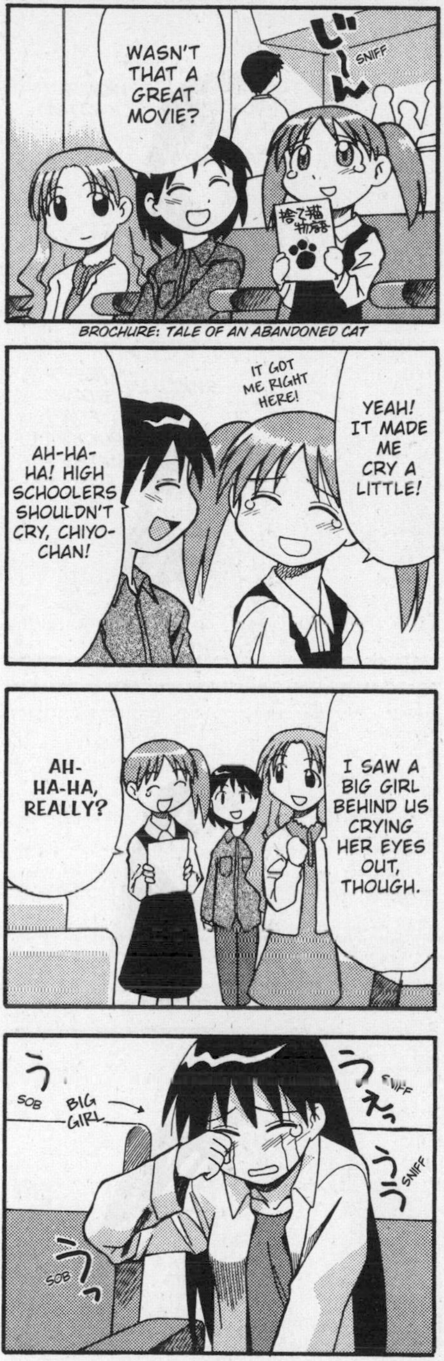
WASN'T THAT A GREAT MOVIE?
じ〜ん
SNIFF
捨て猫物語
BROCHURE: TALE OF AN ABANDONED CAT
YEAH! IT MADE ME CRY A LITTLE!
IT GOT ME RIGHT HERE!
AH-HA-HA! HIGH SCHOOLERS SHOULDN'T CRY, CHIYO-CHAN!
I SAW A BIG GIRL BEHIND US CRYING HER EYES OUT, THOUGH.
AH-HA-HA, REALLY?
うぇっ
SNIFF
うう
SNIFF
う
SOB
BIG GIRL
うっ
SOB

UWAAAAAAH!

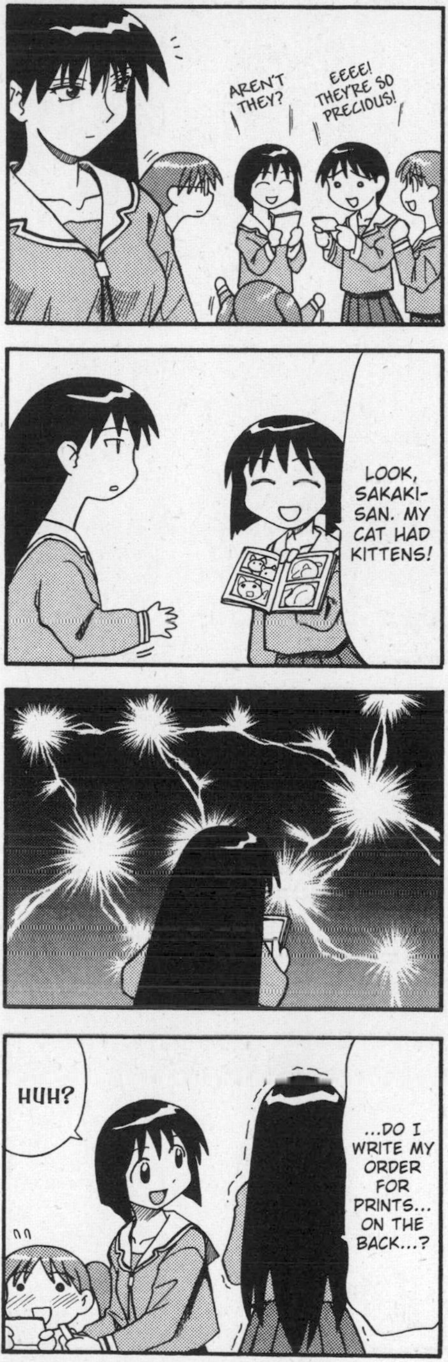
EEEE! THEY'RE SO PRECIOUS!
AREN'T THEY?
LOOK, SAKAKI-SAN. MY CAT HAD KITTENS!
...DO I WRITE MY ORDER FOR PRINTS... ON THE BACK...?
HUH?

WHAT COULD IT BE?

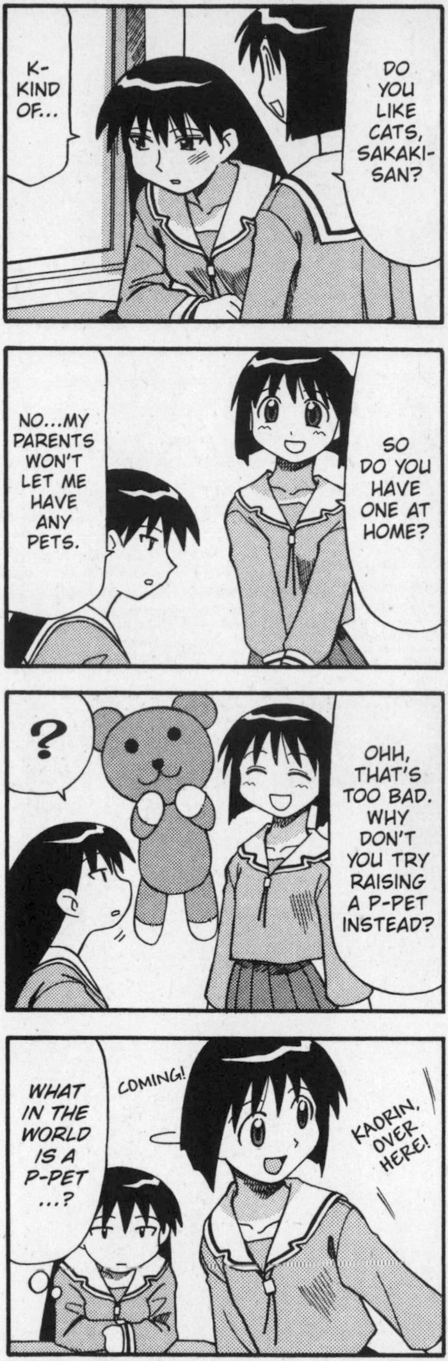
DO YOU LIKE CATS, SAKAKI-SAN?
K-KIND OF...
SO DO YOU HAVE ONE AT HOME?
NO...MY PARENTS WON'T LET ME HAVE ANY PETS.
OHH, THAT'S TOO BAD. WHY DON'T YOU TRY RAISING A P-PET INSTEAD?
?
KAORIN, OVER HERE!
COMING!
WHAT IN THE WORLD IS A P-PET ...?

RECOMMENDED PET

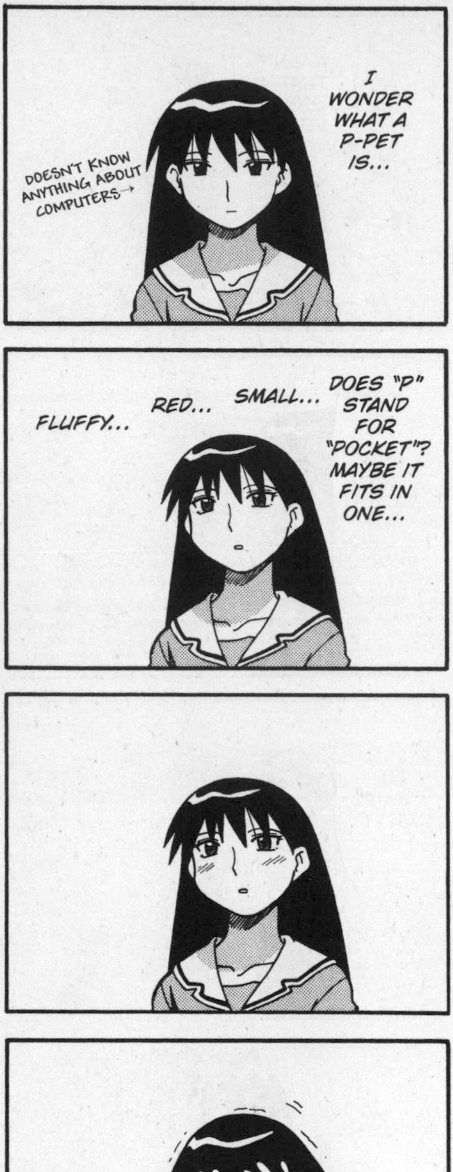
I WONDER WHAT A P-PET IS...
DOESN'T KNOW ANYTHING ABOUT COMPUTERS→
DOES "P" STAND FOR "POCKET"? MAYBE IT FITS IN ONE...
SMALL...
RED...
FLUFFY...
IMAGINING SOMETHING UNBEARABLY CUTE→

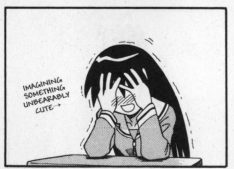

EXPECTATION-DEFYING!

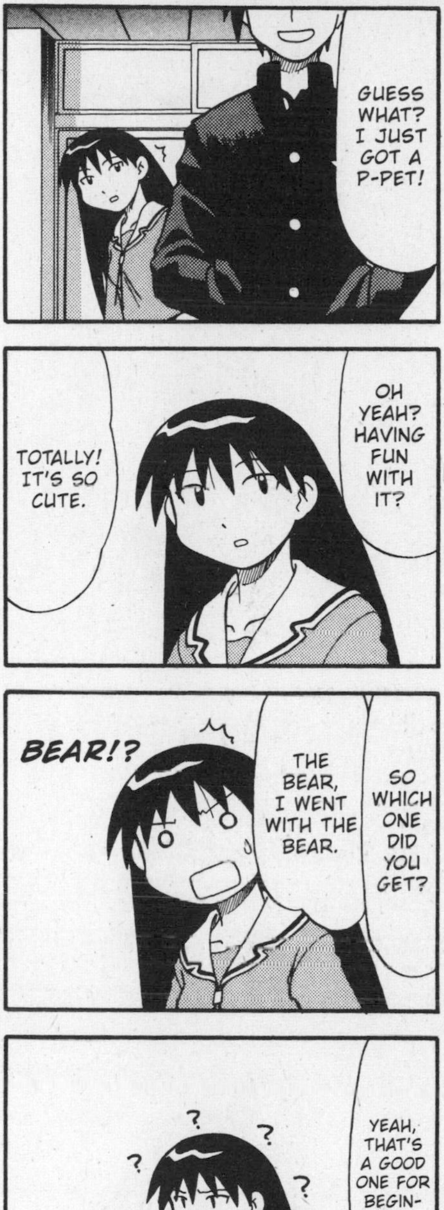
GUESS WHAT? I JUST GOT A P-PET!
OH YEAH? HAVING FUN WITH IT?
TOTALLY! IT'S SO CUTE.
SO WHICH ONE DID YOU GET?
THE BEAR, I WENT WITH THE BEAR.
BEAR!?
YEAH, THAT'S A GOOD ONE FOR BEGINNERS.

ANOTHER ANNOYING PERSON

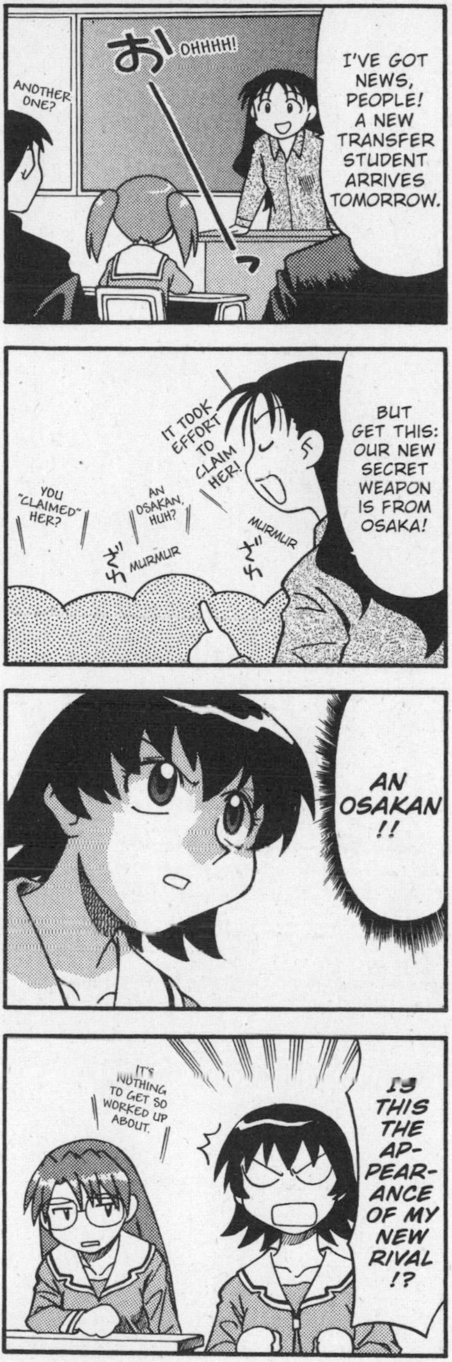
I'VE GOT NEWS, PEOPLE! A NEW TRANSFER STUDENT ARRIVES TOMORROW.
お OHHHH!
ANOTHER ONE?
BUT GET THIS: OUR NEW SECRET WEAPON IS FROM OSAKA!
IT TOOK EFFORT TO CLAIM HER!
MURMUR
AN OSAKAN, HUH?
YOU "CLAIMED" HER?
MURMUR
AN OSAKAN!!
IS THIS THE APPEARANCE OF MY NEW RIVAL!?
IT'S NOTHING TO GET SO WORKED UP ABOUT.

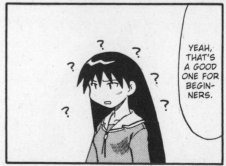

CAN'T LET HER WIN

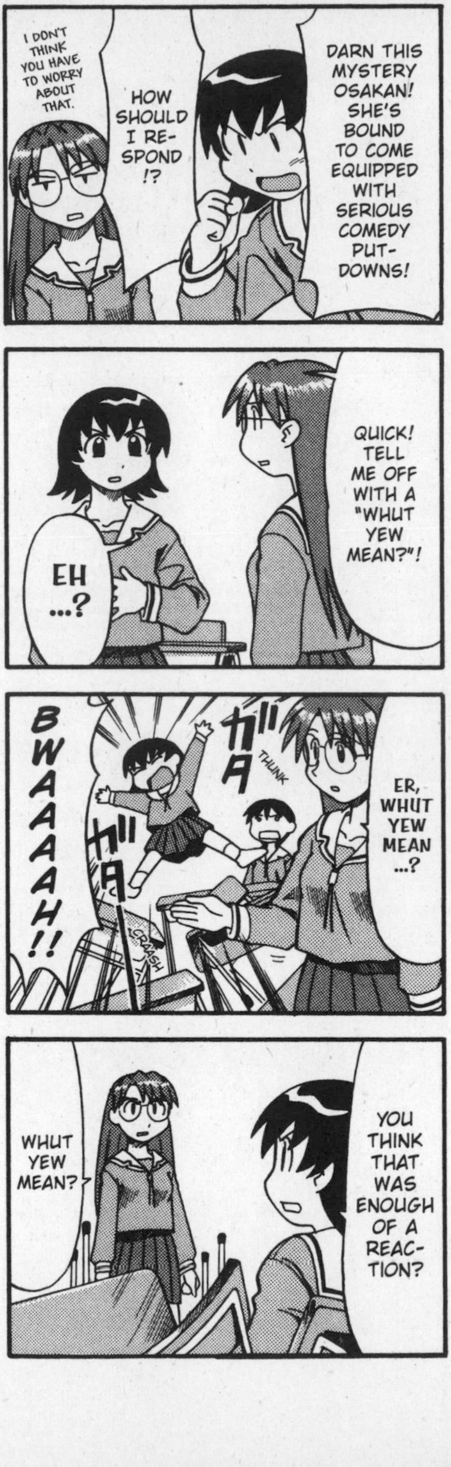
DARN THIS MYSTERY OSAKAN! SHE'S BOUND TO COME EQUIPPED WITH SERIOUS COMEDY PUT-DOWNS!
HOW SHOULD I RESPOND !?
I DON'T THINK YOU HAVE TO WORRY ABOUT THAT.
QUICK! TELL ME OFF WITH A "WHUT YEW MEAN?"!
EH ...?
ER, WHUT YEW MEAN ...?
ガタ
THUNK
ガタ
BWAAAAAH!!
CRASH
YOU THINK THAT WAS ENOUGH OF A REACTION?
WHUT YEW MEAN?

THE OSAKAN'S HERE, Y'ALL.

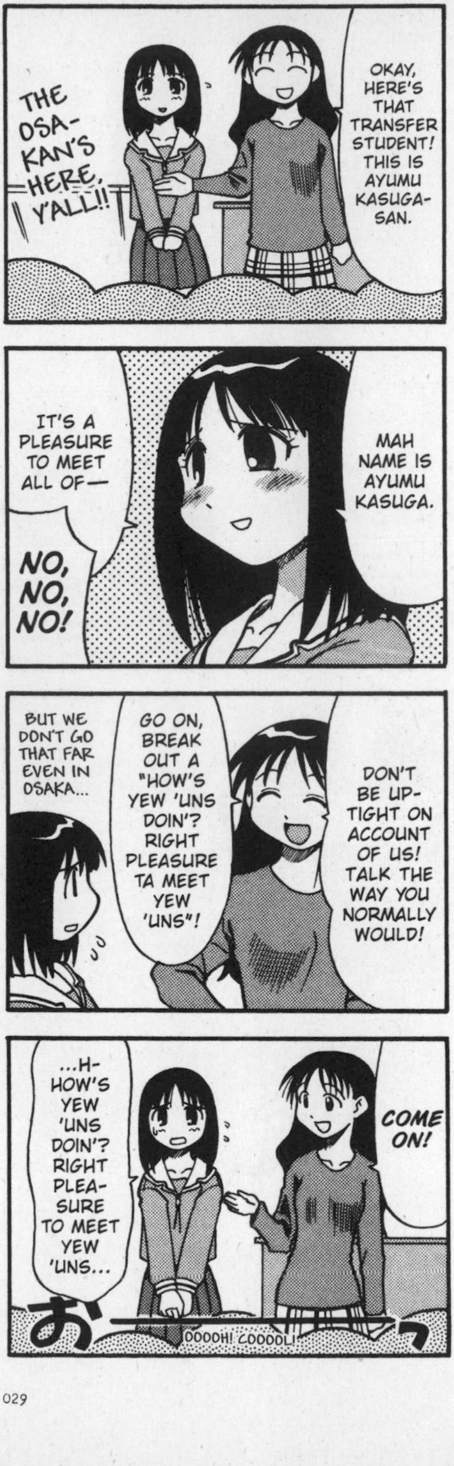
OKAY, HERE'S THAT TRANSFER STUDENT! THIS IS AYUMU KASUGA-SAN.
THE OSAKAN'S HERE, Y'ALL!!
MAH NAME IS AYUMU KASUGA.
IT'S A PLEASURE TO MEET ALL OF—
NO, NO, NO!
DON'T BE UPTIGHT ON ACCOUNT OF US! TALK THE WAY YOU NORMALLY WOULD!
GO ON, BREAK OUT A "HOW'S YEW 'UNS DOIN'? RIGHT PLEASURE TA MEET YEW 'UNS"!
BUT WE DON'T GO THAT FAR EVEN IN OSAKA...
COME ON!
...H-HOW'S YEW 'UNS DOIN'? RIGHT PLEASURE TO MEET YEW 'UNS...
おっ
OOOOH! COOOOL!

WHY'S THAT?

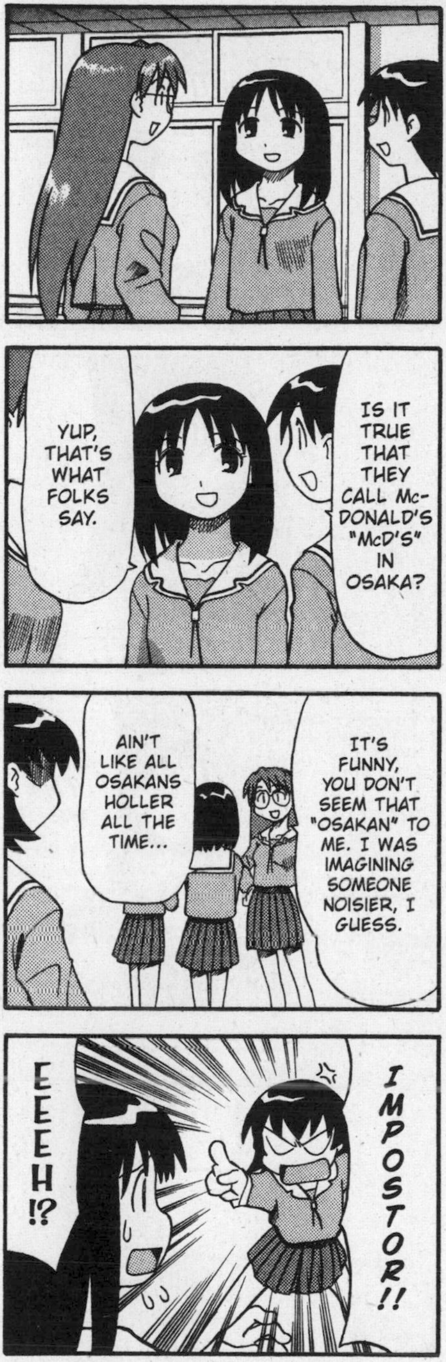
IS IT TRUE THAT THEY CALL McDONALD'S "McD'S" IN OSAKA?
YUP, THAT'S WHAT FOLKS SAY.
IT'S FUNNY, YOU DON'T SEEM THAT "OSAKAN" TO ME. I WAS IMAGINING SOMEONE NOISIER, I GUESS.
AIN'T LIKE ALL OSAKANS HOLLER ALL THE TIME...
IMPOSTOR!!
EEEEH!?

TEST

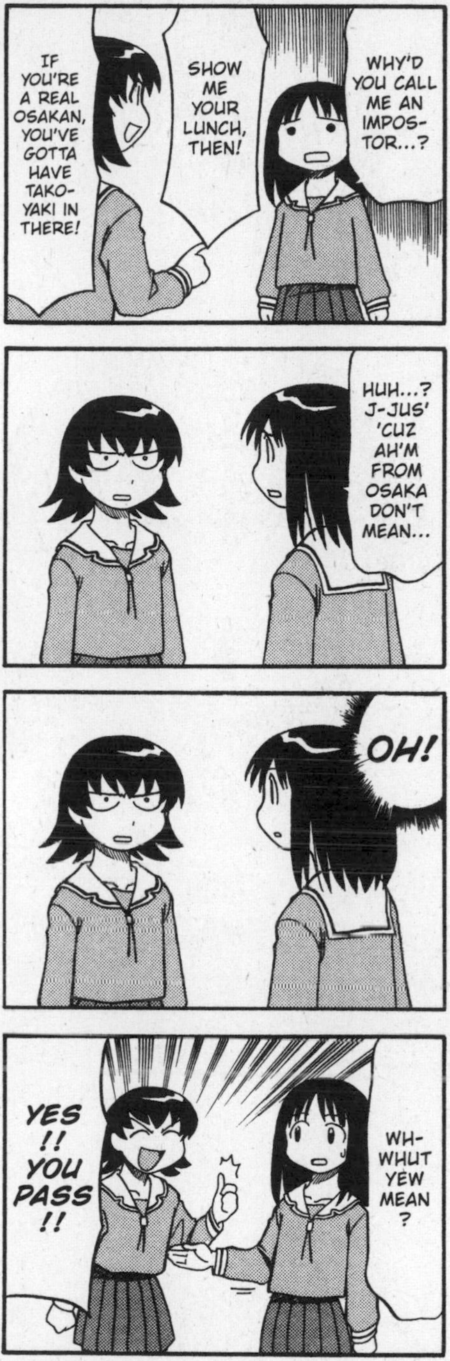
WHY'D YOU CALL ME AN IMPOSTOR...?
SHOW ME YOUR LUNCH, THEN!
IF YOU'RE A REAL OSAKAN, YOU'VE GOTTA HAVE TAKOYAKI IN THERE!
HUH...? J-JUS' 'CUZ AH'M FROM OSAKA DON'T MEAN...
OH!
WH-WHUT YEW MEAN?
YES!! YOU PASS!!

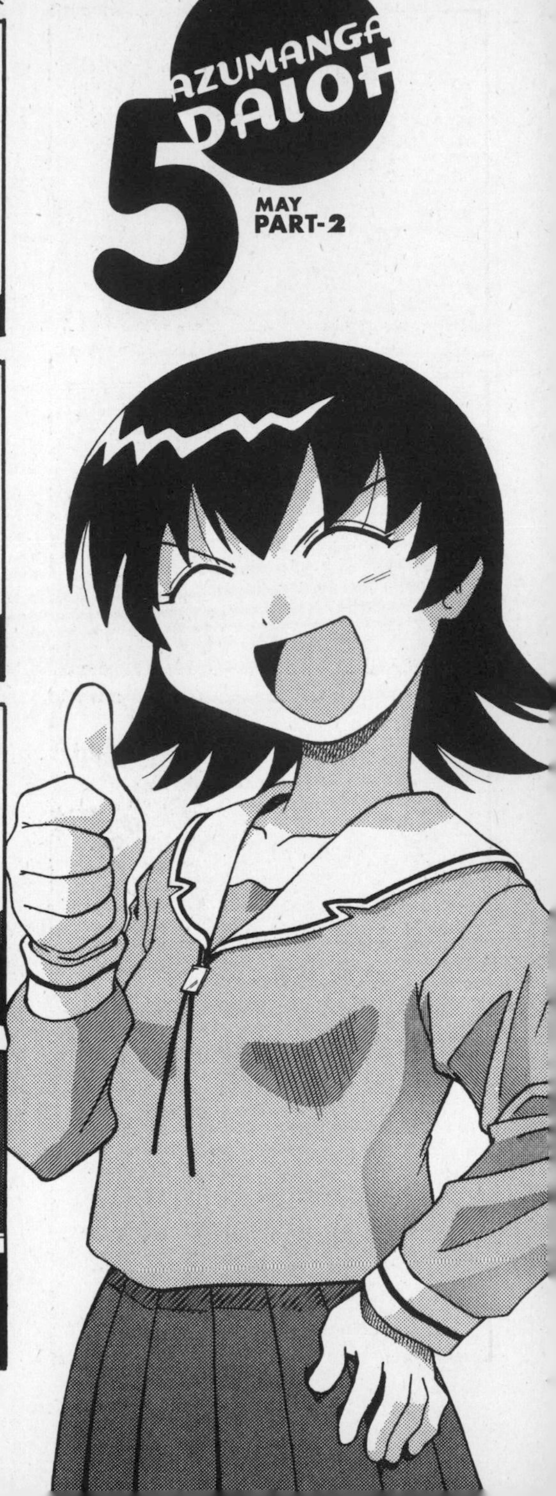
AZUMANGA DAIOH
5
MAY
PART-2

I'M NOT BITTER

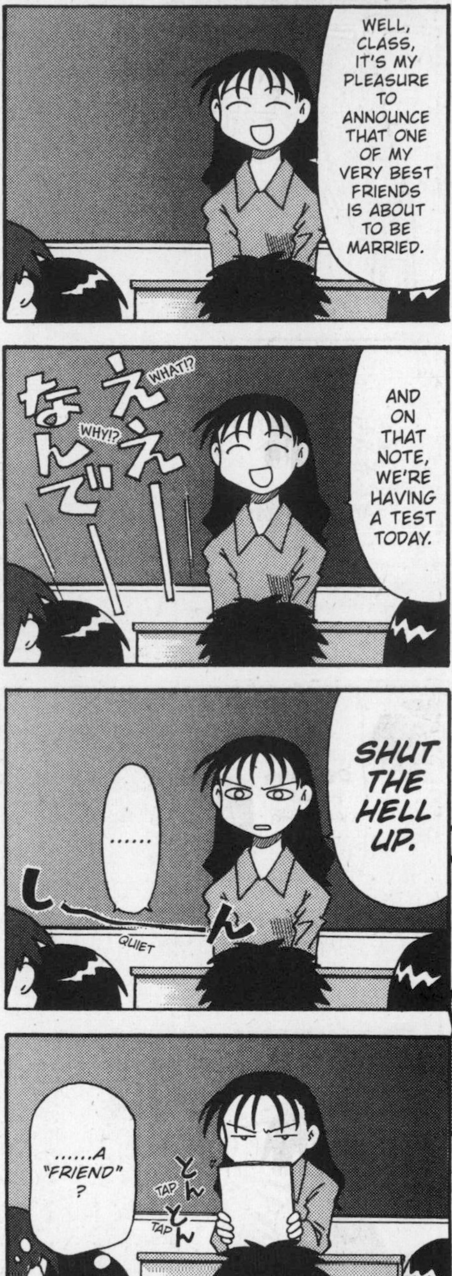
WELL, CLASS, IT'S MY PLEASURE TO ANNOUNCE THAT ONE OF MY VERY BEST FRIENDS IS ABOUT TO BE MARRIED.
AND ON THAT NOTE, WE'RE HAVING A TEST TODAY.
ええー
WHAT!?
なんでー
WHY!?
SHUT THE HELL UP.
......
しーん
QUIET
とん とん
TAP TAP
......A "FRIEND"?

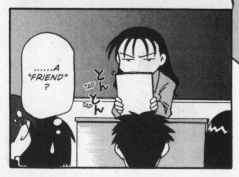

LESSON LEARNED

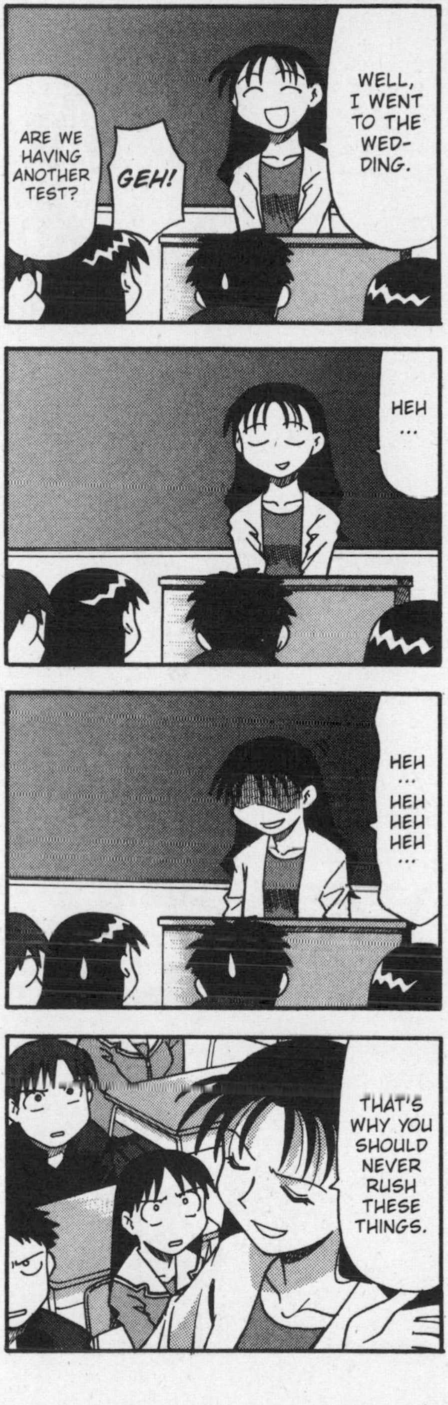
WELL, I WENT TO THE WED-DING.
GEH!
ARE WE HAVING ANOTHER TEST?
HEH ...
HEH ... HEH HEH HEH ...
THAT'S WHY YOU SHOULD NEVER RUSH THESE THINGS.

PATHETIC

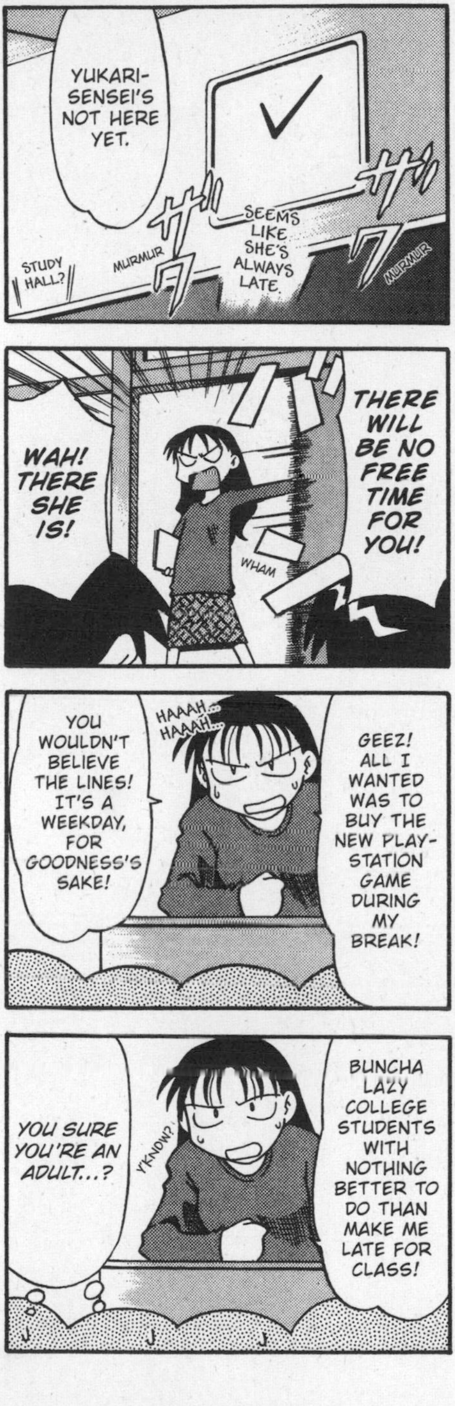
YUKARI-SENSEI'S NOT HERE YET.
ザワ
MURMUR
ザワ
SEEMS LIKE SHE'S ALWAYS LATE.
MURMUR
STUDY HALL?
THERE WILL BE NO FREE TIME FOR YOU!
WHAM
WAH! THERE SHE IS!
GEEZ! ALL I WANTED WAS TO BUY THE NEW PLAY-STATION GAME DURING MY BREAK!
HAAAH... HAAAH...
YOU WOULDN'T BELIEVE THE LINES! IT'S A WEEKDAY, FOR GOODNESS'S SAKE!
BUNCHA LAZY COLLEGE STUDENTS WITH NOTHING BETTER TO DO THAN MAKE ME LATE FOR CLASS!
Y'KNOW?!
YOU SURE YOU'RE AN ADULT...?

TO THE WORLD OF DREAMS

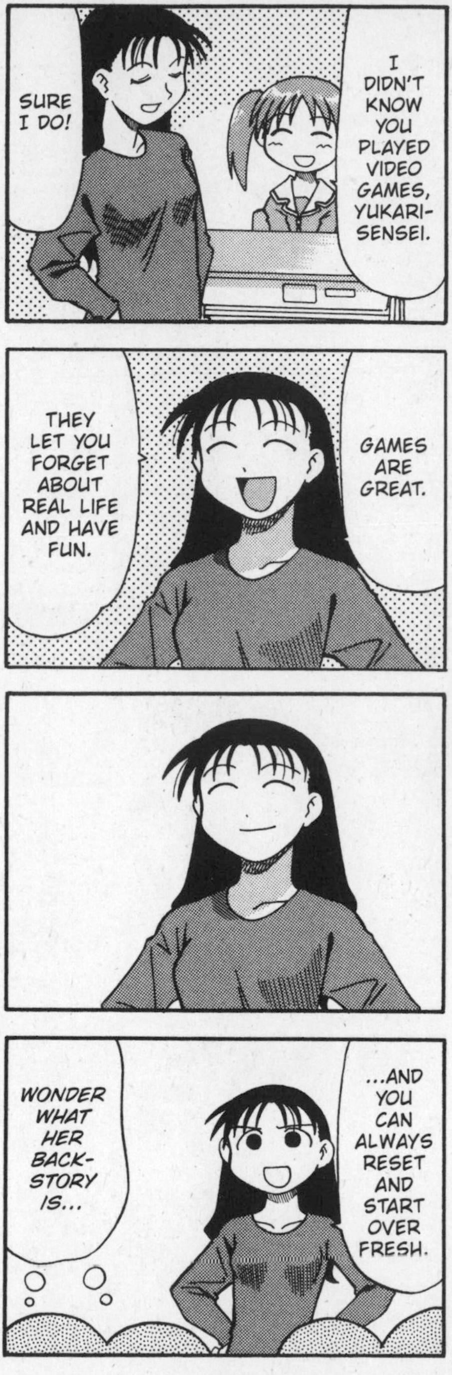
I DIDN'T KNOW YOU PLAYED VIDEO GAMES, YUKARI-SENSEI.
SURE I DO!
GAMES ARE GREAT.
THEY LET YOU FORGET ABOUT REAL LIFE AND HAVE FUN.
...AND YOU CAN ALWAYS RESET AND START OVER FRESH.
WONDER WHAT HER BACK-STORY IS...

GET A GRIP!

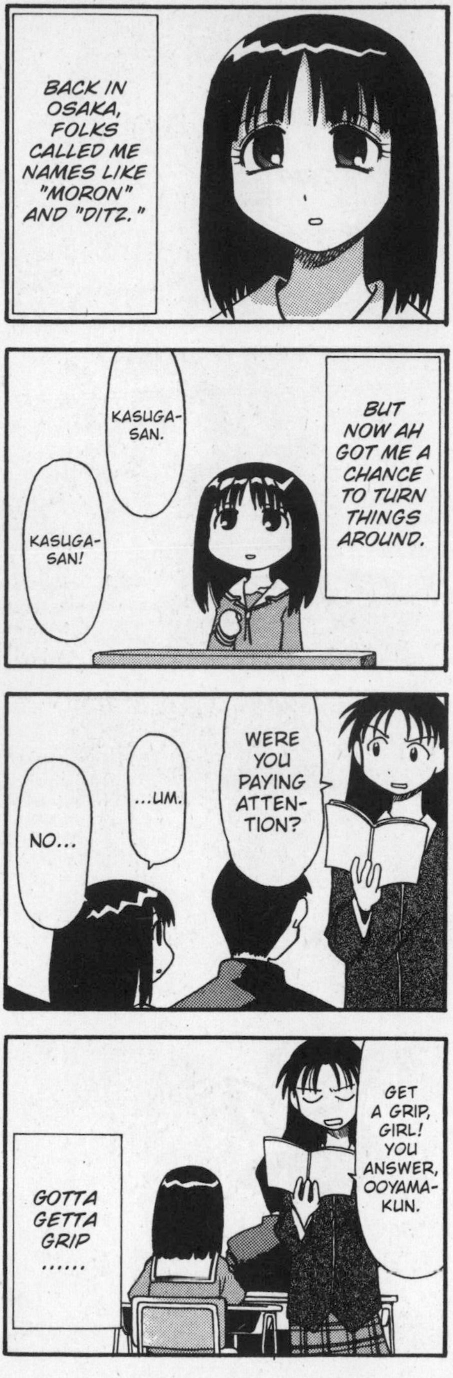
BACK IN OSAKA, FOLKS CALLED ME NAMES LIKE "MORON" AND "DITZ."
BUT NOW AH GOT ME A CHANCE TO TURN THINGS AROUND.
KASUGA-SAN.
KASUGA-SAN!
WERE YOU PAYING ATTEN-TION?
...UM.
NO...
GET A GRIP, GIRL! YOU ANSWER, OOYAMA-KUN.
GOTTA GETTA GRIP ......

OH, AH GET IT, AH GET IT

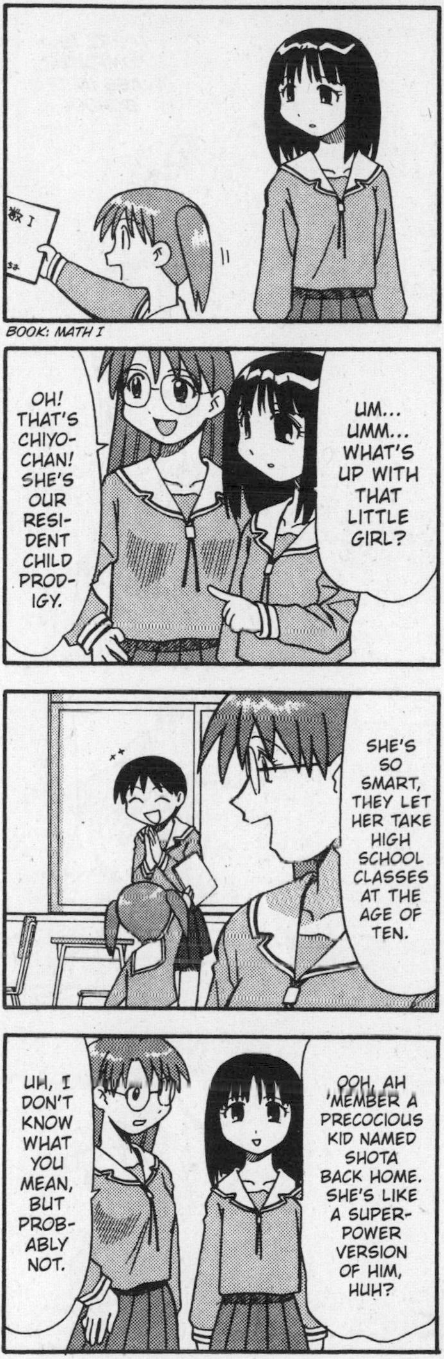
BOOK: MATH I
UM... UMM... WHAT'S UP WITH THAT LITTLE GIRL?
OH! THAT'S CHIYO-CHAN! SHE'S OUR RESI-DENT CHILD PROD-IGY.
SHE'S SO SMART, THEY LET HER TAKE HIGH SCHOOL CLASSES AT THE AGE OF TEN.
OOH, AH 'MEMBER A PRECOCIOUS KID NAMED SHOTA BACK HOME. SHE'S LIKE A SUPER-POWER VERSION OF HIM, HUH?
UH, I DON'T KNOW WHAT YOU MEAN, BUT PROB-ABLY NOT.

GENIUS, Y'ALL...

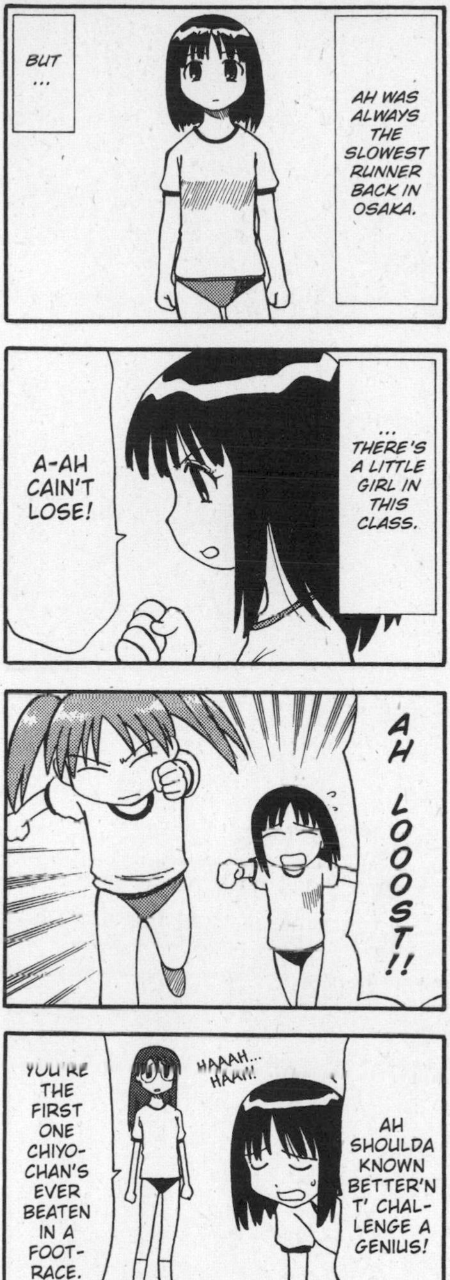
AH WAS ALWAYS THE SLOWEST RUNNER BACK IN OSAKA.
BUT ...
... THERE'S A LITTLE GIRL IN THIS CLASS.
A-AH CAIN'T LOSE!
AH LOOOOST!!
HAAAH... HAAH
AH SHOULDA KNOWN BETTER'N T' CHAL-LENGE A GENIUS!
YOU'RE THE FIRST ONE CHIYO-CHAN'S EVER BEATEN IN A FOOT-RACE.

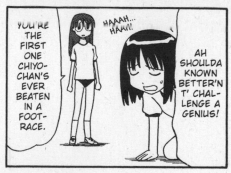

NO SPORTS, PLEASE

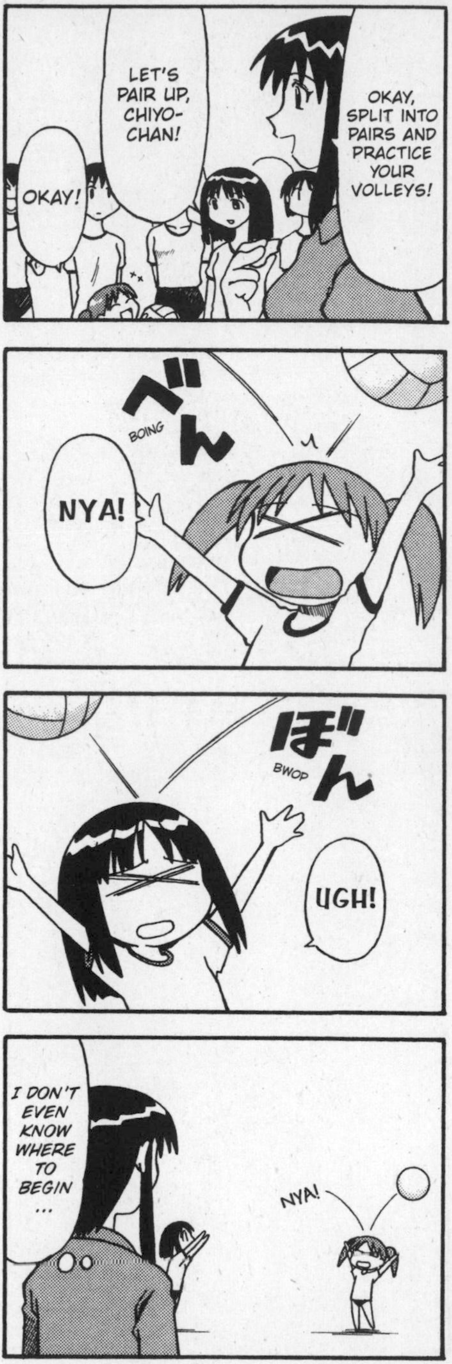
OKAY, SPLIT INTO PAIRS AND PRACTICE YOUR VOLLEYS!
LET'S PAIR UP, CHIYO-CHAN!
OKAY!
べん
BOING
NYA!
ぼん
BWOP
UGH!
NYA!
I DON'T EVEN KNOW WHERE TO BEGIN ...

COMPUTER!

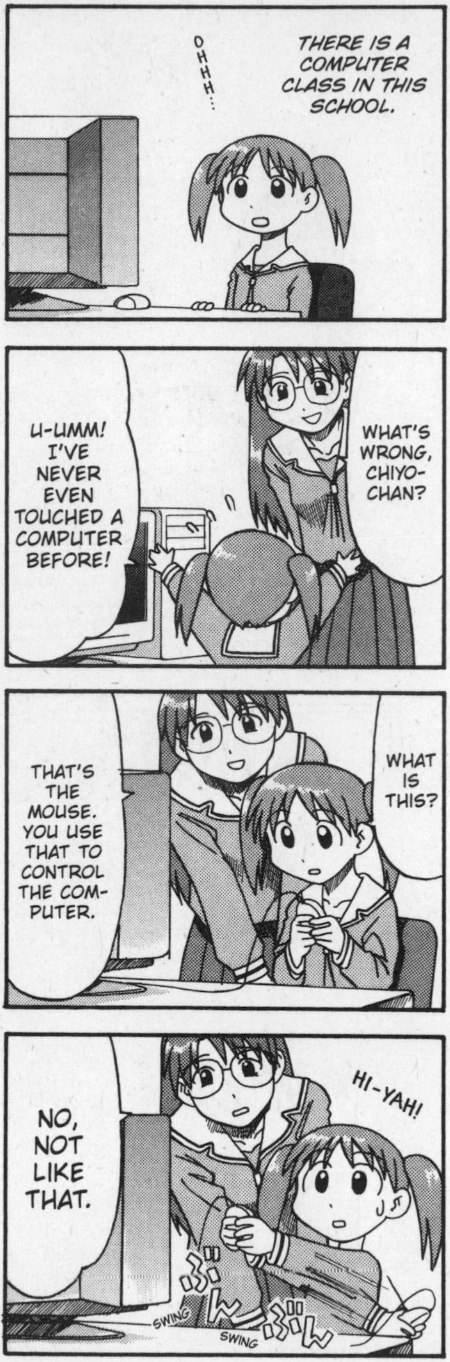
THERE IS A COMPUTER CLASS IN THIS SCHOOL.
OHHH...
WHAT'S WRONG, CHIYO-CHAN?
U-UMM! I'VE NEVER EVEN TOUCHED A COMPUTER BEFORE!
WHAT IS THIS?
THAT'S THE MOUSE. YOU USE THAT TO CONTROL THE COMPUTER.
HI-YAH!
ぶん
SWING
ぶん
SWING
NO, NOT LIKE THAT.

WILL I FIND ONE?

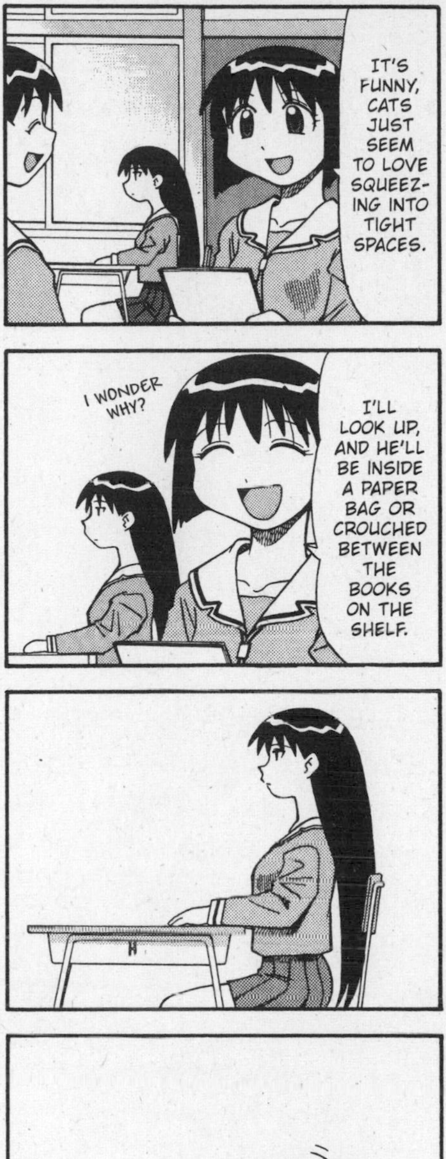

IT'S FUNNY, CATS JUST SEEM TO LOVE SQUEEZING INTO TIGHT SPACES.
I'LL LOOK UP, AND HE'LL BE INSIDE A PAPER BAG OR CROUCHED BETWEEN THE BOOKS ON THE SHELF.
I WONDER WHY?

MR. BUNNY

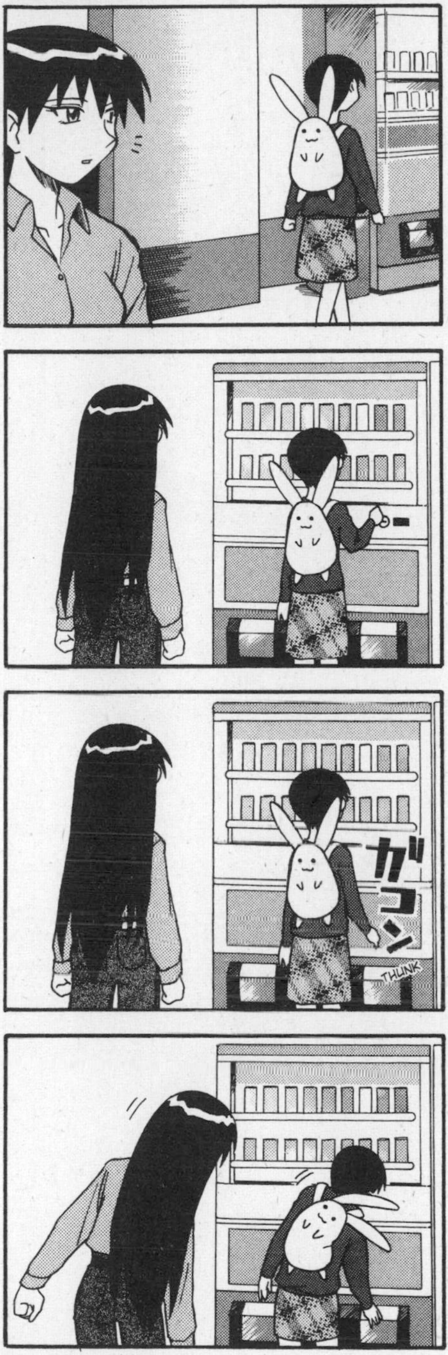

ガコン
THUNK

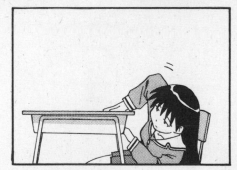

BIG MR. BUNNY

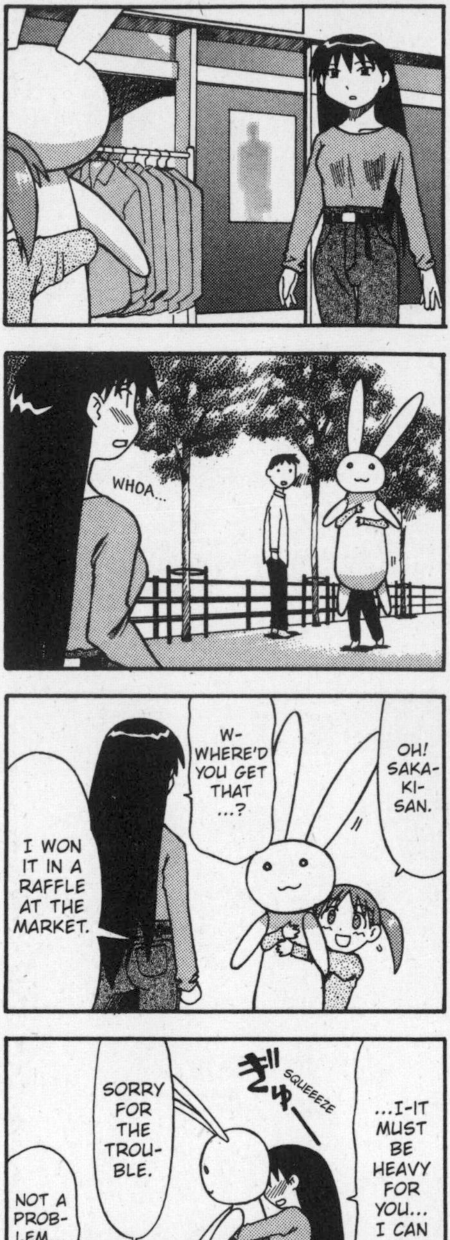
WHOA...
OH! SAKA-KI-SAN.
W-WHERE'D YOU GET THAT ...?
I WON IT IN A RAFFLE AT THE MARKET.
...I-IT MUST BE HEAVY FOR YOU... I CAN CARRY IT...
ぎゅ SQUEEEZE
SORRY FOR THE TROU-BLE.
NOT A PROB-LEM... NO PROB-LEM AT ALL...

DON'T DO THAT

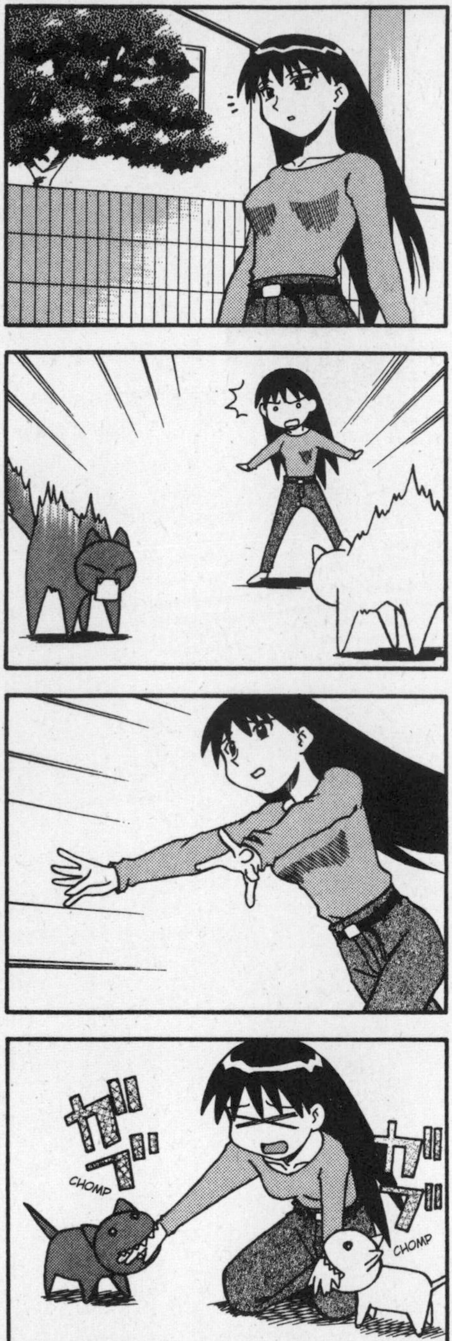
CHOMP
CHOMP

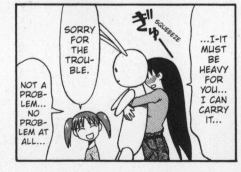

MIDTERMS

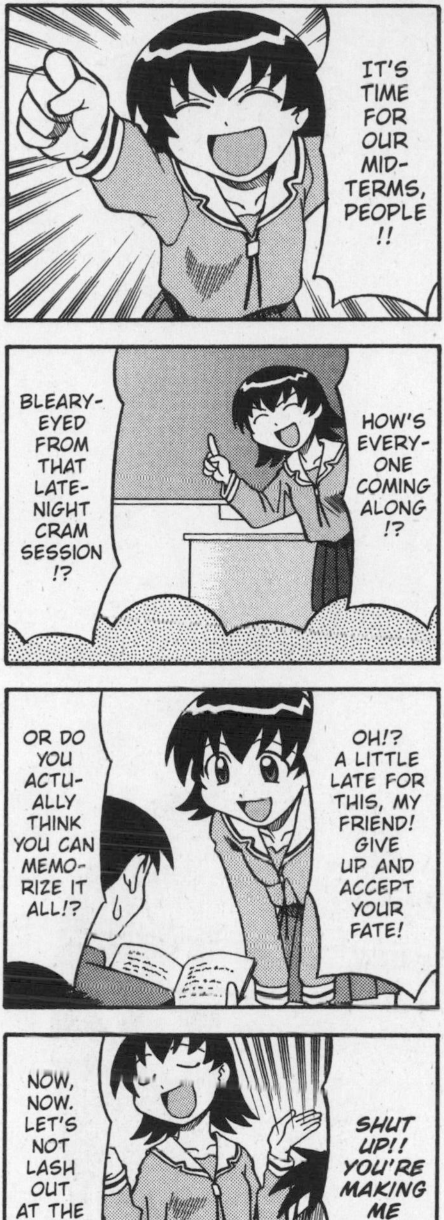
IT'S TIME FOR OUR MIDTERMS, PEOPLE!!
HOW'S EVERYONE COMING ALONG!?
BLEARY-EYED FROM THAT LATE-NIGHT CRAM SESSION!?
OH!? A LITTLE LATE FOR THIS, MY FRIEND! GIVE UP AND ACCEPT YOUR FATE!
OR DO YOU ACTUALLY THINK YOU CAN MEMORIZE IT ALL!?
SHUT UP!! YOU'RE MAKING ME FORGET!!
NOW, NOW. LET'S NOT LASH OUT AT THE INNOCENT, HMM?

I'M TELLING YOU

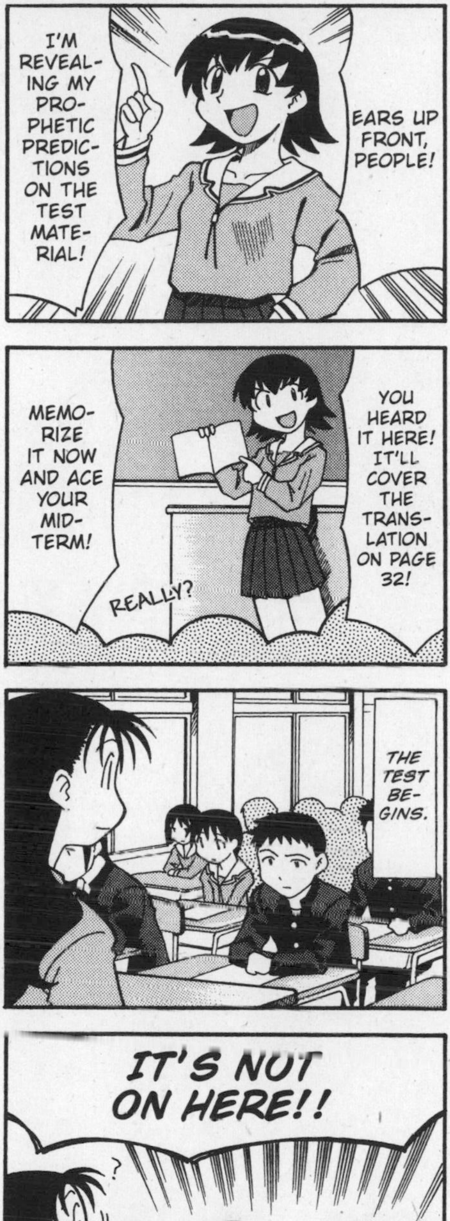
EARS UP FRONT, PEOPLE!
I'M REVEALING MY PROPHETIC PREDICTIONS ON THE TEST MATERIAL!
YOU HEARD IT HERE! IT'LL COVER THE TRANSLATION ON PAGE 32!
MEMORIZE IT NOW AND ACE YOUR MIDTERM!
REALLY?
THE TEST BEGINS.
IT'S NOT ON HERE!!

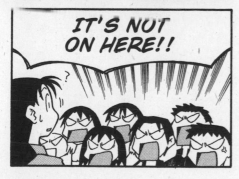

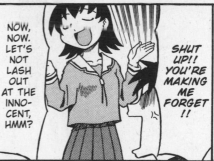

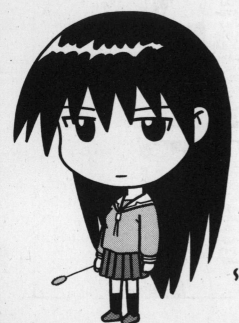

SAKAKI-SAN

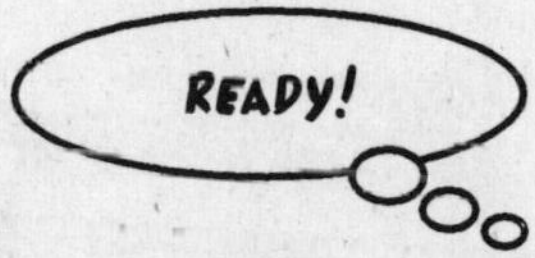
READY!

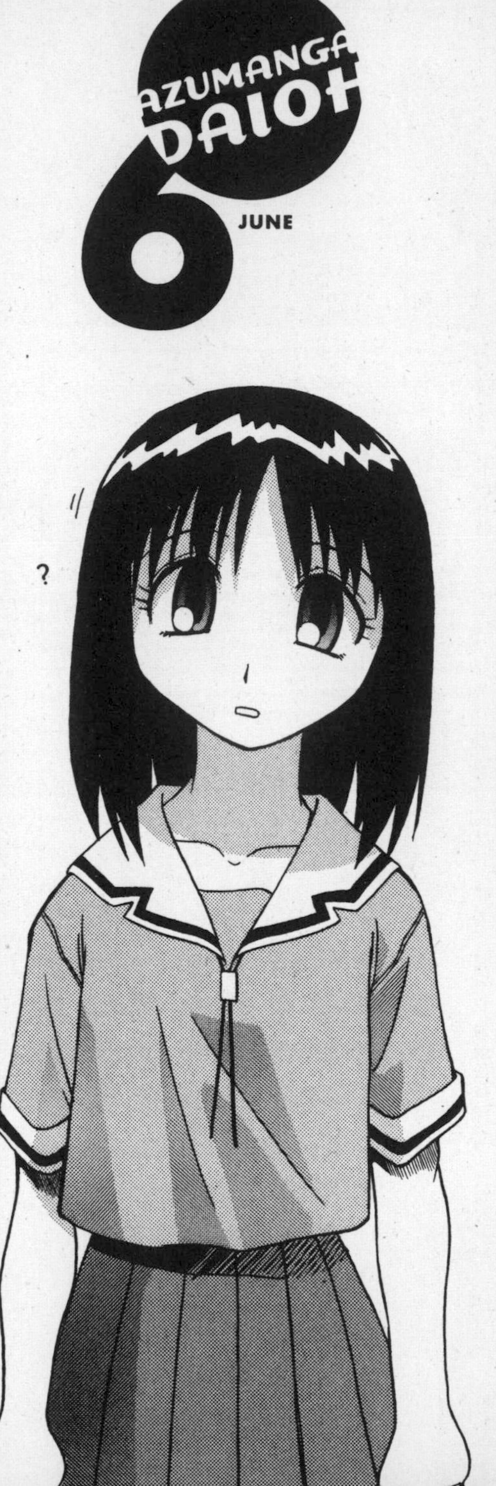
AZUMANGA DAIOH
6
JUNE
?

GROWN UP

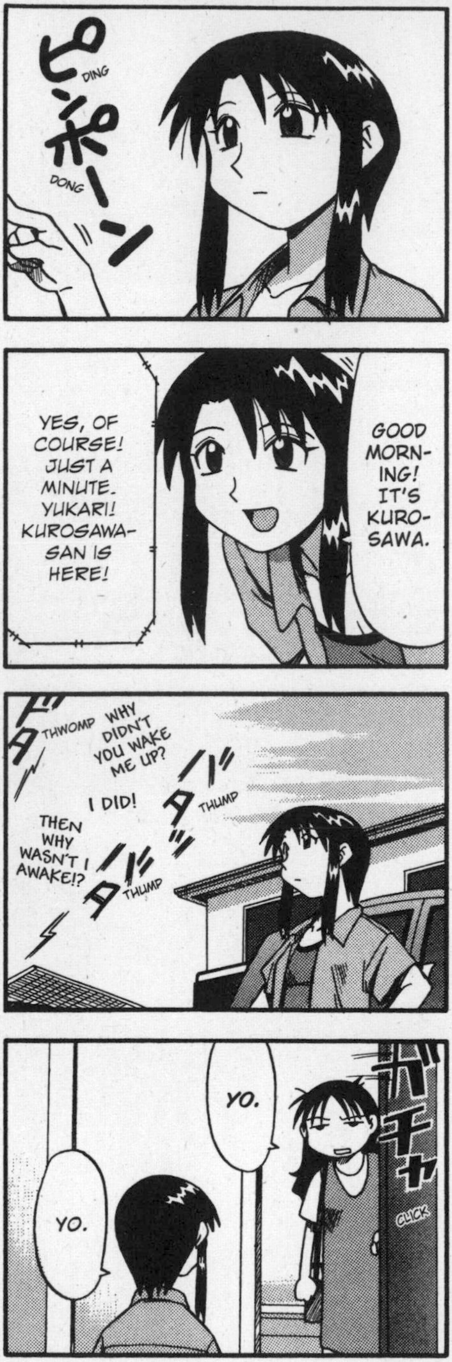
ピンポーン
DING
DONG
GOOD MORNING! IT'S KUROSAWA.
YES, OF COURSE! JUST A MINUTE. YUKARI! KUROSAWA-SAN IS HERE!
WHY DIDN'T YOU WAKE ME UP?
バタッ
THUMP
I DID!
バタ
THUMP
THEN WHY WASN'T I AWAKE!?
ドタ
THWOMP
ガチャ
CLICK
YO.
YO.

COMMUTING

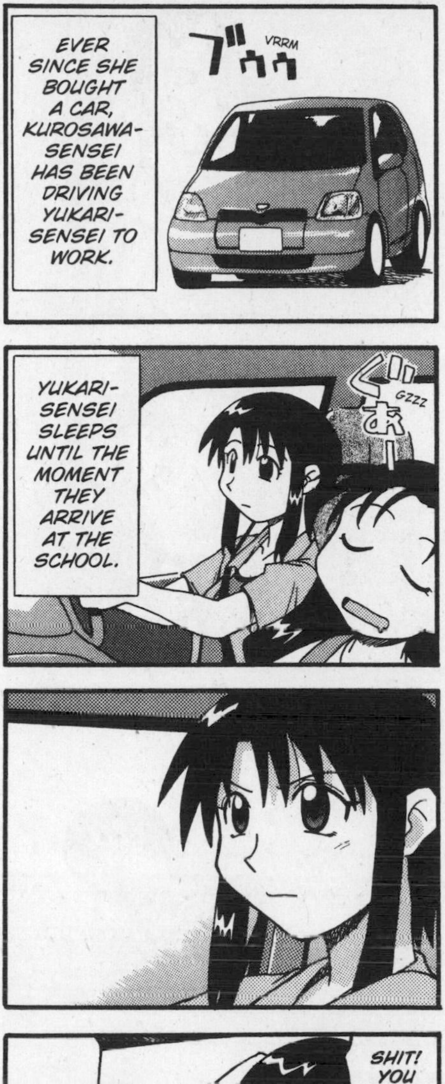
ブウウ VRRM
EVER SINCE SHE BOUGHT A CAR, KUROSAWA-SENSEI HAS BEEN DRIVING YUKARI-SENSEI TO WORK.
ぐぉー GZZZ
YUKARI-SENSEI SLEEPS UNTIL THE MOMENT THEY ARRIVE AT THE SCHOOL.
SHIT! YOU KNOW WHAT? YOU PISS ME OFF SOME-TIMES !!
UUU... WHUT? STOP-PIT!

FRIENDLY

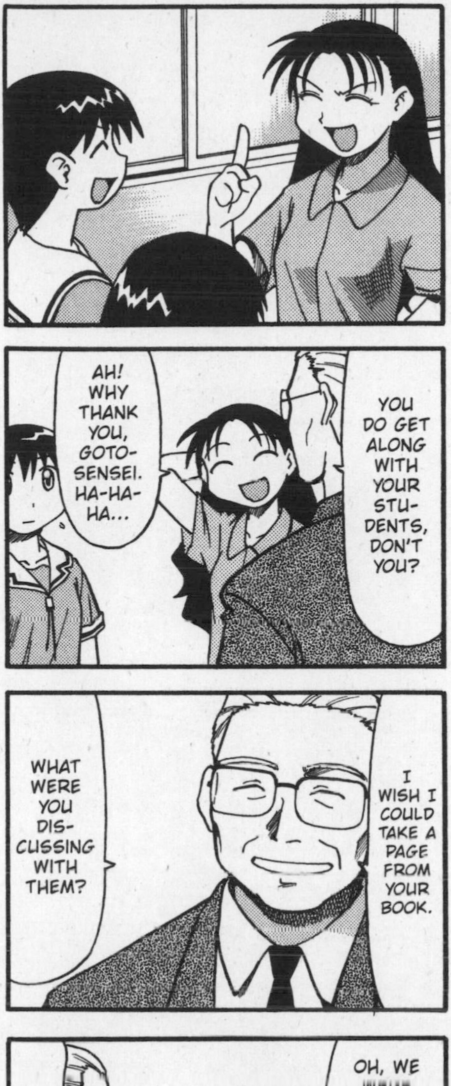
YOU DO GET ALONG WITH YOUR STU-DENTS, DON'T YOU?
AH! WHY THANK YOU, GOTO-SENSEI. HA-HA-HA...
I WISH I COULD TAKE A PAGE FROM YOUR BOOK.
WHAT WERE YOU DIS-CUSSING WITH THEM?
OH, WE WERE JUST ARGUING OVER WHICH BOY IN THE CLASS WE HATE THE MOST.
THAT IS...

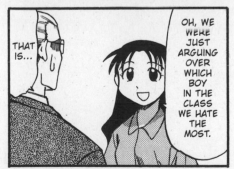

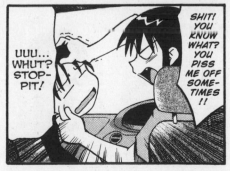

A GENIUS

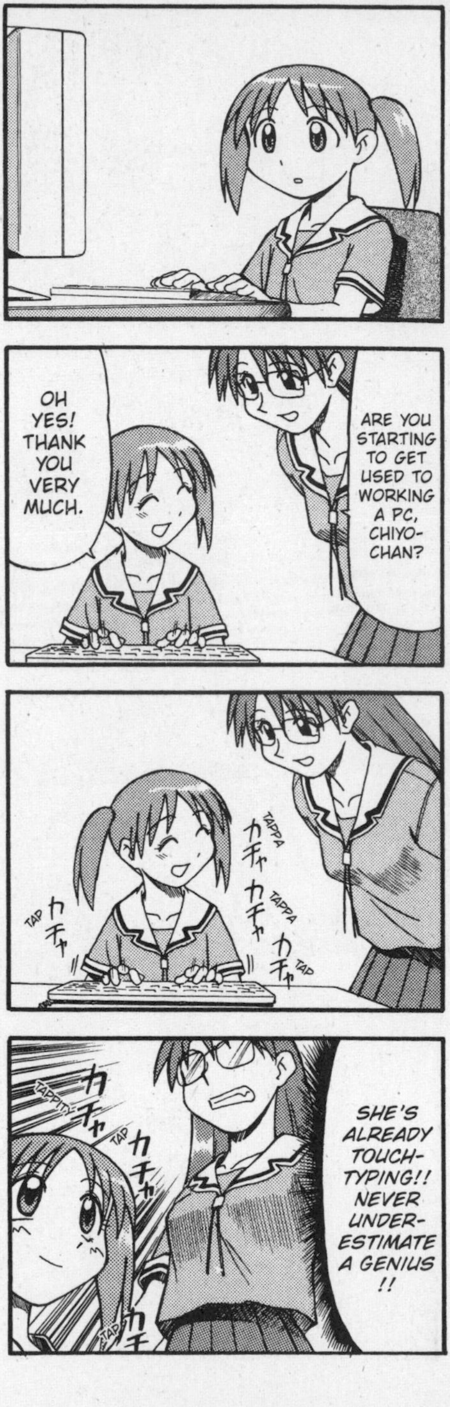
ARE YOU STARTING TO GET USED TO WORKING A PC, CHIYO-CHAN?
OH YES! THANK YOU VERY MUCH.
カチャ TAPPA
カチャ TAPPA
カチャ TAP
カチャ TAP
カチャ TAPPITY
カチャ TAP
カチ TAP
SHE'S ALREADY TOUCH-TYPING!! NEVER UNDER-ESTIMATE A GENIUS!!

HIGH SCHOOL POOL

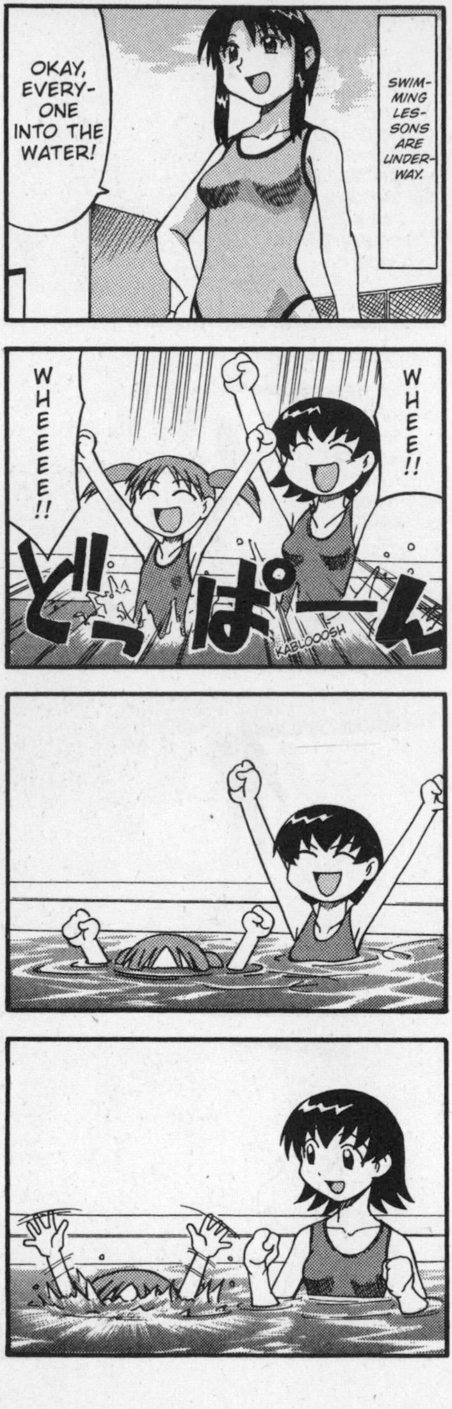
SWIMMING LESSONS ARE UNDERWAY.
OKAY, EVERYONE INTO THE WATER!
WHEE!!
WHEEEEE!!
どっぱーん
KABLOOOSH

IMAGINATION

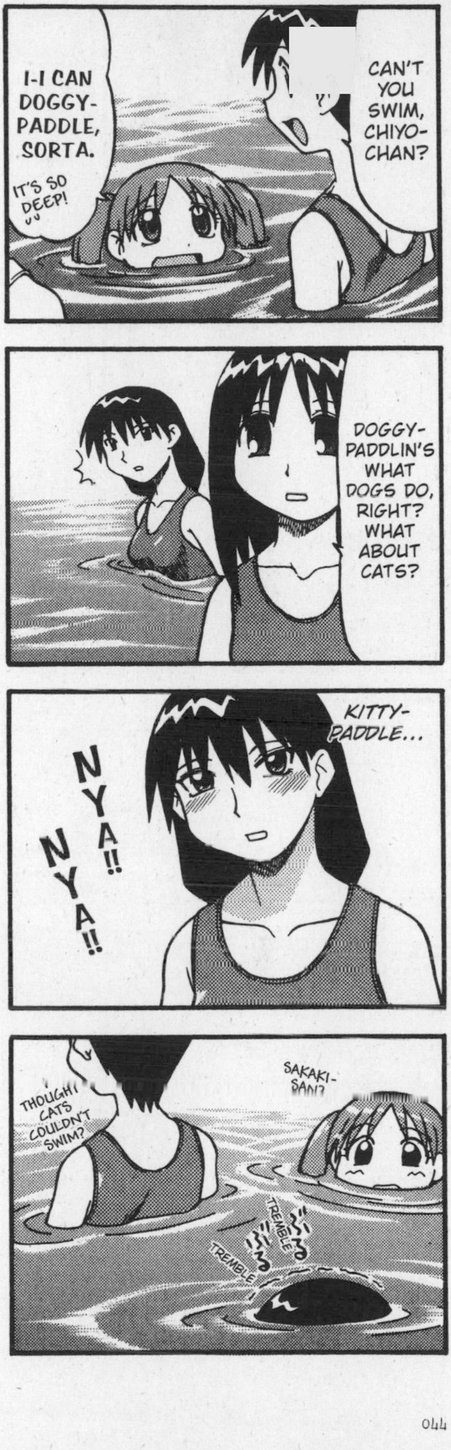
CAN'T YOU SWIM, CHIYO-CHAN?
I-I CAN DOGGY-PADDLE, SORTA.
IT'S SO DEEP!
DOGGY-PADDLIN'S WHAT DOGS DO, RIGHT? WHAT ABOUT CATS?
KITTY-PADDLE...
NYA!!
NYA!!
SAKAKI-SAN!?
THOUGHT CATS COULDN'T SWIM?
TREMBLE
TREMBLE

RIBBONS

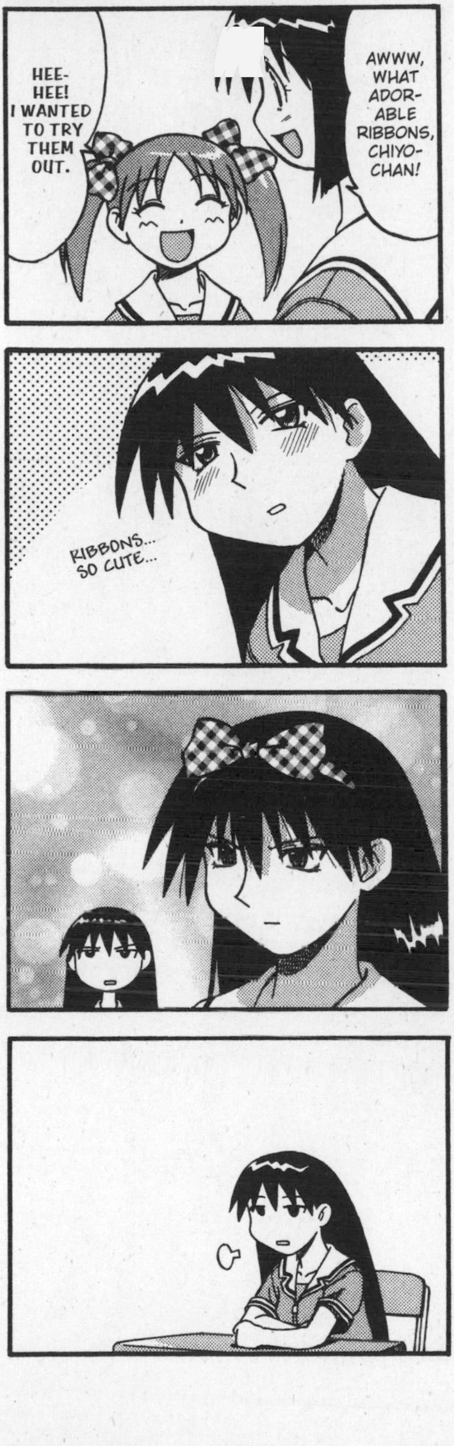
AWWW, WHAT ADOR-ABLE RIBBONS, CHIYO-CHAN!
HEE-HEE! I WANTED TO TRY THEM OUT.
RIBBONS... SO CUTE...

NO FAIR

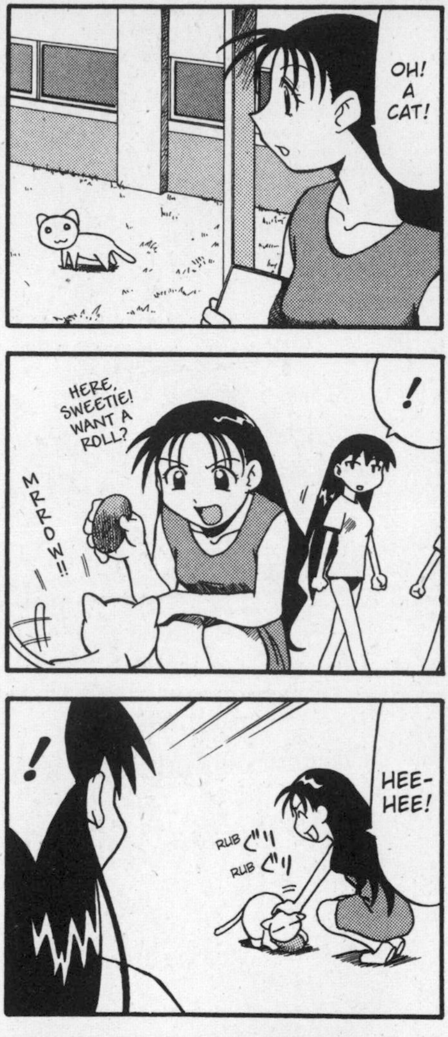
OH! A CAT!
!
HERE, SWEETIE! WANT A ROLL?
MRROW!!
HEE-HEE!
!
RUB ぐり
RUB ぐり
SHE USED BAIT TO CATCH IT!
ARGH...
WHAT'S UP, SAKAKI? YOU LOOK ANGRY.

STILL WANT TO PET IT

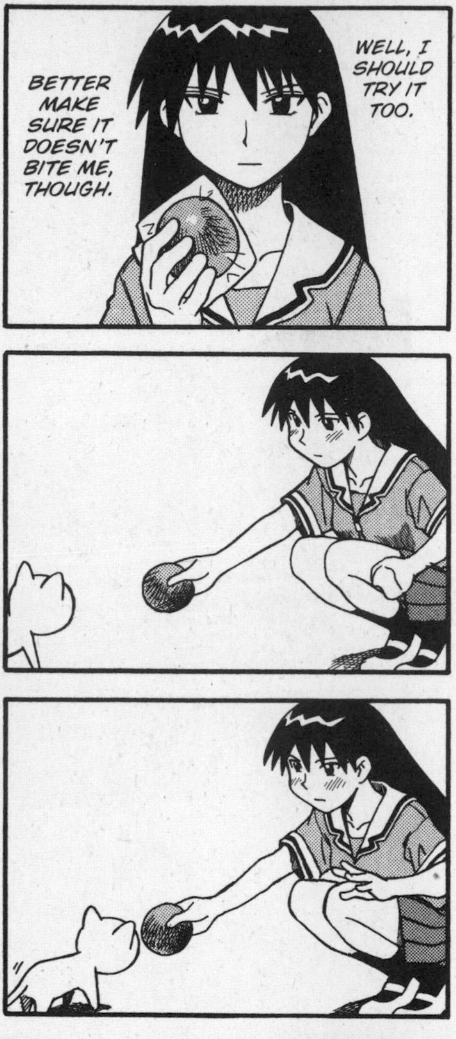
WELL, I SHOULD TRY IT TOO.
BETTER MAKE SURE IT DOESN'T BITE ME, THOUGH.
CHOMP
ぱくっ
しゅっ
ZWEEE

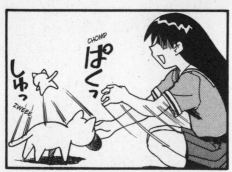

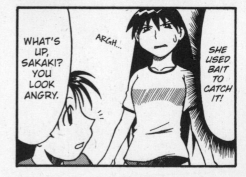

WHAT'LL I DO?

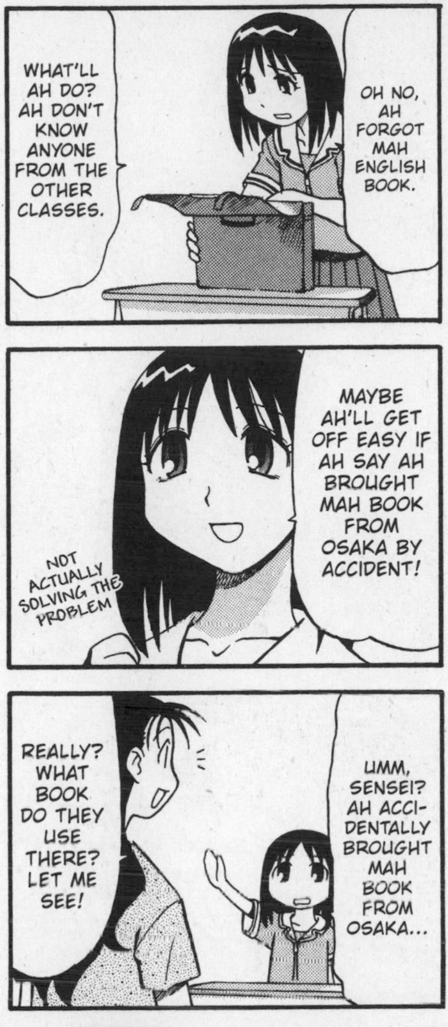
OH NO, AH FORGOT MAH ENGLISH BOOK.
WHAT'LL AH DO? AH DON'T KNOW ANYONE FROM THE OTHER CLASSES.
MAYBE AH'LL GET OFF EASY IF AH SAY AH BROUGHT MAH BOOK FROM OSAKA BY ACCIDENT!
NOT ACTUALLY SOLVING THE PROBLEM
UMM, SENSEI? AH ACCI-DENTALLY BROUGHT MAH BOOK FROM OSAKA...
REALLY? WHAT BOOK DO THEY USE THERE? LET ME SEE!
...... AH... AH DON'T HAVE IT.
HUH?

YES!

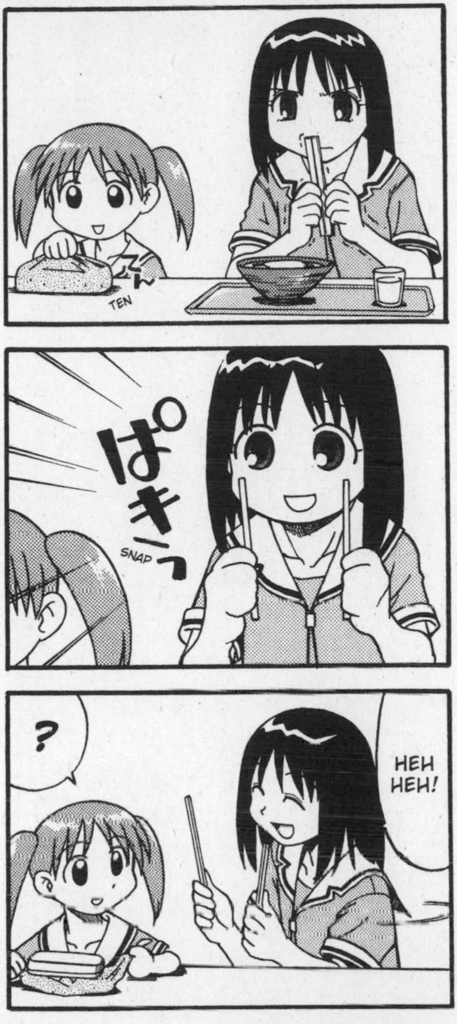
TEN
ぱきっ
SNAP
HEH HEH!
?
HEH HEH!
HMM?
IS SHE HAPPY BECAUSE SHE SPLIT THEM CLEAN-LY?
JUST 'COS OF THAT?

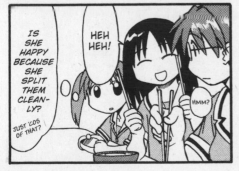

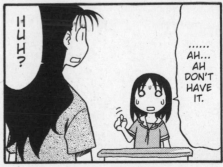

TRAP

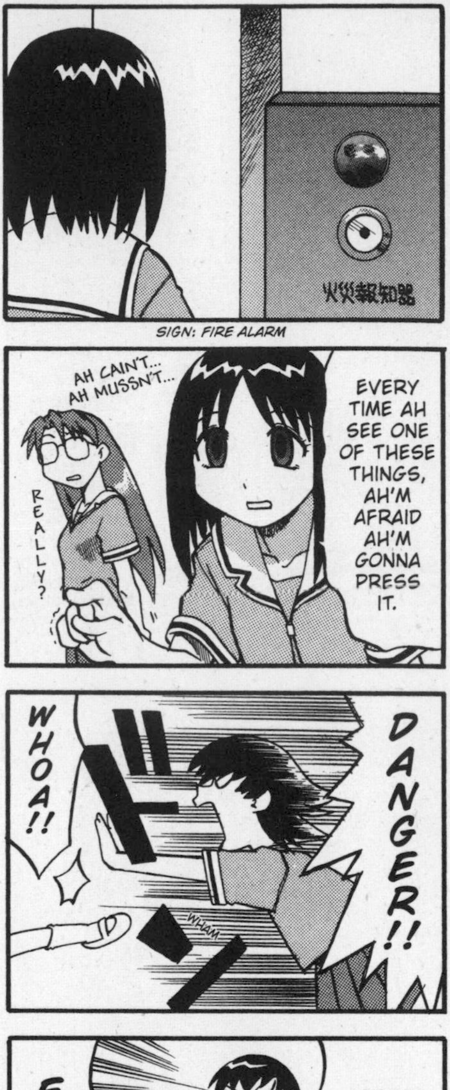
火災報知器
SIGN: FIRE ALARM
EVERY TIME AH SEE ONE OF THESE THINGS, AH'M AFRAID AH'M GONNA PRESS IT.
AH CAIN'T... AH MUSSN'T...
REALLY?
DANGER!!
WHAM
WHOA!!
LEGEND TELLS THAT ONE OF THE SCHOOL'S MANY FIRE ALARMS IS A SELF-DESTRUCT BUTTON!
EEEEEH!?

RUN FOR IT

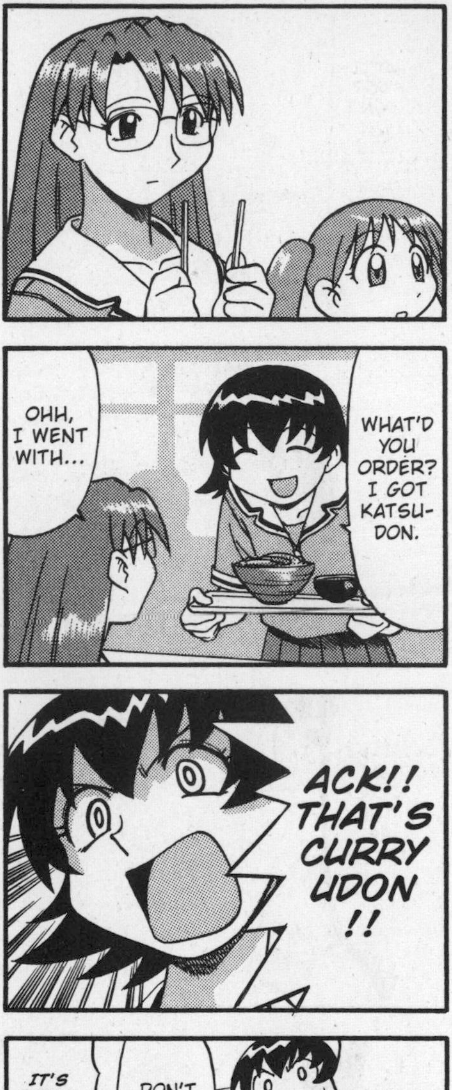
WHAT'D YOU ORDER? I GOT KATSU-DON.
OHH, I WENT WITH...
ACK!! THAT'S CURRY UDON!!
RUN FOR YOUR LIVES! THAT CURRY'S GONNA SPLASH EVERYWHERE!
DON'T WORRY, I'LL BE CAREFUL.
IT'S GONNA SPLASH WHETHER YOU WANT IT TO OR NOT!!

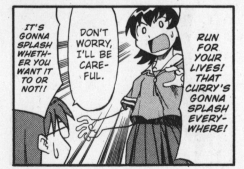

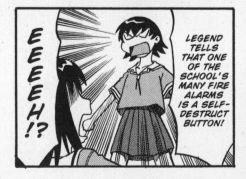

OSAKA

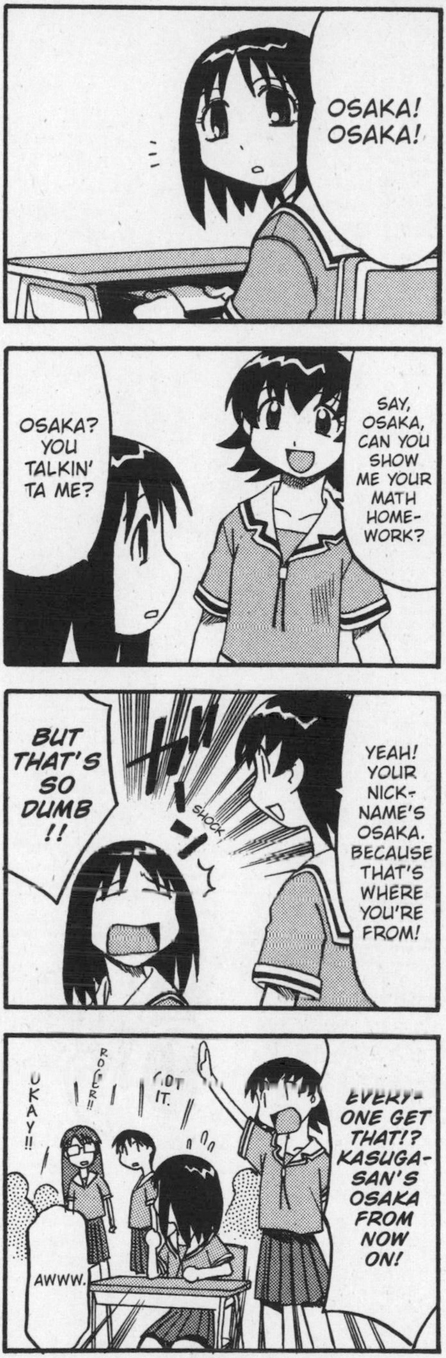
OSAKA! OSAKA!
SAY, OSAKA, CAN YOU SHOW ME YOUR MATH HOME-WORK?
OSAKA? YOU TALKIN' TA ME?
YEAH! YOUR NICK-NAME'S OSAKA. BECAUSE THAT'S WHERE YOU'RE FROM!
SHOCK
BUT THAT'S SO DUMB!!
EVERY-ONE GET THAT!? KASUGA-SAN'S OSAKA FROM NOW ON!
GOT IT.
ROGER!!
OKAY!!
AWWW.

NAMES

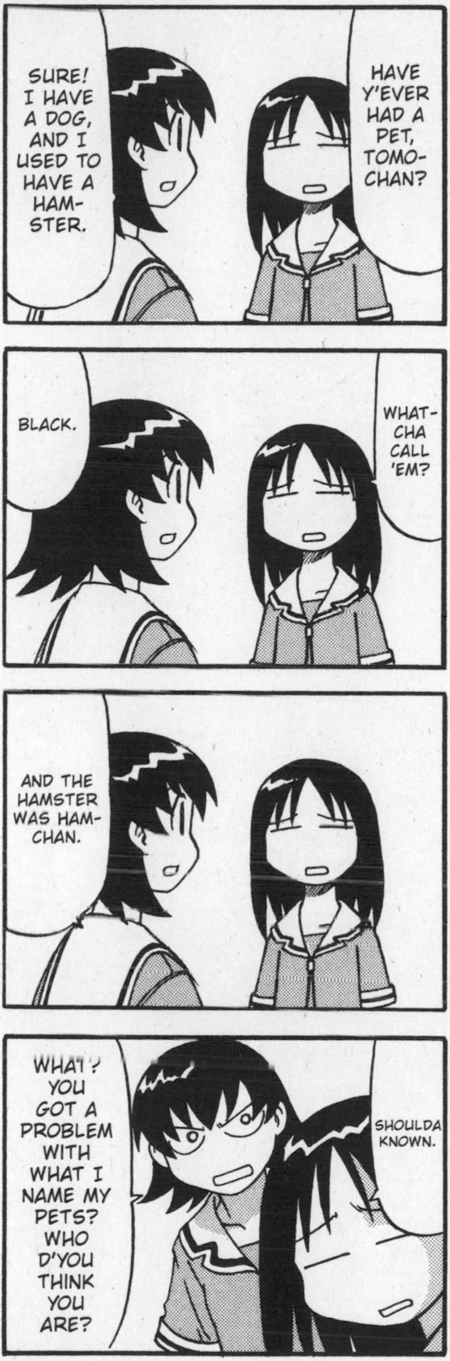
HAVE Y'EVER HAD A PET, TOMO-CHAN?
SURE! I HAVE A DOG, AND I USED TO HAVE A HAM-STER.
WHAT-CHA CALL 'EM?
BLACK.
AND THE HAMSTER WAS HAM-CHAN.
SHOULDA KNOWN.
WHAT? YOU GOT A PROBLEM WITH WHAT I NAME MY PETS? WHO D'YOU THINK YOU ARE?

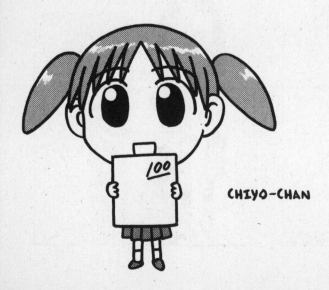

CHIYO-CHAN

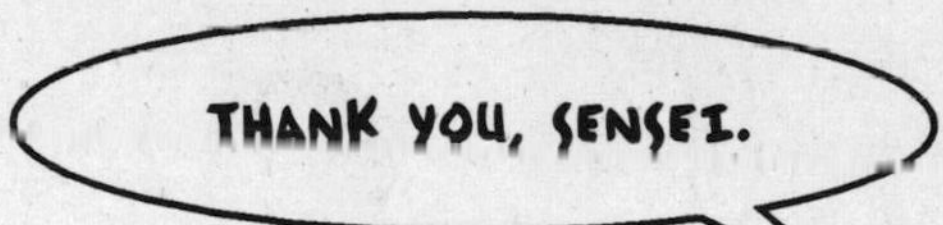
THANK YOU, SENSEI.

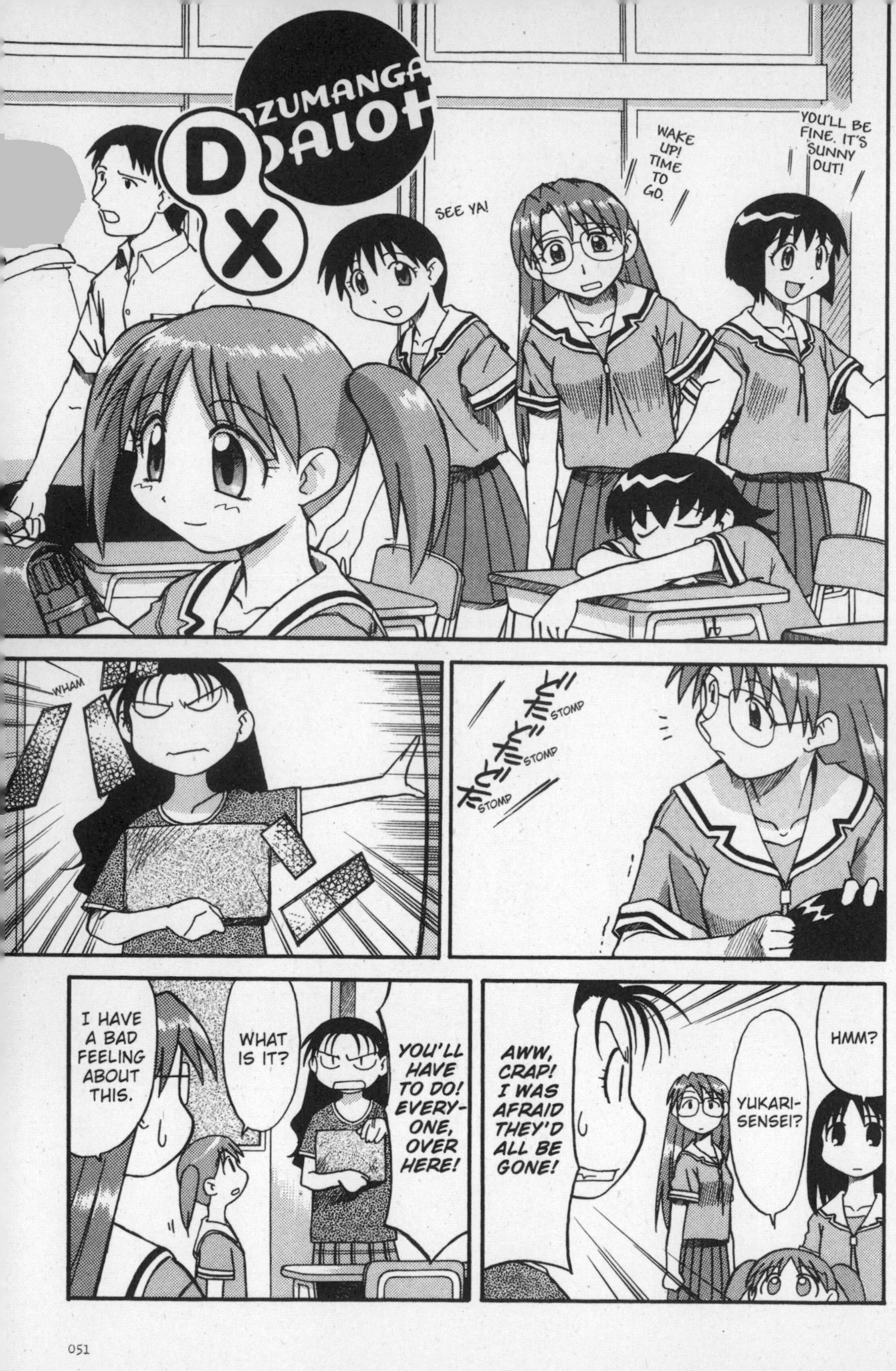
ZUMANGA DAIOH
DX
YOU'LL BE FINE. IT'S SUNNY OUT!
WAKE UP! TIME TO GO.
SEE YA!
STOMP
STOMP
STOMP
WHAM
HMM?
YUKARI-SENSEI?
AWW, CRAP! I WAS AFRAID THEY'D ALL BE GONE!
YOU'LL HAVE TO DO! EVERY-ONE, OVER HERE!
WHAT IS IT?
I HAVE A BAD FEELING ABOUT THIS.

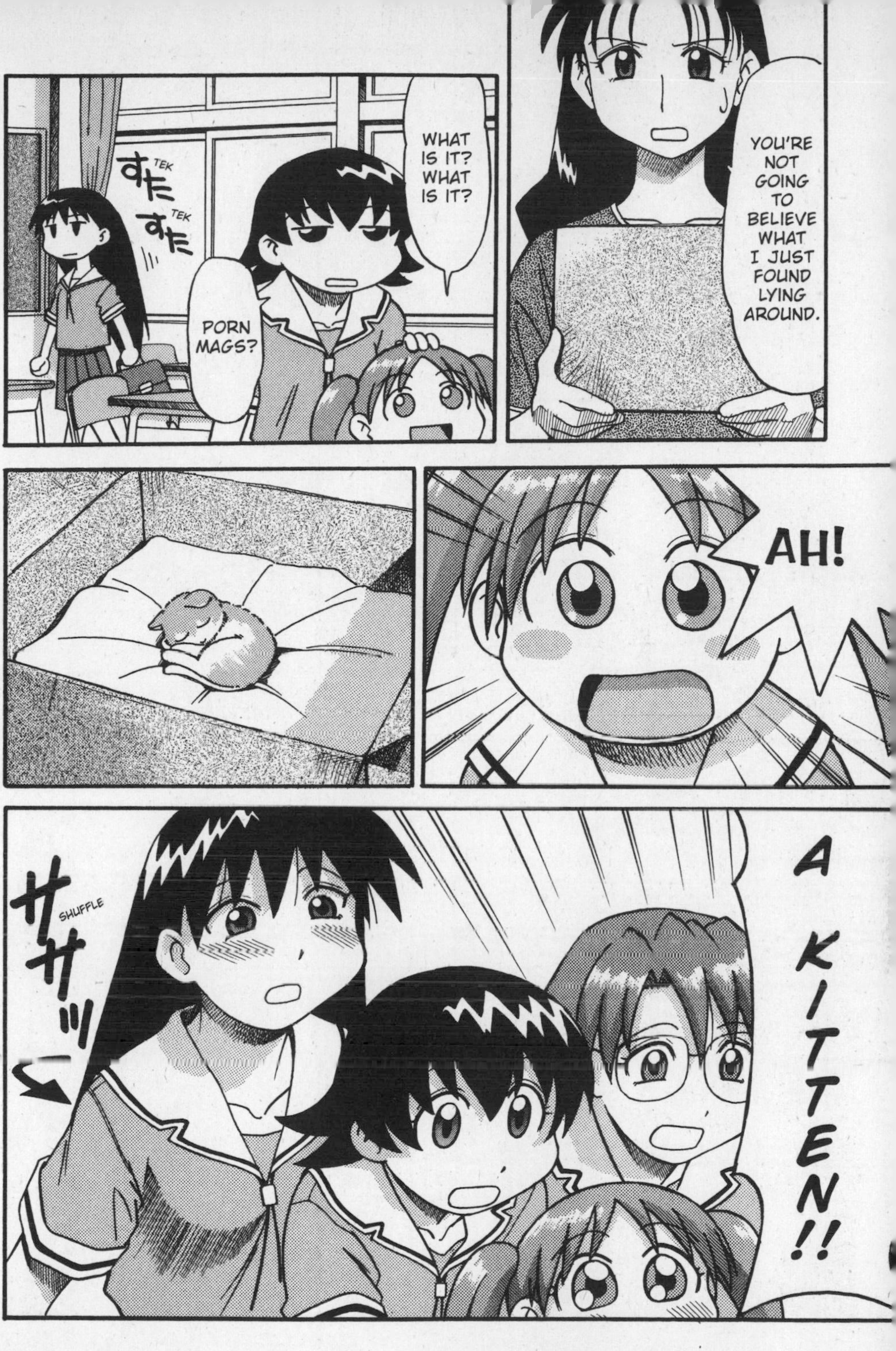
YOU'RE NOT GOING TO BELIEVE WHAT I JUST FOUND LYING AROUND.
WHAT IS IT? WHAT IS IT?
PORN MAGS?
すた TEK すた TEK
AH!
A KITTEN!!
ササッ SHUFFLE

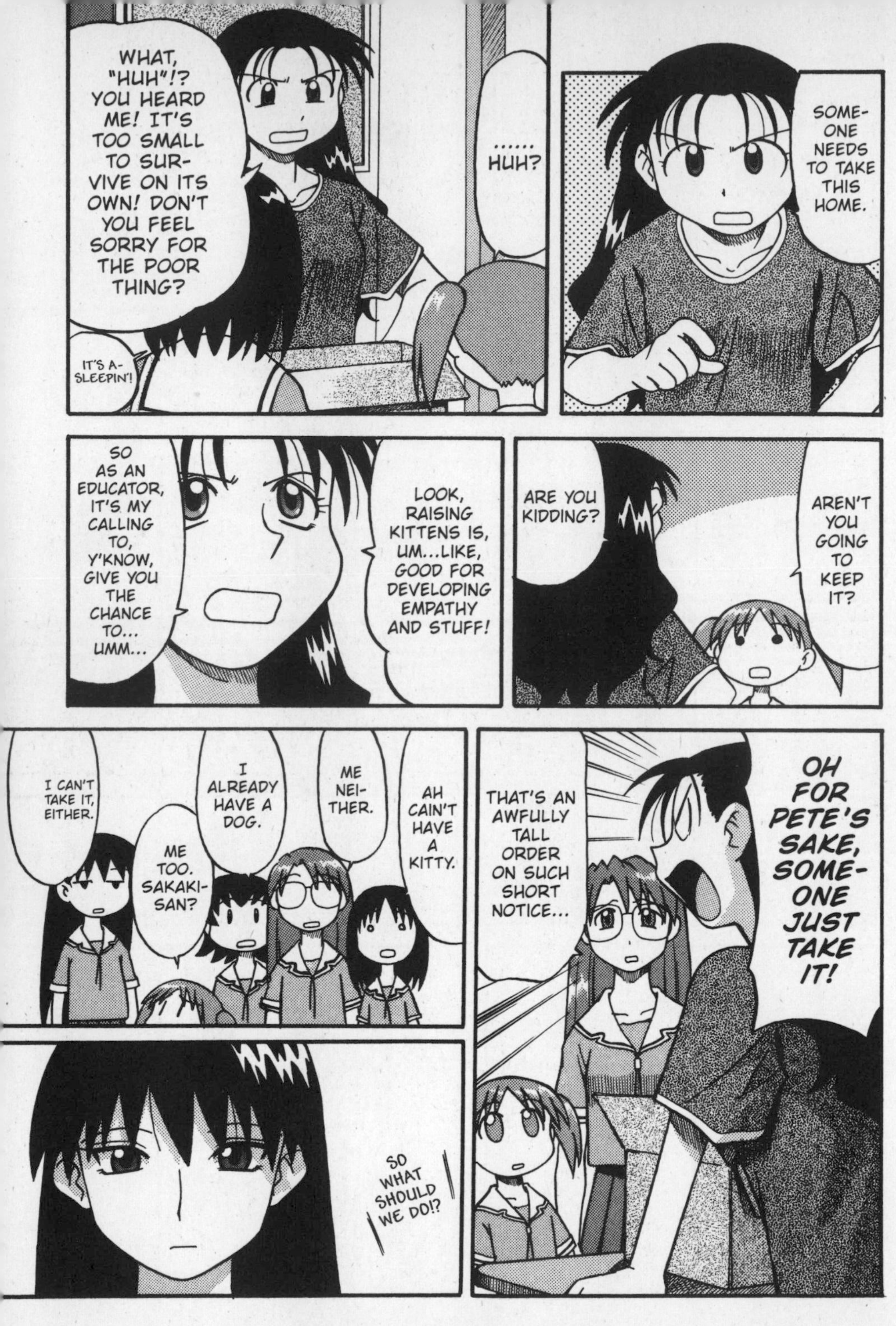
SOME-ONE NEEDS TO TAKE THIS HOME.
......HUH?
WHAT, "HUH"!? YOU HEARD ME! IT'S TOO SMALL TO SUR-VIVE ON ITS OWN! DON'T YOU FEEL SORRY FOR THE POOR THING?
IT'S A-SLEEPIN'!
AREN'T YOU GOING TO KEEP IT?
ARE YOU KIDDING?
LOOK, RAISING KITTENS IS, UM...LIKE, GOOD FOR DEVELOPING EMPATHY AND STUFF!
SO AS AN EDUCATOR, IT'S MY CALLING TO, Y'KNOW, GIVE YOU THE CHANCE TO... UMM...
OH FOR PETE'S SAKE, SOME-ONE JUST TAKE IT!
THAT'S AN AWFULLY TALL ORDER ON SUCH SHORT NOTICE...
AH CAIN'T HAVE A KITTY.
ME NEI-THER.
I ALREADY HAVE A DOG.
ME TOO. SAKAKI-SAN?
I CAN'T TAKE IT, EITHER.
SO WHAT SHOULD WE DO!?

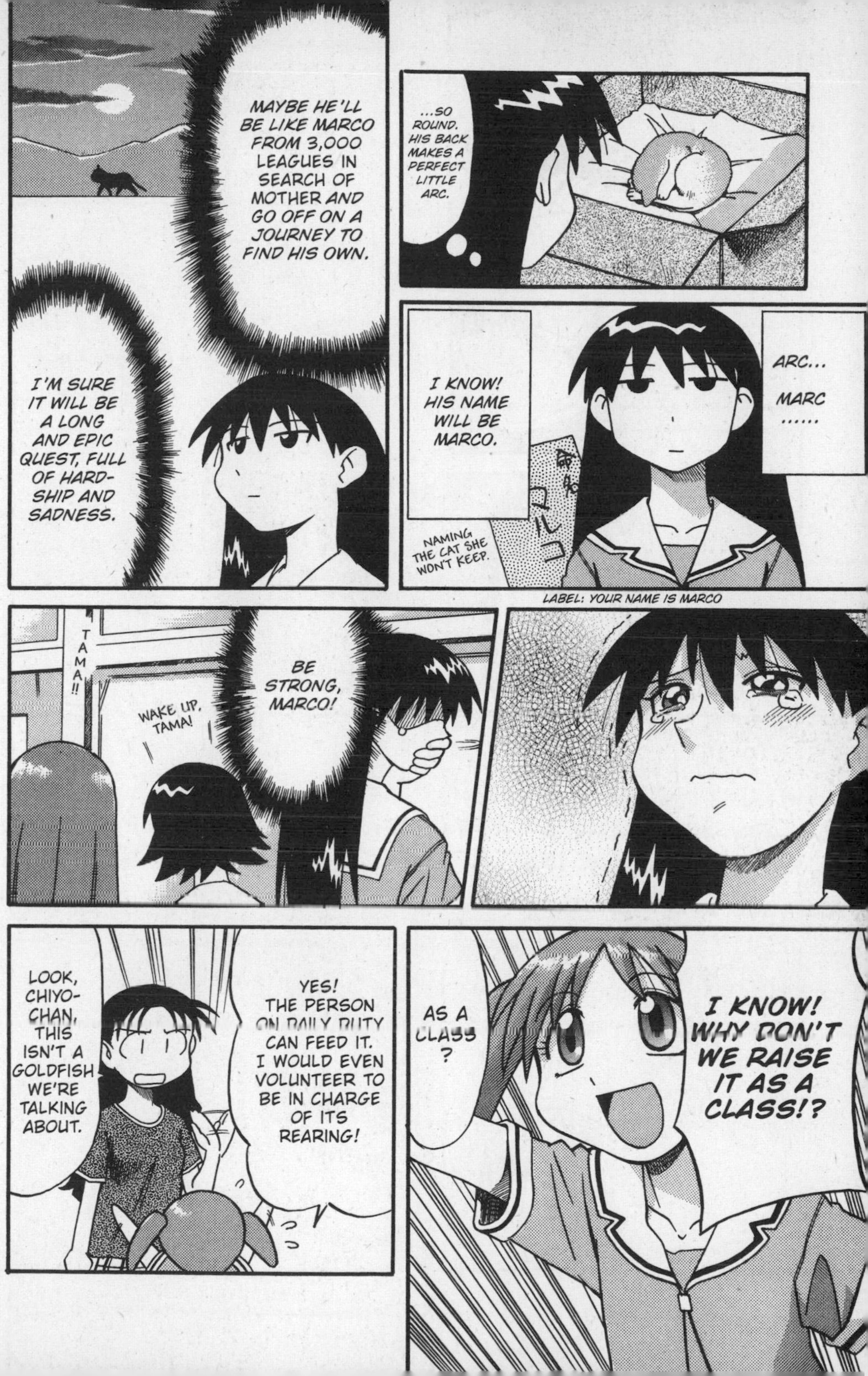
...SO ROUND. HIS BACK MAKES A PERFECT LITTLE ARC.
ARC... MARC ......
I KNOW! HIS NAME WILL BE MARCO.
NAMING THE CAT SHE WON'T KEEP.
LABEL: YOUR NAME IS MARCO
MAYBE HE'LL BE LIKE MARCO FROM 3,000 LEAGUES IN SEARCH OF MOTHER AND GO OFF ON A JOURNEY TO FIND HIS OWN.
I'M SURE IT WILL BE A LONG AND EPIC QUEST, FULL OF HARD-SHIP AND SADNESS.
BE STRONG, MARCO!
WAKE UP, TAMA!
TAMA!!
I KNOW! WHY DON'T WE RAISE IT AS A CLASS!?
AS A CLASS?
YES! THE PERSON ON DAILY DUTY CAN FEED IT. I WOULD EVEN VOLUNTEER TO BE IN CHARGE OF ITS REARING!
LOOK, CHIYO-CHAN, THIS ISN'T A GOLDFISH WE'RE TALKING ABOUT.

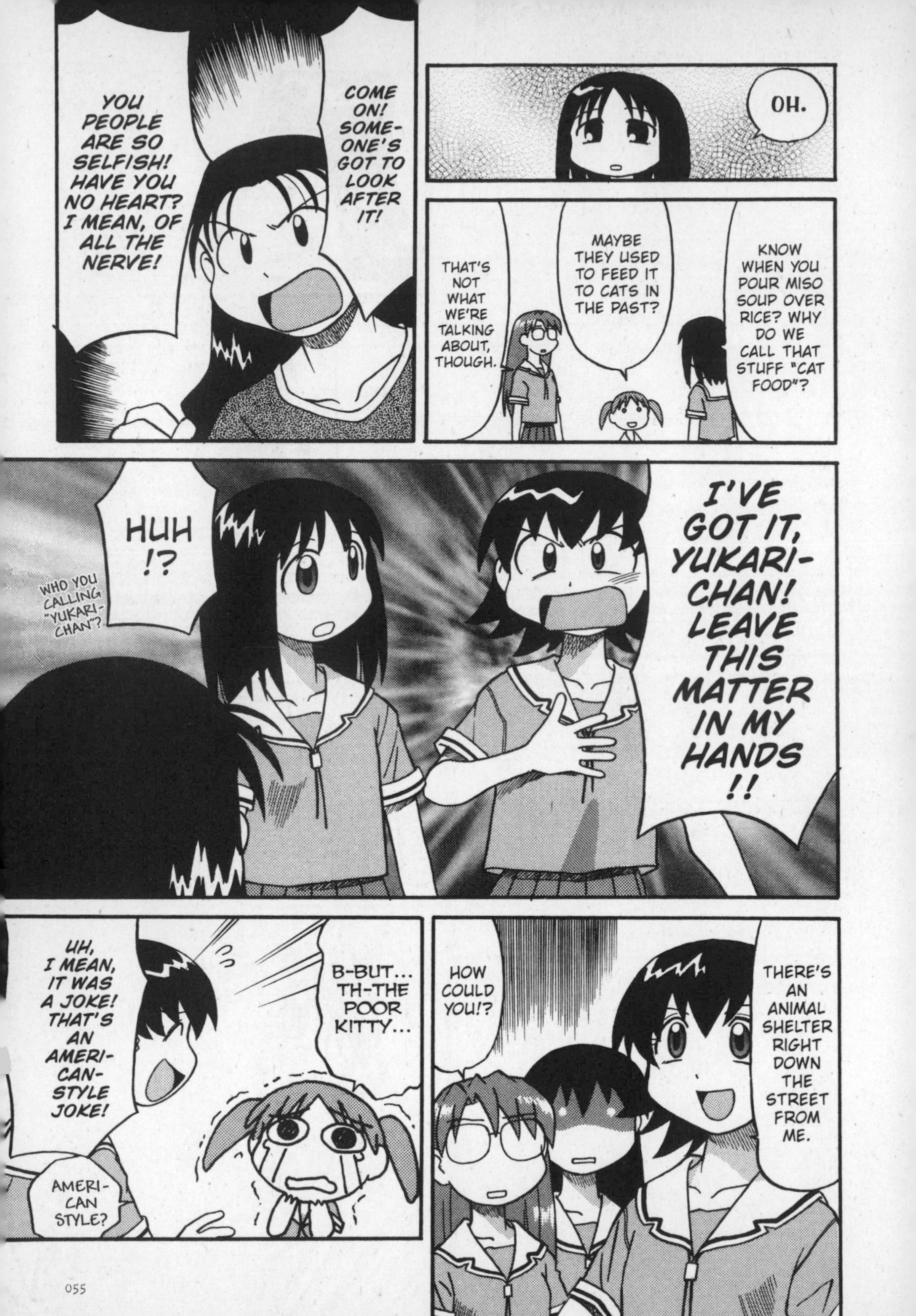

OH.
KNOW WHEN YOU POUR MISO SOUP OVER RICE? WHY DO WE CALL THAT STUFF "CAT FOOD"?
MAYBE THEY USED TO FEED IT TO CATS IN THE PAST?
THAT'S NOT WHAT WE'RE TALKING ABOUT, THOUGH.
COME ON! SOMEONE'S GOT TO LOOK AFTER IT!
YOU PEOPLE ARE SO SELFISH! HAVE YOU NO HEART? I MEAN, OF ALL THE NERVE!
I'VE GOT IT, YUKARI-CHAN! LEAVE THIS MATTER IN MY HANDS!!
HUH!?
WHO YOU CALLING "YUKARI-CHAN"?
THERE'S AN ANIMAL SHELTER RIGHT DOWN THE STREET FROM ME.
HOW COULD YOU!?
B-BUT... TH-THE POOR KITTY...
UH, I MEAN, IT WAS A JOKE! THAT'S AN AMERI-CAN-STYLE JOKE!
AMERI-CAN STYLE?

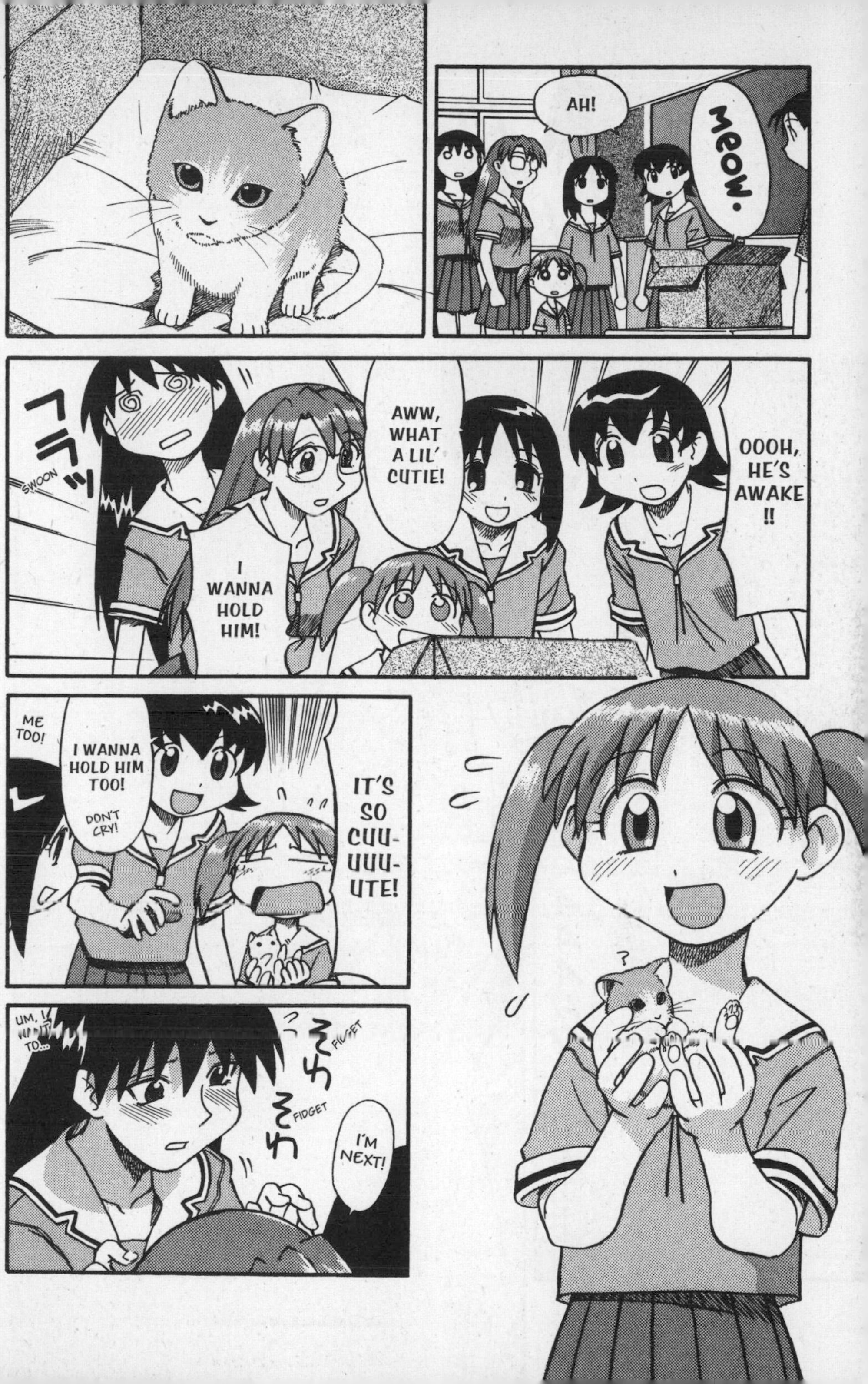
MEOW.
AH!
OOOH, HE'S AWAKE!!
AWW, WHAT A LIL' CUTIE!
フラッ
SWOON
I WANNA HOLD HIM!
IT'S SO CUUUUUUTE!
I WANNA HOLD HIM TOO!
DON'T CRY!
ME TOO!
そわ
FIDGET
そわ
FIDGET
I'M NEXT!
UM, I
TO...

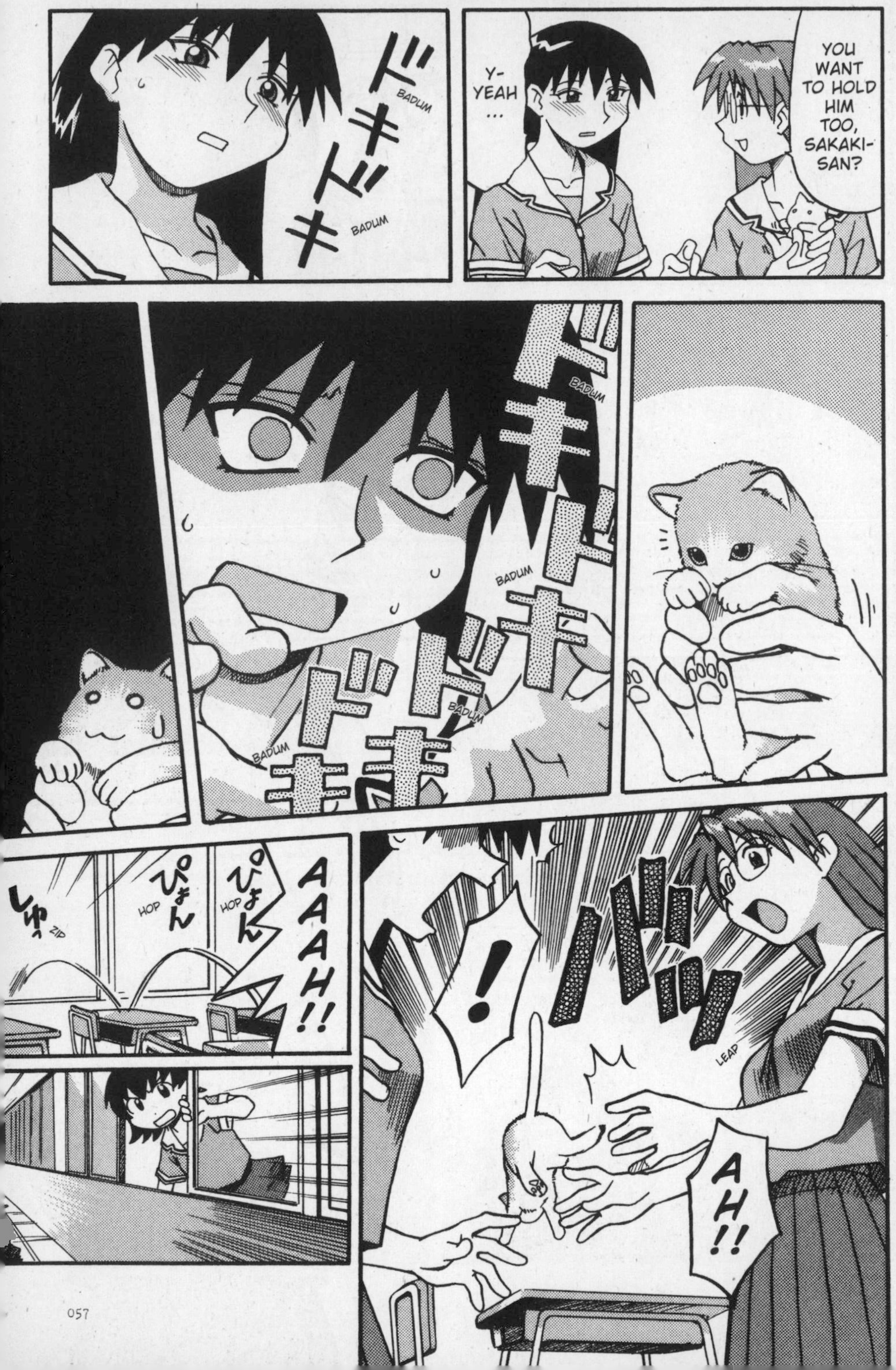
YOU WANT TO HOLD HIM TOO, SAKAKI-SAN?
Y-YEAH ...
ドキドキ
BADUM
BADUM
ドキドキドキドキ
BADUM
BADUM
BADUM
BADUM
!
バッ
LEAP
AH!!
AAAAH!!
ぴょん
HOP
ぴょん
HOP
しゅっ
ZIP

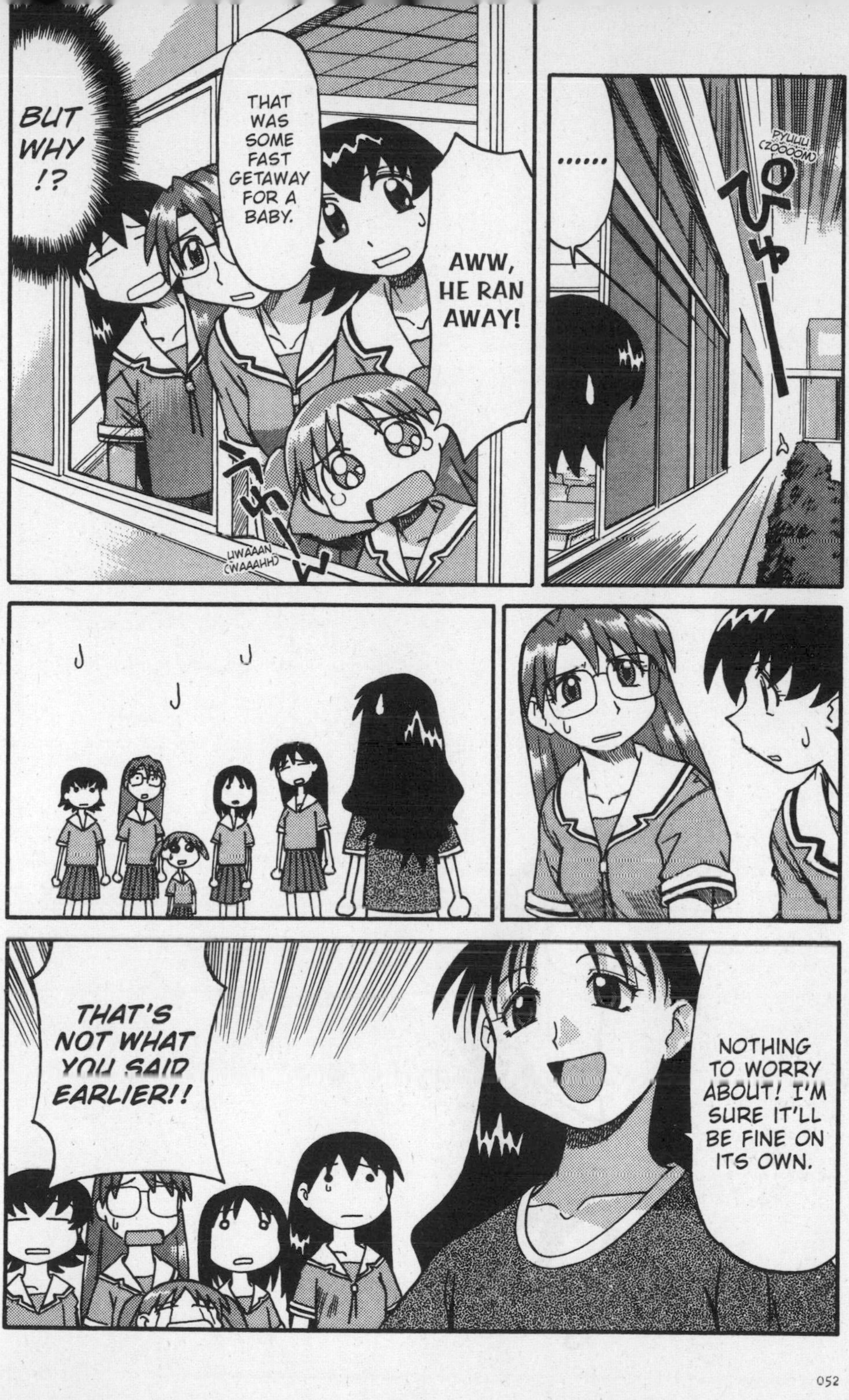
PYUUU (ZOOOOM)
......
AWW, HE RAN AWAY!
THAT WAS SOME FAST GETAWAY FOR A BABY.
BUT WHY !?
UWAAAN (WAAAHH)
NOTHING TO WORRY ABOUT! I'M SURE IT'LL BE FINE ON ITS OWN.
THAT'S NOT WHAT YOU SAID EARLIER!!

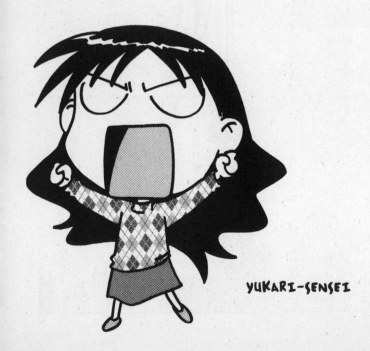

YUKARI-SENSEI

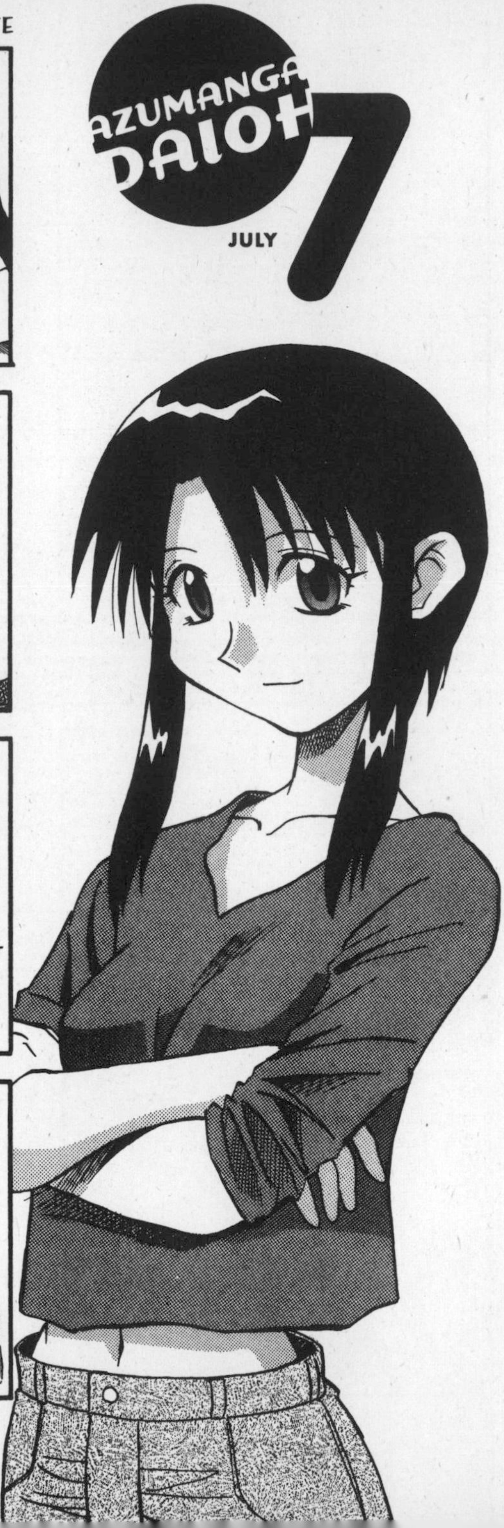
AZUMANGA DAIOH
7
JULY

HATE

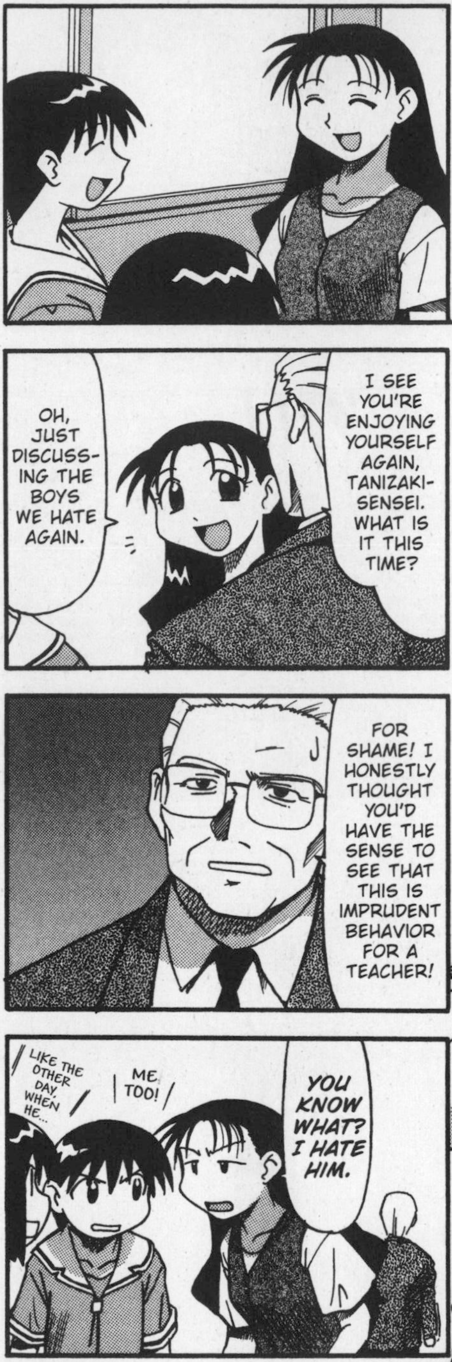
I SEE YOU'RE ENJOYING YOURSELF AGAIN, TANIZAKI-SENSEI. WHAT IS IT THIS TIME?
OH, JUST DISCUSSING THE BOYS WE HATE AGAIN.
FOR SHAME! I HONESTLY THOUGHT YOU'D HAVE THE SENSE TO SEE THAT THIS IS IMPRUDENT BEHAVIOR FOR A TEACHER!
YOU KNOW WHAT? I HATE HIM.
ME, TOO!
LIKE THE OTHER DAY, WHEN HE...

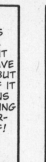

YUKARI-SENSEI GOT SCOLDED

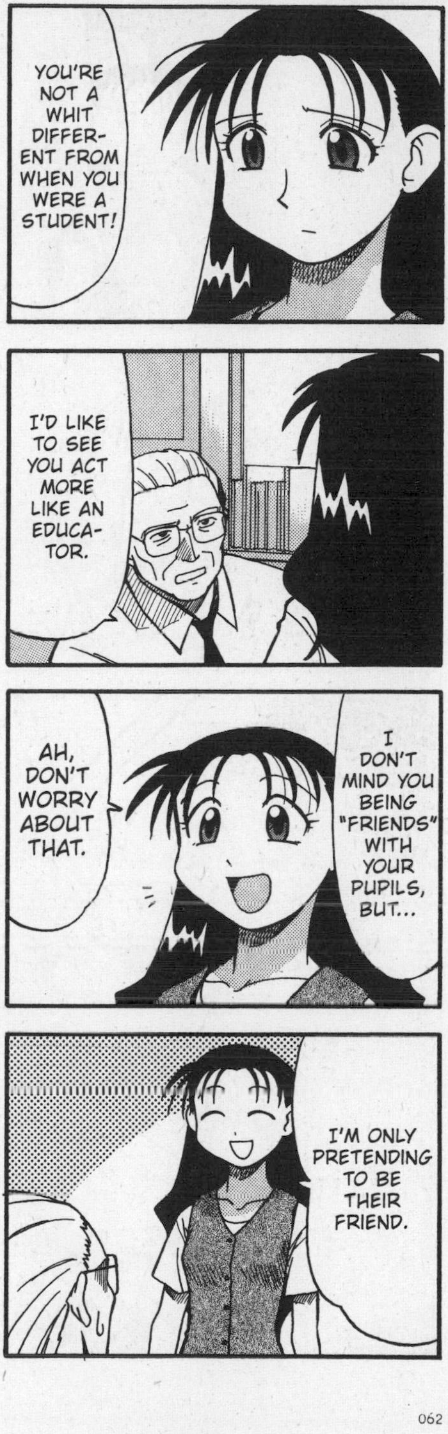
YOU'RE NOT A WHIT DIFFERENT FROM WHEN YOU WERE A STUDENT!
I'D LIKE TO SEE YOU ACT MORE LIKE AN EDUCATOR.
I DON'T MIND YOU BEING "FRIENDS" WITH YOUR PUPILS, BUT...
AH, DON'T WORRY ABOUT THAT.
I'M ONLY PRETENDING TO BE THEIR FRIEND.

KUROSAWA-SENSEI SCOLDS

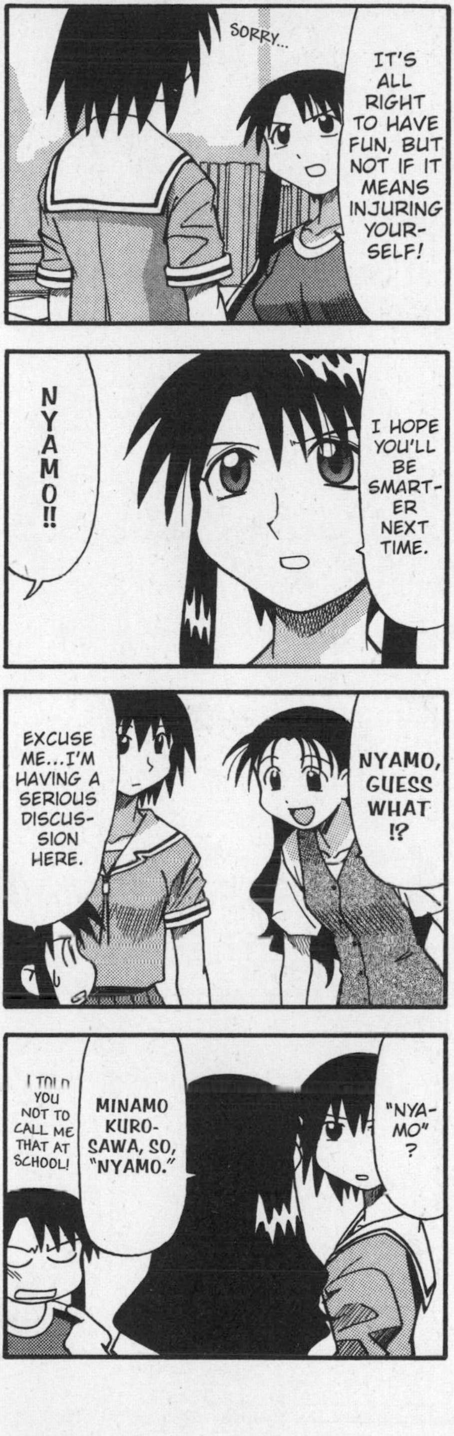
IT'S ALL RIGHT TO HAVE FUN, BUT NOT IF IT MEANS INJURING YOURSELF!
SORRY...
I HOPE YOU'LL BE SMARTER NEXT TIME.
NYAMO!!
NYAMO, GUESS WHAT!?
EXCUSE ME...I'M HAVING A SERIOUS DISCUSSION HERE.
"NYAMO"?
MINAMO KUROSAWA, SO, "NYAMO."
I TOLD YOU NOT TO CALL ME THAT AT SCHOOL!

YUKARI'S DRIVING

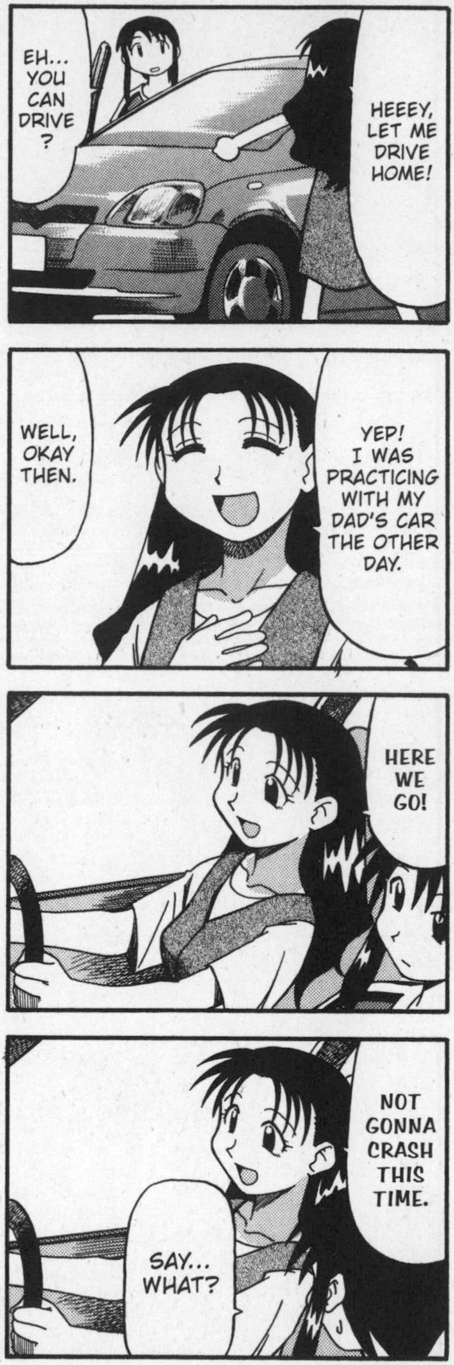
HEEEY, LET ME DRIVE HOME!
EH... YOU CAN DRIVE ?
YEP! I WAS PRACTICING WITH MY DAD'S CAR THE OTHER DAY.
WELL, OKAY THEN.
HERE WE GO!
NOT GONNA CRASH THIS TIME.
SAY... WHAT?

DENIED

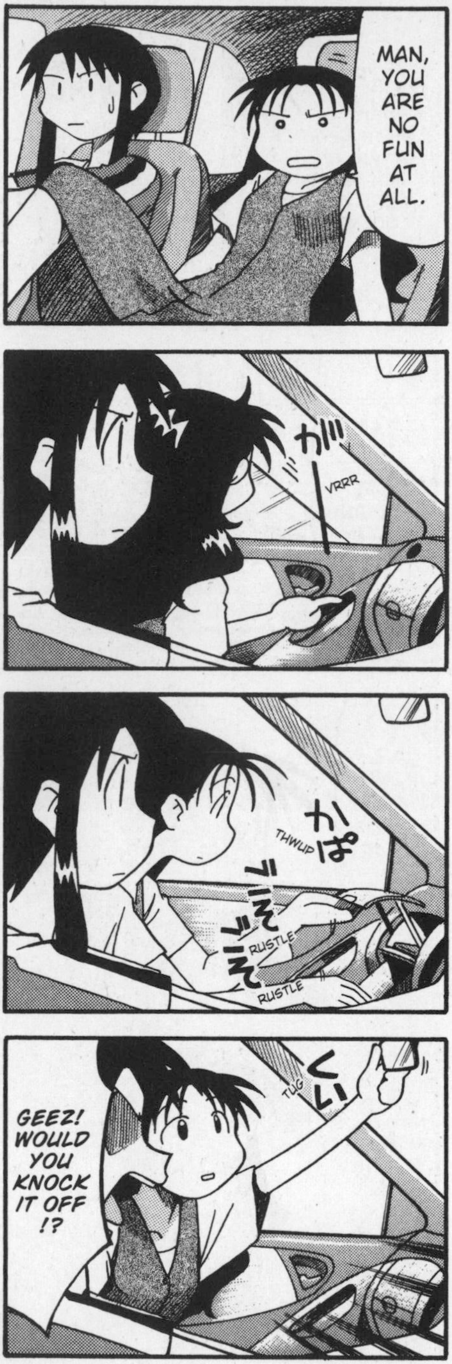
MAN, YOU ARE NO FUN AT ALL.
VRRR
かぱ
THWUP
RUSTLE
RUSTLE
くい
TUG
GEEZ! WOULD YOU KNOCK IT OFF !?

P.E. VOLLEYBALL

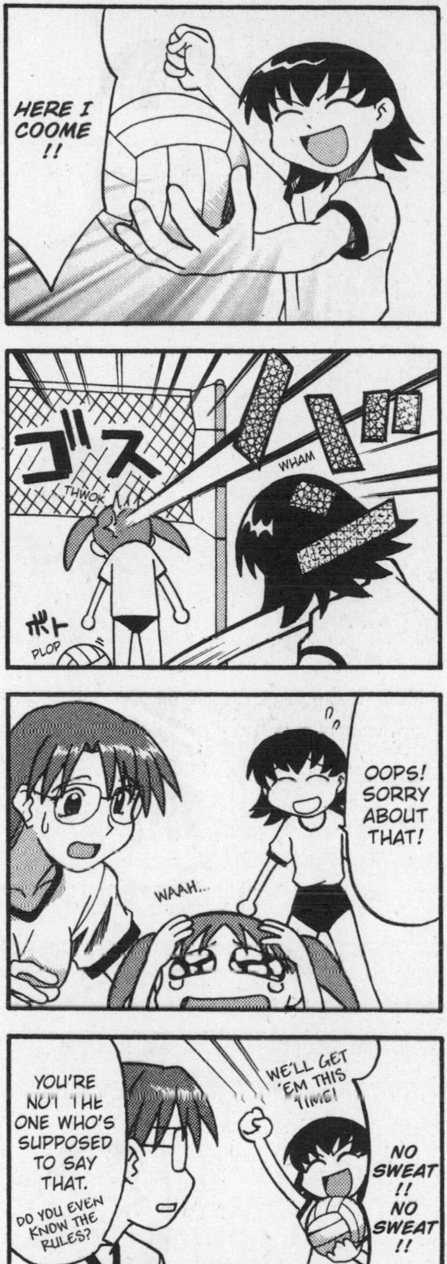
HERE I COOME !!
バッ
WHAM
ゴス
THWOK
ボト
PLOP
OOPS! SORRY ABOUT THAT!
WAAH...
WE'LL GET 'EM THIS TIME!
NO SWEAT !! NO SWEAT !!
YOU'RE NOT THE ONE WHO'S SUPPOSED TO SAY THAT.
DO YOU EVEN KNOW THE RULES?
YOU'RE DONE SERVING.

RIVAL!?

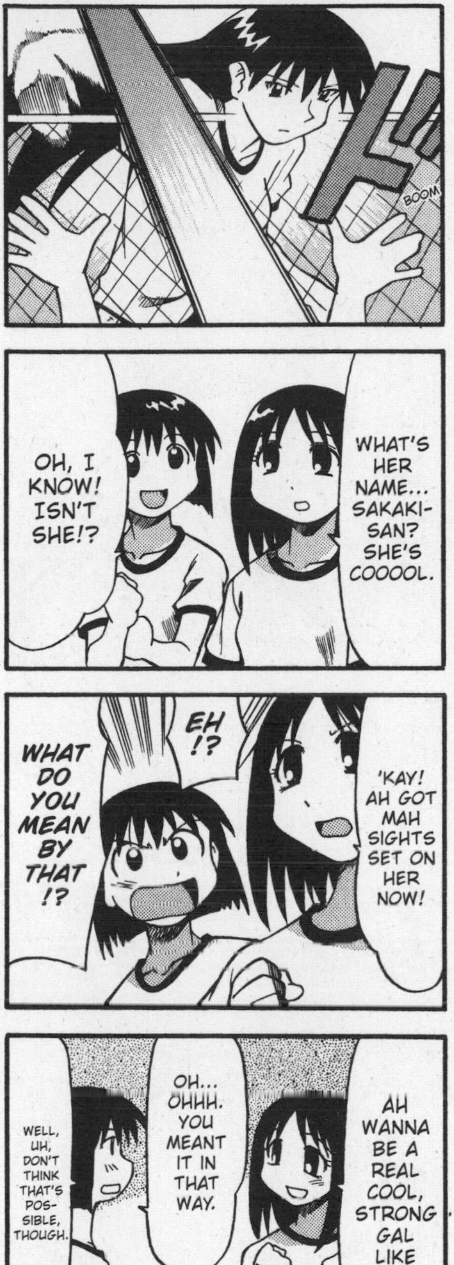
ドッ
BOOM
WHAT'S HER NAME... SAKAKI-SAN? SHE'S COOOOL.
OH, I KNOW! ISN'T SHE!?
'KAY! AH GOT MAH SIGHTS SET ON HER NOW!
EH !?
WHAT DO YOU MEAN BY THAT !?
AH WANNA BE A REAL COOL, STRONG GAL LIKE HER.
OH... OHHH. YOU MEANT IT IN THAT WAY.
WELL, UH, DON'T THINK THAT'S POS-SIBLE, THOUGH.

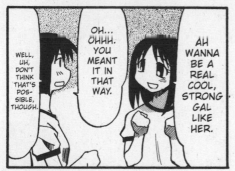

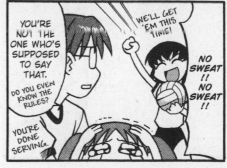

SCARED ME

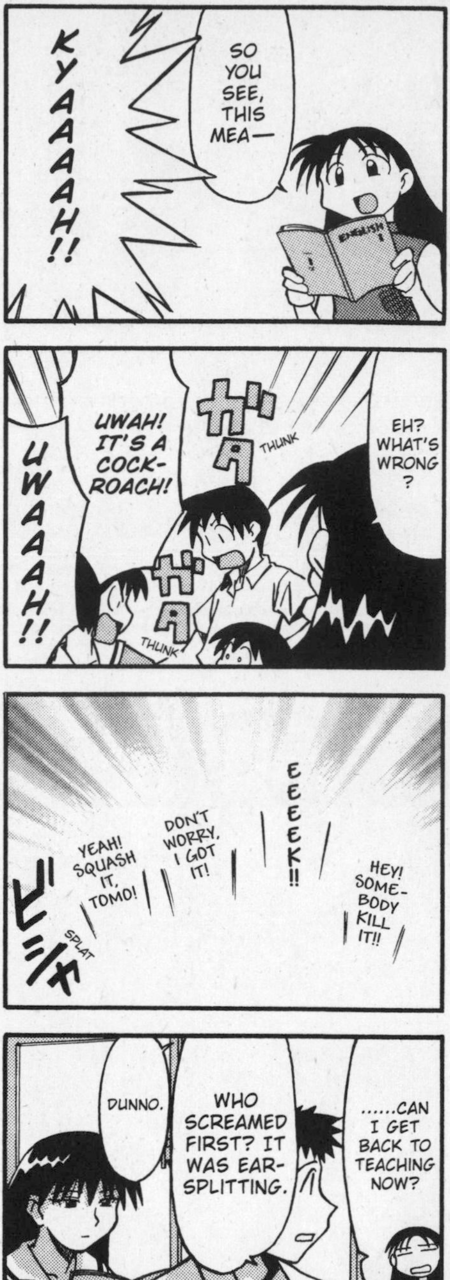
SO YOU SEE, THIS MEA—
KYAAAAAH!!
EH? WHAT'S WRONG?
THUNK
ガタ
UWAH! IT'S A COCKROACH!
UWAAAAAH!!
ガタ
THUNK
HEY! SOMEBODY KILL IT!!
EEEEK!!
DON'T WORRY, I GOT IT!
YEAH! SQUASH IT, TOMO!
ビシャ
SPLAT
......CAN I GET BACK TO TEACHING NOW?
WHO SCREAMED FIRST? IT WAS EAR-SPLITTING.
DUNNO.

WEAPON

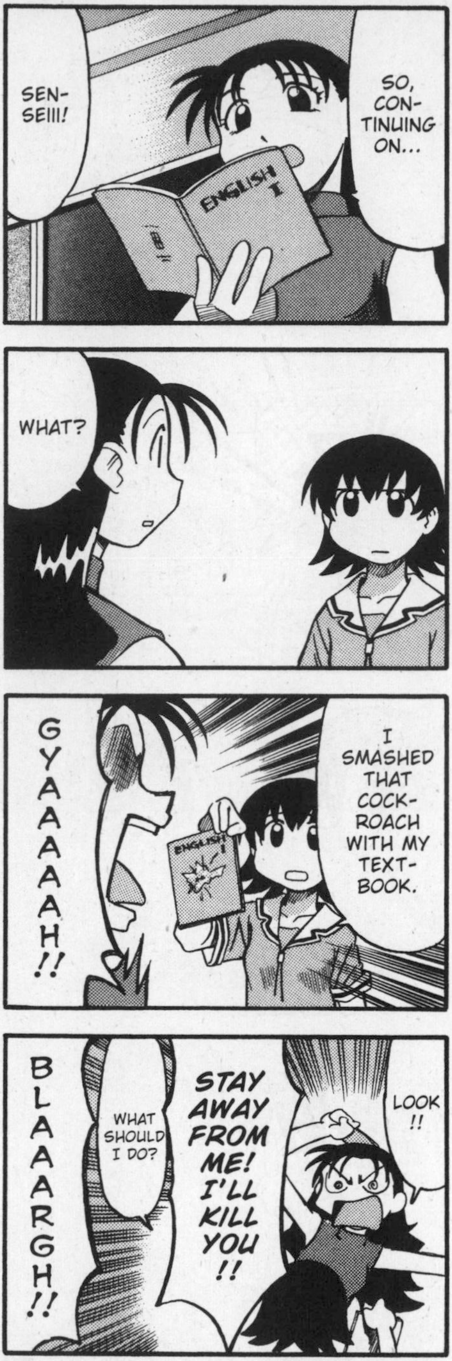
SO, CONTINUING ON...
SEN-SEIII!
ENGLISH I
WHAT?
I SMASHED THAT COCKROACH WITH MY TEXTBOOK.
ENGLISH I
GYAAAAAAH!!
LOOK!!
STAY AWAY FROM ME! I'LL KILL YOU!!
WHAT SHOULD I DO?
BLAAAARGH!!

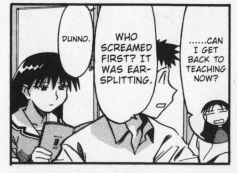

NOT OSAKA

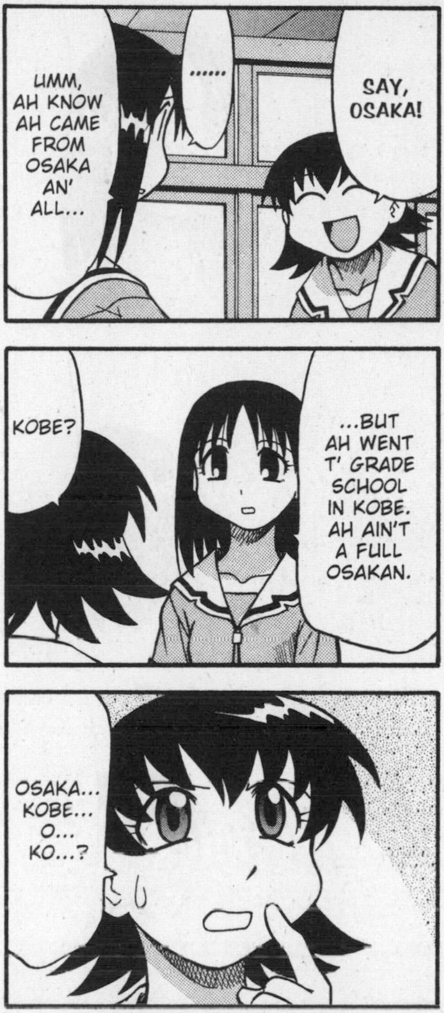
SAY, OSAKA!
......
UMM, AH KNOW AH CAME FROM OSAKA AN' ALL...
...BUT AH WENT T' GRADE SCHOOL IN KOBE. AH AIN'T A FULL OSAKAN.
KOBE?
OSAKA... KOBE... O... KO...?
BUT AH WAS ACTUALLY BORN IN WAKA-YAMA.
I'VE NEVER EVEN HEARD OF WAKA-YAMA!
YOU'RE FROM OSAKA, OKAY!!?

CHOO-CHOO CHRAIN

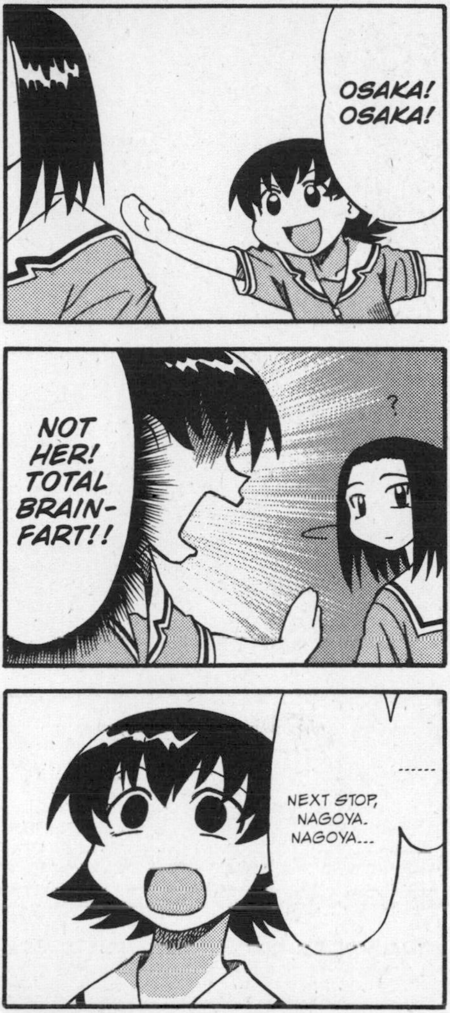
OSAKA! OSAKA!
NOT HER! TOTAL BRAIN-FART!!
?
......
NEXT STOP, NAGOYA. NAGOYA...
TRAIN IS PREPAR-ING TO LEAVE.
PLEASE STAND WELL BEHIND THE WHITE LINE.
UHH..

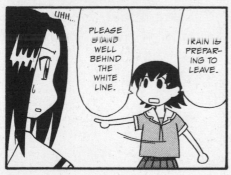

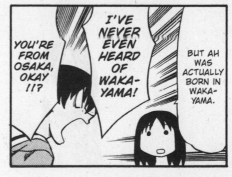

PUNISHMENT

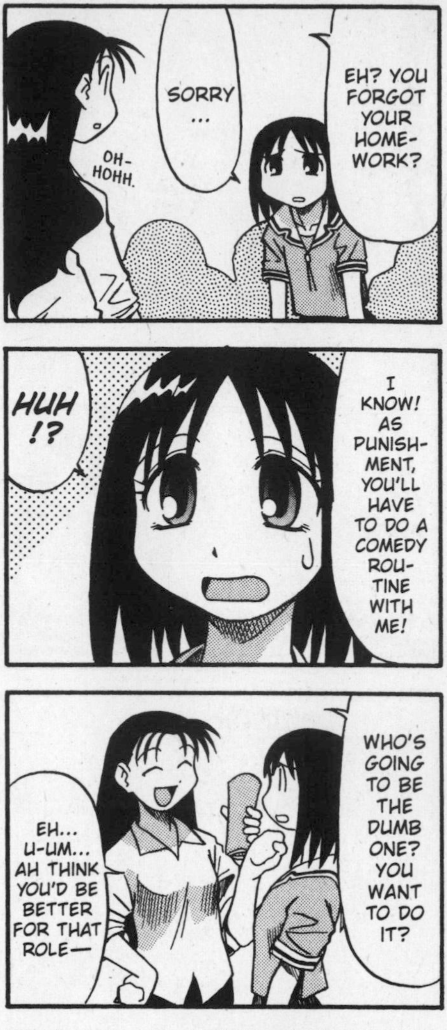
EH? YOU FORGOT YOUR HOMEWORK?
SORRY ...
OH-HOHH.
I KNOW! AS PUNISHMENT, YOU'LL HAVE TO DO A COMEDY ROUTINE WITH ME!
HUH!?
WHO'S GOING TO BE THE DUMB ONE? YOU WANT TO DO IT?
EH... U-UM... AH THINK YOU'D BE BETTER FOR THAT ROLE—
HOW DARE YOU CALL ME DUMB!?
THWAP
HAVE THEY ALREADY STARTED?

PAIRS

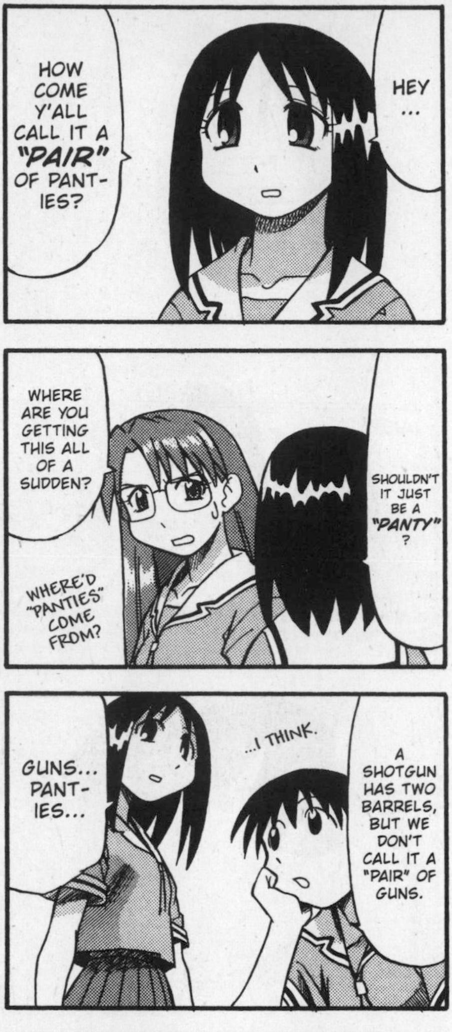
HEY ...
HOW COME Y'ALL CALL IT A "PAIR" OF PANTIES?
SHOULDN'T IT JUST BE A "PANTY"?
WHERE ARE YOU GETTING THIS ALL OF A SUDDEN?
WHERE'D "PANTIES" COME FROM?
A SHOTGUN HAS TWO BARRELS, BUT WE DON'T CALL IT A "PAIR" OF GUNS.
...I THINK.
GUNS... PANTIES...
WHAT'S THE CONNECTION?
PLEASE, JUST SHUT UP.

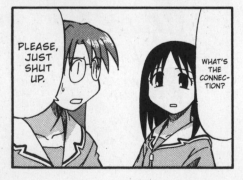

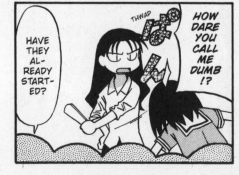

NOT FAIR

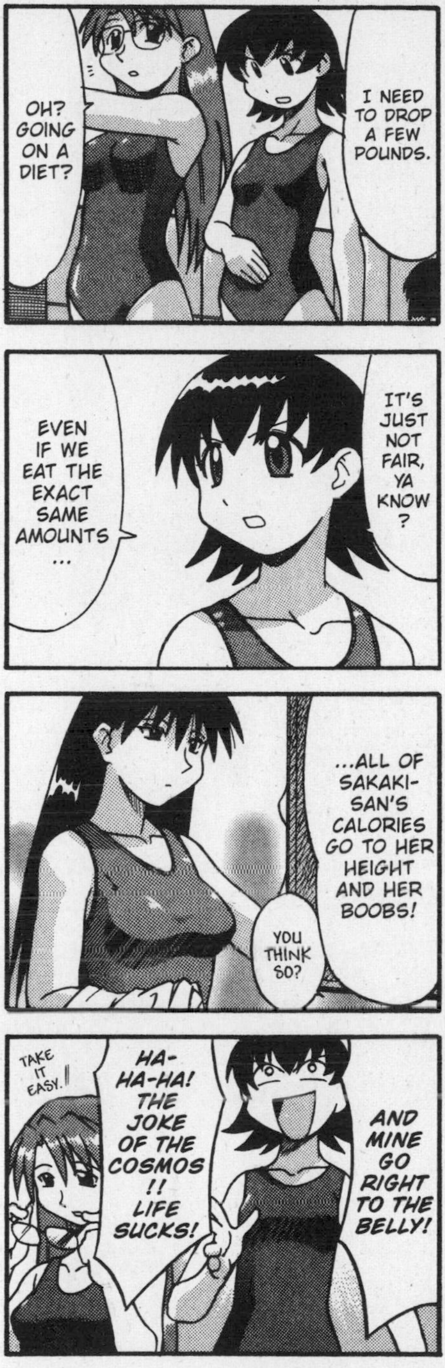
I NEED TO DROP A FEW POUNDS.
OH? GOING ON A DIET?
IT'S JUST NOT FAIR, YA KNOW?
EVEN IF WE EAT THE EXACT SAME AMOUNTS...
...ALL OF SAKAKI-SAN'S CALORIES GO TO HER HEIGHT AND HER BOOBS!
YOU THINK SO?
AND MINE GO RIGHT TO THE BELLY!
HA-HA-HA! THE JOKE OF THE COSMOS!! LIFE SUCKS!
TAKE IT EASY.

FROM KUROSAWA

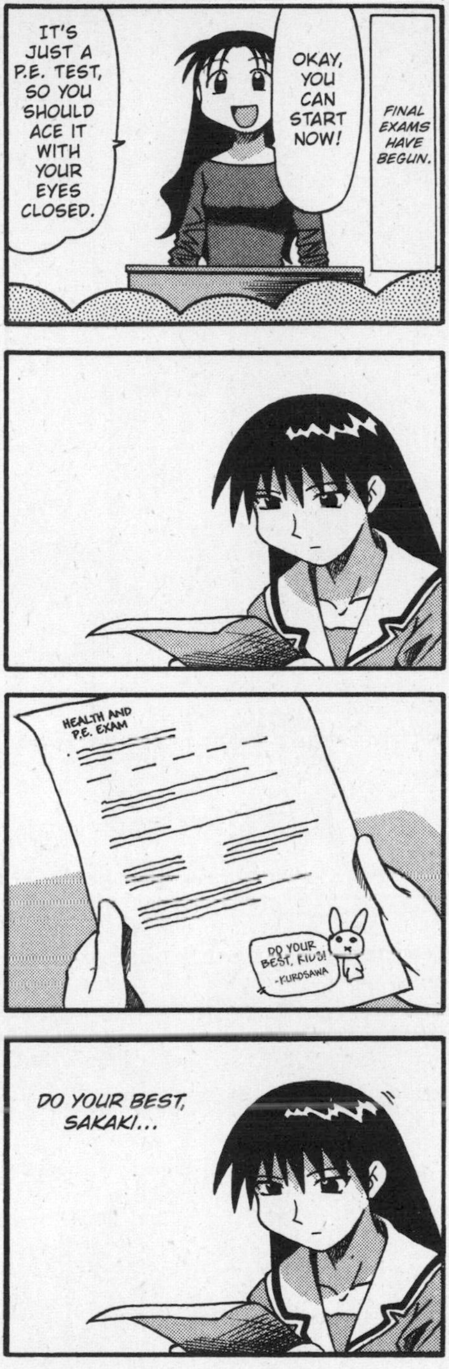
FINAL EXAMS HAVE BEGUN.
OKAY, YOU CAN START NOW!
IT'S JUST A P.E. TEST, SO YOU SHOULD ACE IT WITH YOUR EYES CLOSED.
HEALTH AND P.E. EXAM
DO YOUR BEST, KIDS! -KUROSAWA
DO YOUR BEST, SAKAKI...

LOUD

BREAKTHROUGH

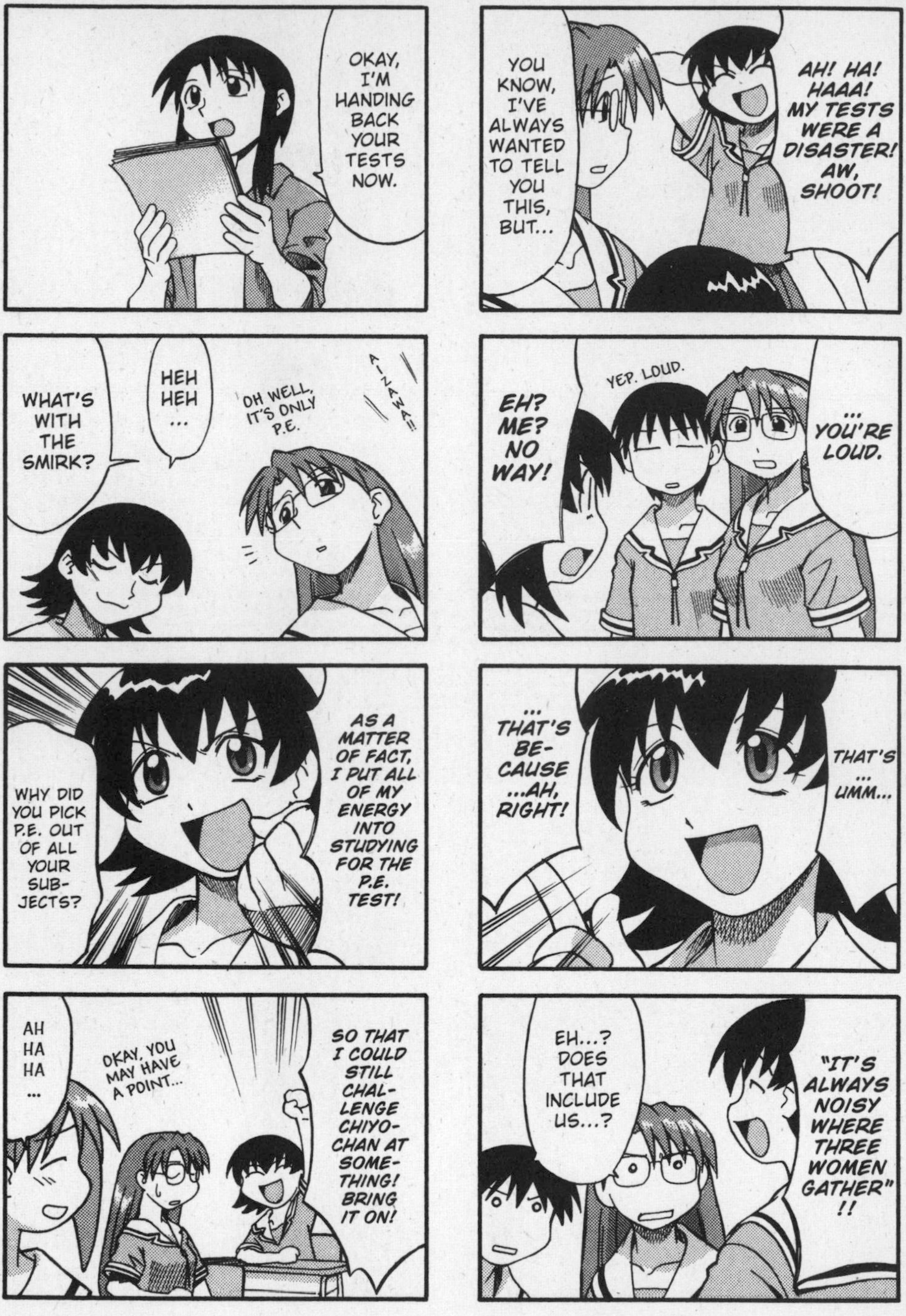

AH! HA! HAAA! MY TESTS WERE A DISASTER! AW, SHOOT!
YOU KNOW, I'VE ALWAYS WANTED TO TELL YOU THIS, BUT...
... YOU'RE LOUD.
YEP. LOUD.
EH? ME? NO WAY!
THAT'S ... UMM...
... THAT'S BE-CAUSE ...AH, RIGHT!
"IT'S ALWAYS NOISY WHERE THREE WOMEN GATHER"!!
EH...? DOES THAT INCLUDE US...?
OKAY, I'M HANDING BACK YOUR TESTS NOW.
AINAWA!!
OH WELL, IT'S ONLY P.E.
HEH HEH ...
WHAT'S WITH THE SMIRK?
AS A MATTER OF FACT, I PUT ALL OF MY ENERGY INTO STUDYING FOR THE P.E. TEST!
WHY DID YOU PICK P.E. OUT OF ALL YOUR SUB-JECTS?
SO THAT I COULD STILL CHAL-LENGE CHIYO-CHAN AT SOME-THING! BRING IT ON!
OKAY, YOU MAY HAVE A POINT...
AH HA HA ...

HATES TO LOSE

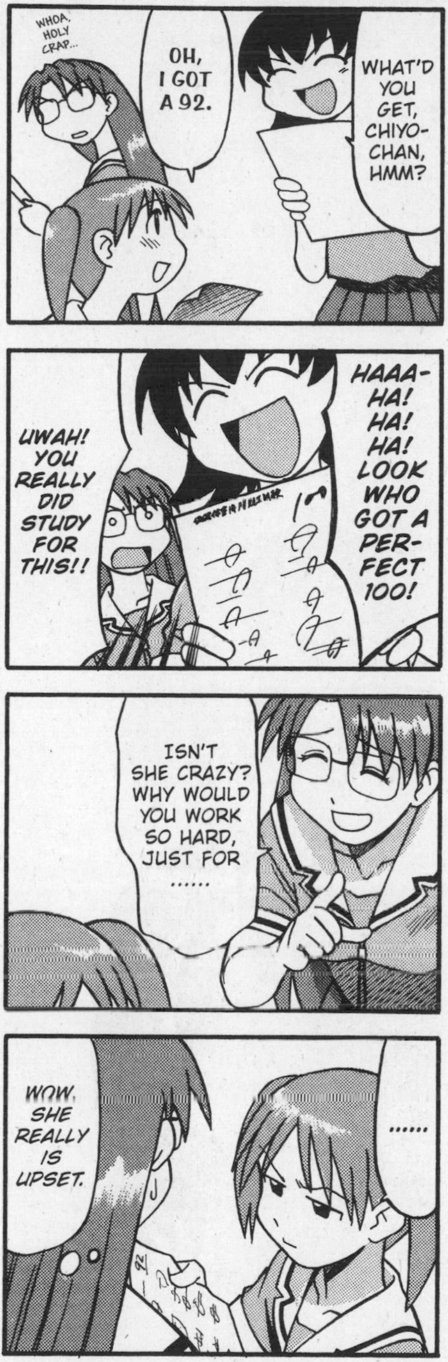
WHAT'D YOU GET, CHIYO-CHAN, HMM?
OH, I GOT A 92.
WHOA, HOLY CRAP...
HAAAA-HA! HA! HA! LOOK WHO GOT A PERFECT 100!
UWAH! YOU REALLY DID STUDY FOR THIS!!
ISN'T SHE CRAZY? WHY WOULD YOU WORK SO HARD, JUST FOR ......
......
WOW. SHE REALLY IS UPSET.

THE TOMO-CHIYO WAR

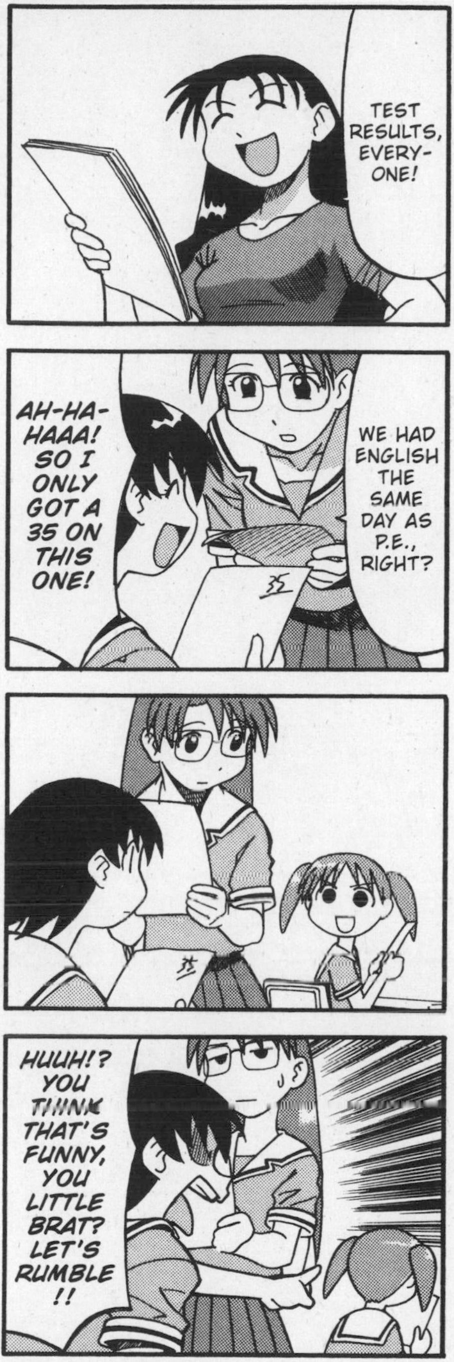
TEST RESULTS, EVERYONE!
WE HAD ENGLISH THE SAME DAY AS P.E., RIGHT?
AH-HA-HAAA! SO I ONLY GOT A 35 ON THIS ONE!
HUUH!? YOU THINK THAT'S FUNNY, YOU LITTLE BRAT? LET'S RUMBLE!!

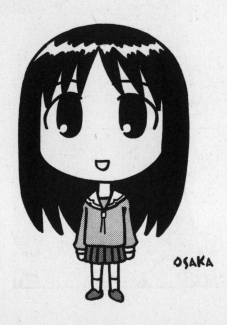

OSAKA

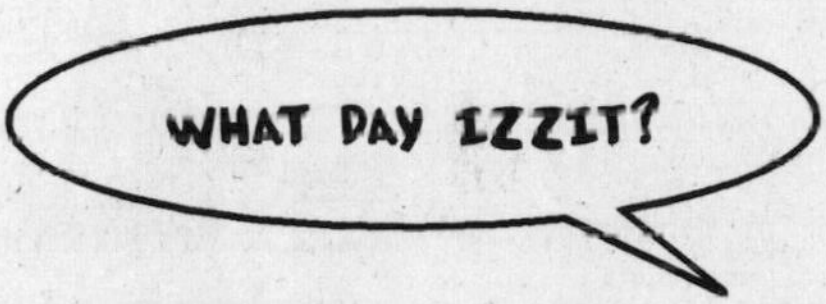
WHAT DAY IZZIT?

8
AUGUST PART-1
AZUMANGA DAIOH

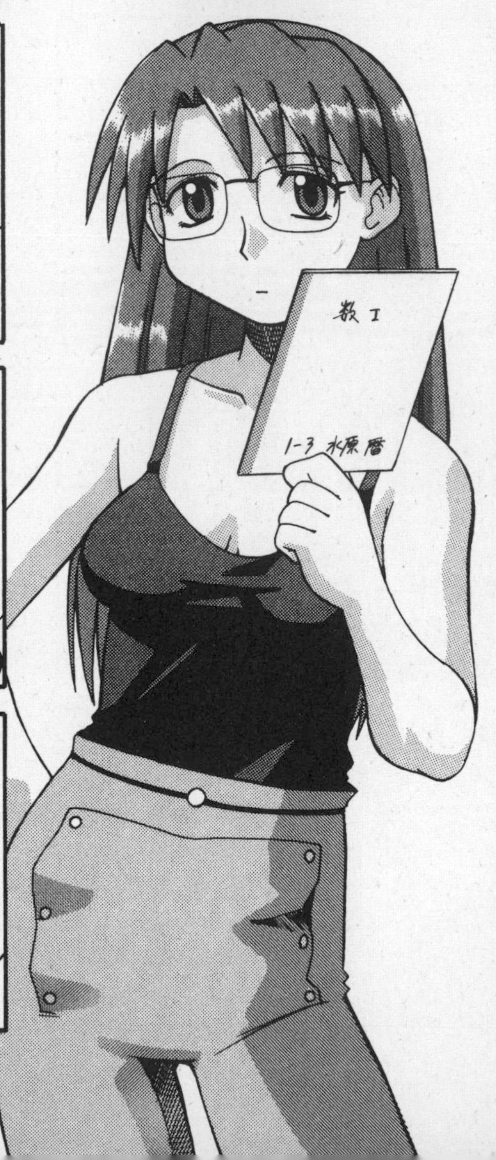
数Ⅰ
1-3 水原暦

YUKARI'S SUMMER BREAK

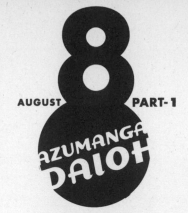

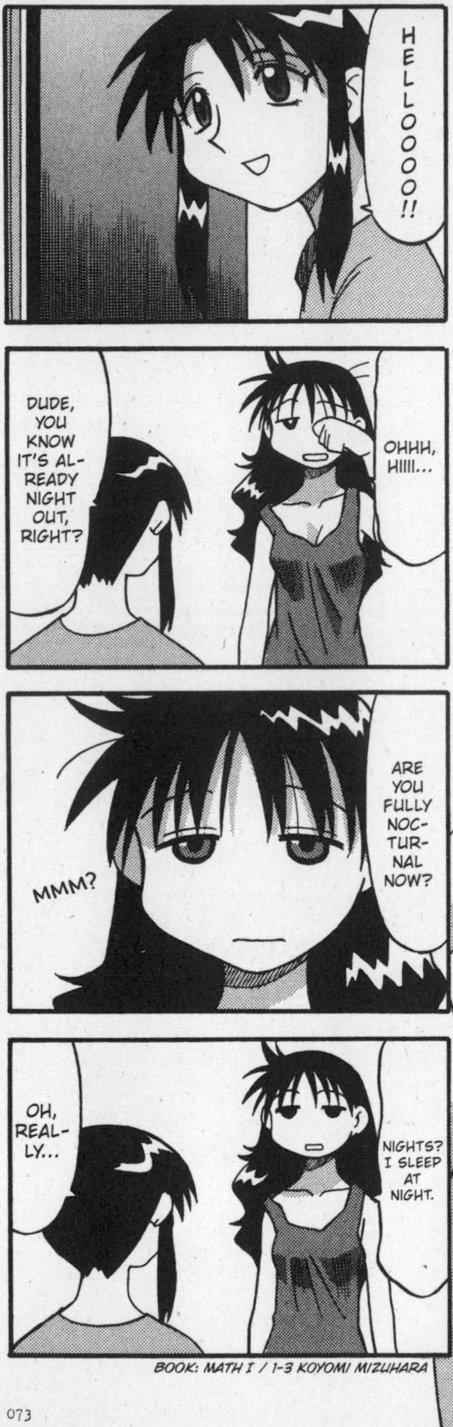
HELLOOOOO!!
OHHH, HIIII...
DUDE, YOU KNOW IT'S ALREADY NIGHT OUT, RIGHT?
ARE YOU FULLY NOCTURNAL NOW?
MMM?
NIGHTS? I SLEEP AT NIGHT.
OH, REALLY...

BOOK: MATH I / 1-3 KOYOMI MIZUHARA

THE YUKARI PLAN

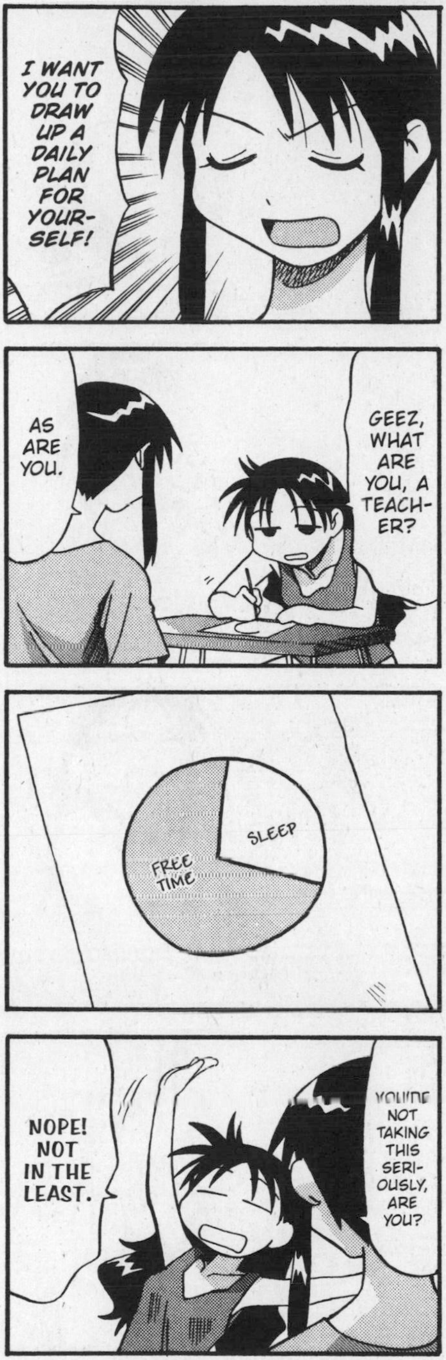
I WANT YOU TO DRAW UP A DAILY PLAN FOR YOURSELF!
GEEZ, WHAT ARE YOU, A TEACHER?
AS ARE YOU.
SLEEP
FREE TIME
YOU'RE NOT TAKING THIS SERIOUSLY, ARE YOU?
NOPE! NOT IN THE LEAST.

LET'S GO TO THE POOL

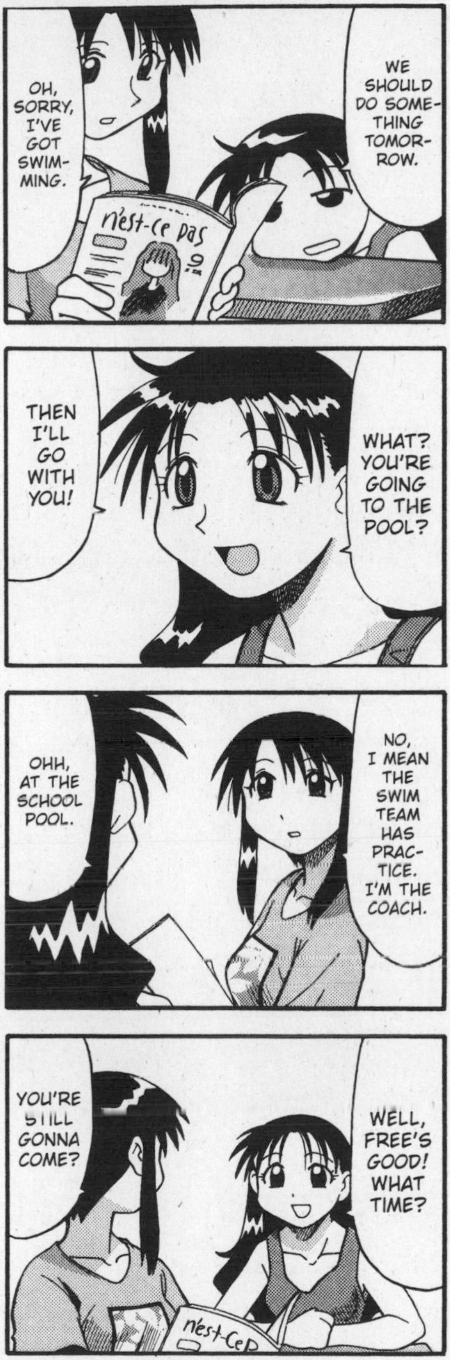
WE SHOULD DO SOMETHING TOMORROW.
OH, SORRY, I'VE GOT SWIMMING.
n'est-ce pas
WHAT? YOU'RE GOING TO THE POOL?
THEN I'LL GO WITH YOU!
NO, I MEAN THE SWIM TEAM HAS PRACTICE. I'M THE COACH.
OHH, AT THE SCHOOL POOL.
WELL, FREE'S GOOD! WHAT TIME?
YOU'RE STILL GONNA COME?
n'est-ceP

BIKINI

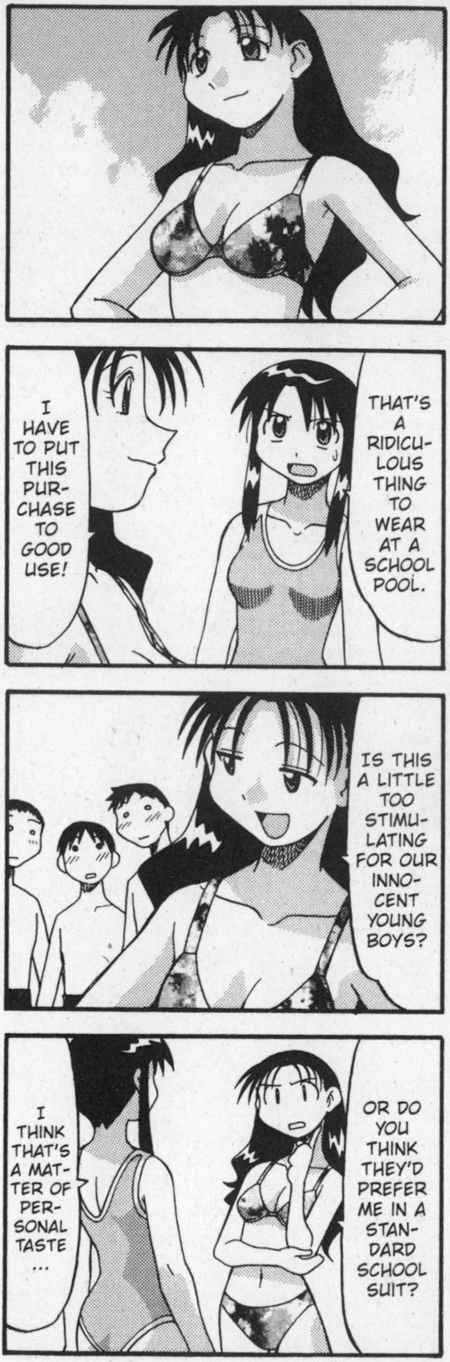
THAT'S A RIDICU-LOUS THING TO WEAR AT A SCHOOL POOL.
I HAVE TO PUT THIS PUR-CHASE TO GOOD USE!
IS THIS A LITTLE TOO STIMU-LATING FOR OUR INNO-CENT YOUNG BOYS?
OR DO YOU THINK THEY'D PREFER ME IN A STAN-DARD SCHOOL SUIT?
I THINK THAT'S A MAT-TER OF PER-SONAL TASTE ...

RESERVED

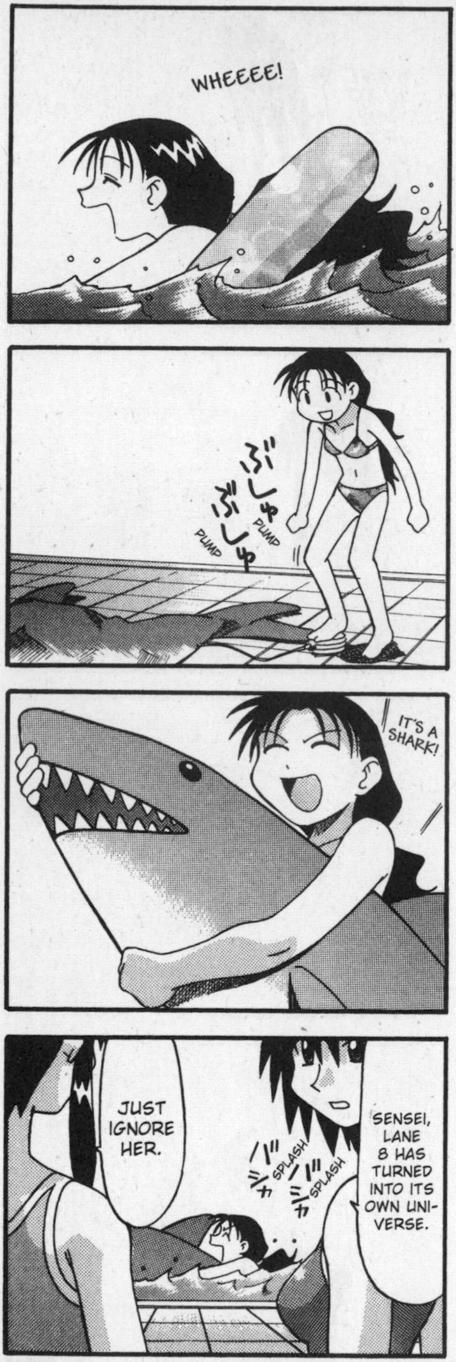
WHEEEE!
ぶしゅ PUMP
ぶしゅ PUMP
IT'S A SHARK!
SENSEI, LANE 8 HAS TURNED INTO ITS OWN UNI-VERSE.
バシャ SPLASH
バシャ SPLASH
JUST IGNORE HER.

TWO CHALLENGERS

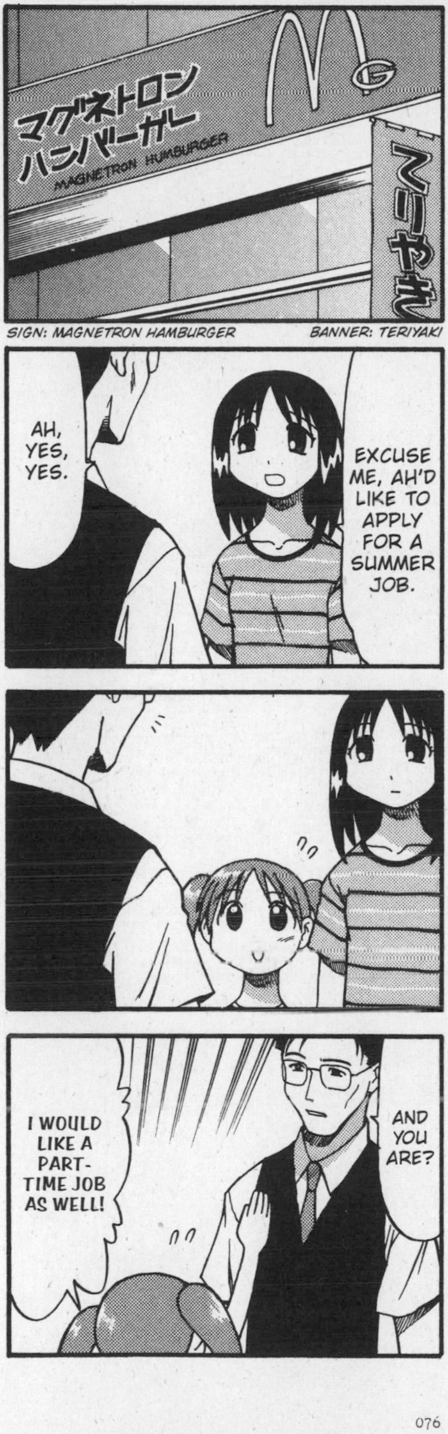
マグネトロン
ハンバーガー
MAGNETRON HUMBURGER
てりやき
SIGN: MAGNETRON HAMBURGER
BANNER: TERIYAKI
EXCUSE ME, AH'D LIKE TO APPLY FOR A SUMMER JOB.
AH, YES, YES.
AND YOU ARE?
I WOULD LIKE A PART-TIME JOB AS WELL!

HANG IN THERE

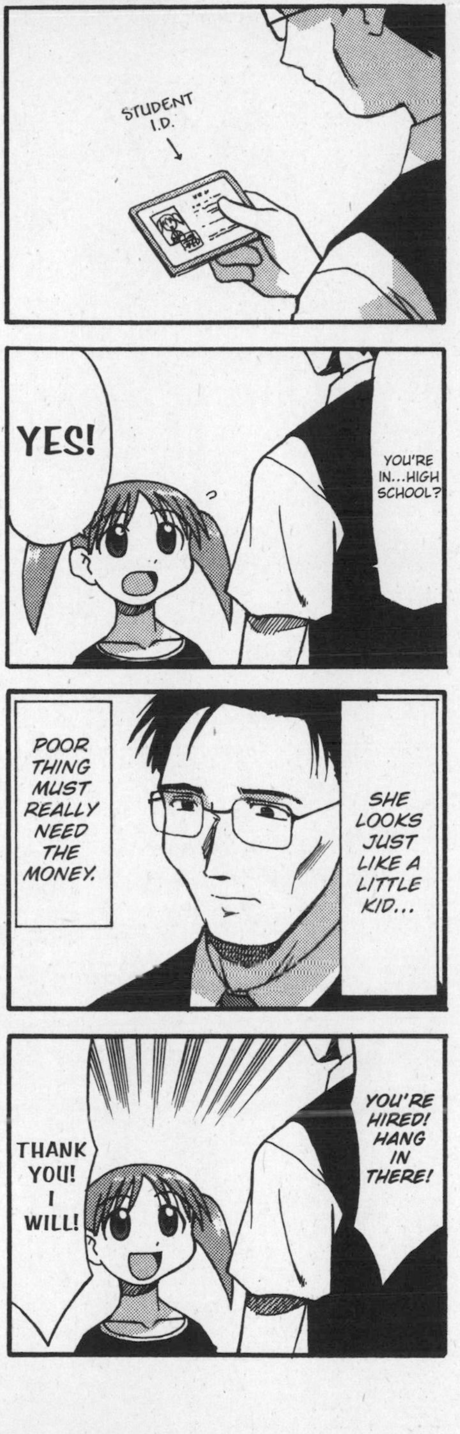
STUDENT I.D.
YOU'RE IN...HIGH SCHOOL?
YES!
SHE LOOKS JUST LIKE A LITTLE KID...
POOR THING MUST REALLY NEED THE MONEY.
YOU'RE HIRED! HANG IN THERE!
THANK YOU! I WILL!

CHILD EMPLOYEE

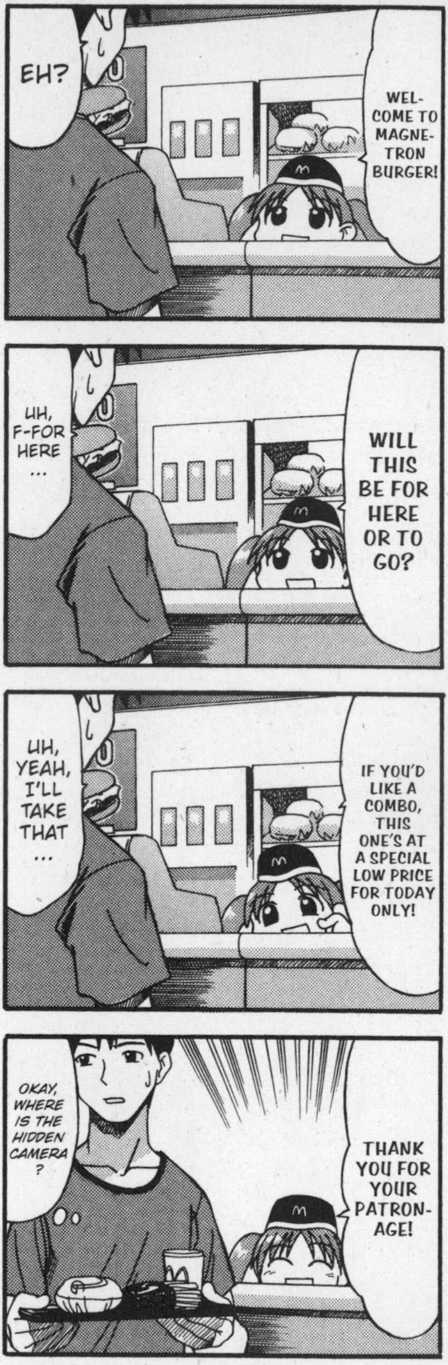
WELCOME TO MAGNETRON BURGER!
EH?
WILL THIS BE FOR HERE OR TO GO?
UH, F-FOR HERE ...
IF YOU'D LIKE A COMBO, THIS ONE'S AT A SPECIAL LOW PRICE FOR TODAY ONLY!
UH, YEAH, I'LL TAKE THAT ...
THANK YOU FOR YOUR PATRONAGE!
OKAY, WHERE IS THE HIDDEN CAMERA?

IT'S NOT FOR ME

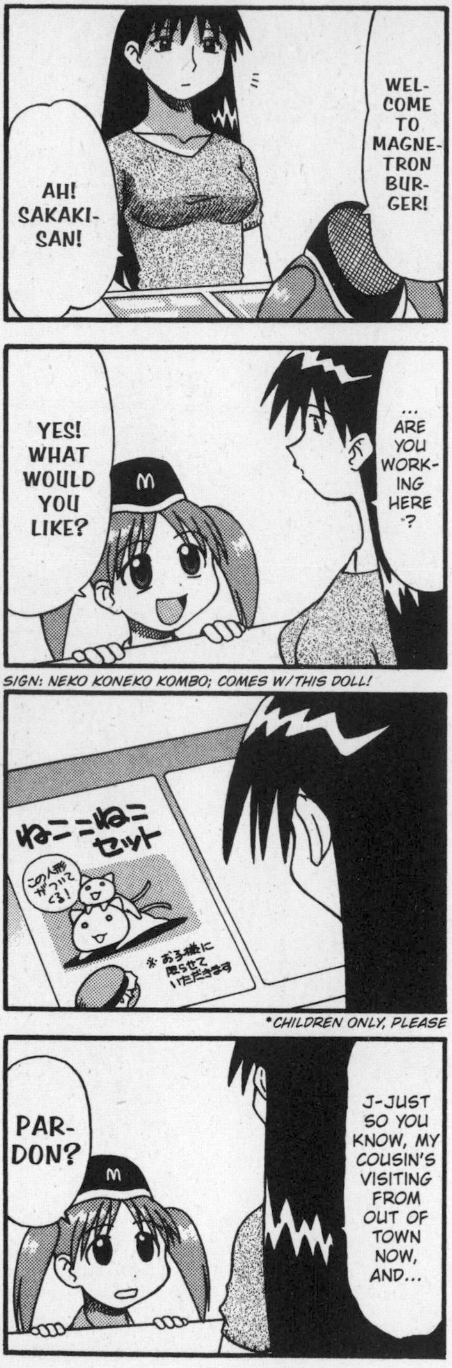
WELCOME TO MAGNETRON BURGER!
AH! SAKAKI-SAN!
... ARE YOU WORKING HERE?
YES! WHAT WOULD YOU LIKE?
ねこねこセット
この人形がついてくる!
※お子様に限らせていただきます
J-JUST SO YOU KNOW, MY COUSIN'S VISITING FROM OUT OF TOWN NOW, AND...
PARDON?

SIGN: NEKO KONEKO KOMBO; COMES W/THIS DOLL!

*CHILDREN ONLY, PLEASE

GOOD TIMING

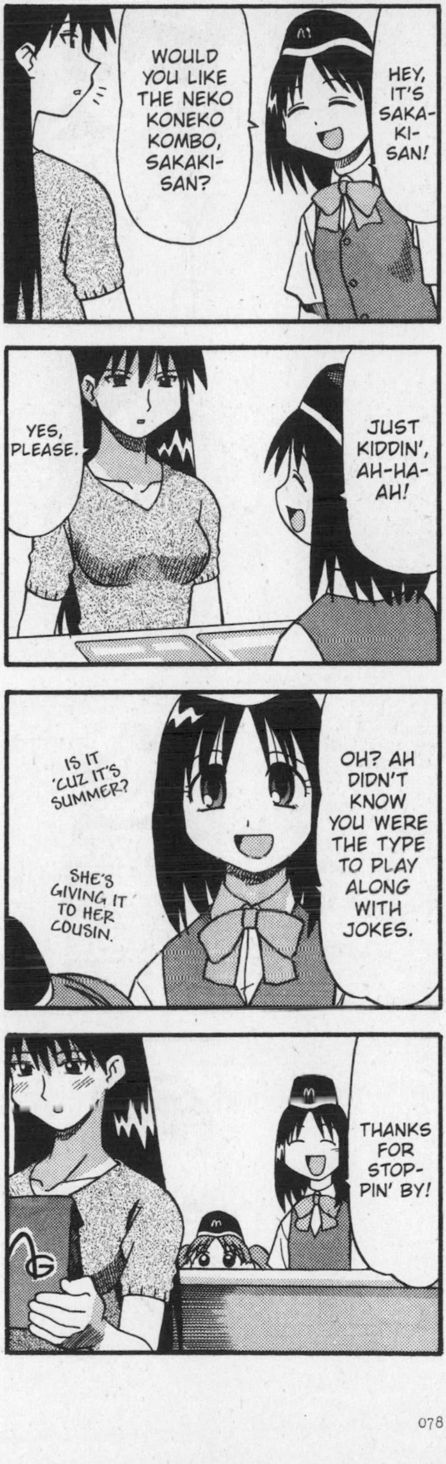
HEY, IT'S SAKA-KI-SAN!
WOULD YOU LIKE THE NEKO KONEKO KOMBO, SAKAKI-SAN?
JUST KIDDIN', AH-HA-AH!
YES, PLEASE.
OH? AH DIDN'T KNOW YOU WERE THE TYPE TO PLAY ALONG WITH JOKES.
IS IT 'CUZ IT'S SUMMER?
SHE'S GIVING IT TO HER COUSIN.
THANKS FOR STOP-PIN' BY!

JAGUAR?

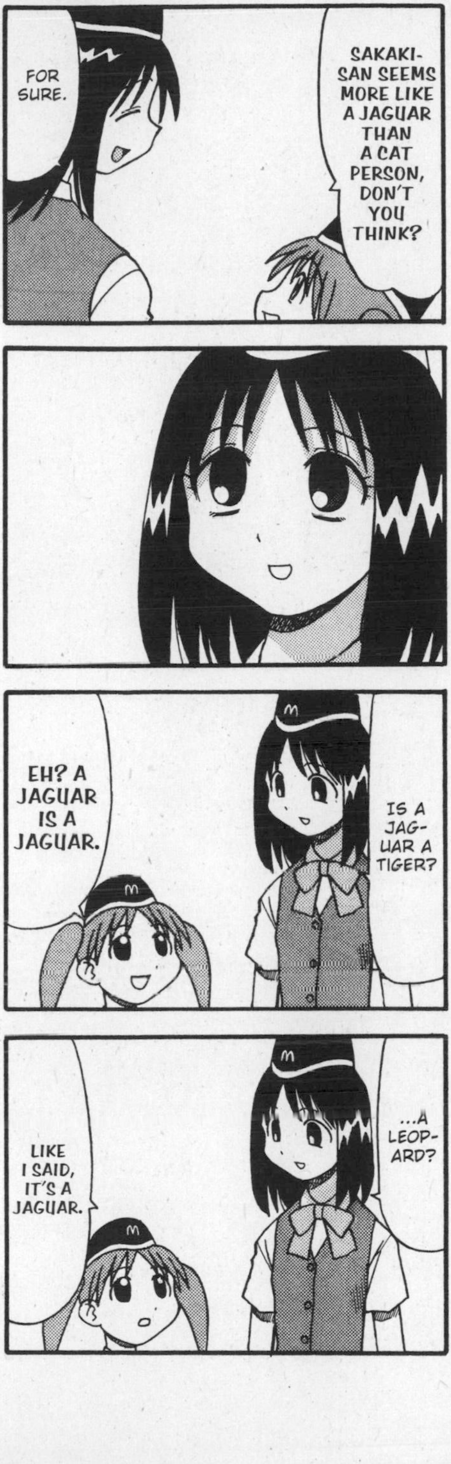
SAKAKI-SAN SEEMS MORE LIKE A JAGUAR THAN A CAT PERSON, DON'T YOU THINK?
FOR SURE.
IS A JAG-UAR A TIGER?
EH? A JAGUAR IS A JAGUAR.
...A LEOP-ARD?
LIKE I SAID, IT'S A JAGUAR.

SUMMER BELONGS TO YOU

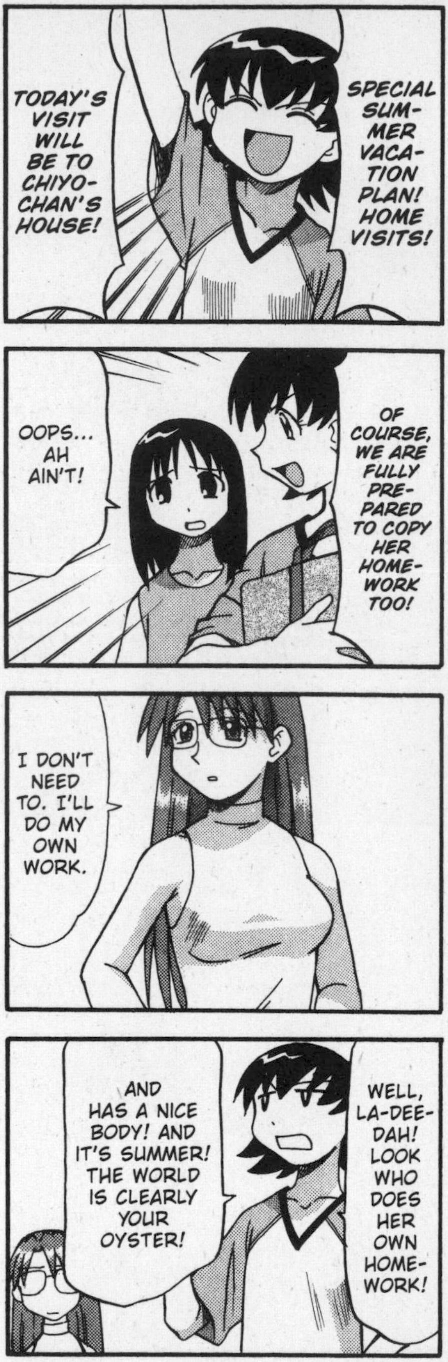
SPECIAL SUMMER VACATION PLAN! HOME VISITS!
TODAY'S VISIT WILL BE TO CHIYO-CHAN'S HOUSE!
OF COURSE, WE ARE FULLY PREPARED TO COPY HER HOMEWORK TOO!
OOPS... AH AIN'T!
I DON'T NEED TO. I'LL DO MY OWN WORK.
WELL, LA-DEE-DAH! LOOK WHO DOES HER OWN HOMEWORK!
AND HAS A NICE BODY! AND IT'S SUMMER! THE WORLD IS CLEARLY YOUR OYSTER!

WORRY

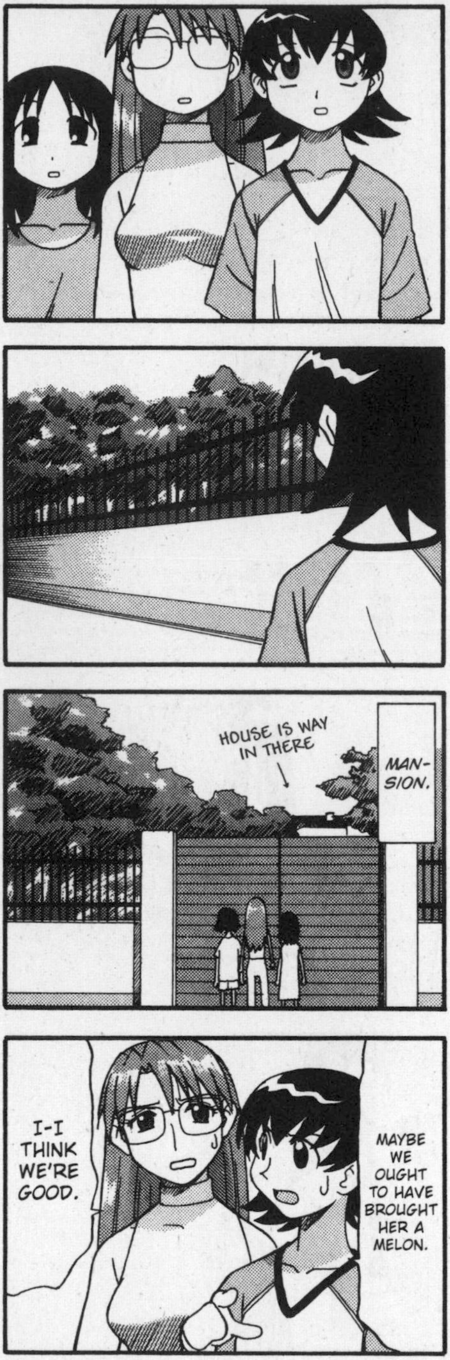
MANSION.
HOUSE IS WAY IN THERE
MAYBE WE OUGHT TO HAVE BROUGHT HER A MELON.
I-I THINK WE'RE GOOD.

WELCOME TO CHIYO'S ROOM

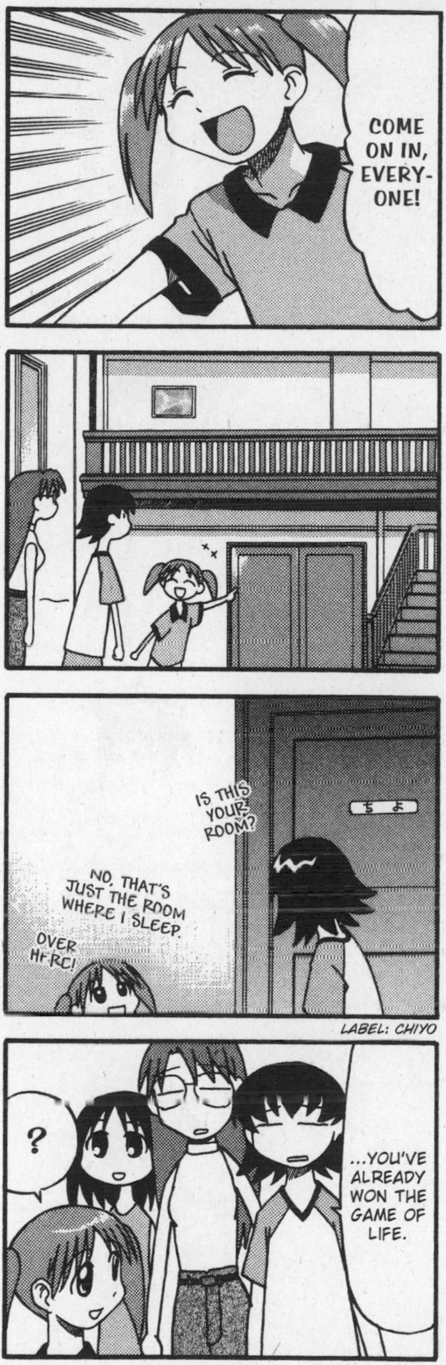
COME ON IN, EVERY-ONE!
IS THIS YOUR ROOM?
NO, THAT'S JUST THE ROOM WHERE I SLEEP.
OVER HERE!
ちよ
LABEL: CHIYO
?
...YOU'VE ALREADY WON THE GAME OF LIFE.

INVITATION

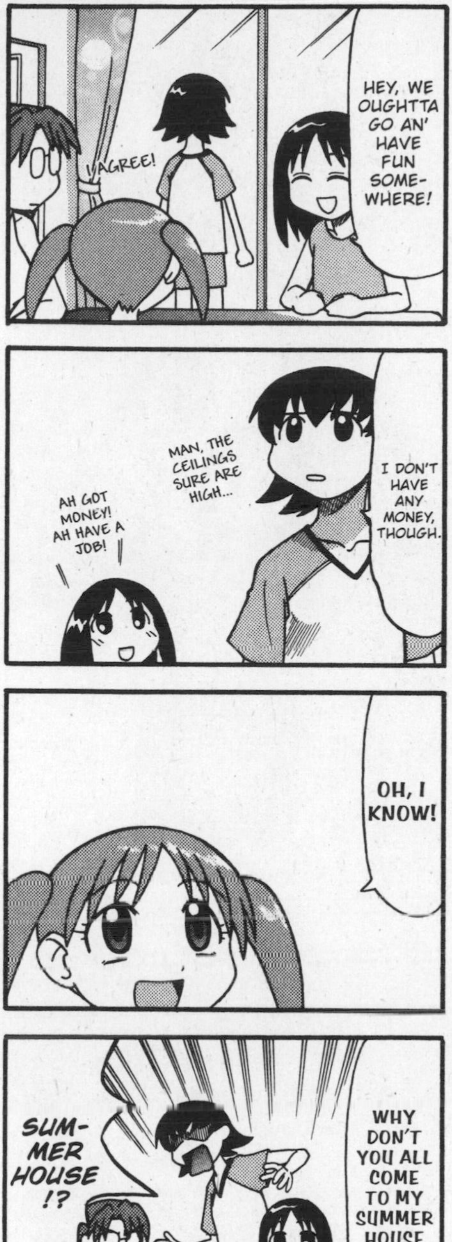
HEY, WE OUGHTTA GO AN' HAVE FUN SOME-WHERE!
I AGREE!
I DON'T HAVE ANY MONEY, THOUGH.
MAN, THE CEILINGS SURE ARE HIGH...
AH GOT MONEY! AH HAVE A JOB!
OH, I KNOW!
WHY DON'T YOU ALL COME TO MY SUMMER HOUSE?
SUM-MER HOUSE !?

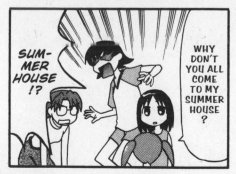

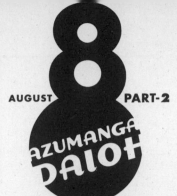

8
AUGUST PART-2
AZUMANGA DAIOH

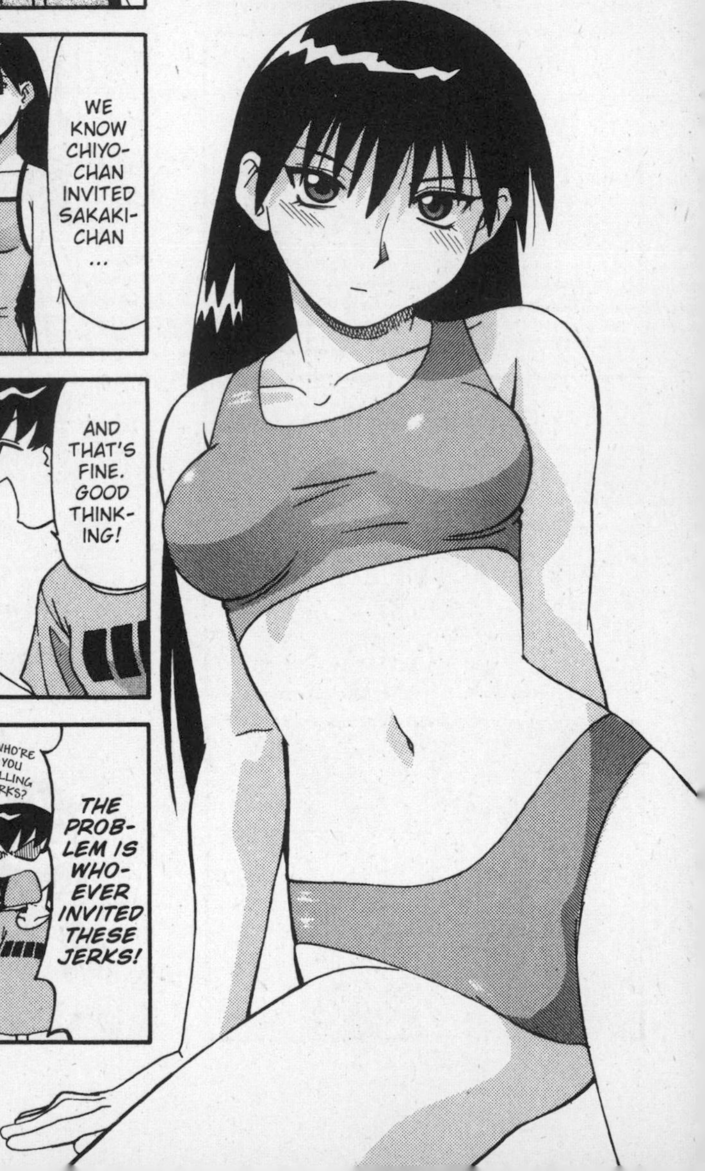

THE GANG

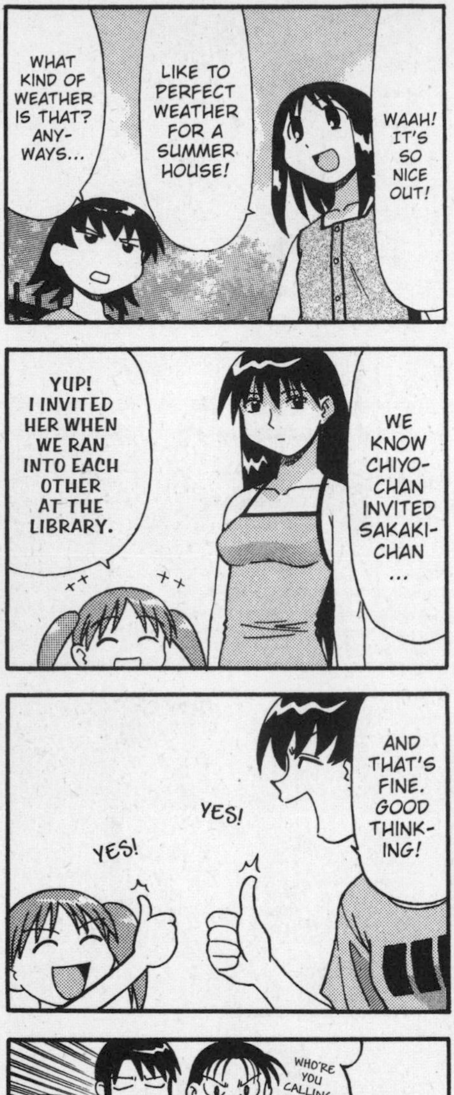

WAAH! IT'S SO NICE OUT!
LIKE TO PERFECT WEATHER FOR A SUMMER HOUSE!
WHAT KIND OF WEATHER IS THAT? ANYWAYS...
WE KNOW CHIYO-CHAN INVITED SAKAKI-CHAN...
YUP! I INVITED HER WHEN WE RAN INTO EACH OTHER AT THE LIBRARY.
AND THAT'S FINE. GOOD THINKING!
YES!
YES!
THE PROBLEM IS WHOEVER INVITED THESE JERKS!
WHO'RE YOU CALLING JERKS?
I CALLED THEM TO ASK FOR PERMISSION, AND THEY SAID THEY HAD TO COME...

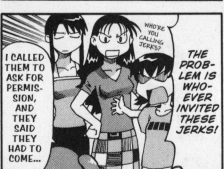

PRACTICE MAKES PERFECT

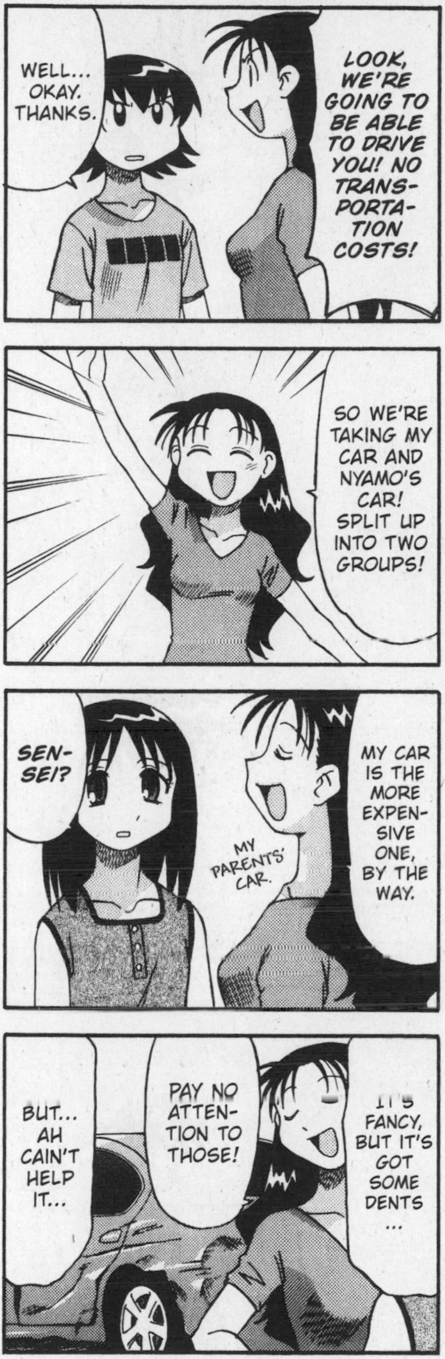
LOOK, WE'RE GOING TO BE ABLE TO DRIVE YOU! NO TRANS-PORTA-TION COSTS!
WELL... OKAY. THANKS.
SO WE'RE TAKING MY CAR AND NYAMO'S CAR! SPLIT UP INTO TWO GROUPS!
MY CAR IS THE MORE EXPEN-SIVE ONE, BY THE WAY.
MY PARENTS' CAR.
SEN-SEI?
IT'S FANCY, BUT IT'S GOT SOME DENTS ...
PAY NO ATTEN-TION TO THOSE!
BUT... AH CAIN'T HELP IT...

HEAVEN AND HELL

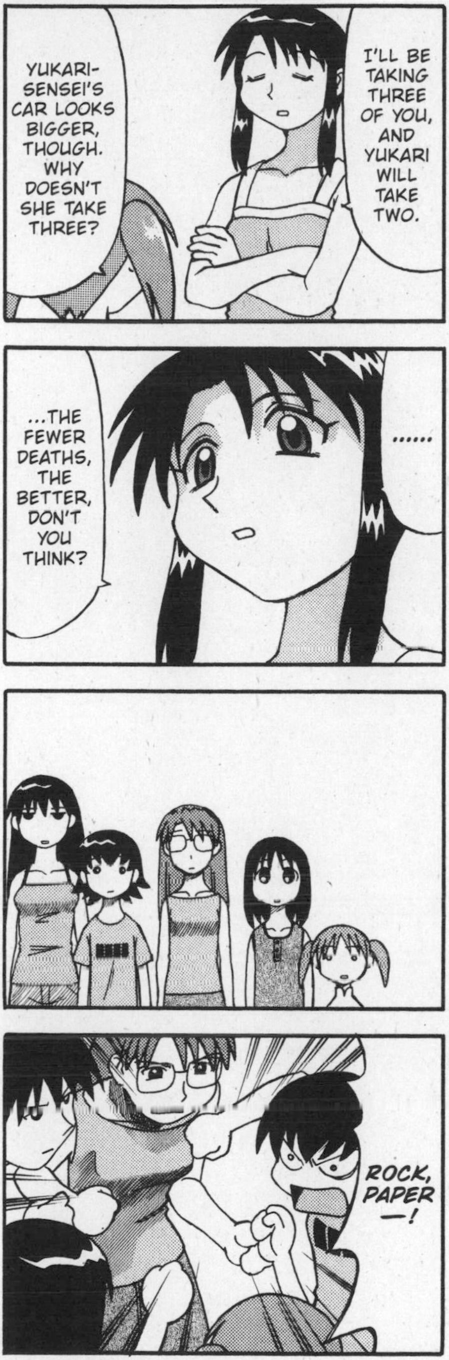
I'LL BE TAKING THREE OF YOU, AND YUKARI WILL TAKE TWO.
YUKARI-SENSEI'S CAR LOOKS BIGGER, THOUGH. WHY DOESN'T SHE TAKE THREE?
......
...THE FEWER DEATHS, THE BETTER, DON'T YOU THINK?
ROCK, PAPER —!

YOMI SAW

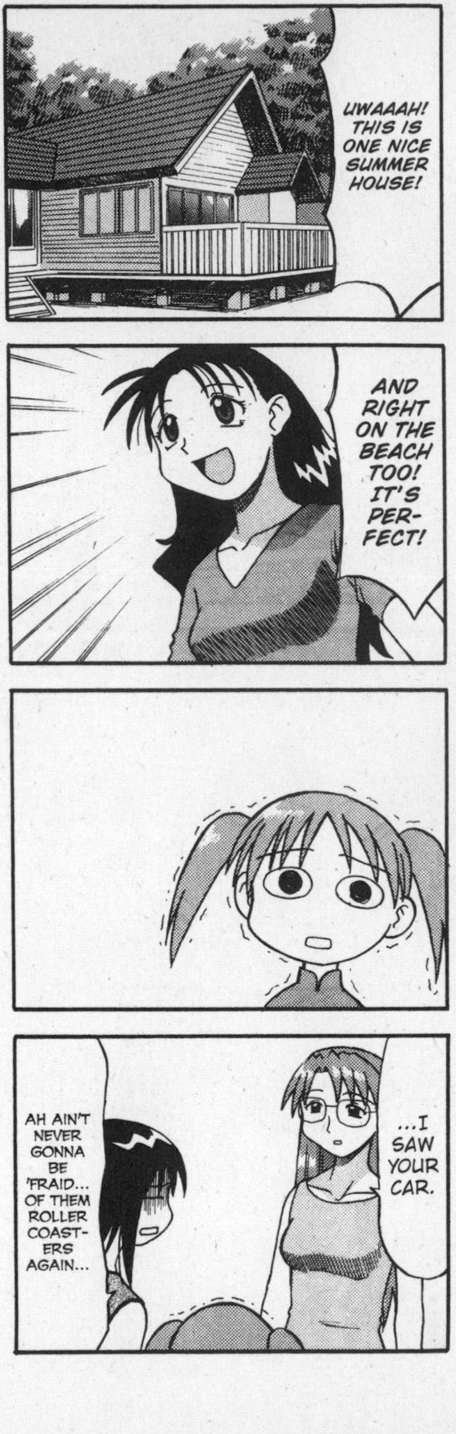
UWAAAH! THIS IS ONE NICE SUMMER HOUSE!
AND RIGHT ON THE BEACH TOO! IT'S PERFECT!
...I SAW YOUR CAR.
AH AIN'T NEVER GONNA BE 'FRAID... OF THEM ROLLER COASTERS AGAIN...

SPLITTING A WATERMELON

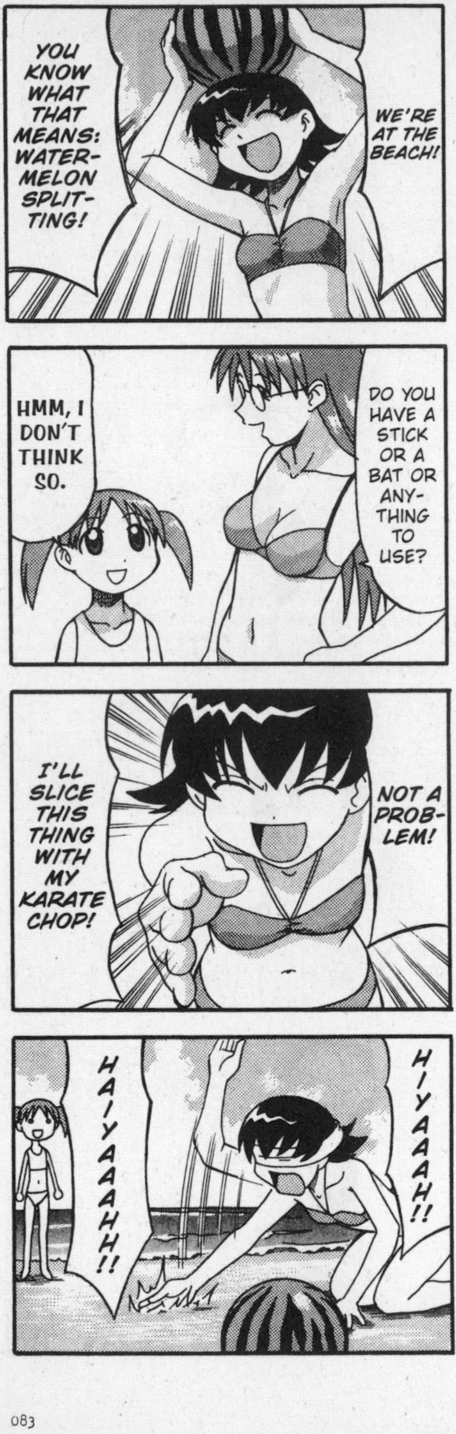
WE'RE AT THE BEACH!
YOU KNOW WHAT THAT MEANS: WATERMELON SPLITTING!
DO YOU HAVE A STICK OR A BAT OR ANYTHING TO USE?
HMM, I DON'T THINK SO.
NOT A PROBLEM!
I'LL SLICE THIS THING WITH MY KARATE CHOP!
HIYAAAAH!!
HAIYAAAAHH!!

RUINING THE MOOD

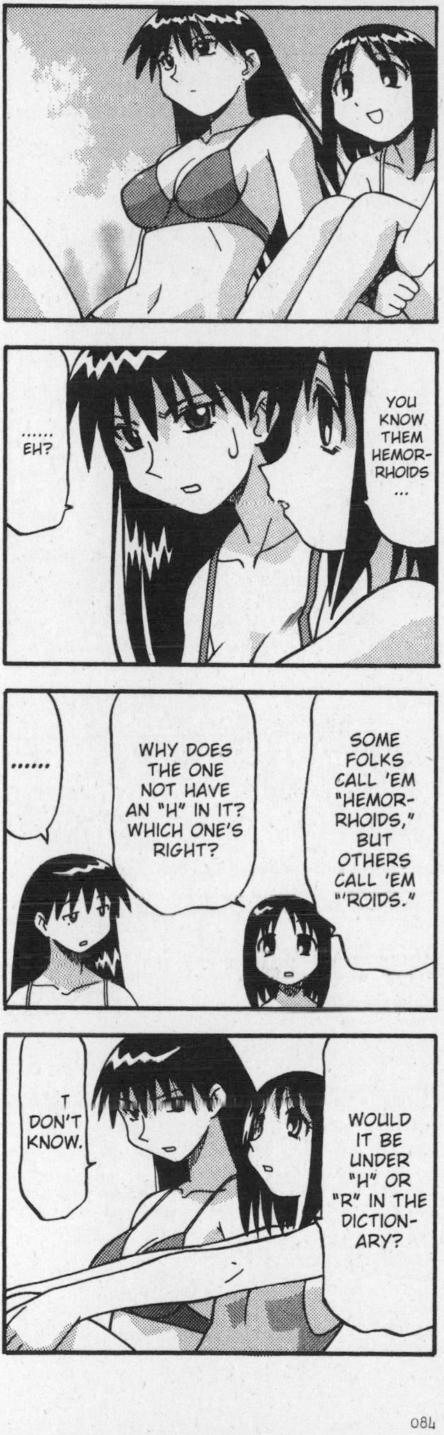
YOU KNOW THEM HEMOR-RHOIDS ...
...... EH?
SOME FOLKS CALL 'EM "HEMOR-RHOIDS," BUT OTHERS CALL 'EM "'ROIDS."
WHY DOES THE ONE NOT HAVE AN "H" IN IT? WHICH ONE'S RIGHT?
......
WOULD IT BE UNDER "H" OR "R" IN THE DICTION-ARY?
I DON'T KNOW.

LET'S GO BY DOLPHIN

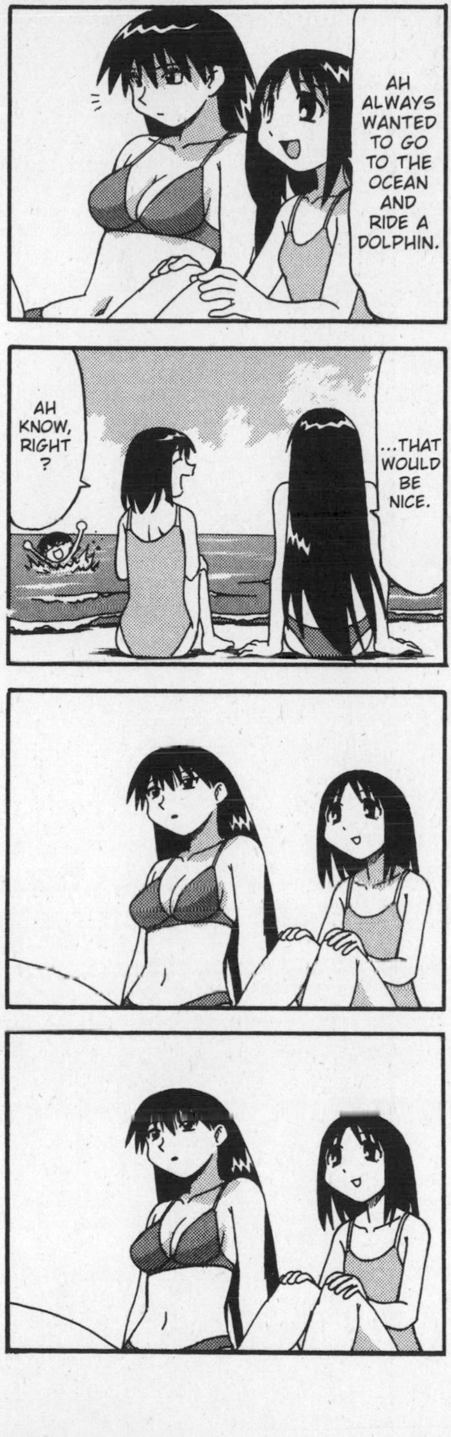
AH ALWAYS WANTED TO GO TO THE OCEAN AND RIDE A DOLPHIN.
...THAT WOULD BE NICE.
AH KNOW, RIGHT?

WHEN DID THEY PART WAYS?

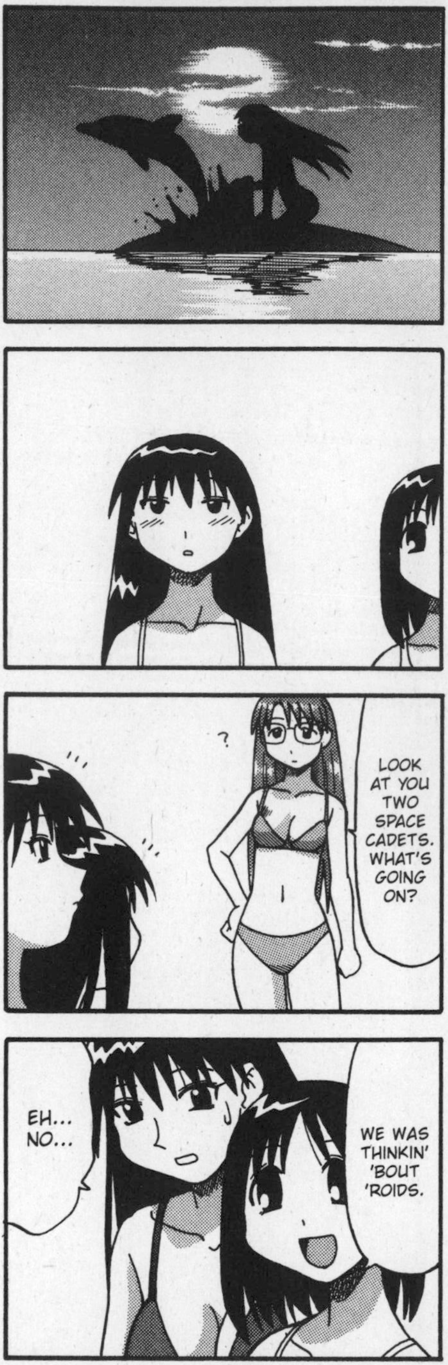
?
LOOK AT YOU TWO SPACE CADETS. WHAT'S GOING ON?
WE WAS THINKIN' 'BOUT 'ROIDS.
EH... NO...

YUKARI GOES WILD

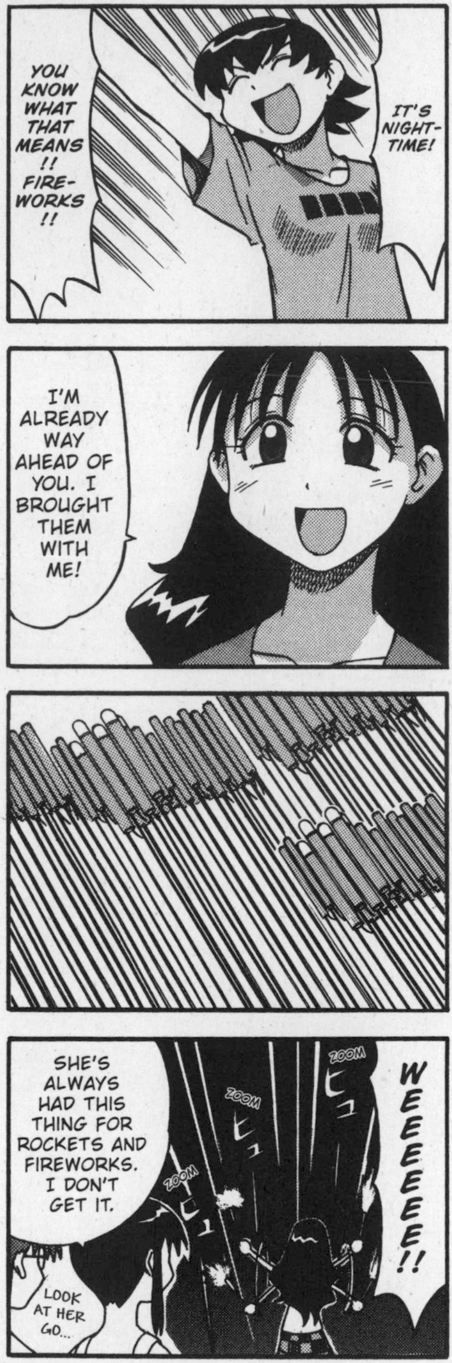
IT'S NIGHT-TIME!
YOU KNOW WHAT THAT MEANS!! FIRE-WORKS!!
I'M ALREADY WAY AHEAD OF YOU. I BROUGHT THEM WITH ME!
WEEEEEEE!!
ZOOM
ZOOM
ZOOM
SHE'S ALWAYS HAD THIS THING FOR ROCKETS AND FIREWORKS. I DON'T GET IT.
LOOK AT HER GO...

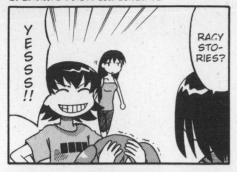

KNOCK IT OFF

SUMMER'S THE SEASON FOR GHOOOST STOOORIES...
KNOW ANY GOOD ONES?
NOOO, AH DOOON'T...
OH!
ONE TIME, AT A SUMMER HOUSE...
...THERE WAS A TERRIBLE SUMMER INFESTATION OF COCKROACHES! THERE WERE ROACHES AS FAR AS THE EYE COULD—!
ゴッ
CHOP
SUMMER'S THE SEASON FOR RACY STORIES!!

SPEAKING FROM EXPERIENCE

RACY STORIES?
YESSS!!
TIME FOR OUR TEACHERS HERE TO SHARE THEIR EXPERIENCES FOR OUR BENEFIT!
A WOMAN CAN GET ALONG JUST FINE ON HER OWN, YOU KNOW.
HOW VERY UNBENEFICIAL!

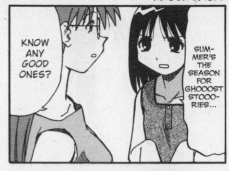

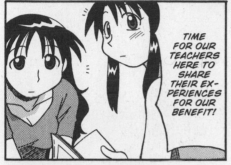

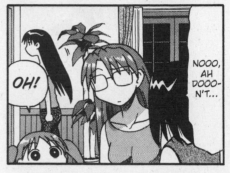

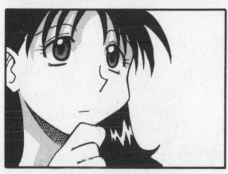

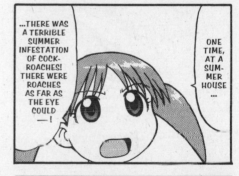

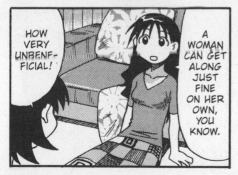

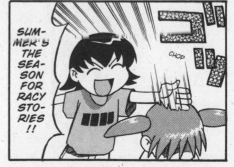

SINGLE SUMMER

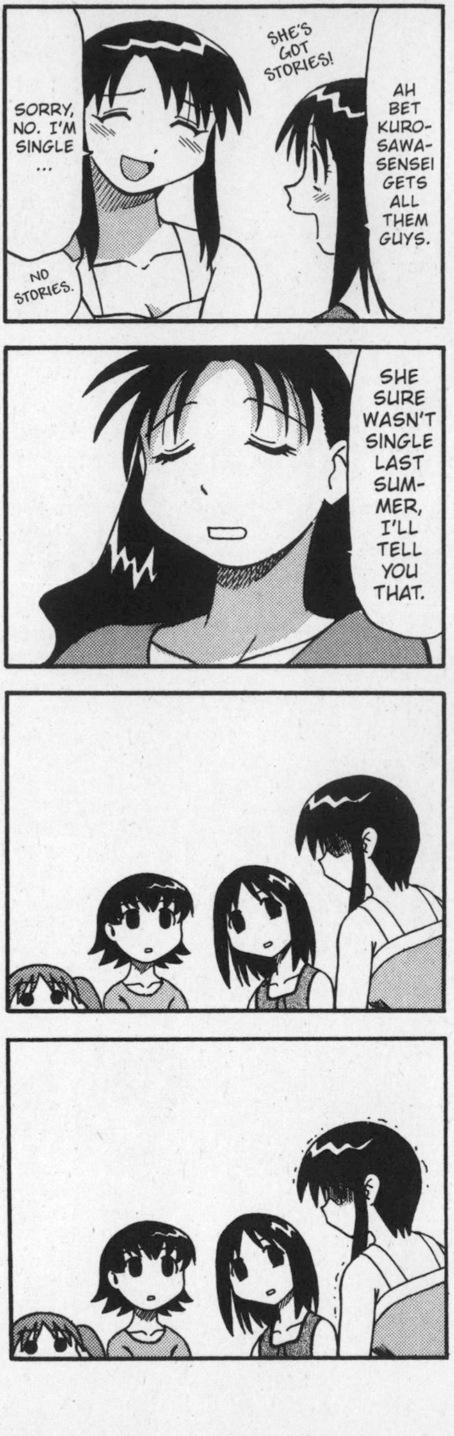
AH BET KUROSAWA-SENSEI GETS ALL THEM GUYS.
SHE'S GOT STORIES!
SORRY, NO. I'M SINGLE ...
NO STORIES.
SHE SURE WASN'T SINGLE LAST SUMMER, I'LL TELL YOU THAT.

CONFESSION

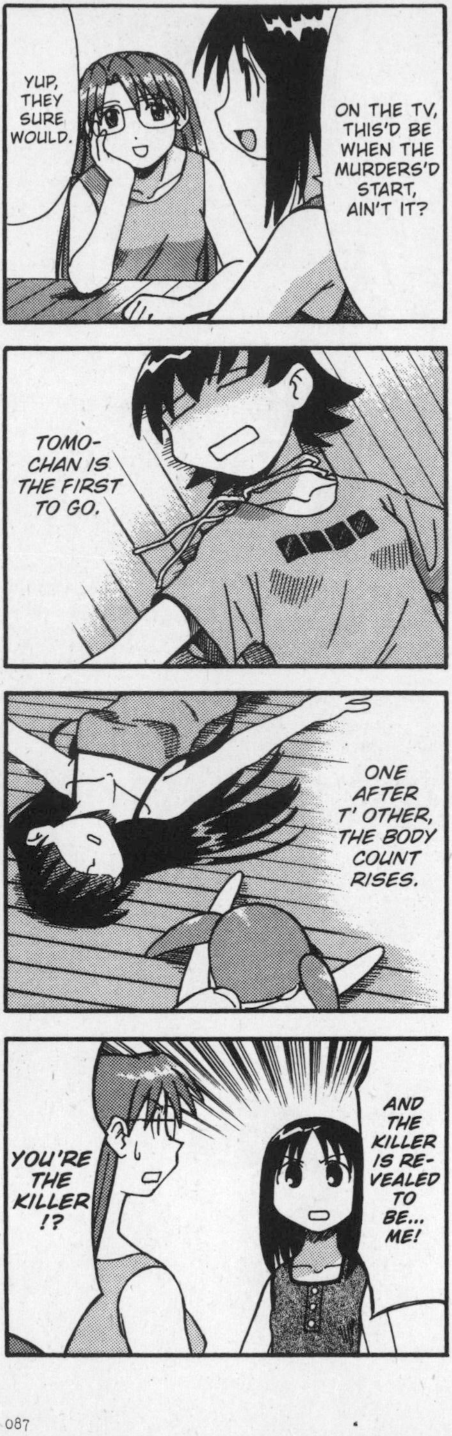
ON THE TV, THIS'D BE WHEN THE MURDERS'D START, AIN'T IT?
YUP, THEY SURE WOULD.
TOMO-CHAN IS THE FIRST TO GO.
ONE AFTER T' OTHER, THE BODY COUNT RISES.
AND THE KILLER IS RE-VEALED TO BE... ME!
YOU'RE THE KILLER !?

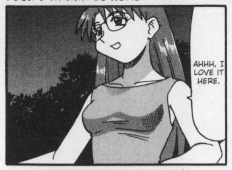

TOO ROWDY

BEFORE WE GO TO SLEEP, IT'S TIME TO GET DRUNK!
NO.
COME ON, NYAMO-CHAN! DON'T BE A HARD-ASS!
IS SHE DRUNK ALREADY?
I'M NOT SAYING THIS TO BE A HARD-ASS.
I'M SAYING IT BECAUSE YUKARI'S WITH US.
...BAD DRUNK?
VERY BAD.
THE WORST.

I DON'T WANNA GO HOME

AHHH, I LOVE IT HERE.
IF ONLY WE COULD STAY HERE FOREVER.
ME TOO!
OR IF NOT, I'D LIKE TO AT LEAST GET HOME ALIVE.
...IN THE YUKARI-MOBILE?
I ALWAYS LOSE AT ROCK-PAPER-SCISSORS!

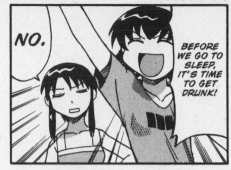

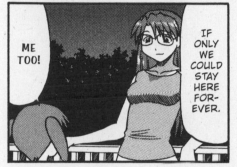

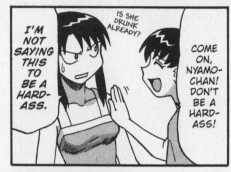

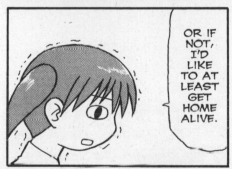

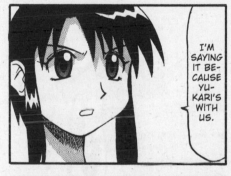

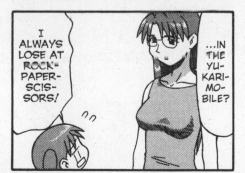

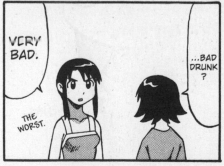

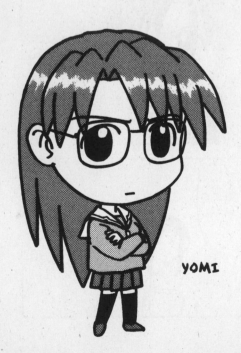

YOMI

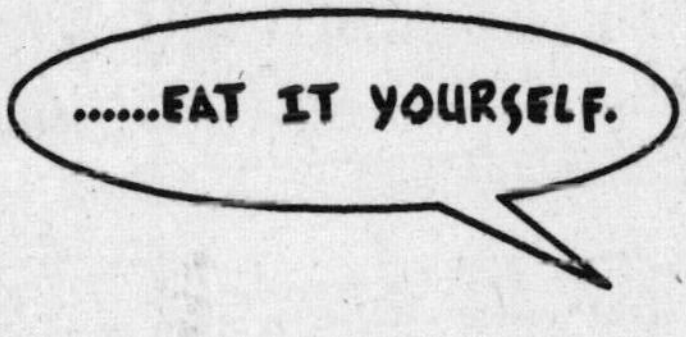
......EAT IT YOURSELF.

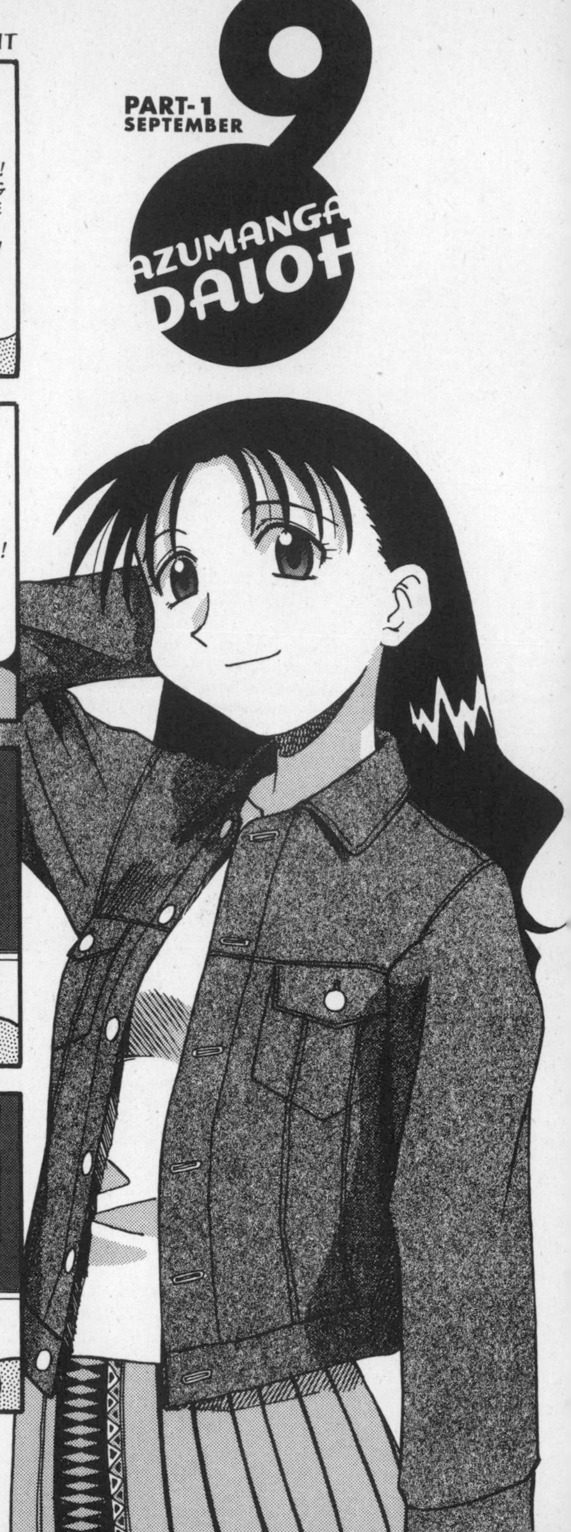
9
PART-1
SEPTEMBER
AZUMANGA DAIOH

I'M NOT GONNA MAKE IT

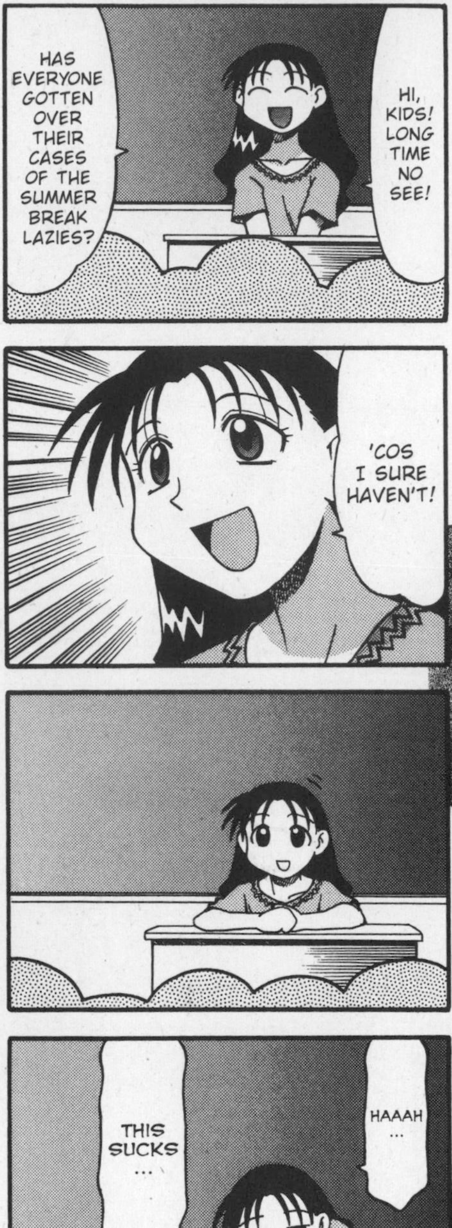
HI, KIDS! LONG TIME NO SEE!
HAS EVERYONE GOTTEN OVER THEIR CASES OF THE SUMMER BREAK LAZIES?
'COS I SURE HAVEN'T!
HAAAH ...
THIS SUCKS ...

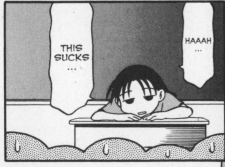

I'LL DO IT!

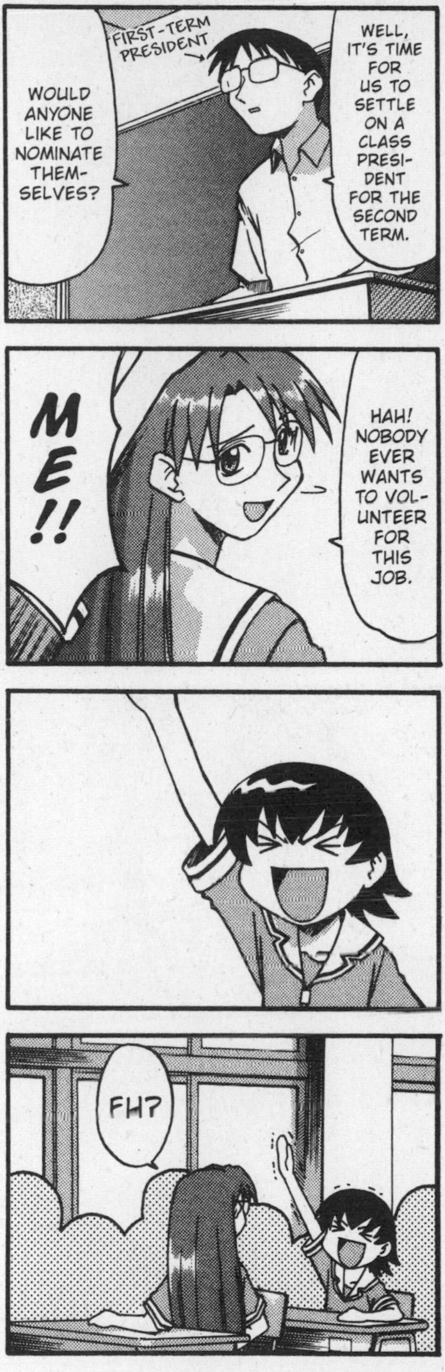
WELL, IT'S TIME FOR US TO SETTLE ON A CLASS PRESI- DENT FOR THE SECOND TERM.
FIRST-TERM PRESIDENT
WOULD ANYONE LIKE TO NOMINATE THEM- SELVES?
HAH! NOBODY EVER WANTS TO VOL- UNTEER FOR THIS JOB.
ME!!
EH?

TELL ME

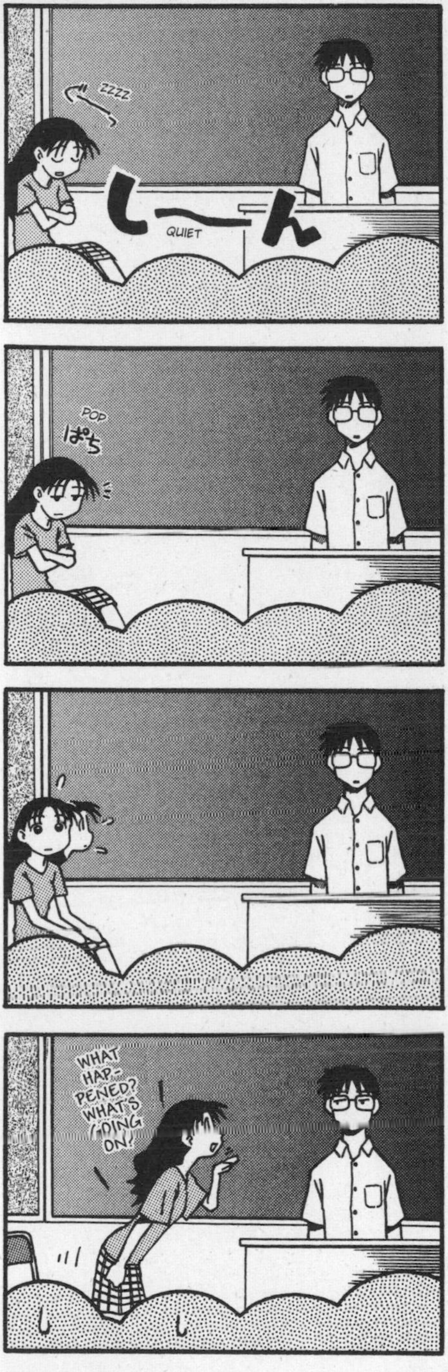
ZZZZ
しーん
QUIET
POP
ぱち
WHAT HAP- PENED? WHAT'S GOING ON!

MISSION

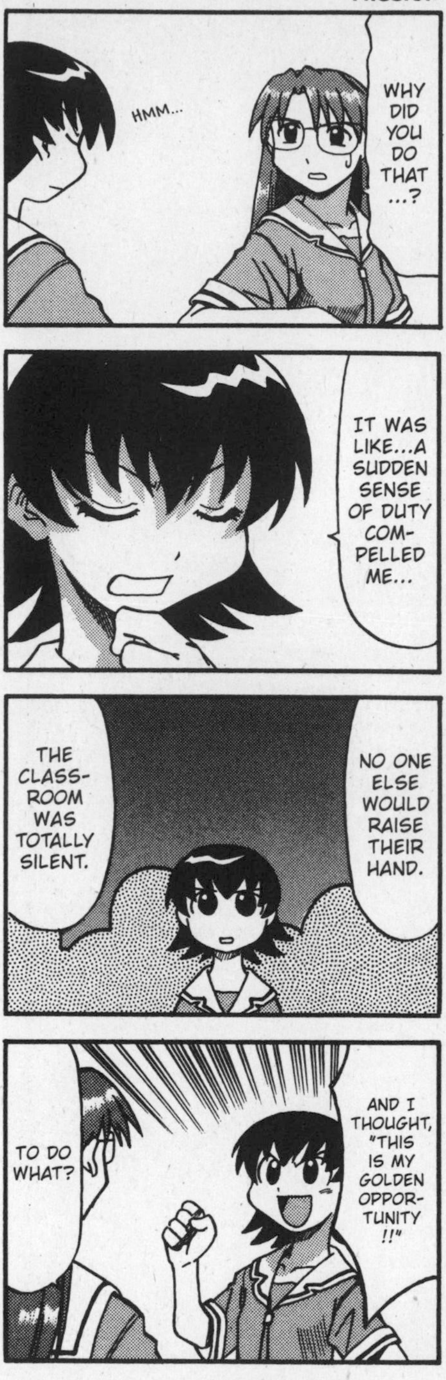
WHY DID YOU DO THAT ...?
HMM...
IT WAS LIKE...A SUDDEN SENSE OF DUTY COMPELLED ME...
NO ONE ELSE WOULD RAISE THEIR HAND.
THE CLASSROOM WAS TOTALLY SILENT.
AND I THOUGHT, "THIS IS MY GOLDEN OPPORTUNITY!!"
TO DO WHAT?

SEEDS OF DISASTER

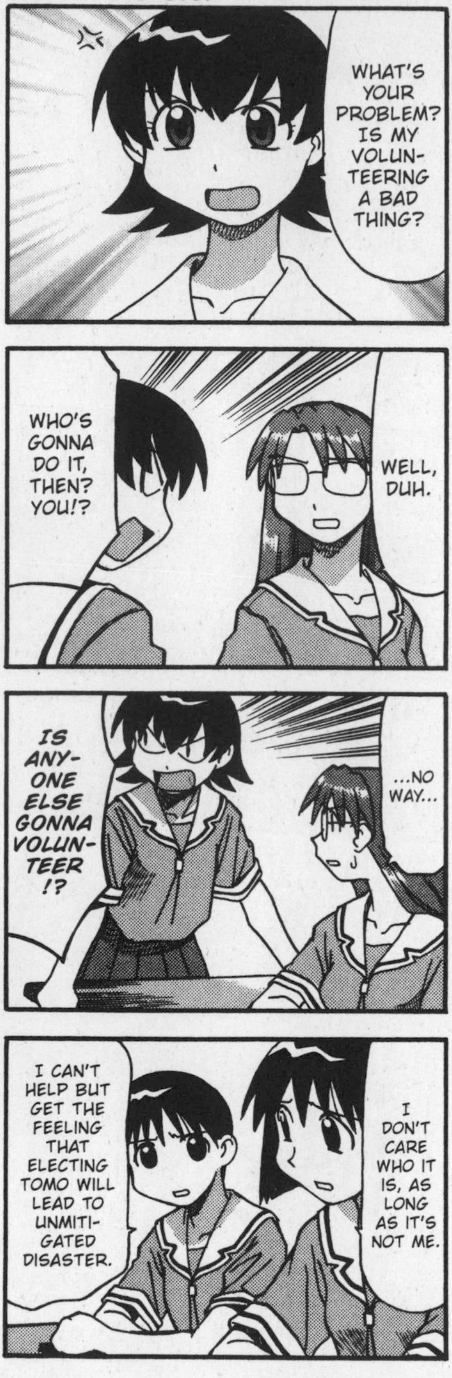
WHAT'S YOUR PROBLEM? IS MY VOLUNTEERING A BAD THING?
WELL, DUH.
WHO'S GONNA DO IT, THEN? YOU!?
...NO WAY...
IS ANYONE ELSE GONNA VOLUNTEER!?
I DON'T CARE WHO IT IS, AS LONG AS IT'S NOT ME.
I CAN'T HELP BUT GET THE FEELING THAT ELECTING TOMO WILL LEAD TO UNMITIGATED DISASTER.

REMEMBER THE SLANDER

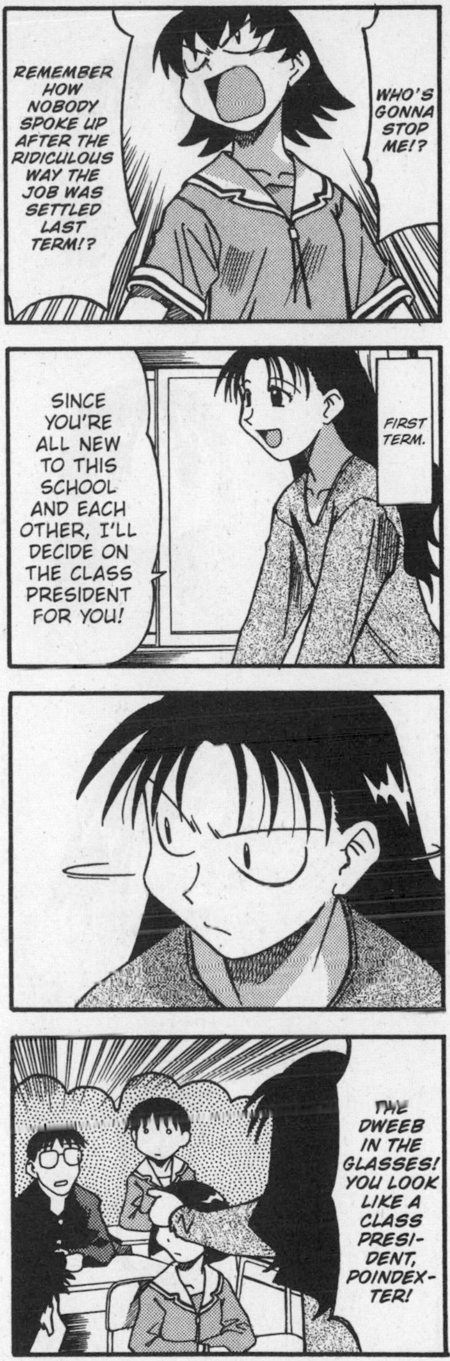
WHO'S GONNA STOP ME!?
REMEMBER HOW NOBODY SPOKE UP AFTER THE RIDICULOUS WAY THE JOB WAS SETTLED LAST TERM!?
FIRST TERM.
SINCE YOU'RE ALL NEW TO THIS SCHOOL AND EACH OTHER, I'LL DECIDE ON THE CLASS PRESIDENT FOR YOU!
THE DWEEB IN THE GLASSES! YOU LOOK LIKE A CLASS PRESIDENT, POINDEXTER!

TOMO-CHIYO WAR II

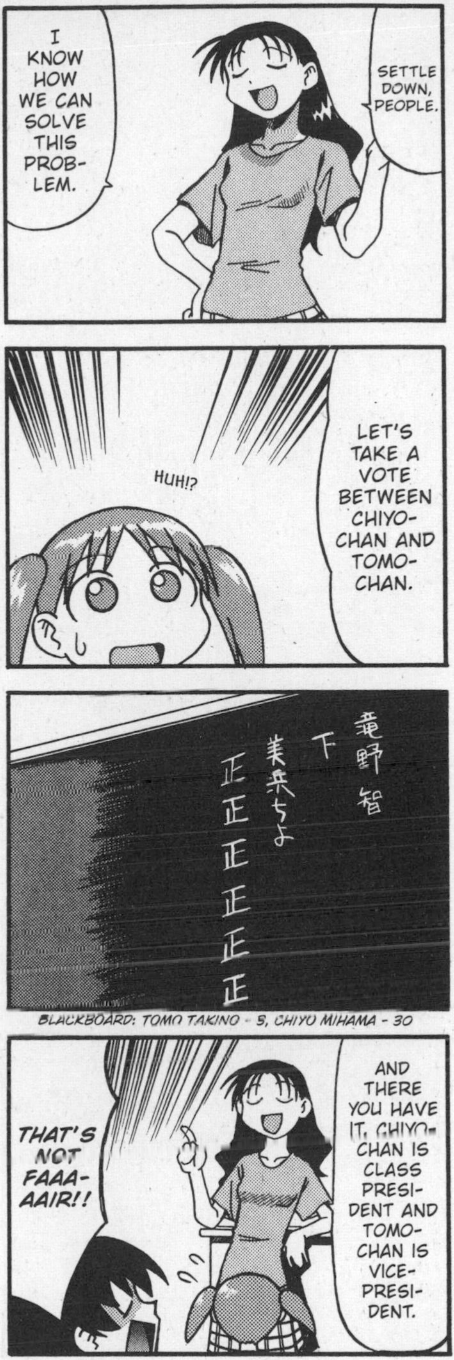
SETTLE DOWN, PEOPLE.
I KNOW HOW WE CAN SOLVE THIS PROBLEM.
LET'S TAKE A VOTE BETWEEN CHIYO-CHAN AND TOMO-CHAN.
HUH!?
滝野智 下
美浜ちよ 正正正正正正
BLACKBOARD: TOMO TAKINO - 5, CHIYO MIHAMA - 30
AND THERE YOU HAVE IT. CHIYO-CHAN IS CLASS PRESIDENT AND TOMO-CHAN IS VICE-PRESIDENT.
THAT'S NOT FAAA-AAIR!!

CHILD PRESIDENT

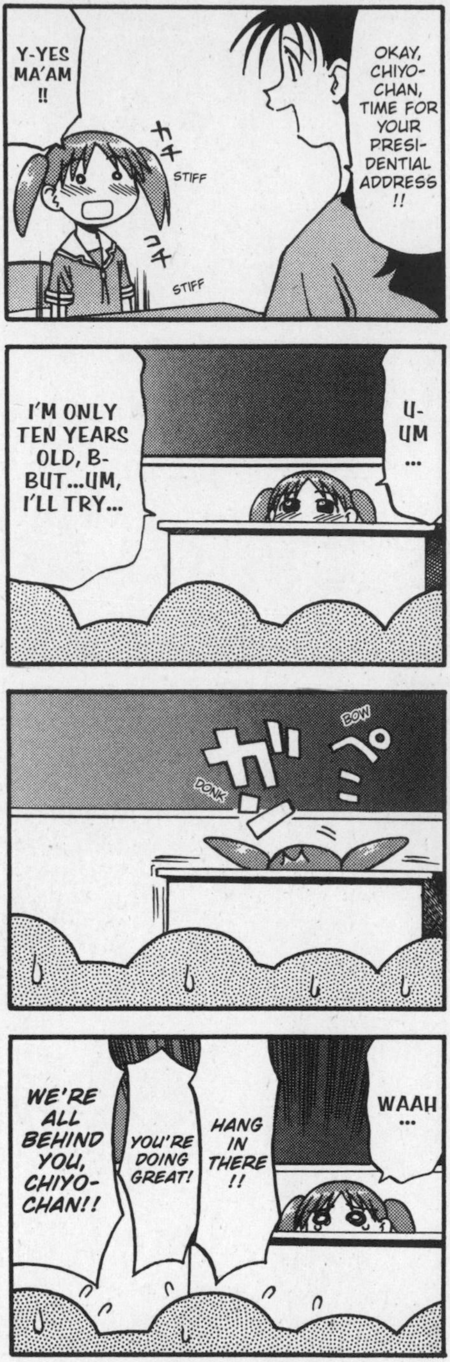
OKAY, CHIYO-CHAN, TIME FOR YOUR PRESI-DENTIAL ADDRESS!!
Y-YES MA'AM!!
カチ
STIFF
コチ
STIFF
U-UM...
I'M ONLY TEN YEARS OLD, B-BUT...UM, I'LL TRY...
ぺこ
BOW
ガン
DONK
WAAH...
HANG IN THERE!!
YOU'RE DOING GREAT!
WE'RE ALL BEHIND YOU, CHIYO-CHAN!!

ANOTHER DAY, ANOTHER OSAKA

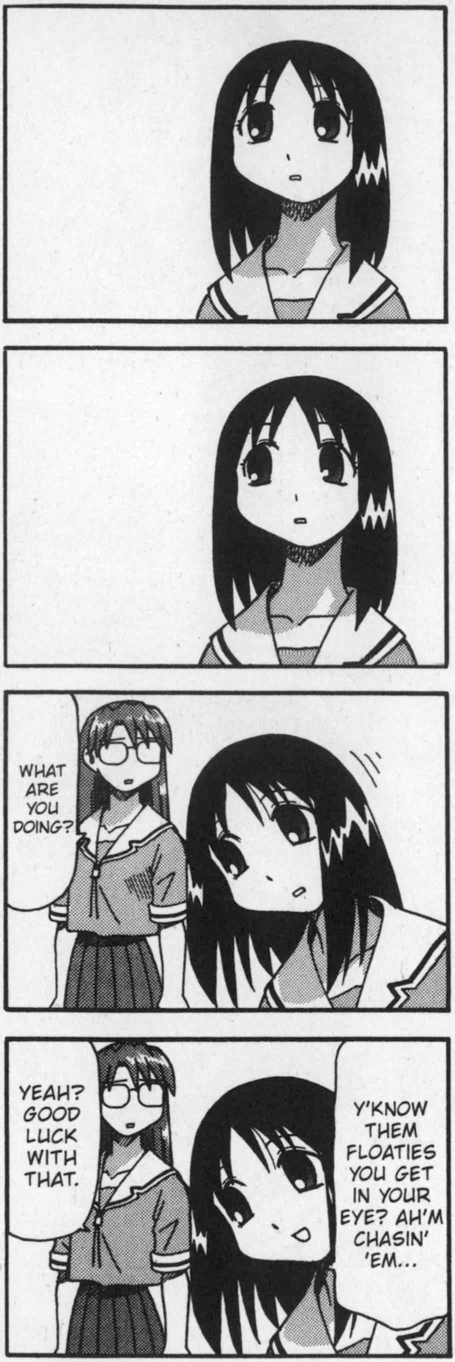
WHAT ARE YOU DOING?
Y'KNOW THEM FLOATIES YOU GET IN YOUR EYE? AH'M CHASIN' 'EM...
YEAH? GOOD LUCK WITH THAT.

NOT LISTENING

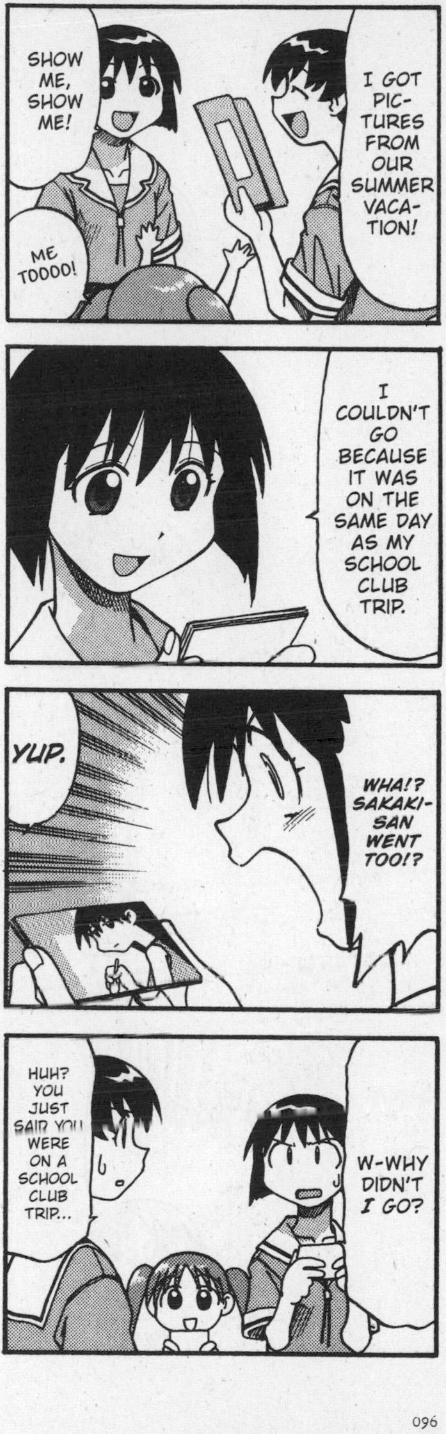
I GOT PIC-TURES FROM OUR SUMMER VACA-TION!
SHOW ME, SHOW ME!
ME TOOOO!
I COULDN'T GO BECAUSE IT WAS ON THE SAME DAY AS MY SCHOOL CLUB TRIP.
WHA!? SAKAKI-SAN WENT TOO!?
YUP.
W-WHY DIDN'T I GO?
HUH? YOU JUST SAID YOU WERE ON A SCHOOL CLUB TRIP...

HOW DARE YOU

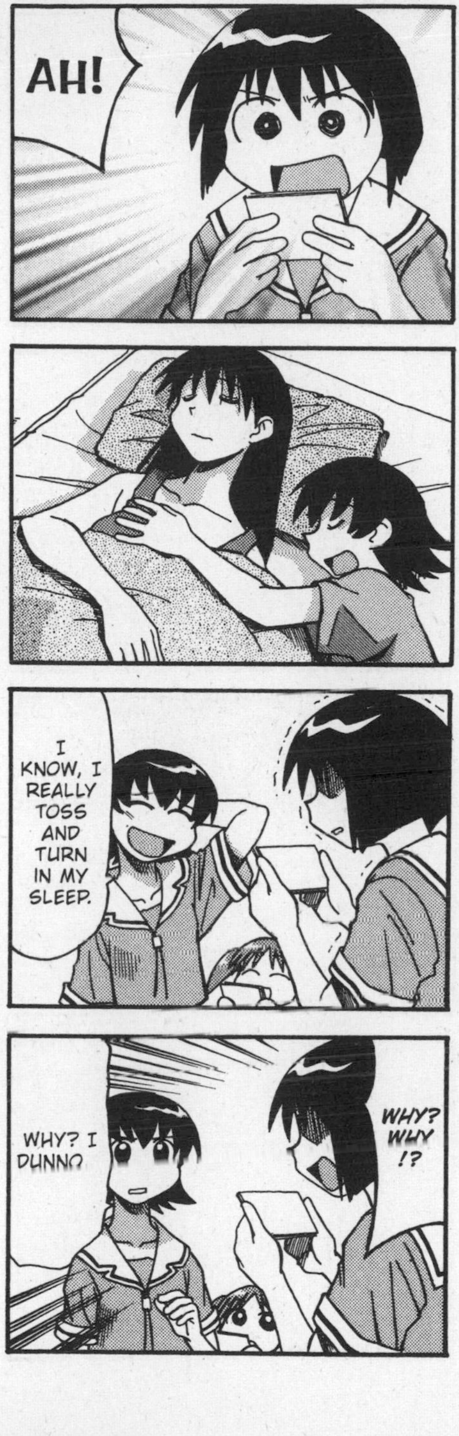
AH!
I KNOW, I REALLY TOSS AND TURN IN MY SLEEP.
WHY? WHY !?
WHY? I DUNNO.

TERROR

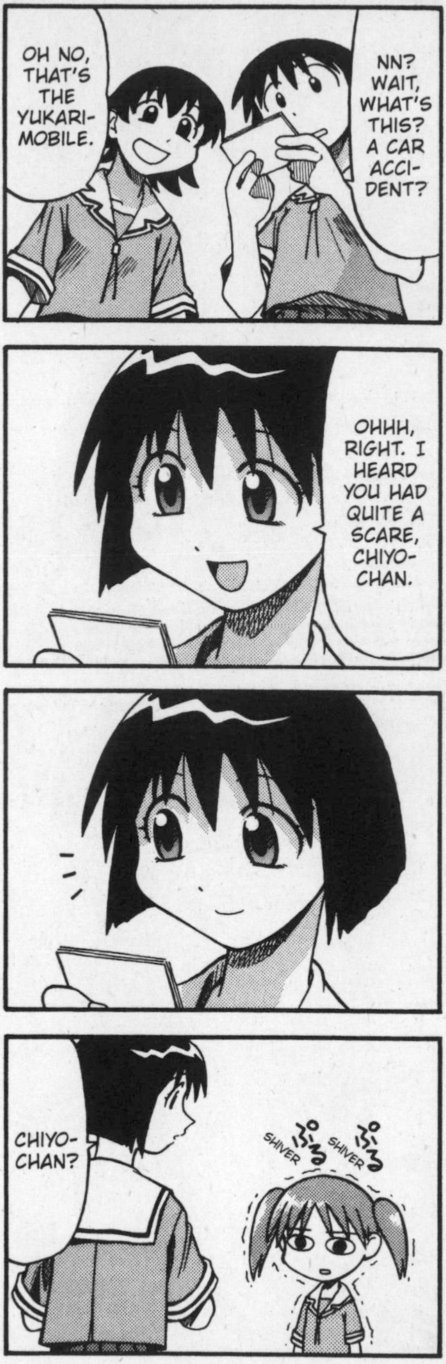
NN? WAIT, WHAT'S THIS? A CAR ACCI-DENT?
OH NO, THAT'S THE YUKARI-MOBILE.
OHHH, RIGHT. I HEARD YOU HAD QUITE A SCARE, CHIYO-CHAN.
SHIVER ぷる SHIVER ぷる
CHIYO-CHAN?

LIFE

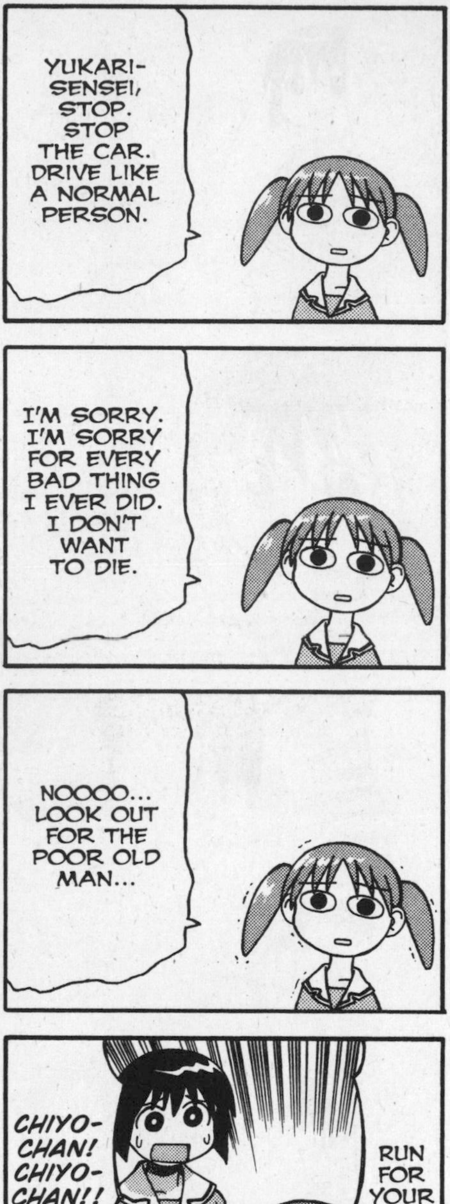
YUKARI-SENSEI, STOP. STOP THE CAR. DRIVE LIKE A NORMAL PERSON.
I'M SORRY. I'M SORRY FOR EVERY BAD THING I EVER DID. I DON'T WANT TO DIE.
NOOOO... LOOK OUT FOR THE POOR OLD MAN...
RUN FOR YOUR LIFE!!
CHIYO-CHAN! CHIYO-CHAN!!

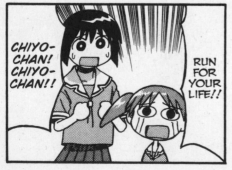

UNKNOWN MAN

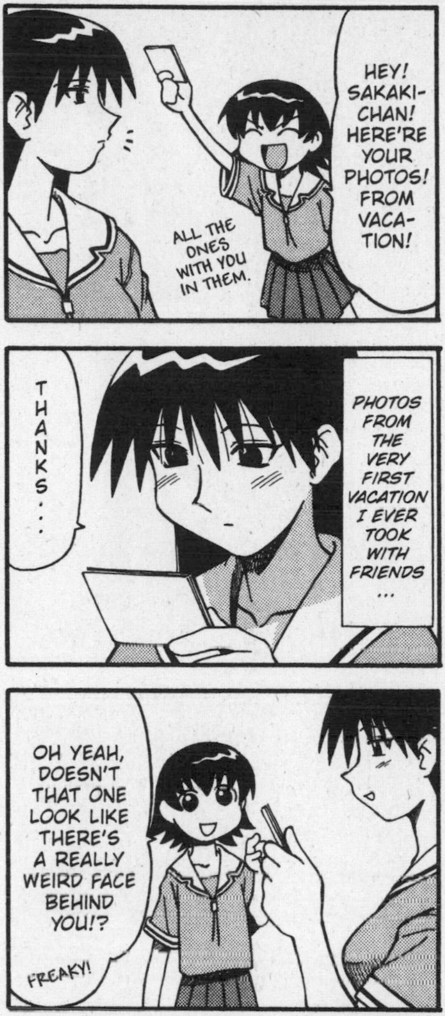
HEY! SAKAKI-CHAN! HERE'RE YOUR PHOTOS! FROM VACATION!
ALL THE ONES WITH YOU IN THEM.
PHOTOS FROM THE VERY FIRST VACATION I EVER TOOK WITH FRIENDS...
THANKS...
OH YEAH, DOESN'T THAT ONE LOOK LIKE THERE'S A REALLY WEIRD FACE BEHIND YOU!?
FREAKY!
OSAKA!!

HE'S SO COOL

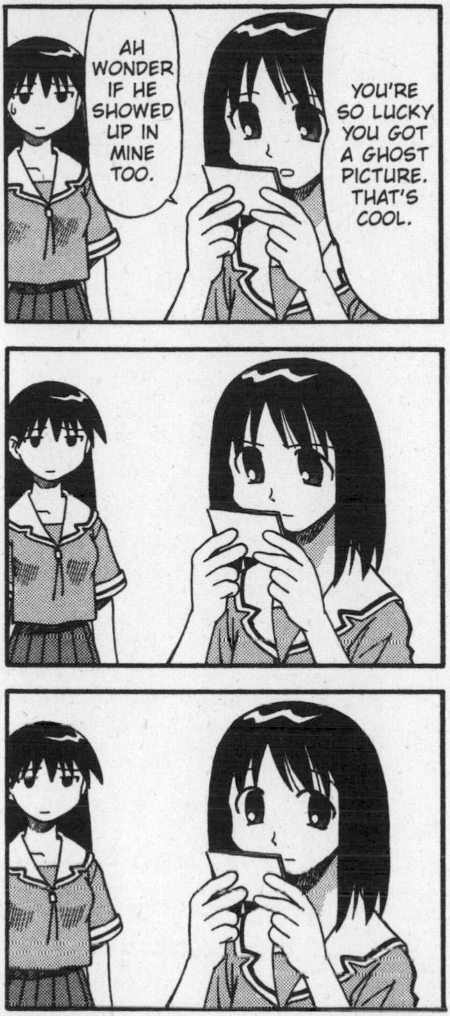
YOU'RE SO LUCKY YOU GOT A GHOST PICTURE. THAT'S COOL.
AH WONDER IF HE SHOWED UP IN MINE TOO.
EH...?

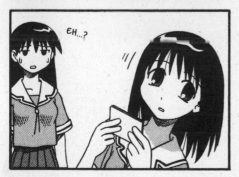

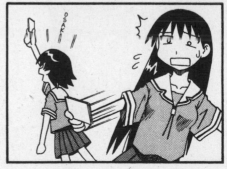

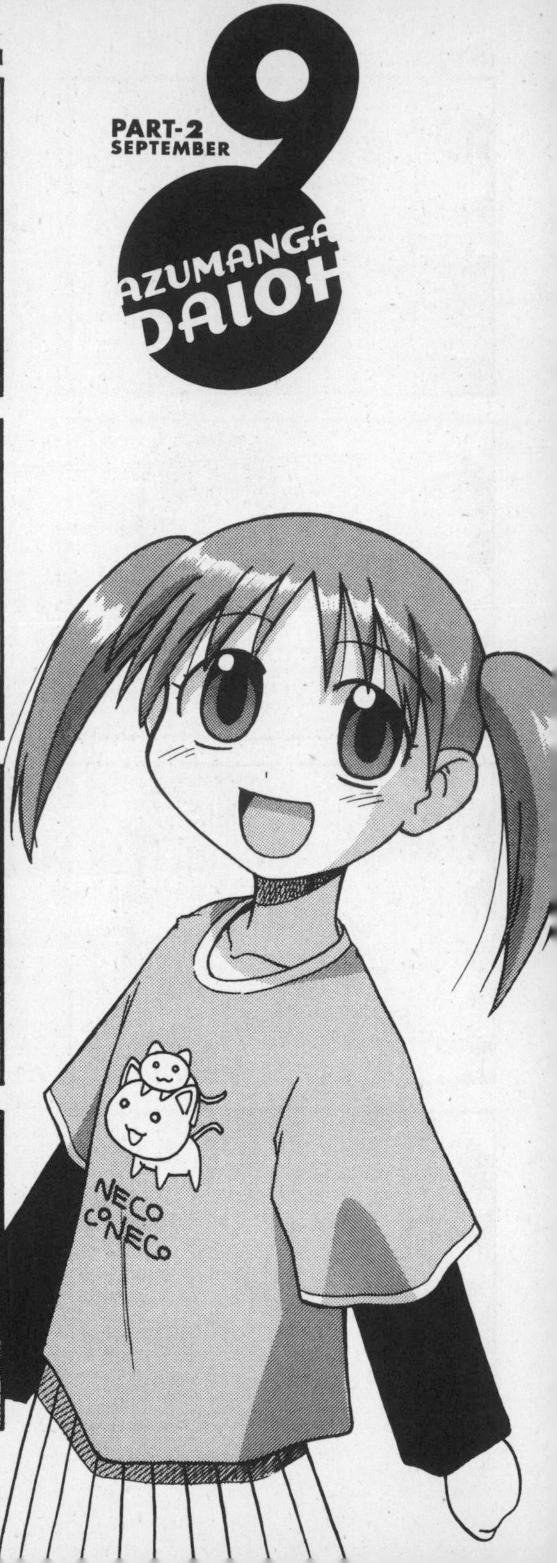
9
PART-2
SEPTEMBER
AZUMANGA DAIOH
NECO CONECO

SCREAM

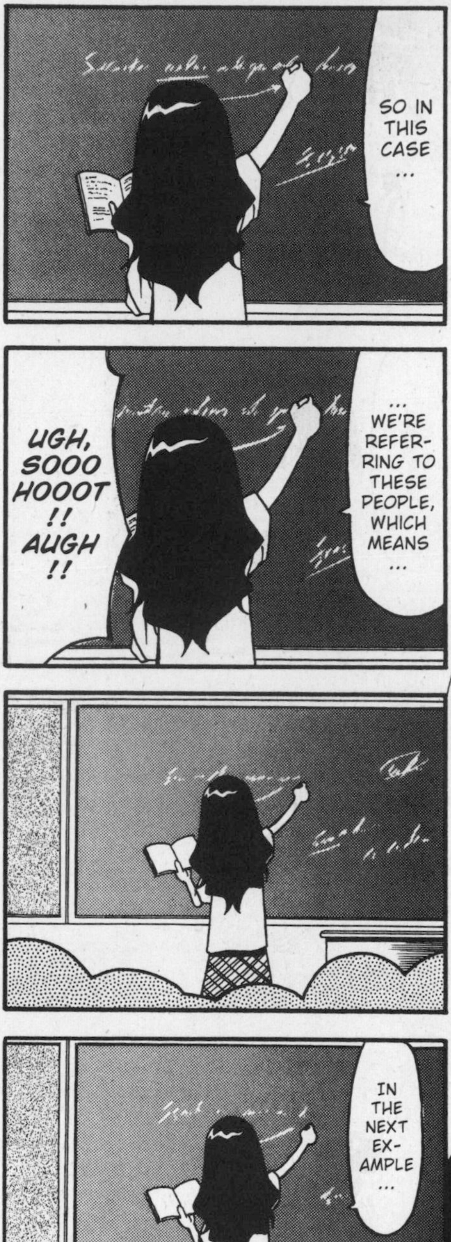
SO IN THIS CASE ...
... WE'RE REFERRING TO THESE PEOPLE, WHICH MEANS ...
UGH, SOOO HOOOT!! AUGH!!
IN THE NEXT EXAMPLE ...

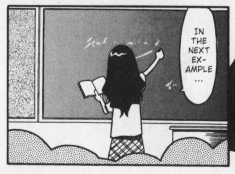

A/C 4 ME

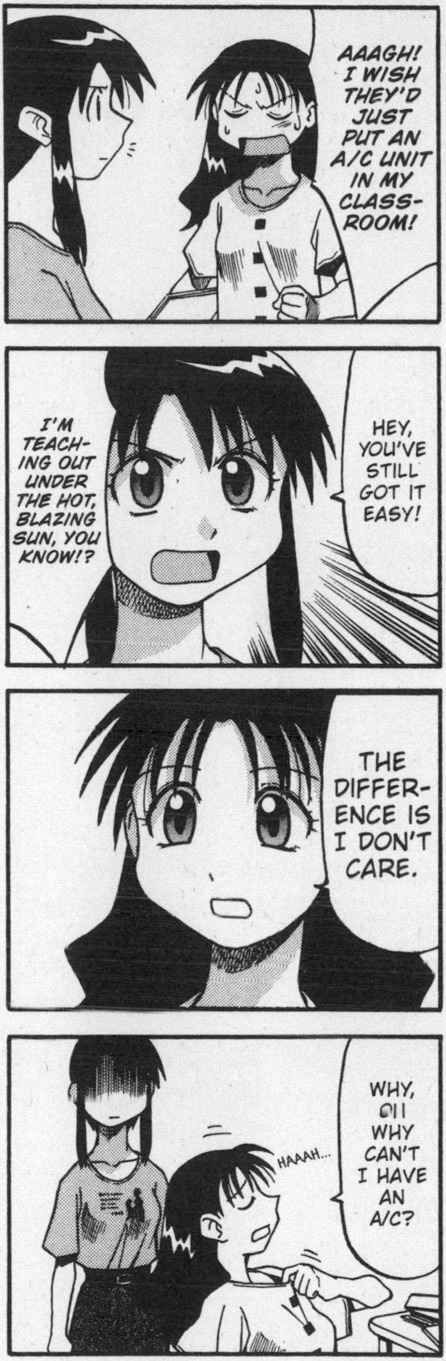

AAAGH! I WISH THEY'D JUST PUT AN A/C UNIT IN MY CLASSROOM!
HEY, YOU'VE STILL GOT IT EASY!
I'M TEACHING OUT UNDER THE HOT, BLAZING SUN, YOU KNOW!?
THE DIFFERENCE IS I DON'T CARE.
WHY, OH WHY CAN'T I HAVE AN A/C?
HAAAH...

DANGER

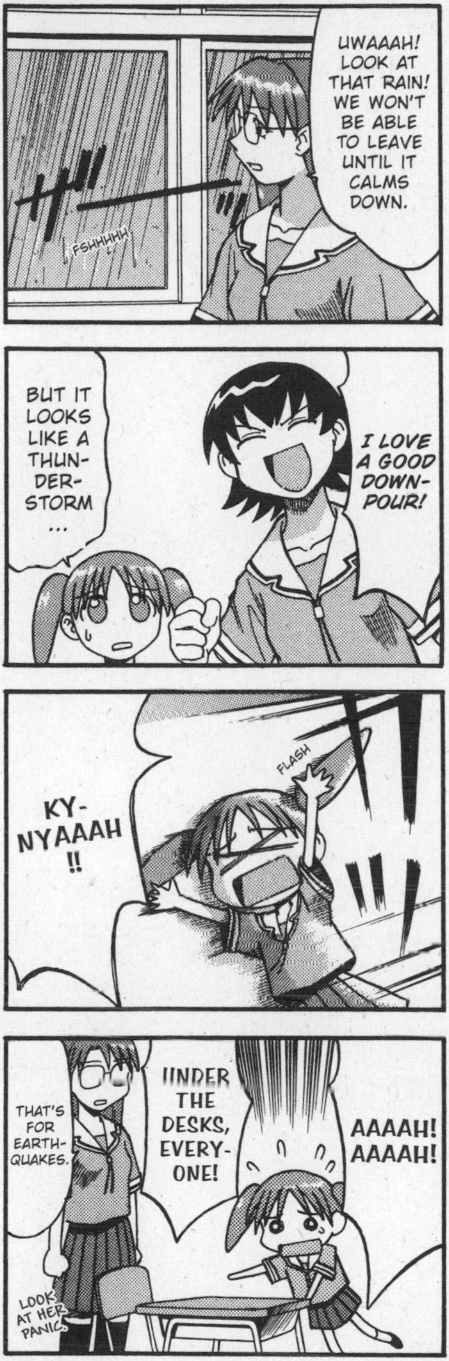

UWAAAH! LOOK AT THAT RAIN! WE WON'T BE ABLE TO LEAVE UNTIL IT CALMS DOWN.
FSHHHHH
I LOVE A GOOD DOWNPOUR!
BUT IT LOOKS LIKE A THUNDERSTORM ...
FLASH
KY-NYAAAH !!
AAAAH! AAAAH!
UNDER THE DESKS, EVERYONE!
THAT'S FOR EARTHQUAKES.
LOOK AT HER PANIC.

NO ESCAPE

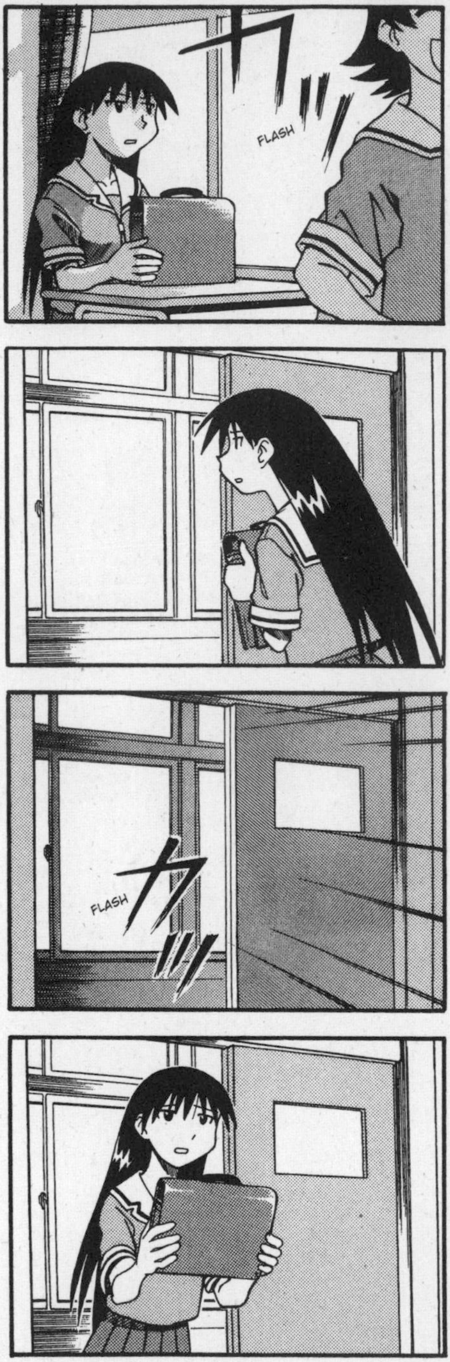
FLASH
FLASH

SCARY

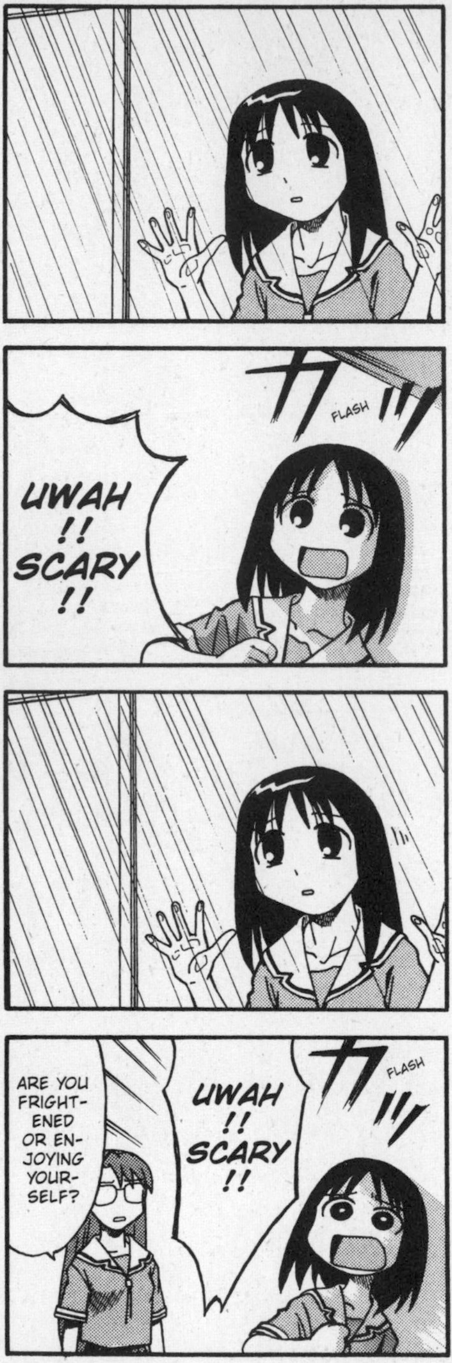
FLASH
UWAH!! SCARY!!
FLASH
UWAH!! SCARY!!
ARE YOU FRIGHT-ENED OR EN-JOYING YOUR-SELF?

UWAAAAHN!

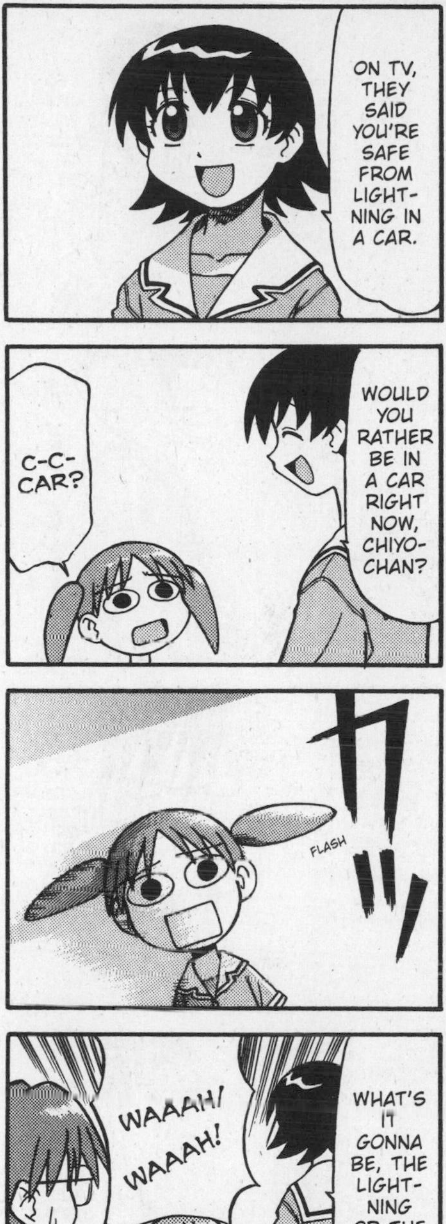
ON TV, THEY SAID YOU'RE SAFE FROM LIGHTNING IN A CAR.
WOULD YOU RATHER BE IN A CAR RIGHT NOW, CHIYO-CHAN?
C-C-CAR?
FLASH
WHAT'S IT GONNA BE, THE LIGHTNING OR THE CAR?
WAAAH! WAAAH!
HEY, STOP THAT.

GONNA DIE

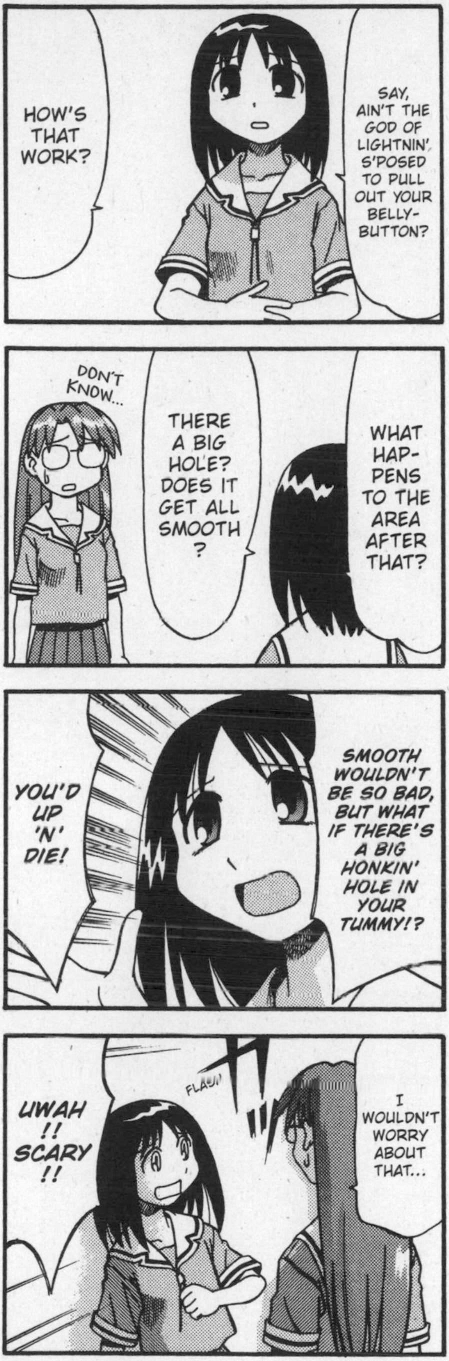
SAY, AIN'T THE GOD OF LIGHTNIN' S'POSED TO PULL OUT YOUR BELLY-BUTTON?
HOW'S THAT WORK?
WHAT HAPPENS TO THE AREA AFTER THAT?
THERE A BIG HOLE? DOES IT GET ALL SMOOTH?
DON'T KNOW...
SMOOTH WOULDN'T BE SO BAD, BUT WHAT IF THERE'S A BIG HONKIN' HOLE IN YOUR TUMMY!?
YOU'D UP 'N' DIE!
I WOULDN'T WORRY ABOUT THAT...
UWAH!! SCARY!!

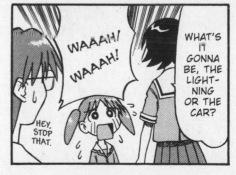

FUN CAREER

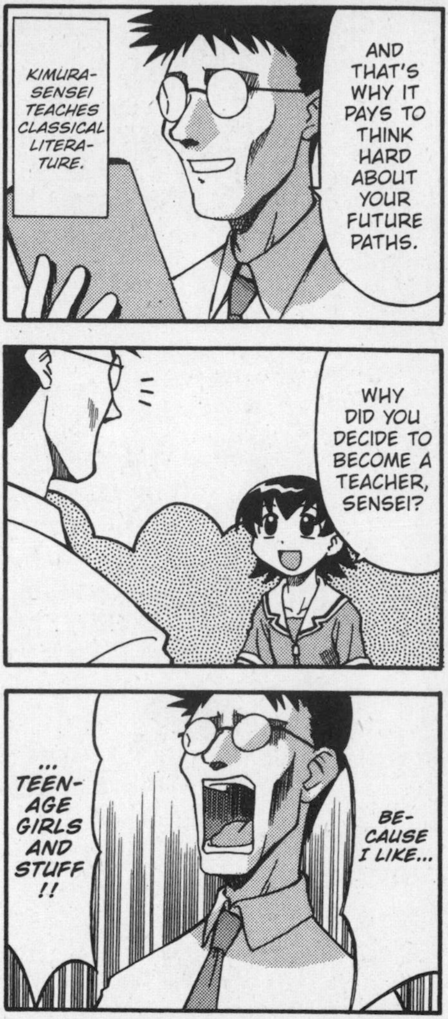
AND THAT'S WHY IT PAYS TO THINK HARD ABOUT YOUR FUTURE PATHS.
KIMURA-SENSEI TEACHES CLASSICAL LITERATURE.
WHY DID YOU DECIDE TO BECOME A TEACHER, SENSEI?
BE-CAUSE I LIKE...
...TEEN-AGE GIRLS AND STUFF!!
キーンコーン
DING
DING
カンコーン
DONG
DONG

HERO

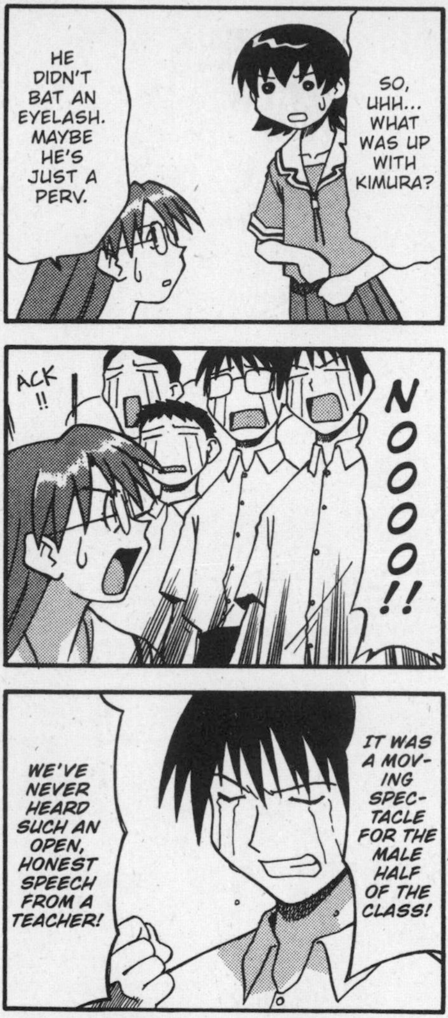
SO, UHH... WHAT WAS UP WITH KIMURA?
HE DIDN'T BAT AN EYELASH. MAYBE HE'S JUST A PERV.
NOOOOO!!
ACK !!
IT WAS A MOVING SPEC-TACLE FOR THE MALE HALF OF THE CLASS!
WE'VE NEVER HEARD SUCH AN OPEN, HONEST SPEECH FROM A TEACHER!
WE'VE NEVER HAD A TEACHER LIKE HIM BEFORE!!
...GUESS YOU COULD SAY THAT.

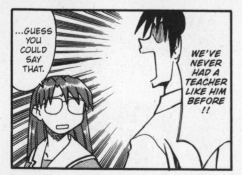

INVITING THE LADIES

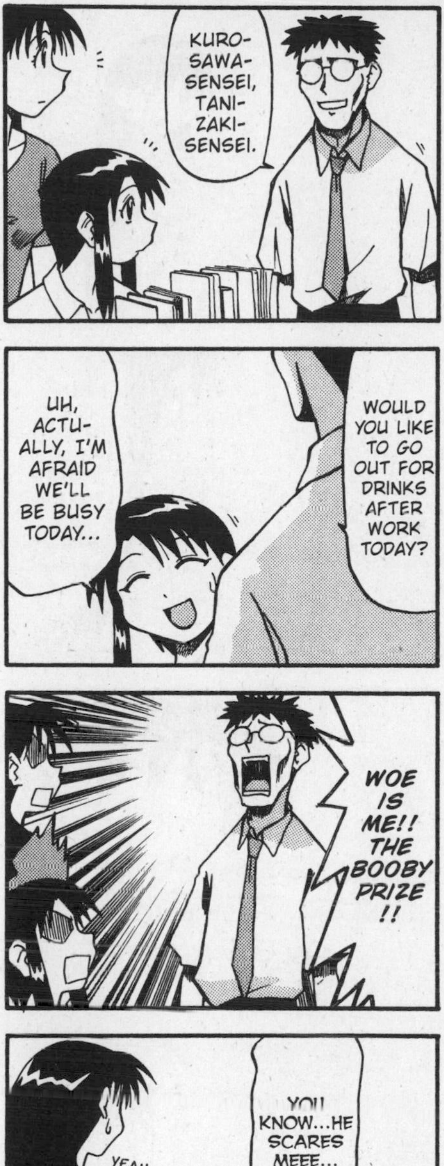
KURO-SAWA-SENSEI, TANI-ZAKI-SENSEI.
WOULD YOU LIKE TO GO OUT FOR DRINKS AFTER WORK TODAY?
UH, ACTU-ALLY, I'M AFRAID WE'LL BE BUSY TODAY...
WOE IS ME!! THE BOOBY PRIZE!!
YOU KNOW...HE SCARES MEEE...
YEAH...... "PRIZE"...?

ASKING SENSEI

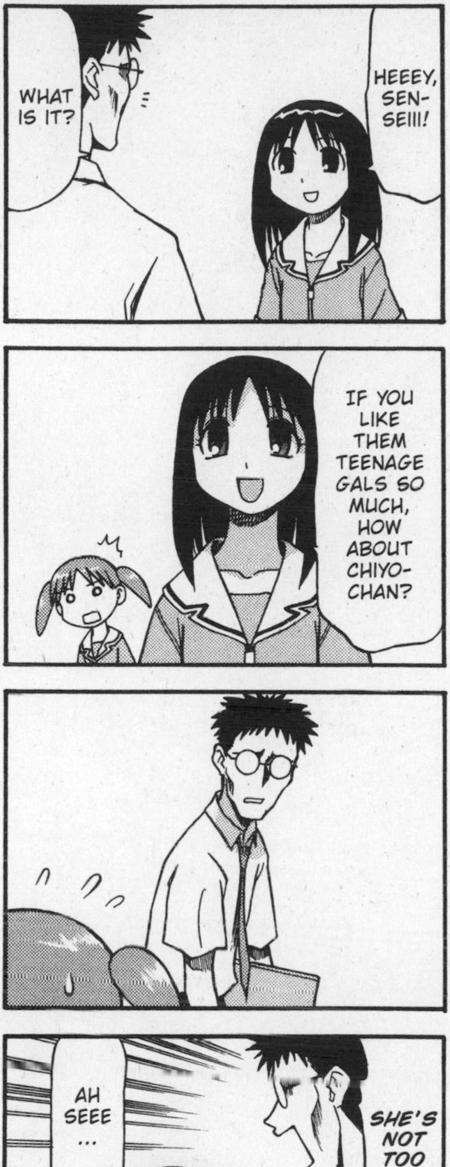
HEEEY, SEN-SEIII!
WHAT IS IT?
IF YOU LIKE THEM TEENAGE GALS SO MUCH, HOW ABOUT CHIYO-CHAN?
SHE'S NOT TOO BAD EI-THER!
AH SEEE ...

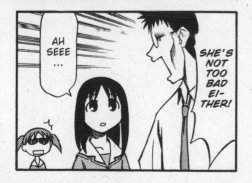

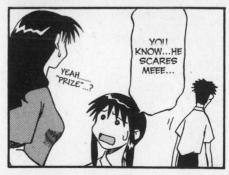

ON A WALK

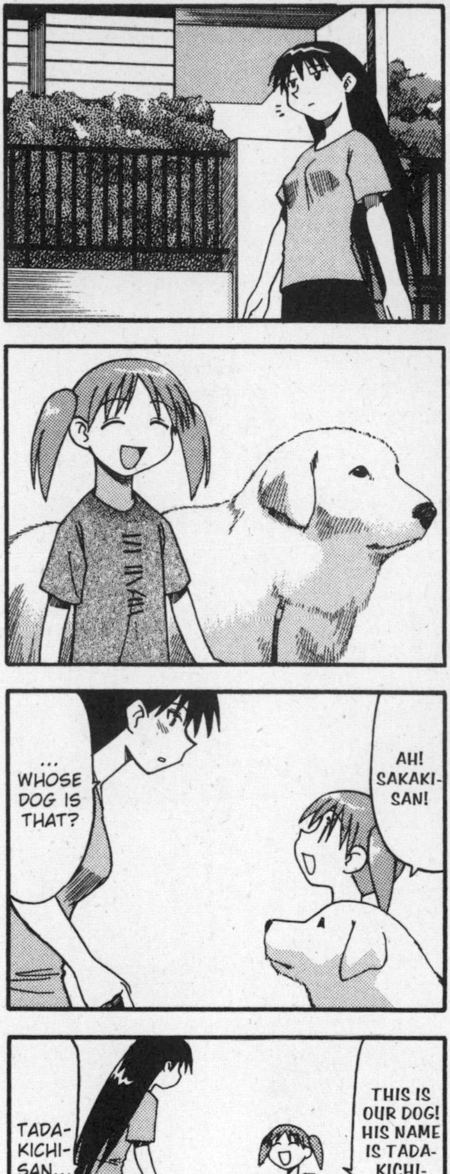
AH! SAKAKI-SAN!
... WHOSE DOG IS THAT?
THIS IS OUR DOG! HIS NAME IS TADA-KICHI-SAN.
TADA-KICHI-SAN...

GENTLEMAN

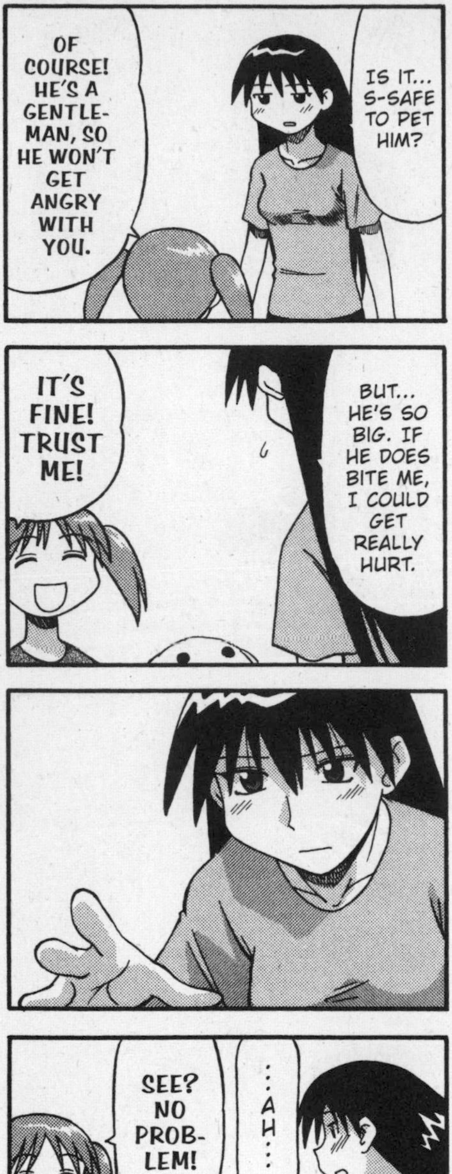
IS IT... S-SAFE TO PET HIM?
OF COURSE! HE'S A GENTLE-MAN, SO HE WON'T GET ANGRY WITH YOU.
BUT... HE'S SO BIG. IF HE DOES BITE ME, I COULD GET REALLY HURT.
IT'S FINE! TRUST ME!
...AH...
SEE? NO PROB-LEM!

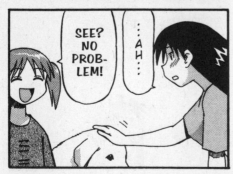

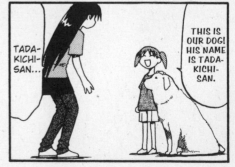

PET PET

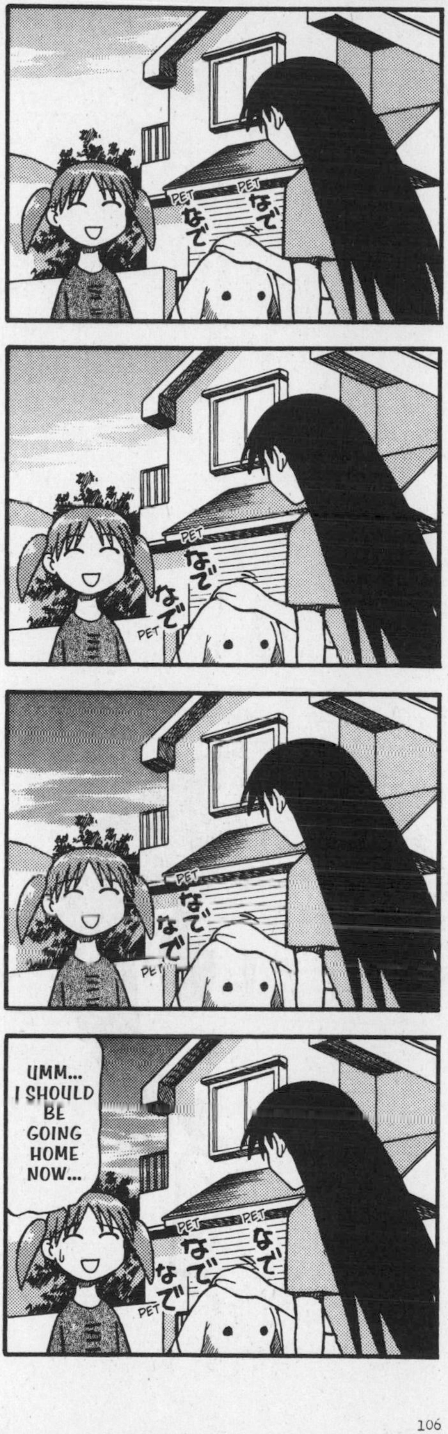
PET
なで
PET
なで
PET
なで
なで
PET
PET
なで
なで
PET
UMM... I SHOULD BE GOING HOME NOW...
PET
なで
PET
なで
なで
PET

HERE WE GO

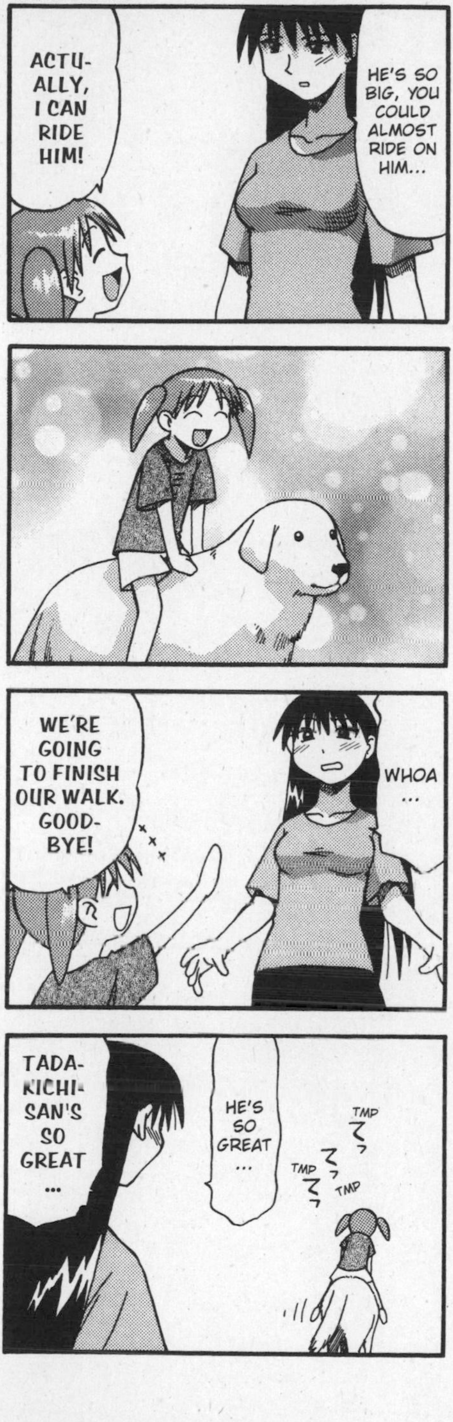
HE'S SO BIG, YOU COULD ALMOST RIDE ON HIM...
ACTU-ALLY, I CAN RIDE HIM!
WHOA ...
WE'RE GOING TO FINISH OUR WALK. GOOD-BYE!
TMP
TMP
TMP
HE'S SO GREAT ...
TADA-KICHI-SAN'S SO GREAT ...

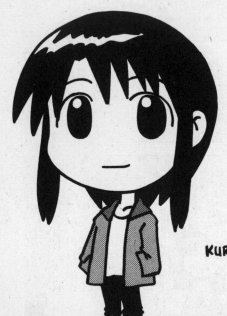

KUROSAWA-SENSEI

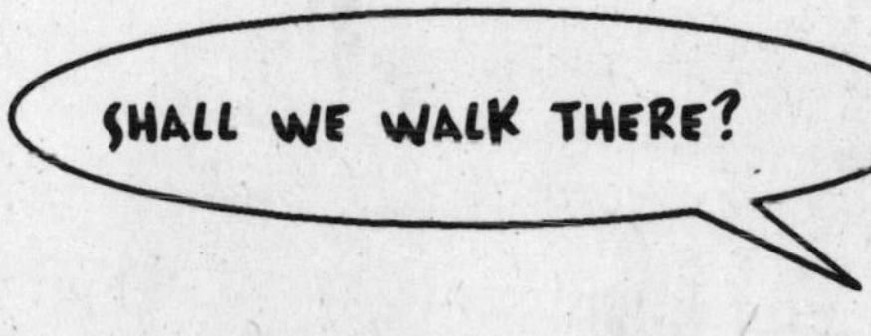

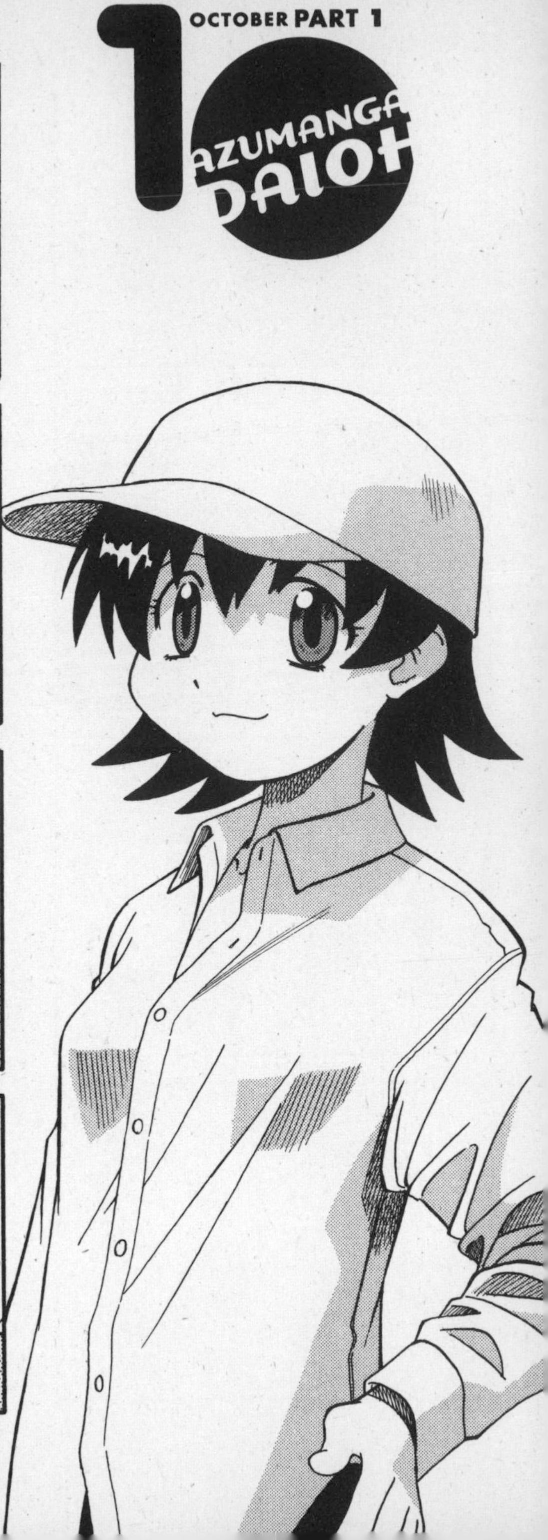
10
OCTOBER PART 1
AZUMANGA DAIOH

WHO CARES

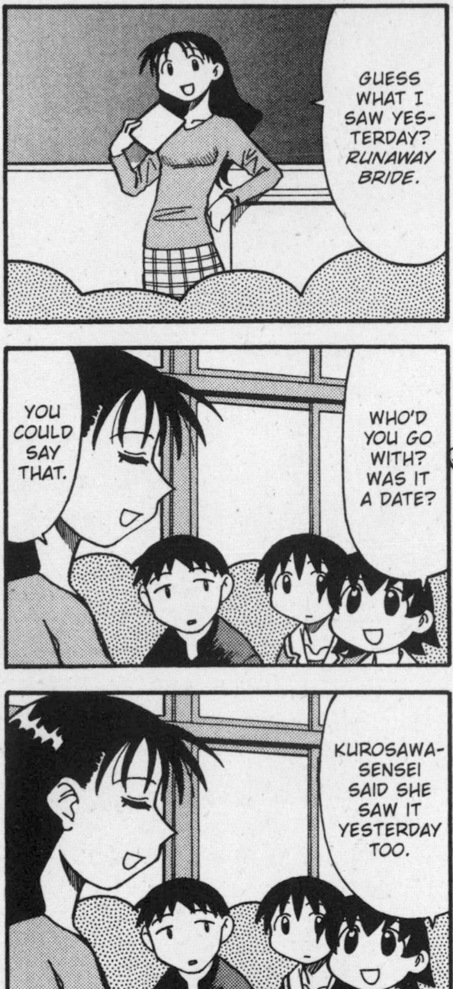
GUESS WHAT I SAW YESTERDAY? *RUNAWAY BRIDE*.
WHO'D YOU GO WITH? WAS IT A DATE?
YOU COULD SAY THAT.
KUROSAWA-SENSEI SAID SHE SAW IT YESTERDAY TOO.
WHO GIVES A DAMN ABOUT MOVIES ANYWAY?
BACK TO THE LESSON.

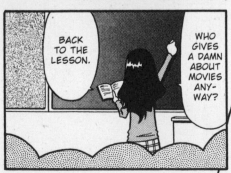

JUMP, CHIYO-CHAN

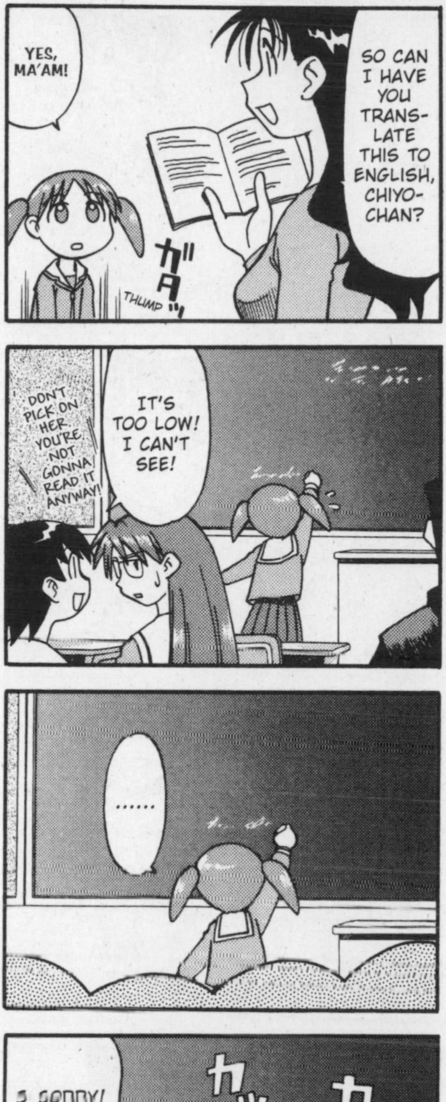
SO CAN I HAVE YOU TRANSLATE THIS TO ENGLISH, CHIYO-CHAN?
YES, MA'AM!
ガタッ
THUMP
IT'S TOO LOW! I CAN'T SEE!
DON'T PICK ON HER. YOU'RE NOT GONNA READ IT ANYWAY!
......
カッ
TEK
カッ
TEK
S-SORRY! IT'S OKAY, YOU DON'T HAVE TO JUMP.
ぴょん
HOP
ぴょん
HOP

ASKING SENSEI

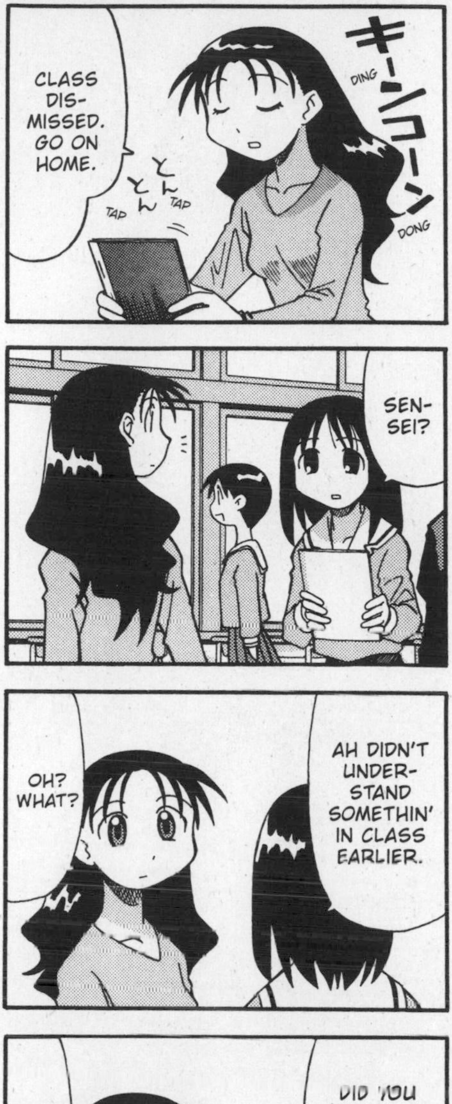
キーンコーン
DING
DONG
CLASS DIS-MISSED. GO ON HOME.
とんとん
TAP
TAP
SEN-SEI?
AH DIDN'T UNDER-STAND SOMETHIN' IN CLASS EARLIER.
OH? WHAT?
DID YOU ACTUALLY SEE THE MOVIE WITH KUROSAWA-SENSEI?
OH, SHUT UP.

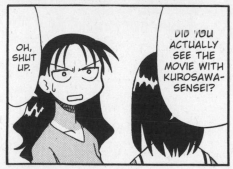

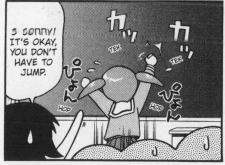

TOO BAD

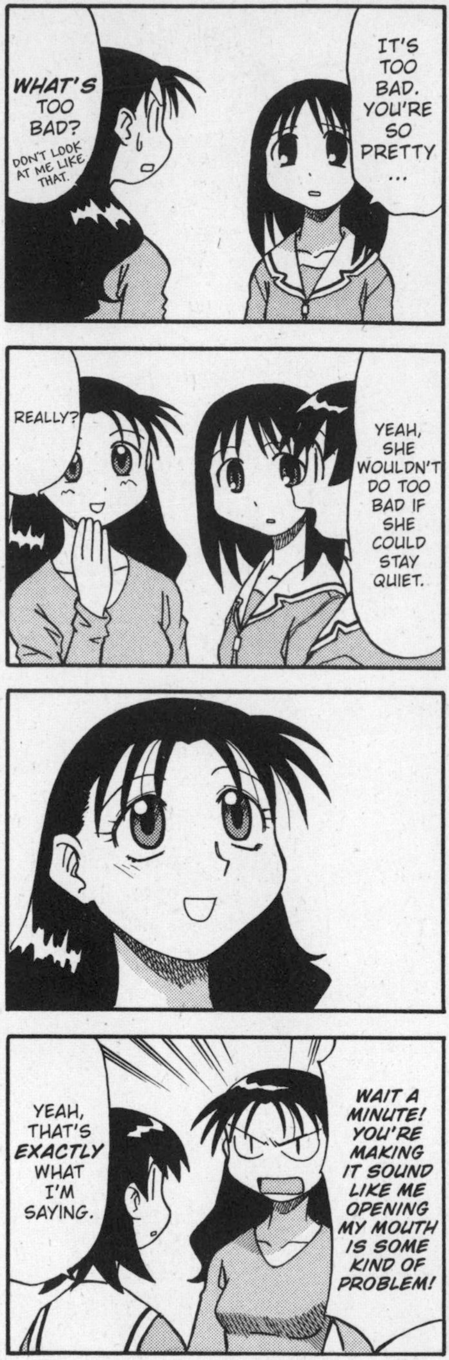
IT'S TOO BAD. YOU'RE SO PRETTY ...
WHAT'S TOO BAD?
DON'T LOOK AT ME LIKE THAT.
YEAH, SHE WOULDN'T DO TOO BAD IF SHE COULD STAY QUIET.
REALLY?
WAIT A MINUTE! YOU'RE MAKING IT SOUND LIKE ME OPENING MY MOUTH IS SOME KIND OF PROBLEM!
YEAH, THAT'S EXACTLY WHAT I'M SAYING.

IT'S THE ONLY WAY

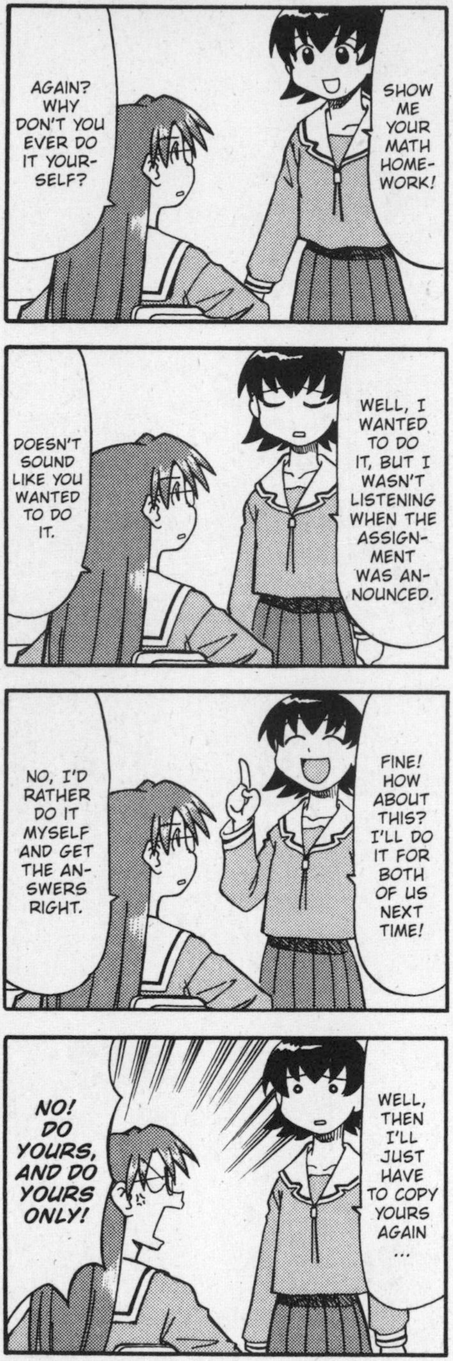
SHOW ME YOUR MATH HOMEWORK!
AGAIN? WHY DON'T YOU EVER DO IT YOURSELF?
WELL, I WANTED TO DO IT, BUT I WASN'T LISTENING WHEN THE ASSIGNMENT WAS ANNOUNCED.
DOESN'T SOUND LIKE YOU WANTED TO DO IT.
FINE! HOW ABOUT THIS? I'LL DO IT FOR BOTH OF US NEXT TIME!
NO, I'D RATHER DO IT MYSELF AND GET THE ANSWERS RIGHT.
WELL, THEN I'LL JUST HAVE TO COPY YOURS AGAIN ...
NO! DO YOURS, AND DO YOURS ONLY!

USE YOUR MANNERS

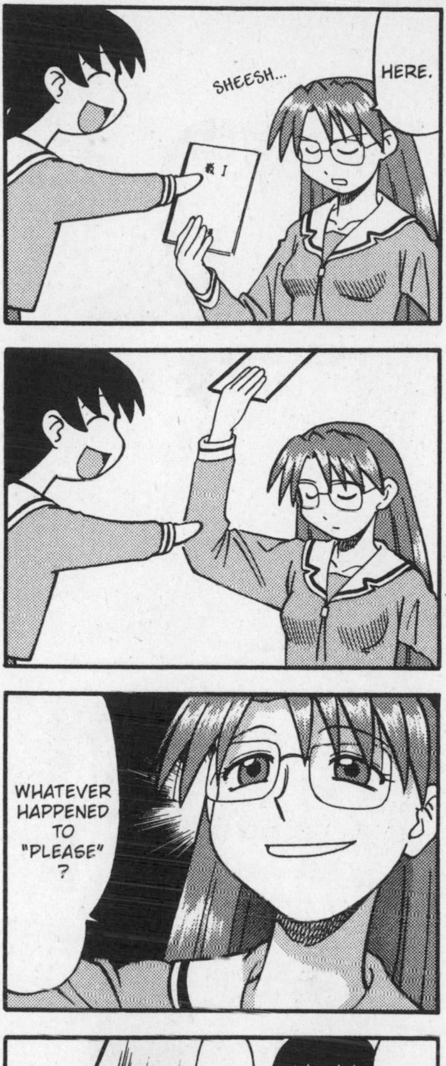
HERE.
SHEESH...
WHATEVER HAPPENED TO "PLEASE"?
HUH? WHAT DOES THAT EVEN MEAN?
ARE YOU STU-PID?
I'M NOT STU-PID! YOU ARE!!

NO-HOLDS-BARRED

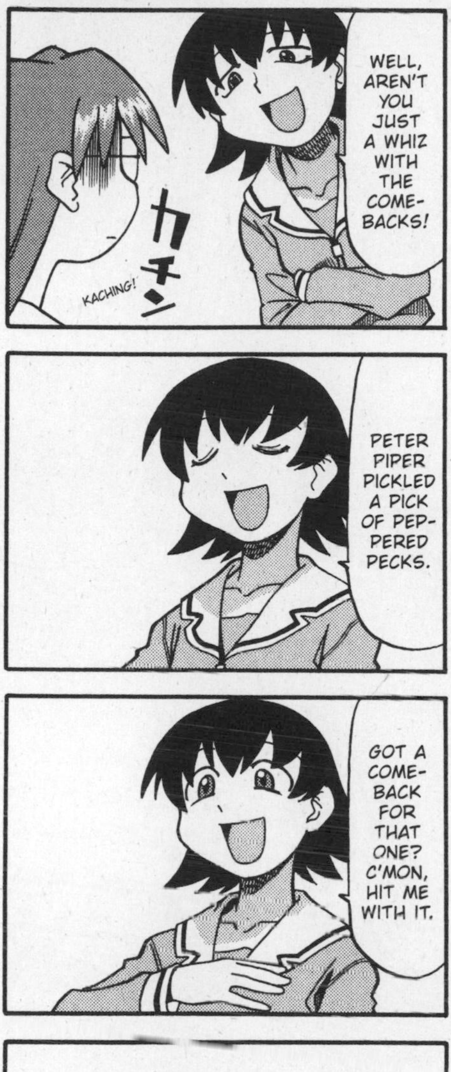
WELL, AREN'T YOU JUST A WHIZ WITH THE COME-BACKS!
カチン
KACHING!
PETER PIPER PICKLED A PICK OF PEP-PERED PECKS.
GOT A COME-BACK FOR THAT ONE? C'MON, HIT ME WITH IT.

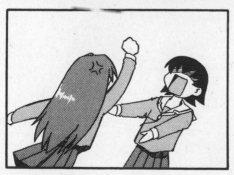

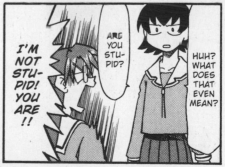

KIMURA'S PREFERENCE

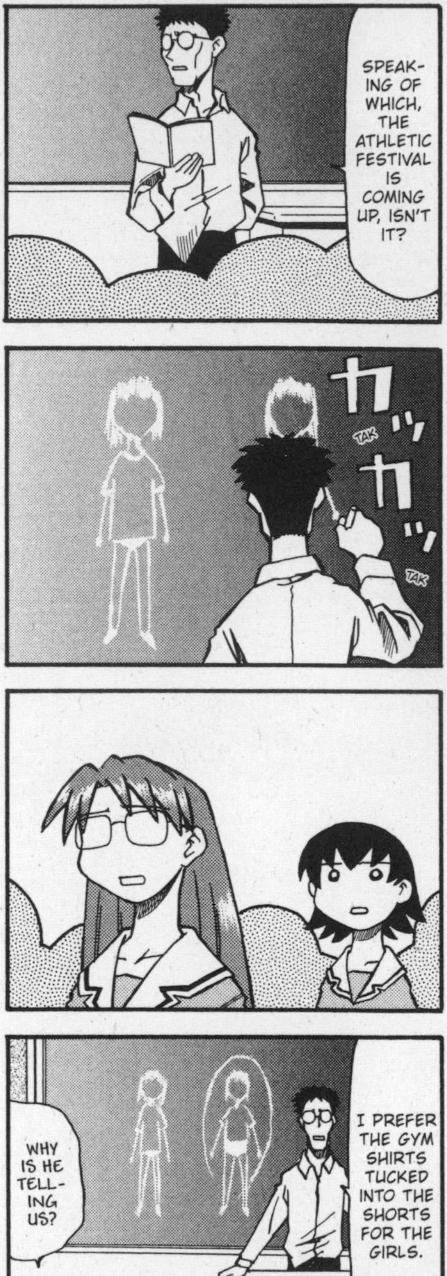
SPEAK-ING OF WHICH, THE ATHLETIC FESTIVAL IS COMING UP, ISN'T IT?
カッ
TAK
カッ
TAK
I PREFER THE GYM SHIRTS TUCKED INTO THE SHORTS FOR THE GIRLS.
WHY IS HE TELL-ING US?

INCOMPREHENSIBLE

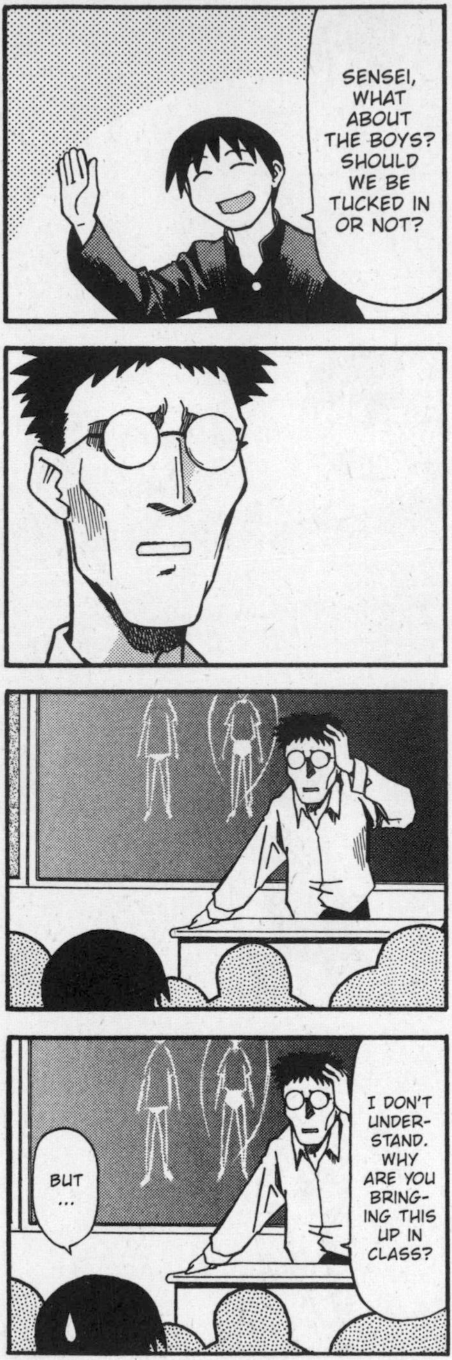
SENSEI, WHAT ABOUT THE BOYS? SHOULD WE BE TUCKED IN OR NOT?
I DON'T UNDER-STAND. WHY ARE YOU BRING-ING THIS UP IN CLASS?
BUT ...

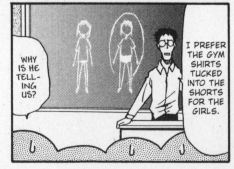

QUEEN OF OBLIVION

HUHHHHH?
CAN AH BORROW YOUR PENCIL? AH THINK AH FORGOT MINE.
SURE THING.
YOU FORGET STUFF A LOT, DON'T YOU?
YEAH. YOU WOULDN'T THINK SO, HUH?
ACTUALLY, I CAN IMAGINE QUITE EASILY.

VICTORY DEMANDED

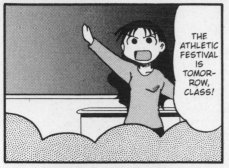

THE ATHLETIC FESTIVAL IS TOMORROW, CLASS!
YOU'VE GOT TO GET IN THE ZONE, PEOPLE! HEAR ME!!?
WIN! VICTORY OVER CLASS 5 AT ALL COSTS!
CLASS 5?
THAT'S KUROSAWA-SENSEI.
DO ANYTHING YOU CAN TO SECURE OUR VICTORY!!
WHAT WOULD THAT ENTAIL, EXACTLY...?

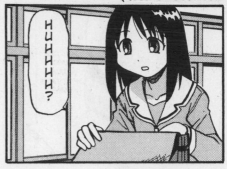

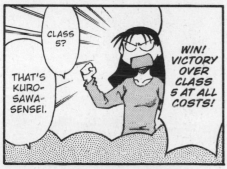

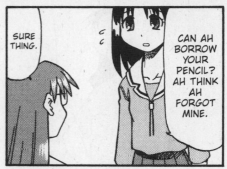

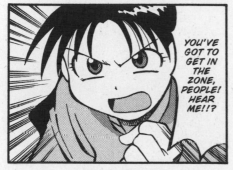

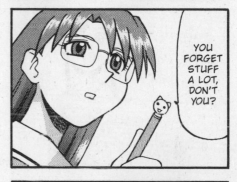

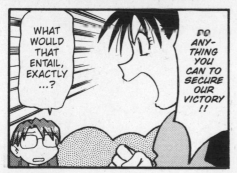

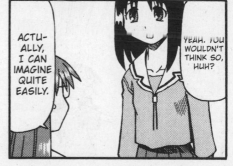

THE EQUATION FOR VICTORY

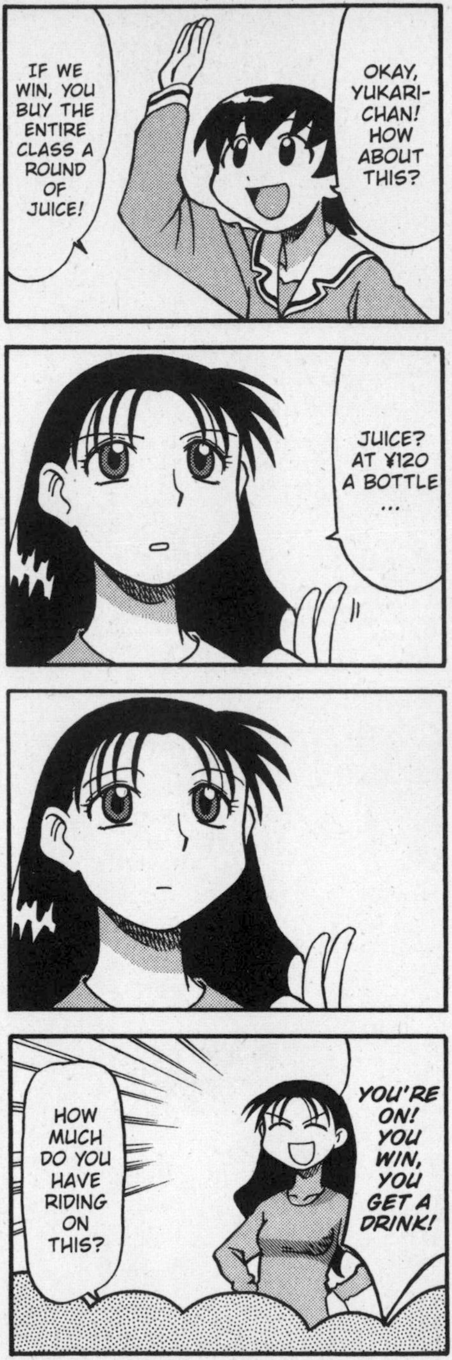
OKAY, YUKARI-CHAN! HOW ABOUT THIS?
IF WE WIN, YOU BUY THE ENTIRE CLASS A ROUND OF JUICE!
JUICE? AT ¥120 A BOTTLE ...
YOU'RE ON! YOU WIN, YOU GET A DRINK!
HOW MUCH DO YOU HAVE RIDING ON THIS?

DECLARATION OF WAR

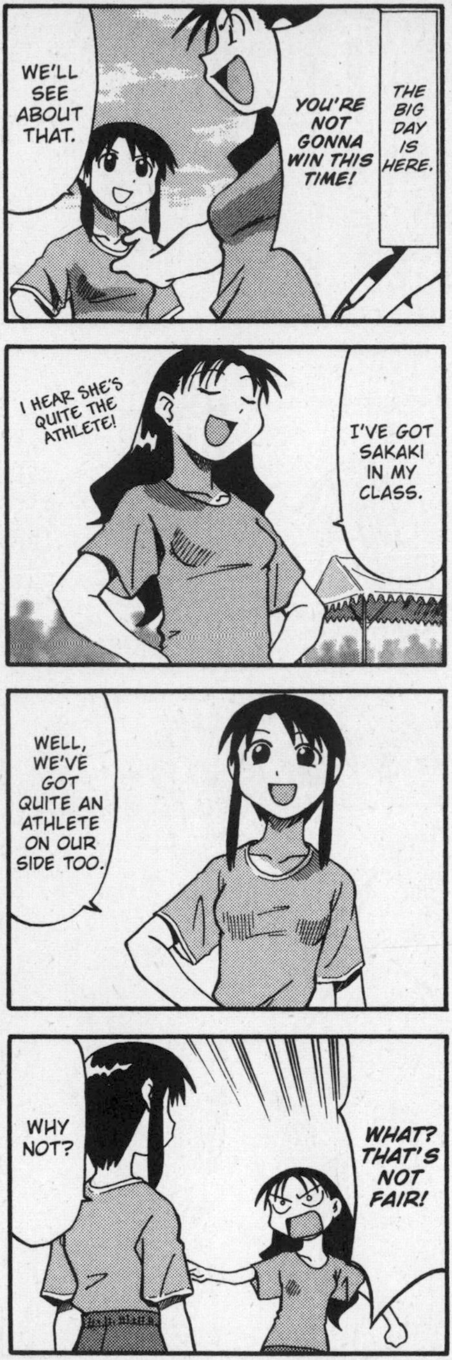
THE BIG DAY IS HERE.
YOU'RE NOT GONNA WIN THIS TIME!
WE'LL SEE ABOUT THAT.
I'VE GOT SAKAKI IN MY CLASS.
I HEAR SHE'S QUITE THE ATHLETE!
WELL, WE'VE GOT QUITE AN ATHLETE ON OUR SIDE TOO.
WHAT? THAT'S NOT FAIR!
WHY NOT?

SAKAKI VS. KAGURA

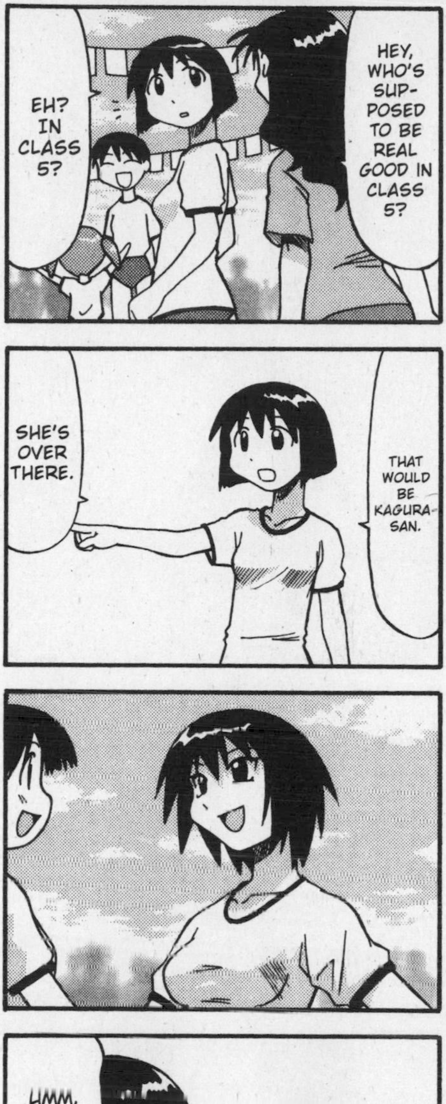
HEY, WHO'S SUP-POSED TO BE REAL GOOD IN CLASS 5?
EH? IN CLASS 5?
THAT WOULD BE KAGURA-SAN.
SHE'S OVER THERE.
UMM, WHY DID YOU ASK? HELLO ...?
SHH

NICE AND TASTY

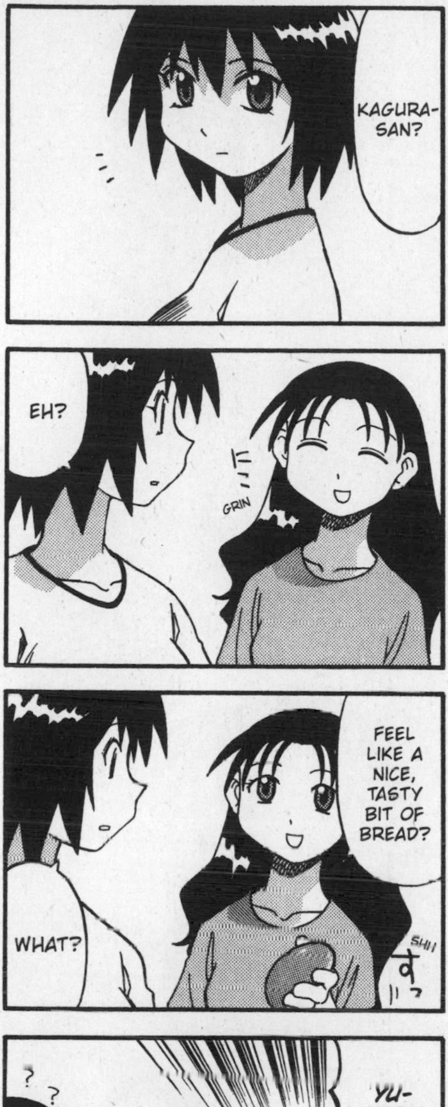
KAGURA-SAN?
EH?
GRIN
FEEL LIKE A NICE, TASTY BIT OF BREAD?
SHII
WHAT?
YU-KARI! WHAT ARE YOU DOING !?
TSK

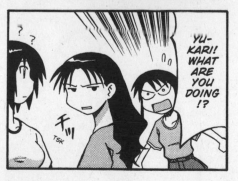

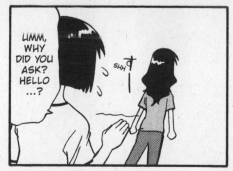

10 OCTOBER PART-2

AZUMANGA DAIOH

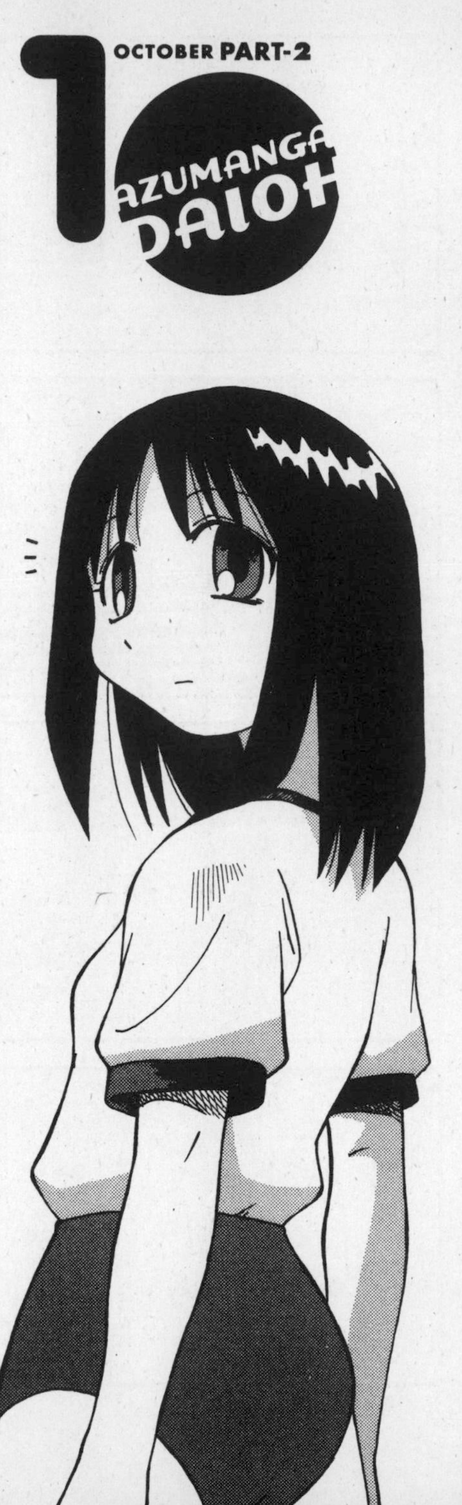

I'LL TRY, BUT I'M SORRY

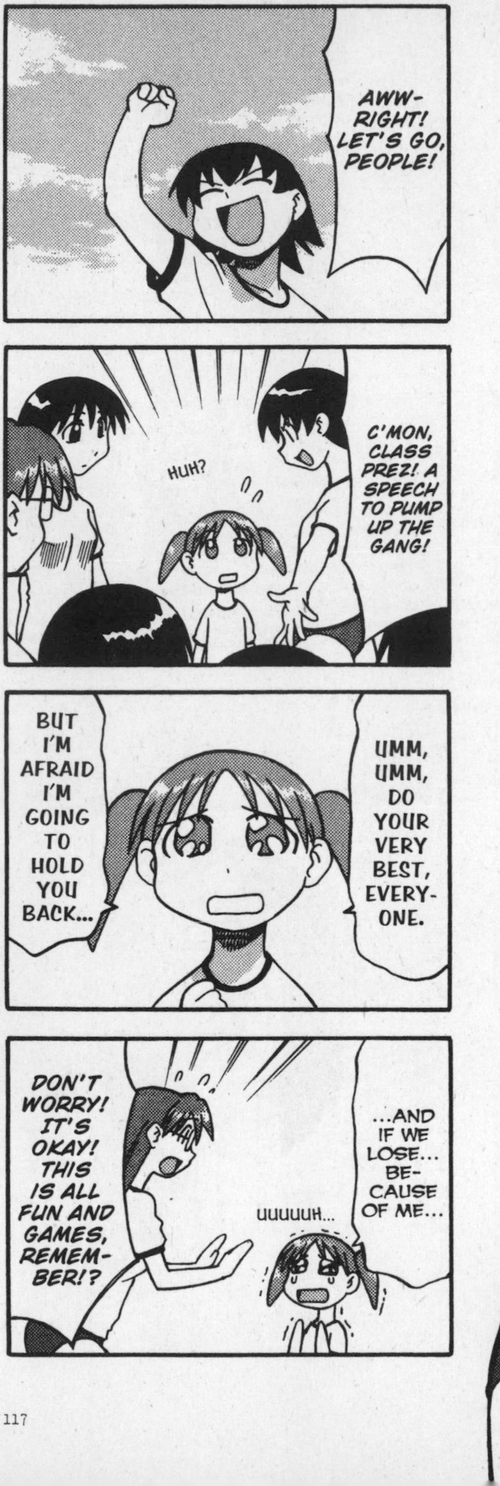
AWW-RIGHT! LET'S GO, PEOPLE!
C'MON, CLASS PREZ! A SPEECH TO PUMP UP THE GANG!
HUH?
UMM, UMM, DO YOUR VERY BEST, EVERY-ONE.
BUT I'M AFRAID I'M GOING TO HOLD YOU BACK...
...AND IF WE LOSE... BE-CAUSE OF ME...
UUUUUH...
DON'T WORRY! IT'S OKAY! THIS IS ALL FUN AND GAMES, REMEM-BER!?

HARDENED STEEL

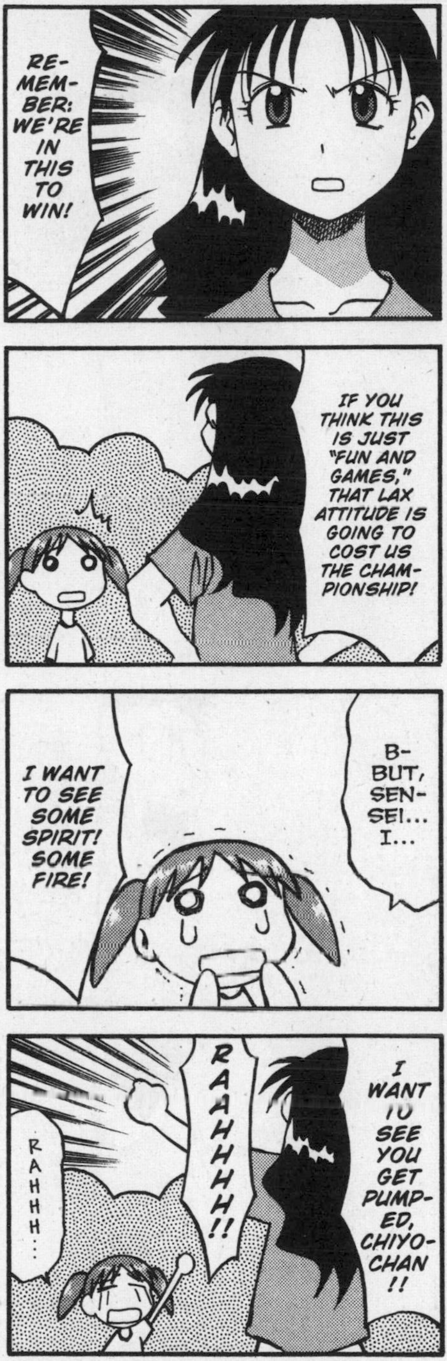
RE-MEMBER: WE'RE IN THIS TO WIN!
IF YOU THINK THIS IS JUST "FUN AND GAMES," THAT LAX ATTITUDE IS GOING TO COST US THE CHAMPIONSHIP!
B-BUT, SENSEI... I...
I WANT TO SEE SOME SPIRIT! SOME FIRE!
I WANT TO SEE YOU GET PUMPED, CHIYO-CHAN!!
RAAHHHH!!
RAHHH...

IT'S OKAY

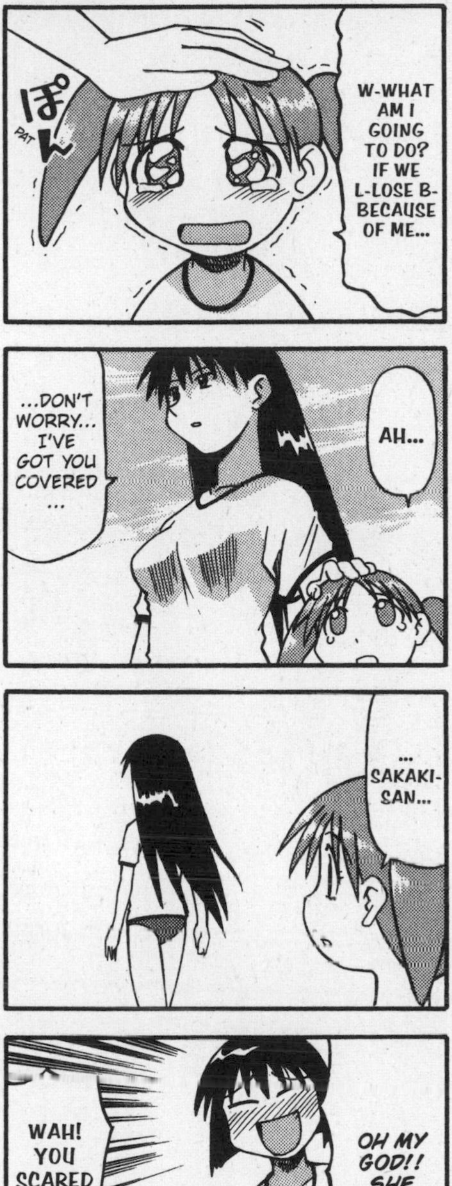
W-WHAT AM I GOING TO DO? IF WE L-LOSE B-BECAUSE OF ME...
ぽん
PAT
AH...
...DON'T WORRY... I'VE GOT YOU COVERED...
...SAKAKI-SAN...
OH MY GOD!! SHE IS THE COOLEST!!
WAH! YOU SCARED ME!

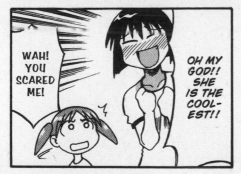

ONE, ONE, ONE

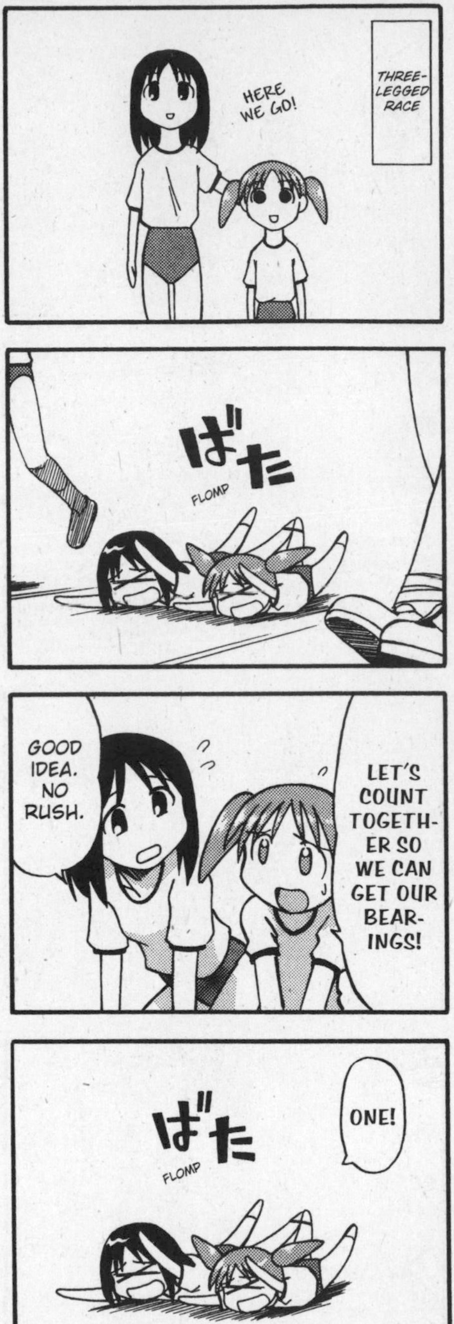
THREE-LEGGED RACE
HERE WE GO!
ばた
FLOMP
LET'S COUNT TOGETHER SO WE CAN GET OUR BEARINGS!
GOOD IDEA. NO RUSH.
ONE!
ばた
FLOMP

WAY IN FRONT

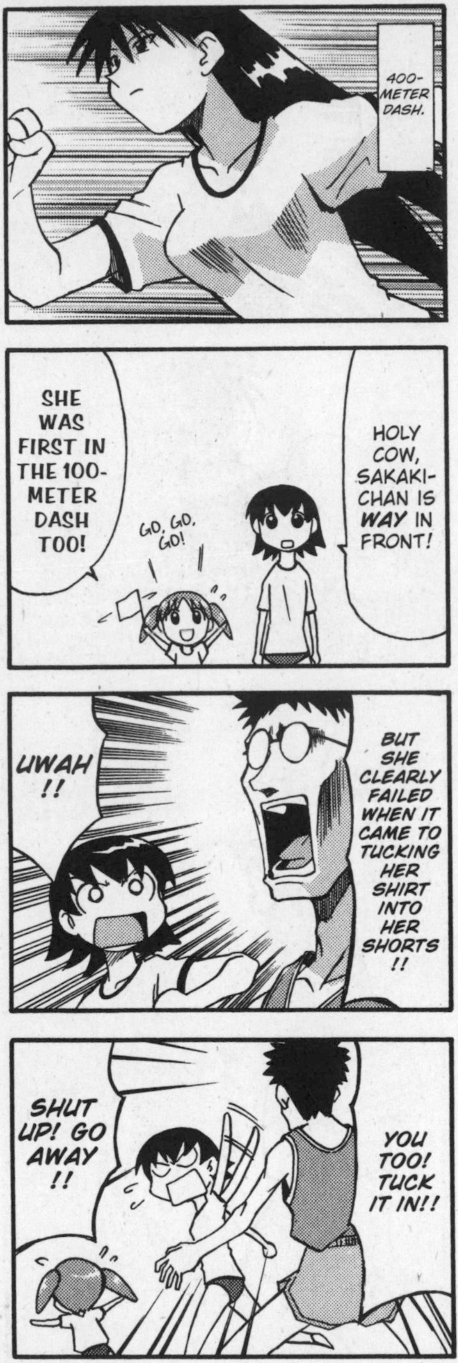
400-METER DASH.
HOLY COW, SAKAKI-CHAN IS WAY IN FRONT!
GO, GO, GO!
SHE WAS FIRST IN THE 100-METER DASH TOO!
BUT SHE CLEARLY FAILED WHEN IT CAME TO TUCKING HER SHIRT INTO HER SHORTS!!
UWAH!!
YOU TOO! TUCK IT IN!!
SHUT UP! GO AWAY!!

PULL, OSAKA

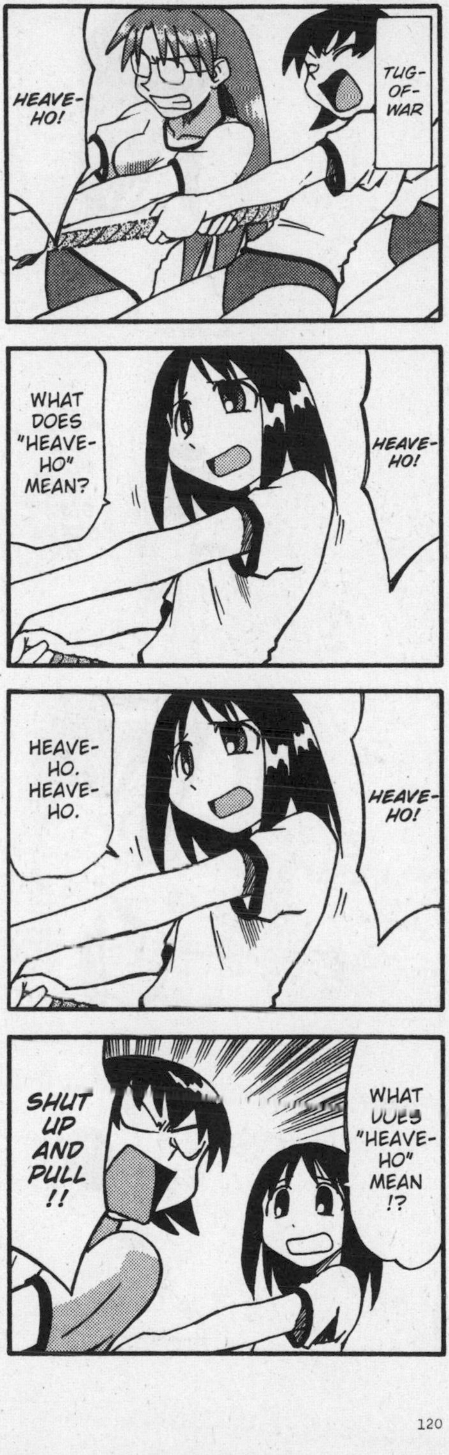
TUG-OF-WAR
HEAVE-HO!
HEAVE-HO!
WHAT DOES "HEAVE-HO" MEAN?
HEAVE-HO!
HEAVE-HO. HEAVE-HO.
WHAT DOES "HEAVE-HO" MEAN !?
SHUT UP AND PULL !!

DON'T LET GO

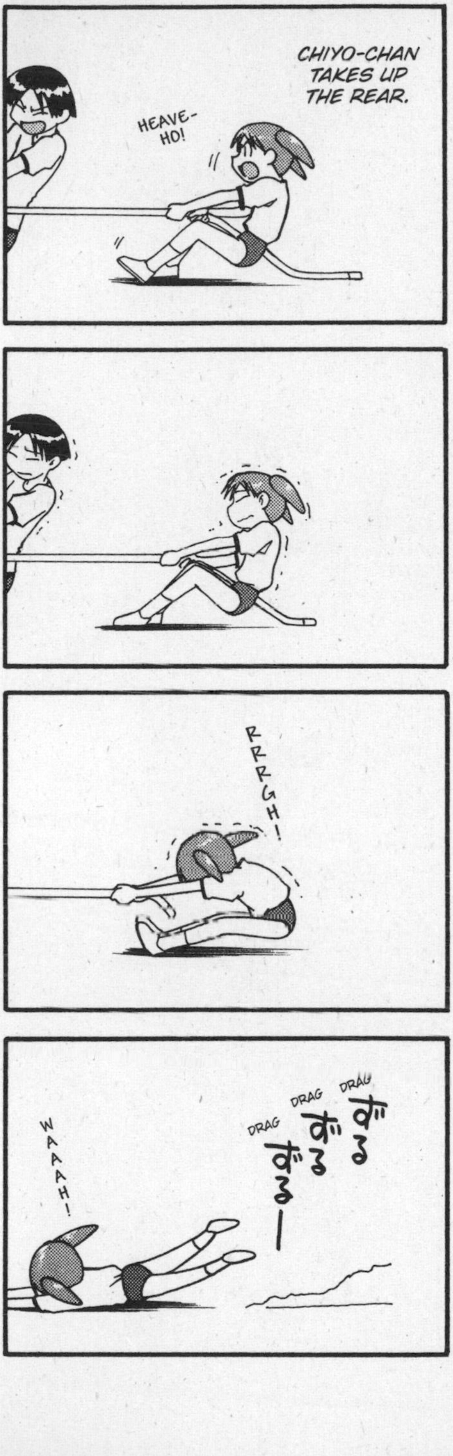
CHIYO-CHAN TAKES UP THE REAR.
HEAVE-HO!
RRRGH!
ずるずるずるー
DRAG DRAG DRAG DRAG
WAAAH!

LET'S TRY IT

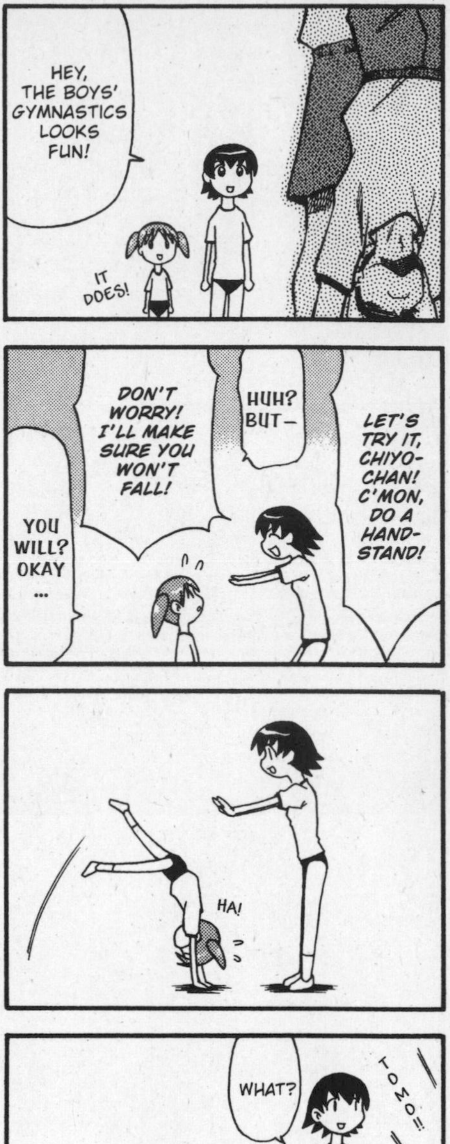
HEY, THE BOYS' GYMNASTICS LOOKS FUN!
IT DOES!
LET'S TRY IT, CHIYO-CHAN! C'MON, DO A HANDSTAND!
HUH? BUT—
DON'T WORRY! I'LL MAKE SURE YOU WON'T FALL!
YOU WILL? OKAY ...
HA!
TOMO!!
WHAT?
びたーん!!
THWAM!!

OSAKA IN GLASSES

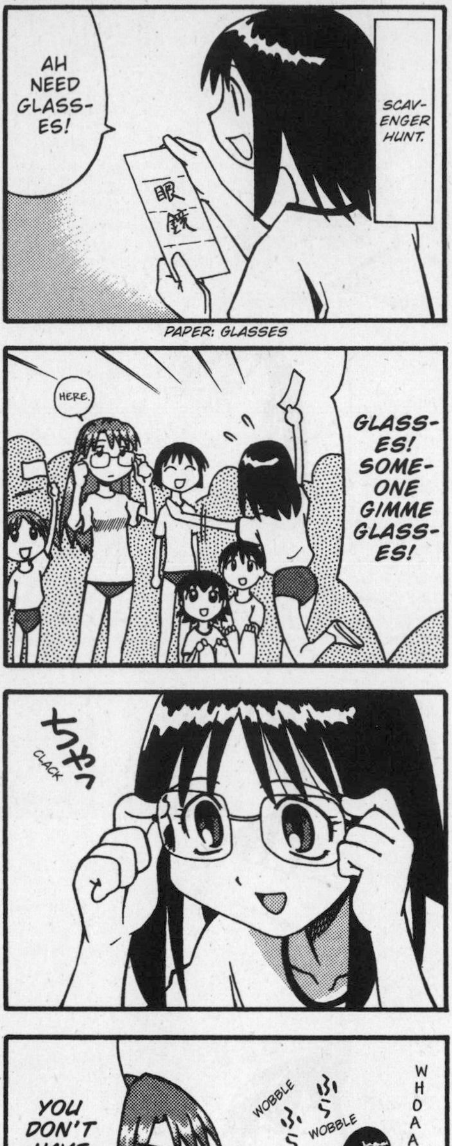
SCAVENGER HUNT.
AH NEED GLASSES!
眼鏡
PAPER: GLASSES
GLASSES! SOMEONE GIMME GLASSES!
HERE.
ちゃっ
CLACK
WHOAAA...
ふら ふら
WOBBLE WOBBLE
YOU DON'T HAVE TO PUT THEM ON!

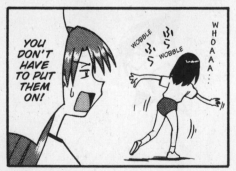

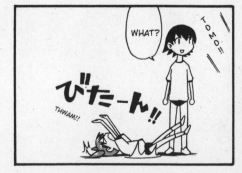

EVERYONE BUT HER

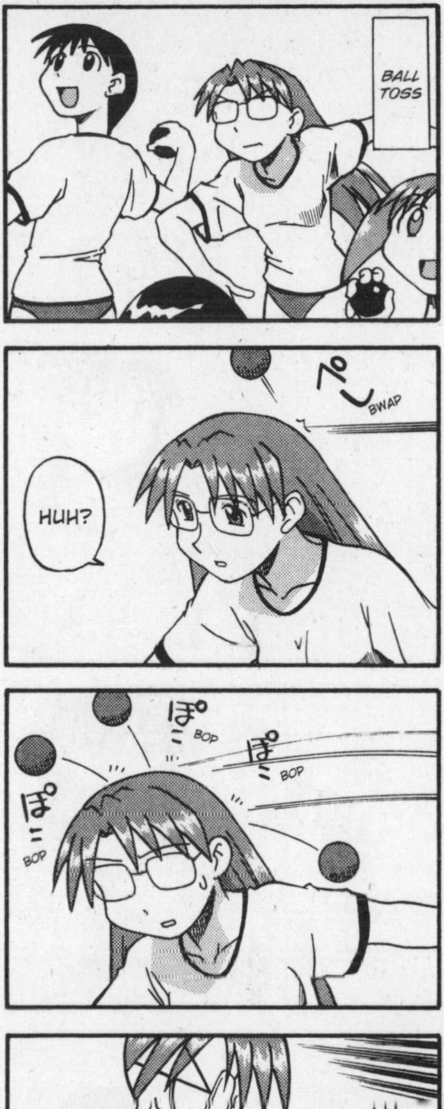
BALL TOSS
ぺし
BWAP
HUH?
ぽこ
BOP
ぽこ
BOP
ぽこ
BOP
KNOCK IT OFF! THIS IS SERIOUS!

SPIN-SPIN, HOP-HOP

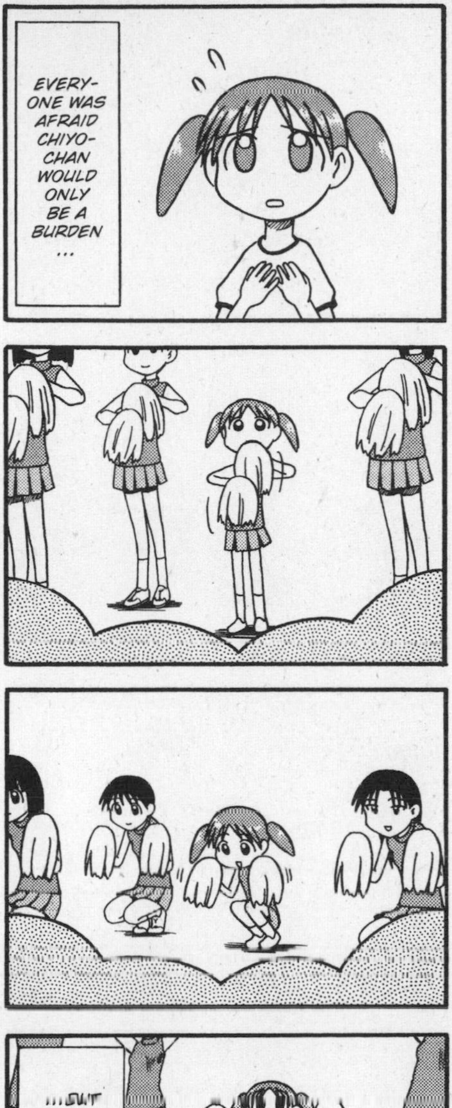
EVERYONE WAS AFRAID CHIYO-CHAN WOULD ONLY BE A BURDEN...
...BUT SHE SCORED BIG IN CHEERLEADING.
OOOH! LOOK AT THAT LITTLE GIRL!
SHE'S SO CUTE!

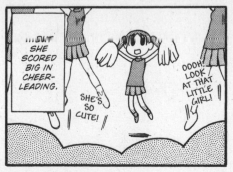

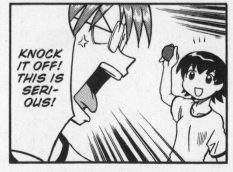

HOORAY

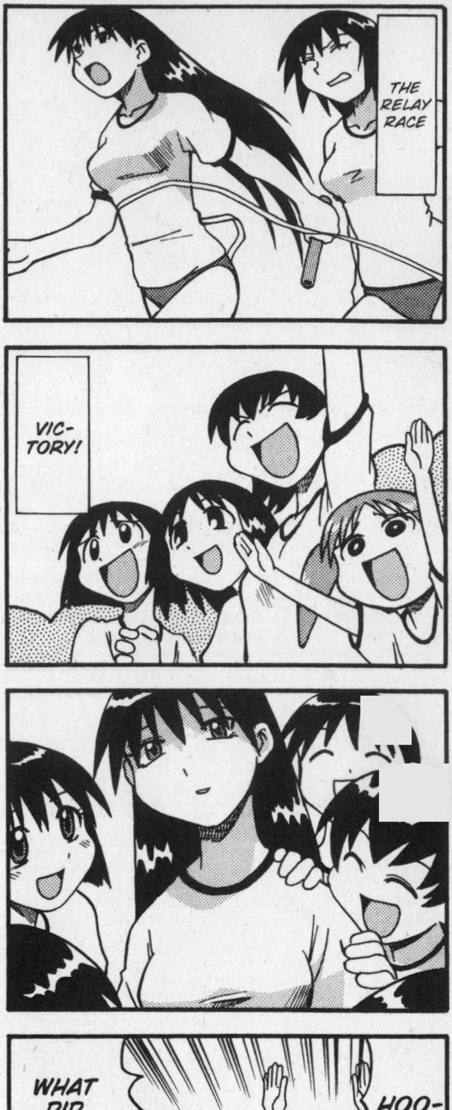
THE RELAY RACE
VIC-TORY!
HOO-RAY!
WHAT DID YOU HAVE TO DO WITH IT!?

THE CLOSING DANCE

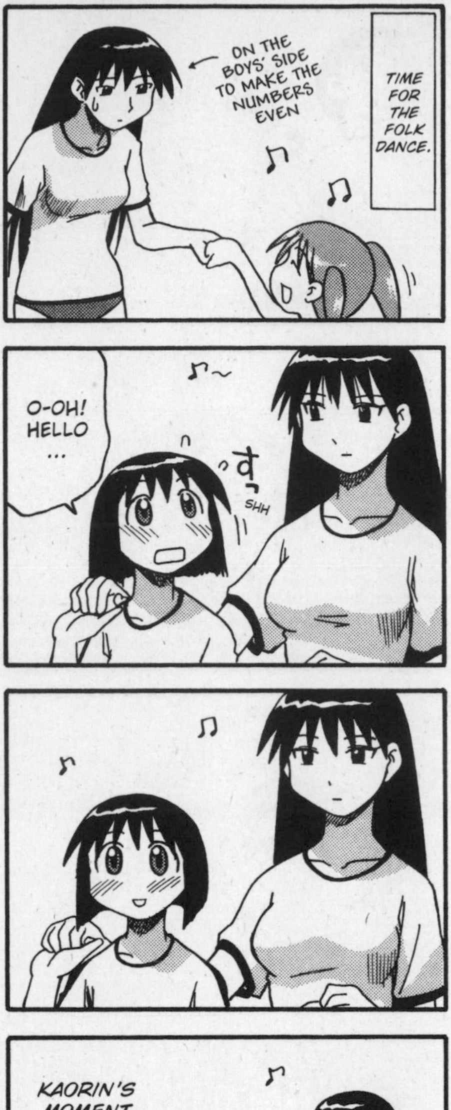
TIME FOR THE FOLK DANCE.
ON THE BOYS' SIDE TO MAKE THE NUMBERS EVEN
す
SHH
O-OH! HELLO ...
KAORIN'S MOMENT OF BLISS

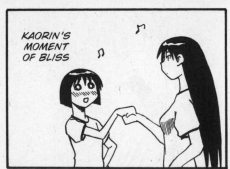

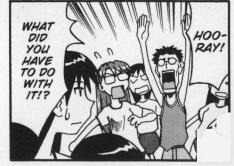

WELCOME

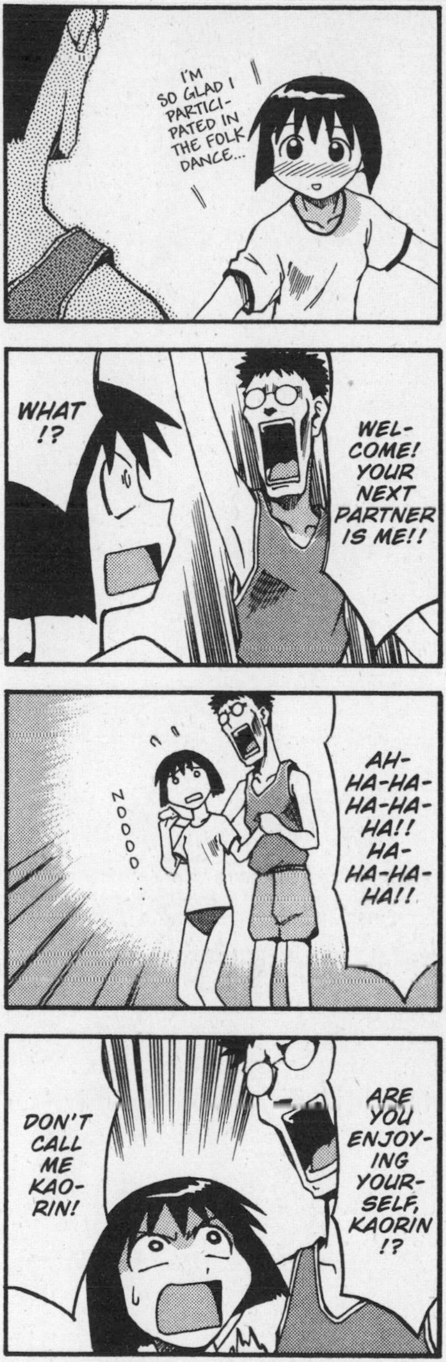
I'M SO GLAD I PARTICI-PATED IN THE FOLK DANCE...
WEL-COME! YOUR NEXT PARTNER IS ME!!
WHAT !?
AH-HA-HA-HA-HA-HA!! HA-HA-HA-HA-HA!!
NOOOO...
ARE YOU ENJOY-ING YOUR-SELF, KAORIN !?
DON'T CALL ME KAO-RIN!

HELLO GOOD-BYE

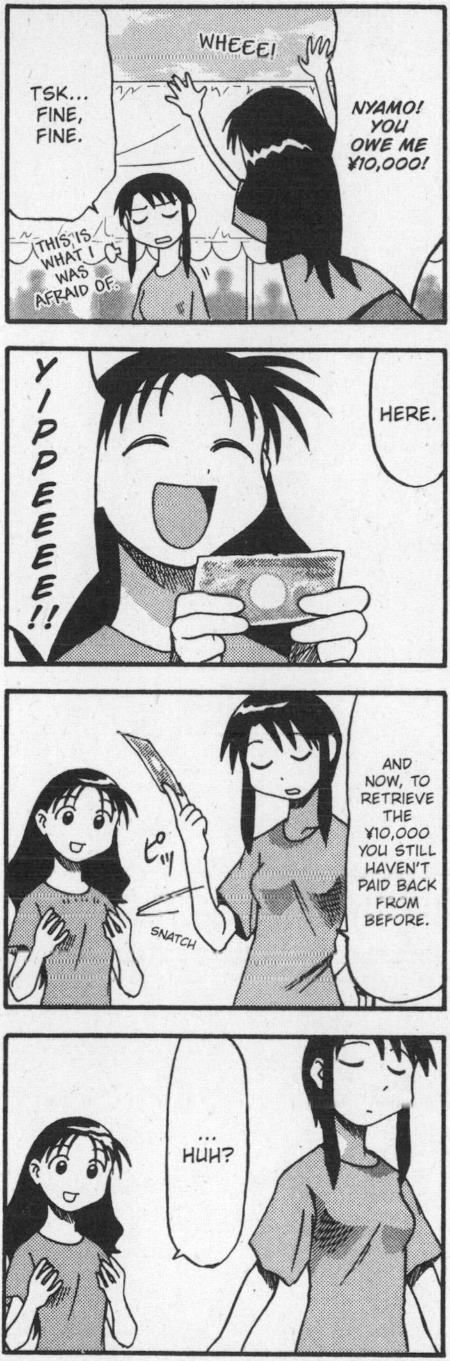
WHEEE!
NYAMO! YOU OWE ME ¥10,000!
TSK... FINE, FINE.
THIS IS WHAT I WAS AFRAID OF.
HERE.
YIPPEEEEE!!
AND NOW, TO RETRIEVE THE ¥10,000 YOU STILL HAVEN'T PAID BACK FROM BEFORE.
ピッ
SNATCH
... HUH?

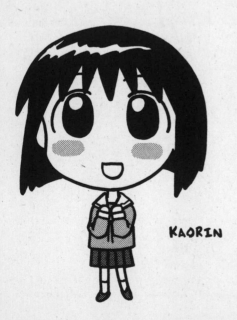

KAORIN

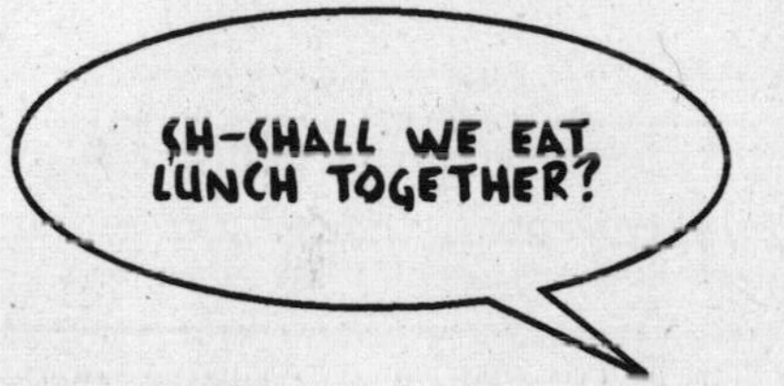

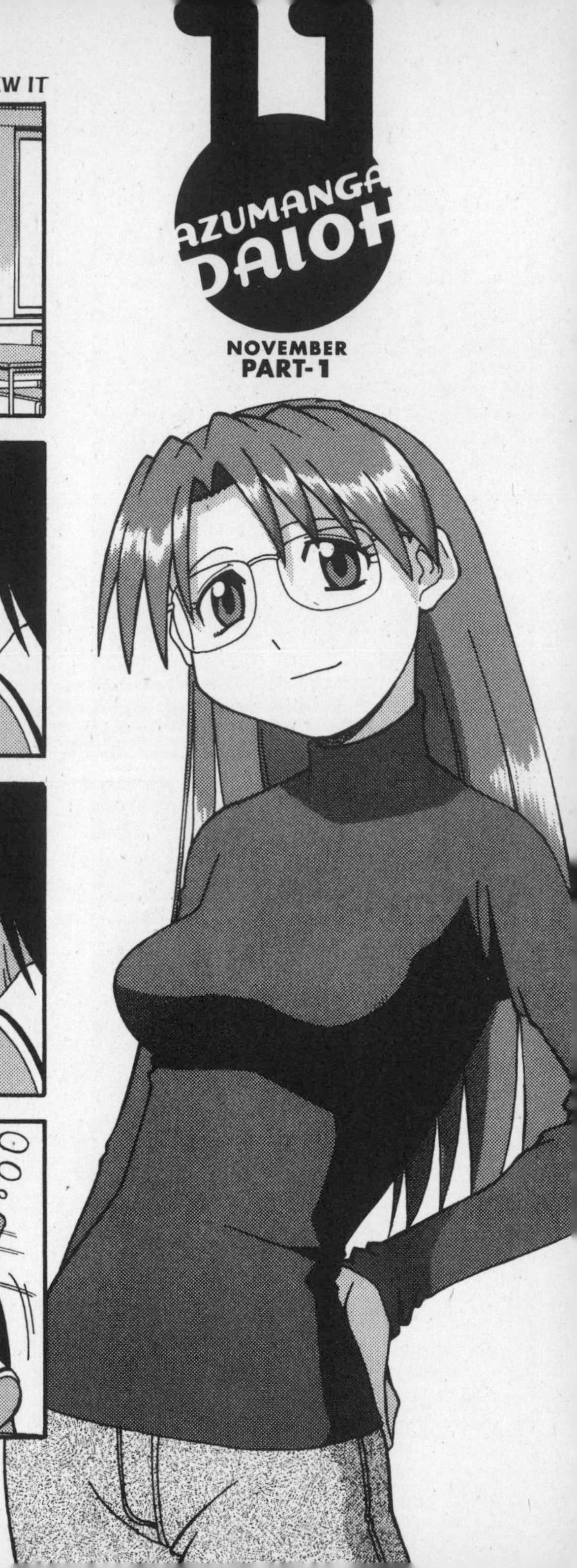
AZUMANGA DAIOH
NOVEMBER
PART-1

I KNEW IT

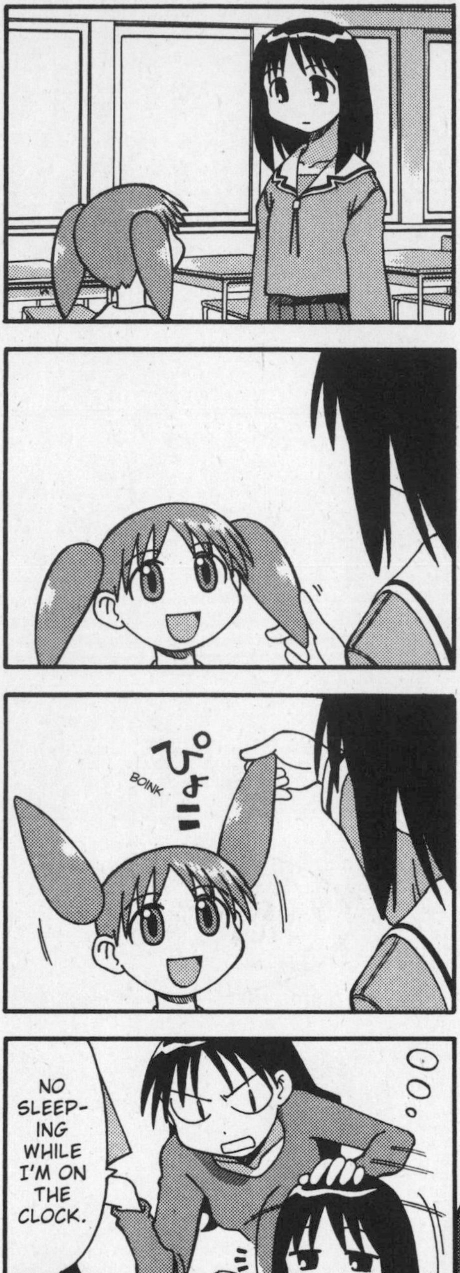
ぴょ
BOINK
NO SLEEPING WHILE I'M ON THE CLOCK.
ENGLISH

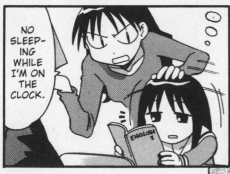

JUST CHECKING

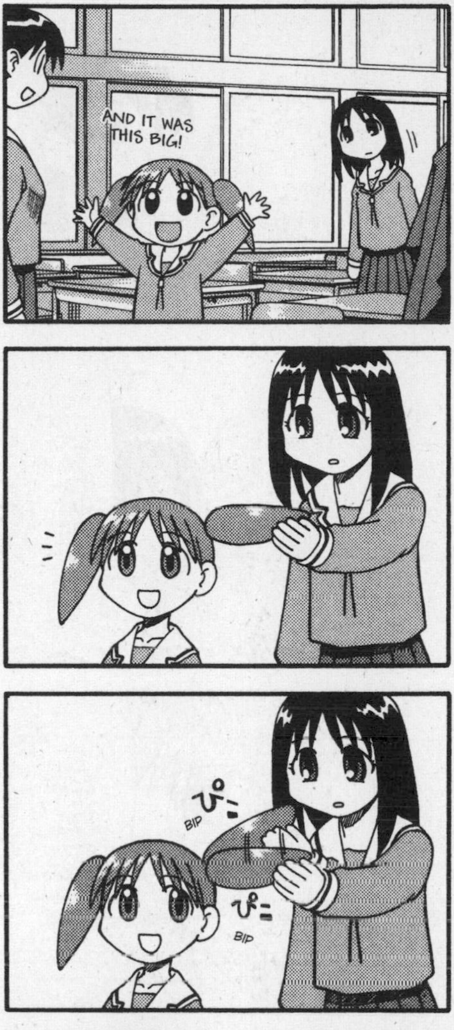
AND IT WAS THIS BIG!
ぴ BIP
ぴ BIP
WHAT'S THE MATTER?
THAT'S WHAT AH THOUGHT.

SHE'D DO IT

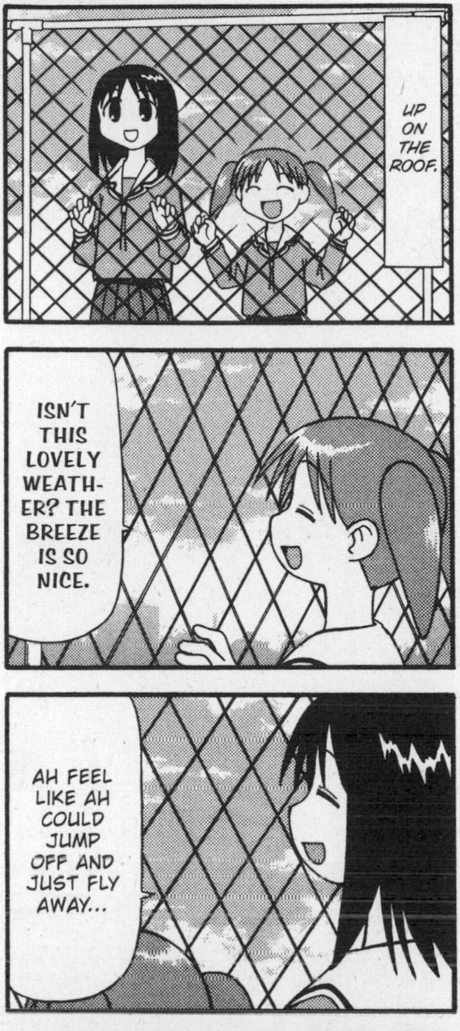
UP ON THE ROOF.
ISN'T THIS LOVELY WEATHER? THE BREEZE IS SO NICE.
AH FEEL LIKE AH COULD JUMP OFF AND JUST FLY AWAY...

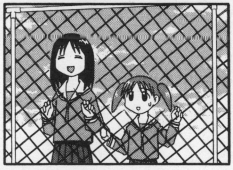

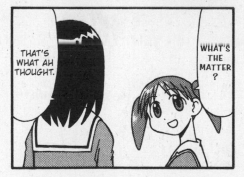

DON'T DO IT

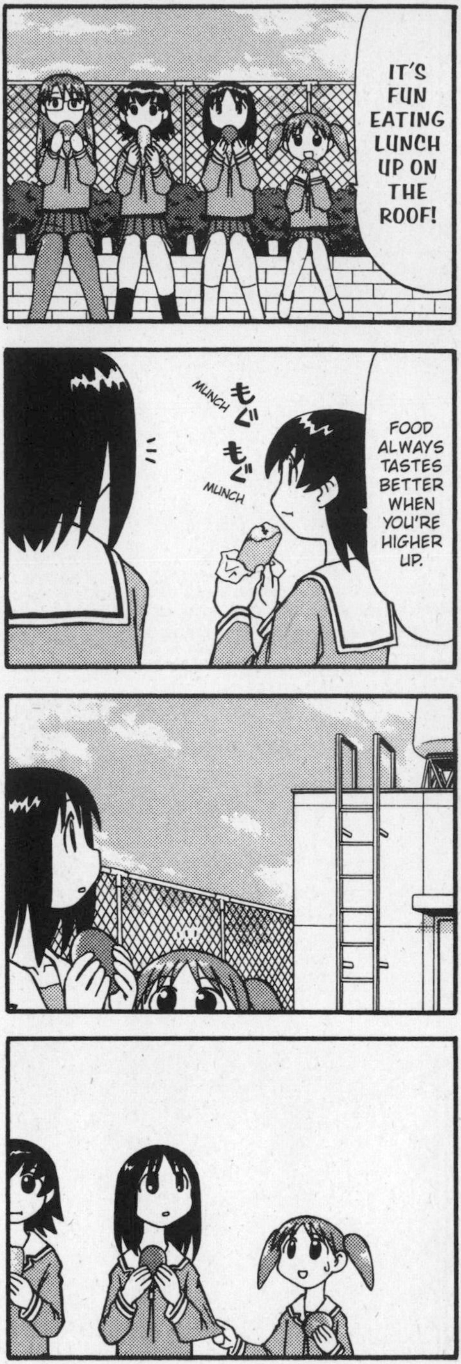
IT'S FUN EATING LUNCH UP ON THE ROOF!
FOOD ALWAYS TASTES BETTER WHEN YOU'RE HIGHER UP.
もぐ
MUNCH
もぐ
MUNCH

GIMME

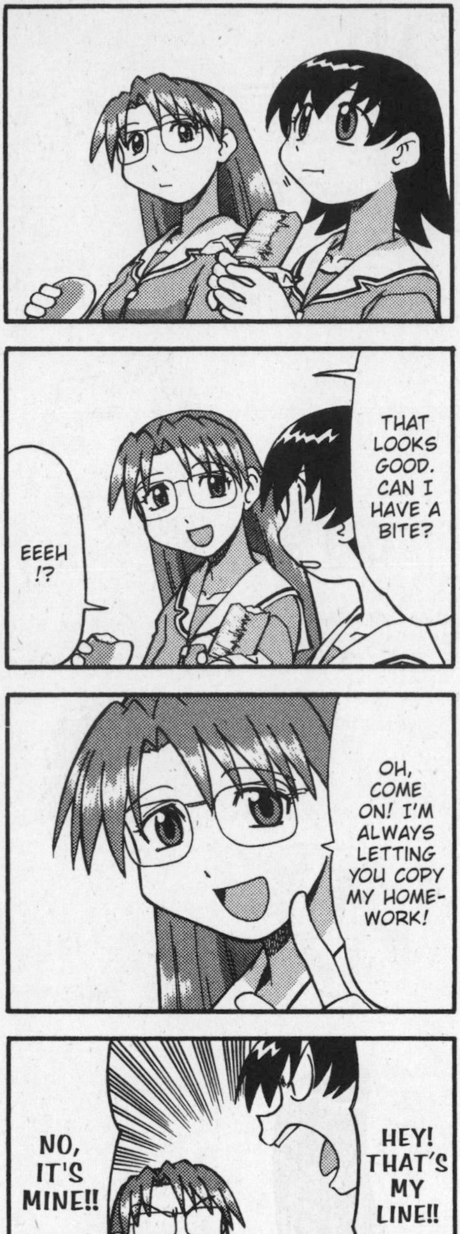
THAT LOOKS GOOD. CAN I HAVE A BITE?
EEEH !?
OH, COME ON! I'M ALWAYS LETTING YOU COPY MY HOME-WORK!
HEY! THAT'S MY LINE!!
NO, IT'S MINE!!

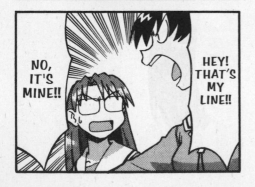

THAT WAS GOOD

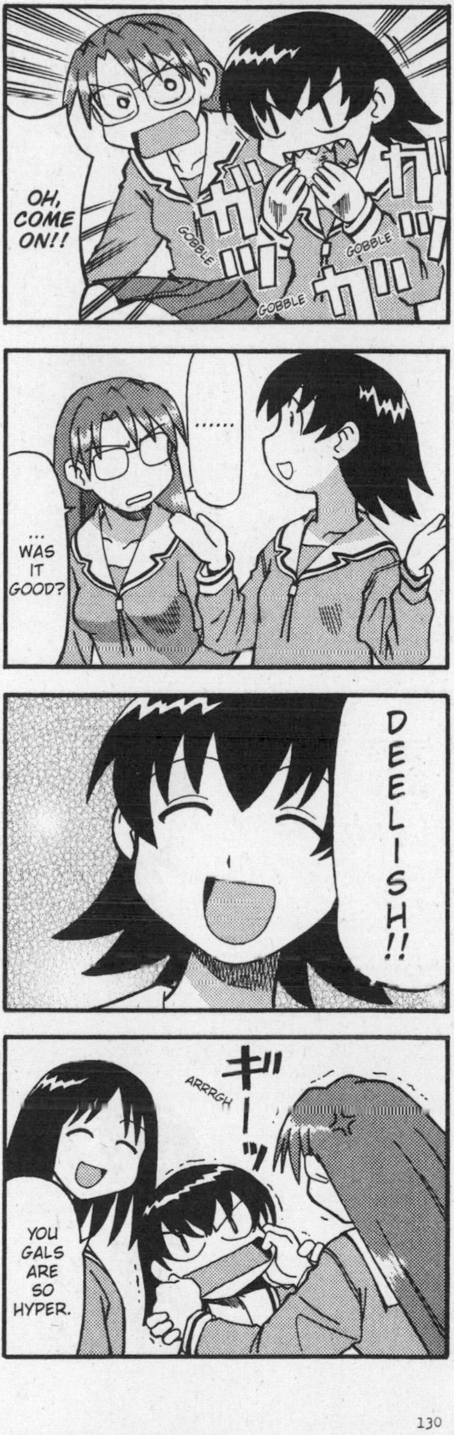
OH, COME ON!!
GOBBLE
GOBBLE
GOBBLE
......
...WAS IT GOOD?
DEELISH!!
ギーッ
ARRRGH
YOU GALS ARE SO HYPER.

COFFEEHOUSE

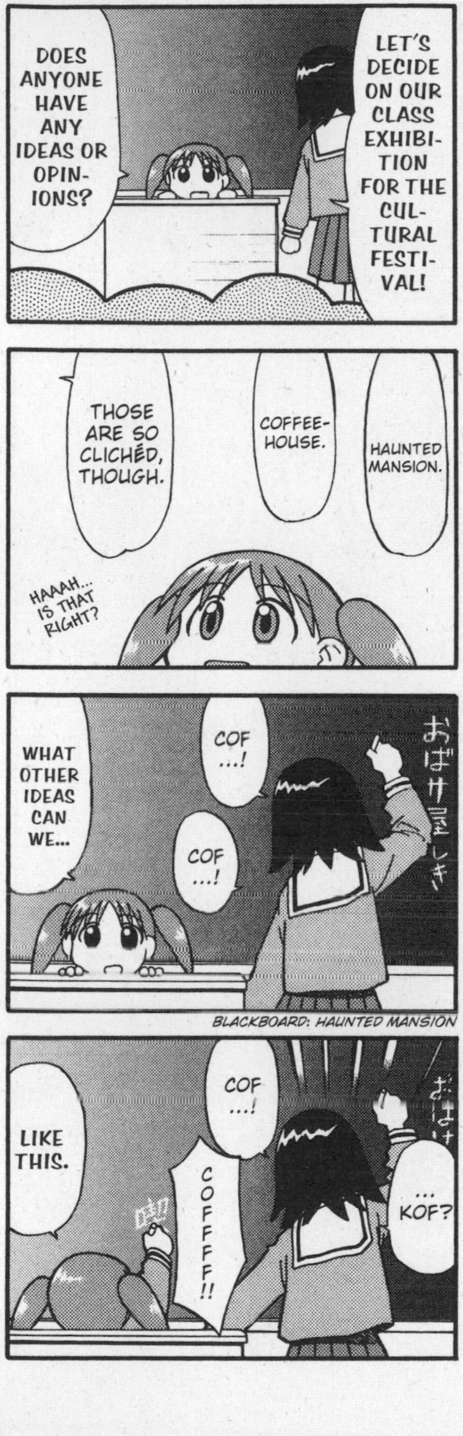
LET'S DECIDE ON OUR CLASS EXHIBITION FOR THE CULTURAL FESTIVAL!
DOES ANYONE HAVE ANY IDEAS OR OPINIONS?
HAUNTED MANSION.
COFFEE-HOUSE.
THOSE ARE SO CLICHÉD, THOUGH.
HAAAH... IS THAT RIGHT?
おばけ屋しき
COF...!
COF...!
WHAT OTHER IDEAS CAN WE...
BLACKBOARD: HAUNTED MANSION
COF...!
...KOF?
COFFFF!!
LIKE THIS.

GRAVEYARD

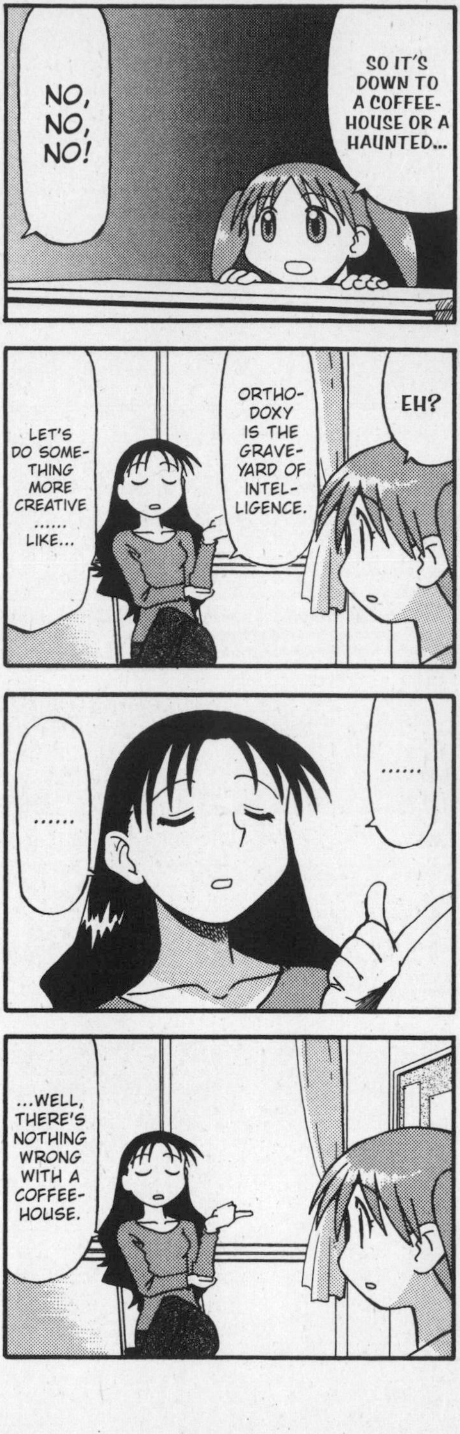
SO IT'S DOWN TO A COFFEE-HOUSE OR A HAUNTED...
NO, NO, NO!
EH?
ORTHODOXY IS THE GRAVEYARD OF INTELLIGENCE.
LET'S DO SOMETHING MORE CREATIVE ...... LIKE...
......
......
...WELL, THERE'S NOTHING WRONG WITH A COFFEE-HOUSE.

MAY YOU HAVE LUCK

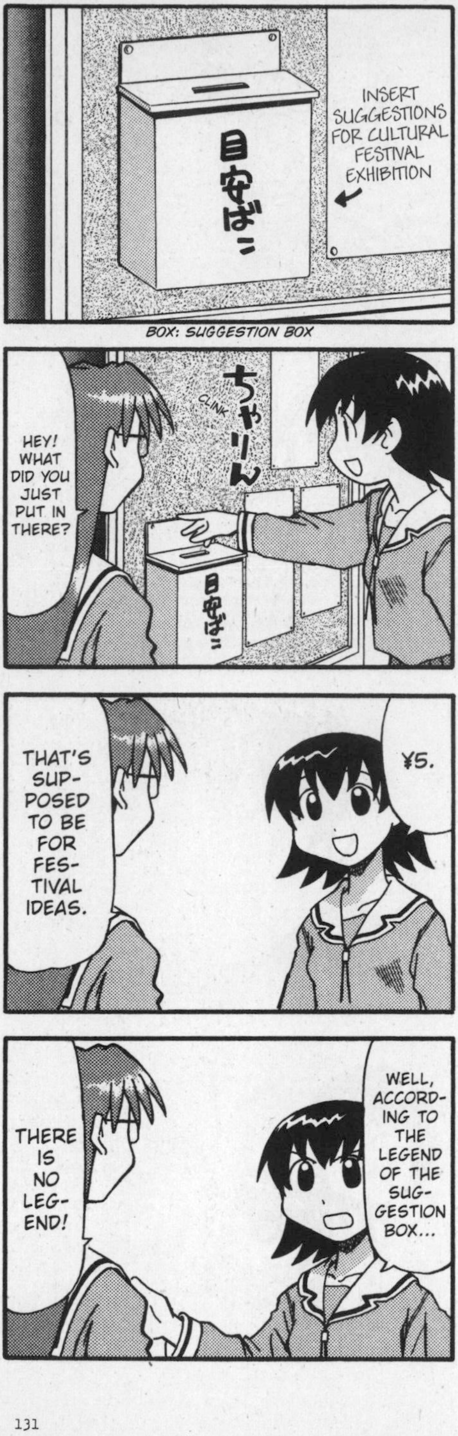
目安ばこ
INSERT SUGGESTIONS FOR CULTURAL FESTIVAL EXHIBITION
ちゃりん
CLINK
目安ばこ
HEY! WHAT DID YOU JUST PUT IN THERE?
¥5.
THAT'S SUPPOSED TO BE FOR FESTIVAL IDEAS.
WELL, ACCORDING TO THE LEGEND OF THE SUGGESTION BOX...
THERE IS NO LEGEND!

BOX: SUGGESTION BOX

OSAKA'S IDEA

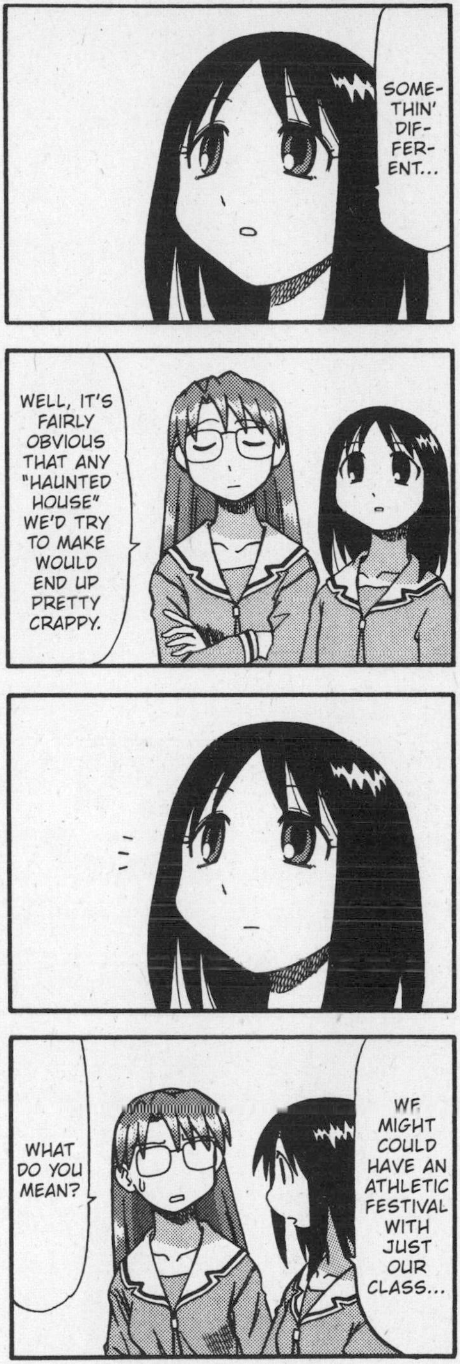
SOMETHIN' DIFFERENT...
WELL, IT'S FAIRLY OBVIOUS THAT ANY "HAUNTED HOUSE" WE'D TRY TO MAKE WOULD END UP PRETTY CRAPPY.
WF MIGHT COULD HAVE AN ATHLETIC FESTIVAL WITH JUST OUR CLASS...
WHAT DO YOU MEAN?

NOT TECHNICALLY STEALING

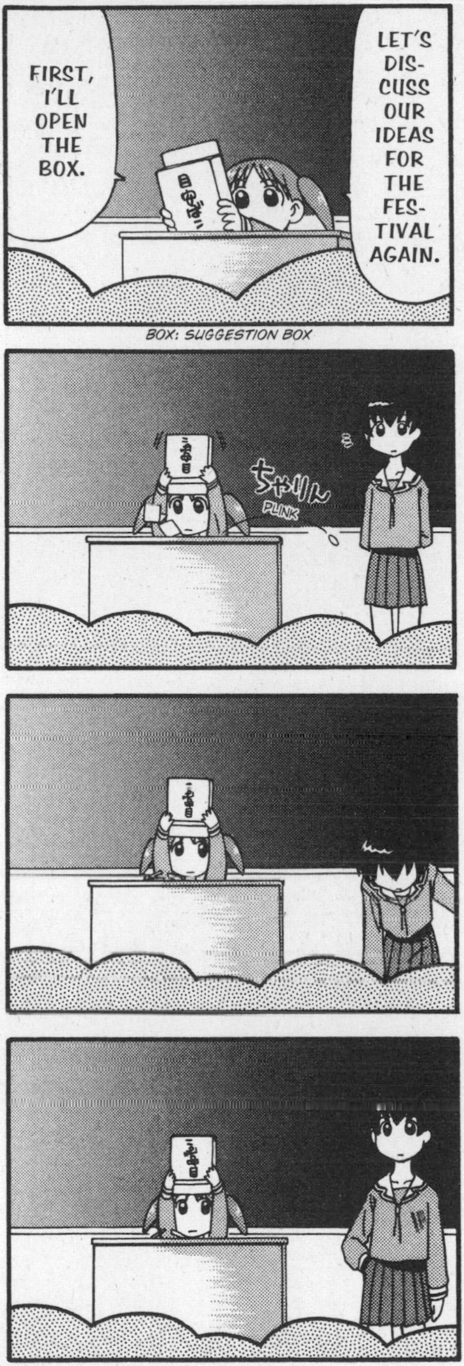
LET'S DISCUSS OUR IDEAS FOR THE FESTIVAL AGAIN.
FIRST, I'LL OPEN THE BOX.
ちゃりん
PLINK

BOX: SUGGESTION BOX

FAIRYLAND CLASS

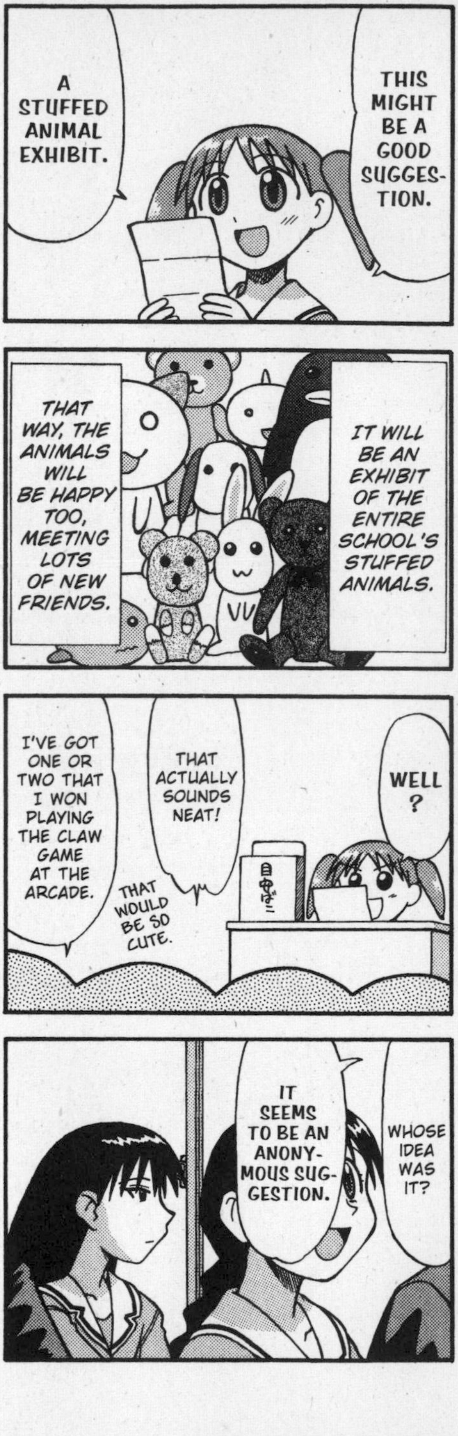
THIS MIGHT BE A GOOD SUGGESTION.
A STUFFED ANIMAL EXHIBIT.
IT WILL BE AN EXHIBIT OF THE ENTIRE SCHOOL'S STUFFED ANIMALS.
THAT WAY, THE ANIMALS WILL BE HAPPY TOO, MEETING LOTS OF NEW FRIENDS.
WELL?
THAT ACTUALLY SOUNDS NEAT!
THAT WOULD BE SO CUTE.
I'VE GOT ONE OR TWO THAT I WON PLAYING THE CLAW GAME AT THE ARCADE.
WHOSE IDEA WAS IT?
IT SEEMS TO BE AN ANONYMOUS SUGGESTION.

BUNNY OUTFIT

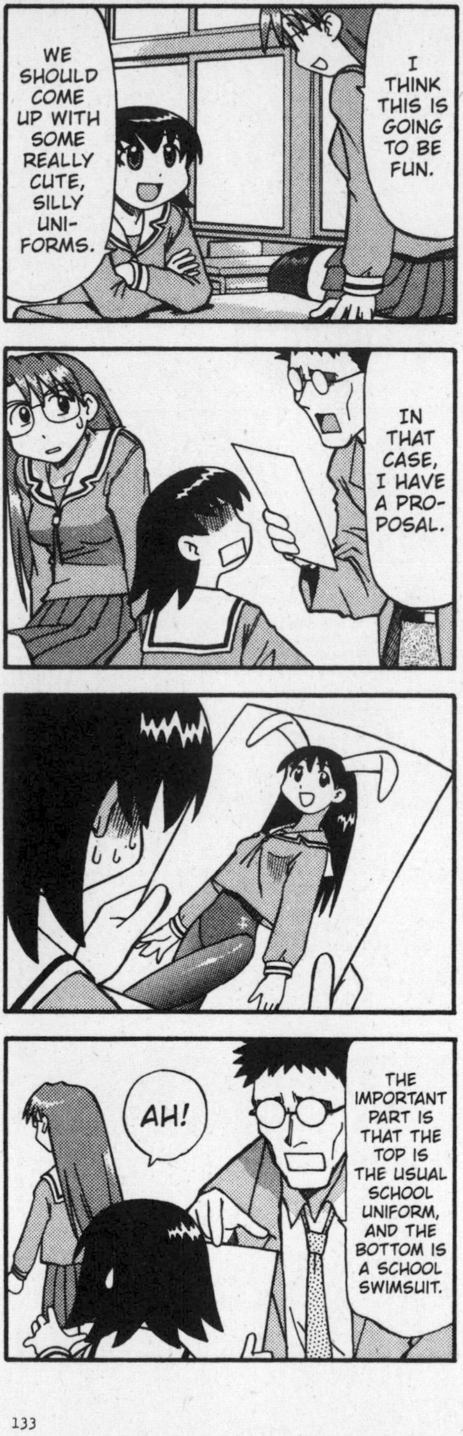
I THINK THIS IS GOING TO BE FUN.
WE SHOULD COME UP WITH SOME REALLY CUTE, SILLY UNIFORMS.
IN THAT CASE, I HAVE A PROPOSAL.
THE IMPORTANT PART IS THAT THE TOP IS THE USUAL SCHOOL UNIFORM, AND THE BOTTOM IS A SCHOOL SWIMSUIT.
AH!

CUTE MASCOT

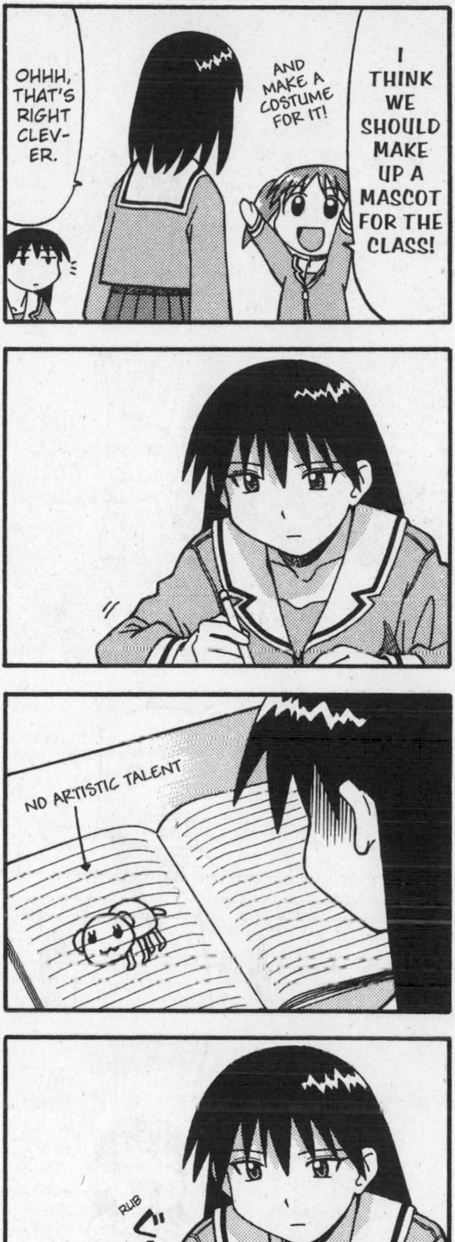
I THINK WE SHOULD MAKE UP A MASCOT FOR THE CLASS!
AND MAKE A COSTUME FOR IT!
OHHH, THAT'S RIGHT CLEVER.
NO ARTISTIC TALENT
RUB
ぐし
RUB
ぐし

MAKE IT LOOK CUTER

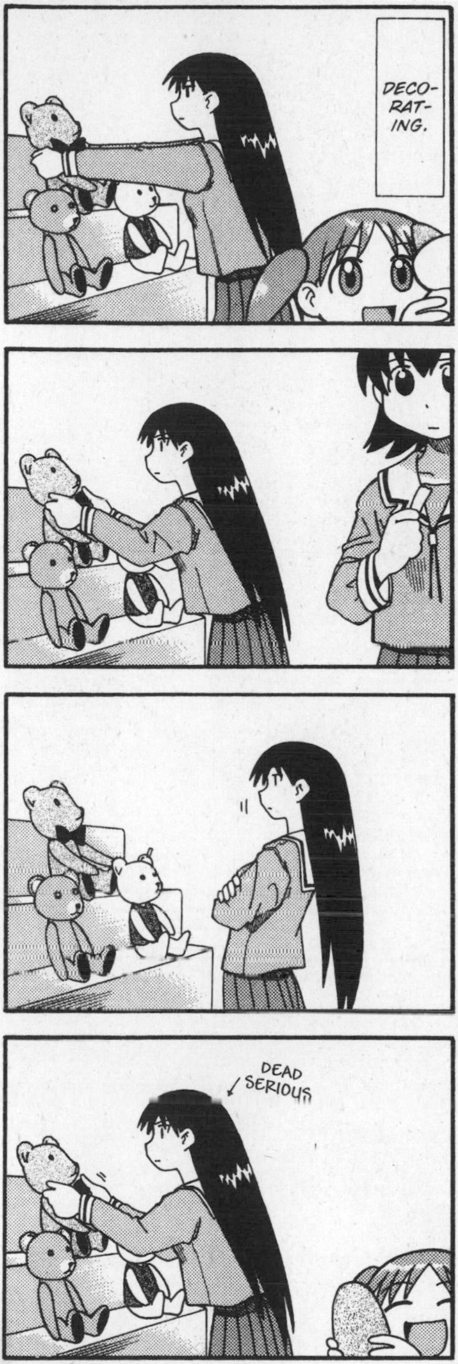
DECO-RATING.
DEAD SERIOUS

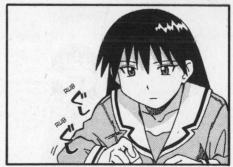

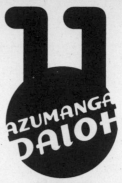

11 AZUMANGA DAIOH

NOVEMBER PART-2

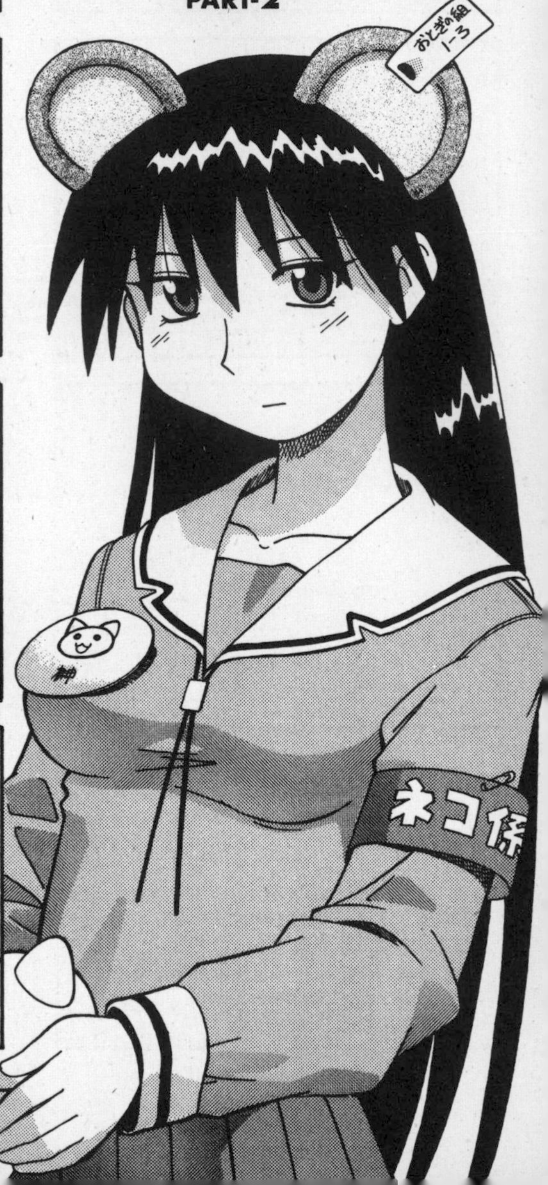
おとぎの組 1-3
ネコ係

EAR TAG: FAIRYLAND CLASS 1-3
BUTTON: SAKAKI
ARM BAND: CAT SQUAD

MASCOT

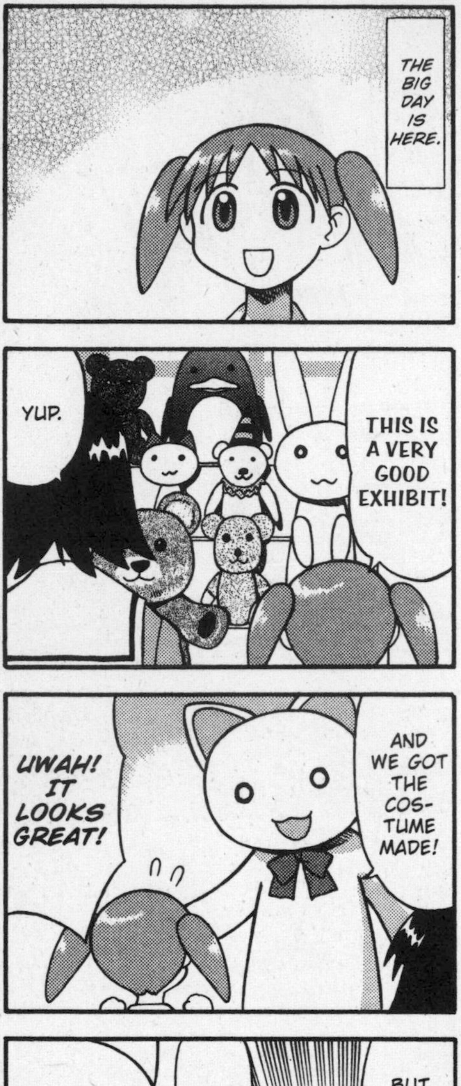
THE BIG DAY IS HERE.
THIS IS A VERY GOOD EXHIBIT!
YUP.
AND WE GOT THE COSTUME MADE!
UWAH! IT LOOKS GREAT!
BUT YOU DON'T HAVE THE HANG OF IT YET.
HERE, LET ME TRY.
HANG OF IT?

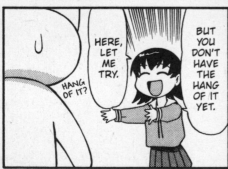

GET IN THE MOOD!

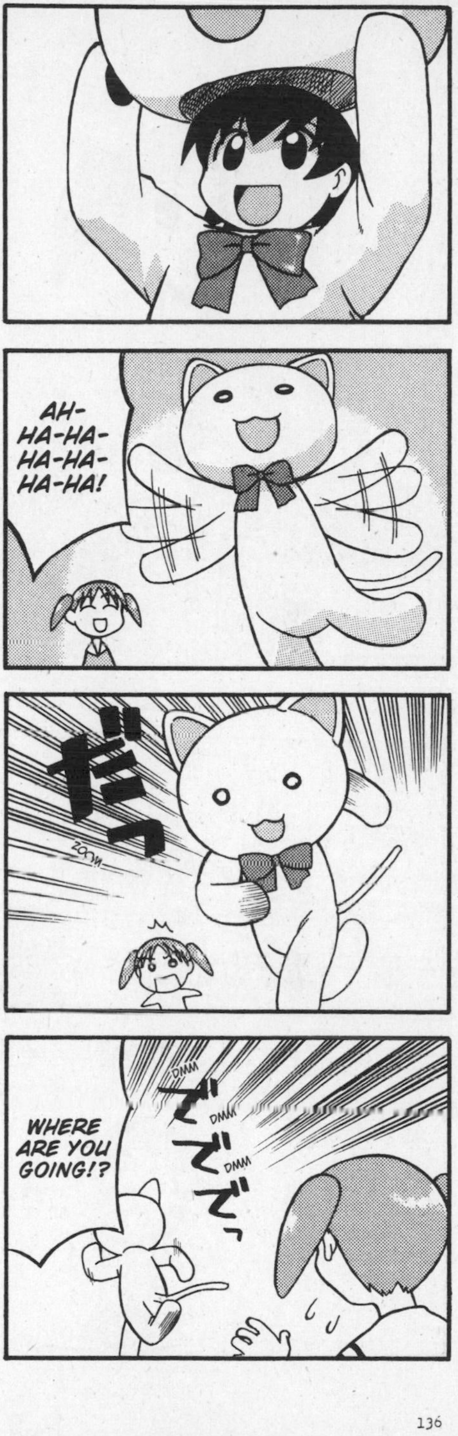
AH-HA-HA-HA-HA-HA-HA!
ZOOM
DMM
DMM
DMM
WHERE ARE YOU GOING!?

FRIENDS

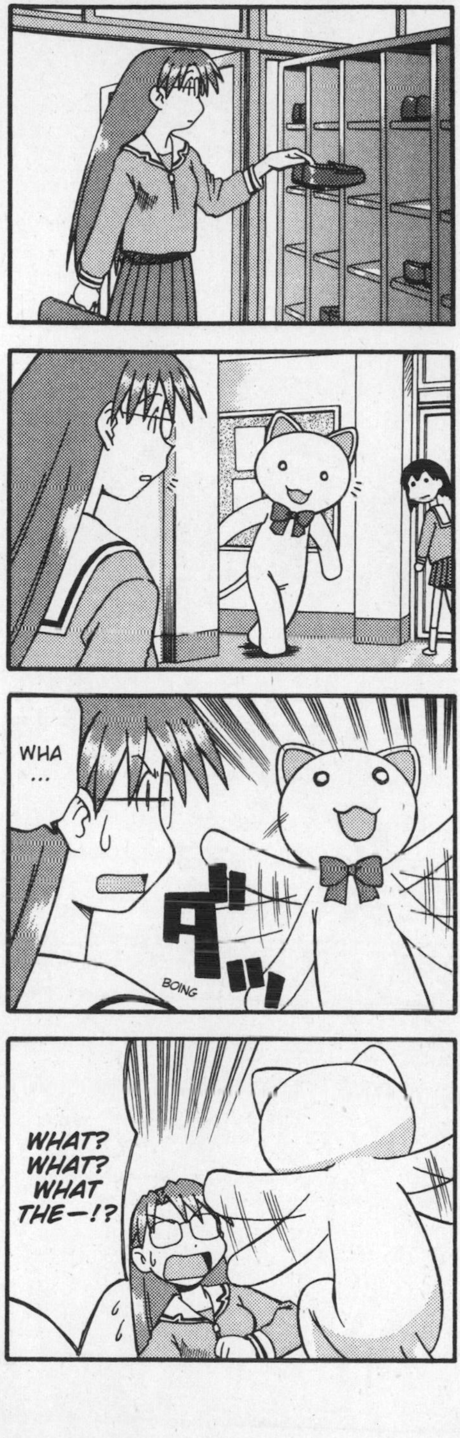
WHA ...
BOING
WHAT? WHAT? WHAT THE—!?

TOMO, AT YOUR SERVICE

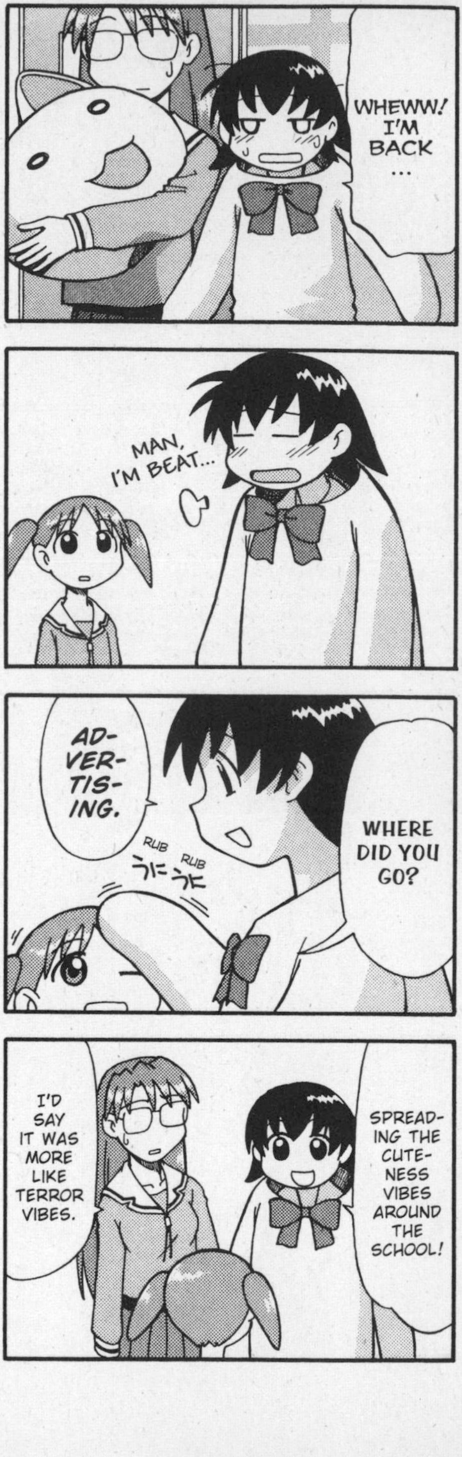
WHEWW! I'M BACK ...
MAN, I'M BEAT...
WHERE DID YOU GO?
AD-VERTIS-ING.
RUB RUB
SPREAD-ING THE CUTE-NESS VIBES AROUND THE SCHOOL!
I'D SAY IT WAS MORE LIKE TERROR VIBES.

MYSTERY CREATURE

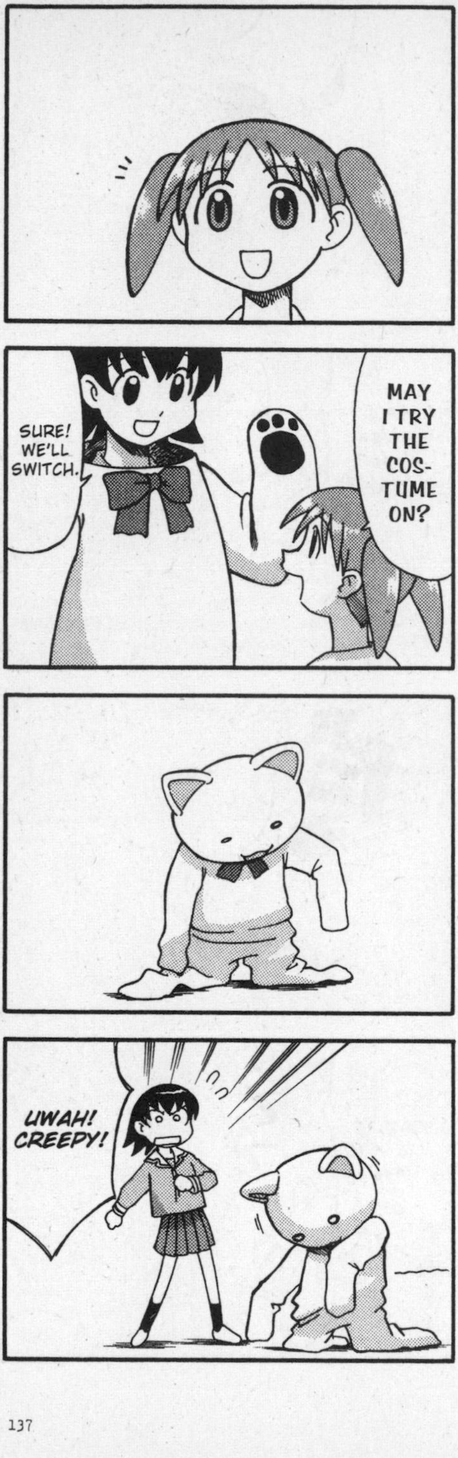
MAY I TRY THE COS-TUME ON?
SURE! WE'LL SWITCH.
UWAH! CREEPY!

THE WATER TRADE

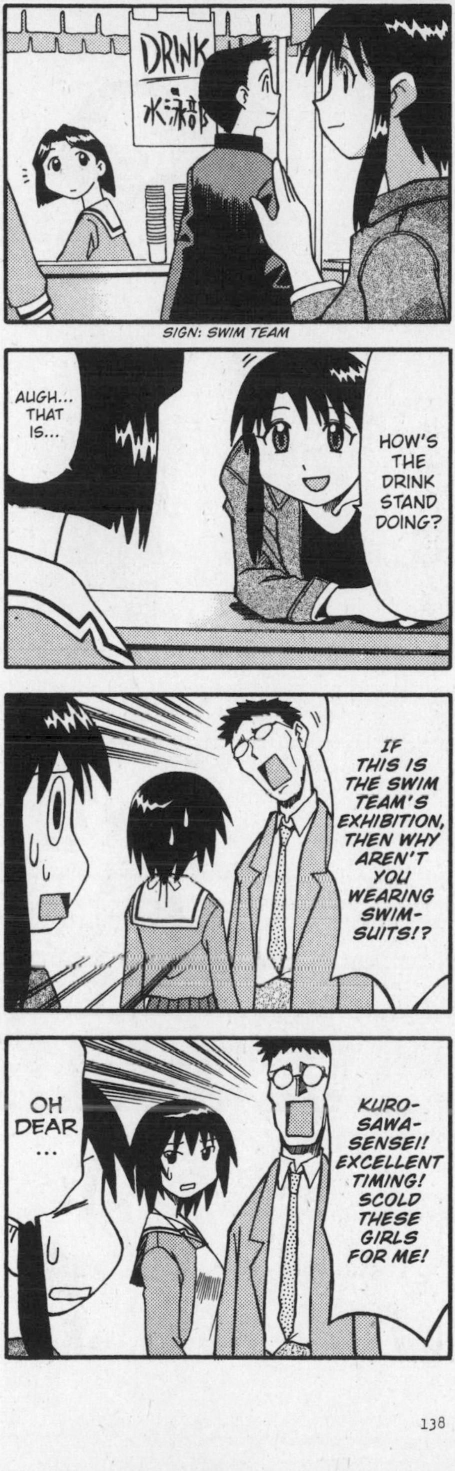
DRINK
水泳部
SIGN: SWIM TEAM
HOW'S THE DRINK STAND DOING?
AUGH... THAT IS...
IF THIS IS THE SWIM TEAM'S EXHIBITION, THEN WHY AREN'T YOU WEARING SWIM-SUITS!?
KURO-SAWA-SENSEI! EXCELLENT TIMING! SCOLD THESE GIRLS FOR ME!
OH DEAR ...

DELICIOUS WATER

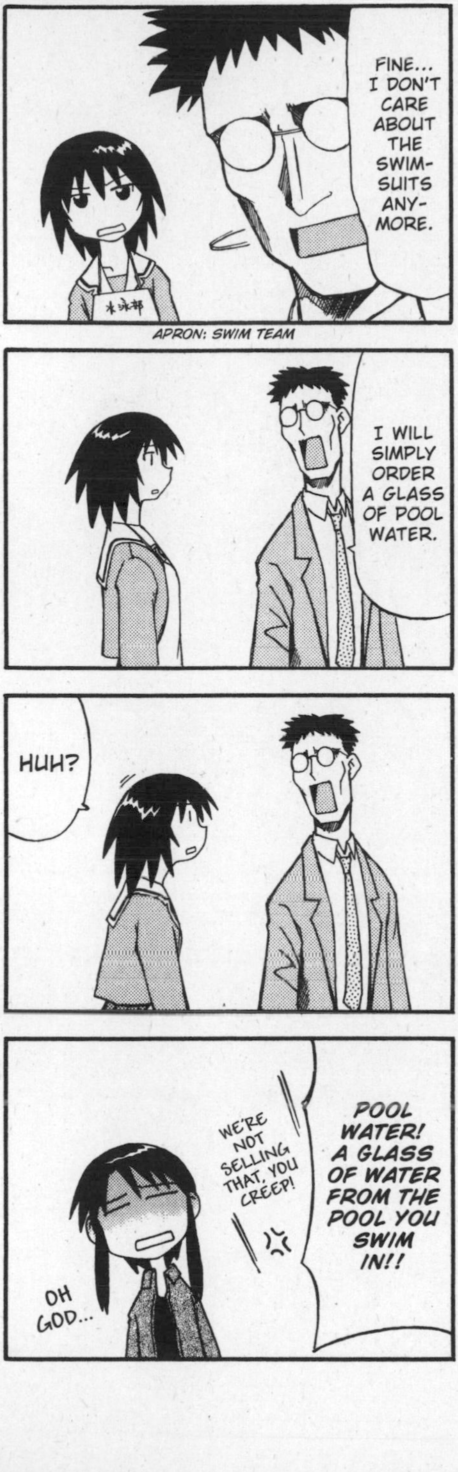
FINE... I DON'T CARE ABOUT THE SWIM-SUITS ANY-MORE.
水泳部
APRON: SWIM TEAM
I WILL SIMPLY ORDER A GLASS OF POOL WATER.
HUH?
POOL WATER! A GLASS OF WATER FROM THE POOL YOU SWIM IN!!
WE'RE NOT SELLING THAT, YOU CREEP!
OH GOD...

DUNNO

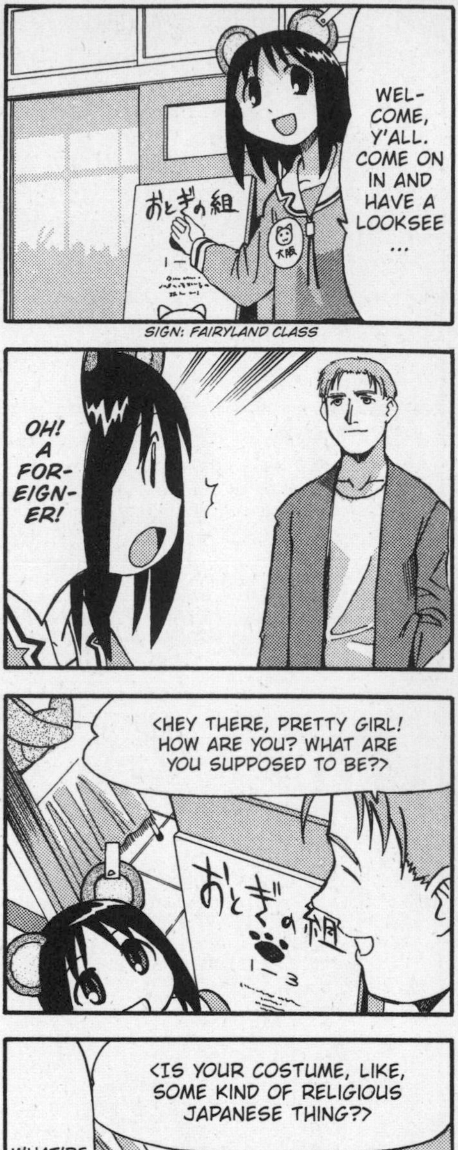

WEL-COME, Y'ALL. COME ON IN AND HAVE A LOOKSEE ...
おとぎの組
SIGN: FAIRYLAND CLASS
OH! A FOR-EIGN-ER!
<HEY THERE, PRETTY GIRL! HOW ARE YOU? WHAT ARE YOU SUPPOSED TO BE?>
おとぎの組
<IS YOUR COSTUME, LIKE, SOME KIND OF RELIGIOUS JAPANESE THING?>
WHAT'RE YOU SAYIN'?
おとぎの組

ENGLISH TEACHER

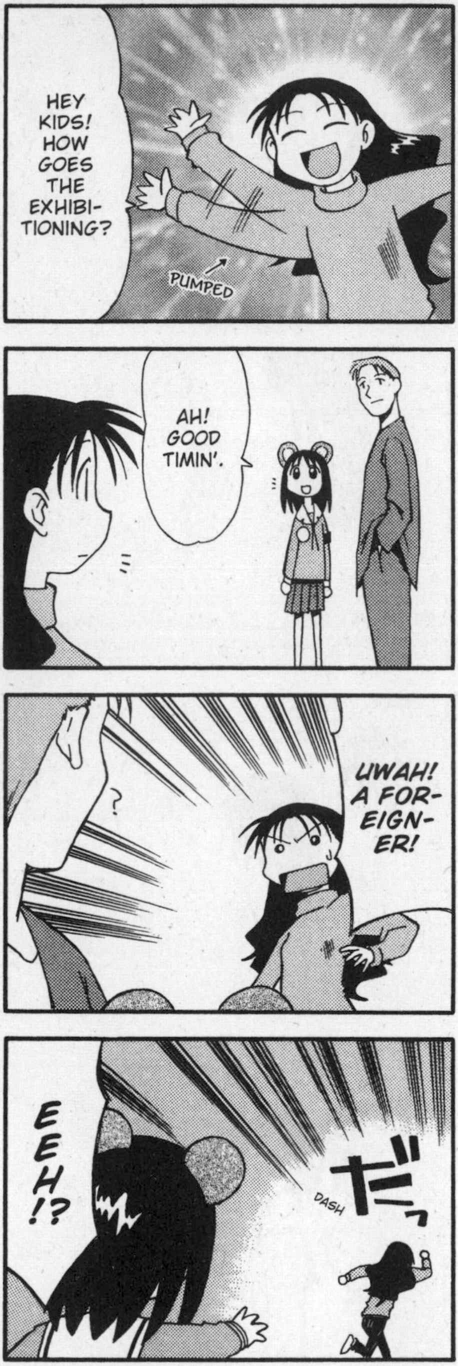

HEY KIDS! HOW GOES THE EXHIBI-TIONING?
PUMPED
AH! GOOD TIMIN'.
UWAH! A FOR-EIGN-ER!
EEH!?
だっ
DASH

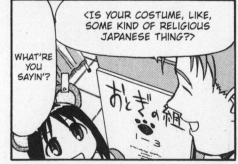

I MADE THEM

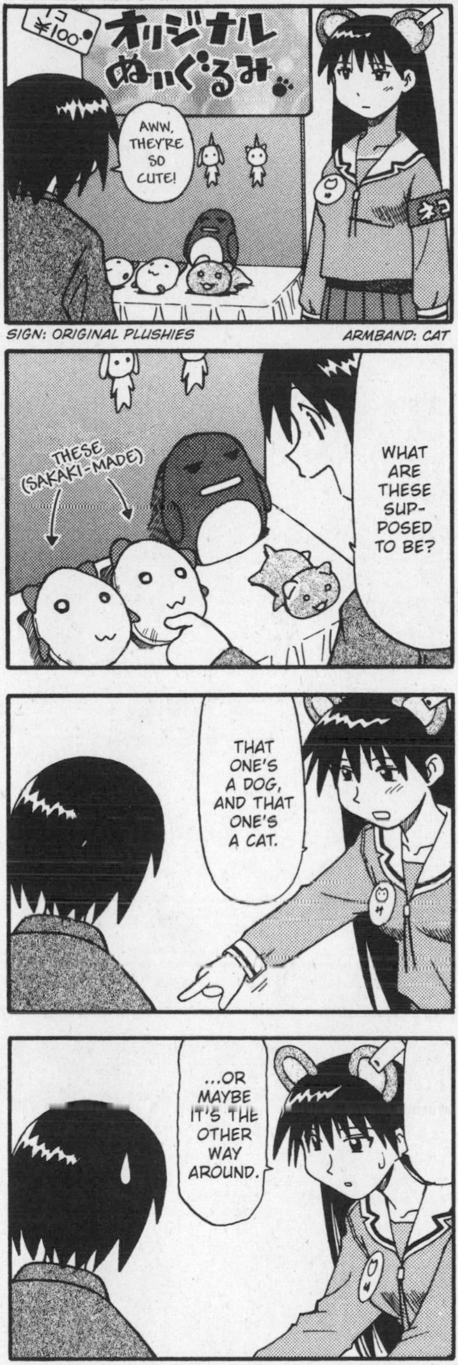
SMALL SIGN: ¥100 EACH
1コ ¥100
オリジナル ぬいぐるみ
AWW, THEY'RE SO CUTE!
ネコ
SIGN: ORIGINAL PLUSHIES
ARMBAND: CAT
WHAT ARE THESE SUP-POSED TO BE?
THESE (SAKAKI-MADE)
THAT ONE'S A DOG, AND THAT ONE'S A CAT.
...OR MAYBE IT'S THE OTHER WAY AROUND.

AT TOMO-CHAN'S REQUEST

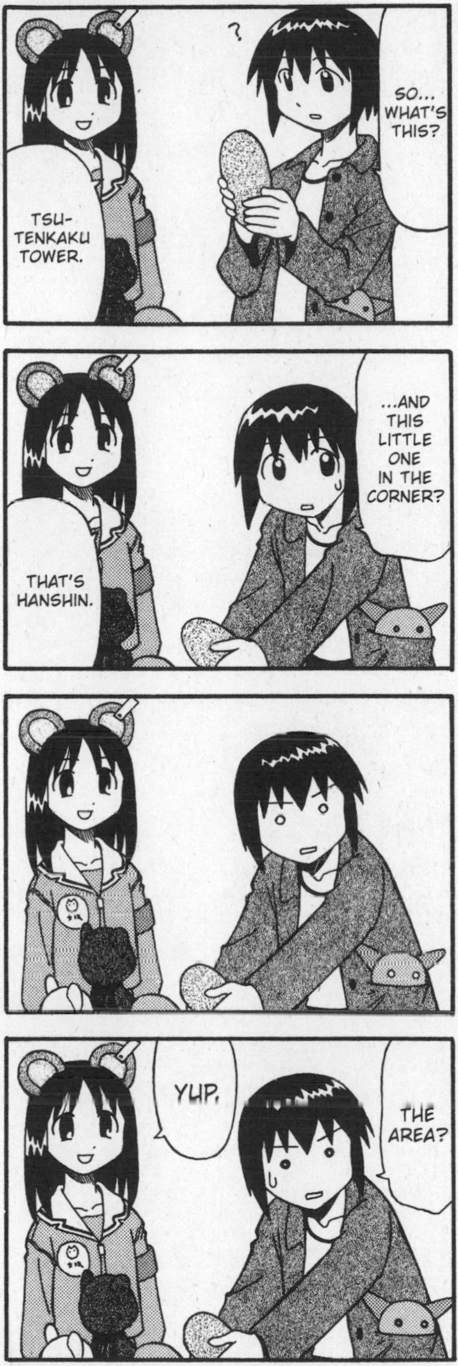
?
SO... WHAT'S THIS?
TSU-TENKAKU TOWER.
...AND THIS LITTLE ONE IN THE CORNER?
THAT'S HANSHIN.
THE AREA?
YUP.

WHILE YOU'RE AT IT

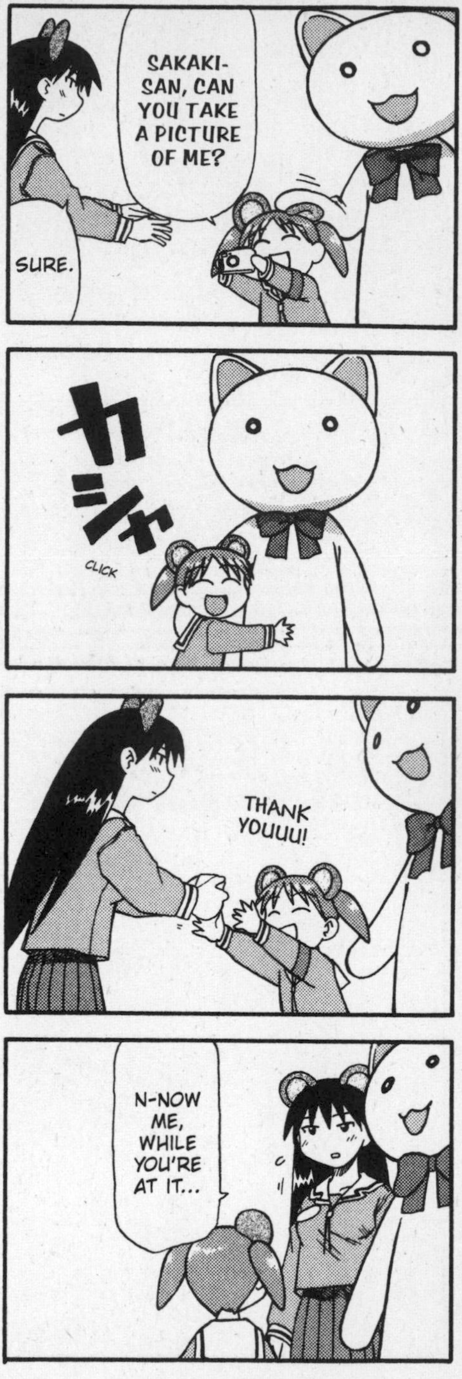
SAKAKI-SAN, CAN YOU TAKE A PICTURE OF ME?
SURE.
カシャ
CLICK
THANK YOUUU!
N-NOW ME, WHILE YOU'RE AT IT...

THERE IS NO INSIDE

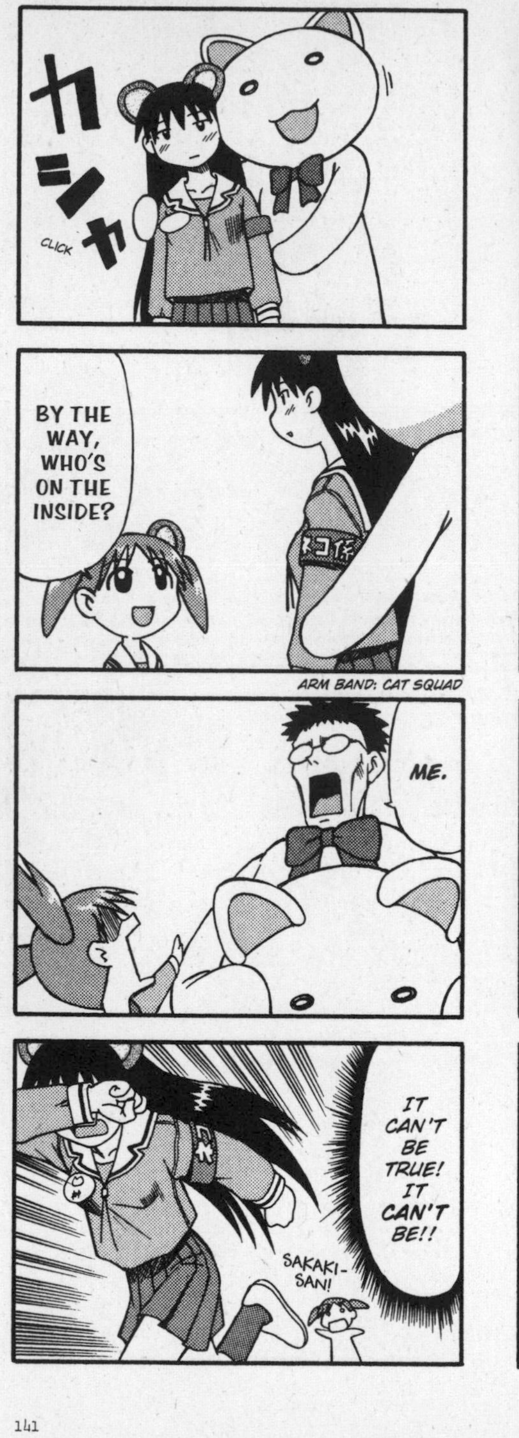
カシャ
CLICK
BY THE WAY, WHO'S ON THE INSIDE?
ME.
IT CAN'T BE TRUE! IT CAN'T BE!!
SAKAKI-SAN!

ARM BAND: CAT SQUAD

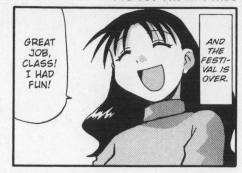

AND THE FESTIVAL IS OVER.
GREAT JOB, CLASS! I HAD FUN!
SO WHAT'S TO BE DONE WITH THESE STUFFED ANIMALS?
BURN 'EM?
EH!?
YOU MEAN WE'RE NOT GONNA BURN THEM ALL FOR A MEMORIAL SERVICE?
MEMORIAL FOR WHAT?

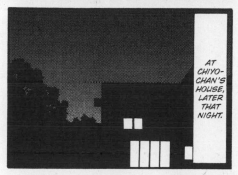

AT CHIYO-CHAN'S HOUSE, LATER THAT NIGHT.
WOOF
WOOF
WOOF
WOOF
TADAKICHI-SAN!
SHE TOOK IT HOME
WOOF
WOOF
WOOF
WOOF

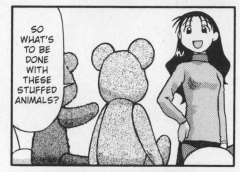

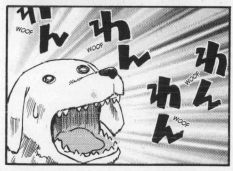

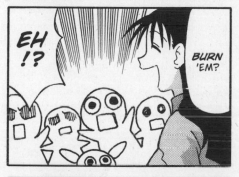

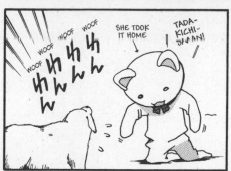

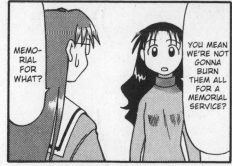

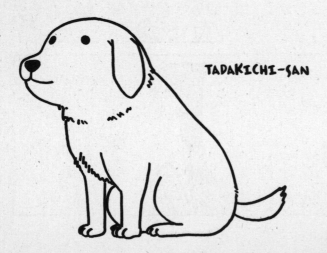

TADAKICHI-SAN

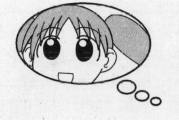

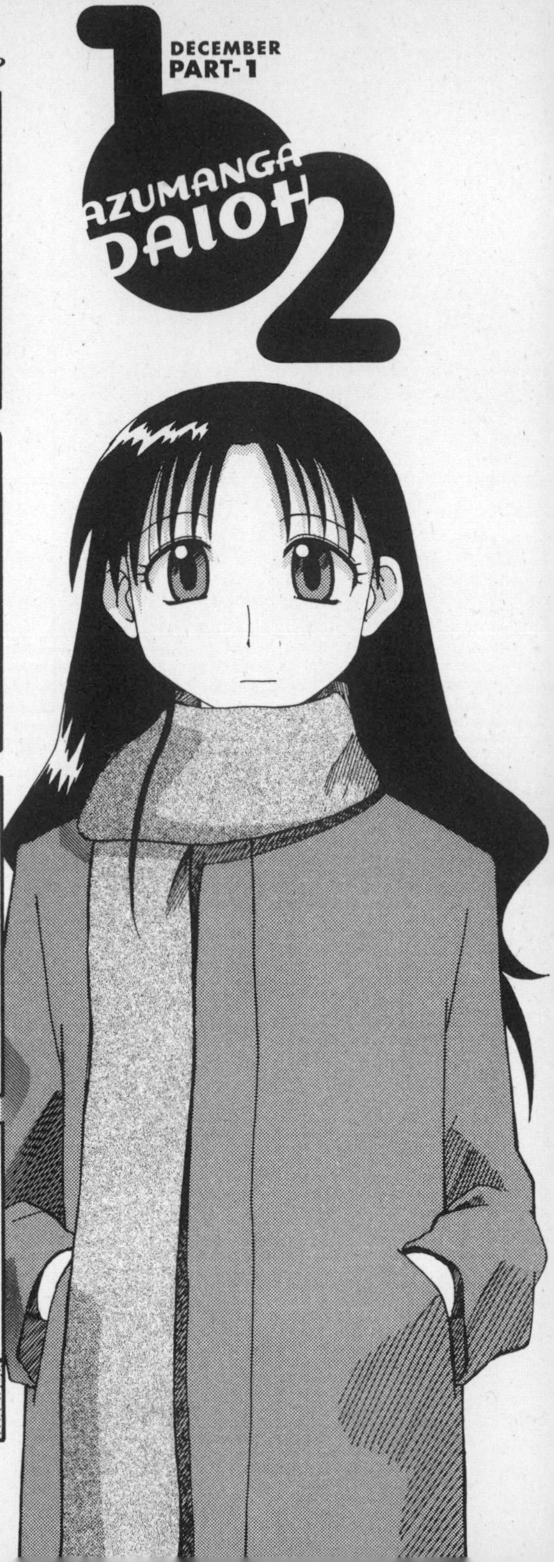
12
DECEMBER
PART-1
AZUMANGA
DAIOH

WHAT HAVE I DONE?

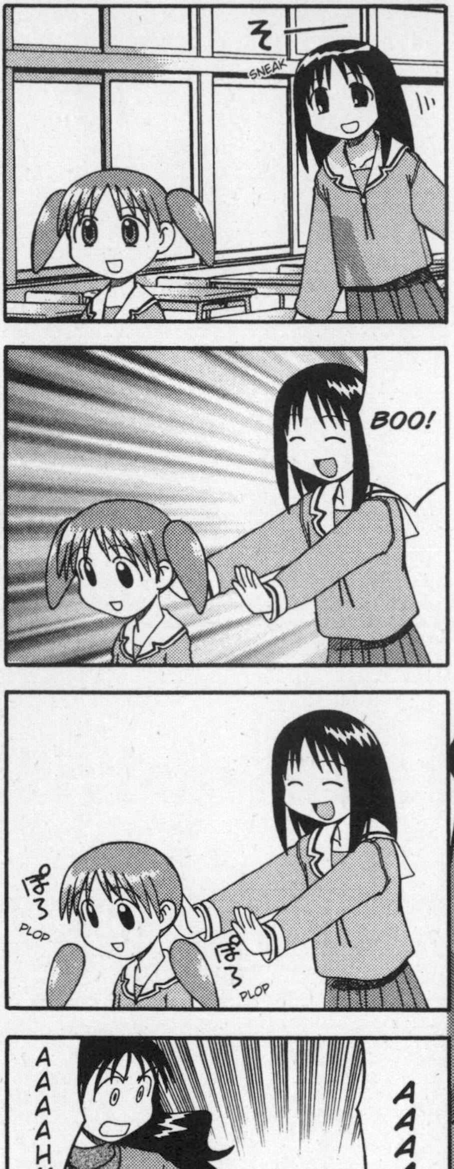
そ〜
SNEAK
BOO!
ぽろ
PLOP
ぽろ
PLOP
AAAAAH!!
AAAAH!!
ENGLISH
I
ENGLISH
I

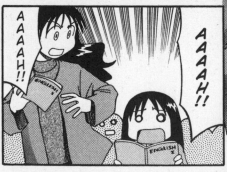

IS THAT TRUE?

READY TO SKE-DADDLE, CHIYO-CHAN?
OH, BUT I WANTED TO STOP BY THE BOOK-STORE ON THE WAY.
THERE'S A VERY CUTE PANDA PICTURE BOOK COMING OUT TODAY.
BUT THE HYPE WAS SO HUGE, IT MIGHT ACTU-ALLY BE SOLD OUT AL-READY.
OHHH. AH RECK-ON WE'LL SEE.
RUN-NING IN THE HALLS!
DM
DM
DM

CHIYO'S PANDA

WAIT, WHICH BITS OF THE PANDA'S WHITE, AND WHICH BITS IS BLACK?
I THINK ...
THAT AIN'T REALLY IT, THOUGH.
HMM...
YOU'RE PROB-ABLY RIGHT.

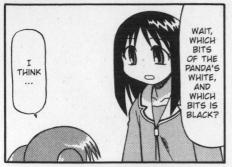

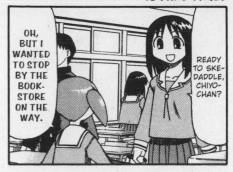

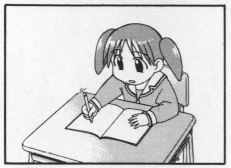

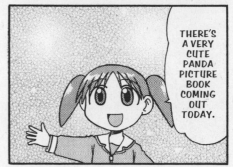

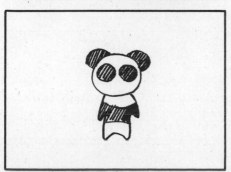

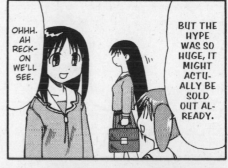

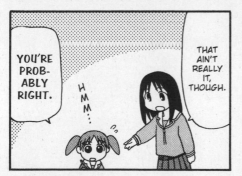

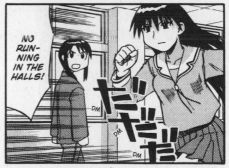

OSAKA'S PANDA

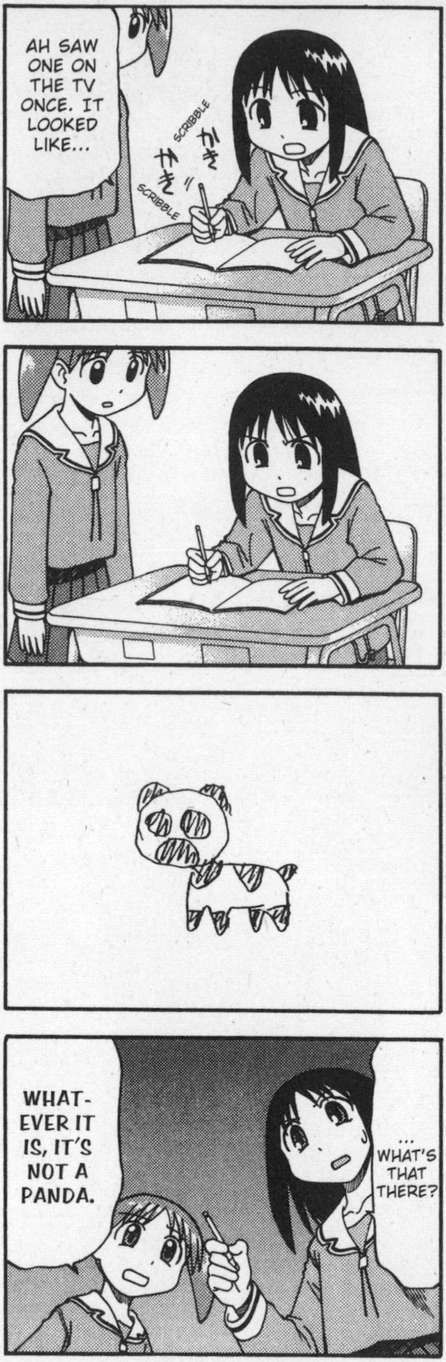
AH SAW ONE ON THE TV ONCE. IT LOOKED LIKE...
かき
SCRIBBLE
かき
SCRIBBLE
...WHAT'S THAT THERE?
WHAT-EVER IT IS, IT'S NOT A PANDA.

CHANGE OF PACE

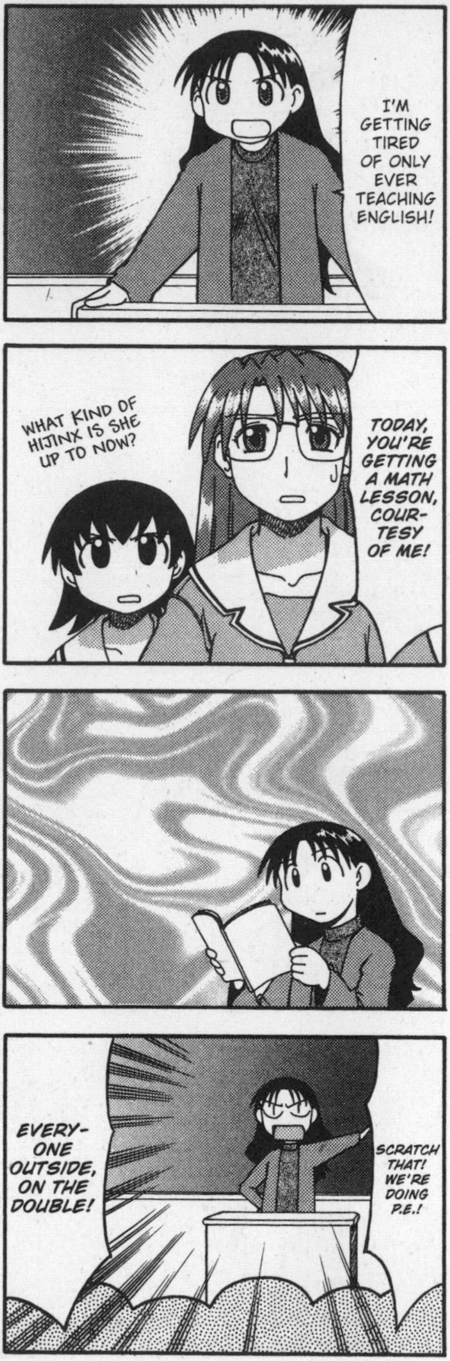
I'M GETTING TIRED OF ONLY EVER TEACHING ENGLISH!
TODAY, YOU'RE GETTING A MATH LESSON, COURTESY OF ME!
WHAT KIND OF HIJINX IS SHE UP TO NOW?
SCRATCH THAT! WE'RE DOING P.E.!
EVERY-ONE OUTSIDE, ON THE DOUBLE!

YUKARI OF THE WIND

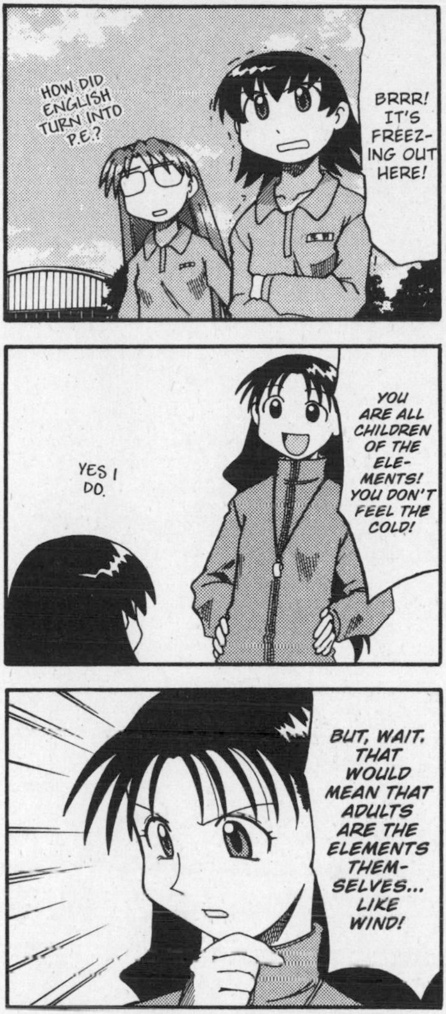
BRRR! IT'S FREEZING OUT HERE!
HOW DID ENGLISH TURN INTO P.E.?
YOU ARE ALL CHILDREN OF THE ELEMENTS! YOU DON'T FEEL THE COLD!
YES I DO.
BUT, WAIT. THAT WOULD MEAN THAT ADULTS ARE THE ELEMENTS THEMSELVES... LIKE WIND!
I AM WIND, HEAR ME ROAR! AS I BLOW FREELY, AND... UH...
WHY'S SHE SO PUMPED UP?

I'M HIDE

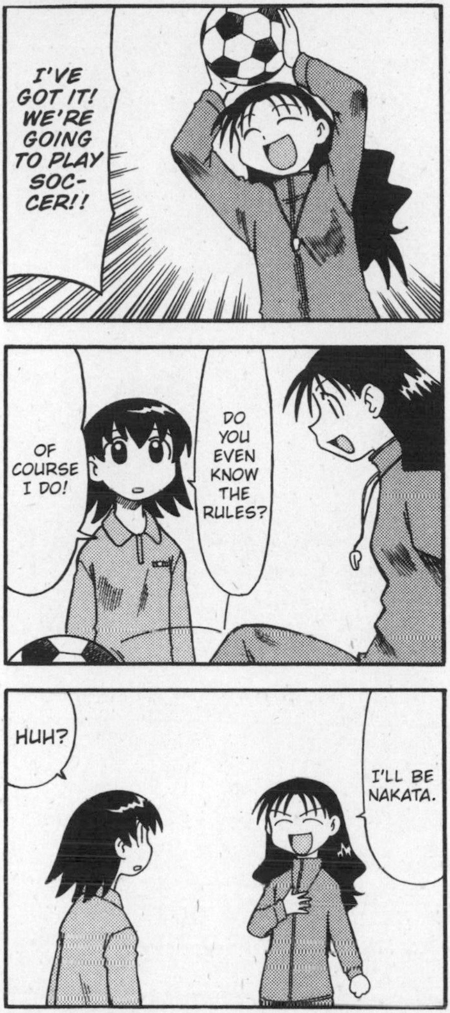
I'VE GOT IT! WE'RE GOING TO PLAY SOCCER!!
DO YOU EVEN KNOW THE RULES?
OF COURSE I DO!
I'LL BE NAKATA.
HUH?
I'M GONNA BE NAKATA.
WHAT DO YOU MEAN?

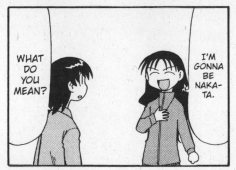

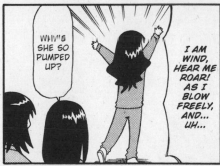

YUKARI THE STRIKER

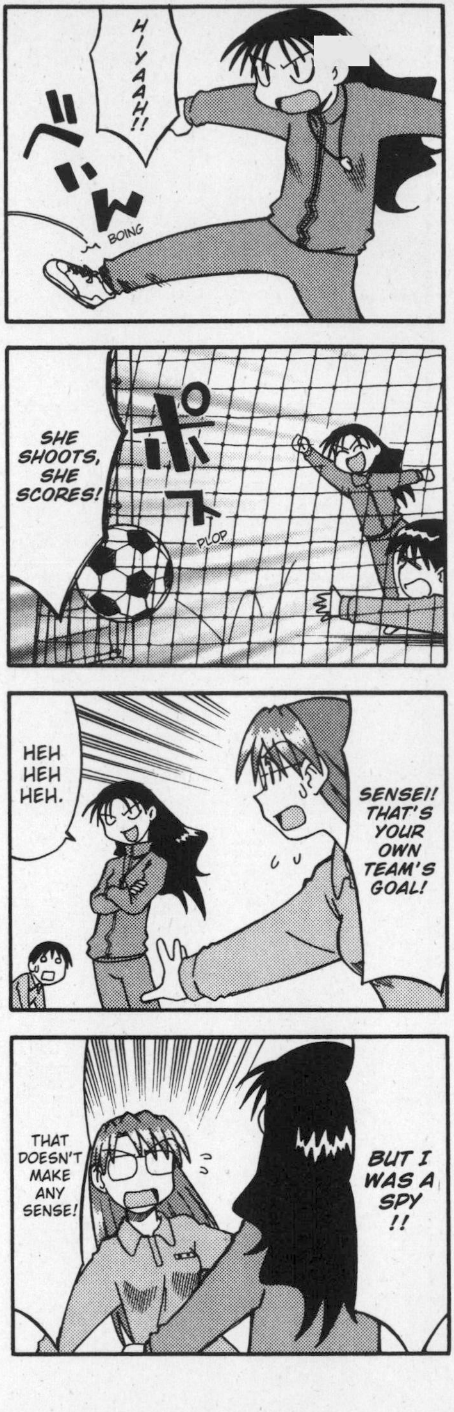
HIYAAAH!!
BOING
SHE SHOOTS, SHE SCORES!
PLOP
SENSEI! THAT'S YOUR OWN TEAM'S GOAL!
HEH HEH HEH.
BUT I WAS A SPY !!
THAT DOESN'T MAKE ANY SENSE!

I TOLD YOU, I'M NAKATA

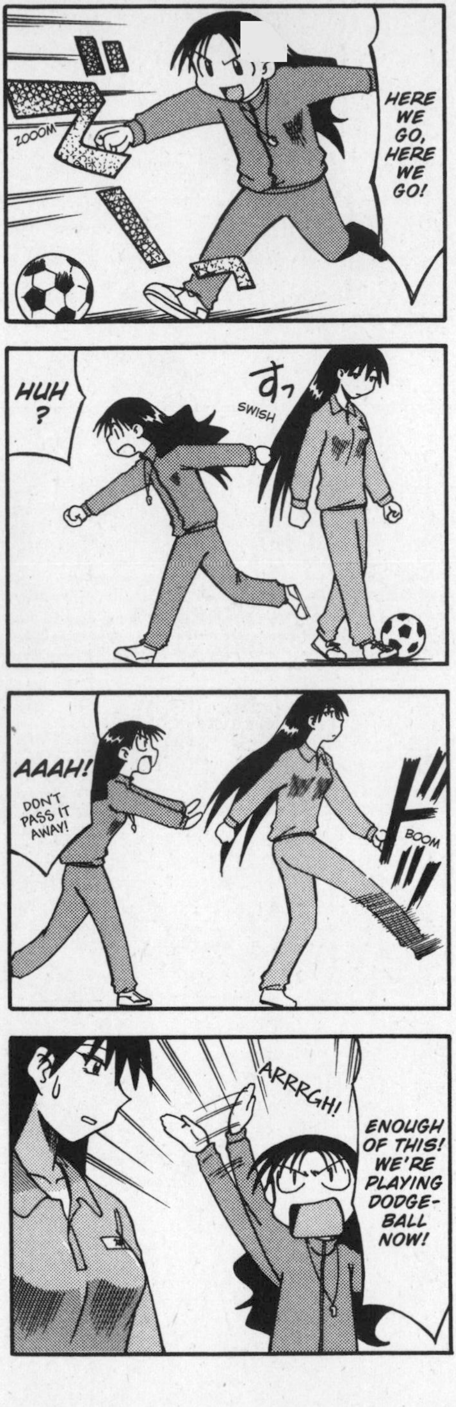
HERE WE GO, HERE WE GO!
ZOOOM
すっ
SWISH
HUH ?
BOOM
AAAH!
DON'T PASS IT AWAY!
ENOUGH OF THIS! WE'RE PLAYING DODGE-BALL NOW!
ARRRGH!

RUN, CHIYO, RUN

YAAAH!
ぱし
FWAP
GET 'EM!
NO! NO!
ぱーん
BWUNG

HITHER AND THITHER

SOMEHOW, CHIYO-CHAN WAS THE LAST ONE LEFT.
LOOK OUT, HERE IT COMES!
JUST HIT HER, ALREADY.

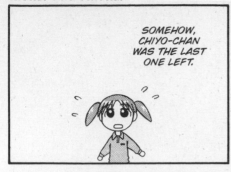

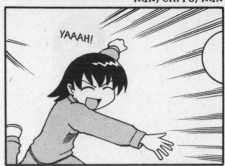

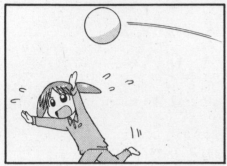

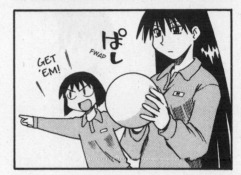

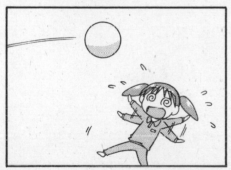

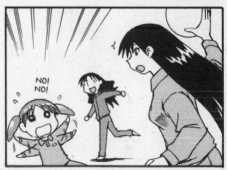

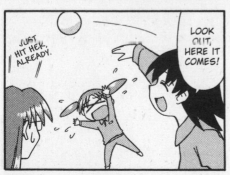

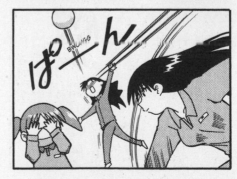

BROKEN VCR

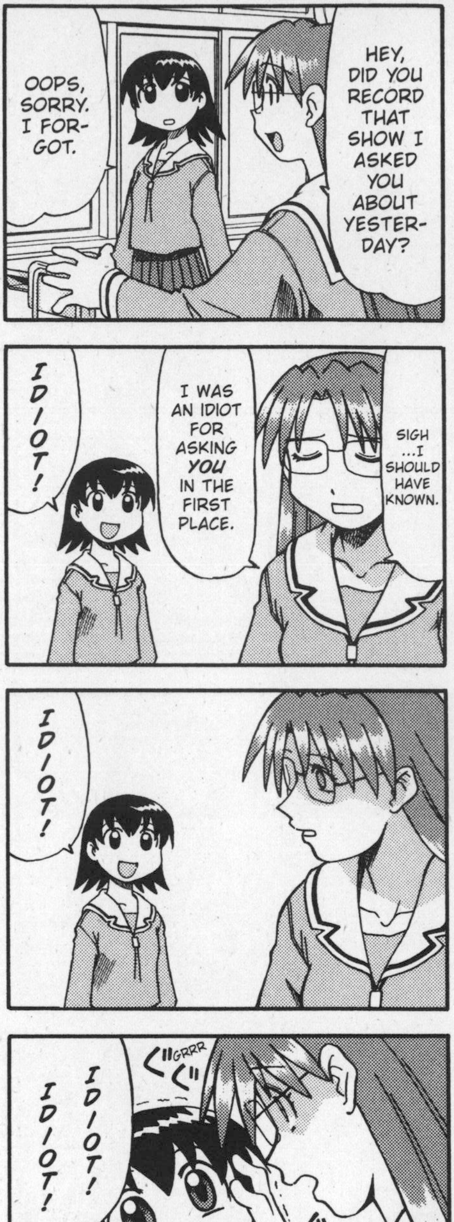
HEY, DID YOU RECORD THAT SHOW I ASKED YOU ABOUT YESTERDAY?
OOPS, SORRY. I FORGOT.
SIGH ...I SHOULD HAVE KNOWN.
I WAS AN IDIOT FOR ASKING *YOU* IN THE FIRST PLACE.
IDIOT!
IDIOT!
ぐ"ぐ" GRRR
IDIOT!
IDIOT!
ぐ" GRRG

VACATION PLANS

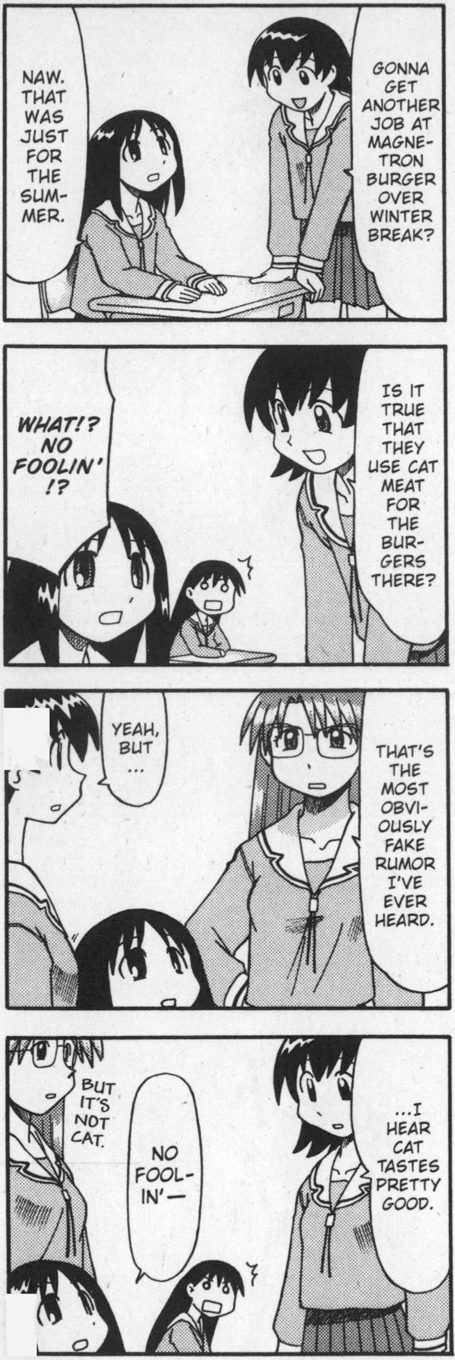
GONNA GET ANOTHER JOB AT MAGNETRON BURGER OVER WINTER BREAK?
NAW. THAT WAS JUST FOR THE SUMMER.
IS IT TRUE THAT THEY USE CAT MEAT FOR THE BURGERS THERE?
WHAT!? NO FOOLIN'!?
THAT'S THE MOST OBVIOUSLY FAKE RUMOR I'VE EVER HEARD.
YEAH, BUT ...
...I HEAR CAT TASTES PRETTY GOOD.
NO FOOLIN'—
BUT IT'S NOT CAT.

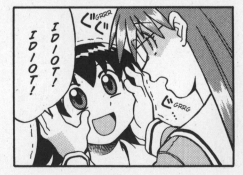

I BOUGHT IT

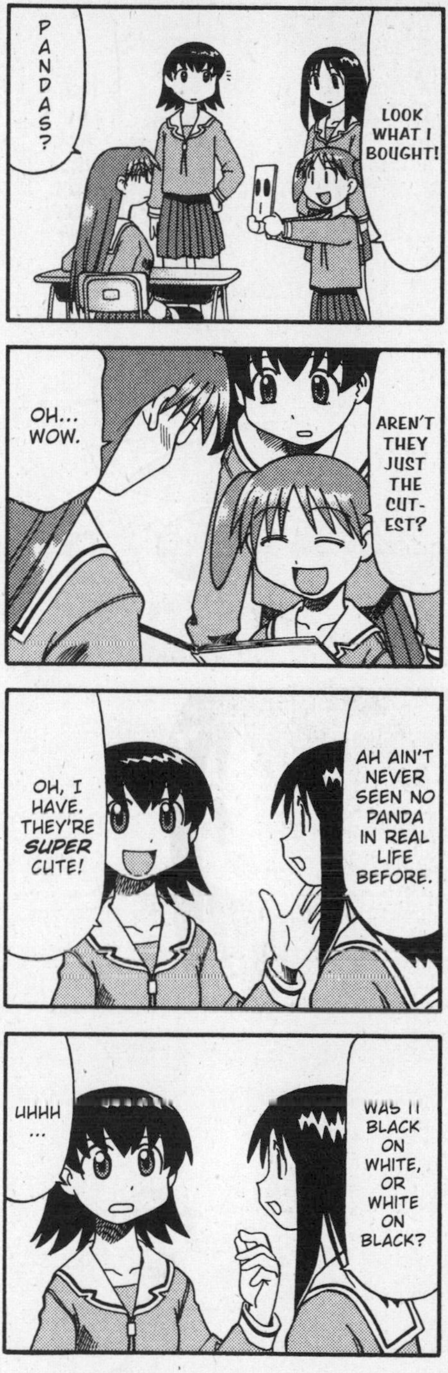
LOOK WHAT I BOUGHT!
PANDAS?
AREN'T THEY JUST THE CUT-EST?
OH... WOW.
AH AIN'T NEVER SEEN NO PANDA IN REAL LIFE BEFORE.
OH, I HAVE. THEY'RE ***SUPER*** CUTE!
WAS IT BLACK ON WHITE, OR WHITE ON BLACK?
UHHH ...

ALWAYS WANTED TO SEE IT

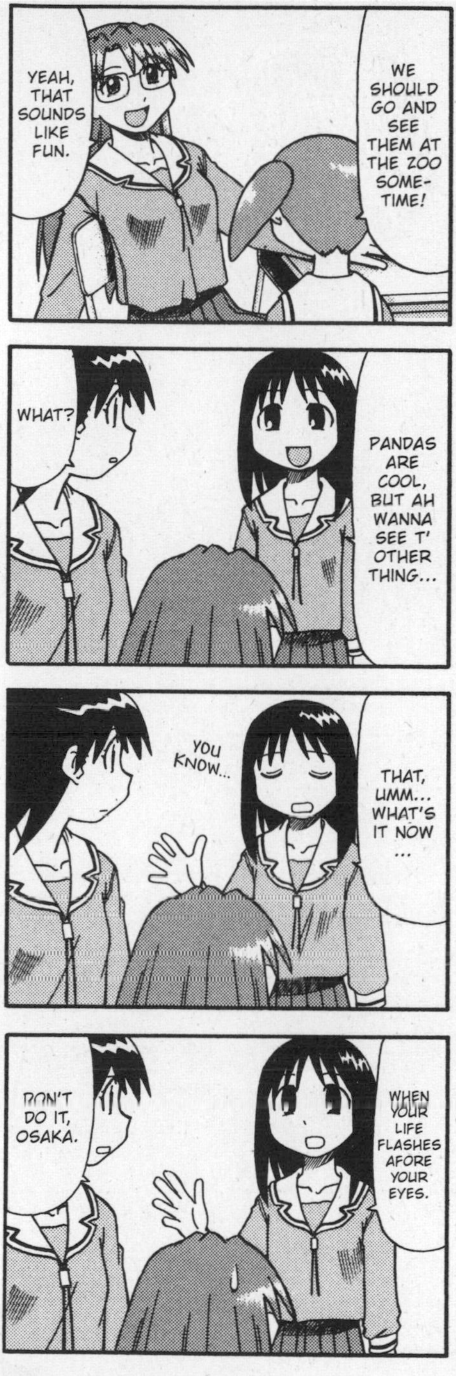
WE SHOULD GO AND SEE THEM AT THE ZOO SOME-TIME!
YEAH, THAT SOUNDS LIKE FUN.
PANDAS ARE COOL, BUT AH WANNA SEE T' OTHER THING...
WHAT?
THAT, UMM... WHAT'S IT NOW ...
YOU KNOW...
WHEN YOUR LIFE FLASHES AFORE YOUR EYES.
DON'T DO IT, OSAKA.

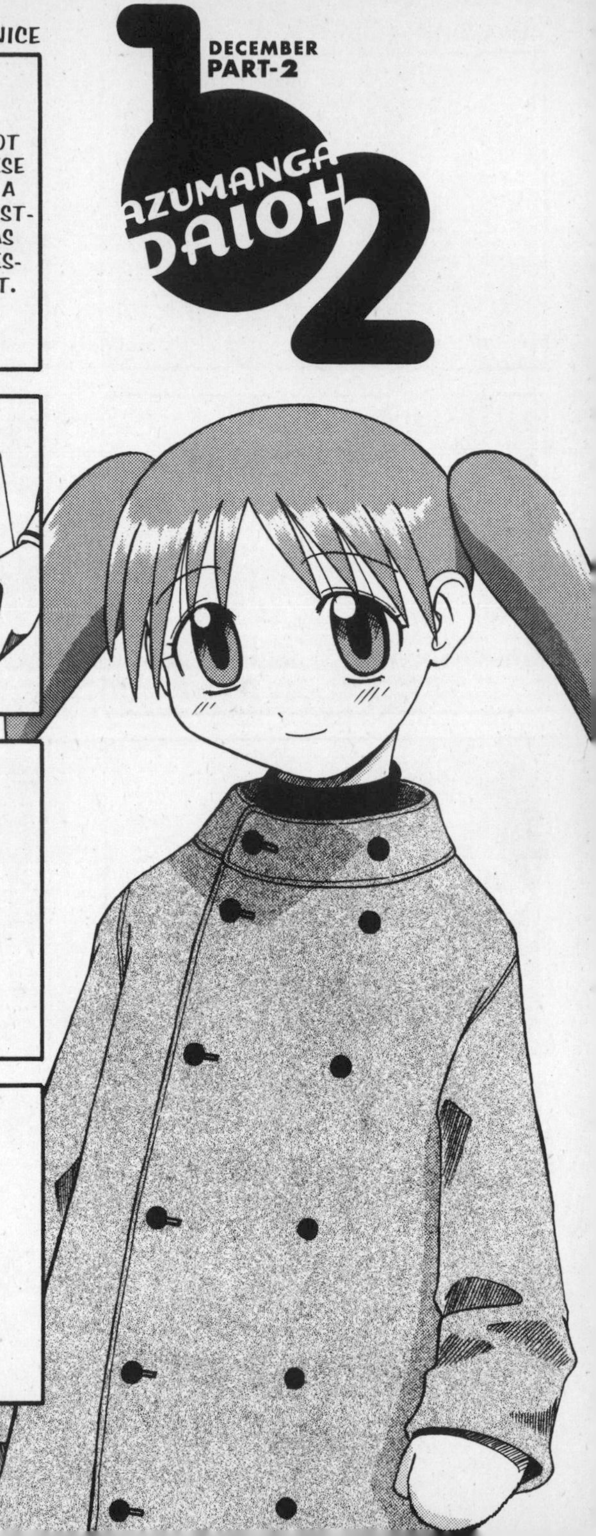
DECEMBER PART-2
AZUMANGA DAIOH
2

SOMETHING NICE

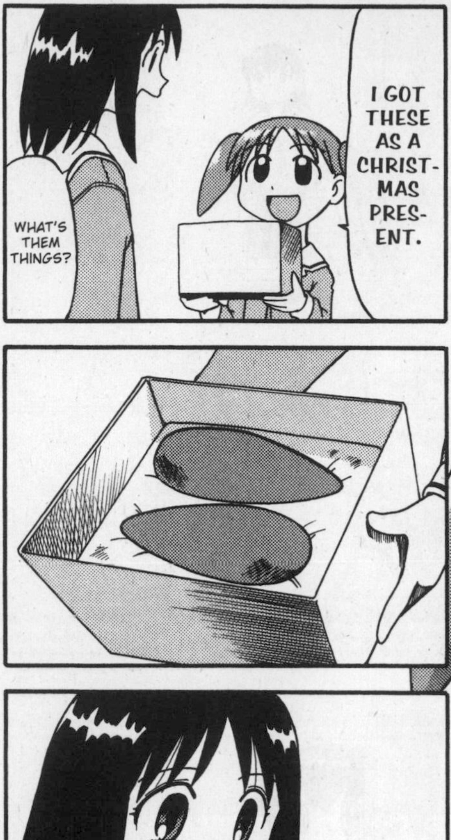
I GOT THESE AS A CHRIST-MAS PRES-ENT.
WHAT'S THEM THINGS?
WHAT'S THEM THINGS?

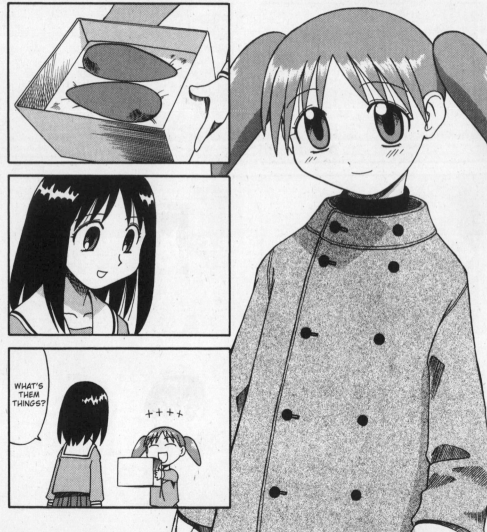

NEW ONES

YOU SEE ...
ぽ POP
ぽ POP
... THEY'RE NEW ONES!
かしゃ CLICK
かしゃ CLICK
NAWWW...
ガタ TREMBLE
?
ENGLISH I

THOUGHTS

NOW, WHO'S GOING TO ANSWER THIS PROBLEM? TOMO-CHAN.
UMMM ...
IN A WORD, "DIFFICULT."
I SEE.
WHAT ABOUT IN TWO WORDS?
"SUPER DIFFICULT," I'D SAY.
I SEE.
WHAT IN THE WORLD...

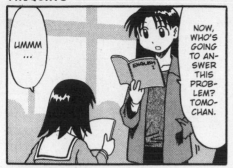

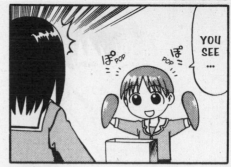

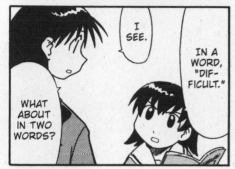

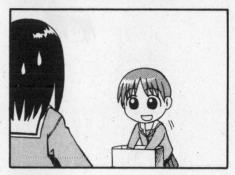

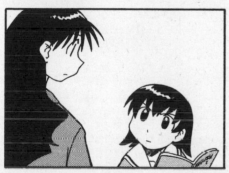

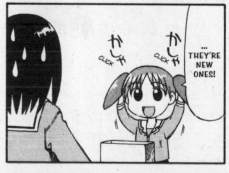

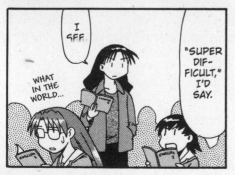

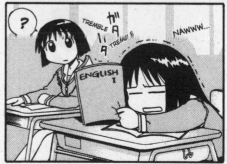

HOW INCONSIDERATE

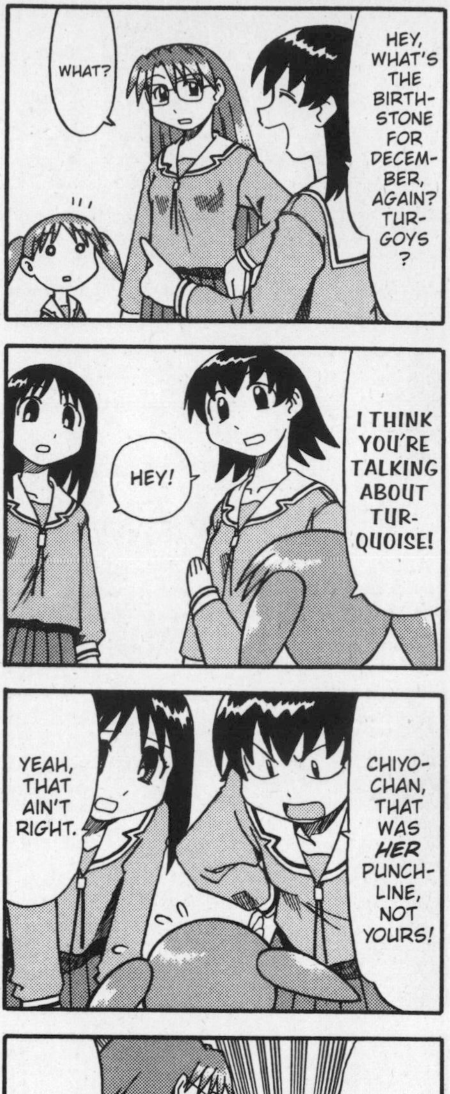
HEY, WHAT'S THE BIRTHSTONE FOR DECEMBER, AGAIN? TURGOYS?
WHAT?
I THINK YOU'RE TALKING ABOUT TURQUOISE!
HEY!
CHIYO-CHAN, THAT WAS *HER* PUNCHLINE, NOT YOURS!
YEAH, THAT AIN'T RIGHT.
I-I'M SO SORRY! I DIDN'T KNOW!
DON'T TAKE THEM SERIOUSLY.

BACK TO WORK

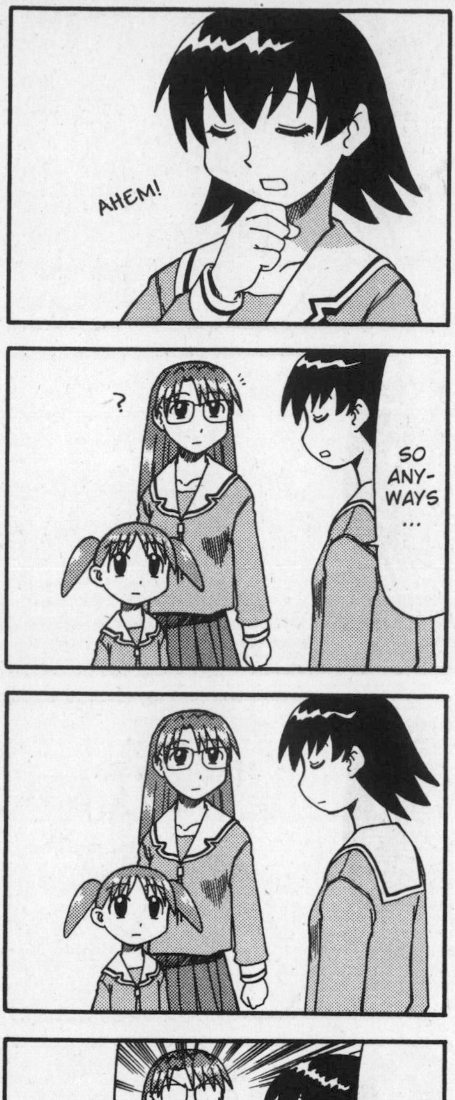
AHEM!
SO ANYWAYS...
WHAT'S THE BIRTHSTONE FOR DECEMBER AGAIN? TUR...
DON'T JUST START OVER!!

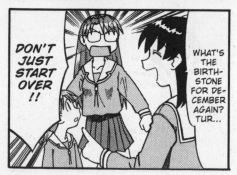

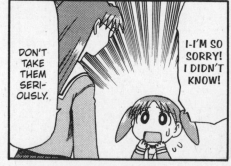

SHAME

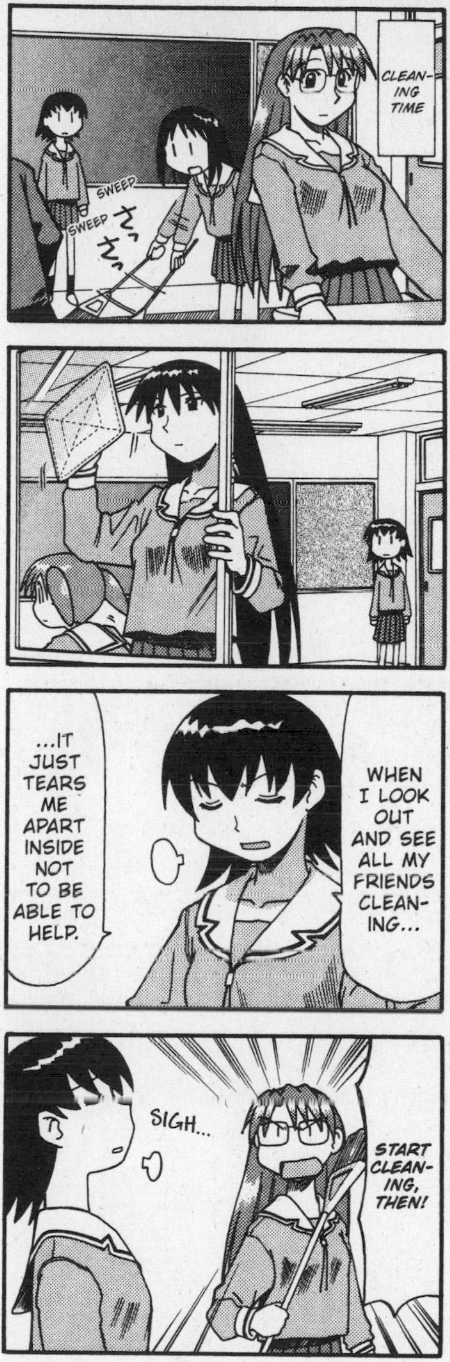

CLEAN-ING TIME
SWEEP
SWEEP
さっさっ
WHEN I LOOK OUT AND SEE ALL MY FRIENDS CLEAN-ING...
...IT JUST TEARS ME APART INSIDE NOT TO BE ABLE TO HELP.
START CLEAN-ING, THEN!
SIGH...

RESULTS

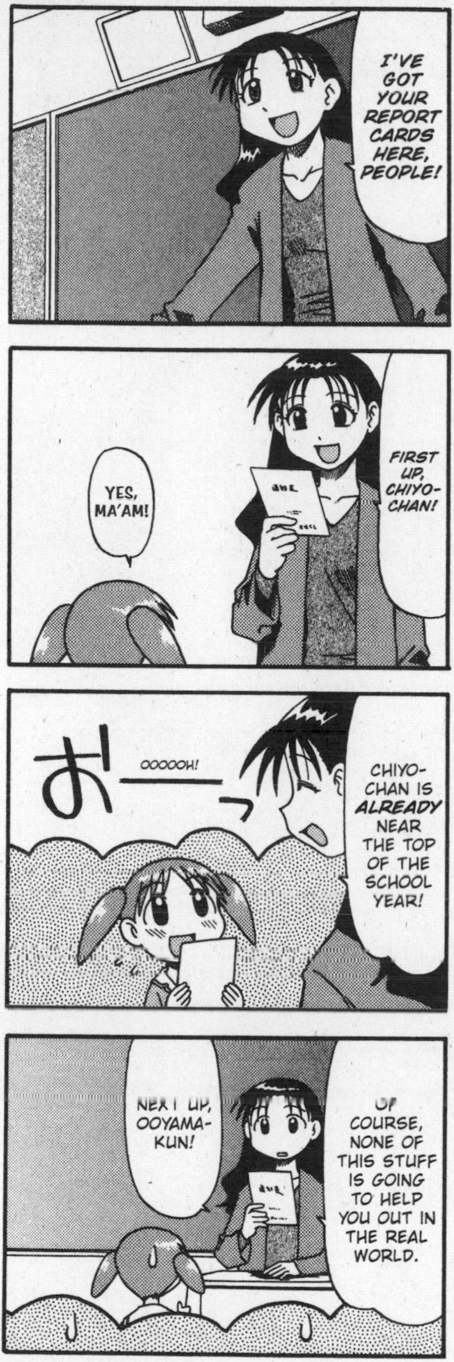

I'VE GOT YOUR REPORT CARDS HERE, PEOPLE!
FIRST UP, CHIYO-CHAN!
YES, MA'AM!
CHIYO-CHAN IS *ALREADY* NEAR THE TOP OF THE SCHOOL YEAR!
おーっ
OOOOOH!
OF COURSE, NONE OF THIS STUFF IS GOING TO HELP YOU OUT IN THE REAL WORLD.
NEXT UP, OOYAMA-KUN!

LEARNING

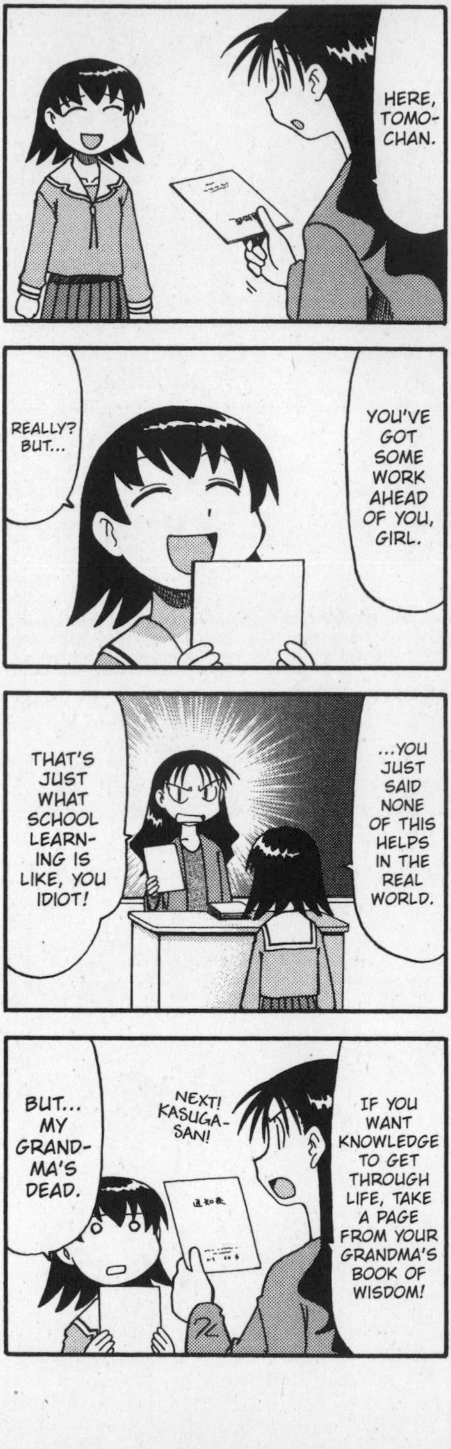
HERE, TOMO-CHAN.
YOU'VE GOT SOME WORK AHEAD OF YOU, GIRL.
REALLY? BUT...
...YOU JUST SAID NONE OF THIS HELPS IN THE REAL WORLD.
THAT'S JUST WHAT SCHOOL LEARNING IS LIKE, YOU IDIOT!
IF YOU WANT KNOWLEDGE TO GET THROUGH LIFE, TAKE A PAGE FROM YOUR GRANDMA'S BOOK OF WISDOM!
NEXT! KASUGA-SAN!
BUT... MY GRANDMA'S DEAD.

CHRISTMAS PARTY

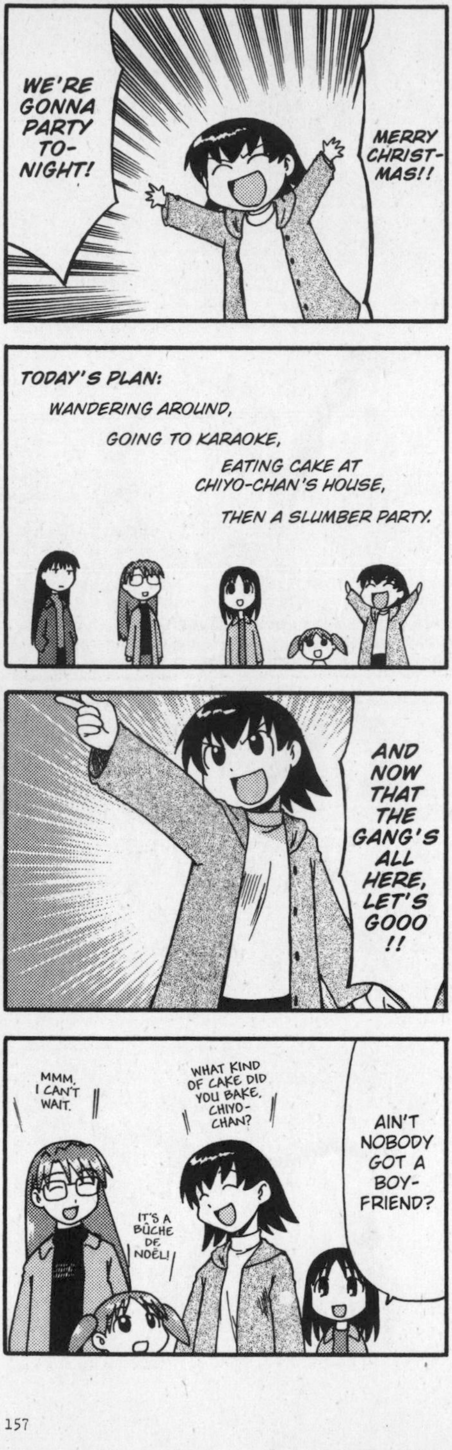
MERRY CHRISTMAS!!
WE'RE GONNA PARTY TONIGHT!
TODAY'S PLAN:
WANDERING AROUND,
GOING TO KARAOKE,
EATING CAKE AT CHIYO-CHAN'S HOUSE,
THEN A SLUMBER PARTY.
AND NOW THAT THE GANG'S ALL HERE, LET'S GOOO!!
AIN'T NOBODY GOT A BOYFRIEND?
WHAT KIND OF CAKE DID YOU BAKE, CHIYO-CHAN?
IT'S A BÛCHE DE NOËL!
MMM, I CAN'T WAIT.

WRONG

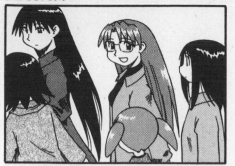

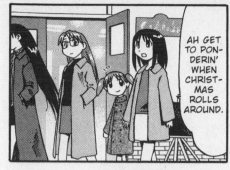

AH GET TO PONDERIN' WHEN CHRISTMAS ROLLS AROUND.
Y'ALL KNOW RUDOLPH THE RED-NOSED REINDEER?
THAT'S MESSED UP, Y'KNOW?
SAYIN' HIS NOSE WILL HELP LIGHT THE WAY AT NIGHT AIN'T NO WAY T'MAKE HIM FEEL BETTER ABOUT IT.
SURE, I GUESS.
IF YOU TOLD A BALD FELLA YOU NEEDED THE LIGHT REFLECTING OFF HIS HEAD TO SEE, HE'D LIKE TO PUNCH YOU.
SANTA'S A CRUEL BULLY.
YOU'RE RIGHT! I NEVER THOUGHT OF IT THAT WAY.

IMPOSTOR?

AND RUDOLPH'S GOT HIS OWN PROBLEMS!
ARE YOU STILL THINKING ABOUT THAT?
WHAT KINDA NOSE LIGHTS THE WAY AT NIGHT!?
HOW'S THAT EVEN WORK!?
WHAT IF RUDOLPH AIN'T EVEN A REAL REINDEER!?
BUT SOMETHIN' ELSE...
WHOA...

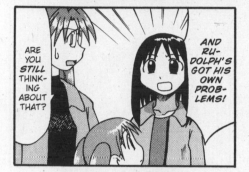

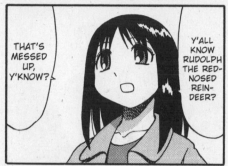

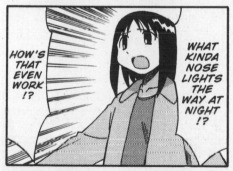

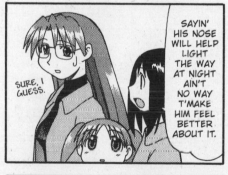

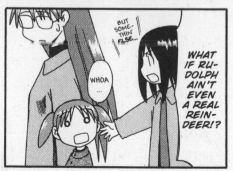

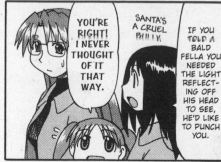

WORK FOR IT

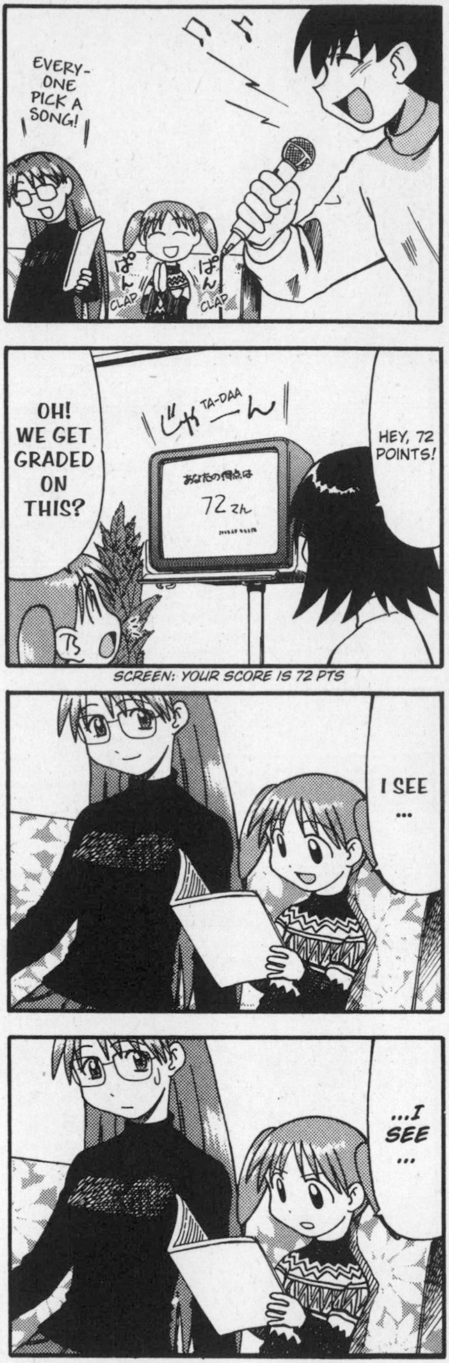
EVERY-ONE PICK A SONG!
ぱん CLAP
ぱん CLAP
HEY, 72 POINTS!
じゃーん TA-DAA
OH! WE GET GRADED ON THIS?
あなたの得点は
72てん
SCREEN: YOUR SCORE IS 72 PTS
I SEE ...
...I SEE ...

GOLDEN PIPES

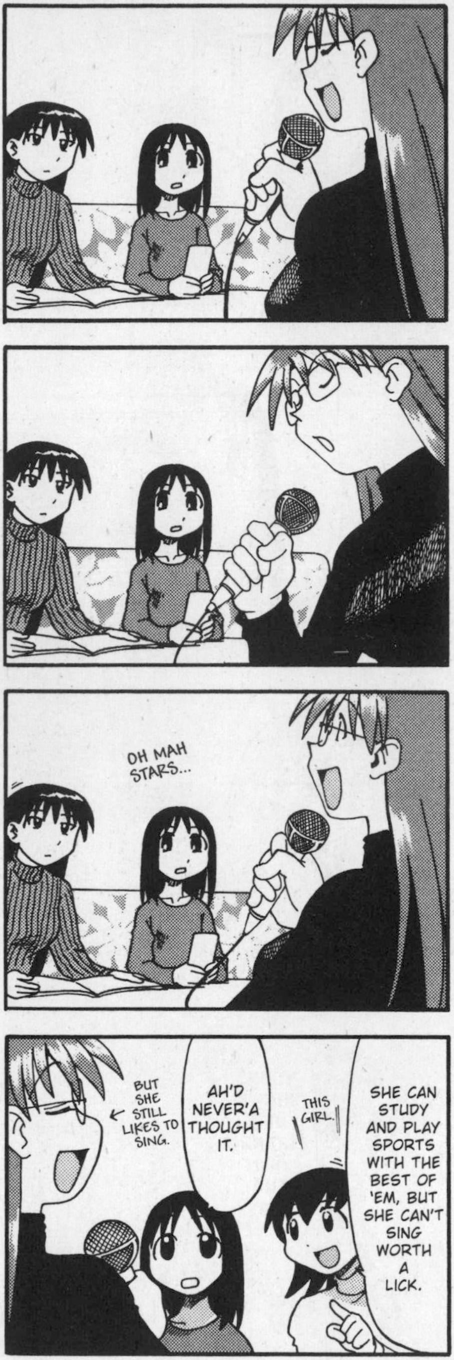
OH MAH STARS...
SHE CAN STUDY AND PLAY SPORTS WITH THE BEST OF 'EM, BUT SHE CAN'T SING WORTH A LICK.
THIS GIRL.
AH'D NEVER'A THOUGHT IT.
BUT SHE STILL LIKES TO SING.

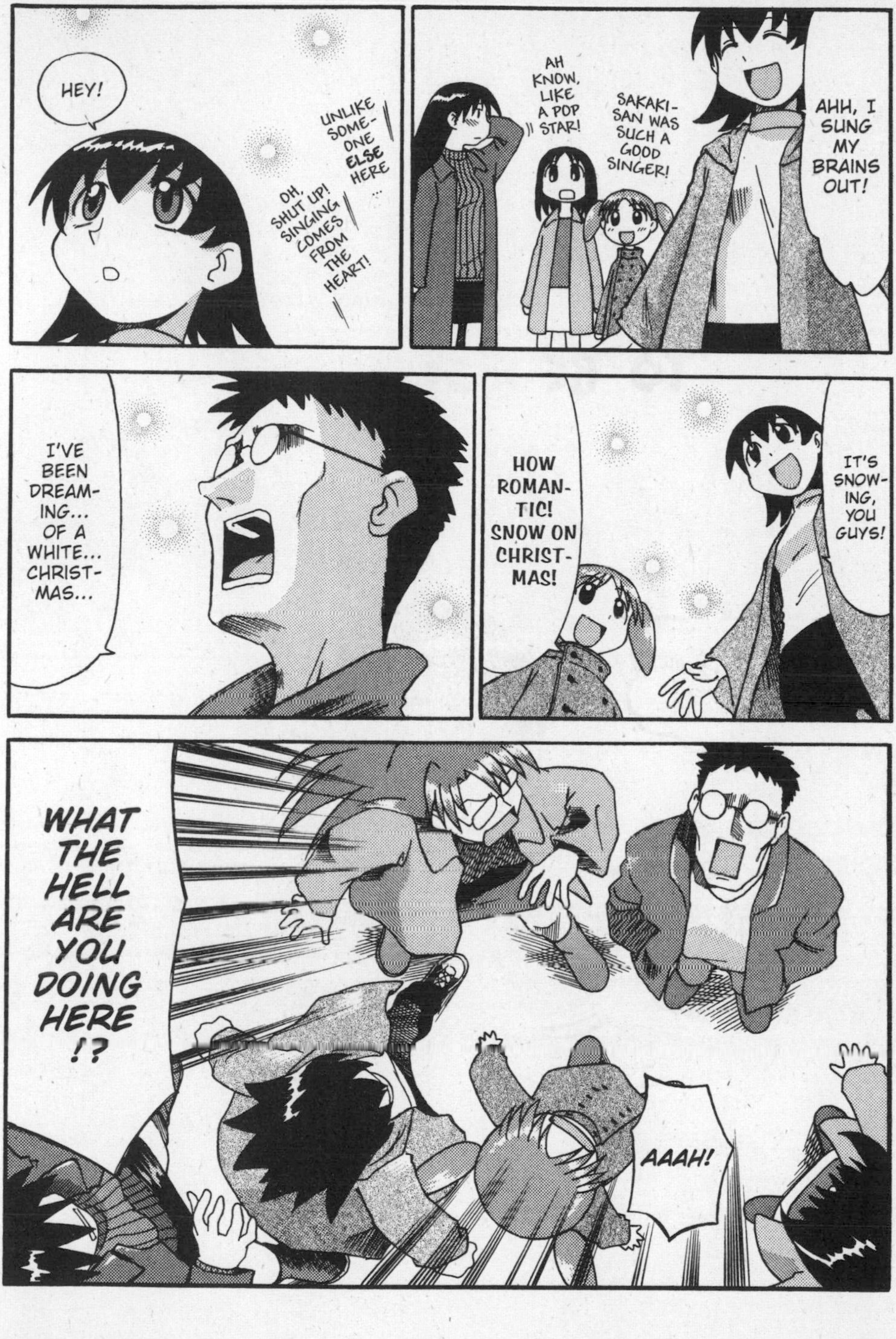
AHH, I SUNG MY BRAINS OUT!
SAKAKI-SAN WAS SUCH A GOOD SINGER!
AH KNOW, LIKE A POP STAR!
UNLIKE SOMEONE ELSE HERE...
OH, SHUT UP! SINGING COMES FROM THE HEART!
HEY!
IT'S SNOWING, YOU GUYS!
HOW ROMANTIC! SNOW ON CHRISTMAS!
I'VE BEEN DREAMING... OF A WHITE... CHRISTMAS...
AAAH!
WHAT THE HELL ARE YOU DOING HERE!?

TO BE CONTINUED.

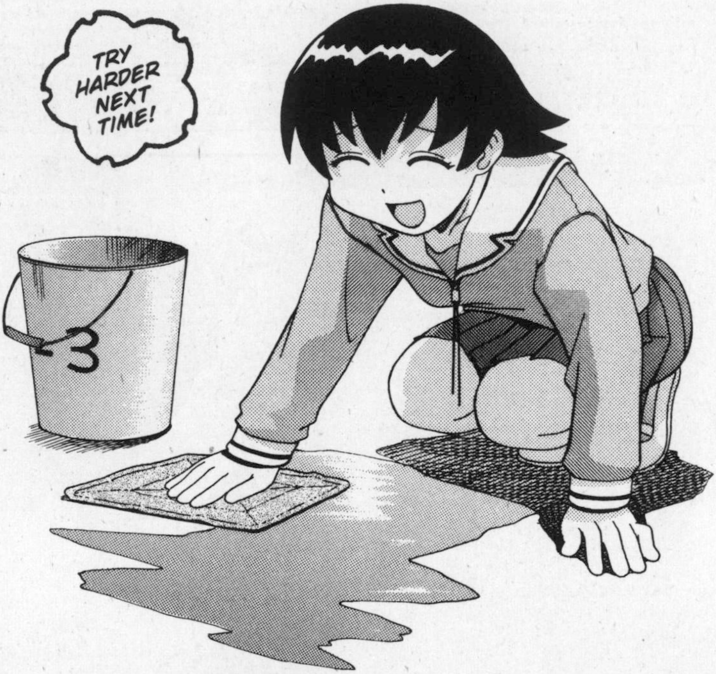
TRY HARDER NEXT TIME!
3

makes a silly or bizarre statement, and the *tsukkomi* corrects him, often fiercely. The routines are fast-paced, punchy, and exaggerated. The audience knows to expect humor from two sources: the cleverness of the *boke*'s misunderstandings and double entendres, and the force with which the *tsukkomi* yells at or hits the boke—with a slap on the top of the head, or more stereotypically, a backhand slap to the chest. Despite this latter source of humor, Tomo's reaction here is clearly way over the top. The interjection *nande ya nen* ("Whut yew mean?") is the most basic and generic form of *tsukkomi* put-down.

Kansai dialect: Japanese has a wide variety of dialects that differ from standard Tokyo Japanese in a number of ways, such as verb forms and conjugation, particle usage, vocabulary, and accent. Out of these, the dialect family of the Kansai (Western Japan) area—particularly the Osaka dialect—is the most widely recognized and understood nationwide, thanks in part to the comedy industry. To speakers of standard Japanese, Osakan speech sounds faster, rougher, and livelier. The irony, of course, is that the students of Class 3 expect these qualities from their Osakan transfer student, when in fact her personality and demeanor are the exact opposite. In translation, we opted to have Osaka speak with something of a Southern accent, which is the largest accent group in the United States.

PAGE 30
Takoyaki: Octopus dumplings that are rounded into spheres, with special sauce dribbled on top. A specialty from Osaka and extremely popular.

PAGE 47
Katsudon: Literally meaning "cutlet bowl," this dish features deep-fried pork cutlet topped with egg and served over a bowl of rice.

Curry udon: Udon is a type of wheat noodle, typically much thicker than ramen. One popular udon dish served in a soup broth made with Japanese curry powder. Because the udon noodles are larger and heavier than most, they can be difficult to control, and curry, of course, will stain anything.

PAGE 54
Marco: The protagonist of *3,000 Leagues in Search of Mother*, a well-known anime series from the 1970s based on Edmondo de Amicis' *From the Apennines to the Andes*. Marco is a young boy living in Genoa, Italy, whose mother goes to work in wealthy Argentina to make money for the family. Worried for her safety, Marco decides to stow away on a ship across the Atlantic to find her.

Tama: An extremely generic name for a pet, along the lines of "Spot" or "Kitty."

PAGE 55
"Cat food": The act of adding miso soup or some other kind of broth to a bowl of rice is called *neko manma*, or "cat food," particularly in Western Japan, which includes Osaka.

American Joke: As the Japanese don't particularly have an equivalent to the typical question-and-answer joke, attempts to explain the humor in "why did the chicken cross the road?" are rarely ever able to transcend the culture barrier. The term "American joke" is often used in Japanese to describe the concept of a joke, but due to the impenetrability of the humor, "American joke" is used equally often to describe some sort of jest that nobody understands or finds funny.

PAGE 67
Pairs: The original joke in this strip refers to linguistic counters. In English, we have a simple plural system (with exceptions) that makes it easy to count objects. In Japanese, however, multiple objects must be quantified by a counter, of which there are a great number, many being related to the size or shape of the object being counted, i.e. -*hon* counts long, thin objects such as pencils, rivers, etc. The counter word -*cho* is one of the most unusual of all, representing cast metal objects such as guns, tools and scissors, but also tofu blocks, town blocks, and yes, panties. Osaka was originally wondering why they use that counter, and what connection there could be between panties and weapons.

PAGE 77
Neko Koneko: This brand found within the world of *Azumanga Daioh* means "cat and kitten."

PAGE 79
Home visit gifts: The giving of gifts when visiting a home for the first time is traditional. It's not such a big deal for the girls, since they're not that old, but the signs of wealth are clearly intimidating Tomo.

COMMON HONORIFICS

no honorific: Indicates familiarity or closeness; if used without permission or reason, addresssing someone in this manner would constitute an insult.

-san: The Japanese equivalent of Mr./Mrs./Miss. If a situation calls for politeness, this is the fail-safe honorific.

-sama: Conveys great respect; may also indicate that the social status of the speaker is lower than that of the addressee.

-kun: Used most often when referring to boys, this indicates affection or familiarity.

-chan: An affectionate honorific indicating familiarity used mostly in reference to girls; also used in reference to cute persons or animals of either gender.

-sensei: A respectful term for teachers, artists, or high-level professionals.

MONETARY CONVERSION

Though exchange rates fluctuate daily, a good estimate to use is 100 JPY to 1 USD.

TITLE

Azumanga Daioh: The first part of the title is a meld of the author's name, Azuma, with the word manga. The second part comes from the magazine in which the series originally ran, *Dengeki Daioh*.

PAGE 5

Japanese school year: Unlike the American custom of starting the school year in the fall, the Japanese school year rolls over in the spring. In high school and below, there are generally three terms or trimesters in a school year: the first from spring to summer followed by summer vacation, the second from fall to winter followed by winter break, and the third and final term from the new year to spring break. Most Japanese schools split secondary education (7th to 12th grades) into three years each at junior and senior high.

Homeroom: Homeroom in Japanese schools is a more central feature than we're used to here. A class will often spend several periods of the day in their homeroom classroom, while the teachers move from class to class to teach their subjects. In addition, these homeroom classes work together on a variety of school duties, such as cleaning the campus and organizing exhibitions for student festivals. Therefore, class arrangements play a significant role in a student's education, as they can potentially be placed in the same class of 20–30 students for their entire time in high school. Another note: Classes are often labeled by year and then room, i.e., Class 1-4 would refer to the first-year class in Room 4.

PAGE 9

Daily helper: Part of the student responsibilities within the Japanese class system is the *nicchoku*, or "day duty," a role that places certain tasks—such as assisting the teacher or cleaning up the classroom or campus—on a student within the class. This responsibility is rotated each day between the students of the class.

PAGE 11

Standing in the hallway: This form of punishment, involving holding heavy buckets full of water in the hallway, is a throwback to the days when corporal punishment was regularly practiced in schools. They don't do it anymore, of course.

PAGE 27

P-Pet: A reference to the Japanese e-mail service, "PostPet," a comprehensive program that gives its users the ability to raise electronic "pets" who interact and deliver mail. PostPet started in the late 1990s and gained popularity right around the turn of the century, when this part of *Azumanga Daioh* was originally drawn. The author most likely abbreviated the name out of copyright concerns. The most popular pet and overall mascot of PostPet is a pink teddy bear named "Momo."

PAGE 28

Osaka: As the second most populated metropolitan area in Japan, Osaka represents the most significant and recognizable source of culture outside of Tokyo. Long considered the major center of commerce in Japan, Osaka does some of the most brisk business in the nation. If Tokyo is the place where people call the shots, Osaka is where they make their money. Because of this, Osakans are often stereotyped as being loud, lively, and fast-paced. Thanks to the aggressive efforts of the Osakan comedy business, the Kansai area that encompasses Osaka—along with the Kansai dialect of the Japanese language—is virtually synonymous with stand-up humor (see *manzai* below).

PAGE 29

Manzai: The most popular form of comedy in Japan, *manzai* is typically performed by two people, the *boke* (clown) and the *tsukkomi* (straight man). The humor is derived by a simple pattern: The *boke*

Watermelon is a decadent and particularly expensive midsummer treat suited for gifts and special occasions.

PAGE 83
Watermelon splitting: A common game played at the beach, similar to piñata, in which the player is blindfolded, given a stick or bat, spun around until dizzy, then attempts to break the melon.

PAGE 86
Ghost stories: In Japan, telling ghost stories is considered a summertime activity. The reasoning is that the spine-chilling terror it provokes will help cool you down. Sounds like as good a reason as any!

PAGE 102
Lightning: The Japanese god of lightning, Raijin, is said to eat or steal the bellybuttons of exposed stomachs. This is mostly a folklore warning against the danger of sleeping with the stomach exposed in the summer. It's a general belief in Japan that sleeping with one's stomach exposed, especially in conditions of sudden chill such as the onset of thunderstorms, can lead to ailments like colds and diarrhea. Therefore, it became common to frighten children into sleeping fully covered by warning them that the god of lightning would come to steal their bellybuttons.

PAGE 116
Bread: What Yukari offered Kagura was an *anpan*, a roll filled with jam made from sweet red beans.

PAGE 124
Kaorin: Her regular name is Kaori. It's a common practice to make nicknames by adding "n" on the end (especially if they end with *-ri*).

PAGE 130
Coffeehouse: The Japanese word for café, *kissaten*, starts with a somewhat complicated and seldom-used Chinese character. Still, it's not much excuse for a high-school student...

PAGE 140
Hanshin, Tsutenkaku: Hanshin is a nickname for the area comprising Osaka and Kobe, based on altered readings of the kanji in those cities' names. While it's not an official title for any city or region, it appears in several widely recognizable places, such as the baseball team, Hanshin Tigers, and the Great Hanshin Earthquake that rocked Kobe in 1995. Tsutenkaku, meanwhile, is a recognizable landmark in Osaka modeled after the Eiffel Tower.

PAGE 148
Nakata: Hidetoshi Nakata, nicknamed "Hide," was the most prominent soccer player in Japan during the '90s and '00s. He attracted attention not only for his great skill, but his fashion sense and haircuts.

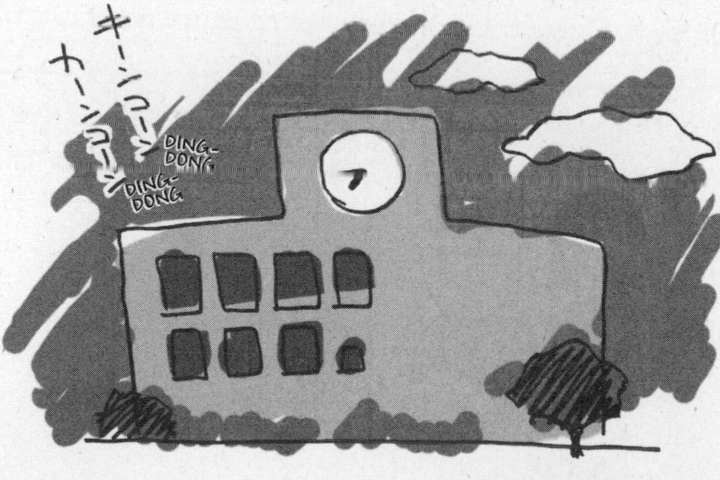
キーンコーン
DING-DONG
カーンコーン
DING-DONG

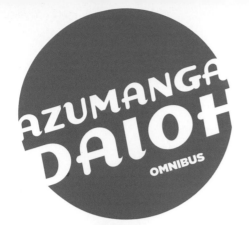

AZUMANGA DAIOH

OMNIBUS

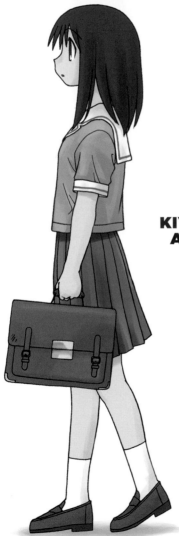

**KIYOHIKO
AZUMA**

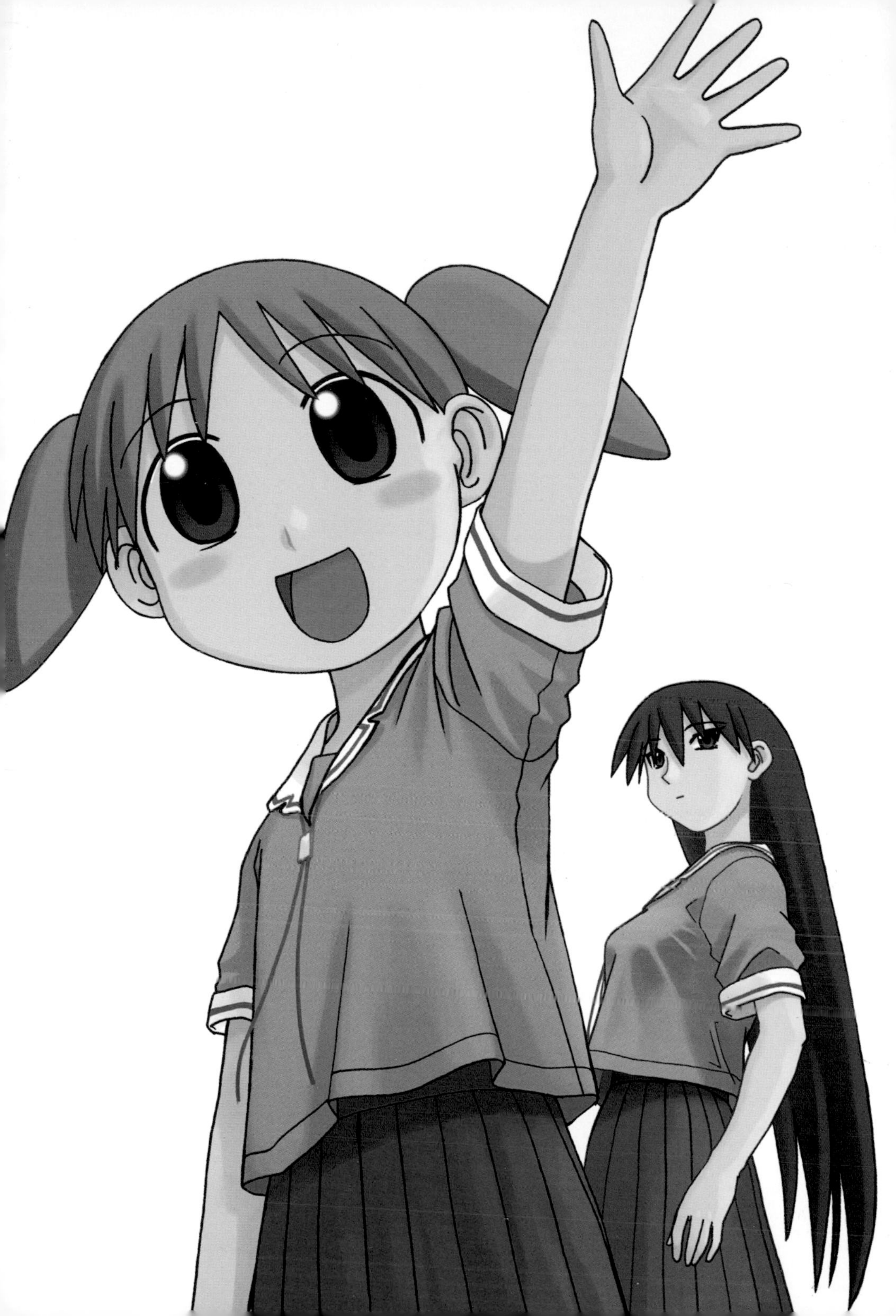

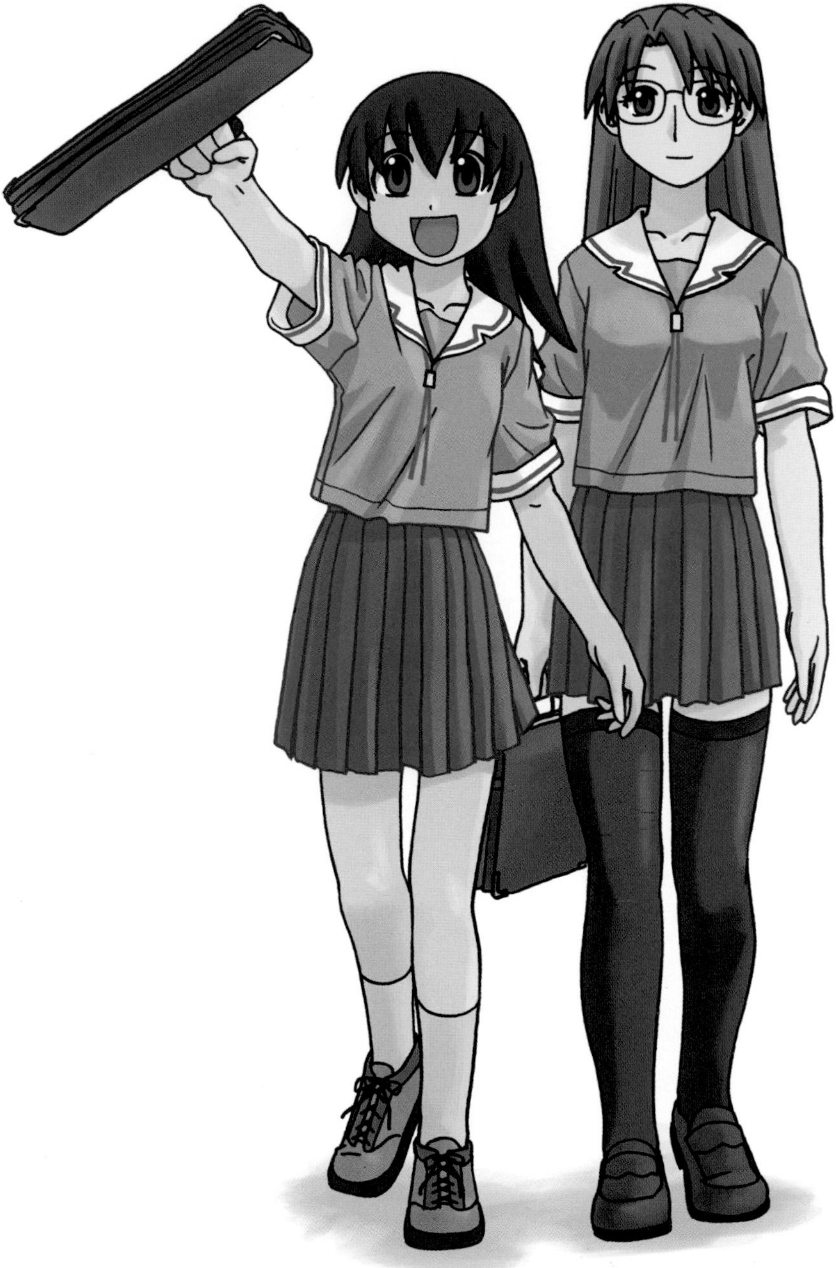

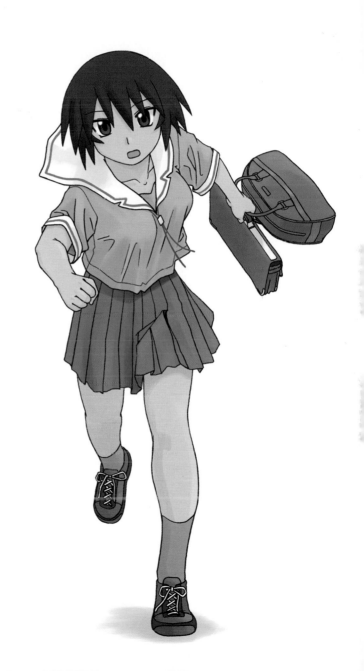

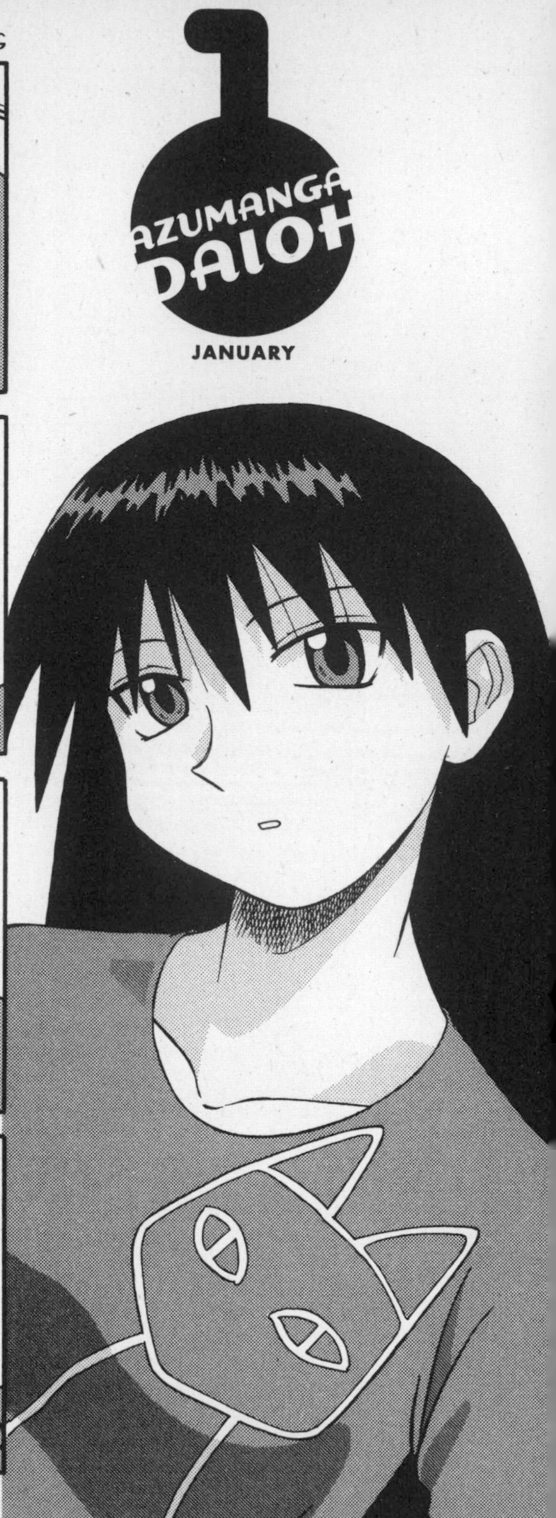
AZUMANGA DAIOH
JANUARY

WINTER MORNING

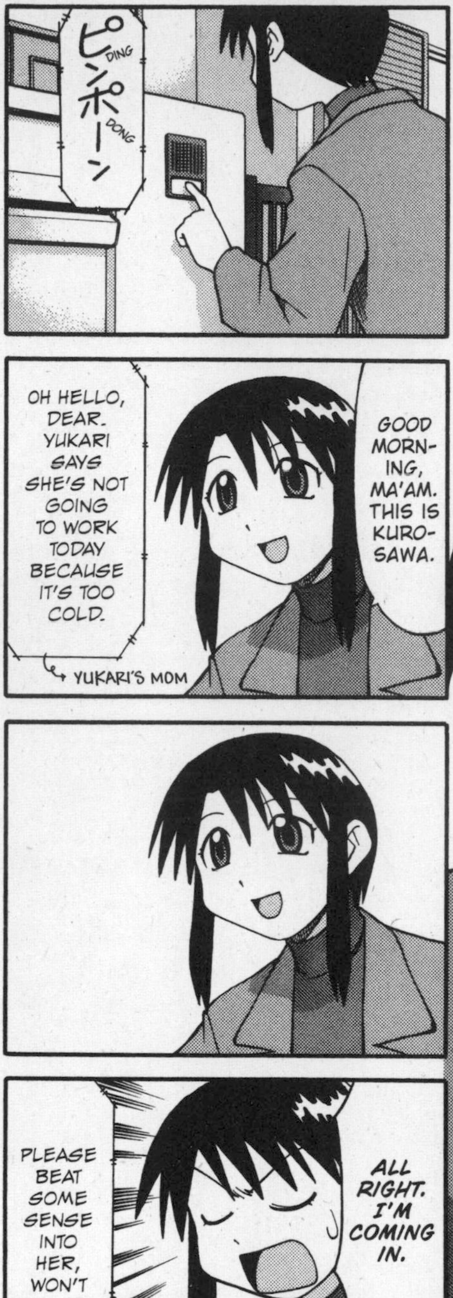
ピンポーン
DING DONG
GOOD MORNING, MA'AM. THIS IS KUROSAWA.
OH HELLO, DEAR. YUKARI SAYS SHE'S NOT GOING TO WORK TODAY BECAUSE IT'S TOO COLD.
YUKARI'S MOM
ALL RIGHT. I'M COMING IN.
PLEASE BEAT SOME SENSE INTO HER, WON'T YOU?

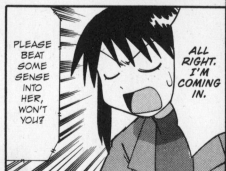

TWINS

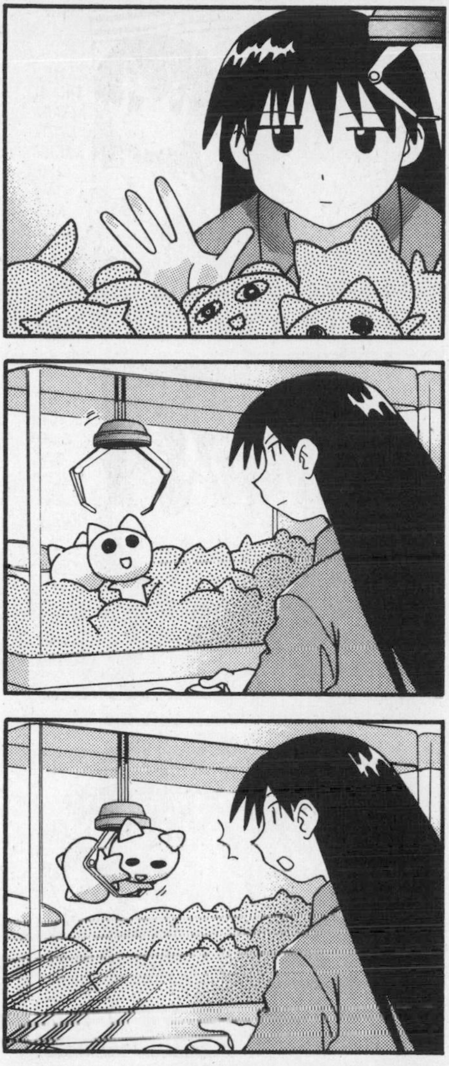
IT'S GOING TO BE A GOOD YEAR!
A GOOD YEAR!

CAT REPELLENT

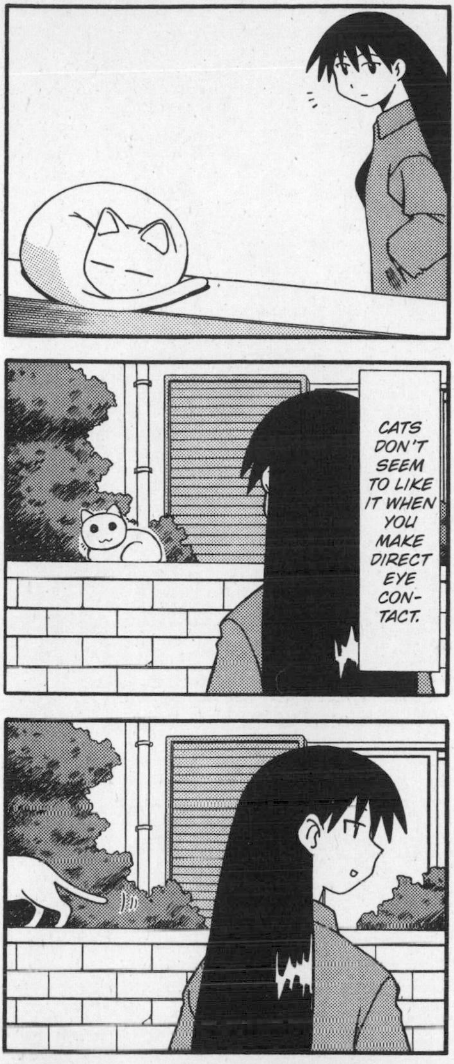
CATS DON'T SEEM TO LIKE IT WHEN YOU MAKE DIRECT EYE CON-TACT.

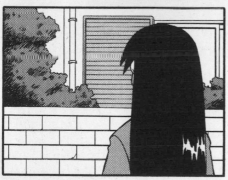

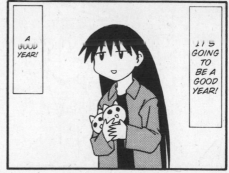

EVERYTHING'S FINE, RIGHT?

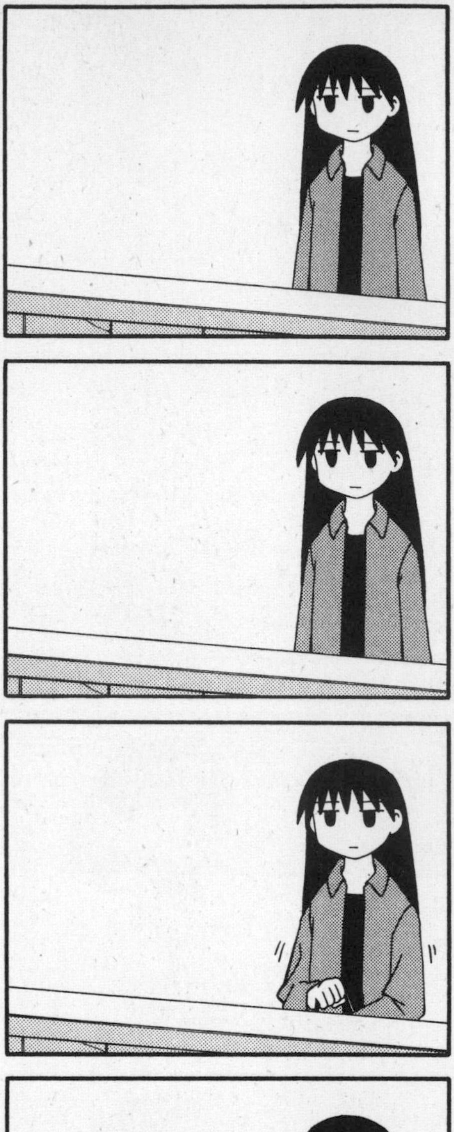
HUG...

BLOB

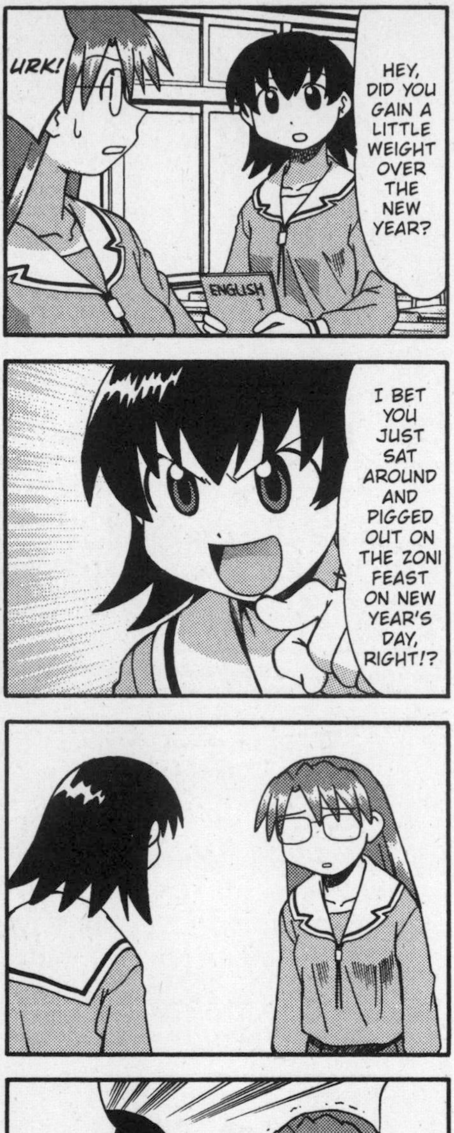
HEY, DID YOU GAIN A LITTLE WEIGHT OVER THE NEW YEAR?
URK!
ENGLISH I
I BET YOU JUST SAT AROUND AND PIGGED OUT ON THE ZONI FEAST ON NEW YEAR'S DAY, RIGHT!?
...ACTUALLY, IT WAS THE SWEET BEAN SOUP...
THE BEAN SOUP GOTCHA, HUH!!?
I CAN SEE THAT...

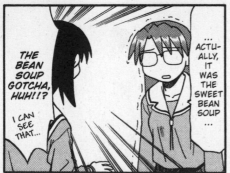

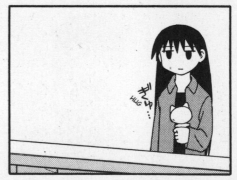

NAKED JEALOUSY

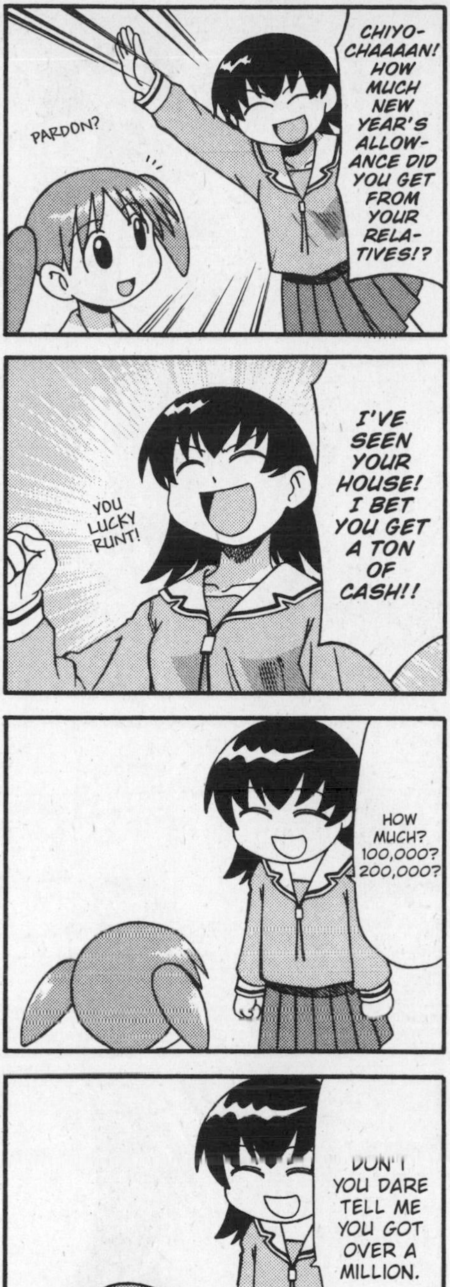
CHIYO-CHAAAAN! HOW MUCH NEW YEAR'S ALLOWANCE DID YOU GET FROM YOUR RELATIVES!?
PARDON?
I'VE SEEN YOUR HOUSE! I BET YOU GET A TON OF CASH!!
YOU LUCKY RUNT!
HOW MUCH? 100,000? 200,000?
DON'T YOU DARE TELL ME YOU GOT OVER A MILLION.

A VERY GOOD GIRL

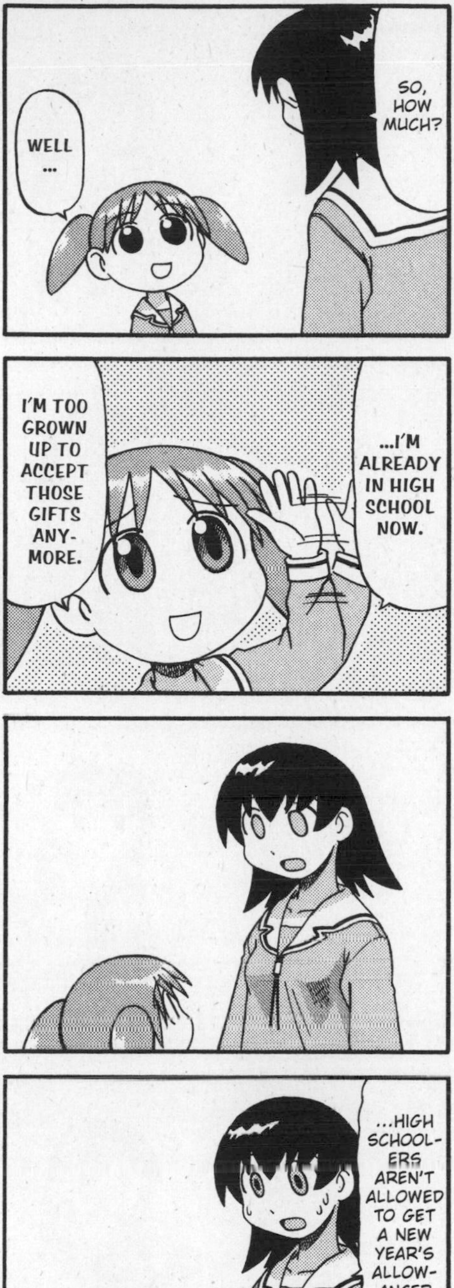
SO, HOW MUCH?
WELL ...
...I'M ALREADY IN HIGH SCHOOL NOW.
I'M TOO GROWN UP TO ACCEPT THOSE GIFTS ANYMORE.
...HIGH SCHOOLERS AREN'T ALLOWED TO GET A NEW YEAR'S ALLOWANCE?

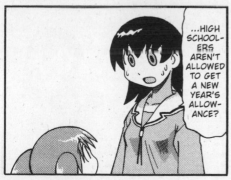

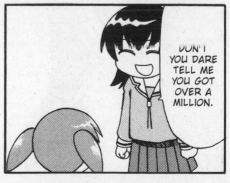

NEWBORN

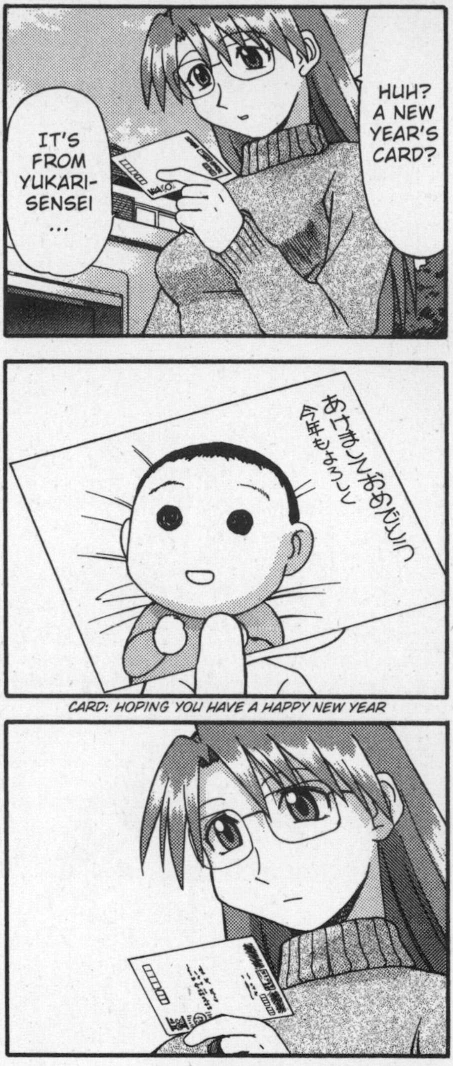
HUH? A NEW YEAR'S CARD?
IT'S FROM YUKARI-SENSEI ...
あけましておめでとう
今年もよろしく
CARD: HOPING YOU HAVE A HAPPY NEW YEAR
WAIT, WHAT !?

MRS. YUKARI

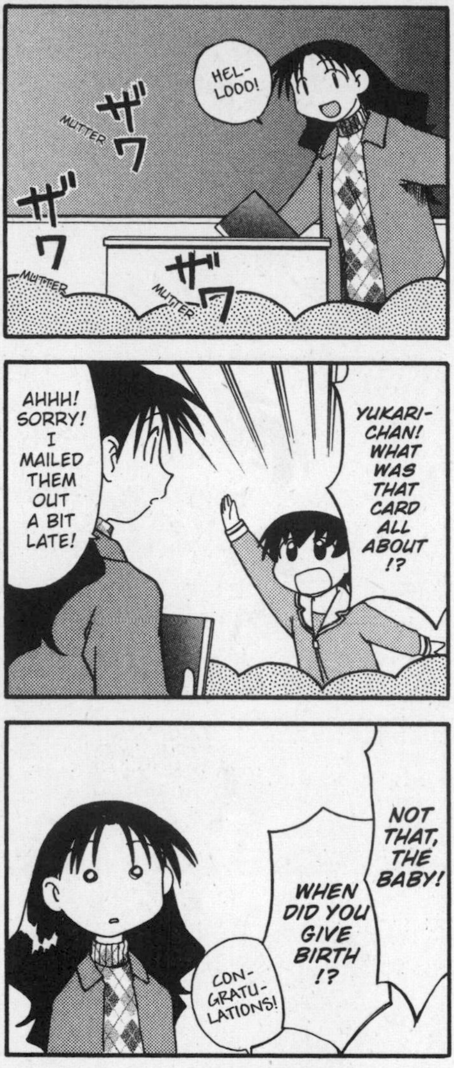
HEL-LOOO!
ザワ
MUTTER
ザワ
MUTTER
ザワ
MUTTER
YUKARI-CHAN! WHAT WAS THAT CARD ALL ABOUT !?
AHHH! SORRY! I MAILED THEM OUT A BIT LATE!
NOT THAT, THE BABY!
WHEN DID YOU GIVE BIRTH !?
CON-GRATU-LATIONS!
THAT'S MY COUSIN'S BABY.
STOP CONFUSING US LIKE THAT!!

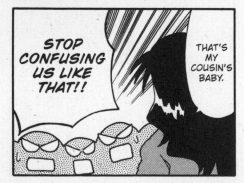

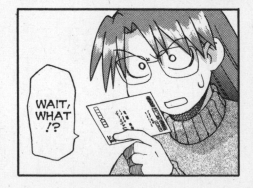

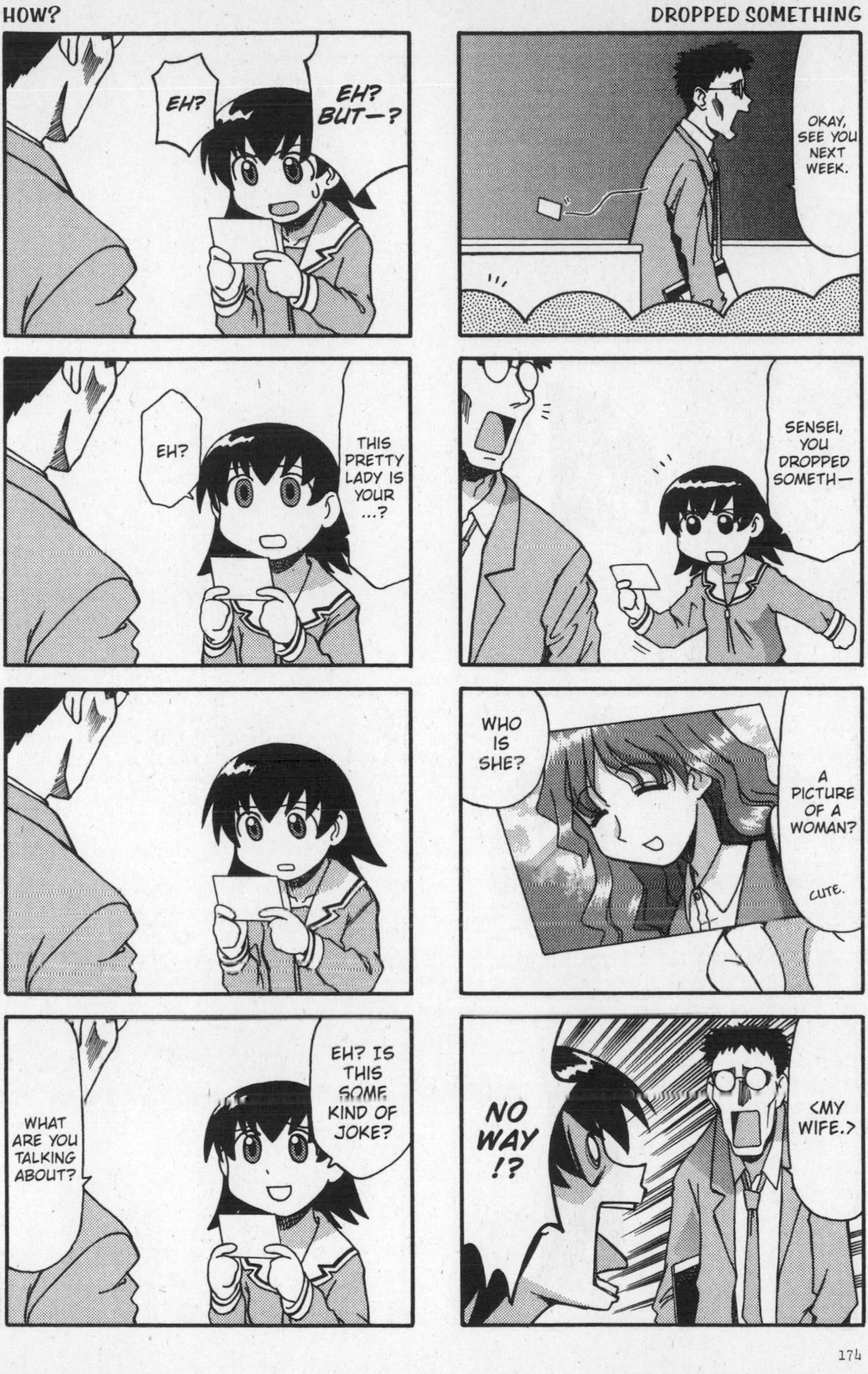
DROPPED SOMETHING
OKAY, SEE YOU NEXT WEEK.
SENSEI, YOU DROPPED SOMETH—
A PICTURE OF A WOMAN?
CUTE.
WHO IS SHE?
<MY WIFE.>
NO WAY!?
HOW?
EH? BUT—?
EH?
THIS PRETTY LADY IS YOUR ...?
EH?
EH? IS THIS SOME KIND OF JOKE?
WHAT ARE YOU TALKING ABOUT?

THE KIMURA FAMILY

HERE'S A PHOTO OF US TOGETHER.
UM... AND THIS KID...
OH. THAT'S MY DAUGHTER.
BUT SHE LOOKS SO SMART!!

INCOMPREHENSIBLE

I STILL CAN'T ACCEPT THAT KIMURA HAS A WIFE LIKE HER. IT'S TOO WEIRD.
YEAH, REALLY.
MAYBE WE OUGHTA CALL THE POLICE OR SOMETHIN'!
Y-YES! GOOD IDEA!

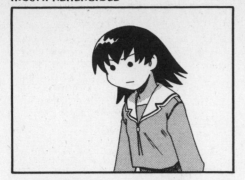

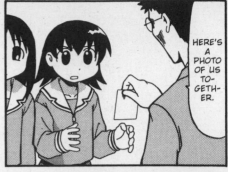

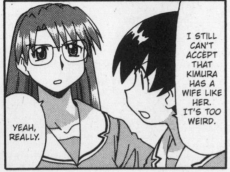

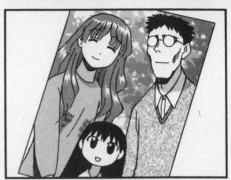

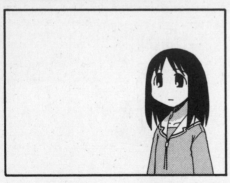

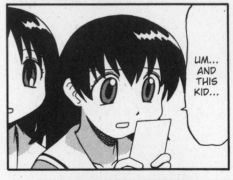

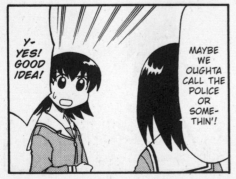

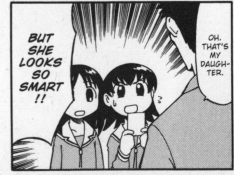

CHIYO THE LAWYER

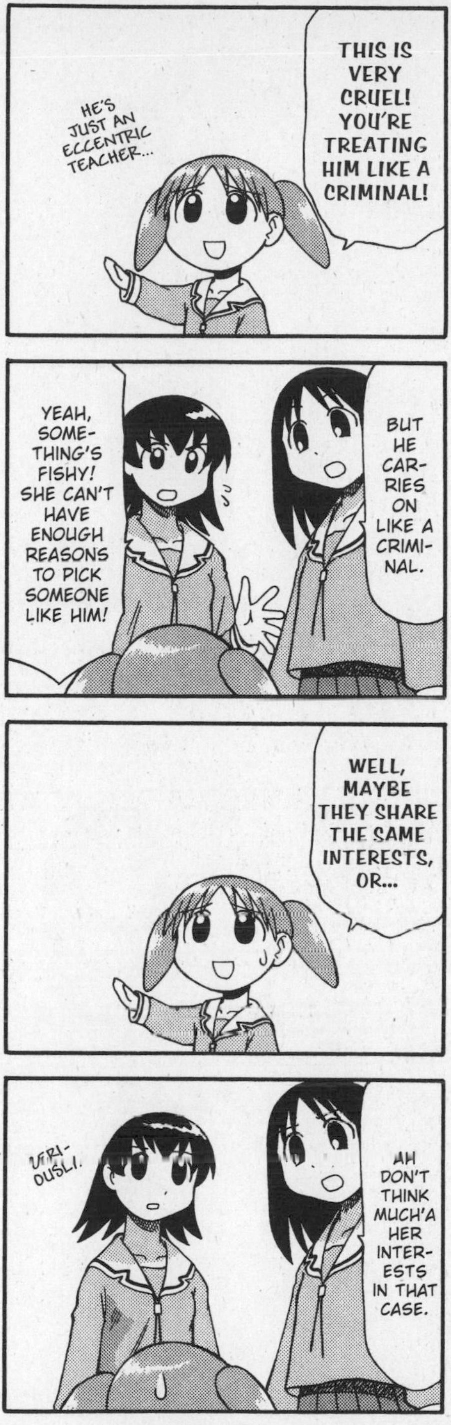
THIS IS VERY CRUEL! YOU'RE TREATING HIM LIKE A CRIMINAL!
HE'S JUST AN ECCENTRIC TEACHER...
BUT HE CARRIES ON LIKE A CRIMINAL.
YEAH, SOMETHING'S FISHY! SHE CAN'T HAVE ENOUGH REASONS TO PICK SOMEONE LIKE HIM!
WELL, MAYBE THEY SHARE THE SAME INTERESTS, OR...
AH DON'T THINK MUCH'A HER INTERESTS IN THAT CASE.

THE LADY'S SECRET

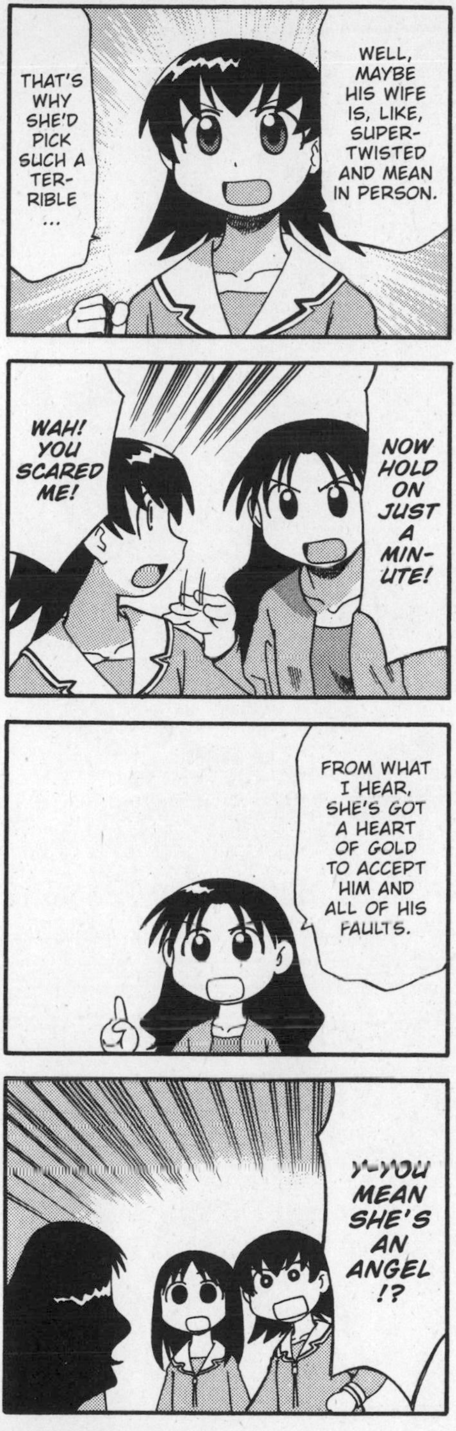
WELL, MAYBE HIS WIFE IS, LIKE, SUPER-TWISTED AND MEAN IN PERSON.
THAT'S WHY SHE'D PICK SUCH A TERRIBLE ...
NOW HOLD ON JUST A MINUTE!
WAH! YOU SCARED ME!
FROM WHAT I HEAR, SHE'S GOT A HEART OF GOLD TO ACCEPT HIM AND ALL OF HIS FAULTS.
Y-YOU MEAN SHE'S AN ANGEL !?

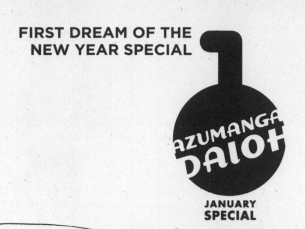

FIRST DREAM OF THE NEW YEAR SPECIAL

AZUMANGA DAIOH

JANUARY SPECIAL

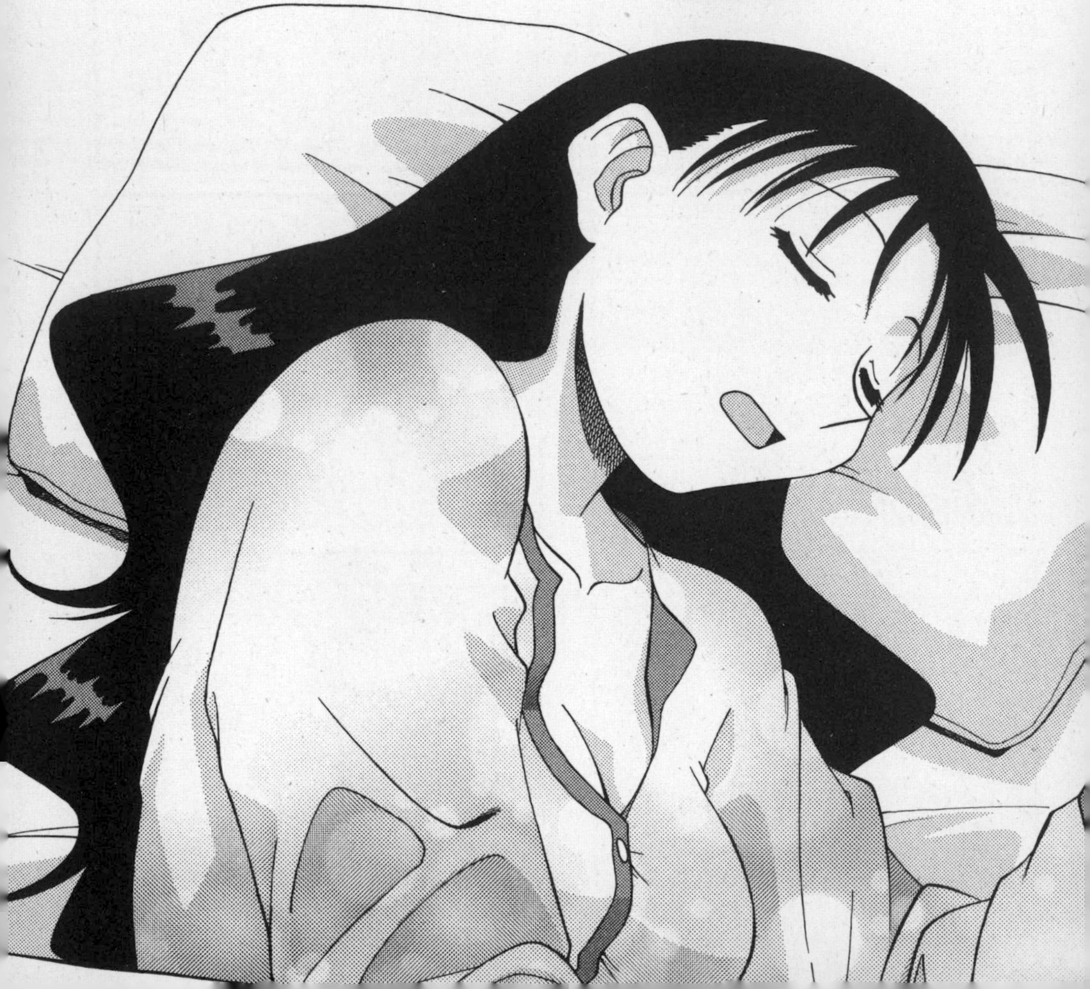

OSAKA'S FIRST DREAM

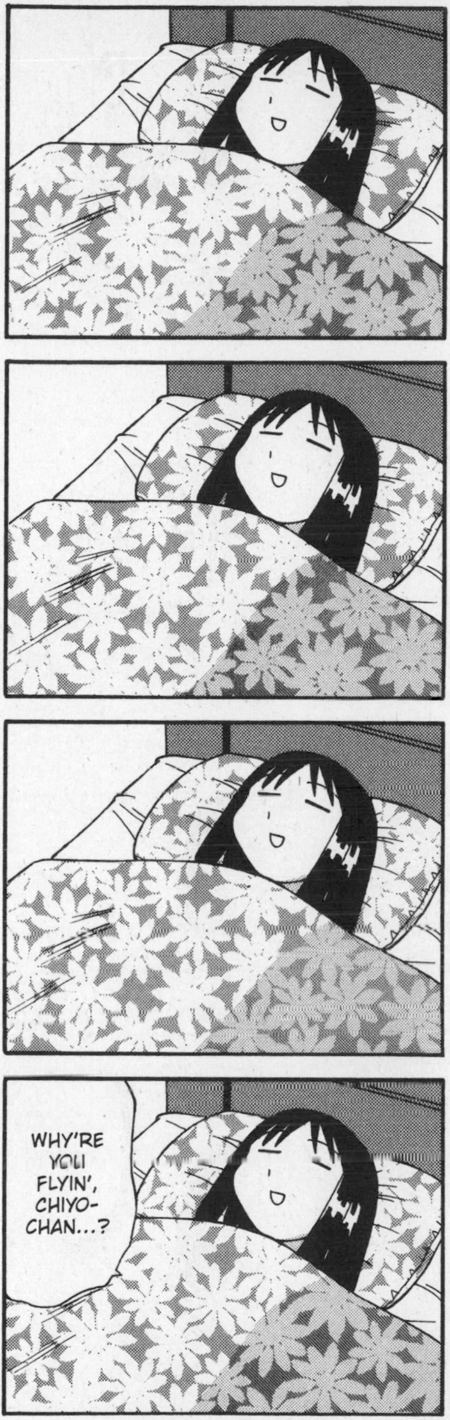
WHY'RE YOU FLYIN', CHIYO-CHAN...?

FLYING CHIYO

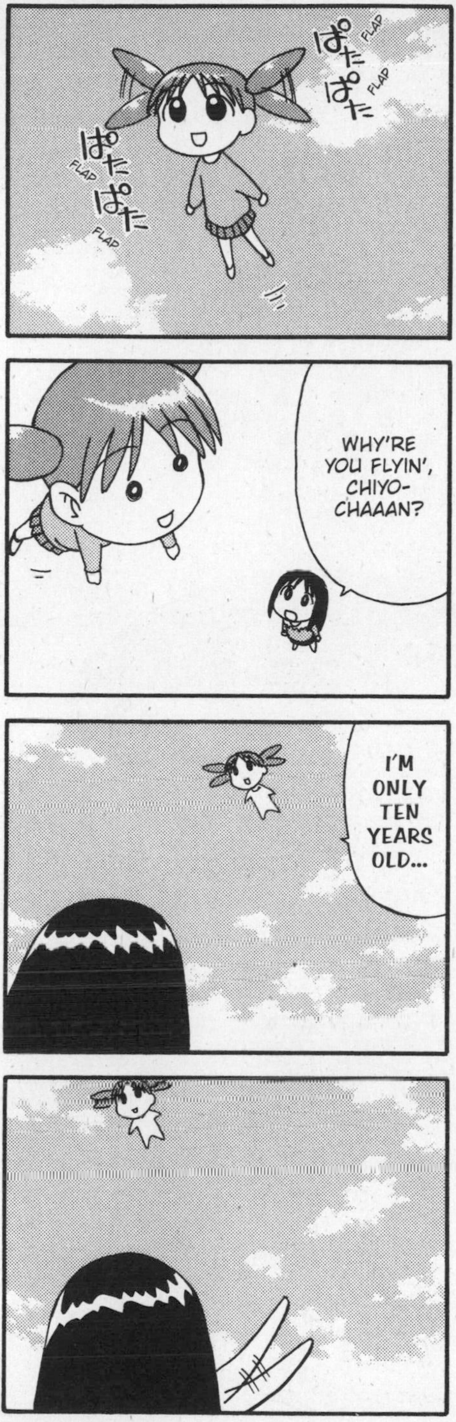
ぱたぱた
FLAP FLAP
ぱたぱた
FLAP FLAP
WHY'RE YOU FLYIN', CHIYO-CHAAAN?
I'M ONLY TEN YEARS OLD...

IN THE FLESH

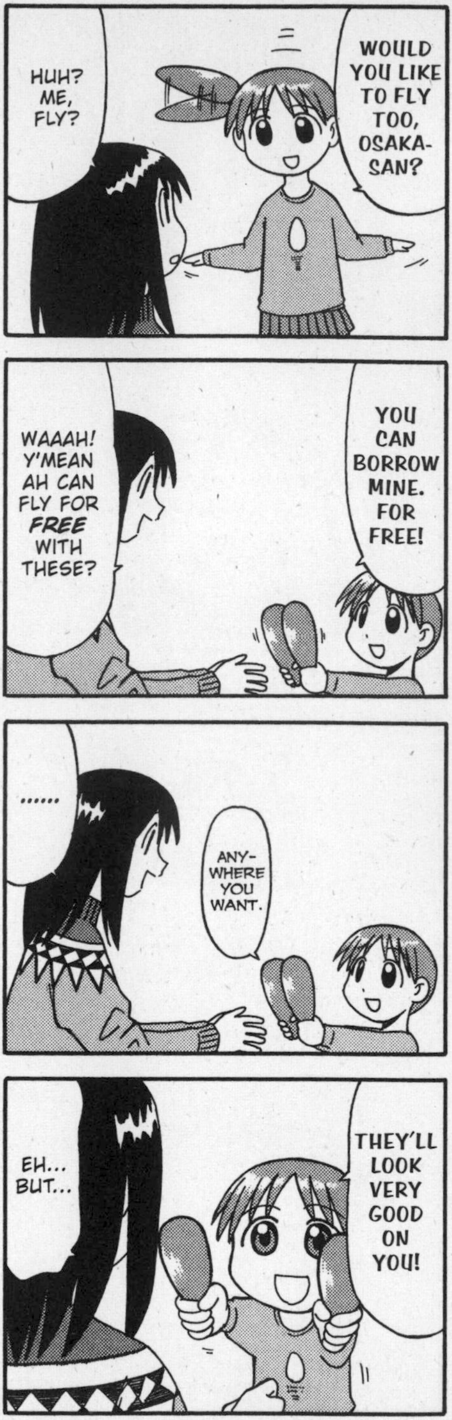
WOULD YOU LIKE TO FLY TOO, OSAKA-SAN?
HUH? ME, FLY?
YOU CAN BORROW MINE. FOR FREE!
WAAAH! Y'MEAN AH CAN FLY FOR *FREE* WITH THESE?
ANY-WHERE YOU WANT.
......
THEY'LL LOOK VERY GOOD ON YOU!
EH... BUT...

PARASITES

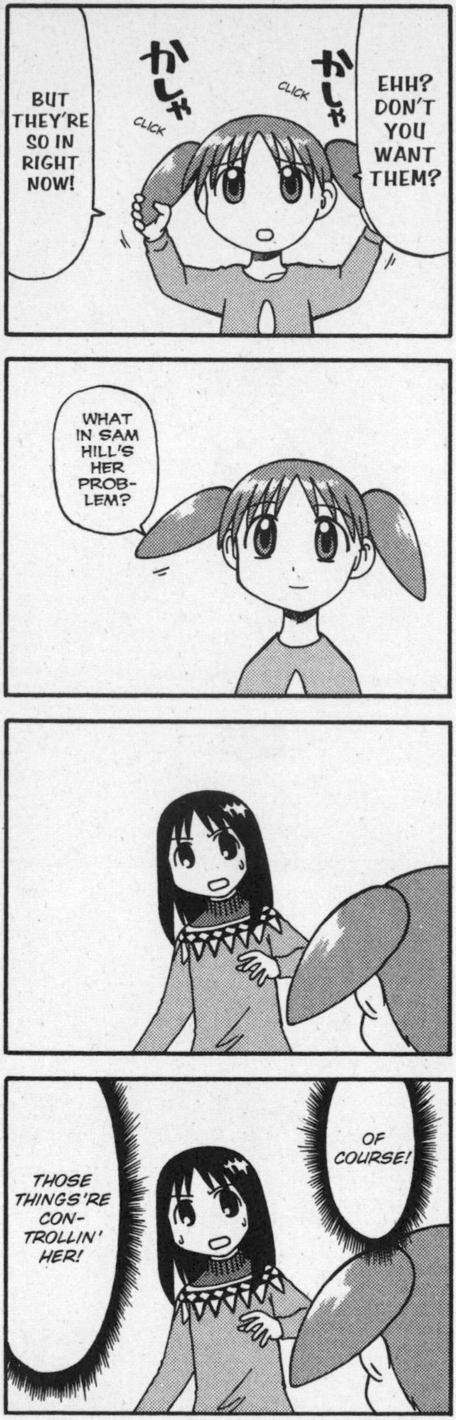
EHH? DON'T YOU WANT THEM?
かしゃ
CLICK
かしゃ
CLICK
BUT THEY'RE SO IN RIGHT NOW!
WHAT IN SAM HILL'S HER PROBLEM?
OF COURSE!
THOSE THINGS'RE CON-TROLLIN' HER!

DESTRUCTION

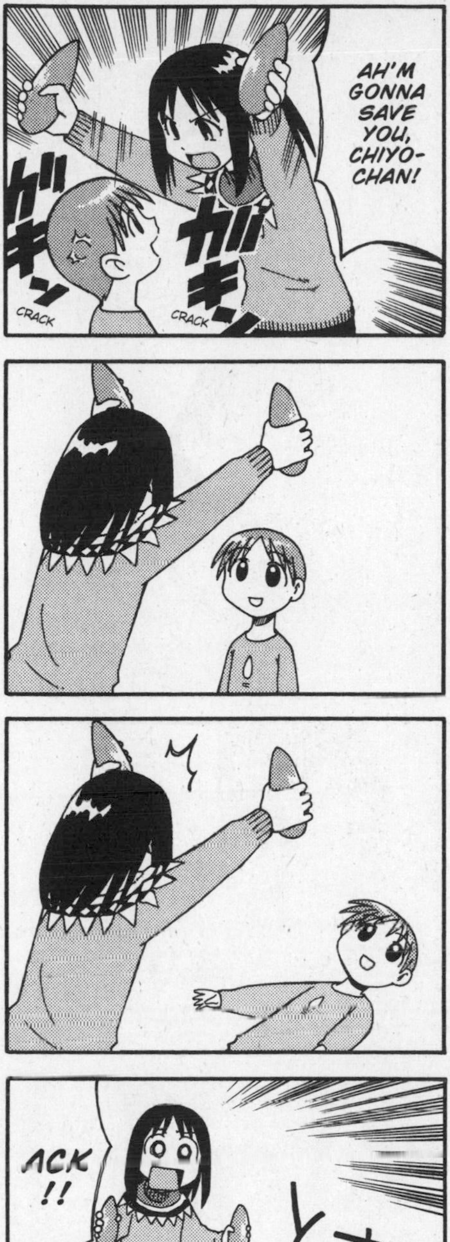
AH'M GONNA SAVE YOU, CHIYO-CHAN!
CRACK
CRACK
ACK!!
とす…
FL'OP

GO AWAY

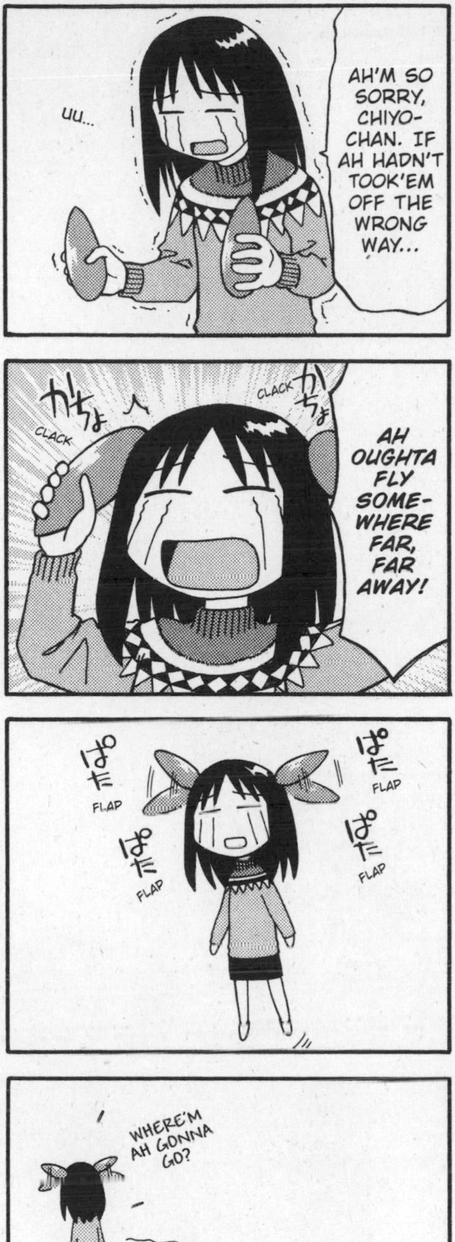
AH'M SO SORRY, CHIYO-CHAN. IF AH HADN'T TOOK'EM OFF THE WRONG WAY...
UU...
かちょ
CLACK
かちょ
CLACK
AH OUGHTA FLY SOMEWHERE FAR, FAR AWAY!
ぱた
FLAP
ぱた
FLAP
ぱた
FLAP
ぱた
FLAP
WHERE'M AH GONNA GO?

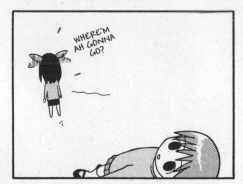

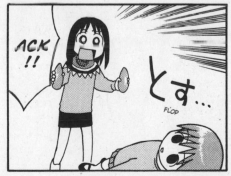

IN TOMO'S CASE

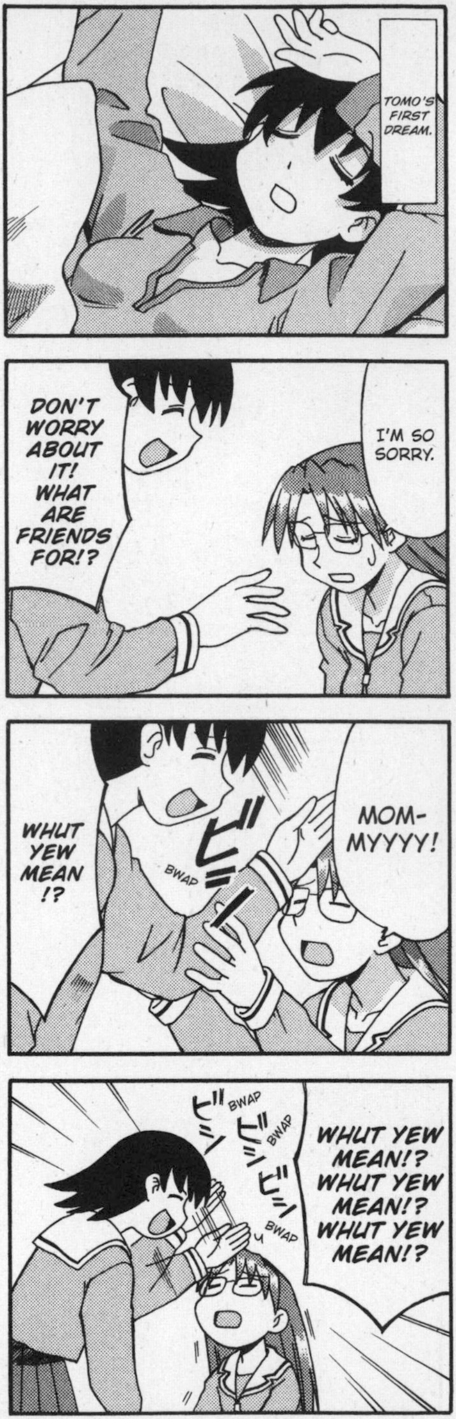
TOMO'S FIRST DREAM.
I'M SO SORRY.
DON'T WORRY ABOUT IT! WHAT ARE FRIENDS FOR!?
MOM-MYYYY!
BWAP
WHUT YEW MEAN!?
BWAP
BWAP
BWAP
WHUT YEW MEAN!? WHUT YEW MEAN!? WHUT YEW MEAN!?

HIGH-LEVEL 100

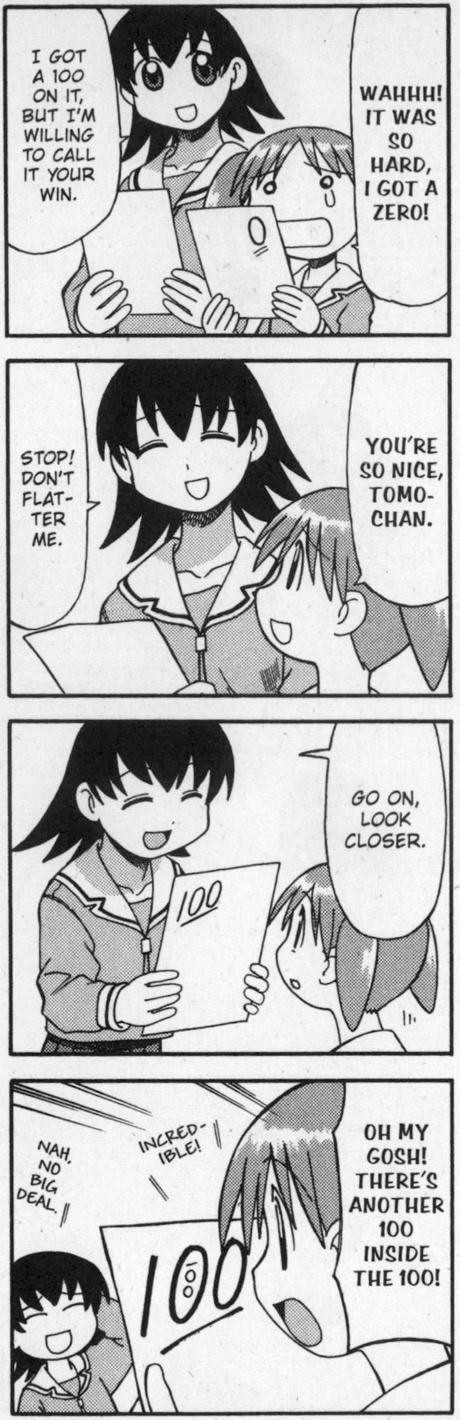
WAHHH! IT WAS SO HARD, I GOT A ZERO!
I GOT A 100 ON IT, BUT I'M WILLING TO CALL IT YOUR WIN.
YOU'RE SO NICE, TOMO-CHAN.
STOP! DON'T FLATTER ME.
GO ON, LOOK CLOSER.
100
OH MY GOSH! THERE'S ANOTHER 100 INSIDE THE 100!
INCREDIBLE!
NAH, NO BIG DEAL.
100

FAST

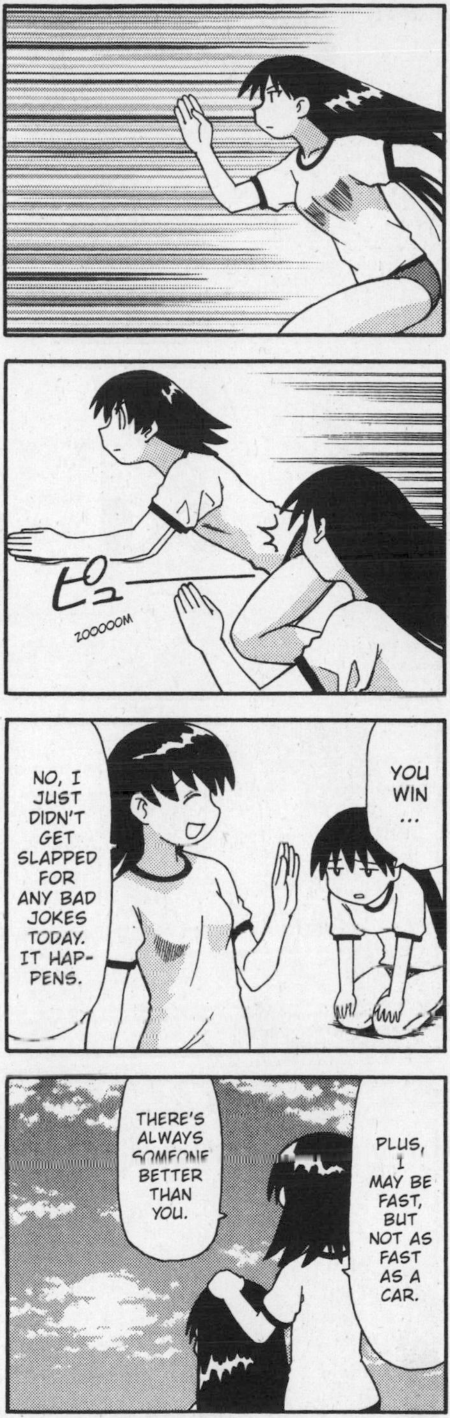
ピュー
ZOOOOOM
YOU WIN ...
NO, I JUST DIDN'T GET SLAPPED FOR ANY BAD JOKES TODAY. IT HAPPENS.
PLUS, I MAY BE FAST, BUT NOT AS FAST AS A CAR.
THERE'S ALWAYS SOMEONE BETTER THAN YOU.

IN SAKAKI'S CASE

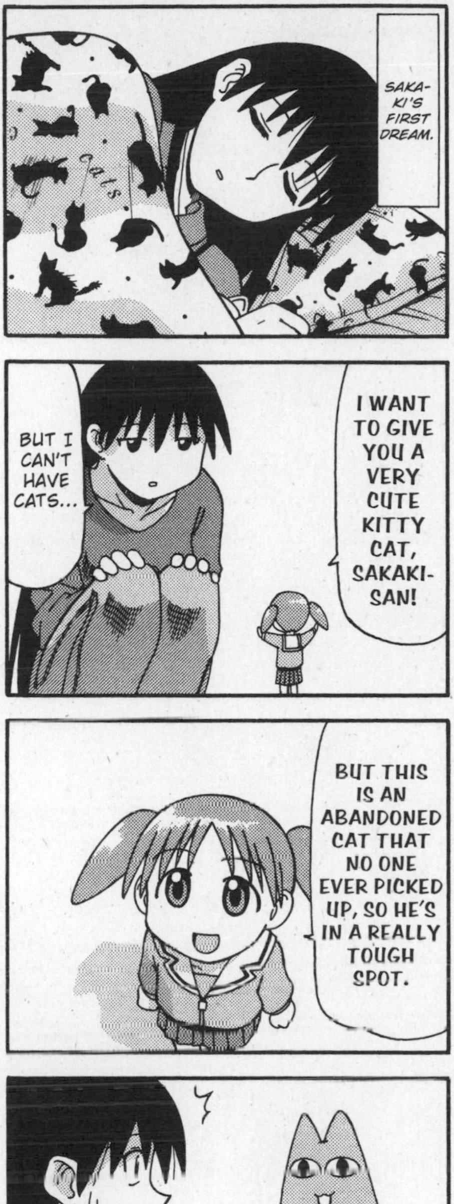
SAKAKI'S FIRST DREAM.
cats
I WANT TO GIVE YOU A VERY CUTE KITTY CAT, SAKAKI-SAN!
BUT I CAN'T HAVE CATS...
BUT THIS IS AN ABANDONED CAT THAT NO ONE EVER PICKED UP, SO HE'S IN A REALLY TOUGH SPOT.

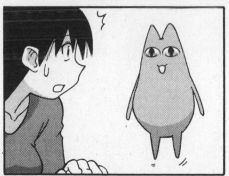

ON A WALK

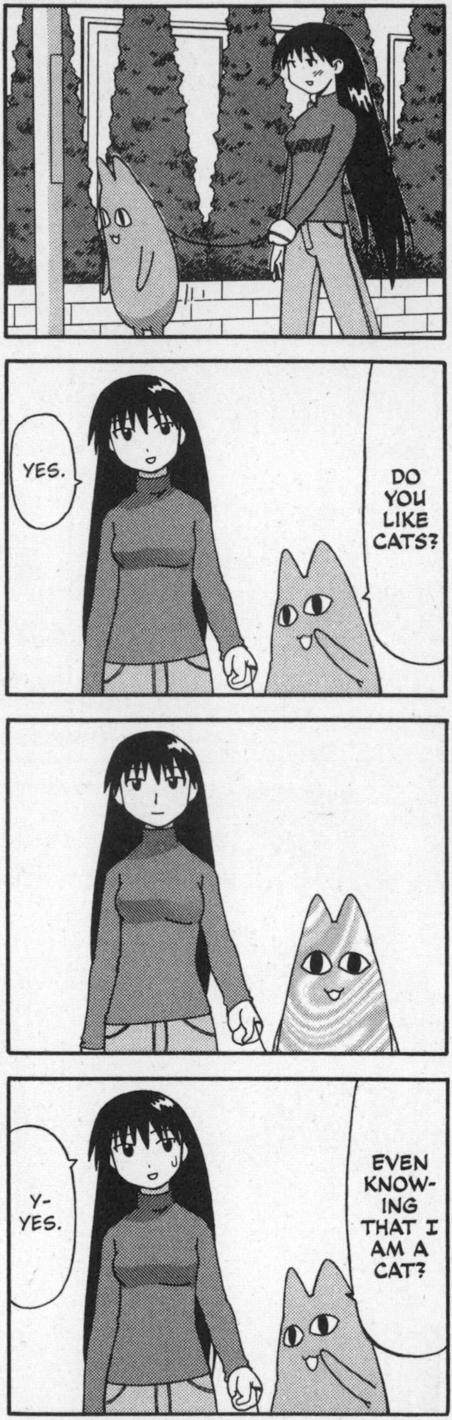
DO YOU LIKE CATS?
YES.
EVEN KNOWING THAT I AM A CAT?
Y-YES.

CAT-STYLE

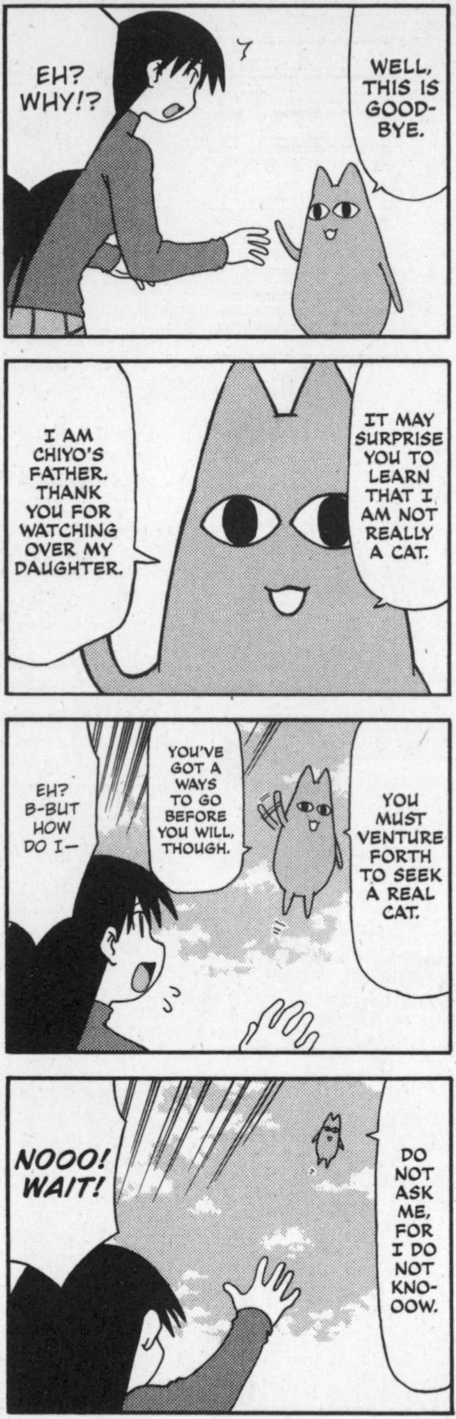
WELL, THIS IS GOOD-BYE.
EH? WHY!?
IT MAY SURPRISE YOU TO LEARN THAT I AM NOT REALLY A CAT.
I AM CHIYO'S FATHER. THANK YOU FOR WATCHING OVER MY DAUGHTER.
YOU MUST VENTURE FORTH TO SEEK A REAL CAT.
YOU'VE GOT A WAYS TO GO BEFORE YOU WILL, THOUGH.
EH? B-BUT HOW DO I—
DO NOT ASK ME, FOR I DO NOT KNOO-OOW.
NOOO! WAIT!

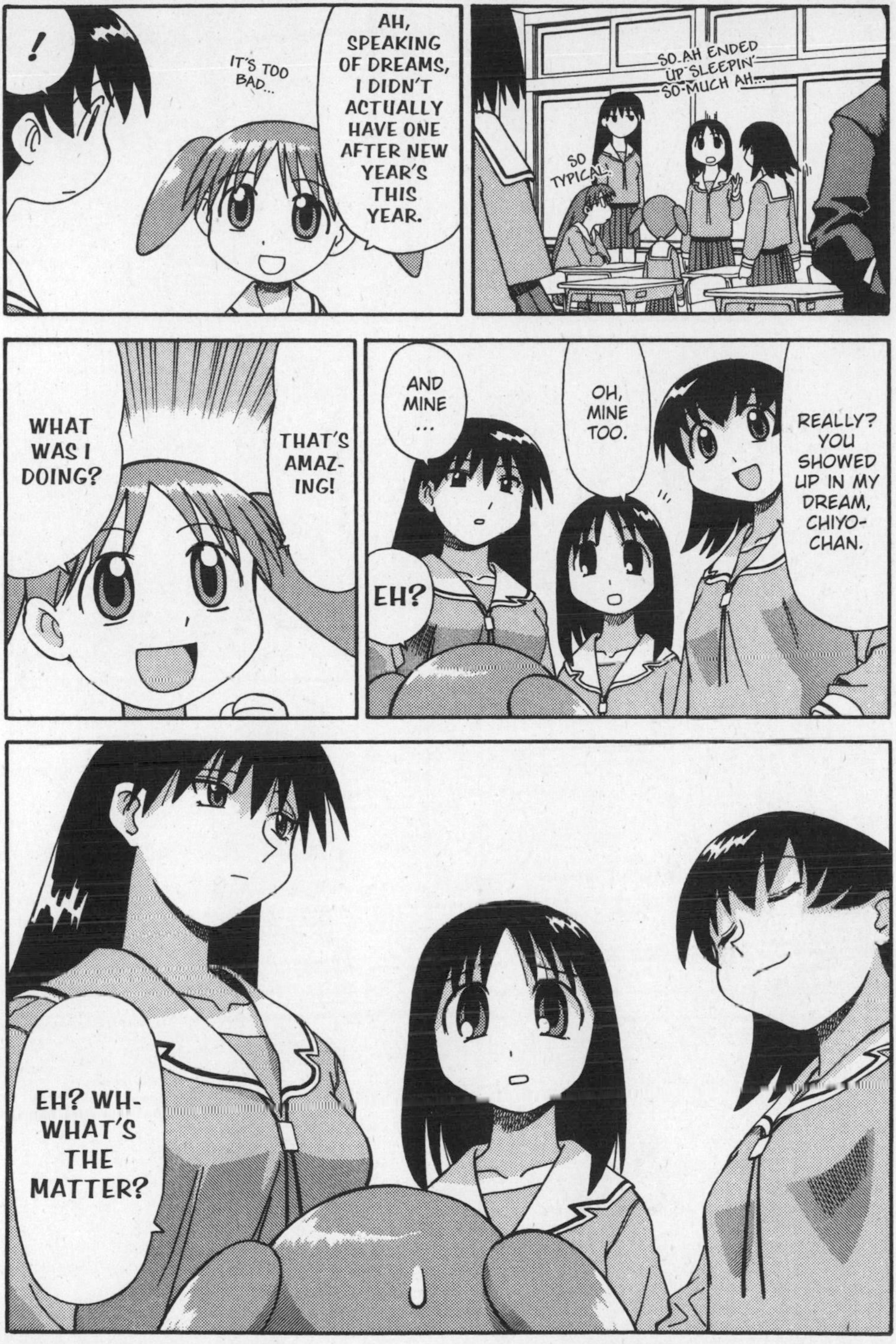
SO AH ENDED UP SLEEPIN' SO MUCH AH...
SO TYPICAL.
AH, SPEAKING OF DREAMS, I DIDN'T ACTUALLY HAVE ONE AFTER NEW YEAR'S THIS YEAR.
IT'S TOO BAD...
!
REALLY? YOU SHOWED UP IN MY DREAM, CHIYO-CHAN.
OH, MINE TOO.
AND MINE ...
EH?
THAT'S AMAZ-ING!
WHAT WAS I DOING?
EH? WH-WHAT'S THE MATTER?

154

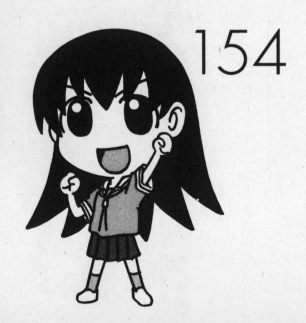

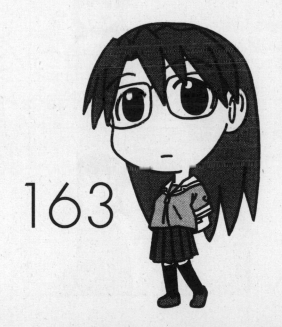

163

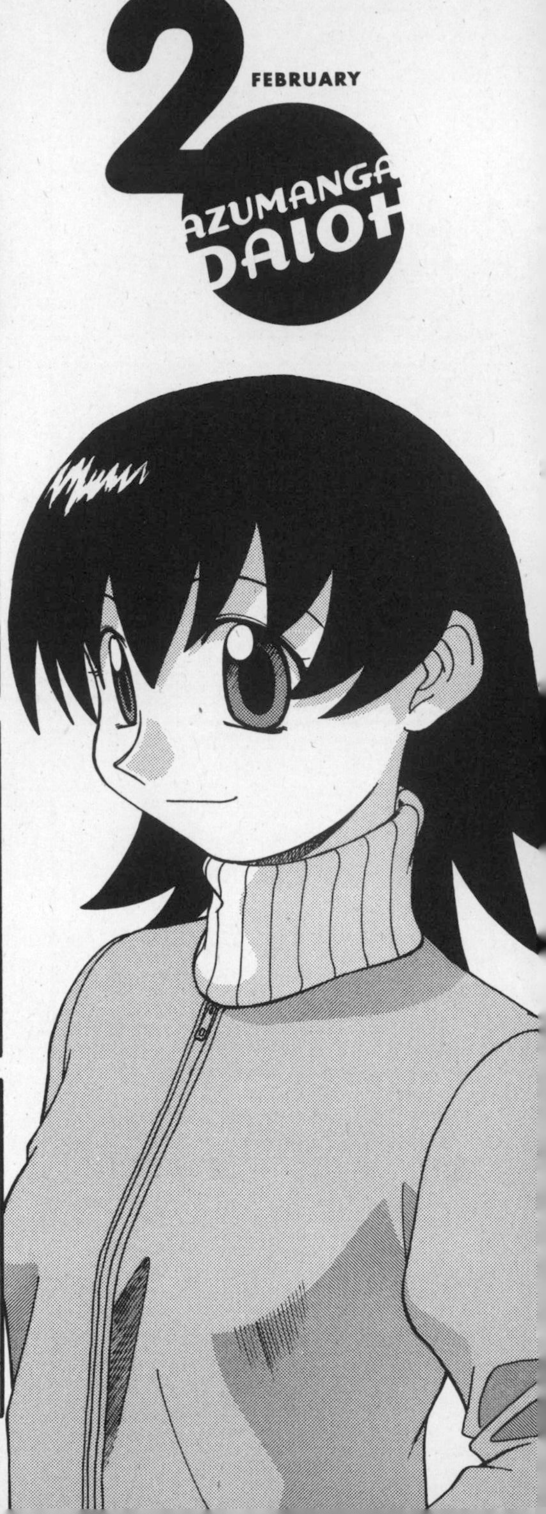
2
FEBRUARY
AZUMANGA DAIOH

THE TAIYAKI SPIRIT

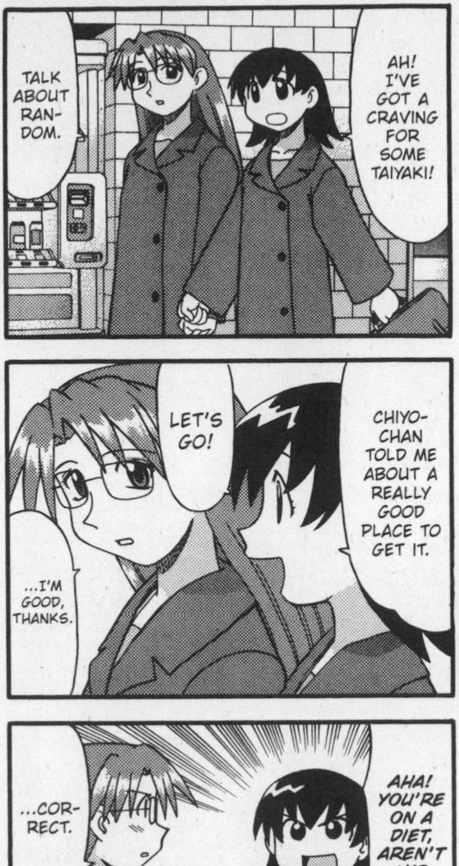
AH! I'VE GOT A CRAVING FOR SOME TAIYAKI!
TALK ABOUT RAN-DOM.
CHIYO-CHAN TOLD ME ABOUT A REALLY GOOD PLACE TO GET IT.
LET'S GO!
...I'M GOOD, THANKS.
AHA! YOU'RE ON A DIET, AREN'T YA? YOU SUCK-ER!
...COR-RECT.
LET'S GO!
WELL, YOU CAN SIT THERE AND WATCH ME EAT!

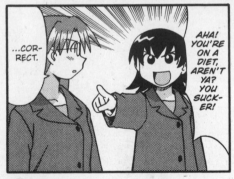

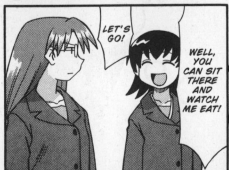

JUST WATCH

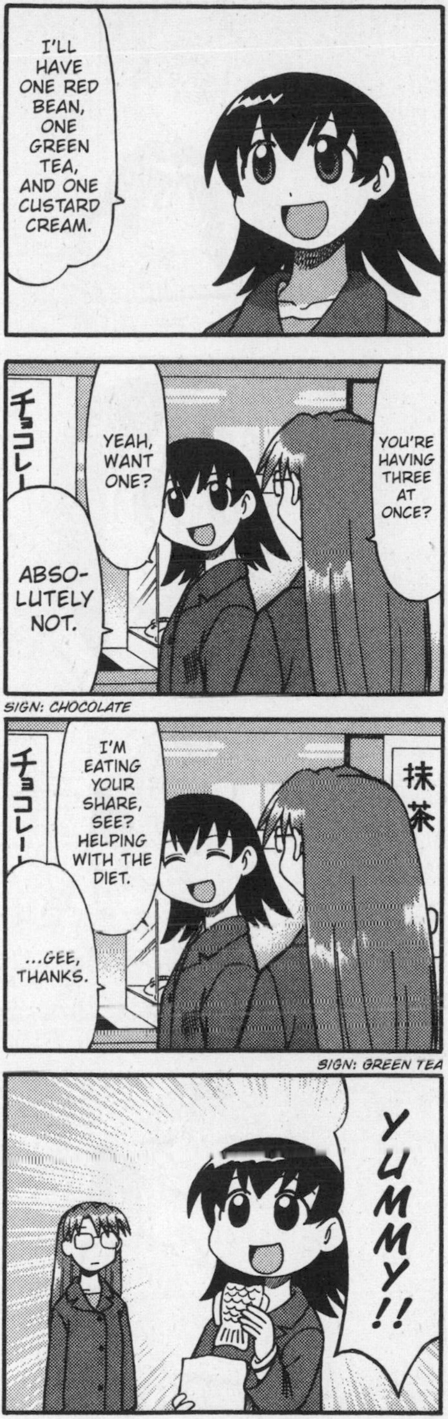
I'LL HAVE ONE RED BEAN, ONE GREEN TEA, AND ONE CUSTARD CREAM.
YOU'RE HAVING THREE AT ONCE?
チョコレー
YEAH, WANT ONE?
ABSO-LUTELY NOT.
SIGN: CHOCOLATE
抹茶
チョコレー
I'M EATING YOUR SHARE, SEE? HELPING WITH THE DIET.
...GEE, THANKS.
SIGN: GREEN TEA
YUMMY!!

JUST FOR TODAY

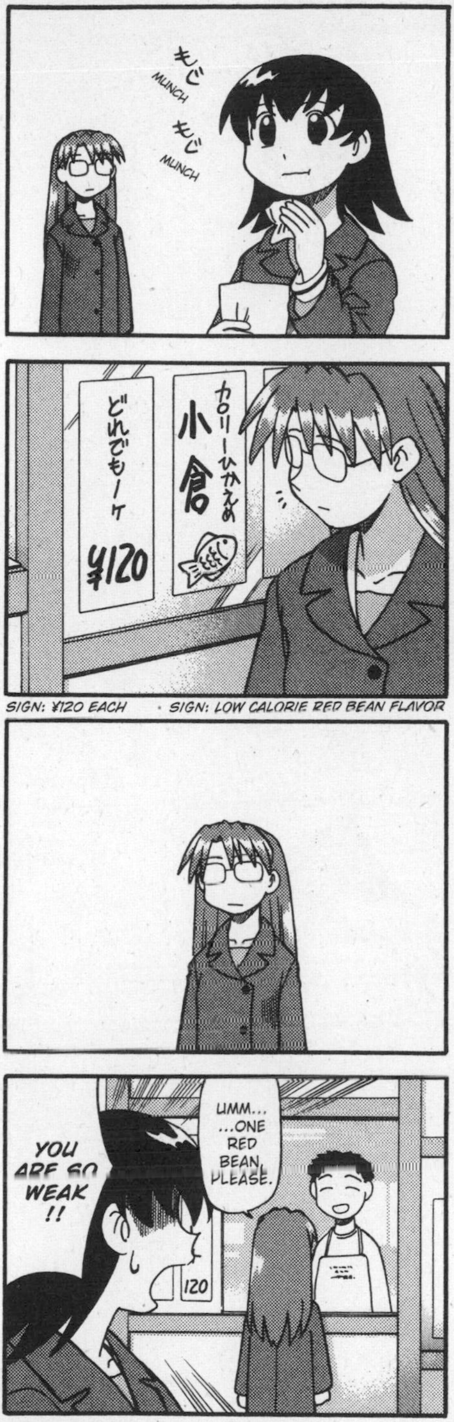
もぐ
MUNCH
もぐ
MUNCH
カロリーひかえめ
小倉
どれでも1ケ
¥120
SIGN: ¥120 EACH
SIGN: LOW CALORIE RED BEAN FLAVOR
UMM... ...ONE RED BEAN, PLEASE.
120
YOU ARE SO WEAK!!

CAN'T TAKE IT

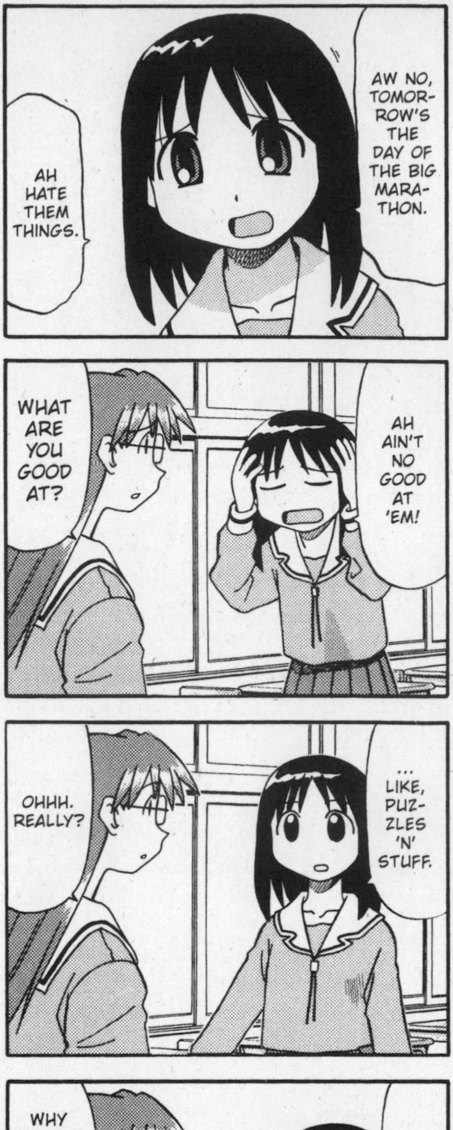
AW NO, TOMORROW'S THE DAY OF THE BIG MARATHON.
AH HATE THEM THINGS.
AH AIN'T NO GOOD AT 'EM!
WHAT ARE YOU GOOD AT?
...LIKE, PUZZLES 'N' STUFF.
OHHH. REALLY?
NO, SORRY.
NO GOOD AT PUZZLES.
WHY MAKE A JOKE IF YOU'RE NOT GONNA STICK WITH IT?

TERU TERU CHIYO

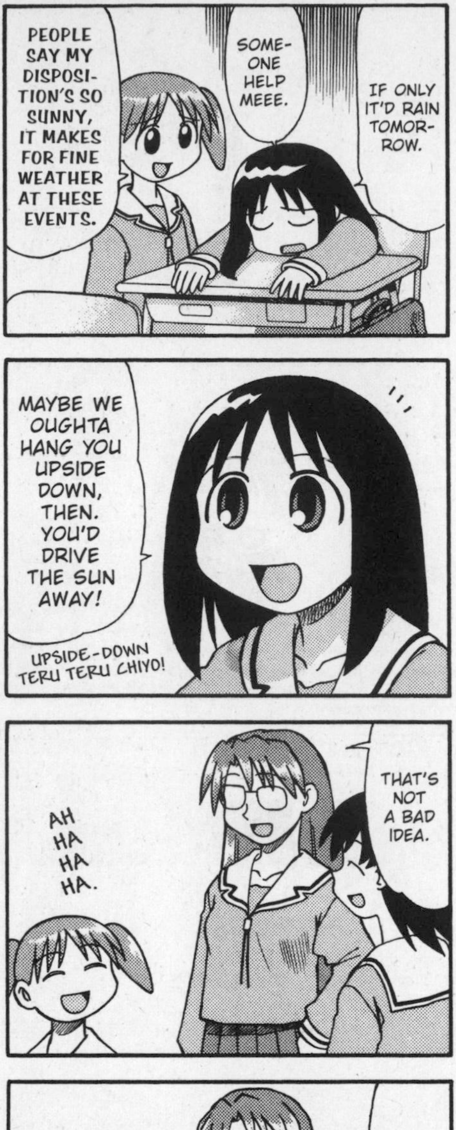
IF ONLY IT'D RAIN TOMORROW.
SOMEONE HELP MEEE.
PEOPLE SAY MY DISPOSITION'S SO SUNNY, IT MAKES FOR FINE WEATHER AT THESE EVENTS.
MAYBE WE OUGHTA HANG YOU UPSIDE DOWN, THEN. YOU'D DRIVE THE SUN AWAY!
UPSIDE-DOWN TERU TERU CHIYO!
THAT'S NOT A BAD IDEA.
AH HA HA HA HA.
...MAYBE WE OUGHTA TRY IT.
HUH?

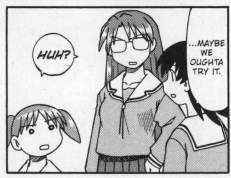

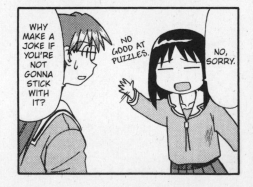

TORTURE ISLAND

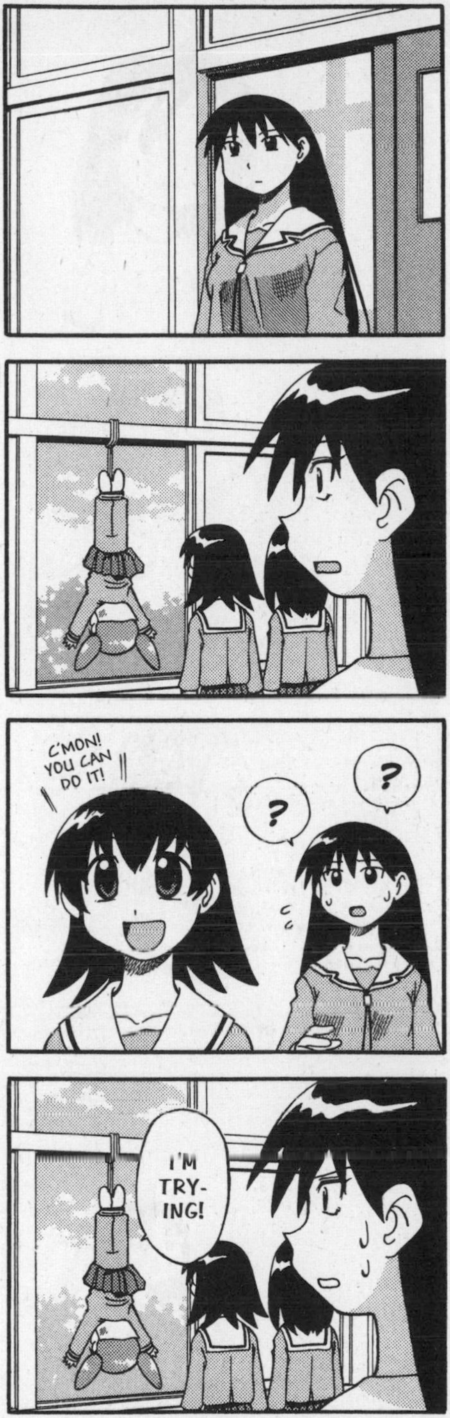
C'MON! YOU CAN DO IT!
?
?
I'M TRY-ING!

DIZZY

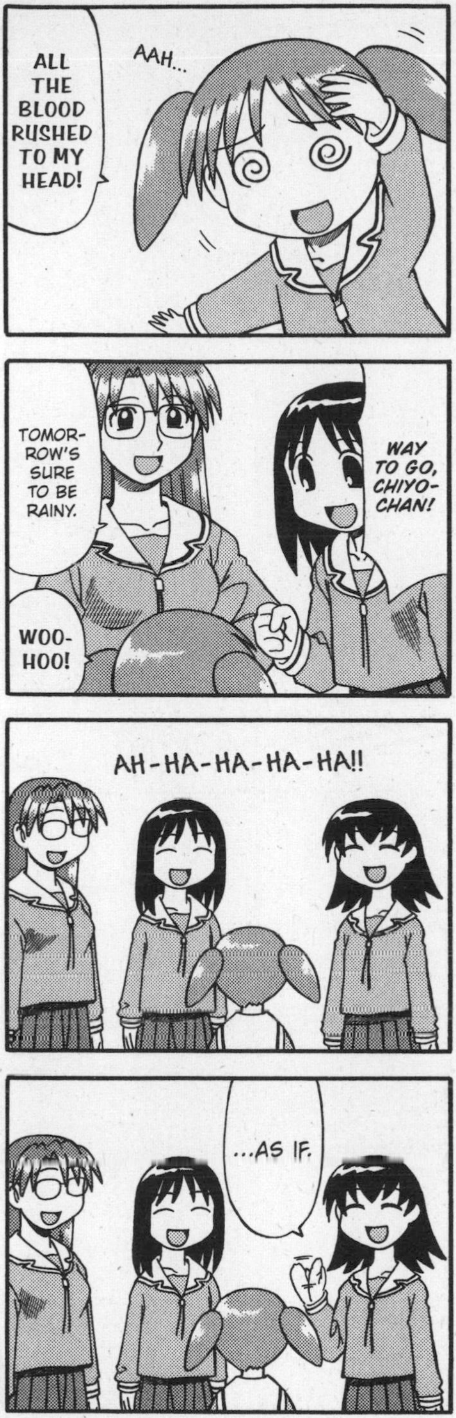
ALL THE BLOOD RUSHED TO MY HEAD!
AAH...
WAY TO GO, CHIYO-CHAN!
TOMORROW'S SURE TO BE RAINY.
WOO-HOO!
AH-HA-HA-HA-HA!!
...AS IF.

SUNNY SKIES

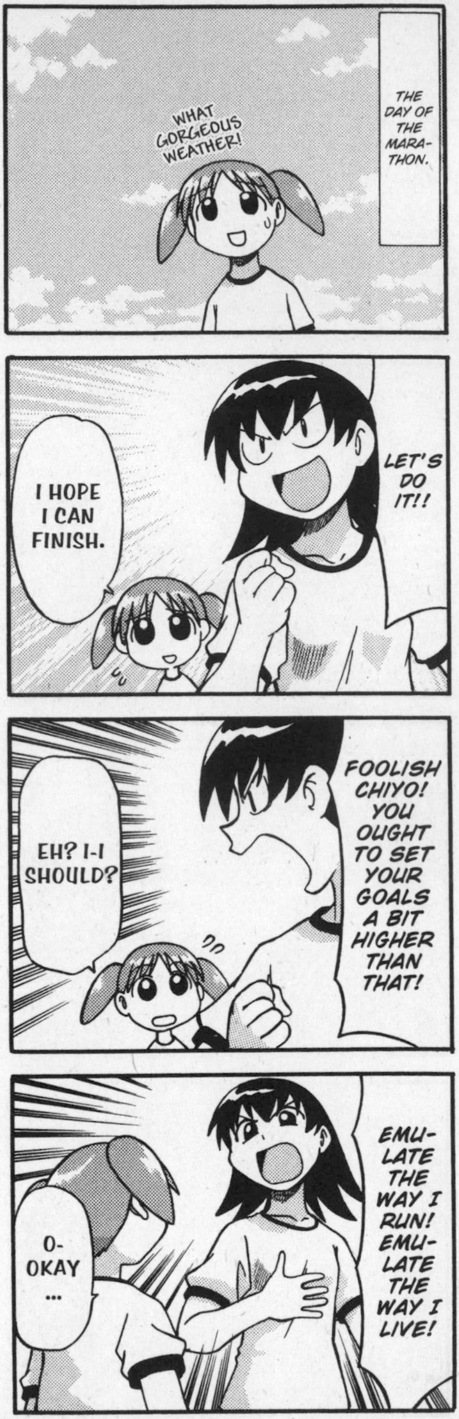
THE DAY OF THE MARA-THON.
WHAT GORGEOUS WEATHER!
LET'S DO IT!!
I HOPE I CAN FINISH.
FOOLISH CHIYO! YOU OUGHT TO SET YOUR GOALS A BIT HIGHER THAN THAT!
EH? I-I SHOULD?
EMU-LATE THE WAY I RUN! EMU-LATE THE WAY I LIVE!
O-OKAY ...

AEROBIC EXERCISE

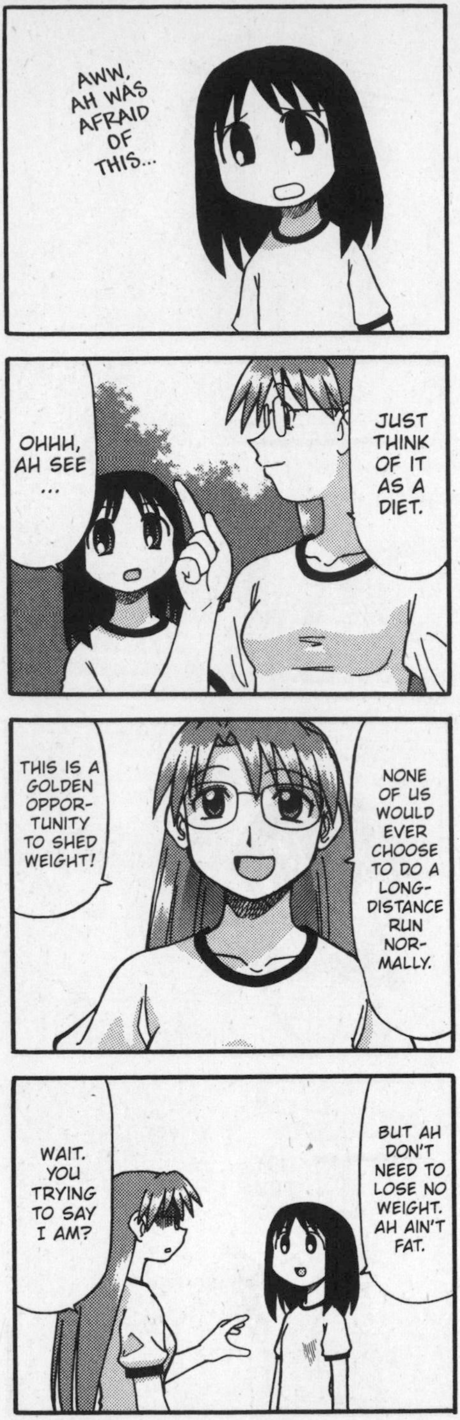
AWW, AH WAS AFRAID OF THIS...
JUST THINK OF IT AS A DIET.
OHHH, AH SEE ...
NONE OF US WOULD EVER CHOOSE TO DO A LONG-DISTANCE RUN NOR-MALLY.
THIS IS A GOLDEN OPPOR-TUNITY TO SHED WEIGHT!
BUT AH DON'T NEED TO LOSE NO WEIGHT. AH AIN'T FAT.
WAIT. YOU TRYING TO SAY I AM?

AND SHE RAN OVER THE HORIZON

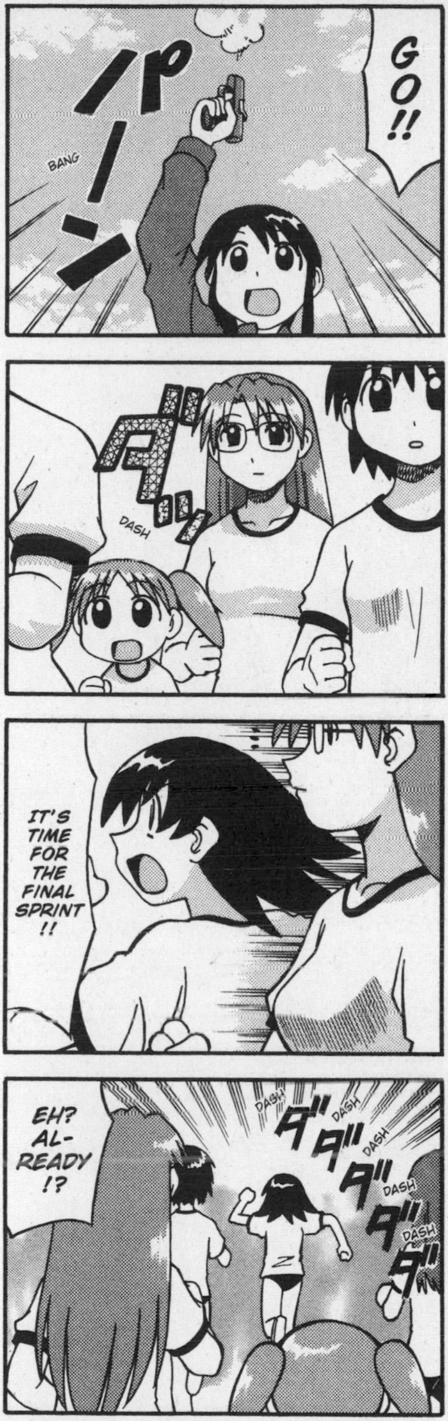
GO!!
パーン
BANG
ダッ
DASH
IT'S TIME FOR THE FINAL SPRINT!!
EH? AL-READY!?
ダッダッダッダッダッ
DASH DASH DASH DASH DASH

I WILL

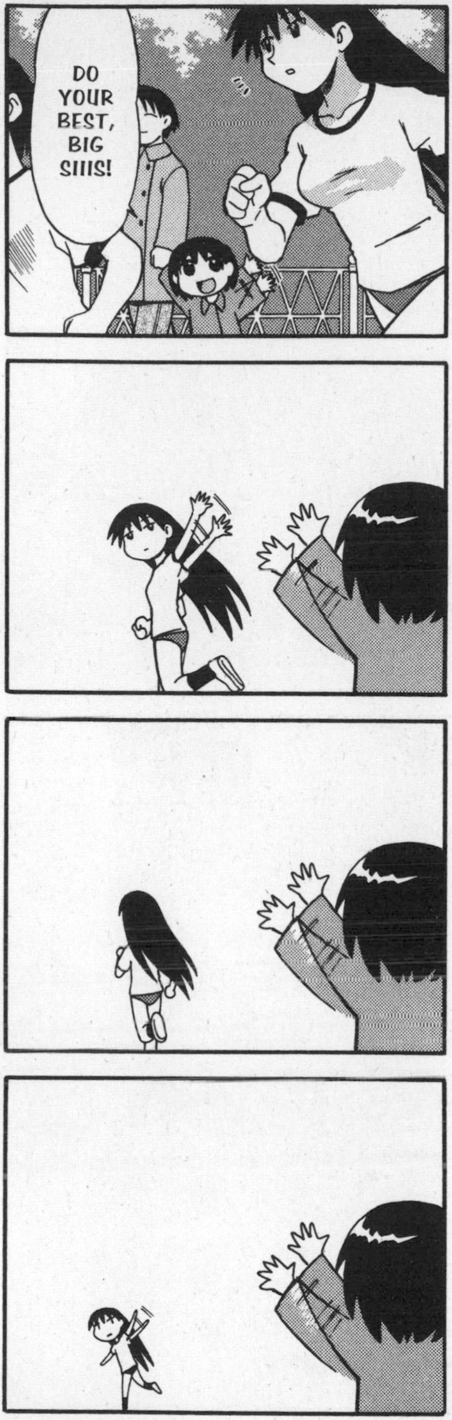
DO YOUR BEST, BIG SIIIS!

YOU OKAY?

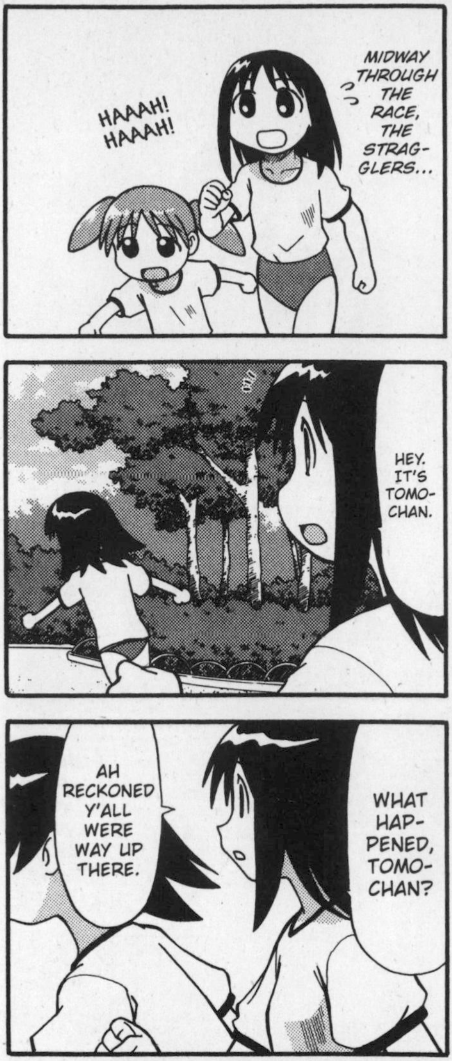
MIDWAY THROUGH THE RACE, THE STRAGGLERS...
HAAAH! HAAAH!
HEY. IT'S TOMO-CHAN.
WHAT HAPPENED, TOMO-CHAN?
AH RECKONED Y'ALL WERE WAY UP THERE.
WHEEZE
WHEEZE
WHEEZE
...WHY DON'TCHA CATCH YOUR BREATH FIRST.

THE LIGHT

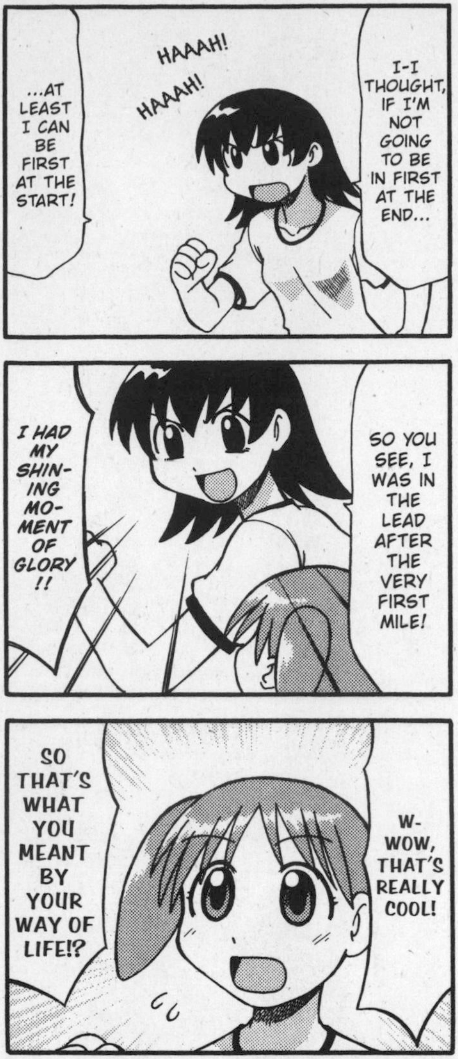
I-I THOUGHT, IF I'M NOT GOING TO BE IN FIRST AT THE END...
HAAAH!
HAAAH!
...AT LEAST I CAN BE FIRST AT THE START!
SO YOU SEE, I WAS IN THE LEAD AFTER THE VERY FIRST MILE!
I HAD MY SHINING MOMENT OF GLORY!!
W-WOW, THAT'S REALLY COOL!
SO THAT'S WHAT YOU MEANT BY YOUR WAY OF LIFE!?
I-I CAN DO IT TOO!
DASH
HEY! CHIYO-CHAN!?

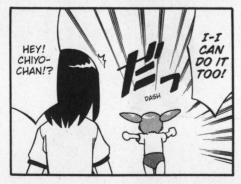

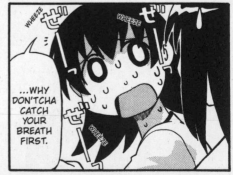

OH DEAR, OH DEAR

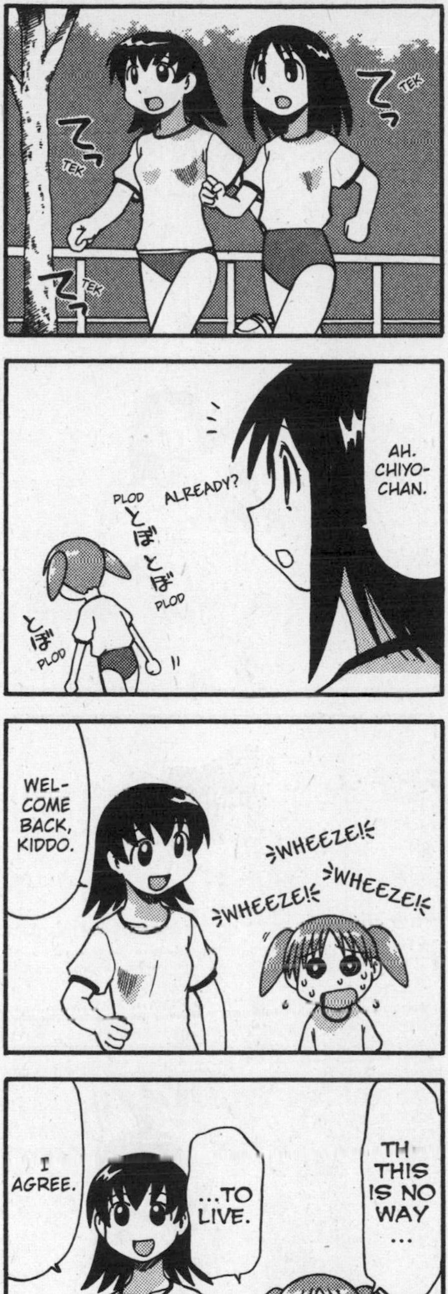
TEK
TEK
TEK
AH. CHIYO-CHAN.
ALREADY?
PLOD とぼとぼ PLOD
とぼ PLOD
WEL-COME BACK, KIDDO.
WHEEZE!
WHEEZE!
WHEEZE!
TH THIS IS NO WAY ...
...TO LIVE.
I AGREE.

ONE WIN, ONE LOSS

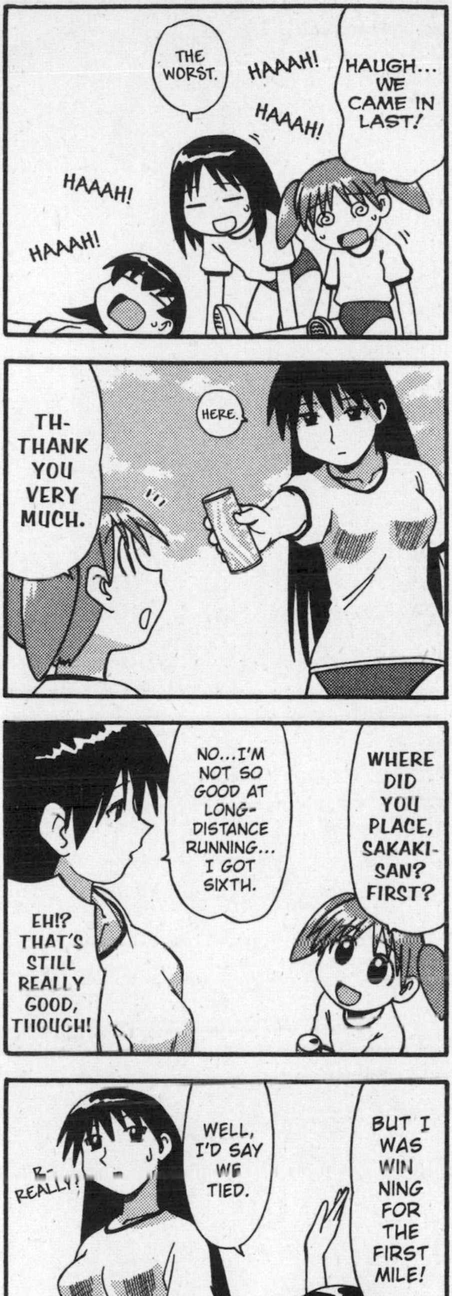
HAUGH... WE CAME IN LAST!
HAAAH!
HAAAH!
THE WORST.
HAAAH!
HAAAH!
HERE.
TH-THANK YOU VERY MUCH.
WHERE DID YOU PLACE, SAKAKI-SAN? FIRST?
NO...I'M NOT SO GOOD AT LONG-DISTANCE RUNNING... I GOT SIXTH.
EH!? THAT'S STILL REALLY GOOD, THOUGH!
BUT I WAS WIN NING FOR THE FIRST MILE!
WELL, I'D SAY WE TIED.
R-REALLY!

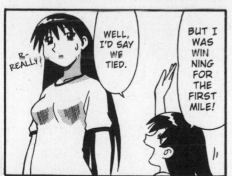

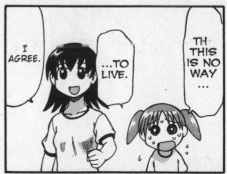

CHECKING RESULTS

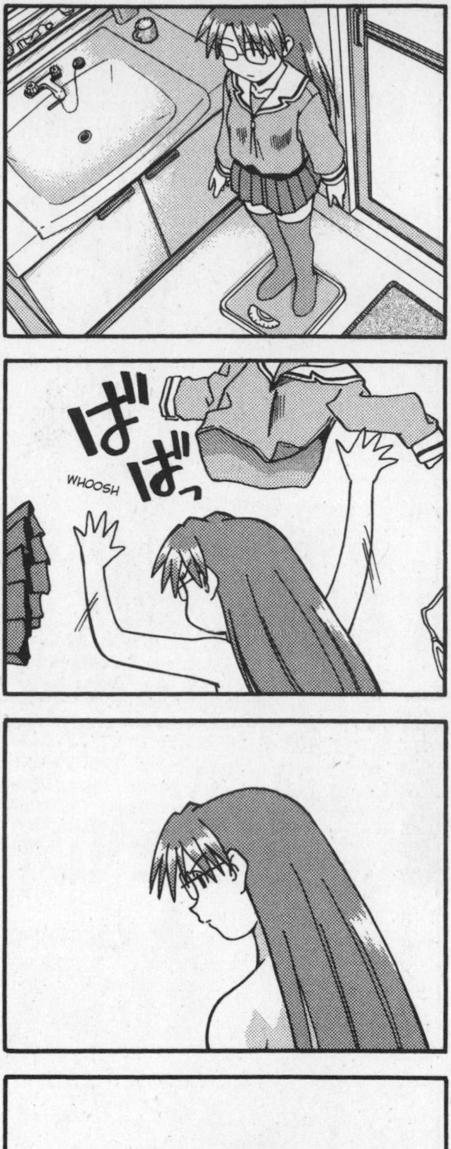
ばばっ
WHOOSH

SPRING

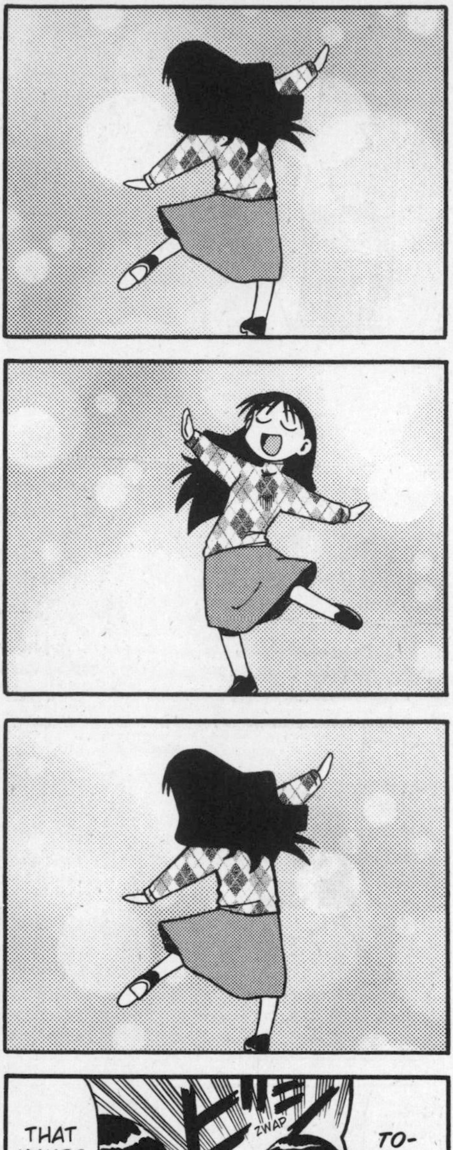
TO-DAY'S MY PAY-DAY!!
ZWAP
THAT MAKES TWO OF US.

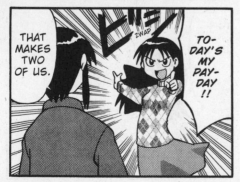

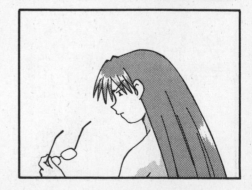

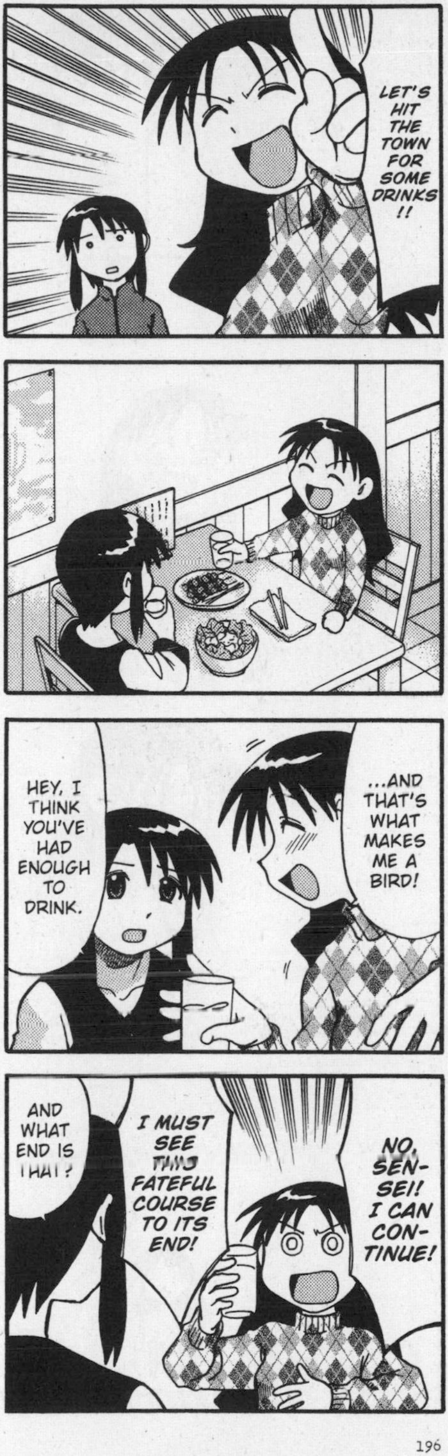
LET'S HIT THE TOWN FOR SOME DRINKS!!
...AND THAT'S WHAT MAKES ME A BIRD!
HEY, I THINK YOU'VE HAD ENOUGH TO DRINK.
NO, SENSEI! I CAN CONTINUE!
I MUST SEE THIS FATEFUL COURSE TO ITS END!
AND WHAT END IS THAT?

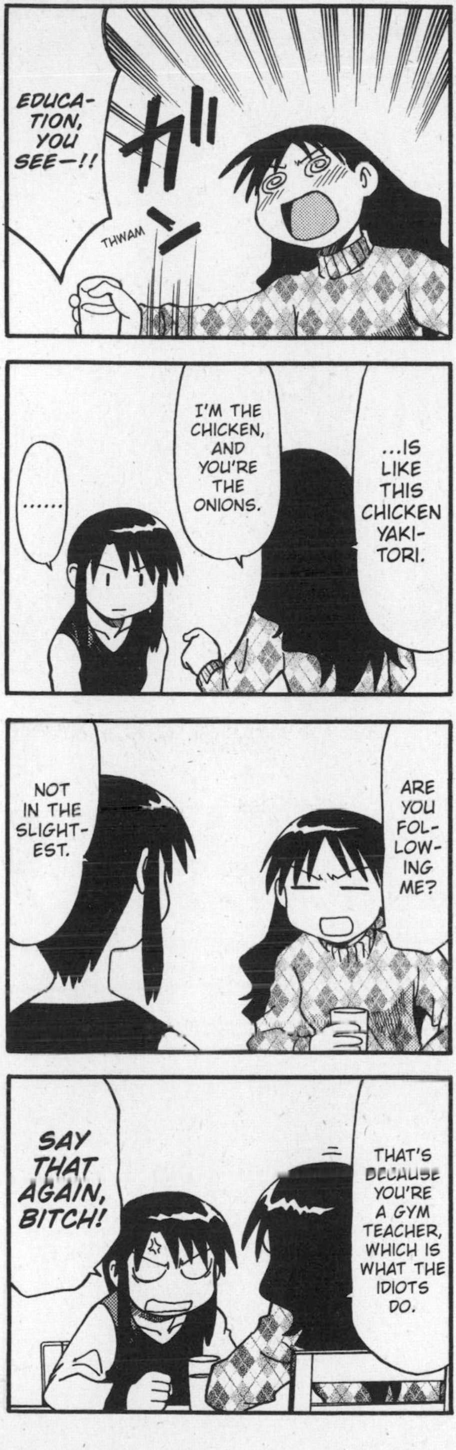
EDUCATION, YOU SEE—!!
ガン
THWAM
...IS LIKE THIS CHICKEN YAKITORI.
I'M THE CHICKEN, AND YOU'RE THE ONIONS.
……
ARE YOU FOLLOWING ME?
NOT IN THE SLIGHTEST.
THAT'S BECAUSE YOU'RE A GYM TEACHER, WHICH IS WHAT THE IDIOTS DO.
SAY THAT AGAIN, BITCH!

OVERCONFIDENCE

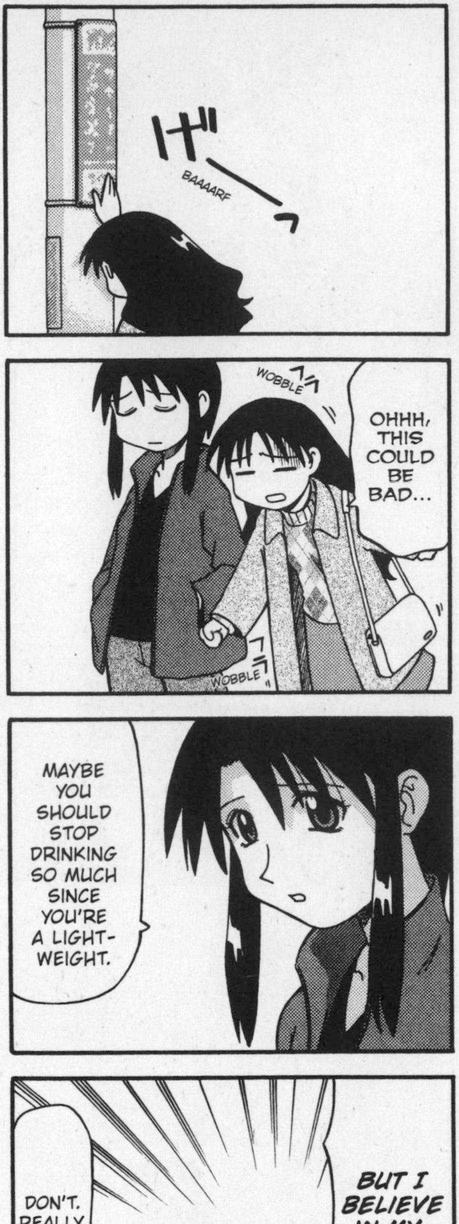
BAAAARF
WOBBLE
OHHH, THIS COULD BE BAD...
WOBBLE
MAYBE YOU SHOULD STOP DRINKING SO MUCH SINCE YOU'RE A LIGHT-WEIGHT.
BUT I BELIEVE IN MY-SELF!!
DON'T. REALLY.

DOING GOOD

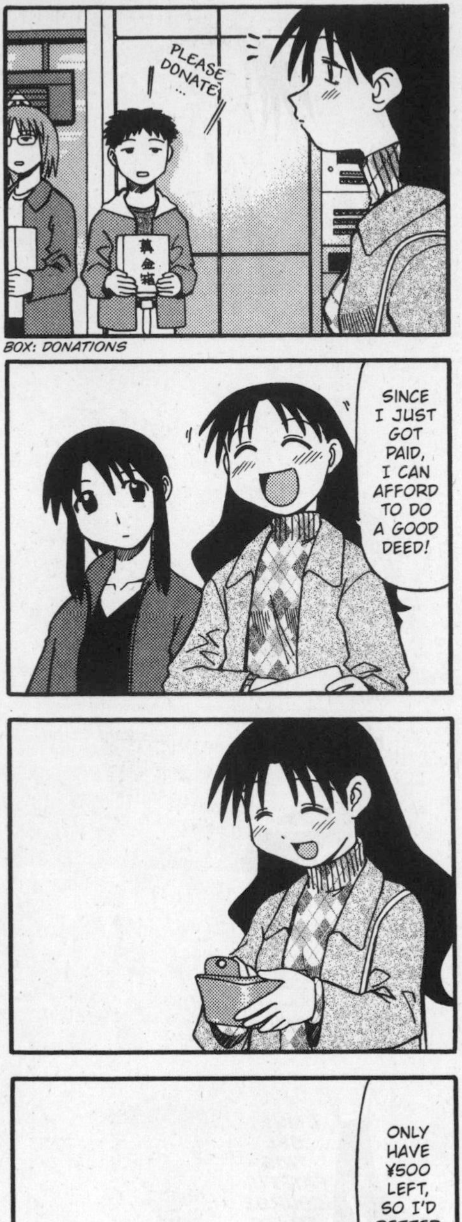
PLEASE DONATE...
SINCE I JUST GOT PAID, I CAN AFFORD TO DO A GOOD DEED!
ONLY HAVE ¥500 LEFT, SO I'D BETTER NOT.

BOX: DONATIONS

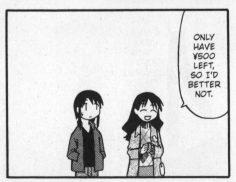

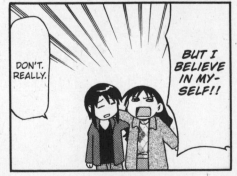

TEACHER

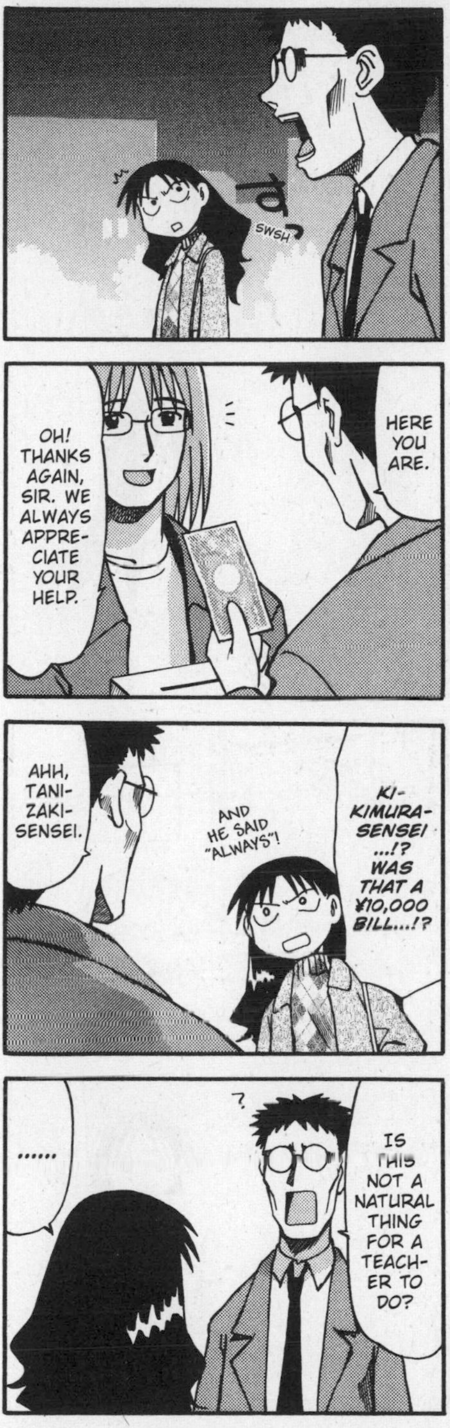
SWSH
HERE YOU ARE.
OH! THANKS AGAIN, SIR. WE ALWAYS APPRECIATE YOUR HELP.
KI-KIMURA-SENSEI ...!? WAS THAT A ¥10,000 BILL...!?
AND HE SAID "ALWAYS"!
AHH, TANI-ZAKI-SENSEI.
IS THIS NOT A NATURAL THING FOR A TEACH-ER TO DO?
......

CREEP

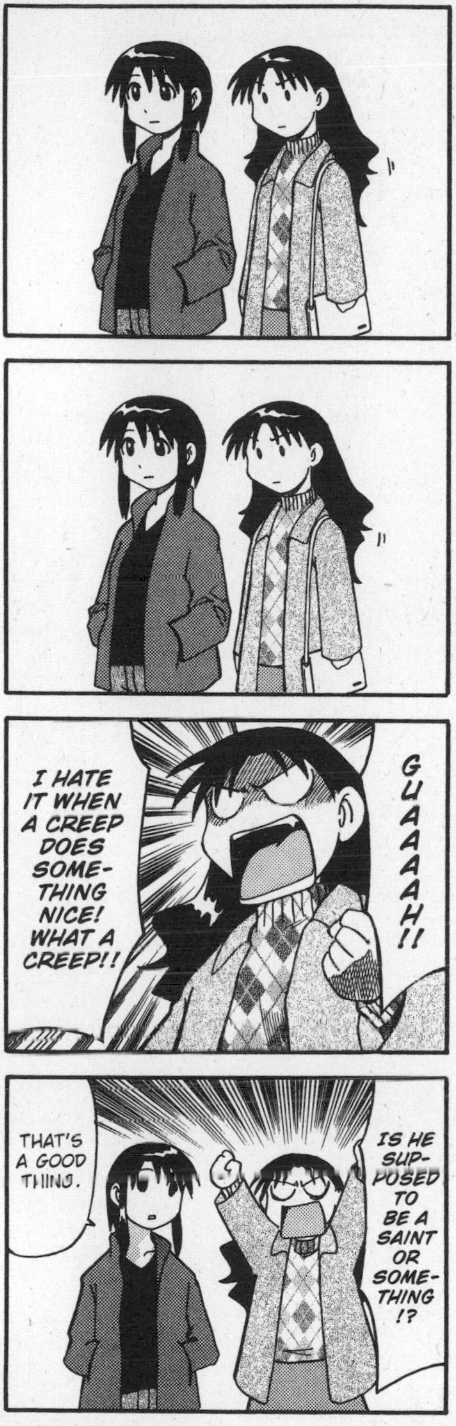
GUAAAAAAH!!
I HATE IT WHEN A CREEP DOES SOME-THING NICE! WHAT A CREEP!!
IS HE SUP-POSED TO BE A SAINT OR SOME-THING !?
THAT'S A GOOD THING.

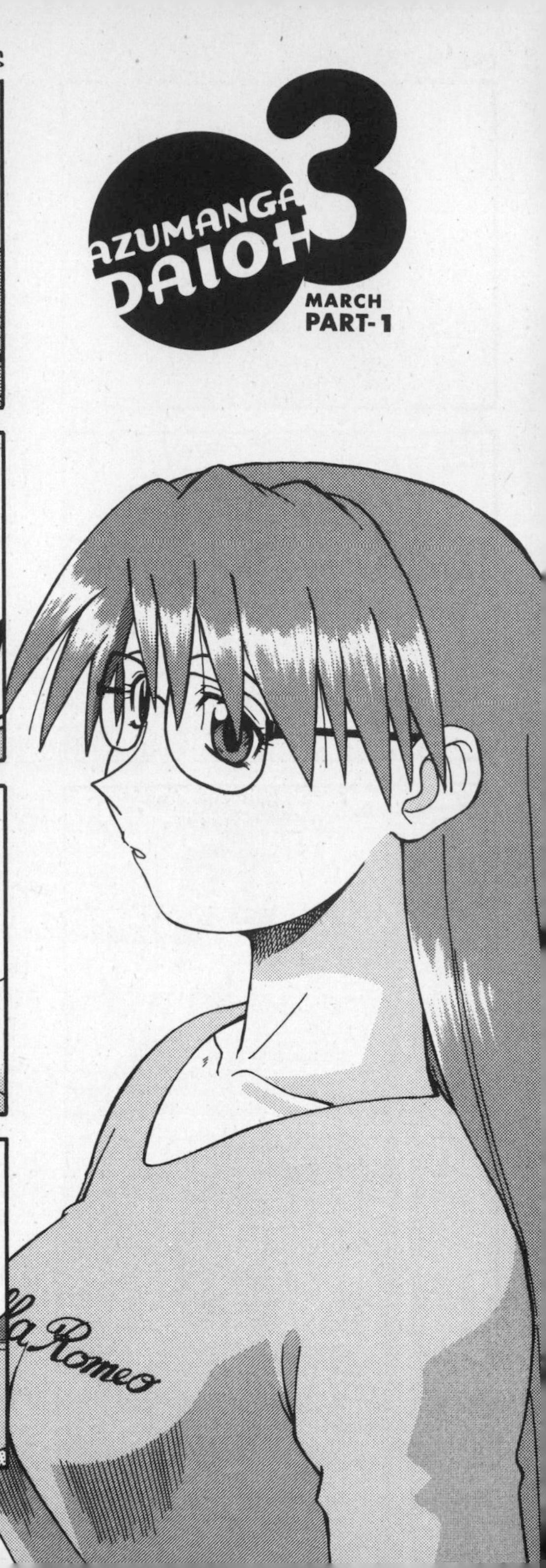
AZUMANGA DAIOH 3
MARCH
PART-1
lla Romeo

READ BETWEEN THE LINES

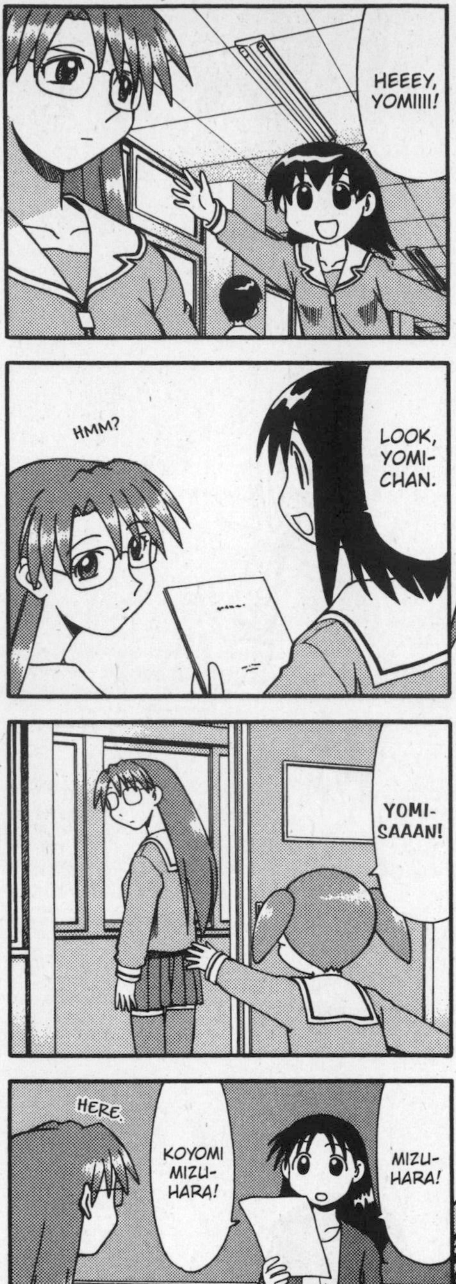
HEEEY, YOMIIII!
LOOK, YOMI-CHAN.
HMM?
YOMI-SAAAN!
MIZU-HARA!
KOYOMI MIZU-HARA!
HERE.

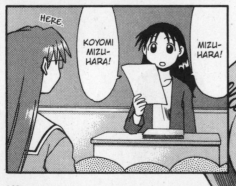

ELEVEN YEARS OLD

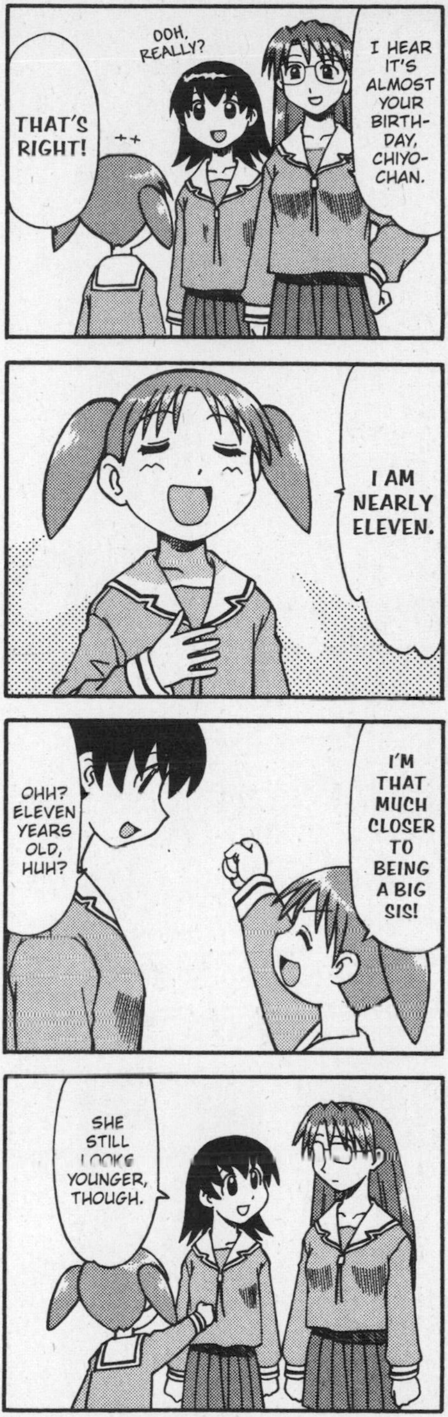
I HEAR IT'S ALMOST YOUR BIRTHDAY, CHIYO-CHAN.
OOH, REALLY?
THAT'S RIGHT!
I AM NEARLY ELEVEN.
I'M THAT MUCH CLOSER TO BEING A BIG SIS!
OHH? ELEVEN YEARS OLD, HUH?
SHE STILL LOOKS YOUNGER, THOUGH.

LIKE CHIYO-CHAN

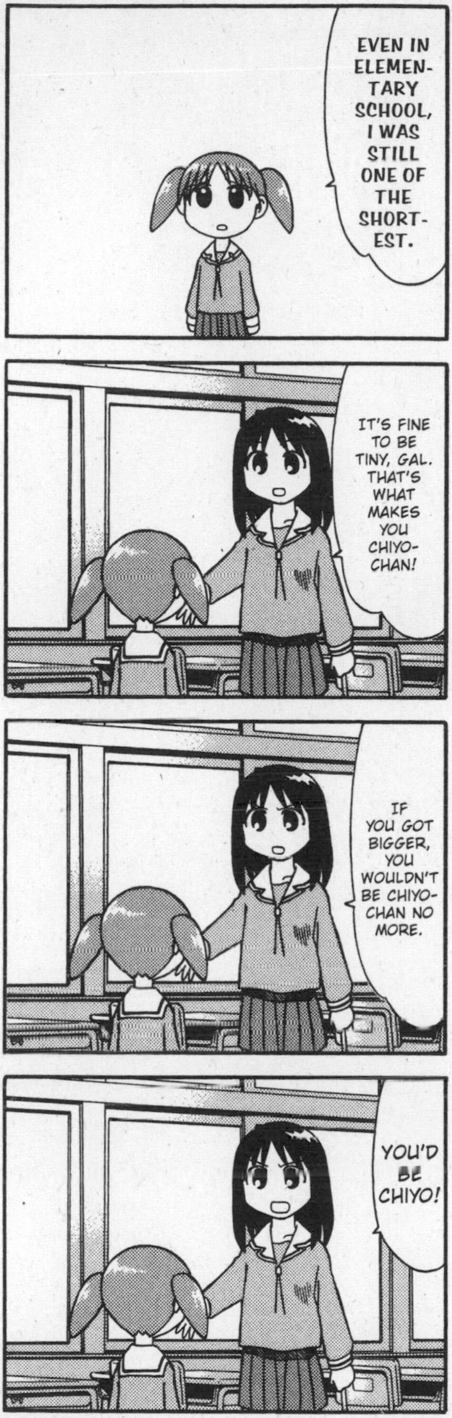
EVEN IN ELEMENTARY SCHOOL, I WAS STILL ONE OF THE SHORTEST.
IT'S FINE TO BE TINY, GAL. THAT'S WHAT MAKES YOU CHIYO-CHAN!
IF YOU GOT BIGGER, YOU WOULDN'T BE CHIYO-CHAN NO MORE.
YOU'D BE CHIYO!

POOR TALKER

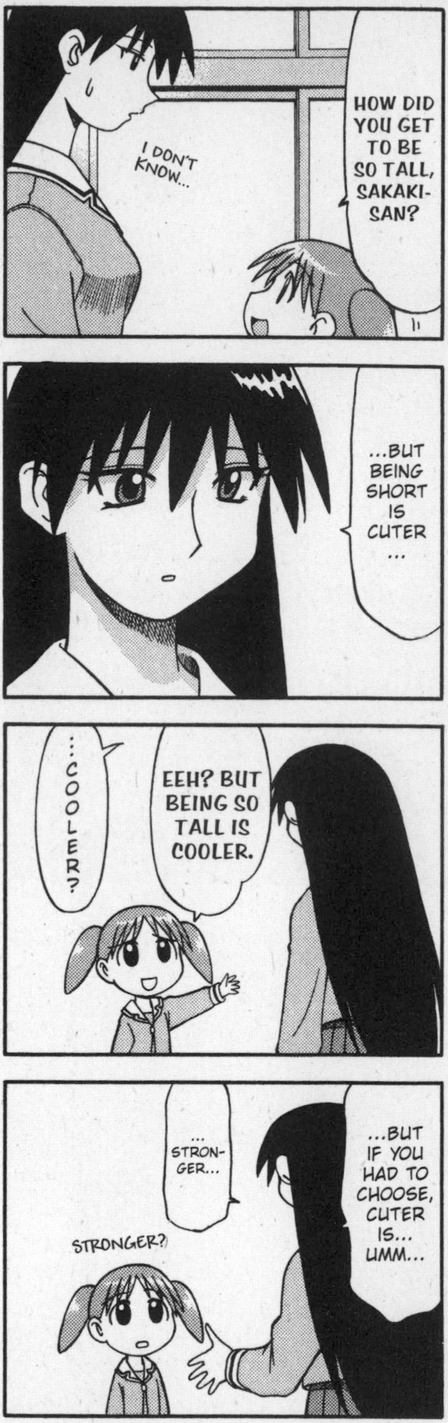
HOW DID YOU GET TO BE SO TALL, SAKAKI-SAN?
I DON'T KNOW...
...BUT BEING SHORT IS CUTER...
EEH? BUT BEING SO TALL IS COOLER.
...COOLER?
...BUT IF YOU HAD TO CHOOSE, CUTER IS... UMM...
...STRONGER...
STRONGER?

GROWTH SPURT

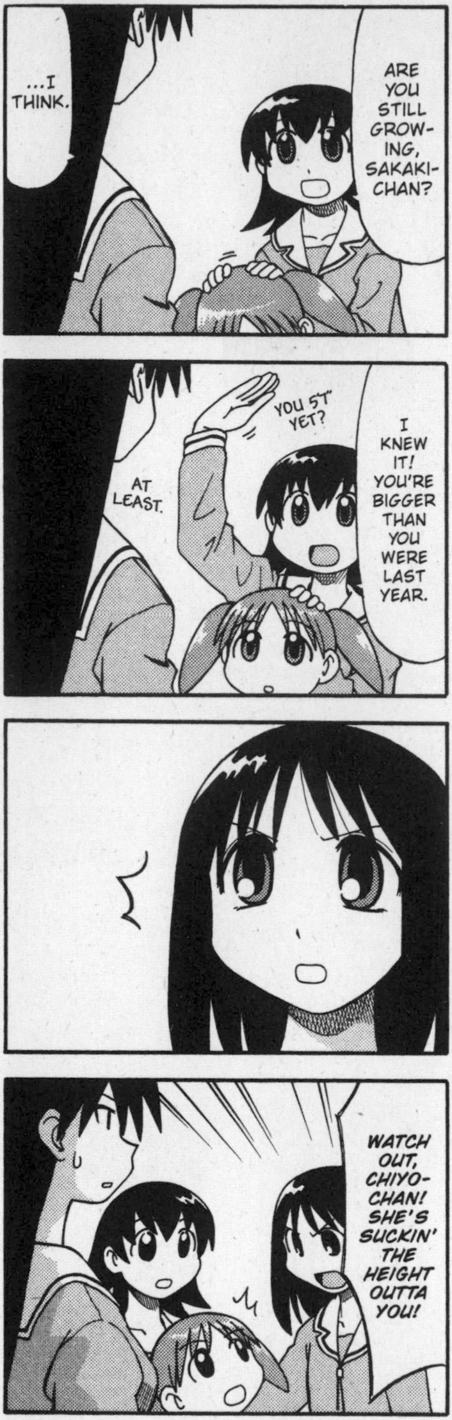
ARE YOU STILL GROWING, SAKAKI-CHAN?
...I THINK.
I KNEW IT! YOU'RE BIGGER THAN YOU WERE LAST YEAR.
YOU 5'1" YET?
AT LEAST.
WATCH OUT, CHIYO-CHAN! SHE'S SUCKIN' THE HEIGHT OUTTA YOU!

GIVE IT BACK

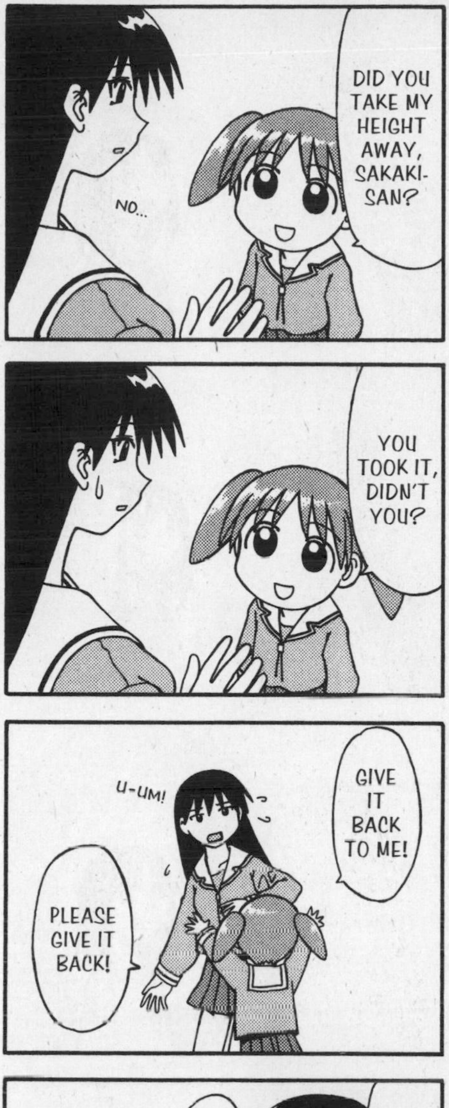
DID YOU TAKE MY HEIGHT AWAY, SAKAKI-SAN?
NO...
YOU TOOK IT, DIDN'T YOU?
GIVE IT BACK TO ME!
U-UM!
PLEASE GIVE IT BACK!
GIVE IT BACK!
GIVE IT BACK!
LOOK AT SAKAKI! SHE'S FREAKIN' OUT!
CHIYO-CHAN SURE KNOWS HOW TO ATTACK LIKE AN ELEVEN-YEAR-OLD...

HONEST THOUGHTS

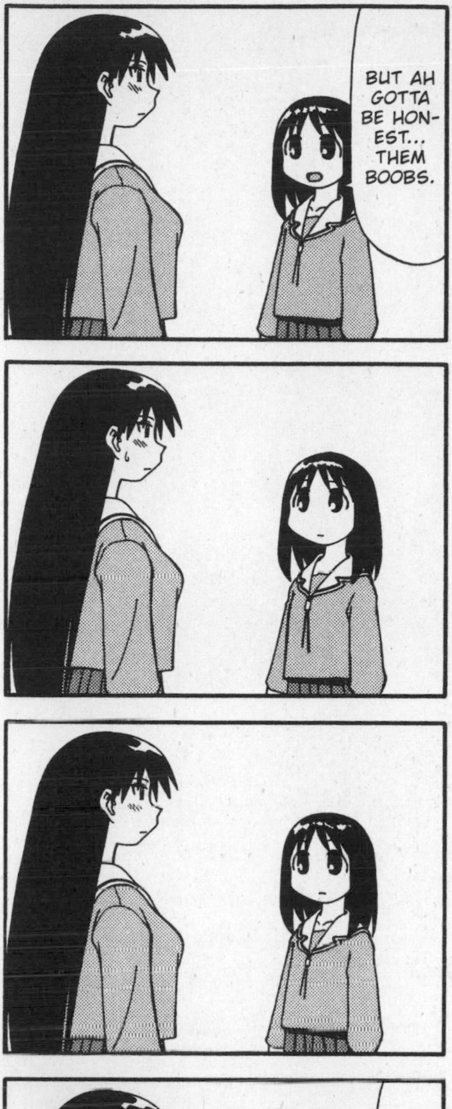
BUT AH GOTTA BE HON-EST... THEM BOOBS.
VERY NICE!

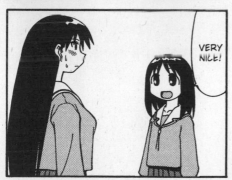

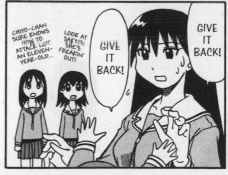

BOOM

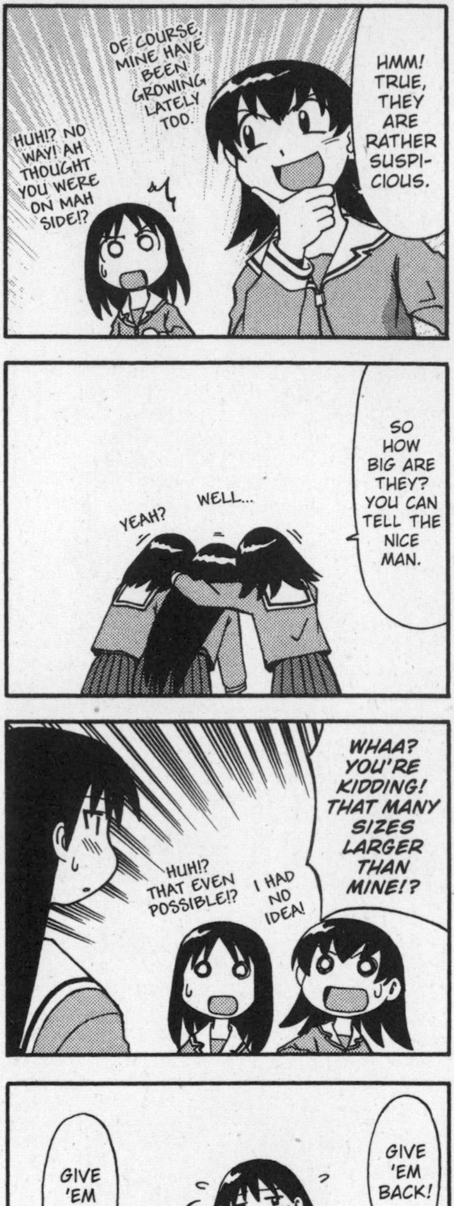
HMM! TRUE, THEY ARE RATHER SUSPICIOUS.
OF COURSE, MINE HAVE BEEN GROWING LATELY TOO.
HUH!? NO WAY! AH THOUGHT YOU WERE ON MAH SIDE!?
SO HOW BIG ARE THEY? YOU CAN TELL THE NICE MAN.
WELL...
YEAH?
WHAA? YOU'RE KIDDING! THAT MANY SIZES LARGER THAN MINE!?
I HAD NO IDEA!
HUH!? THAT EVEN POSSIBLE!?
GIVE 'EM BACK!
GIVE 'EM BACK!

PROPORTION

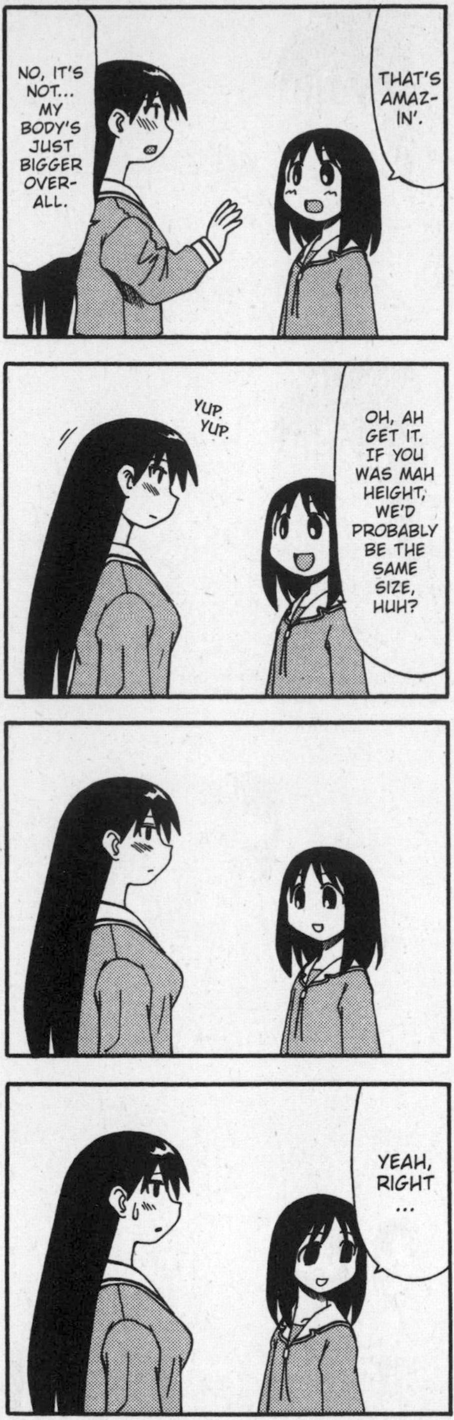
THAT'S AMAZIN'.
NO, IT'S NOT... MY BODY'S JUST BIGGER OVERALL.
OH, AH GET IT. IF YOU WAS MAH HEIGHT, WE'D PROBABLY BE THE SAME SIZE, HUH?
YUP. YUP.
YEAH, RIGHT ...

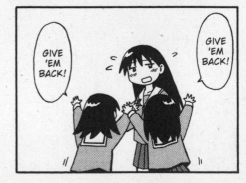

UDW (UNIDENTIFIED DRIVING WIFE)

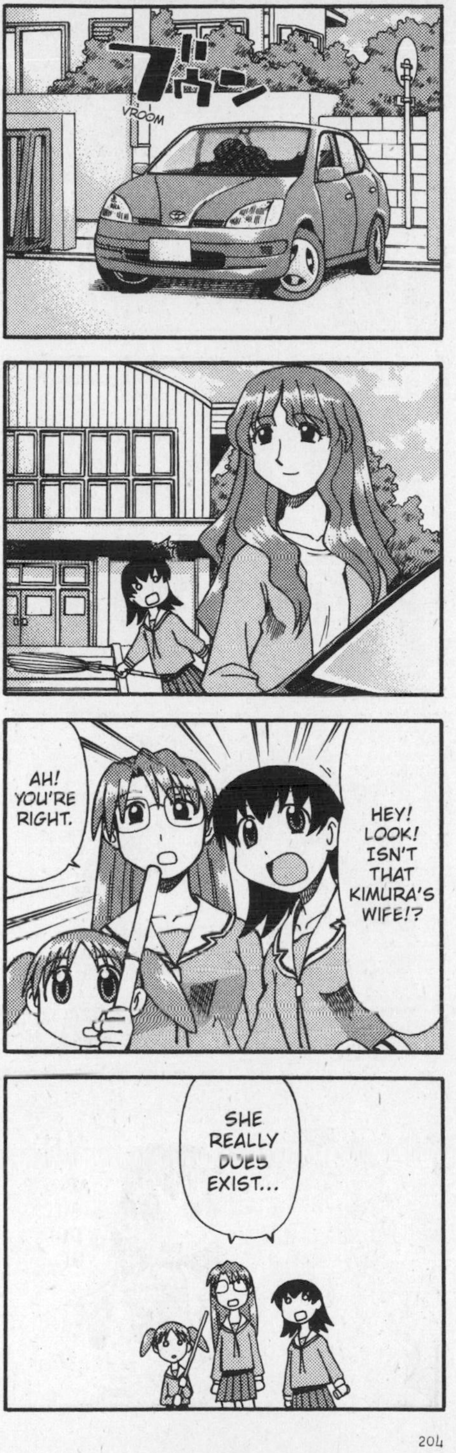
VROOM
HEY! LOOK! ISN'T THAT KIMURA'S WIFE!?
AH! YOU'RE RIGHT.
SHE REALLY DOES EXIST...

EXPERIMENT

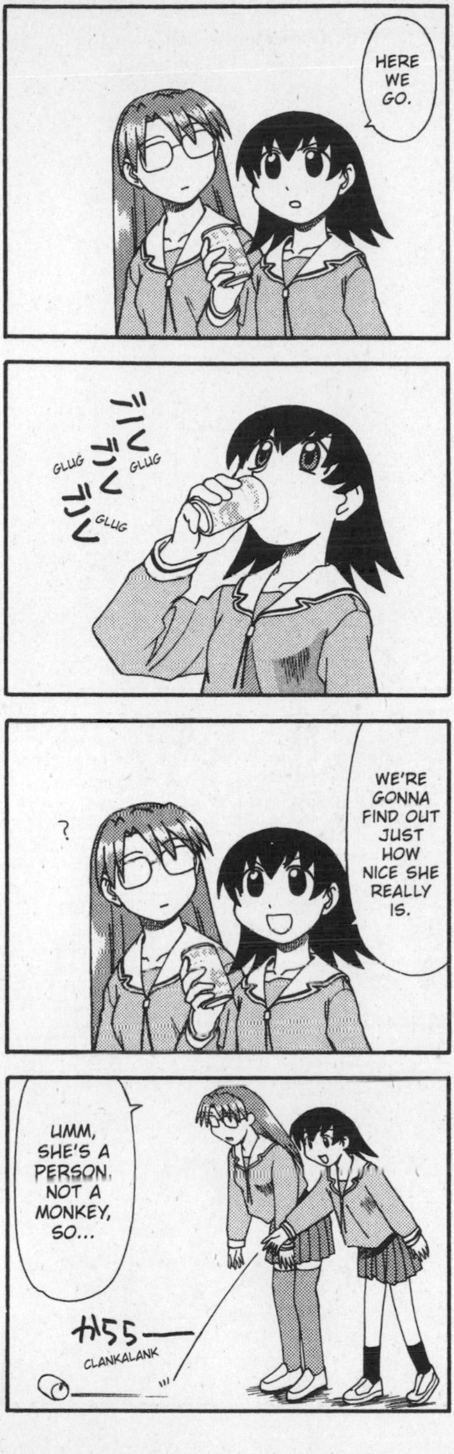
HERE WE GO.
GLUG GLUG
GLUG
WE'RE GONNA FIND OUT JUST HOW NICE SHE REALLY IS.
?
UMM, SHE'S A PERSON, NOT A MONKEY, SO...
CLANKALANK

VERY NICE

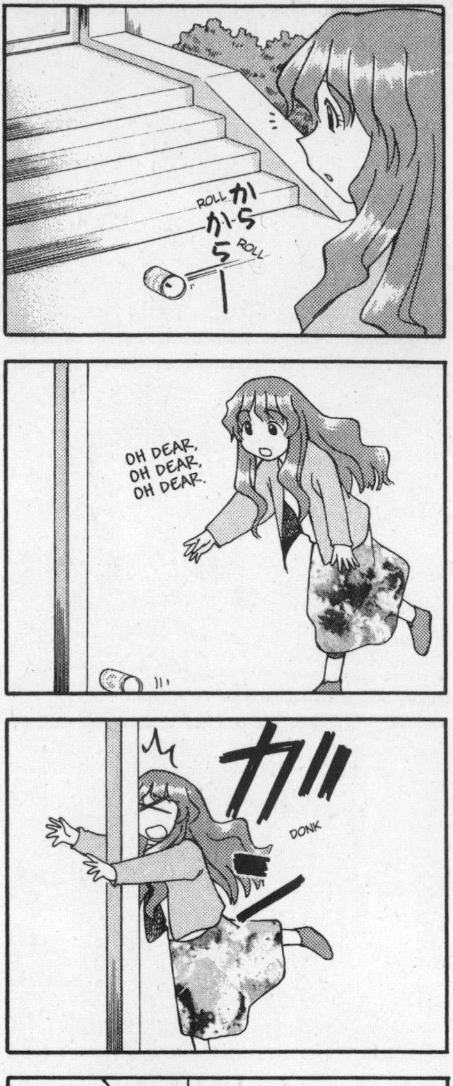

ROLL から
から ROLL
OH DEAR, OH DEAR, OH DEAR.
ガッ
DONK
UWAH! SHE IS REALLY NICE!
OWWIE...
ぽい
TOSS

WARNING SIGNAL

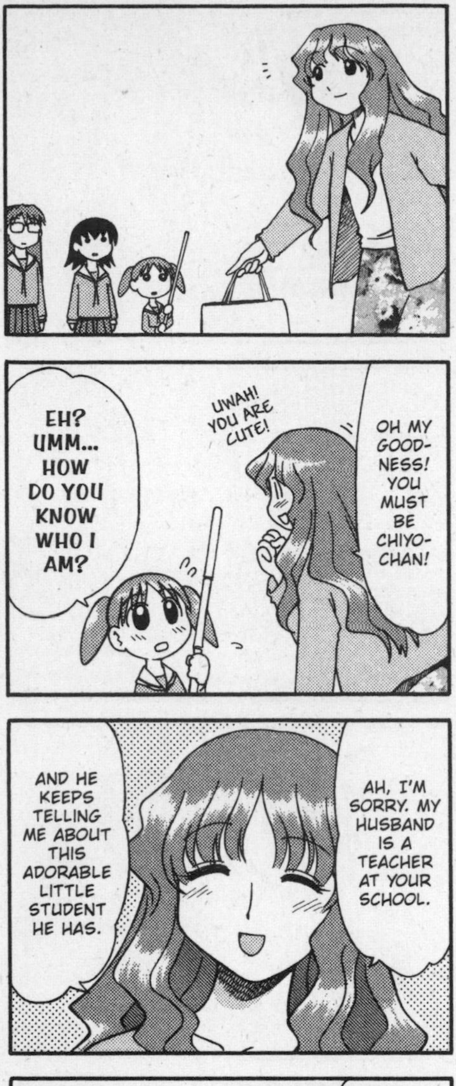

OH MY GOODNESS! YOU MUST BE CHIYO-CHAN!
UWAH! YOU ARE CUTE!
EH? UMM... HOW DO YOU KNOW WHO I AM?
AH, I'M SORRY. MY HUSBAND IS A TEACHER AT YOUR SCHOOL.
AND HE KEEPS TELLING ME ABOUT THIS ADORABLE LITTLE STUDENT HE HAS.
......H-HE TELLS YOU ABOUT ME... DOES HE...?
YIKES!

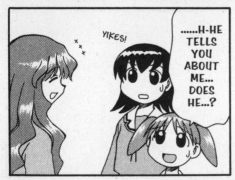

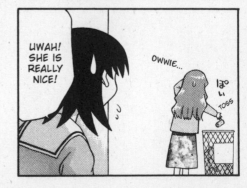

SHOWDOWN REDUX

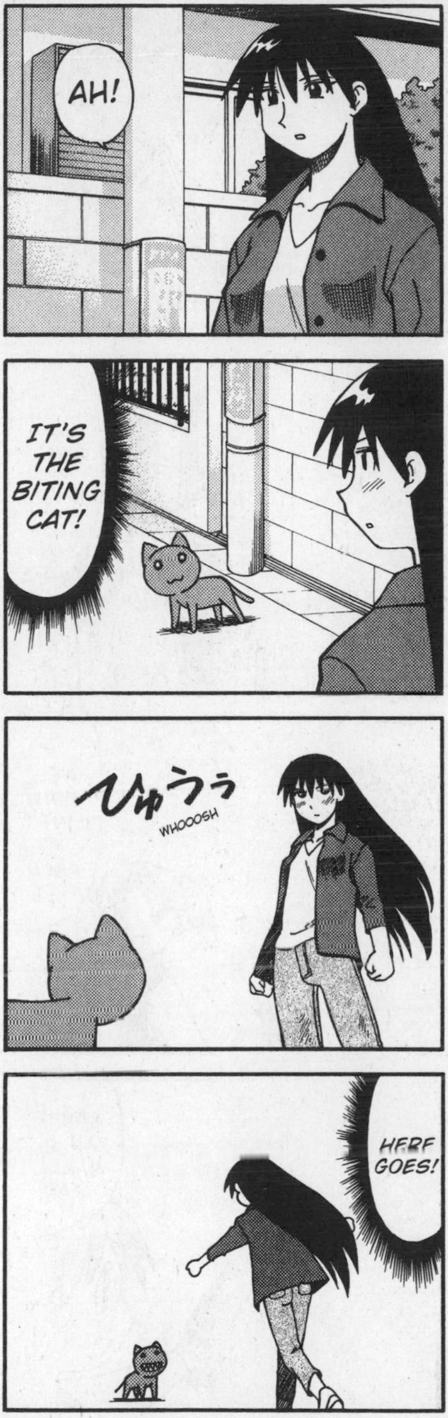
AH!
IT'S THE BITING CAT!
ひゅうぅ
WHOOOSH
HERE GOES!

SECRET PLAN

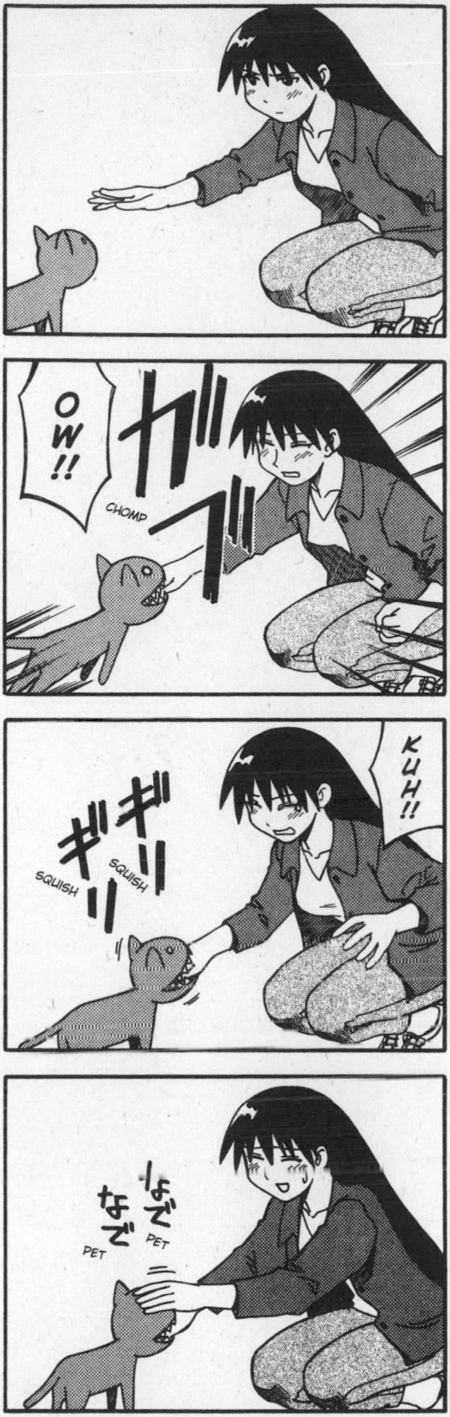
OW!!
ガブ
CHOMP
KUH!!
ギリギリ
SQUISH
SQUISH
なでなで
PET
PET

<TRAP>

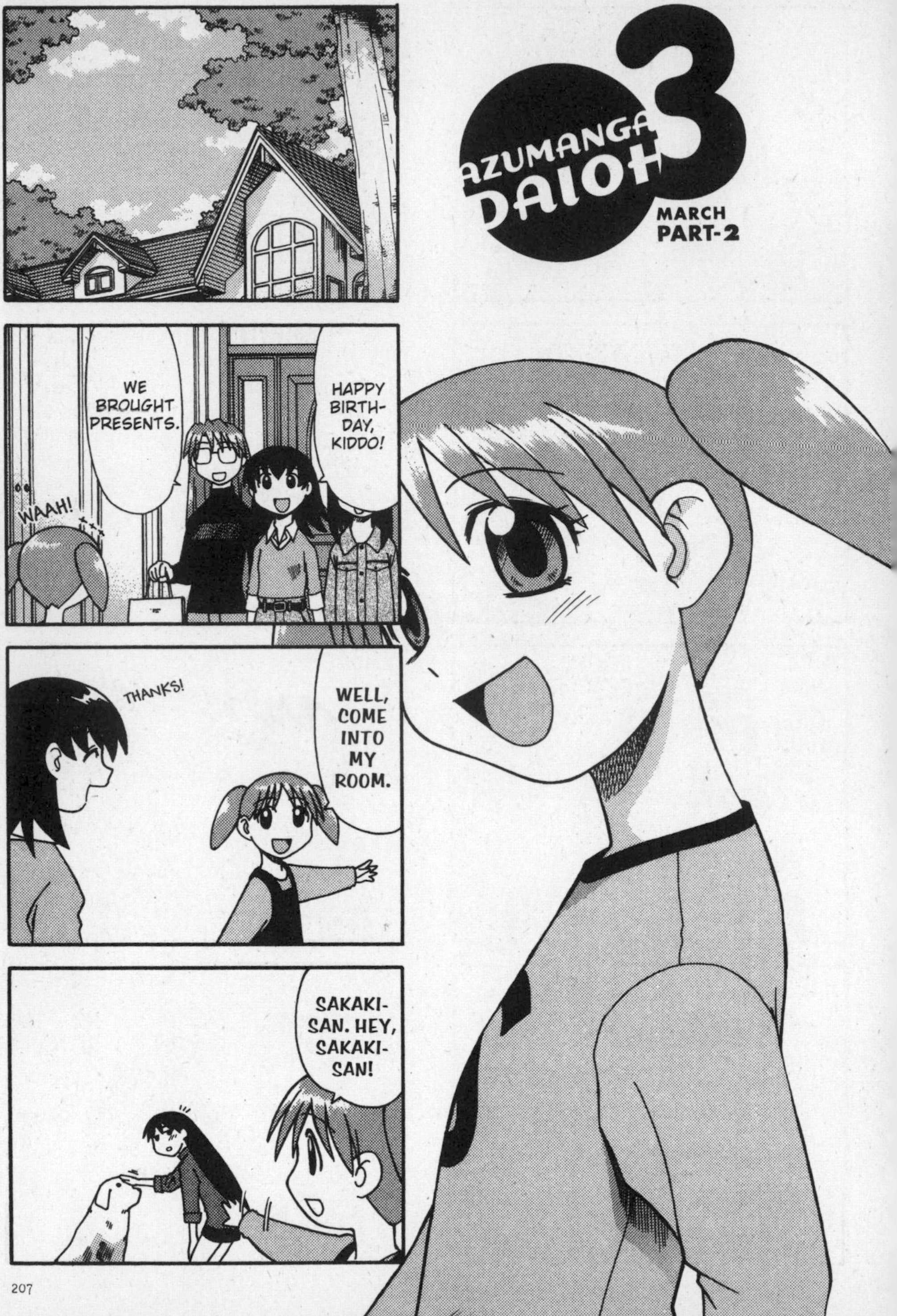
AZUMANGA DAIOH 3
MARCH PART-2
HAPPY BIRTH-DAY, KIDDO!
WE BROUGHT PRESENTS.
WAAH!
WELL, COME INTO MY ROOM.
THANKS!
SAKAKI-SAN. HEY, SAKAKI-SAN!

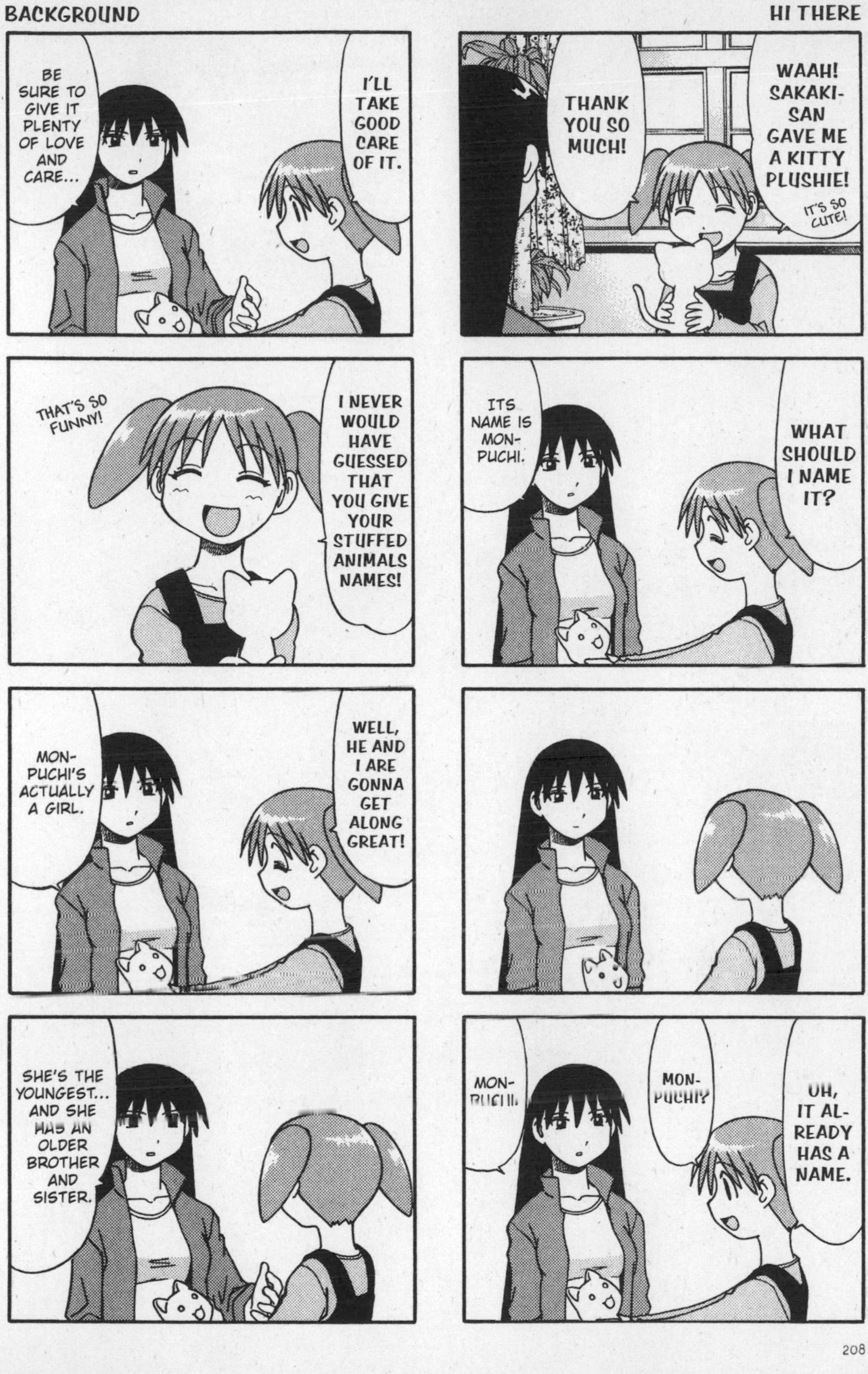
HI THERE
WAAH! SAKAKI-SAN GAVE ME A KITTY PLUSHIE!
IT'S SO CUTE!
THANK YOU SO MUCH!
WHAT SHOULD I NAME IT?
ITS NAME IS MON-PUCHI.
UH, IT AL-READY HAS A NAME.
MON-PUCHI?
MON-PUCHI.
BACKGROUND
I'LL TAKE GOOD CARE OF IT.
BE SURE TO GIVE IT PLENTY OF LOVE AND CARE...
I NEVER WOULD HAVE GUESSED THAT YOU GIVE YOUR STUFFED ANIMALS NAMES!
THAT'S SO FUNNY!
WELL, HE AND I ARE GONNA GET ALONG GREAT!
MON-PUCHI'S ACTUALLY A GIRL.
SHE'S THE YOUNGEST... AND SHE HAS AN OLDER BROTHER AND SISTER.

NAMES

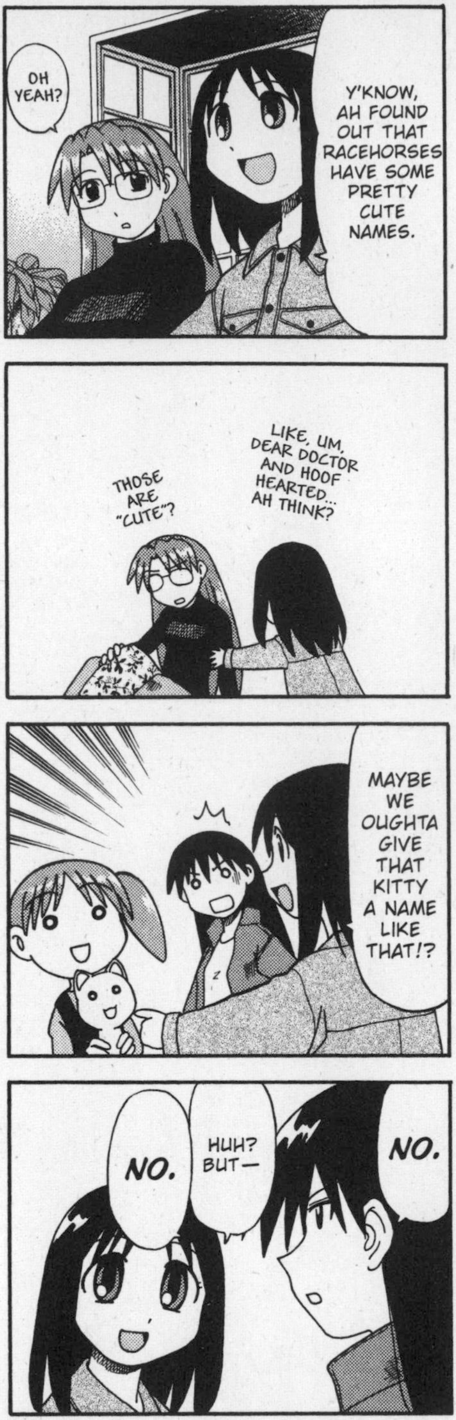
Y'KNOW, AH FOUND OUT THAT RACEHORSES HAVE SOME PRETTY CUTE NAMES.
OH YEAH?
LIKE, UM, DEAR DOCTOR AND HOOF HEARTED... AH THINK?
THOSE ARE "CUTE"?
MAYBE WE OUGHTA GIVE THAT KITTY A NAME LIKE THAT!?
NO.
HUH? BUT—
NO.

REUNION

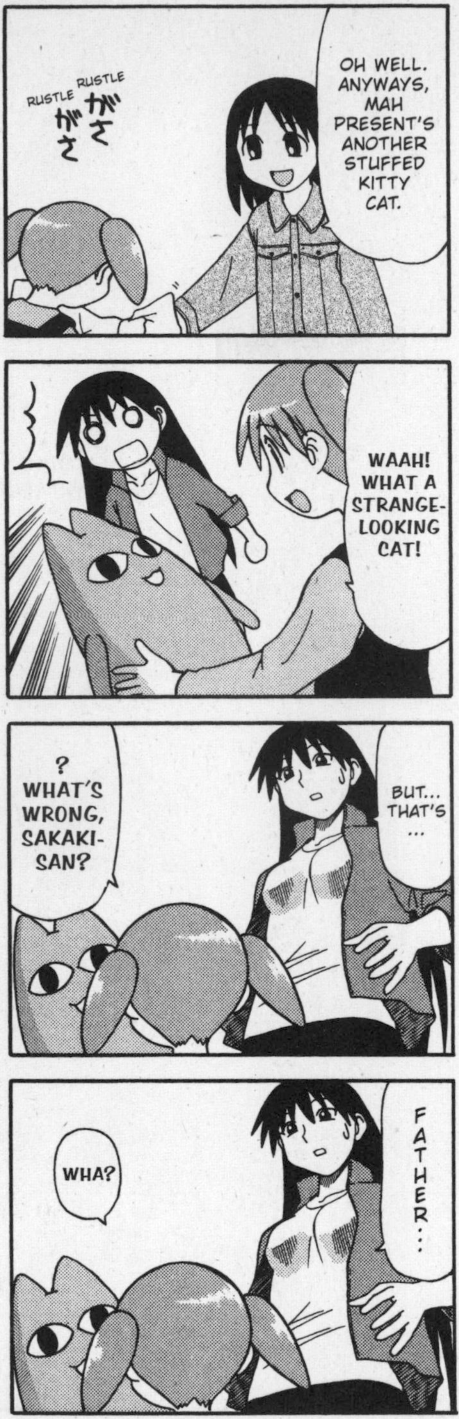
OH WELL. ANYWAYS, MAH PRESENT'S ANOTHER STUFFED KITTY CAT.
RUSTLE RUSTLE
がさがさ
WAAH! WHAT A STRANGE-LOOKING CAT!
BUT... THAT'S ...
? WHAT'S WRONG, SAKAKI-SAN?
FATHER...
WHA?

WHAT COULD THIS MEAN?

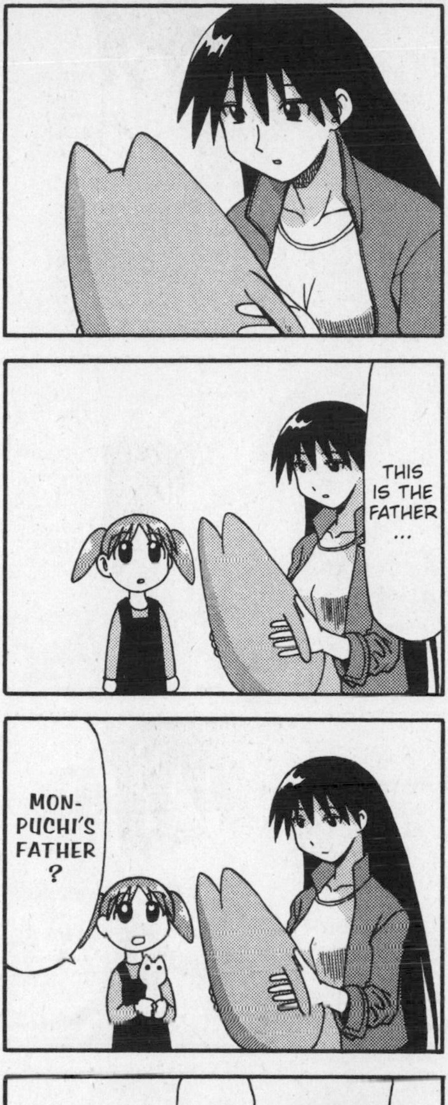
THIS IS THE FATHER ...
MON-PUCHI'S FATHER ?
......
NO, CHIYO-CHAN'S ...
MINE ?

COFFEE TIME

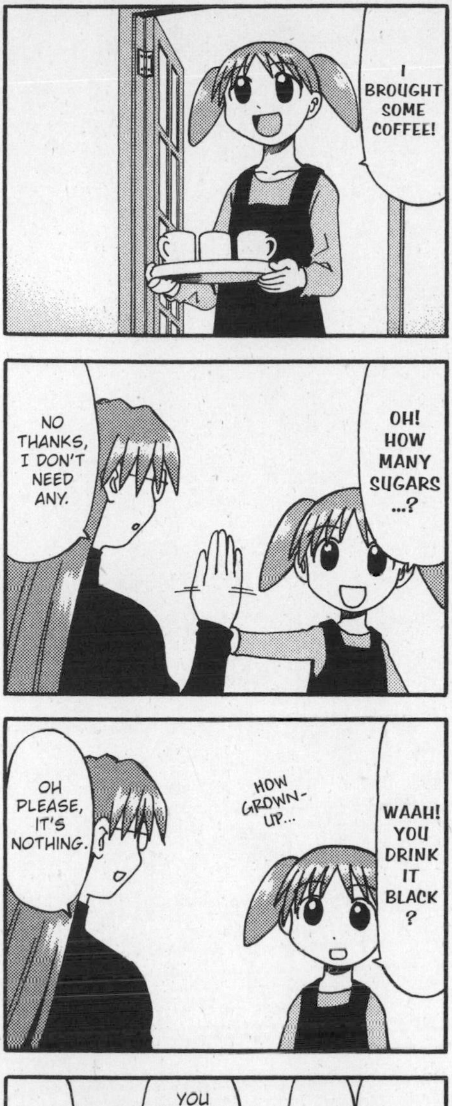
I BROUGHT SOME COFFEE!
OH! HOW MANY SUGARS ...?
NO THANKS, I DON'T NEED ANY.
WAAH! YOU DRINK IT BLACK ?
HOW GROWN-UP...
OH PLEASE, IT'S NOTHING.
NO WAY! HAVE YOU ALWAYS DRUNK IT BLACK? I THOUGHT YOU—
YUP.
YOU AREN'T DOING THIS FOR YOUR DIET?
NO.

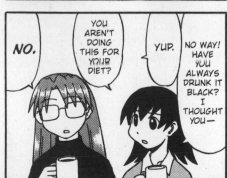

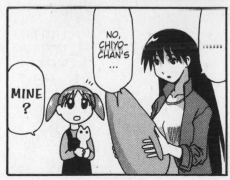

WHAT IS THIS STUFF?

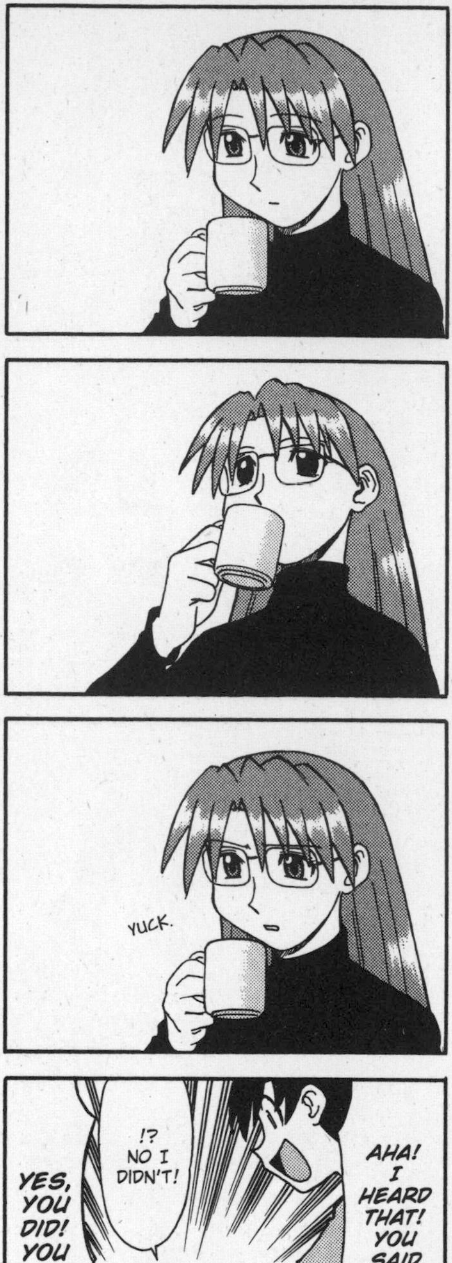
YUCK.
AHA! I HEARD THAT! YOU SAID "YUCK"!
!? NO I DIDN'T!
YES, YOU DID! YOU DID!!

THEY WILL WIN

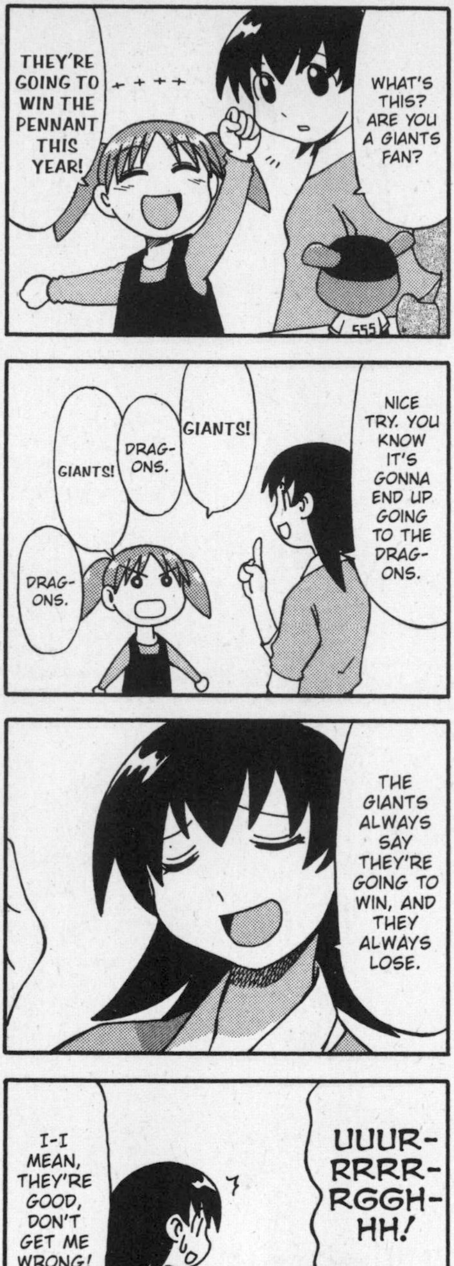
WHAT'S THIS? ARE YOU A GIANTS FAN?
THEY'RE GOING TO WIN THE PENNANT THIS YEAR!
555
NICE TRY. YOU KNOW IT'S GONNA END UP GOING TO THE DRAGONS.
GIANTS!
DRAGONS.
GIANTS!
DRAGONS.
THE GIANTS ALWAYS SAY THEY'RE GOING TO WIN, AND THEY ALWAYS LOSE.
UUURRRRRRGGHHH!
I-I MEAN, THEY'RE GOOD, DON'T GET ME WRONG!

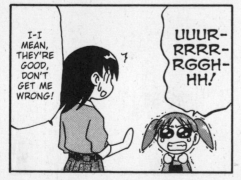

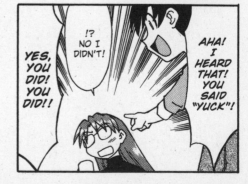

FLYING TREASURE

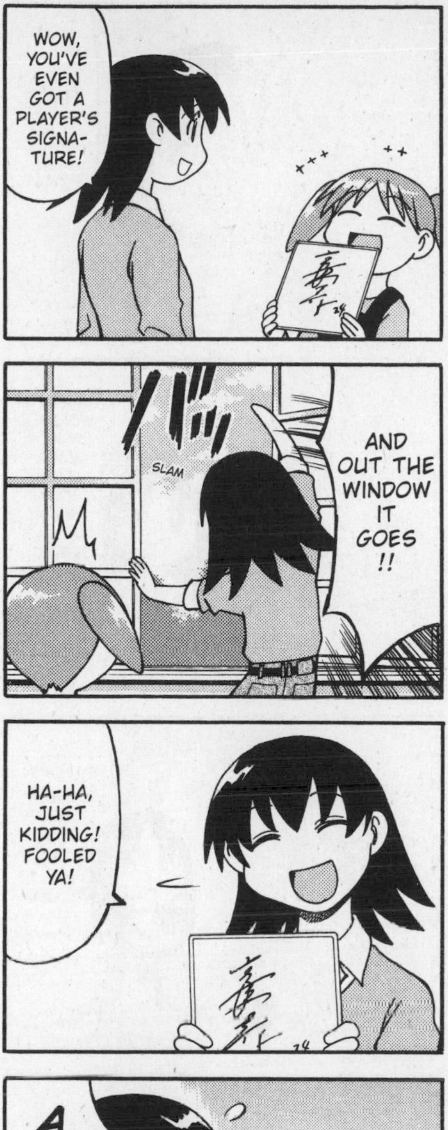
WOW, YOU'VE EVEN GOT A PLAYER'S SIGNA-TURE!
SLAM
AND OUT THE WINDOW IT GOES !!
HA-HA, JUST KIDDING! FOOLED YA!
AAH!

WHAT WAS THAT?

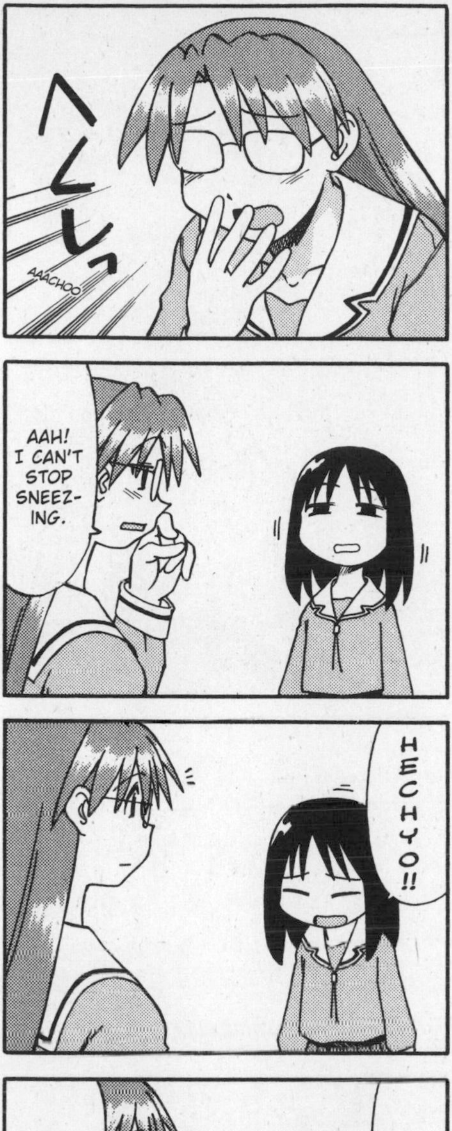
AAACHOO
AAH! I CAN'T STOP SNEEZ-ING.
HECHYO!!
ME NEI-THER.
WAIT, THAT WAS A SNEEZE?

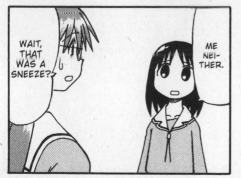

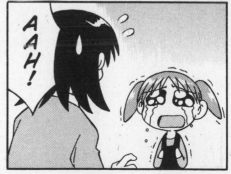

OHH

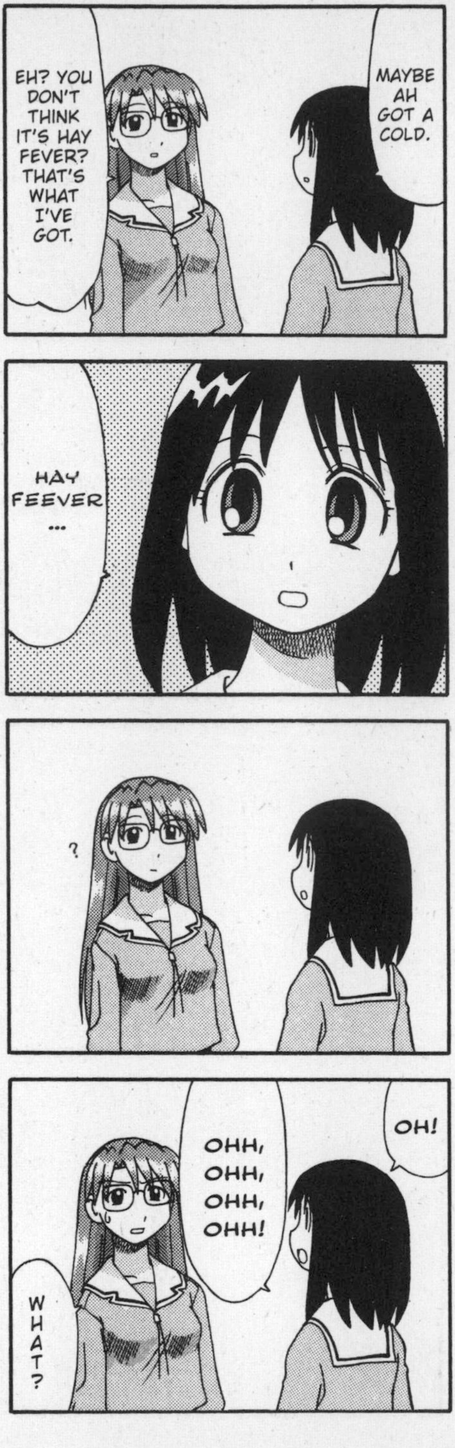
MAYBE AH GOT A COLD.
EH? YOU DON'T THINK IT'S HAY FEVER? THAT'S WHAT I'VE GOT.
HAY FEEVER ...
?
OH!
OHH, OHH, OHH, OHH!
WHAT?

I UNDERSTAND

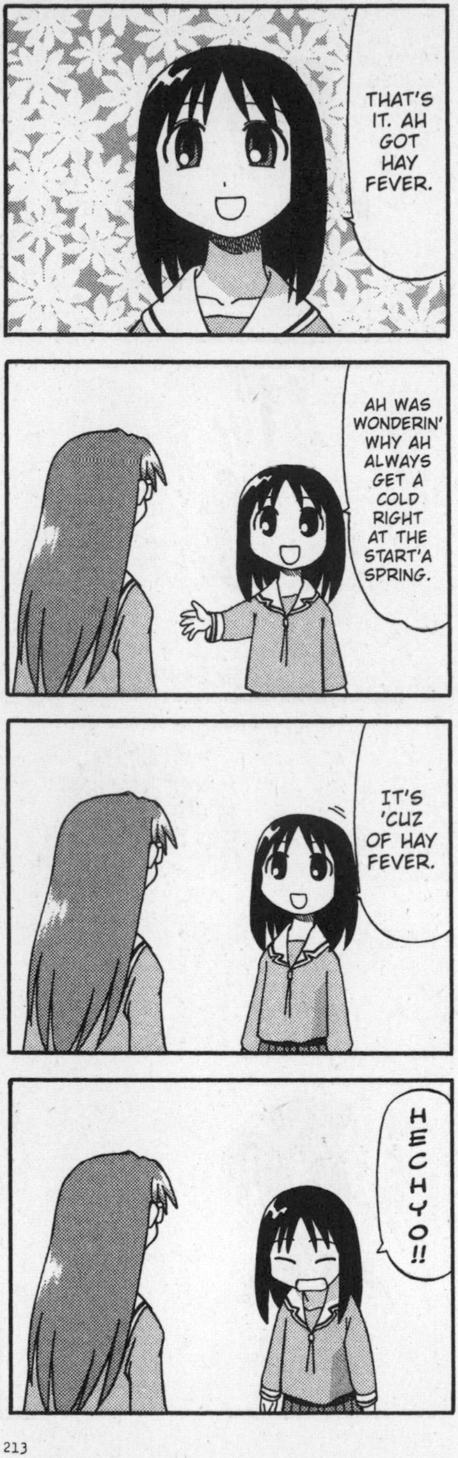
THAT'S IT. AH GOT HAY FEVER.
AH WAS WONDERIN' WHY AH ALWAYS GET A COLD RIGHT AT THE START'A SPRING.
IT'S 'CUZ OF HAY FEVER.
HECHYO!!

FAD

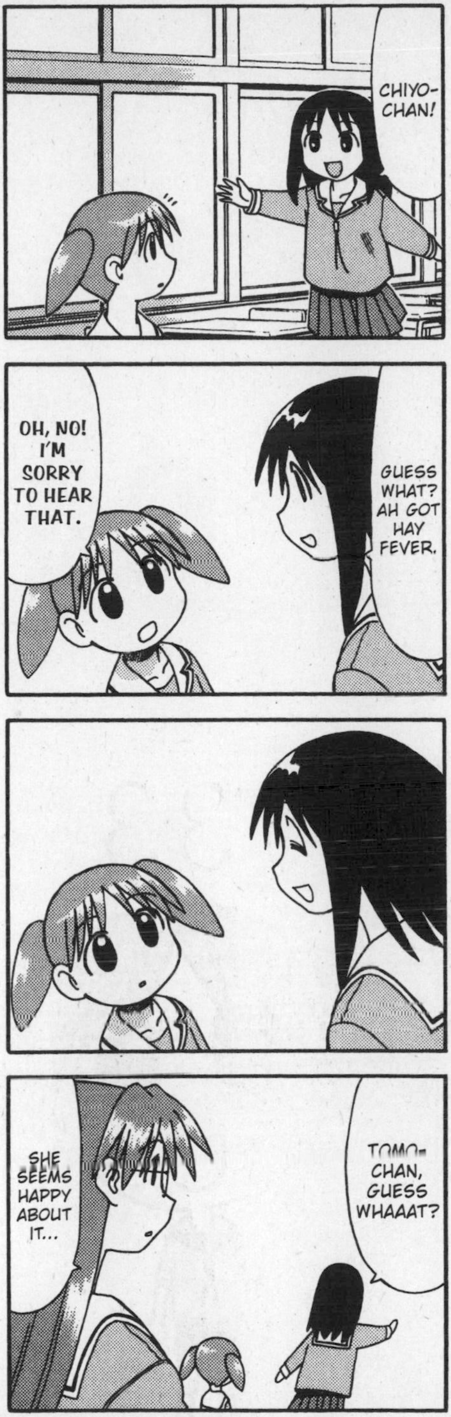
CHIYO-CHAN!
GUESS WHAT? AH GOT HAY FEVER.
OH, NO! I'M SORRY TO HEAR THAT.
TOMO-CHAN, GUESS WHAAAT?
SHE SEEMS HAPPY ABOUT IT...

GETTING DRAFTED

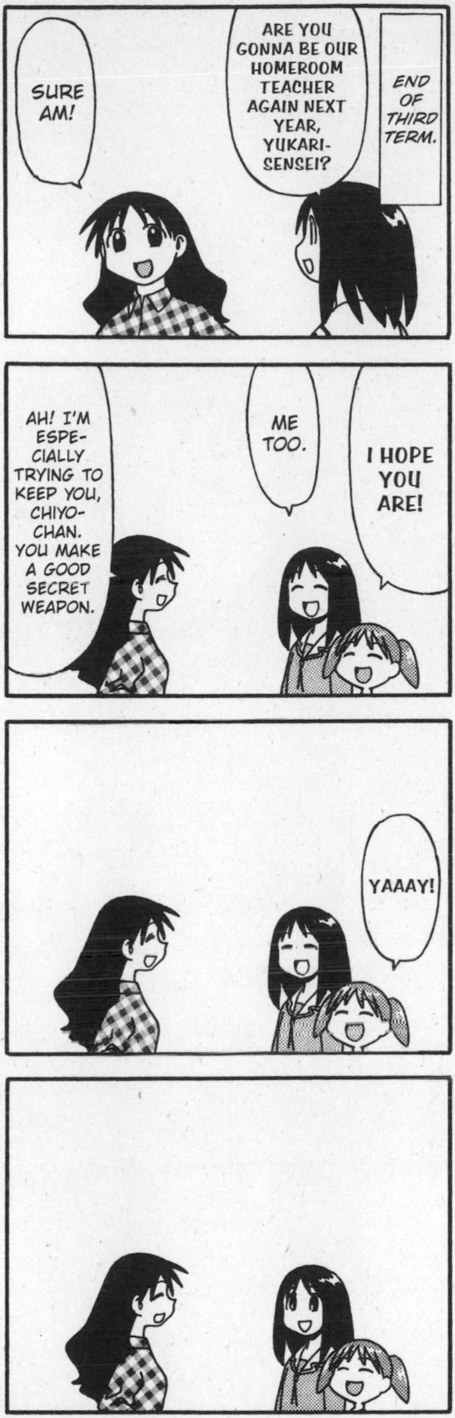
END OF THIRD TERM.
ARE YOU GONNA BE OUR HOMEROOM TEACHER AGAIN NEXT YEAR, YUKARI-SENSEI?
SURE AM!
I HOPE YOU ARE!
ME TOO.
AH! I'M ESPE-CIALLY TRYING TO KEEP YOU, CHIYO-CHAN. YOU MAKE A GOOD SECRET WEAPON.
YAAAY!

133

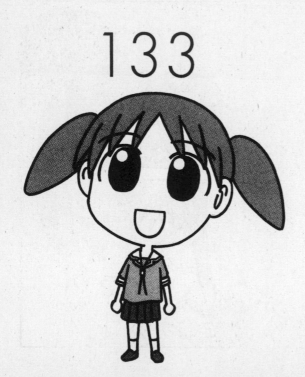

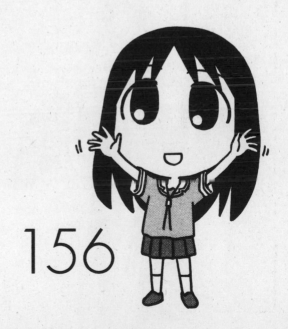

156

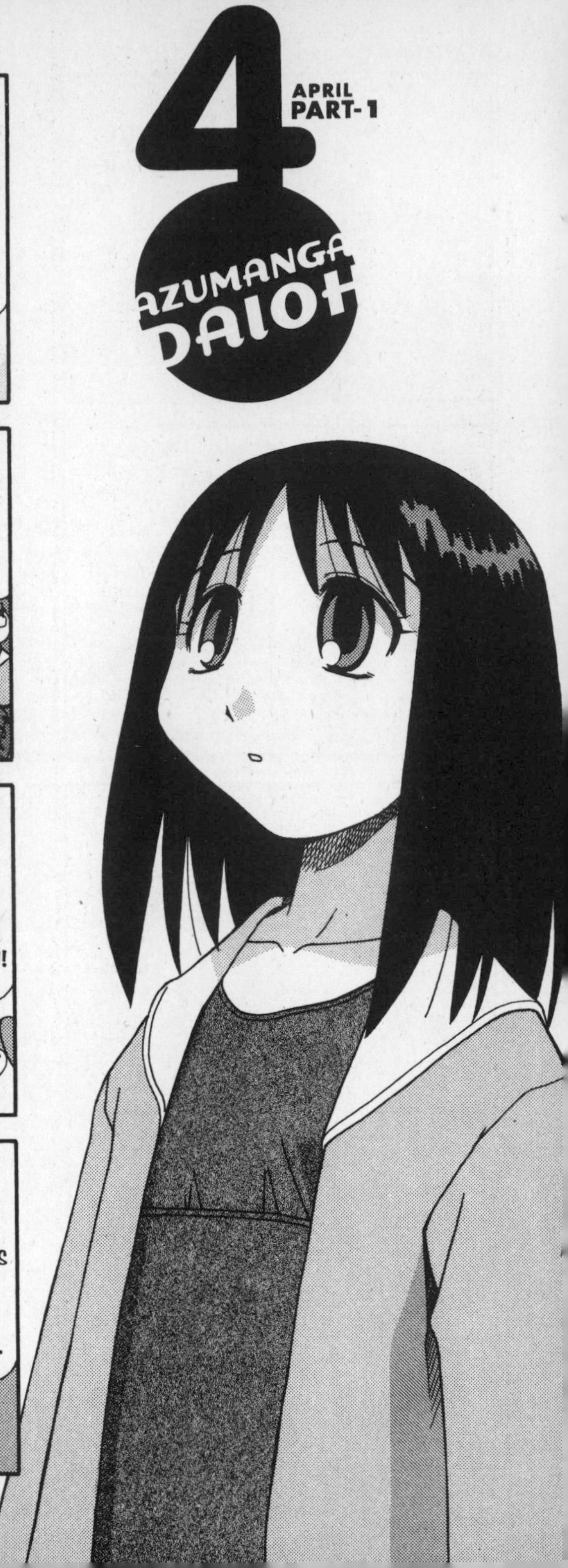
4
APRIL
PART-1
AZUMANGA DAIOH

CHANGING CLASSES

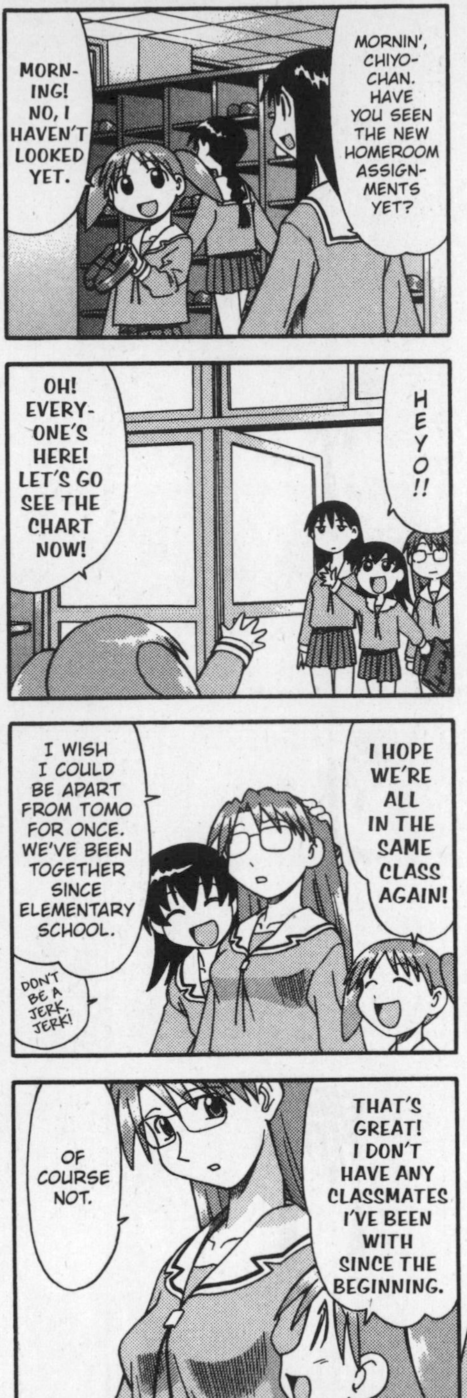
MORNIN', CHIYO-CHAN. HAVE YOU SEEN THE NEW HOMEROOM ASSIGNMENTS YET?
MORNING! NO, I HAVEN'T LOOKED YET.
HEYO!!
OH! EVERYONE'S HERE! LET'S GO SEE THE CHART NOW!
I HOPE WE'RE ALL IN THE SAME CLASS AGAIN!
I WISH I COULD BE APART FROM TOMO FOR ONCE. WE'VE BEEN TOGETHER SINCE ELEMENTARY SCHOOL.
DON'T BE A JERK, JERK!
THAT'S GREAT! I DON'T HAVE ANY CLASSMATES I'VE BEEN WITH SINCE THE BEGINNING.
OF COURSE NOT.

TOGETHER

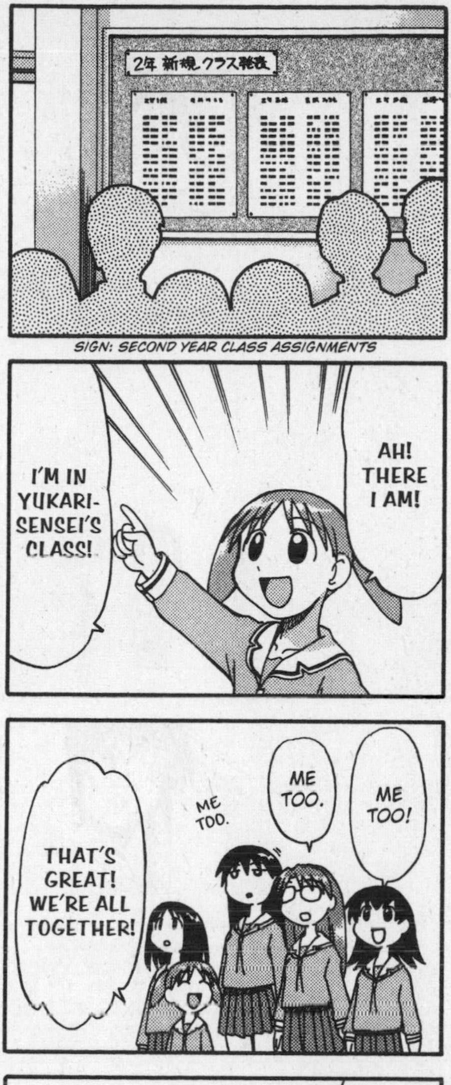
2年 新規クラス発表
SIGN: SECOND YEAR CLASS ASSIGNMENTS
AH! THERE I AM!
I'M IN YUKARI-SENSEI'S CLASS!
ME TOO!
ME TOO.
ME TOO.
THAT'S GREAT! WE'RE ALL TOGETHER!
AH AIN'T.
HUH?

REDEEMING FEATURES

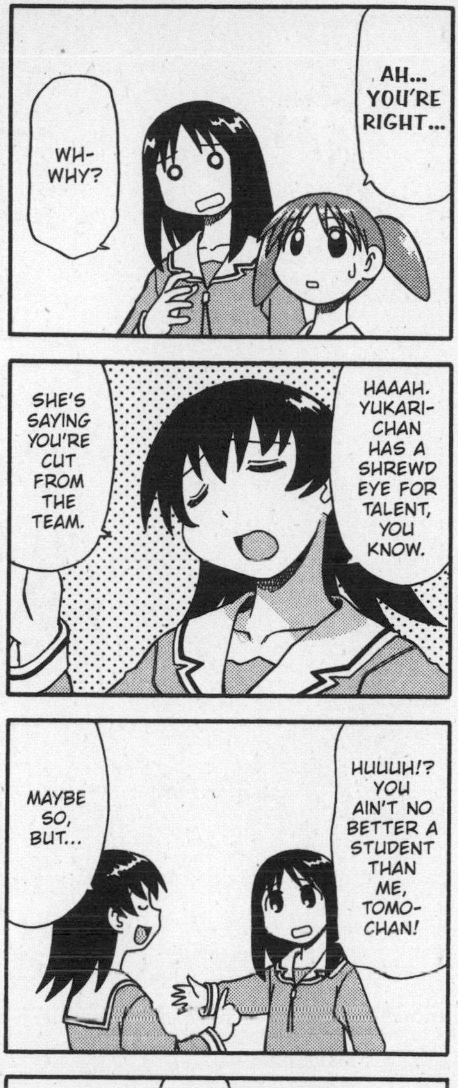
AH... YOU'RE RIGHT...
WH- WHY?
HAAAH. YUKARI-CHAN HAS A SHREWD EYE FOR TALENT, YOU KNOW.
SHE'S SAYING YOU'RE CUT FROM THE TEAM.
HUUUH!? YOU AIN'T NO BETTER A STUDENT THAN ME, TOMO-CHAN!
MAYBE SO, BUT...
... I GOT PEP ON MY SIDE!

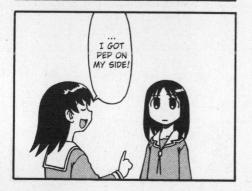

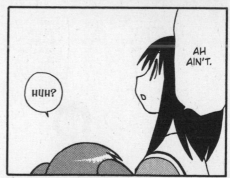

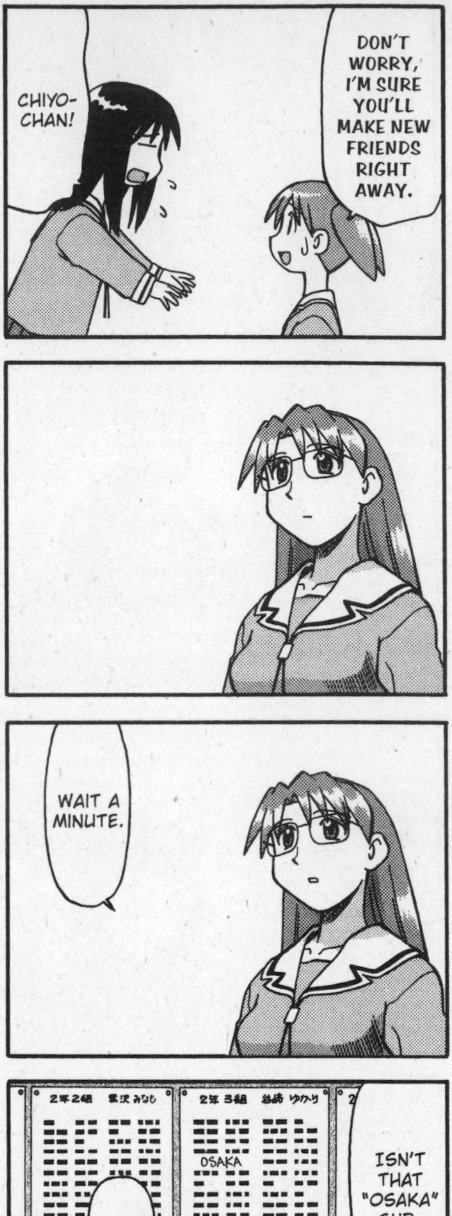
DON'T WORRY, I'M SURE YOU'LL MAKE NEW FRIENDS RIGHT AWAY.
CHIYO-CHAN!
WAIT A MINUTE.
2年2組 黒沢 みなも
2年3組 谷崎 ゆかり
ISN'T THAT "OSAKA" SUPPOSED TO BE YOU?
OSAKA
HUH?

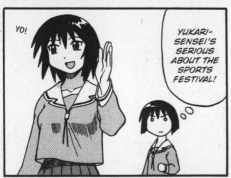

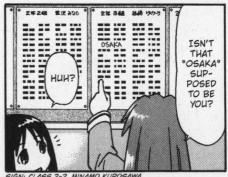

SIGN: CLASS 2-2, MINAMO KUROSAWA
SIGN: CLASS 2-3, YUKARI TANIZAKI

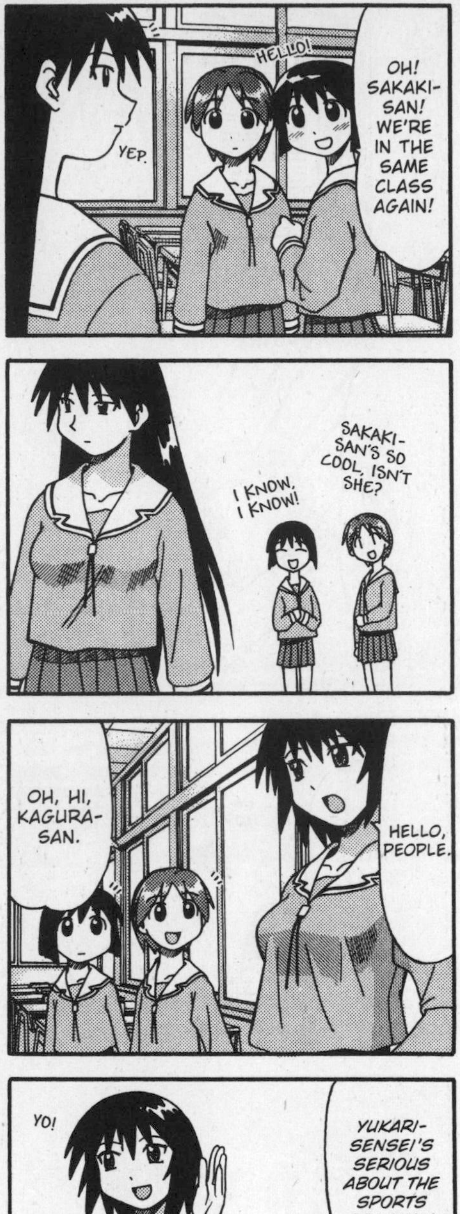
OH! SAKAKI-SAN! WE'RE IN THE SAME CLASS AGAIN!
HELLO!
YEP.
SAKAKI-SAN'S SO COOL, ISN'T SHE?
I KNOW, I KNOW!
HELLO, PEOPLE.
OH, HI, KAGURA-SAN.
YUKARI-SENSEI'S SERIOUS ABOUT THE SPORTS FESTIVAL!
YO!

RIVALS

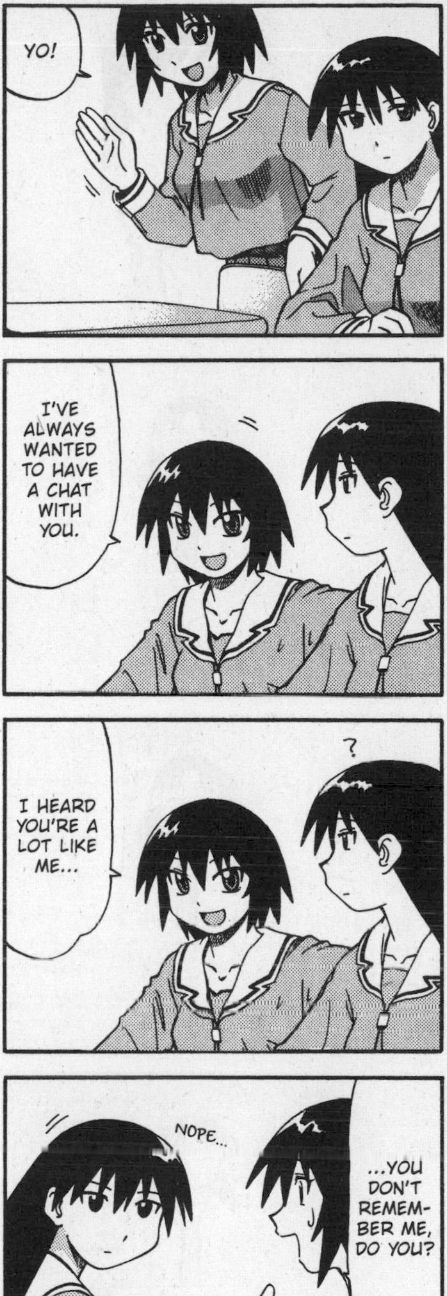
YO!
I'VE ALWAYS WANTED TO HAVE A CHAT WITH YOU.
?
I HEARD YOU'RE A LOT LIKE ME...
...YOU DON'T REMEMBER ME, DO YOU?
NOPE...

PUT 'ER THERE

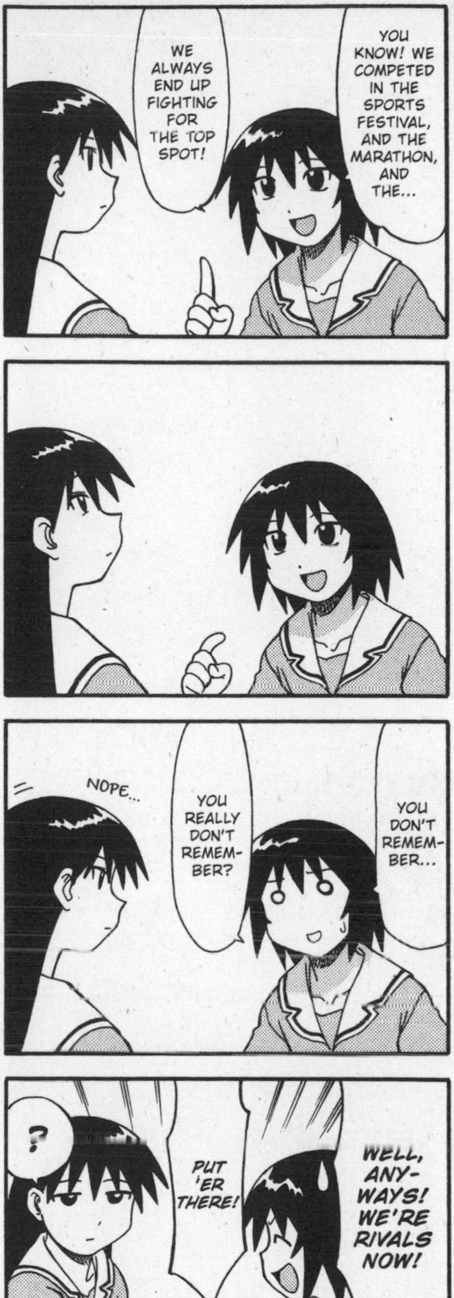
YOU KNOW! WE COMPETED IN THE SPORTS FESTIVAL, AND THE MARATHON, AND THE...
WE ALWAYS END UP FIGHTING FOR THE TOP SPOT!
YOU DON'T REMEMBER...
YOU REALLY DON'T REMEMBER?
NOPE...
WELL, ANYWAYS! WE'RE RIVALS NOW!
PUT 'ER THERE!
?

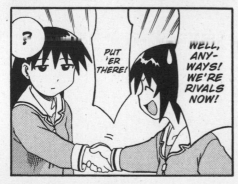

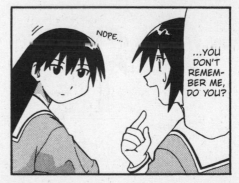

FAMOUS IDIOT

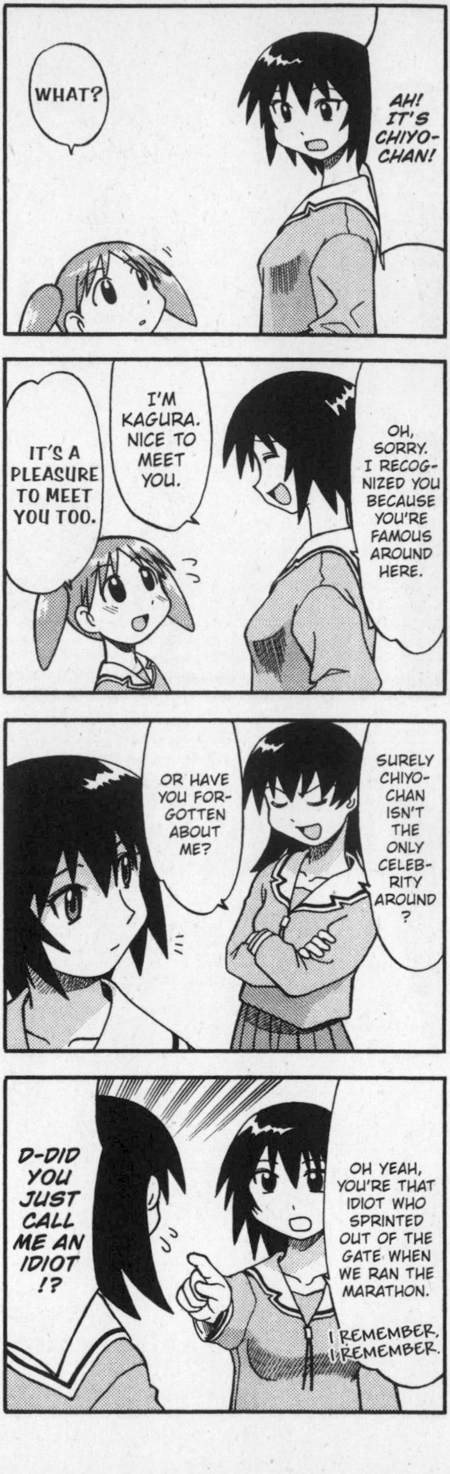
AH! IT'S CHIYO-CHAN!
WHAT?
OH, SORRY. I RECOGNIZED YOU BECAUSE YOU'RE FAMOUS AROUND HERE.
I'M KAGURA. NICE TO MEET YOU.
IT'S A PLEASURE TO MEET YOU TOO.
SURELY CHIYO-CHAN ISN'T THE ONLY CELEBRITY AROUND?
OR HAVE YOU FORGOTTEN ABOUT ME?
OH YEAH, YOU'RE THAT IDIOT WHO SPRINTED OUT OF THE GATE WHEN WE RAN THE MARATHON.
I REMEMBER, I REMEMBER.
D-DID YOU JUST CALL ME AN IDIOT!?

NO LESSONS LEARNED

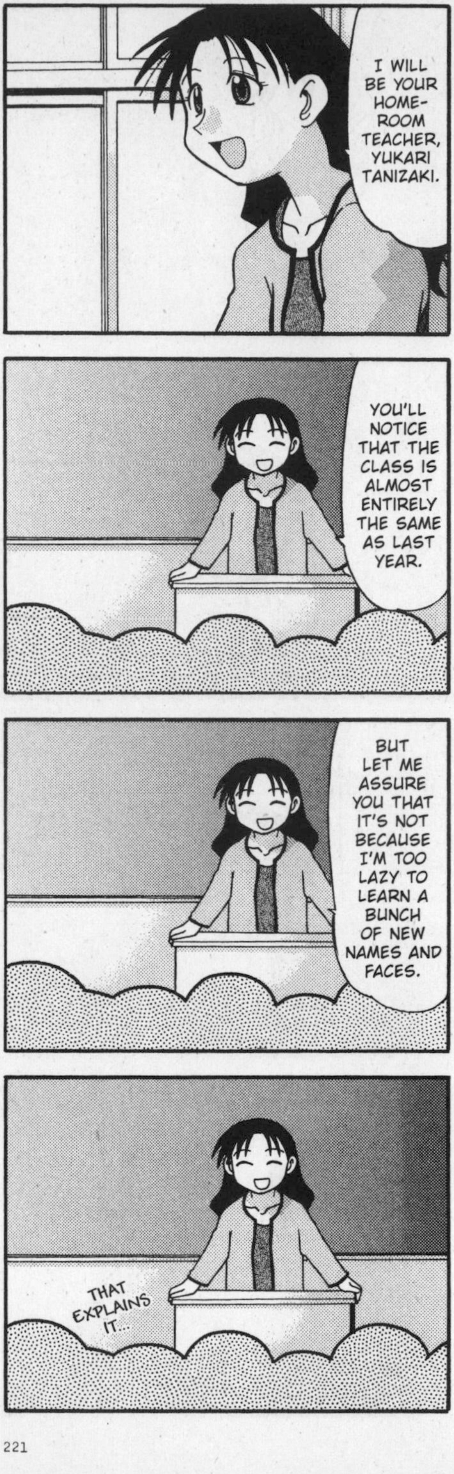
I WILL BE YOUR HOMEROOM TEACHER, YUKARI TANIZAKI.
YOU'LL NOTICE THAT THE CLASS IS ALMOST ENTIRELY THE SAME AS LAST YEAR.
BUT LET ME ASSURE YOU THAT IT'S NOT BECAUSE I'M TOO LAZY TO LEARN A BUNCH OF NEW NAMES AND FACES.
THAT EXPLAINS IT...

WOLF

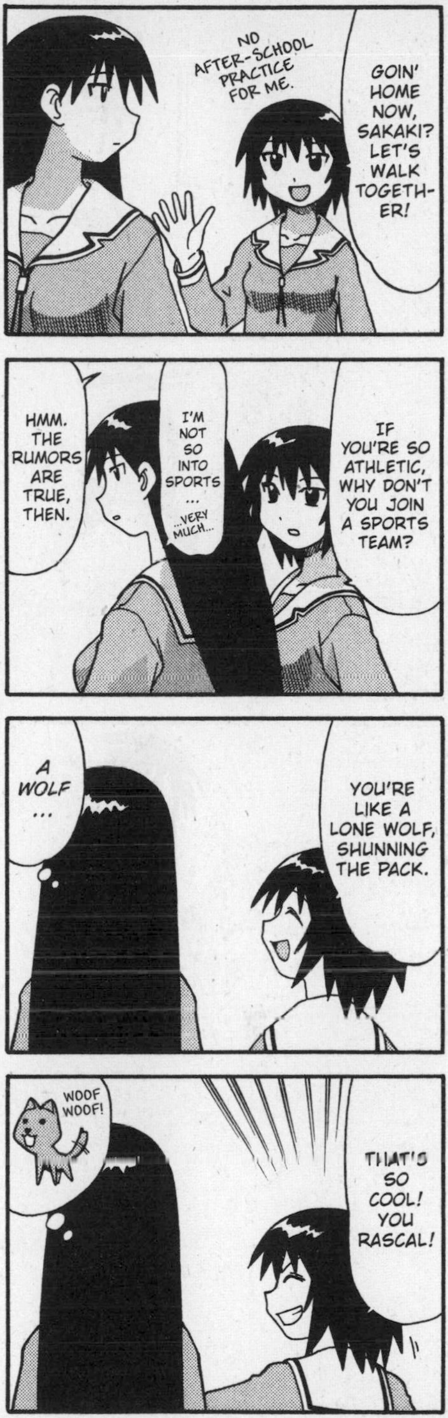
GOIN' HOME NOW, SAKAKI? LET'S WALK TOGETHER!
NO AFTER-SCHOOL PRACTICE FOR ME.
IF YOU'RE SO ATHLETIC, WHY DON'T YOU JOIN A SPORTS TEAM?
I'M NOT SO INTO SPORTS ... ...VERY MUCH...
HMM. THE RUMORS ARE TRUE, THEN.
YOU'RE LIKE A LONE WOLF, SHUNNING THE PACK.
A WOLF ...
THAT'S SO COOL! YOU RASCAL!
WOOF WOOF!

HOW COULD YOU?

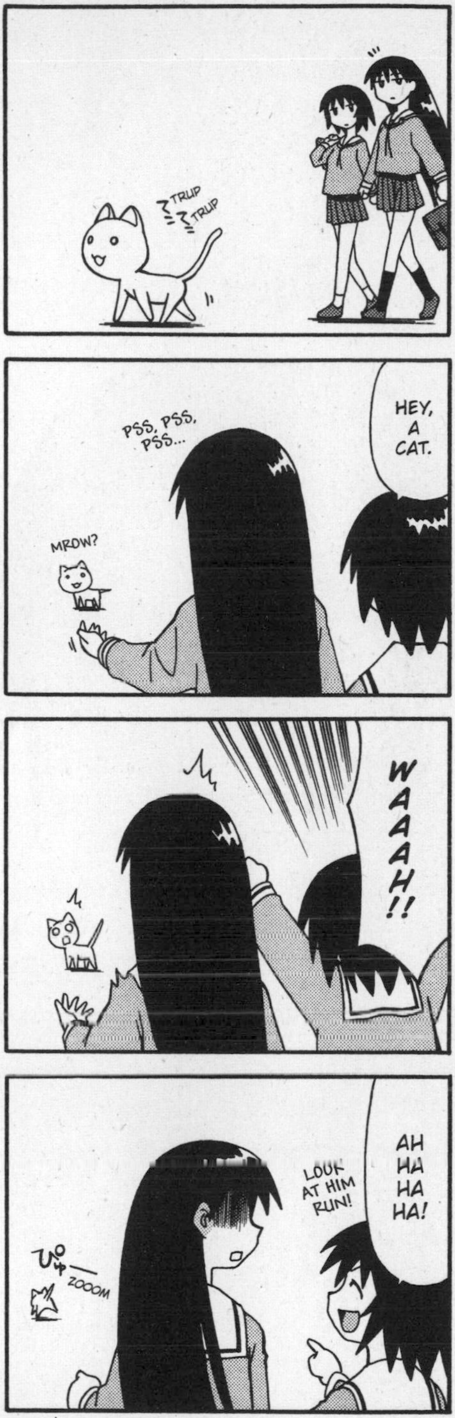
TRUP TRUP
HEY, A CAT.
PSS, PSS, PSS...
MROW?
WAAAAH!!
AH HA HA HA!
LOOK AT HIM RUN!
ぴゅー
ZOOOM

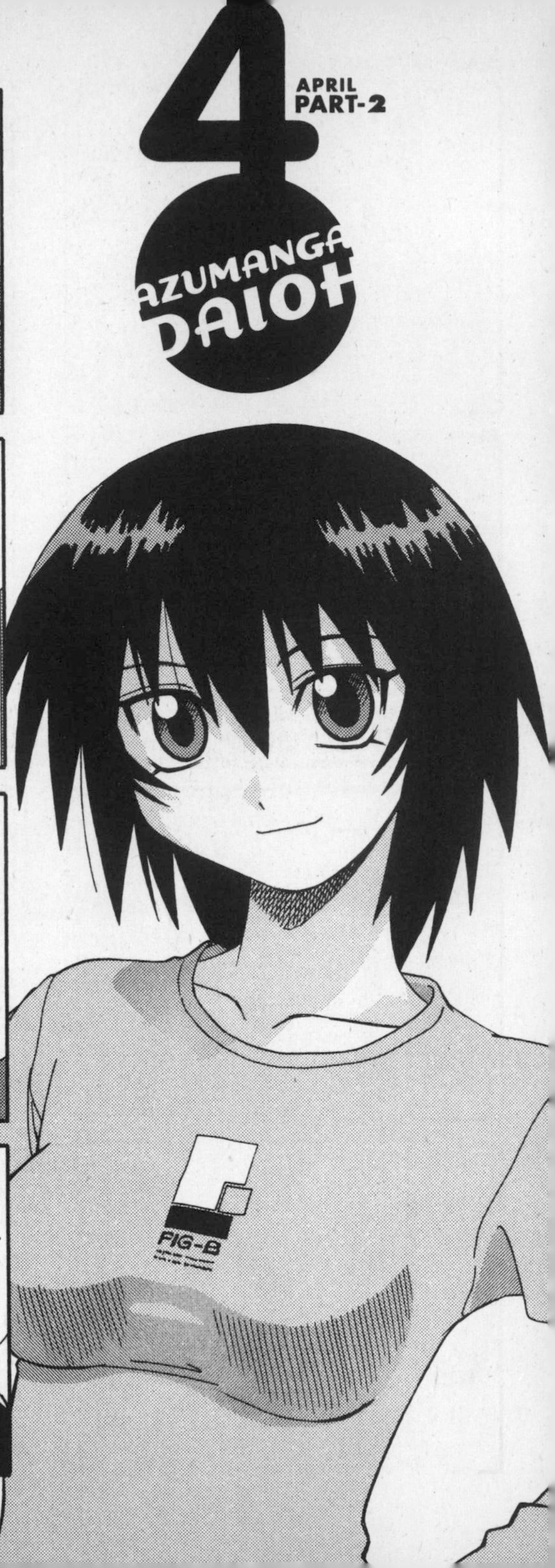
4
APRIL PART-2
AZUMANGA DAIOH
FIG-B

NYAMO'S PLACE

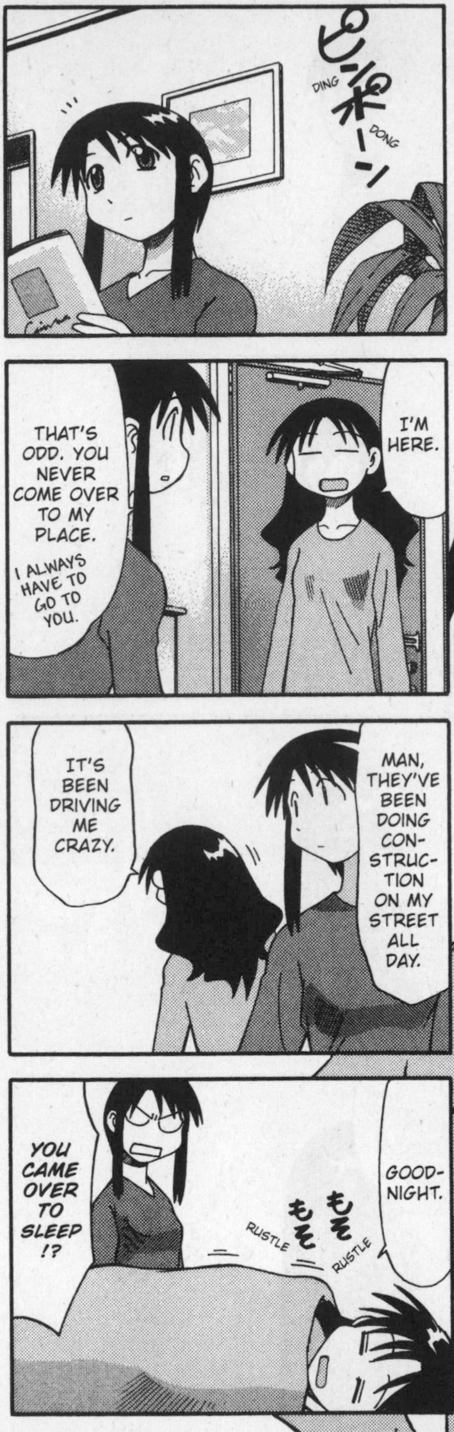
ピンポーン
DING DONG
I'M HERE.
THAT'S ODD. YOU NEVER COME OVER TO MY PLACE.
I ALWAYS HAVE TO GO TO YOU.
MAN, THEY'VE BEEN DOING CONSTRUCTION ON MY STREET ALL DAY.
IT'S BEEN DRIVING ME CRAZY.
GOOD-NIGHT.
もそもそ
RUSTLE RUSTLE
YOU CAME OVER TO SLEEP!?

MORNING

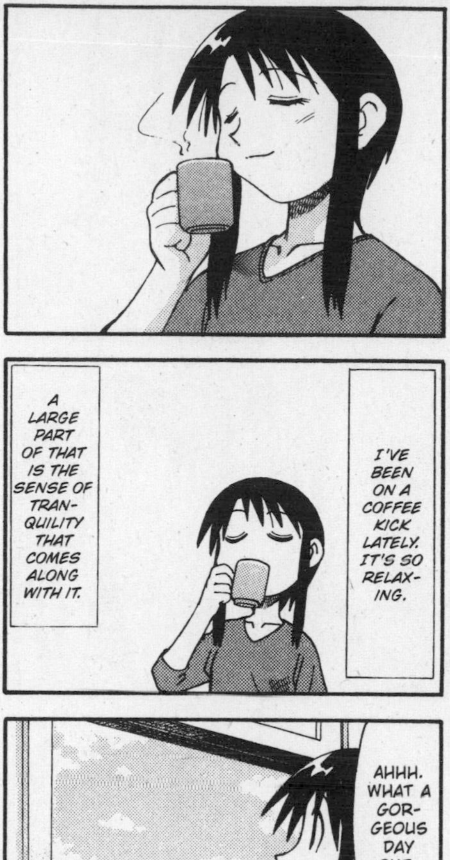
I'VE BEEN ON A COFFEE KICK LATELY. IT'S SO RELAX-ING.
A LARGE PART OF THAT IS THE SENSE OF TRAN-QUILITY THAT COMES ALONG WITH IT.
AHHH. WHAT A GOR-GEOUS DAY OUT-SIDE.
THE SUUUUN... CLOSE THE DAMN CURTAINS!
AAAH! WOULD YOU SHUT UP!!?

MORNING COFFEE

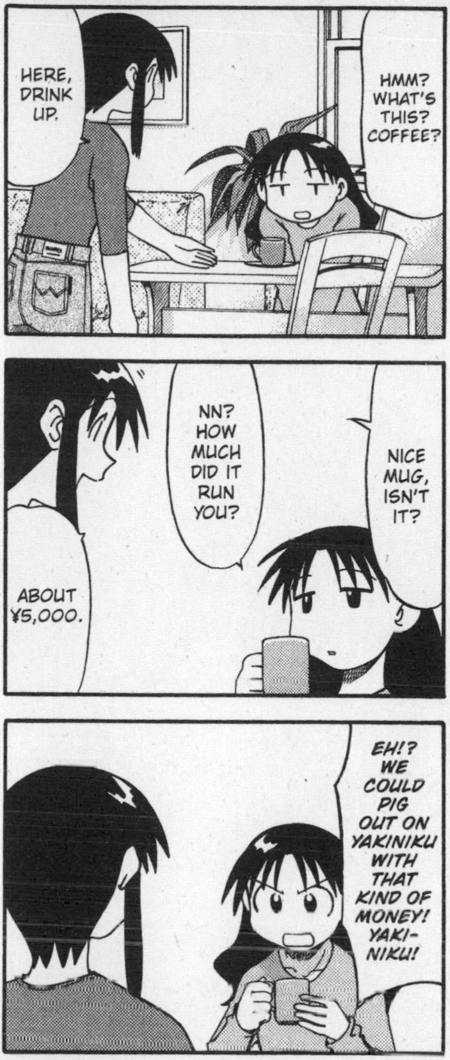
HMM? WHAT'S THIS? COFFEE?
HERE, DRINK UP.
NICE MUG, ISN'T IT?
NN? HOW MUCH DID IT RUN YOU?
ABOUT ¥5,000.
EH!? WE COULD PIG OUT ON YAKINIKU WITH THAT KIND OF MONEY! YAKI-NIKU!
I'VE GOT A GREAT IDEA! LET'S GO OUT FOR YAKINIKU TONIGHT! YAKINIKU!

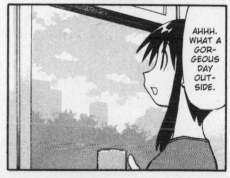

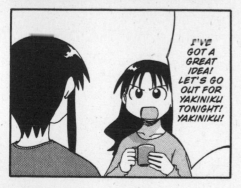

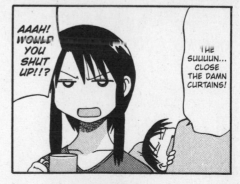

DIFFERENCE IN VALUES

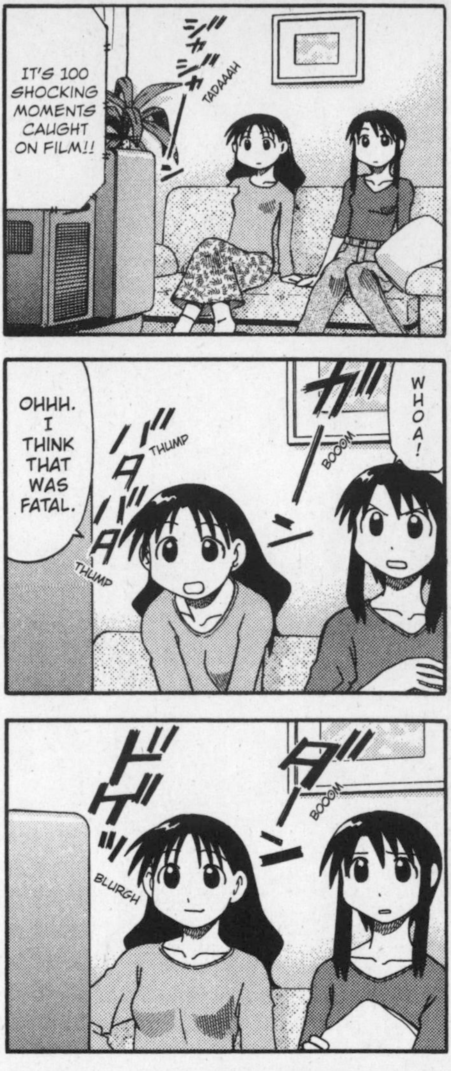
ジャジャーン
TADAAAH
IT'S 100 SHOCKING MOMENTS CAUGHT ON FILM!!
WHOA!
ガーン
BOOOM
バタバタ
THUMP
THUMP
OHHH. I THINK THAT WAS FATAL.
ダーン
BOOOM
ドゲッ
BLURGH
UGH ...
グシャ
SPLAT
AH-HA-HA-HA! WHATTA BUNCH OF IDIOTS!

TOO CORNY

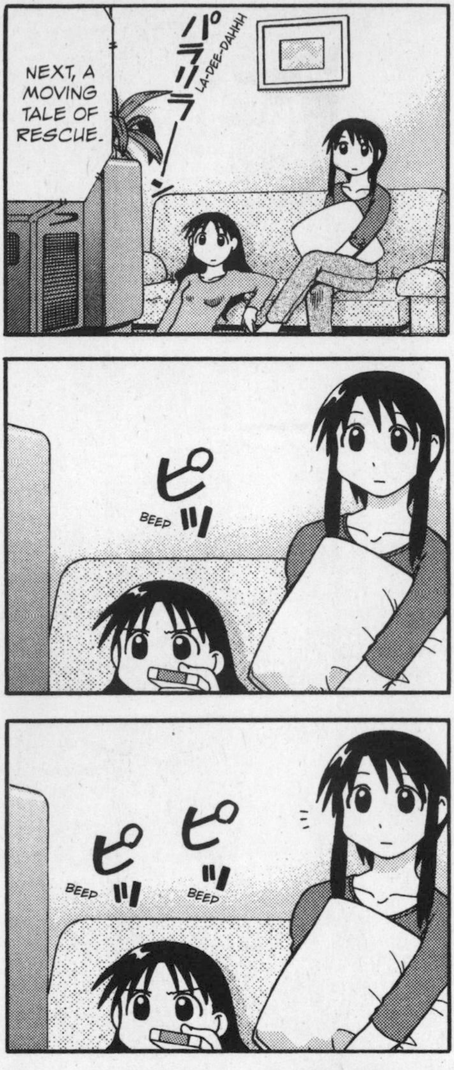
パラリラーン
LA-DEE-DAHHH
NEXT, A MOVING TALE OF RESCUE.
ピッ
BEEP
ピッ
BEEP
ピッ
BEEP
WHY'D YOU CHANGE THE CHAN-NEL?
I HATE RESCUE STORIES.

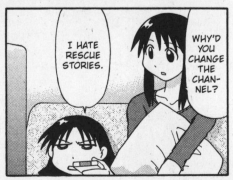

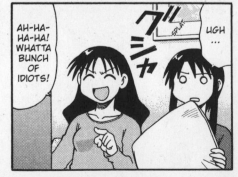

SENIORITY SUPERIORITY

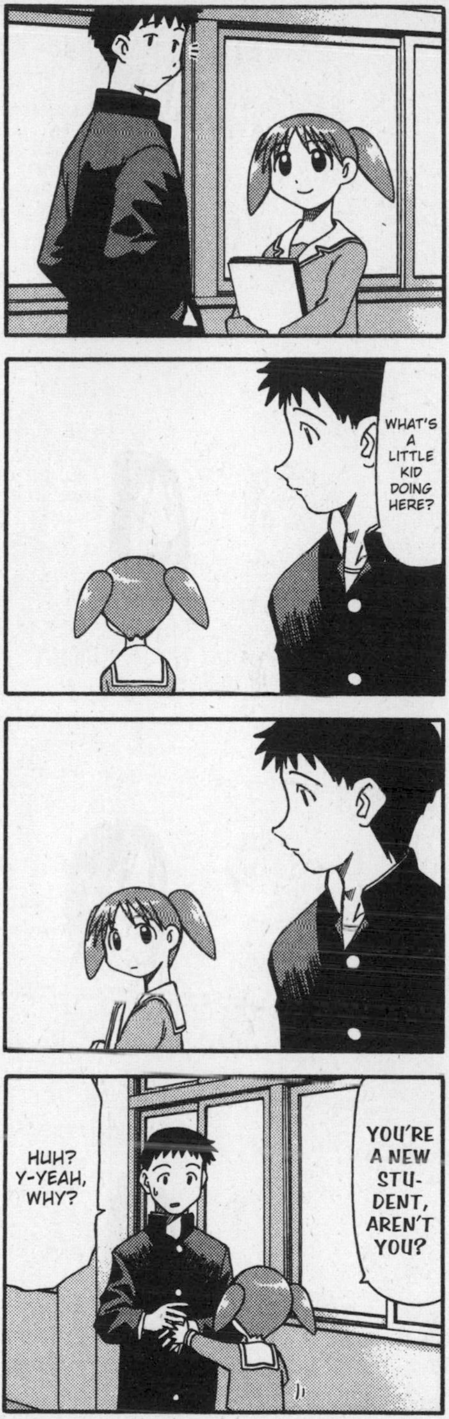
WHAT'S A LITTLE KID DOING HERE?
YOU'RE A NEW STU-DENT, AREN'T YOU?
HUH? Y-YEAH, WHY?

COMMANDING RESPECT

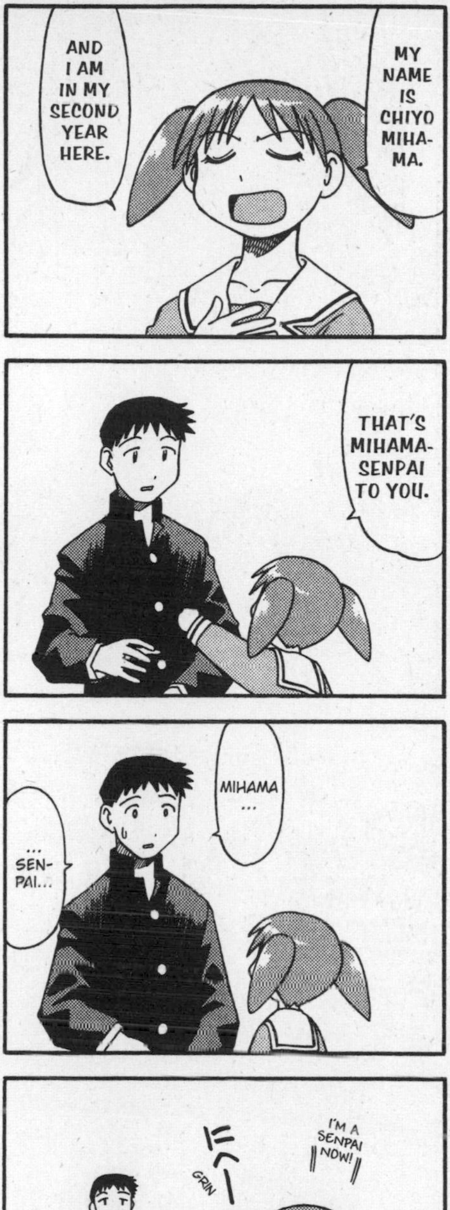
MY NAME IS CHIYO MIHA-MA.
AND I AM IN MY SECOND YEAR HERE.
THAT'S MIHAMA-SENPAI TO YOU.
MIHAMA ...
... SEN-PAI...
I'M A SENPAI NOW!
にへー
GRIN

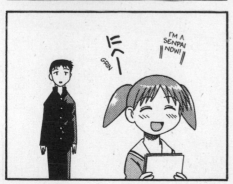

TAKINO TOMO

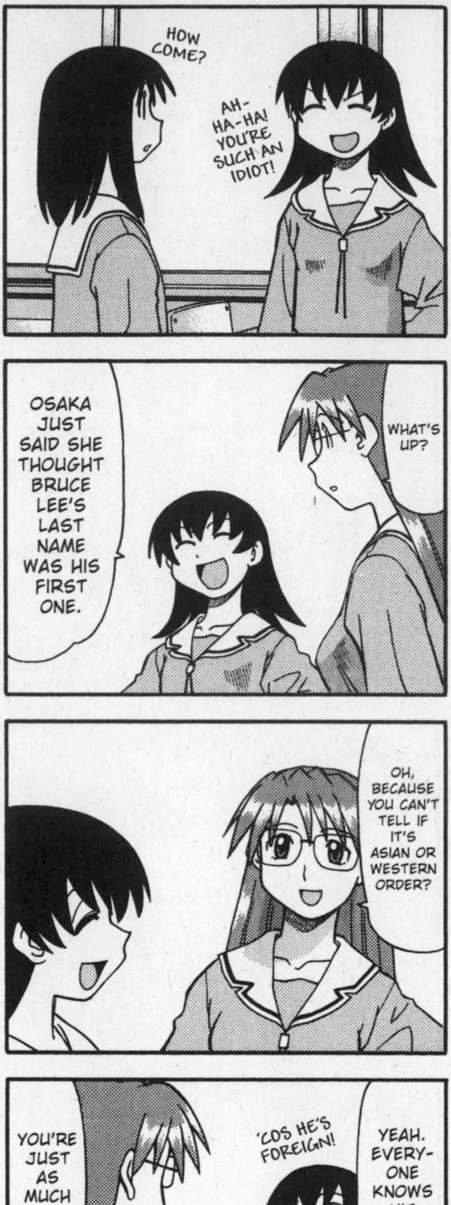
HOW COME?
AH-HA-HA! YOU'RE SUCH AN IDIOT!
WHAT'S UP?
OSAKA JUST SAID SHE THOUGHT BRUCE LEE'S LAST NAME WAS HIS FIRST ONE.
OH, BECAUSE YOU CAN'T TELL IF IT'S ASIAN OR WESTERN ORDER?
YEAH. EVERY-ONE KNOWS HIS FAMILY NAME IS "SLEE."
'COS HE'S FOREIGN!
YOU'RE JUST AS MUCH OF AN IDIOT AS SHE IS.

TIPSY PEOPLE

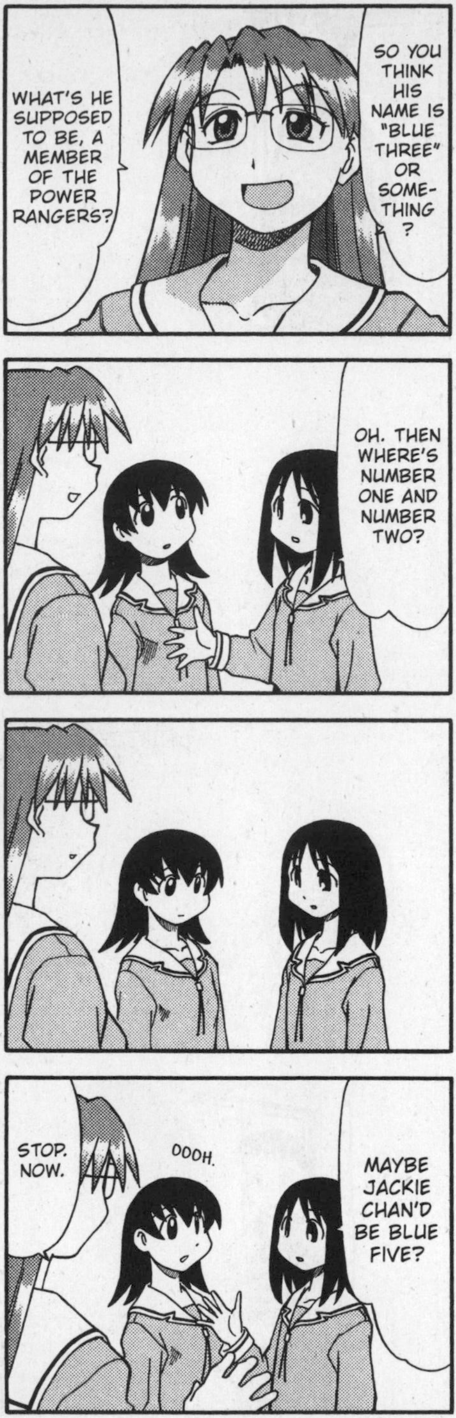
SO YOU THINK HIS NAME IS "BLUE THREE" OR SOME-THING ?
WHAT'S HE SUPPOSED TO BE, A MEMBER OF THE POWER RANGERS?
OH. THEN WHERE'S NUMBER ONE AND NUMBER TWO?
MAYBE JACKIE CHAN'D BE BLUE FIVE?
OOOH.
STOP. NOW.

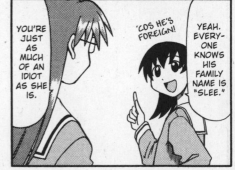

OH MY...

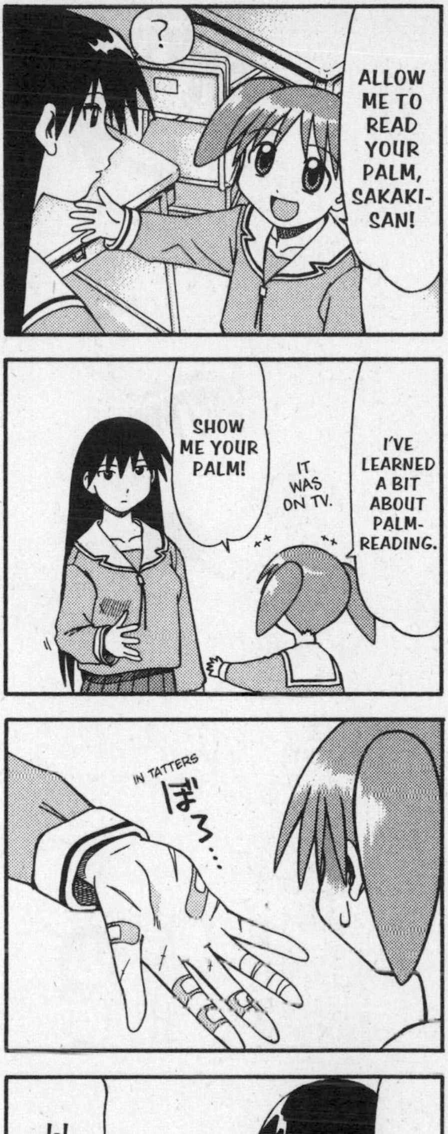
?
ALLOW ME TO READ YOUR PALM, SAKAKI-SAN!
I'VE LEARNED A BIT ABOUT PALM-READING.
IT WAS ON TV.
SHOW ME YOUR PALM!
IN TATTERS
ぼろ…
WELL ...?
I-I DON'T KNOW... UM...

SO CURIOUS

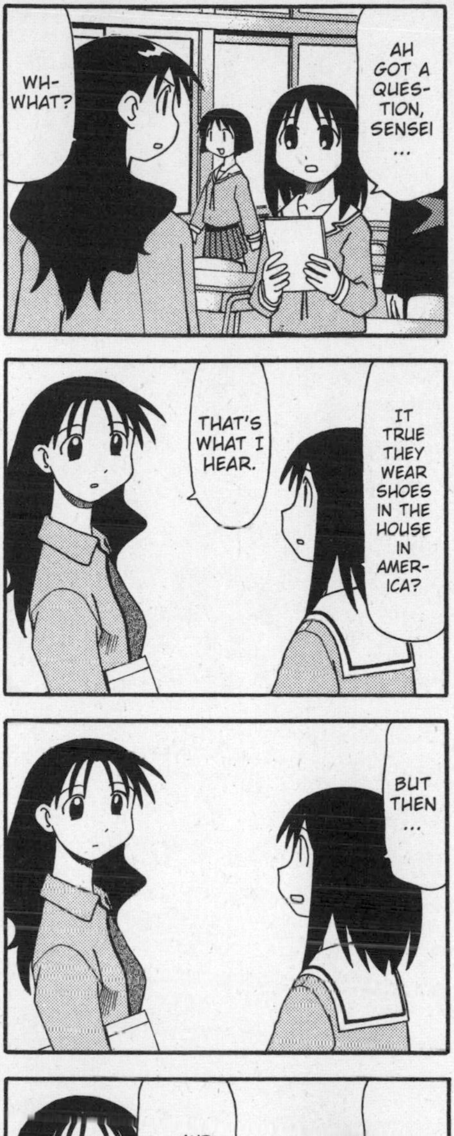
AH GOT A QUESTION, SENSEI ...
WH-WHAT?
IT TRUE THEY WEAR SHOES IN THE HOUSE IN AMERICA?
THAT'S WHAT I HEAR.
BUT THEN ...
...WH-WHAT IF YOU STEPPED IN DOG POO OUTSIDE...
...AND YOU NEVER NOTICED? AND THEN...

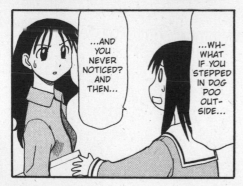

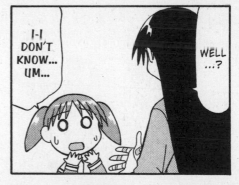

SHOWDOWN

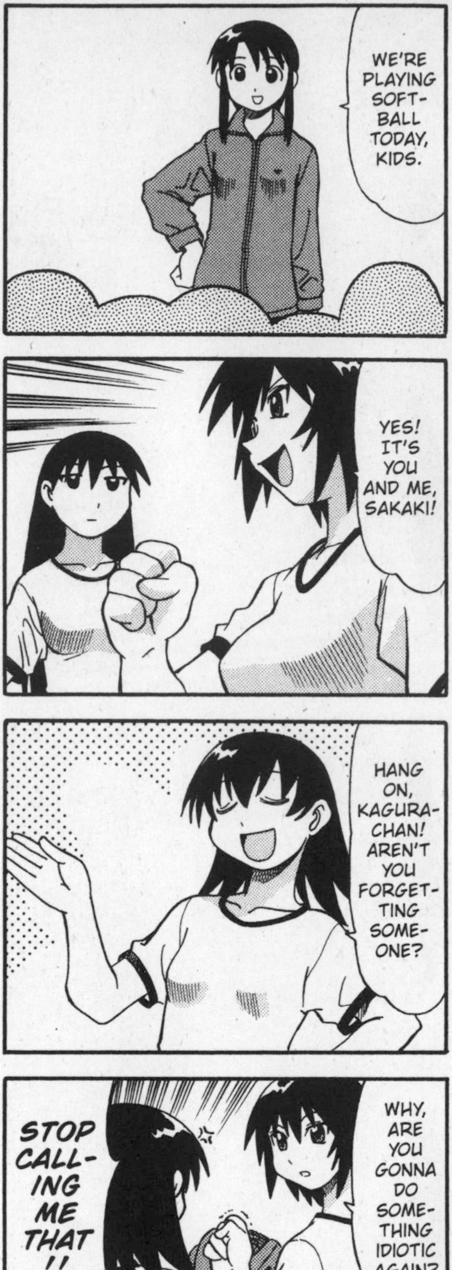
WE'RE PLAYING SOFT-BALL TODAY, KIDS.
YES! IT'S YOU AND ME, SAKAKI!
HANG ON, KAGURA-CHAN! AREN'T YOU FORGET-TING SOME-ONE?
WHY, ARE YOU GONNA DO SOME-THING IDIOTIC AGAIN?
STOP CALL-ING ME THAT!!

A THREE-POINTER, I SUPPOSE

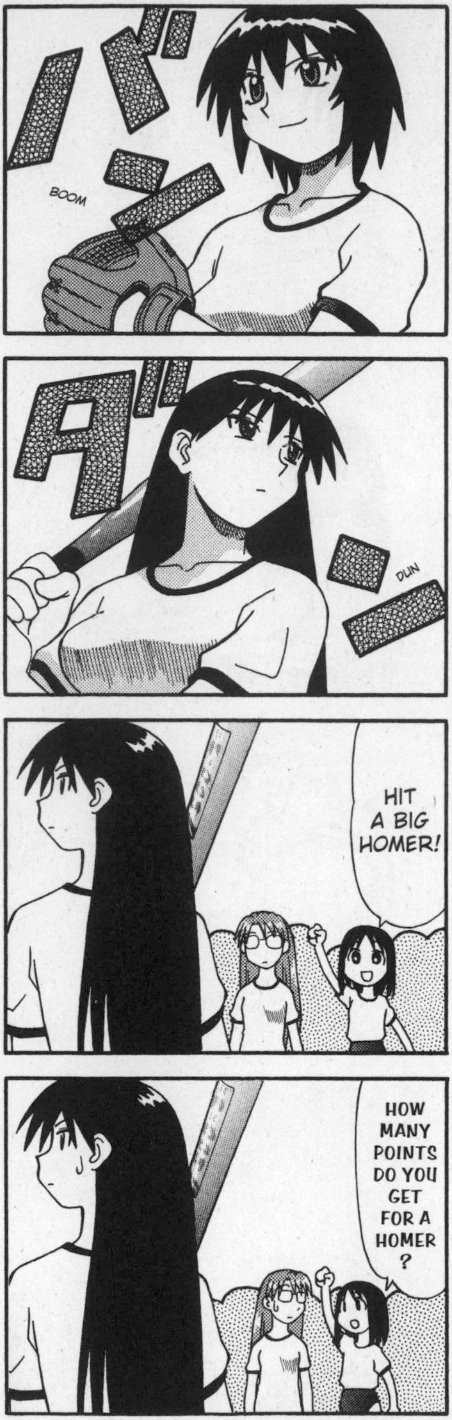
BOOM
DUN
HIT A BIG HOMER!
HOW MANY POINTS DO YOU GET FOR A HOMER?

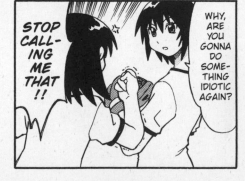

GOLD GLOVER

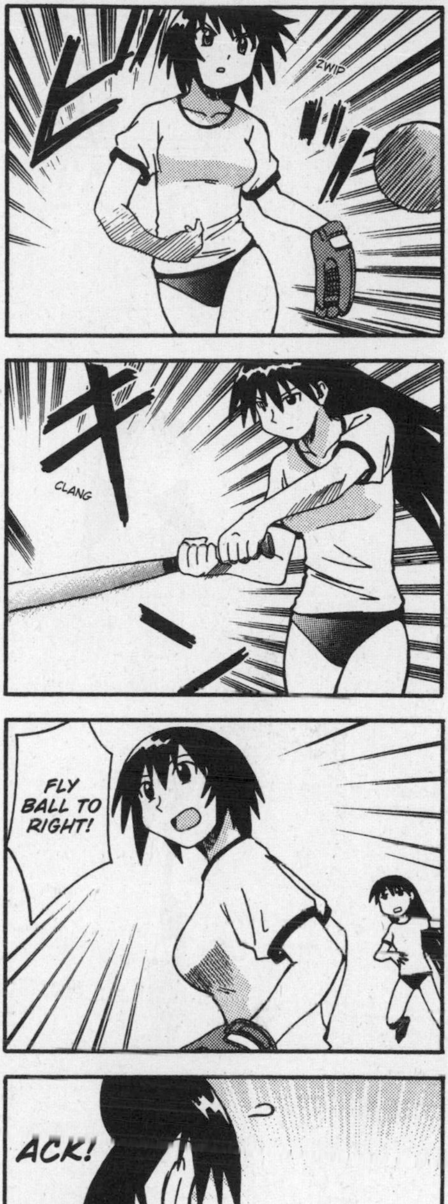
ZWIP
CLANG
FLY BALL TO RIGHT!
ACK!

HIT

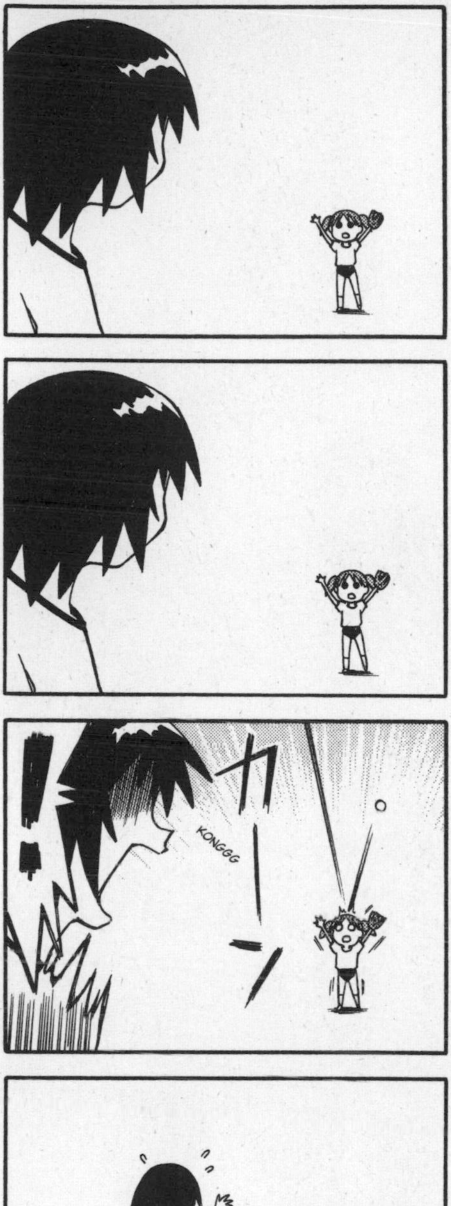
KONGGG

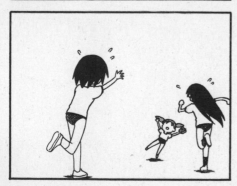

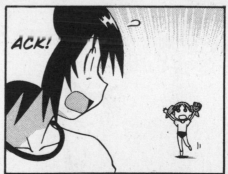

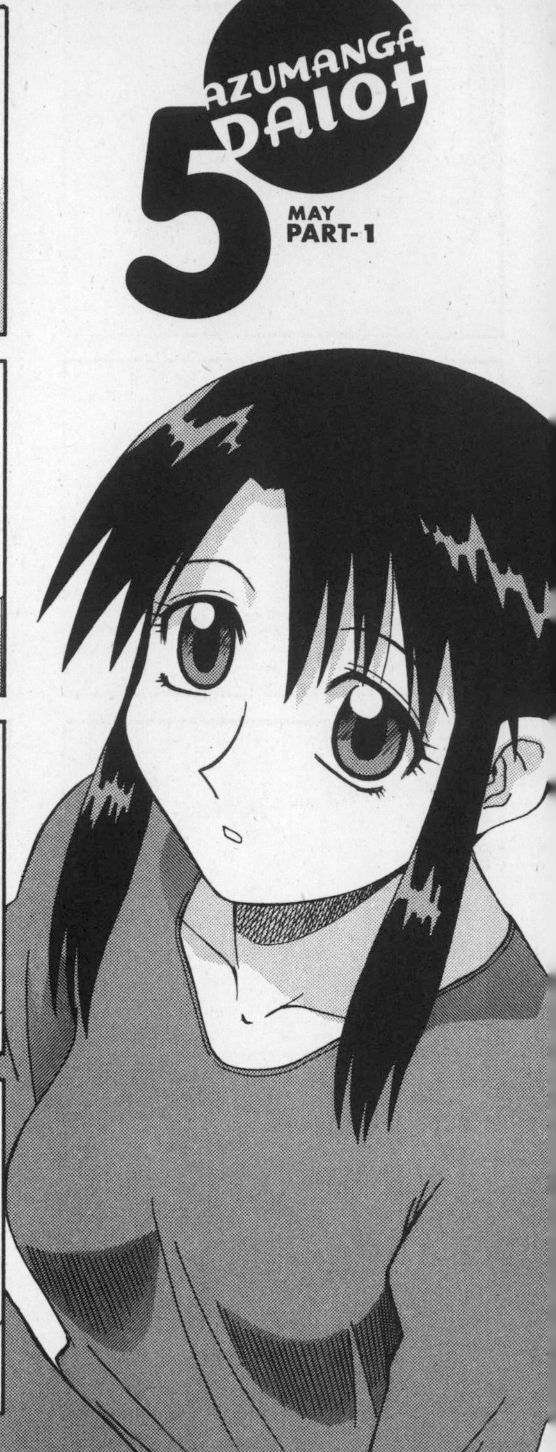
AZUMANGA DAIOH
5
MAY
PART-1

YUKARI'S HERE

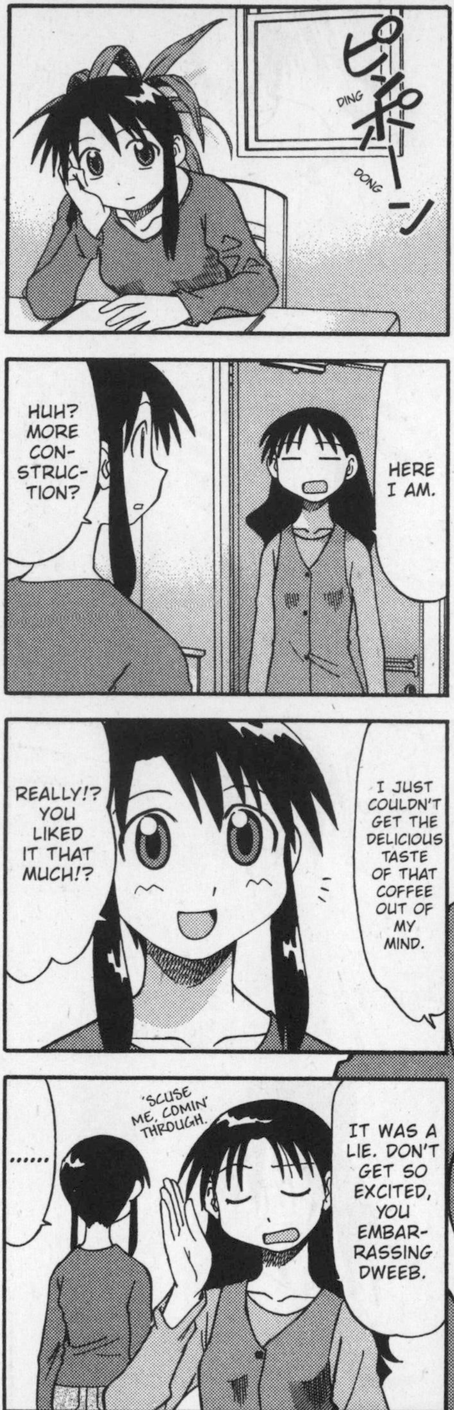
ピンポーン
DING
DONG
HERE I AM.
HUH? MORE CON-STRUC-TION?
I JUST COULDN'T GET THE DELICIOUS TASTE OF THAT COFFEE OUT OF MY MIND.
REALLY!? YOU LIKED IT THAT MUCH!?
IT WAS A LIE. DON'T GET SO EXCITED, YOU EMBAR-RASSING DWEEB.
'SCUSE ME, COMIN' THROUGH.
......

A GOOD NIGHT'S SLEEP

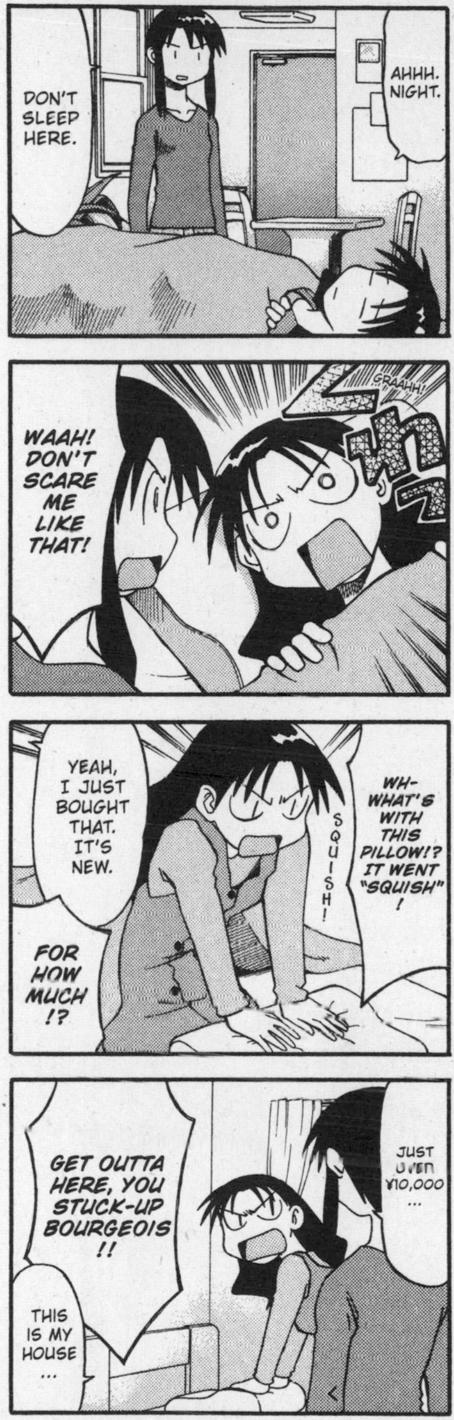
AHHH. NIGHT.
DON'T SLEEP HERE.
GRAAHH!
WAAH! DON'T SCARE ME LIKE THAT!
WH- WHAT'S WITH THIS PILLOW!? IT WENT "SQUISH"!
SQUISH!
YEAH, I JUST BOUGHT THAT. IT'S NEW.
FOR HOW MUCH!?
JUST OVER ¥10,000...
GET OUTTA HERE, YOU STUCK-UP BOURGEOIS!!
THIS IS MY HOUSE...

SQUISHY

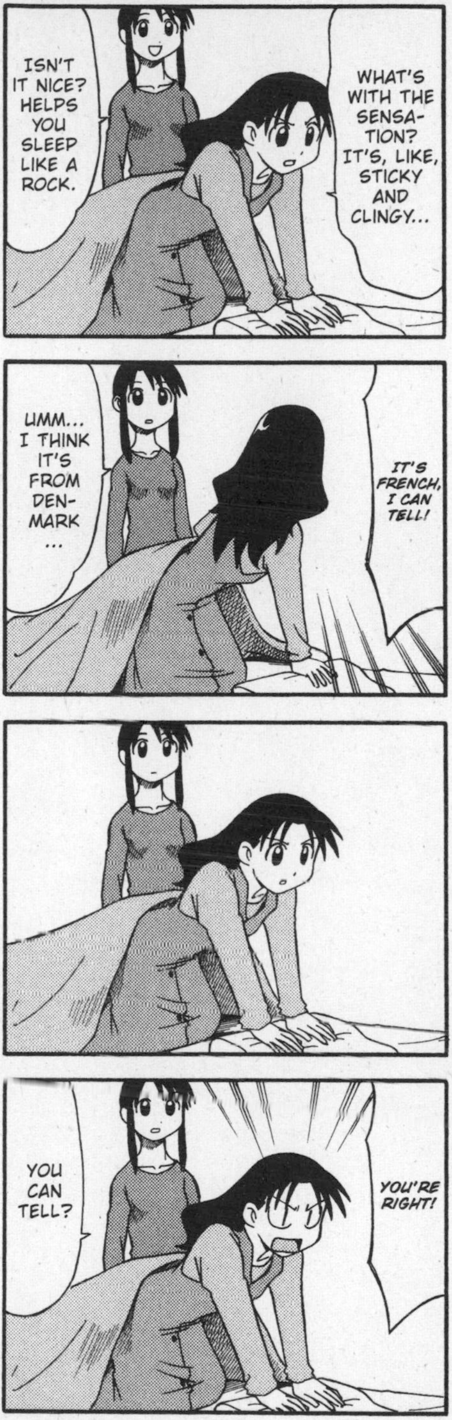
WHAT'S WITH THE SENSATION? IT'S, LIKE, STICKY AND CLINGY...
ISN'T IT NICE? HELPS YOU SLEEP LIKE A ROCK.
IT'S FRENCH, I CAN TELL!
UMM... I THINK IT'S FROM DENMARK...
YOU'RE RIGHT!
YOU CAN TELL?

FAST ASLEEP

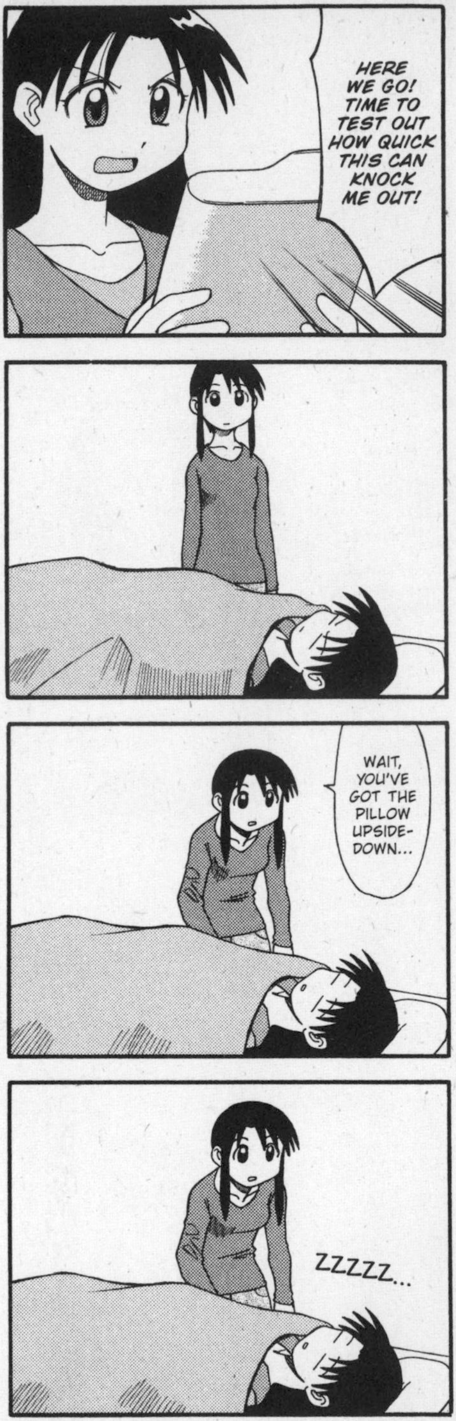
HERE WE GO! TIME TO TEST OUT HOW QUICK THIS CAN KNOCK ME OUT!
WAIT, YOU'VE GOT THE PILLOW UPSIDE-DOWN...
ZZZZZ...

WHAT ARE YOU DOING?

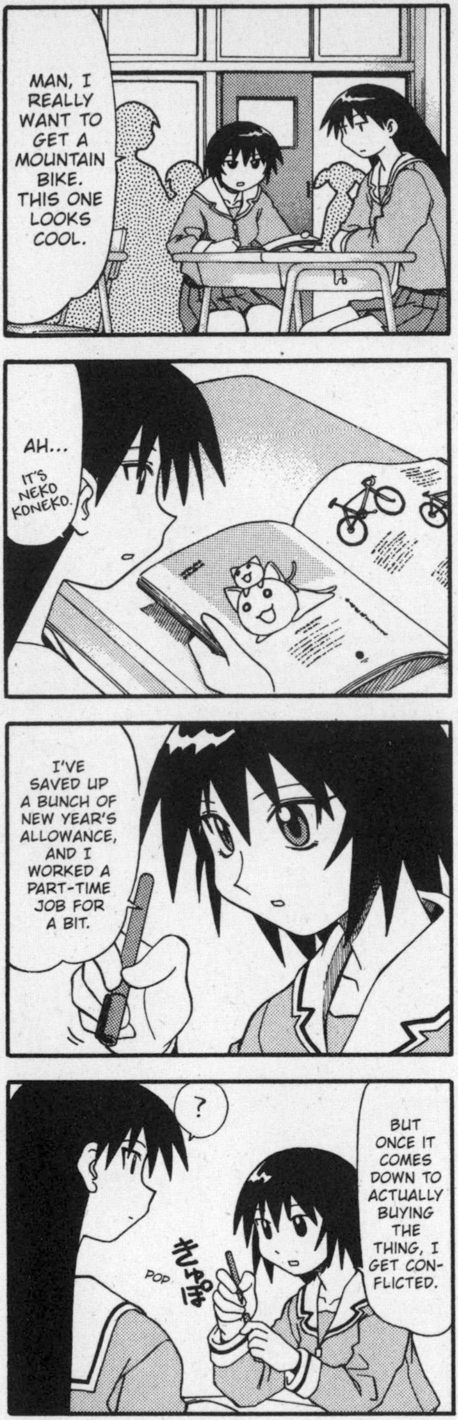
MAN, I REALLY WANT TO GET A MOUNTAIN BIKE. THIS ONE LOOKS COOL.
AH...
IT'S NEKO KONEKO.
I'VE SAVED UP A BUNCH OF NEW YEAR'S ALLOWANCE, AND I WORKED A PART-TIME JOB FOR A BIT.
BUT ONCE IT COMES DOWN TO ACTUALLY BUYING THE THING, I GET CONFLICTED.
?
きゅぽ
POP

TRANSFORMATION

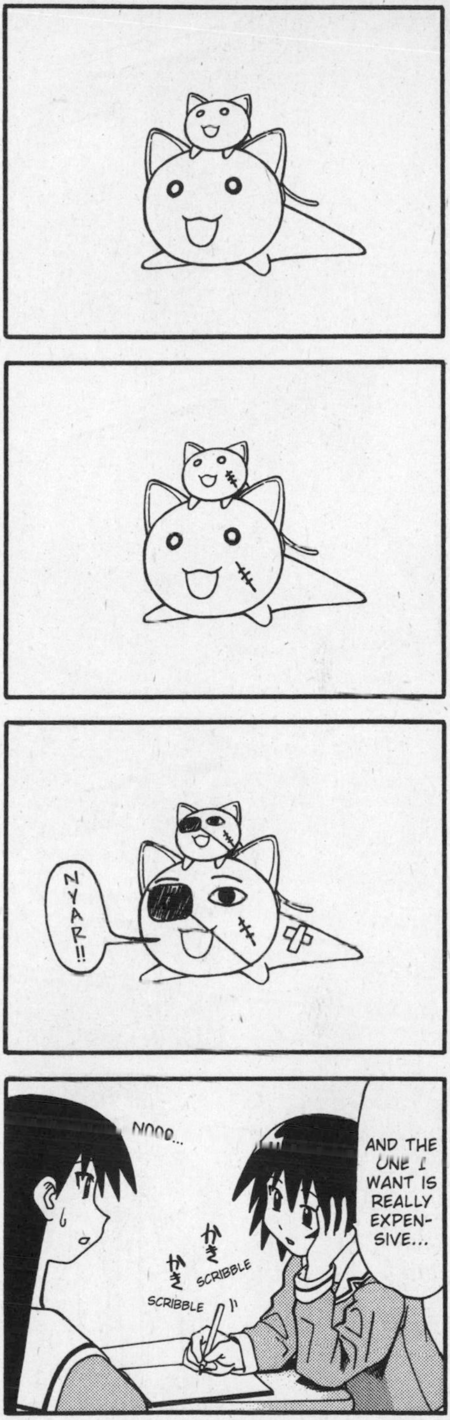
NYAR!!
AND THE ONE I WANT IS REALLY EXPENSIVE...
NOOO...
かき
SCRIBBLE
かき
SCRIBBLE

LOOKS TOUGH

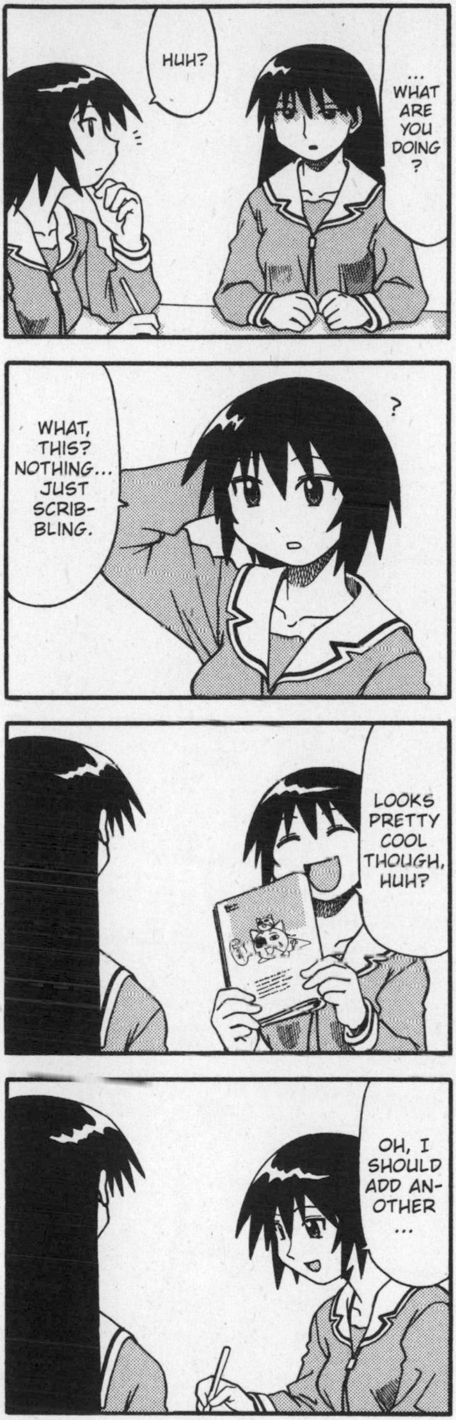
...WHAT ARE YOU DOING?
HUH?
?
WHAT, THIS? NOTHING... JUST SCRIB-BLING.
LOOKS PRETTY COOL THOUGH, HUH?
OH, I SHOULD ADD AN-OTHER...

SUCCESSFUL DIET

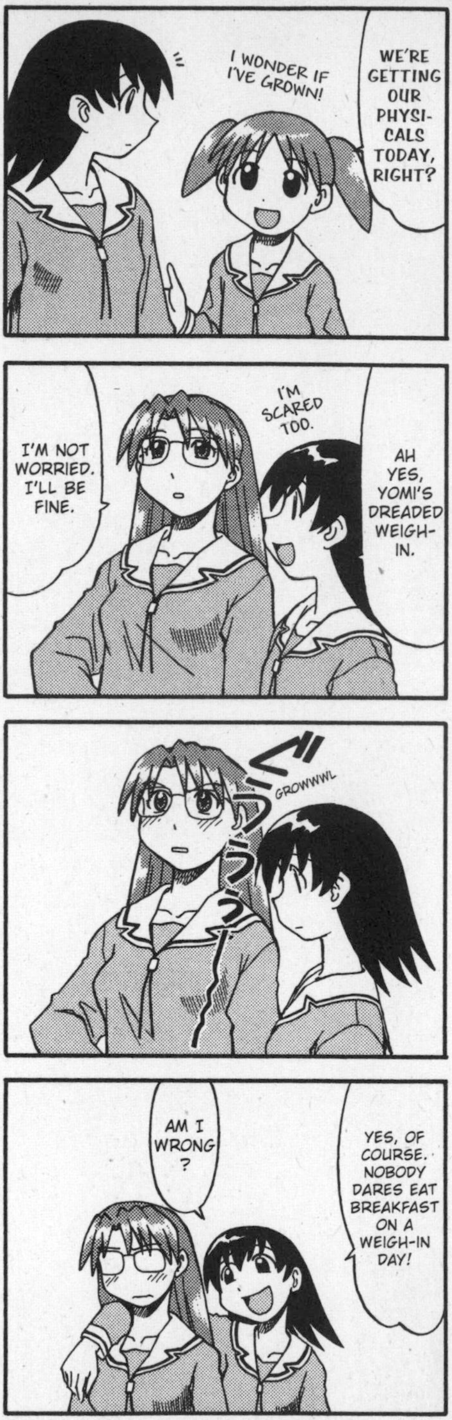

WE'RE GETTING OUR PHYSICALS TODAY, RIGHT?
I WONDER IF I'VE GROWN!
AH YES, YOMI'S DREADED WEIGH-IN.
I'M SCARED TOO.
I'M NOT WORRIED. I'LL BE FINE.
GROWWWL
YES, OF COURSE. NOBODY DARES EAT BREAKFAST ON A WEIGH-IN DAY!
AM I WRONG?

JUST CURIOUS

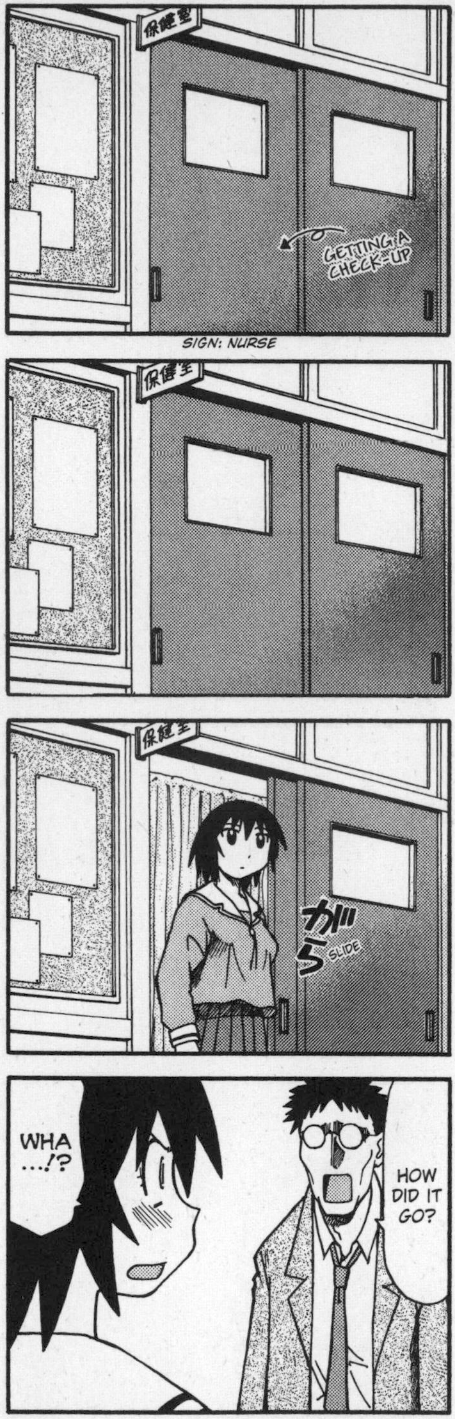

保健室
GETTING A CHECK-UP
SIGN: NURSE
SLIDE
HOW DID IT GO?
WHA ...!?

ONCE MORE PLEASE

AH DON'T UNDER-STAND THIS ENGLISH QUES-TION, CHIYO-CHAN.
WELL, IN THIS CASE...
UH-HUH?
YOU'D...
DID YOU GET ALL THAT?
U-UMM...
<ONE AGAIN?>
...I THINK YOU MEAN <ONCE AGAIN>?
AND MAYBE A <PLEASE> ON THE END.

WHAT'S GOING ON!?

LET'S STOP BY THE BOOKSTORE!
OKAY.
<EXCUSE ME.>
WHOA!
JABBER
JIBBER
JIBBER
JIBBER
WHOA!
JABBER
JABBER

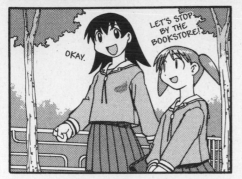

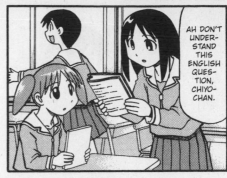

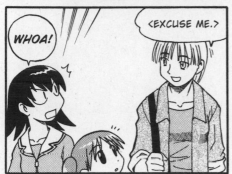

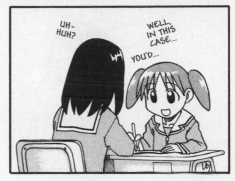

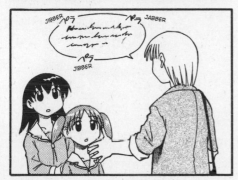

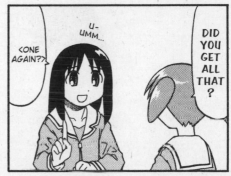

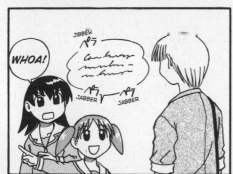

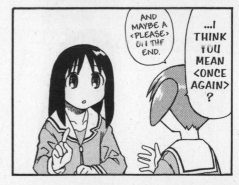

THE INCREDIBLE CHIYO

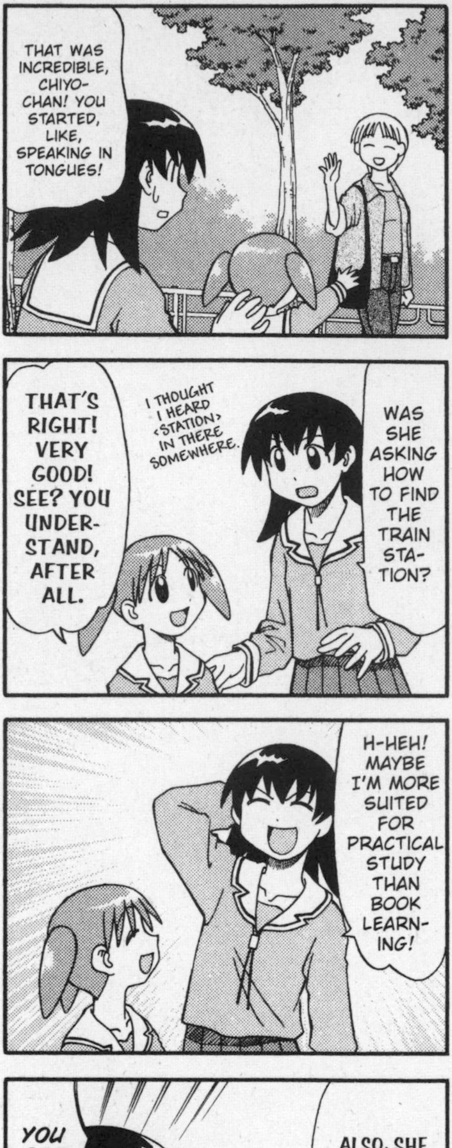
THAT WAS INCREDIBLE, CHIYO-CHAN! YOU STARTED, LIKE, SPEAKING IN TONGUES!
WAS SHE ASKING HOW TO FIND THE TRAIN STATION?
I THOUGHT I HEARD <STATION> IN THERE SOMEWHERE.
THAT'S RIGHT! VERY GOOD! SEE? YOU UNDERSTAND, AFTER ALL.
H-HEH! MAYBE I'M MORE SUITED FOR PRACTICAL STUDY THAN BOOK LEARNING!
ALSO, SHE FLEW HERE FROM NORTH CAROLINA ON BUSINESS, AND APPARENTLY IT'S HER FIRST TIME IN JAPAN.
AND SHE SAID SHE WANTED TO FIND SOME GOOD SUSHI TONIGHT.
YOU GOT ALL THAT!?

HERE I GO

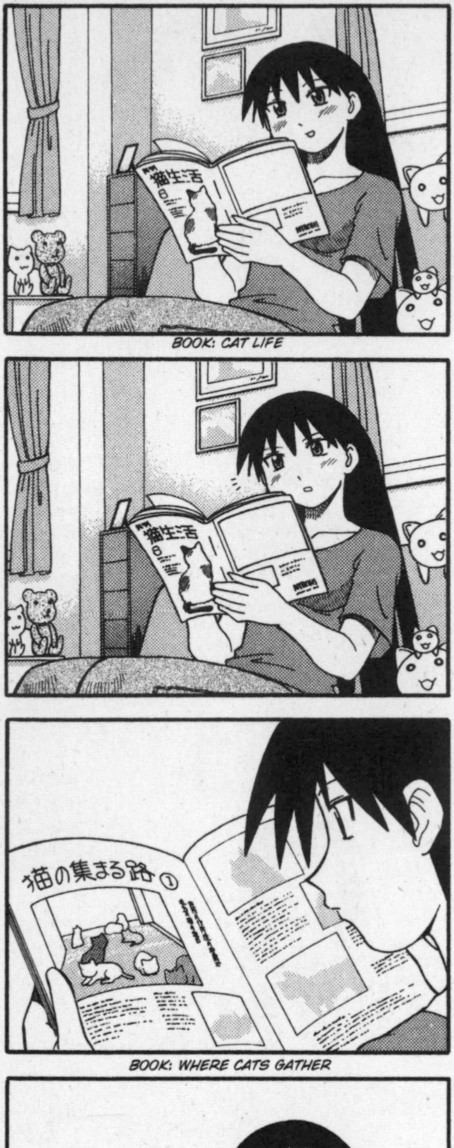
猫生活
猫の集まる路①
バン
SLAM

BOOK: CAT LIFE

BOOK: WHERE CATS GATHER

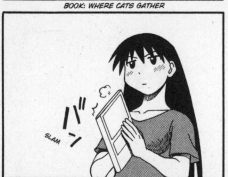

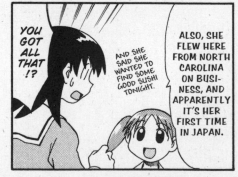

IN A RUSH

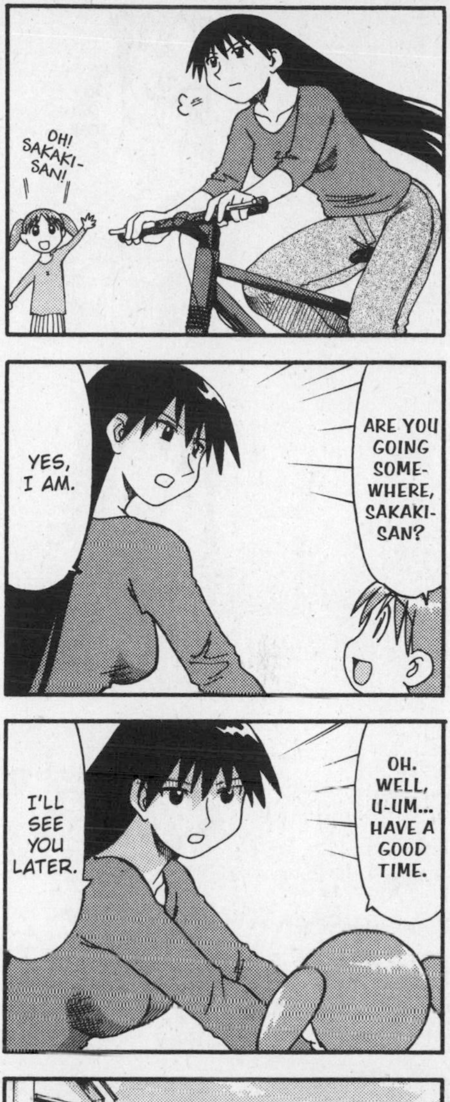
OH! SAKAKI-SAN!
ARE YOU GOING SOME-WHERE, SAKAKI-SAN?
YES, I AM.
OH. WELL, U-UM... HAVE A GOOD TIME.
I'LL SEE YOU LATER.
?
FZZZZ.

COVERED IN CATS

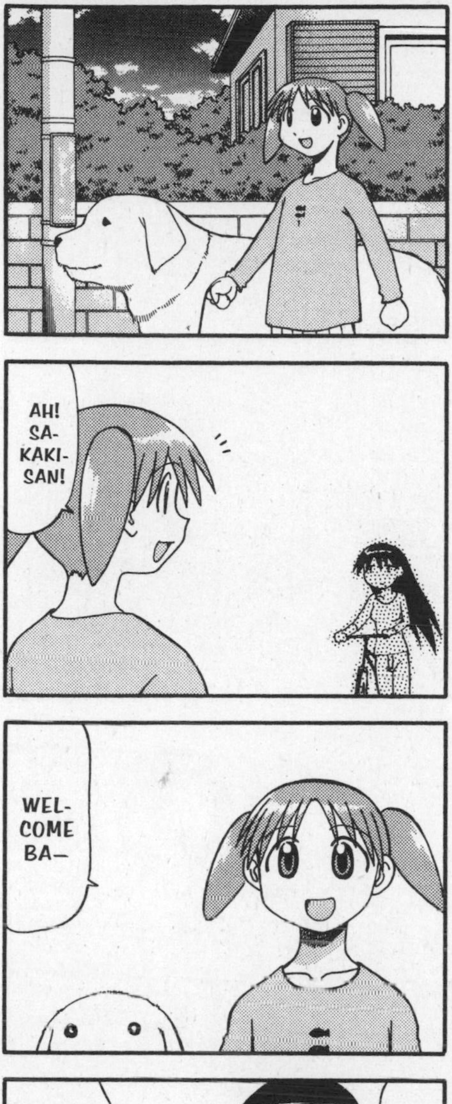
AH! SA-KAKI-SAN!
WEL-COME BA—
THEY JUMPED ME...
HUH? BUT... HUH?

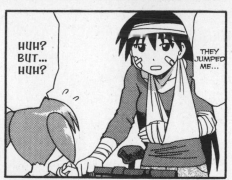

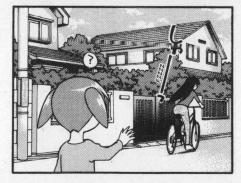

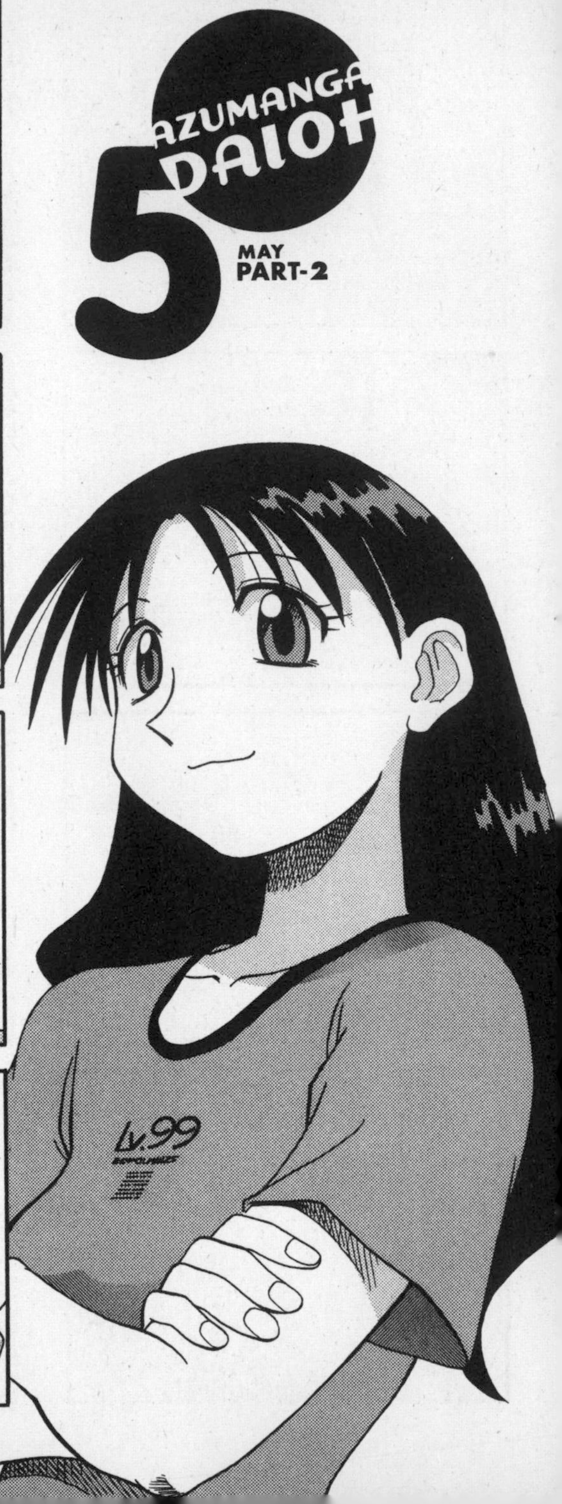
AZUMANGA DAIOH
5
MAY
PART-2
Lv.99

TOMORROW'S A VACATION DAY

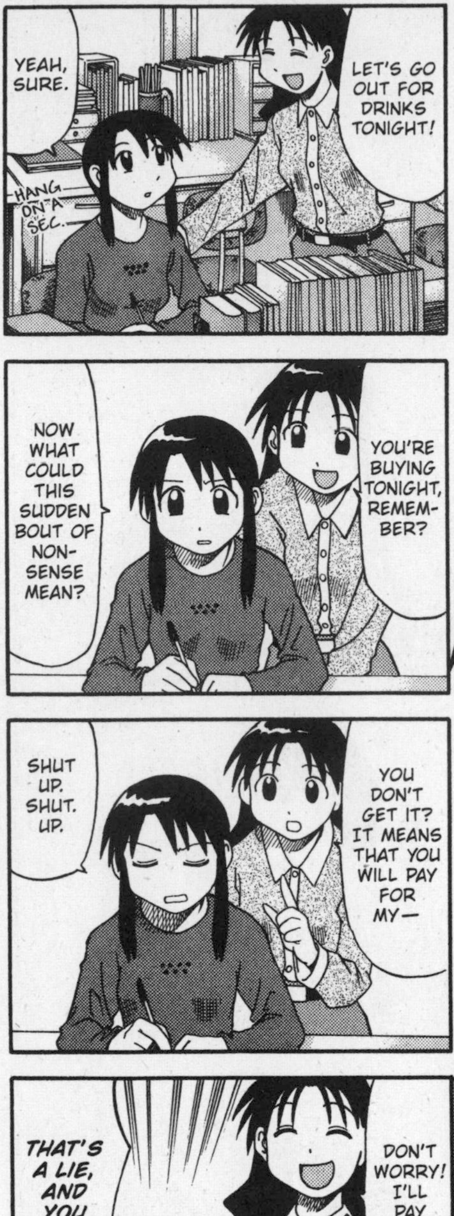
LET'S GO OUT FOR DRINKS TONIGHT!
YEAH, SURE.
HANG ON A SEC.
YOU'RE BUYING TONIGHT, REMEMBER?
NOW WHAT COULD THIS SUDDEN BOUT OF NONSENSE MEAN?
YOU DON'T GET IT? IT MEANS THAT YOU WILL PAY FOR MY—
SHUT UP. SHUT. UP.
DON'T WORRY! I'LL PAY NEXT TIME!
THAT'S A LIE, AND YOU DAMN WELL KNOW IT!!

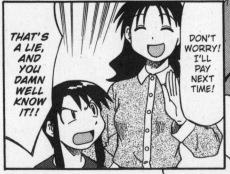

POINTER

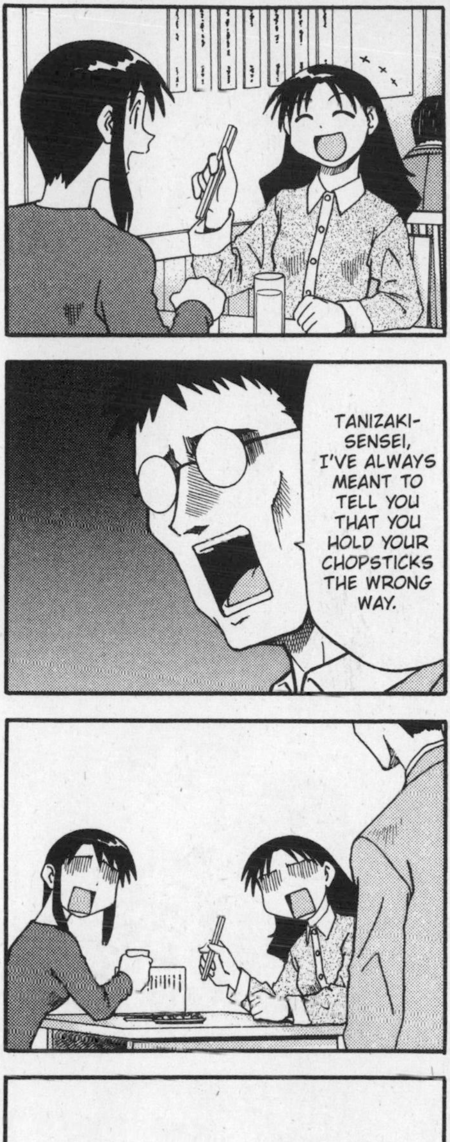
TANIZAKI-SENSEI, I'VE ALWAYS MEANT TO TELL YOU THAT YOU HOLD YOUR CHOPSTICKS THE WRONG WAY.

I'LL FIX IT

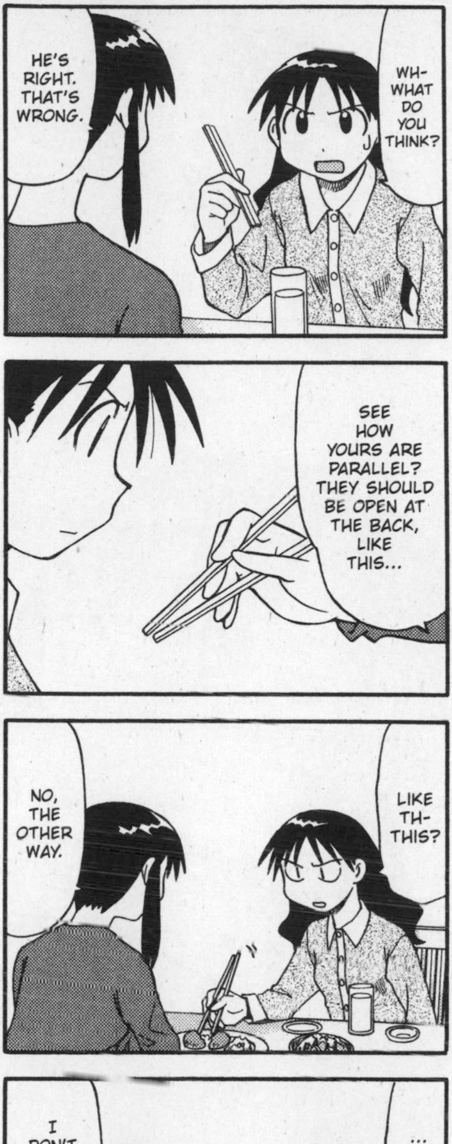
WH-WHAT DO YOU THINK?
HE'S RIGHT. THAT'S WRONG.
SEE HOW YOURS ARE PARALLEL? THEY SHOULD BE OPEN AT THE BACK, LIKE THIS...
LIKE TH-THIS?
NO, THE OTHER WAY.
...LIKE THIS?
I DON'T REALLY CARE, JUST STOP DEMOLISHING THE FOOD.

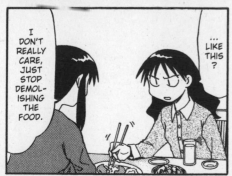

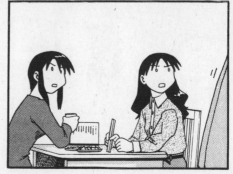

EXAMPLE

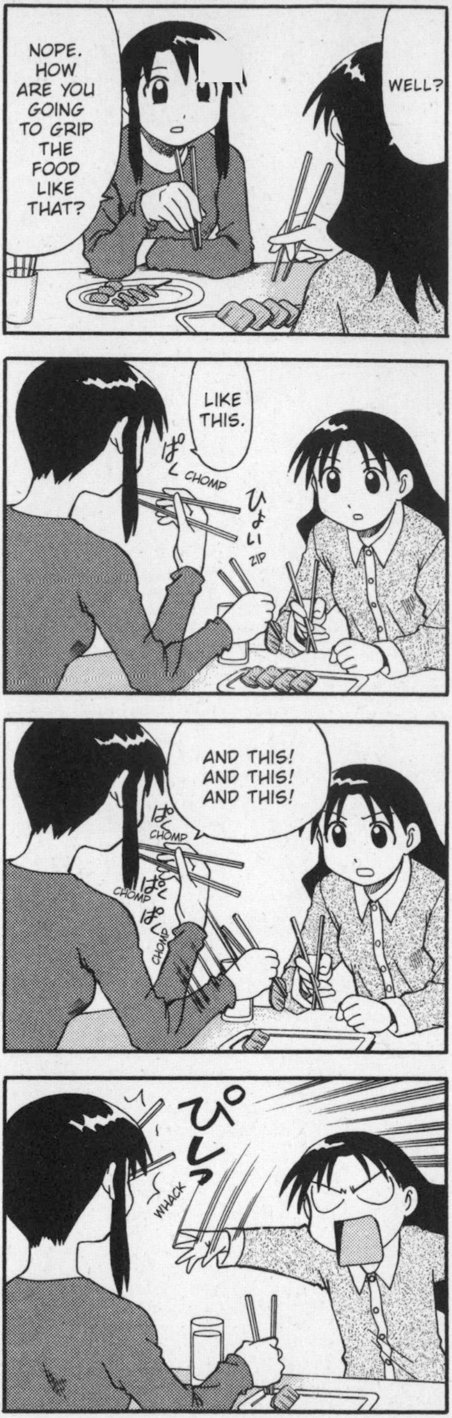
WELL?
NOPE. HOW ARE YOU GOING TO GRIP THE FOOD LIKE THAT?
LIKE THIS.
ぱく CHOMP
ひょい ZIP
AND THIS! AND THIS! AND THIS!
ぱく CHOMP
ぱく CHOMP
ぱく CHOMP
ぴしっ
WHACK

SLEEPY

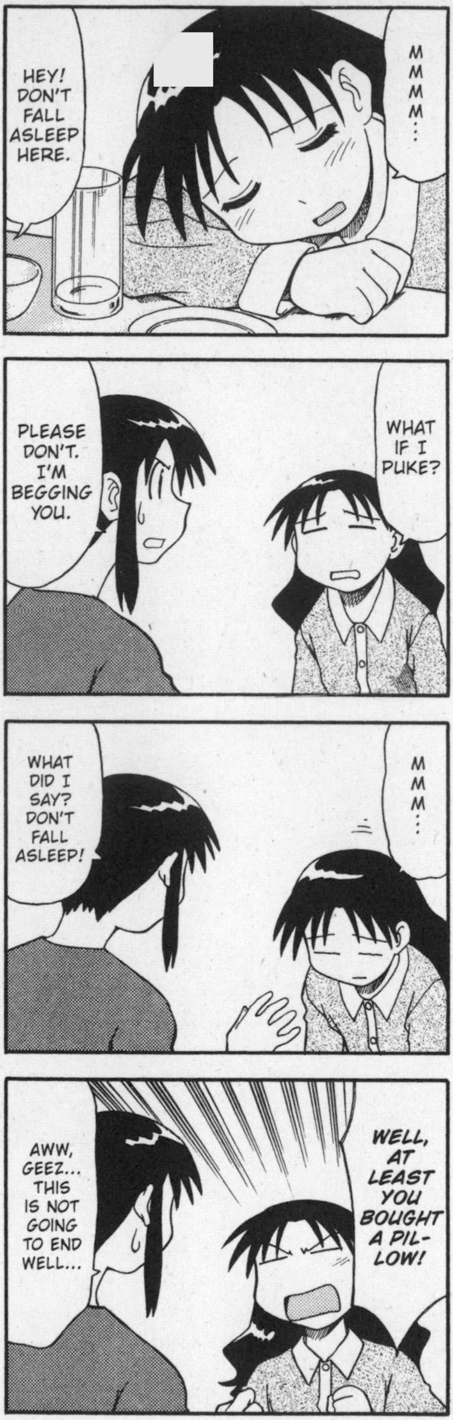
MMMM...
HEY! DON'T FALL ASLEEP HERE.
WHAT IF I PUKE?
PLEASE DON'T. I'M BEGGING YOU.
MMM...
WHAT DID I SAY? DON'T FALL ASLEEP!
WELL, AT LEAST YOU BOUGHT A PIL-LOW!
AWW, GEEZ... THIS IS NOT GOING TO END WELL...

AN ADULT'S EYES

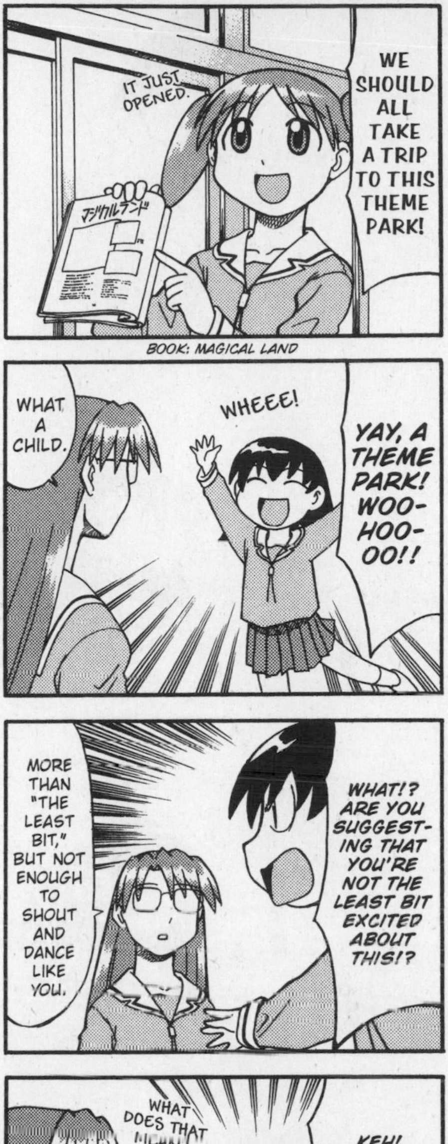
WE SHOULD ALL TAKE A TRIP TO THIS THEME PARK!
IT JUST OPENED.
マジカルランド
BOOK: MAGICAL LAND
YAY, A THEME PARK! WOO-HOO-OO!!
WHEEE!
WHAT A CHILD.
WHAT!? ARE YOU SUGGESTING THAT YOU'RE NOT THE LEAST BIT EXCITED ABOUT THIS!?
MORE THAN "THE LEAST BIT," BUT NOT ENOUGH TO SHOUT AND DANCE LIKE YOU.
KEH! LOOK AT MISS GROWN-UP! YOUR EYES HAVE ALREADY LOST THE SPARKLE AND SHINE OF CHILDHOOD!
WHAT DOES THAT MEAN!?

EXCITING

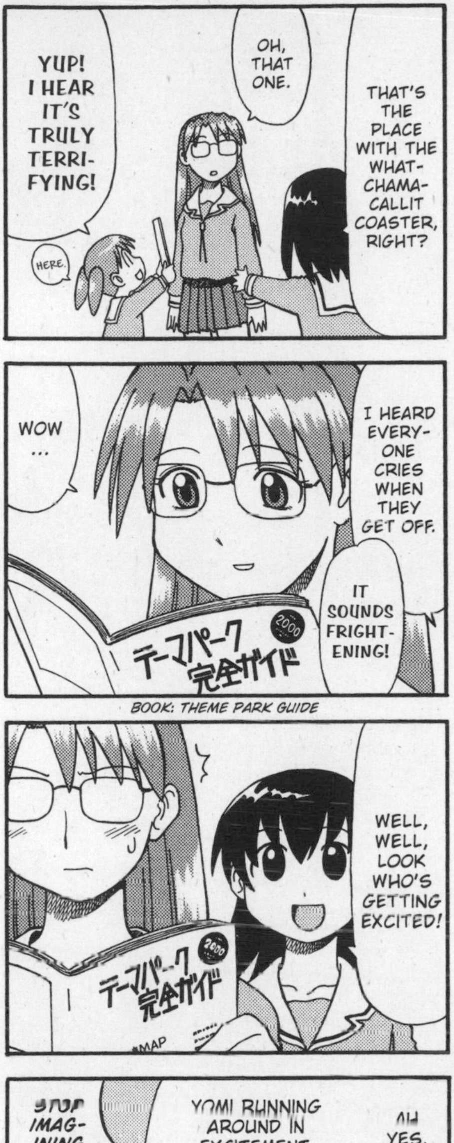
THAT'S THE PLACE WITH THE WHAT-CHAMA-CALLIT COASTER, RIGHT?
OH, THAT ONE.
YUP! I HEAR IT'S TRULY TERRI-FYING!
HERE.
I HEARD EVERY-ONE CRIES WHEN THEY GET OFF.
IT SOUNDS FRIGHT-ENING!
WOW ...
2000
テーマパーク完全ガイド
BOOK: THEME PARK GUIDE
WELL, WELL, LOOK WHO'S GETTING EXCITED!
2000
テーマパーク完全ガイド
MAP
AH YES, I CAN SEE IT NOW.
YOMI RUNNING AROUND IN EXCITEMENT, LIKE A LITTLE CHILD! OH NO, SHE FELL DOWN! THERE, THERE, LITTLE YOMI! DON'T CRY!
STOP IMAG-INING ME IN HUMILI-ATING SITUA-TIONS !!

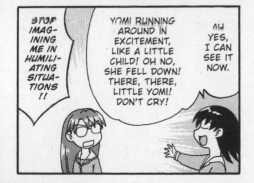

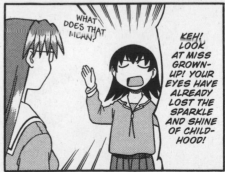

REALLY EXCITING

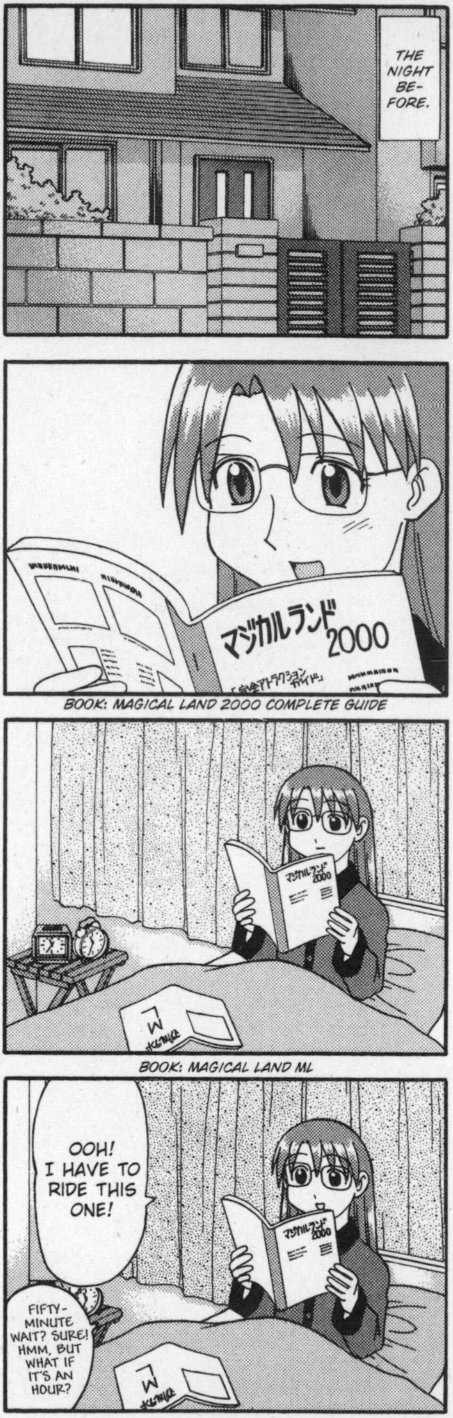
THE NIGHT BEFORE.
マジカルランド 2000
「完全アトラクションガイド」
BOOK: MAGICAL LAND 2000 COMPLETE GUIDE
BOOK: MAGICAL LAND ML
OOH! I HAVE TO RIDE THIS ONE!
FIFTY-MINUTE WAIT? SURE! HMM, BUT WHAT IF IT'S AN HOUR?

I WAS SO LOOKING FORWARD TO IT

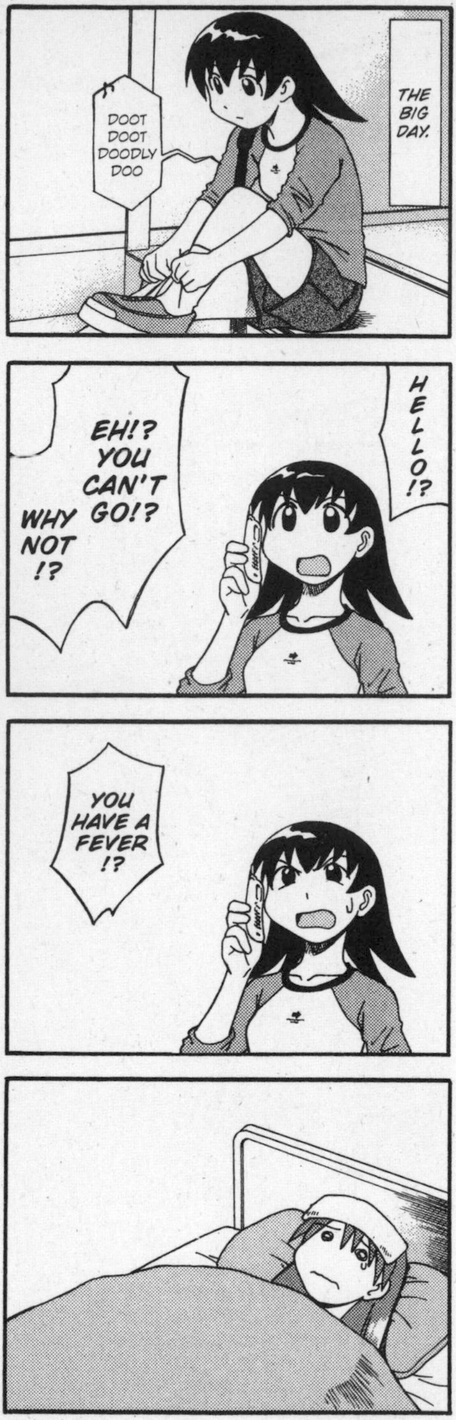
THE BIG DAY.
DOOT DOOT DOODLY DOO
HELLO!?
EH!? YOU CAN'T GO!?
WHY NOT!?
YOU HAVE A FEVER!?

ADULT OPINION

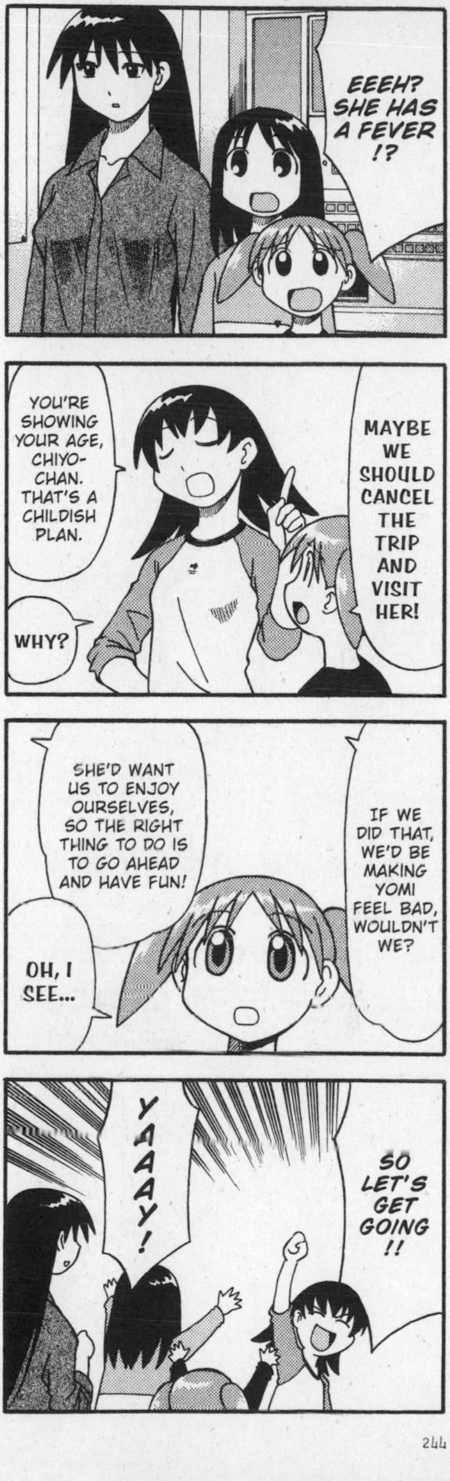
EEEH? SHE HAS A FEVER !?
MAYBE WE SHOULD CANCEL THE TRIP AND VISIT HER!
YOU'RE SHOWING YOUR AGE, CHIYO-CHAN. THAT'S A CHILDISH PLAN.
WHY?
IF WE DID THAT, WE'D BE MAKING YOMI FEEL BAD, WOULDN'T WE?
SHE'D WANT US TO ENJOY OURSELVES, SO THE RIGHT THING TO DO IS TO GO AHEAD AND HAVE FUN!
OH, I SEE...
SO LET'S GET GOING !!
YAAAY!

THRILLING REPORT

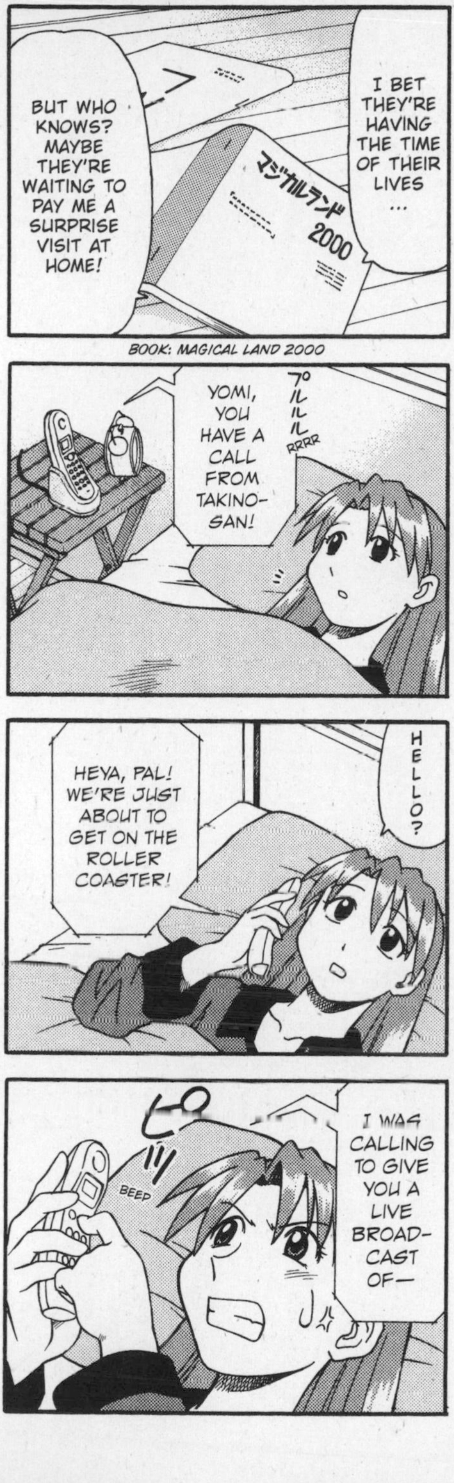
I BET THEY'RE HAVING THE TIME OF THEIR LIVES ...
BUT WHO KNOWS? MAYBE THEY'RE WAITING TO PAY ME A SURPRISE VISIT AT HOME!
マジカルランド 2000
BOOK: MAGICAL LAND 2000
プルルル RRRR
YOMI, YOU HAVE A CALL FROM TAKINO-SAN!
HELLO?
HEYA, PAL! WE'RE JUST ABOUT TO GET ON THE ROLLER COASTER!
I WAS CALLING TO GIVE YOU A LIVE BROADCAST OF—
ピッ
BEEP

I HEARD

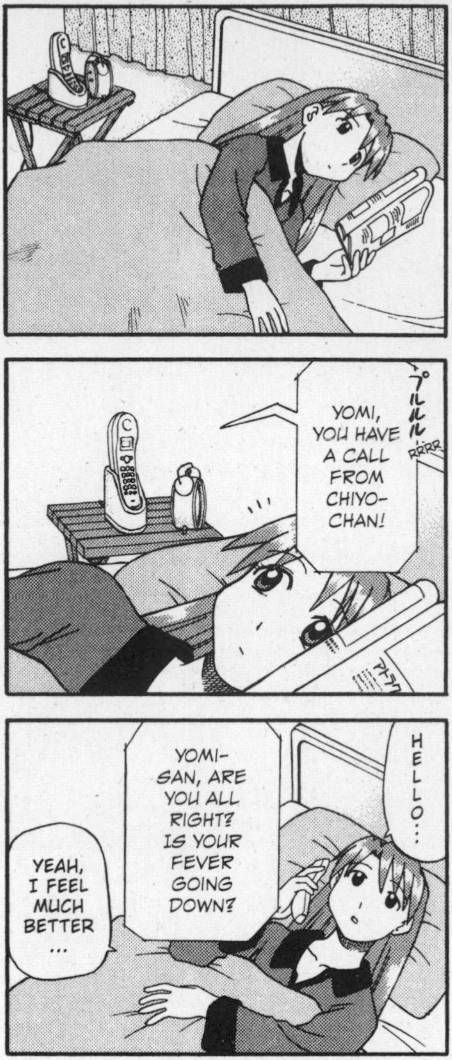
YOMI, YOU HAVE A CALL FROM CHIYO-CHAN!
プルルル RRRR
HELLO...
YOMI-SAN, ARE YOU ALL RIGHT? IS YOUR FEVER GOING DOWN?
YEAH, I FEEL MUCH BETTER ...
PLEASE DON'T SLEEP NAKED NEXT TIME. IT'S NOT GOOD FOR YOU!
BAD!
E-EXCUSE ME!? WHAT WAS THAT? DID TOMO TELL YOU THAT? DID SHE!?
DON'T SCOLD ME!

AMBIANCE

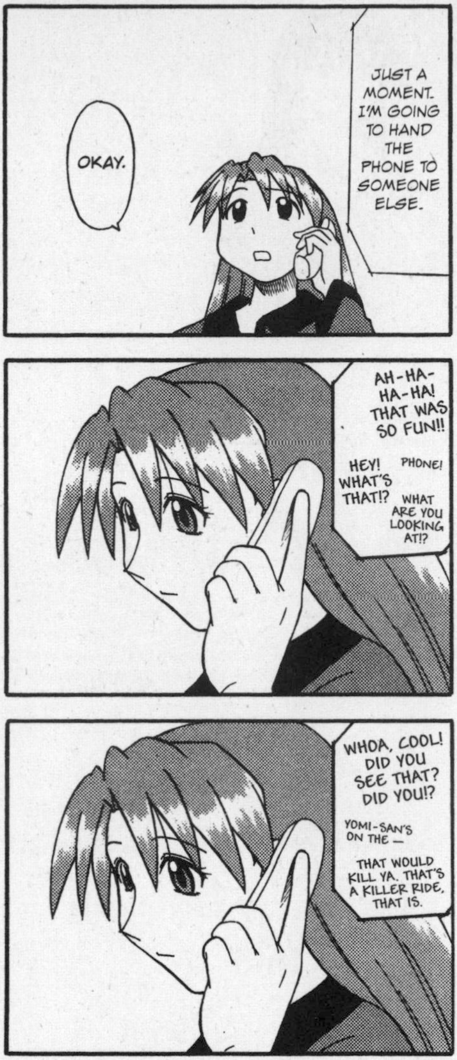
JUST A MOMENT. I'M GOING TO HAND THE PHONE TO SOMEONE ELSE.
OKAY.
AH-HA-HA-HA! THAT WAS SO FUN!!
PHONE!
HEY! WHAT'S THAT!?
WHAT ARE YOU LOOKING AT!?
WHOA, COOL! DID YOU SEE THAT? DID YOU!?
YOMI-SAN'S ON THE —
THAT WOULD KILL YA. THAT'S A KILLER RIDE, THAT IS.
LET'S RIDE THAT ONE NEXT! C'MON, LET'S GO! <GO!>
...PHONE!
AH-HA-HA-HA-HA!

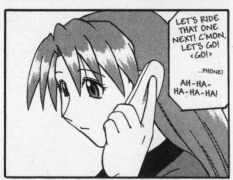

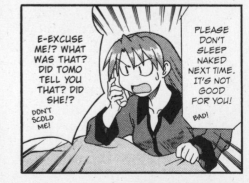

HONEST

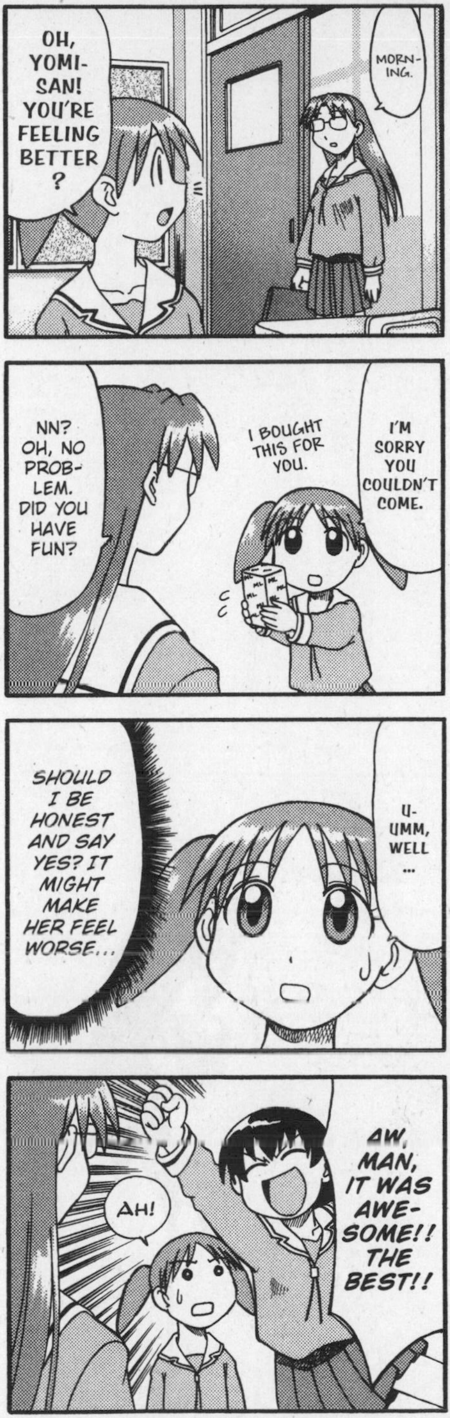
MORN-ING.
OH, YOMI-SAN! YOU'RE FEELING BETTER?
I'M SORRY YOU COULDN'T COME.
I BOUGHT THIS FOR YOU.
NN? OH, NO PROB-LEM. DID YOU HAVE FUN?
U-UMM, WELL...
SHOULD I BE HONEST AND SAY YES? IT MIGHT MAKE HER FEEL WORSE...
AW, MAN, IT WAS AWE-SOME!! THE BEST!!
AH!

OUT OF THE LOOP

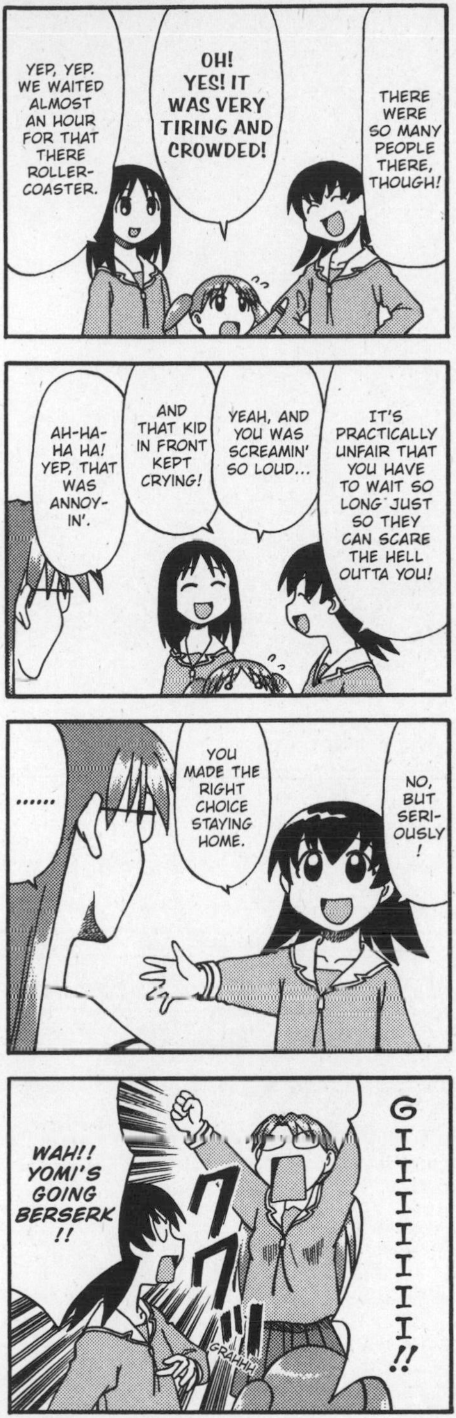
THERE WERE SO MANY PEOPLE THERE, THOUGH!
OH! YES! IT WAS VERY TIRING AND CROWDED!
YEP, YEP. WE WAITED ALMOST AN HOUR FOR THAT THERE ROLLER-COASTER.
IT'S PRACTICALLY UNFAIR THAT YOU HAVE TO WAIT SO LONG JUST SO THEY CAN SCARE THE HELL OUTTA YOU!
YEAH, AND YOU WAS SCREAMIN' SO LOUD...
AND THAT KID IN FRONT KEPT CRYING!
AH-HA-HA HA! YEP, THAT WAS ANNOY-IN'.
NO, BUT SERI-OUSLY!
YOU MADE THE RIGHT CHOICE STAYING HOME.
......
GIIIIIIIII!!
GRAHHH
WAH!! YOMI'S GOING BERSERK!!

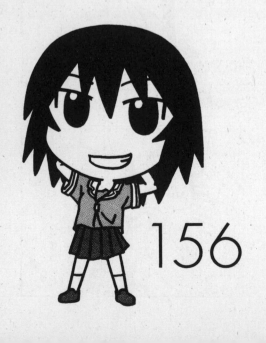

156

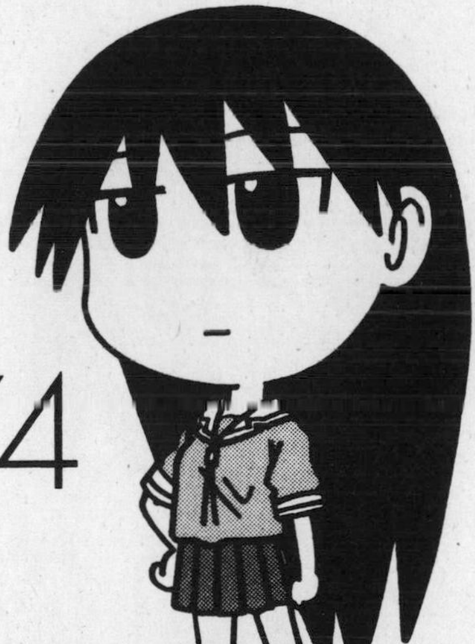

174

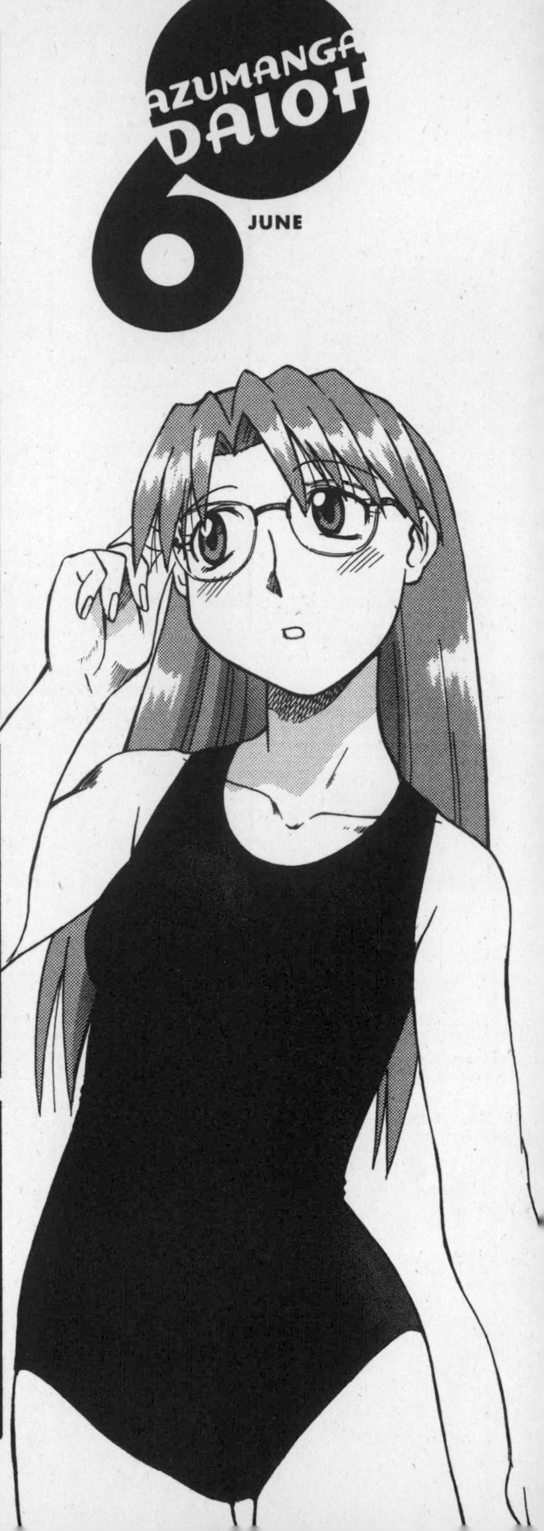
AZUMANGA DAIOH
6
JUNE

NYAMO FOOD

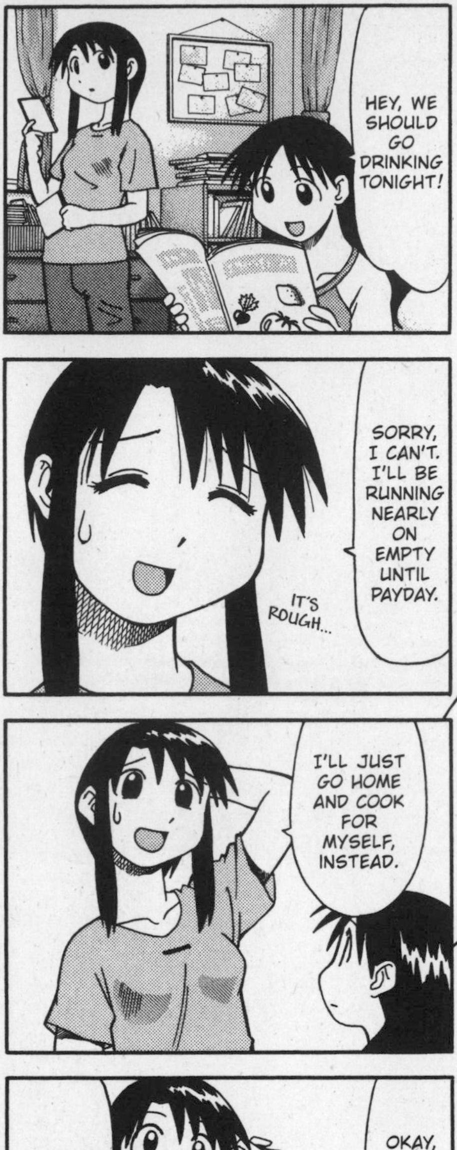
HEY, WE SHOULD GO DRINKING TONIGHT!
SORRY, I CAN'T. I'LL BE RUNNING NEARLY ON EMPTY UNTIL PAYDAY.
IT'S ROUGH...
I'LL JUST GO HOME AND COOK FOR MYSELF, INSTEAD.
OKAY, I'LL JOIN YOU.
EH!? YOU WANNA COME TO EAT!?

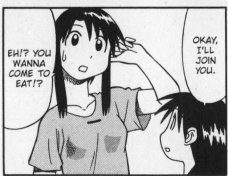

THE IDEAL WIFE

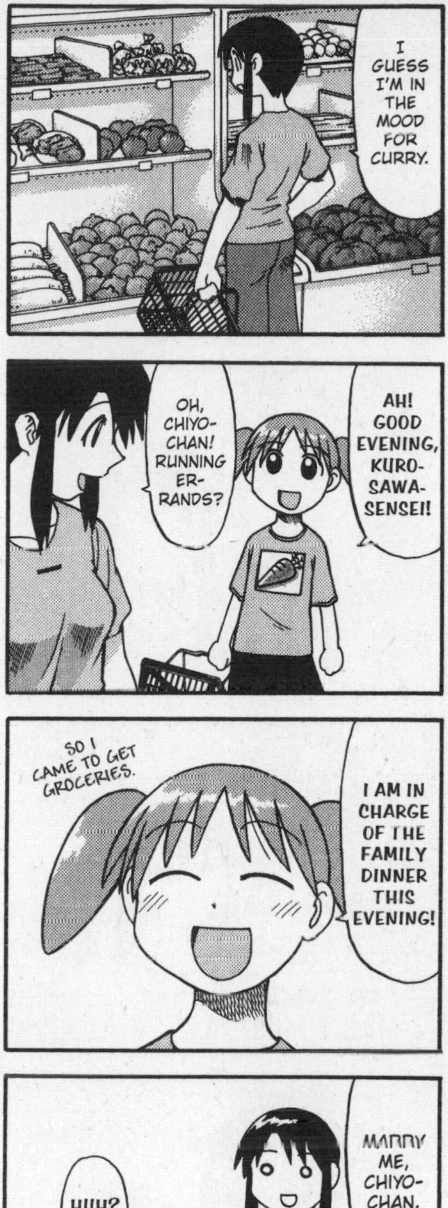
I GUESS I'M IN THE MOOD FOR CURRY.
AH! GOOD EVENING, KURO-SAWA-SENSEI!
OH, CHIYO-CHAN! RUNNING ER-RANDS?
I AM IN CHARGE OF THE FAMILY DINNER THIS EVENING!
SO I CAME TO GET GROCERIES.
MARRY ME, CHIYO-CHAN.
HUH?

MENU

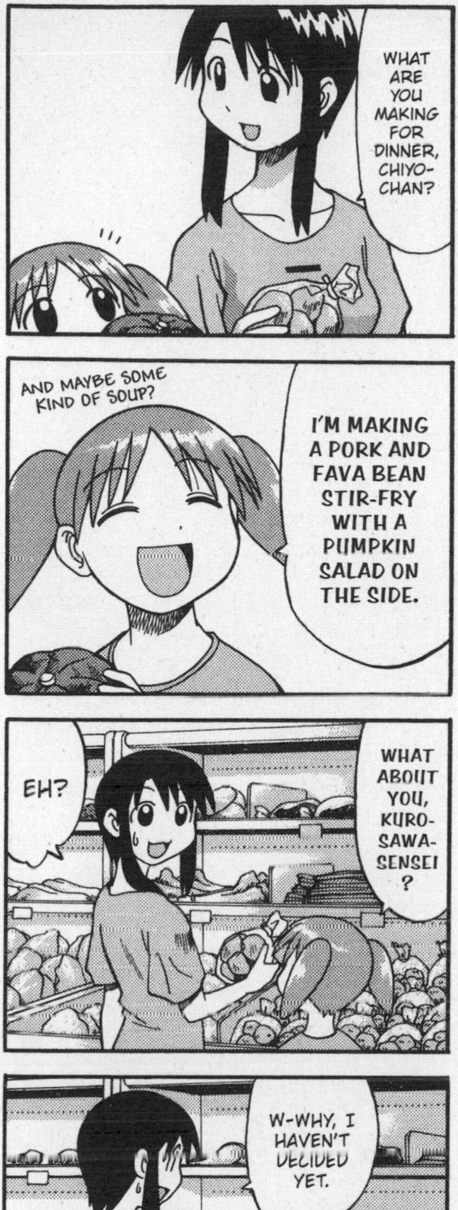
WHAT ARE YOU MAKING FOR DINNER, CHIYO-CHAN?
I'M MAKING A PORK AND FAVA BEAN STIR-FRY WITH A PUMPKIN SALAD ON THE SIDE.
AND MAYBE SOME KIND OF SOUP?
WHAT ABOUT YOU, KURO-SAWA-SENSEI?
EH?
W-WHY, I HAVEN'T DECIDED YET.

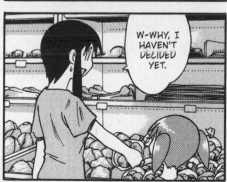

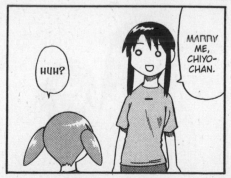

ACT YOUR AGE

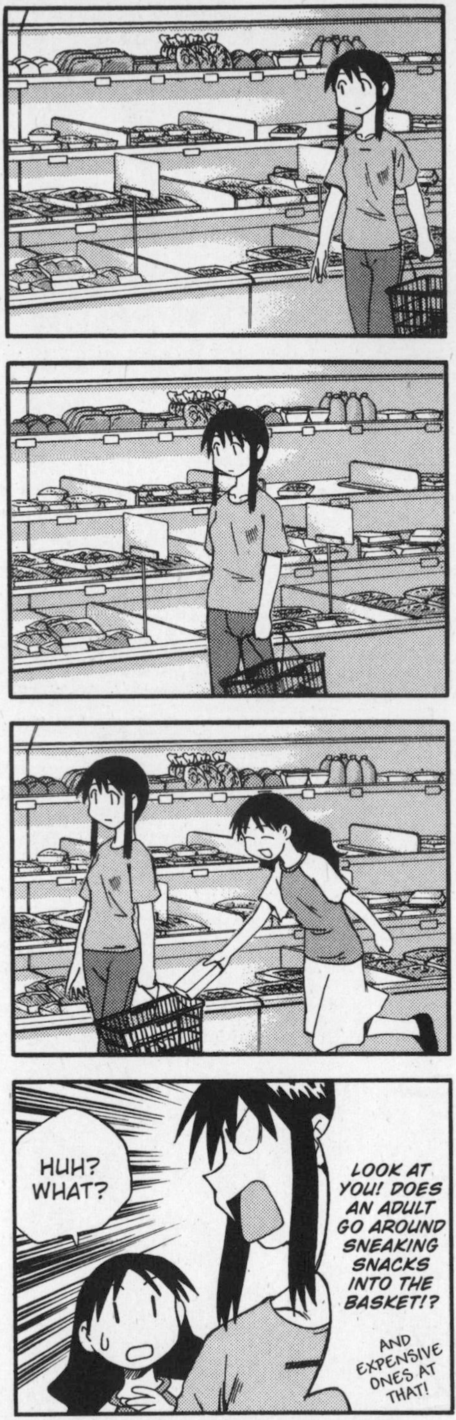
LOOK AT YOU! DOES AN ADULT GO AROUND SNEAKING SNACKS INTO THE BASKET!?
HUH? WHAT?
AND EXPENSIVE ONES AT THAT!

IN BLOOM

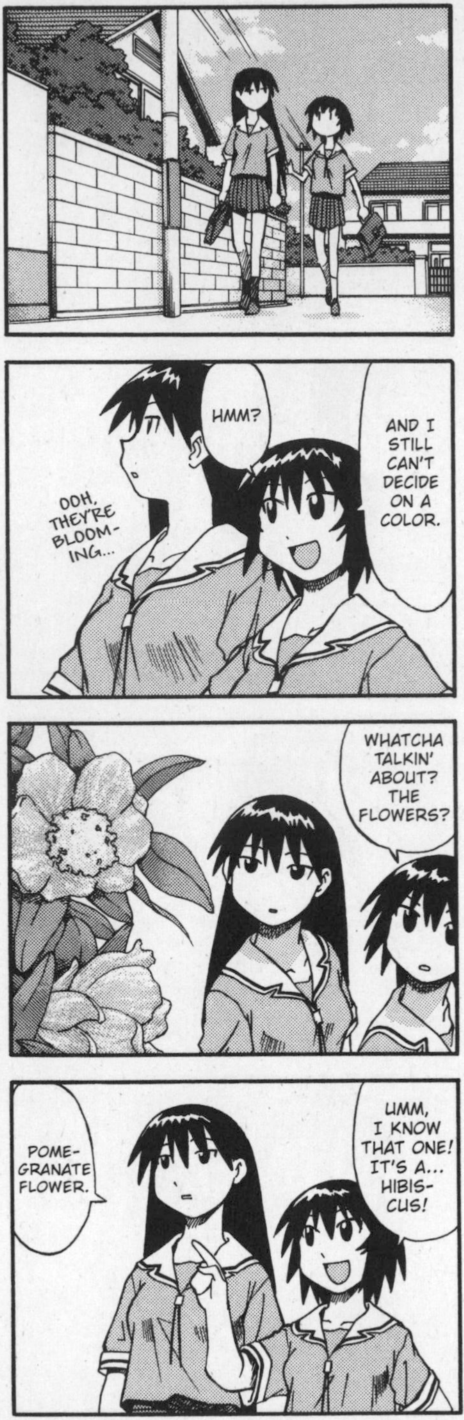
AND I STILL CAN'T DECIDE ON A COLOR.
HMM?
OOH, THEY'RE BLOOMING...
WHATCHA TALKIN' ABOUT? THE FLOWERS?
UMM, I KNOW THAT ONE! IT'S A... HIBISCUS!
POMEGRANATE FLOWER.

CLEYERA JAPONICA

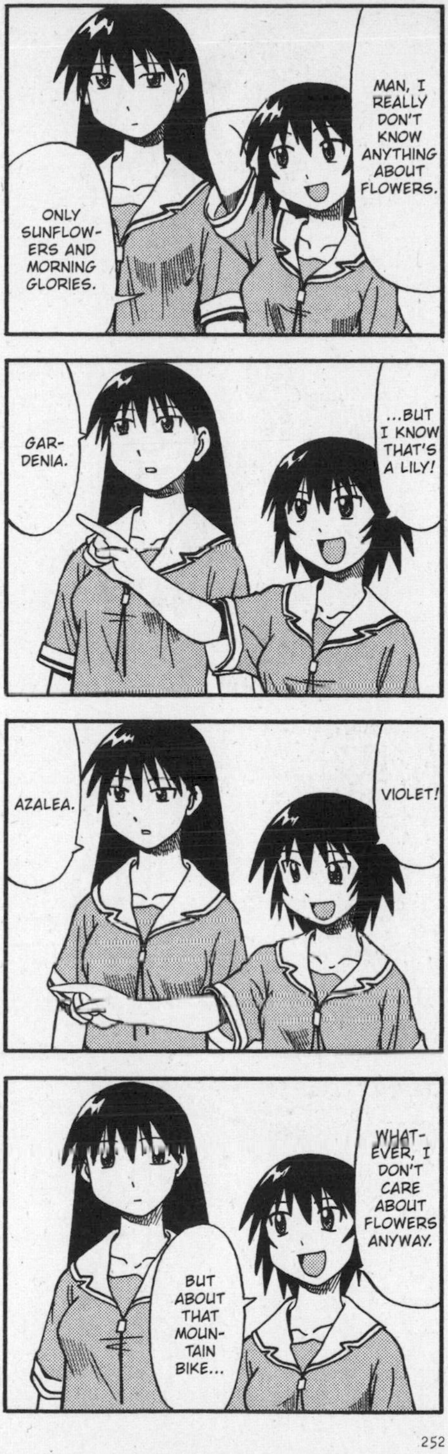
MAN, I REALLY DON'T KNOW ANYTHING ABOUT FLOWERS.
ONLY SUNFLOWERS AND MORNING GLORIES.
...BUT I KNOW THAT'S A LILY!
GARDENIA.
VIOLET!
AZALEA.
WHATEVER, I DON'T CARE ABOUT FLOWERS ANYWAY.
BUT ABOUT THAT MOUNTAIN BIKE...

ANALYSIS

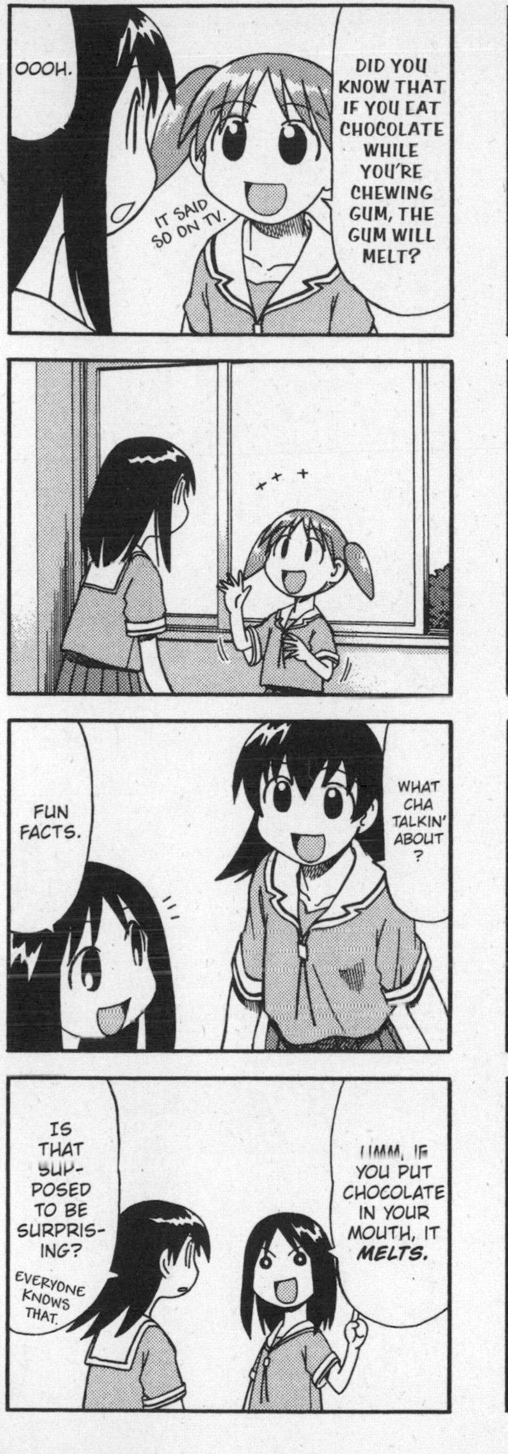
DID YOU KNOW THAT IF YOU EAT CHOCOLATE WHILE YOU'RE CHEWING GUM, THE GUM WILL MELT?
IT SAID SO ON TV.
OOOH.
WHATCHA TALKIN' ABOUT?
FUN FACTS.
UMM, IF YOU PUT CHOCOLATE IN YOUR MOUTH, IT *MELTS.*
IS THAT SUPPOSED TO BE SURPRISING?
EVERYONE KNOWS THAT.

CORRECTION

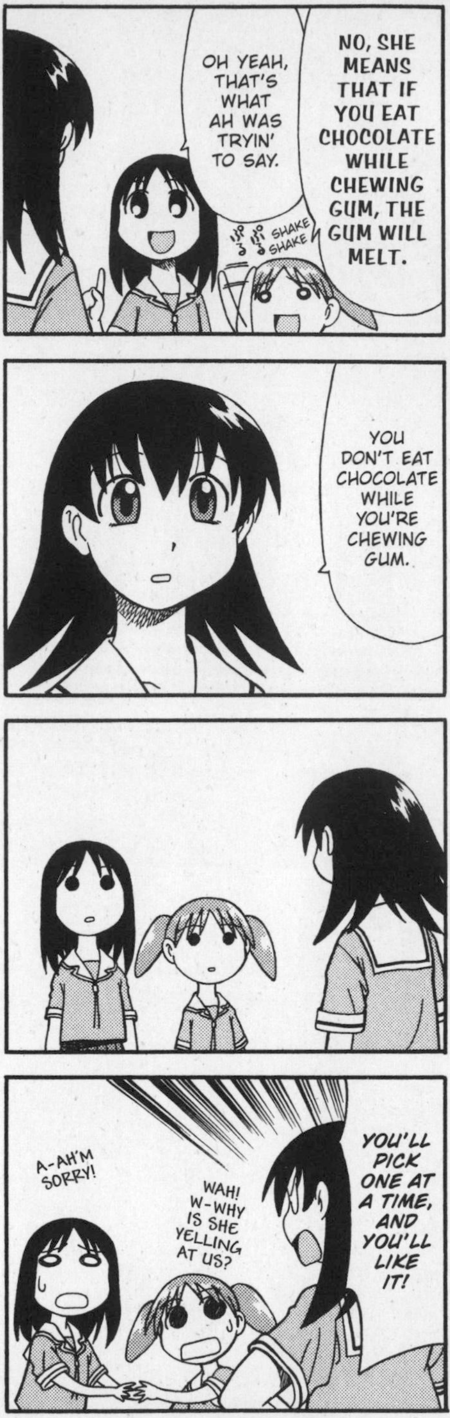
NO, SHE MEANS THAT IF YOU EAT CHOCOLATE WHILE CHEWING GUM, THE GUM WILL MELT.
SHAKE SHAKE
OH YEAH, THAT'S WHAT AH WAS TRYIN' TO SAY.
YOU DON'T EAT CHOCOLATE WHILE YOU'RE CHEWING GUM.
YOU'LL PICK ONE AT A TIME, AND YOU'LL LIKE IT!
WAH! W-WHY IS SHE YELLING AT US?
A-AH'M SORRY!

POOL POOL POOL

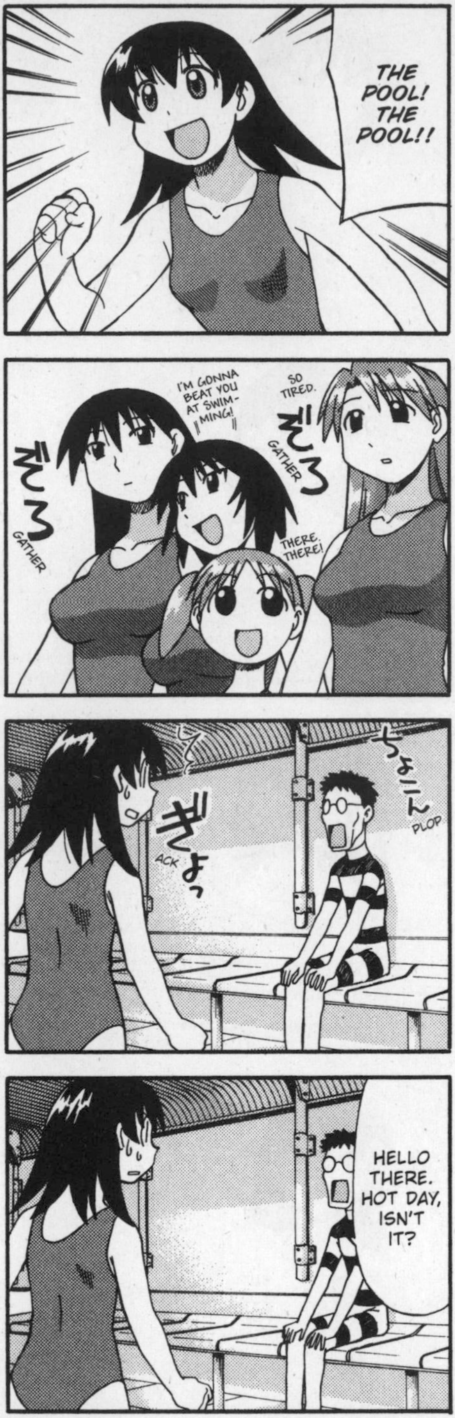
THE POOL! THE POOL!!
ぞろ
GATHER
SO TIRED.
I'M GONNA BEAT YOU AT SWIMMING!
THERE, THERE!
ぞろ
GATHER
ちょこん
PLOP
ぎょっ
ACK
HELLO THERE. HOT DAY, ISN'T IT?

GLISTENING

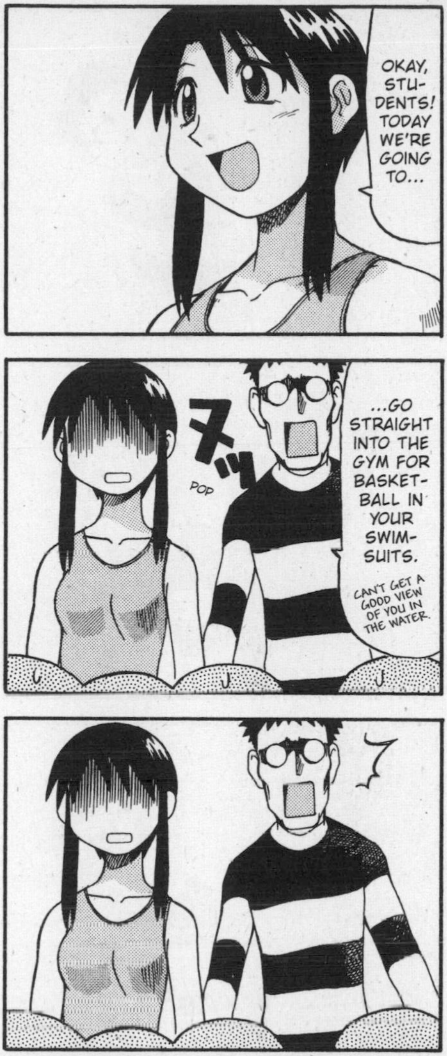
OKAY, STU-DENTS! TODAY WE'RE GOING TO...
...GO STRAIGHT INTO THE GYM FOR BASKET-BALL IN YOUR SWIM-SUITS.
CAN'T GET A GOOD VIEW OF YOU IN THE WATER.
POP
OH! BUT WHAT ABOUT THE SIGHT OF THEIR YOUNG BODIES, DRIPPING WET...?
WHICH-EVER AM I TO CHOOSE !?

RESOLUTION

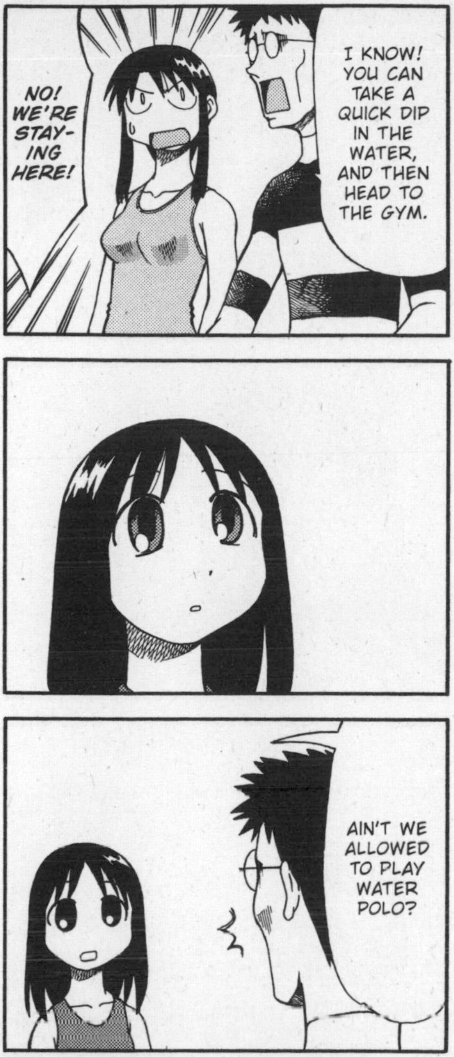
I KNOW! YOU CAN TAKE A QUICK DIP IN THE WATER, AND THEN HEAD TO THE GYM.
NO! WE'RE STAY-ING HERE!
AIN'T WE ALLOWED TO PLAY WATER POLO?
SO WHAT DO YOU WANT ME TO DO!?
EH?

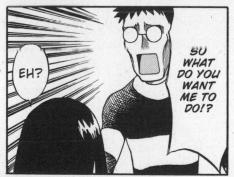

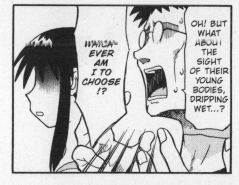

WARNING

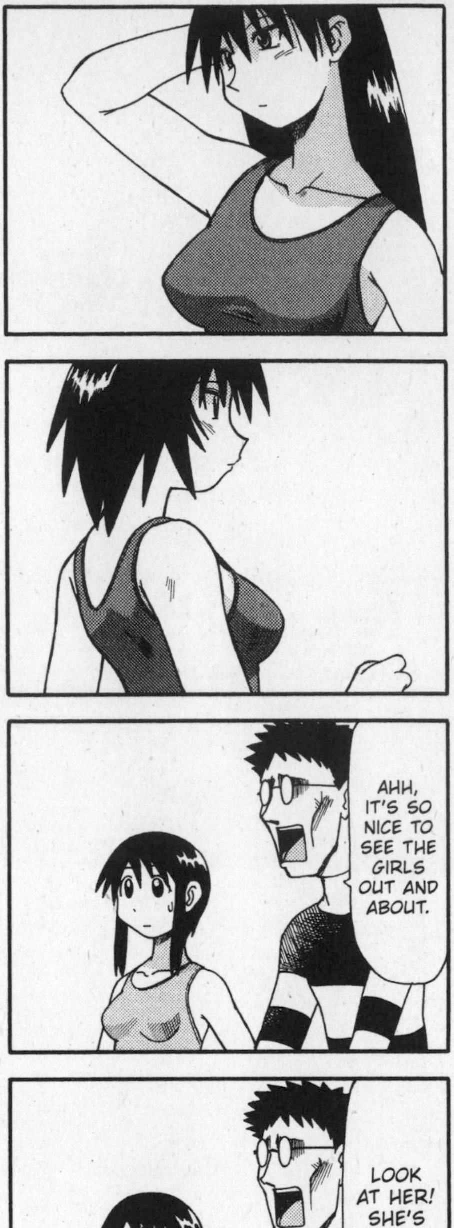
AHH, IT'S SO NICE TO SEE THE GIRLS OUT AND ABOUT.
LOOK AT HER! SHE'S BARELY LEGAL!

FRIENDLY CONCERN

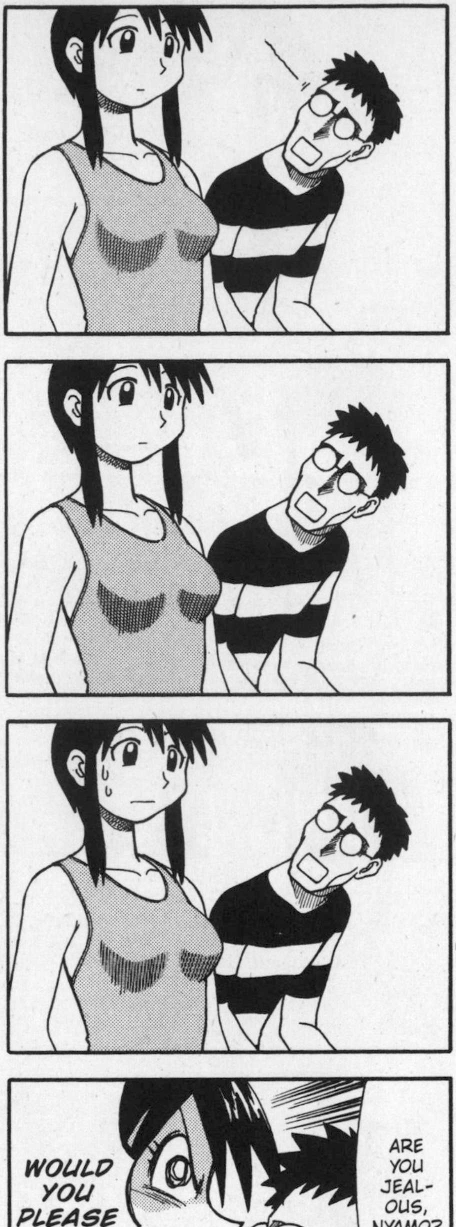
ARE YOU JEAL-OUS, NYAMO?
WOULD YOU PLEASE GET OUT OF HERE !!?

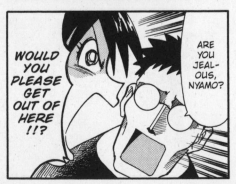

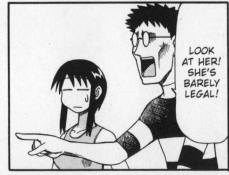

SPECIALTY

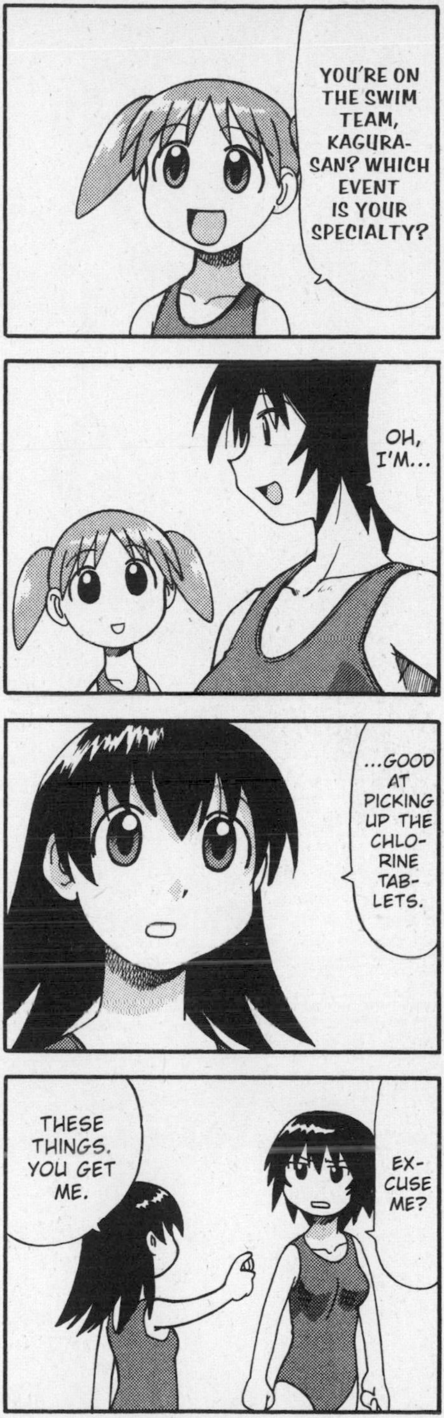
YOU'RE ON THE SWIM TEAM, KAGURA-SAN? WHICH EVENT IS YOUR SPECIALTY?
OH, I'M...
...GOOD AT PICKING UP THE CHLORINE TABLETS.
EXCUSE ME?
THESE THINGS. YOU GET ME.

FASTER, FASTER

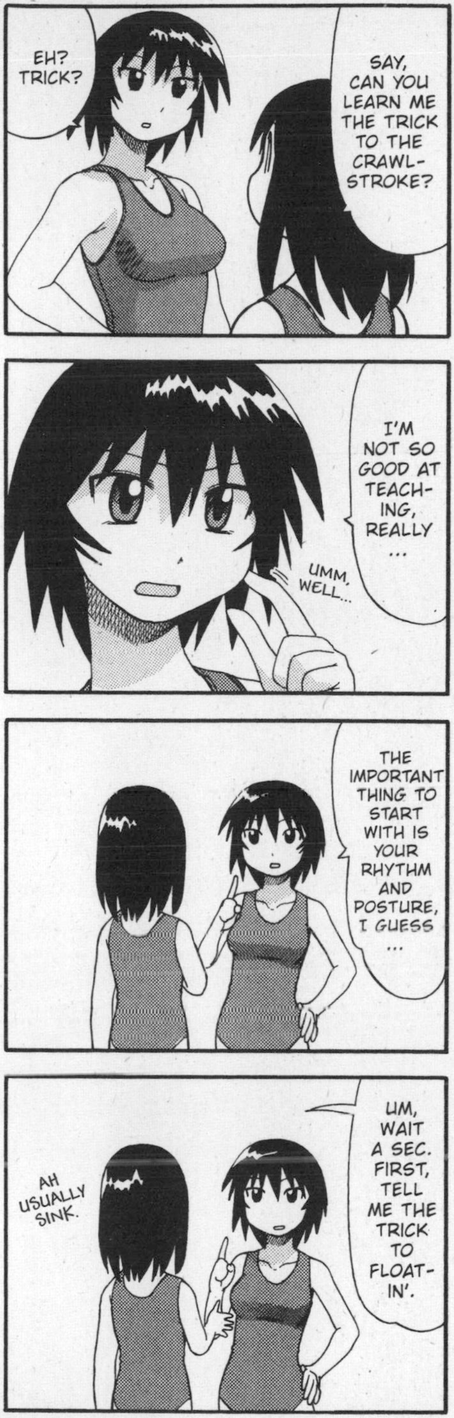
SAY, CAN YOU LEARN ME THE TRICK TO THE CRAWL-STROKE?
EH? TRICK?
I'M NOT SO GOOD AT TEACHING, REALLY...
UMM, WELL...
THE IMPORTANT THING TO START WITH IS YOUR RHYTHM AND POSTURE, I GUESS...
UM, WAIT A SEC. FIRST, TELL ME THE TRICK TO FLOATIN'.
AH USUALLY SINK.

OSAKA'S HALF-DAY

AZUMANGA DAIOH

6

JUNE SPECIAL

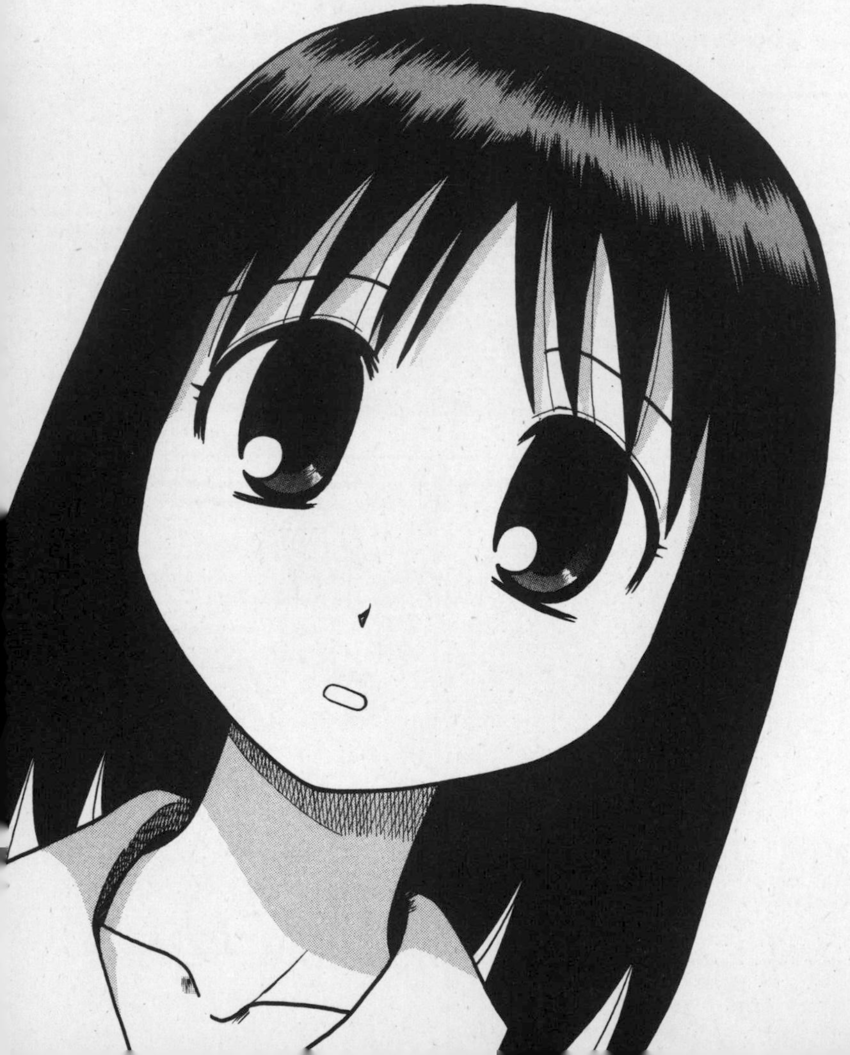

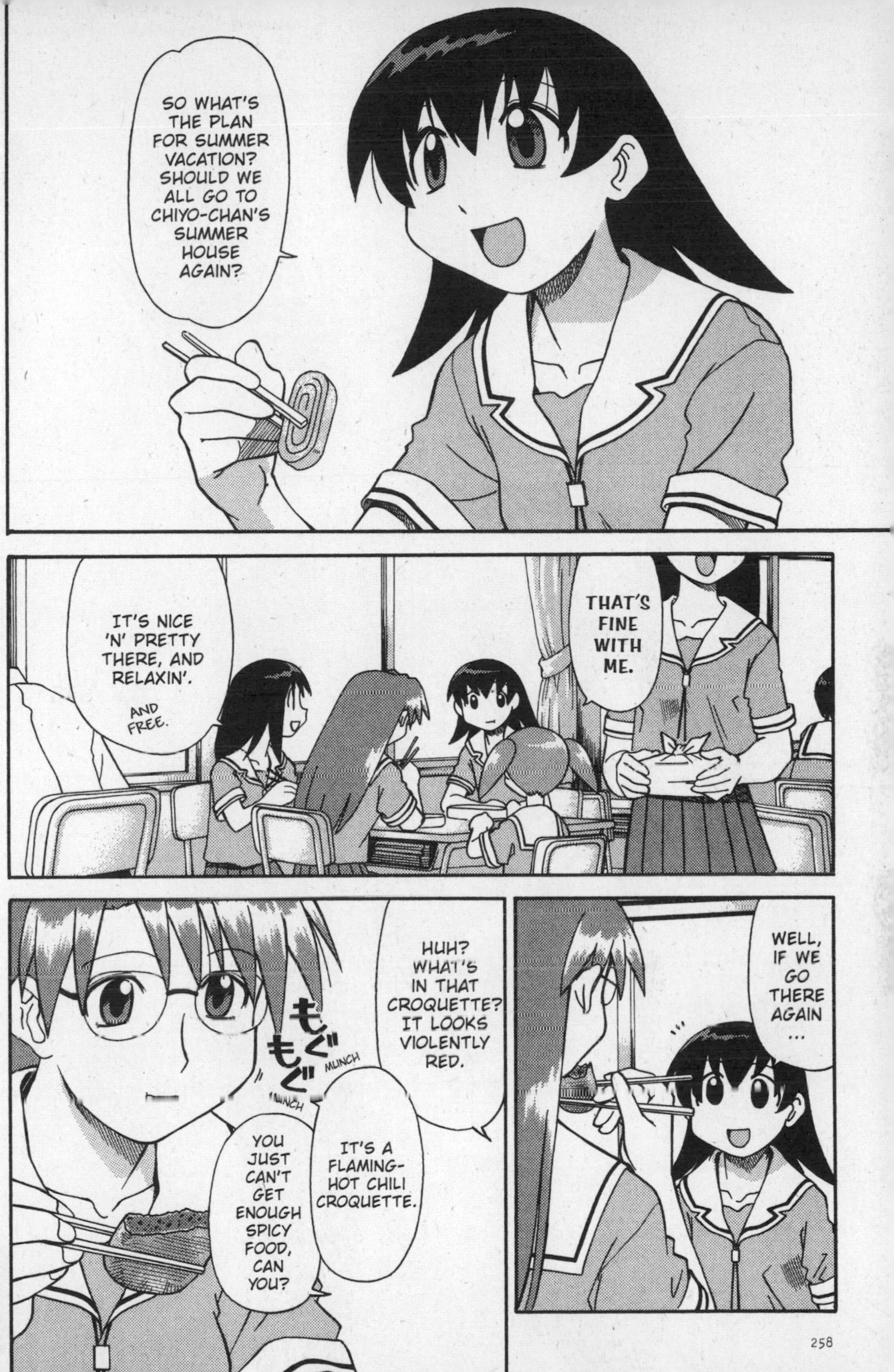
SO WHAT'S THE PLAN FOR SUMMER VACATION? SHOULD WE ALL GO TO CHIYO-CHAN'S SUMMER HOUSE AGAIN?
THAT'S FINE WITH ME.
IT'S NICE 'N' PRETTY THERE, AND RELAXIN'.
AND FREE.
WELL, IF WE GO THERE AGAIN ...
HUH? WHAT'S IN THAT CROQUETTE? IT LOOKS VIOLENTLY RED.
もぐもぐ
MUNCH MUNCH
IT'S A FLAMING-HOT CHILI CROQUETTE.
YOU JUST CAN'T GET ENOUGH SPICY FOOD, CAN YOU?

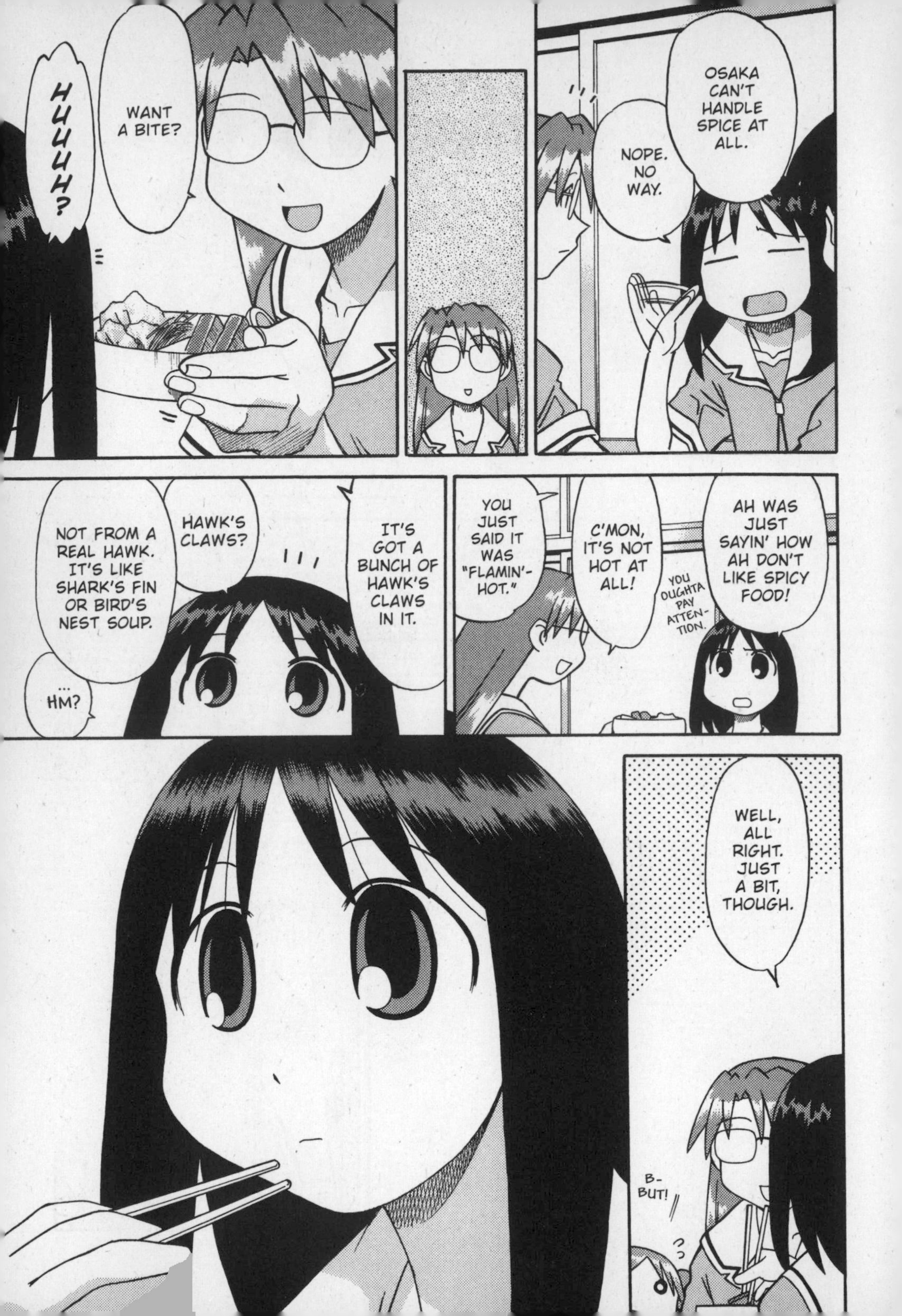
OSAKA CAN'T HANDLE SPICE AT ALL.
NOPE. NO WAY.
WANT A BITE?
HUUUH?
AH WAS JUST SAYIN' HOW AH DON'T LIKE SPICY FOOD!
C'MON, IT'S NOT HOT AT ALL!
YOU OUGHTA PAY ATTEN-TION.
YOU JUST SAID IT WAS "FLAMIN'-HOT."
IT'S GOT A BUNCH OF HAWK'S CLAWS IN IT.
HAWK'S CLAWS?
NOT FROM A REAL HAWK. IT'S LIKE SHARK'S FIN OR BIRD'S NEST SOUP.
... HM?
WELL, ALL RIGHT. JUST A BIT, THOUGH.
B-BUT!

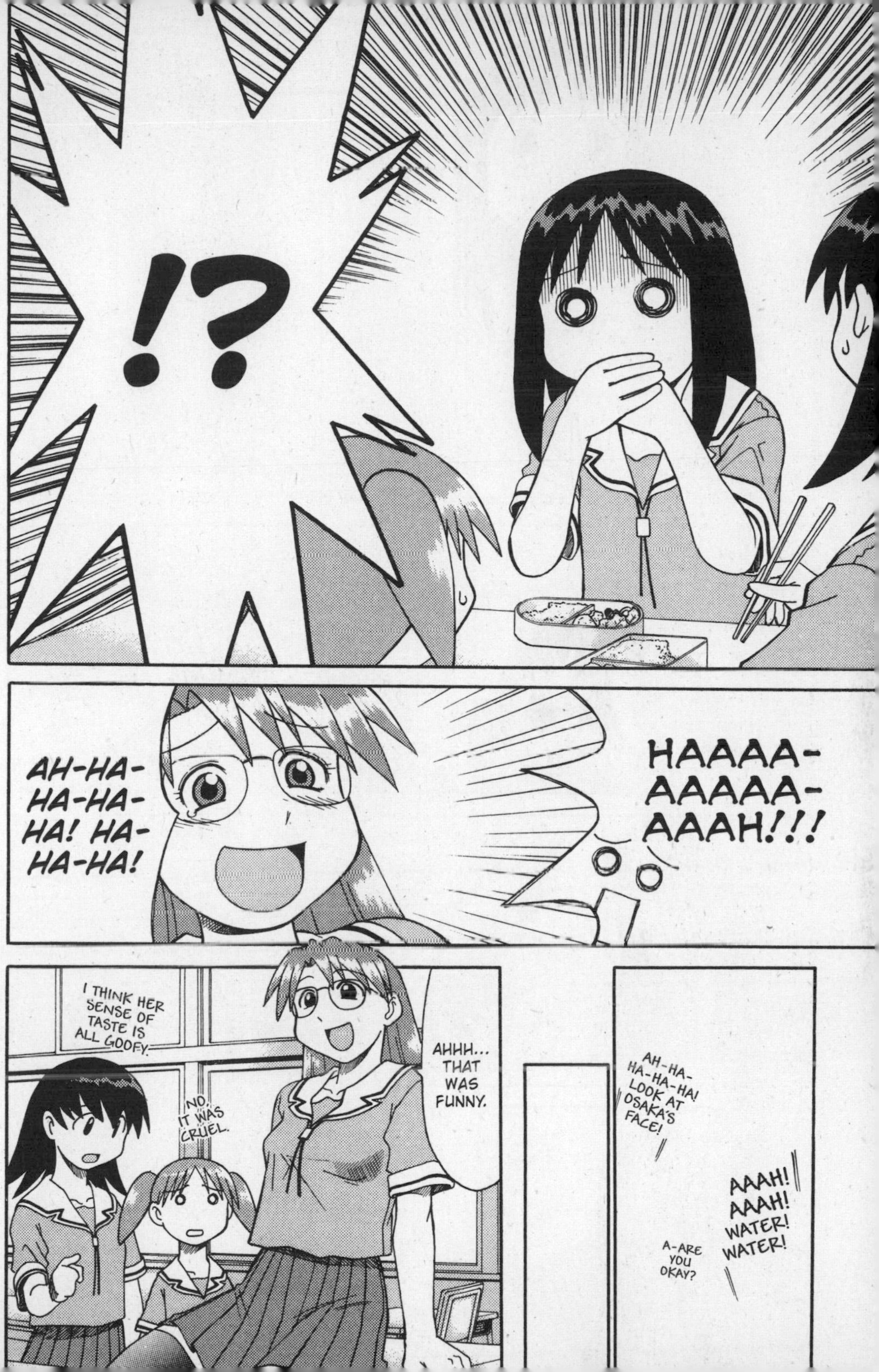
!?
HAAAA-AAAAA-AAAH!!!
AH-HA-HA-HA-HA! HA-HA-HA!
AH-HA-HA-HA! LOOK AT OSAKA'S FACE!
AAAH! AAAH! WATER! WATER!
A-ARE YOU OKAY?
AHHH... THAT WAS FUNNY.
I THINK HER SENSE OF TASTE IS ALL GOOFY.
NO, IT WAS CRUEL.

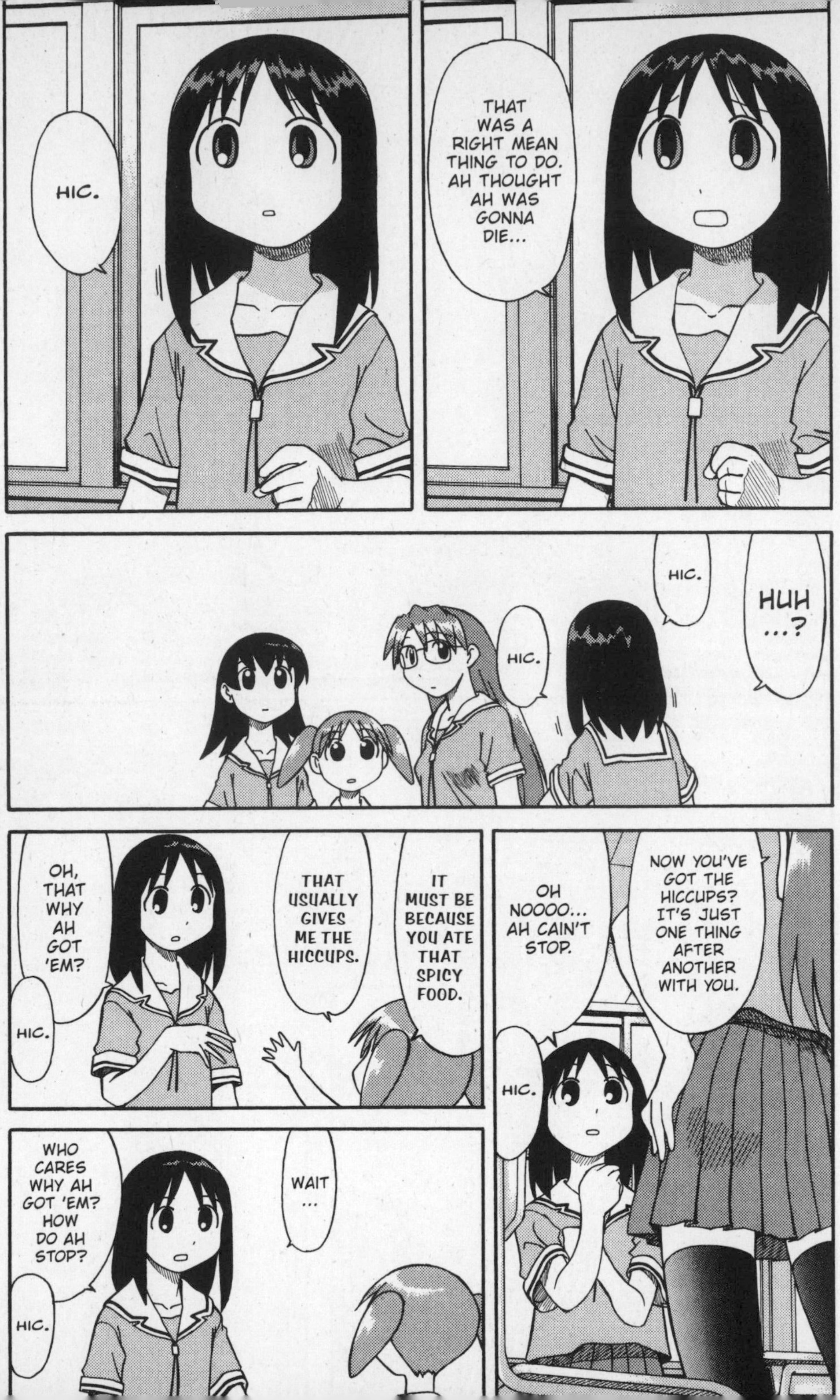
THAT WAS A RIGHT MEAN THING TO DO. AH THOUGHT AH WAS GONNA DIE...
HIC.
HUH ...?
HIC.
HIC.
NOW YOU'VE GOT THE HICCUPS? IT'S JUST ONE THING AFTER ANOTHER WITH YOU.
OH NOOOO... AH CAIN'T STOP.
HIC.
IT MUST BE BECAUSE YOU ATE THAT SPICY FOOD.
THAT USUALLY GIVES ME THE HICCUPS.
OH, THAT WHY AH GOT 'EM?
HIC.
WAIT ...
WHO CARES WHY AH GOT 'EM? HOW DO AH STOP?
HIC.

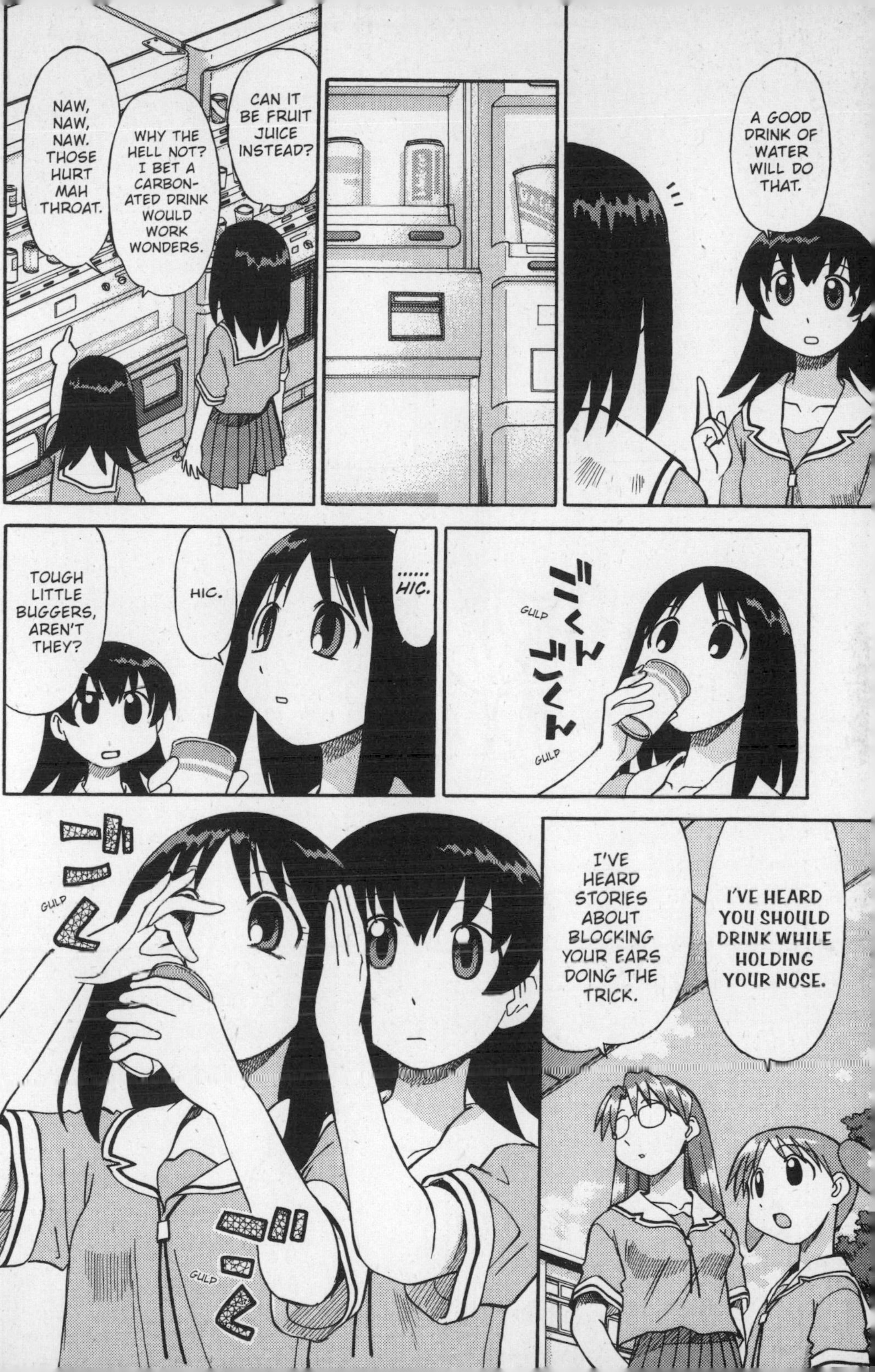
A GOOD DRINK OF WATER WILL DO THAT.
CAN IT BE FRUIT JUICE INSTEAD?
WHY THE HELL NOT? I BET A CARBON-ATED DRINK WOULD WORK WONDERS.
NAW, NAW, NAW. THOSE HURT MAH THROAT.
ごくん ごくん
GULP
GULP
......HIC.
HIC.
TOUGH LITTLE BUGGERS, AREN'T THEY?
I'VE HEARD YOU SHOULD DRINK WHILE HOLDING YOUR NOSE.
I'VE HEARD STORIES ABOUT BLOCKING YOUR EARS DOING THE TRICK.
GULP
GULP

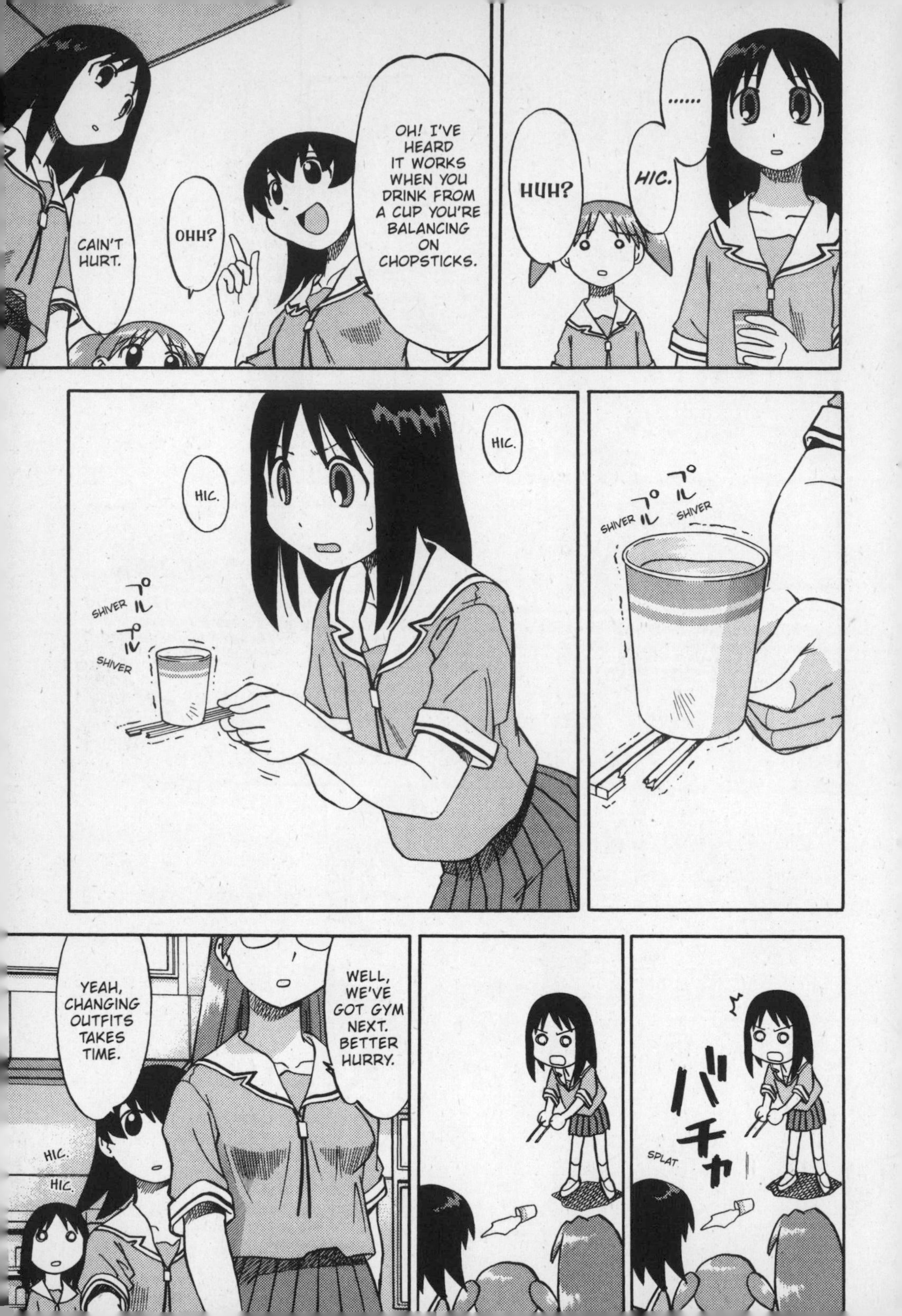
......
HIC.
HUH?
OH! I'VE HEARD IT WORKS WHEN YOU DRINK FROM A CUP YOU'RE BALANCING ON CHOPSTICKS.
OHH?
CAIN'T HURT.
プル SHIVER
プル SHIVER
HIC.
HIC.
プル SHIVER
プル SHIVER
バチャ
SPLAT
WELL, WE'VE GOT GYM NEXT. BETTER HURRY.
YEAH, CHANGING OUTFITS TAKES TIME.
HIC.
HIC.

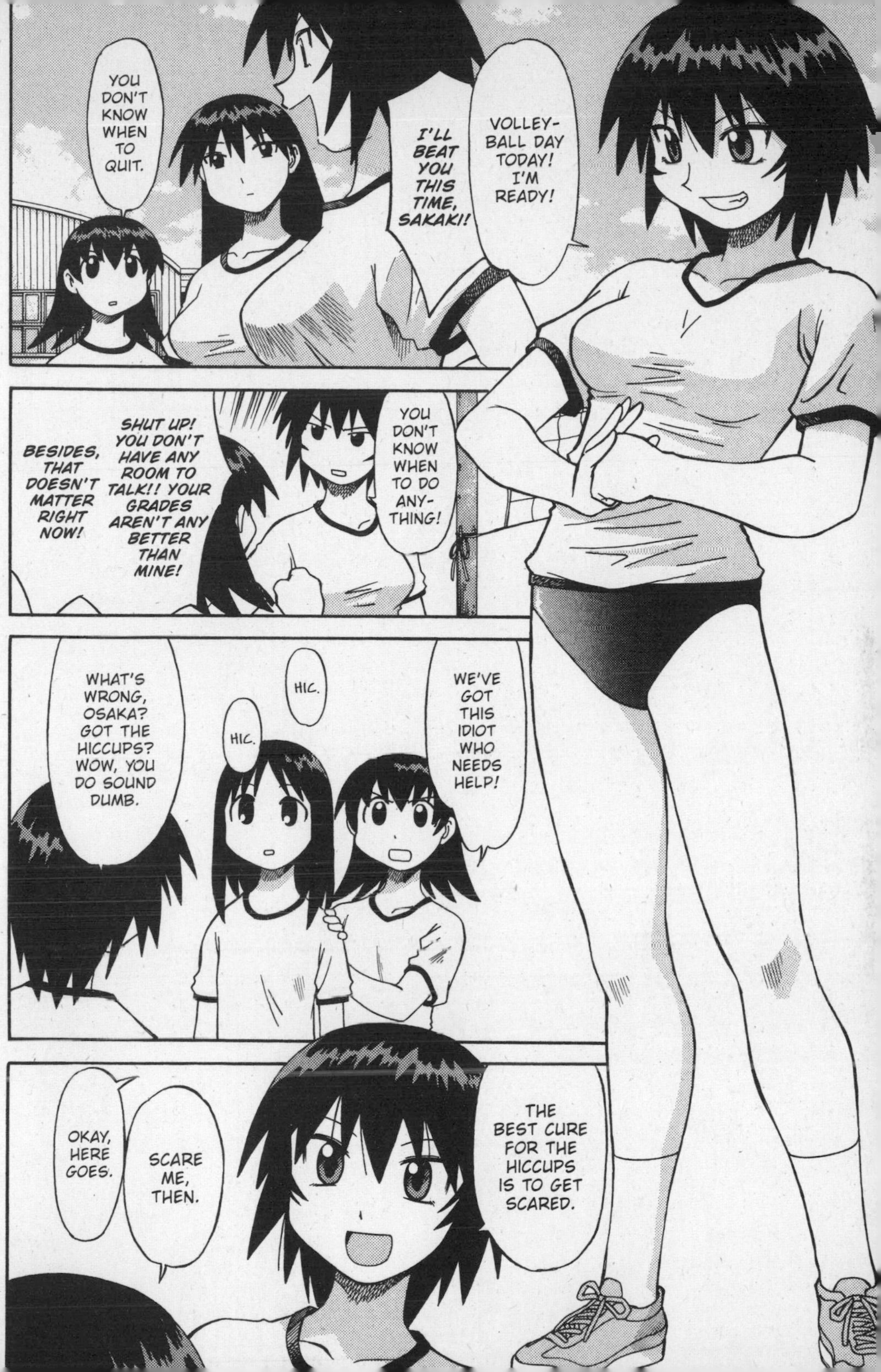
VOLLEY-BALL DAY TODAY! I'M READY!
I'LL BEAT YOU THIS TIME, SAKAKI!
YOU DON'T KNOW WHEN TO QUIT.
YOU DON'T KNOW WHEN TO DO ANYTHING!
SHUT UP! YOU DON'T HAVE ANY ROOM TO TALK!! YOUR GRADES AREN'T ANY BETTER THAN MINE!
BESIDES, THAT DOESN'T MATTER RIGHT NOW!
WE'VE GOT THIS IDIOT WHO NEEDS HELP!
HIC.
HIC.
WHAT'S WRONG, OSAKA? GOT THE HICCUPS? WOW, YOU DO SOUND DUMB.
THE BEST CURE FOR THE HICCUPS IS TO GET SCARED.
SCARE ME, THEN.
OKAY, HERE GOES.

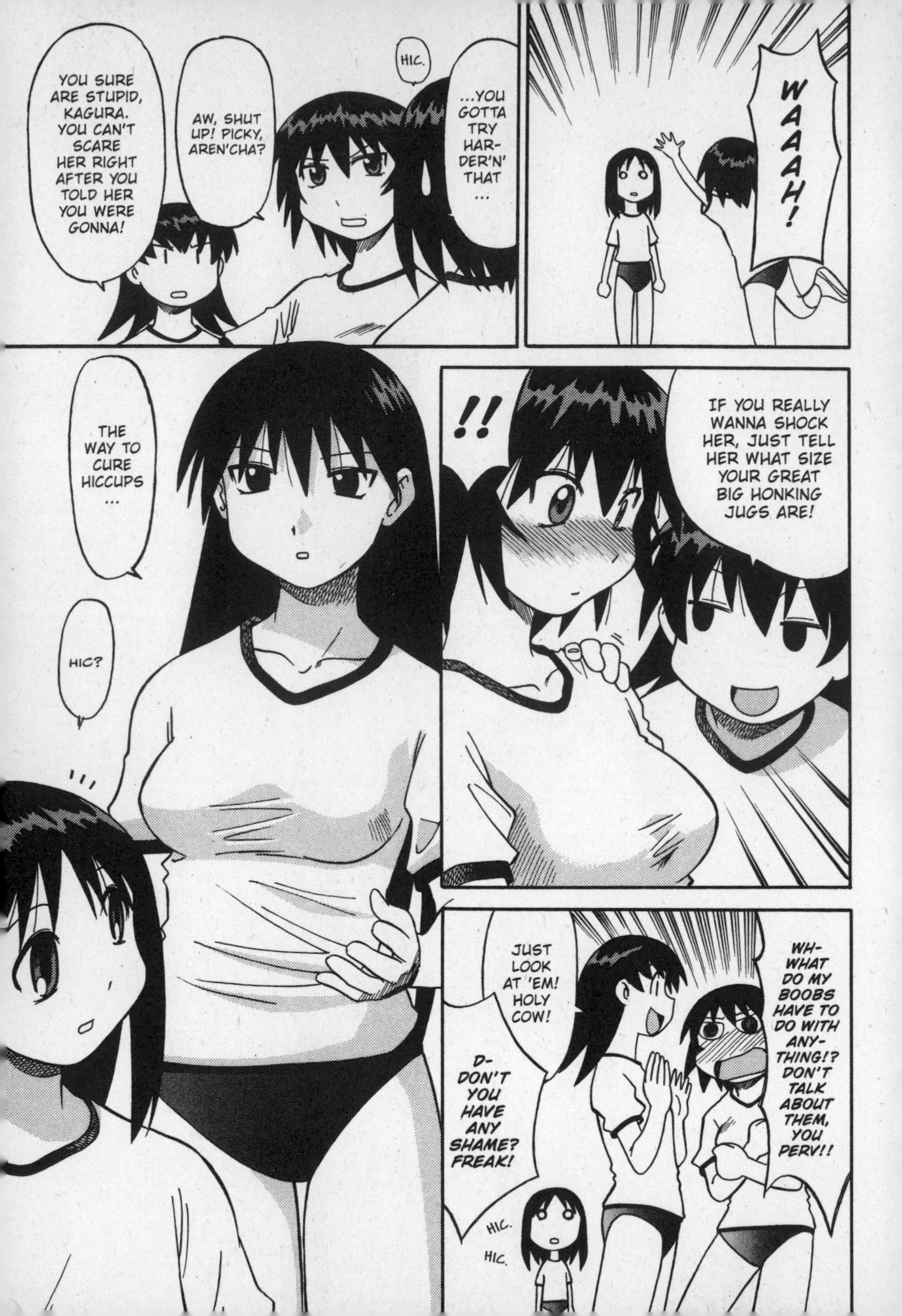
WAAAH!
...YOU GOTTA TRY HARDER'N' THAT...
HIC.
AW, SHUT UP! PICKY, AREN'CHA?
YOU SURE ARE STUPID, KAGURA. YOU CAN'T SCARE HER RIGHT AFTER YOU TOLD HER YOU WERE GONNA!
IF YOU REALLY WANNA SHOCK HER, JUST TELL HER WHAT SIZE YOUR GREAT BIG HONKING JUGS ARE!
!!
WH-WHAT DO MY BOOBS HAVE TO DO WITH ANYTHING!? DON'T TALK ABOUT THEM, YOU PERV!!
JUST LOOK AT 'EM! HOLY COW!
D-DON'T YOU HAVE ANY SHAME? FREAK!
HIC.
HIC.
THE WAY TO CURE HICCUPS...
HIC?

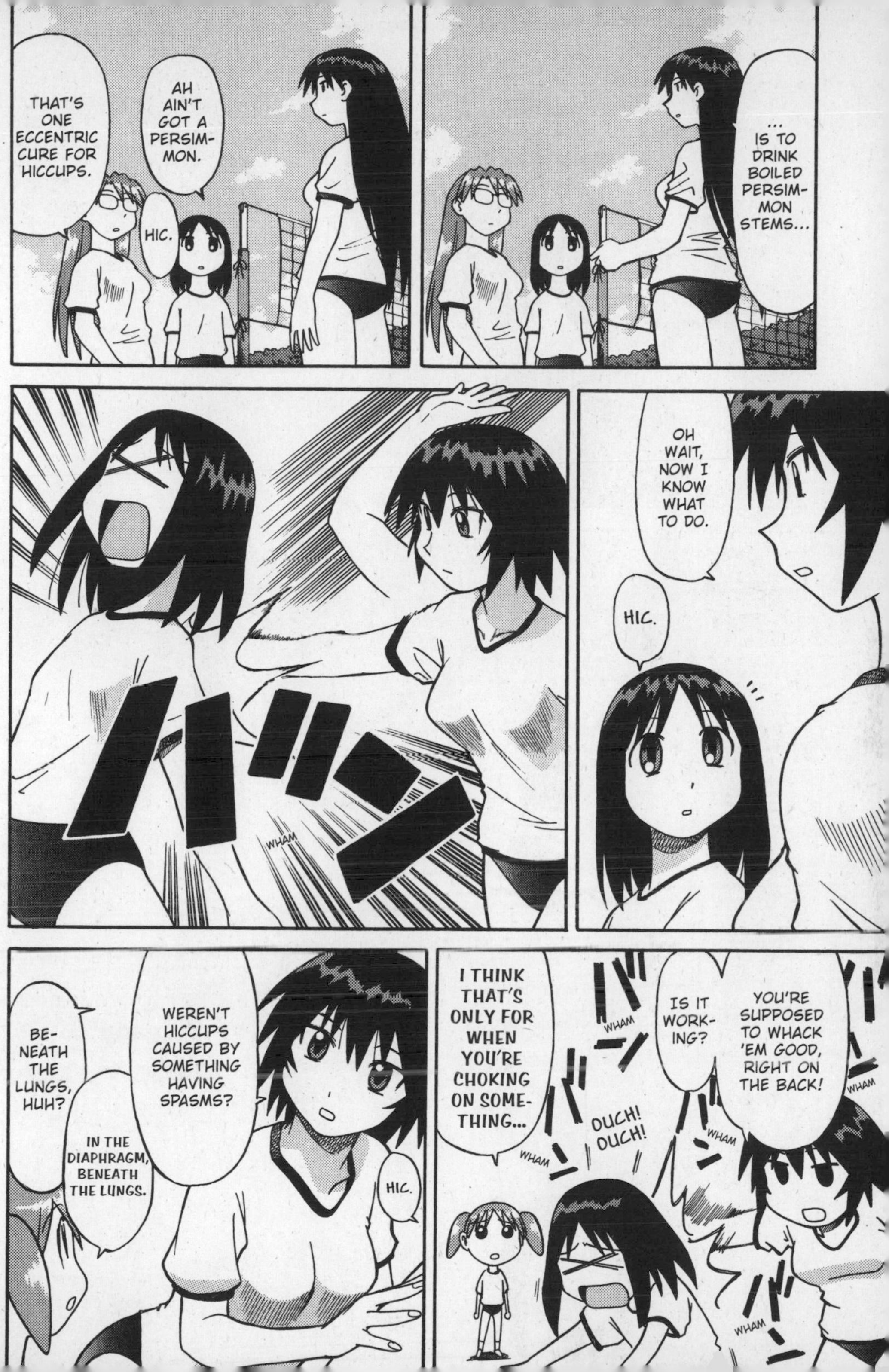

... IS TO DRINK BOILED PERSIM-MON STEMS...
AH AIN'T GOT A PERSIM-MON.
HIC.
THAT'S ONE ECCENTRIC CURE FOR HICCUPS.
OH WAIT, NOW I KNOW WHAT TO DO.
HIC.
WHAM
YOU'RE SUPPOSED TO WHACK 'EM GOOD, RIGHT ON THE BACK!
WHAM
IS IT WORK-ING?
WHAM
I THINK THAT'S ONLY FOR WHEN YOU'RE CHOKING ON SOME-THING...
OUCH! OUCH!
WHAM
WHAM
WEREN'T HICCUPS CAUSED BY SOMETHING HAVING SPASMS?
IN THE DIAPHRAGM, BENEATH THE LUNGS.
BE-NEATH THE LUNGS, HUH?
HIC.

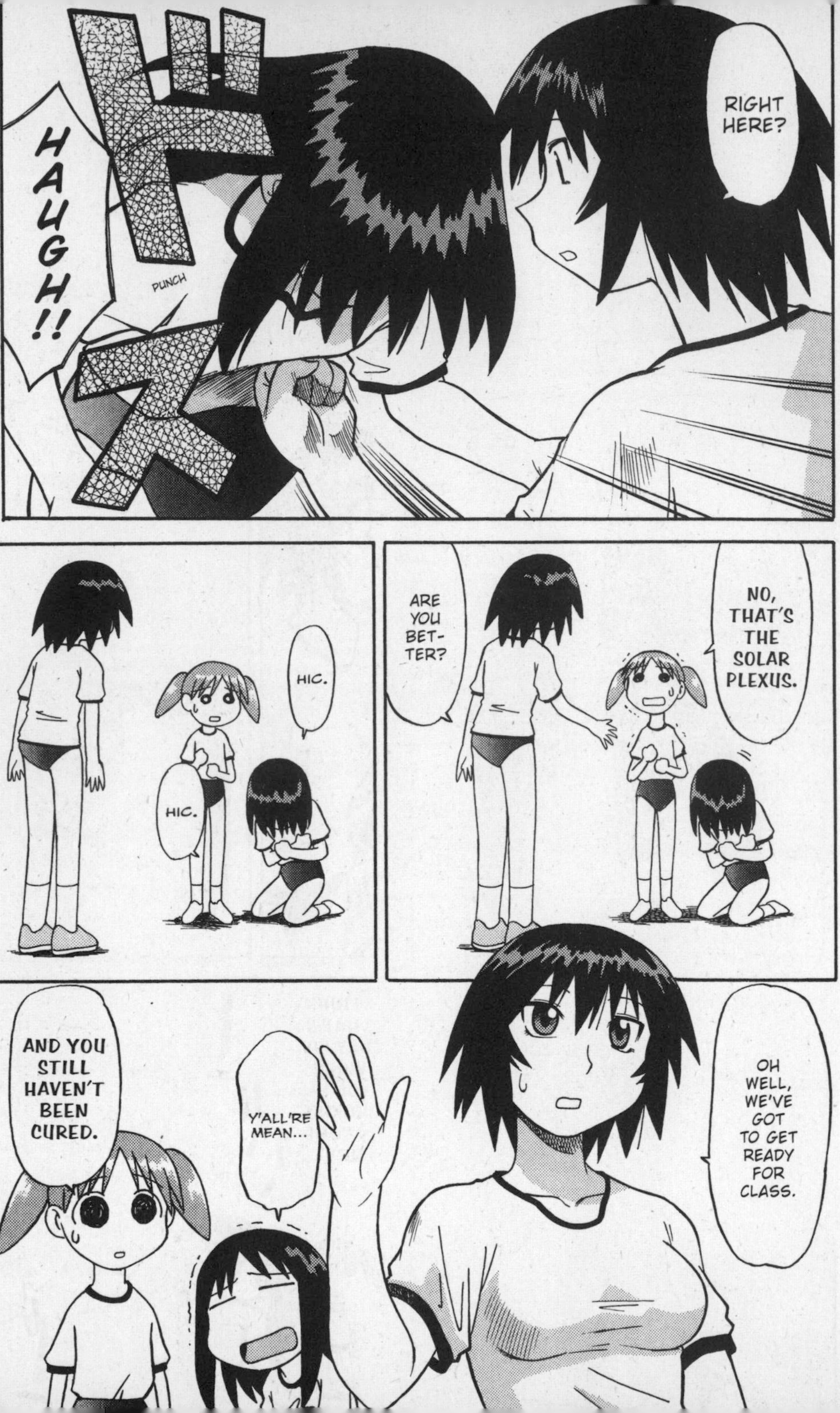
RIGHT HERE?
HAUGH!!
PUNCH
NO, THAT'S THE SOLAR PLEXUS.
ARE YOU BET-TER?
HIC.
HIC.
OH WELL, WE'VE GOT TO GET READY FOR CLASS.
Y'ALL'RE MEAN...
AND YOU STILL HAVEN'T BEEN CURED.

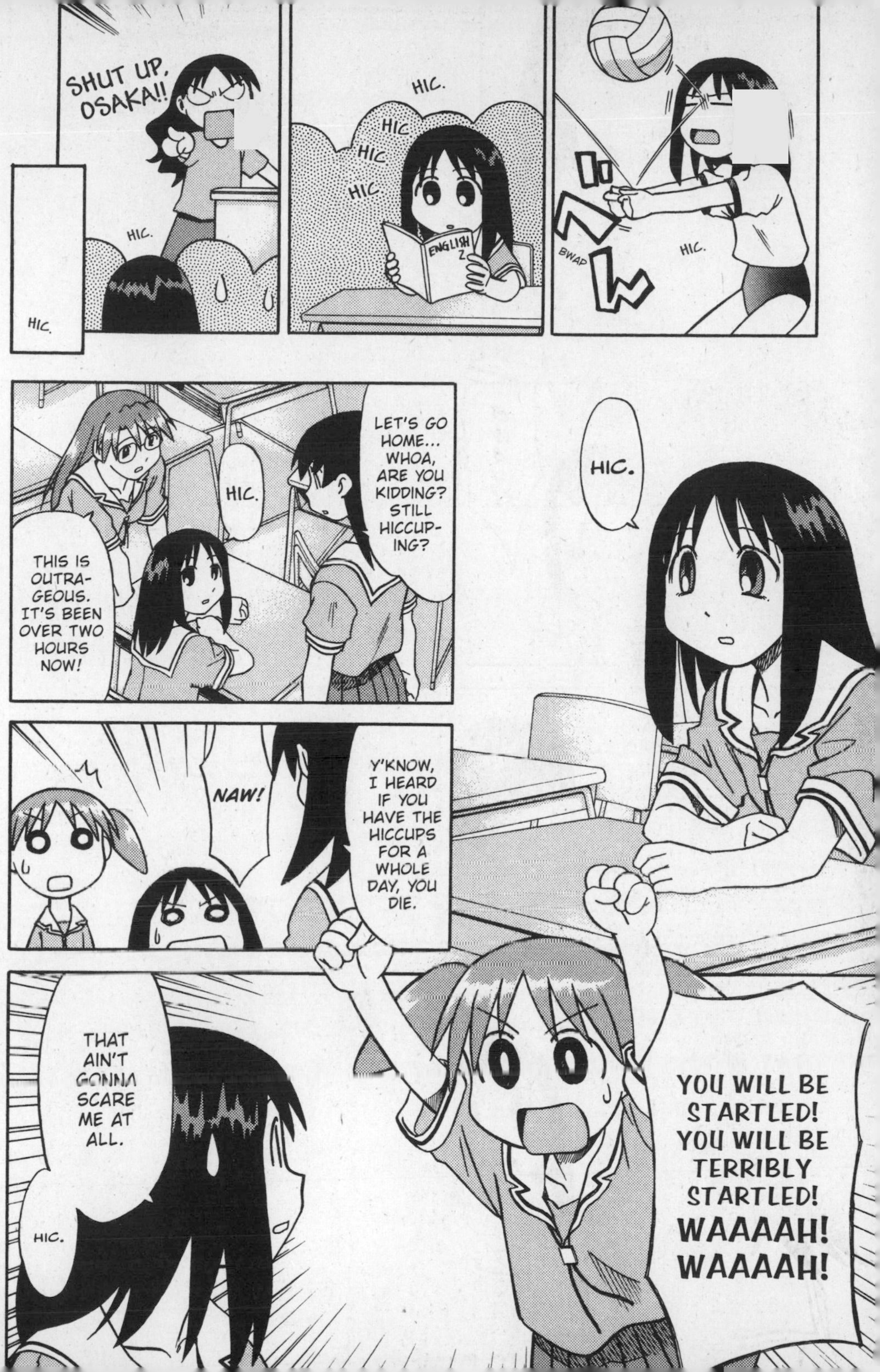
BWAP
HIC.
HIC.
HIC.
HIC.
HIC.
ENGLISH Z
SHUT UP, OSAKA!!
HIC.
HIC.
HIC.
LET'S GO HOME... WHOA, ARE YOU KIDDING? STILL HICCUP-ING?
HIC.
THIS IS OUTRA-GEOUS. IT'S BEEN OVER TWO HOURS NOW!
Y'KNOW, I HEARD IF YOU HAVE THE HICCUPS FOR A WHOLE DAY, YOU DIE.
NAW!
YOU WILL BE STARTLED! YOU WILL BE TERRIBLY STARTLED! WAAAAH! WAAAAH!
THAT AIN'T GONNA SCARE ME AT ALL.
HIC.

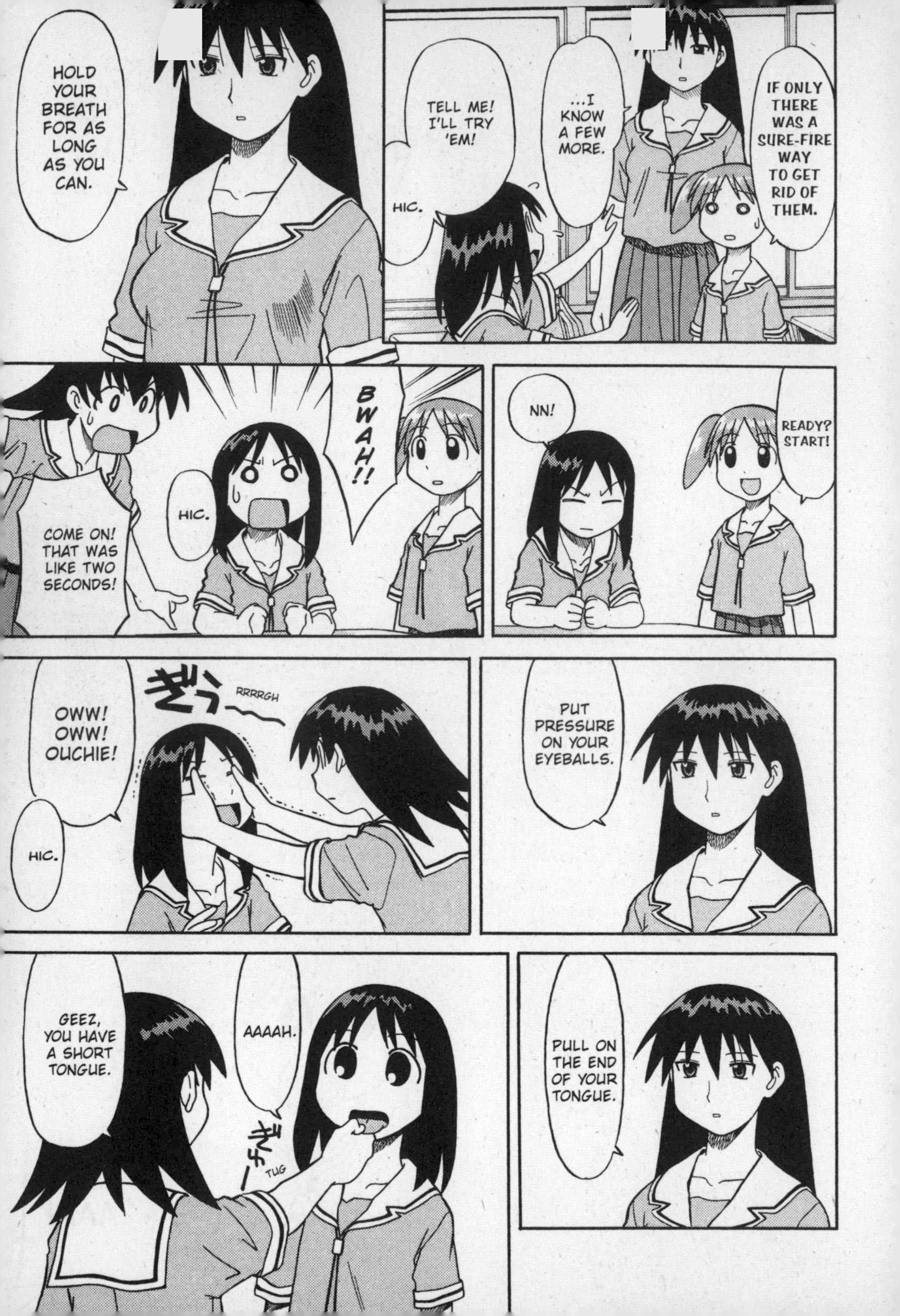
IF ONLY THERE WAS A SURE-FIRE WAY TO GET RID OF THEM.
...I KNOW A FEW MORE.
TELL ME! I'LL TRY 'EM!
HIC.
HOLD YOUR BREATH FOR AS LONG AS YOU CAN.
READY? START!
NN!
BWAH!!
HIC.
COME ON! THAT WAS LIKE TWO SECONDS!
PUT PRESSURE ON YOUR EYEBALLS.
RRRRGH
OWW! OWW! OUCHIE!
HIC.
PULL ON THE END OF YOUR TONGUE.
AAAAH.
TUG
GEEZ, YOU HAVE A SHORT TONGUE.

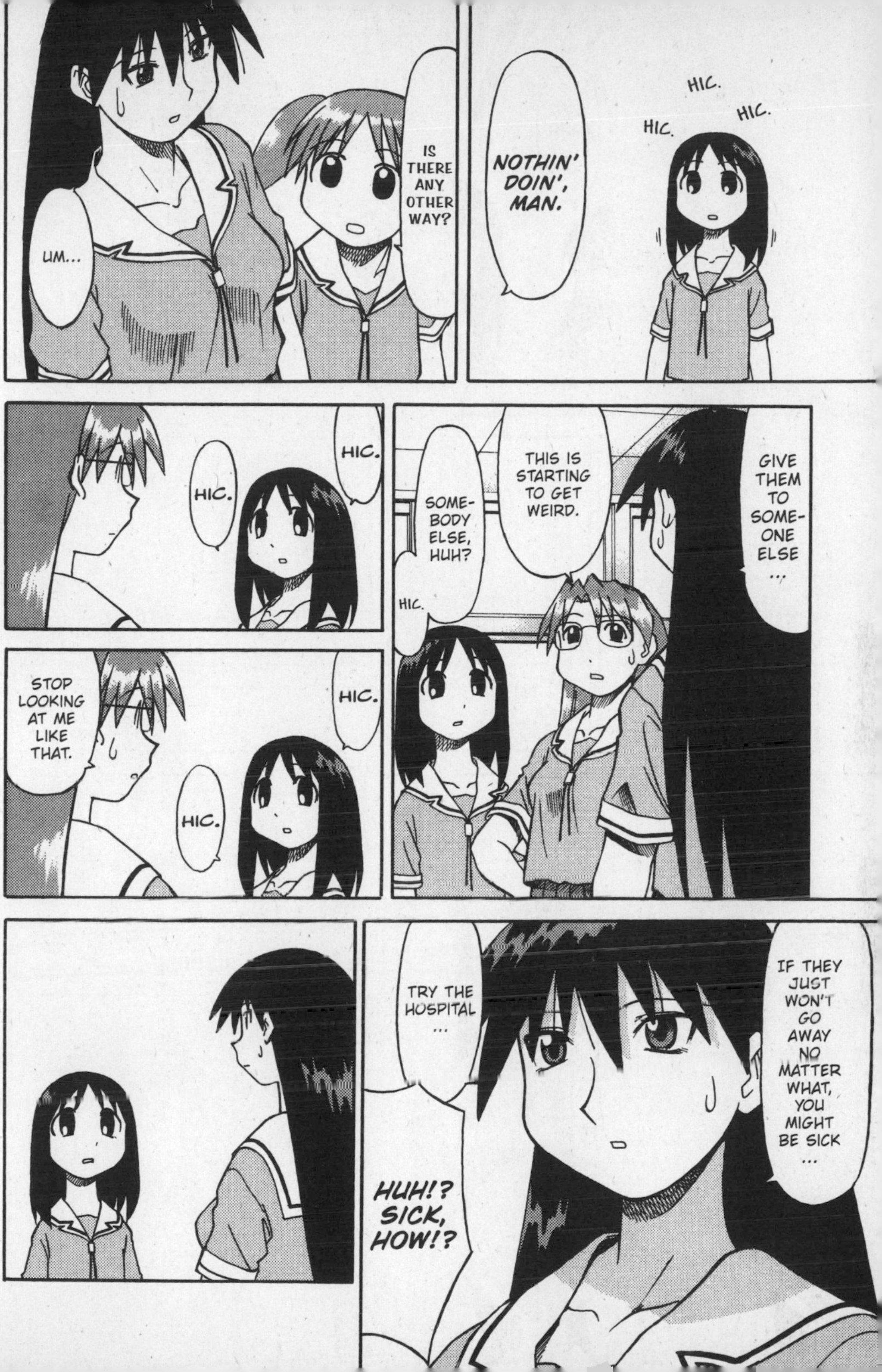
HIC.
HIC.
HIC.
NOTHIN' DOIN', MAN.
IS THERE ANY OTHER WAY?
UM...
GIVE THEM TO SOMEONE ELSE...
THIS IS STARTING TO GET WEIRD.
SOMEBODY ELSE, HUH?
HIC.
HIC.
HIC.
HIC.
STOP LOOKING AT ME LIKE THAT.
HIC.
IF THEY JUST WON'T GO AWAY NO MATTER WHAT, YOU MIGHT BE SICK...
TRY THE HOSPITAL...
HUH!? SICK, HOW!?

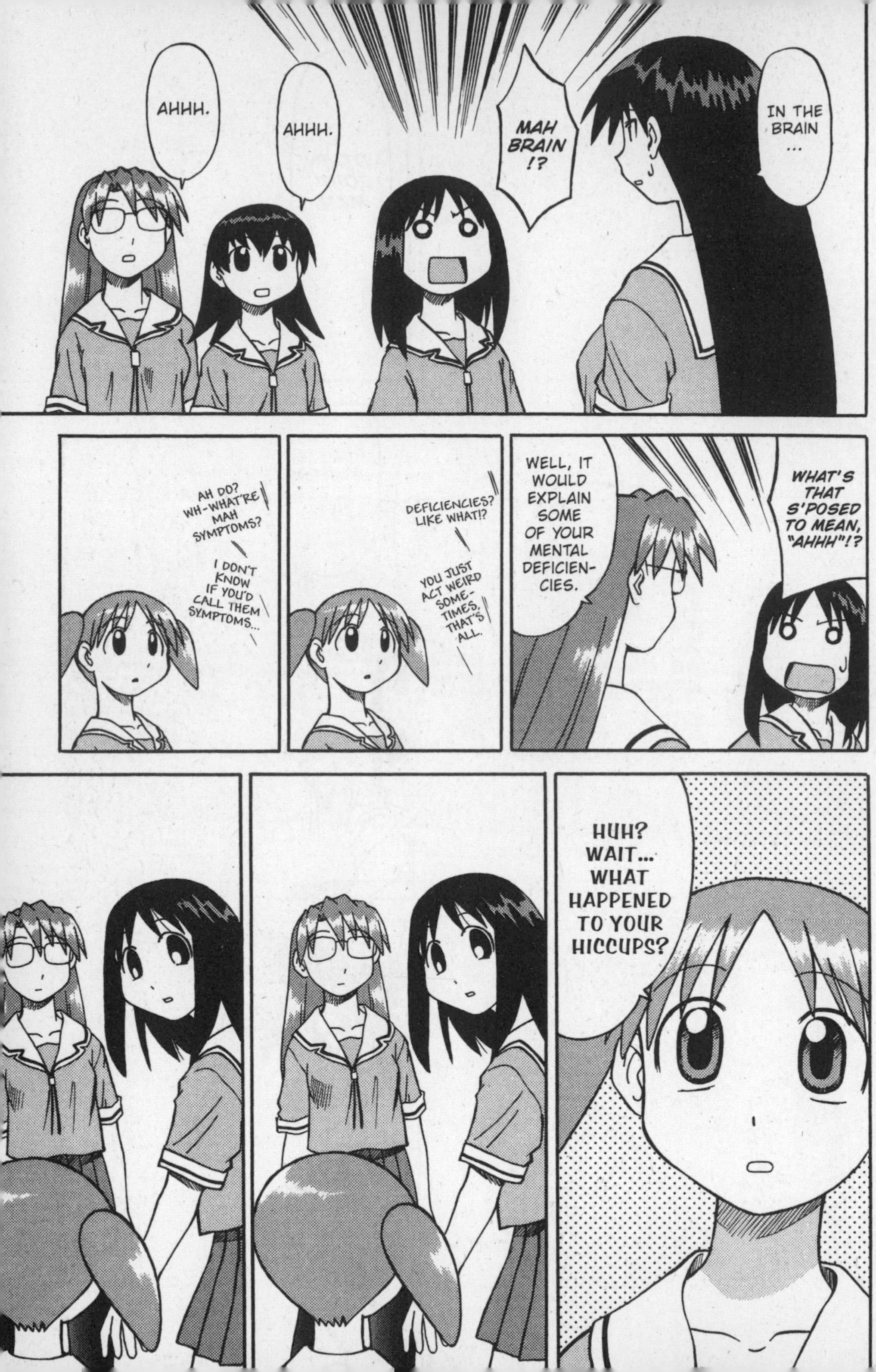
IN THE BRAIN ...
MAH BRAIN !?
AHHH.
AHHH.
WHAT'S THAT S'POSED TO MEAN, "AHHH"!?
WELL, IT WOULD EXPLAIN SOME OF YOUR MENTAL DEFICIENCIES.
DEFICIENCIES? LIKE WHAT!?
YOU JUST ACT WEIRD SOMETIMES, THAT'S ALL.
AH DO? WH-WHAT'RE MAH SYMPTOMS?
I DON'T KNOW IF YOU'D CALL THEM SYMPTOMS...
HUH? WAIT... WHAT HAPPENED TO YOUR HICCUPS?

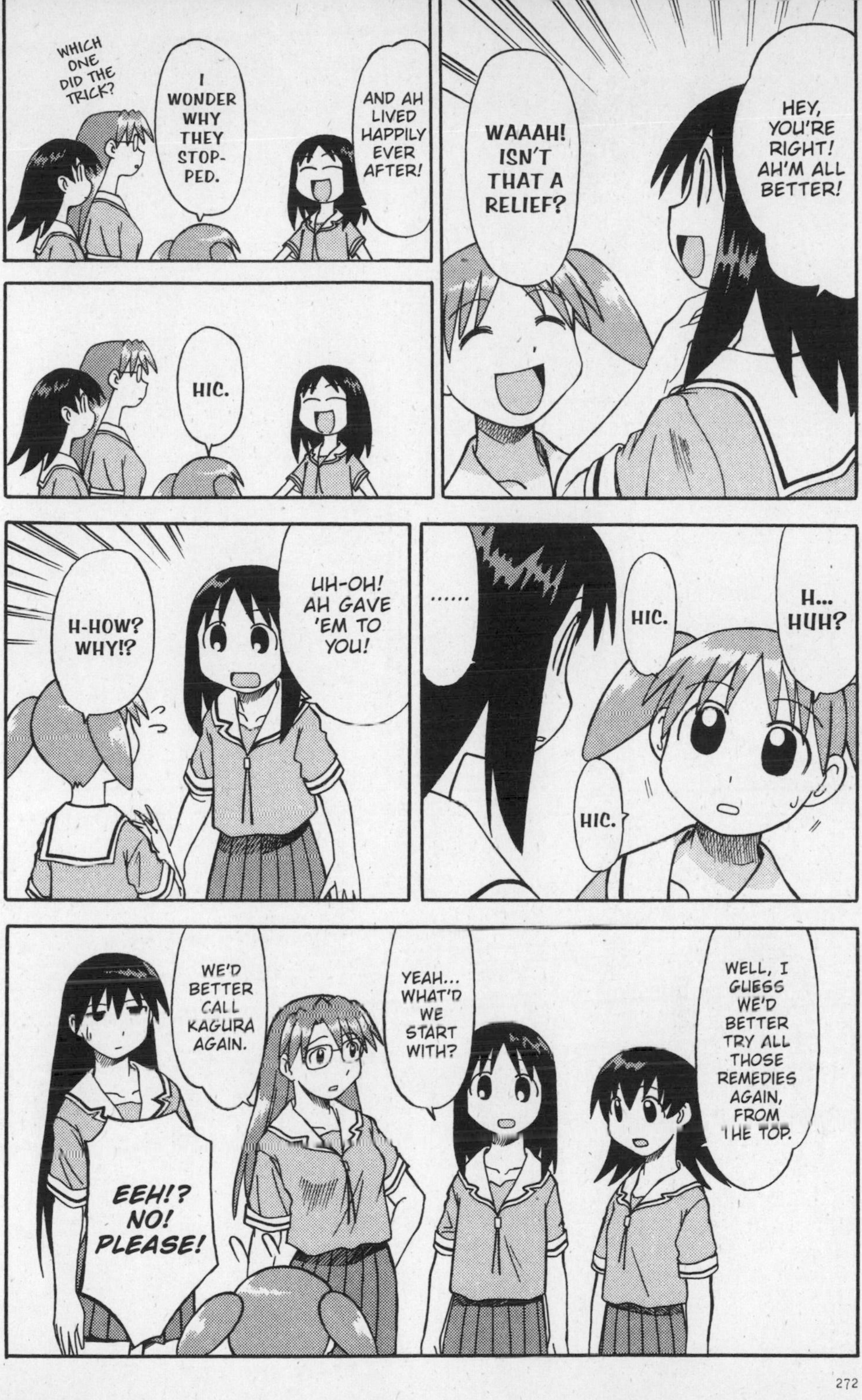
HEY, YOU'RE RIGHT! AH'M ALL BETTER!
WAAAH! ISN'T THAT A RELIEF?
AND AH LIVED HAPPILY EVER AFTER!
I WONDER WHY THEY STOP-PED.
WHICH ONE DID THE TRICK?
HIC.
H... HUH?
HIC.
......
HIC.
UH-OH! AH GAVE 'EM TO YOU!
H-HOW? WHY!?
WELL, I GUESS WE'D BETTER TRY ALL THOSE REMEDIES AGAIN, FROM THE TOP.
YEAH... WHAT'D WE START WITH?
WE'D BETTER CALL KAGURA AGAIN.
EEH!? NO! PLEASE!

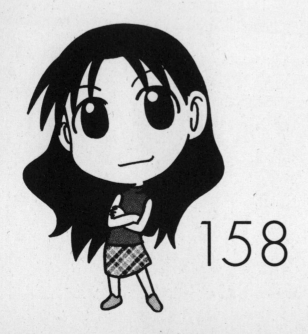

158

161

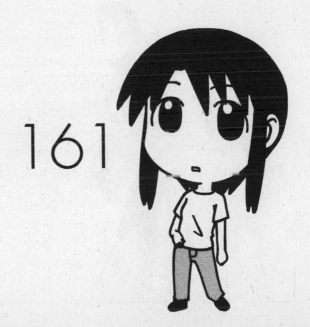

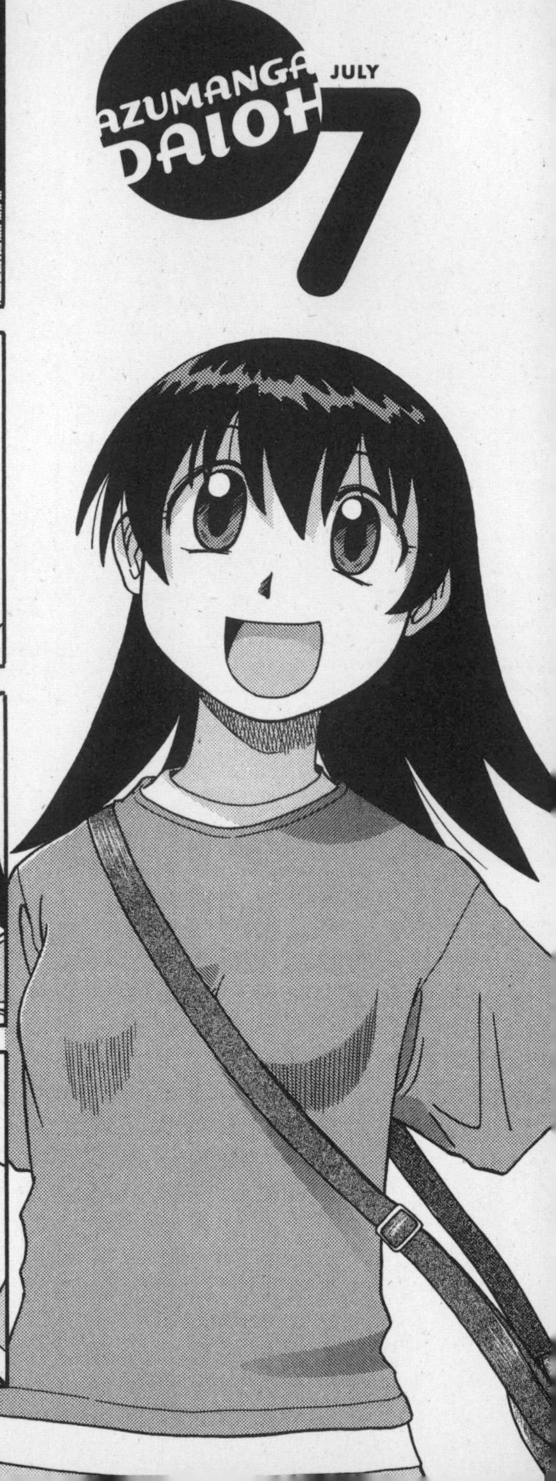
AZUMANGA DAIOH
JULY
7

TEACHER'S SO SMART

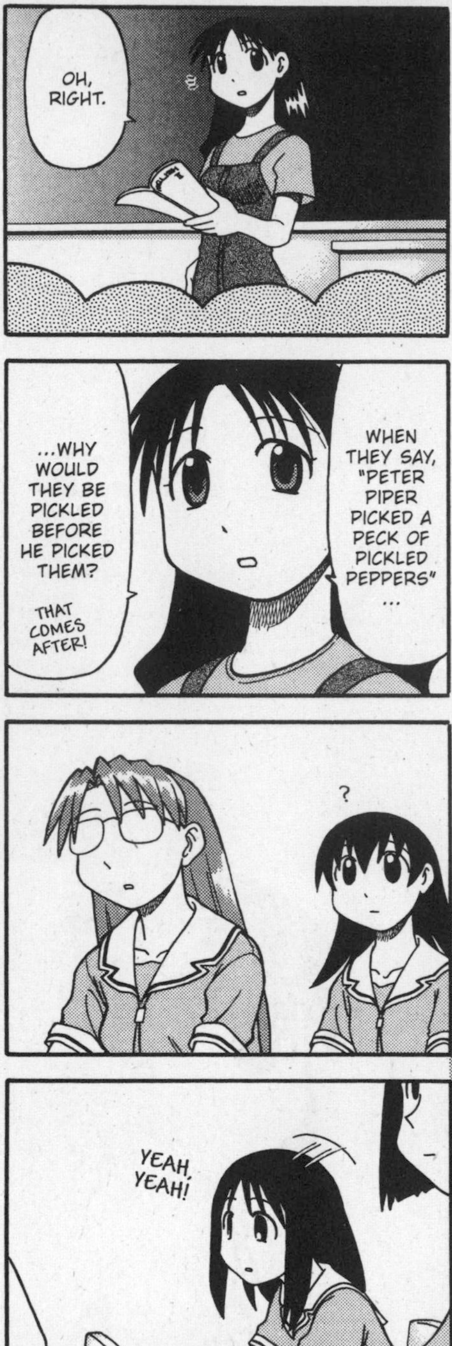
OH, RIGHT.
WHEN THEY SAY, "PETER PIPER PICKED A PECK OF PICKLED PEPPERS" ...
...WHY WOULD THEY BE PICKLED BEFORE HE PICKED THEM?
THAT COMES AFTER!
?
YEAH, YEAH!

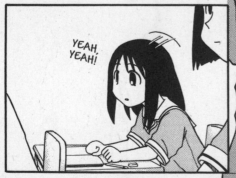

A DREAM

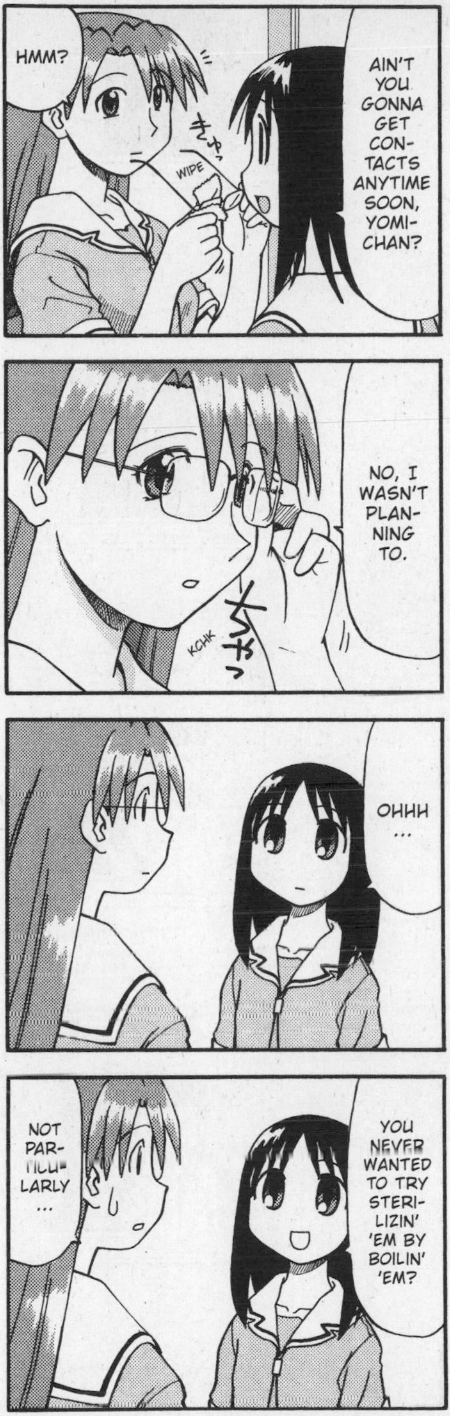
AIN'T YOU GONNA GET CON- TACTS ANYTIME SOON, YOMI- CHAN?
HMM?
WIPE
NO, I WASN'T PLAN- NING TO.
KCHK
OHHH ...
YOU NEVER WANTED TO TRY STERI- LIZIN' 'EM BY BOILIN' 'EM?
NOT PAR- TICU- LARLY ...

TRICKY

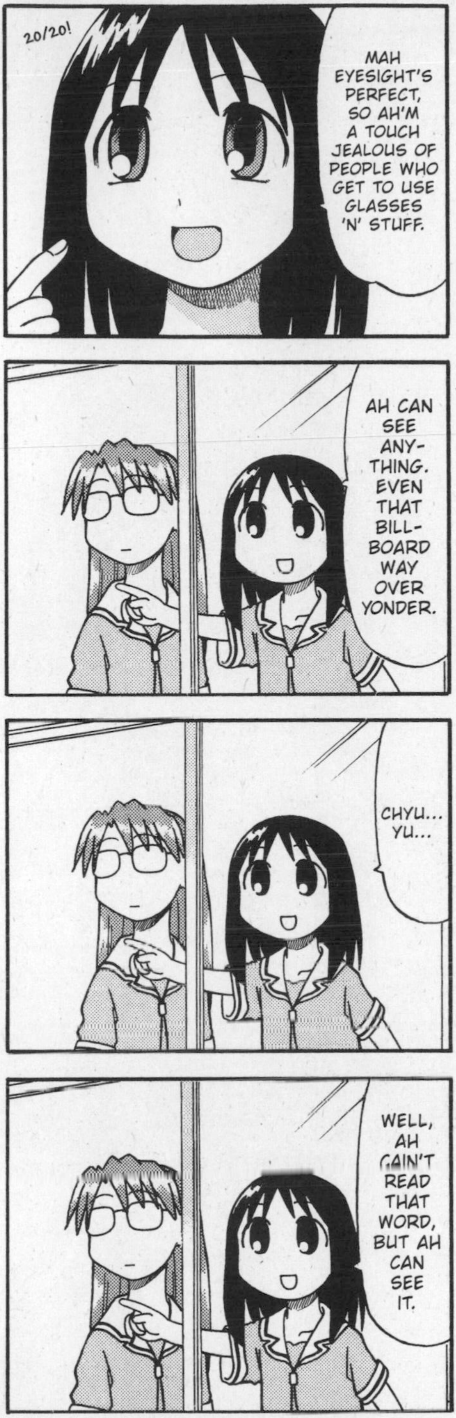
MAH EYESIGHT'S PERFECT, SO AH'M A TOUCH JEALOUS OF PEOPLE WHO GET TO USE GLASSES 'N' STUFF.
20/20!
AH CAN SEE ANY- THING. EVEN THAT BILL- BOARD WAY OVER YONDER.
CHYU... YU...
WELL, AH CAIN'T READ THAT WORD, BUT AH CAN SEE IT.

GENTLEMEN

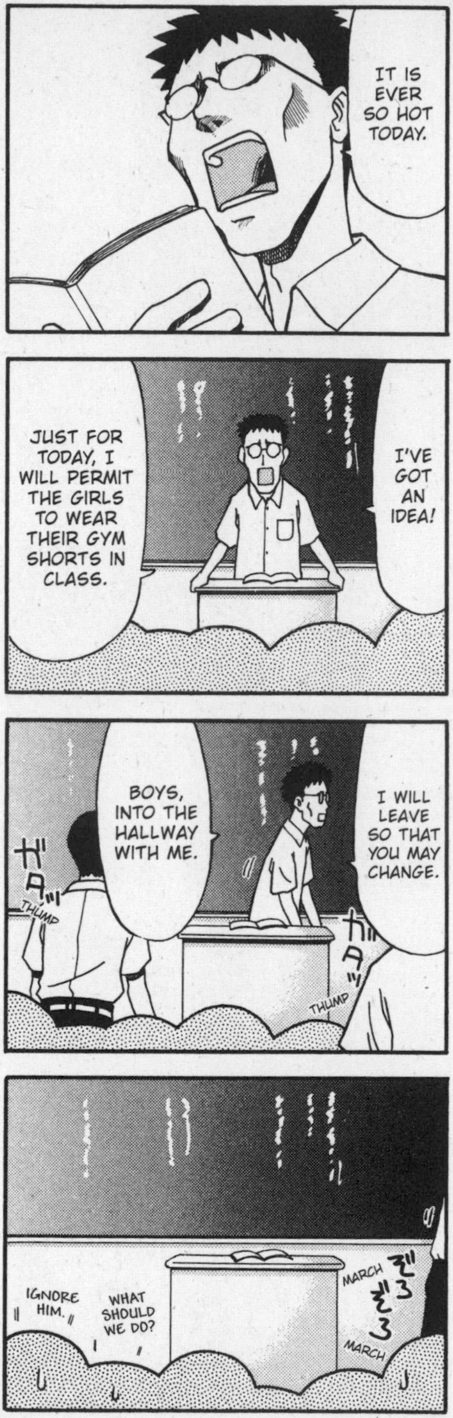
IT IS EVER SO HOT TODAY.
I'VE GOT AN IDEA!
JUST FOR TODAY, I WILL PERMIT THE GIRLS TO WEAR THEIR GYM SHORTS IN CLASS.
I WILL LEAVE SO THAT YOU MAY CHANGE.
ガタッ
THUMP
BOYS, INTO THE HALLWAY WITH ME.
ガタッ
THUMP
ぞろぞろ
MARCH
MARCH
WHAT SHOULD WE DO?
IGNORE HIM.

COMPLETELY UNEXPECTED

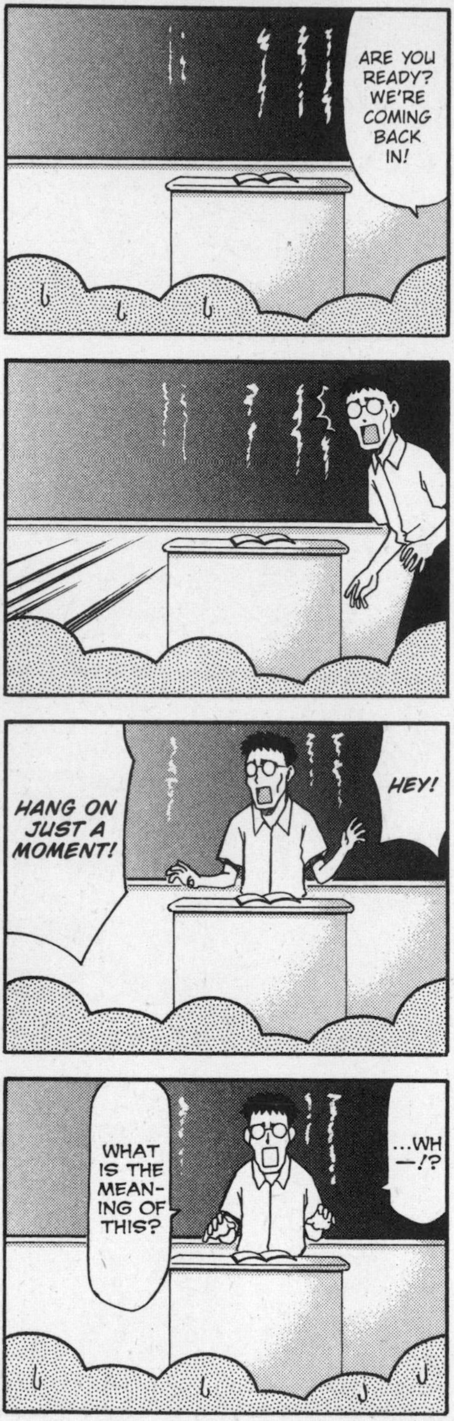
ARE YOU READY? WE'RE COMING BACK IN!
HEY!
HANG ON JUST A MOMENT!
...WH—!?
WHAT IS THE MEANING OF THIS?

MORON

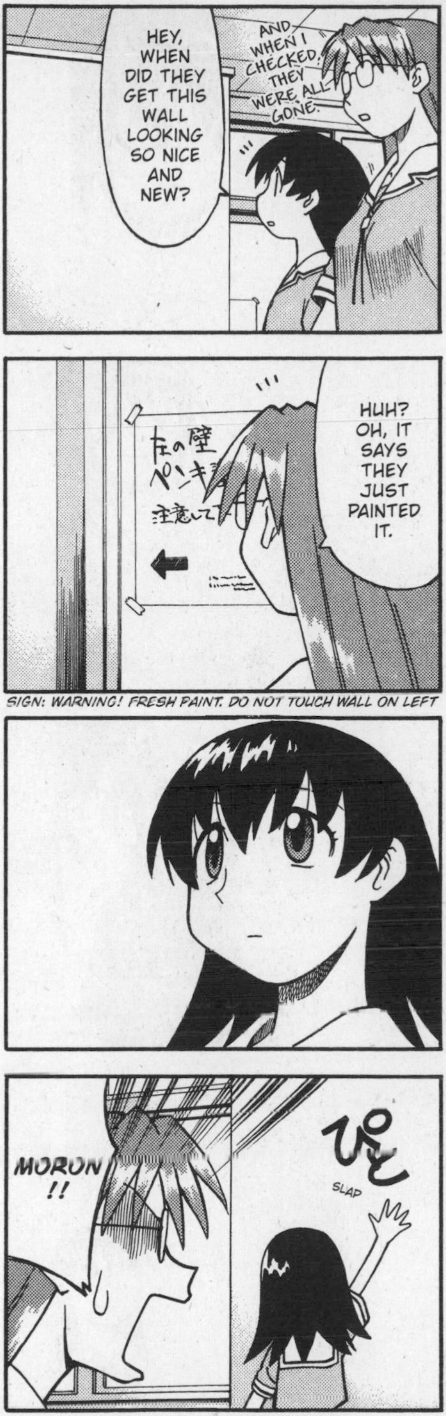
AND WHEN I CHECKED, THEY WERE ALL GONE.
HEY, WHEN DID THEY GET THIS WALL LOOKING SO NICE AND NEW?
HUH? OH, IT SAYS THEY JUST PAINTED IT.
左の壁
ペンキ
注意して
ぴと
SLAP
MORON!!

SIGN: WARNING! FRESH PAINT. DO NOT TOUCH WALL ON LEFT

WHY?

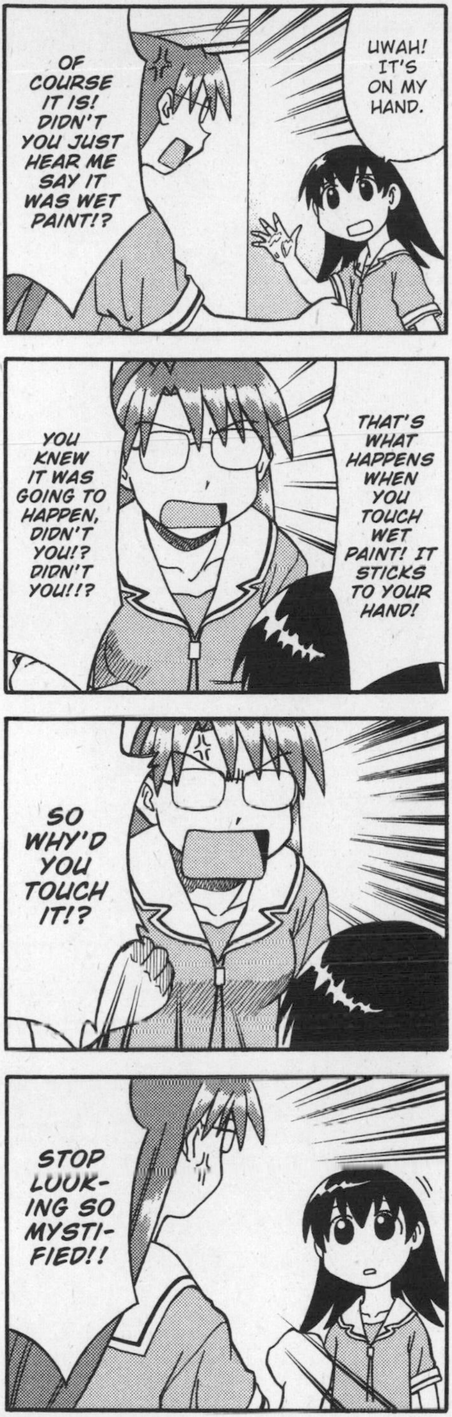
UWAH! IT'S ON MY HAND.
OF COURSE IT IS! DIDN'T YOU JUST HEAR ME SAY IT WAS WET PAINT!?
THAT'S WHAT HAPPENS WHEN YOU TOUCH WET PAINT! IT STICKS TO YOUR HAND!
YOU KNEW IT WAS GOING TO HAPPEN, DIDN'T YOU!? DIDN'T YOU!!?
SO WHY'D YOU TOUCH IT!?
STOP LOOKING SO MYSTIFIED!!

SCOLDED

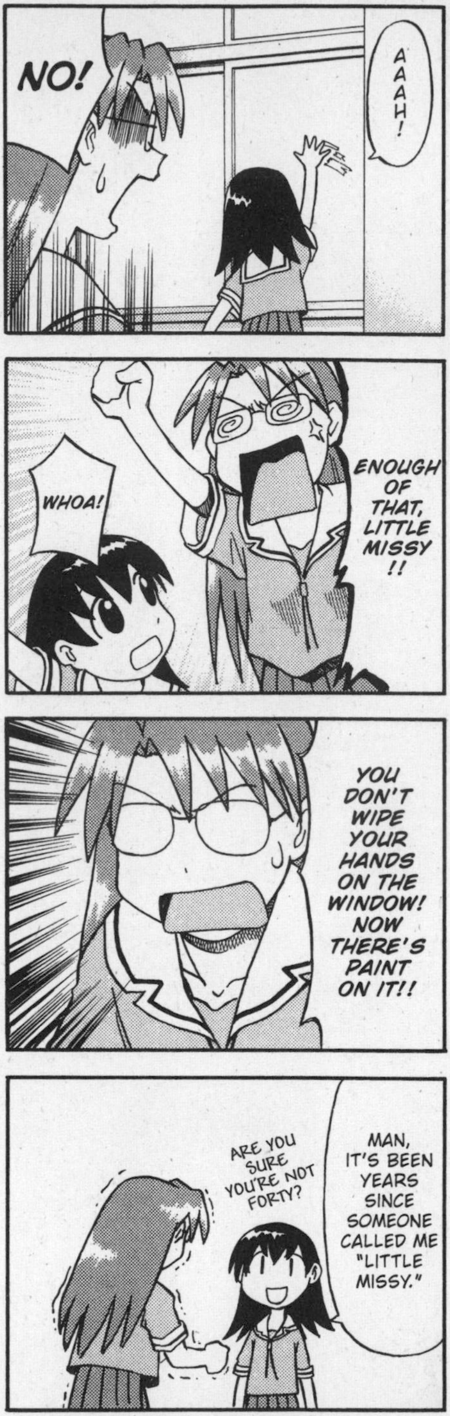
AAAH!
NO!
ENOUGH OF THAT, LITTLE MISSY!!
WHOA!
YOU DON'T WIPE YOUR HANDS ON THE WINDOW! NOW THERE'S PAINT ON IT!!
MAN, IT'S BEEN YEARS SINCE SOMEONE CALLED ME "LITTLE MISSY."
ARE YOU SURE YOU'RE NOT FORTY?

I WAS PRESUMPTUOUS

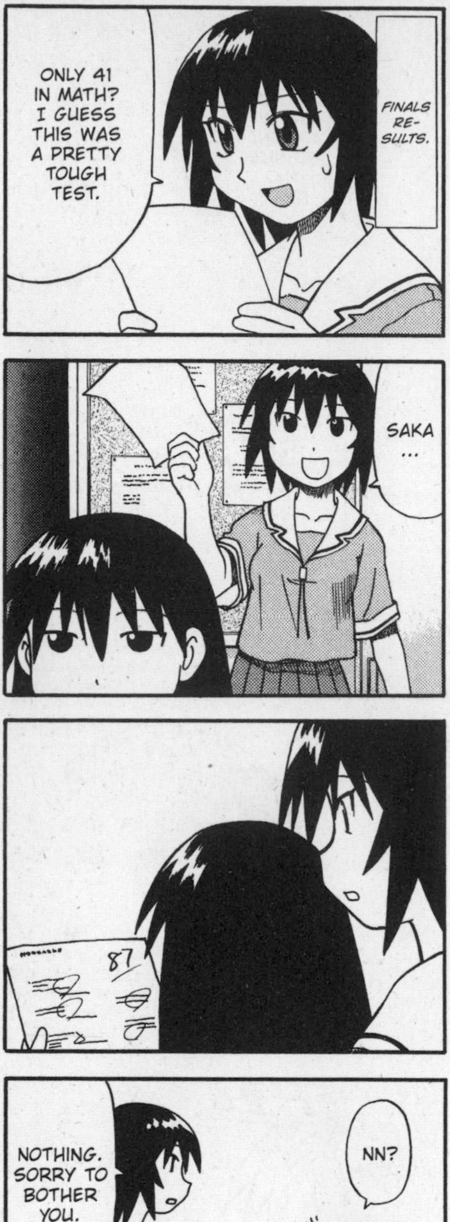
FINALS RESULTS.
ONLY 41 IN MATH? I GUESS THIS WAS A PRETTY TOUGH TEST.
SAKA...
87
NN?
NOTHING. SORRY TO BOTHER YOU.

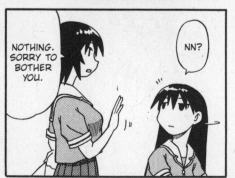

AM I JUST DUMB?

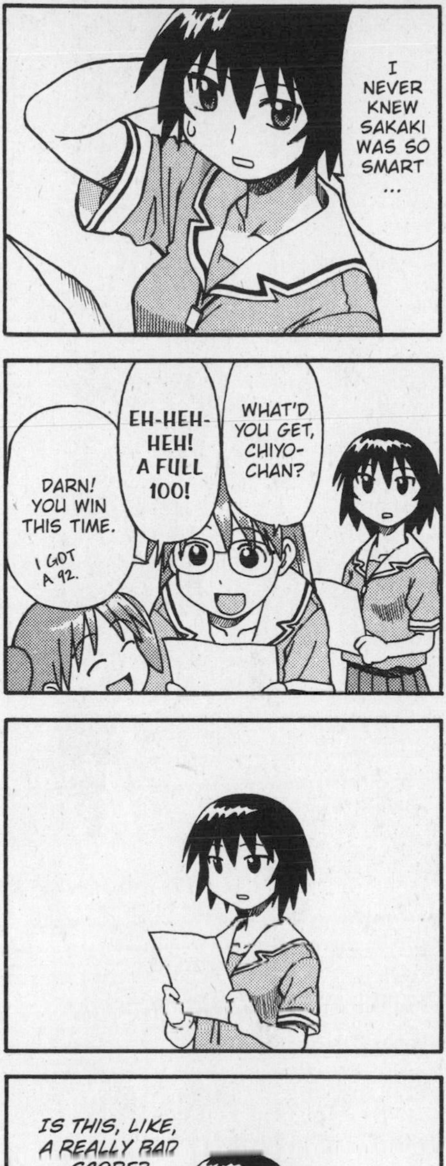
I NEVER KNEW SAKAKI WAS SO SMART ...
WHAT'D YOU GET, CHIYO-CHAN?
EH-HEH-HEH! A FULL 100!
DARN! YOU WIN THIS TIME.
I GOT A 92.
IS THIS, LIKE, A REALLY BAD SCORE?

MY FRIENDS

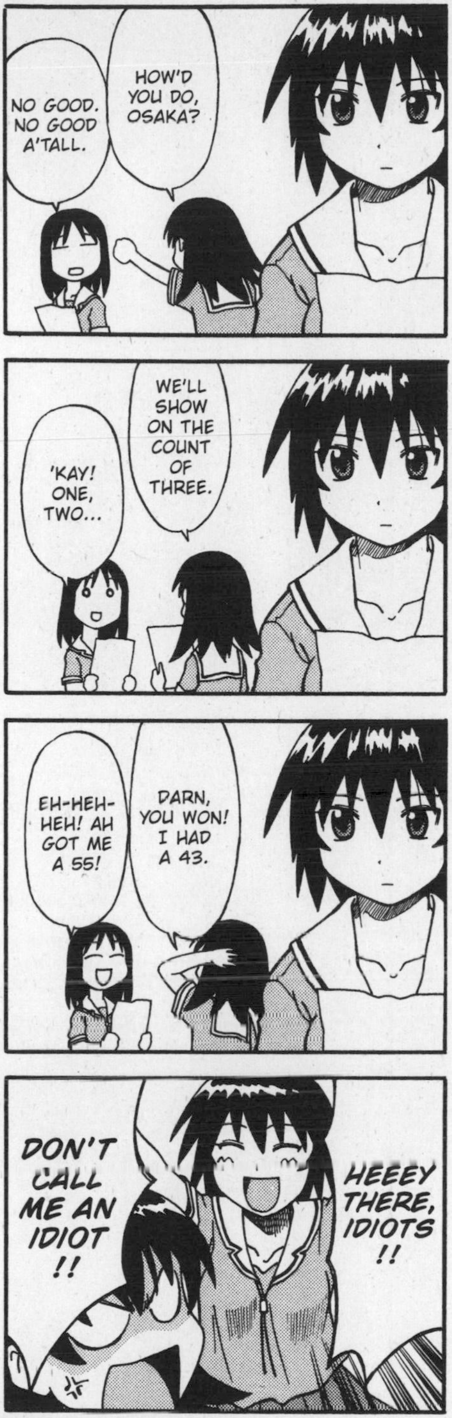
HOW'D YOU DO, OSAKA?
NO GOOD. NO GOOD A'TALL.
WE'LL SHOW ON THE COUNT OF THREE.
'KAY! ONE, TWO...
DARN, YOU WON! I HAD A 43.
EH-HEH-HEH! AH GOT ME A 55!
HEEEY THERE, IDIOTS!!
DON'T CALL ME AN IDIOT!!

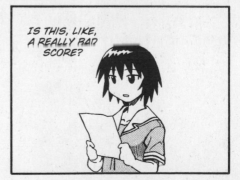

IT WAS CLOSE

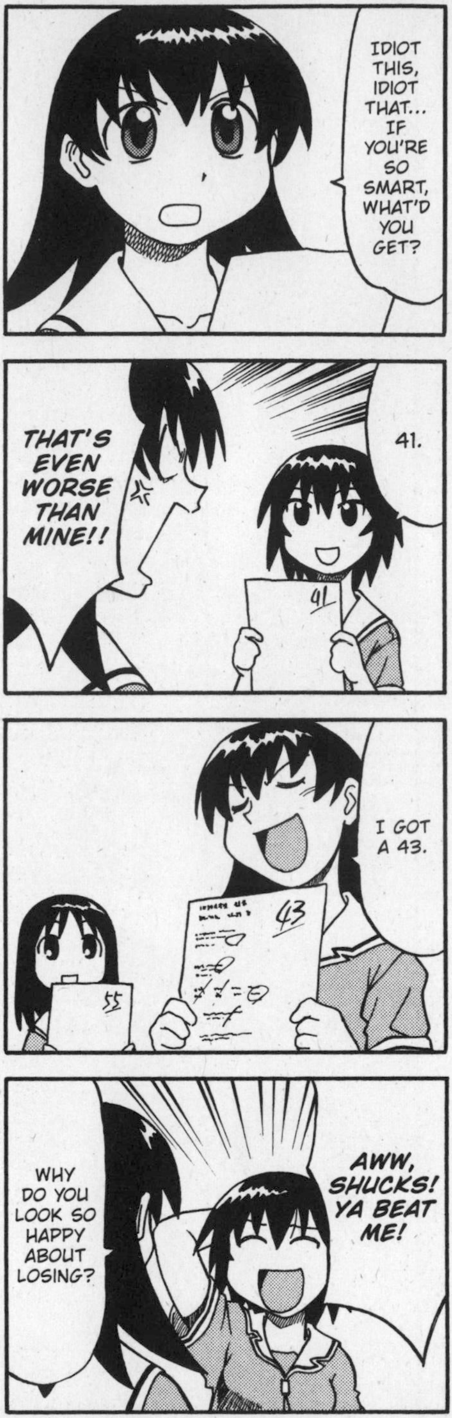
IDIOT THIS, IDIOT THAT... IF YOU'RE SO SMART, WHAT'D YOU GET?
41.
THAT'S EVEN WORSE THAN MINE!!
I GOT A 43.
AWW, SHUCKS! YA BEAT ME!
WHY DO YOU LOOK SO HAPPY ABOUT LOSING?

PERV

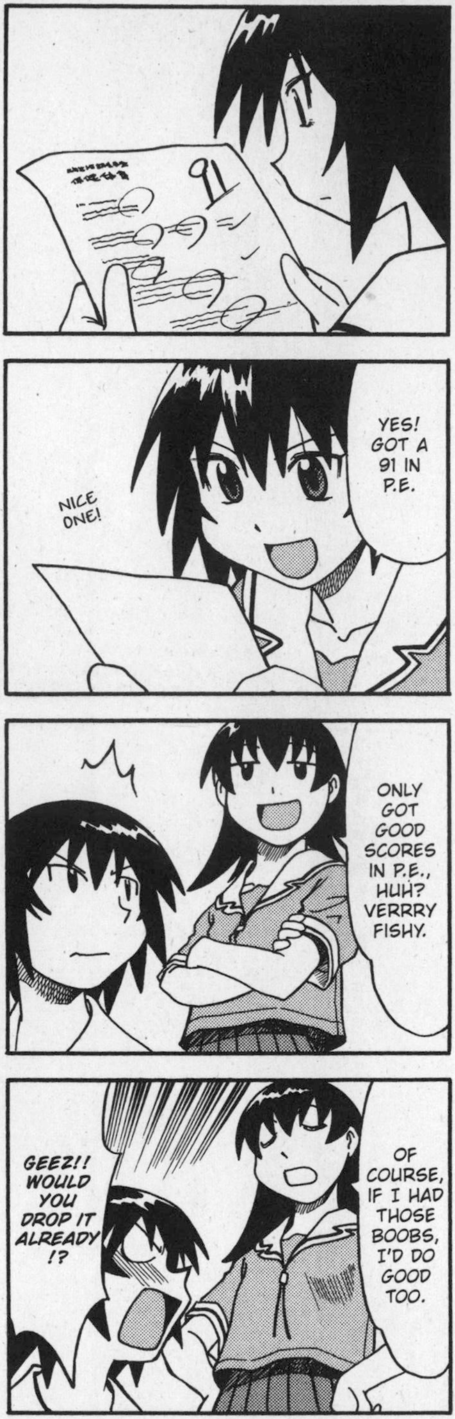
YES! GOT A 91 IN P.E.
NICE ONE!
ONLY GOT GOOD SCORES IN P.E., HUH? VERRRY FISHY.
OF COURSE, IF I HAD THOSE BOOBS, I'D DO GOOD TOO.
GEEZ!! WOULD YOU DROP IT ALREADY!?

THE REASON FOR OBSESSION

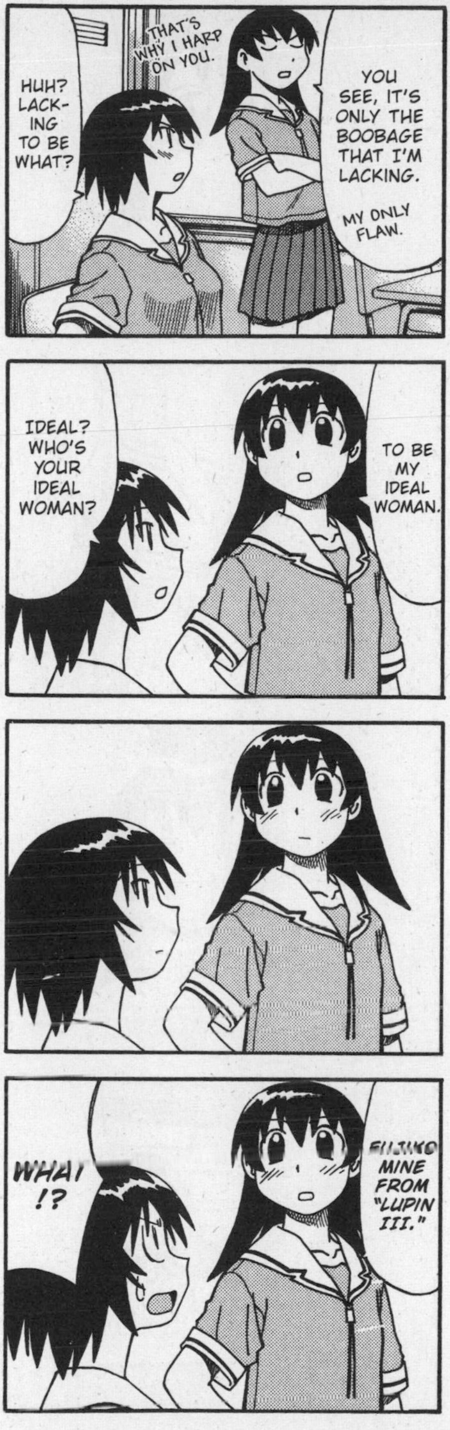
YOU SEE, IT'S ONLY THE BOOBAGE THAT I'M LACKING.
MY ONLY FLAW.
THAT'S WHY I HARP ON YOU.
HUH? LACKING TO BE WHAT?
TO BE MY IDEAL WOMAN.
IDEAL? WHO'S YOUR IDEAL WOMAN?
FUJIKO MINE FROM "LUPIN III."
WHAT !?

NOT EVEN CLOSE

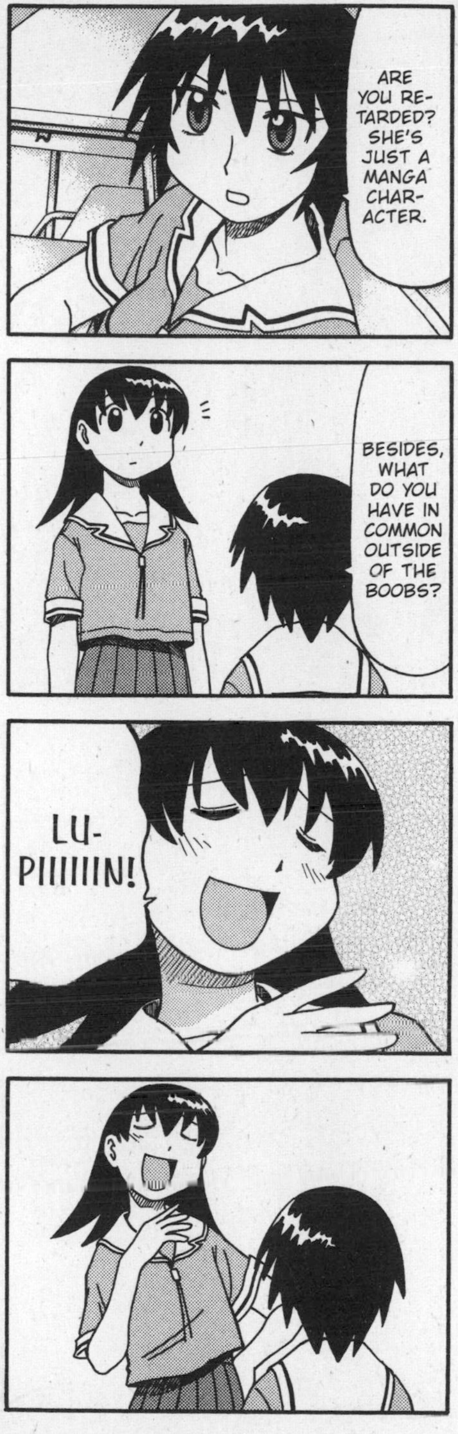
ARE YOU RE-TARDED? SHE'S JUST A MANGA CHAR-ACTER.
BESIDES, WHAT DO YOU HAVE IN COMMON OUTSIDE OF THE BOOBS?
LU-PIIIIIIN!

HIP HIP HOORAY

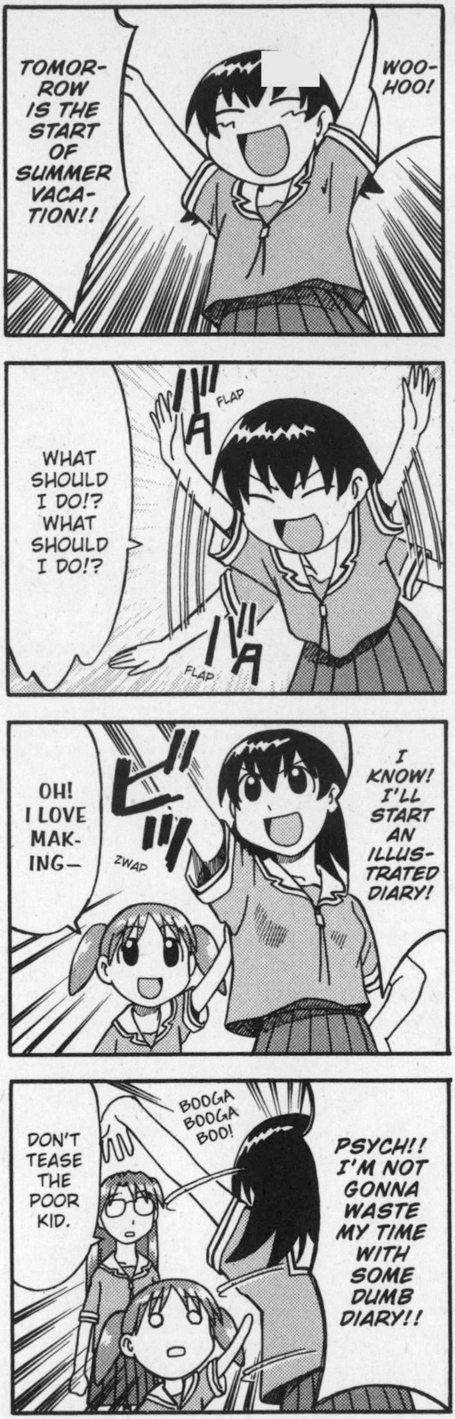
WOO-HOO!
TOMORROW IS THE START OF SUMMER VACATION!!
WHAT SHOULD I DO!? WHAT SHOULD I DO!?
FLAP
FLAP
I KNOW! I'LL START AN ILLUSTRATED DIARY!
ZWAP
OH! I LOVE MAKING—
PSYCH!! I'M NOT GONNA WASTE MY TIME WITH SOME DUMB DIARY!!
BOOGA BOOGA BOO!
DON'T TEASE THE POOR KID.

McB'S

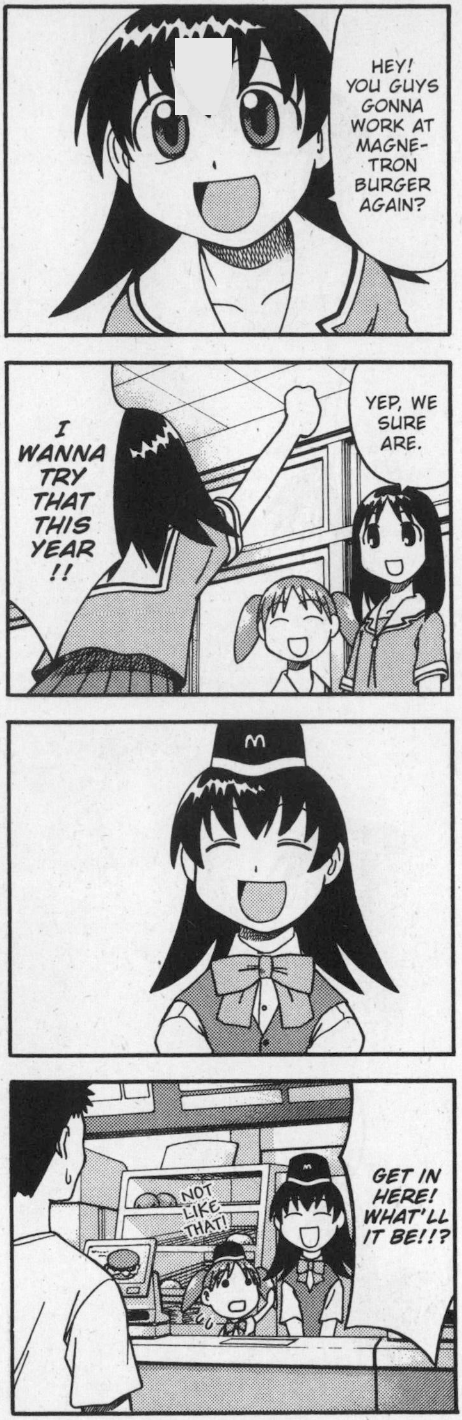
HEY! YOU GUYS GONNA WORK AT MAGNETRON BURGER AGAIN?
YEP, WE SURE ARE.
I WANNA TRY THAT THIS YEAR!!
GET IN HERE! WHAT'LL IT BE!!?
NOT LIKE THAT!

IT'S MY SECOND TIME TOO

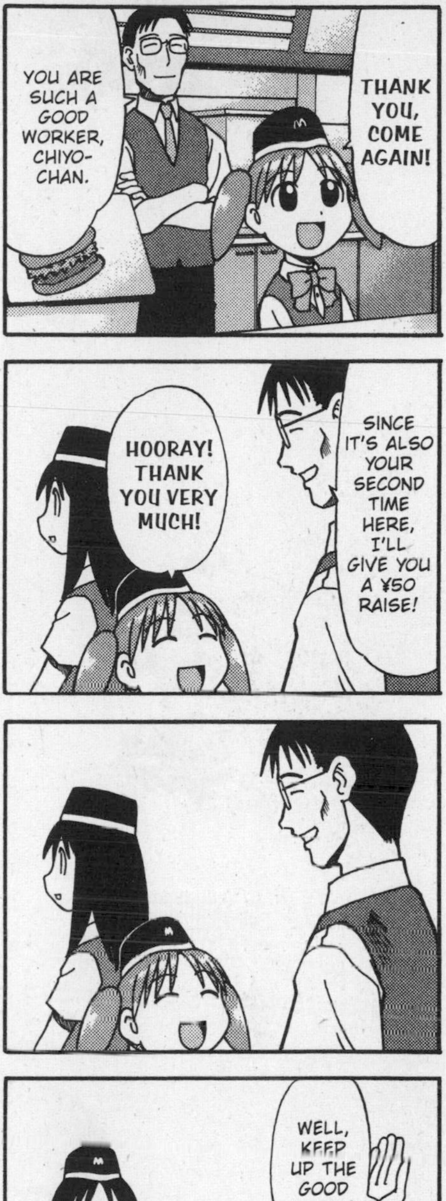
THANK YOU, COME AGAIN!
YOU ARE SUCH A GOOD WORKER, CHIYO-CHAN.
SINCE IT'S ALSO YOUR SECOND TIME HERE, I'LL GIVE YOU A ¥50 RAISE!
HOORAY! THANK YOU VERY MUCH!
WELL, KEEP UP THE GOOD WORK!

IS SHE EXCITED?

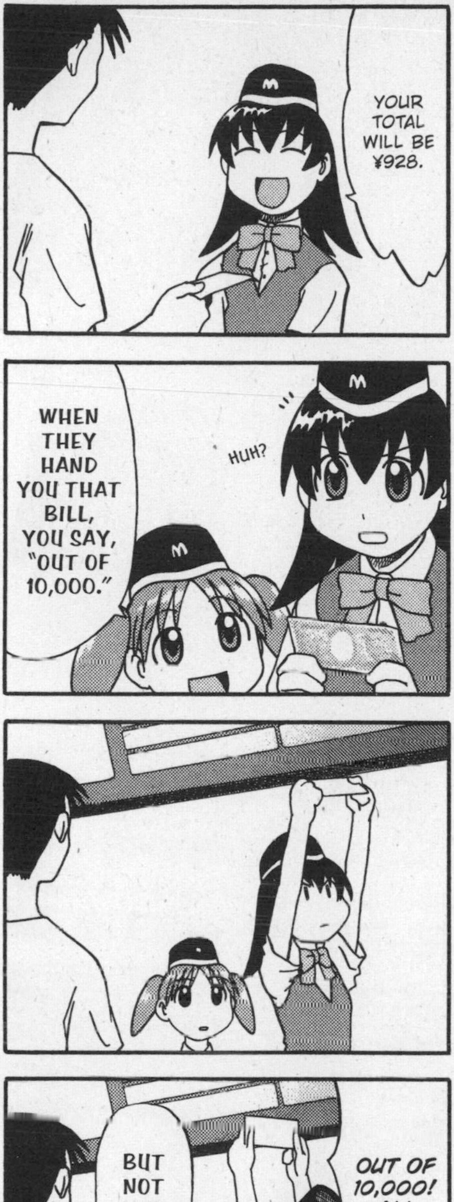
YOUR TOTAL WILL BE ¥928.
WHEN THEY HAND YOU THAT BILL, YOU SAY, "OUT OF 10,000."
HUH?
OUT OF 10,000! ALL HAIL THE ¥10,000 BILL!
BUT NOT LIKE THAT.

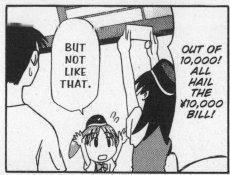

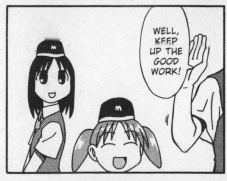

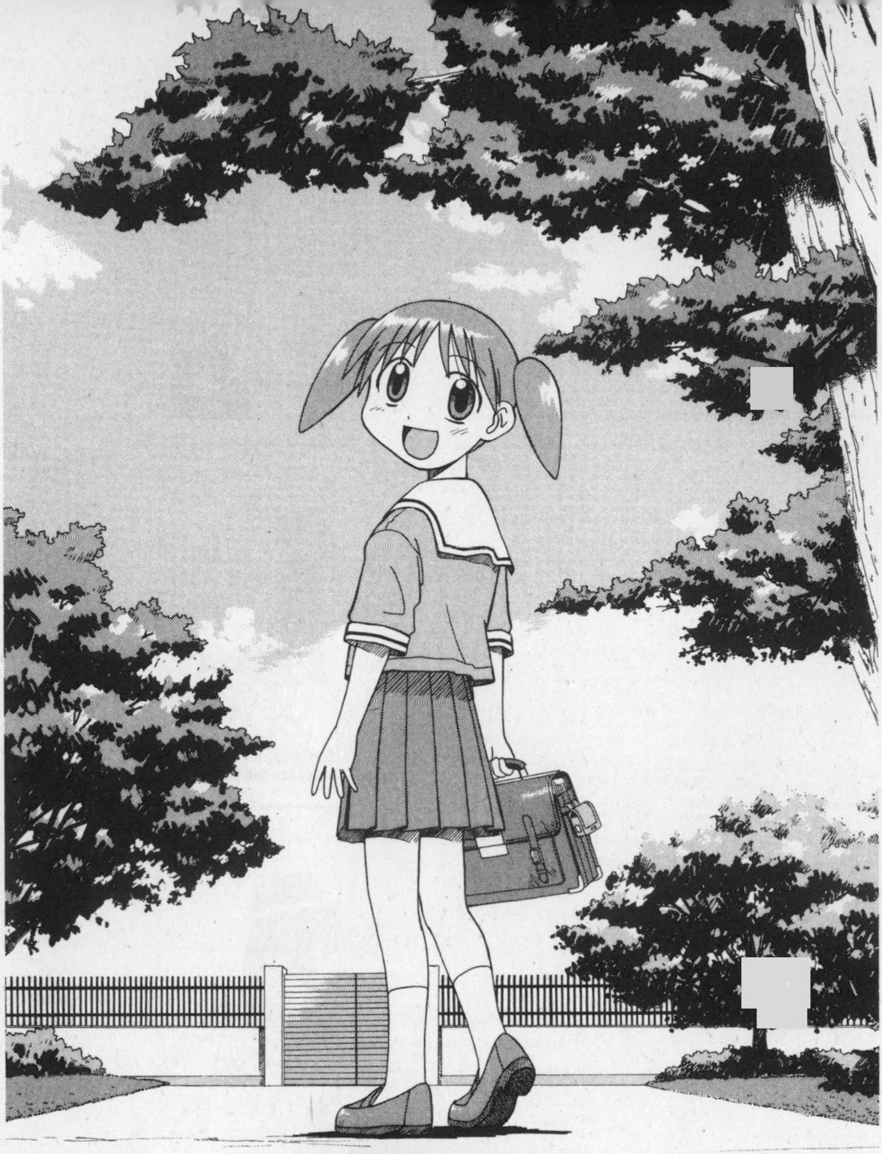

AZUMANGA DAIOH JULY SPECIAL 7

A DAY IN THE LIFE OF CHIYO-CHAN

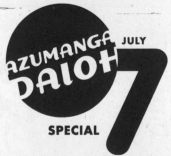

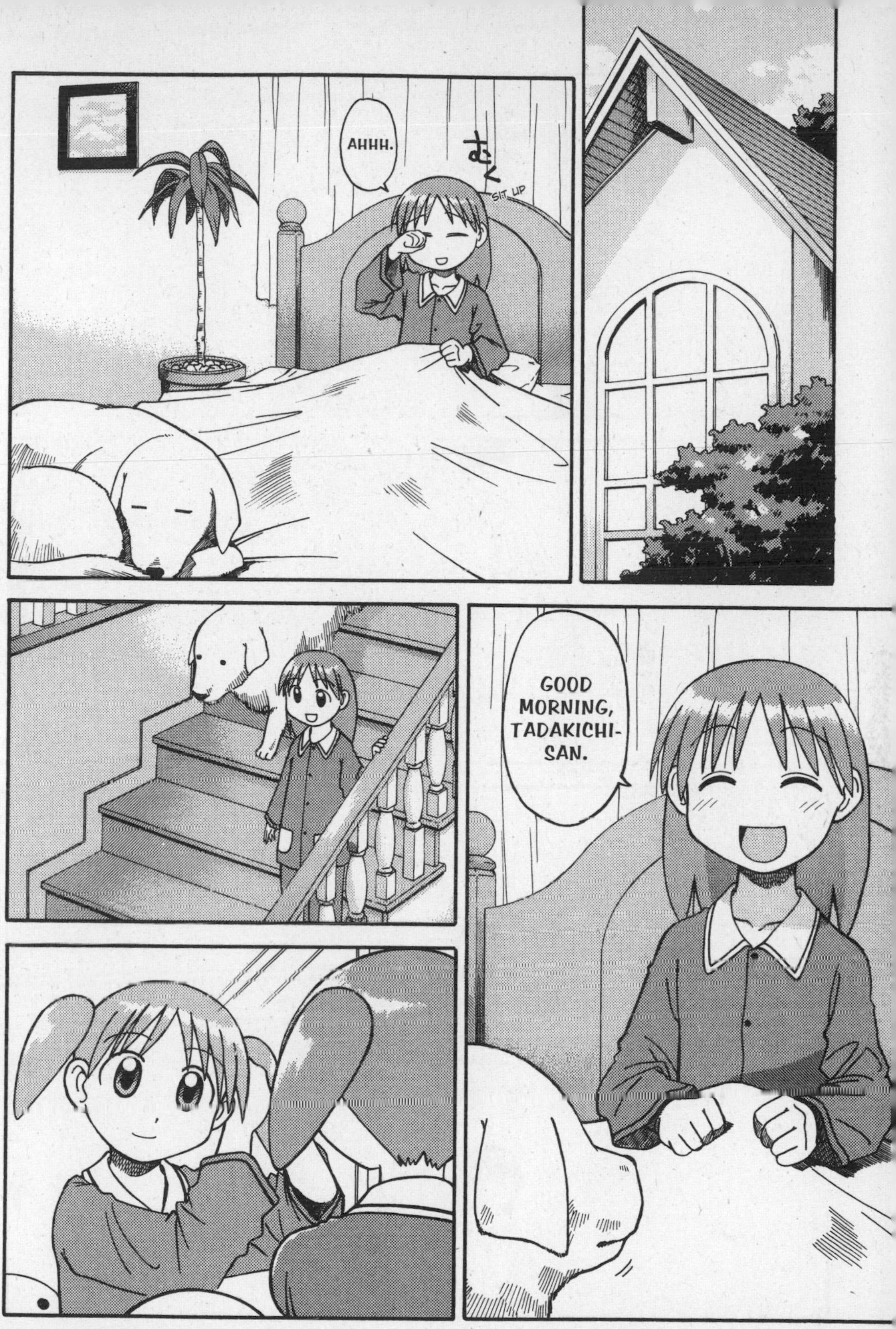
AHHH.
むく
SIT UP
GOOD MORNING, TADAKICHI-SAN.

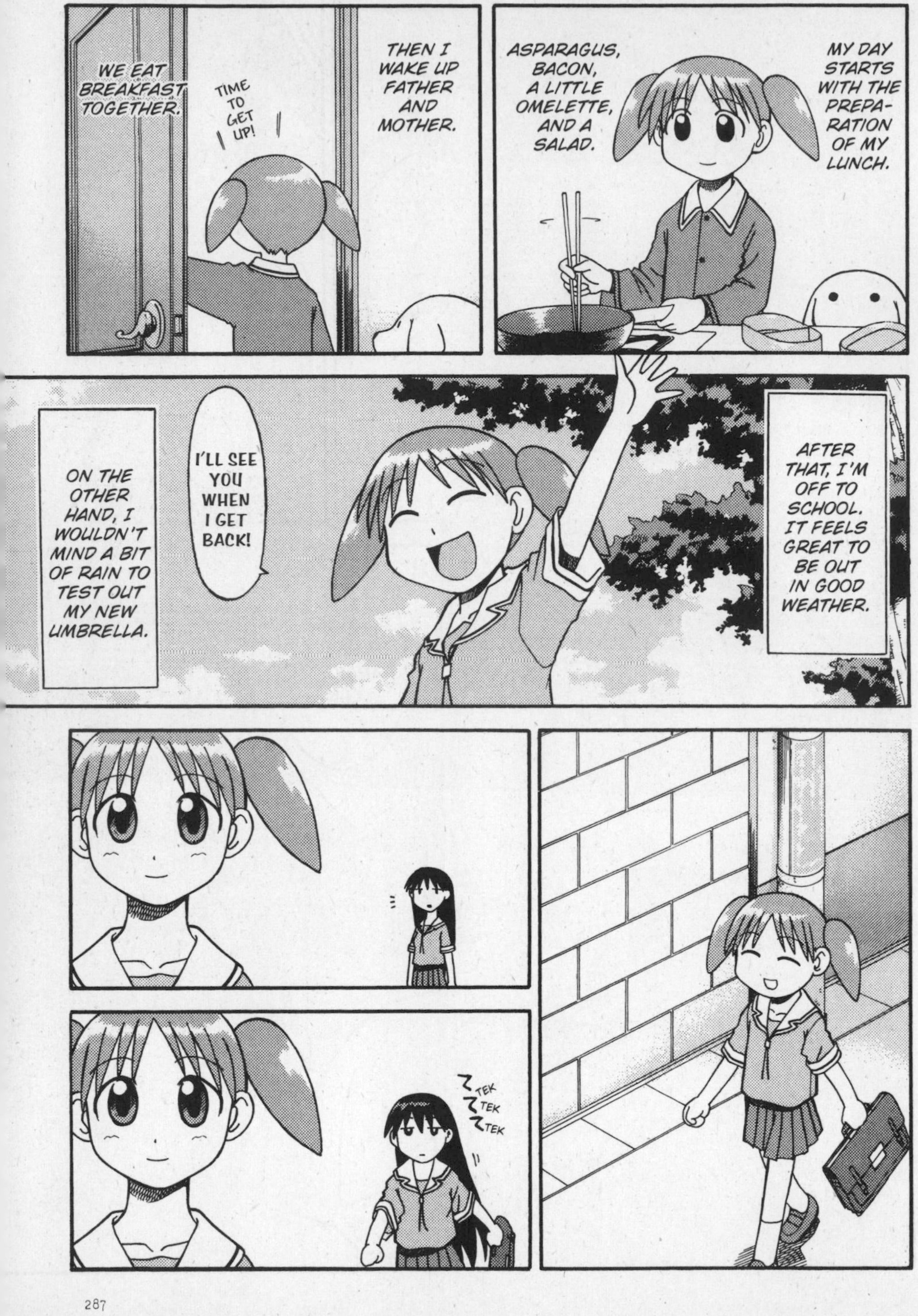
MY DAY STARTS WITH THE PREPARATION OF MY LUNCH.
ASPARAGUS, BACON, A LITTLE OMELETTE, AND A SALAD.
THEN I WAKE UP FATHER AND MOTHER.
TIME TO GET UP!
WE EAT BREAKFAST TOGETHER.
AFTER THAT, I'M OFF TO SCHOOL. IT FEELS GREAT TO BE OUT IN GOOD WEATHER.
I'LL SEE YOU WHEN I GET BACK!
ON THE OTHER HAND, I WOULDN'T MIND A BIT OF RAIN TO TEST OUT MY NEW UMBRELLA.
TEK TEK TEK

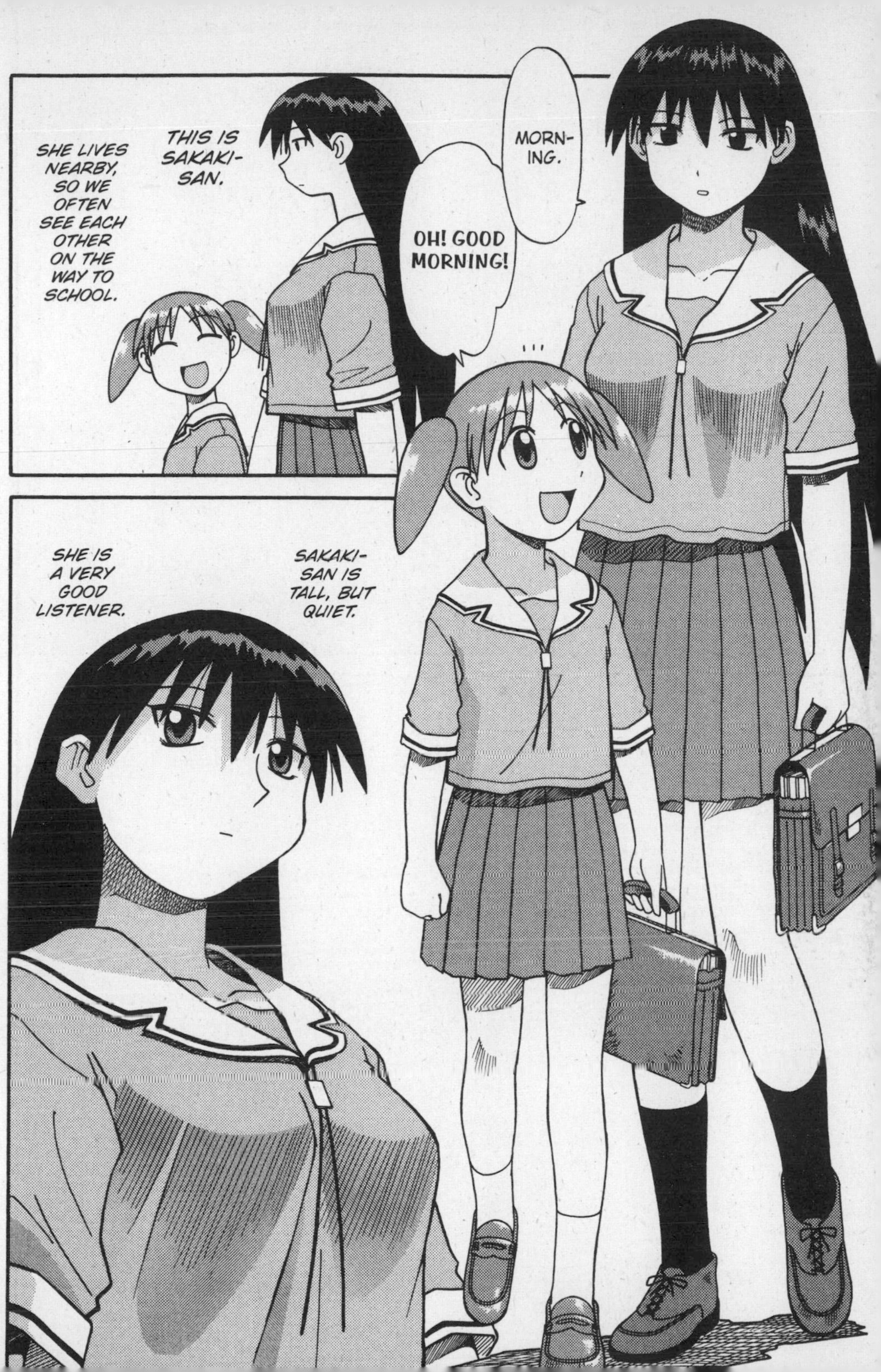
MORN-
ING.
OH! GOOD
MORNING!
THIS IS
SAKAKI-
SAN.
SHE LIVES
NEARBY,
SO WE
OFTEN
SEE EACH
OTHER
ON THE
WAY TO
SCHOOL.
SAKAKI-
SAN IS
TALL, BUT
QUIET.
SHE IS
A VERY
GOOD
LISTENER.

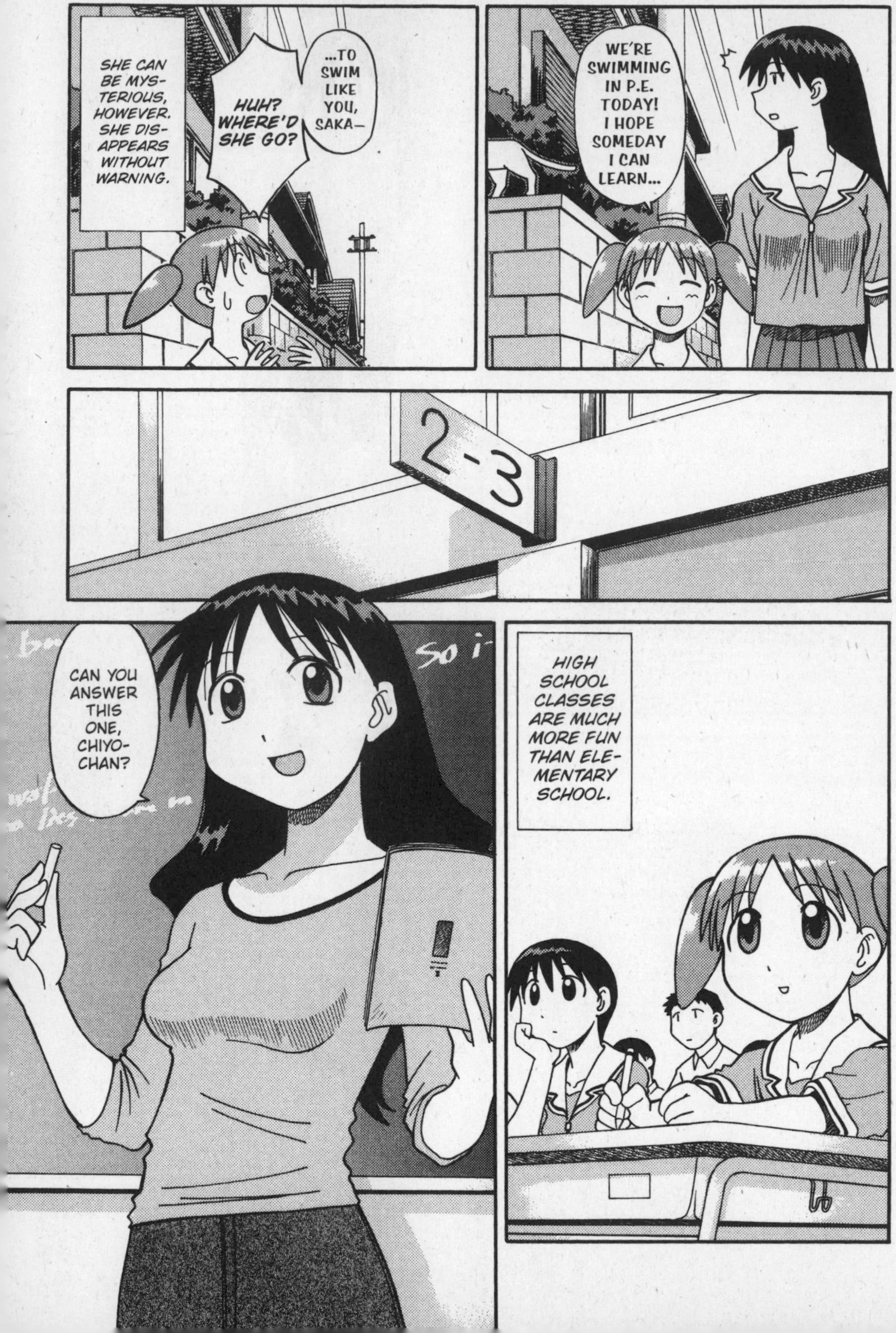
WE'RE SWIMMING IN P.E. TODAY! I HOPE SOMEDAY I CAN LEARN...
...TO SWIM LIKE YOU, SAKA—
HUH? WHERE'D SHE GO?
SHE CAN BE MYS-TERIOUS, HOWEVER. SHE DIS-APPEARS WITHOUT WARNING.
2-3
HIGH SCHOOL CLASSES ARE MUCH MORE FUN THAN ELE-MENTARY SCHOOL.
CAN YOU ANSWER THIS ONE, CHIYO-CHAN?

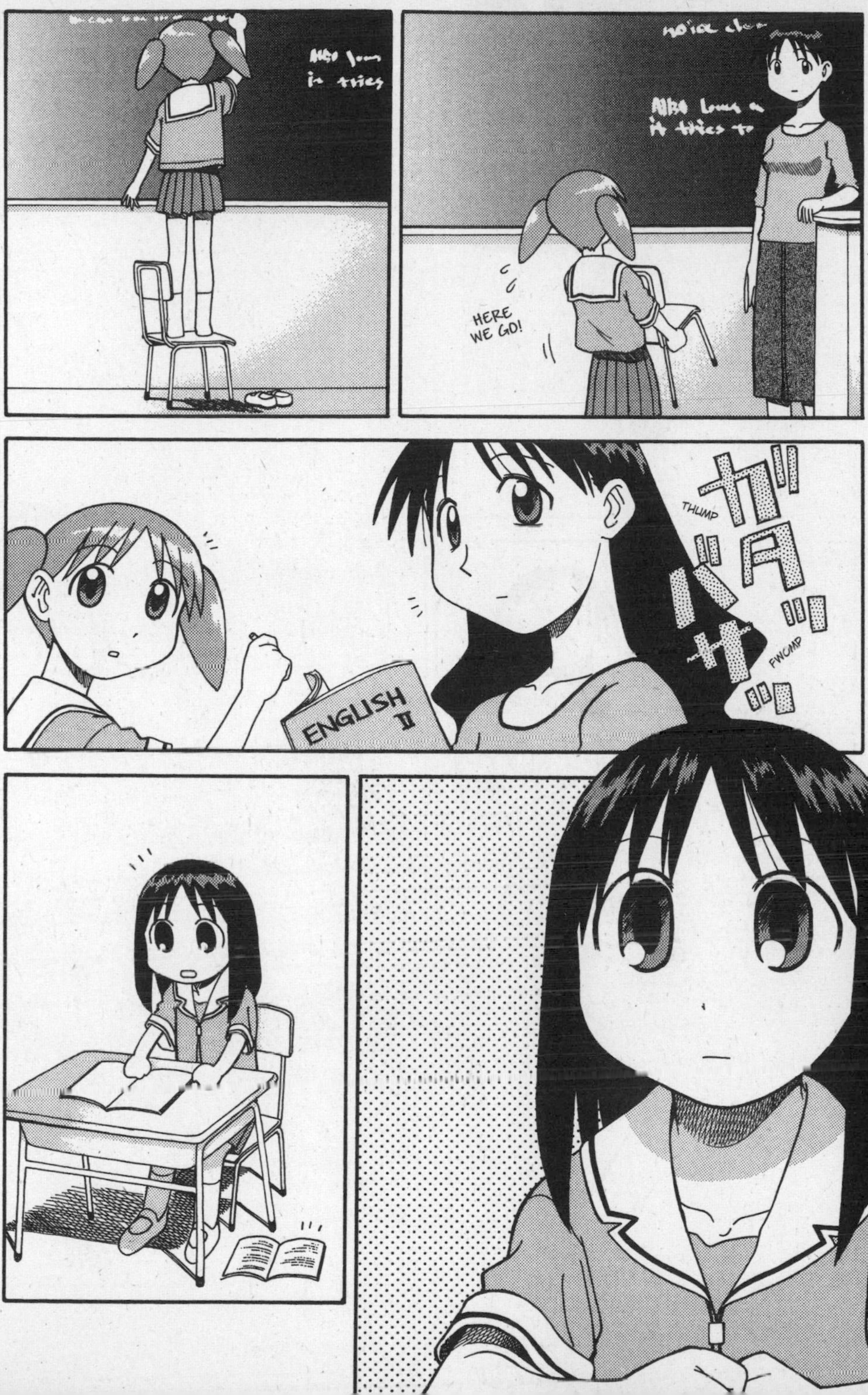
HERE WE GO!
ガタッ
THUMP
バサッ
FWOMP

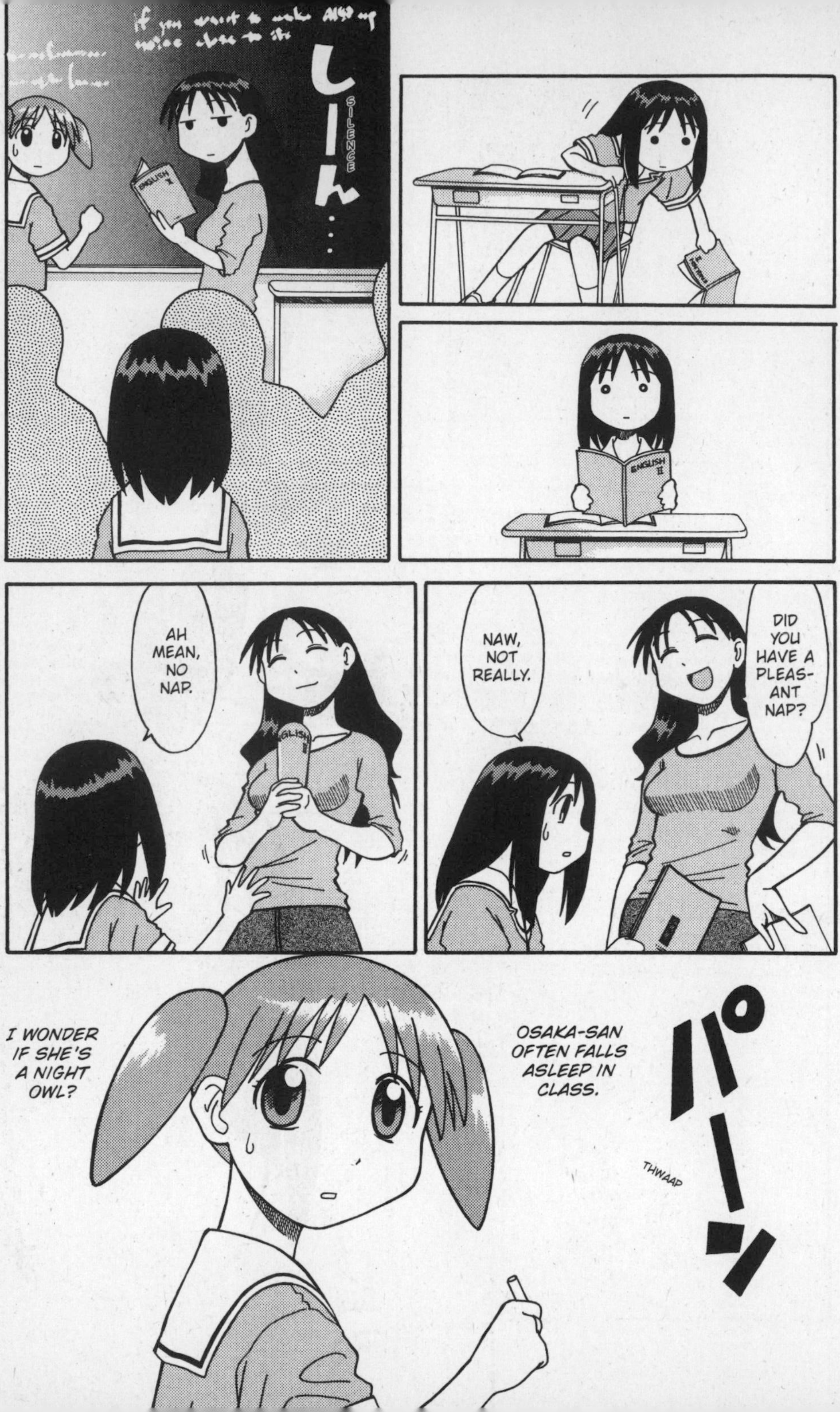
しーん…
SILENCE
DID YOU HAVE A PLEASANT NAP?
NAW, NOT REALLY.
AH MEAN, NO NAP.
パーッ
THWAAP
OSAKA-SAN OFTEN FALLS ASLEEP IN CLASS.
I WONDER IF SHE'S A NIGHT OWL?

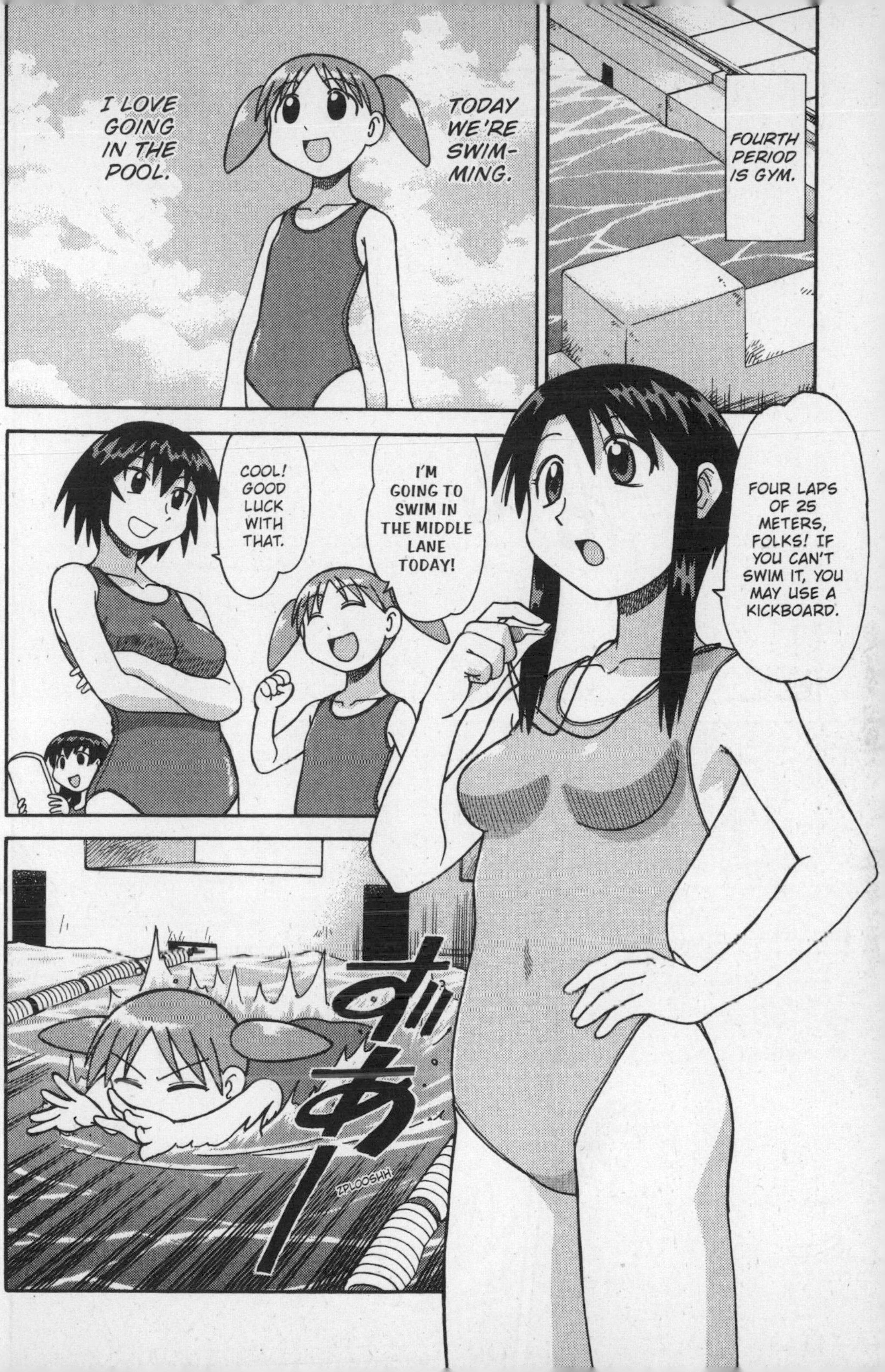
FOURTH PERIOD IS GYM.
TODAY WE'RE SWIMMING.
I LOVE GOING IN THE POOL.
FOUR LAPS OF 25 METERS, FOLKS! IF YOU CAN'T SWIM IT, YOU MAY USE A KICKBOARD.
I'M GOING TO SWIM IN THE MIDDLE LANE TODAY!
COOL! GOOD LUCK WITH THAT.
ZPLOOSHH

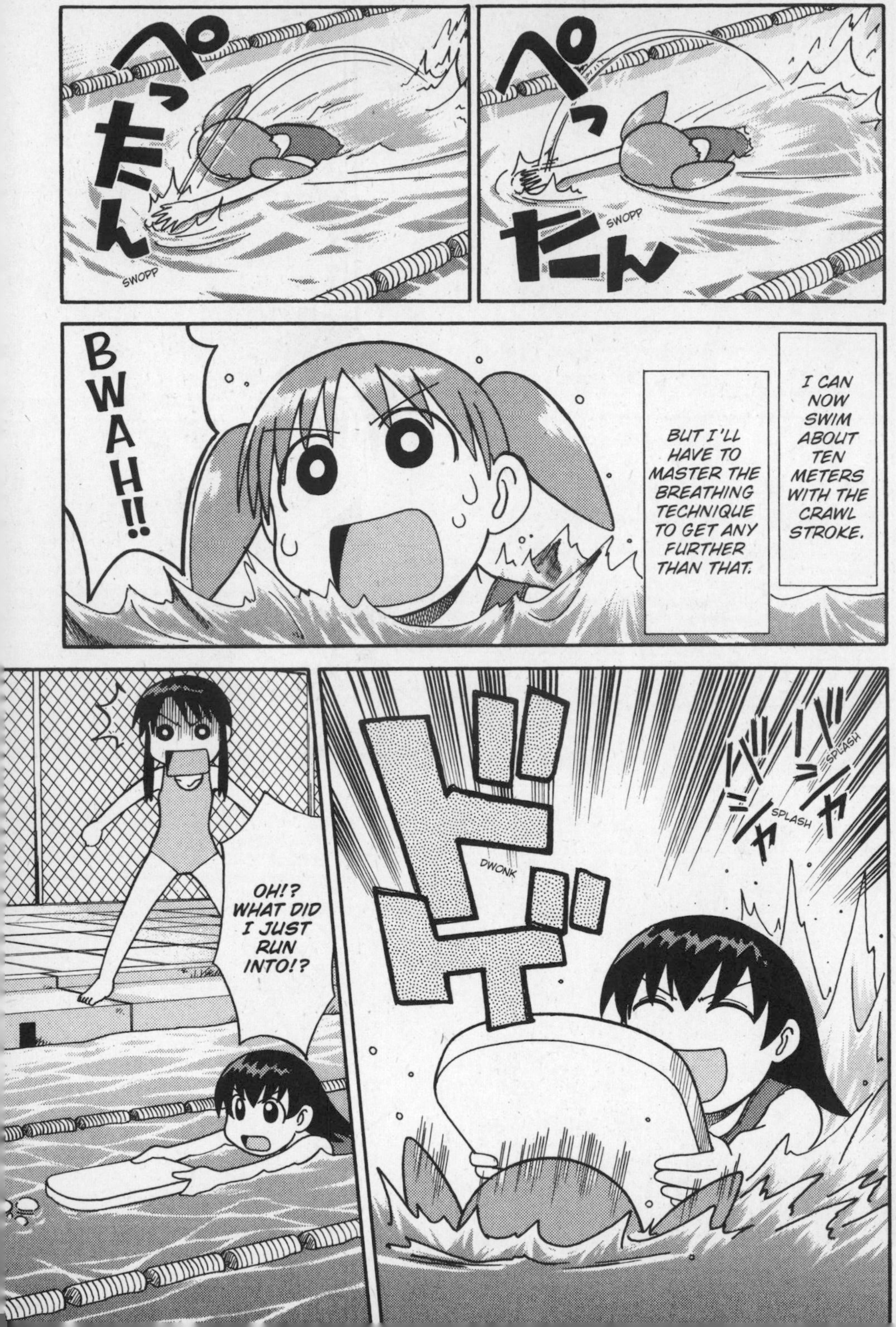
ぺったん
SWOPP
ぺったん
SWOPP
I CAN NOW SWIM ABOUT TEN METERS WITH THE CRAWL STROKE.
BUT I'LL HAVE TO MASTER THE BREATHING TECHNIQUE TO GET ANY FURTHER THAN THAT.
BWAH!!
ドゴ
DWONK
バシャバシャ
SPLASH
SPLASH
OH!? WHAT DID I JUST RUN INTO!?

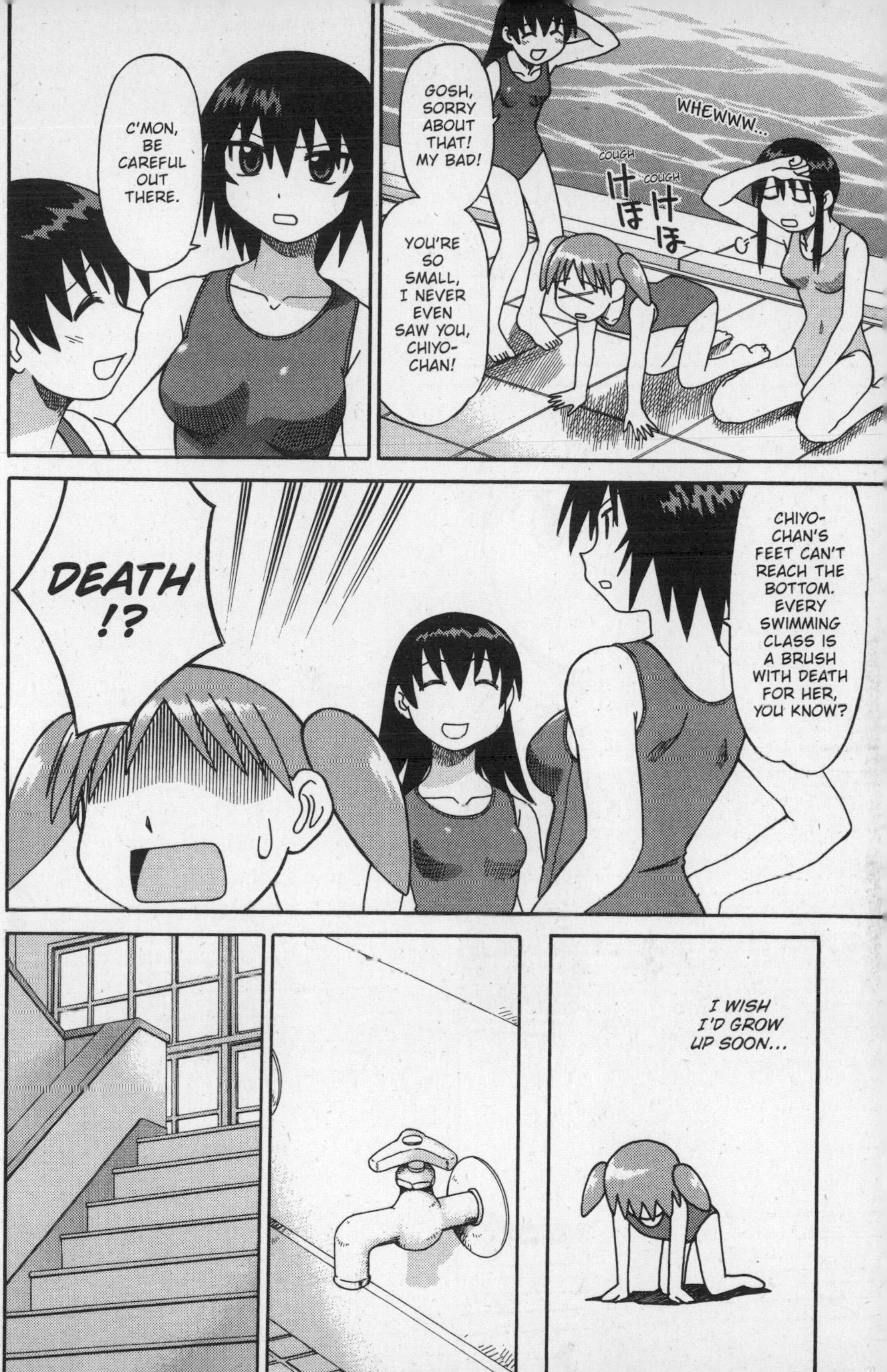
WHEWWW...
COUGH
けほ
COUGH
けほ
GOSH, SORRY ABOUT THAT! MY BAD!
YOU'RE SO SMALL, I NEVER EVEN SAW YOU, CHIYO-CHAN!
C'MON, BE CAREFUL OUT THERE.
CHIYO-CHAN'S FEET CAN'T REACH THE BOTTOM. EVERY SWIMMING CLASS IS A BRUSH WITH DEATH FOR HER, YOU KNOW?
DEATH!?
I WISH I'D GROW UP SOON...

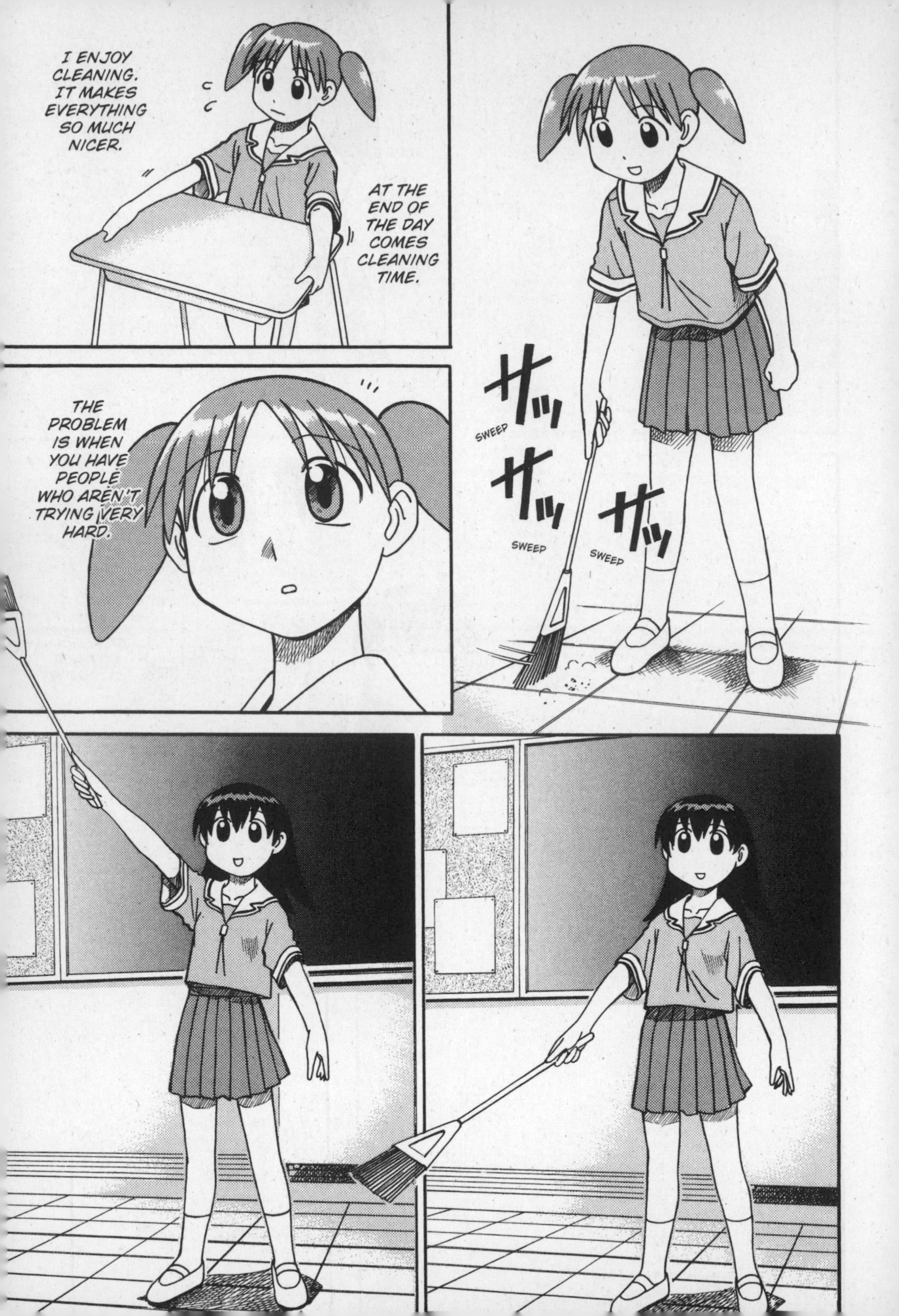

サッ
SWEEP
サッ
SWEEP
サッ
SWEEP
AT THE END OF THE DAY COMES CLEANING TIME.
I ENJOY CLEANING. IT MAKES EVERYTHING SO MUCH NICER.
THE PROBLEM IS WHEN YOU HAVE PEOPLE WHO AREN'T TRYING VERY HARD.

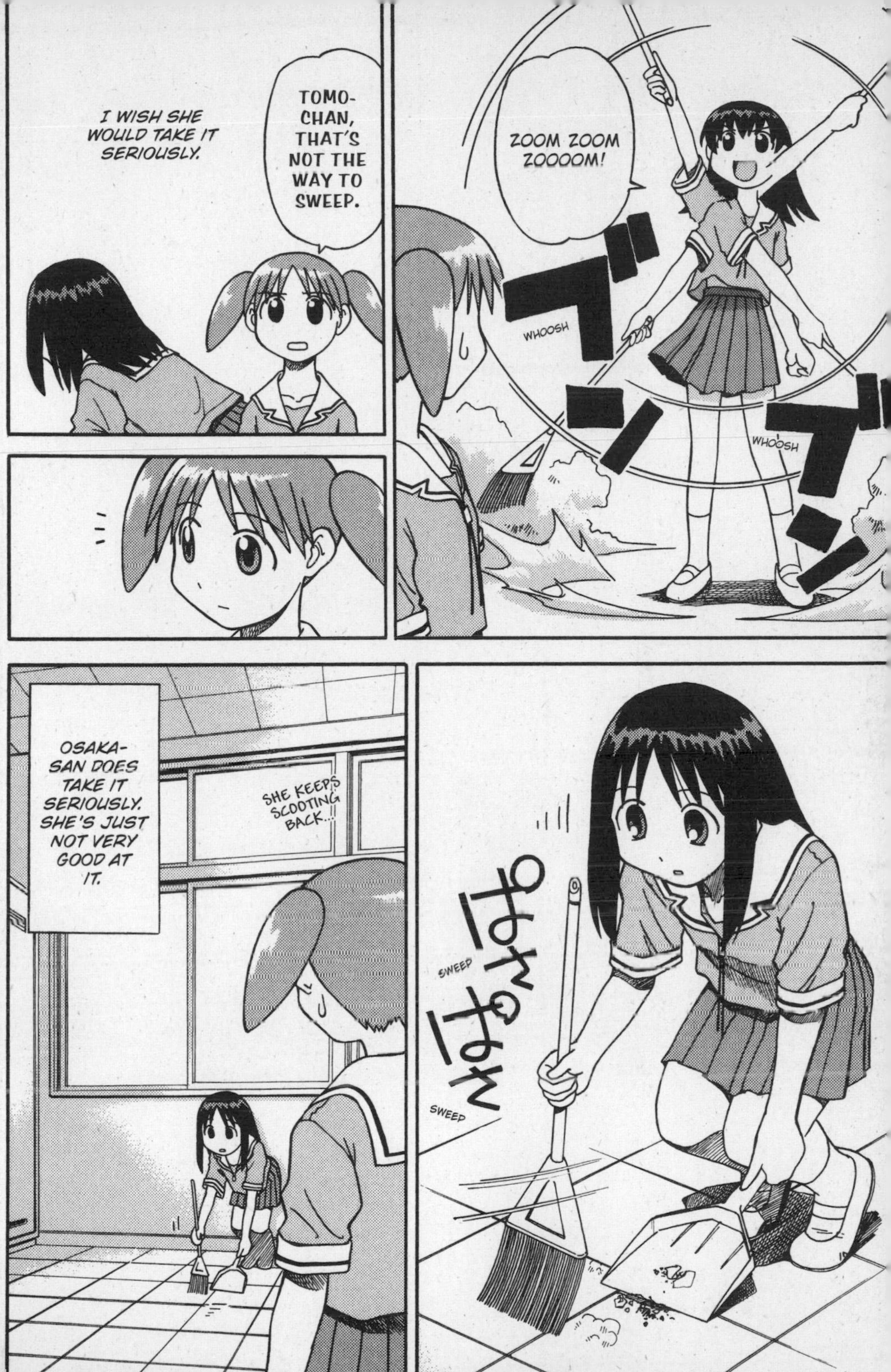
ZOOM ZOOM ZOOOOM!
WHOOSH
WHOOSH
TOMO-CHAN, THAT'S NOT THE WAY TO SWEEP.
I WISH SHE WOULD TAKE IT SERIOUSLY.
SWEEP
SWEEP
OSAKA-SAN DOES TAKE IT SERIOUSLY. SHE'S JUST NOT VERY GOOD AT IT.
SHE KEEPS SCOOTING BACK...

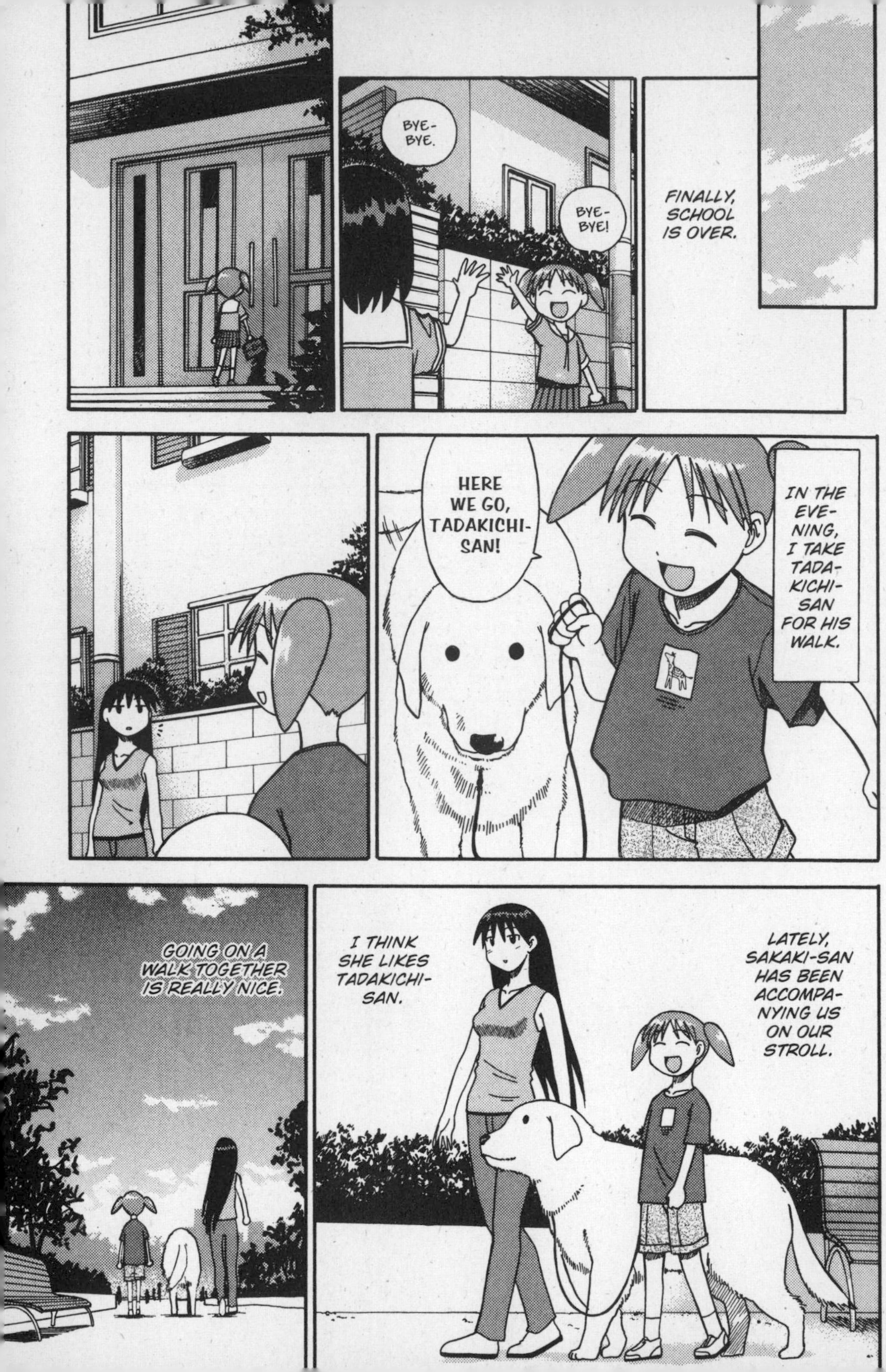
FINALLY, SCHOOL IS OVER.
BYE-BYE.
BYE-BYE!
IN THE EVENING, I TAKE TADAKICHI-SAN FOR HIS WALK.
HERE WE GO, TADAKICHI-SAN!
LATELY, SAKAKI-SAN HAS BEEN ACCOMPANYING US ON OUR STROLL.
I THINK SHE LIKES TADAKICHI-SAN.
GOING ON A WALK TOGETHER IS REALLY NICE.

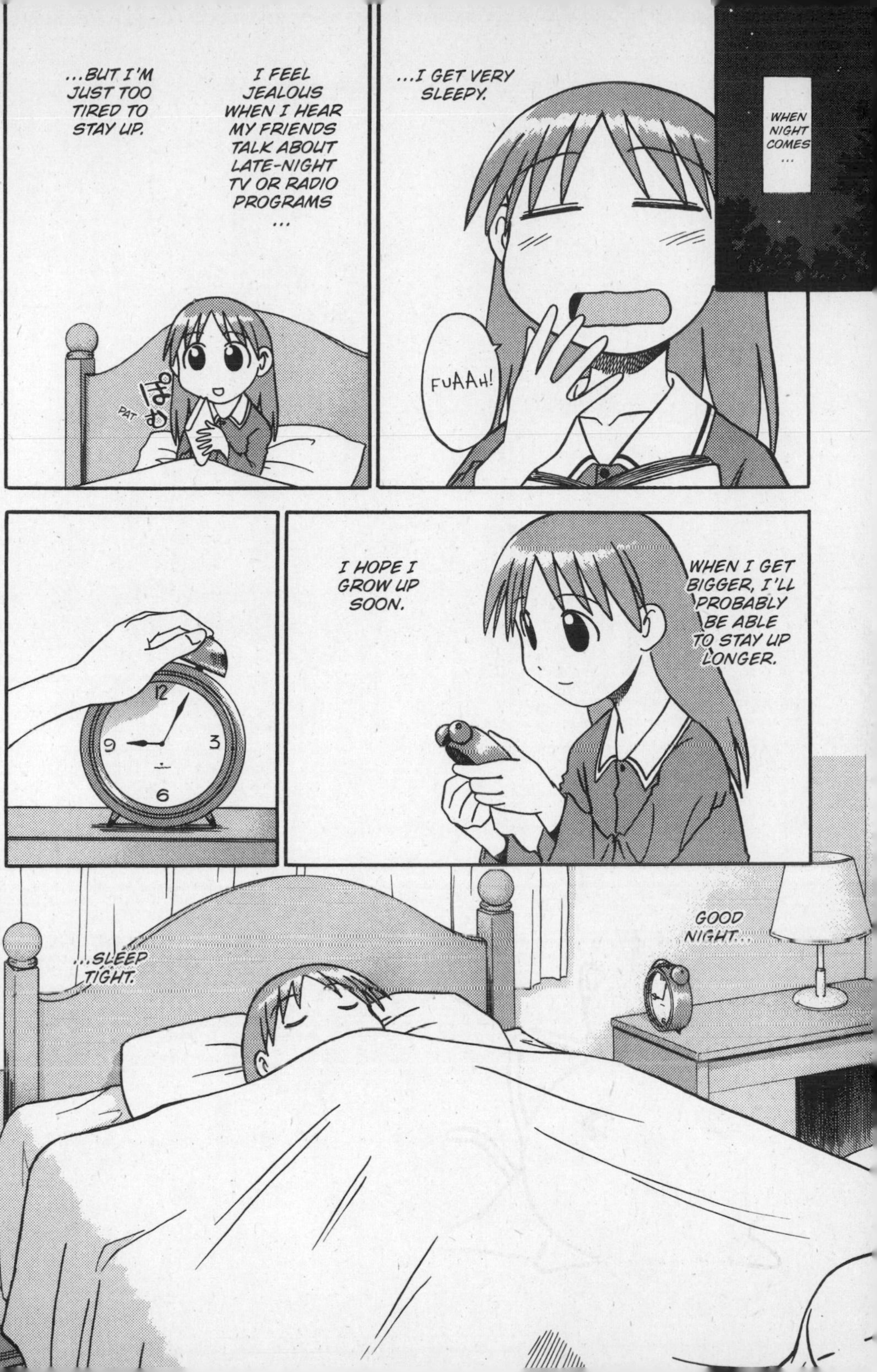
WHEN NIGHT COMES ...
...I GET VERY SLEEPY.
FUAAH!
I FEEL JEALOUS WHEN I HEAR MY FRIENDS TALK ABOUT LATE-NIGHT TV OR RADIO PROGRAMS ...
...BUT I'M JUST TOO TIRED TO STAY UP.
ぽむ
PAT
WHEN I GET BIGGER, I'LL PROBABLY BE ABLE TO STAY UP LONGER.
I HOPE I GROW UP SOON.
GOOD NIGHT...
...SLEEP TIGHT.

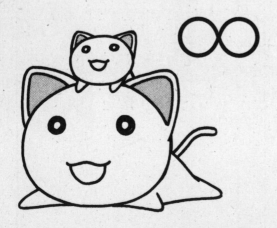

51461367522

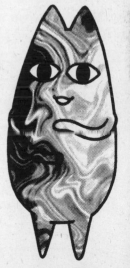

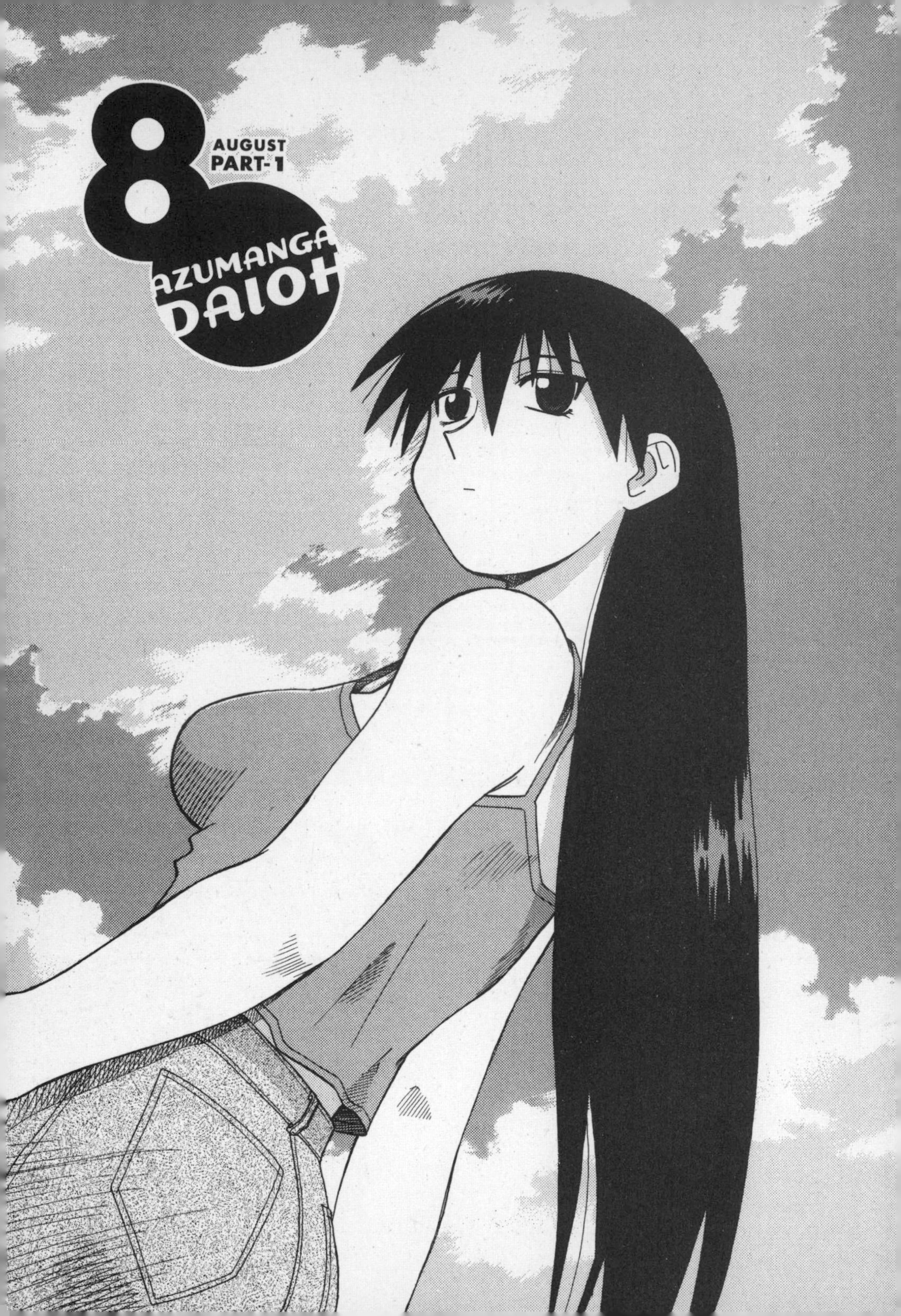
8
AUGUST
PART-1
AZUMANGA
DAIOH

FREE TISSUES

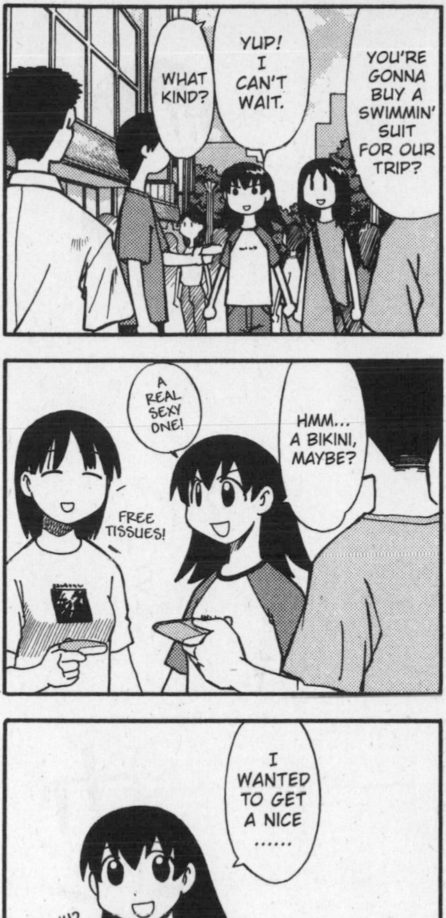
YOU'RE GONNA BUY A SWIMMIN' SUIT FOR OUR TRIP?
YUP! I CAN'T WAIT.
WHAT KIND?
HMM... A BIKINI, MAYBE?
A REAL SEXY ONE!
FREE TISSUES!
I WANTED TO GET A NICE ......
HUH?
WILD
AW NOOOO! AH CAIN'T HOLD NO MORE!
THEN DON'T ACCEPT TISSUES FROM EVERY SINGLE PERSON HANDING THEM OUT!

GIVE & TAKE

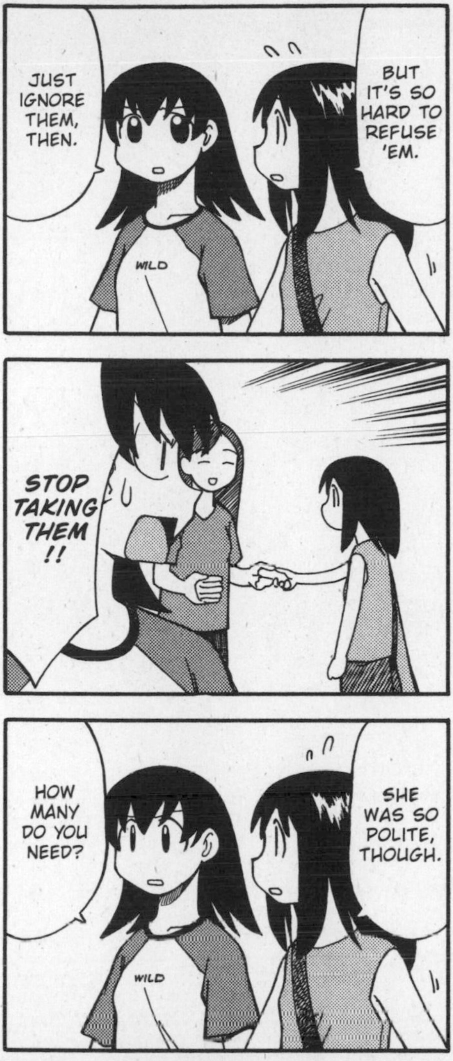
BUT IT'S SO HARD TO REFUSE 'EM.
JUST IGNORE THEM, THEN.
WILD
STOP TAKING THEM!!
SHE WAS SO POLITE, THOUGH.
HOW MANY DO YOU NEED?
WILD
UWAH! AND NOW YOU'RE GIVING SOME-ONE SOME-THING!!?

BOX: DONATIONS

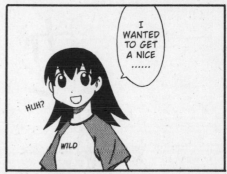

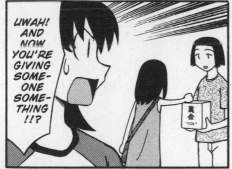

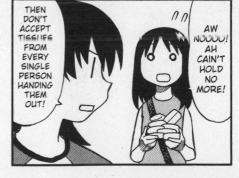

SHOPPING

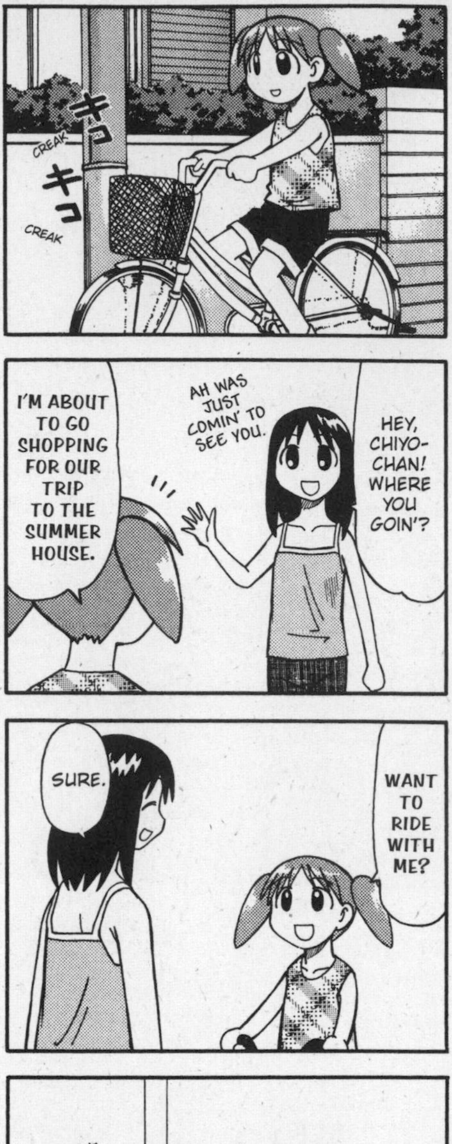
キコ
CREAK
キコ
CREAK
HEY, CHIYO-CHAN! WHERE YOU GOIN'?
AH WAS JUST COMIN' TO SEE YOU.
I'M ABOUT TO GO SHOPPING FOR OUR TRIP TO THE SUMMER HOUSE.
WANT TO RIDE WITH ME?
SURE.
ふら
SWISH
ふら
SWISH
ガン
DONK

FORGET IT

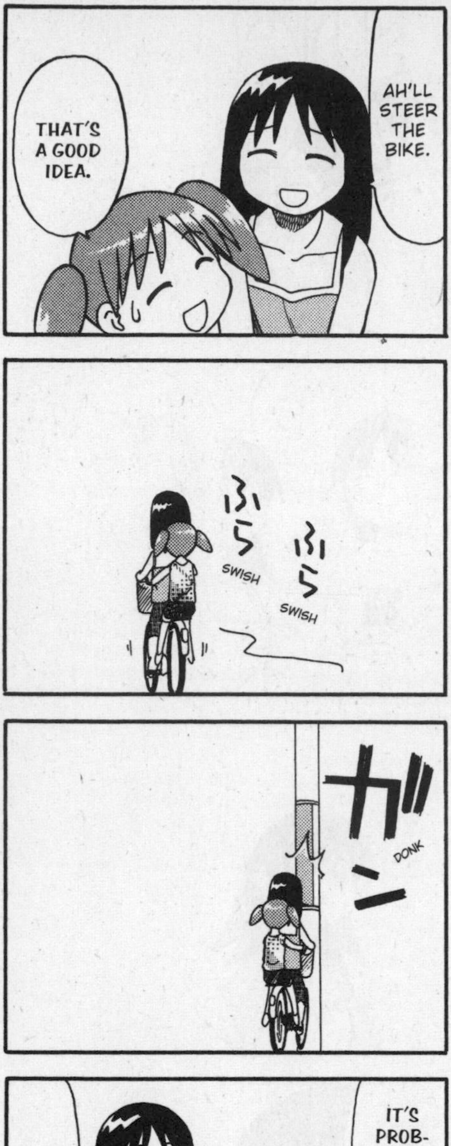
AH'LL STEER THE BIKE.
THAT'S A GOOD IDEA.
ふら
SWISH
ふら
SWISH
ガン
DONK
IT'S PROB-ABLY NOT SAFE TO RIDE TWO TO A BIKE.
DEFI-NITELY NOT.

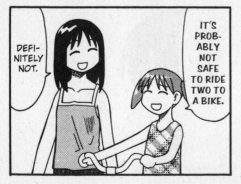

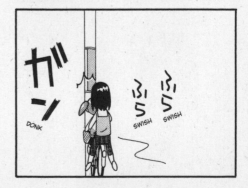

MOVING STAIRS

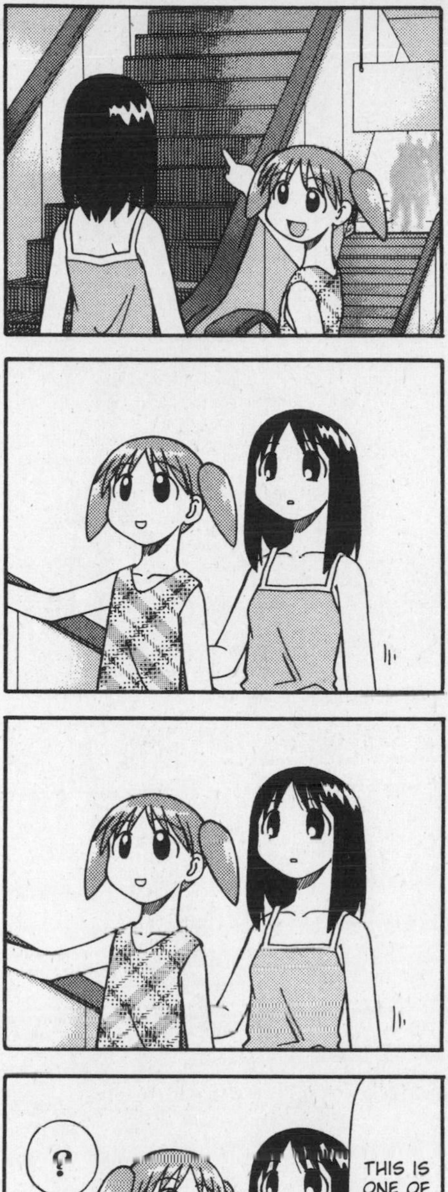
?
THIS IS ONE OF THEM ESCALATORS...

MOVING BOX

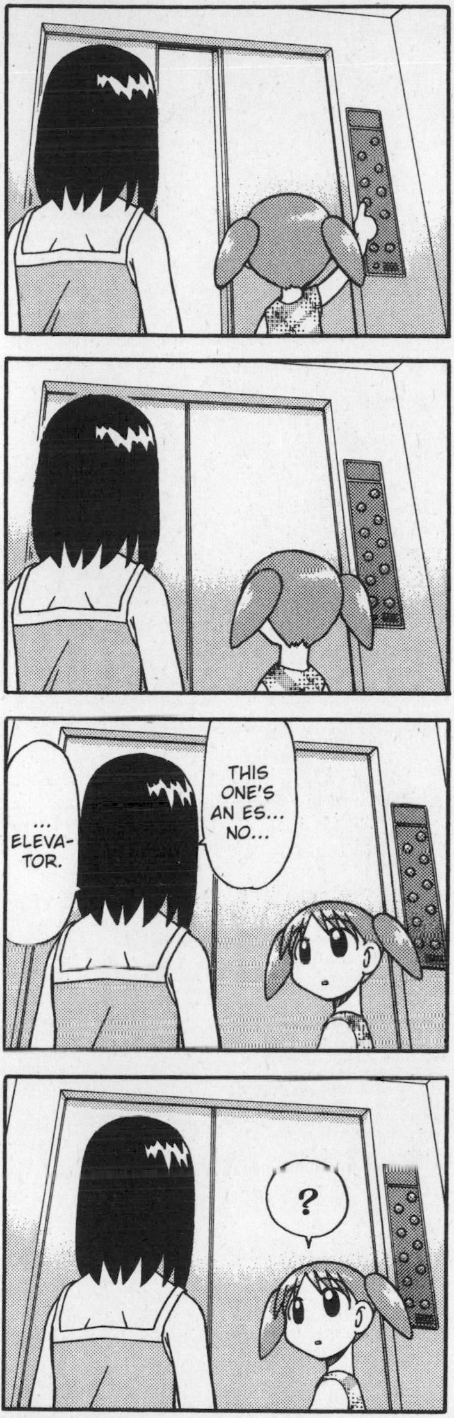
THIS ONE'S AN ES... NO...
...ELEVATOR.
?

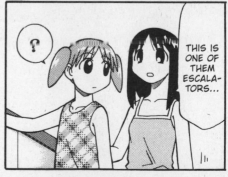

—ATORS

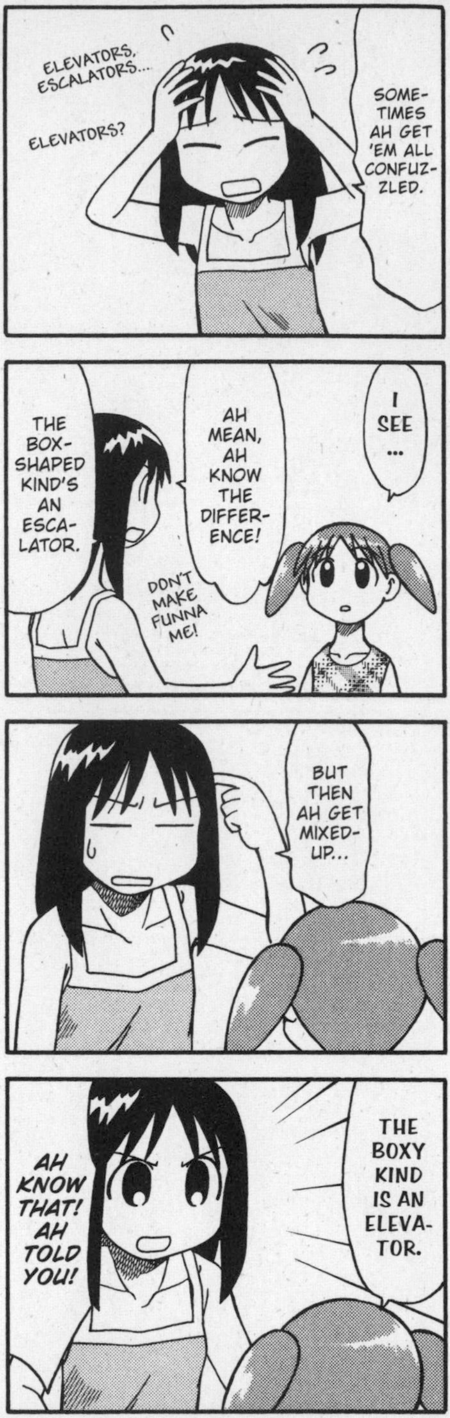
SOMETIMES AH GET 'EM ALL CONFUZZLED.
ELEVATORS, ESCALATORS...
ELEVATORS?
I SEE...
AH MEAN, AH KNOW THE DIFFERENCE!
THE BOX-SHAPED KIND'S AN ESCALATOR.
DON'T MAKE FUNNA ME!
BUT THEN AH GET MIXED-UP...
THE BOXY KIND IS AN ELEVATOR.
AH KNOW THAT! AH TOLD YOU!

SO MUCH FUN

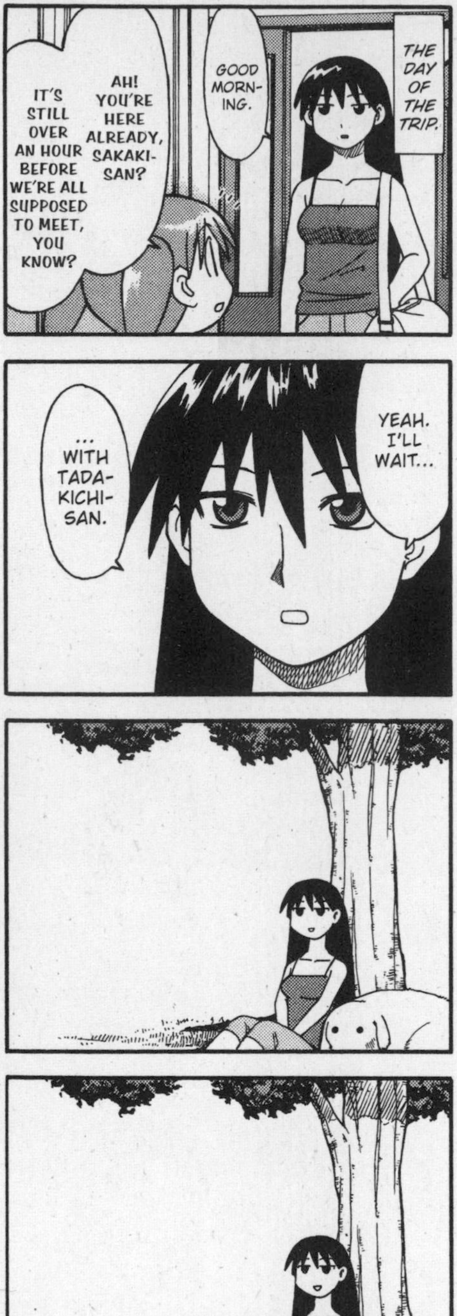
THE DAY OF THE TRIP.
GOOD MORNING.
AH! YOU'RE HERE ALREADY, SAKAKI-SAN?
IT'S STILL OVER AN HOUR BEFORE WE'RE ALL SUPPOSED TO MEET, YOU KNOW?
YEAH. I'LL WAIT...
... WITH TADAKICHI-SAN.

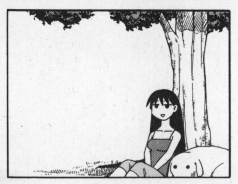

MEETING

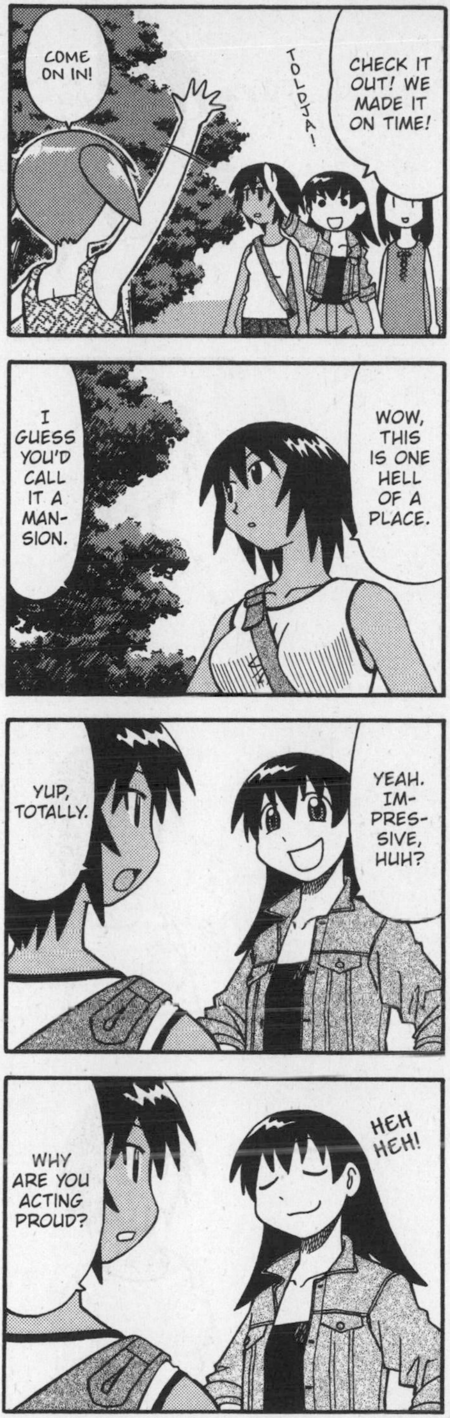
CHECK IT OUT! WE MADE IT ON TIME!
TOLDJA!
COME ON IN!
WOW, THIS IS ONE HELL OF A PLACE.
I GUESS YOU'D CALL IT A MAN-SION.
YEAH. IM-PRES-SIVE, HUH?
YUP, TOTALLY.
HEH HEH!
WHY ARE YOU ACTING PROUD?

PLAYER

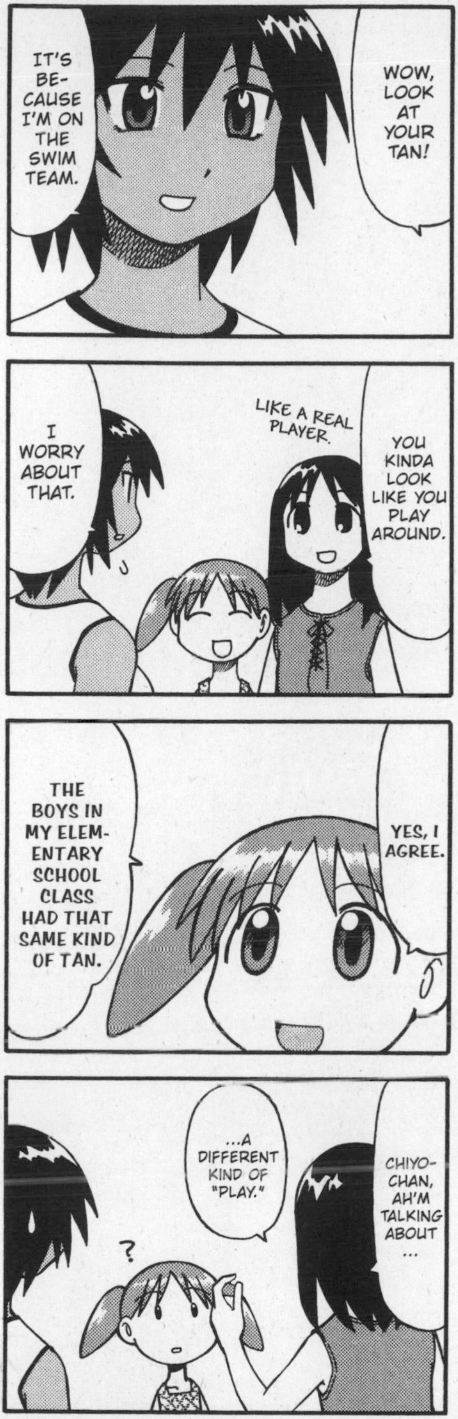
WOW, LOOK AT YOUR TAN!
IT'S BE-CAUSE I'M ON THE SWIM TEAM.
YOU KINDA LOOK LIKE YOU PLAY AROUND.
LIKE A REAL PLAYER.
I WORRY ABOUT THAT.
YES, I AGREE.
THE BOYS IN MY ELEM-ENTARY SCHOOL CLASS HAD THAT SAME KIND OF TAN.
CHIYO-CHAN, AH'M TALKING ABOUT ...
...A DIFFERENT KIND OF "PLAY."
?

JUST ONE DRIVER

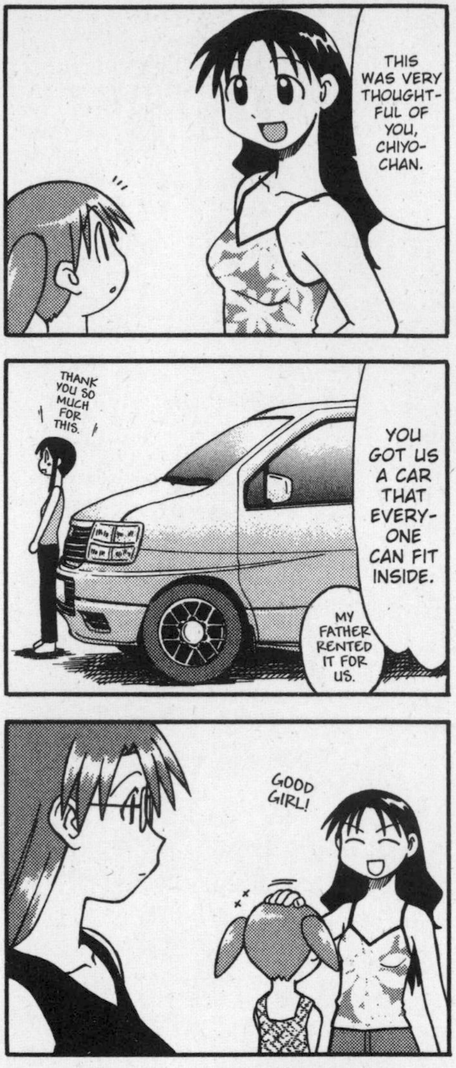
THIS WAS VERY THOUGHTFUL OF YOU, CHIYO-CHAN.
YOU GOT US A CAR THAT EVERYONE CAN FIT INSIDE.
MY FATHER RENTED IT FOR US.
THANK YOU SO MUCH FOR THIS.
GOOD GIRL!
A PLAN TO AVOID THE YUKARI-MOBILE, HUH?
NICE WORK, CHIYO-CHAN.
YUKARI-CHAN HAS NO IDEA WHY SHE RENTED IT, HUH?

SCARS

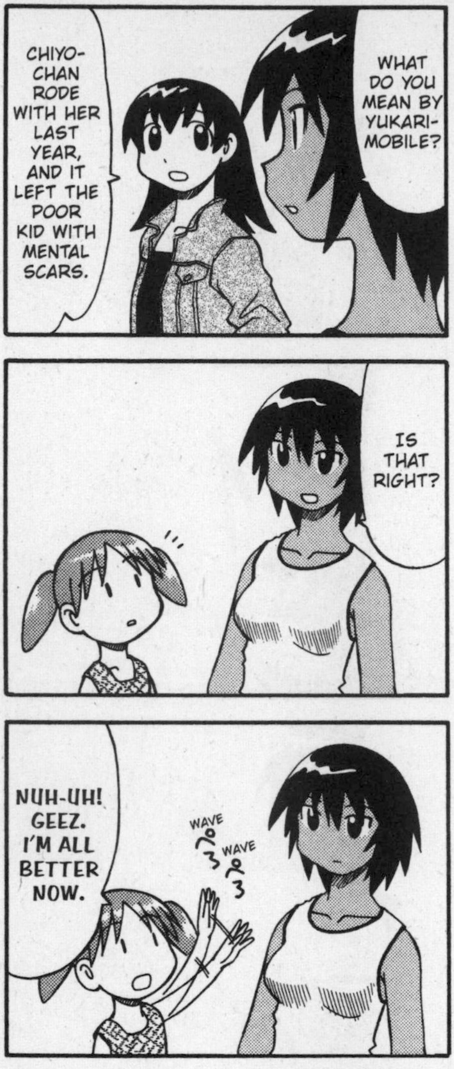
WHAT DO YOU MEAN BY YUKARI-MOBILE?
CHIYO-CHAN RODE WITH HER LAST YEAR, AND IT LEFT THE POOR KID WITH MENTAL SCARS.
IS THAT RIGHT?
WAVE
WAVE
NUH-UH! GEEZ. I'M ALL BETTER NOW.

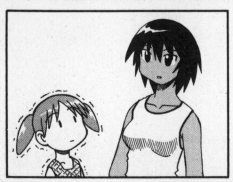

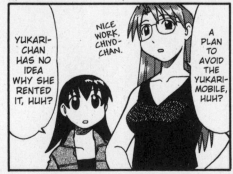

TESTIMONY

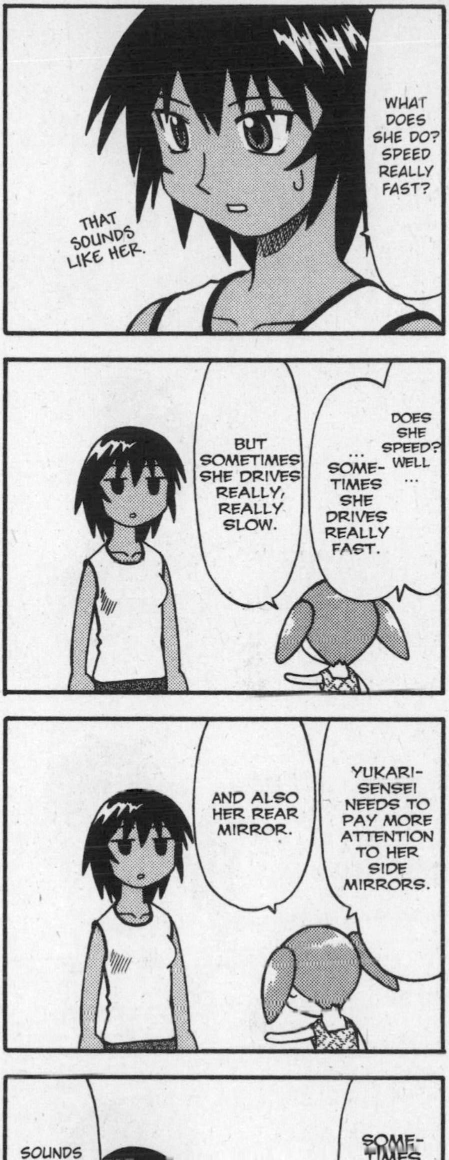
WHAT DOES SHE DO? SPEED REALLY FAST?
THAT SOUNDS LIKE HER.
DOES SHE SPEED? WELL ...
... SOMETIMES SHE DRIVES REALLY FAST.
BUT SOMETIMES SHE DRIVES REALLY, REALLY SLOW.
YUKARI-SENSEI NEEDS TO PAY MORE ATTENTION TO HER SIDE MIRRORS.
AND ALSO HER REAR MIRROR.
SOMETIMES I THINK SHE DOESN'T NOTICE TRAFFIC LIGHTS OR PEDESTRIANS ...
SOUNDS LIKE SHE DOESN'T KNOW HOW TO DRIVE AT ALL.

NOT YOU

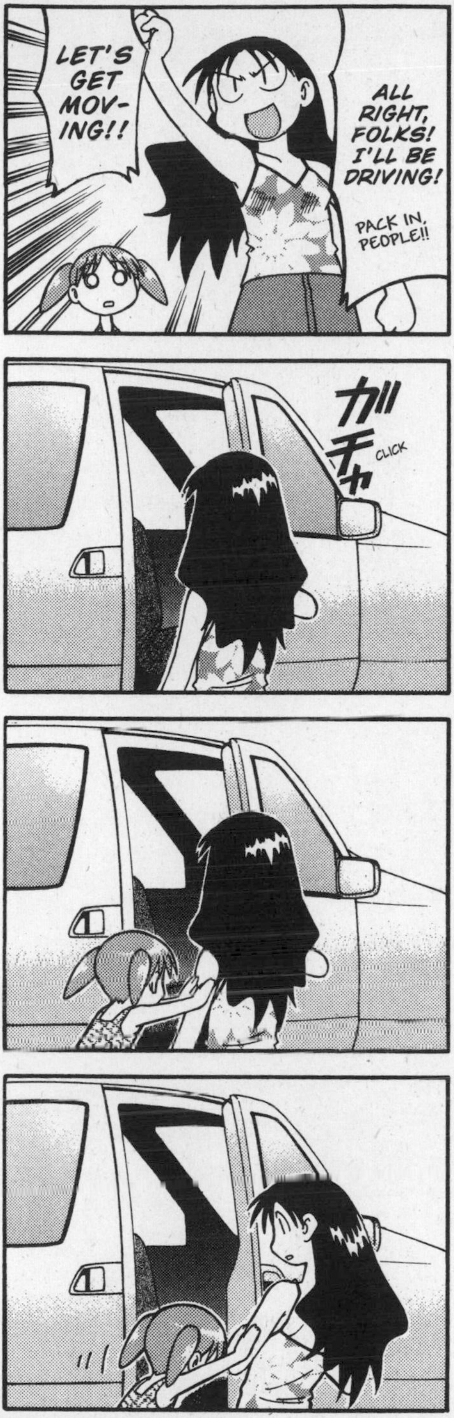
ALL RIGHT, FOLKS! I'LL BE DRIVING!
PACK IN, PEOPLE!!
LET'S GET MOVING!!
ガチャ
CLICK

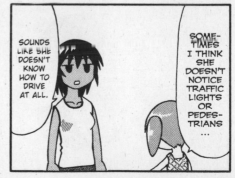

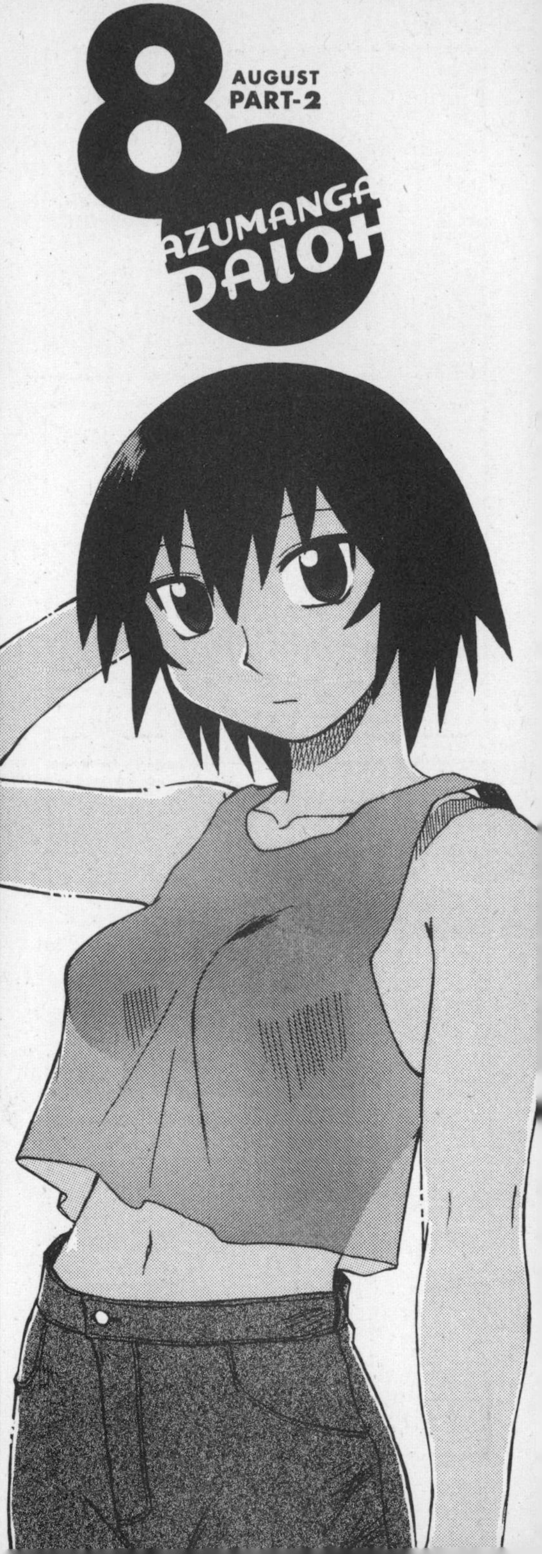
8
AUGUST
PART-2
AZUMANGA DAIOH

OPEN YOUR HEART

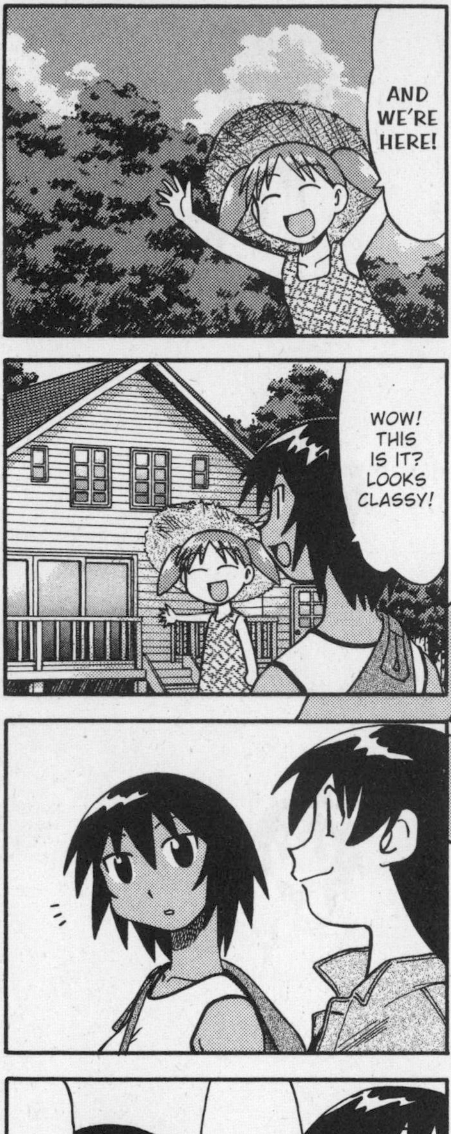
AND WE'RE HERE!
WOW! THIS IS IT? LOOKS CLASSY!
YOU STILL HAVEN'T EXPLAINED WHAT YOU HAVE TO BE PROUD OF.
SERI-OUSLY, I'D LIKE TO KNOW.

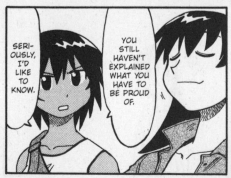

SPASM

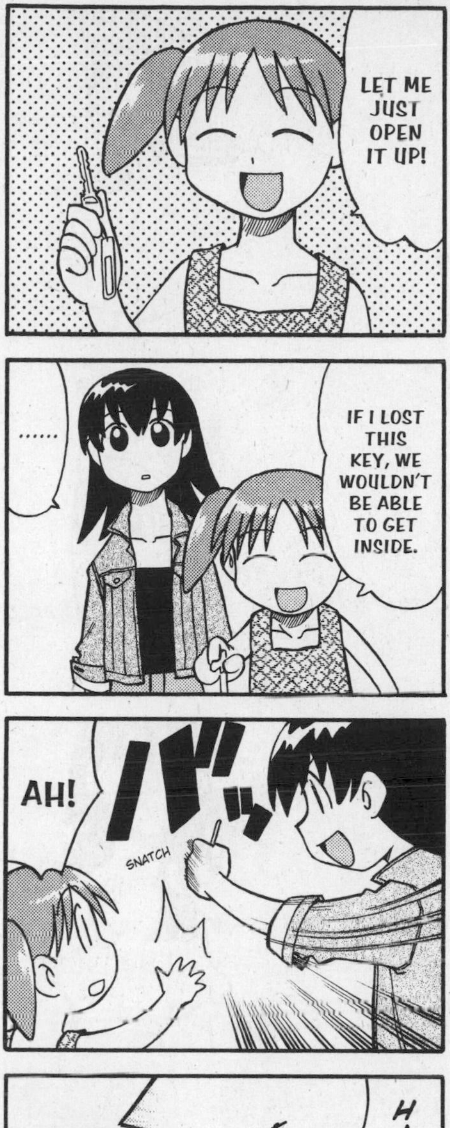
LET ME JUST OPEN IT UP!
IF I LOST THIS KEY, WE WOULDN'T BE ABLE TO GET INSIDE.
......
バッ
AH!
SNATCH
HIYAAAH!!
!?

TOSSED

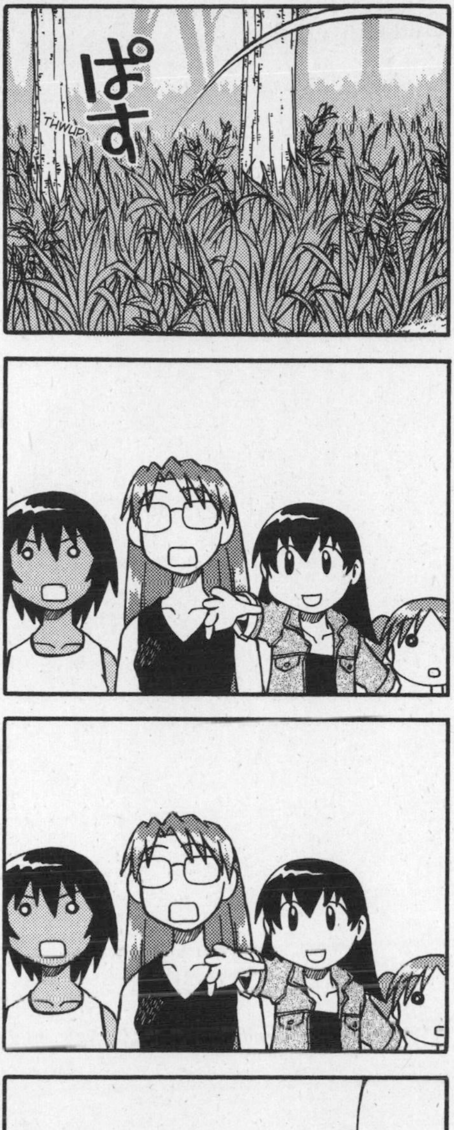
ぱす
THWUP
OOPS ......

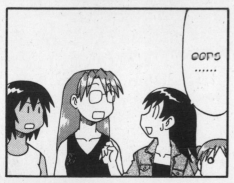

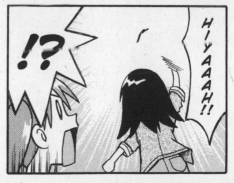

LOL

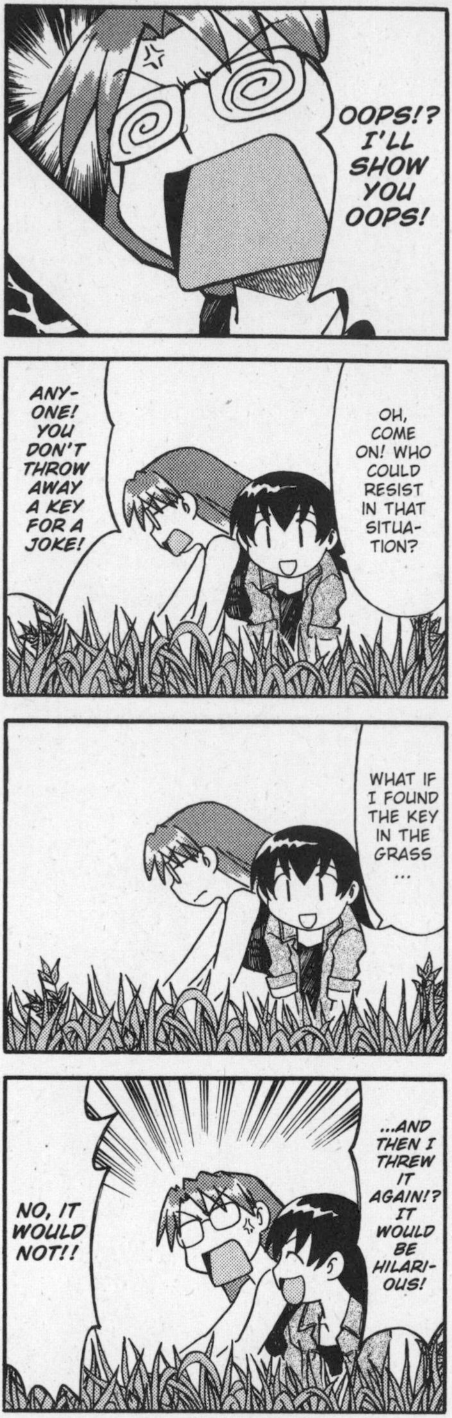
OOPS!? I'LL SHOW YOU OOPS!
OH, COME ON! WHO COULD RESIST IN THAT SITUATION?
ANYONE! YOU DON'T THROW AWAY A KEY FOR A JOKE!
WHAT IF I FOUND THE KEY IN THE GRASS ...
...AND THEN I THREW IT AGAIN!? IT WOULD BE HILARIOUS!
NO, IT WOULD NOT!!

TEAMWORK

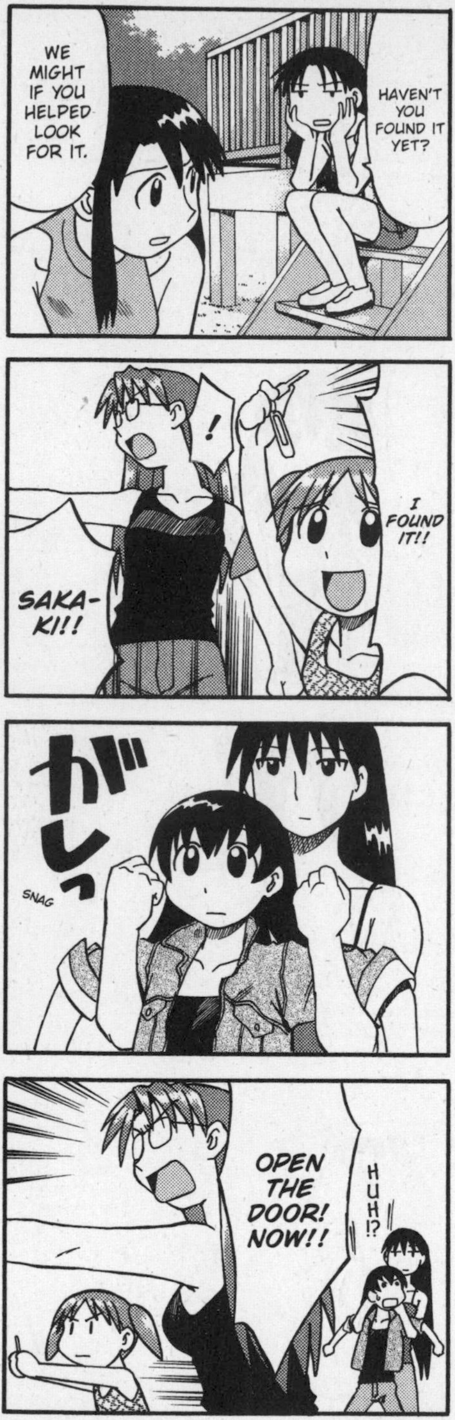
HAVEN'T YOU FOUND IT YET?
WE MIGHT IF YOU HELPED LOOK FOR IT.
I FOUND IT!!
!
SAKAKI!!
がしっ
SNAG
HUH!?
OPEN THE DOOR! NOW!!

STRATEGY

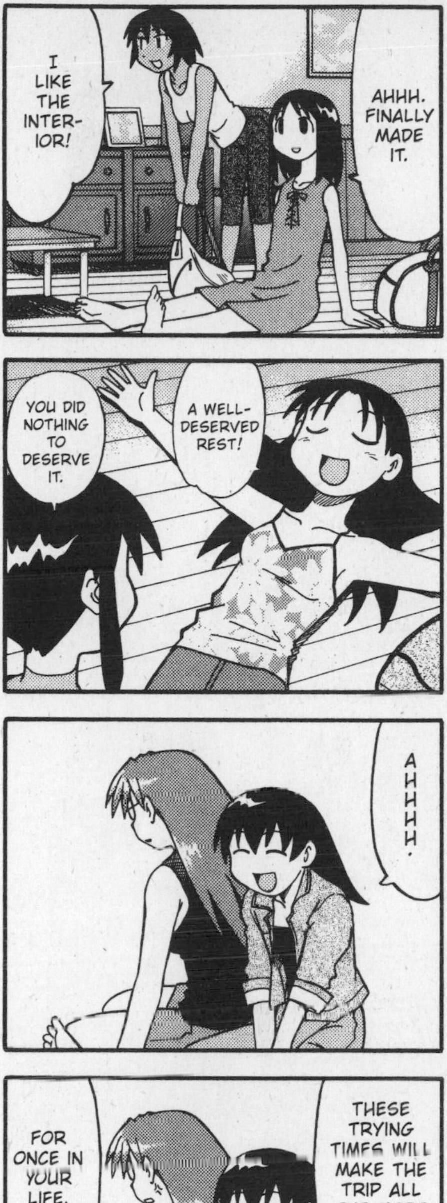
AHHH. FINALLY MADE IT.
I LIKE THE INTER-IOR!
A WELL-DESERVED REST!
YOU DID NOTHING TO DESERVE IT.
AHHHH.
THESE TRYING TIMES WILL MAKE THE TRIP ALL THE MORE MEMOR-ABLE ...
FOR ONCE IN YOUR LIFE, SHUT UP.

CHOP DENIED

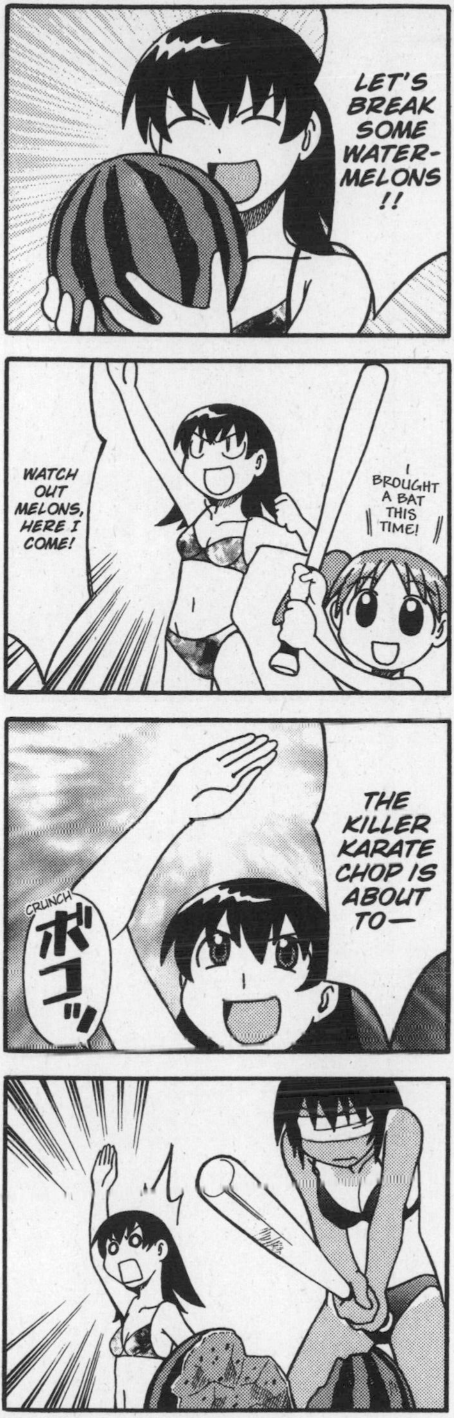
LET'S BREAK SOME WATER-MELONS !!
I BROUGHT A BAT THIS TIME!
WATCH OUT MELONS, HERE I COME!
THE KILLER KARATE CHOP IS ABOUT TO—
CRUNCH
ボコッ

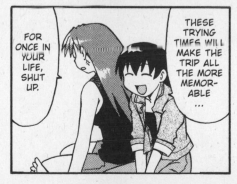

BUT I WANTED TO DO IT

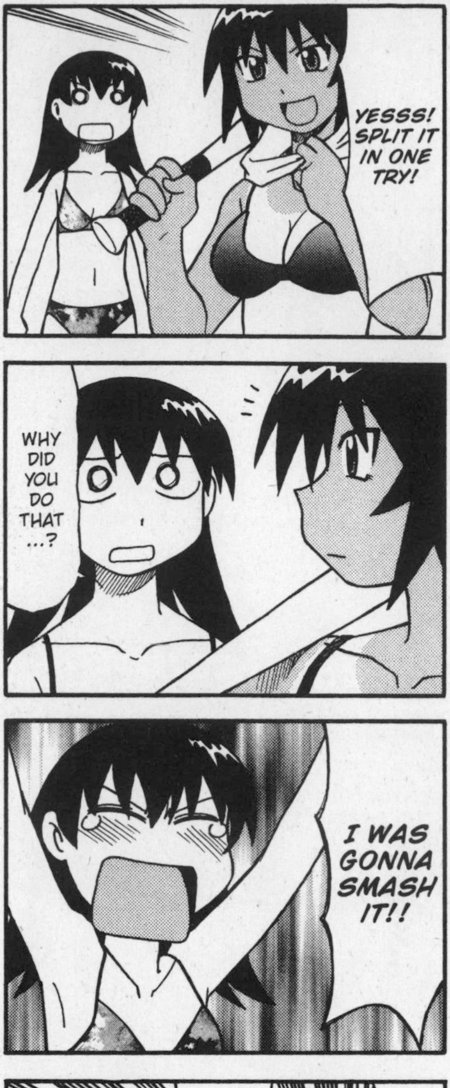
YESSS! SPLIT IT IN ONE TRY!
WHY DID YOU DO THAT ...?
I WAS GONNA SMASH IT!!
I WAS GONNA SMASH IT!!
I WAS GONNA SMASH IT!!
OH, STOP CRY-ING.

OSAKA IN THE CURRENT

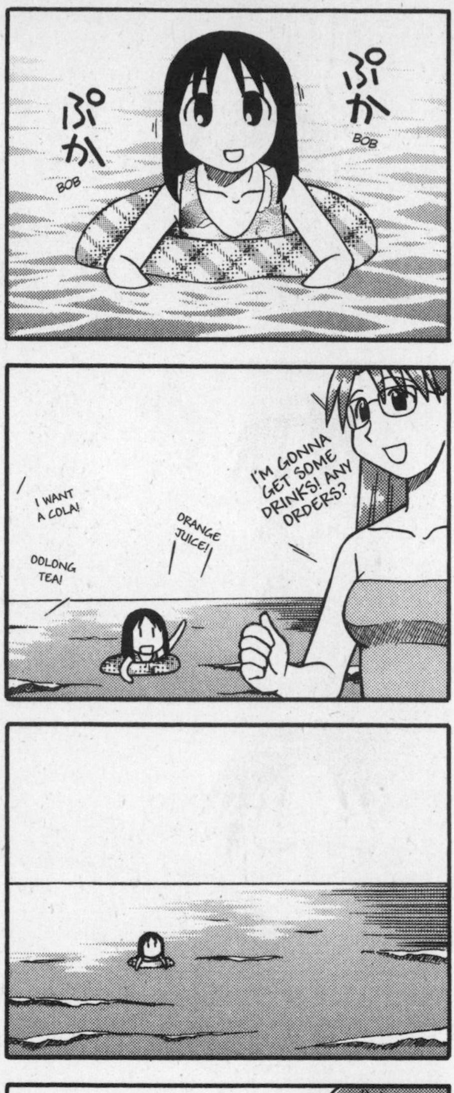
ぷか
BOB
ぷか
BOB
I'M GONNA GET SOME DRINKS! ANY ORDERS?
ORANGE JUICE!
I WANT A COLA!
OOLONG TEA!

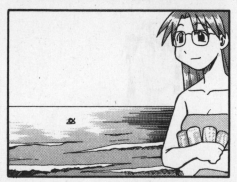

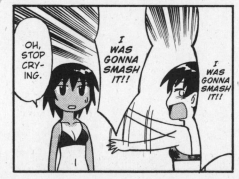

OFF-DUTY

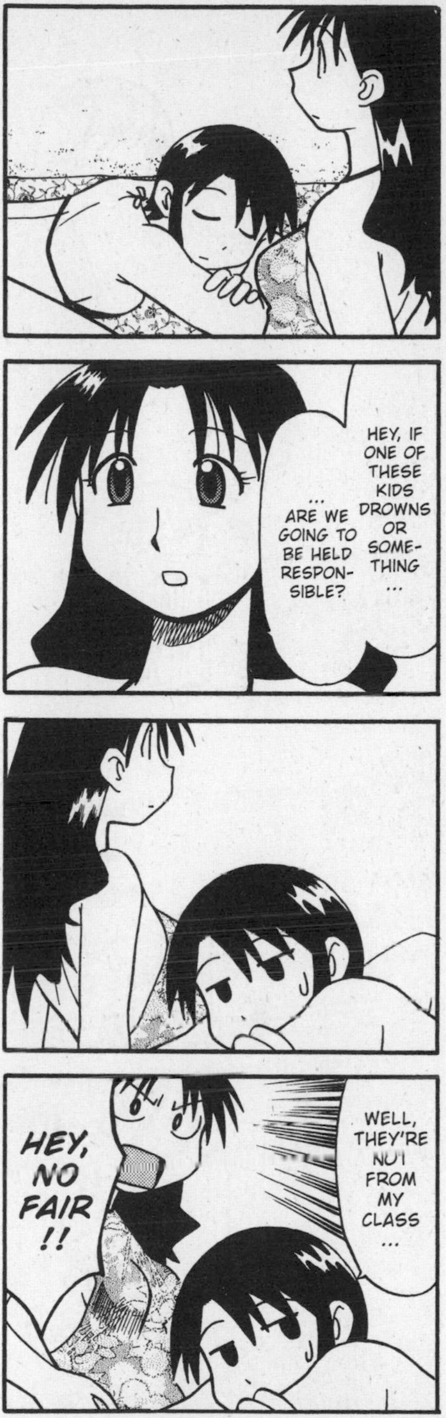
HEY, IF ONE OF THESE KIDS DROWNS OR SOMETHING ...
... ARE WE GOING TO BE HELD RESPONSIBLE?
WELL, THEY'RE NOT FROM MY CLASS ...
HEY, NO FAIR !!

I'M BACK

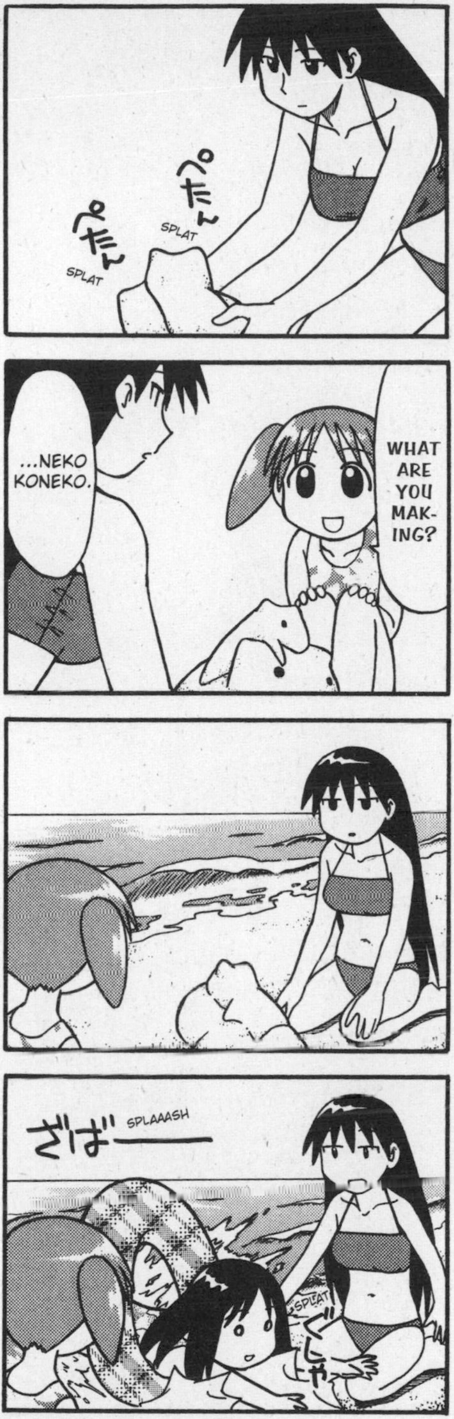
ぺたん
SPLAT
ぺたん
SPLAT
WHAT ARE YOU MAKING?
...NEKO KONEKO.
ざばー
SPLAAASH
ぐしゃ
SPLAT

SNEAKING AHEAD

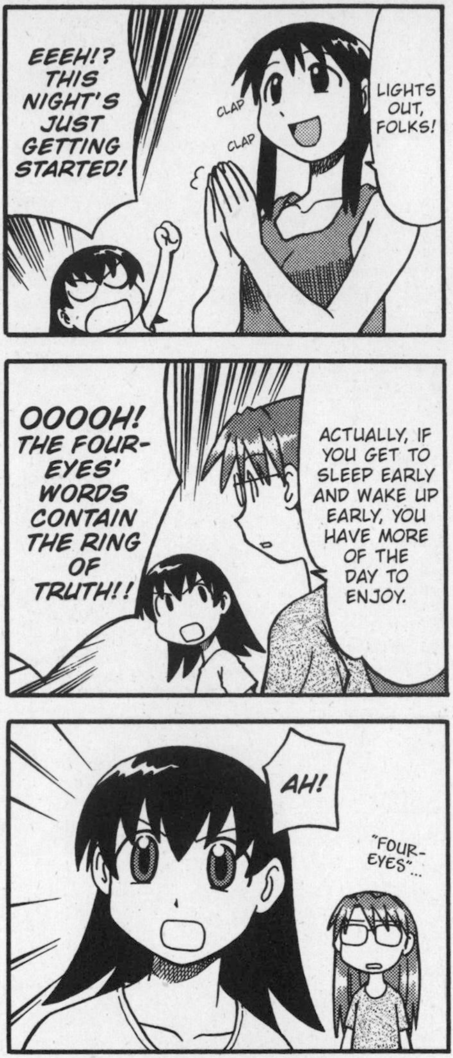
LIGHTS OUT, FOLKS!
CLAP
CLAP
EEEH!? THIS NIGHT'S JUST GETTING STARTED!
ACTUALLY, IF YOU GET TO SLEEP EARLY AND WAKE UP EARLY, YOU HAVE MORE OF THE DAY TO ENJOY.
OOOOH! THE FOUR-EYES' WORDS CONTAIN THE RING OF TRUTH!!
AH!
"FOUR-EYES"...
こっくり
NOD
こっくり
NOD
SHE'S TRYING TO GET THE JUMP ON US BEFORE WE CAN GET TO BED!!
NO FAIR!

PUNISHMENT

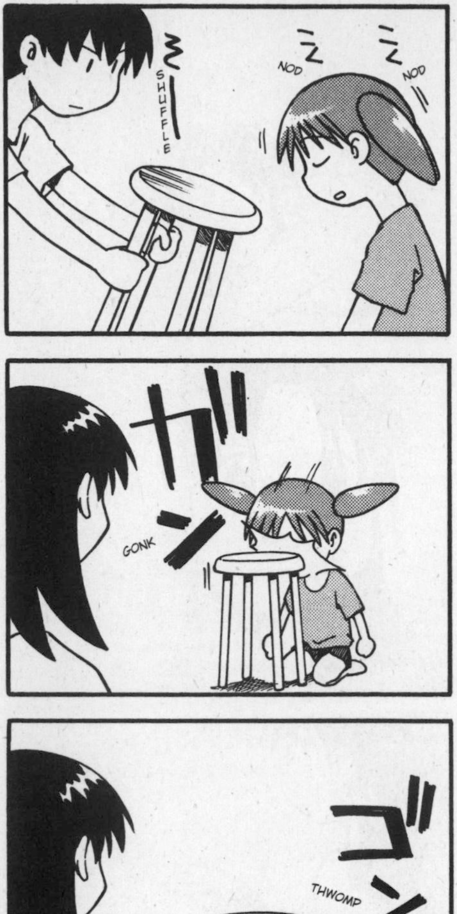
NOD
NOD
SHUFFLE
GONK
THWOMP
!?
!?
AH-HA-HA-HA! HA-HA!
THAT'S MESSED UP, MAN.

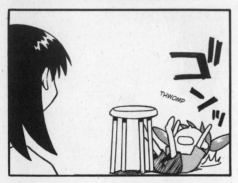

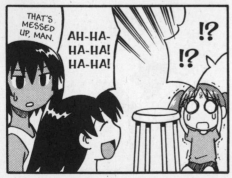

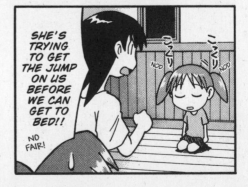

HERE COMES TOMO

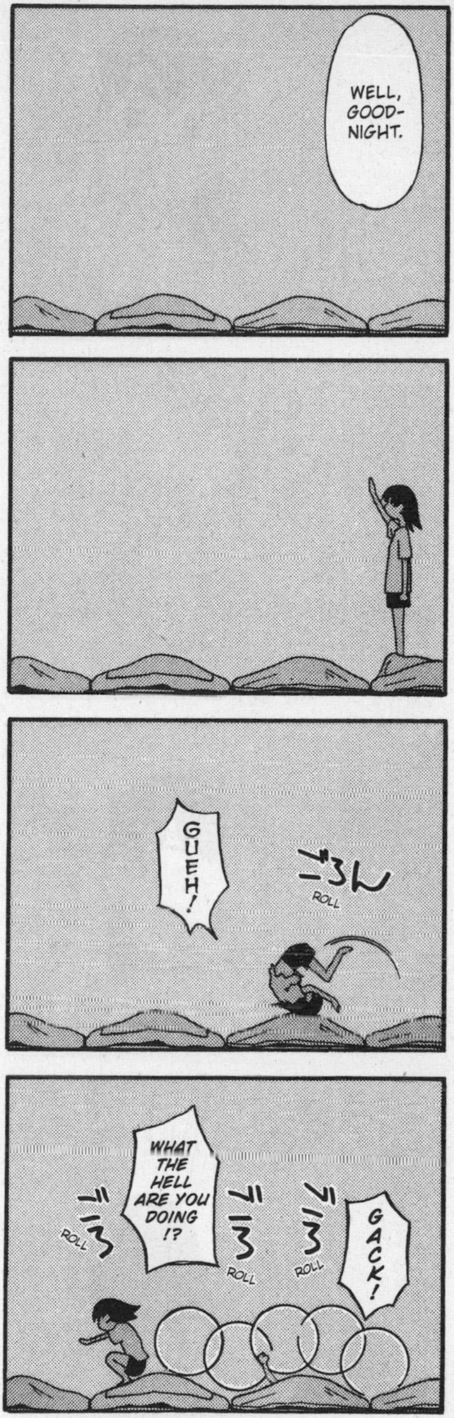
WELL, GOOD-NIGHT.
GUEH!
ごろん
ROLL
GACK!
ごろ
ROLL
WHAT THE HELL ARE YOU DOING!?
ごろ
ROLL
ごろ
ROLL

WAKE UP, PEOPLE!

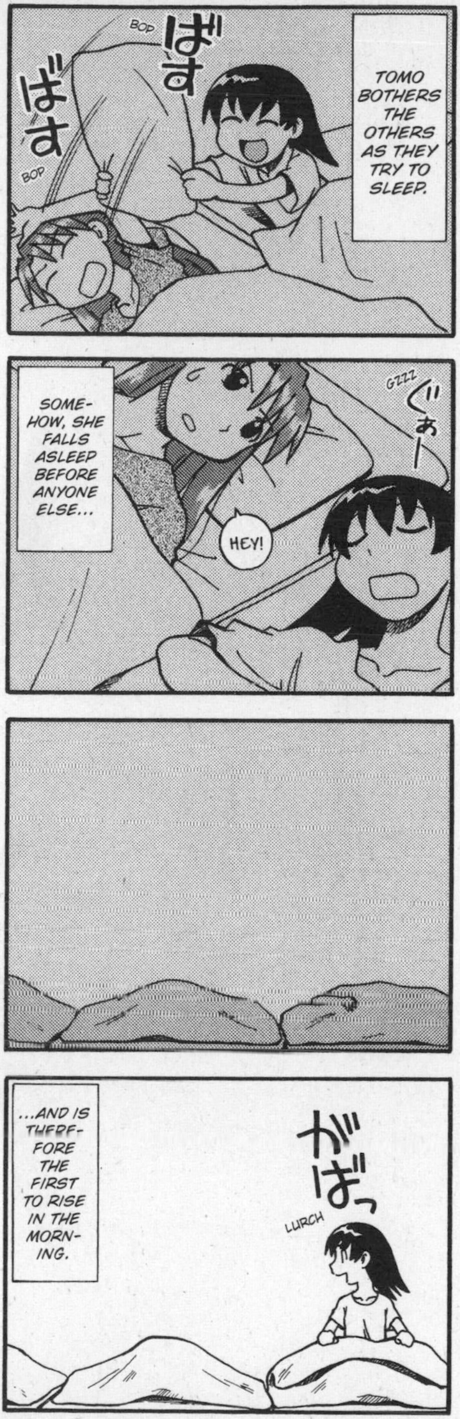
TOMO BOTHERS THE OTHERS AS THEY TRY TO SLEEP.
ばす
BOP
ばす
BOP
ぐぁー
GZZZ
SOME-HOW, SHE FALLS ASLEEP BEFORE ANYONE ELSE...
HEY!
がばっ
LURCH
...AND IS THERE-FORE THE FIRST TO RISE IN THE MORNING.

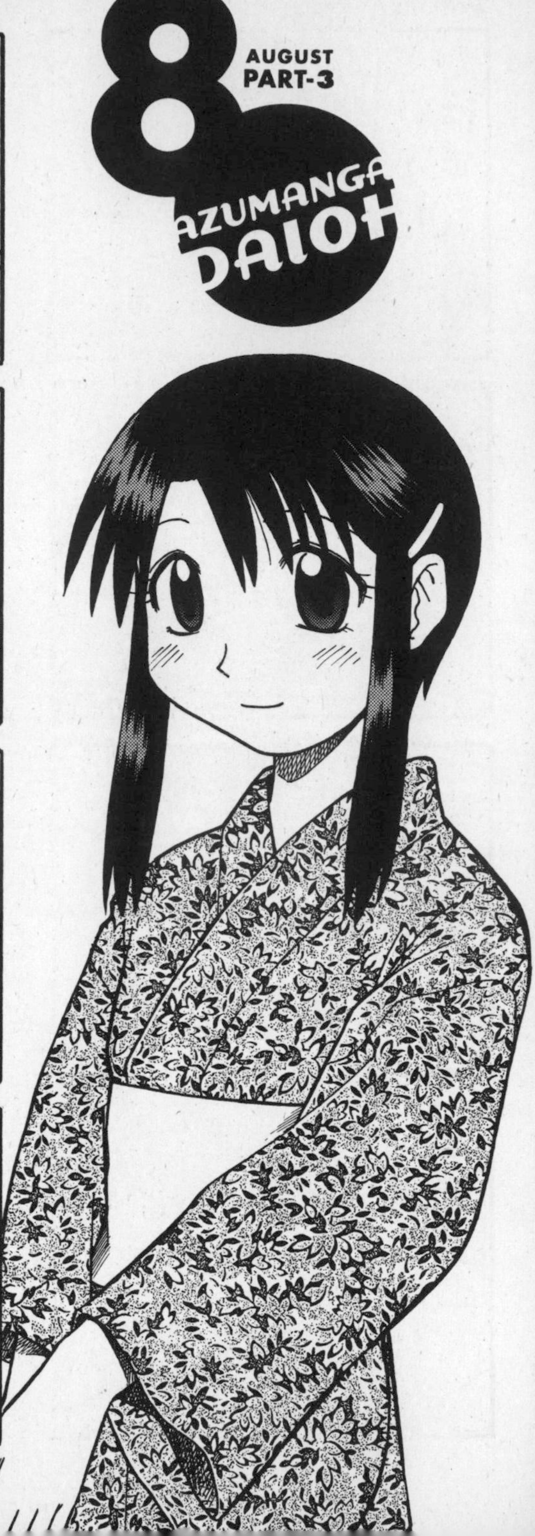
8
AUGUST PART-3
AZUMANGA DAIOH

RESCUE OPERATION

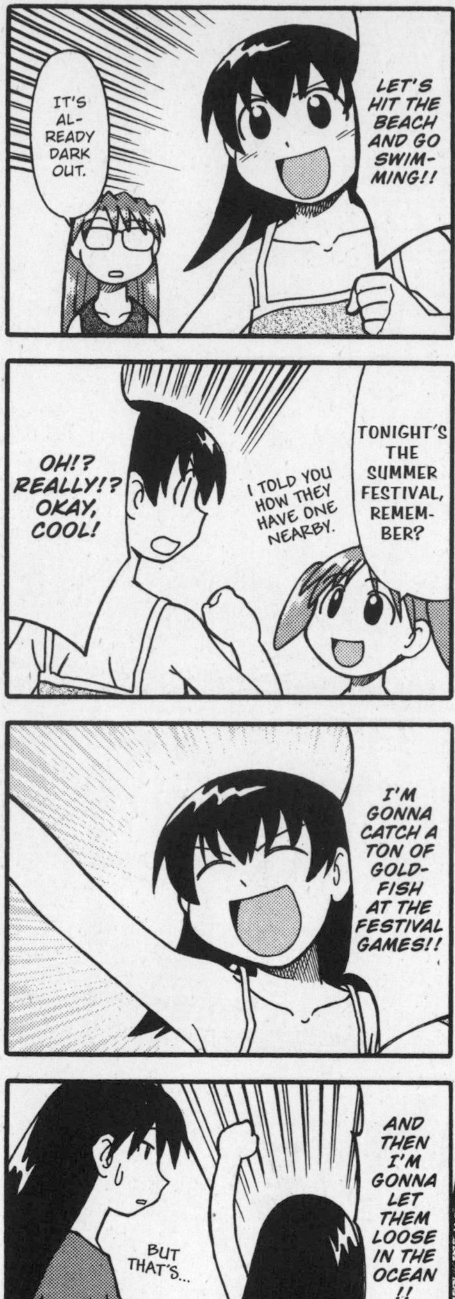
LET'S HIT THE BEACH AND GO SWIMMING!!
IT'S ALREADY DARK OUT.
TONIGHT'S THE SUMMER FESTIVAL, REMEMBER?
I TOLD YOU HOW THEY HAVE ONE NEARBY.
OH!? REALLY!? OKAY, COOL!
I'M GONNA CATCH A TON OF GOLDFISH AT THE FESTIVAL GAMES!!
AND THEN I'M GONNA LET THEM LOOSE IN THE OCEAN!!
BUT THAT'S...

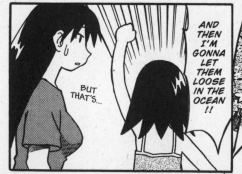

LET ME SHOW YOU

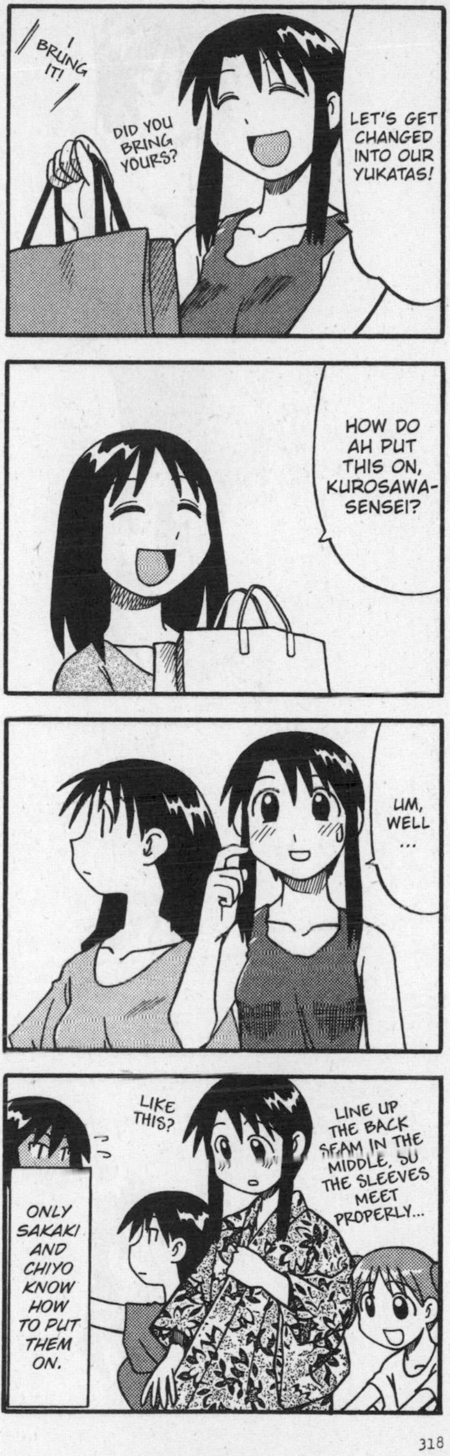
LET'S GET CHANGED INTO OUR YUKATAS!
DID YOU BRING YOURS?
I BRUNG IT!
HOW DO AH PUT THIS ON, KUROSAWA-SENSEI?
UM, WELL ...
LINE UP THE BACK SEAM IN THE MIDDLE, SO THE SLEEVES MEET PROPERLY...
LIKE THIS?
ONLY SAKAKI AND CHIYO KNOW HOW TO PUT THEM ON.

GOOD-NIGHT, SENSEI

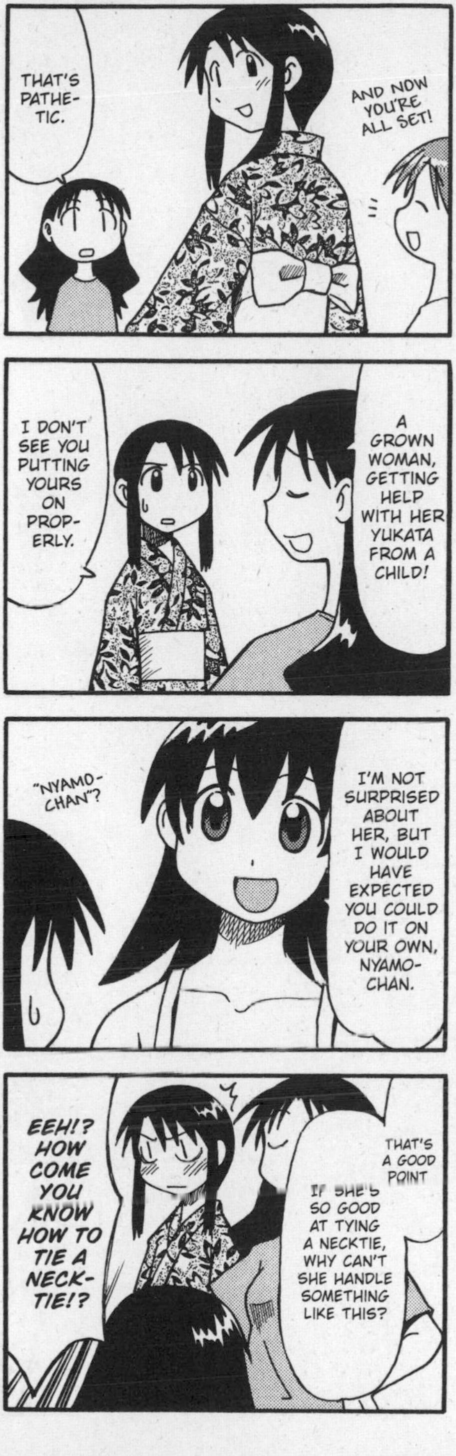
AND NOW YOU'RE ALL SET!
THAT'S PATHETIC.
A GROWN WOMAN, GETTING HELP WITH HER YUKATA FROM A CHILD!
I DON'T SEE YOU PUTTING YOURS ON PROPERLY.
I'M NOT SURPRISED ABOUT HER, BUT I WOULD HAVE EXPECTED YOU COULD DO IT ON YOUR OWN, NYAMO-CHAN.
"NYAMO-CHAN"?
THAT'S A GOOD POINT
IF SHE'S SO GOOD AT TYING A NECKTIE, WHY CAN'T SHE HANDLE SOMETHING LIKE THIS?
EEH!? HOW COME YOU KNOW HOW TO TIE A NECKTIE!?

THE BIG REVEAL

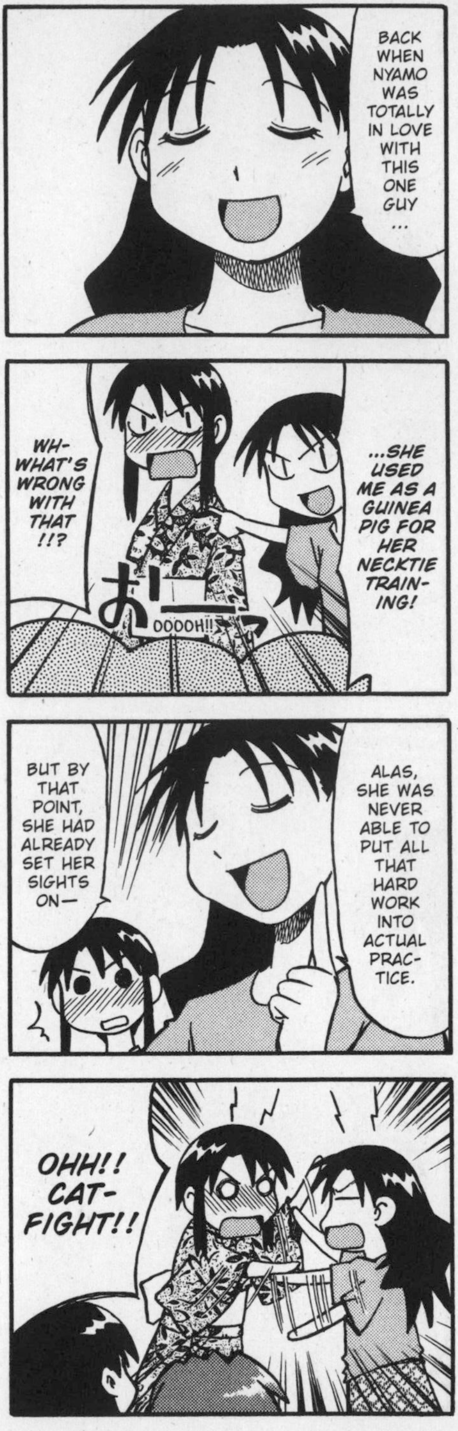
BACK WHEN NYAMO WAS TOTALLY IN LOVE WITH THIS ONE GUY ...
...SHE USED ME AS A GUINEA PIG FOR HER NECKTIE TRAINING!
WH-WHAT'S WRONG WITH THAT !!?
おー OOOOH!!
ALAS, SHE WAS NEVER ABLE TO PUT ALL THAT HARD WORK INTO ACTUAL PRAC-TICE.
BUT BY THAT POINT, SHE HAD ALREADY SET HER SIGHTS ON—
OHH!! CAT-FIGHT!!

FEMININE

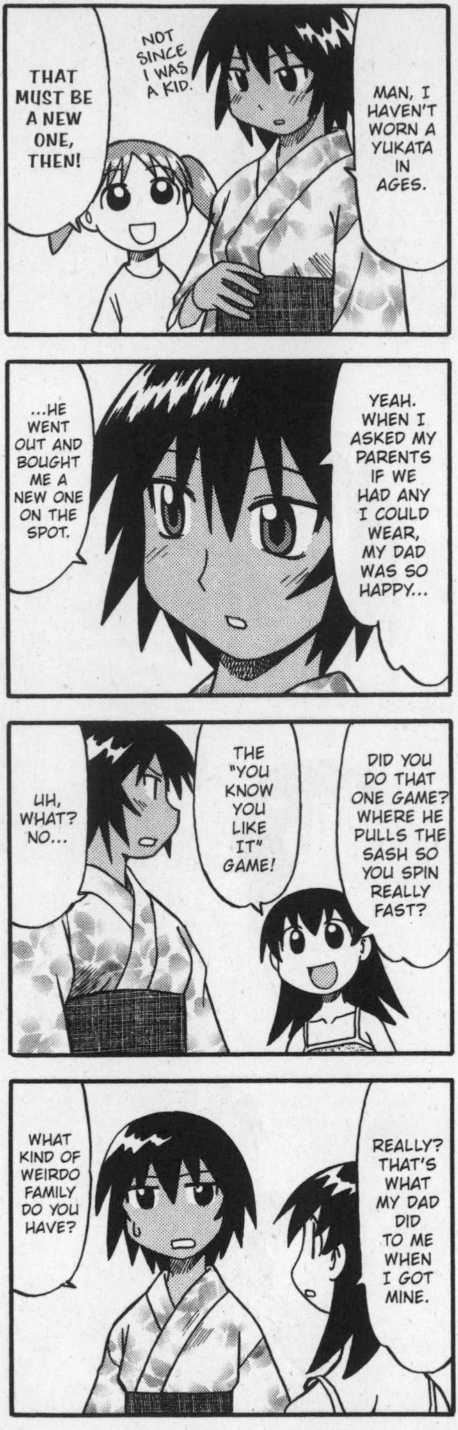
MAN, I HAVEN'T WORN A YUKATA IN AGES.
NOT SINCE I WAS A KID.
THAT MUST BE A NEW ONE, THEN!
YEAH. WHEN I ASKED MY PARENTS IF WE HAD ANY I COULD WEAR, MY DAD WAS SO HAPPY...
...HE WENT OUT AND BOUGHT ME A NEW ONE ON THE SPOT.
DID YOU DO THAT ONE GAME? WHERE HE PULLS THE SASH SO YOU SPIN REALLY FAST?
THE "YOU KNOW YOU LIKE IT" GAME!
UH, WHAT? NO...
REALLY? THAT'S WHAT MY DAD DID TO ME WHEN I GOT MINE.
WHAT KIND OF WEIRDO FAMILY DO YOU HAVE?

WON'T KEEP IT

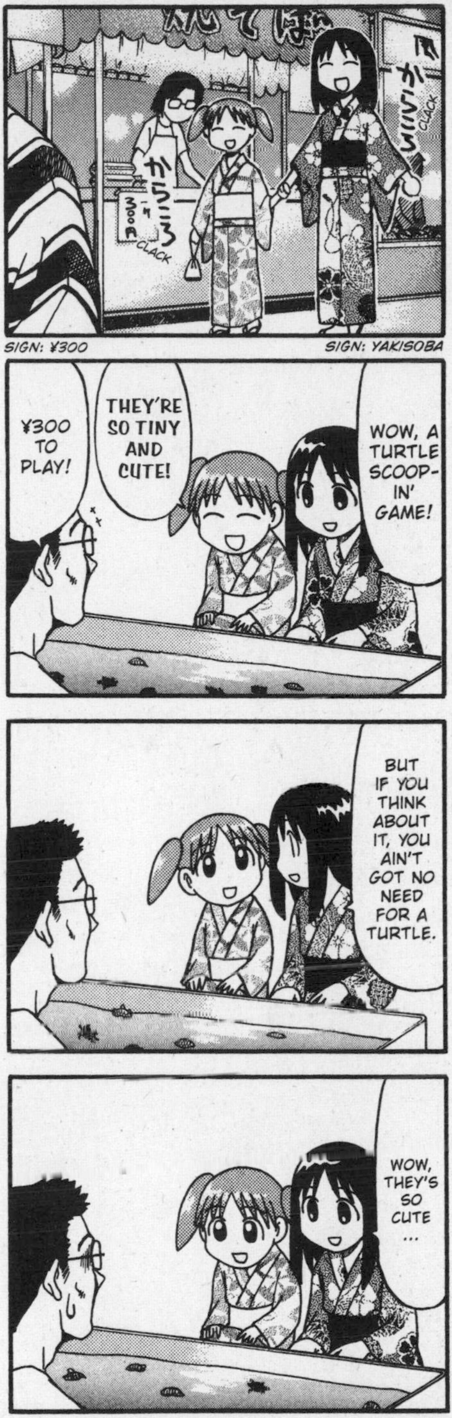
からころ
CLACK
からころ
300円
CLACK
SIGN: ¥300
SIGN: YAKISOBA
WOW, A TURTLE SCOOP-IN' GAME!
THEY'RE SO TINY AND CUTE!
¥300 TO PLAY!
BUT IF YOU THINK ABOUT IT, YOU AIN'T GOT NO NEED FOR A TURTLE.
WOW, THEY'S SO CUTE ...

ON THE HUNT

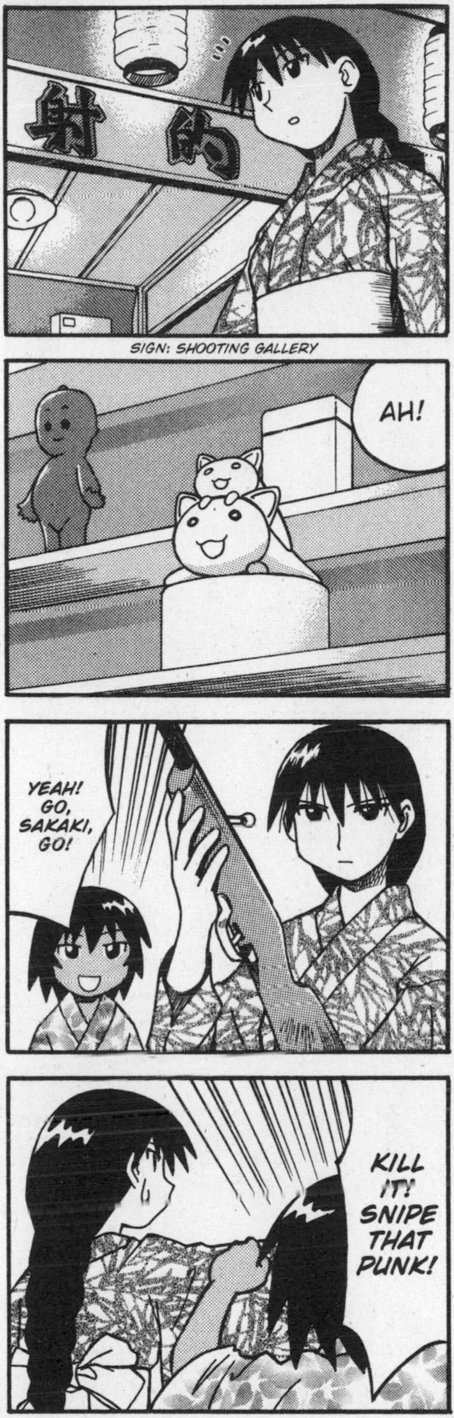
SIGN: SHOOTING GALLERY
AH!
YEAH! GO, SAKAKI, GO!
KILL IT! SNIPE THAT PUNK!

NEKO KONEKO ASSASSINATION ORDER

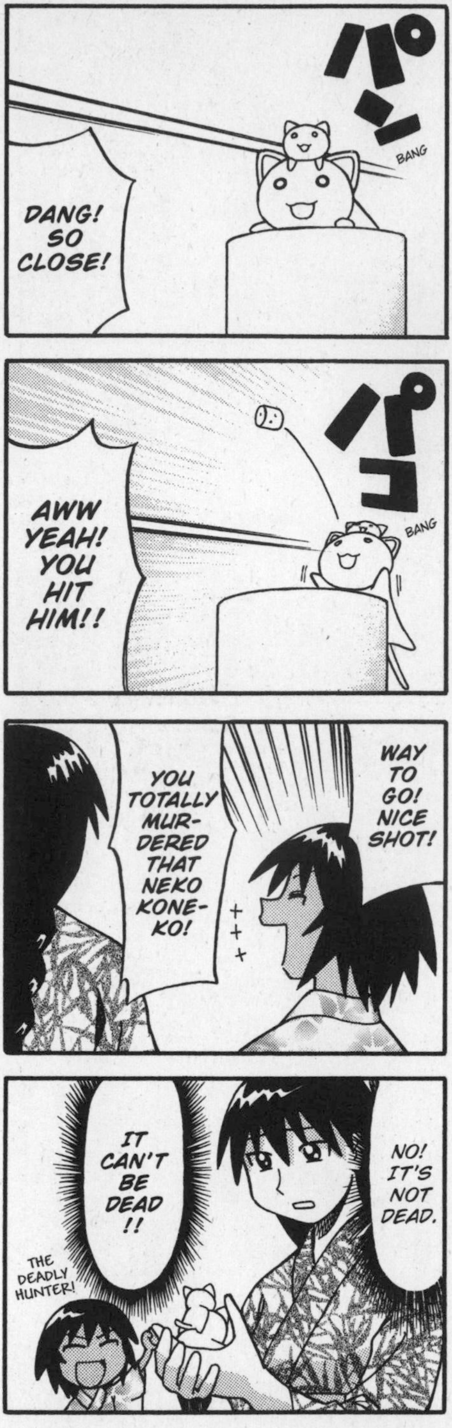
パン
BANG
DANG! SO CLOSE!
パコ
BANG
AWW YEAH! YOU HIT HIM!!
WAY TO GO! NICE SHOT!
YOU TOTALLY MUR-DERED THAT NEKO KONE-KO!
NO! IT'S NOT DEAD.
IT CAN'T BE DEAD!!
THE DEADLY HUNTER!

PROHIBITION

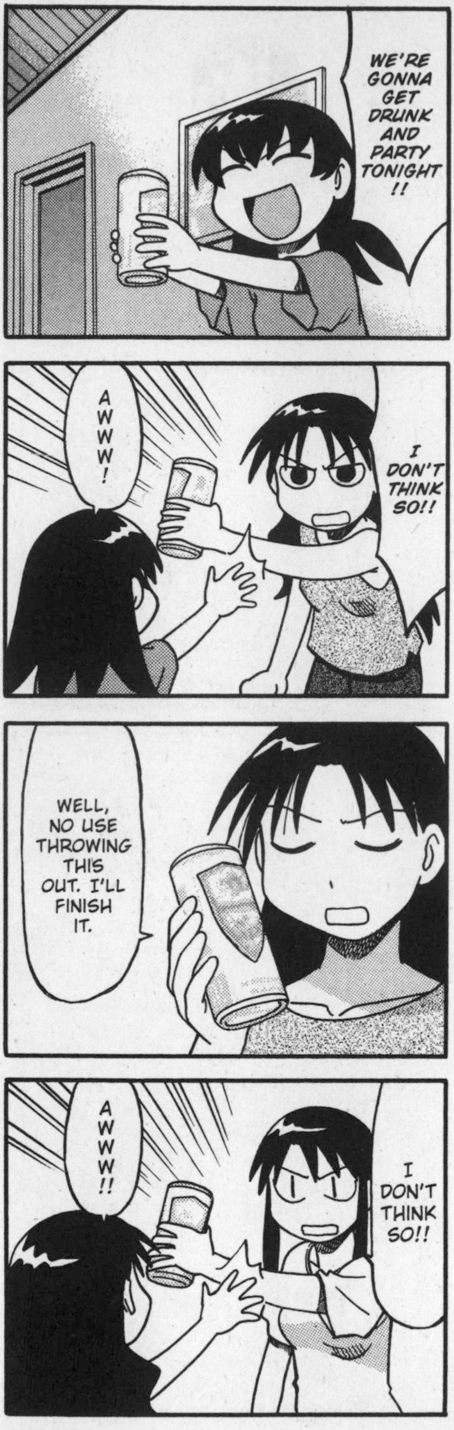
WE'RE GONNA GET DRUNK AND PARTY TONIGHT!!
I DON'T THINK SO!!
AWWW!
WELL, NO USE THROWING THIS OUT. I'LL FINISH IT.
I DON'T THINK SO!!
AWWW!!

SELF-SACRIFICE

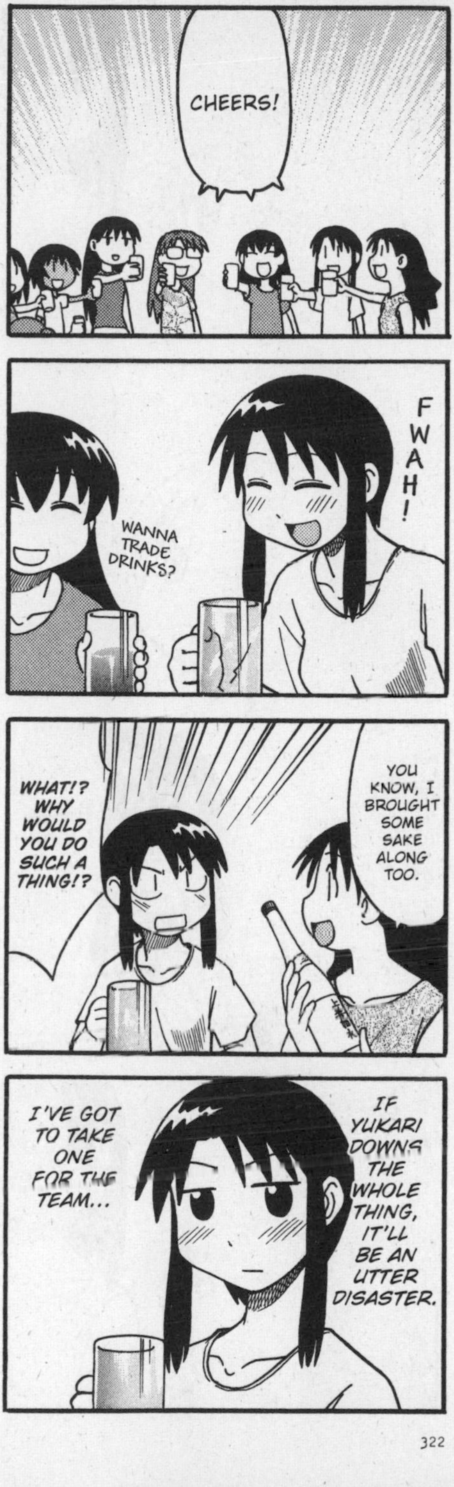
CHEERS!
FWAH!
WANNA TRADE DRINKS?
YOU KNOW, I BROUGHT SOME SAKE ALONG TOO.
WHAT!? WHY WOULD YOU DO SUCH A THING!?
IF YUKARI DOWNS THE WHOLE THING, IT'LL BE AN UTTER DISASTER.
I'VE GOT TO TAKE ONE FOR THE TEAM...

SMASHED

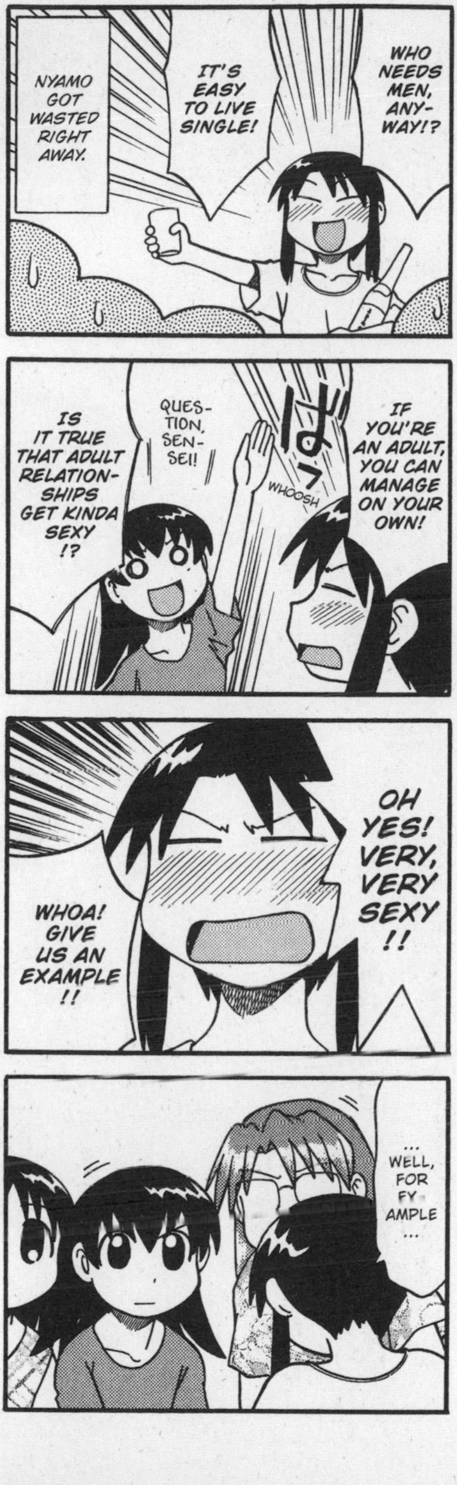
WHO NEEDS MEN, ANYWAY!?
IT'S EASY TO LIVE SINGLE!
NYAMO GOT WASTED RIGHT AWAY.
IF YOU'RE AN ADULT, YOU CAN MANAGE ON YOUR OWN!
ぱっ
WHOOSH
QUESTION, SENSEI!
IS IT TRUE THAT ADULT RELATIONSHIPS GET KINDA SEXY!?
OH YES! VERY, VERY SEXY!!
WHOA! GIVE US AN EXAMPLE!!
... WELL, FOR EX-AMPLE ...

THE WORLD OF ADULTS

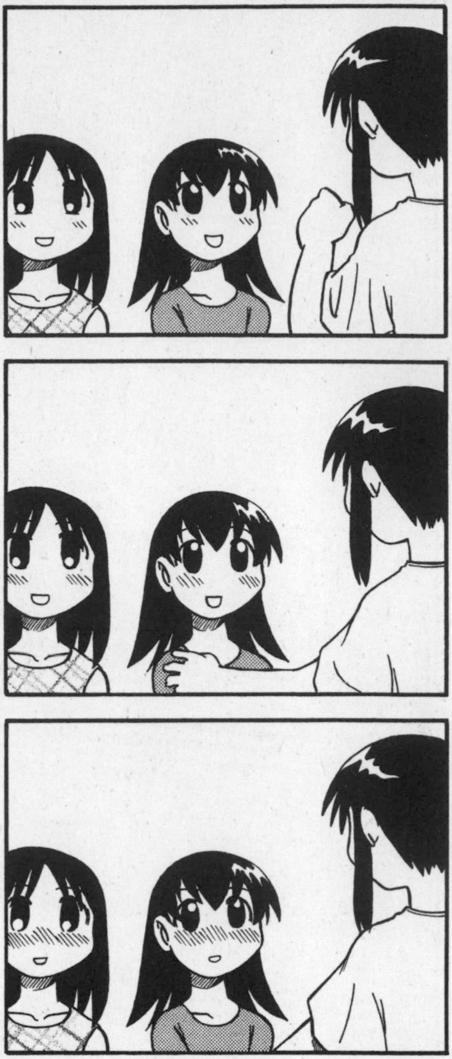

I DON'T UNDERSTAND

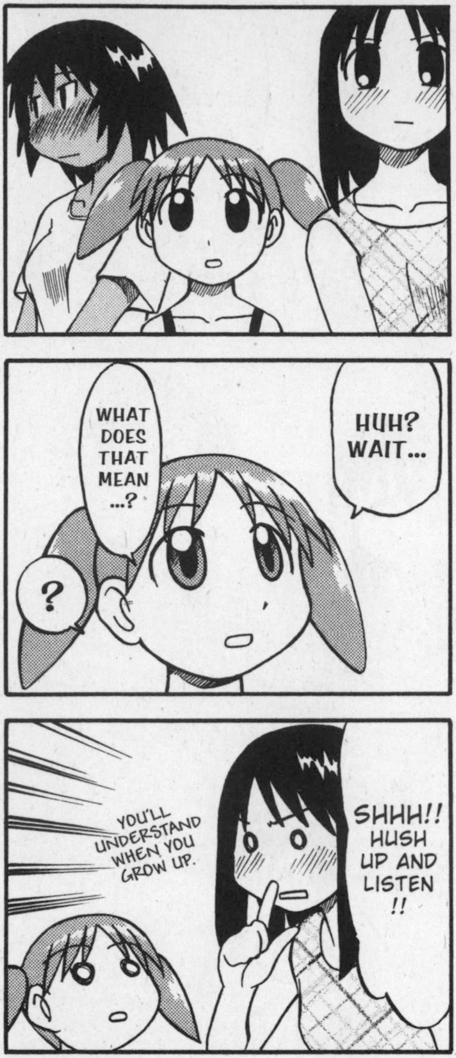
HUH? WAIT...
WHAT DOES THAT MEAN ...?
?
SHHH!! HUSH UP AND LISTEN !!
YOU'LL UNDERSTAND WHEN YOU GROW UP.

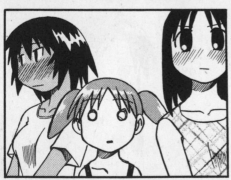

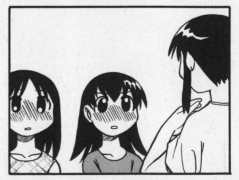

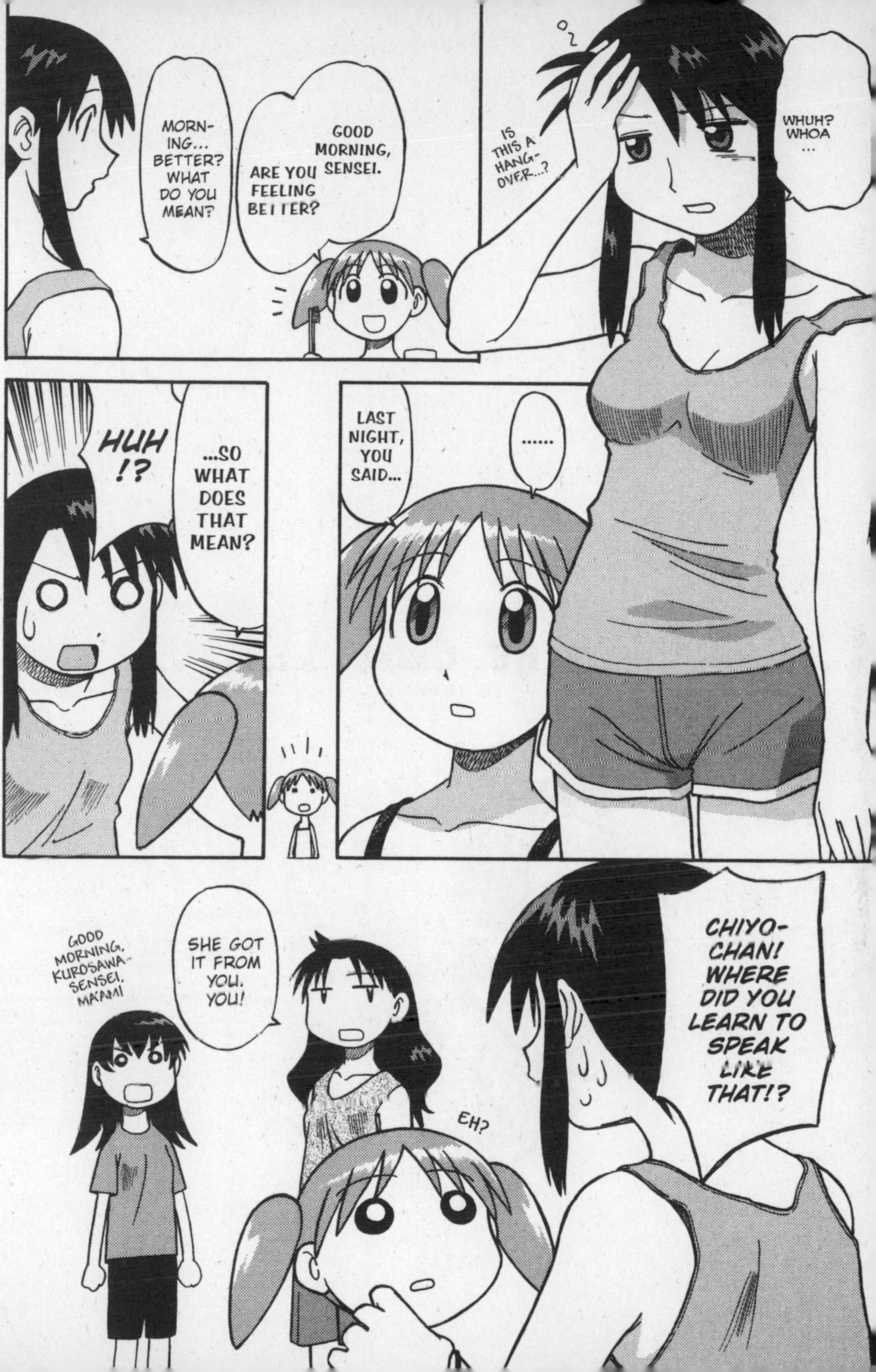
WHUH? WHOA ...
IS THIS A HANG-OVER...?
GOOD MORNING, SENSEI.
ARE YOU FEELING BETTER?
MORN-ING... BETTER? WHAT DO YOU MEAN?
......
LAST NIGHT, YOU SAID...
...SO WHAT DOES THAT MEAN?
HUH!?
CHIYO-CHAN! WHERE DID YOU LEARN TO SPEAK LIKE THAT!?
EH?
SHE GOT IT FROM YOU. YOU!
GOOD MORNING, KUROSAWA-SENSEI, MA'AM!

TO BE CONTINUED.

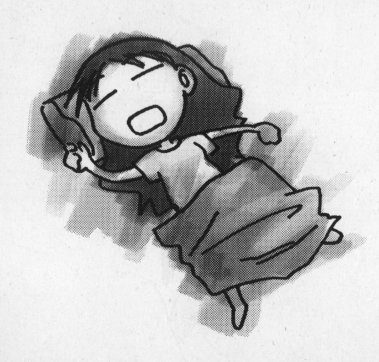

PAGE 317
Festivals: Japan has a number of holidays in the summer in which visiting a temple is customary, and on those occasions the temple often holds a festival featuring food stands, fireworks, and games. One of these games is the goldfish catch, in which a basin is filled with water and goldfish, and for a small price, the player is given a fragile paper net with which to scoop out a fish. If they manage to do it without the net breaking, they will receive a bag full of water to put the goldfish inside and take home.

PAGE 318
Yukata: A summer version of the traditional *kimono* that is lighter and draftier for use in the hot and muggy Japanese summer.

PAGE 320
Yakisoba: A popular summer dish consisting of fried noodles with pork and cabbage. You can invariably find it at any summer festival in Japan.

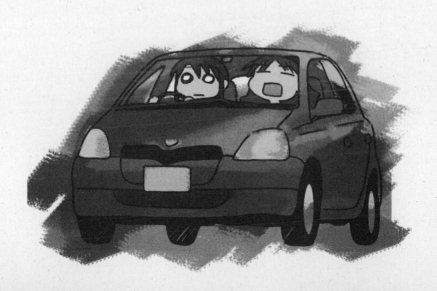

TRANSLATION NOTES 1 *AZUMANGA DAIOH VOLUME 2*

PAGE 171

Zoni: A traditional dish eaten around New Year's. *Zoni* is a light soup with mochi rice cakes, some type of meat such as chicken, fish, or meatballs, leafy greens, and carrots. The sweet bean soup mentioned in the strip is *zenzai*, a winter treat consisting of a thick, warm soup made with sweet red beans and sticky, half-melted *mochi*. Yomi must have really eaten a lot of it....

PAGE 172

New Year's allowance: Another feature of the Japanese New Year, *otoshidama* is a gift of money given from older relatives to young children. The money is usually placed in decorative paper pouches called *otoshidama-bukuro*.

PAGE 177

First dream: In Japan, the first dream that one sees in the New Year is thought to foretell the year ahead. Traditionally, a dream that combined Mt. Fuji, a hawk, and an eggplant was considered a sign of great fortune ahead.

PAGE 185

The numbers listed on the dividing pages between chapters here are the heights of the characters in centimeters. If you were to convert into inches, you'd find the following measurements:

Tomo	154 cm	5'0"
Yomi	163 cm	5'4"
Chiyo	133 cm	4'4"
Osaka	156 cm	5'1"
Kagura	156 cm	5'1"
Sakaki	174 cm	5'8"
Yukari	158 cm	5'2"
Nyamo	161 cm	5'3"

PAGE 187

Taiyaki: A delicious pastry shaped like a fish (no actual fish involved) and filled with sweet red bean jam. The dish is served warm, but be careful not to bite into it too fast, because the filling inside is hot!

PAGE 189

Teru teru bozu: A good luck charm made from cloth or tissue paper that is intended to bring good weather. The name means "shiny priest," and with the appearance of a round head tied off with the ends hanging loose, the charm resembles a simple Halloween "ghost" hanging. While the charm is meant to keep rain away, some will hang them upside down to encourage the rain instead.

PAGE 211

Giants: The Tokyo Yomiuri Giants are the most successful baseball team in Japan, the equivalent of the New York Yankees. Tomo is arguing on behalf of the Chunichi Dragons, another team in the same league, though nowhere near as successful.

PAGE 224

Yakiniku: Literally "grilled meat," *yakiniku* is often called Korean barbecue. *Yakiniku* restaurants have little grills built into the tables, from which the customers order servings of bite-sized beef that they can cook to their own liking.

PAGE 227

Name order: While the characters in this translation are presented with their names in the Western order (given, family), Far East countries like Japan, China, and Korea use the opposite order (family, given). Within Japan, it's common knowledge that the "rest of the world" places their names in the opposite order, so for example, they would say "Brad Pitt" rather than "Pitt Brad." Because the Japanese alphabet must fit certain distinct sounds from foreign languages (such as "R" and "L", and "S" and "Th") into the same pronunciation, the name "Bruce Lee" sounds exactly the same as "Blue Three."

PAGE 259

Hawk's claws: The literal translation of the Japanese name (*taka no tsume*) for a type of small chile pepper that got its name from the curved shape it comes in.

PAGE 282

Fujiko Mine: An iconic femme fatale from the *Lupin III* manga and anime series. She uses her voluptuous body and charms to seduce the mystery thief Lupin into divulging important information or acting on her whims. Even her name references her sexy body—it has often been suggested that if Fujiko's name was translated into English, it would be "Twin Peaks."

PAGE 302

Tissues: In Japan, a common form of promotion for certain businesses is to wrap packets of tissues with an advertisement, then pay people to hand them out in crowded areas such as malls or outside train stations. If you don't learn to ignore them, you'll soon find your hands full.

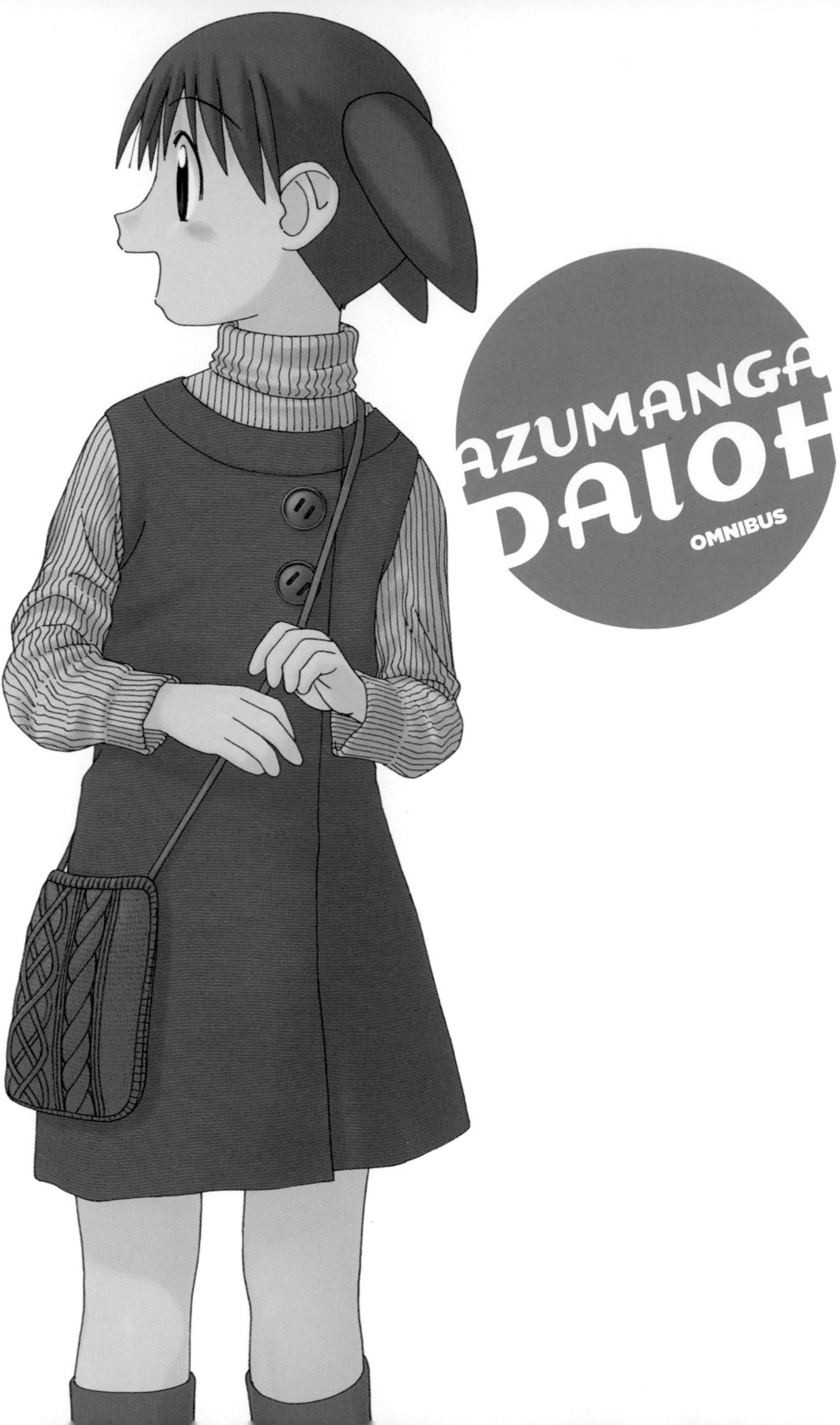

AZUMANGA DAIOH

OMNIBUS

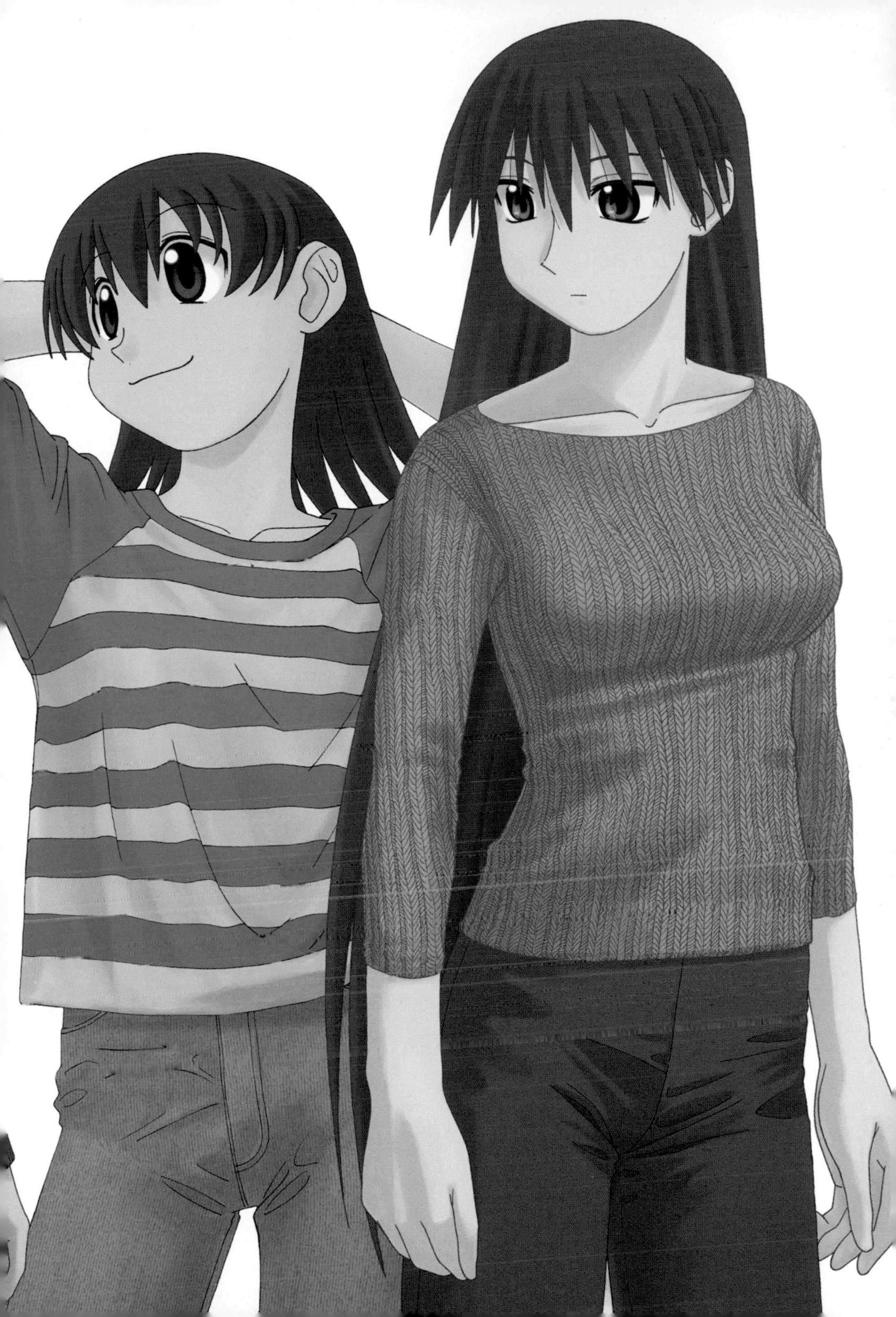

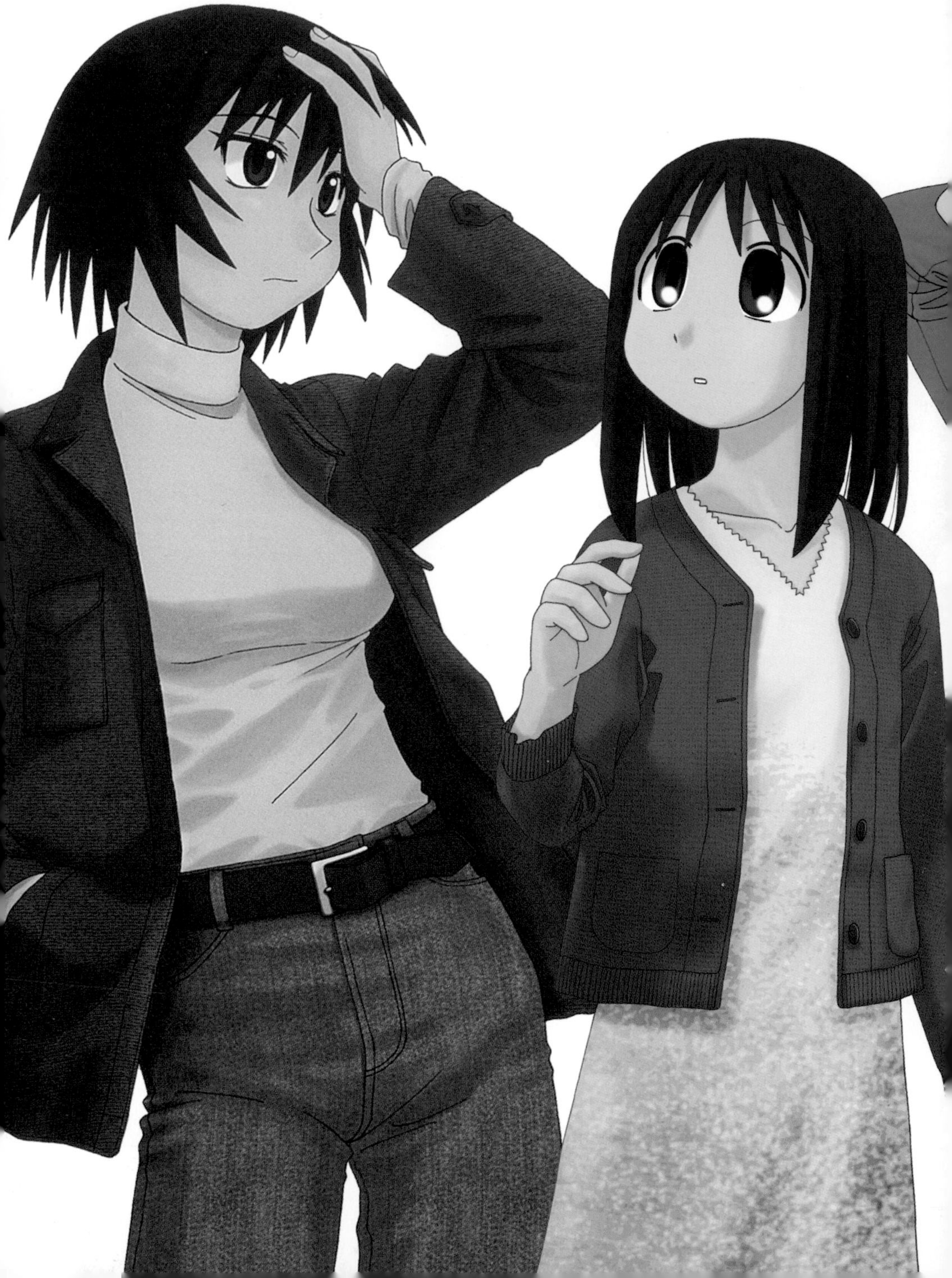

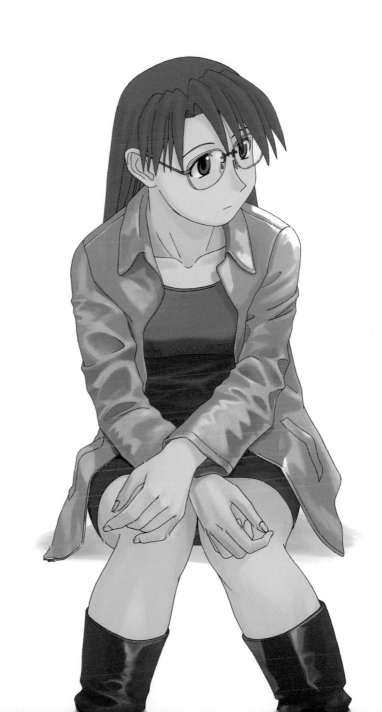

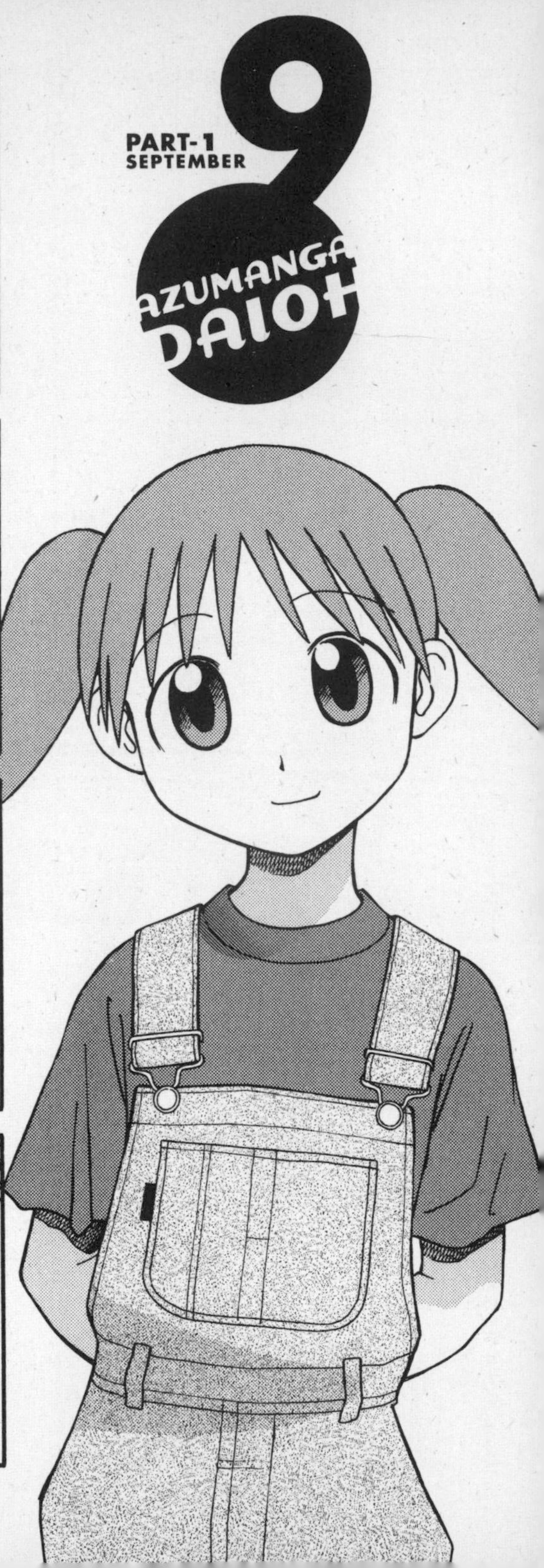
PART-1
SEPTEMBER
AZUMANGA
DAIOH

HIP HIP HOORAY

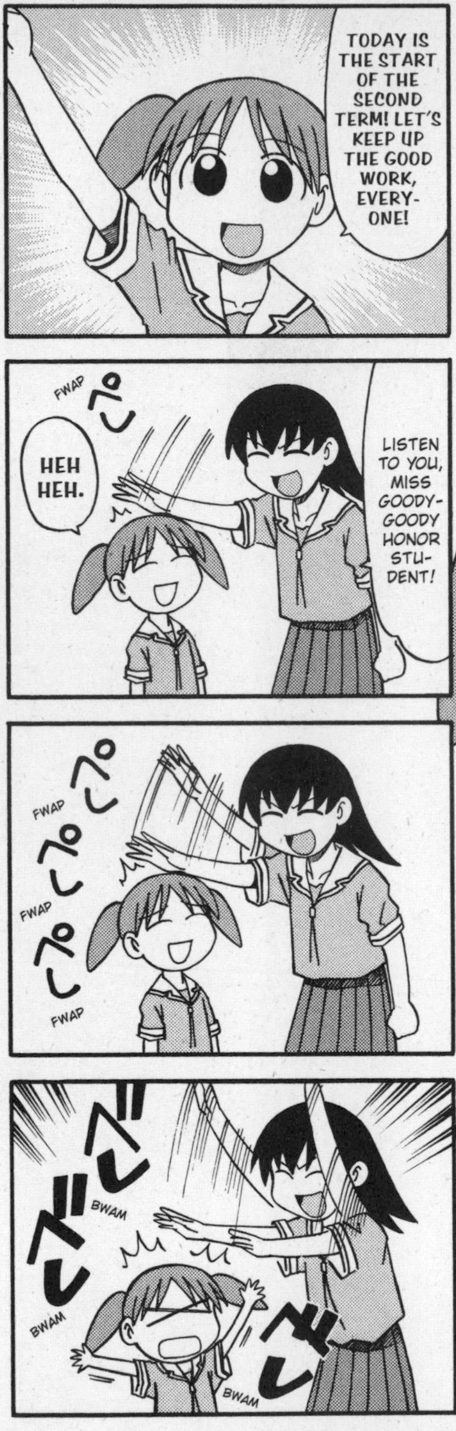
TODAY IS THE START OF THE SECOND TERM! LET'S KEEP UP THE GOOD WORK, EVERYONE!
LISTEN TO YOU, MISS GOODY-GOODY HONOR STUDENT!
ぺし
FWAP
HEH HEH.
ぺし
FWAP
ぺし
FWAP
ぺし
FWAP
べし
BWAM
べし
BWAM
べし
BWAM

"S"

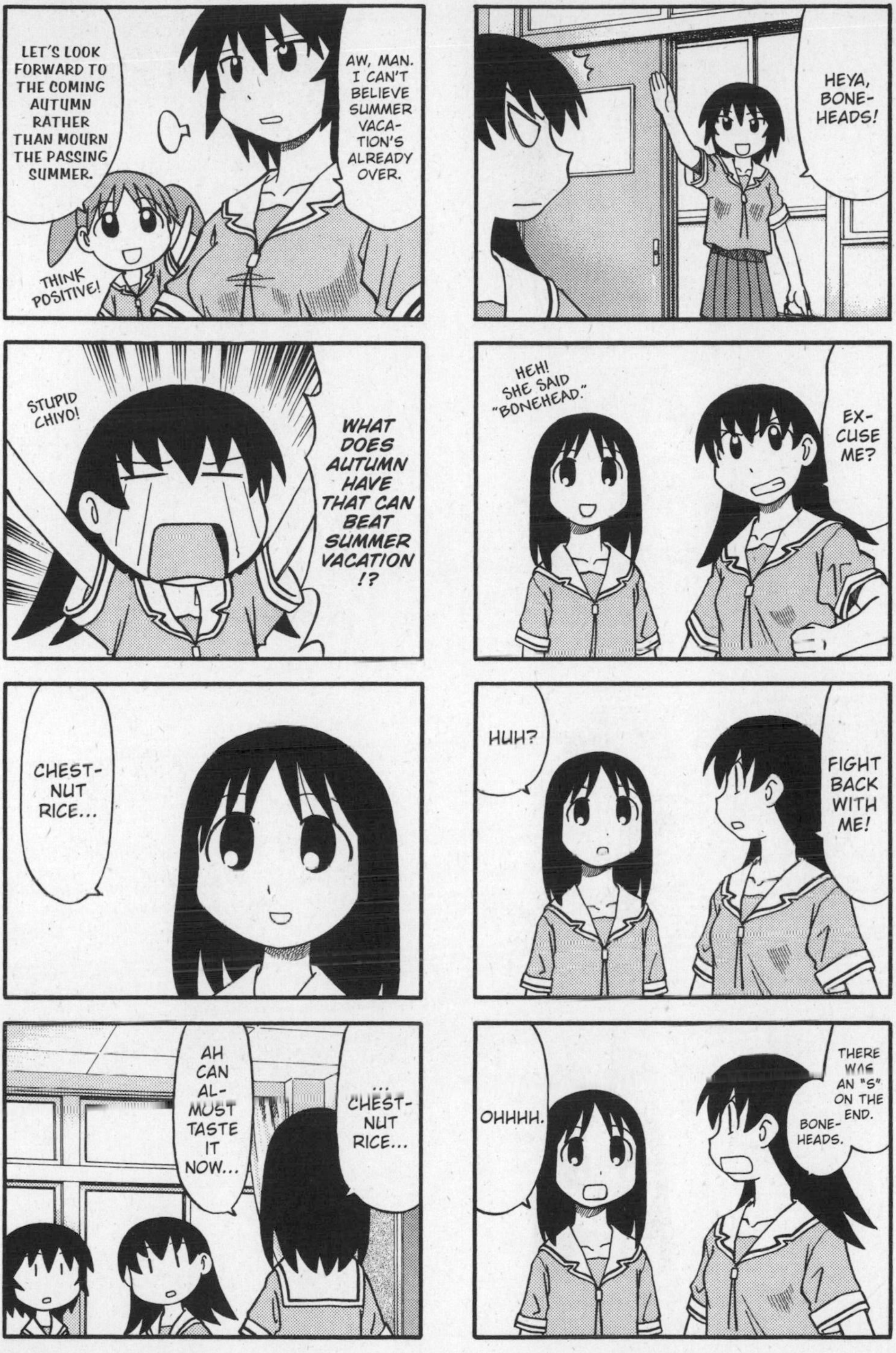
HEYA, BONE-HEADS!
EX-CUSE ME?
HEH! SHE SAID "BONEHEAD."
FIGHT BACK WITH ME!
HUH?
THERE WAS AN "S" ON THE END.
BONE-HEADS.
OHHHH.
AW, MAN. I CAN'T BELIEVE SUMMER VACA-TION'S ALREADY OVER.
LET'S LOOK FORWARD TO THE COMING AUTUMN RATHER THAN MOURN THE PASSING SUMMER.
THINK POSITIVE!
WHAT DOES AUTUMN HAVE THAT CAN BEAT SUMMER VACATION !?
STUPID CHIYO!
CHEST-NUT RICE...
... CHEST-NUT RICE...
AH CAN AL-MUST TASTE IT NOW...

CHESTNUT RICE

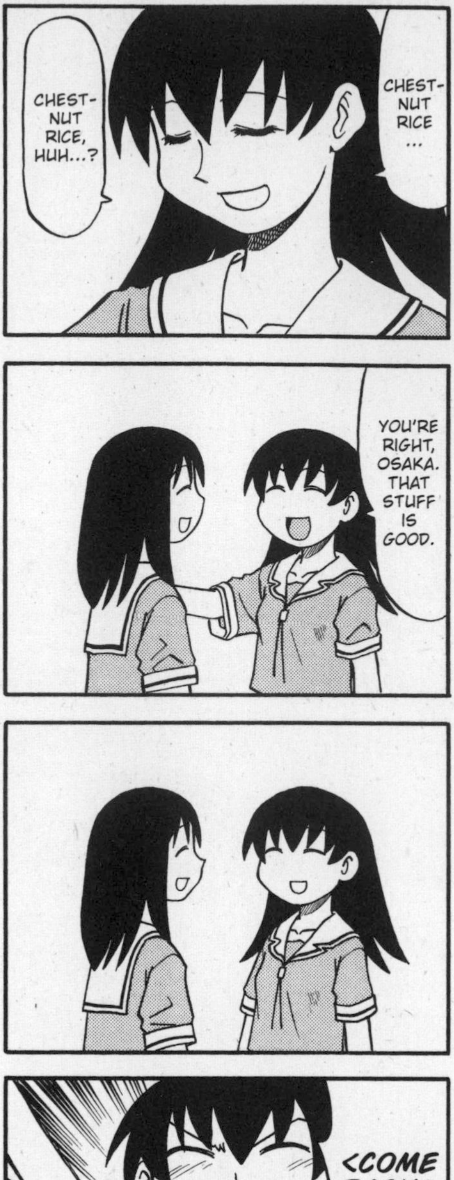
CHESTNUT RICE...
CHESTNUT RICE, HUH...?
YOU'RE RIGHT, OSAKA. THAT STUFF IS GOOD.
<COME BACK,> SUMMER VACATION!!
?

OSAKA-MAN

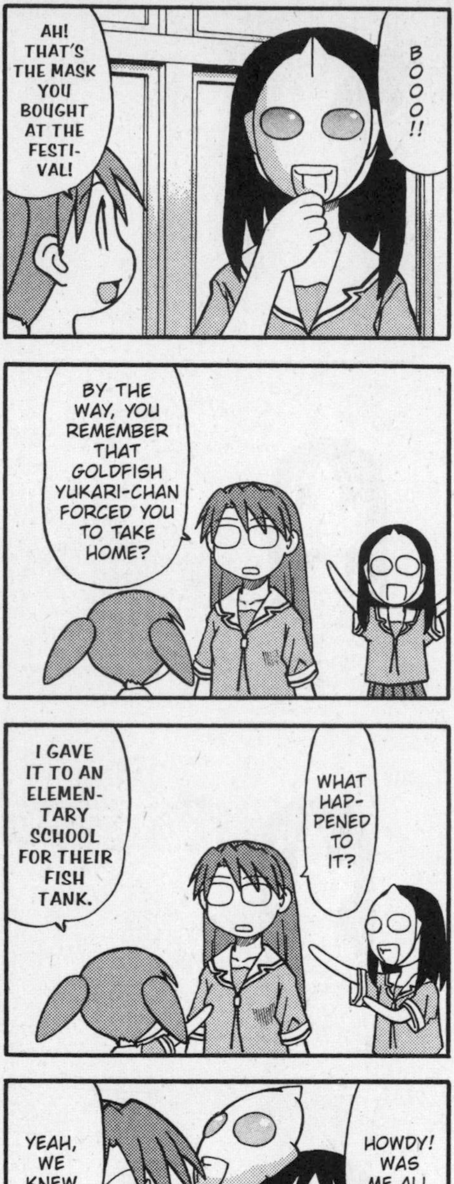
BOOOO!!
AH! THAT'S THE MASK YOU BOUGHT AT THE FESTIVAL!
BY THE WAY, YOU REMEMBER THAT GOLDFISH YUKARI-CHAN FORCED YOU TO TAKE HOME?
WHAT HAPPENED TO IT?
I GAVE IT TO AN ELEMENTARY SCHOOL FOR THEIR FISH TANK.
HOWDY! WAS ME ALL ALONG.
YEAH, WE KNEW THAT.

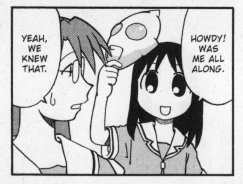

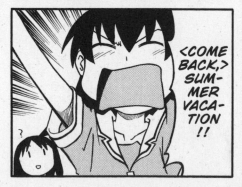

HONESTY IS THE BEST POLICY

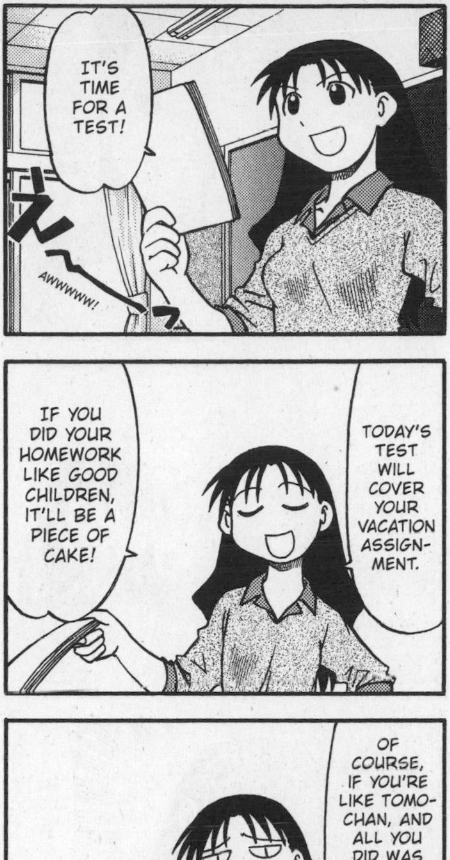
IT'S TIME FOR A TEST!
AWWWWW!
TODAY'S TEST WILL COVER YOUR VACATION ASSIGNMENT.
IF YOU DID YOUR HOMEWORK LIKE GOOD CHILDREN, IT'LL BE A PIECE OF CAKE!
OF COURSE, IF YOU'RE LIKE TOMO-CHAN, AND ALL YOU DID WAS COPY CHIYO-CHAN'S HOME-WORK, IT MAY BE OVER YOUR HEAD.
NOT ONLY HERS. YOMI'S TOO.
SHUT UP, MORON!!

SUMMER VACATION IS...

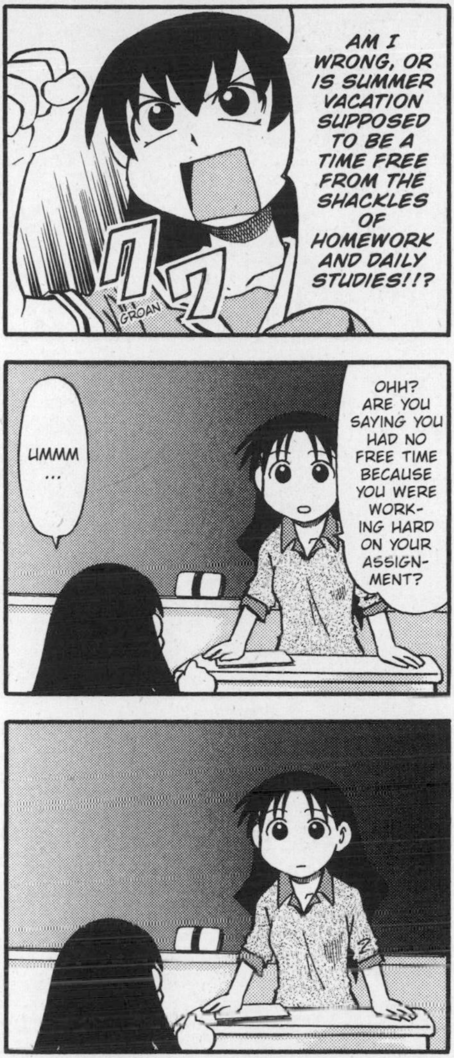
AM I WRONG, OR IS SUMMER VACATION SUPPOSED TO BE A TIME FREE FROM THE SHACKLES OF HOMEWORK AND DAILY STUDIES!!?
GROAN
OHH? ARE YOU SAYING YOU HAD NO FREE TIME BECAUSE YOU WERE WORK-ING HARD ON YOUR ASSIGN-MENT?
UMMM ...
ALL RIGHT, I ADMIT IT! I HAD LOTS AND LOTS OF FREE TIME!!
AND WITH THAT, LET'S GET THIS TEST START-ED!

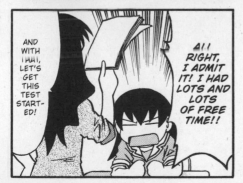

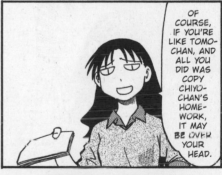

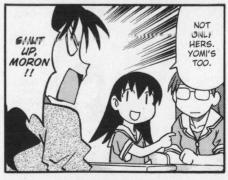

ATROCIOUS

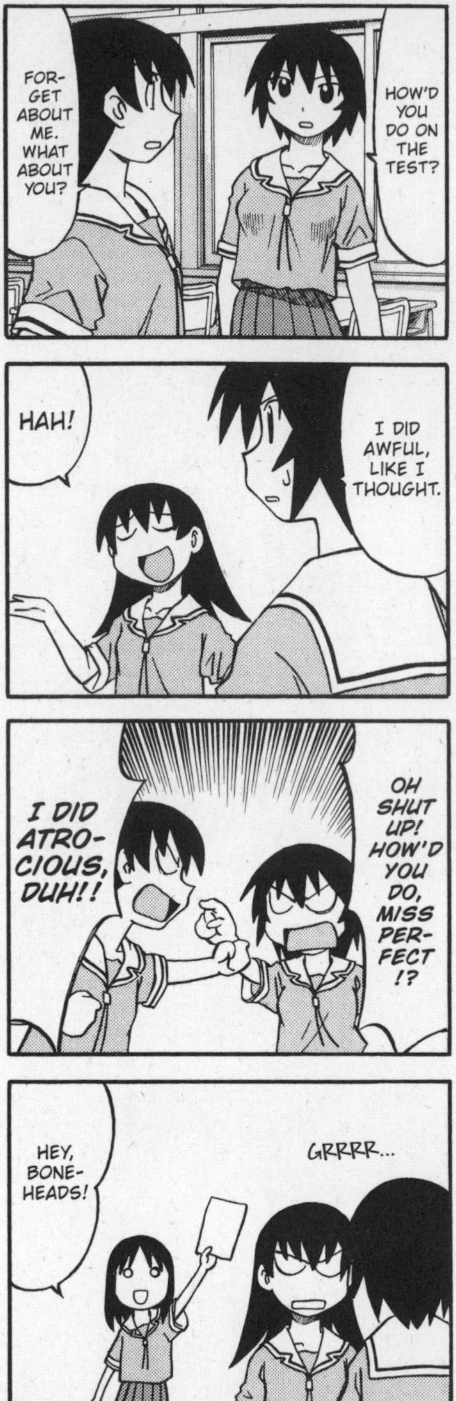
HOW'D YOU DO ON THE TEST?
FOR-GET ABOUT ME. WHAT ABOUT YOU?
I DID AWFUL, LIKE I THOUGHT.
HAH!
OH SHUT UP! HOW'D YOU DO, MISS PER-FECT!?
I DID ATRO-CIOUS, DUH!!
GRRRR...
HEY, BONE-HEADS!

TERRIBLE

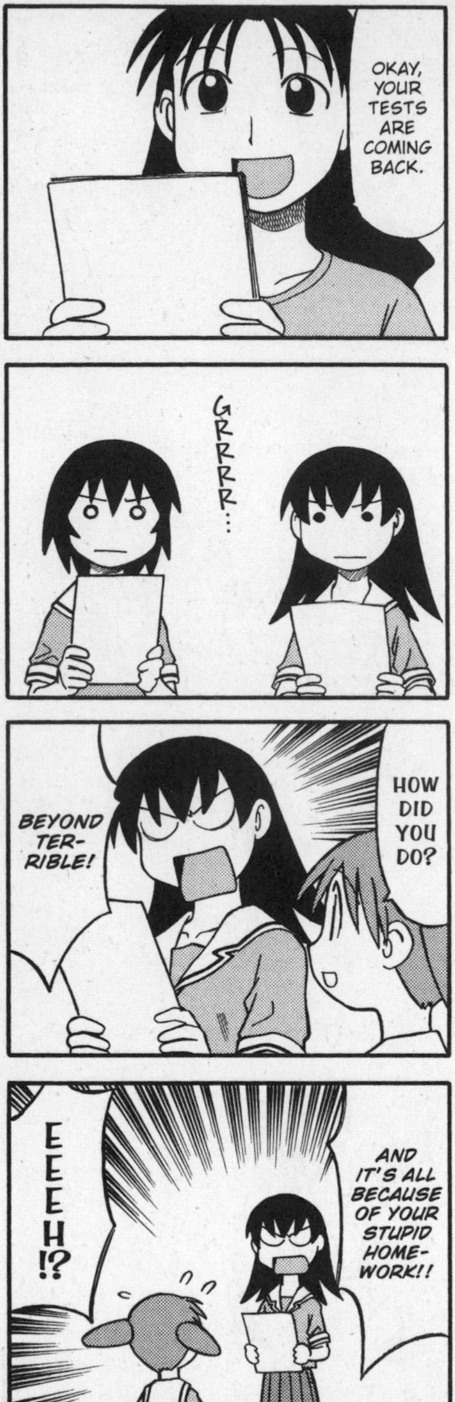
OKAY, YOUR TESTS ARE COMING BACK.
GRRRR...
HOW DID YOU DO?
BEYOND TER-RIBLE!
AND IT'S ALL BECAUSE OF YOUR STUPID HOME-WORK!!
EEEEH!?

IN FORMATION

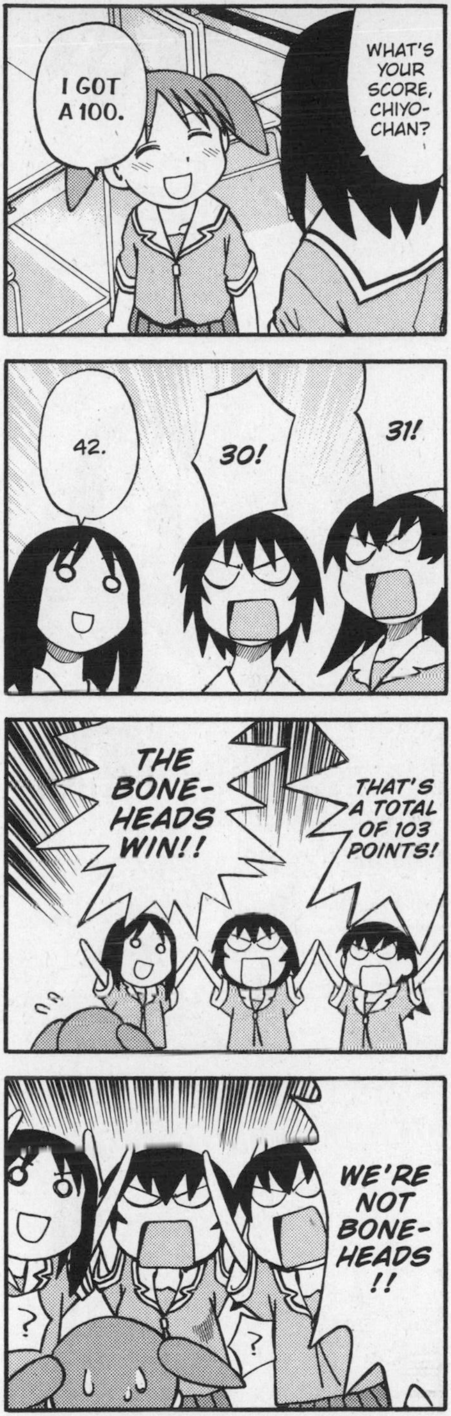
WHAT'S YOUR SCORE, CHIYO-CHAN?
I GOT A 100.
31!
30!
42.
THAT'S A TOTAL OF 103 POINTS!
THE BONE-HEADS WIN!!
WE'RE NOT BONE-HEADS !!

IF I CAN'T PET THEM...

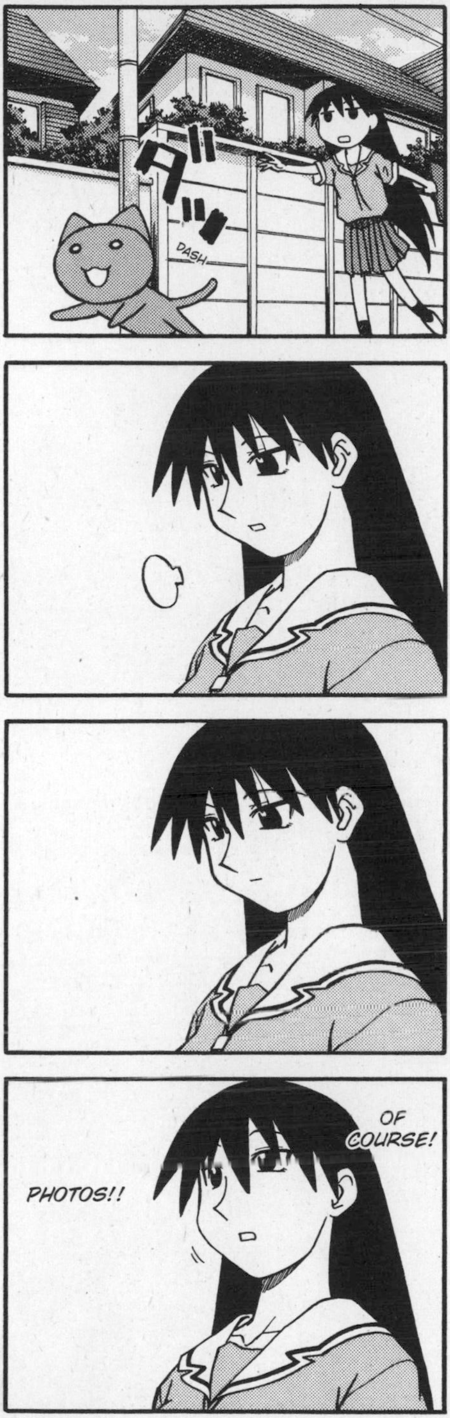
ダッ
DASH
OF COURSE!
PHOTOS!!

日本の猫
BOOK: CATS OF JAPAN
I'LL TAKE LOTS OF PICTURES OF THEM!
THAT WAY, THEY WON'T TRY TO...
... ES-CAPE.

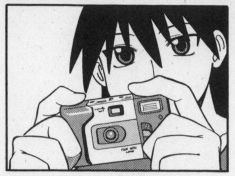

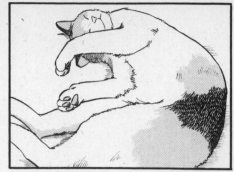

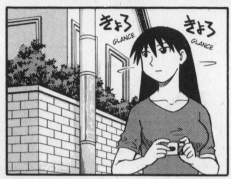

きょろ
GLANCE
きょろ
GLANCE
ちゃ
KCHK
ザッ
ZWISH

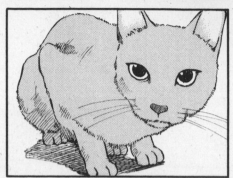

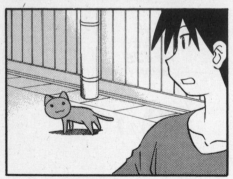

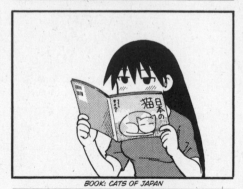

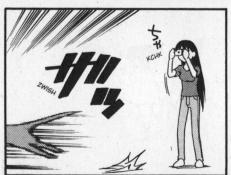

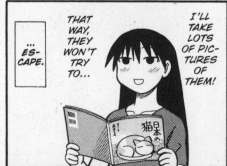

PHOTOS OF THE BITING CAT

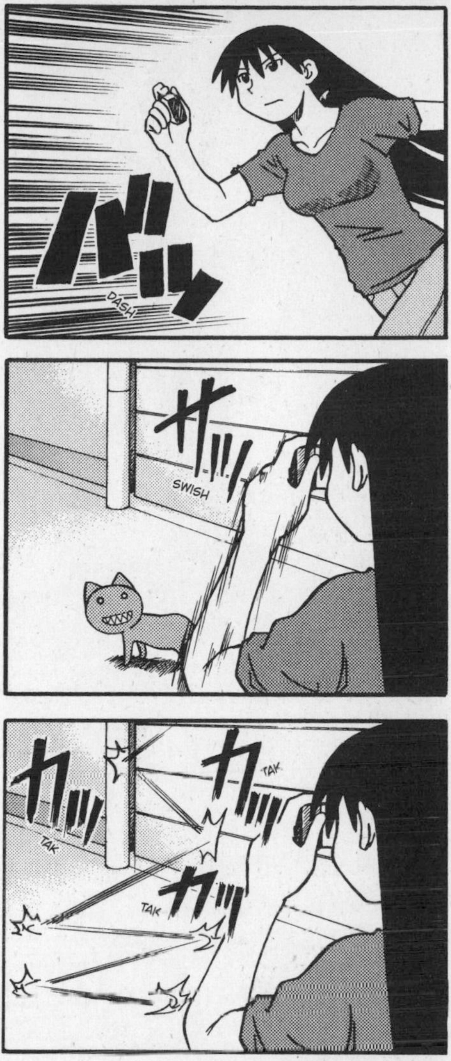
DASH
SWISH
TAK
TAK
TAK

RESULTS

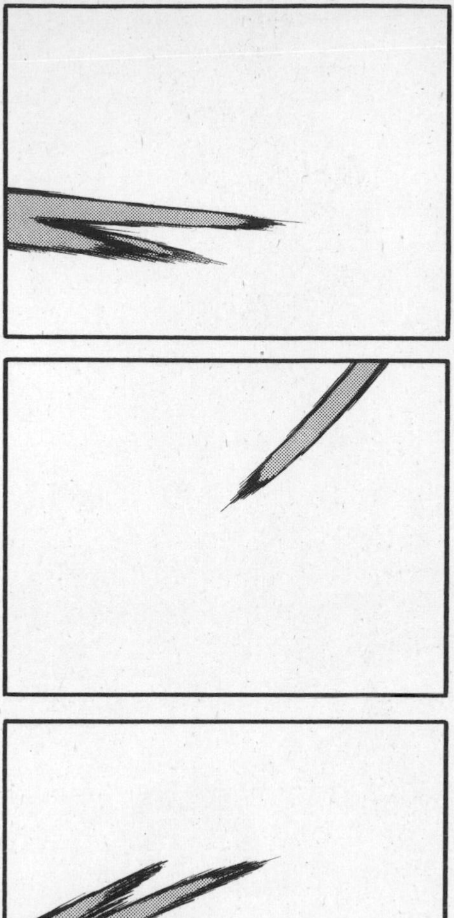
ARE YOU SURE YOU WANT TO KEEP THESE?
......
...YES.

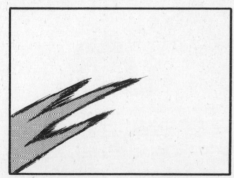

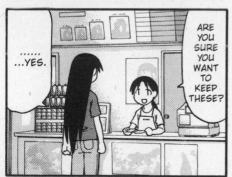

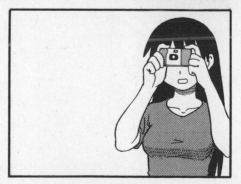

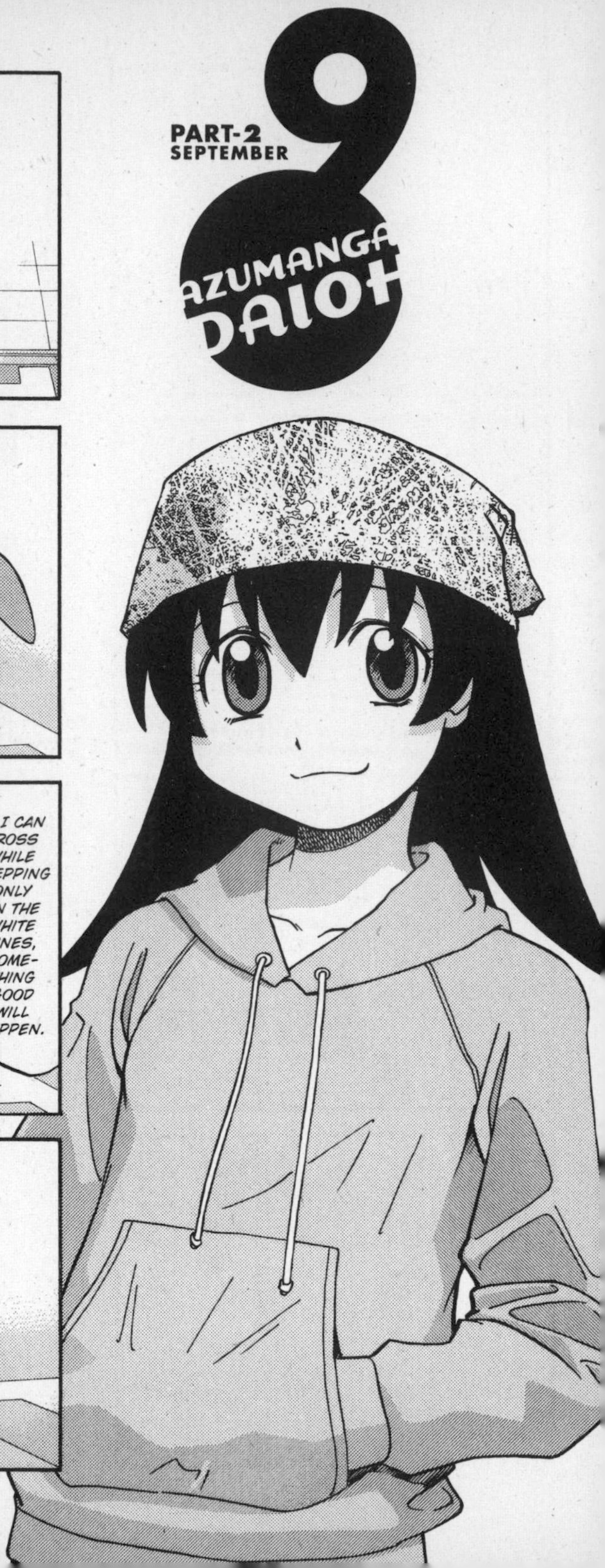
9
PART-2
SEPTEMBER
AZUMANGA
DAIOH

LET'S GO, CHIYO-CHAN

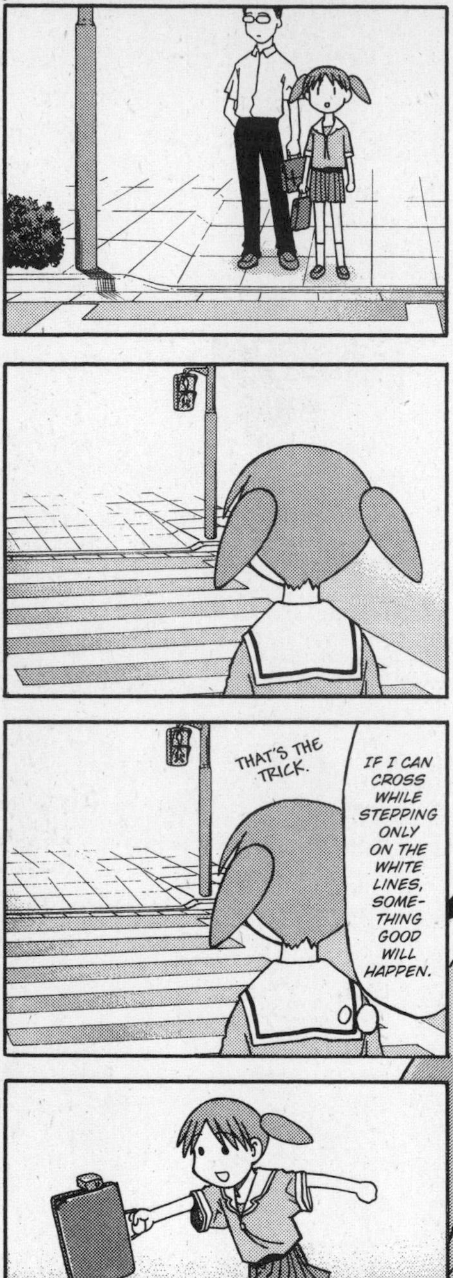
IF I CAN CROSS WHILE STEPPING ONLY ON THE WHITE LINES, SOMETHING GOOD WILL HAPPEN.
THAT'S THE TRICK.

TODAY'S FORTUNE IS...

HUP!
HUP!
AH ...
YO!
....
HIYA.

CAUGHT IN THE ACT

TEK
TEK
TEK
TEK
BY THE WAY...
... WHAT WERE YOU WISHING FOR?
...SO YOU KNEW, AND YOU STILL BLOCKED ME?

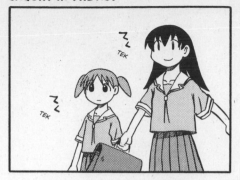

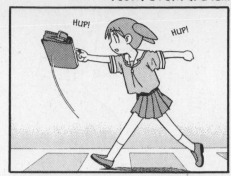

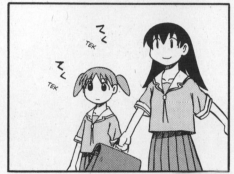

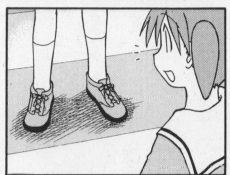

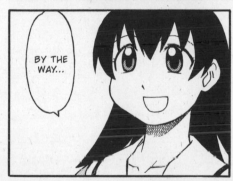

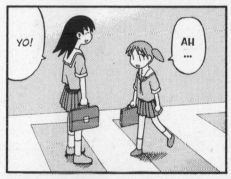

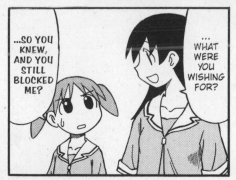

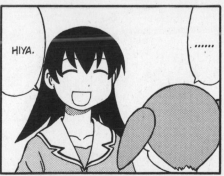

EARLY WARNING

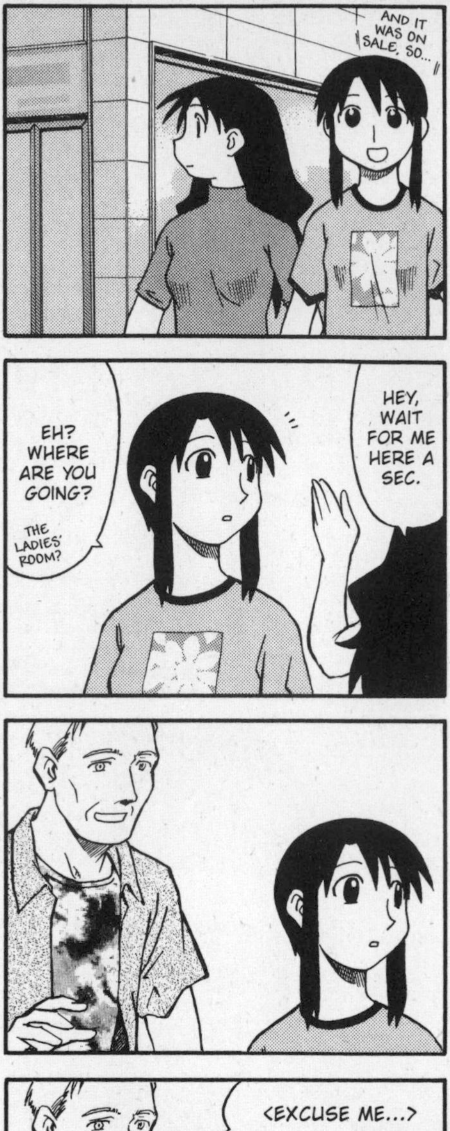
AND IT WAS ON SALE, SO...
HEY, WAIT FOR ME HERE A SEC.
EH? WHERE ARE YOU GOING?
THE LADIES' ROOM?
<EXCUSE ME...>
AAH!!

TRICKY QUESTION

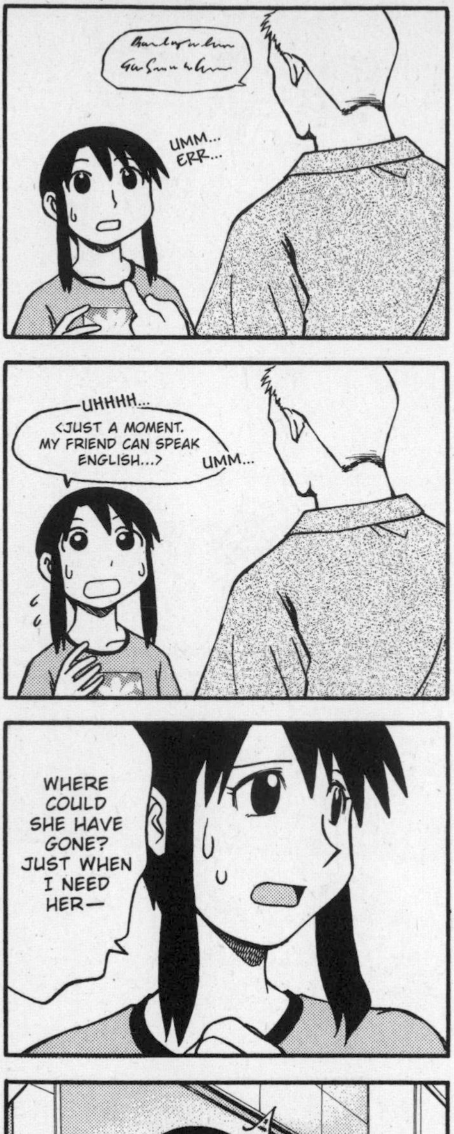
UMM... ERR...
UHHHH...
<JUST A MOMENT. MY FRIEND CAN SPEAK ENGLISH...>
UMM...
WHERE COULD SHE HAVE GONE? JUST WHEN I NEED HER—

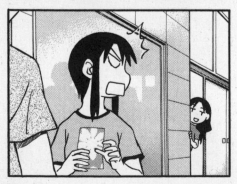

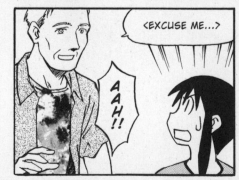

I'M A TEACHER

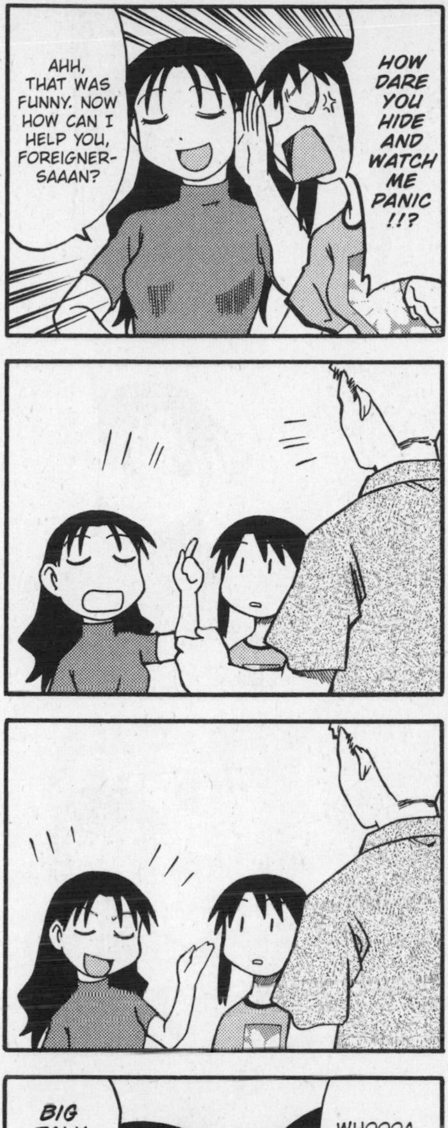
HOW DARE YOU HIDE AND WATCH ME PANIC !!?
AHH, THAT WAS FUNNY. NOW HOW CAN I HELP YOU, FOREIGNER-SAAAN?
WHOOOA... YOU ACTUALLY DON'T SEEM THAT STUPID FOR ONCE.
BIG TALK FROM A GYM TEACHER.

NO, I'M NOT!

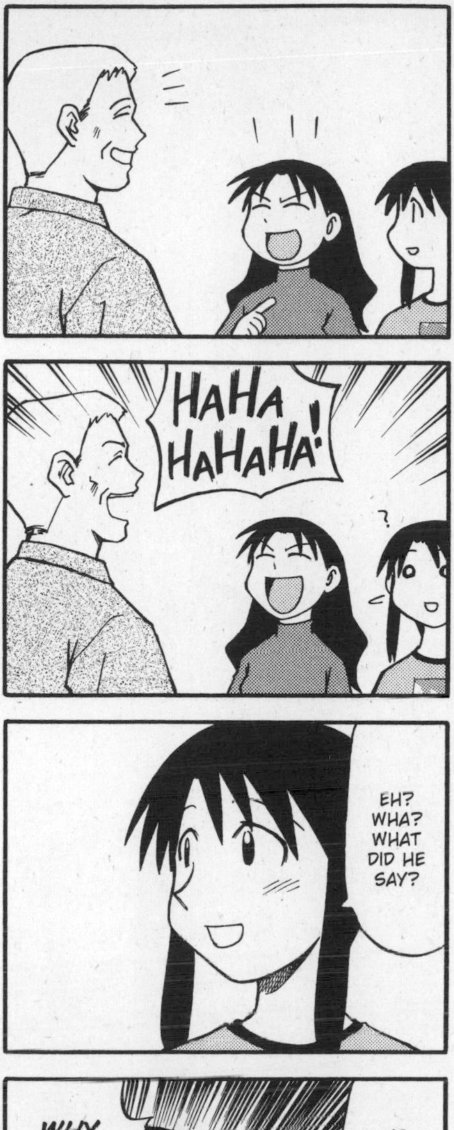
HAHA HAHAHA!
EH? WHA? WHAT DID HE SAY?
HE SAID, "GYM TEACHERS ARE STUPID IN MY COUNTRY TOO."
WHY ARE YOU DISCUSSING THAT WITH HIM !!?

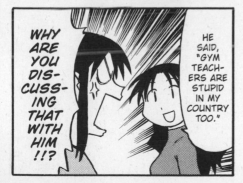

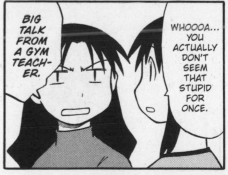

UNRECOMMENDED MENU

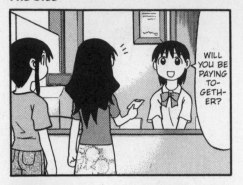

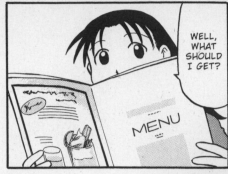

WELL, WHAT SHOULD I GET?
MENU
WHOA! NYAMO, LOOK AT THIS!
YOU HAVE TO GET THIS SPRING ROLL COMBO!
WHY?
SEE, ISN'T THAT WEIRD? IT'S THE ONLY ONE THAT DOESN'T HAVE THE "MANAGER'S CHOICE" SIGN ON IT!
EVERYTHING ELSE HAS ONE!
IF YOU'RE THAT CURIOUS, GET IT YOURSELF.

THE BILL

WILL YOU BE PAYING TOGETHER?
ROCK-PAPER-SCISSORS FOR THE BILL.
YOU'RE ON!
ROCK! PAPER!
SCISSORS!
WE'LL BE PAYING SEPARATELY.
EH!?

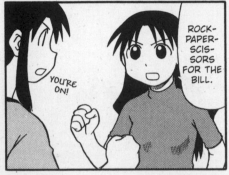

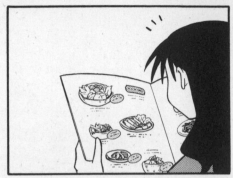

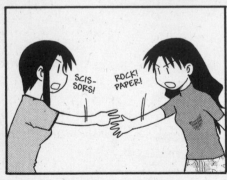

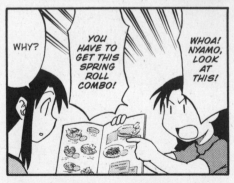

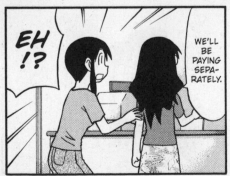

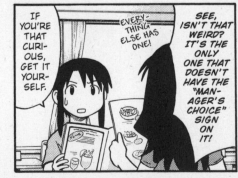

ATTACK

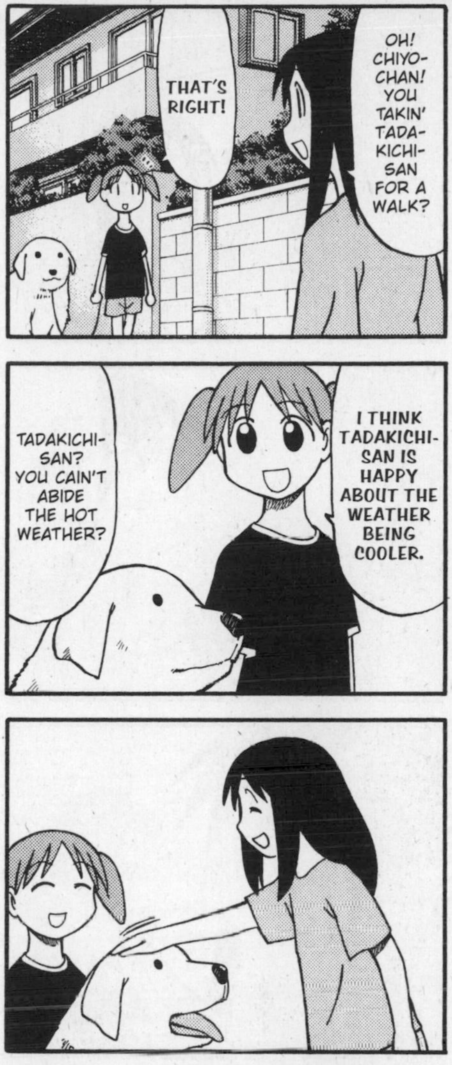
OH! CHIYO-CHAN! YOU TAKIN' TADA-KICHI-SAN FOR A WALK?
THAT'S RIGHT!
I THINK TADAKICHI-SAN IS HAPPY ABOUT THE WEATHER BEING COOLER.
TADAKICHI-SAN? YOU CAIN'T ABIDE THE HOT WEATHER?
しゅっ しゅっ
RUB RUB
HOW'S ABOUT THAT? FEELIN' THE HEAT?

<GREAT>

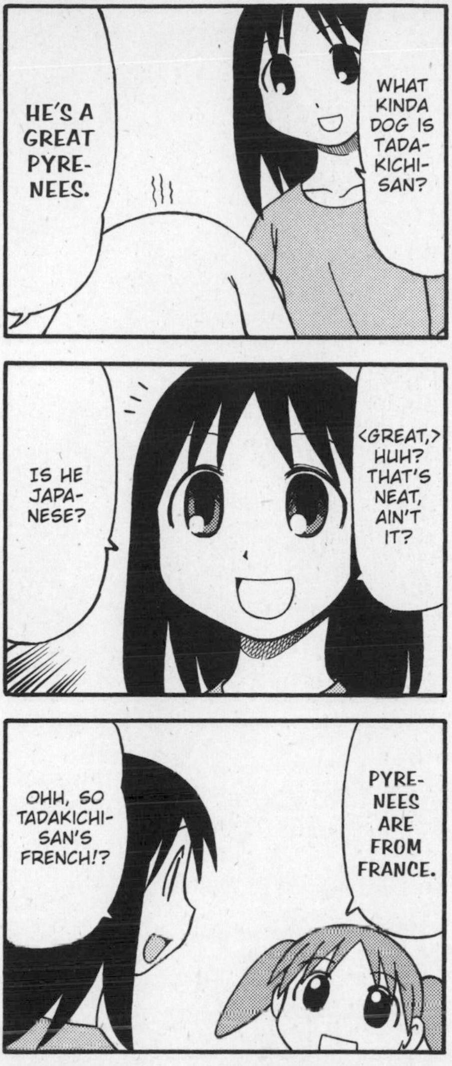
WHAT KINDA DOG IS TADA-KICHI-SAN?
HE'S A GREAT PYRE-NEES.
<GREAT,> HUH? THAT'S NEAT, AIN'T IT?
IS HE JAPA-NESE?
PYRE-NEES ARE FROM FRANCE.
OHH, SO TADAKICHI-SAN'S FRENCH!?
<S'IL VOUS PLAÎT, TADA-KICHI!>

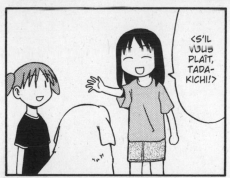

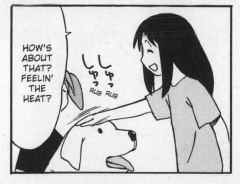

EYES

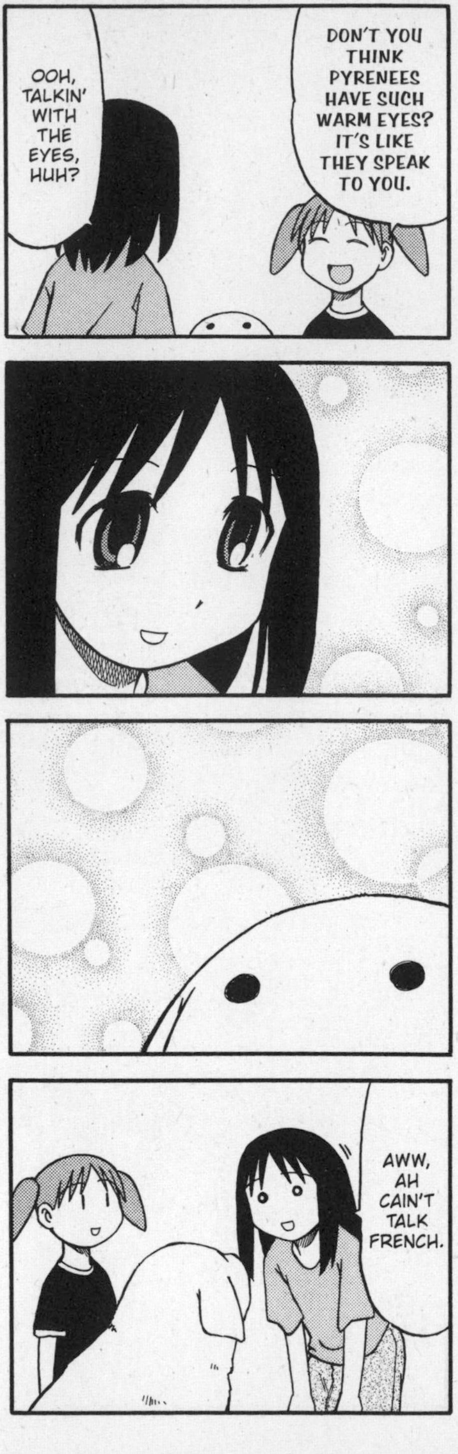
DON'T YOU THINK PYRENEES HAVE SUCH WARM EYES? IT'S LIKE THEY SPEAK TO YOU.
OOH, TALKIN' WITH THE EYES, HUH?
AWW, AH CAIN'T TALK FRENCH.

HAPPY

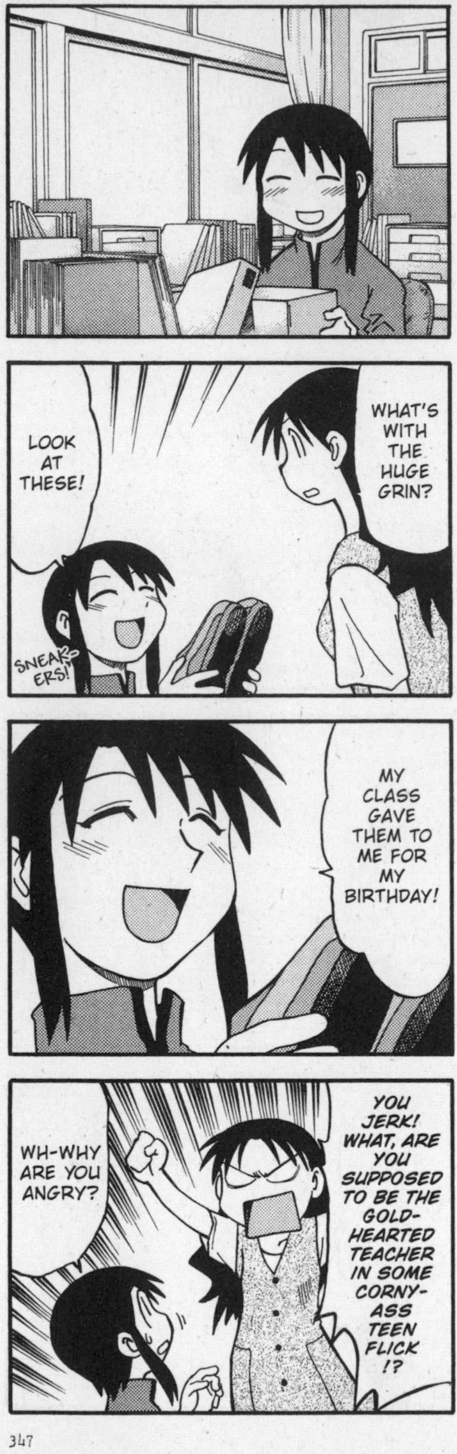
WHAT'S WITH THE HUGE GRIN?
LOOK AT THESE!
SNEAK-ERS!
MY CLASS GAVE THEM TO ME FOR MY BIRTHDAY!
YOU JERK! WHAT, ARE YOU SUPPOSED TO BE THE GOLD-HEARTED TEACHER IN SOME CORNY-ASS TEEN FLICK !?
WH-WHY ARE YOU ANGRY?

OH, NOTHING

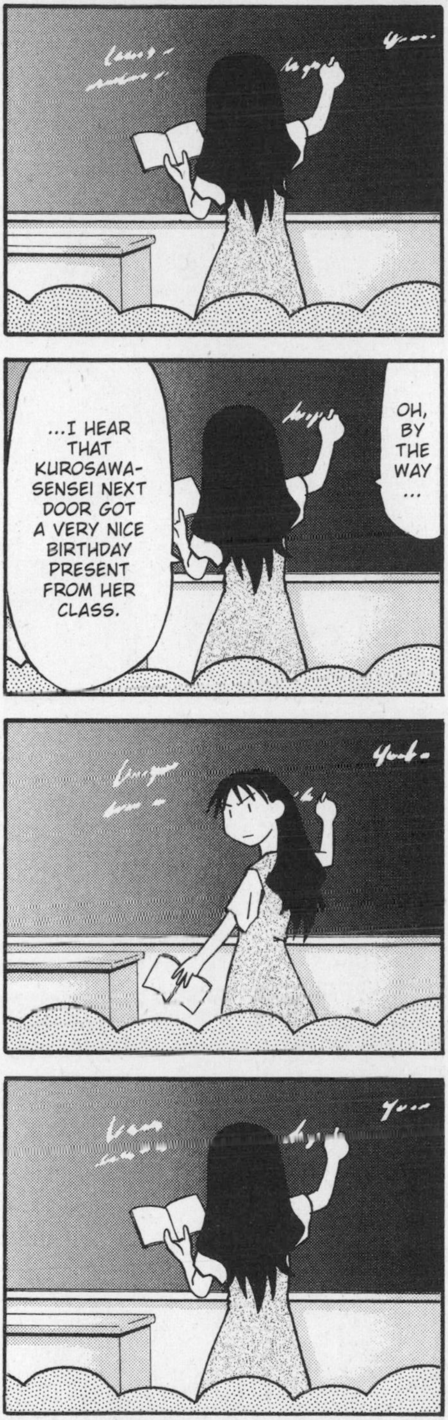
OH, BY THE WAY ...
...I HEAR THAT KUROSAWA-SENSEI NEXT DOOR GOT A VERY NICE BIRTHDAY PRESENT FROM HER CLASS.

BIRTHDAY

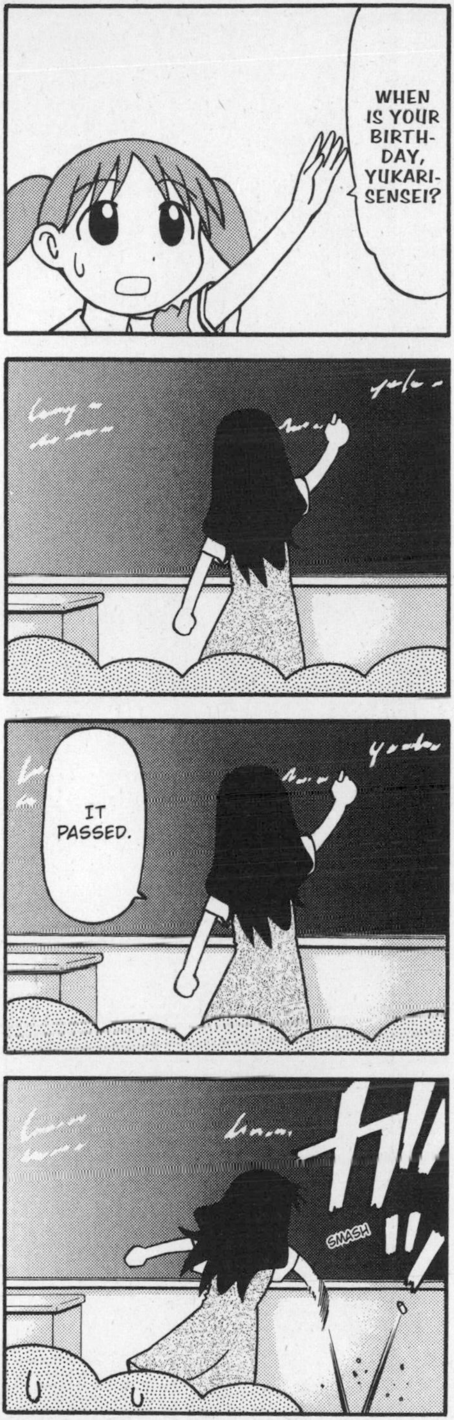
WHEN IS YOUR BIRTH-DAY, YUKARI-SENSEI?
IT PASSED.
SMASH

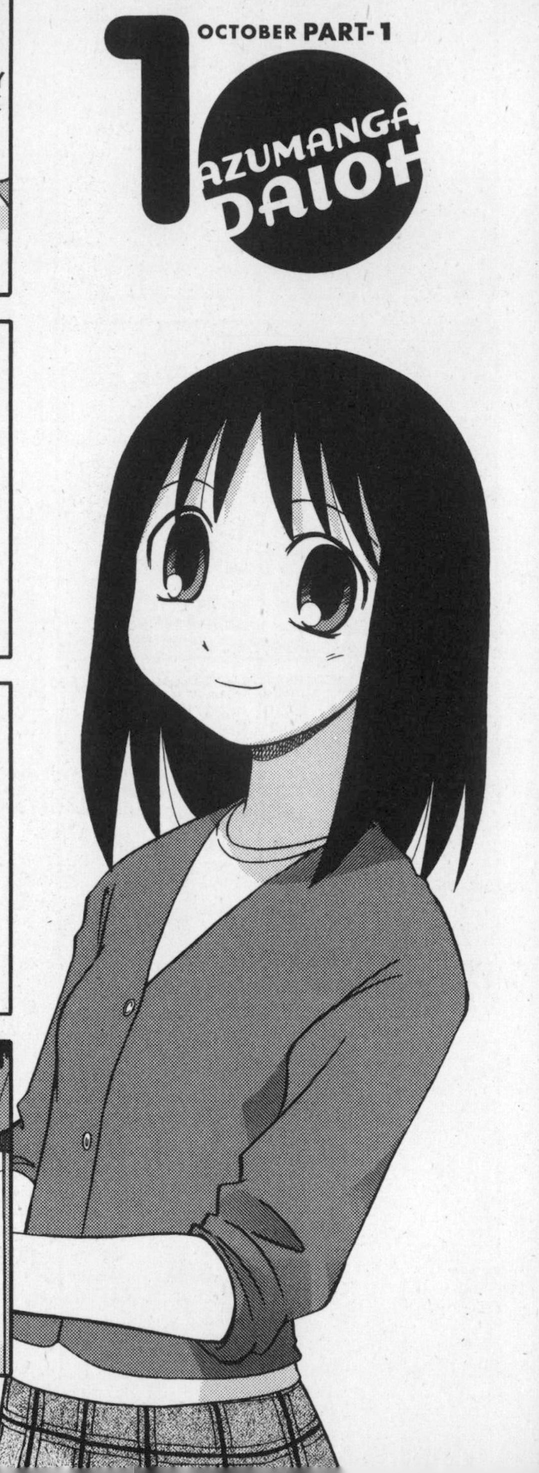
10
OCTOBER PART-1
AZUMANGA DAIOH

AUTUMN SKY

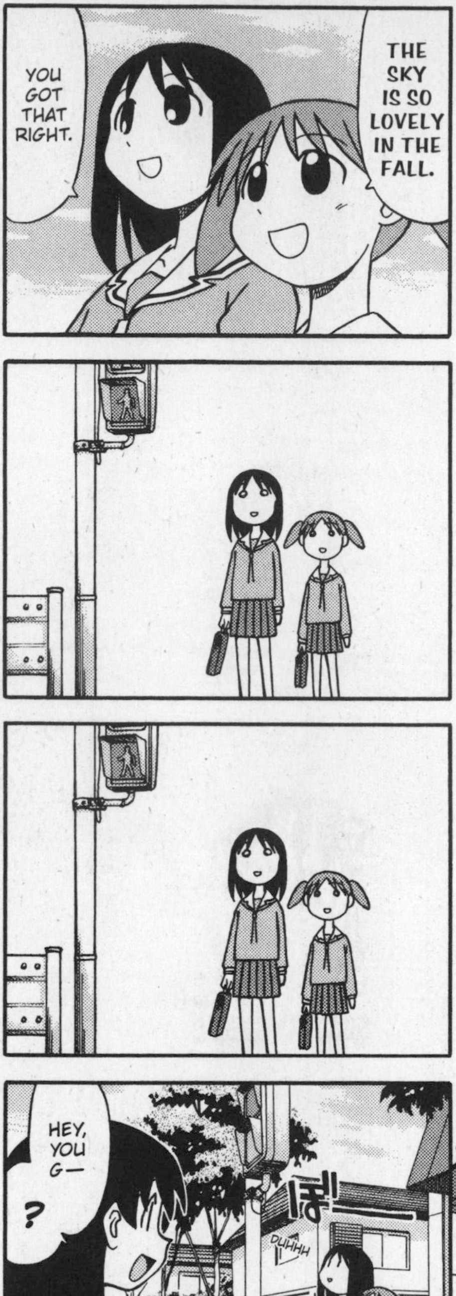
THE SKY IS SO LOVELY IN THE FALL.
YOU GOT THAT RIGHT.
HEY, YOU G—
?
DUHHH

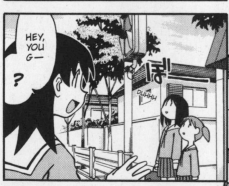

CHECK THE RANKING

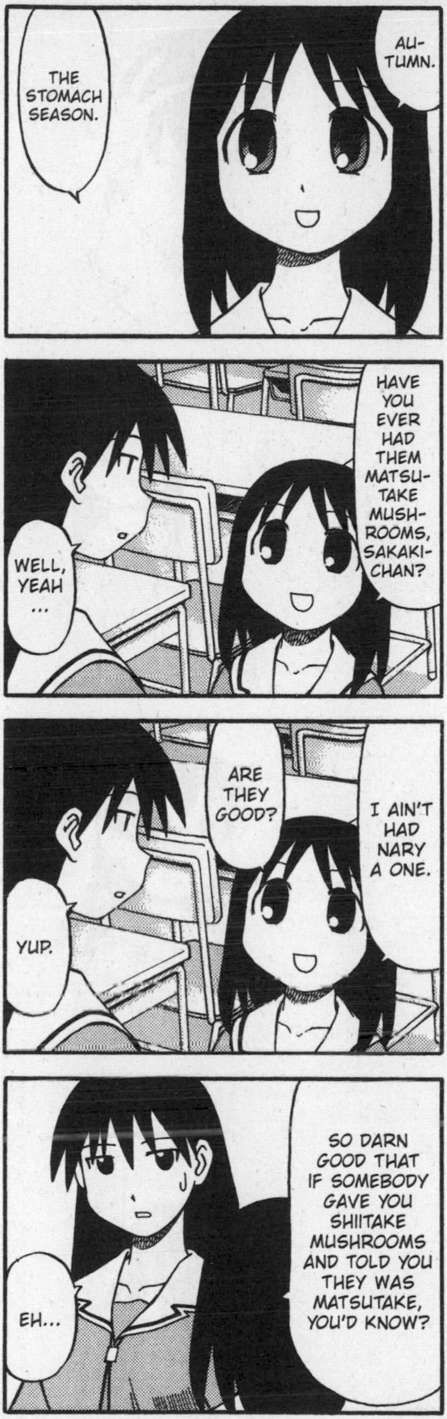
AUTUMN.
THE STOMACH SEASON.
HAVE YOU EVER HAD THEM MATSUTAKE MUSHROOMS, SAKAKI-CHAN?
WELL, YEAH ...
I AIN'T HAD NARY A ONE.
ARE THEY GOOD?
YUP.
SO DARN GOOD THAT IF SOMEBODY GAVE YOU SHIITAKE MUSHROOMS AND TOLD YOU THEY WAS MATSUTAKE, YOU'D KNOW?
EH...

IMAGINARY MATSUTAKE

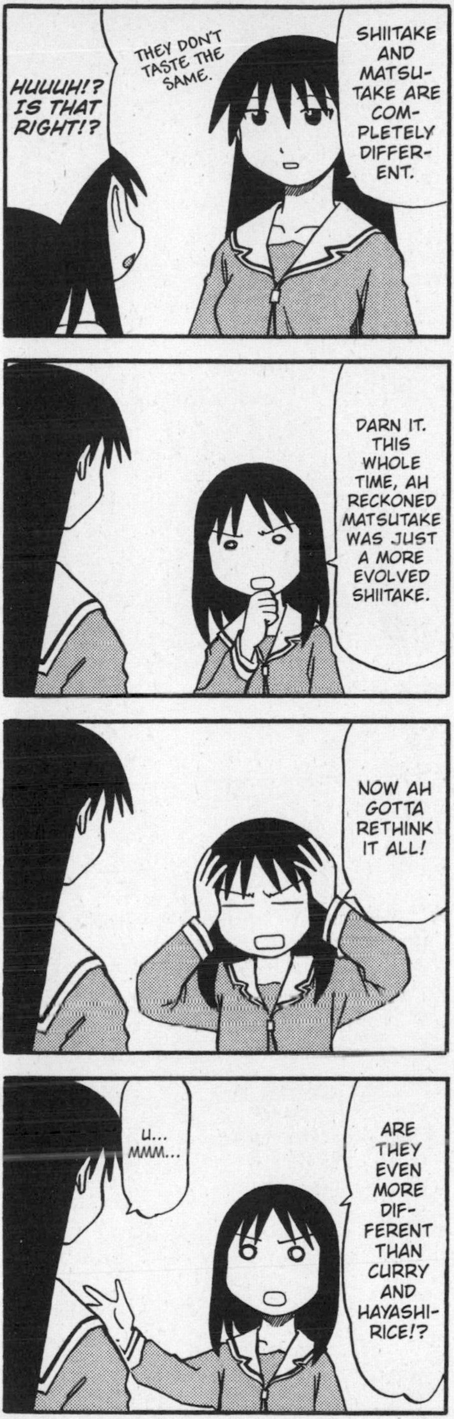
SHIITAKE AND MATSUTAKE ARE COMPLETELY DIFFERENT.
THEY DON'T TASTE THE SAME.
HUUUH!? IS THAT RIGHT!?
DARN IT. THIS WHOLE TIME, AH RECKONED MATSUTAKE WAS JUST A MORE EVOLVED SHIITAKE.
NOW AH GOTTA RETHINK IT ALL!
ARE THEY EVEN MORE DIFFERENT THAN CURRY AND HAYASHI-RICE!?
U... MMM...

GROWTH SPURT

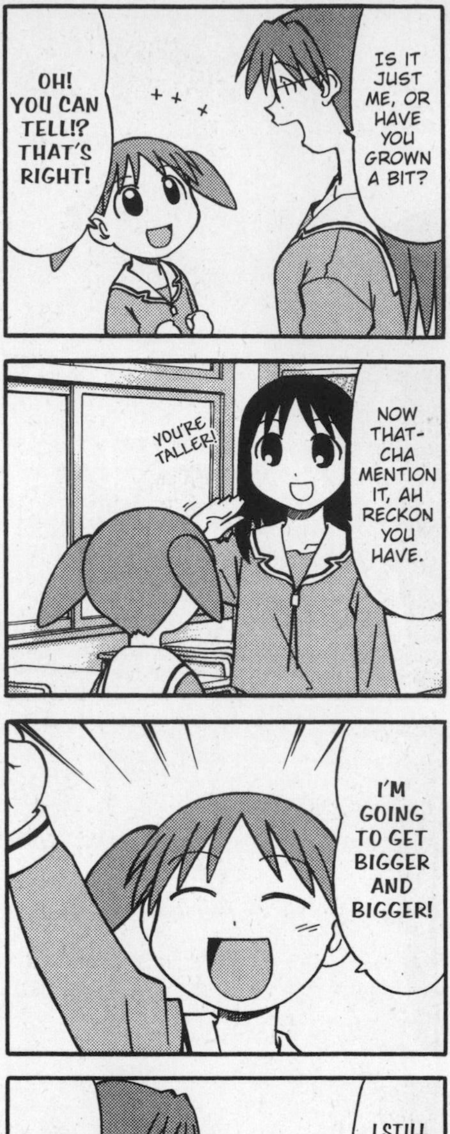
IS IT JUST ME, OR HAVE YOU GROWN A BIT?
OH! YOU CAN TELL!? THAT'S RIGHT!
NOW THAT-CHA MENTION IT, AH RECKON YOU HAVE.
YOU'RE TALLER!
I'M GOING TO GET BIGGER AND BIGGER!
I STILL GET MIS-TAKEN FOR AN ELEMEN-TARY SCHOOL STU-DENT, THOUGH.
THERE'S NOT A WHOLE LOT YOU CAN DO ABOUT THAT, I'M AFRAID.

I WANT TO BE BIGGER

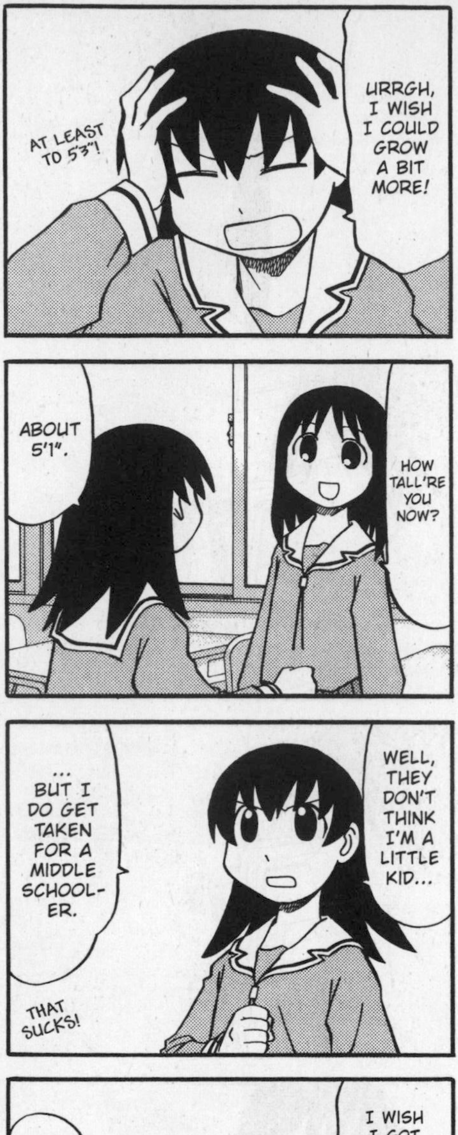
URRGH, I WISH I COULD GROW A BIT MORE!
AT LEAST TO 5'3"!
HOW TALL'RE YOU NOW?
ABOUT 5'1".
WELL, THEY DON'T THINK I'M A LITTLE KID...
... BUT I DO GET TAKEN FOR A MIDDLE SCHOOL-ER.
THAT SUCKS!
I WISH I GOT CONFUSED FOR A COLLEGE STUDENT OR A SECRETARY, LIKE YOMI!
OH, SHUT UP.

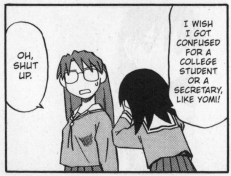

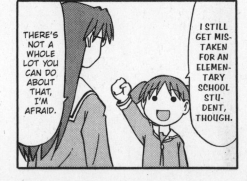

FAMILY

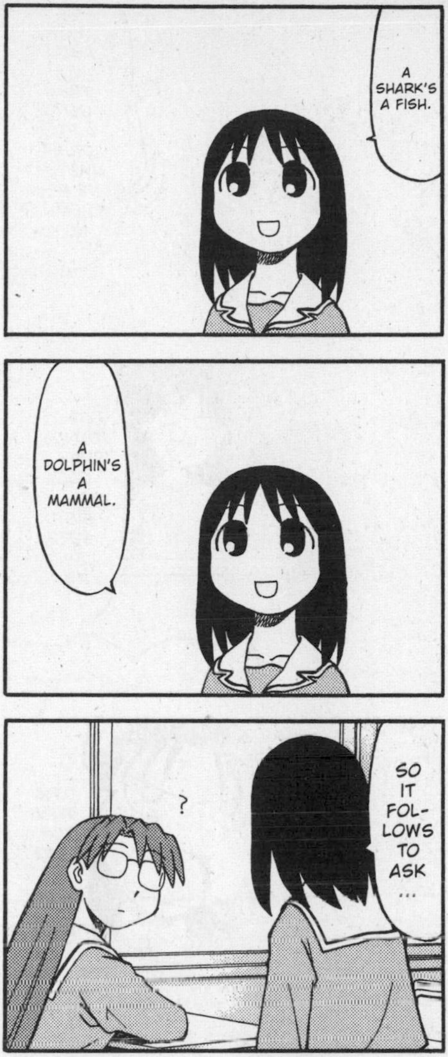
A SHARK'S A FISH.
A DOLPHIN'S A MAMMAL.
SO IT FOLLOWS TO ASK...
?
...IS A SNAIL A INSECT?
EH...

IS ANYTHING IN A GARDEN AN INSECT?

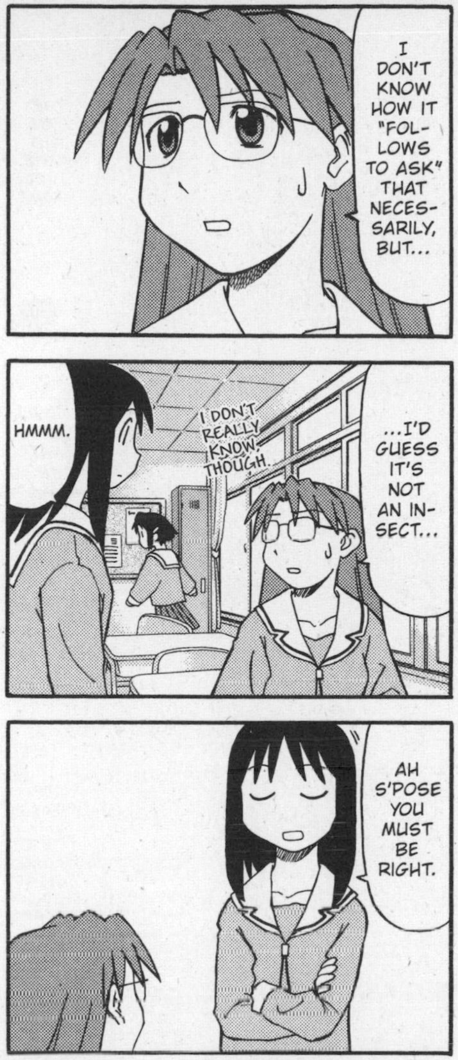
I DON'T KNOW HOW IT "FOLLOWS TO ASK" THAT NECESSARILY, BUT...
...I'D GUESS IT'S NOT AN INSECT...
I DON'T REALLY KNOW, THOUGH.
HMMM.
AH S'POSE YOU MUST BE RIGHT.
IT'D BE WEIRD IF YOU WENT AND STUCK ONE IN THE MIDDLE OF A BUG COLLECTION...
THAT'S NOT REALLY THE POINT...

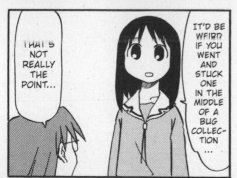

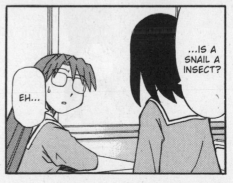

CALCULATIONS

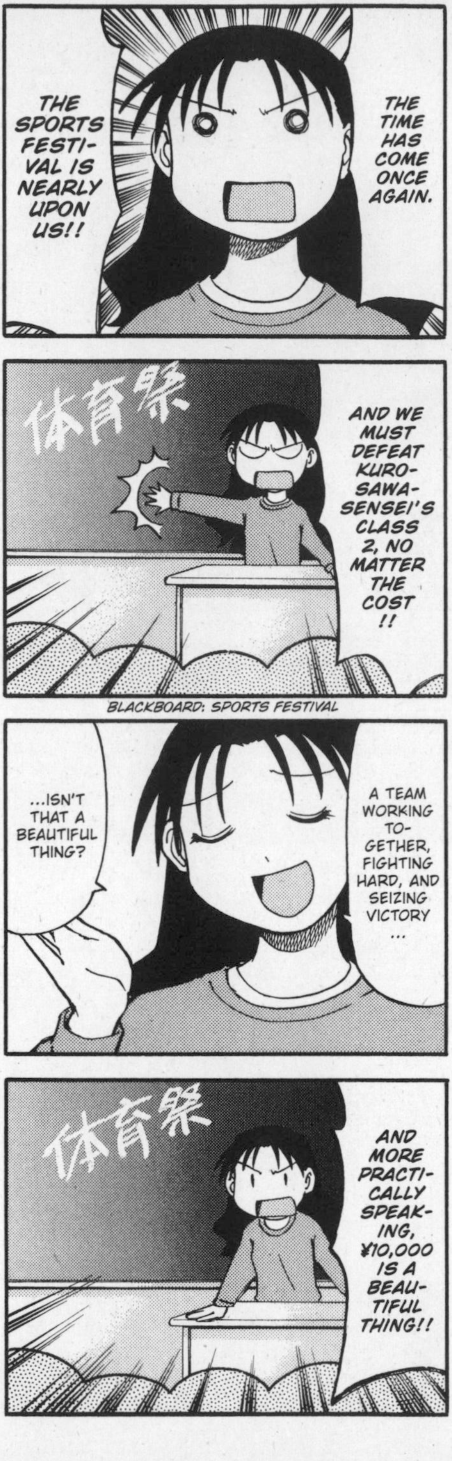
THE TIME HAS COME ONCE AGAIN.
THE SPORTS FESTI-VAL IS NEARLY UPON US!!
AND WE MUST DEFEAT KURO-SAWA-SENSEI'S CLASS 2, NO MATTER THE COST!!
体育祭
BLACKBOARD: SPORTS FESTIVAL
A TEAM WORKING TO-GETHER, FIGHTING HARD, AND SEIZING VICTORY...
...ISN'T THAT A BEAUTIFUL THING?
体育祭
AND MORE PRACTI-CALLY SPEAK-ING, ¥10,000 IS A BEAU-TIFUL THING!!

<OPTIONS>

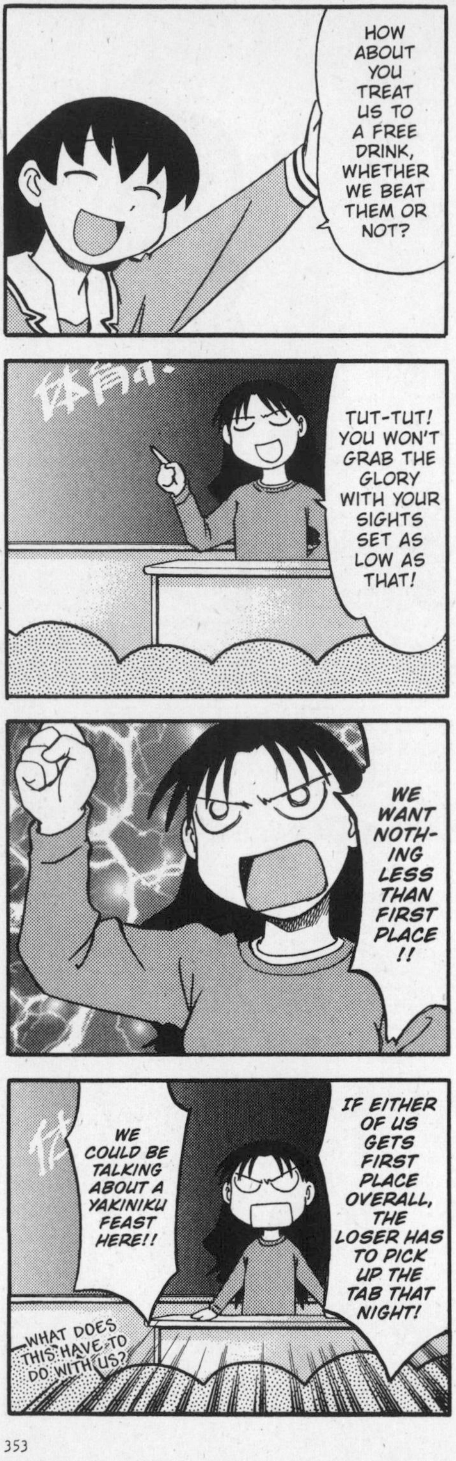
HOW ABOUT YOU TREAT US TO A FREE DRINK, WHETHER WE BEAT THEM OR NOT?
TUT-TUT! YOU WON'T GRAB THE GLORY WITH YOUR SIGHTS SET AS LOW AS THAT!
WE WANT NOTH-ING LESS THAN FIRST PLACE!!
IF EITHER OF US GETS FIRST PLACE OVERALL, THE LOSER HAS TO PICK UP THE TAB THAT NIGHT!
WE COULD BE TALKING ABOUT A YAKINIKU FEAST HERE!!
WHAT DOES THIS HAVE TO DO WITH US?

WORK FOR IT, KAGURA

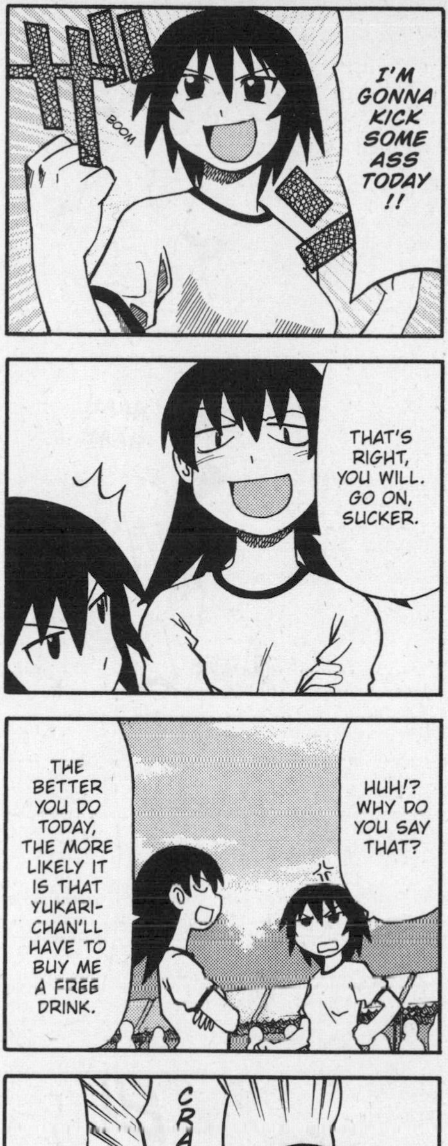
I'M GONNA KICK SOME ASS TODAY!!
BOOM
THAT'S RIGHT, YOU WILL. GO ON, SUCKER.
HUH!? WHY DO YOU SAY THAT?
THE BETTER YOU DO TODAY, THE MORE LIKELY IT IS THAT YUKARI-CHAN'LL HAVE TO BUY ME A FREE DRINK.
WORK! WORK FOR ME, SLAVE!!
CRAP!!
THEY ARE SO LAME...

SCAVENGER HUNT

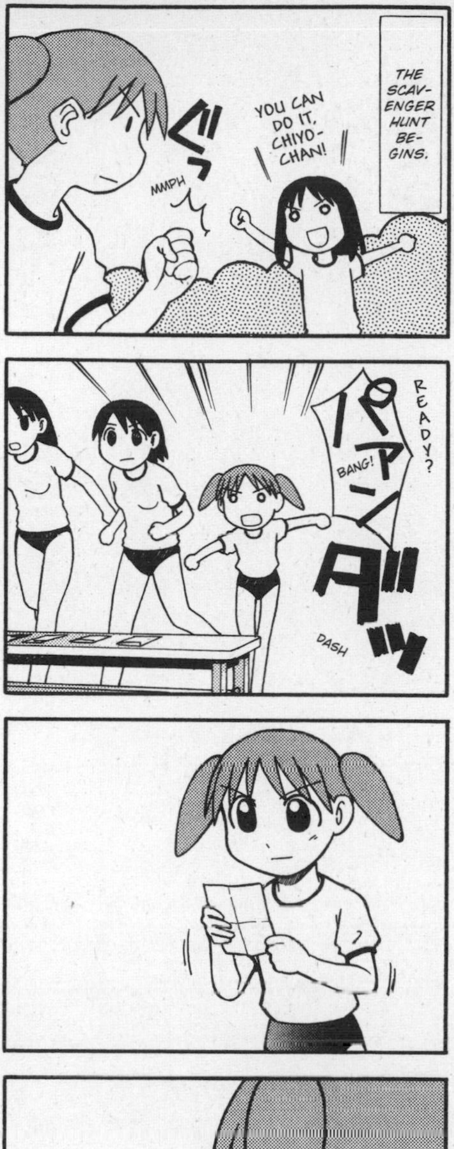
THE SCAVENGER HUNT BEGINS.
YOU CAN DO IT, CHIYO-CHAN!
MMPH
READY?
BANG!
DASH

PAPER: IDIOT

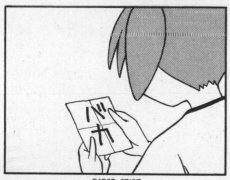

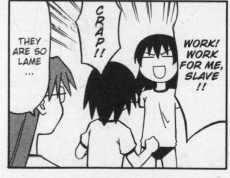

FOUND ONE

WHAT IS IT?

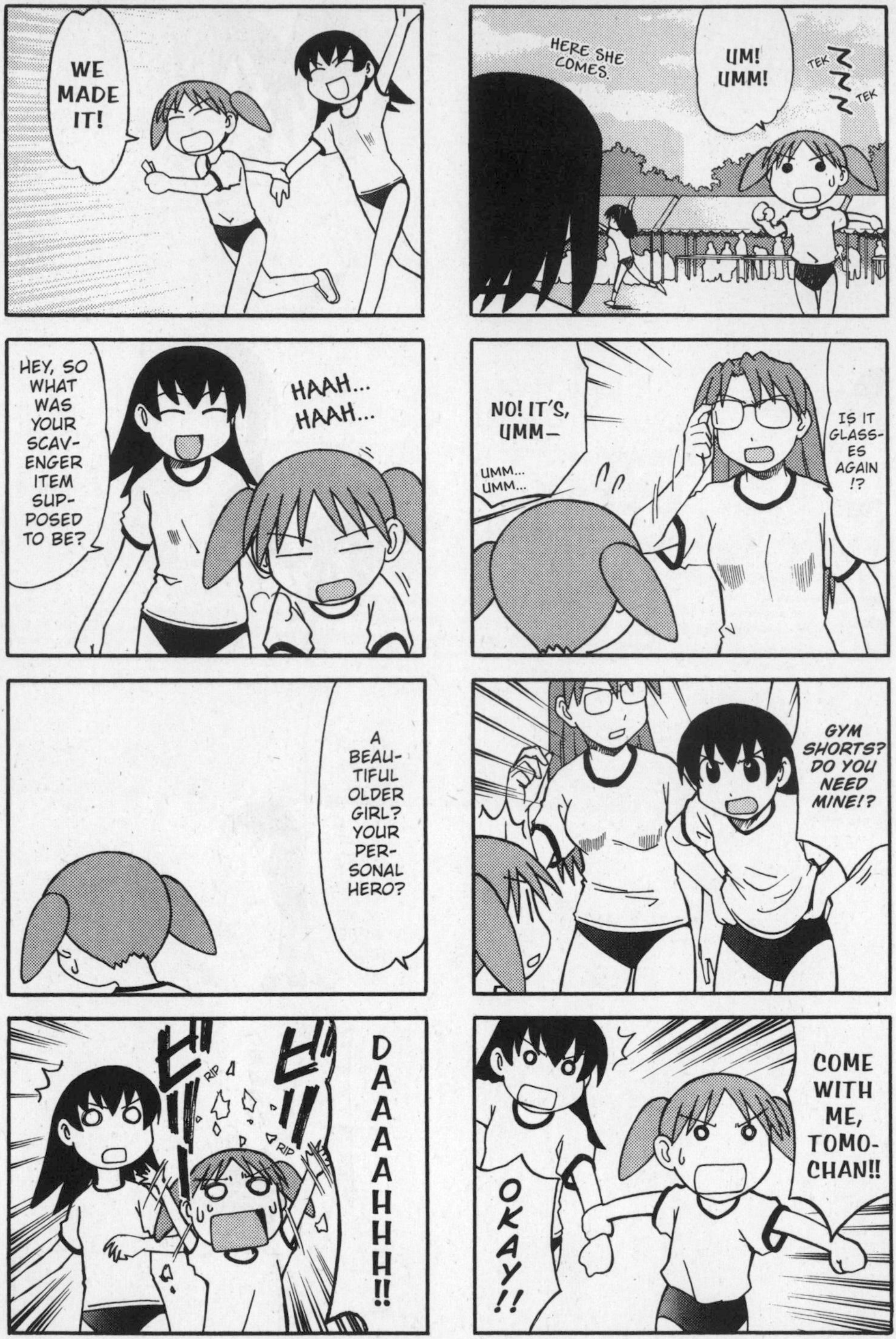

HERE SHE COMES.
UM! UMM!
TEK
TEK
IS IT GLASSES AGAIN!?
NO! IT'S, UMM—
UMM... UMM...
GYM SHORTS? DO YOU NEED MINE!?
COME WITH ME, TOMO-CHAN!!
OKAY!!
WE MADE IT!
HEY, SO WHAT WAS YOUR SCAVENGER ITEM SUPPOSED TO BE?
HAAH... HAAH...
A BEAUTIFUL OLDER GIRL? YOUR PERSONAL HERO?
DAAAAAHHH!!
RIP
RIP

CAIN'T GET THROUGH

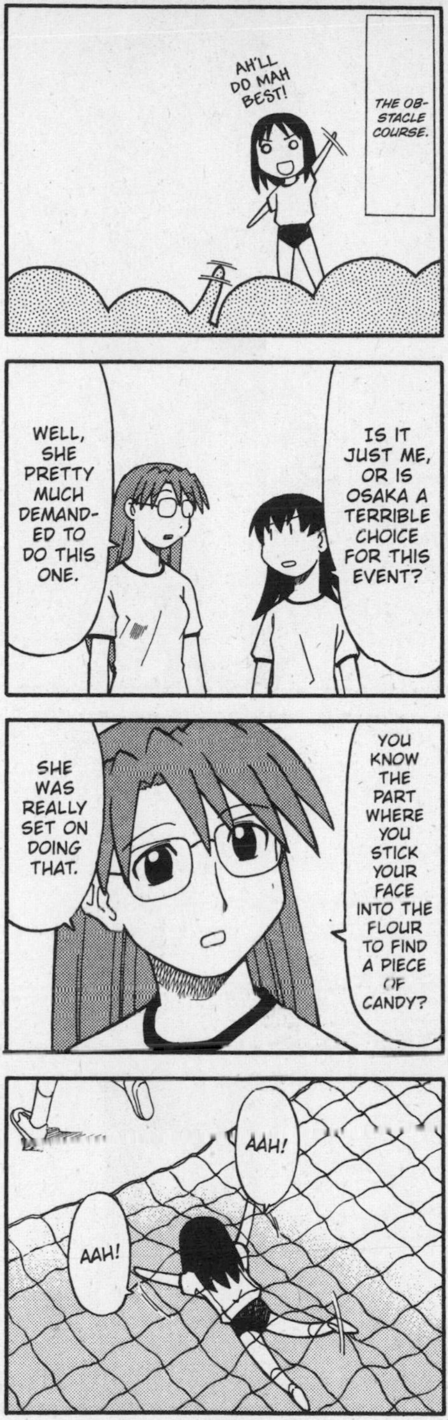
THE OB-STACLE COURSE.
AH'LL DO MAH BEST!
IS IT JUST ME, OR IS OSAKA A TERRIBLE CHOICE FOR THIS EVENT?
WELL, SHE PRETTY MUCH DEMANDED-ED TO DO THIS ONE.
YOU KNOW THE PART WHERE YOU STICK YOUR FACE INTO THE FLOUR TO FIND A PIECE OF CANDY?
SHE WAS REALLY SET ON DOING THAT.
AAH!
AAH!

WHERE'D IT GET TO?

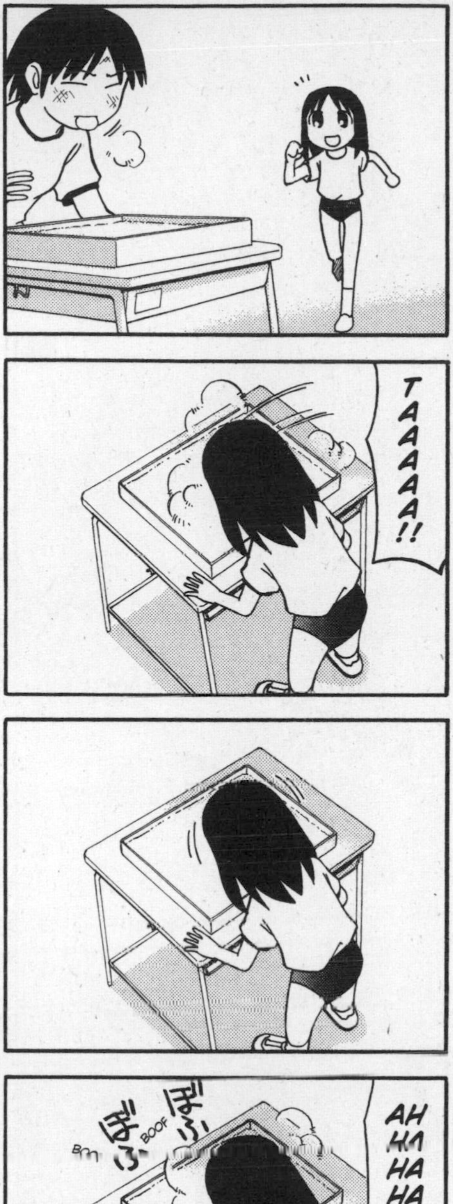
TAAAAAA!!
AH HA HA HA!!
ぼふ
BOOF
ぼふ
AH HA HA HA HA HA!!

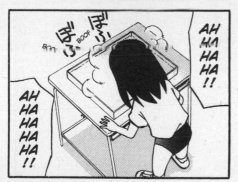

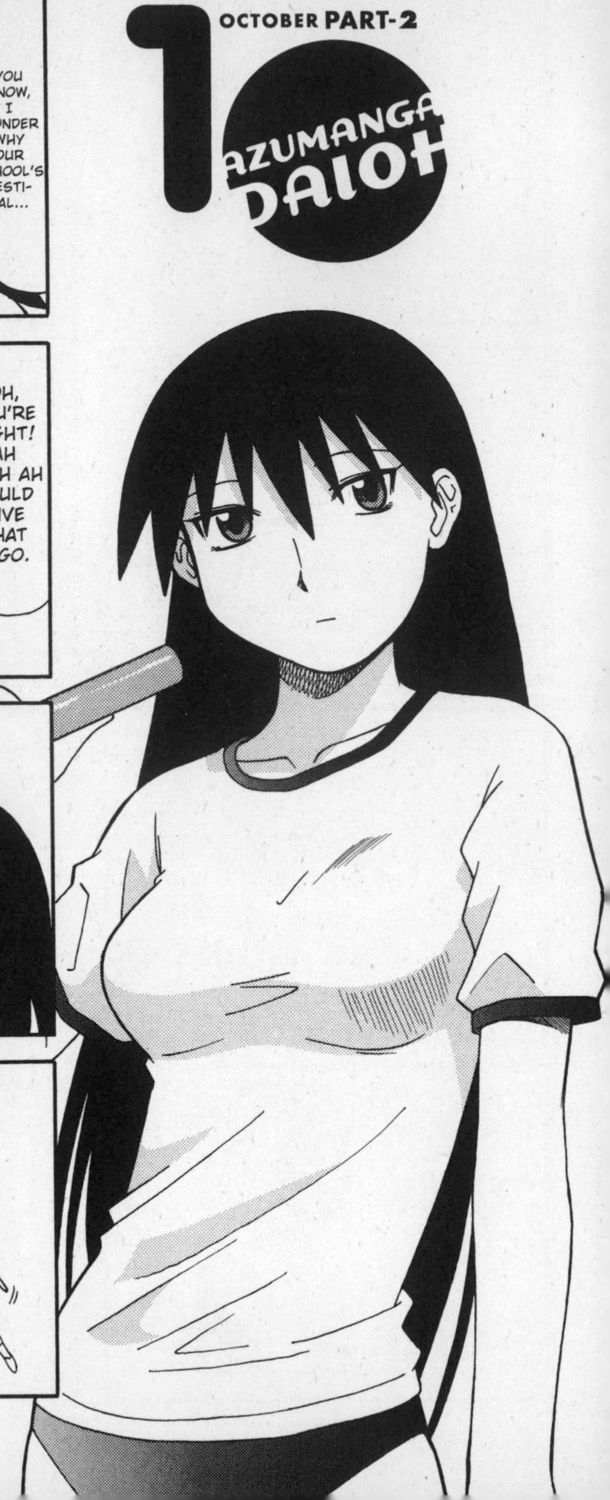
10
OCTOBER PART-2
AZUMANGA DAIOH

BREAD

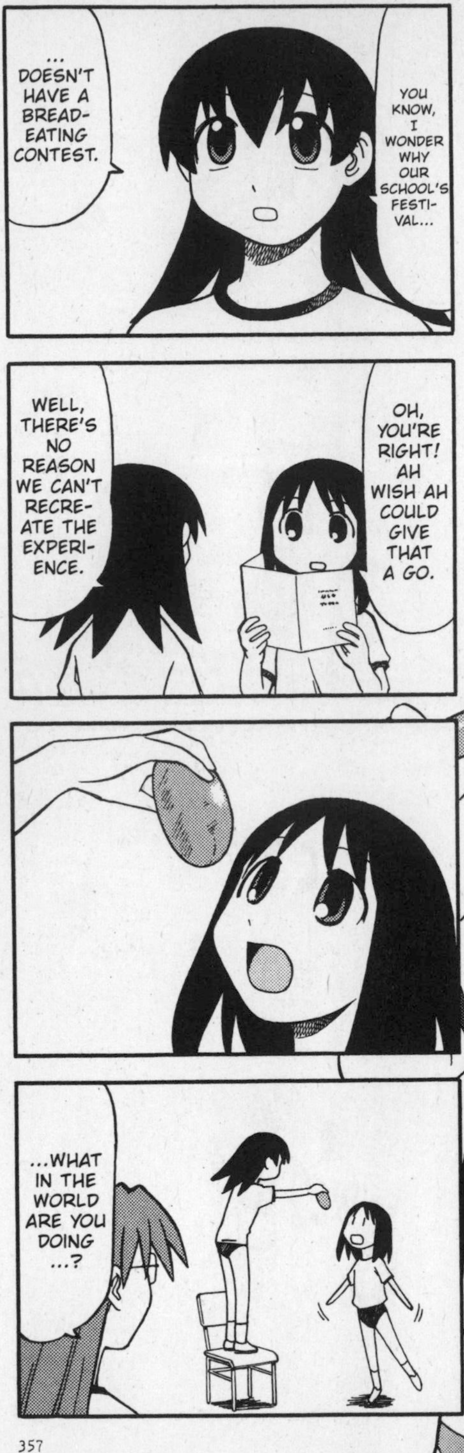
YOU KNOW, I WONDER WHY OUR SCHOOL'S FESTI-VAL...
...DOESN'T HAVE A BREAD-EATING CONTEST.
OH, YOU'RE RIGHT! AH WISH AH COULD GIVE THAT A GO.
WELL, THERE'S NO REASON WE CAN'T RECRE-ATE THE EXPERI-ENCE.
...WHAT IN THE WORLD ARE YOU DOING ...?

SHE VANISHED

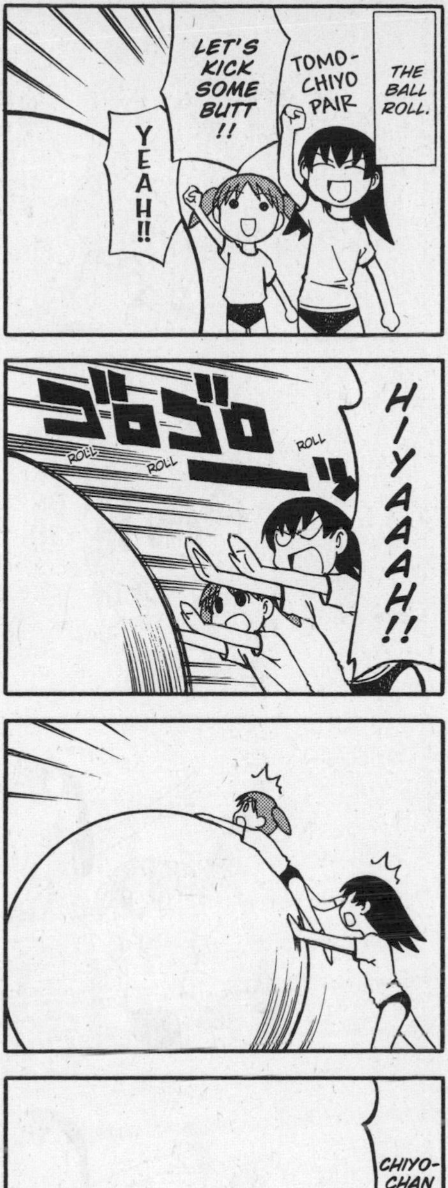
THE BALL ROLL.
TOMO-CHIYO PAIR
LET'S KICK SOME BUTT !!
YEAH!!
HIYAAAAH!!
ゴロゴローーッ
ROLL
ROLL
ROLL
CHIYO-CHAN !?

DOUBLE THE PAIN

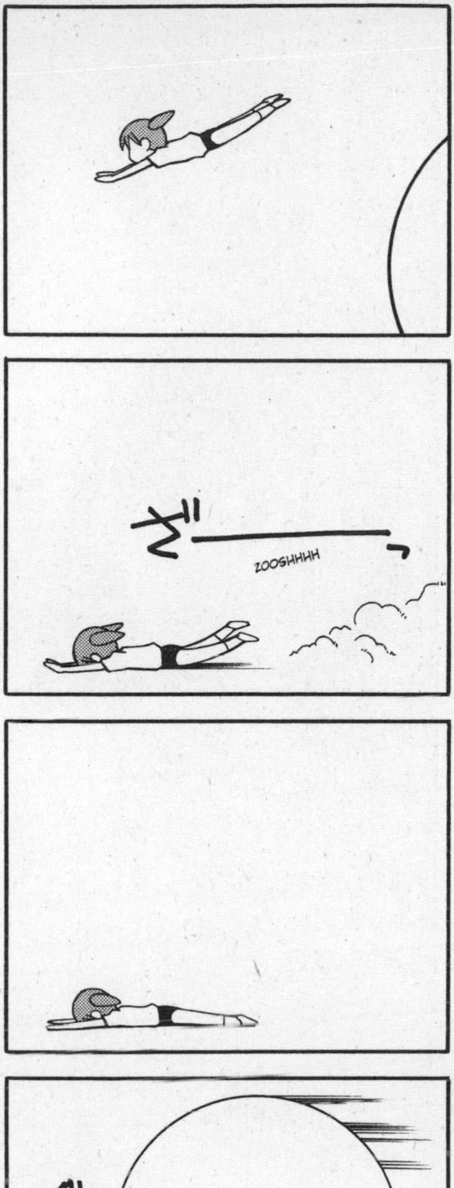
ざーーーっ
ZOOSHHHH
ぐしゃ
SPLAT

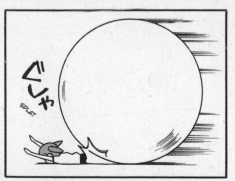

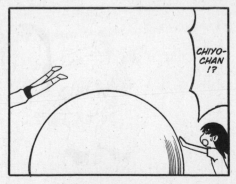

DETERMINATION

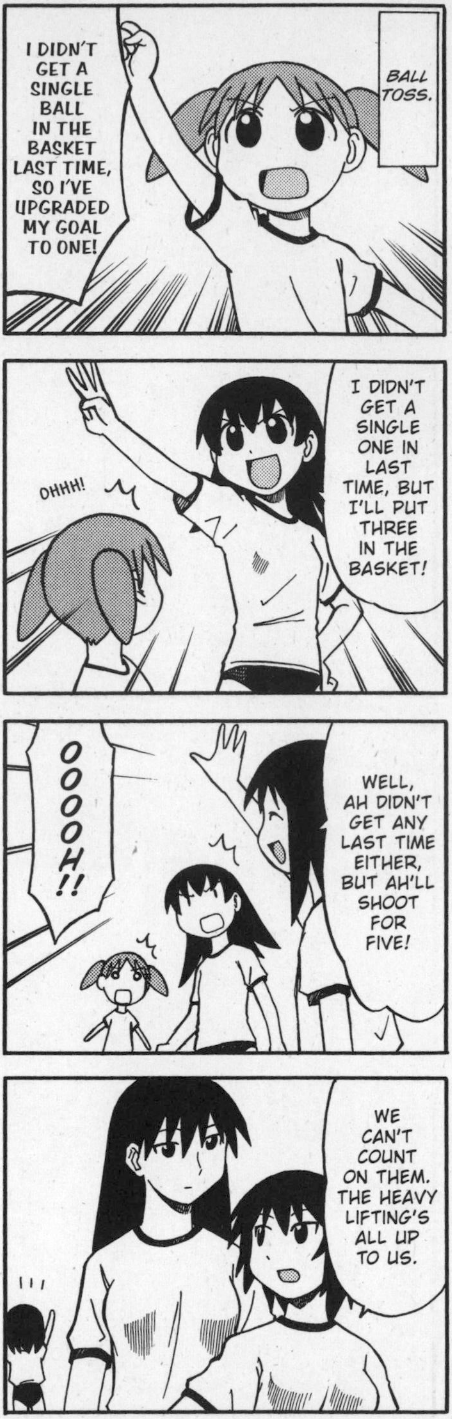
BALL TOSS.
I DIDN'T GET A SINGLE BALL IN THE BASKET LAST TIME, SO I'VE UPGRADED MY GOAL TO ONE!
I DIDN'T GET A SINGLE ONE IN LAST TIME, BUT I'LL PUT THREE IN THE BASKET!
OHHH!
WELL, AH DIDN'T GET ANY LAST TIME EITHER, BUT AH'LL SHOOT FOR FIVE!
OOOOOH!!
WE CAN'T COUNT ON THEM. THE HEAVY LIFTING'S ALL UP TO US.

DID YOU SEE THAT?

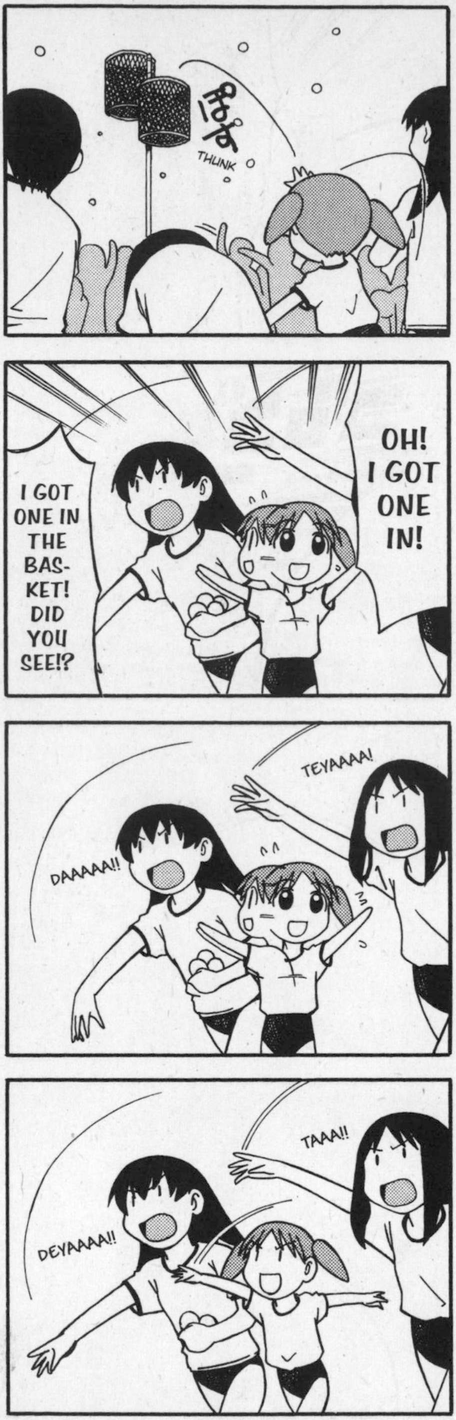
ぽす
THUNK
OH! I GOT ONE IN!
I GOT ONE IN THE BAS-KET! DID YOU SEE!?
TEYAAAA!
DAAAAA!!
TAAA!!
DEYAAAA!!

NO WAY!

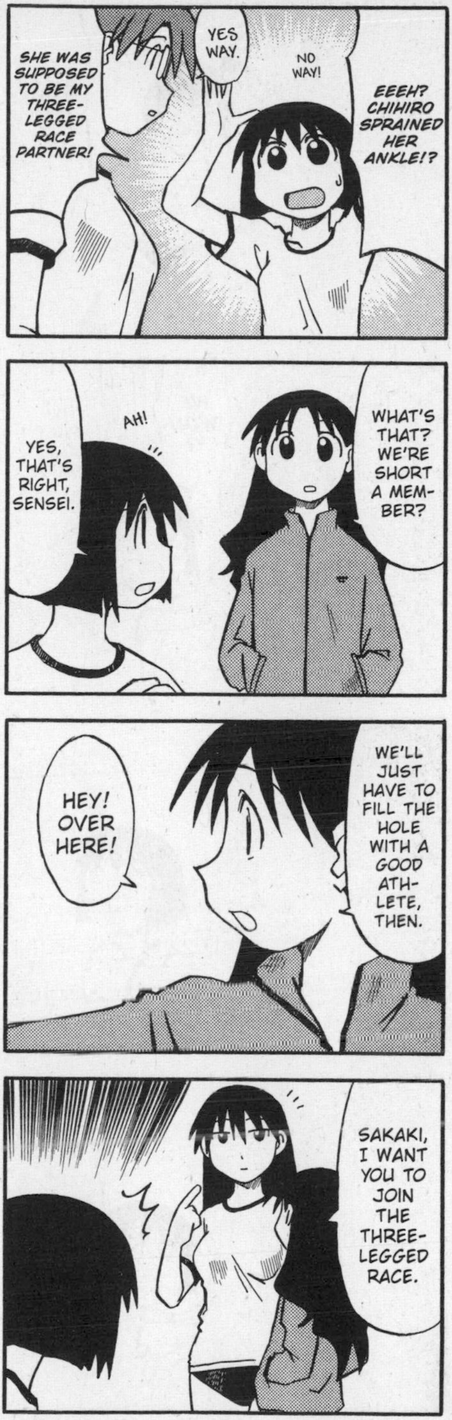
EEEH? CHIHIRO SPRAINED HER ANKLE!?
NO WAY!
YES WAY.
SHE WAS SUPPOSED TO BE MY THREE-LEGGED RACE PARTNER!
WHAT'S THAT? WE'RE SHORT A MEMBER?
AH!
YES, THAT'S RIGHT, SENSEI.
WE'LL JUST HAVE TO FILL THE HOLE WITH A GOOD ATHLETE, THEN.
HEY! OVER HERE!
SAKAKI, I WANT YOU TO JOIN THE THREE-LEGGED RACE.

DON'T TRY

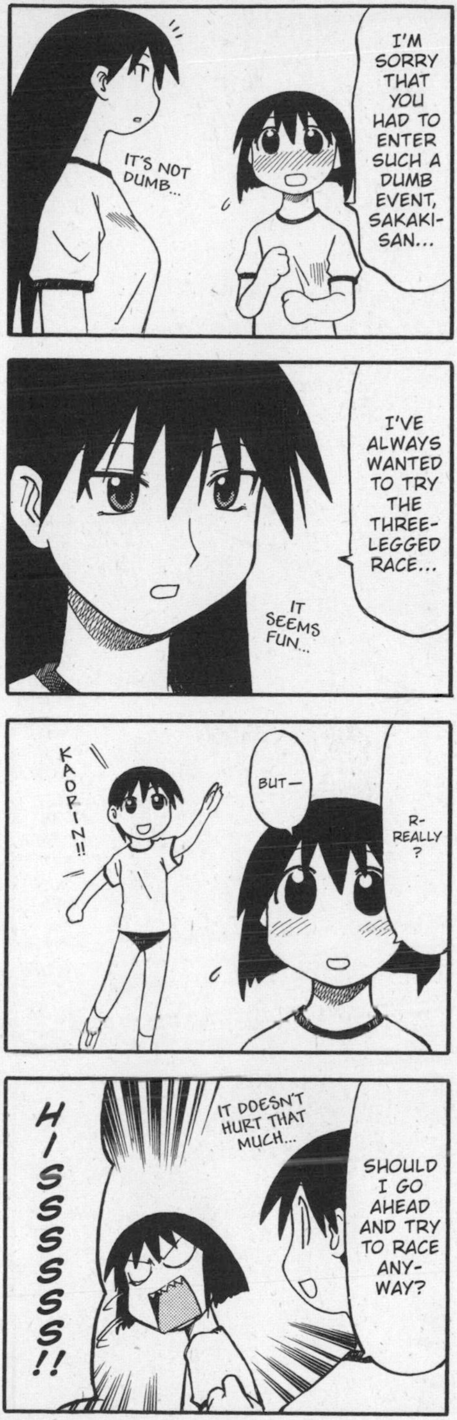
I'M SORRY THAT YOU HAD TO ENTER SUCH A DUMB EVENT, SAKAKI-SAN...
IT'S NOT DUMB...
I'VE ALWAYS WANTED TO TRY THE THREE-LEGGED RACE...
IT SEEMS FUN...
R-REALLY?
BUT—
KAORIN!!
SHOULD I GO AHEAD AND TRY TO RACE ANYWAY?
IT DOESN'T HURT THAT MUCH...
HISSSSSS!!

DESPERATION

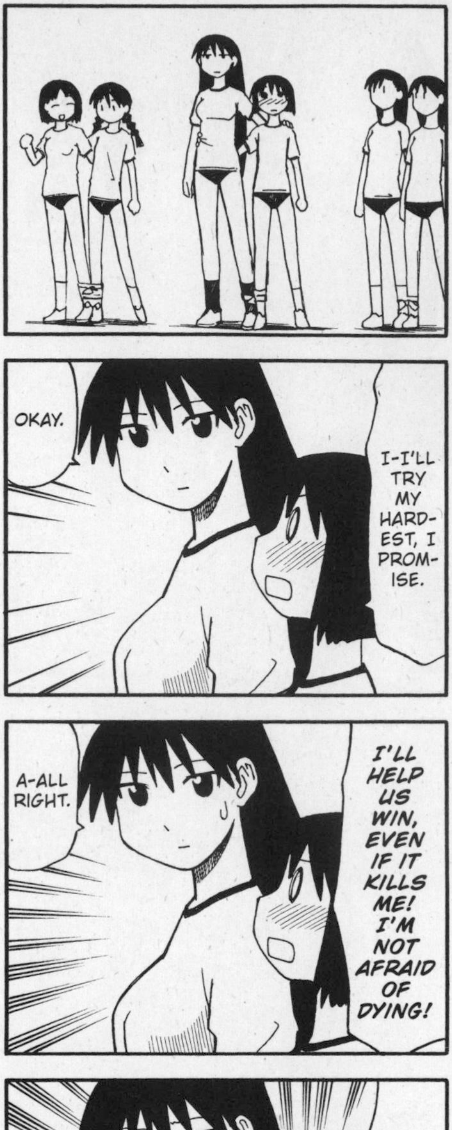
I-I'LL TRY MY HARDEST, I PROMISE.
OKAY.
I'LL HELP US WIN, EVEN IF IT KILLS ME! I'M NOT AFRAID OF DYING!
A-ALL RIGHT.
I-I'LL DIE!

TROPHY

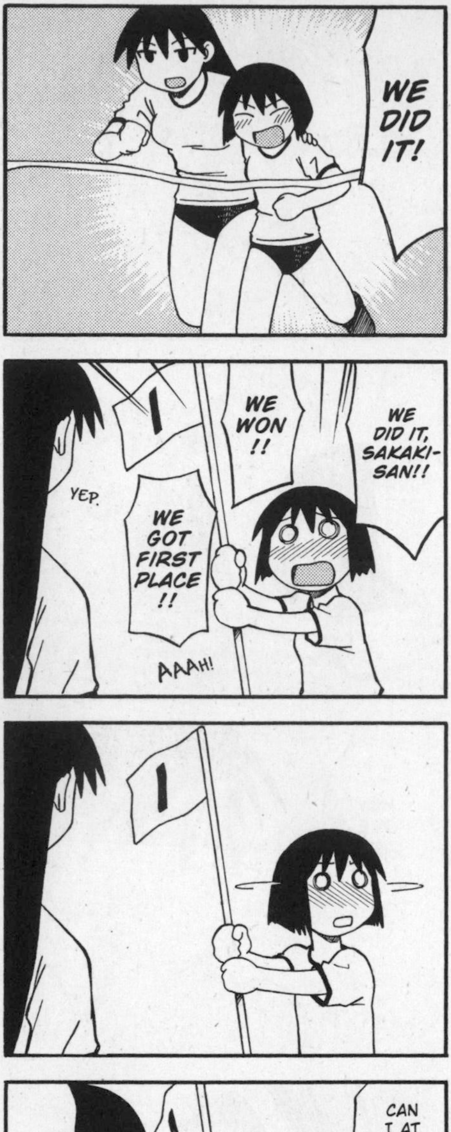
WE DID IT!
WE DID IT, SAKAKI-SAN!!
WE WON!!
WE GOT FIRST PLACE!!
AAAH!
YEP.
CAN I AT LEAST OFFER YOU THIS FLAG AS A MEMORIAL OF OUR—
N-NO THANKS.

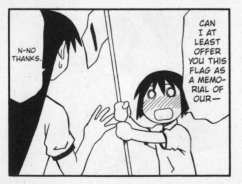

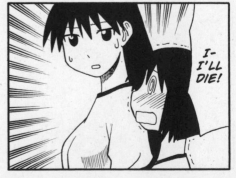

TOO TIGHT

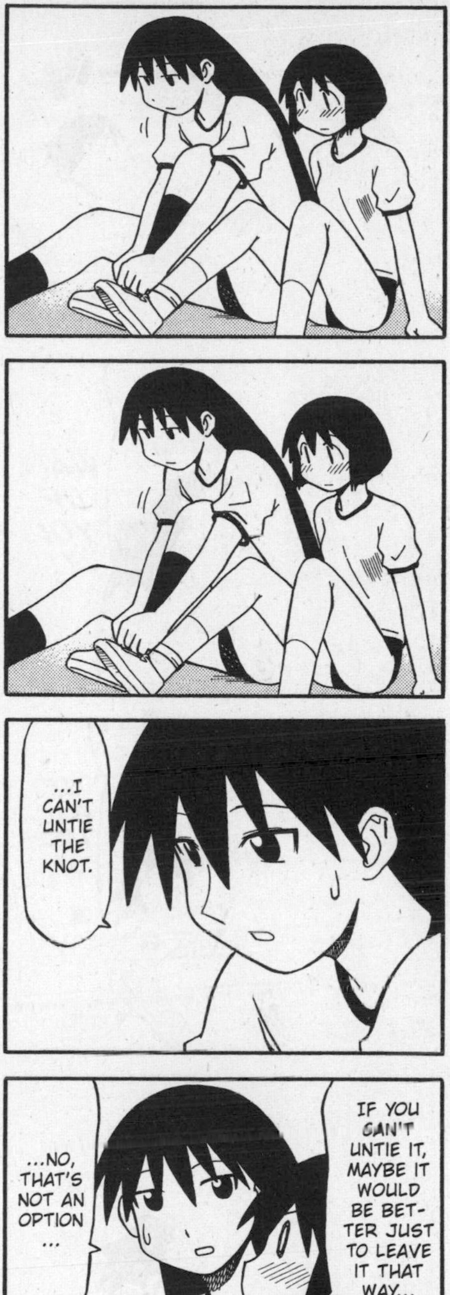
...I CAN'T UNTIE THE KNOT.
IF YOU CAN'T UNTIE IT, MAYBE IT WOULD BE BETTER JUST TO LEAVE IT THAT WAY...
...NO, THAT'S NOT AN OPTION ...

FINAL BOSS

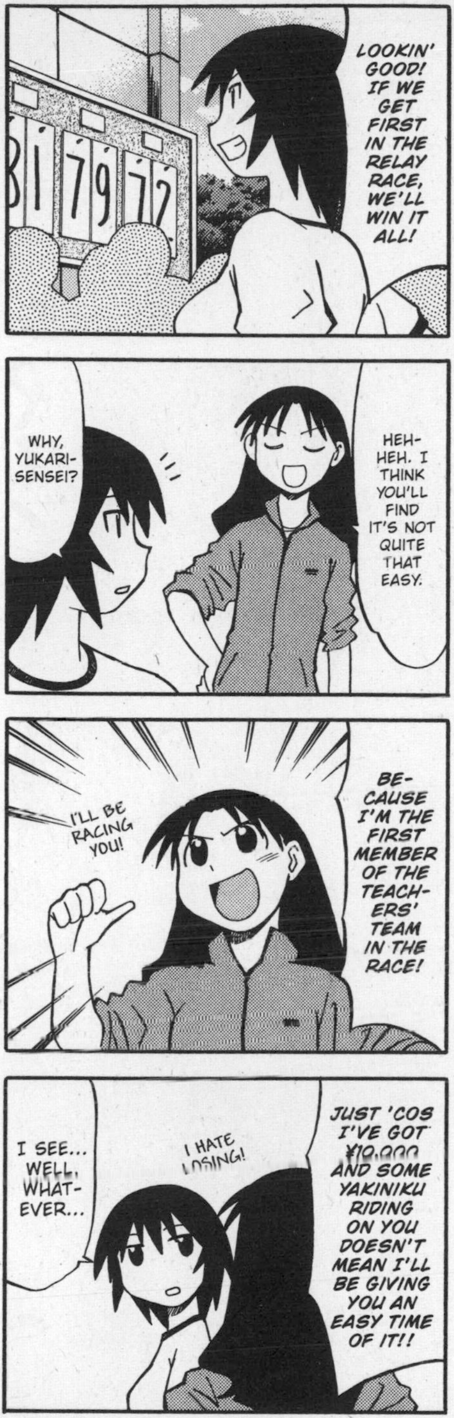
LOOKIN' GOOD! IF WE GET FIRST IN THE RELAY RACE, WE'LL WIN IT ALL!
HEH-HEH. I THINK YOU'LL FIND IT'S NOT QUITE THAT EASY.
WHY, YUKARI-SENSEI?
BE-CAUSE I'M THE FIRST MEMBER OF THE TEACHERS' TEAM IN THE RACE!
I'LL BE RACING YOU!
JUST 'COS I'VE GOT ¥10,000 AND SOME YAKINIKU RIDING ON YOU DOESN'T MEAN I'LL BE GIVING YOU AN EASY TIME OF IT!!
I HATE LOSING!
I SEE... WELL, WHATEVER...

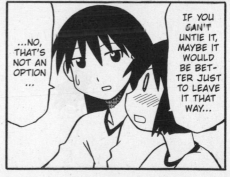

WHAT THE—!?

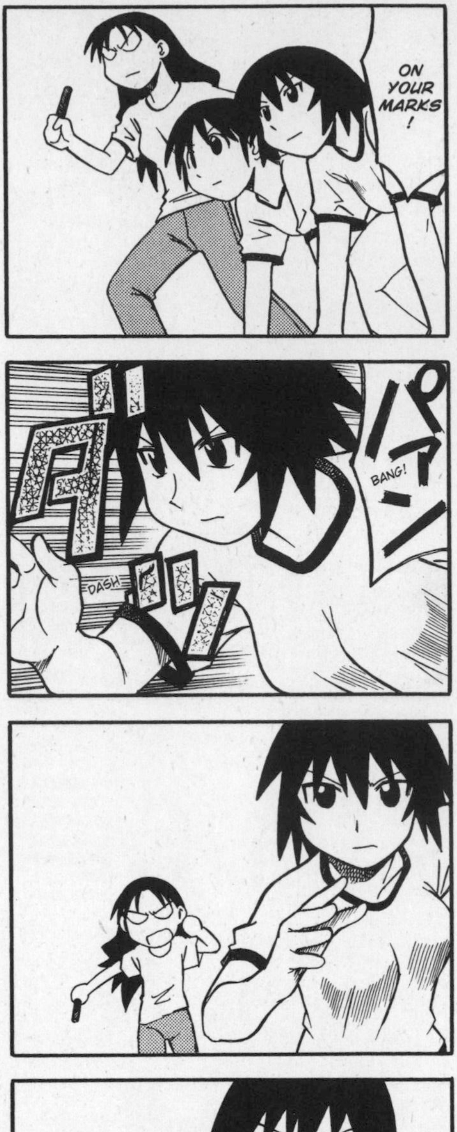
ON YOUR MARKS!
パァーン
BANG!
ダッ
DASH

YOU LITTLE JERK

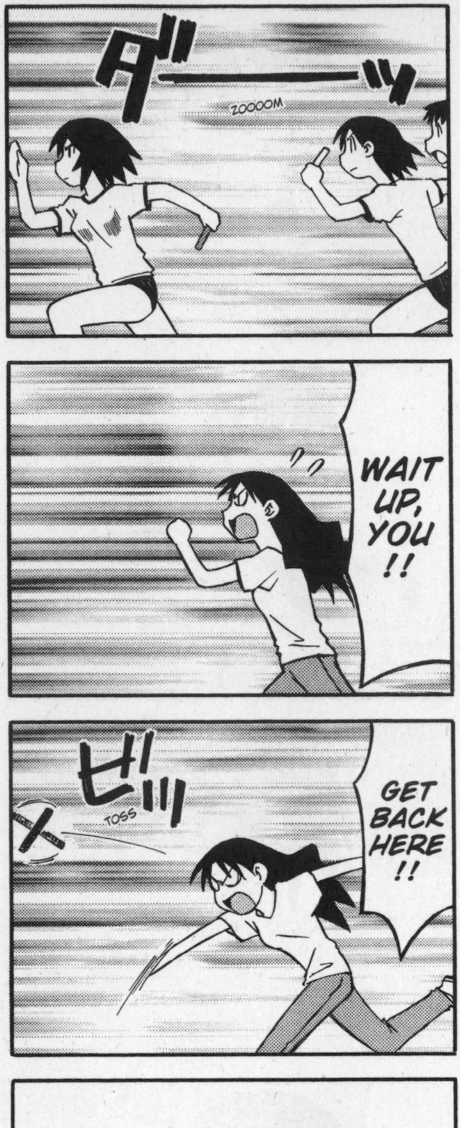
ダーーッ
ZOOOOM
WAIT UP, YOU!!
ビッ
TOSS
GET BACK HERE!!
ARGH!
ころころ
ROLL ROLL

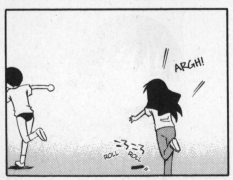

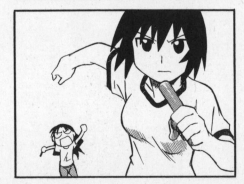

TWO-PEAT

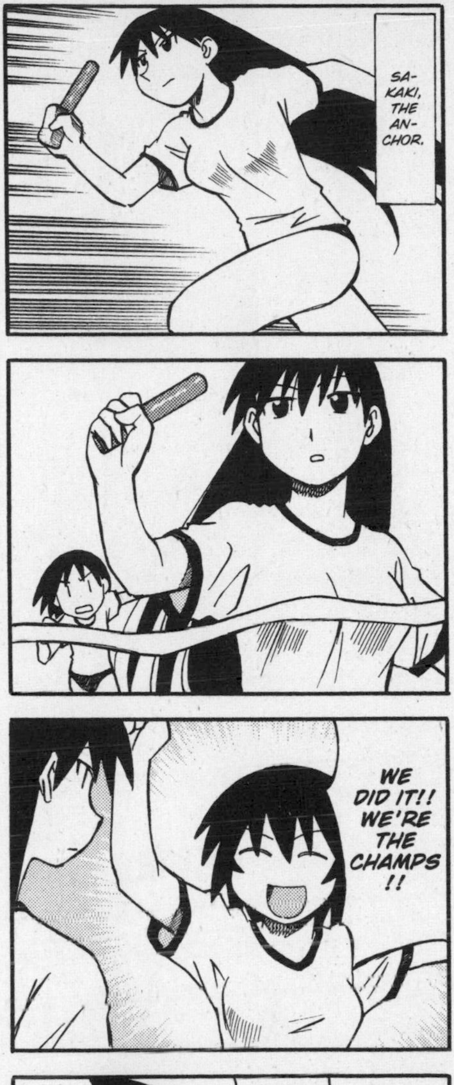
SA-KAKI, THE AN-CHOR.
WE DID IT!! WE'RE THE CHAMPS!!
HAAAH!
HAAAH!
DON'T THINK THIS IS OVER YET, CHUMP!!
UH... IT IS OVER. WE WON.
HAAAH!
HAAAH!

LOSERLY

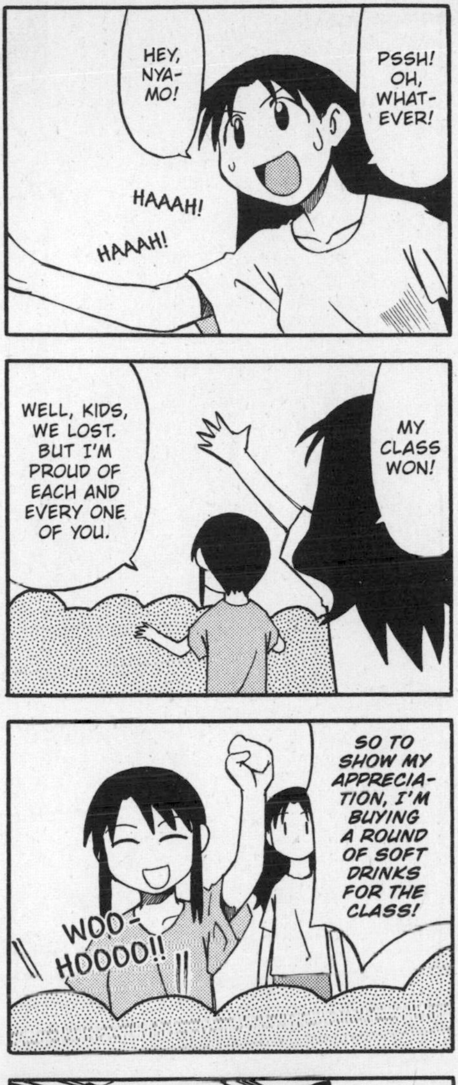
PSSH! OH, WHAT-EVER!
HEY, NYA-MO!
HAAAH!
HAAAH!
MY CLASS WON!
WELL, KIDS, WE LOST. BUT I'M PROUD OF EACH AND EVERY ONE OF YOU.
SO TO SHOW MY APPRECIA-TION, I'M BUYING A ROUND OF SOFT DRINKS FOR THE CLASS!
WOO-HOOOO!!
OH, COME ON! YOU DON'T GET TO ACT GRACEFUL AFTER LOSING!!
YOU'RE LOSERS! LOSERS!!
NYAH NYAH!

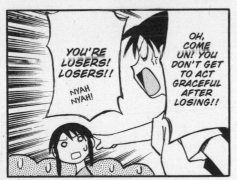

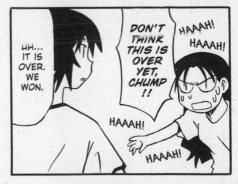

AZUMANGA-DAIOH

037

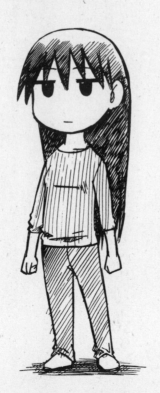

You belong.

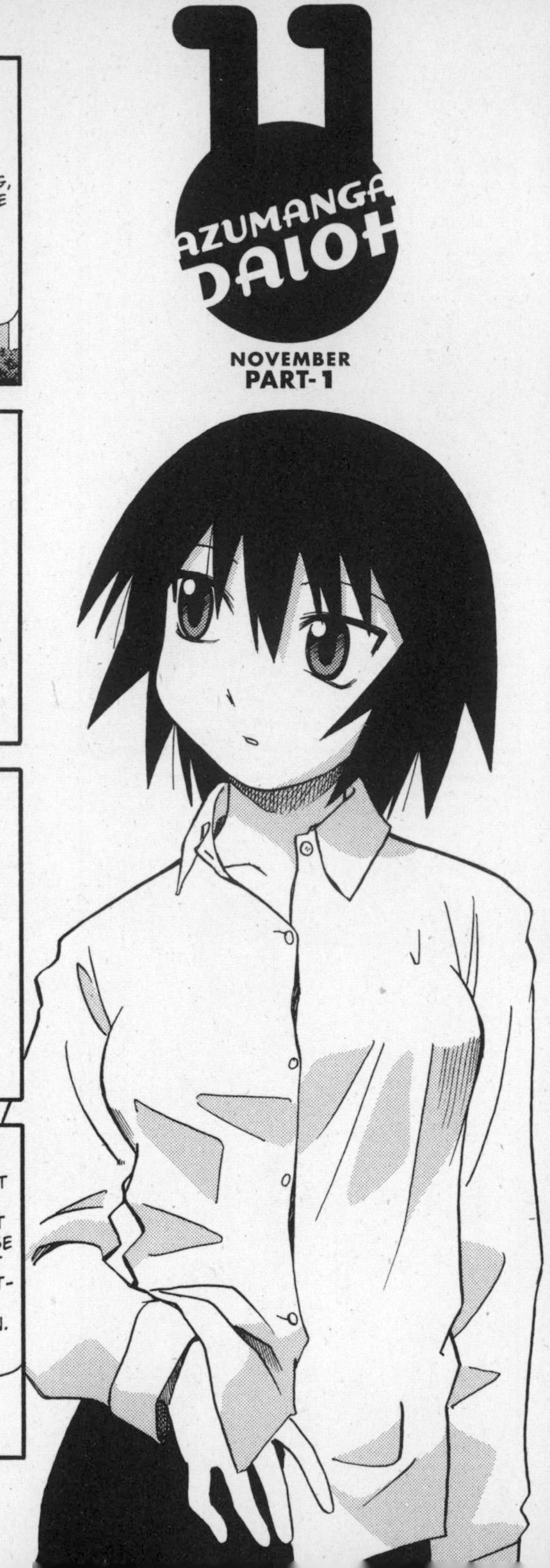
11
AZUMANGA DAIOH
NOVEMBER
PART-1

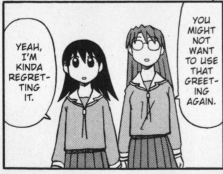

FAIL

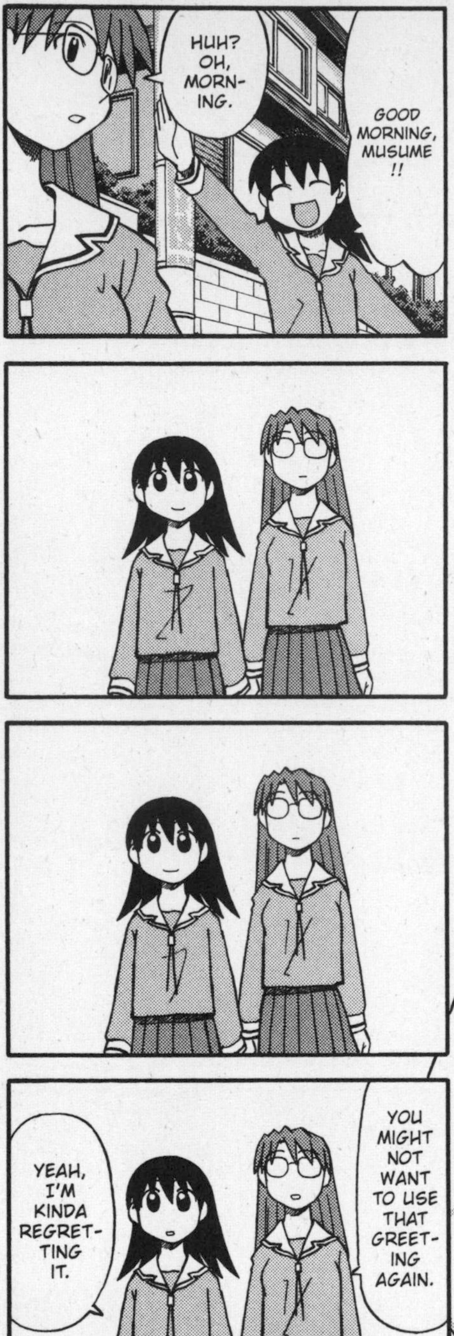
GOOD MORNING, MUSUME !!
HUH? OH, MORNING.
YOU MIGHT NOT WANT TO USE THAT GREET-ING AGAIN.
YEAH, I'M KINDA REGRET-TING IT.

ABANDONING DUTY

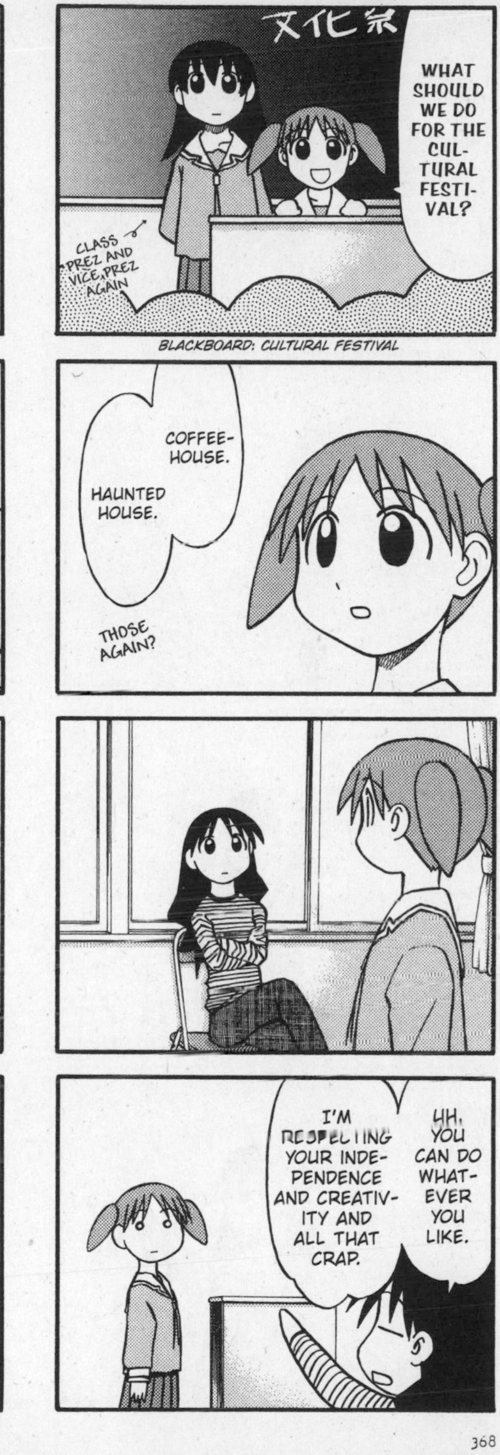
文化祭
WHAT SHOULD WE DO FOR THE CULTURAL FESTIVAL?
CLASS PREZ AND VICE PREZ AGAIN
BLACKBOARD: CULTURAL FESTIVAL
COFFEE-HOUSE.
HAUNTED HOUSE.
THOSE AGAIN?
UH, YOU CAN DO WHATEVER YOU LIKE.
I'M RESPECTING YOUR INDEPENDENCE AND CREATIVITY AND ALL THAT CRAP.

MILK

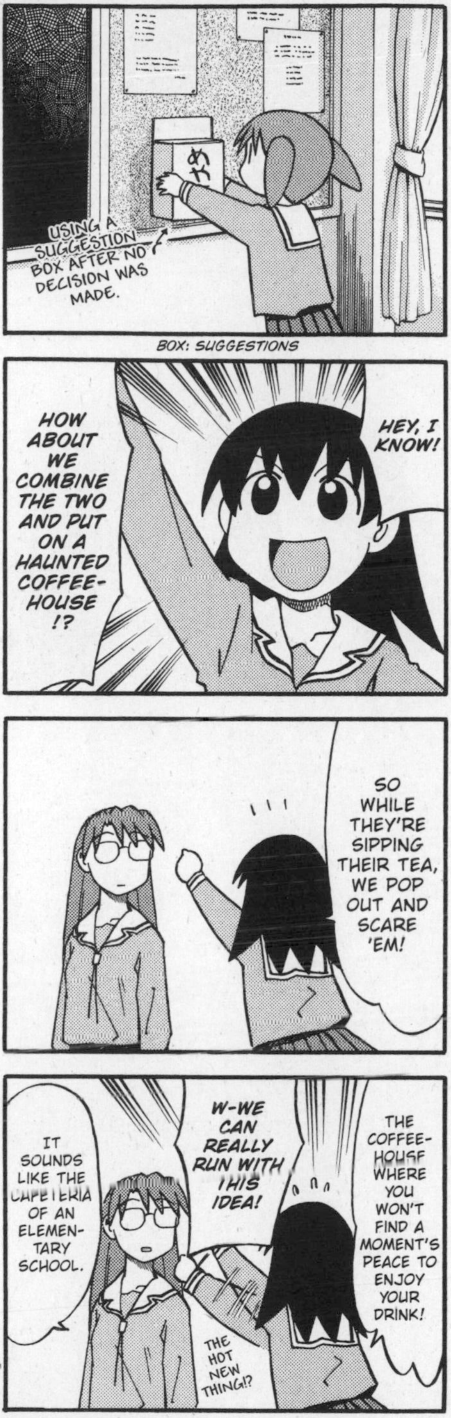
USING A SUGGESTION BOX AFTER NO DECISION WAS MADE.
BOX: SUGGESTIONS
HEY, I KNOW!
HOW ABOUT WE COMBINE THE TWO AND PUT ON A HAUNTED COFFEE-HOUSE!?
SO WHILE THEY'RE SIPPING THEIR TEA, WE POP OUT AND SCARE 'EM!
THE COFFEE-HOUSE WHERE YOU WON'T FIND A MOMENT'S PEACE TO ENJOY YOUR DRINK!
W-WE CAN REALLY RUN WITH THIS IDEA!
THE HOT NEW THING!?
IT SOUNDS LIKE THE CAFETERIA OF AN ELEMENTARY SCHOOL.

PRANKHOUSE

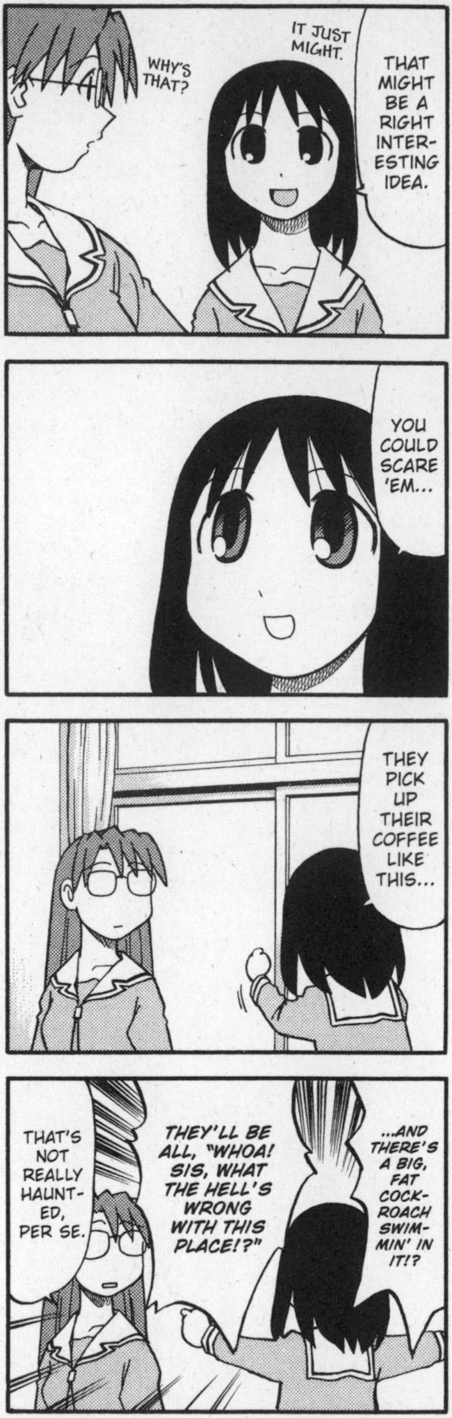
THAT MIGHT BE A RIGHT INTERESTING IDEA.
IT JUST MIGHT.
WHY'S THAT?
YOU COULD SCARE 'EM...
THEY PICK UP THEIR COFFEE LIKE THIS...
...AND THERE'S A BIG, FAT COCKROACH SWIMMIN' IN IT!?
THEY'LL BE ALL, "WHOA! SIS, WHAT THE HELL'S WRONG WITH THIS PLACE!?"
THAT'S NOT REALLY HAUNTED, PER SE.

HAUNTED COFFEEHOUSE

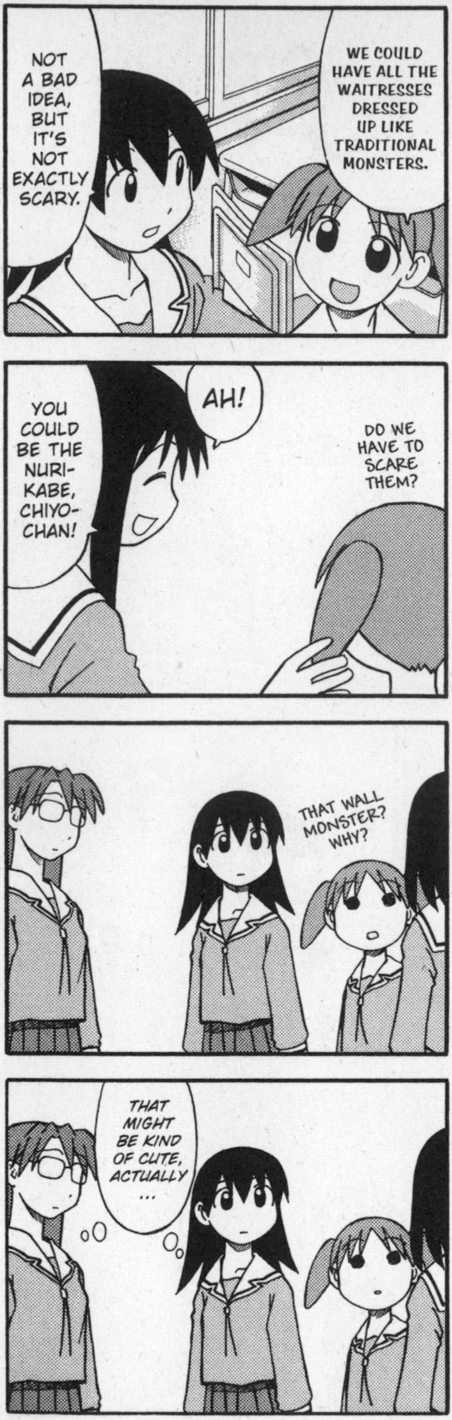
WE COULD HAVE ALL THE WAITRESSES DRESSED UP LIKE TRADITIONAL MONSTERS.
NOT A BAD IDEA, BUT IT'S NOT EXACTLY SCARY.
AH!
YOU COULD BE THE NURI-KABE, CHIYO-CHAN!
DO WE HAVE TO SCARE THEM?
THAT WALL MONSTER? WHY?
THAT MIGHT BE KIND OF CUTE, ACTUALLY ...

NURIKABE CHIYO

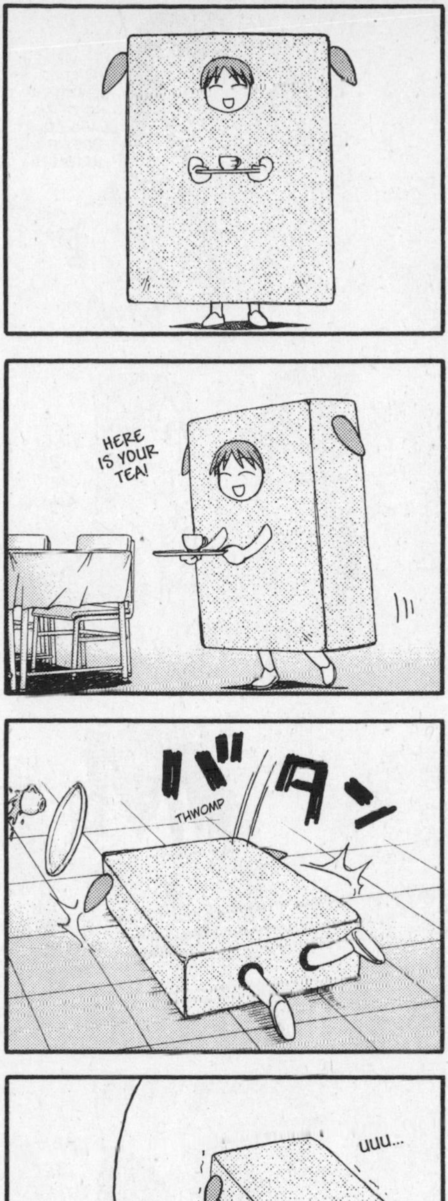
HERE IS YOUR TEA!
バタン
THWOMP
UUU...

FLAWED COFFEEHOUSE

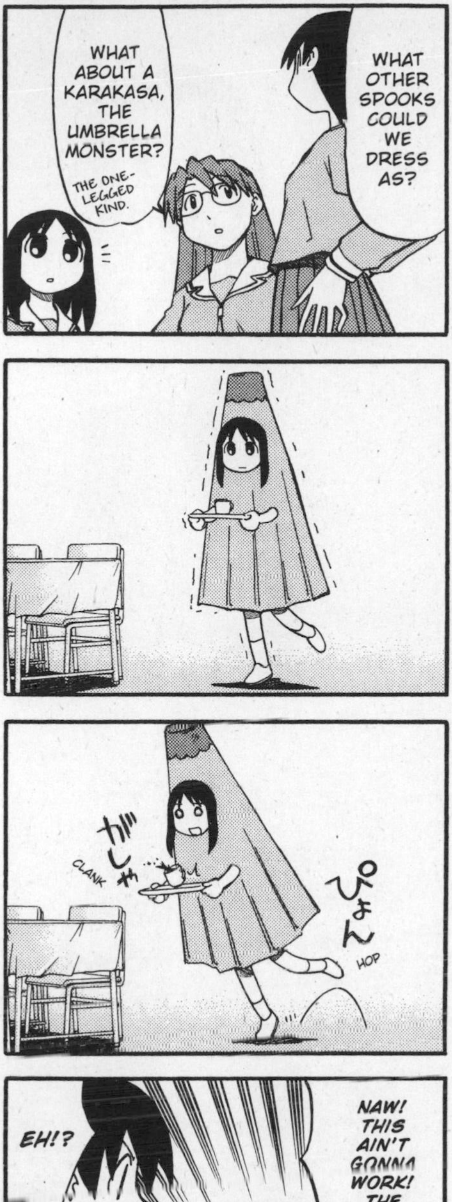
WHAT OTHER SPOOKS COULD WE DRESS AS?
WHAT ABOUT A KARAKASA, THE UMBRELLA MONSTER?
THE ONE-LEGGED KIND.
がしゃ
CLANK
ぴょん
HOP
NAW! THIS AIN'T GONNA WORK! THE HAUNTED COFFEE-HOUSE IDEA'S FATALLY FLAWED!
EH!?

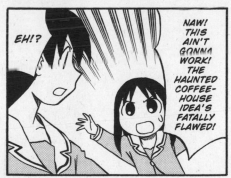

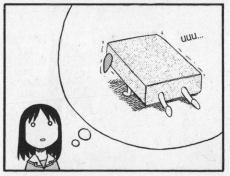

ROUND AND ROUND

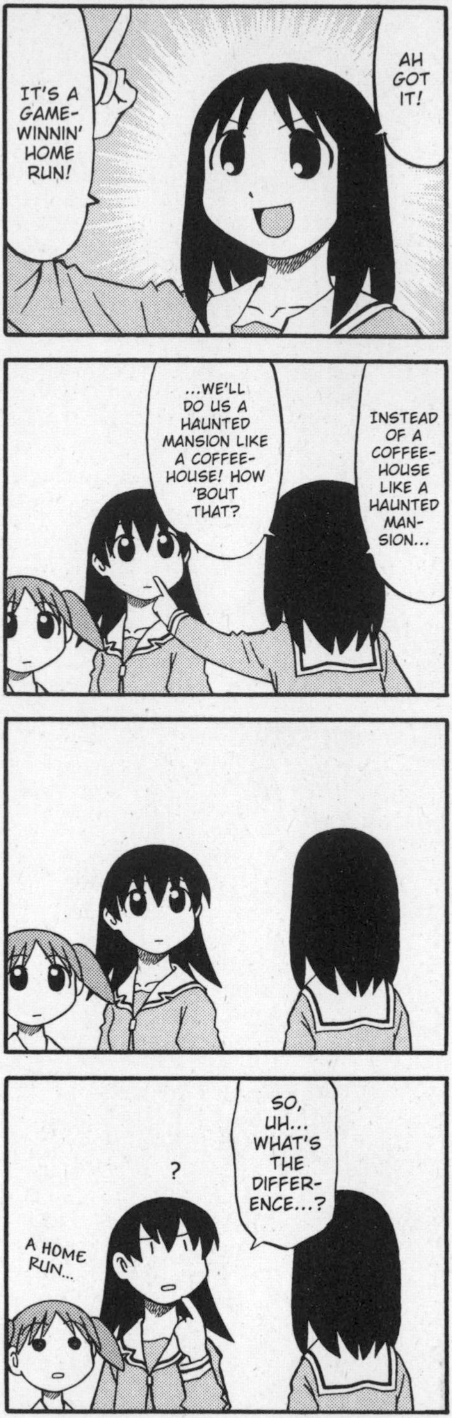
AH GOT IT!
IT'S A GAME-WINNIN' HOME RUN!
INSTEAD OF A COFFEE-HOUSE LIKE A HAUNTED MANSION...
...WE'LL DO US A HAUNTED MANSION LIKE A COFFEE-HOUSE! HOW 'BOUT THAT?
SO, UH... WHAT'S THE DIFFERENCE...?
?
A HOME RUN...

REPRODUCE THE ORIGINAL MATERIAL

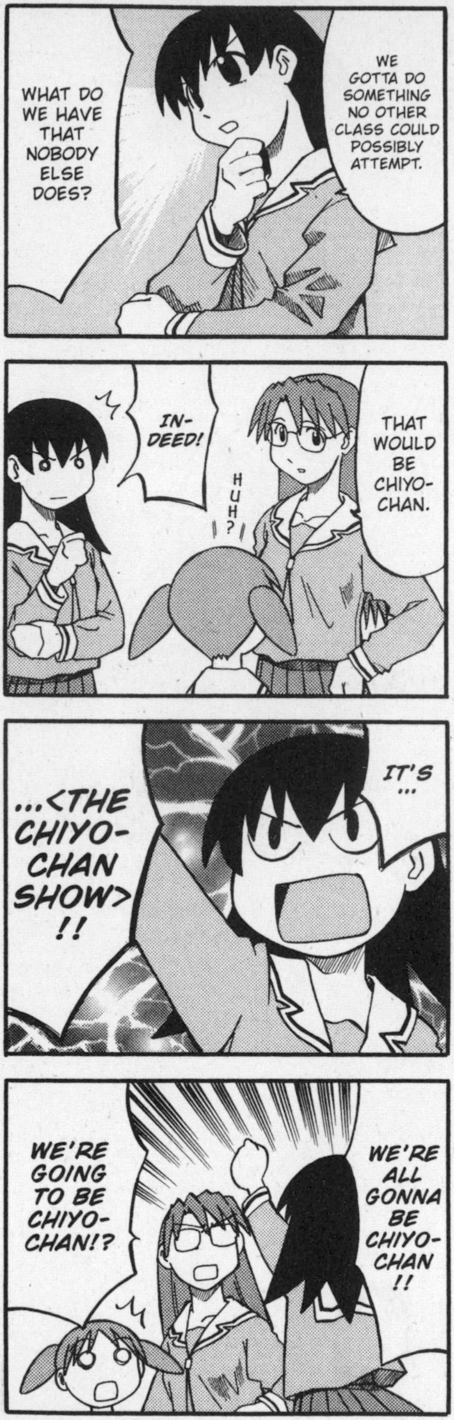
WE GOTTA DO SOMETHING NO OTHER CLASS COULD POSSIBLY ATTEMPT.
WHAT DO WE HAVE THAT NOBODY ELSE DOES?
THAT WOULD BE CHIYO-CHAN.
HUH?
IN-DEED!
IT'S...
...<THE CHIYO-CHAN SHOW>!!
WE'RE ALL GONNA BE CHIYO-CHAN!!
WE'RE GOING TO BE CHIYO-CHAN!?

LOOK AT ME

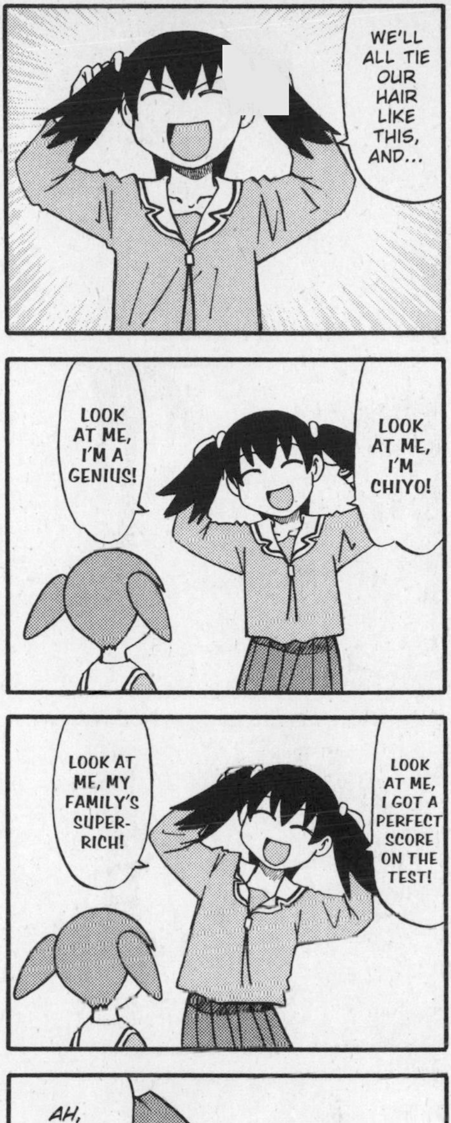

WE'LL ALL TIE OUR HAIR LIKE THIS, AND...
LOOK AT ME, I'M CHIYO!
LOOK AT ME, I'M A GENIUS!
LOOK AT ME, I GOT A PERFECT SCORE ON THE TEST!
LOOK AT ME, MY FAMILY'S SUPER-RICH!
AH, SHE'S MAD. SHE'S MAD!
GRRR...

I AM NOT

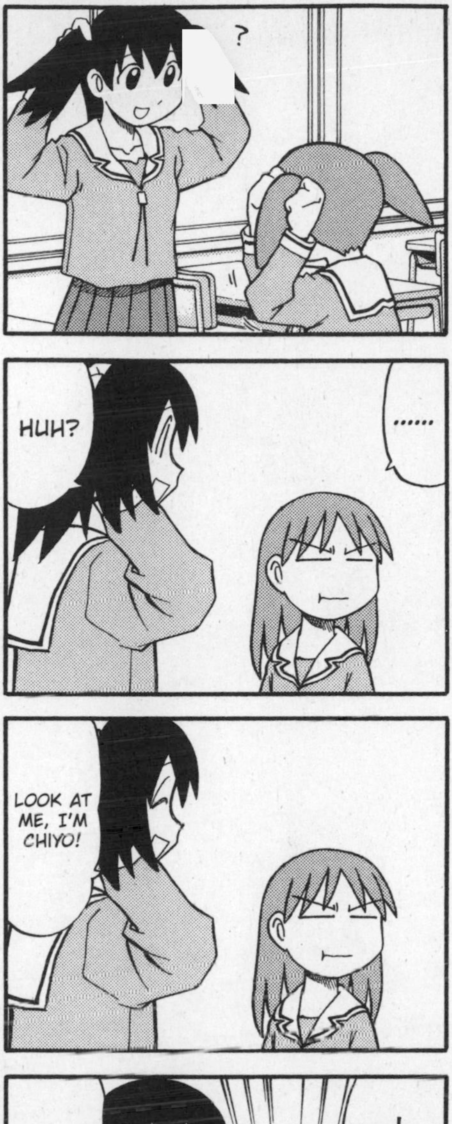

?
......
HUH?
LOOK AT ME, I'M CHIYO!
I AIN'T TALK LIKE THAT ONE BIT!
"AIN'T TALK" ...?

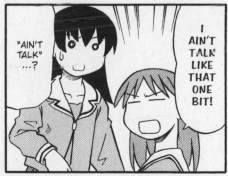

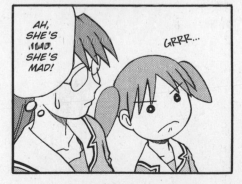

BIRDS OF A FEATHER

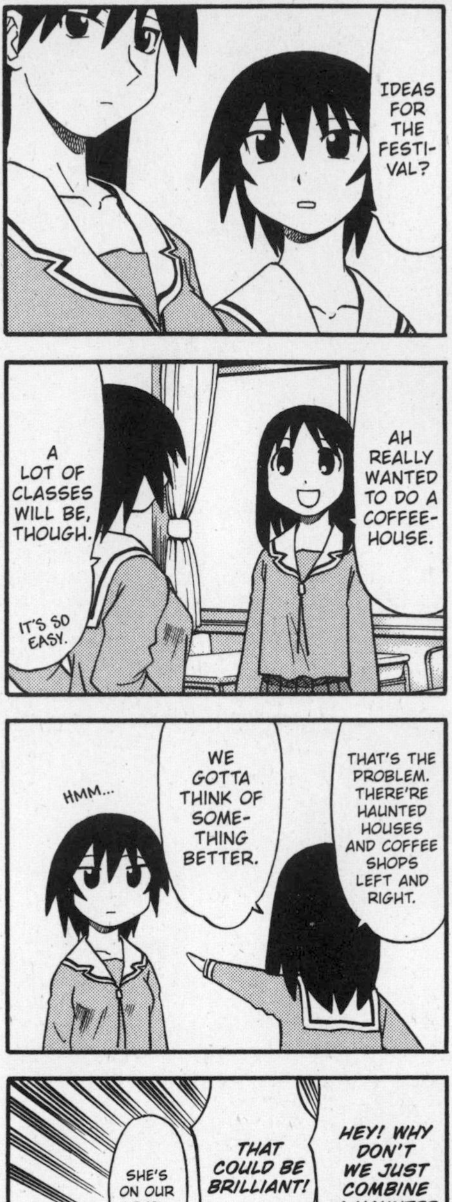
IDEAS FOR THE FESTI-VAL?
AH REALLY WANTED TO DO A COFFEE-HOUSE.
A LOT OF CLASSES WILL BE, THOUGH.
IT'S SO EASY.
THAT'S THE PROBLEM. THERE'RE HAUNTED HOUSES AND COFFEE SHOPS LEFT AND RIGHT.
WE GOTTA THINK OF SOME-THING BETTER.
HMM...
HEY! WHY DON'T WE JUST COMBINE A HAUNTED HOUSE AND COFFEE SHOP!?
THAT COULD BE BRILLIANT!
SHE'S ON OUR LEVEL.
UGH...

COMBINATIONS

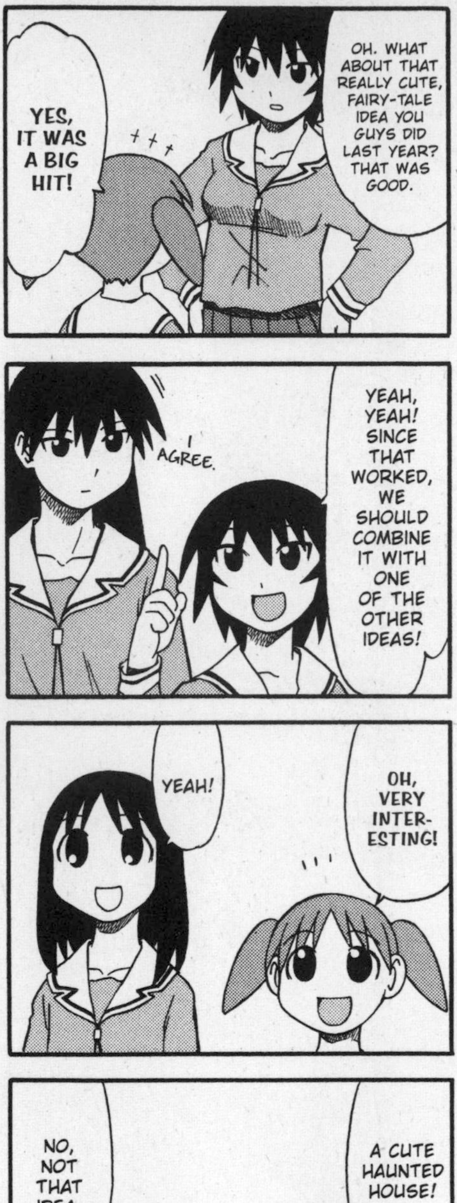
OH. WHAT ABOUT THAT REALLY CUTE, FAIRY-TALE IDEA YOU GUYS DID LAST YEAR? THAT WAS GOOD.
YES, IT WAS A BIG HIT!
YEAH, YEAH! SINCE THAT WORKED, WE SHOULD COMBINE IT WITH ONE OF THE OTHER IDEAS!
I AGREE.
OH, VERY INTERESTING!
YEAH!
A CUTE HAUNTED HOUSE!
NO, NOT THAT IDEA.

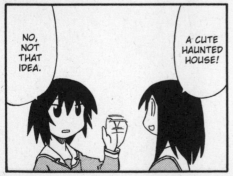

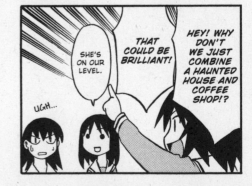

ALL MIXED UP

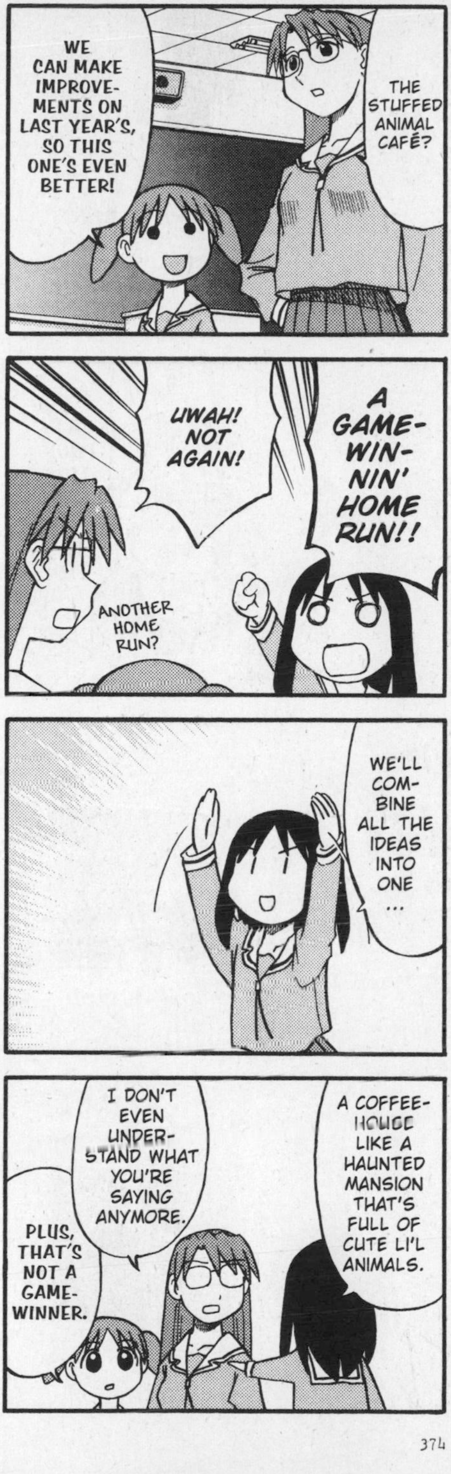
THE STUFFED ANIMAL CAFÉ?
WE CAN MAKE IMPROVEMENTS ON LAST YEAR'S, SO THIS ONE'S EVEN BETTER!
A GAME-WINNIN' HOME RUN!!
UWAH! NOT AGAIN!
ANOTHER HOME RUN?
WE'LL COMBINE ALL THE IDEAS INTO ONE ...
A COFFEEHOUSE LIKE A HAUNTED MANSION THAT'S FULL OF CUTE LI'L ANIMALS.
I DON'T EVEN UNDERSTAND WHAT YOU'RE SAYING ANYMORE.
PLUS, THAT'S NOT A GAME-WINNER.

OH MY GOD

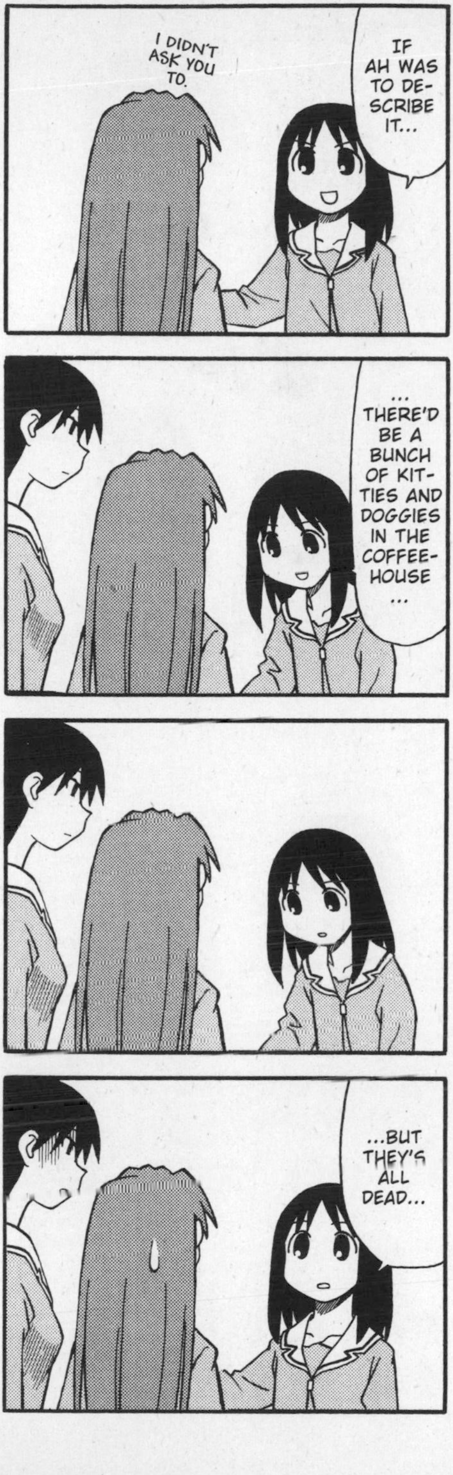
IF AH WAS TO DESCRIBE IT...
I DIDN'T ASK YOU TO.
... THERE'D BE A BUNCH OF KITTIES AND DOGGIES IN THE COFFEEHOUSE ...
...BUT THEY'S ALL DEAD...

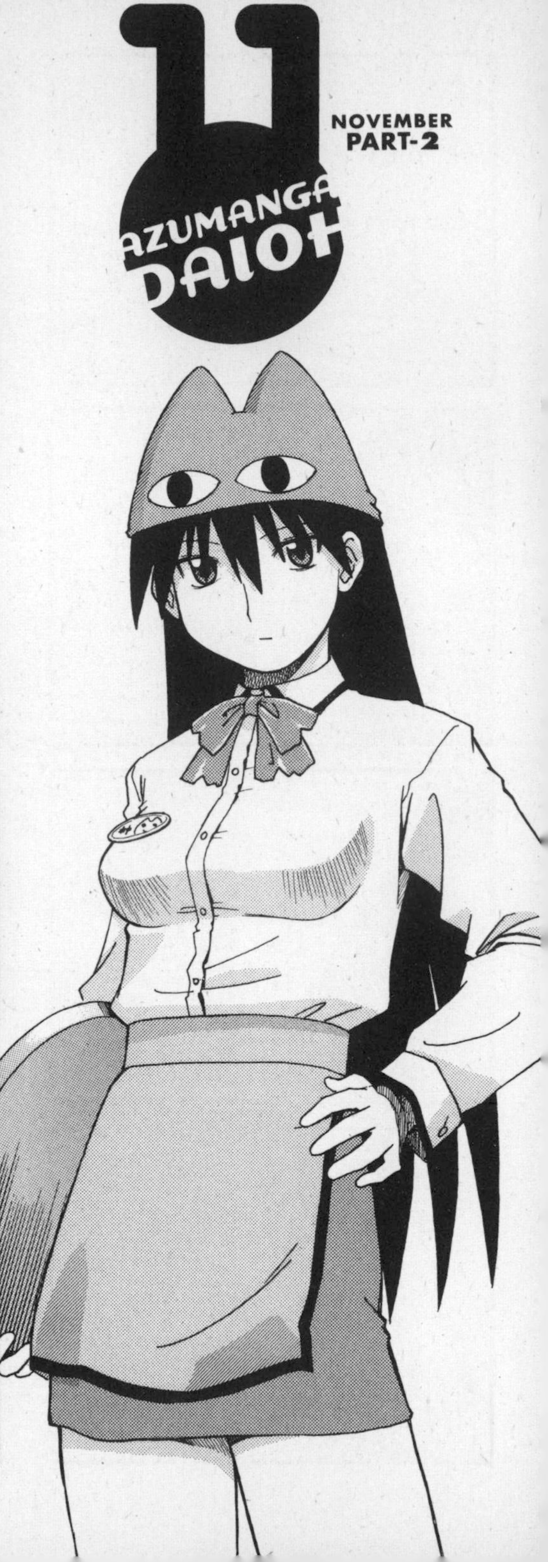
11
NOVEMBER
PART-2
AZUMANGA DAIOH

TO THE LETTER

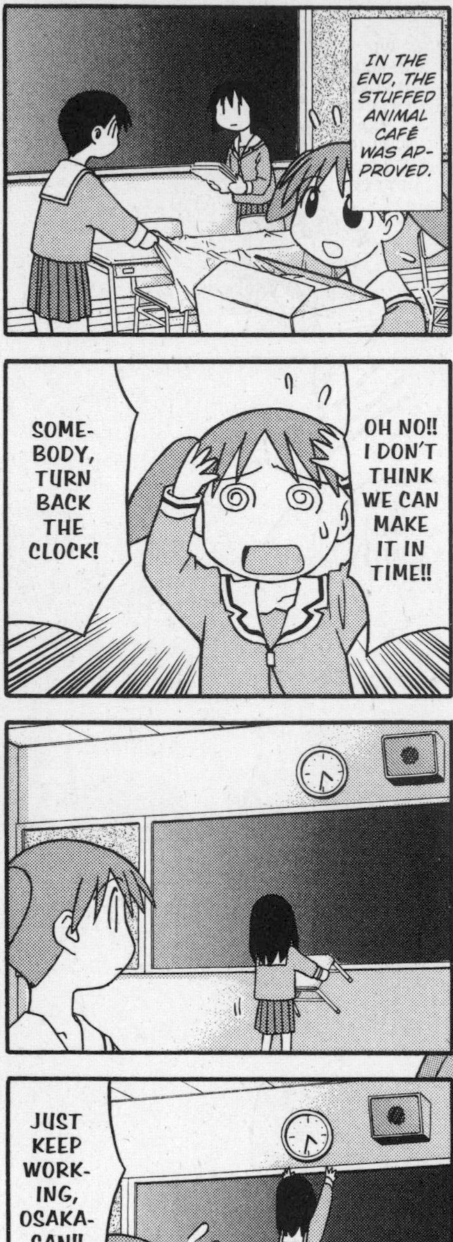
IN THE END, THE STUFFED ANIMAL CAFÉ WAS AP-PROVED.
OH NO!! I DON'T THINK WE CAN MAKE IT IN TIME!!
SOME-BODY, TURN BACK THE CLOCK!
JUST KEEP WORK-ING, OSAKA-SAN!!

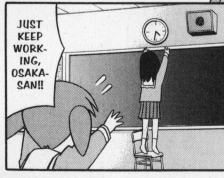

SHOWDOWN

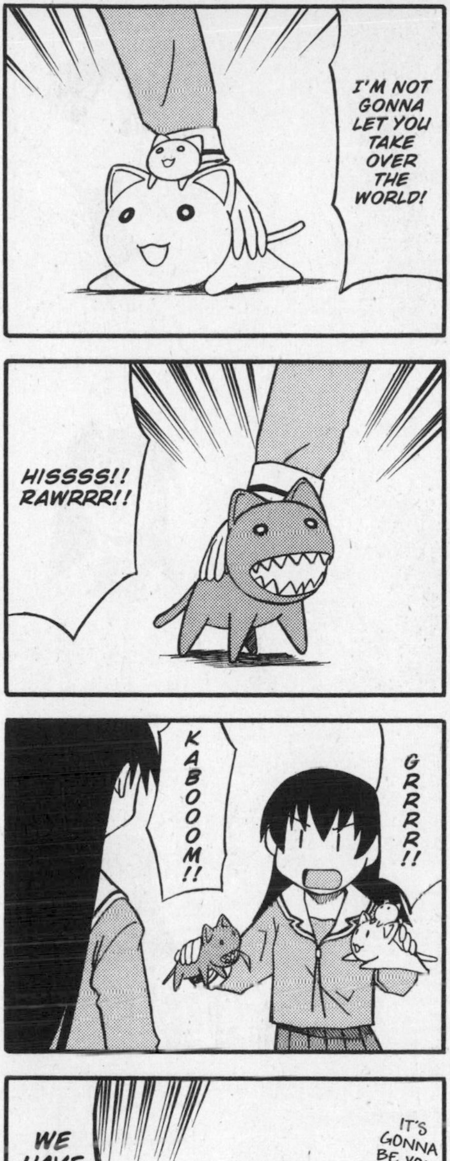
I'M NOT GONNA LET YOU TAKE OVER THE WORLD!
HISSSS!! RAWRRR!!
GRRRR!!
KABOOOOM!!
IT'S GONNA BE YOU OR ME, PAL!
WE HAVE WORK TO DO!!

THE ADVENT

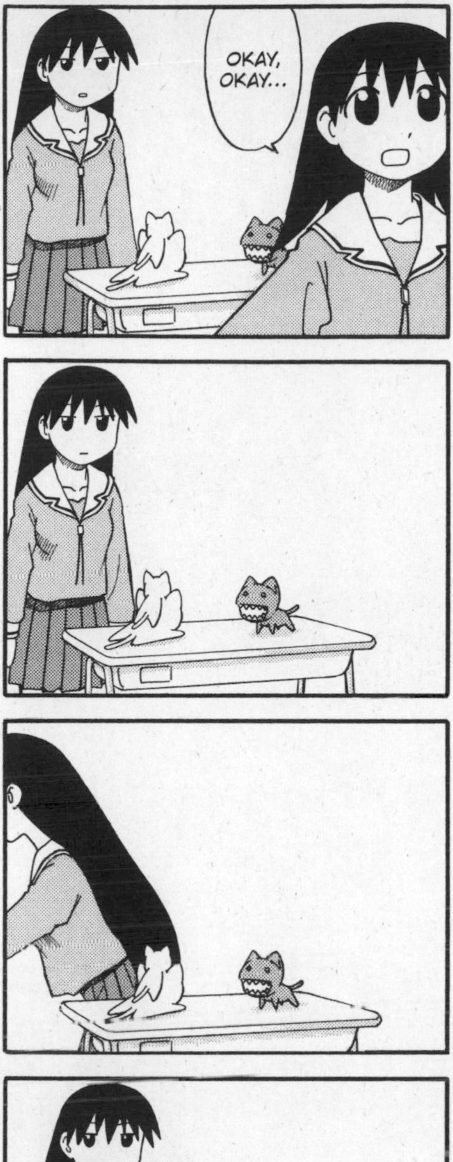
OKAY, OKAY...

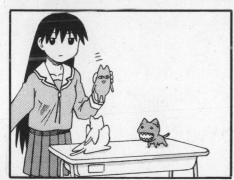

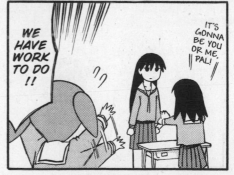

THE CHIYO'S DAD HAT

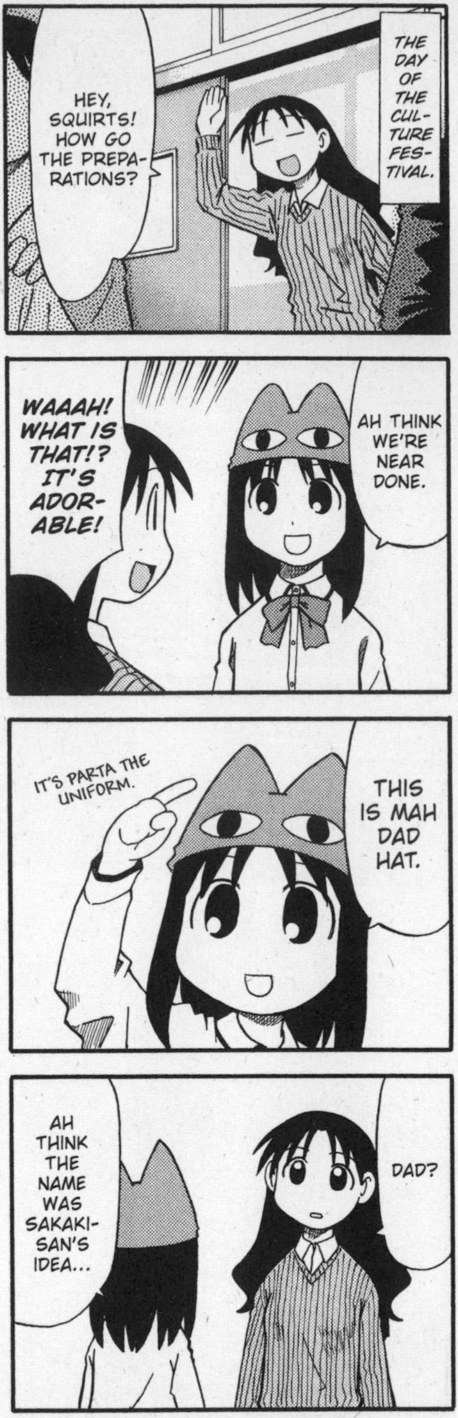
THE DAY OF THE CULTURE FESTIVAL.
HEY, SQUIRTS! HOW GO THE PREPARATIONS?
AH THINK WE'RE NEAR DONE.
WAAAH! WHAT IS THAT!? IT'S ADORABLE!
THIS IS MAH DAD HAT.
IT'S PARTA THE UNIFORM.
DAD?
AH THINK THE NAME WAS SAKAKI-SAN'S IDEA...

ON YOUR HEAD

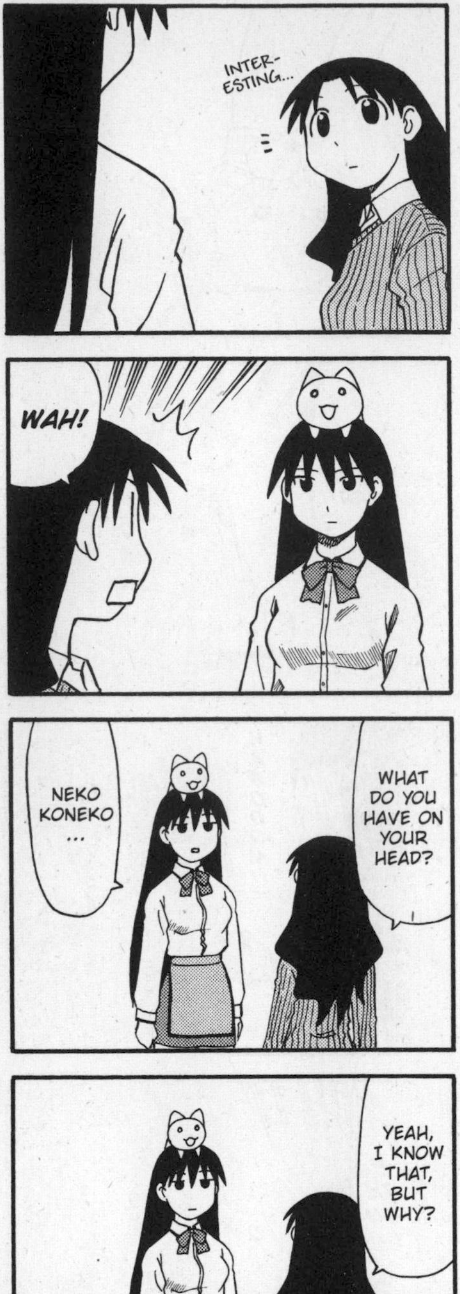
INTERESTING...
WAH!
WHAT DO YOU HAVE ON YOUR HEAD?
NEKO KONEKO ...
YEAH, I KNOW THAT, BUT WHY?

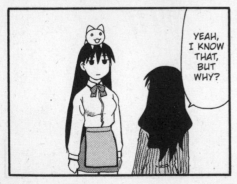

I LIKE IT

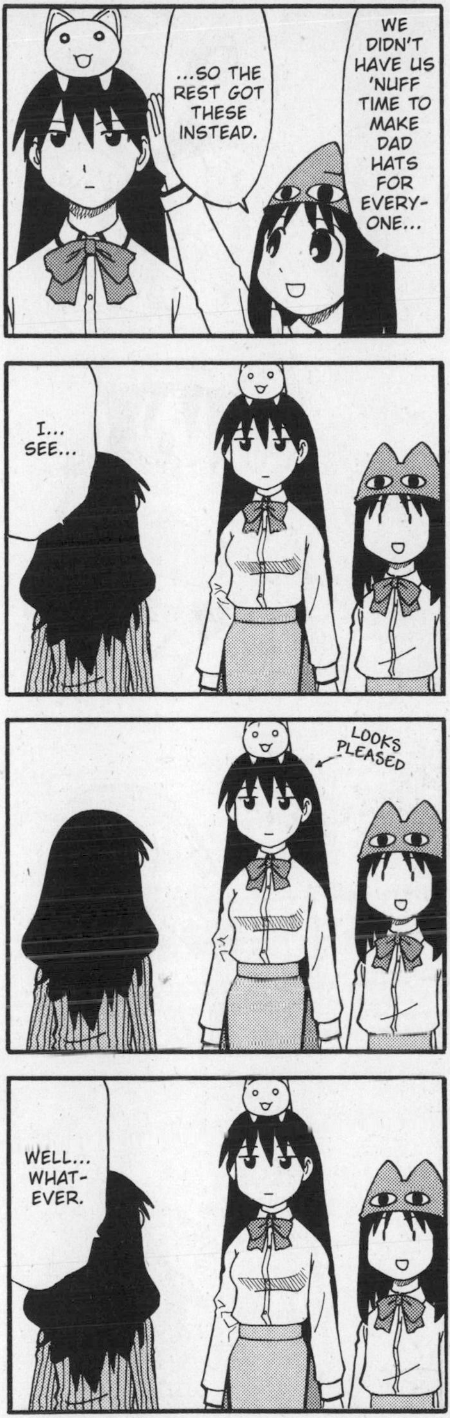

WE DIDN'T HAVE US 'NUFF TIME TO MAKE DAD HATS FOR EVERYONE...
...SO THE REST GOT THESE INSTEAD.
I... SEE...
LOOKS PLEASED
WELL... WHATEVER.

CAPTAIN

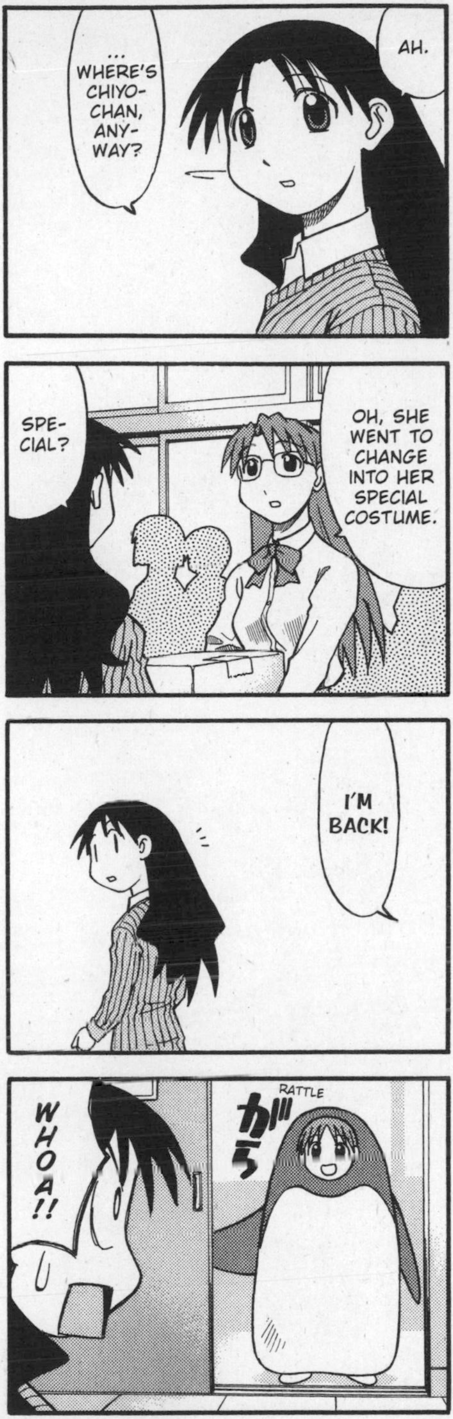

AH.
...WHERE'S CHIYO-CHAN, ANYWAY?
OH, SHE WENT TO CHANGE INTO HER SPECIAL COSTUME.
SPECIAL?
I'M BACK!
RATTLE
がら
WHOA!!

ADORABLE

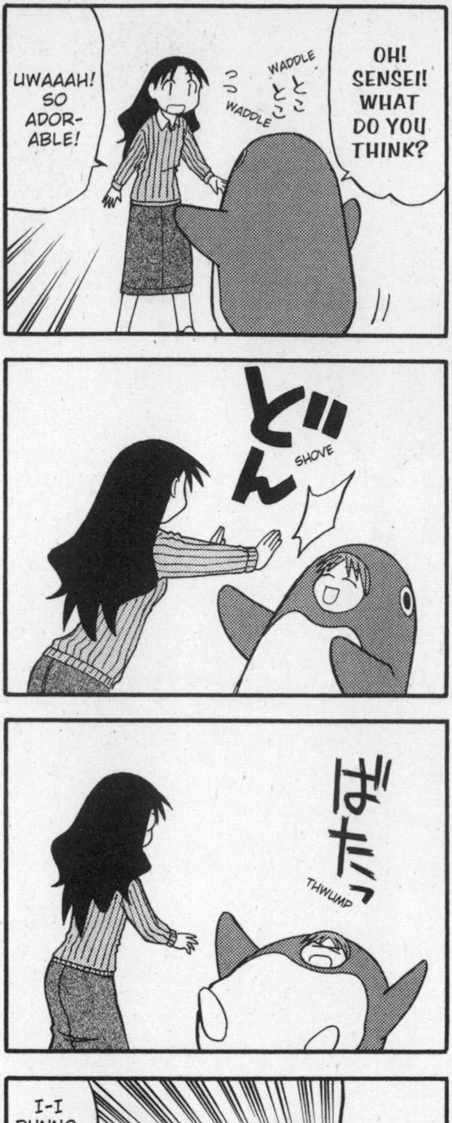
OH! SENSEI! WHAT DO YOU THINK?
とことこ
WADDLE WADDLE
UWAAAH! SO ADOR-ABLE!
どん
SHOVE
ばたっ
THWUMP
WHY DID YOU DO THAAAT?
ばたばた
FLOP FLOP
I-I DUNNO, MY HANDS JUST POPPED OUT...

GEEZ

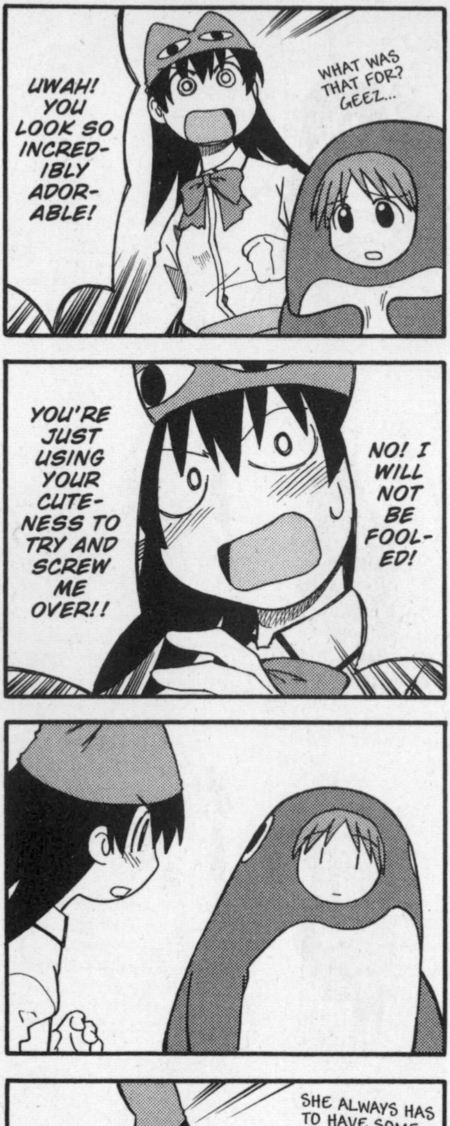
WHAT WAS THAT FOR? GEEZ...
UWAH! YOU LOOK SO INCRED-IBLY ADOR-ABLE!
NO! I WILL NOT BE FOOL-ED!
YOU'RE JUST USING YOUR CUTE-NESS TO TRY AND SCREW ME OVER!!
SHE ALWAYS HAS TO HAVE SOME-THING MEAN TO SAY...GEEZ...
たぺたぺ
SPLOT SPLOT
AH! ARRGH! SO... MUCH... CUTE...

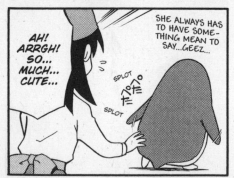

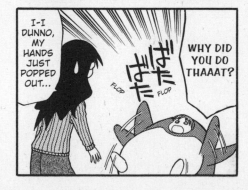

S'OKAY

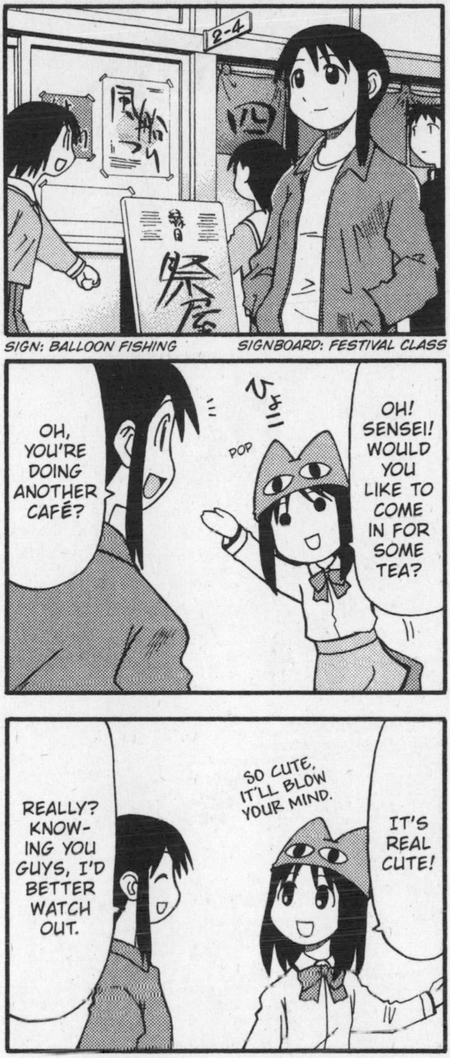
SIGN: BALLOON FISHING
SIGNBOARD: FESTIVAL CLASS
OH! SENSEI! WOULD YOU LIKE TO COME IN FOR SOME TEA?
POP
OH, YOU'RE DOING ANOTHER CAFÉ?
IT'S REAL CUTE!
SO CUTE, IT'LL BLOW YOUR MIND.
REALLY? KNOWING YOU GUYS, I'D BETTER WATCH OUT.
OH, DUN'CHA WORRY. THERE AIN'T A SINGLE DEAD CAT IN HERE.
EH...

OH MY...

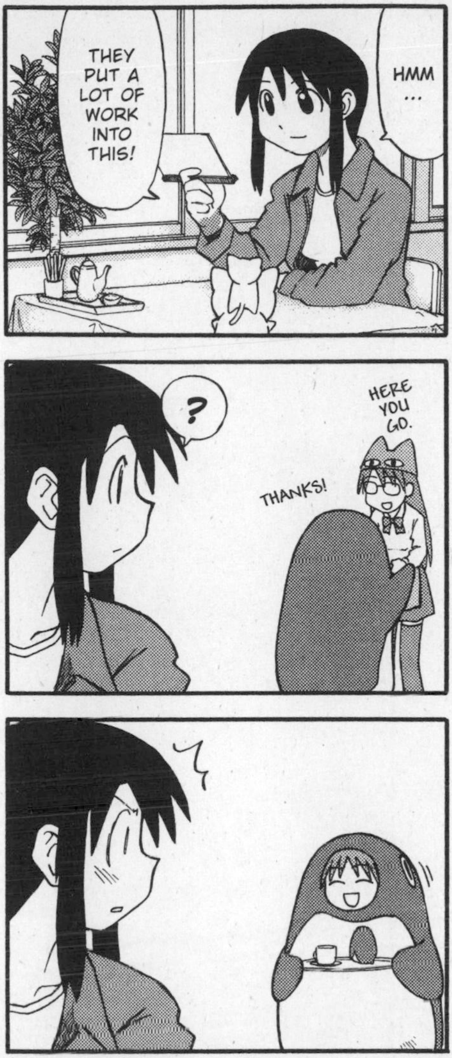
HMM ...
THEY PUT A LOT OF WORK INTO THIS!
?
HERE YOU GO.
THANKS!
HERE'S YOUR COFFEE!
EEEP!
HOW ADORABLE!

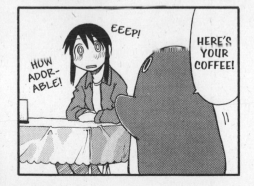

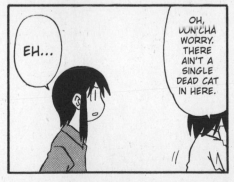

ORDER

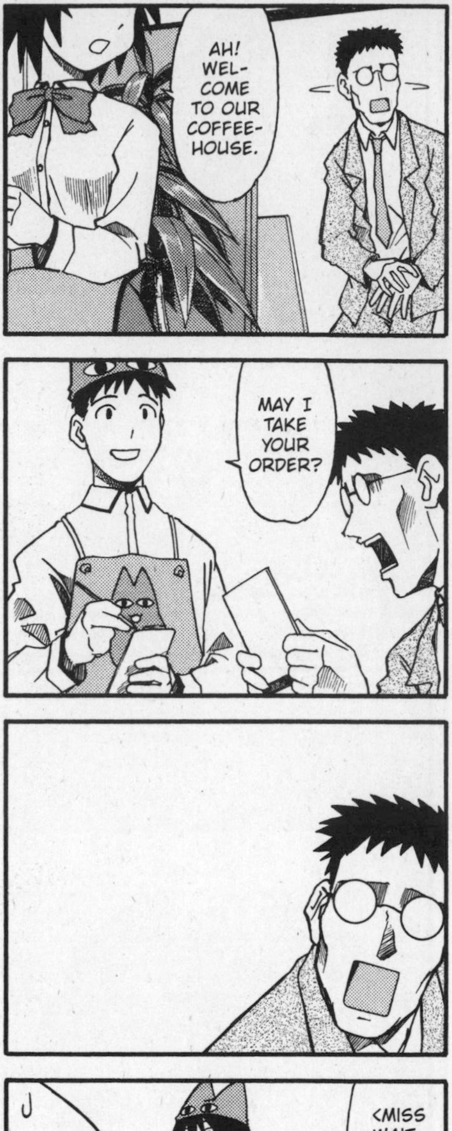
AH! WELCOME TO OUR COFFEEHOUSE.
MAY I TAKE YOUR ORDER?
<MISS WAITRESS?> I'M READY TO ORDER NOW.

ALLOW ME!

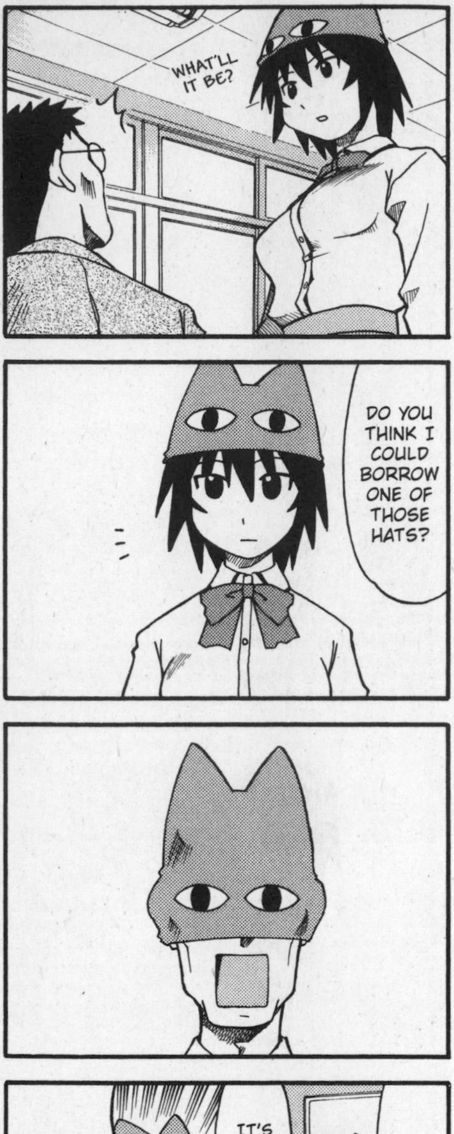
WHAT'LL IT BE?
DO YOU THINK I COULD BORROW ONE OF THOSE HATS?
COME ON IN, STUDENTS!
IT'S TERRIBLY CUTE INSIDE!
WE DON'T NEED HELP PULLING IN CUSTOMERS, THANK YOU VERY MUCH!!

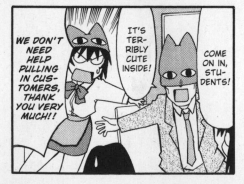

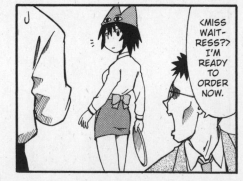

IT'S MISSING SOMETHING

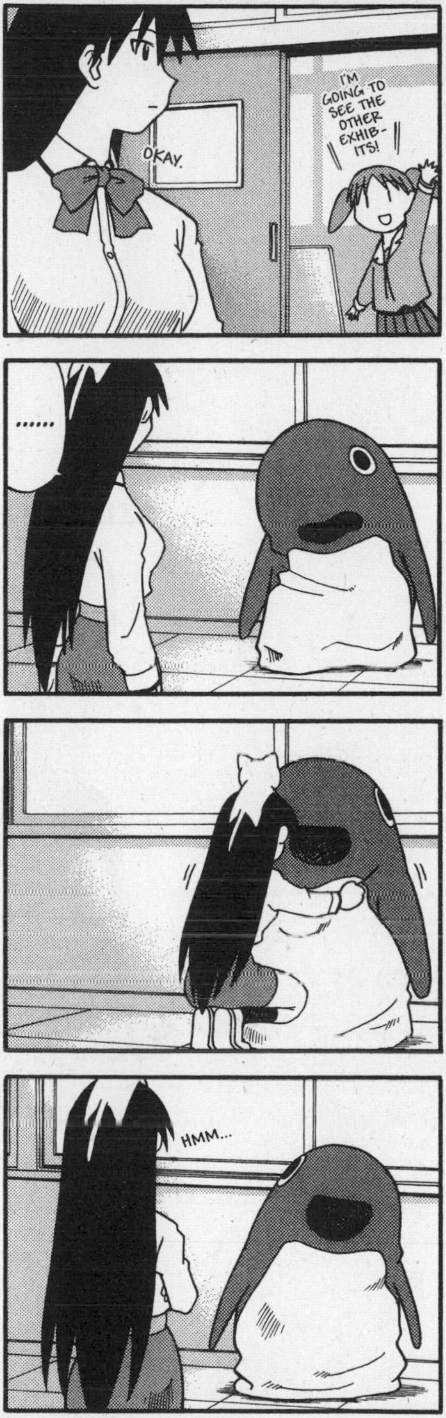
I'M GOING TO SEE THE OTHER EXHIB-ITS!
OKAY.
......
HMM...

GOT IT

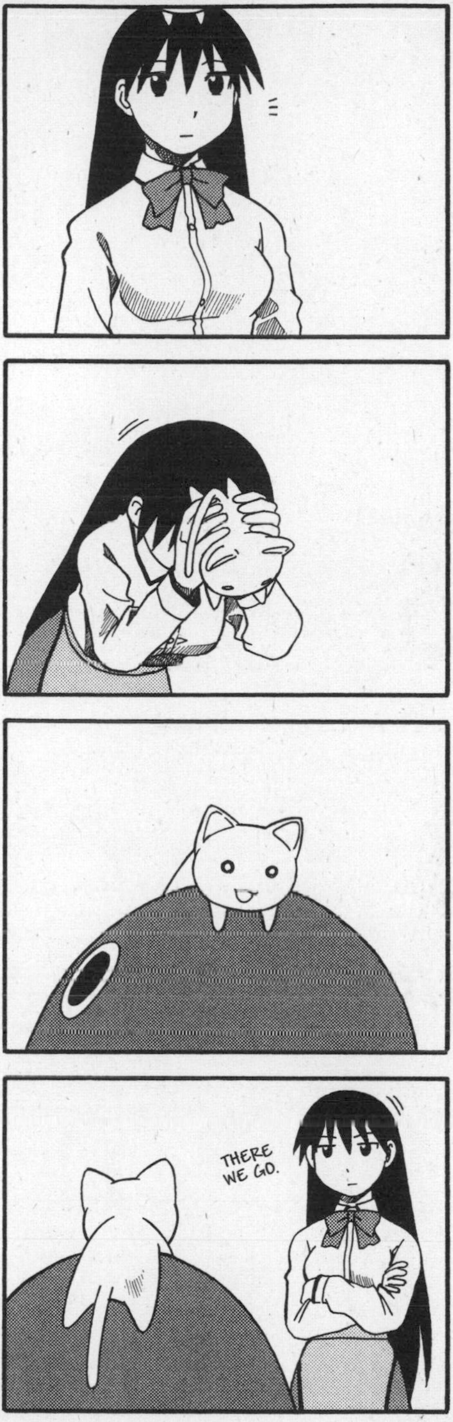
THERE WE GO.

AZUMANGA-DAIOH
055

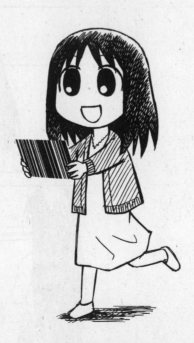

You belong.

DECEMBER PART-1

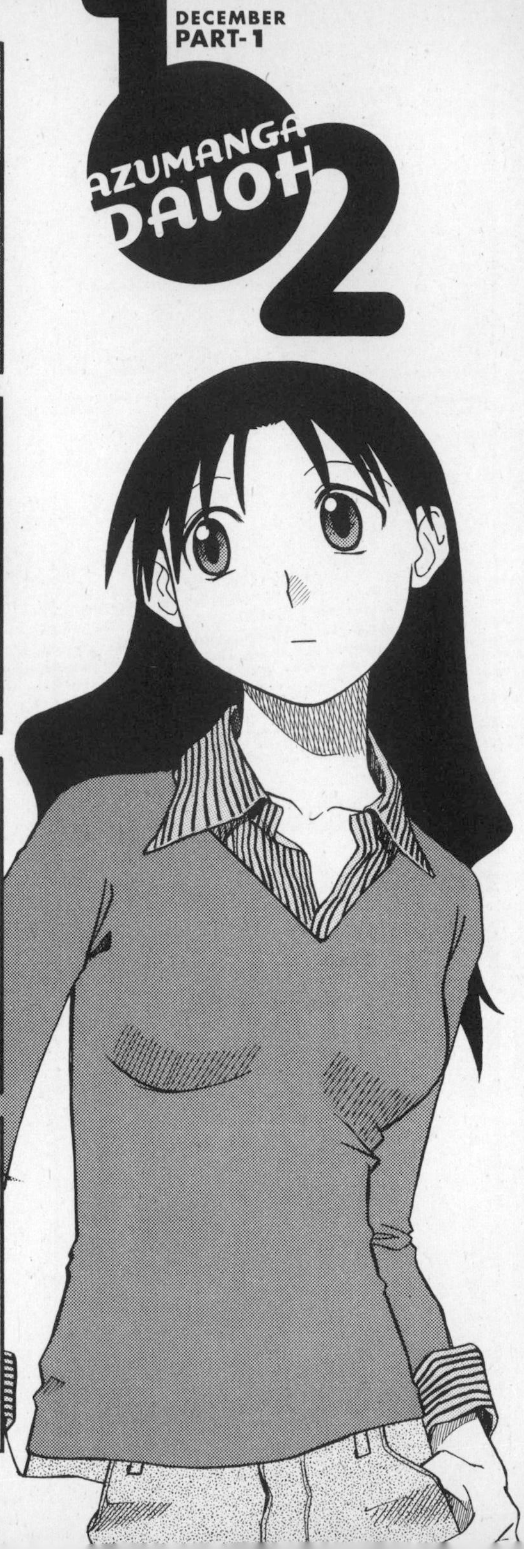
AZUMANGA DAIOH
2

POOR DECISION

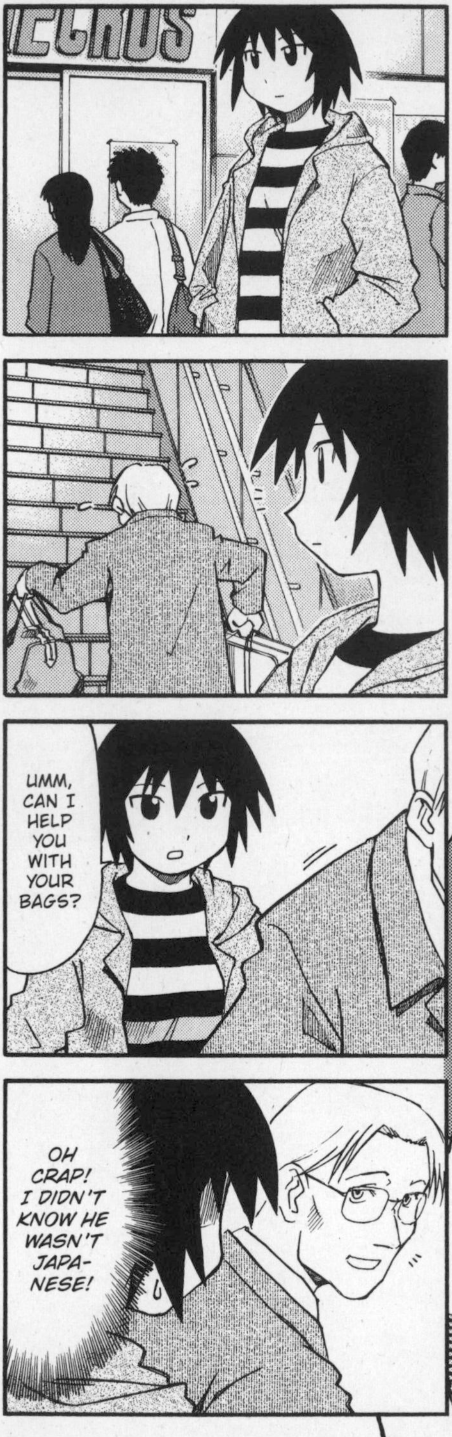
UMM, CAN I HELP YOU WITH YOUR BAGS?
OH CRAP! I DIDN'T KNOW HE WASN'T JAPANESE!

I WANT TO

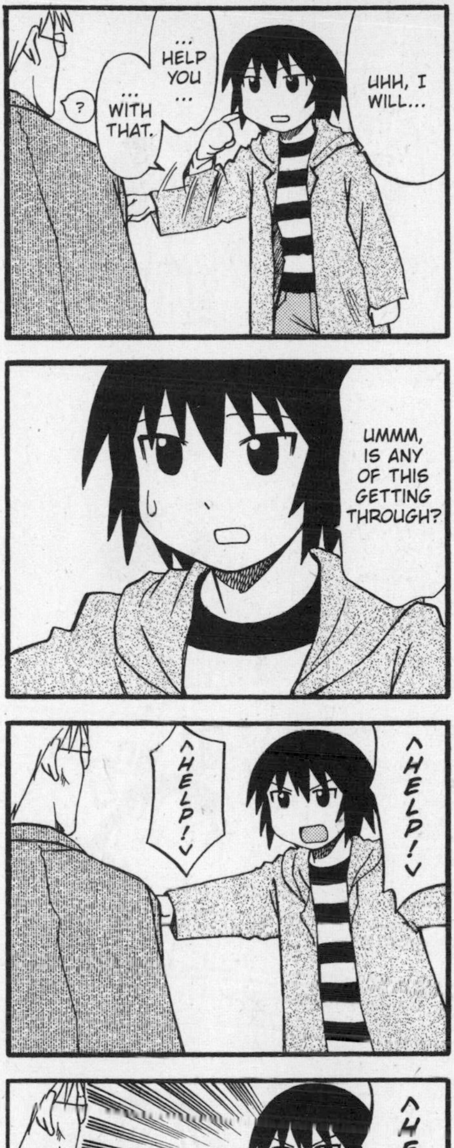
UHH, I WILL...
... HELP YOU ...
... WITH THAT.
?
UMMM, IS ANY OF THIS GETTING THROUGH?
HELP!
HELP!
HELP ME!!

HAVE A NICE TRIP

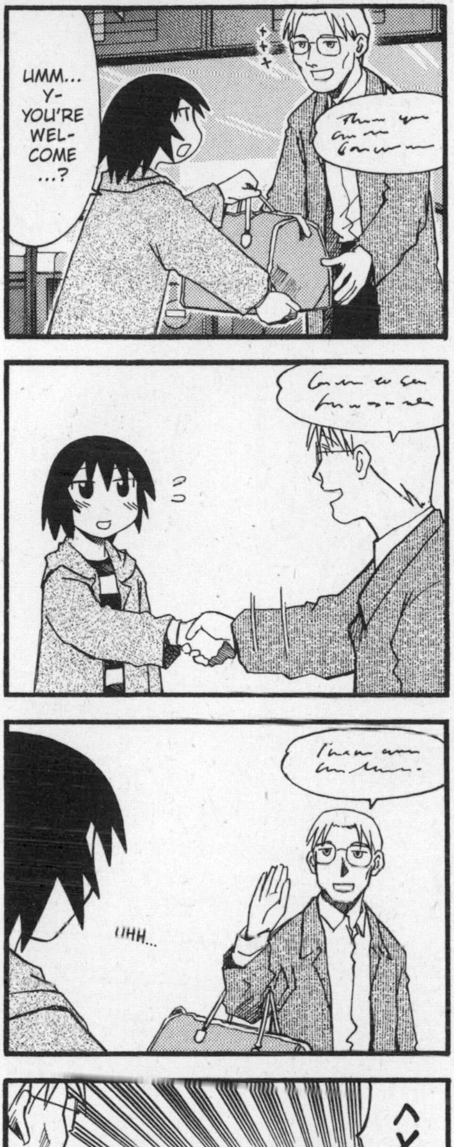
UMM... Y-YOU'RE WEL-COME ...?
UHH...
YAY!!

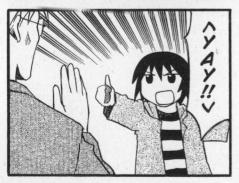

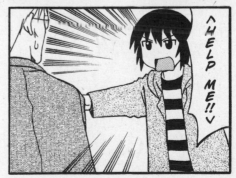

INTERNATIONAL METROPOLIS

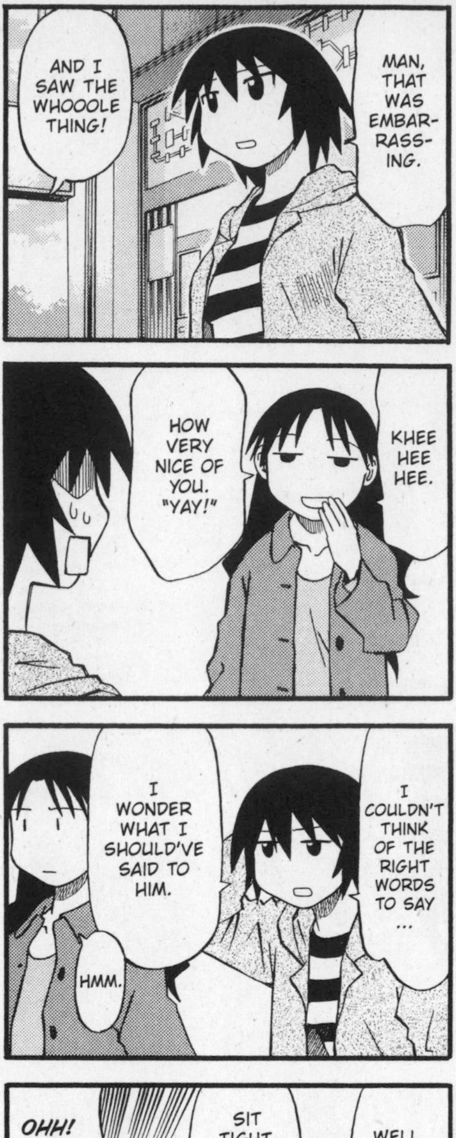
MAN, THAT WAS EMBARRASSING.
AND I SAW THE WHOOOLE THING!
KHEE HEE HEE.
HOW VERY NICE OF YOU. "YAY!"
I COULDN'T THINK OF THE RIGHT WORDS TO SAY ...
I WONDER WHAT I SHOULD'VE SAID TO HIM.
HMM.
WELL, HERE YOU GO. THERE'S ANOTHER SUCKER IN TROUBLE OVER THERE.
SIT TIGHT. I'LL SHOW YOU HOW IT'S DONE.
OHH! LEAD THE WAY, SEN-SEI!!

HIT-AND-RUN

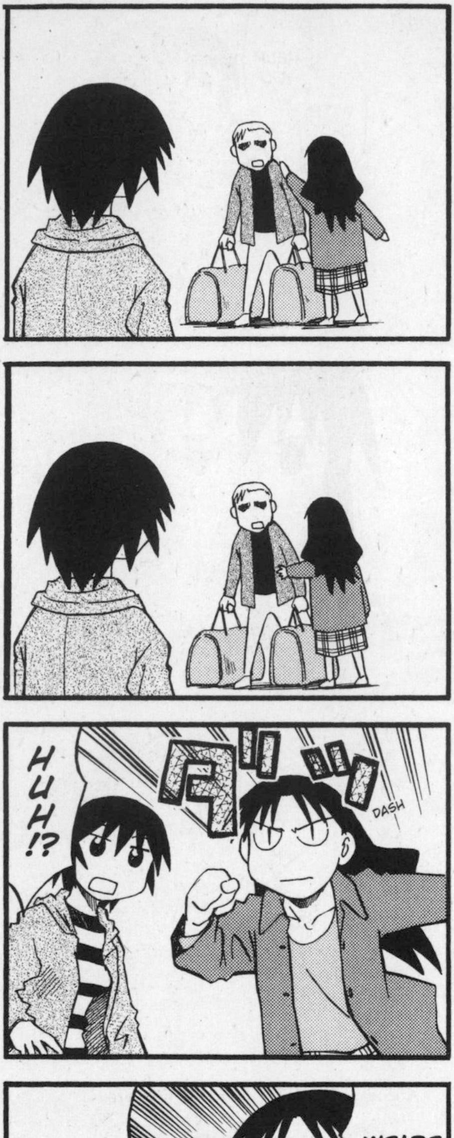
DASH
HUH!?
WE'RE DONE FOR! HE'S GER-MAN!!
EEEH!? YOU'RE JUST GONNA RUN AWAY!?

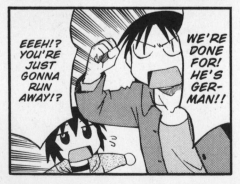

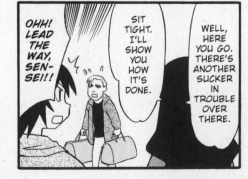

SHOTPUT

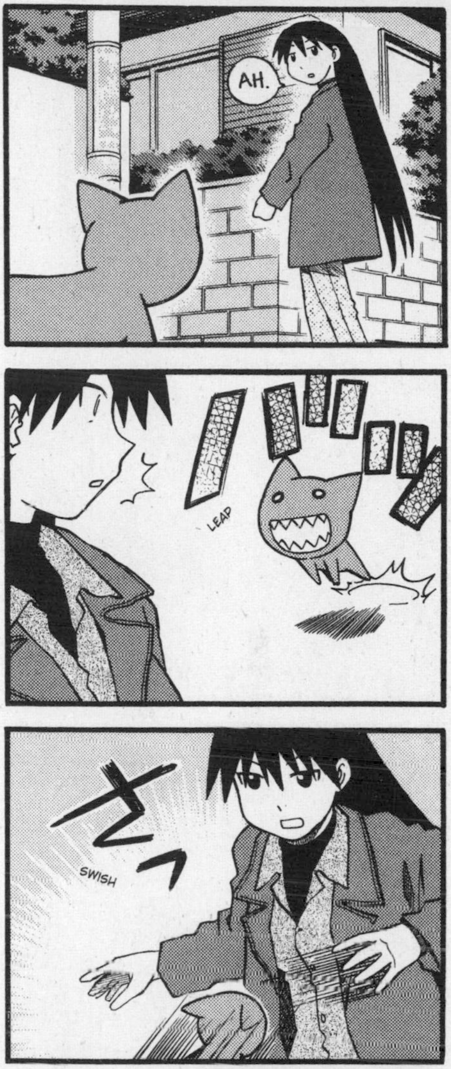
AH.
LEAP
SWISH
OOMPH!!
THUDD

FINISHING BLOW

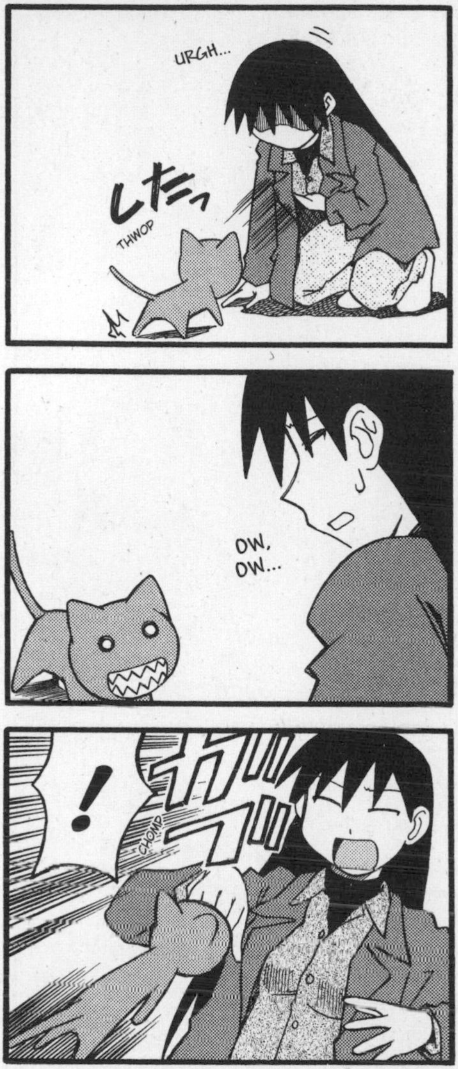
URGH...
THWOP
OW,
OW...
!
CHOMP
!?
SPIN
SPIN

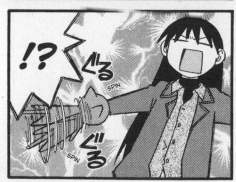

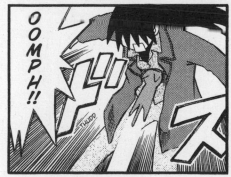

DISCIPLINE

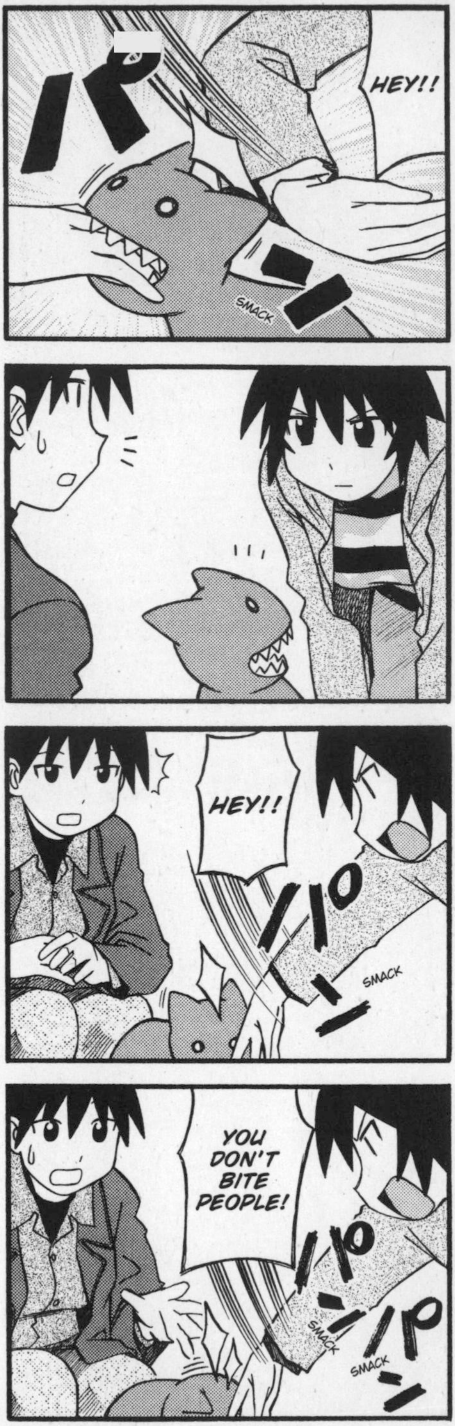
HEY!!
SMACK
HEY!!
SMACK
YOU DON'T BITE PEOPLE!
SMACK
SMACK

YOU DON'T HAVE TO HIT IT

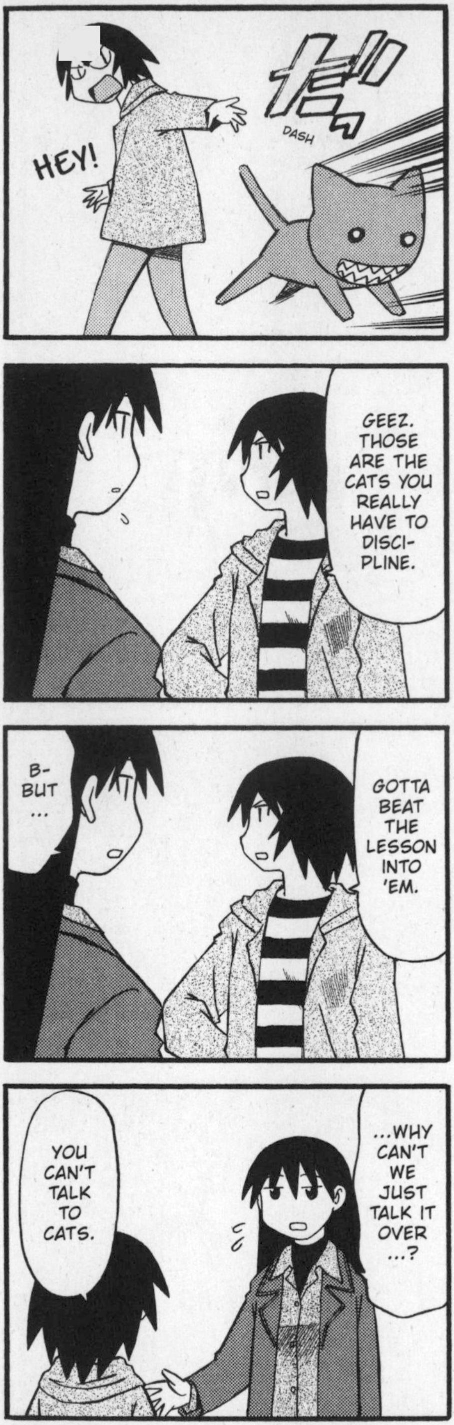
HEY!
DASH
GEEZ. THOSE ARE THE CATS YOU REALLY HAVE TO DISCI-PLINE.
GOTTA BEAT THE LESSON INTO 'EM.
B-BUT...
...WHY CAN'T WE JUST TALK IT OVER...?
YOU CAN'T TALK TO CATS.

GIFT SEASON

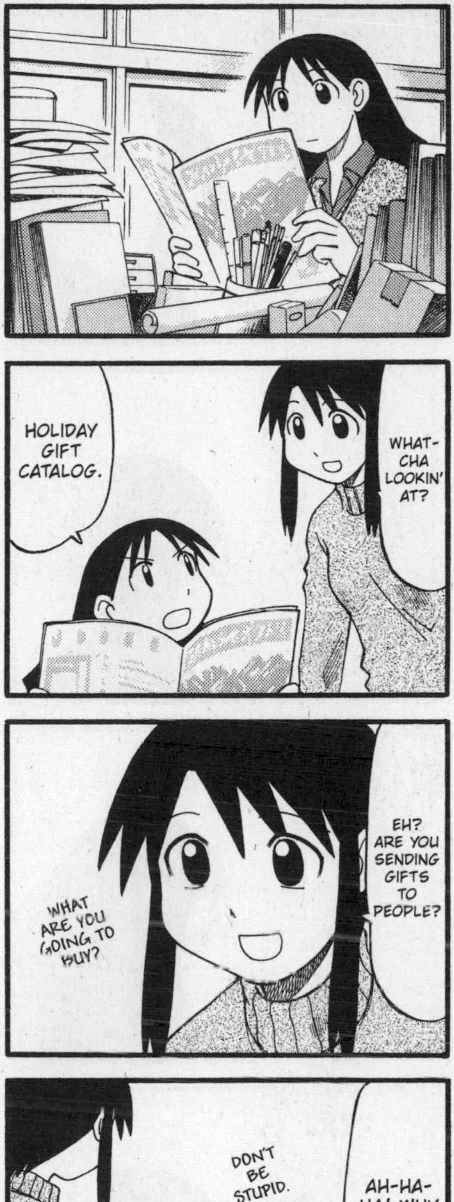
WHAT-CHA LOOKIN' AT?
HOLIDAY GIFT CATALOG.
EH? ARE YOU SENDING GIFTS TO PEOPLE?
WHAT ARE YOU GOING TO BUY?
AH-HA-HA! WHY WOULD I BE THE ONE BUYING GIFTS?
DON'T BE STUPID.
HUH?

WARMTH

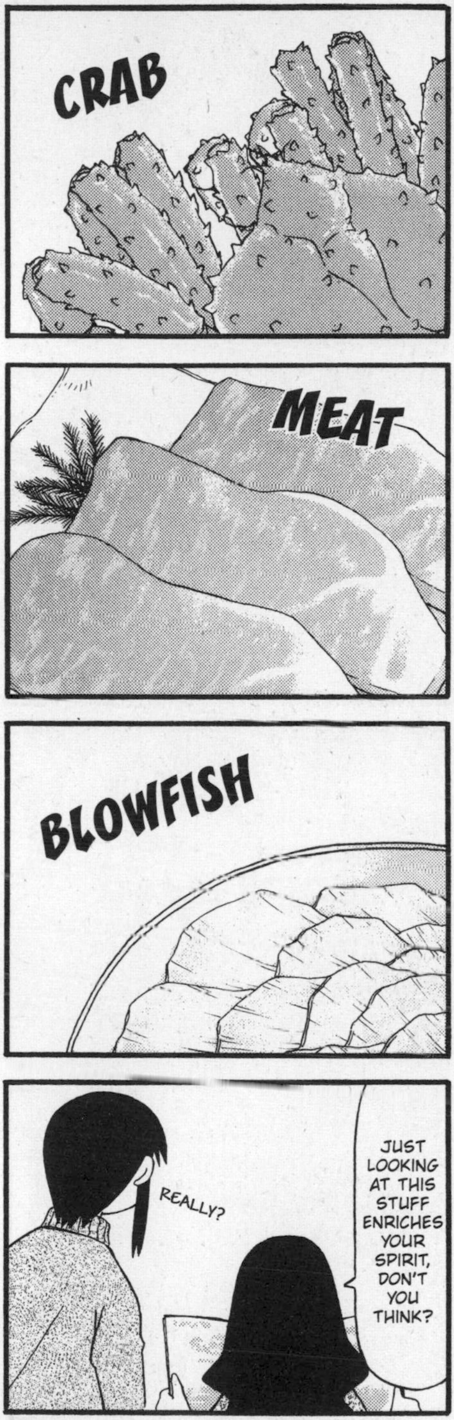
CRAB
MEAT
BLOWFISH
JUST LOOKING AT THIS STUFF ENRICHES YOUR SPIRIT, DON'T YOU THINK?
REALLY?

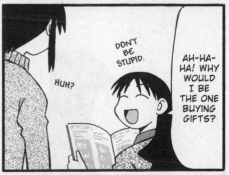

OPEN YOUR EYES

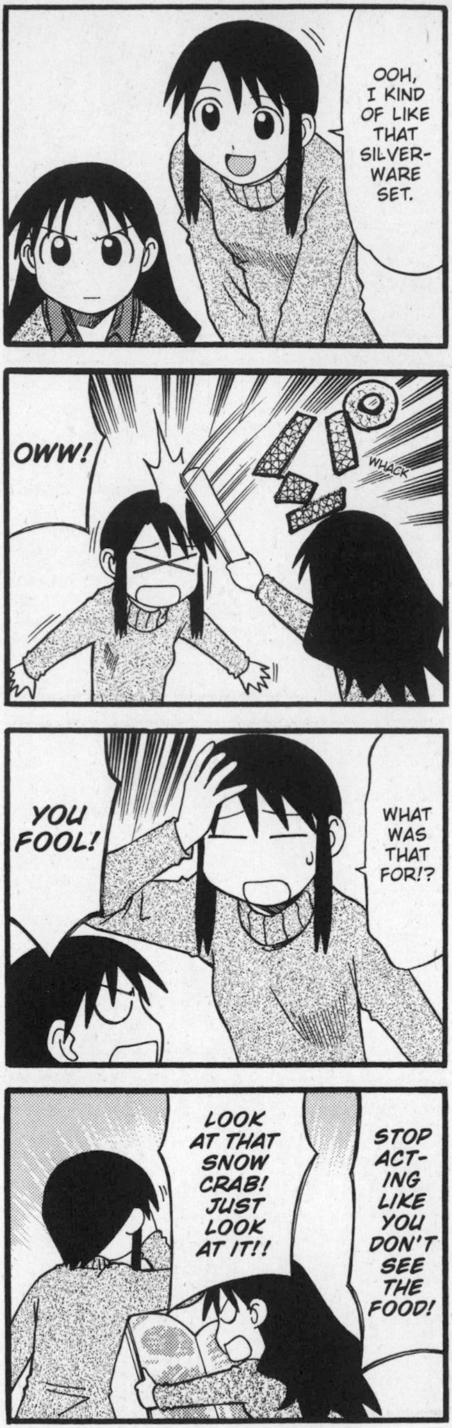
OOH, I KIND OF LIKE THAT SILVER-WARE SET.
OWW!
WHACK
WHAT WAS THAT FOR!?
YOU FOOL!
STOP ACT-ING LIKE YOU DON'T SEE THE FOOD!
LOOK AT THAT SNOW CRAB! JUST LOOK AT IT!!

THE BEEF

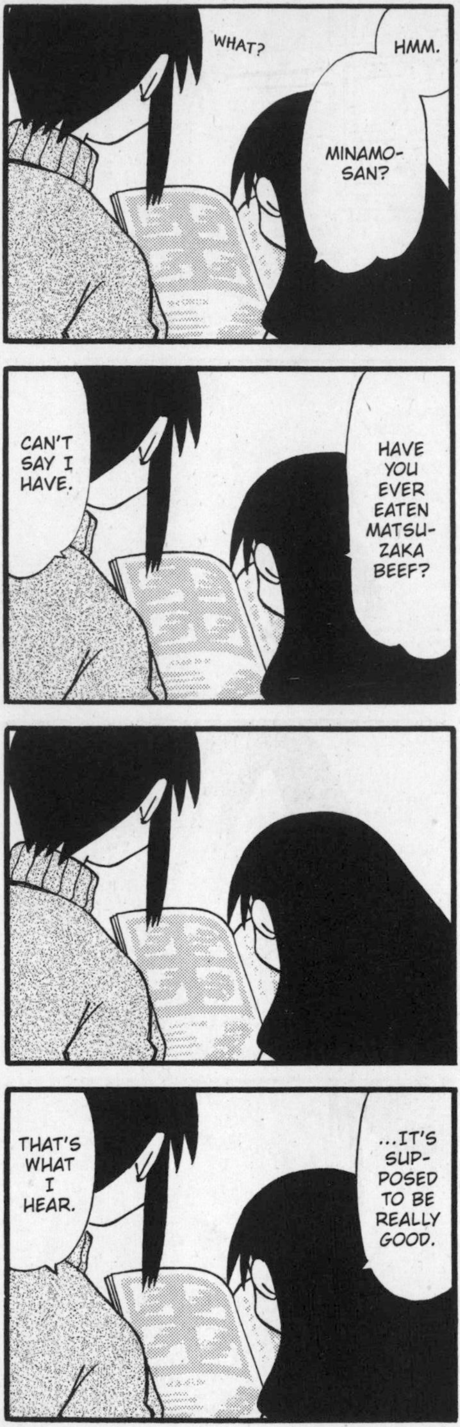
HMM.
MINAMO-SAN?
WHAT?
HAVE YOU EVER EATEN MATSU-ZAKA BEEF?
CAN'T SAY I HAVE.
...IT'S SUP-POSED TO BE REALLY GOOD.
THAT'S WHAT I HEAR.

RAGE

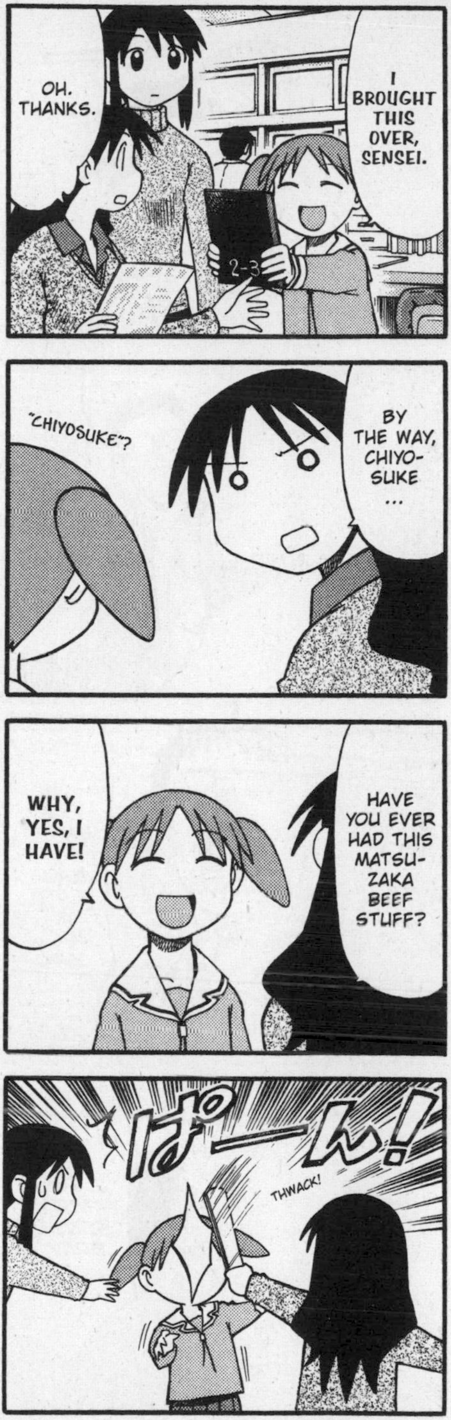
I BROUGHT THIS OVER, SENSEI.
OH. THANKS.
BY THE WAY, CHIYOSUKE ...
"CHIYOSUKE"?
HAVE YOU EVER HAD THIS MATSUZAKA BEEF STUFF?
WHY, YES, I HAVE!
ぱーん!
THWACK!

STOP PLAYING COY

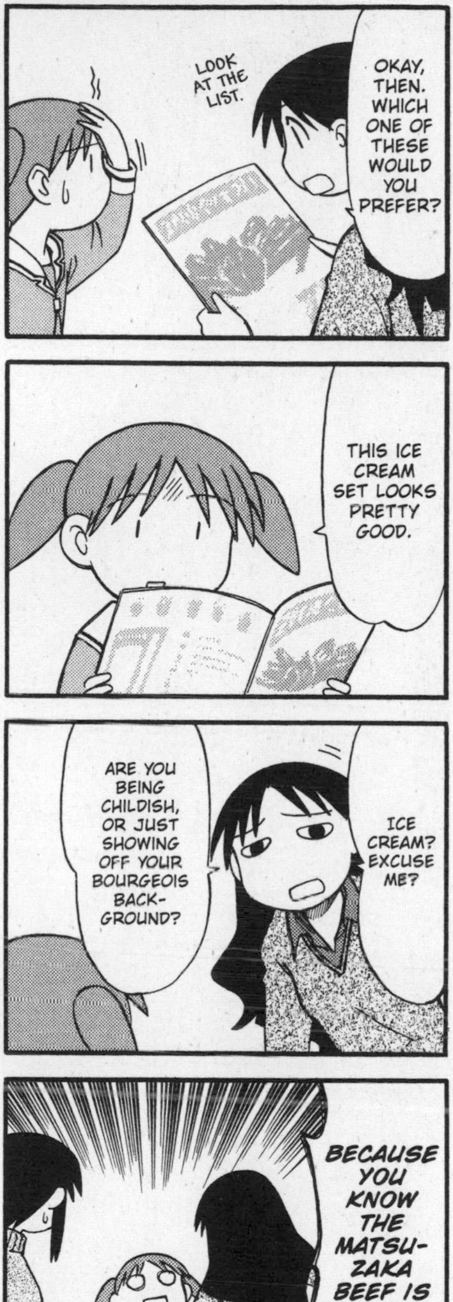
OKAY, THEN. WHICH ONE OF THESE WOULD YOU PREFER?
LOOK AT THE LIST.
THIS ICE CREAM SET LOOKS PRETTY GOOD.
ICE CREAM? EXCUSE ME?
ARE YOU BEING CHILDISH, OR JUST SHOWING OFF YOUR BOURGEOIS BACKGROUND?
BECAUSE YOU KNOW THE MATSUZAKA BEEF IS BETTER, RIGHT!?

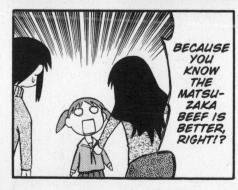

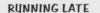

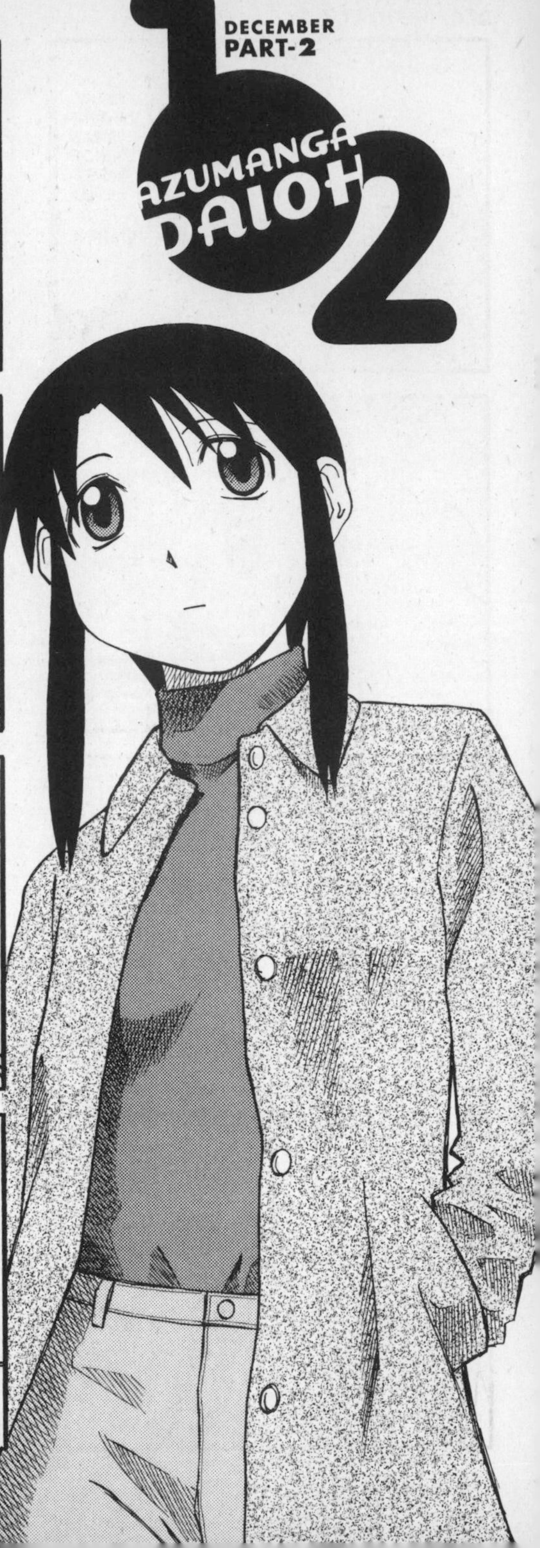
DECEMBER
PART-2
AZUMANGA DAIOH
2

RUNNING LATE

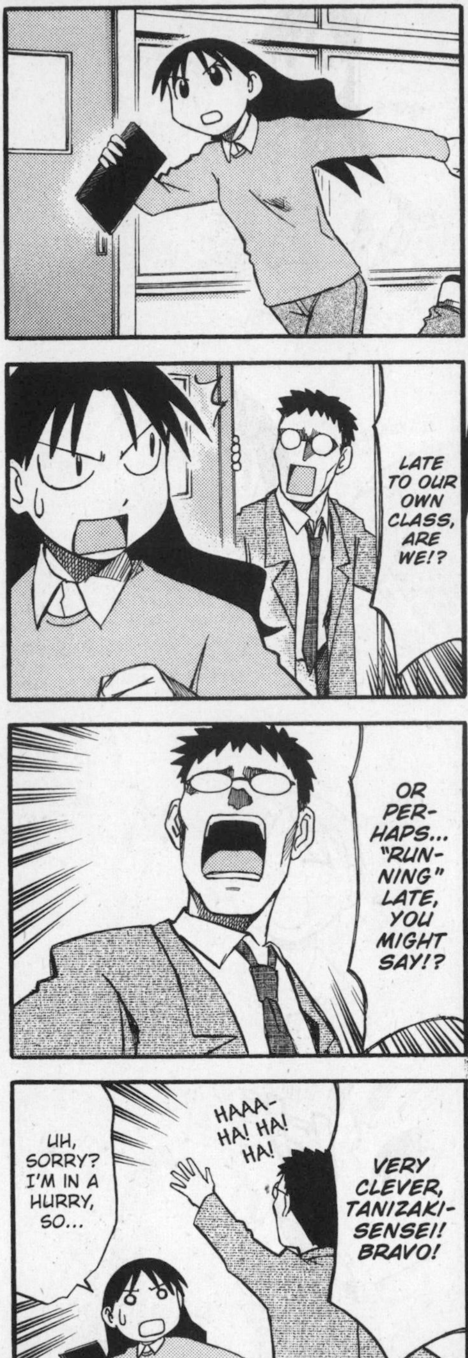
LATE TO OUR OWN CLASS, ARE WE!?
OR PERHAPS... "RUNNING" LATE, YOU MIGHT SAY!?
VERY CLEVER, TANIZAKI-SENSEI! BRAVO!
HAAA-HA! HA! HA!
UH, SORRY? I'M IN A HURRY, SO...

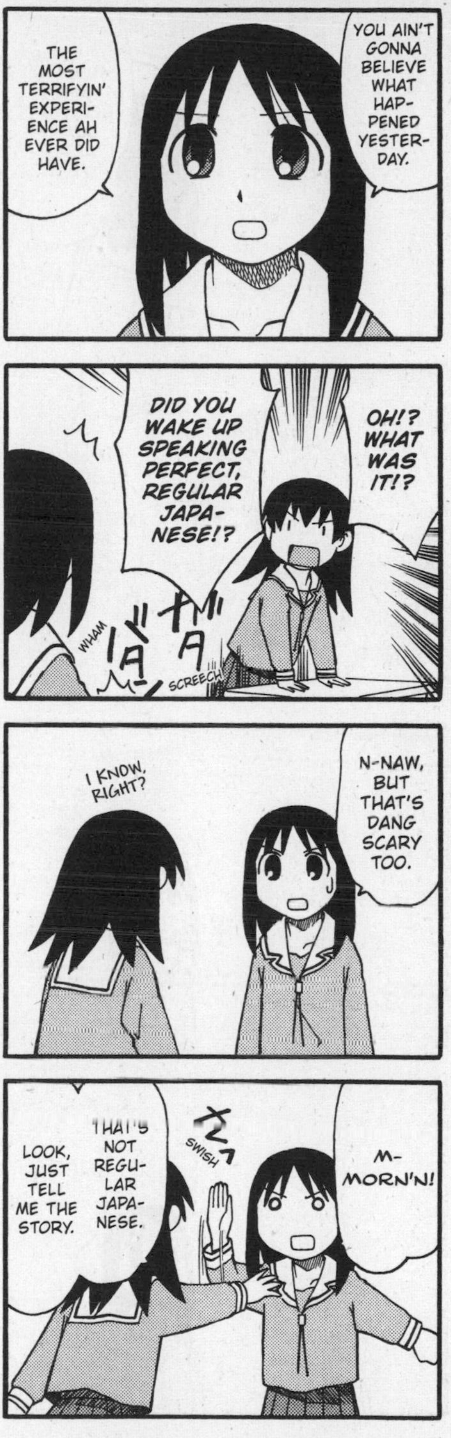
YOU AIN'T GONNA BELIEVE WHAT HAP-PENED YESTER-DAY.
THE MOST TERRIFYIN' EXPERI-ENCE AH EVER DID HAVE.
OH!? WHAT WAS IT!?
DID YOU WAKE UP SPEAKING PERFECT, REGULAR JAPA-NESE!?
WHAM
SCREECH
N-NAW, BUT THAT'S DANG SCARY TOO.
I KNOW, RIGHT?
M-MORN'N!
SWISH
THAT'S NOT REGU-LAR JAPA-NESE.
LOOK, JUST TELL ME THE STORY.

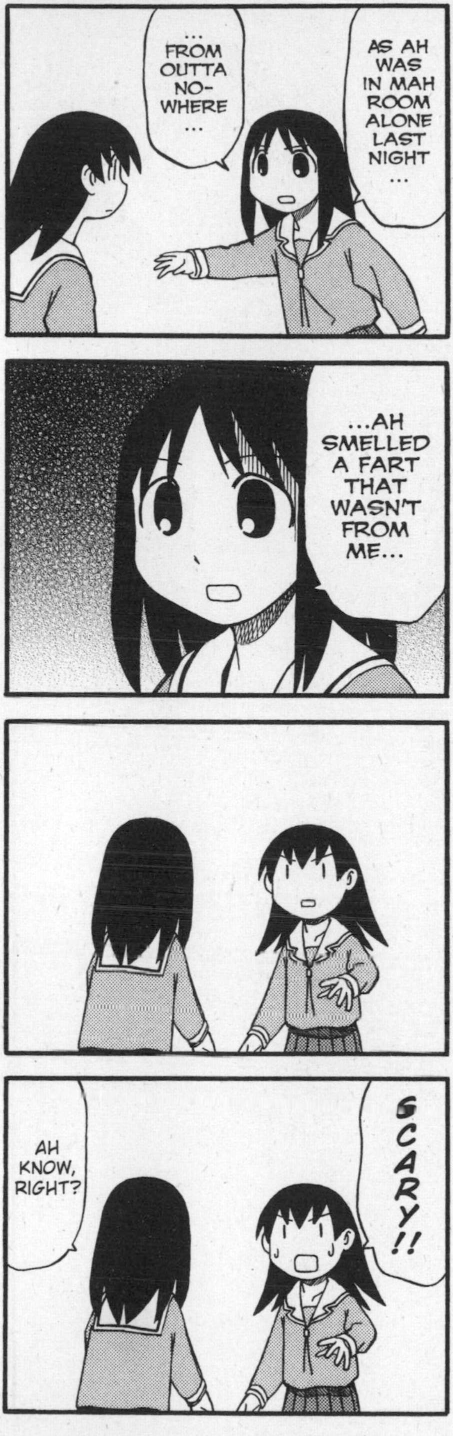
AS AH WAS IN MAH ROOM ALONE LAST NIGHT ...
... FROM OUTTA NO-WHERE ...
...AH SMELLED A FART THAT WASN'T FROM ME...
SCARY!!
AH KNOW, RIGHT?

GONNA DRAW

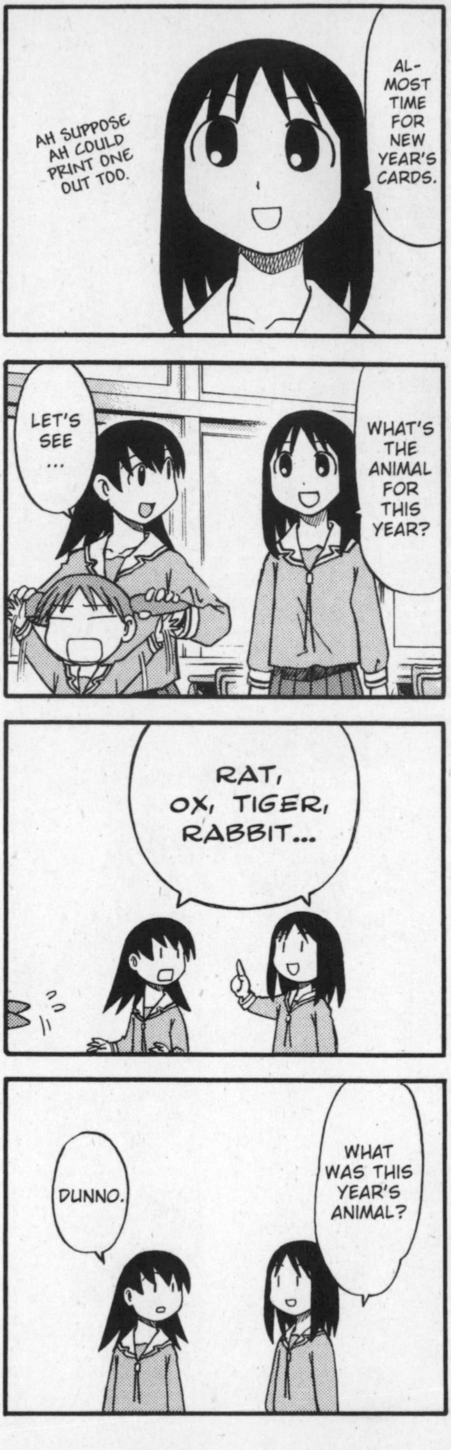
AL-MOST TIME FOR NEW YEAR'S CARDS.
AH SUPPOSE AH COULD PRINT ONE OUT TOO.
WHAT'S THE ANIMAL FOR THIS YEAR?
LET'S SEE ...
RAT, OX, TIGER, RABBIT...
WHAT WAS THIS YEAR'S ANIMAL?
DUNNO.

UMM

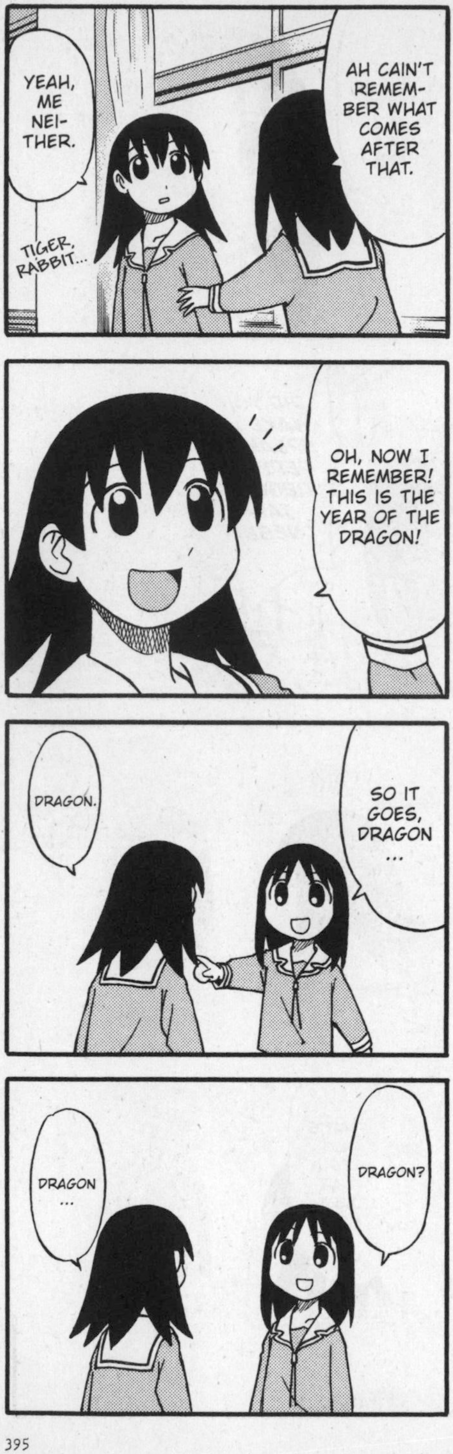
AH CAIN'T REMEM-BER WHAT COMES AFTER THAT.
YEAH, ME NEI-THER.
TIGER, RABBIT...
OH, NOW I REMEMBER! THIS IS THE YEAR OF THE DRAGON!
SO IT GOES, DRAGON ...
DRAGON.
DRAGON?
DRAGON ...

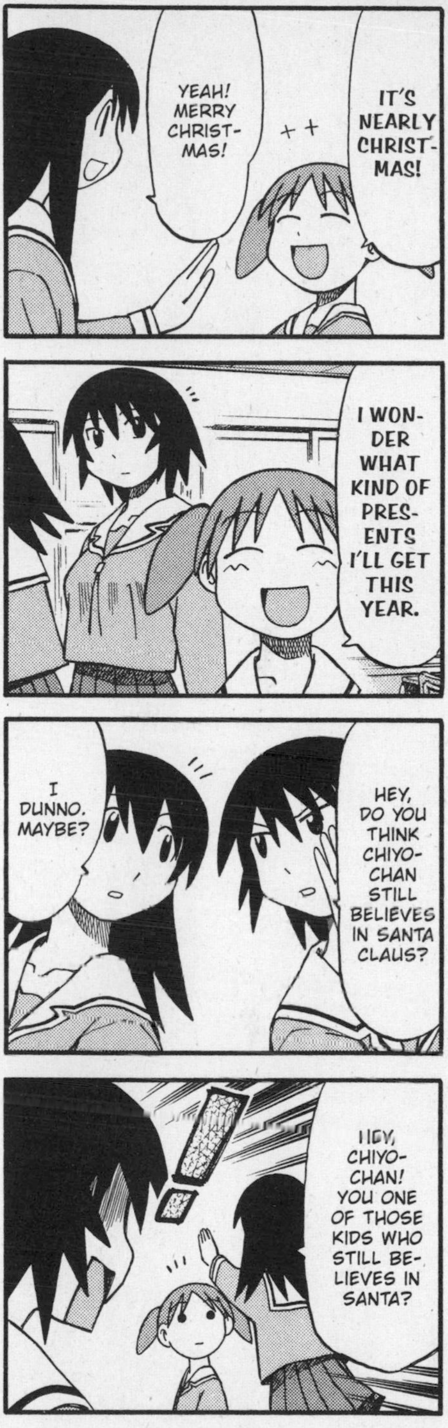
IT'S NEARLY CHRISTMAS!
YEAH! MERRY CHRISTMAS!
I WONDER WHAT KIND OF PRESENTS I'LL GET THIS YEAR.
HEY, DO YOU THINK CHIYO-CHAN STILL BELIEVES IN SANTA CLAUS?
I DUNNO. MAYBE?
HEY, CHIYO-CHAN! YOU ONE OF THOSE KIDS WHO STILL BELIEVES IN SANTA?

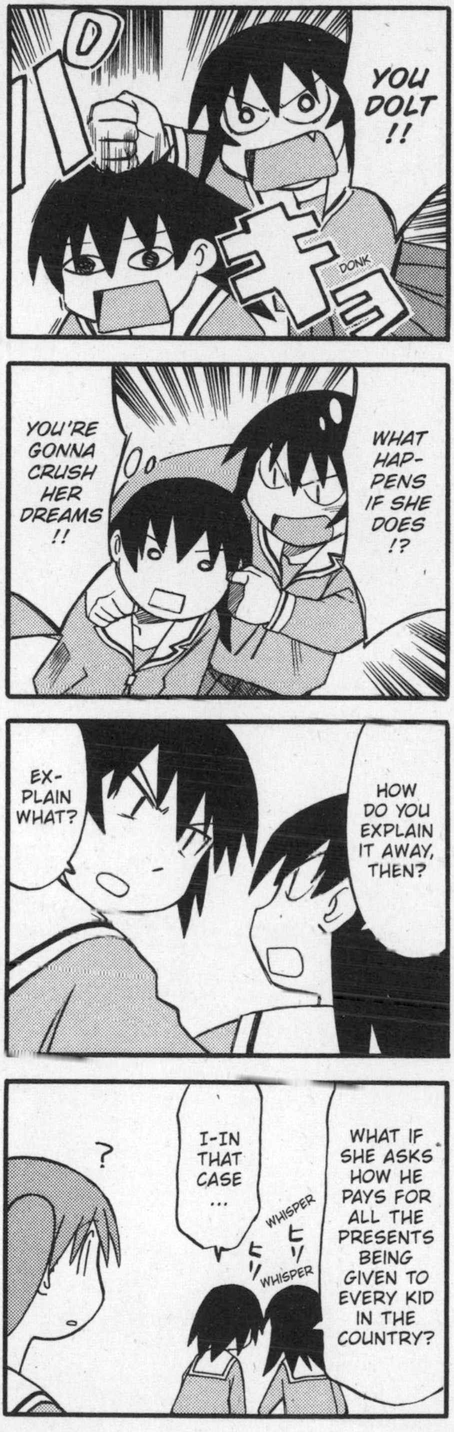
YOU DOLT!!
DONK
WHAT HAPPENS IF SHE DOES!?
YOU'RE GONNA CRUSH HER DREAMS!!
HOW DO YOU EXPLAIN IT AWAY, THEN?
EXPLAIN WHAT?
WHAT IF SHE ASKS HOW HE PAYS FOR ALL THE PRESENTS BEING GIVEN TO EVERY KID IN THE COUNTRY?
WHISPER
WHISPER
I-IN THAT CASE ...
?

SANTA

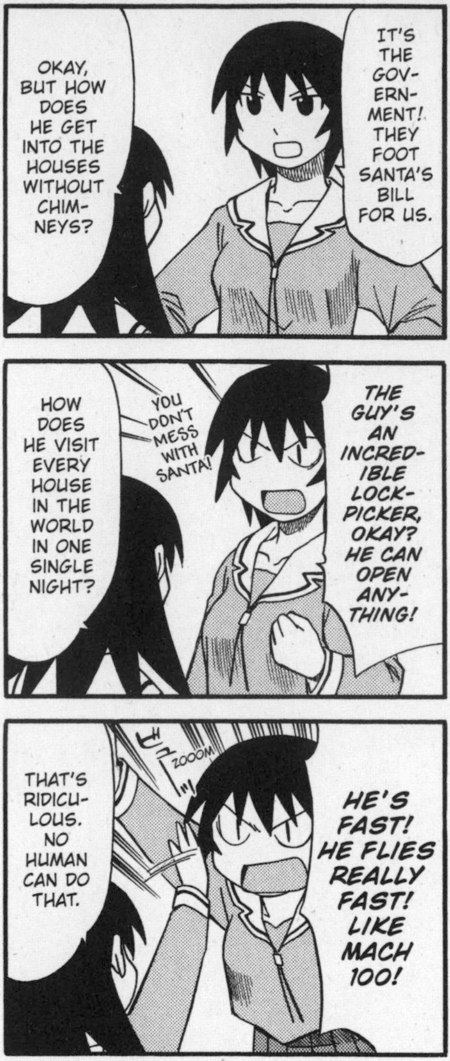
IT'S THE GOVERNMENT! THEY FOOT SANTA'S BILL FOR US.
OKAY, BUT HOW DOES HE GET INTO THE HOUSES WITHOUT CHIMNEYS?
YOU DON'T MESS WITH SANTA!
THE GUY'S AN INCREDIBLE LOCK-PICKER, OKAY? HE CAN OPEN ANYTHING!
HOW DOES HE VISIT EVERY HOUSE IN THE WORLD IN ONE SINGLE NIGHT?
ZOOOM
HE'S FAST! HE FLIES REALLY FAST! LIKE MACH 100!
THAT'S RIDICULOUS. NO HUMAN CAN DO THAT.
THAT'S BECAUSE SANTA ISN'T HUMAN!!
WHAT IS HE, AN ALIEN!?
UM, IT'S OKAY, I ALREADY KNOW...

TRUE IDENTITY

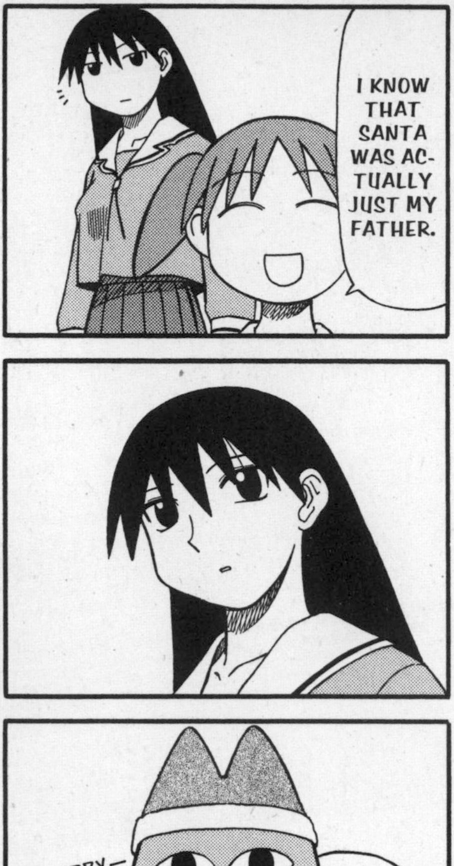
I KNOW THAT SANTA WAS ACTUALLY JUST MY FATHER.
MERRRRY—
WHAT'S WRONG?

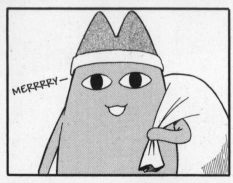

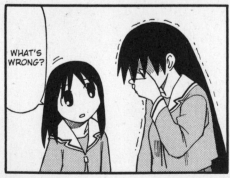

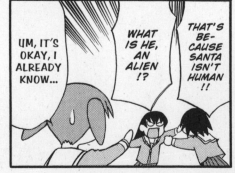

INCREDIBLE SANTA

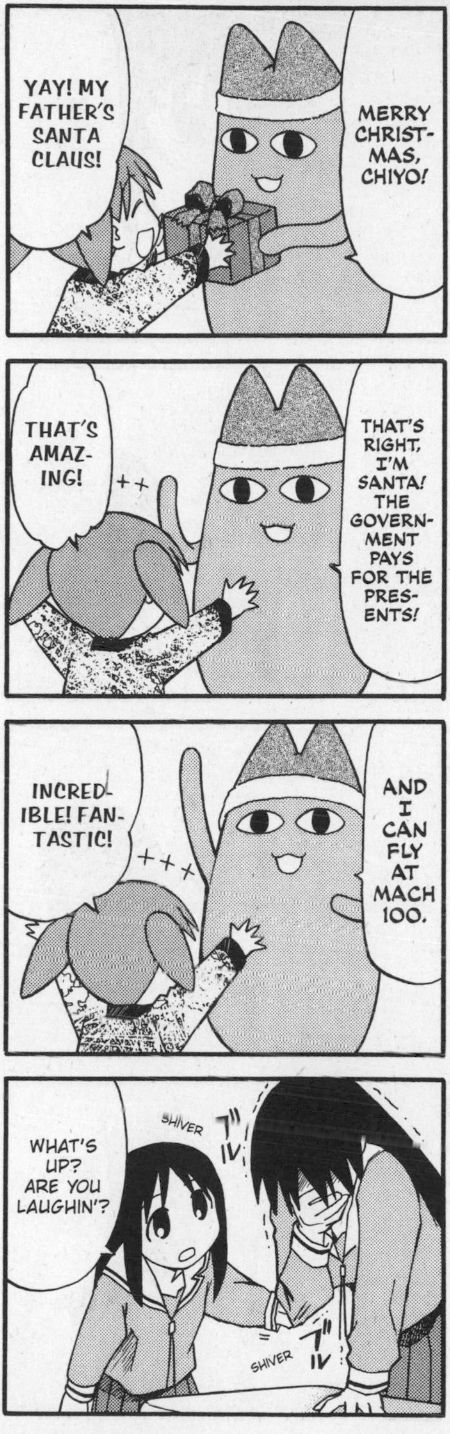
MERRY CHRISTMAS, CHIYO!
YAY! MY FATHER'S SANTA CLAUS!
THAT'S RIGHT, I'M SANTA! THE GOVERNMENT PAYS FOR THE PRESENTS!
THAT'S AMAZING!
AND I CAN FLY AT MACH 100.
INCREDIBLE! FANTASTIC!
SHIVER
WHAT'S UP? ARE YOU LAUGHIN'?
SHIVER

WISH

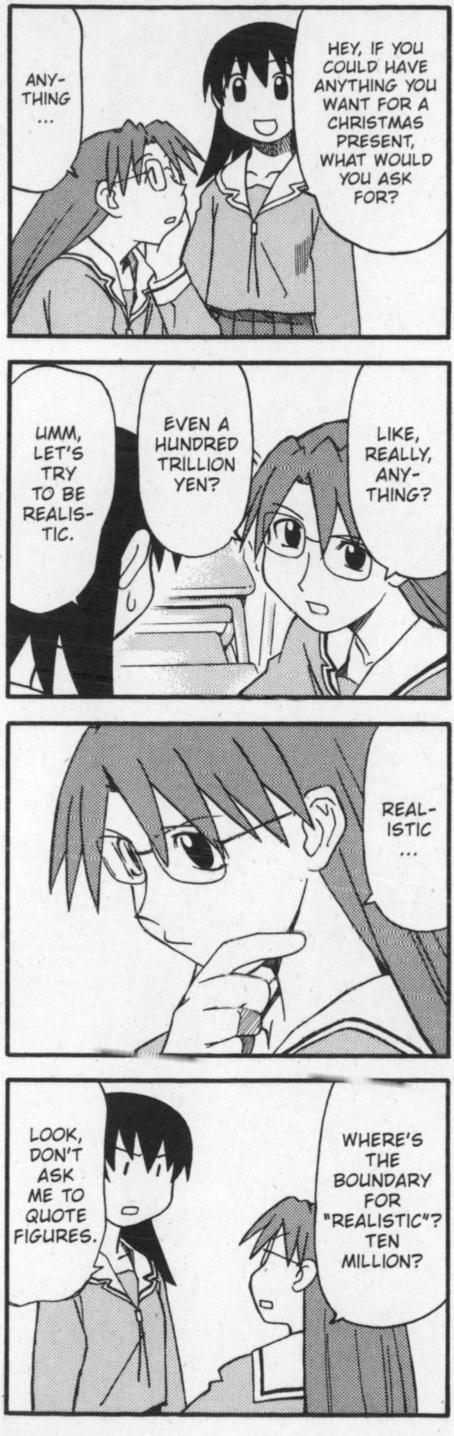
HEY, IF YOU COULD HAVE ANYTHING YOU WANT FOR A CHRISTMAS PRESENT, WHAT WOULD YOU ASK FOR?
ANYTHING ...
LIKE, REALLY, ANYTHING?
EVEN A HUNDRED TRILLION YEN?
UMM, LET'S TRY TO BE REALISTIC.
REALISTIC ...
WHERE'S THE BOUNDARY FOR "REALISTIC"? TEN MILLION?
LOOK, DON'T ASK ME TO QUOTE FIGURES.

DESIRE

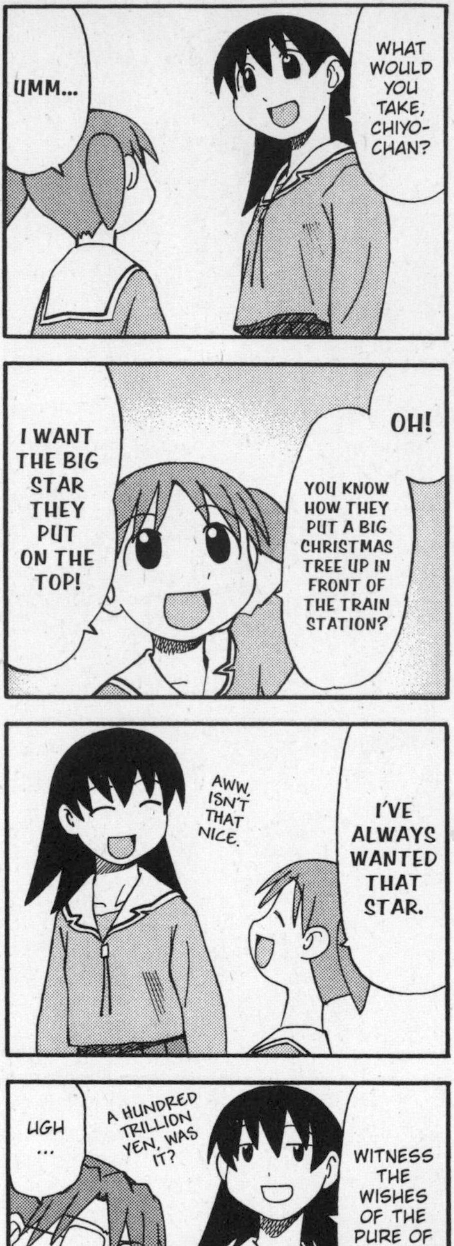
WHAT WOULD YOU TAKE, CHIYO-CHAN?
UMM...
OH!
YOU KNOW HOW THEY PUT A BIG CHRISTMAS TREE UP IN FRONT OF THE TRAIN STATION?
I WANT THE BIG STAR THEY PUT ON THE TOP!
I'VE ALWAYS WANTED THAT STAR.
AWW, ISN'T THAT NICE.
WITNESS THE WISHES OF THE PURE OF HEART, YOMI.
A HUNDRED TRILLION YEN, WAS IT?
UGH ...

DO THEY EXIST?

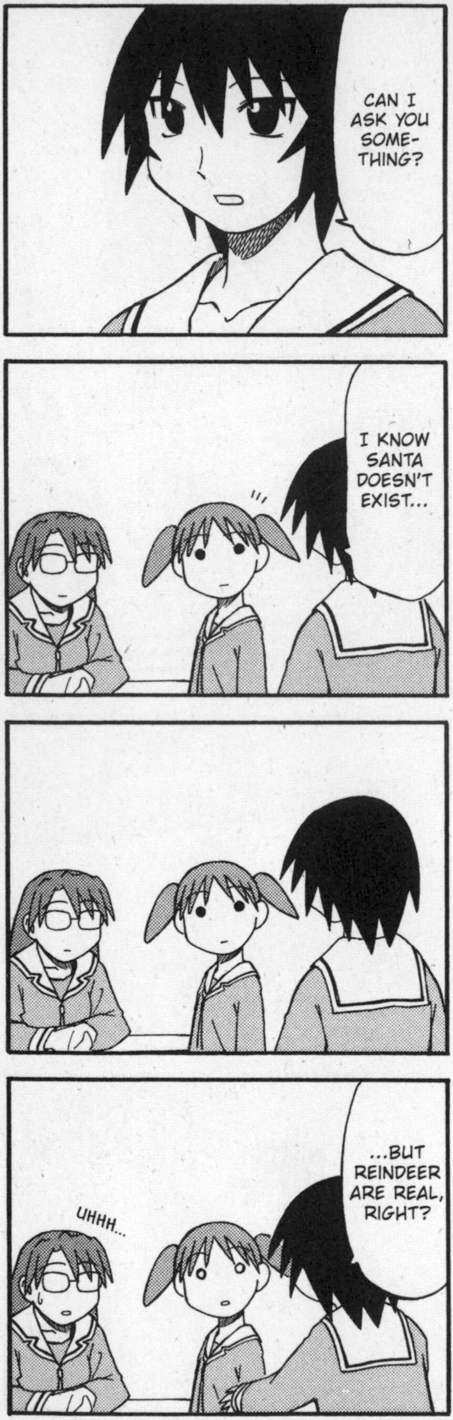
CAN I ASK YOU SOMETHING?
I KNOW SANTA DOESN'T EXIST...
...BUT REINDEER ARE REAL, RIGHT?
UHHH...

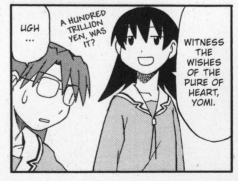

REINDEER

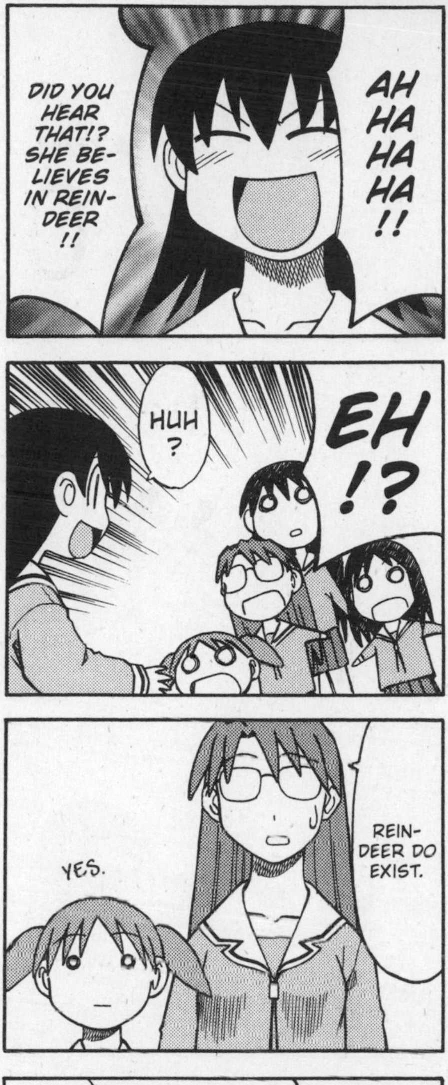
AH HA HA HA!!
DID YOU HEAR THAT!? SHE BELIEVES IN REINDEER!!
EH!?
HUH?
REINDEER DO EXIST.
YES.
YOU GOTTA BE KIDDING! I'VE NEVER SEEN A FLYING DEER BEFORE!!
YOU GUYS CAN'T FOOL ME!
UWAH! SHE'S SO DENSE...

DON'T STARE AT ME

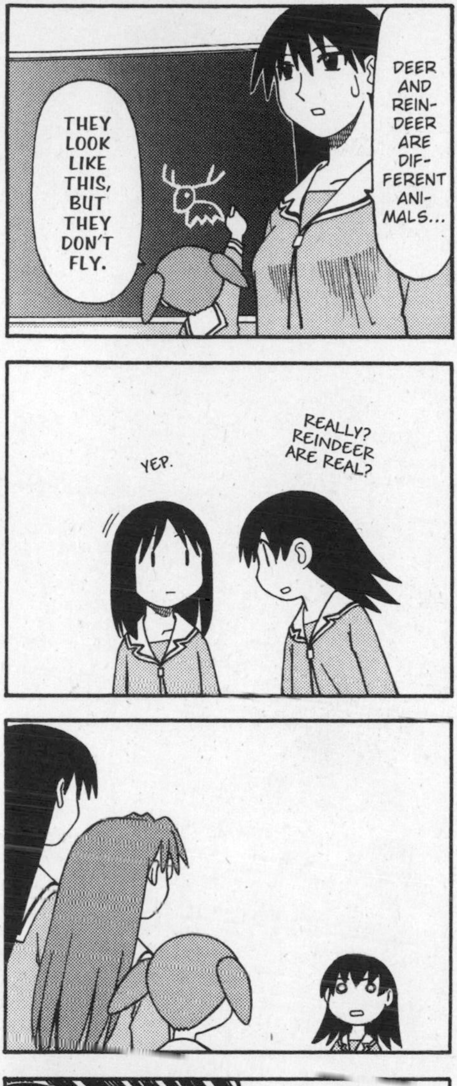
DEER AND REINDEER ARE DIFFERENT ANIMALS...
THEY LOOK LIKE THIS, BUT THEY DON'T FLY.
REALLY? REINDEER ARE REAL?
YEP.
WH-WHAT? WHAT'S YOUR PROBLEM!! I'M NOT STUPID!! I'M NOT!!

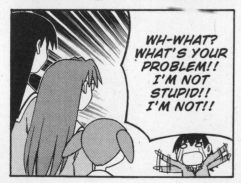

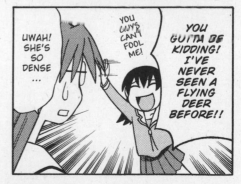

AZUMANGA-DAIOH
073

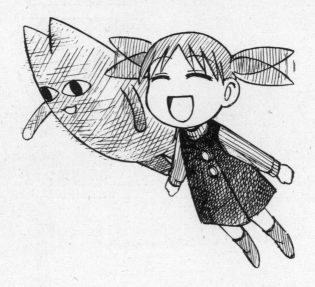

You belong.

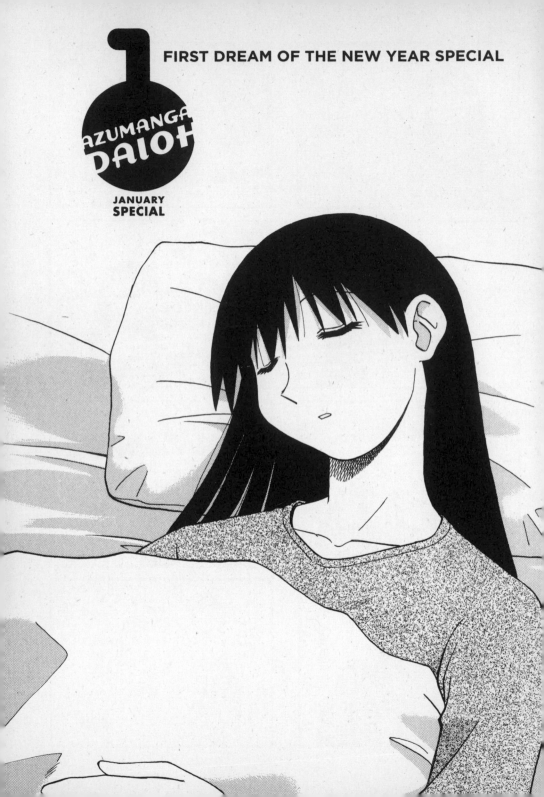

FIRST DREAM OF THE NEW YEAR SPECIAL

AZUMANGA DAIOH

JANUARY
SPECIAL

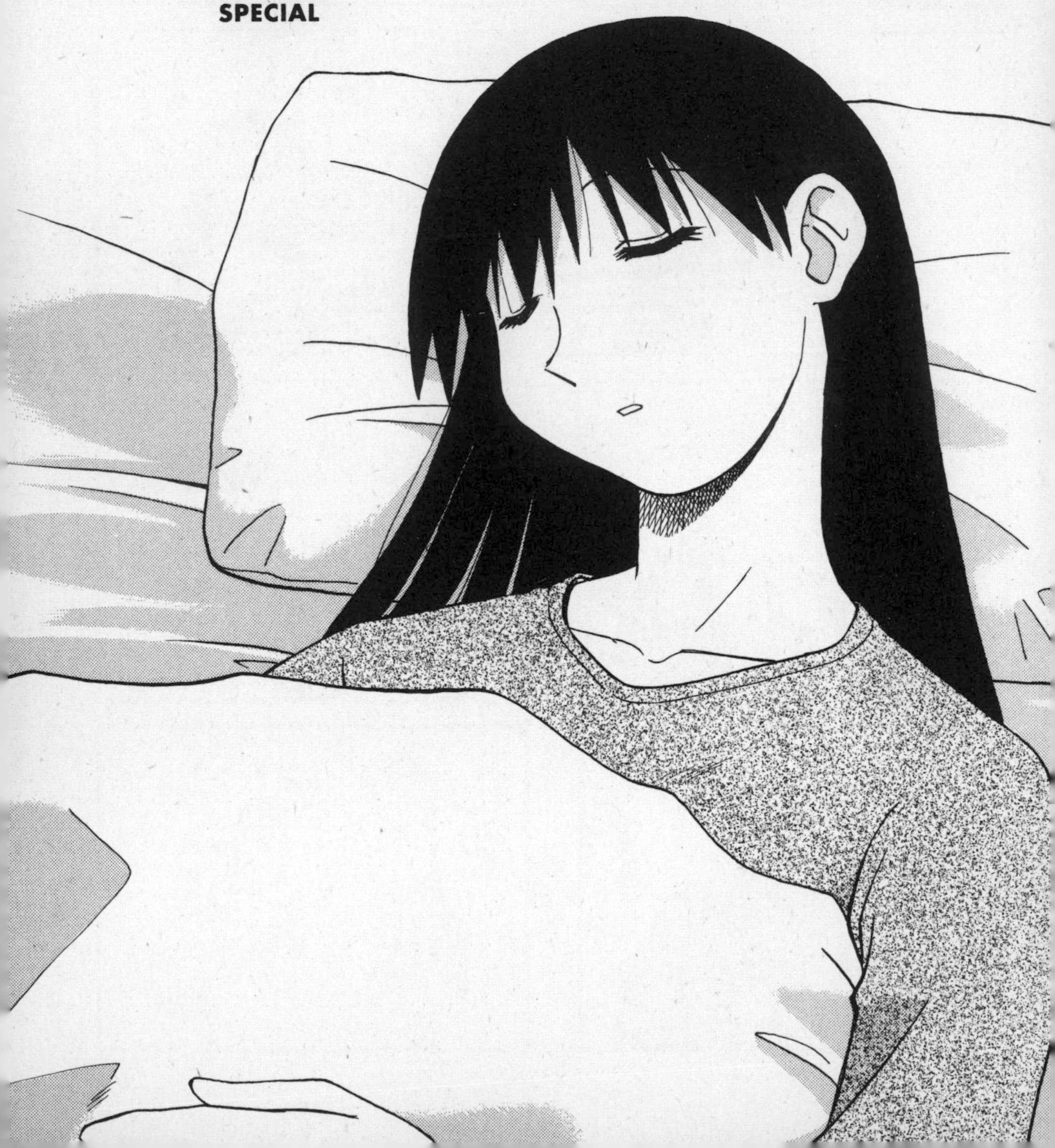

WELCOME

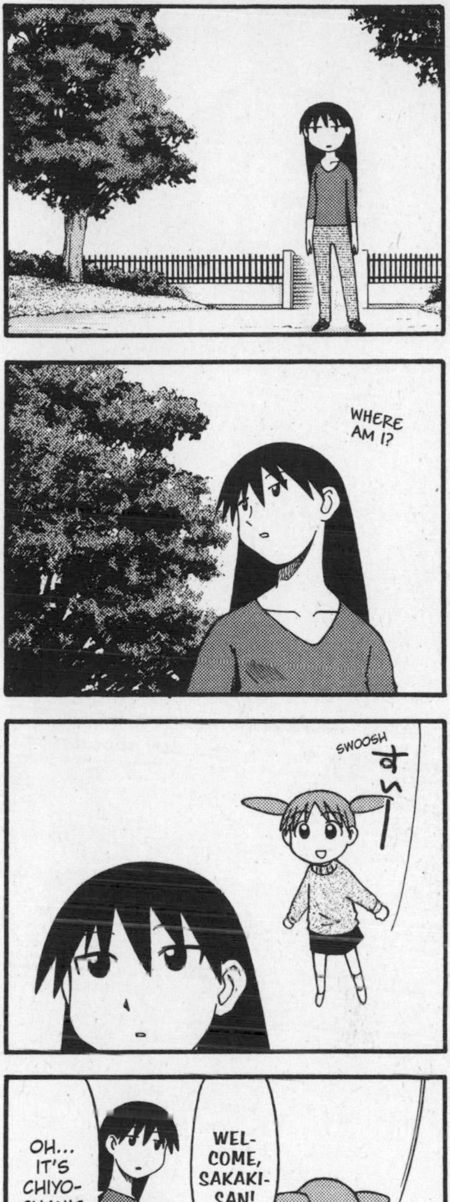
WHERE AM I?
SWOOSH
すいー
WEL-COME, SAKAKI-SAN!
OH... IT'S CHIYO-CHAN'S HOUSE.

WHO?

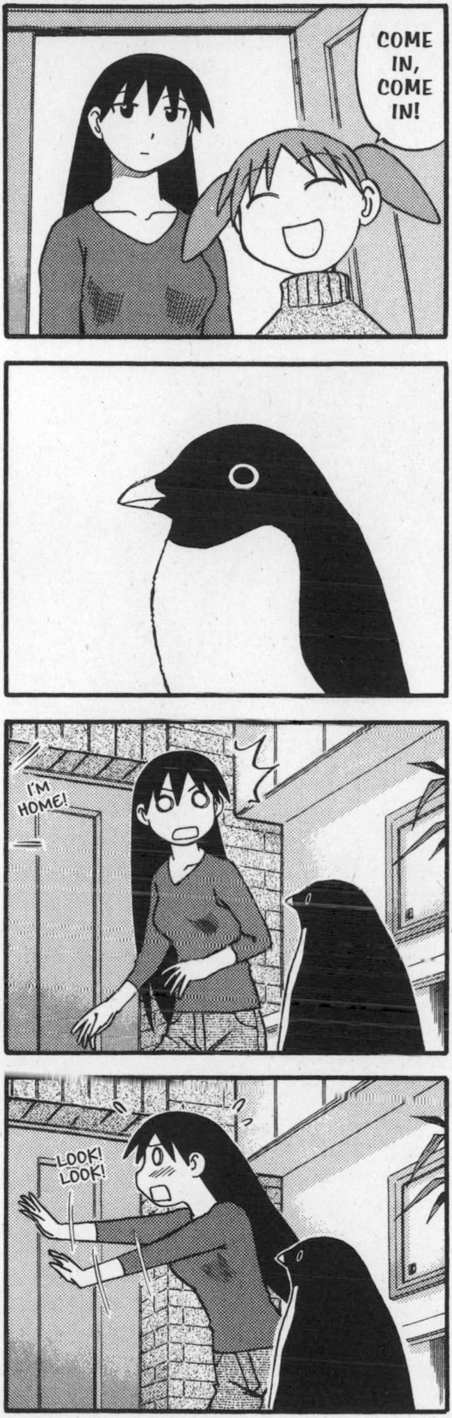
COME IN, COME IN!
I'M HOME!
LOOK! LOOK!

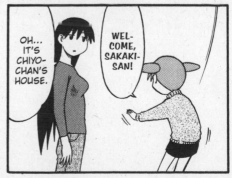

GOTTA CLEAN

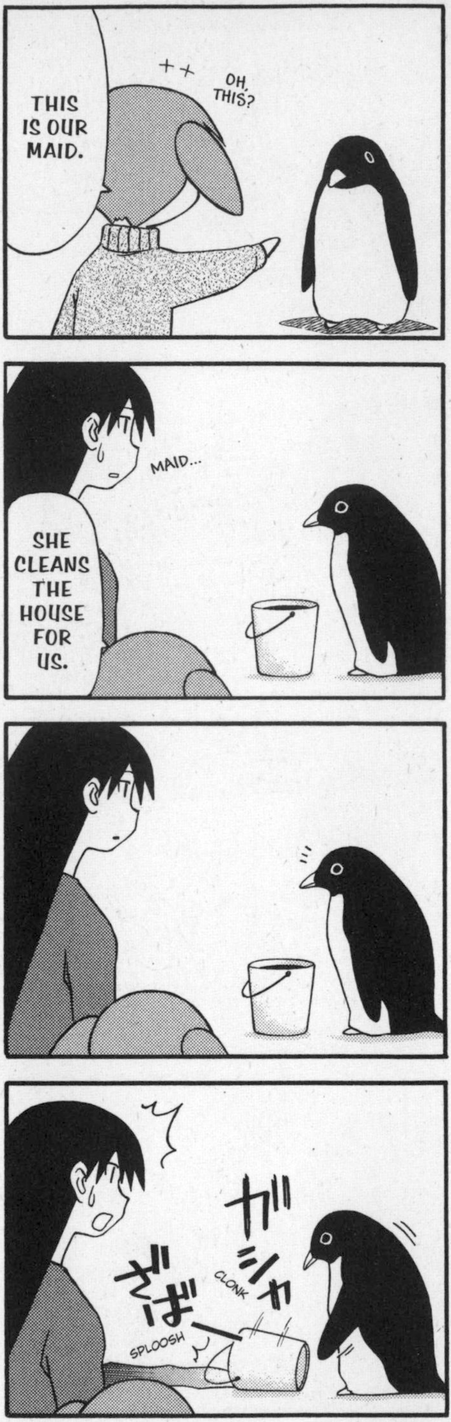
OH, THIS?
THIS IS OUR MAID.
MAID...
SHE CLEANS THE HOUSE FOR US.
ガシャ
CLONK
ざばー
SPLOOSH

WHAT SHOULD I DO?

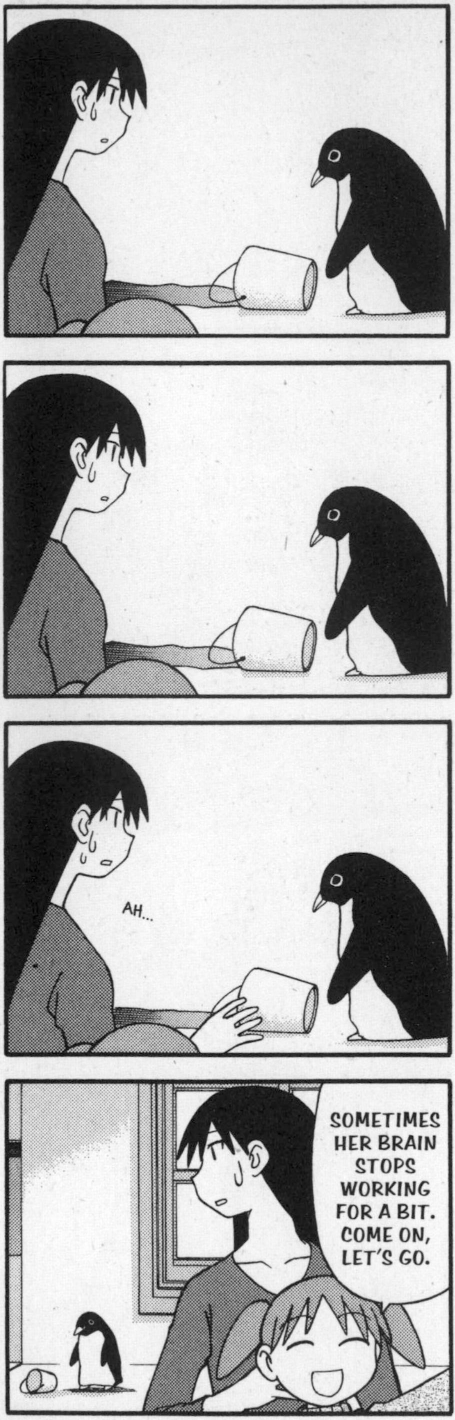
AH...
SOMETIMES HER BRAIN STOPS WORKING FOR A BIT. COME ON, LET'S GO.

INVITATION

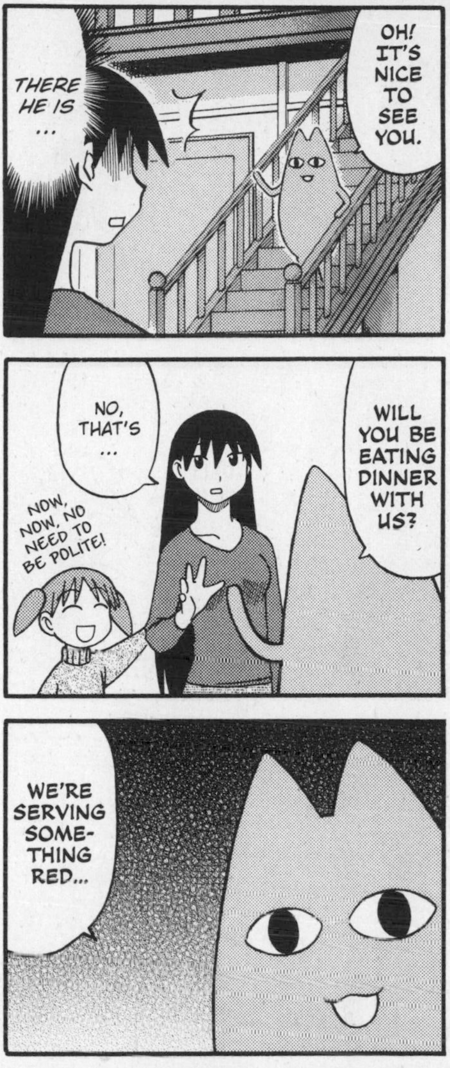
OH! IT'S NICE TO SEE YOU.
THERE HE IS ...
WILL YOU BE EATING DINNER WITH US?
NO, THAT'S ...
NOW, NOW, NO NEED TO BE POLITE!
WE'RE SERVING SOME-THING RED...
...BUT I DO HOPE YOU WILL JOIN US.
SOMETHING RED?

WHAT SHOULD I DO?

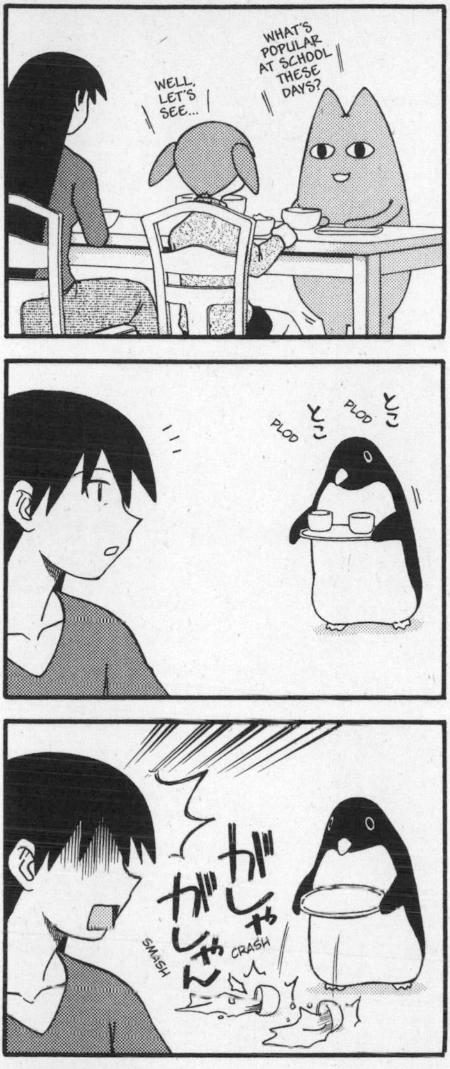
WHAT'S POPULAR AT SCHOOL THESE DAYS?
WELL, LET'S SEE...
とこ
PLOD
とこ
PLOD
がしゃ
CRASH
がしゃん
SMASH

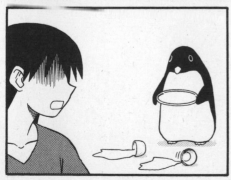

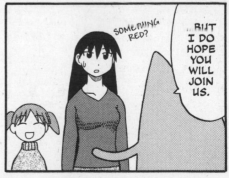

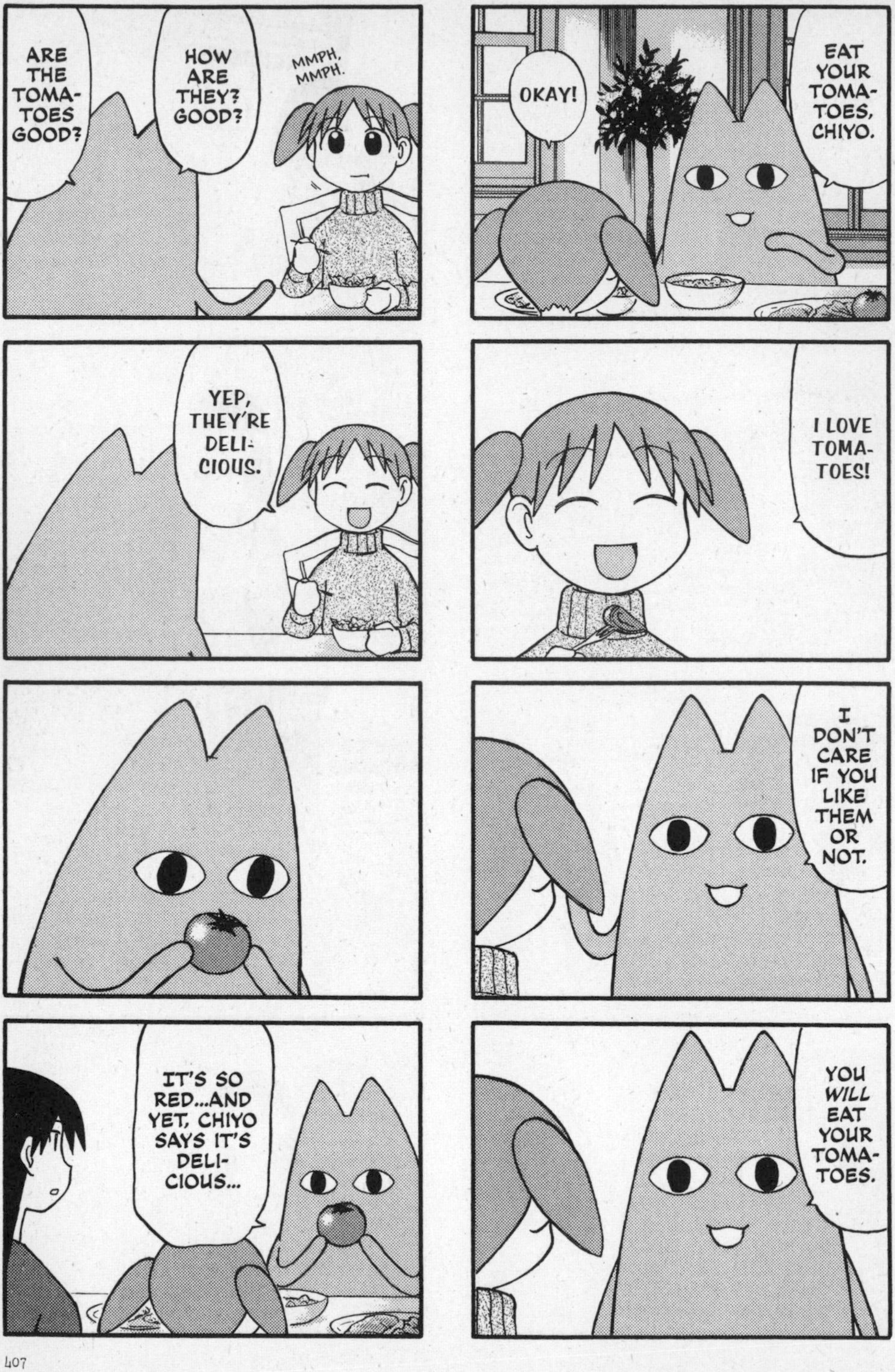
EAT YOUR TOMATOES, CHIYO.
OKAY!
MMPH, MMPH.
HOW ARE THEY? GOOD?
ARE THE TOMATOES GOOD?
I LOVE TOMATOES!
YEP, THEY'RE DELICIOUS.
I DON'T CARE IF YOU LIKE THEM OR NOT.
YOU *WILL* EAT YOUR TOMATOES.
IT'S SO RED...AND YET, CHIYO SAYS IT'S DELICIOUS...

MORE ADVICE

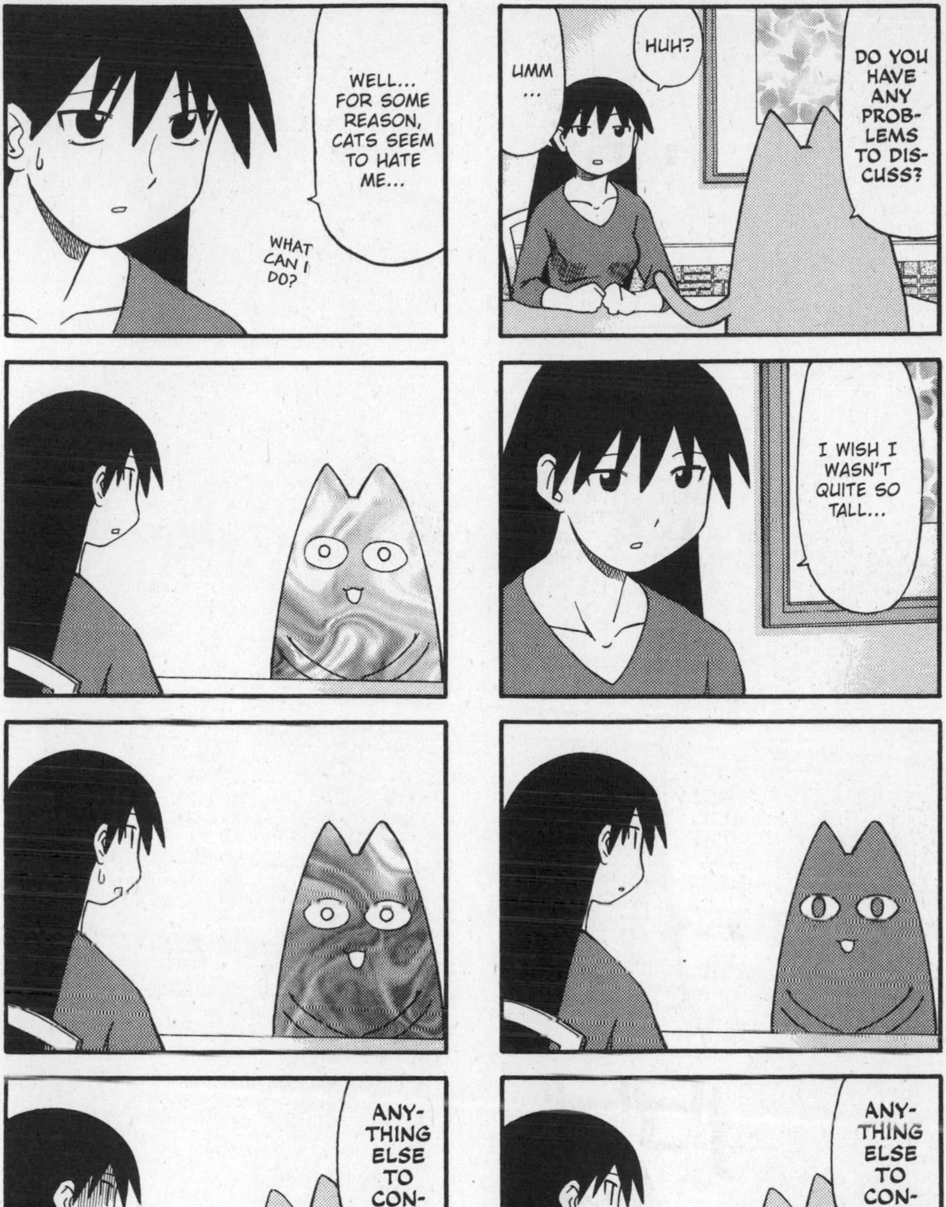
DO YOU HAVE ANY PROB-LEMS TO DIS-CUSS?
HUH?
UMM ...
WELL... FOR SOME REASON, CATS SEEM TO HATE ME...
WHAT CAN I DO?
I WISH I WASN'T QUITE SO TALL...
ANY-THING ELSE TO CON-FESS?
ANY-THING ELSE TO CON-FESS?

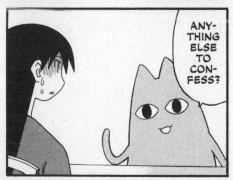

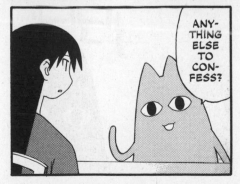

FEELINGS

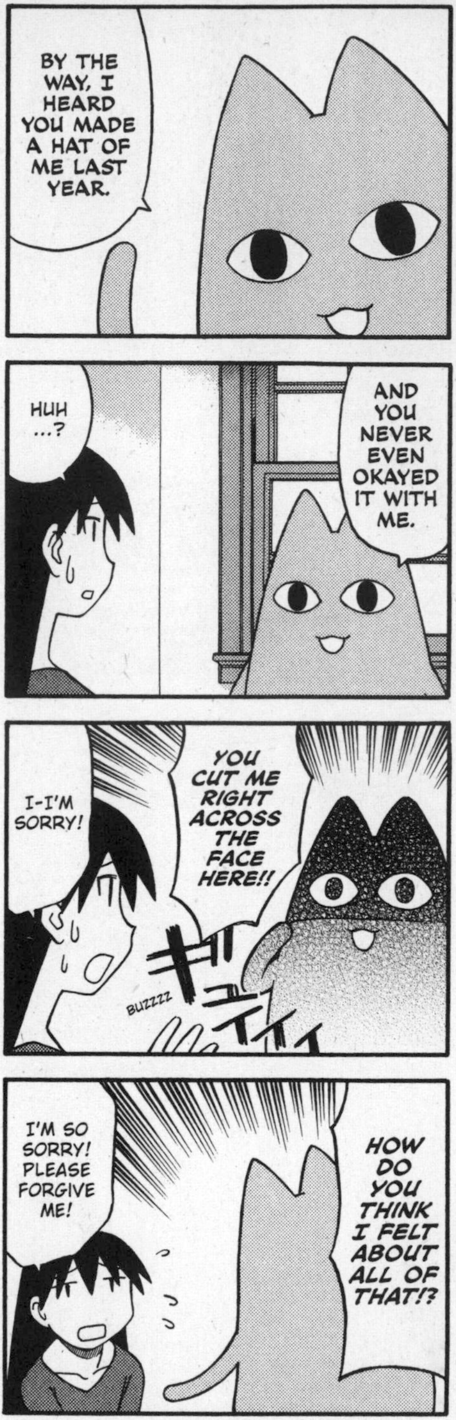
BY THE WAY, I HEARD YOU MADE A HAT OF ME LAST YEAR.
AND YOU NEVER EVEN OKAYED IT WITH ME.
HUH ...?
YOU CUT ME RIGHT ACROSS THE FACE HERE!!
I-I'M SORRY!
BUZZZZ
HOW DO YOU THINK I FELT ABOUT ALL OF THAT!?
I'M SO SORRY! PLEASE FORGIVE ME!

WHAT HAPPENS

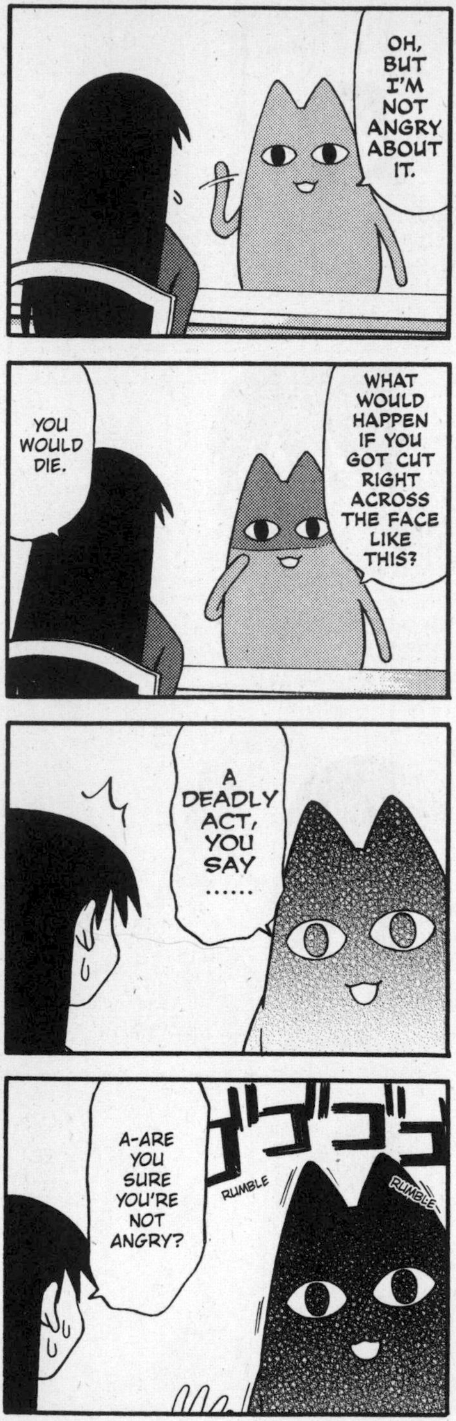
OH, BUT I'M NOT ANGRY ABOUT IT.
WHAT WOULD HAPPEN IF YOU GOT CUT RIGHT ACROSS THE FACE LIKE THIS?
YOU WOULD DIE.
A DEADLY ACT, YOU SAY ......
RUMBLE
RUMBLE
A-ARE YOU SURE YOU'RE NOT ANGRY?

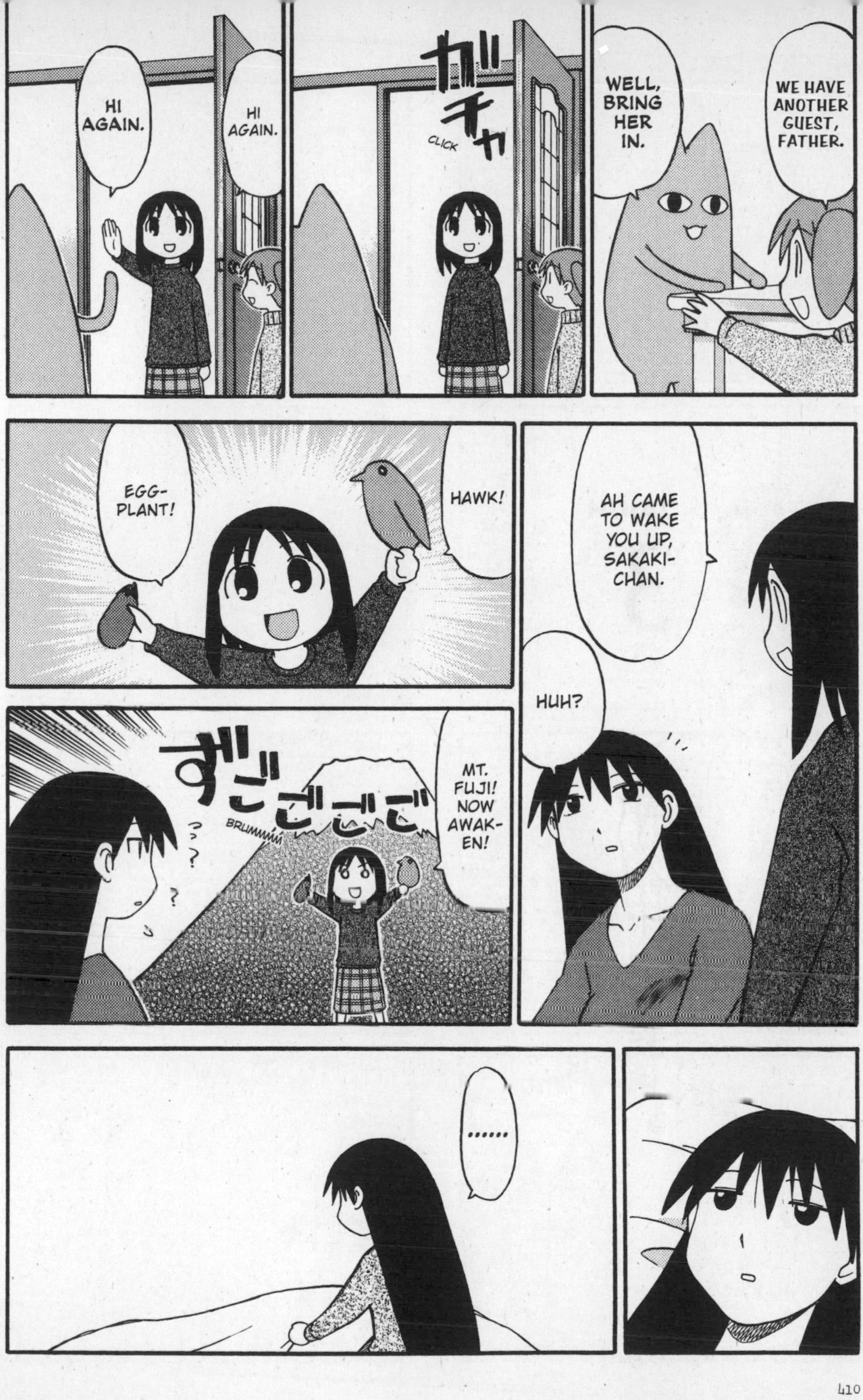
WE HAVE ANOTHER GUEST, FATHER.
WELL, BRING HER IN.
ガチャ
CLICK
HI AGAIN.
HI AGAIN.
AH CAME TO WAKE YOU UP, SAKAKI-CHAN.
HUH?
HAWK!
EGG-PLANT!
MT. FUJI! NOW AWAKEN!
すごごご
BRUMMMM
......

AZUMANGA-DAIOH

083

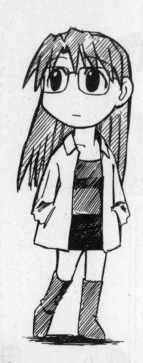

You belong.

AZUMANGA DAIOH

JANUARY

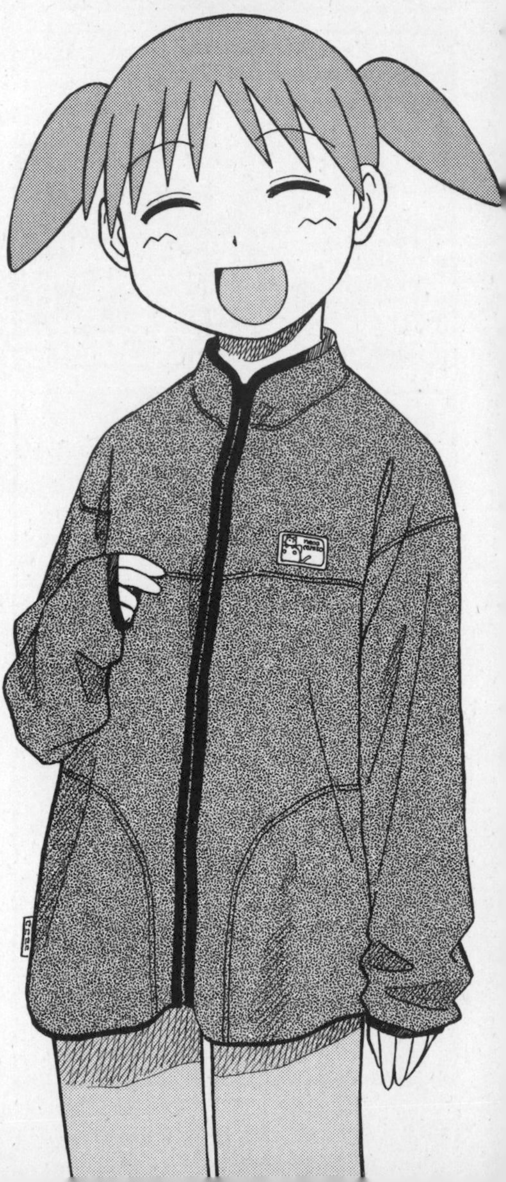

HOW TO SPEND YOUR NEW YEAR'S

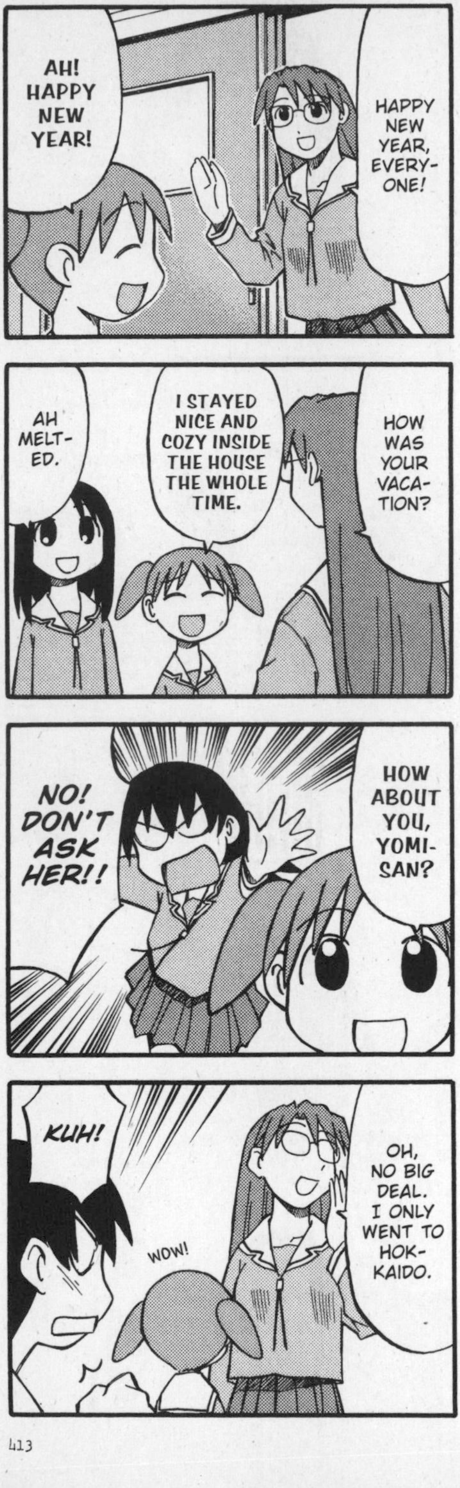
HAPPY NEW YEAR, EVERY-ONE!
AH! HAPPY NEW YEAR!
HOW WAS YOUR VACA-TION?
I STAYED NICE AND COZY INSIDE THE HOUSE THE WHOLE TIME.
AH MELT-ED.
HOW ABOUT YOU, YOMI-SAN?
NO! DON'T ASK HER!!
OH, NO BIG DEAL. I ONLY WENT TO HOK-KAIDO.
KUH!
WOW!

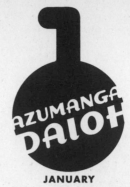

GLOATING YOMI

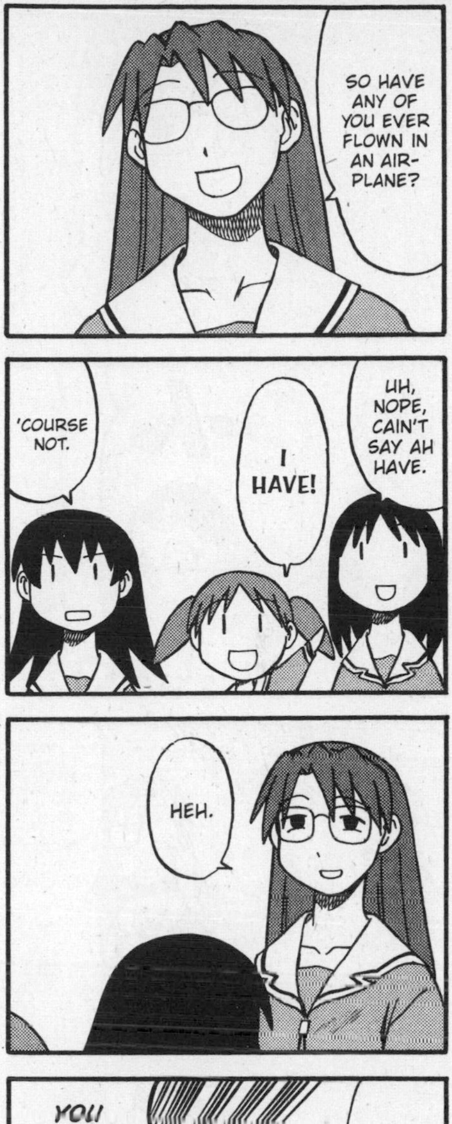
SO HAVE ANY OF YOU EVER FLOWN IN AN AIR-PLANE?
UH, NOPE, CAIN'T SAY AH HAVE.
I HAVE!
'COURSE NOT.
HEH.
WOULD YOU LIKE TO TALK OVER THERE, CHIYO-CHAN?
YOU HADN'T EITHER BEFORE JUST NOW!!

BEARS IN HOKKAIDO

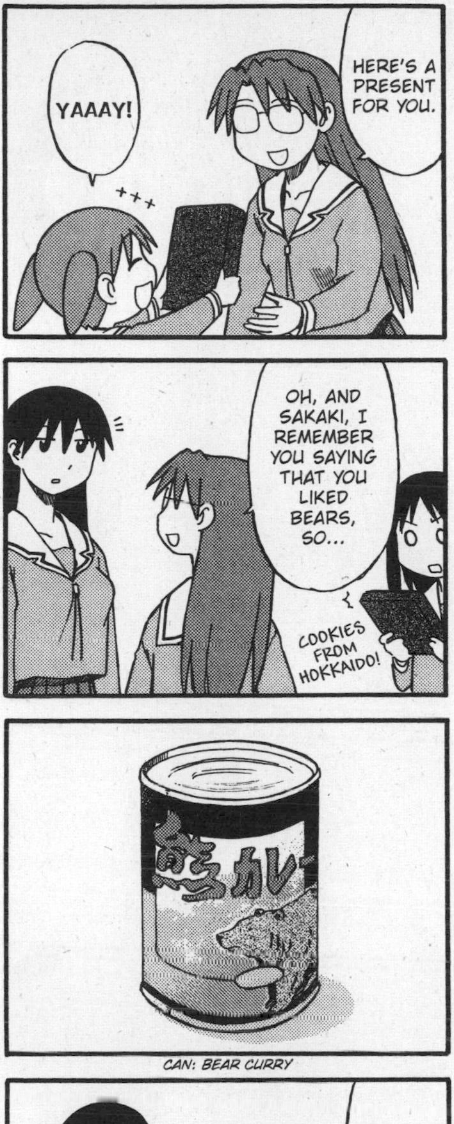
HERE'S A PRESENT FOR YOU.
YAAAY!
OH, AND SAKAKI, I REMEMBER YOU SAYING THAT YOU LIKED BEARS, SO...
COOKIES FROM HOKKAIDO!
CAN: BEAR CURRY
THAT'S GOT BEAR IN IT.
AWW, LUCKYYY!

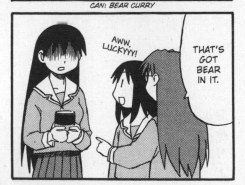

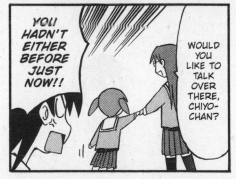

MOCHI

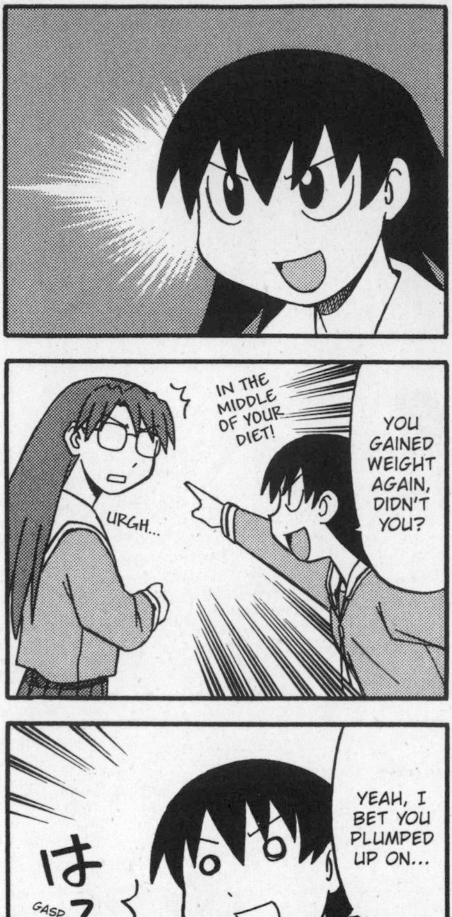
YOU GAINED WEIGHT AGAIN, DIDN'T YOU?
IN THE MIDDLE OF YOUR DIET!
URGH...
YEAH, I BET YOU PLUMPED UP ON...
はっ
GASP
......
NO! IT COULDN'T BE!!

HOW DARE YOU

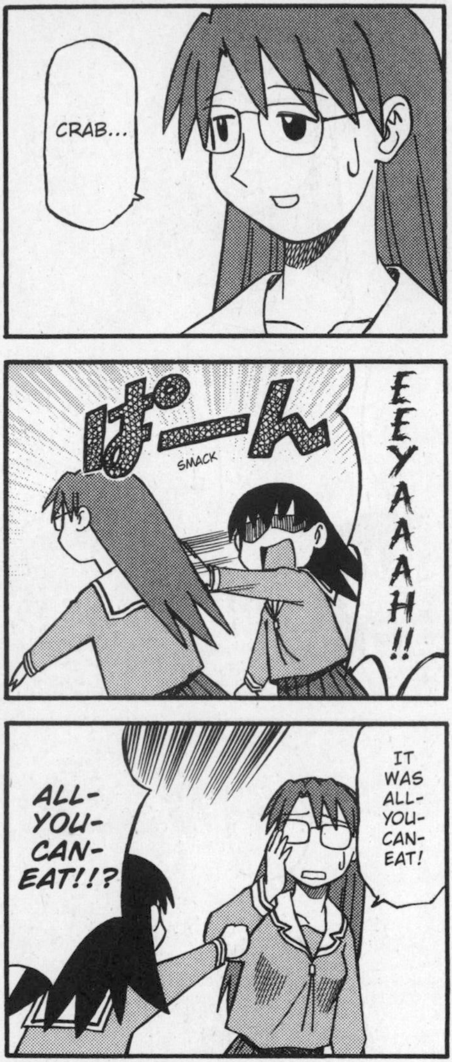
CRAB...
EEYAAAAH!!
ぱーん
SMACK
IT WAS ALL-YOU-CAN-EAT!
ALL-YOU-CAN-EAT!!?
I'M GONNA TELL THE TEACHER!!
だッ
DASH
WHA—?

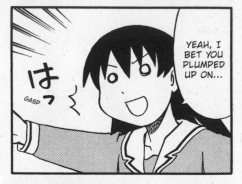

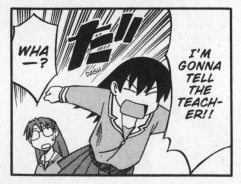

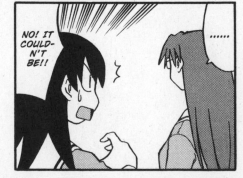

HERE SHE COMES

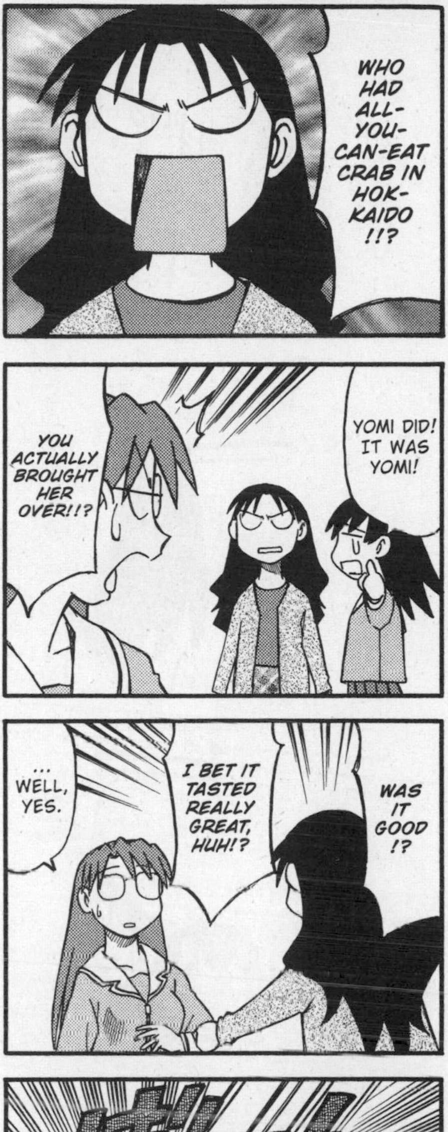
WHO HAD ALL-YOU-CAN-EAT CRAB IN HOKKAIDO!!?
YOMI DID! IT WAS YOMI!
YOU ACTUALLY BROUGHT HER OVER!!?
WAS IT GOOD!?
I BET IT TASTED REALLY GREAT, HUH!?
...WELL, YES.
ばーん
WHAM

ALSO ALL-YOU-CAN-EAT

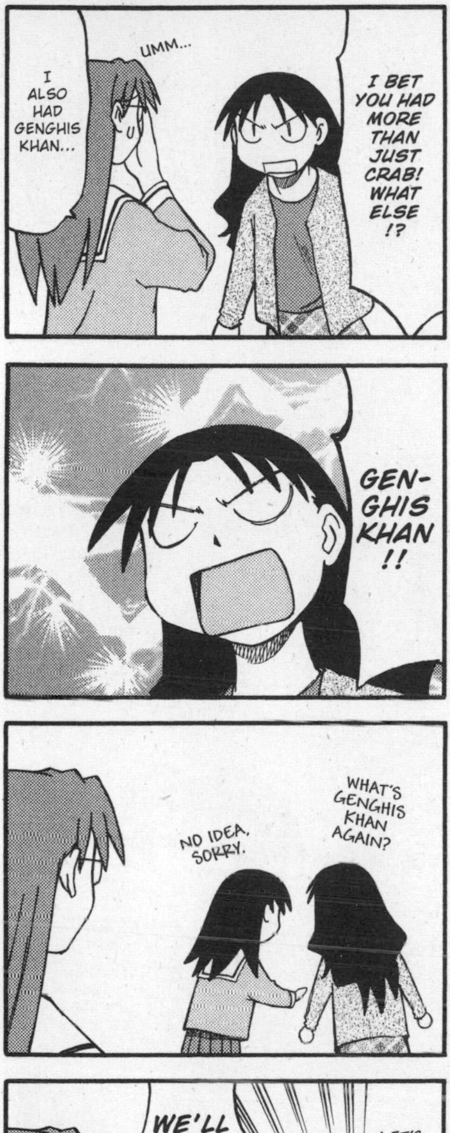
I BET YOU HAD MORE THAN JUST CRAB! WHAT ELSE!?
UMM...
I ALSO HAD GENGHIS KHAN...
GENGHIS KHAN!!
WHAT'S GENGHIS KHAN AGAIN?
NO IDEA, SORRY.
LET'S ASK CHIYO-CHAN!
WE'LL BE BACK FOR YOU!!

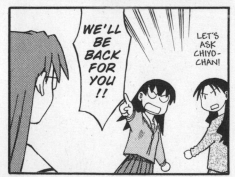

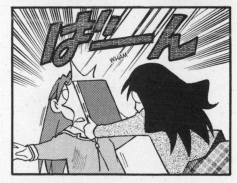

DEFINITION

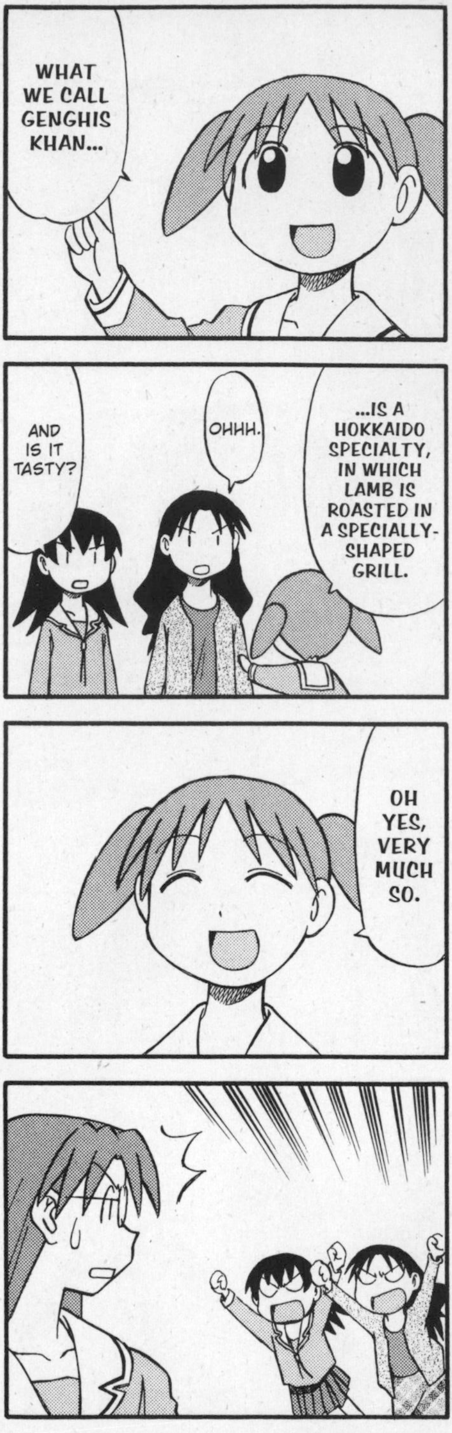
WHAT WE CALL GENGHIS KHAN...
...IS A HOKKAIDO SPECIALTY, IN WHICH LAMB IS ROASTED IN A SPECIALLY-SHAPED GRILL.
OHHH.
AND IS IT TASTY?
OH YES, VERY MUCH SO.

KNOCK KNOCK

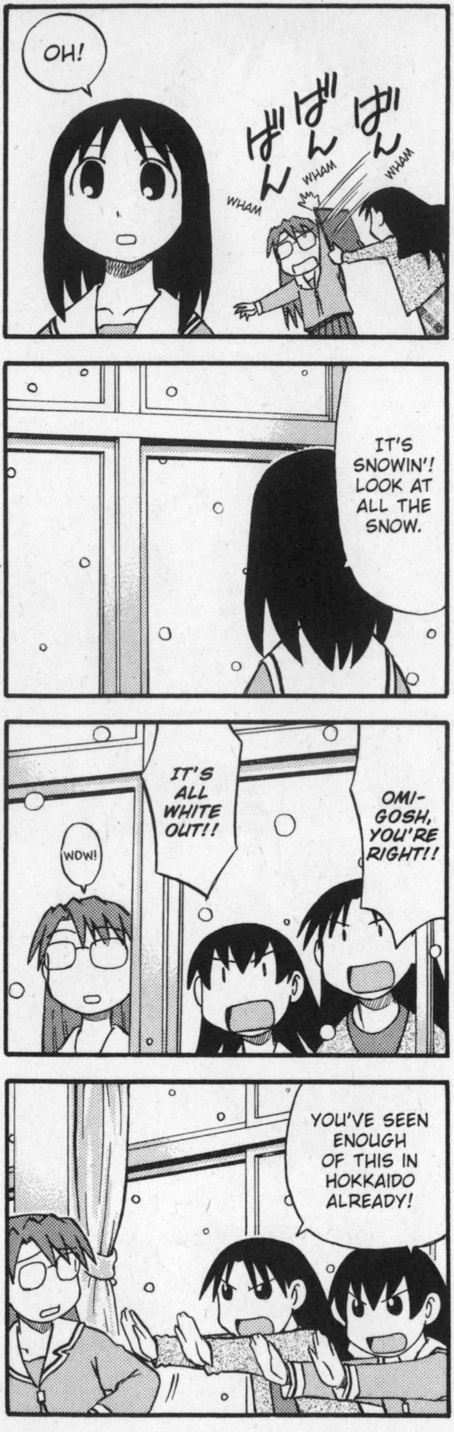
OH!
ばん
WHAM
ばん
WHAM
ばん
WHAM
IT'S SNOWIN'! LOOK AT ALL THE SNOW.
OMI-GOSH, YOU'RE RIGHT!!
IT'S ALL WHITE OUT!!
WOW!
YOU'VE SEEN ENOUGH OF THIS IN HOKKAIDO ALREADY!

AMPLE JUSTICE

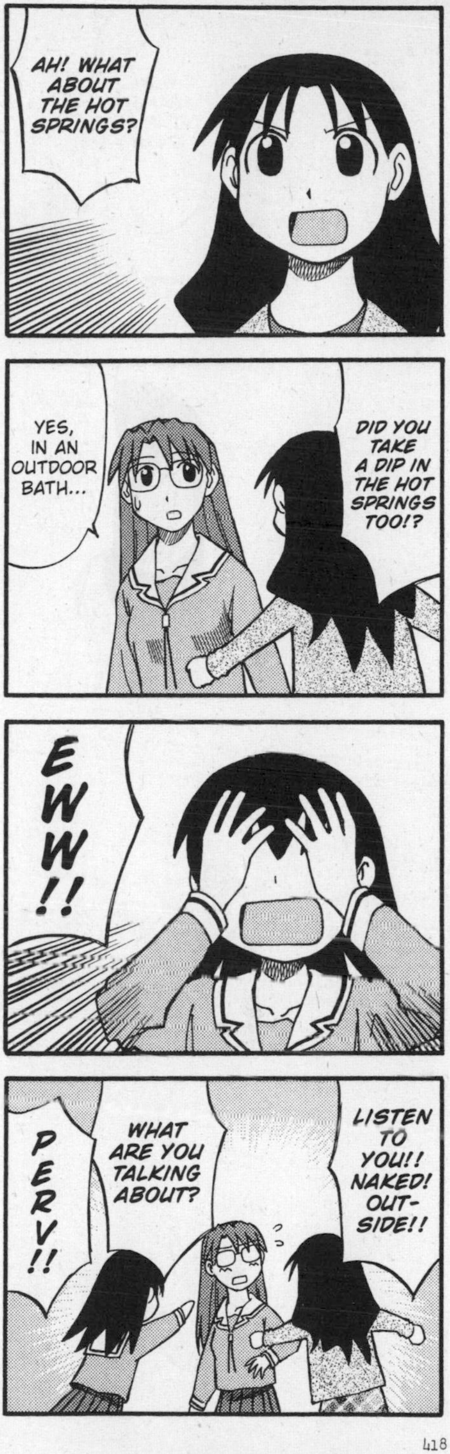
AH! WHAT ABOUT THE HOT SPRINGS?
DID YOU TAKE A DIP IN THE HOT SPRINGS TOO!?
YES, IN AN OUTDOOR BATH...
EWW!!
LISTEN TO YOU!! NAKED! OUT-SIDE!!
WHAT ARE YOU TALKING ABOUT?
PERV!!

PALS

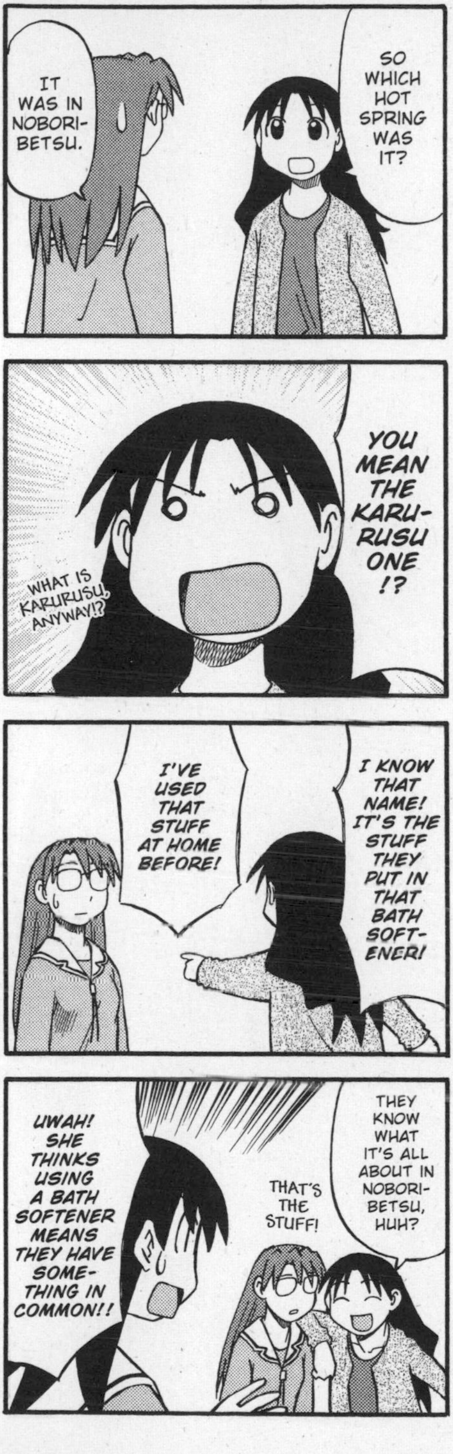
SO WHICH HOT SPRING WAS IT?
IT WAS IN NOBORI-BETSU.
YOU MEAN THE KARU-RUSU ONE !?
WHAT IS KARURUSU, ANYWAY!?
I KNOW THAT NAME! IT'S THE STUFF THEY PUT IN THAT BATH SOFT-ENER!
I'VE USED THAT STUFF AT HOME BEFORE!
THEY KNOW WHAT IT'S ALL ABOUT IN NOBORI-BETSU, HUH?
THAT'S THE STUFF!
UWAH! SHE THINKS USING A BATH SOFTENER MEANS THEY HAVE SOME-THING IN COMMON!!

DANGER

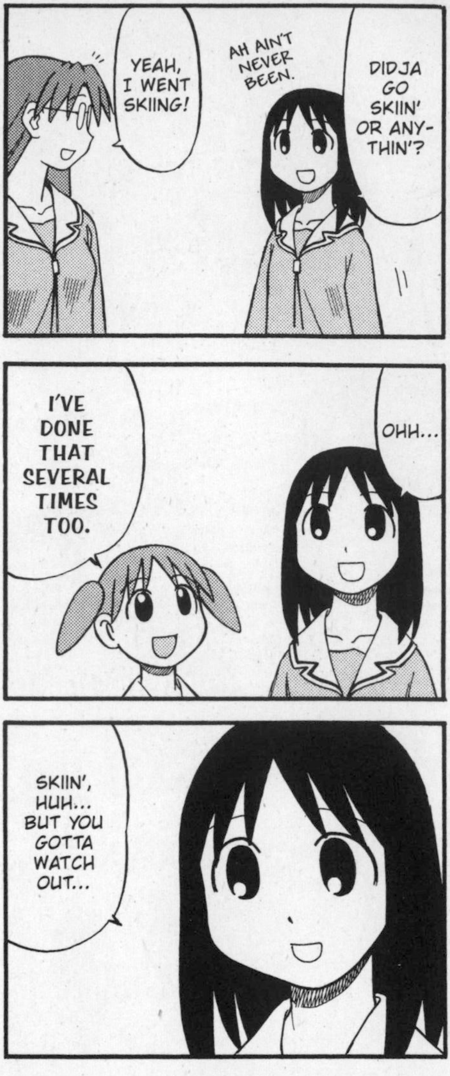
DIDJA GO SKIIN' OR ANYTHIN'?
AH AIN'T NEVER BEEN.
YEAH, I WENT SKIING!
OHH...
I'VE DONE THAT SEVERAL TIMES TOO.
SKIIN', HUH... BUT YOU GOTTA WATCH OUT...
THAT SNOW'S MIGHTY SLIPPERY.
THAT'S RIGHT! YOU CAN REALLY HURT YOURSELF IF YOU SLIP AND FALL.

GO!

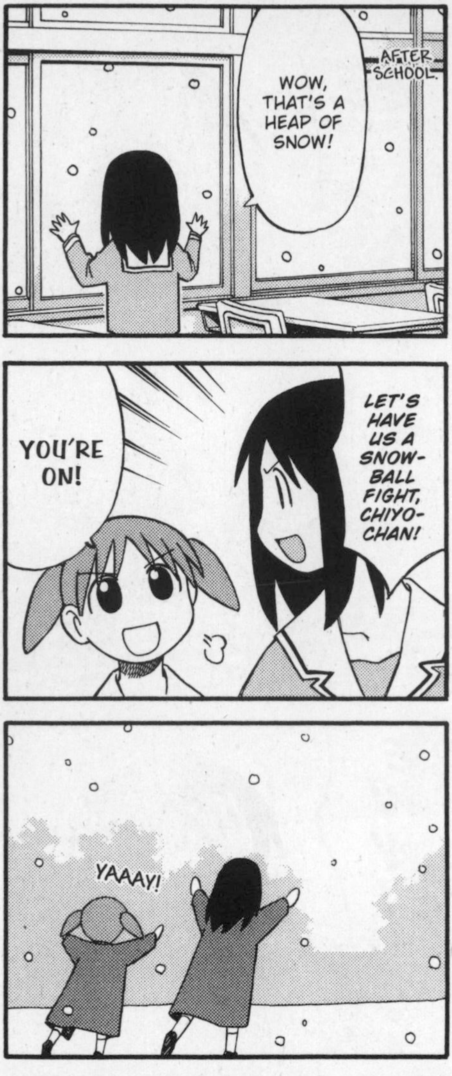
AFTER SCHOOL
WOW, THAT'S A HEAP OF SNOW!
LET'S HAVE US A SNOWBALL FIGHT, CHIYO-CHAN!
YOU'RE ON!
YAAAY!

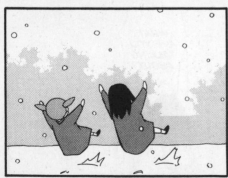

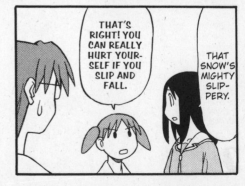

THIS IS FUN

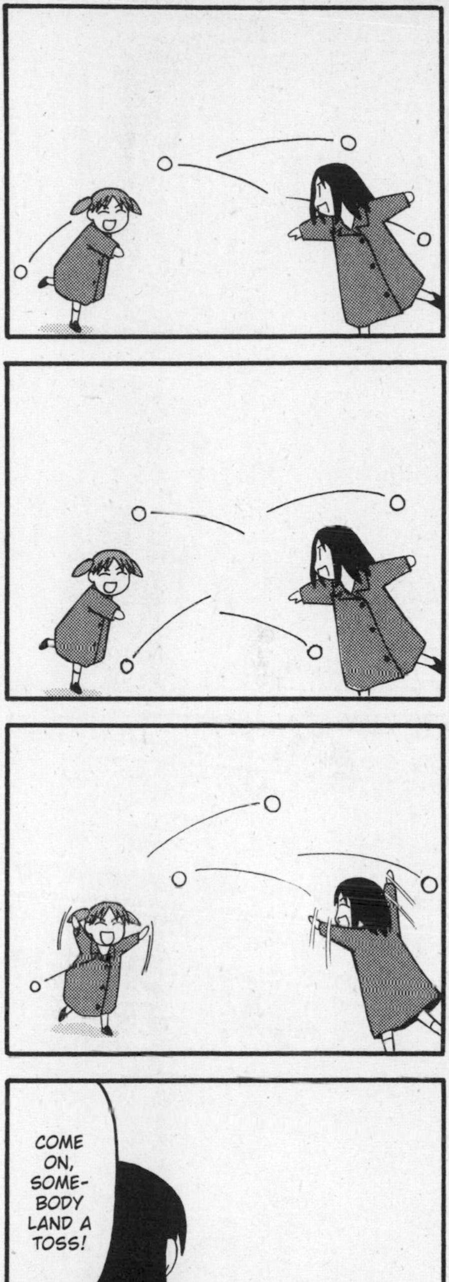
COME ON, SOME-BODY LAND A TOSS!

VICTORY

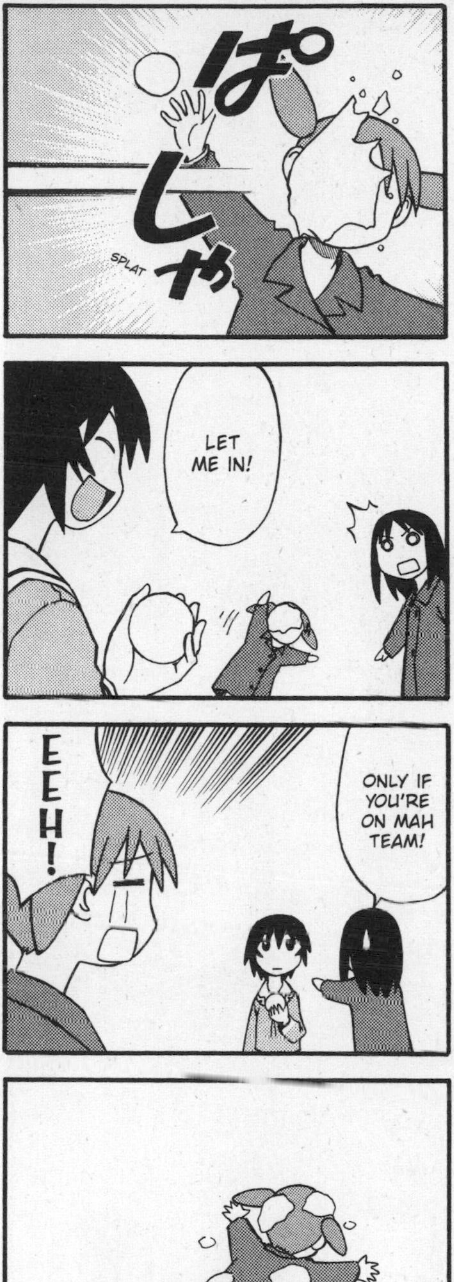
ぱしゃ
SPLAT
LET ME IN!
ONLY IF YOU'RE ON MAH TEAM!
EEH!

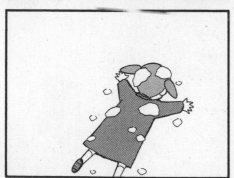

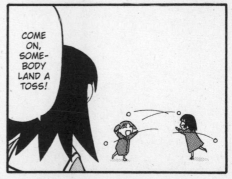

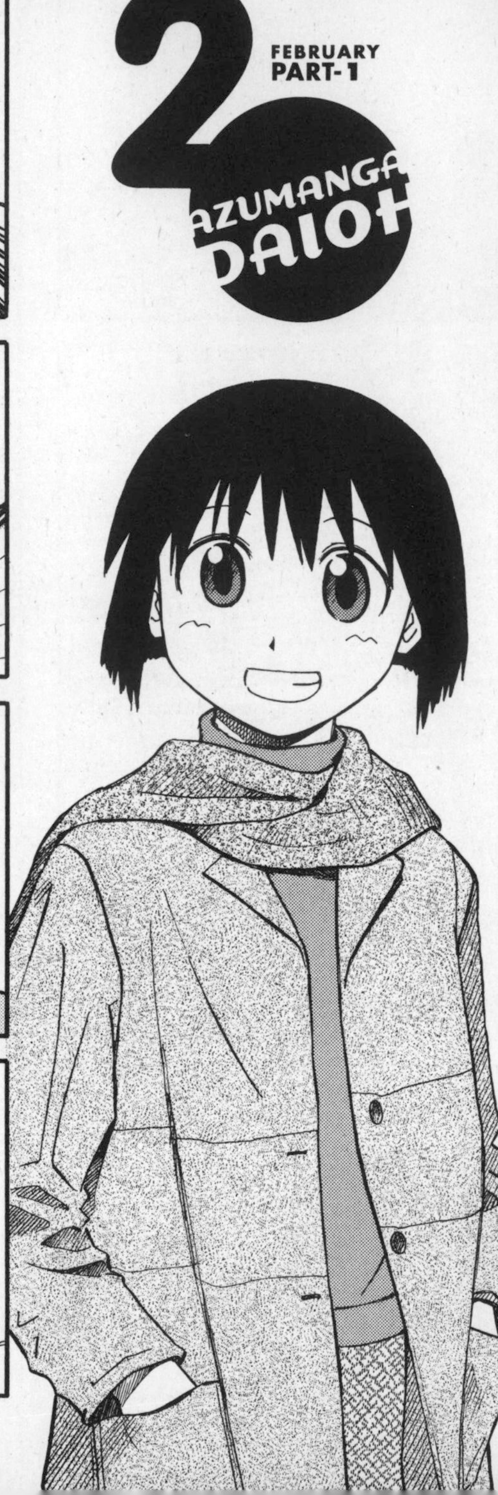
2
FEBRUARY PART-1
AZUMANGA DAIOH

FUTON-MAN

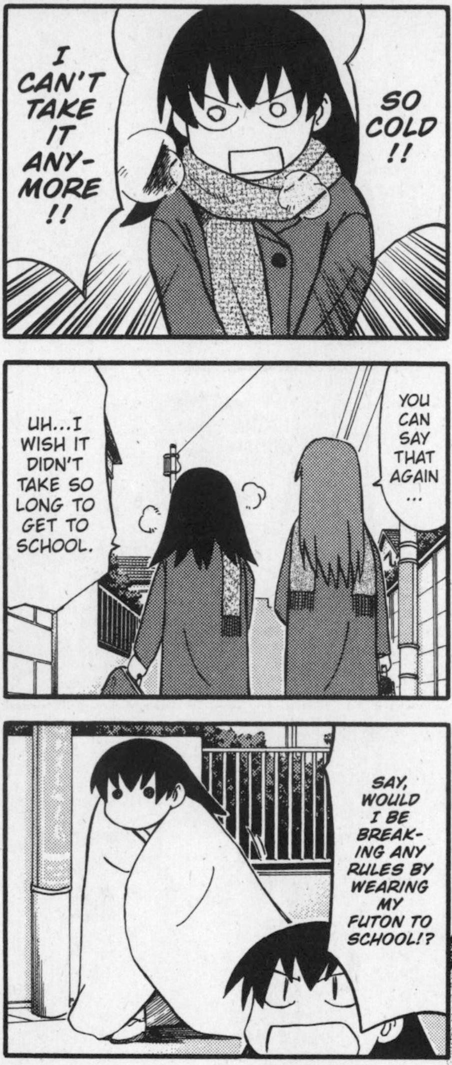
I CAN'T TAKE IT ANYMORE!!
SO COLD!!
YOU CAN SAY THAT AGAIN...
UH...I WISH IT DIDN'T TAKE SO LONG TO GET TO SCHOOL.
SAY, WOULD I BE BREAKING ANY RULES BY WEARING MY FUTON TO SCHOOL!?
AS LONG AS IT DOESN'T HAVE ANY FLASHY PATTERNS, I'LL BE IN THE CLEAR, RIGHT!?
SURE, WHATEVER.

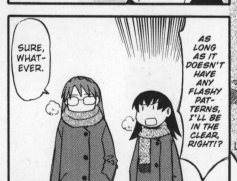

PLAN

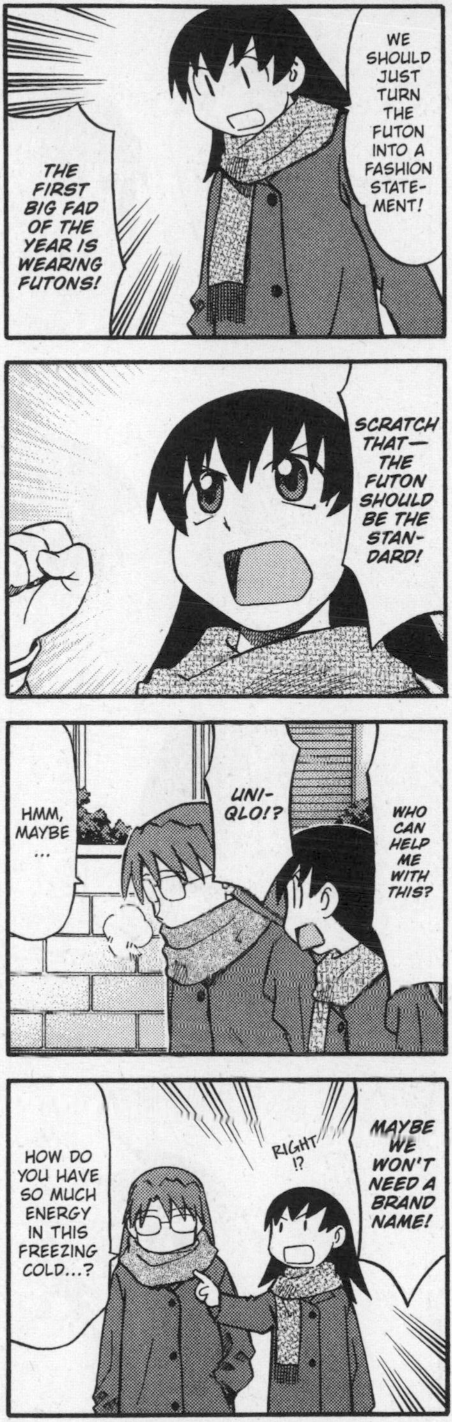
WE SHOULD JUST TURN THE FUTON INTO A FASHION STATE-MENT!
THE FIRST BIG FAD OF THE YEAR IS WEARING FUTONS!
SCRATCH THAT—THE FUTON SHOULD BE THE STAN-DARD!
WHO CAN HELP ME WITH THIS?
UNI-QLO!?
HMM, MAYBE ...
MAYBE WE WON'T NEED A BRAND NAME!
RIGHT !?
HOW DO YOU HAVE SO MUCH ENERGY IN THIS FREEZING COLD...?

WAKE UP, KAORIN

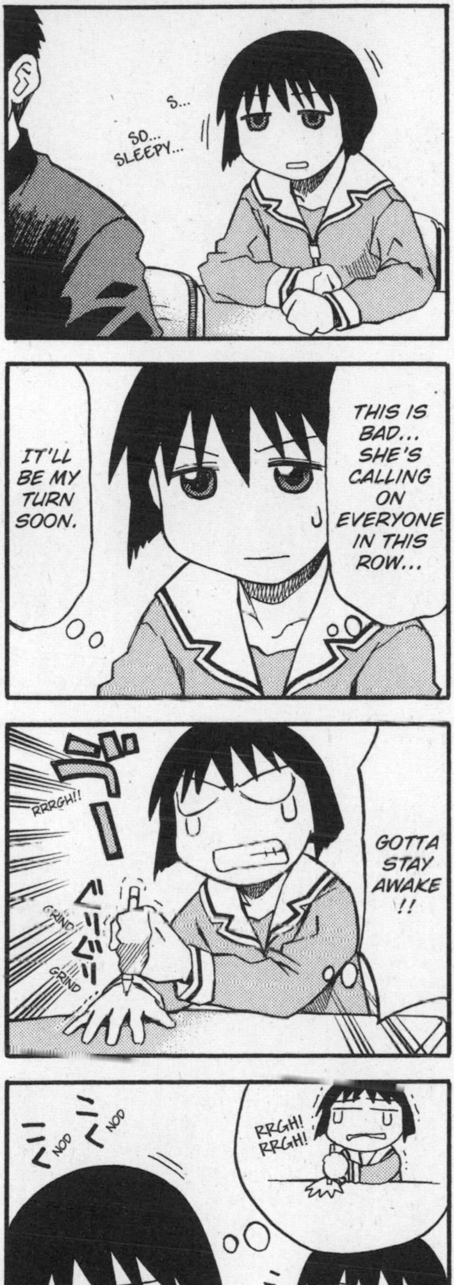
S...
SO... SLEEPY...
THIS IS BAD... SHE'S CALLING ON EVERYONE IN THIS ROW...
IT'LL BE MY TURN SOON.
GOTTA STAY AWAKE !!
RRRGH!!
GRIND
GRIND
RRGH! RRGH!
NOD
NOD

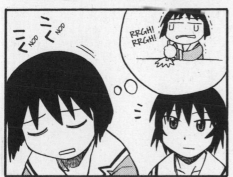

MECHANICAL PENCIL POINT

ZZZ...
つん POKE
つん POKE
HEY! KAORIN! YOU'RE UP NEXT!
つん POKE
つん POKE
プス PSHHK

SORRY

?
DRIIIP...
HAUGH!!

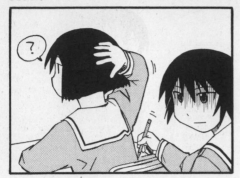

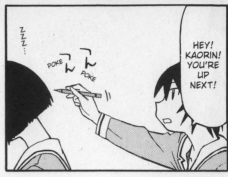

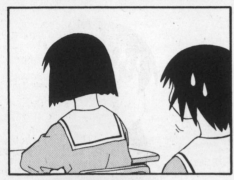

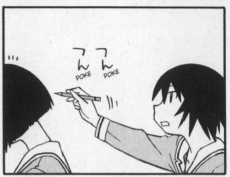

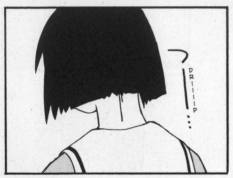

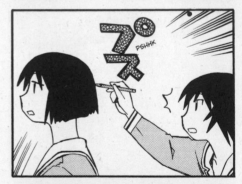

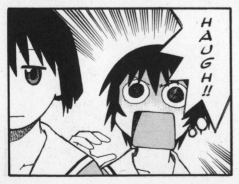

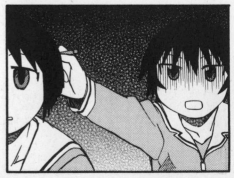

GYM SHORTS

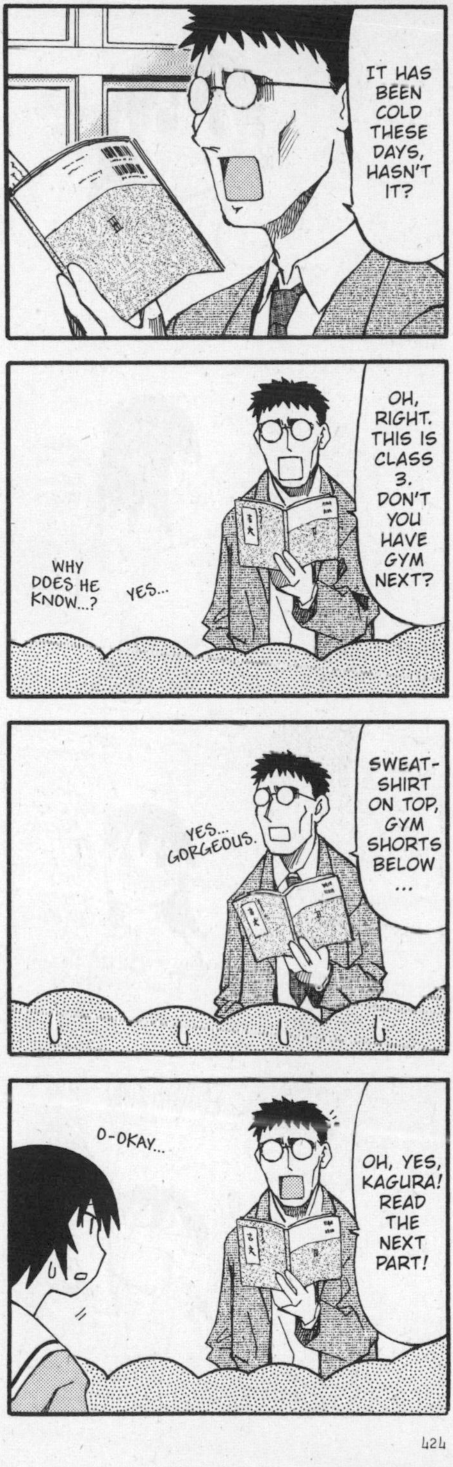
IT HAS BEEN COLD THESE DAYS, HASN'T IT?
OH, RIGHT. THIS IS CLASS 3. DON'T YOU HAVE GYM NEXT?
YES...
WHY DOES HE KNOW...?
SWEATSHIRT ON TOP, GYM SHORTS BELOW...
YES... GORGEOUS.
OH, YES, KAGURA! READ THE NEXT PART!
O-OKAY...

SPEAKING FROM THE HEART

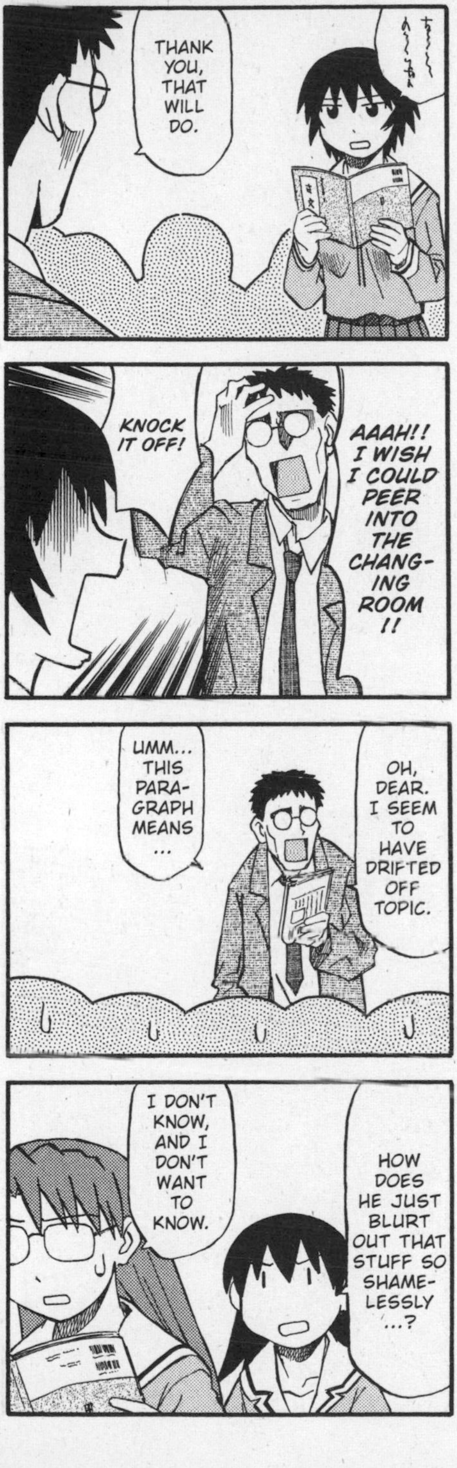
THANK YOU, THAT WILL DO.
AAAH!! I WISH I COULD PEER INTO THE CHANGING ROOM!!
KNOCK IT OFF!
OH, DEAR. I SEEM TO HAVE DRIFTED OFF TOPIC.
UMM... THIS PARAGRAPH MEANS...
HOW DOES HE JUST BLURT OUT THAT STUFF SO SHAMELESSLY...?
I DON'T KNOW, AND I DON'T WANT TO KNOW.

ALL-GIRLS' SCHOOL

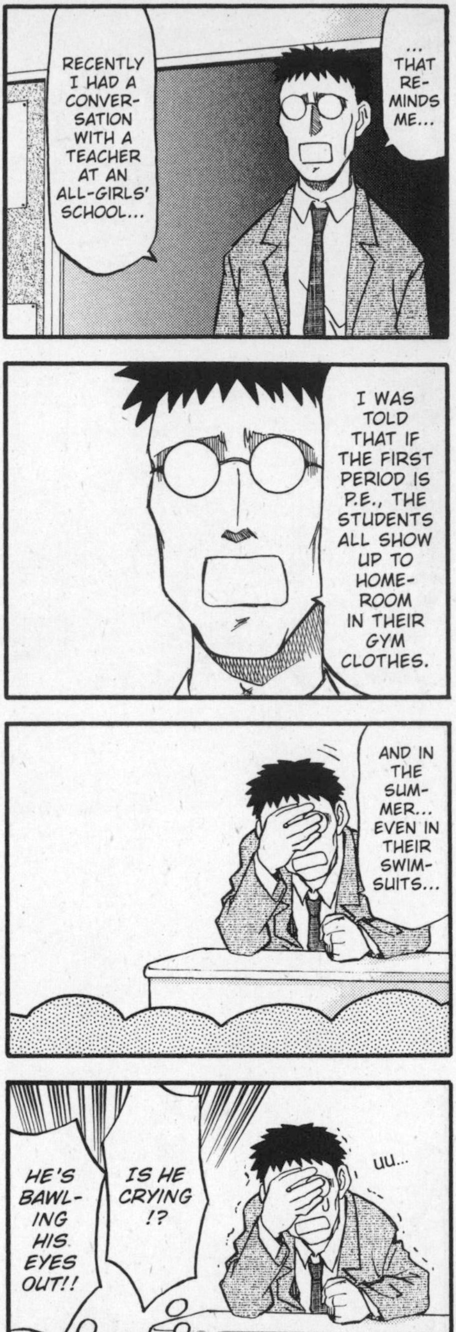
... THAT REMINDS ME...
RECENTLY I HAD A CONVERSATION WITH A TEACHER AT AN ALL-GIRLS' SCHOOL...
I WAS TOLD THAT IF THE FIRST PERIOD IS P.E., THE STUDENTS ALL SHOW UP TO HOMEROOM IN THEIR GYM CLOTHES.
AND IN THE SUMMER... EVEN IN THEIR SWIMSUITS...
UU...
IS HE CRYING!?
HE'S BAWLING HIS EYES OUT!!

STABILITY

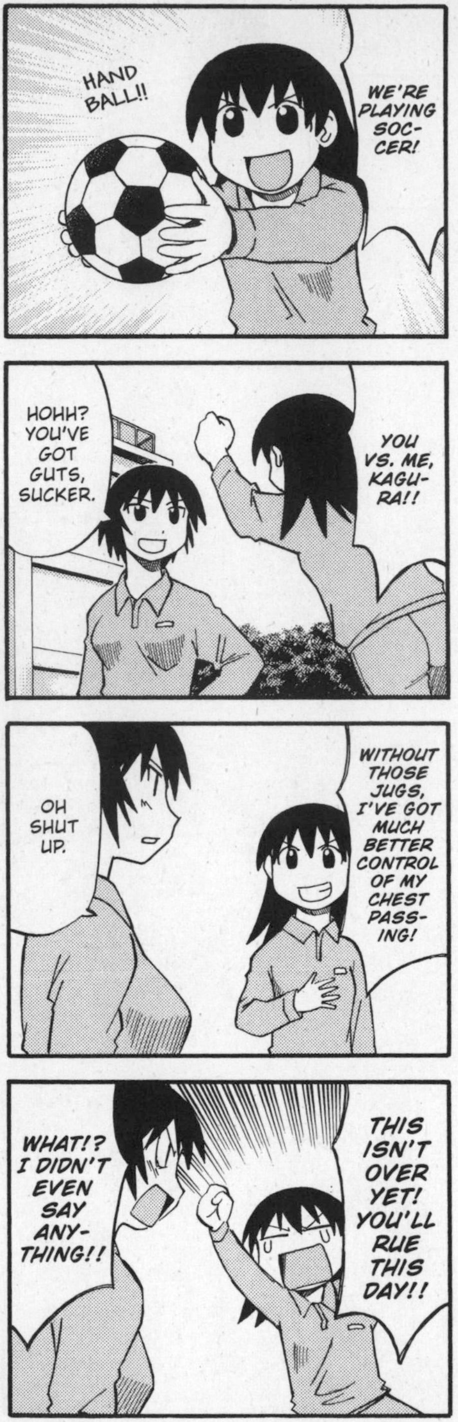
WE'RE PLAYING SOCCER!
HAND BALL!!
YOU VS. ME, KAGURA!!
HOHH? YOU'VE GOT GUTS, SUCKER.
WITHOUT THOSE JUGS, I'VE GOT MUCH BETTER CONTROL OF MY CHEST PASSING!
OH SHUT UP.
THIS ISN'T OVER YET! YOU'LL RUE THIS DAY!!
WHAT!? I DIDN'T EVEN SAY ANYTHING!!

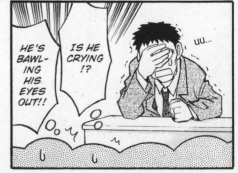

HEADING TO THE FRONT

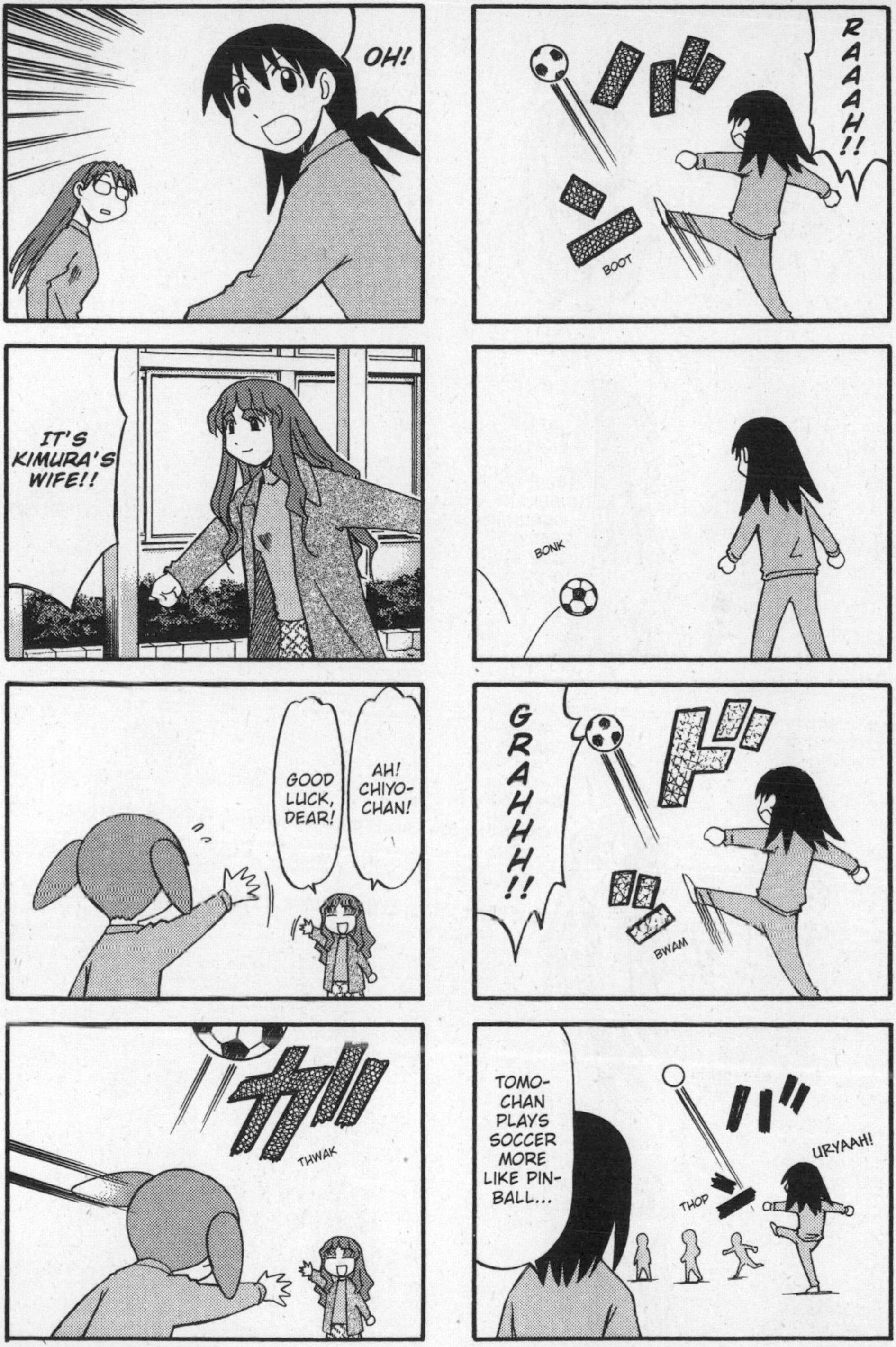
RAAAAH!!
BOOT
BONK
GRAHHHH!!
BWAM
TOMO-CHAN PLAYS SOCCER MORE LIKE PIN-BALL...
URYAAH!
THOP
OH!
IT'S KIMURA'S WIFE!!
AH! CHIYO-CHAN!
GOOD LUCK, DEAR!
THWAK

OBEY THE RULES

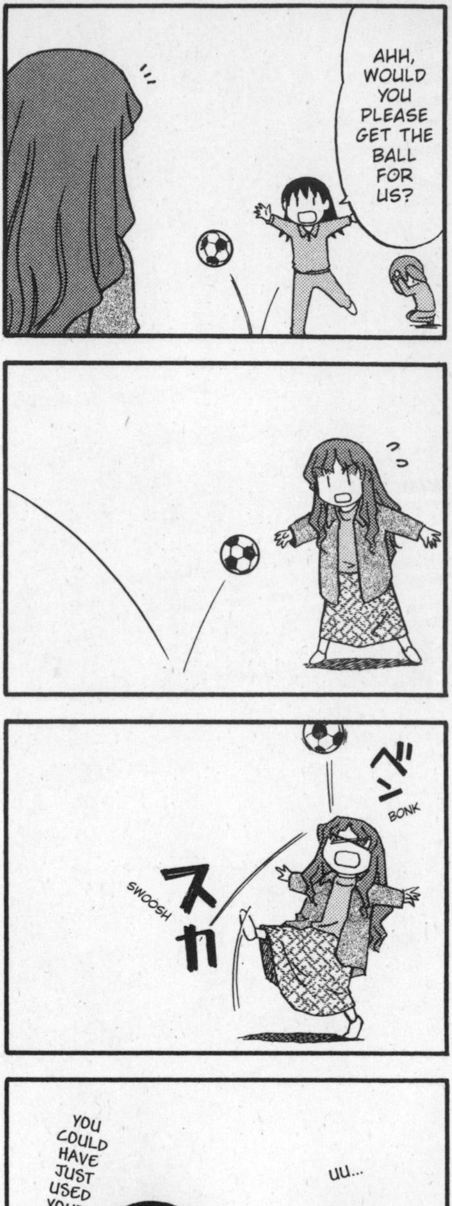
AHH, WOULD YOU PLEASE GET THE BALL FOR US?
ベン
BONK
スカ
SWOOSH
UU...
YOU COULD HAVE JUST USED YOUR HANDS.

SEASONED WITH LOVE

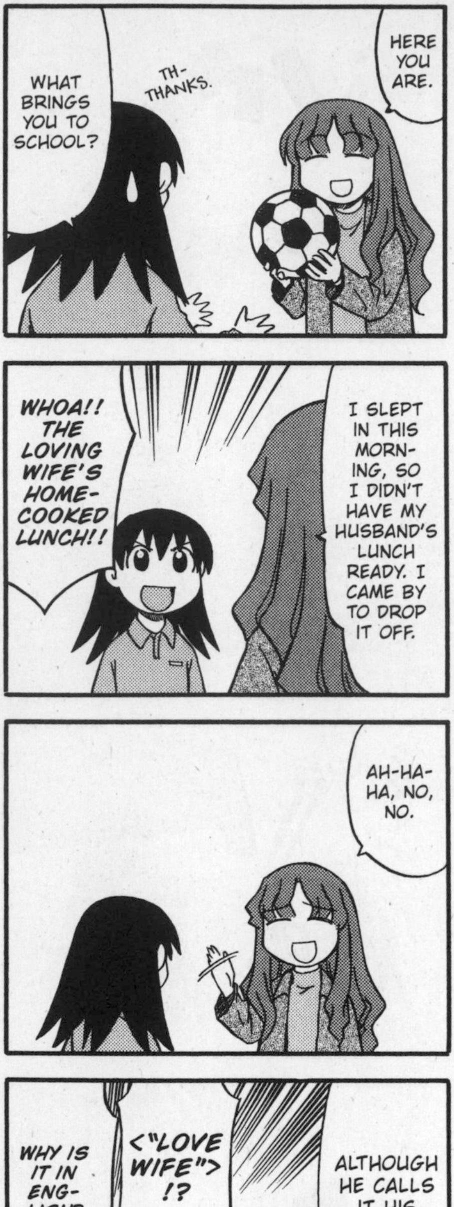
HERE YOU ARE.
TH-THANKS.
WHAT BRINGS YOU TO SCHOOL?
I SLEPT IN THIS MORNING, SO I DIDN'T HAVE MY HUSBAND'S LUNCH READY. I CAME BY TO DROP IT OFF.
WHOA!! THE LOVING WIFE'S HOME-COOKED LUNCH!!
AH-HA-HA, NO, NO.
ALTHOUGH HE CALLS IT HIS <"LOVE WIFE"> LUNCH.
<"LOVE WIFE">!?
WHY IS IT IN ENGLISH? AND ON TOP OF THAT, IT SEEMS WRONG!!

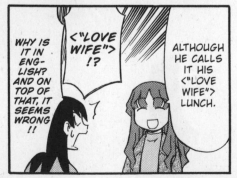

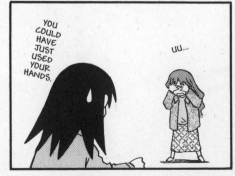

SO MANY THINGS

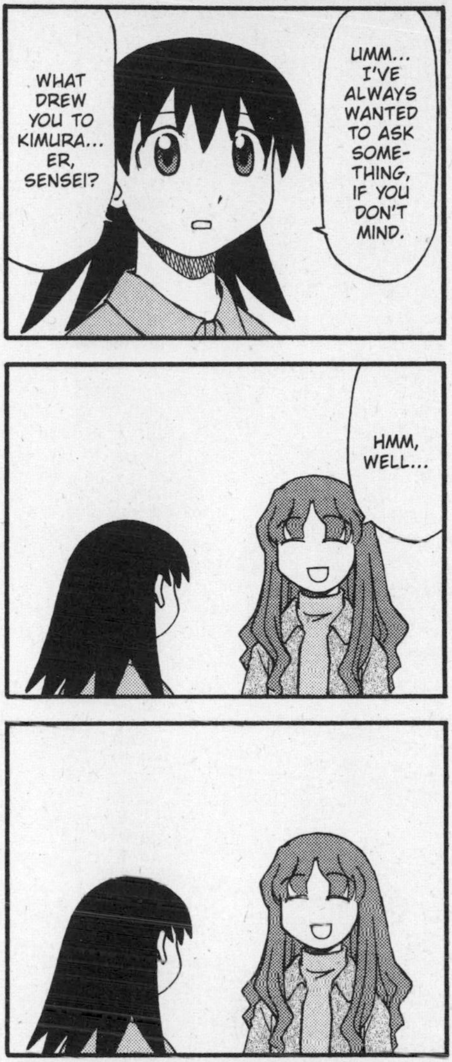
UMM... I'VE ALWAYS WANTED TO ASK SOME-THING, IF YOU DON'T MIND.
WHAT DREW YOU TO KIMURA... ER, SENSEI?
HMM, WELL...
...HOW ABOUT HIS HAND-SOME LOOKS?
UWAH!! SHE HAS NO TASTE IN MEN!!

ROUND AND ROUND

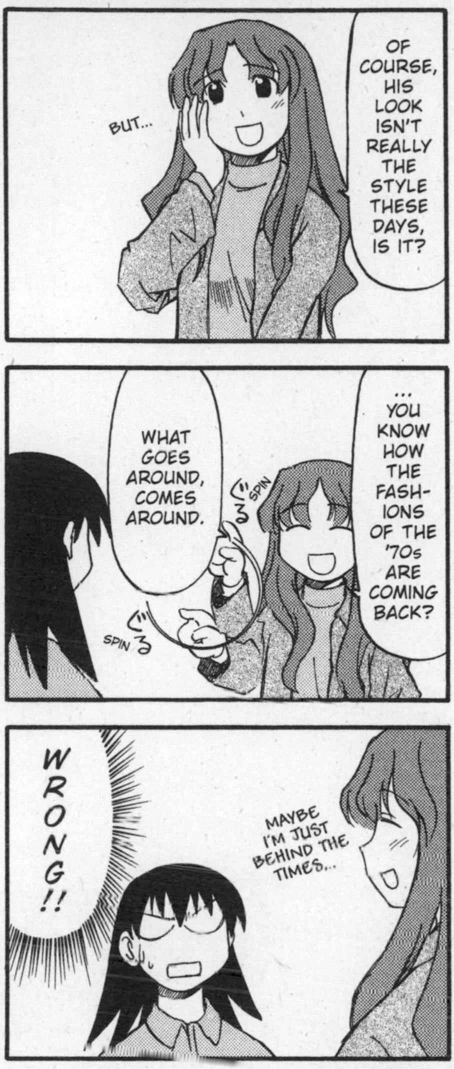
OF COURSE, HIS LOOK ISN'T REALLY THE STYLE THESE DAYS, IS IT?
BUT...
...YOU KNOW HOW THE FASH-IONS OF THE '70s ARE COMING BACK?
SPIN
WHAT GOES AROUND, COMES AROUND.
SPIN
MAYBE I'M JUST BEHIND THE TIMES...
WRONG!!
NO MATTER HOW MANY TIMES THE CYCLE GOES 'ROUND, KIMURA'S TURN NEVER COMES UP!
?

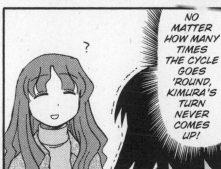

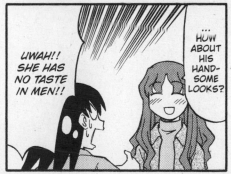

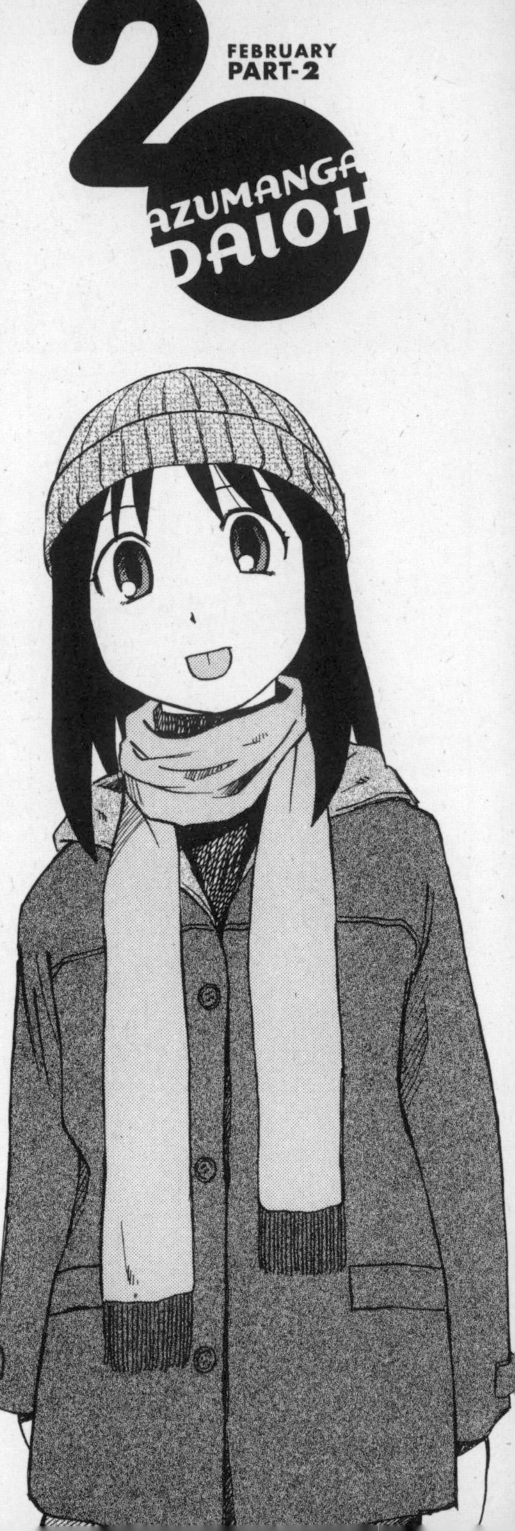
2
FEBRUARY
PART-2
AZUMANGA DAIOH

GOURMET YUKARI

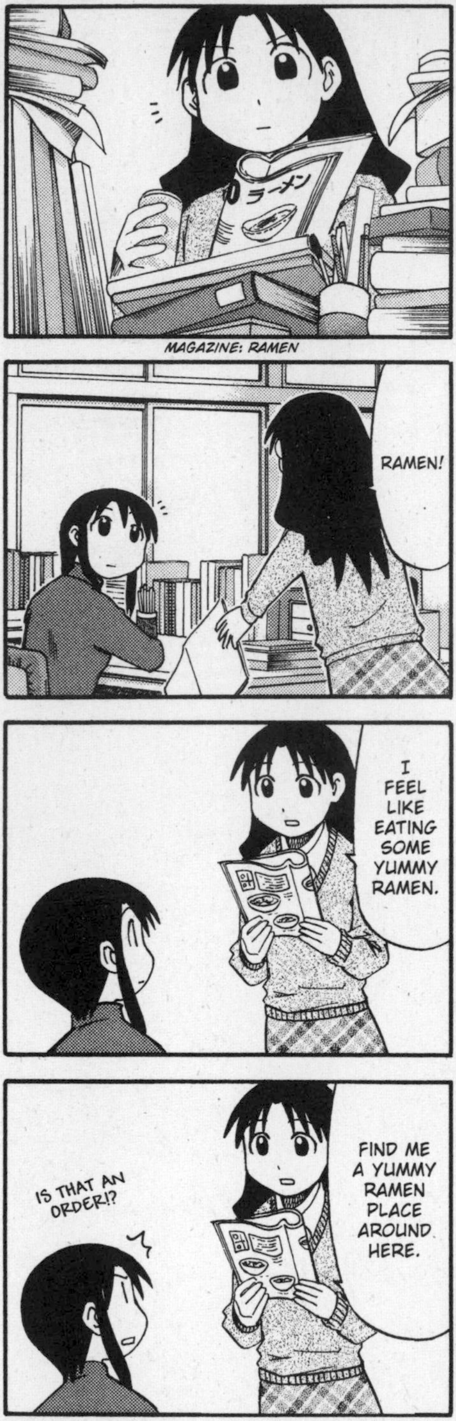
MAGAZINE: RAMEN
RAMEN!
I FEEL LIKE EATING SOME YUMMY RAMEN.
FIND ME A YUMMY RAMEN PLACE AROUND HERE.
IS THAT AN ORDER!?

WHAT?

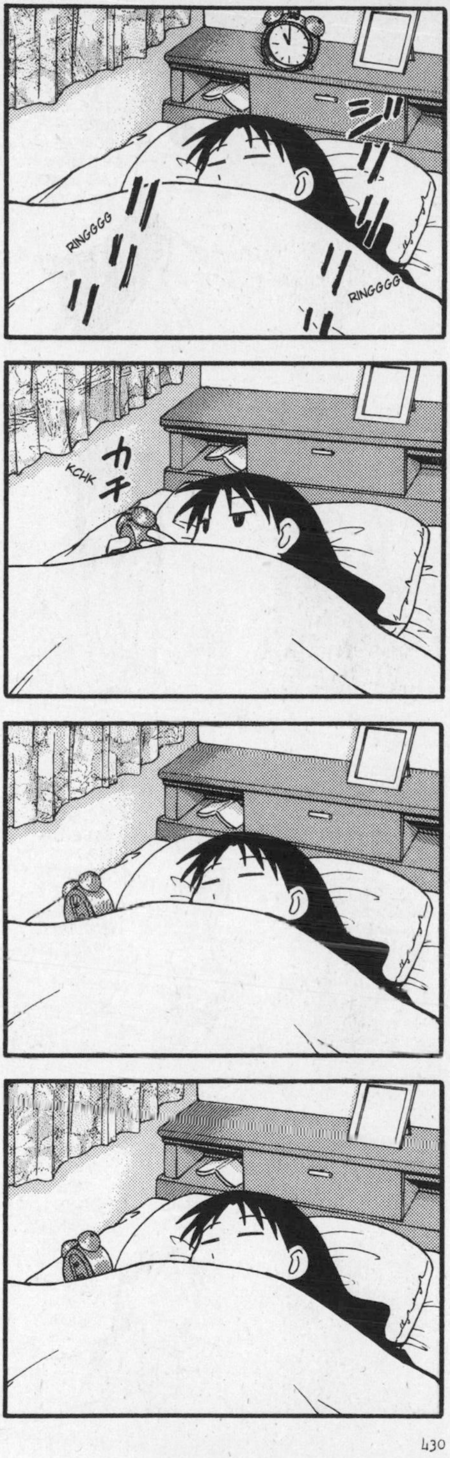

ジジ
RINGGGG
RINGGGG
カチ
KCHK

LEAVE ME ALONE

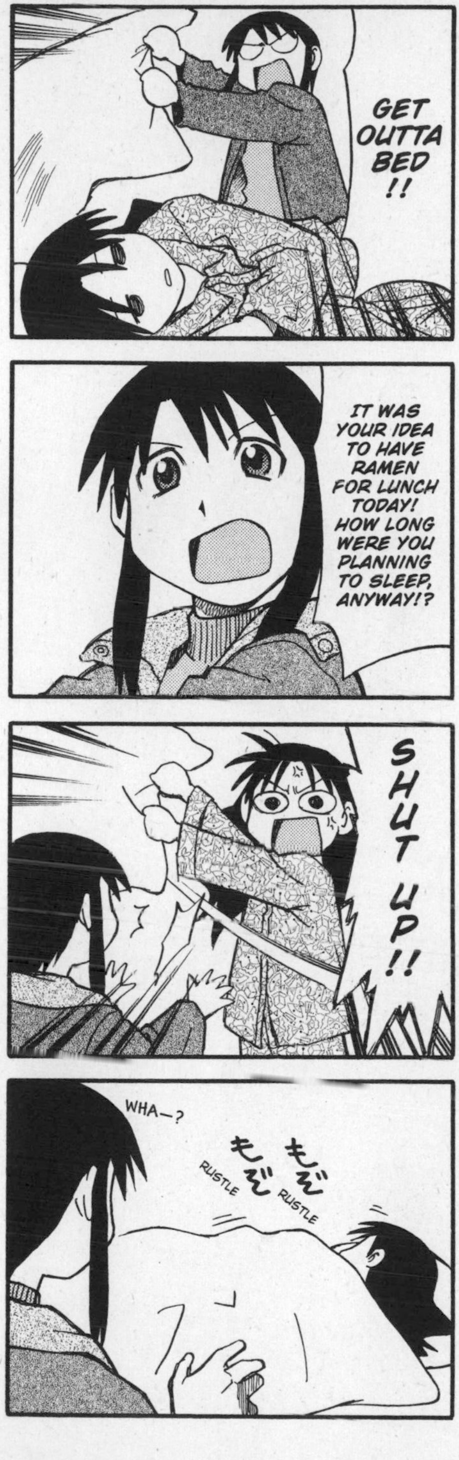

GET OUTTA BED !!
IT WAS YOUR IDEA TO HAVE RAMEN FOR LUNCH TODAY! HOW LONG WERE YOU PLANNING TO SLEEP, ANYWAY!?
SHUT UP!!
WHA—?
もぞもぞ
RUSTLE
RUSTLE

LET'S PLAY

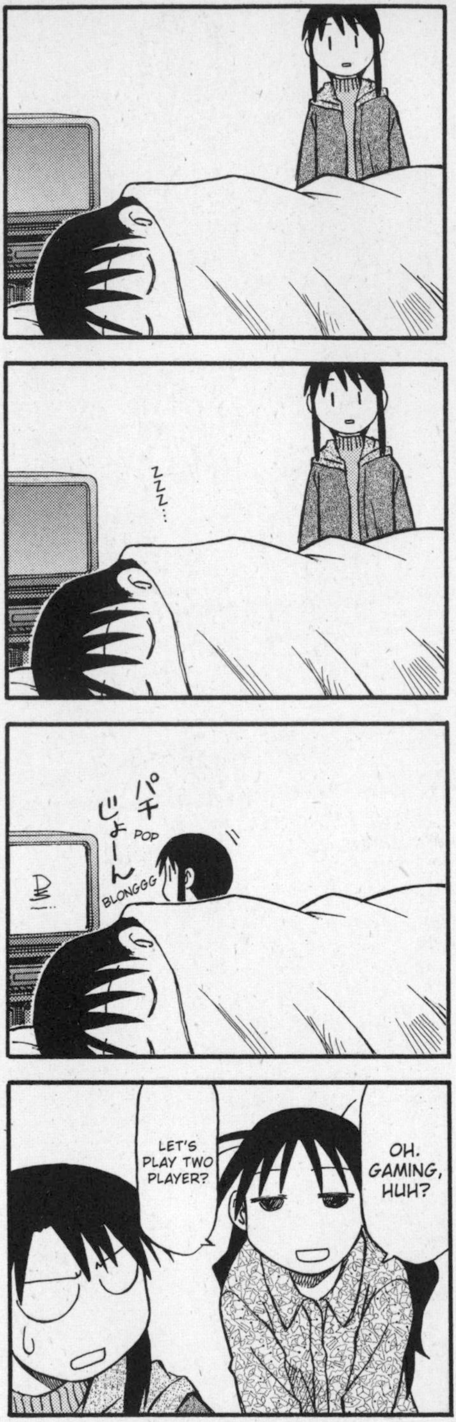
ZZZ...
パチ
POP
じょーん
BLONGGG
OH. GAMING, HUH?
LET'S PLAY TWO PLAYER?

CAN'T GET UP

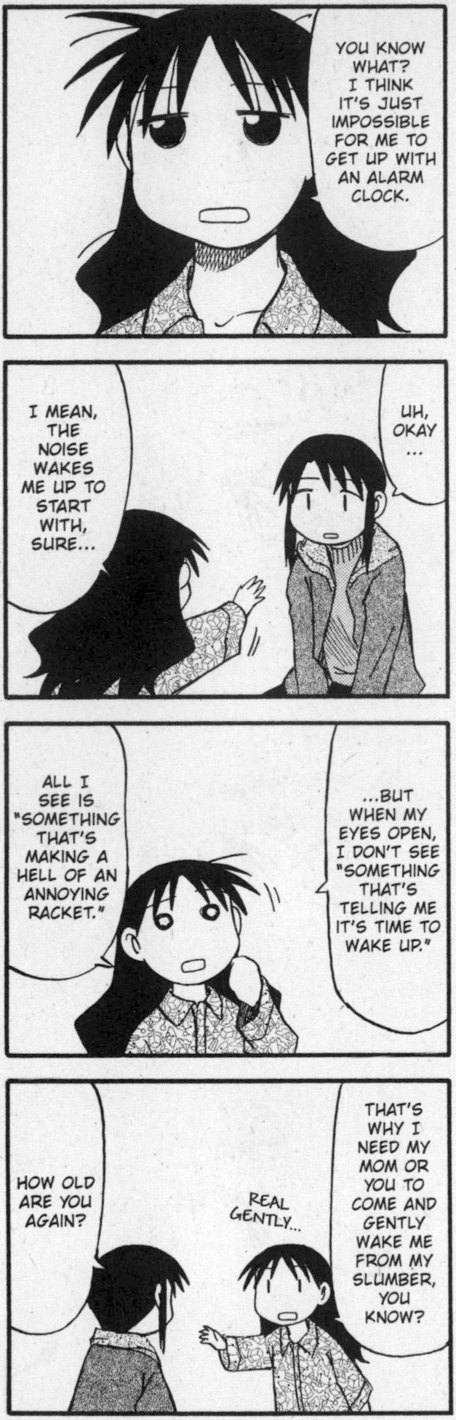
YOU KNOW WHAT? I THINK IT'S JUST IMPOSSIBLE FOR ME TO GET UP WITH AN ALARM CLOCK.
UH, OKAY ...
I MEAN, THE NOISE WAKES ME UP TO START WITH, SURE...
...BUT WHEN MY EYES OPEN, I DON'T SEE "SOMETHING THAT'S TELLING ME IT'S TIME TO WAKE UP."
ALL I SEE IS "SOMETHING THAT'S MAKING A HELL OF AN ANNOYING RACKET."
THAT'S WHY I NEED MY MOM OR YOU TO COME AND GENTLY WAKE ME FROM MY SLUMBER, YOU KNOW?
REAL GENTLY...
HOW OLD ARE YOU AGAIN?

NOT IN THE MOOD

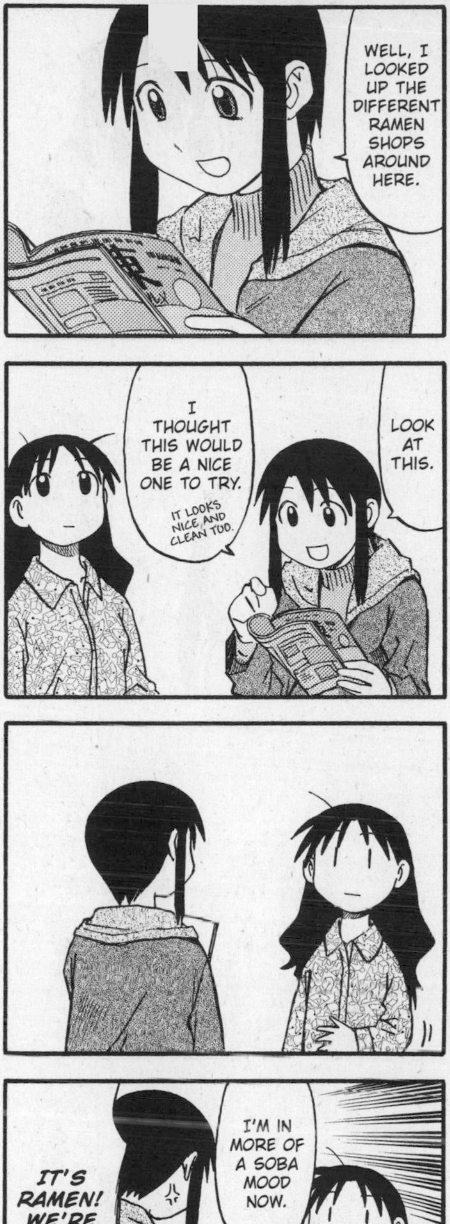
WELL, I LOOKED UP THE DIFFERENT RAMEN SHOPS AROUND HERE.
LOOK AT THIS.
I THOUGHT THIS WOULD BE A NICE ONE TO TRY.
IT LOOKS NICE AND CLEAN TOO.
I'M IN MORE OF A SOBA MOOD NOW.
IT'S RAMEN! WE'RE HAVING RAMEN TODAY!!

FORGOTTEN

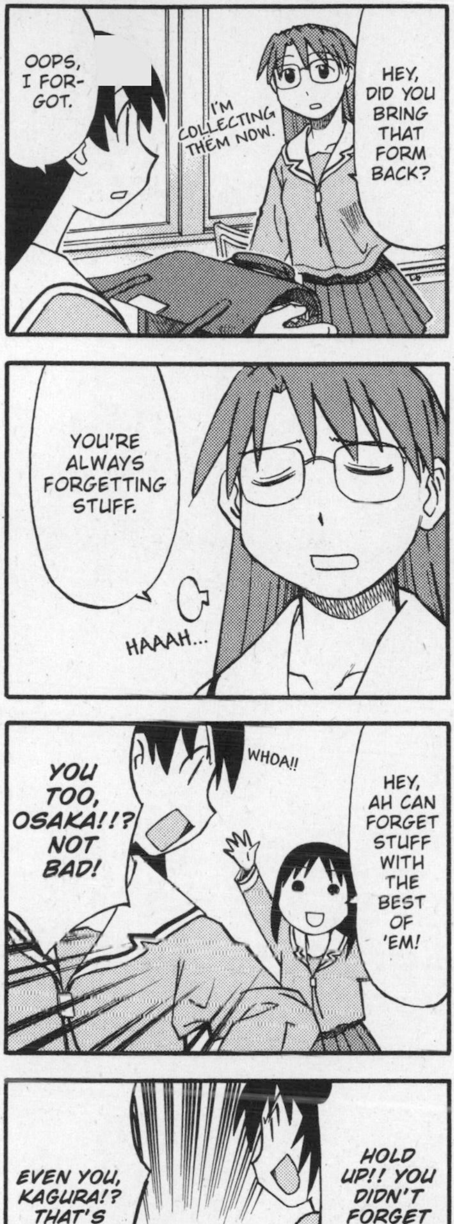
HEY, DID YOU BRING THAT FORM BACK?
I'M COLLECTING THEM NOW.
OOPS, I FORGOT.
YOU'RE ALWAYS FORGETTING STUFF.
HAAAH...
HEY, AH CAN FORGET STUFF WITH THE BEST OF 'EM!
WHOA!!
YOU TOO, OSAKA!!? NOT BAD!
HOLD UP!! YOU DIDN'T FORGET ABOUT ME, DID YOU!!?
EVEN YOU, KAGURA!? THAT'S RIGHT!! WE SHOULDN'T BE FORGETTING!!

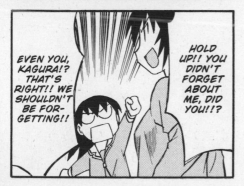

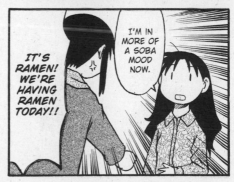

THE EMPRESS

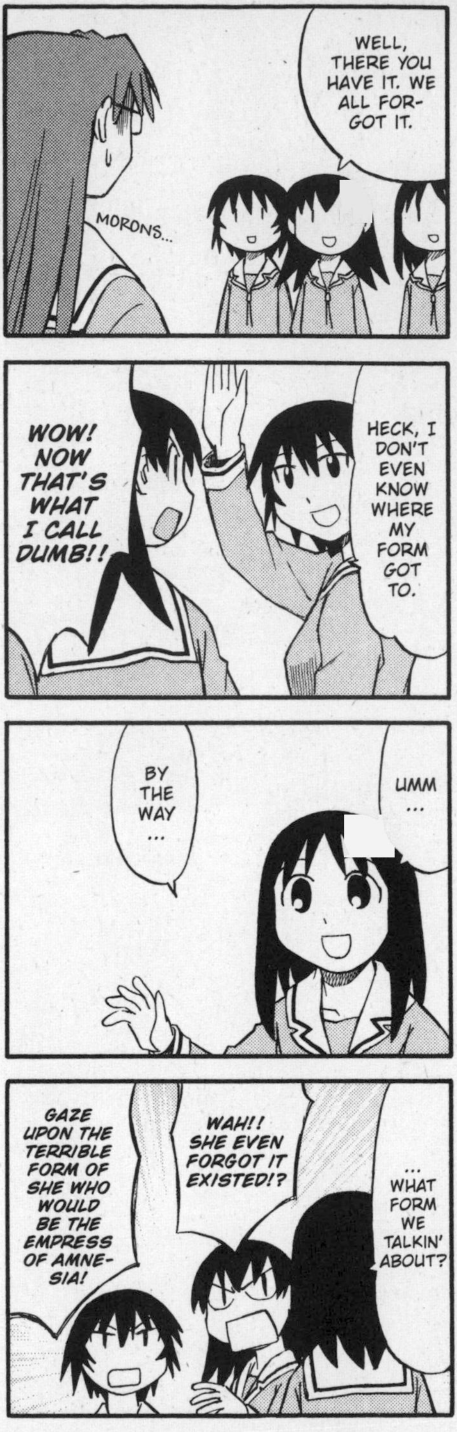
WELL, THERE YOU HAVE IT. WE ALL FOR-GOT IT.
MORONS...
HECK, I DON'T EVEN KNOW WHERE MY FORM GOT TO.
WOW! NOW THAT'S WHAT I CALL DUMB!!
UMM ...
BY THE WAY ...
... WHAT FORM WE TALKIN' ABOUT?
WAH!! SHE EVEN FORGOT IT EXISTED!?
GAZE UPON THE TERRIBLE FORM OF SHE WHO WOULD BE THE EMPRESS OF AMNE-SIA!

HEART OF OSAKA

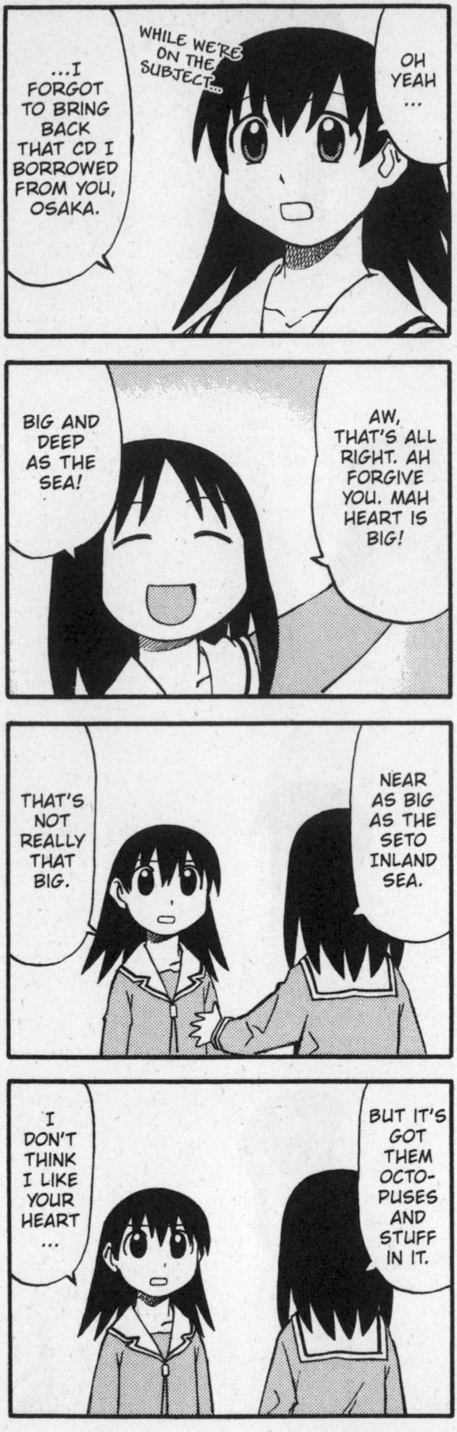
OH YEAH ...
WHILE WE'RE ON THE SUBJECT...
...I FORGOT TO BRING BACK THAT CD I BORROWED FROM YOU, OSAKA.
AW, THAT'S ALL RIGHT. AH FORGIVE YOU. MAH HEART IS BIG!
BIG AND DEEP AS THE SEA!
NEAR AS BIG AS THE SETO INLAND SEA.
THAT'S NOT REALLY THAT BIG.
BUT IT'S GOT THEM OCTO-PUSES AND STUFF IN IT.
I DON'T THINK I LIKE YOUR HEART ...

SUSPICION

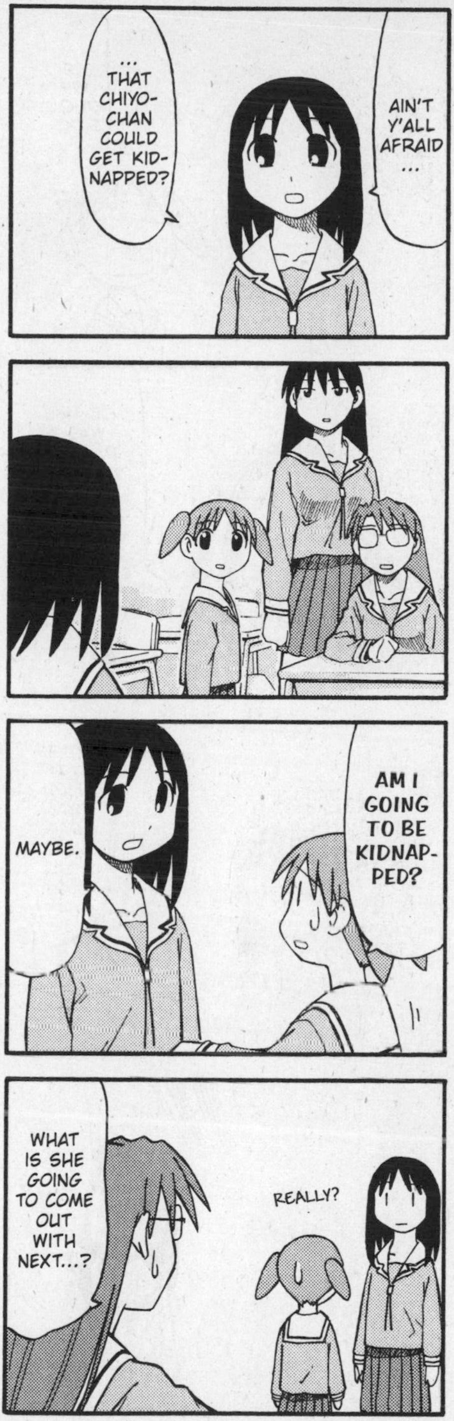

AIN'T Y'ALL AFRAID ...
... THAT CHIYO-CHAN COULD GET KID-NAPPED?
AM I GOING TO BE KIDNAP-PED?
MAYBE.
REALLY?
WHAT IS SHE GOING TO COME OUT WITH NEXT...?

CAPTURE

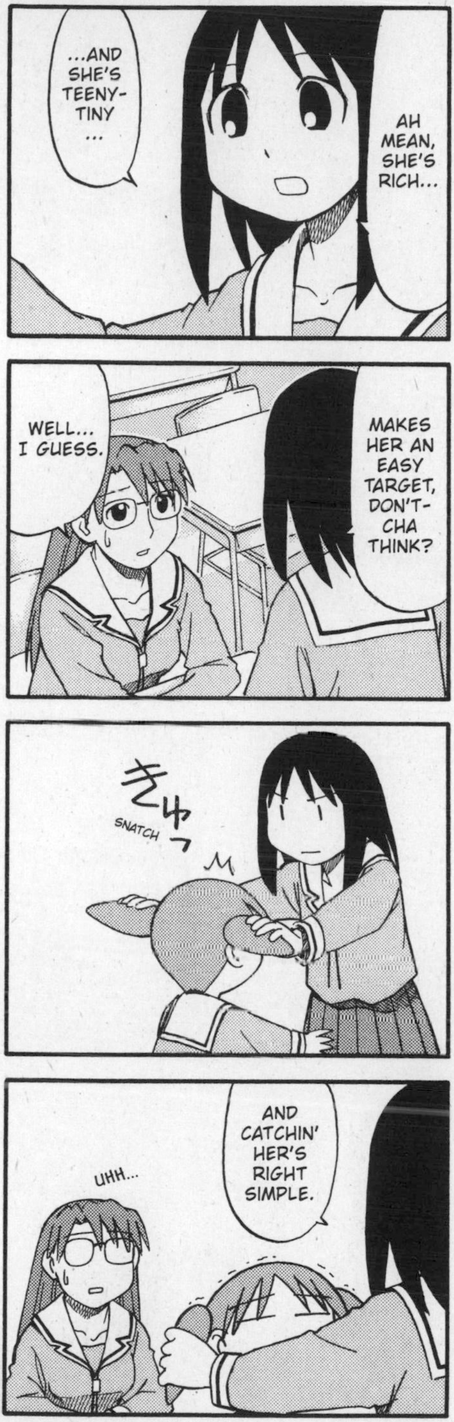

AH MEAN, SHE'S RICH...
...AND SHE'S TEENY-TINY ...
MAKES HER AN EASY TARGET, DON'T-CHA THINK?
WELL... I GUESS.
きゅっ
SNATCH
AND CATCHIN' HER'S RIGHT SIMPLE.
UHH...

GIRL'S BEST FRIEND

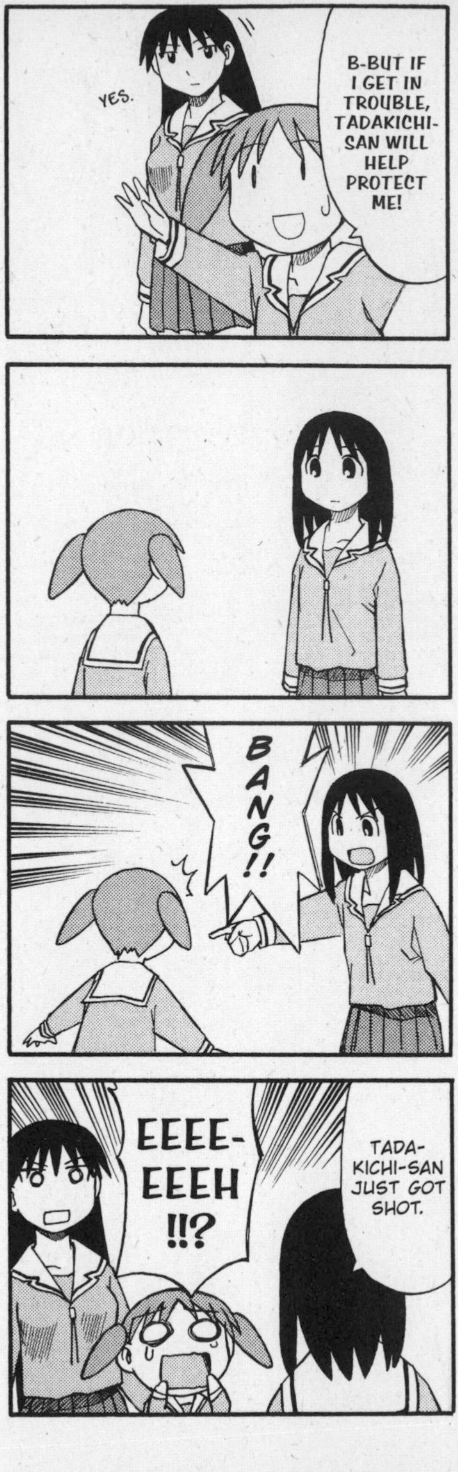
B-BUT IF I GET IN TROUBLE, TADAKICHI-SAN WILL HELP PROTECT ME!
YES.
BANG!!
TADA-KICHI-SAN JUST GOT SHOT.
EEEE-EEEH!!?

CHIYO-CHAN

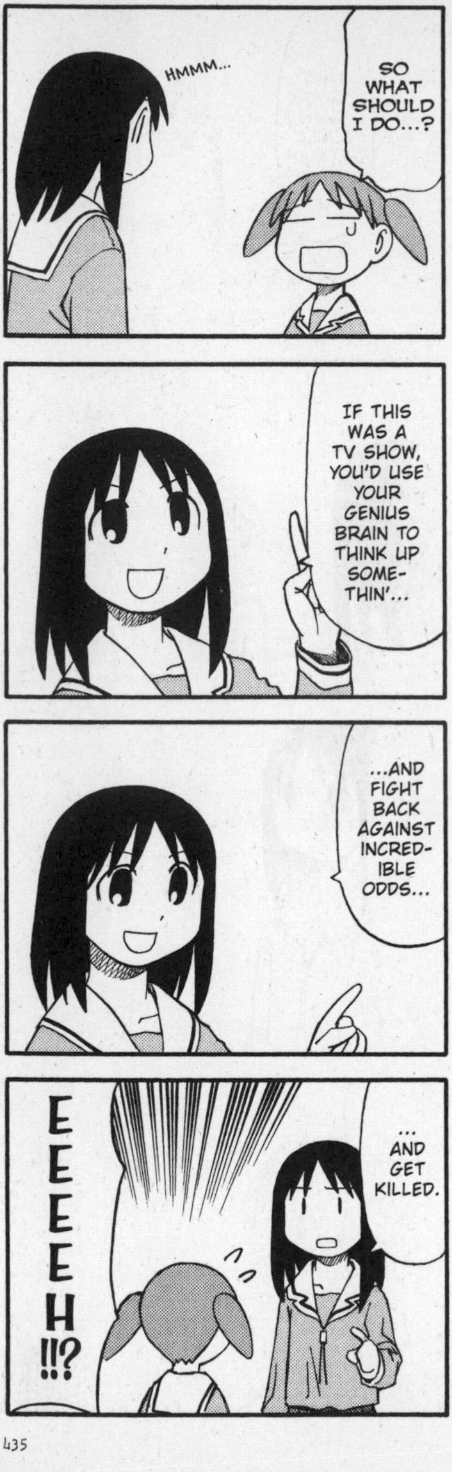
SO WHAT SHOULD I DO...?
HMMM...
IF THIS WAS A TV SHOW, YOU'D USE YOUR GENIUS BRAIN TO THINK UP SOME-THIN'...
...AND FIGHT BACK AGAINST INCRED-IBLE ODDS...
...AND GET KILLED.
EEEEEH!!?

FLIGHT

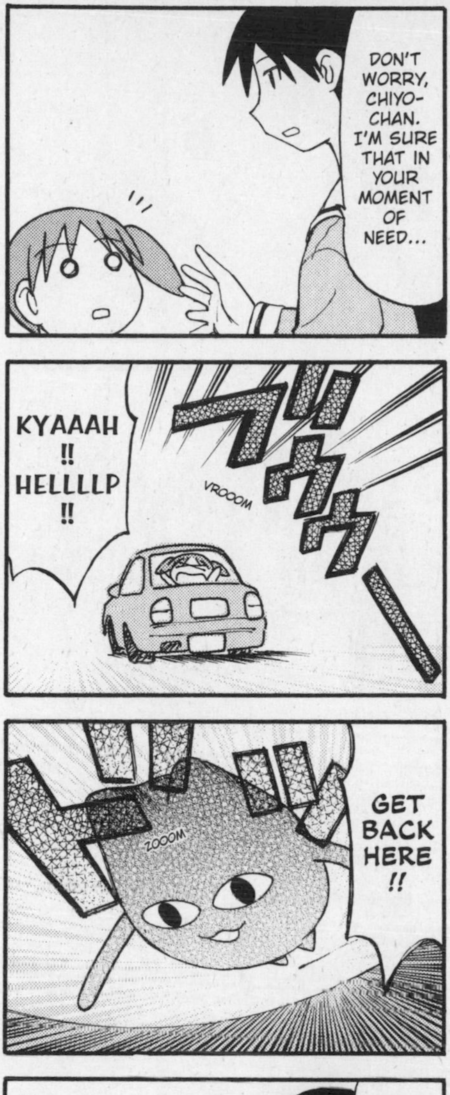
DON'T WORRY, CHIYO-CHAN. I'M SURE THAT IN YOUR MOMENT OF NEED...
KYAAAH!! HELLLLP!!
VROOOM
GET BACK HERE!!
ZOOOM
...YOUR FATHER WILL COME FLYING TO THE RESCUE.
Y-YOU THINK SO?

FATHER!!

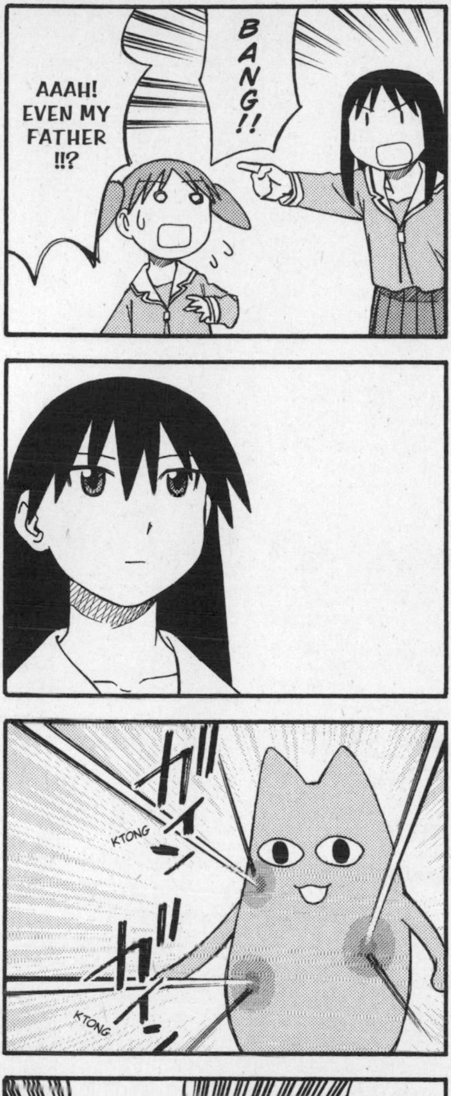
BANG!!
AAAH! EVEN MY FATHER!!?
KTONG
KTONG
DON'T WORRY, HE BOUNCED THEM OFF.
NO WAY!!

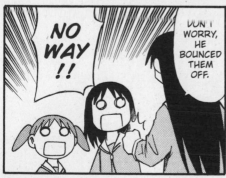

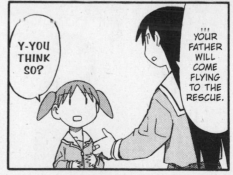

AZUMANGA-DAIOH

109

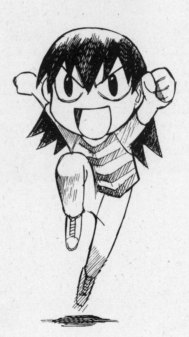

You belong.

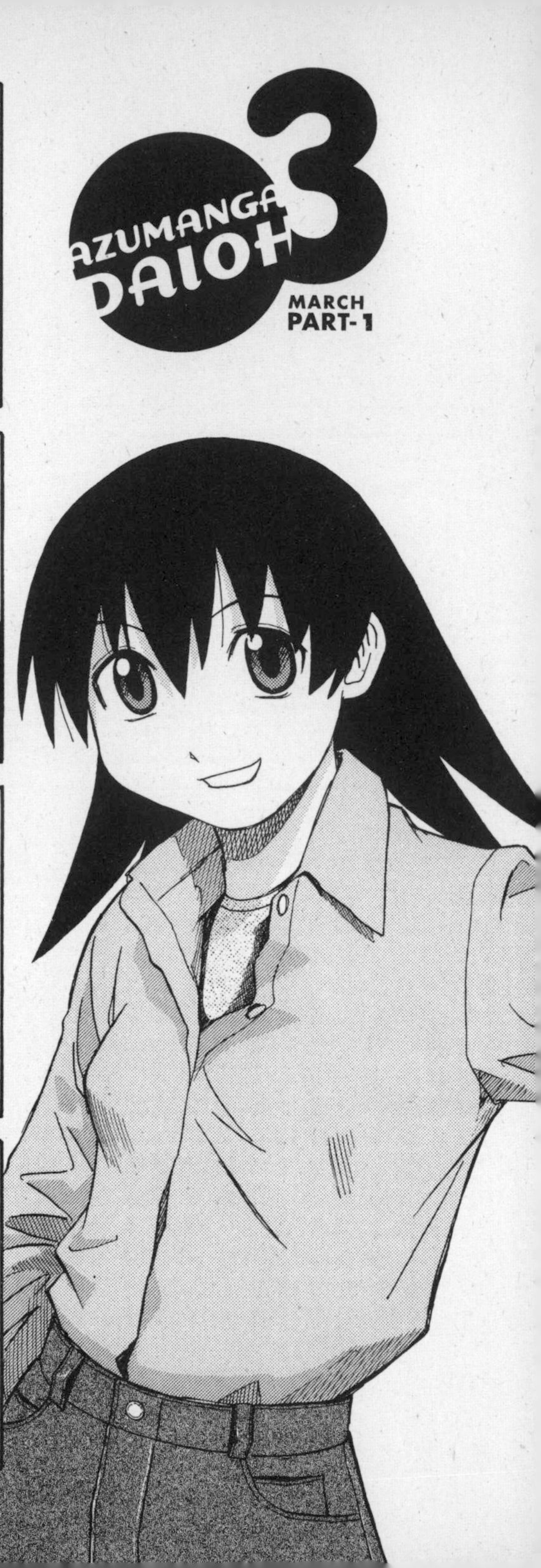
AZUMANGA DAIOH 3
MARCH PART-1

OF COURSE

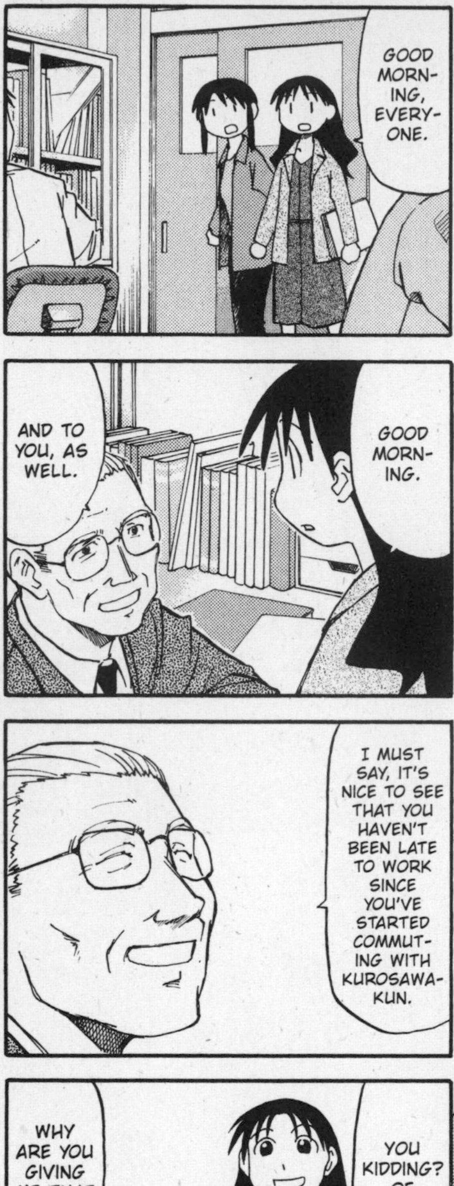
GOOD MORNING, EVERYONE.
GOOD MORNING.
AND TO YOU, AS WELL.
I MUST SAY, IT'S NICE TO SEE THAT YOU HAVEN'T BEEN LATE TO WORK SINCE YOU'VE STARTED COMMUTING WITH KUROSAWA-KUN.
YOU KIDDING? OF COURSE NOT!
WHY ARE YOU GIVING ME THAT ATTITUDE?

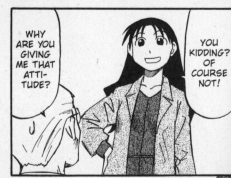

IT FINALLY HAPPENED

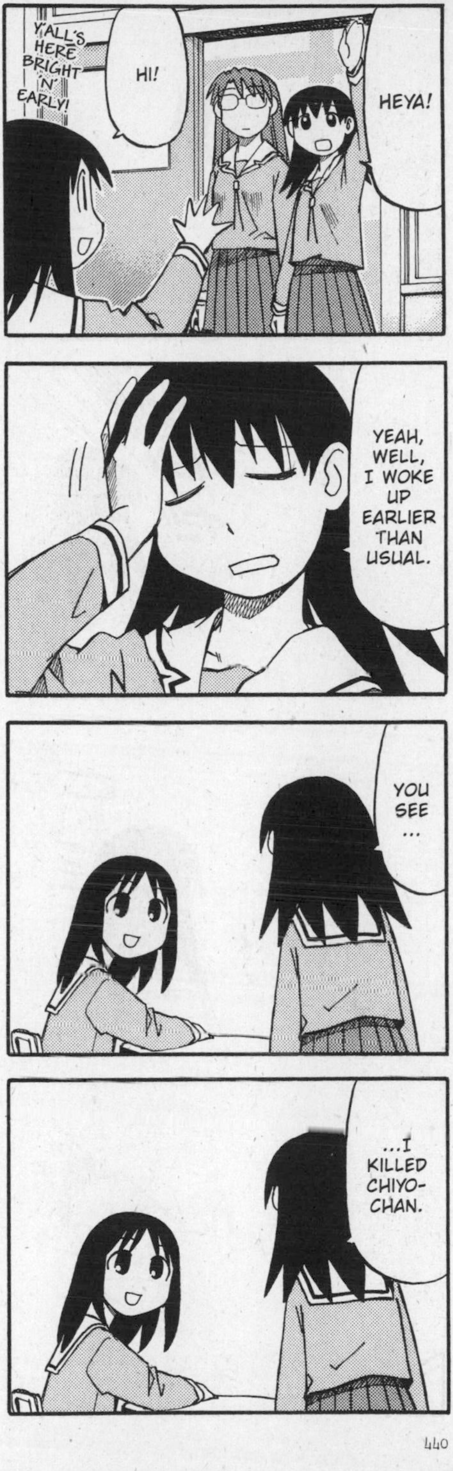
HEYA!
HI!
Y'ALL'S HERE BRIGHT 'N' EARLY!
YEAH, WELL, I WOKE UP EARLIER THAN USUAL.
YOU SEE ...
...I KILLED CHIYO-CHAN.

MURDERER

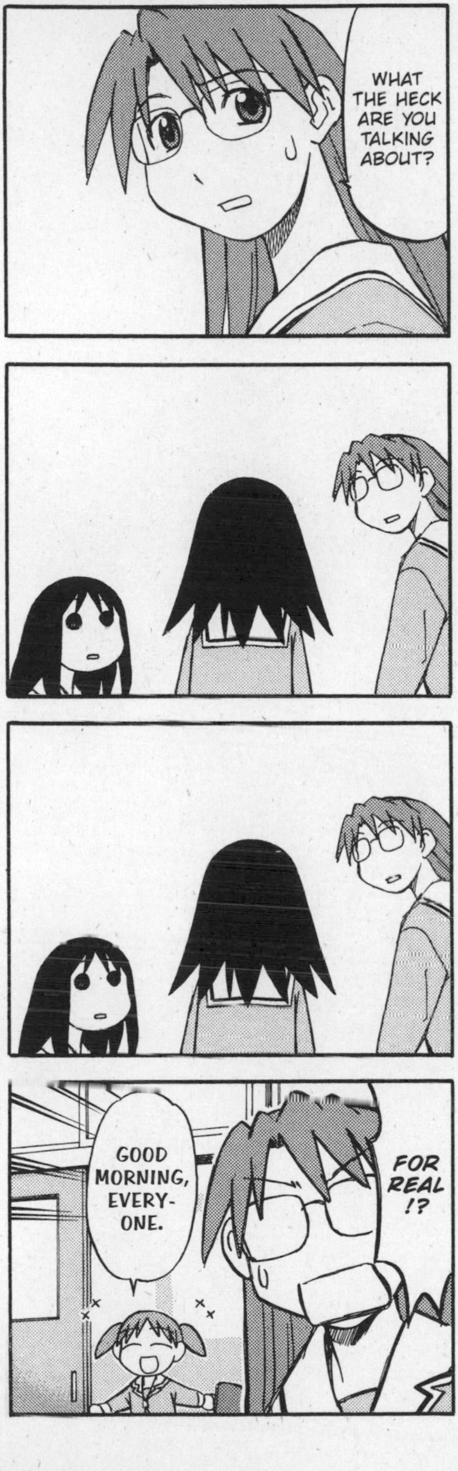
WHAT THE HECK ARE YOU TALKING ABOUT?
FOR REAL!?
GOOD MORNING, EVERY-ONE.

DEFENSE

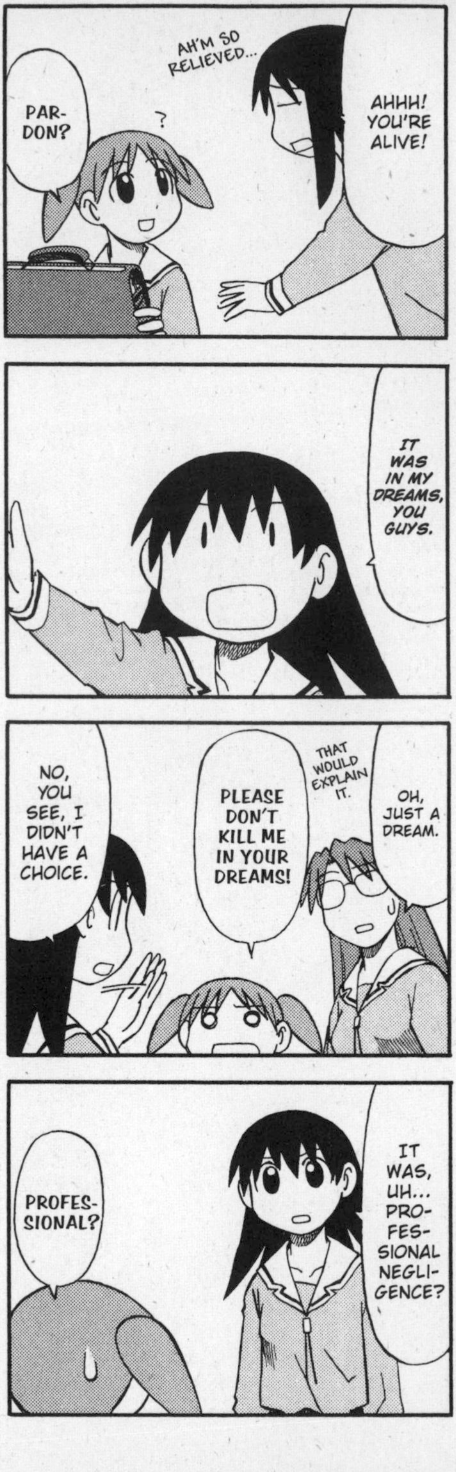

AHHH! YOU'RE ALIVE!
AH'M SO RELIEVED...
?
PAR-DON?
IT WAS IN MY DREAMS, YOU GUYS.
OH, JUST A DREAM.
THAT WOULD EXPLAIN IT.
PLEASE DON'T KILL ME IN YOUR DREAMS!
NO, YOU SEE, I DIDN'T HAVE A CHOICE.
IT WAS, UH... PRO-FES-SIONAL NEGLI-GENCE?
PROFES-SIONAL?

BUTTON

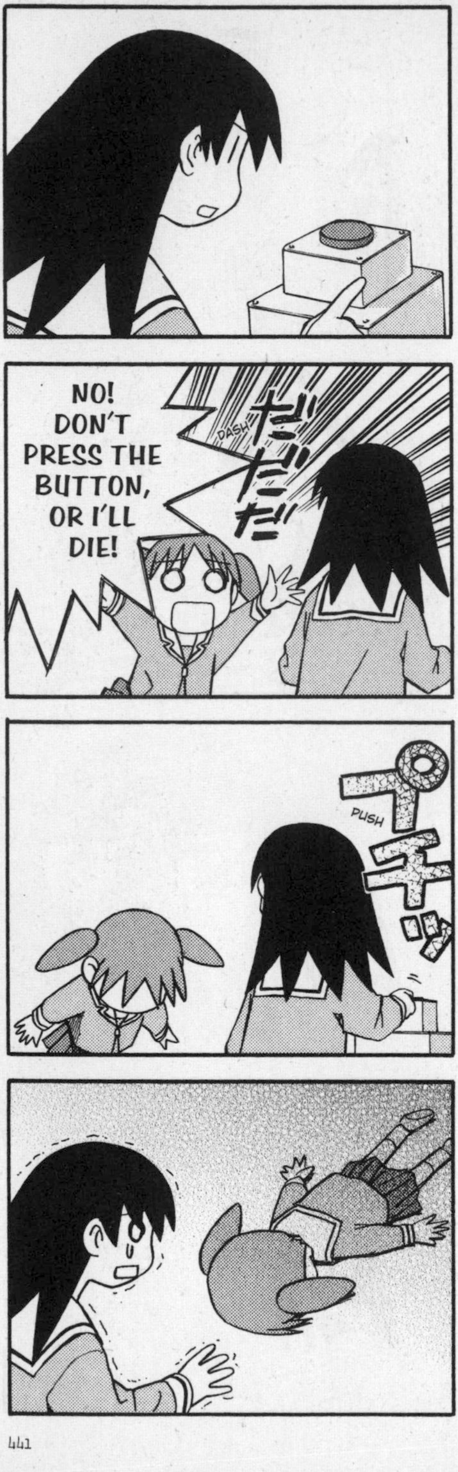

だだだだ
DASH
NO! DON'T PRESS THE BUTTON, OR I'LL DIE!
プチッ
PUSH

CLOSE ONE

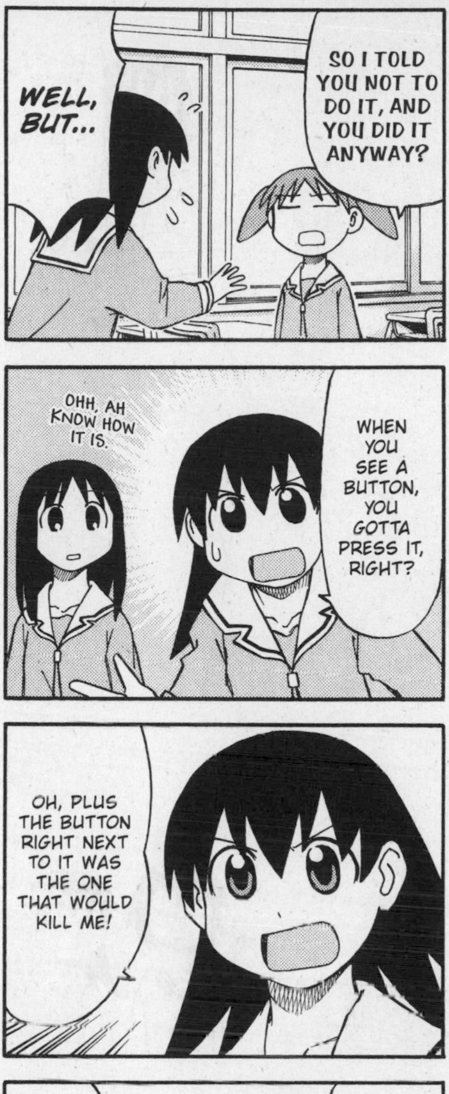
SO I TOLD YOU NOT TO DO IT, AND YOU DID IT ANYWAY?
WELL, BUT...
WHEN YOU SEE A BUTTON, YOU GOTTA PRESS IT, RIGHT?
OHH, AH KNOW HOW IT IS.
OH, PLUS THE BUTTON RIGHT NEXT TO IT WAS THE ONE THAT WOULD KILL ME!
AND I COULDN'T BRING MYSELF TO PRESS THAT ONE, YOU KNOW.
WHEW!
BUT YOU COULD PRESS MINE...?

COMMON CONTEMPORARY TERMS

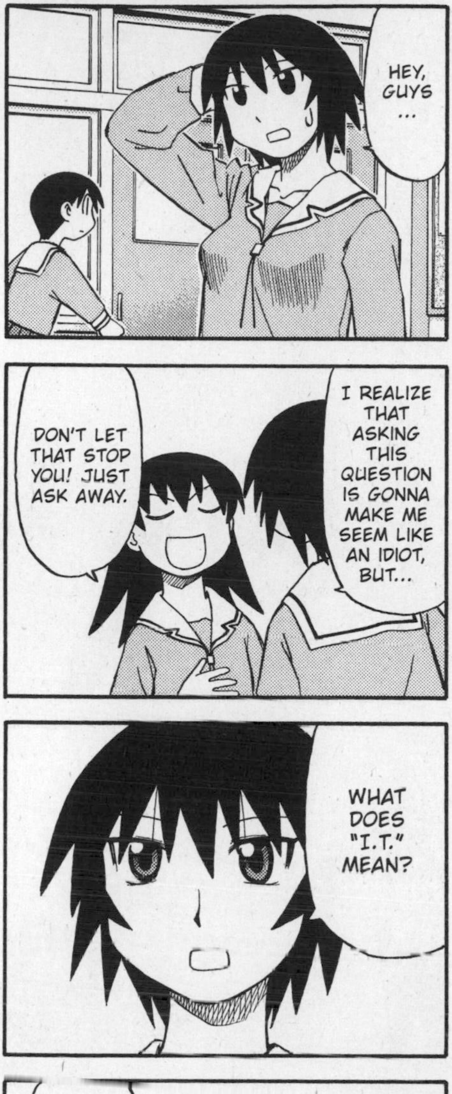
HEY, GUYS ...
I REALIZE THAT ASKING THIS QUESTION IS GONNA MAKE ME SEEM LIKE AN IDIOT, BUT...
DON'T LET THAT STOP YOU! JUST ASK AWAY.
WHAT DOES "I.T." MEAN?
DON'T LOOK AWAY.

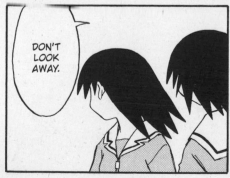

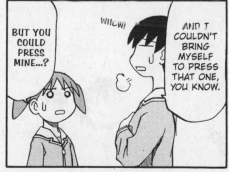

SORTA LIKE...

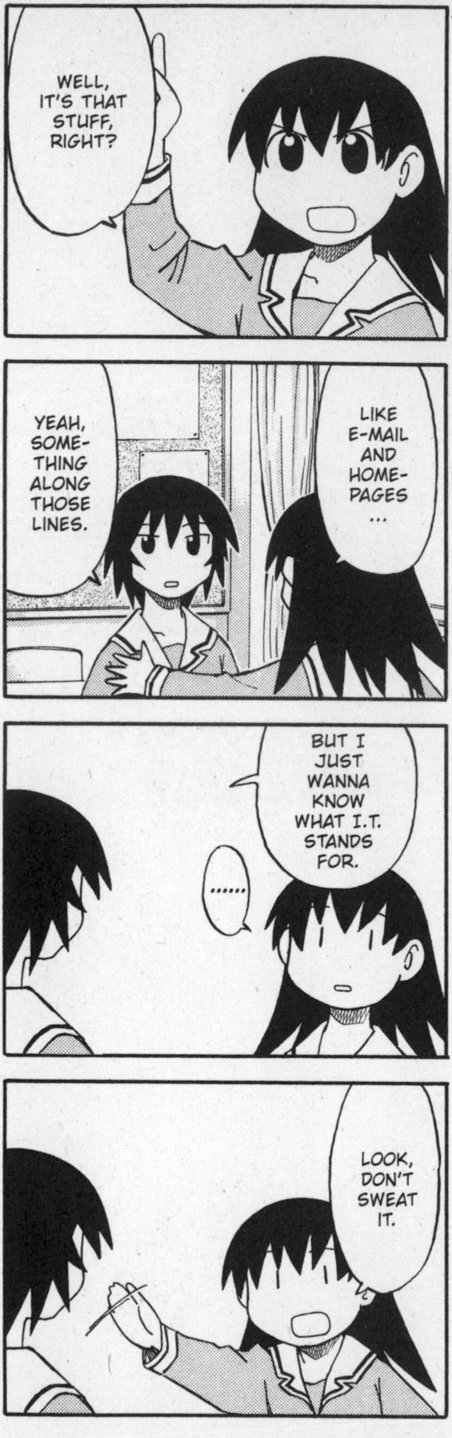
WELL, IT'S THAT STUFF, RIGHT?
LIKE E-MAIL AND HOME-PAGES...
YEAH, SOME-THING ALONG THOSE LINES.
BUT I JUST WANNA KNOW WHAT I.T. STANDS FOR.
......
LOOK, DON'T SWEAT IT.

I.T.

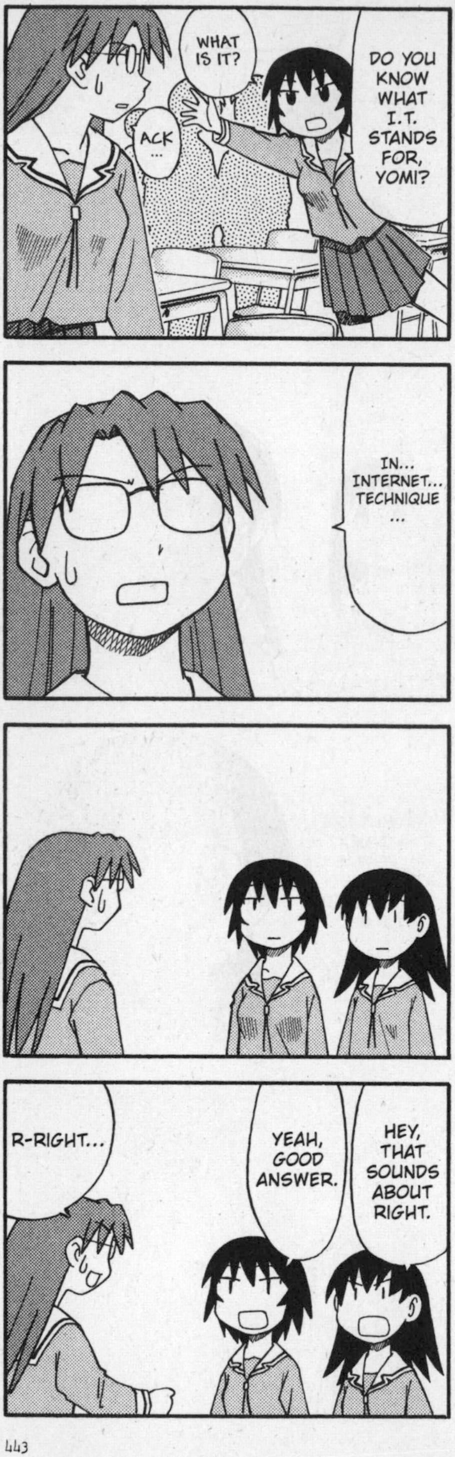
DO YOU KNOW WHAT I.T. STANDS FOR, YOMI?
WHAT IS IT?
ACK...
IN... INTERNET... TECHNIQUE...
HEY, THAT SOUNDS ABOUT RIGHT.
YEAH, GOOD ANSWER.
R-RIGHT...

THE REAL I.T.

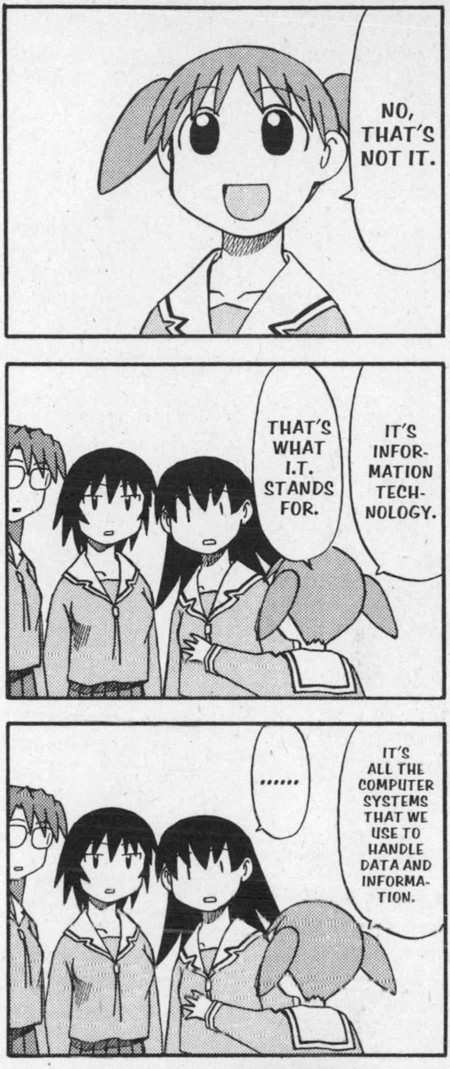
NO, THAT'S NOT IT.
IT'S INFORMATION TECHNOLOGY.
THAT'S WHAT I.T. STANDS FOR.
IT'S ALL THE COMPUTER SYSTEMS THAT WE USE TO HANDLE DATA AND INFORMATION.
......
WHERE DO YOU LEARN STUFF LIKE THAT?
UMM... I DON'T KNOW.

THE LAW

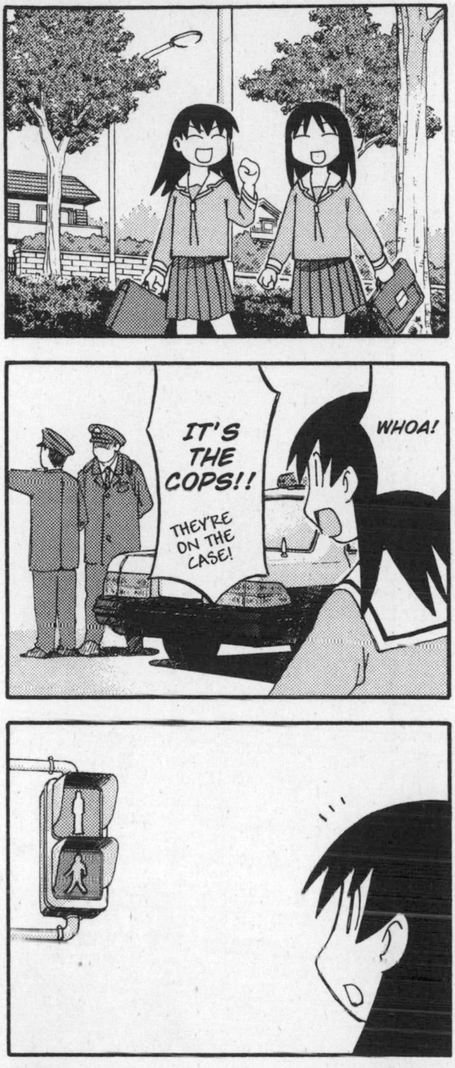
WHOA!
IT'S THE COPS!!
THEY'RE ON THE CASE!
BEST WE FOLLOW THE TRAFFIC LIGHT.
YEAH.

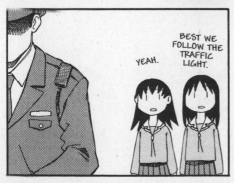

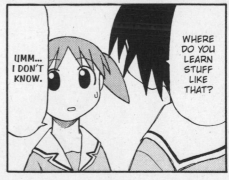

APPEAL

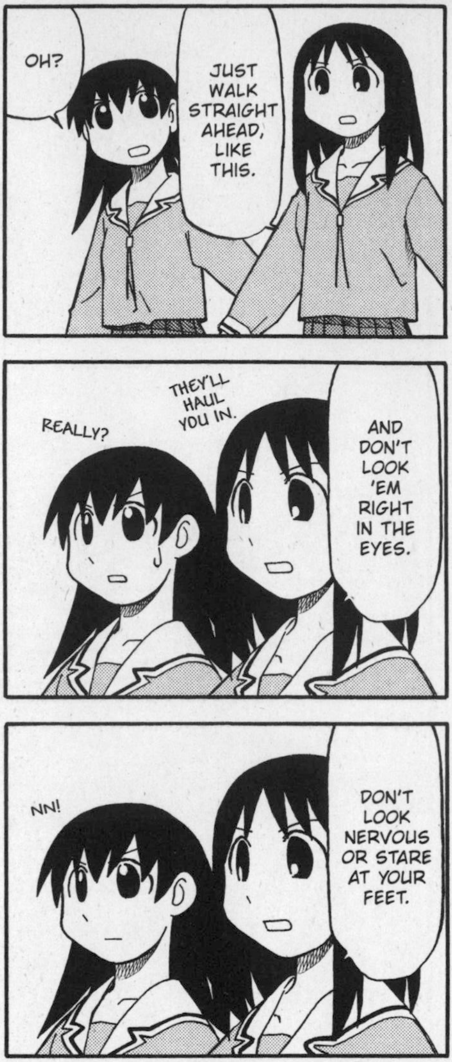
JUST WALK STRAIGHT AHEAD, LIKE THIS.
OH?
AND DON'T LOOK 'EM RIGHT IN THE EYES.
THEY'LL HAUL YOU IN.
REALLY?
DON'T LOOK NERVOUS OR STARE AT YOUR FEET.
NN!
GOTTA ACT LIKE YOU AIN'T A CRIMINAL.
GOT IT!

GROWING PAINS

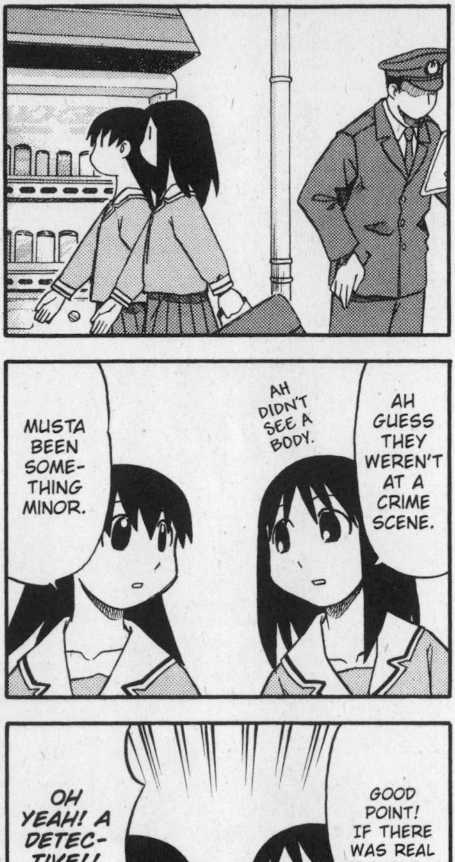
AH GUESS THEY WEREN'T AT A CRIME SCENE.
AH DIDN'T SEE A BODY.
MUSTA BEEN SOME-THING MINOR.
GOOD POINT! IF THERE WAS REAL TROUBLE, A DETECTIVE'D BE AT THE SCENE!
OH YEAH! A DETEC-TIVE!!
AH WONDER IF THEM BACK THERE'LL TURN INTO DETECTIVES WHEN THEY GROW UP.
IS THAT HOW IT WORKS?

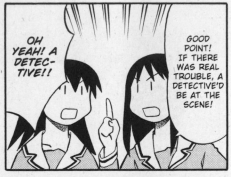

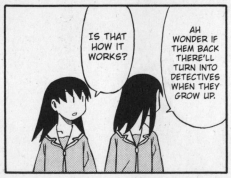

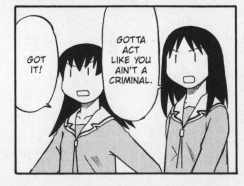

MEMO

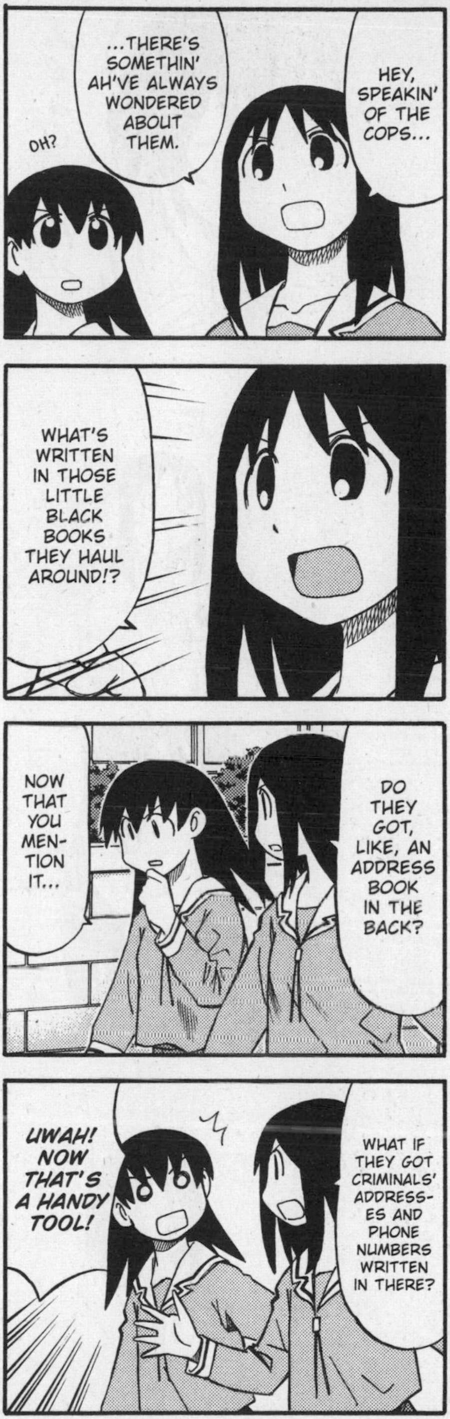
HEY, SPEAKIN' OF THE COPS...
...THERE'S SOMETHIN' AH'VE ALWAYS WONDERED ABOUT THEM.
OH?
WHAT'S WRITTEN IN THOSE LITTLE BLACK BOOKS THEY HAUL AROUND!?
DO THEY GOT, LIKE, AN ADDRESS BOOK IN THE BACK?
NOW THAT YOU MEN-TION IT...
WHAT IF THEY GOT CRIMINALS' ADDRESS-ES AND PHONE NUMBERS WRITTEN IN THERE?
UWAH! NOW THAT'S A HANDY TOOL!

REALITY

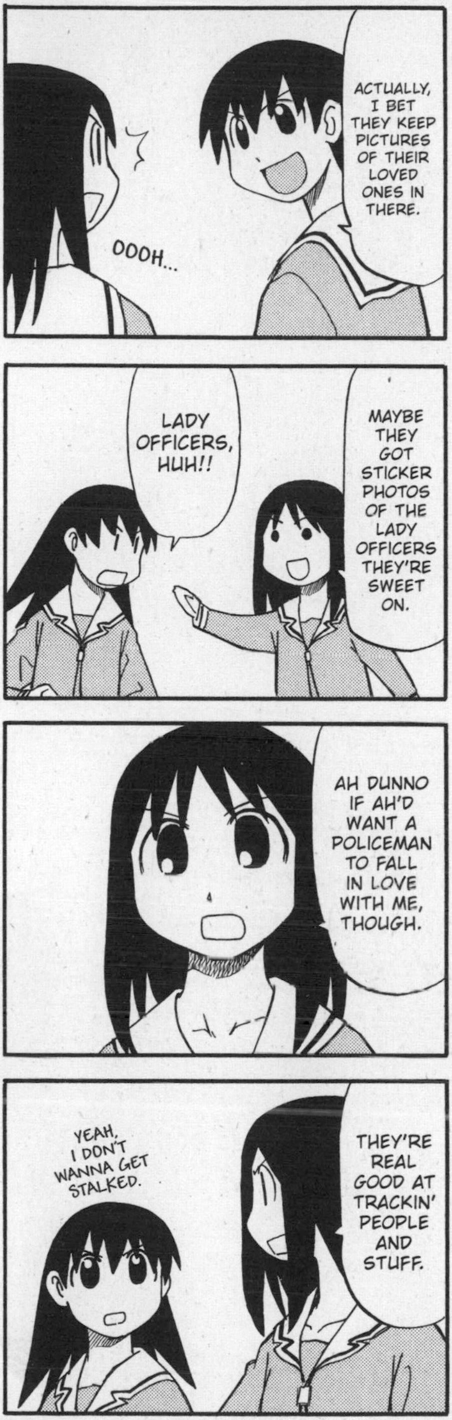
ACTUALLY, I BET THEY KEEP PICTURES OF THEIR LOVED ONES IN THERE.
OOOH...
MAYBE THEY GOT STICKER PHOTOS OF THE LADY OFFICERS THEY'RE SWEET ON.
LADY OFFICERS, HUH!!
AH DUNNO IF AH'D WANT A POLICEMAN TO FALL IN LOVE WITH ME, THOUGH.
THEY'RE REAL GOOD AT TRACKIN' PEOPLE AND STUFF.
YEAH, I DON'T WANNA GET STALKED.

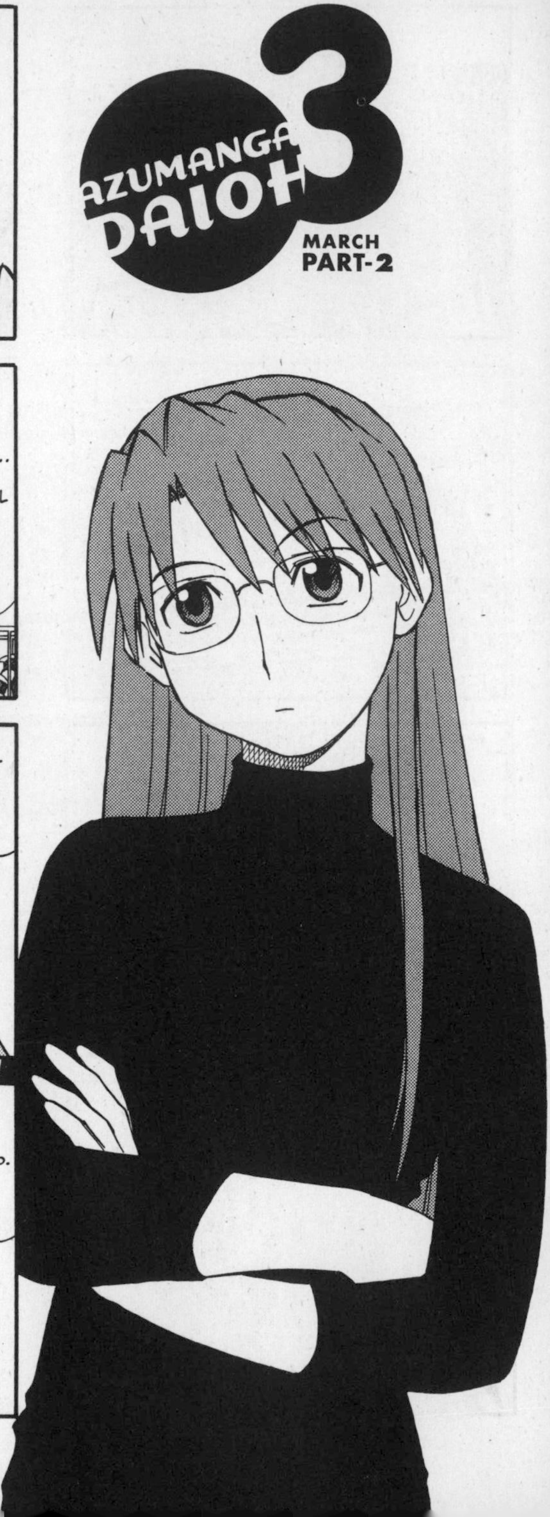
AZUMANGA DAIOH 3
MARCH PART-2

DESIRE

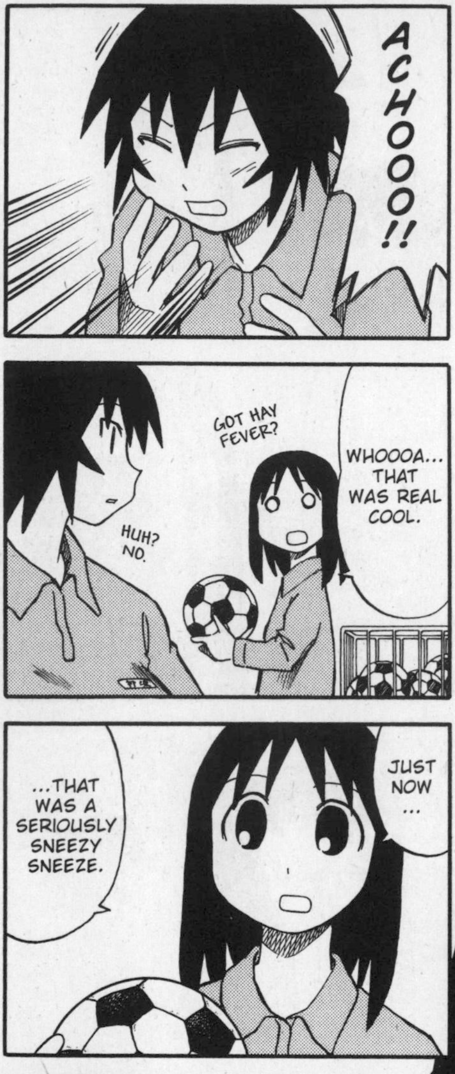
ACHOOOO!!
WHOOOA... THAT WAS REAL COOL.
GOT HAY FEVER?
HUH? NO.
JUST NOW ...
...THAT WAS A SERIOUSLY SNEEZY SNEEZE.
HECHYO.

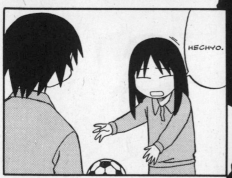

HECHYO

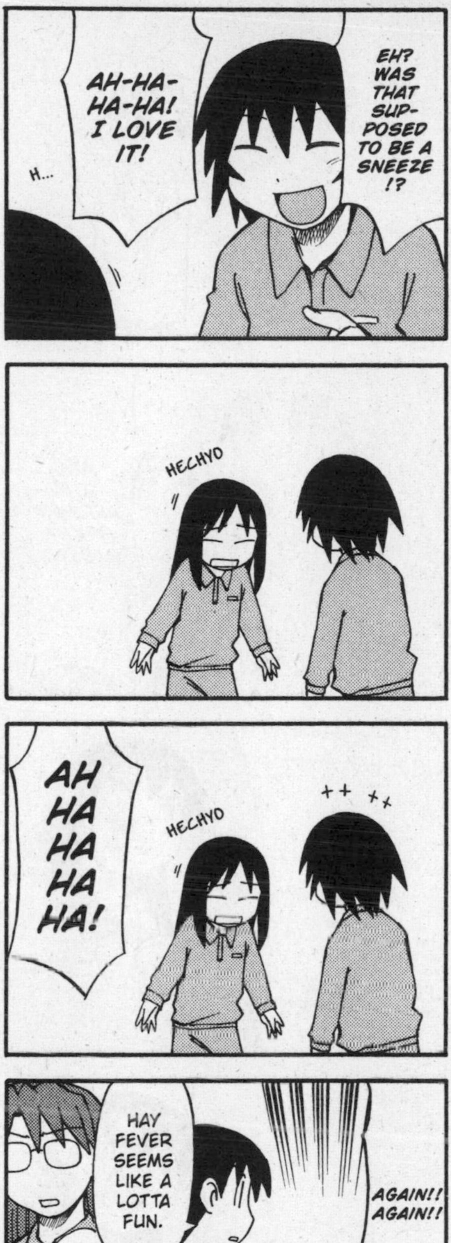
EH? WAS THAT SUP-POSED TO BE A SNEEZE !?
AH-HA-HA-HA! I LOVE IT!
H...
HECHYO
AH HA HA HA HA HA!
HECHYO
AGAIN!! AGAIN!!
HAY FEVER SEEMS LIKE A LOTTA FUN.
HECHYO.
NO, IT'S NOT.

<SPEAK ILL OF>

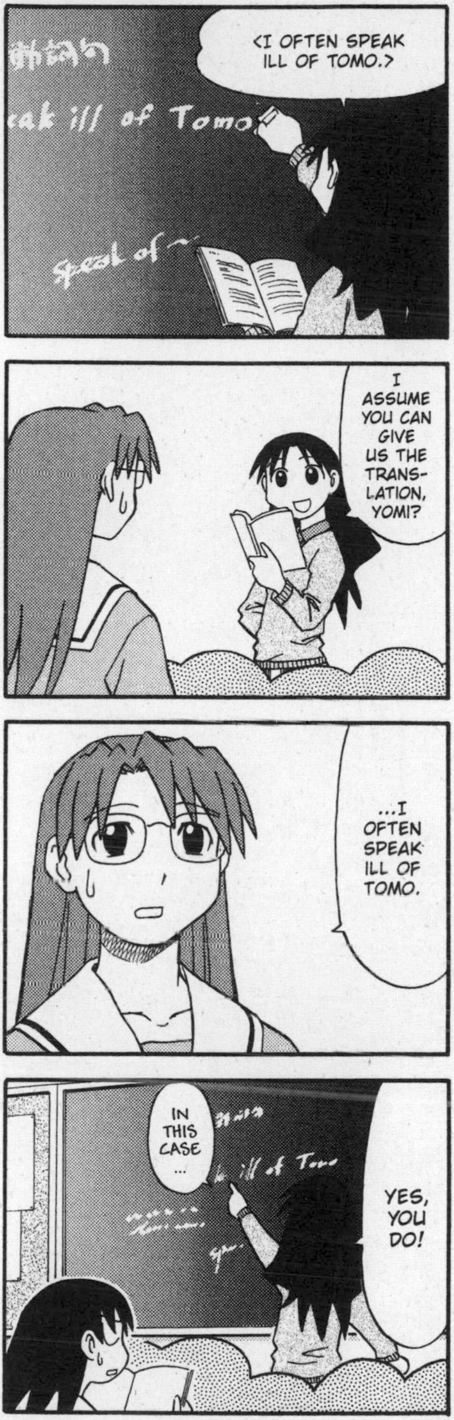
<I OFTEN SPEAK ILL OF TOMO.>
I ASSUME YOU CAN GIVE US THE TRANS-LATION, YOMI?
...I OFTEN SPEAK ILL OF TOMO.
YES, YOU DO!
IN THIS CASE ...

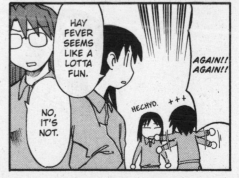

INDEFINITE ARTICLE

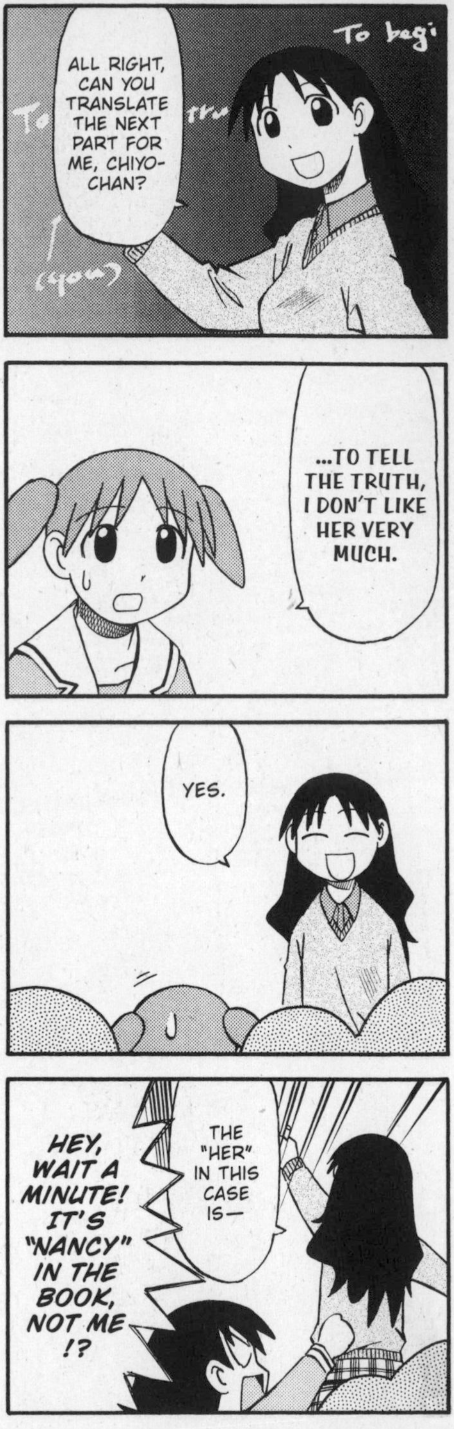
To begi
To
tru
(you)
ALL RIGHT, CAN YOU TRANSLATE THE NEXT PART FOR ME, CHIYO-CHAN?
...TO TELL THE TRUTH, I DON'T LIKE HER VERY MUCH.
YES.
THE "HER" IN THIS CASE IS—
HEY, WAIT A MINUTE! IT'S "NANCY" IN THE BOOK, NOT ME!?

NICE TRY

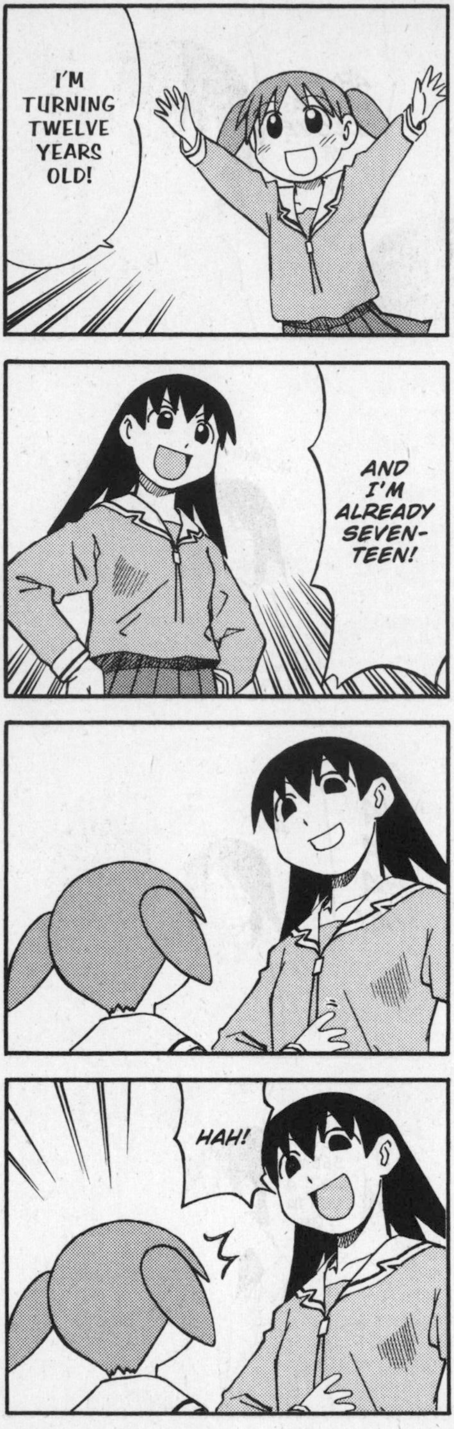
I'M TURNING TWELVE YEARS OLD!
AND I'M ALREADY SEVEN-TEEN!
HAH!

HAPPY BIRTHDAY

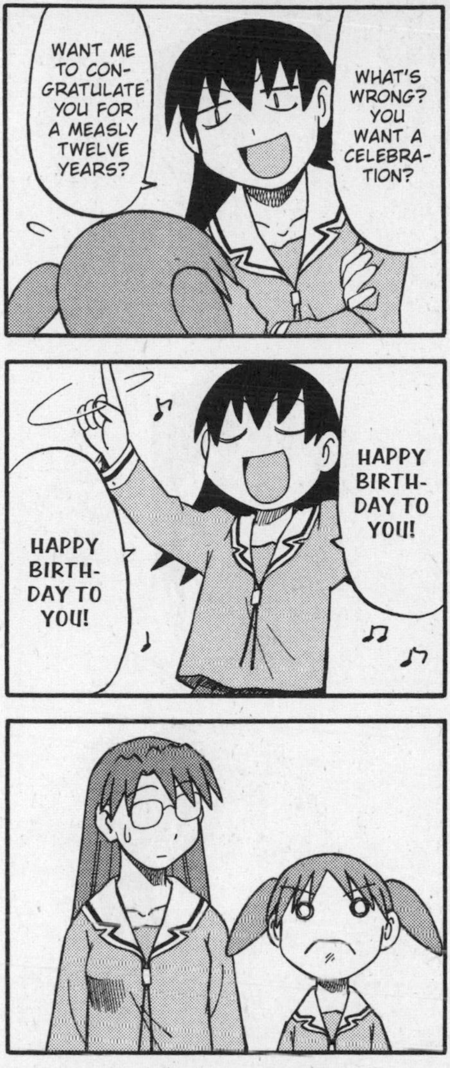
WHAT'S WRONG? YOU WANT A CELEBRA-TION?
WANT ME TO CON-GRATULATE YOU FOR A MEASLY TWELVE YEARS?
HAPPY BIRTH-DAY TO YOU!
HAPPY BIRTH-DAY TO YOU!
I'M NOT GOING TO INVITE YOU TO MY BIRTH-DAY PARTY!
WHAT!!? THINK OF ALL THE CAKE I'LL BE MISS-ING OUT ON!!

INVITATION

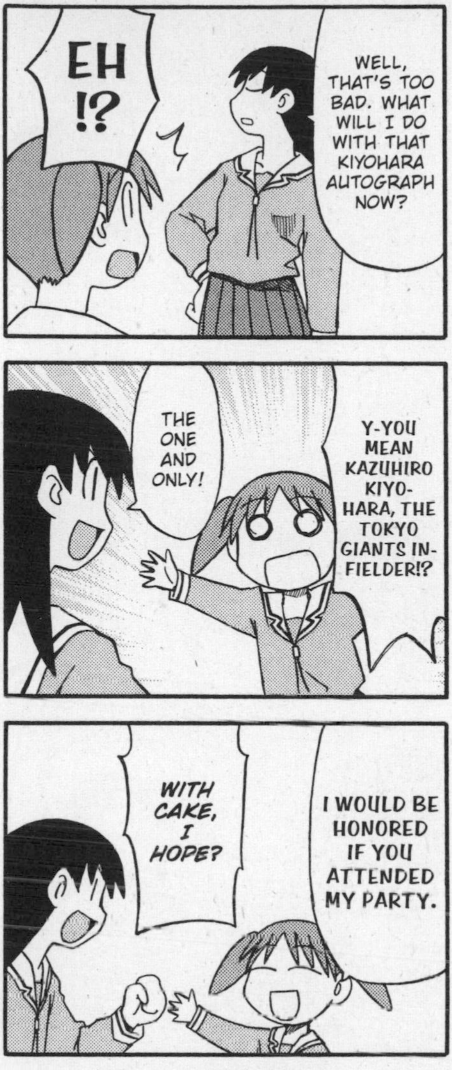
WELL, THAT'S TOO BAD. WHAT WILL I DO WITH THAT KIYOHARA AUTOGRAPH NOW?
EH !?
Y-YOU MEAN KAZUHIRO KIYO-HARA, THE TOKYO GIANTS IN-FIELDER!?
THE ONE AND ONLY!
I WOULD BE HONORED IF YOU ATTENDED MY PARTY.
WITH CAKE, I HOPE?
YOU CAN EVEN HAVE THE SLICE WITH THE LITTLE HOUSE ON TOP.
WOO-HOO! SCORE!
LUCKY ...

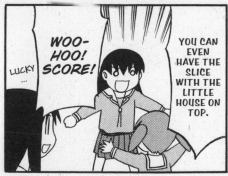

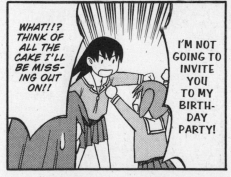

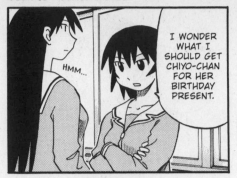

MESSED UP

WELL, HERE YOU GO!
W-WOW, THANK YOU SO MUCH!
YOU HAVE IT HERE!?
......
HUH?
THAT'S KIYOHARA'S AUTO-GRAPH...
清原
BOARD: KIYOHARA
...AS SIGNED BY ME.
ブル
SHAKE
ブル
SHAKE
WHAT!? YOU DON'T WANT IT!?
ブル
SHAKE

GENIUS MERCHANDISE

I WONDER WHAT I SHOULD GET CHIYO-CHAN FOR HER BIRTHDAY PRESENT.
HMM...
CHIYO-CHAN'S SO SMART, I FIGURED SOMETHING SMART WOULD SUIT HER.
WHAT KIND OF PRESENT'S SMART, ANYWAY?
NO IDEA...

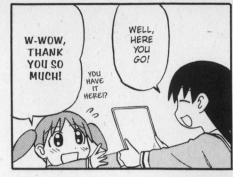

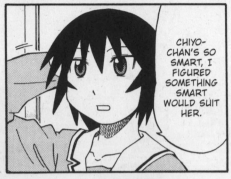

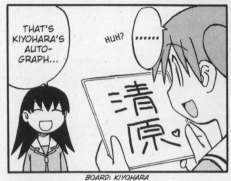

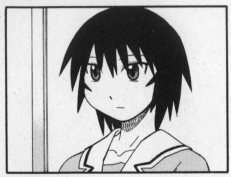

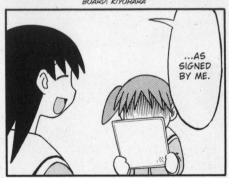

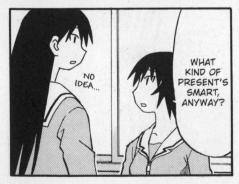

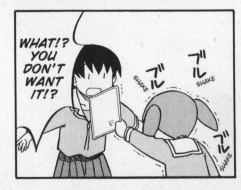

UNBEARABLY SO

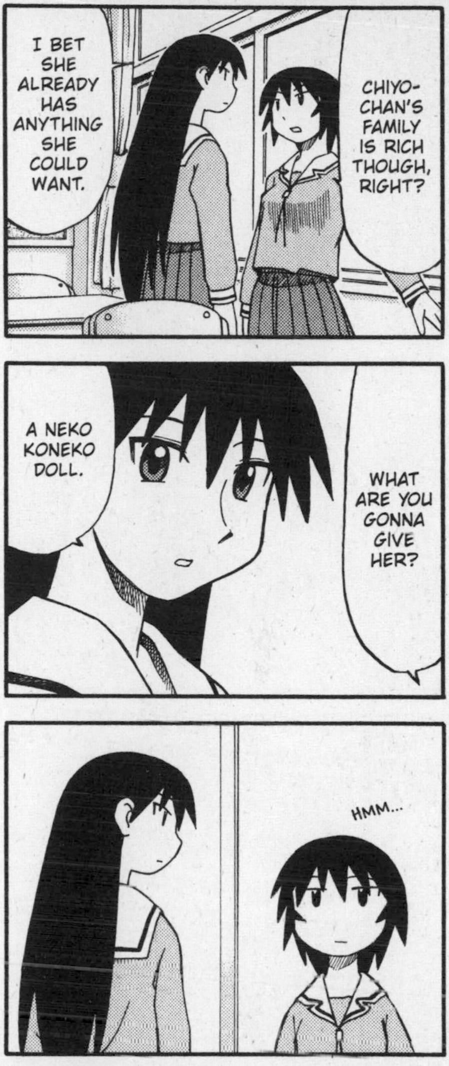

CHIYO-CHAN'S FAMILY IS RICH THOUGH, RIGHT?
I BET SHE ALREADY HAS ANYTHING SHE COULD WANT.
WHAT ARE YOU GONNA GIVE HER?
A NEKO KONEKO DOLL.
HMM...
IT'S REALLY CUTE!

WHEN LESS IS MORE

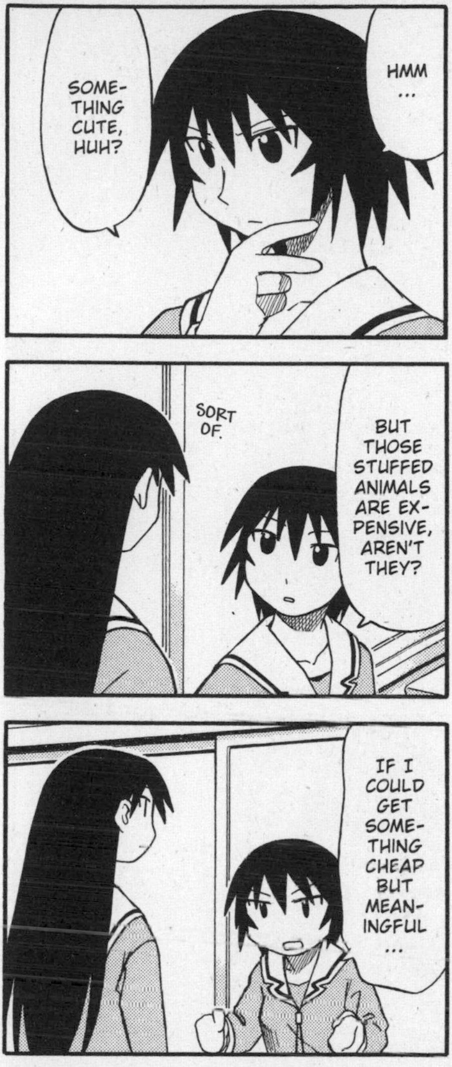

HMM ...
SOMETHING CUTE, HUH?
BUT THOSE STUFFED ANIMALS ARE EXPENSIVE, AREN'T THEY?
SORT OF.
IF I COULD GET SOMETHING CHEAP BUT MEANINGFUL ...
THAT'S IT! LET'S MAKE HER ONE OF THOSE!!
FROM BOTH OF US!
BOTH?

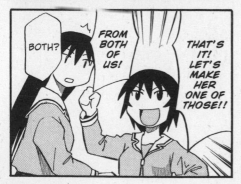

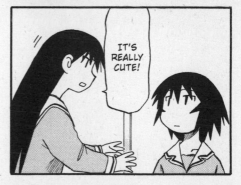

SO WHAT?

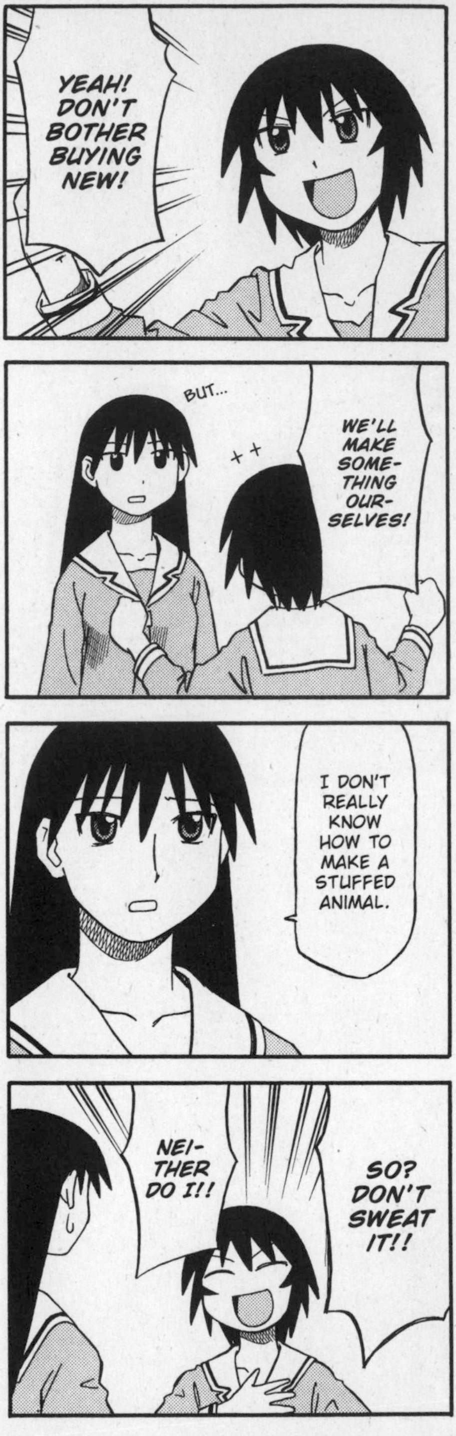
YEAH! DON'T BOTHER BUYING NEW!
WE'LL MAKE SOME-THING OUR-SELVES!
BUT...
I DON'T REALLY KNOW HOW TO MAKE A STUFFED ANIMAL.
SO? DON'T SWEAT IT!!
NEI-THER DO I!!

WITH HEART

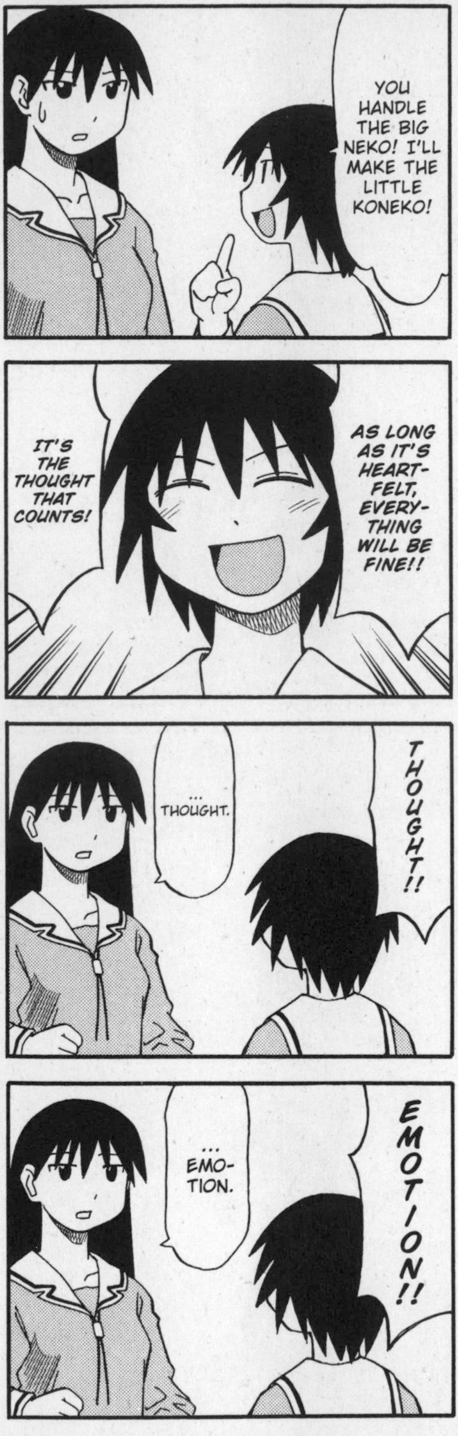
YOU HANDLE THE BIG NEKO! I'LL MAKE THE LITTLE KONEKO!
AS LONG AS IT'S HEART-FELT, EVERY-THING WILL BE FINE!!
IT'S THE THOUGHT THAT COUNTS!
THOUGHT!!
... THOUGHT.
EMOTION!!
... EMO-TION.

BLOBS OF FEELING

COMPLETE

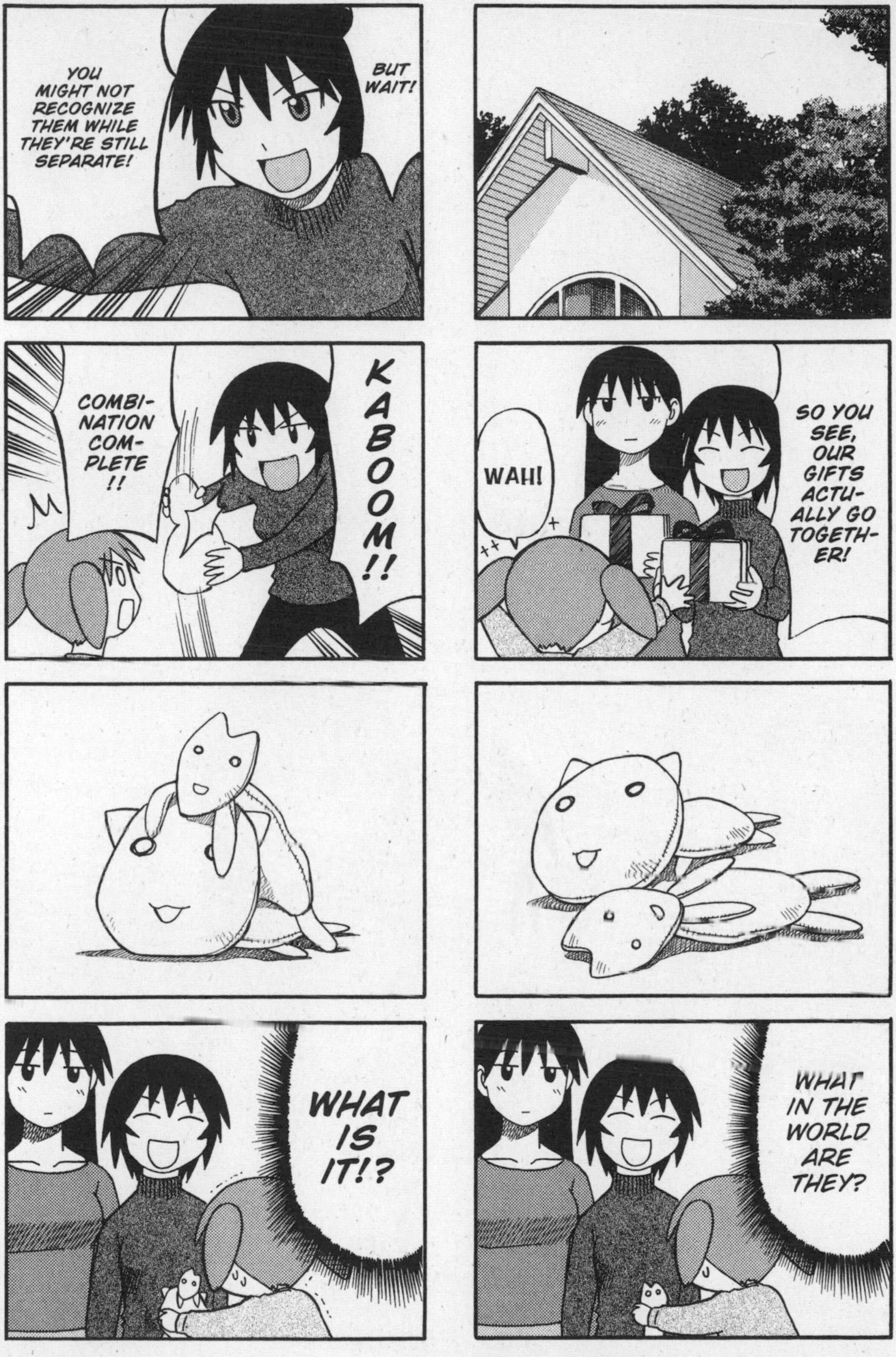
WAH!
SO YOU SEE, OUR GIFTS ACTUALLY GO TOGETHER!
WHAT IN THE WORLD ARE THEY?
BUT WAIT!
YOU MIGHT NOT RECOGNIZE THEM WHILE THEY'RE STILL SEPARATE!
KABOOOM!!
COMBINATION COMPLETE!!
WHAT IS IT!?

AZUMANGA-DAIOH
127

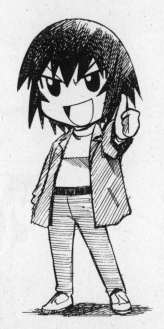

You belong.

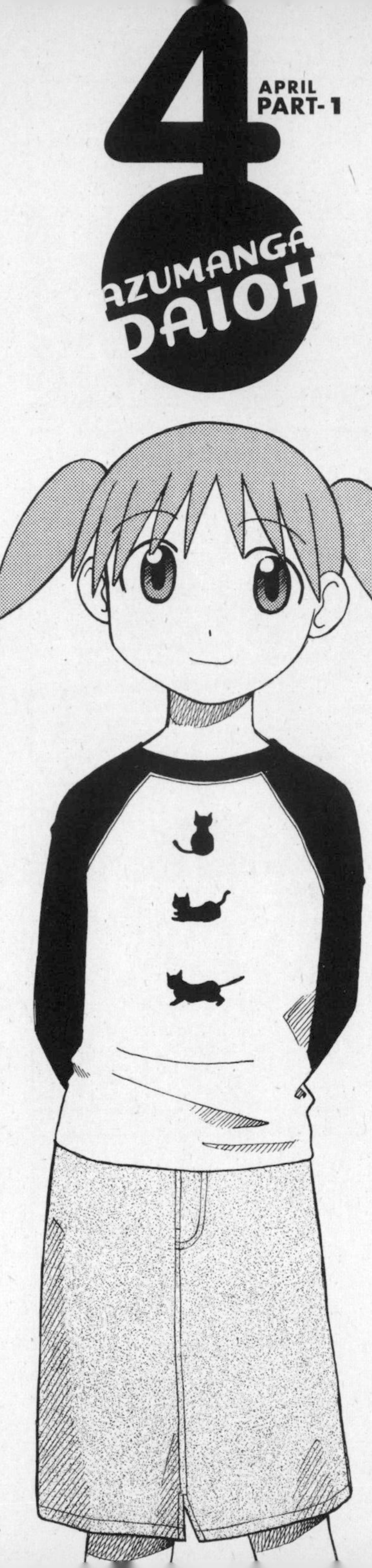
4
APRIL
PART-1
AZUMANGA DAIOH

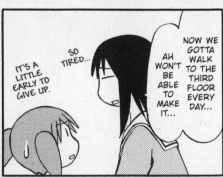

THIRD YEAR

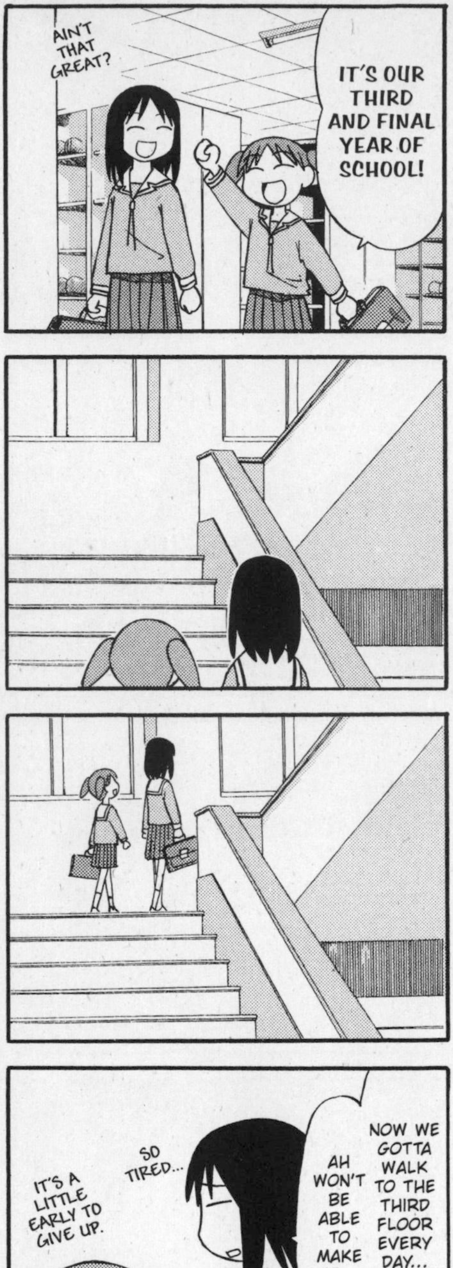
IT'S OUR THIRD AND FINAL YEAR OF SCHOOL!
AIN'T THAT GREAT?
NOW WE GOTTA WALK TO THE THIRD FLOOR EVERY DAY...
AH WON'T BE ABLE TO MAKE IT...
SO TIRED...
IT'S A LITTLE EARLY TO GIVE UP.

SEPARATION

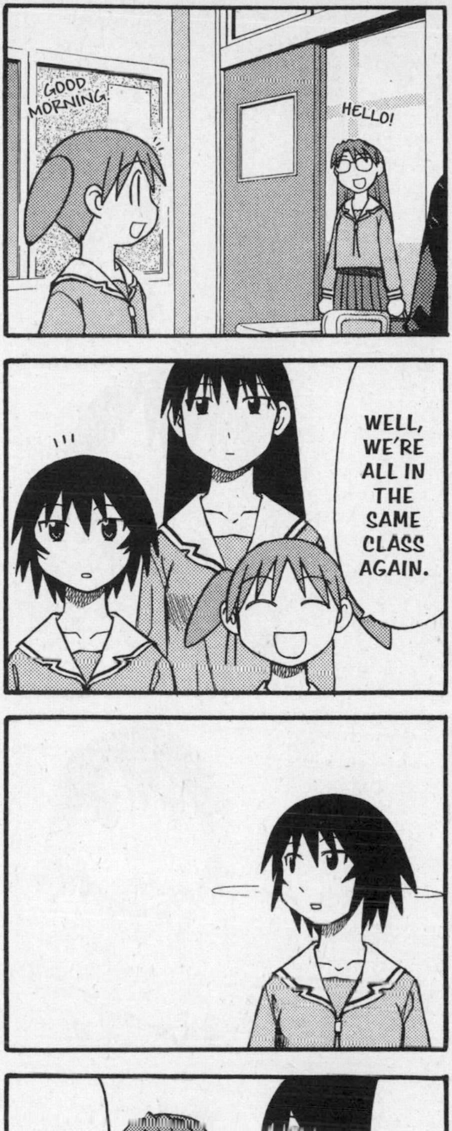
HELLO!
GOOD MORNING.
WELL, WE'RE ALL IN THE SAME CLASS AGAIN.
WHERE'S KAORIN?
OH, SHE'S IN A DIFFERENT CLASS THIS TIME.

LIKE SPRING FLOWERS BLOOMING

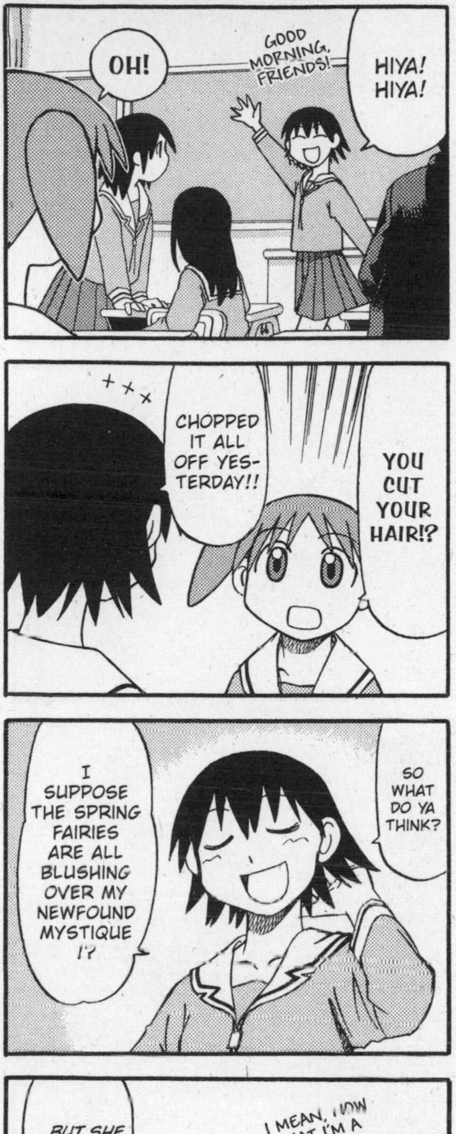
HIYA! HIYA!
GOOD MORNING, FRIENDS!
OH!
YOU CUT YOUR HAIR!?
CHOPPED IT ALL OFF YES-TERDAY!!
SO WHAT DO YA THINK?
I SUPPOSE THE SPRING FAIRIES ARE ALL BLUSHING OVER MY NEWFOUND MYSTIQUE!?
I MEAN, NOW THAT I'M A SENIOR...
...BUT SHE LOOKS JUST LIKE SHE DID BACK IN OUR FIRST YEAR HERE...

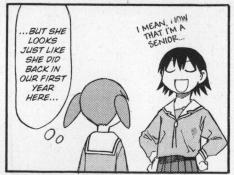

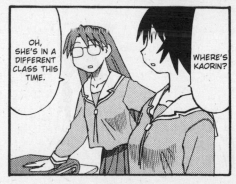

SKIRTING THE DARKNESS

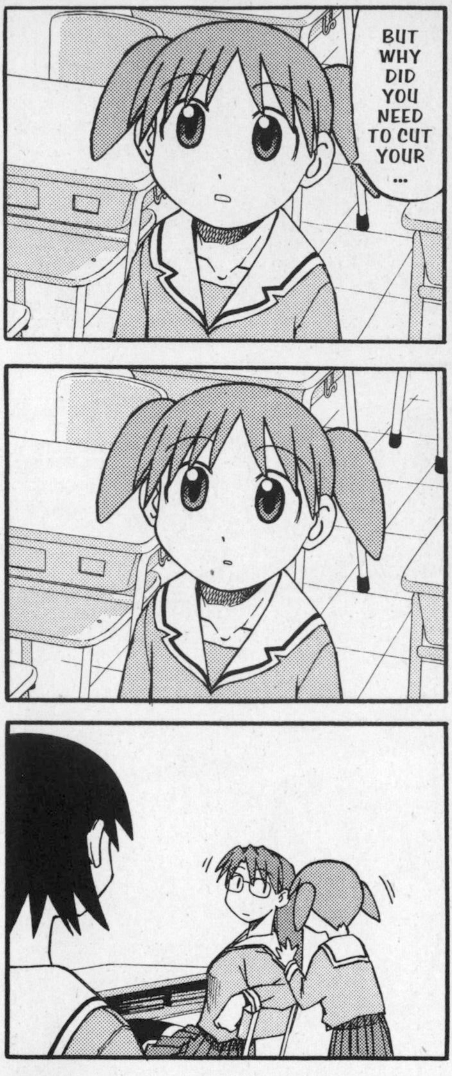
BUT WHY DID YOU NEED TO CUT YOUR ...
AH HA HA!
HER, IN LOVE!? NEVER!!

A TOWER TO REACH THE HEAVENS

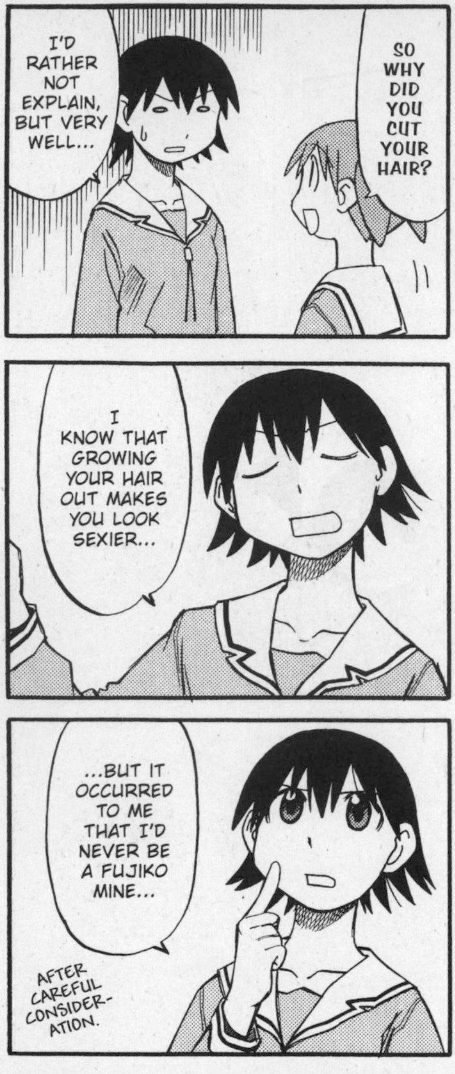
SO WHY DID YOU CUT YOUR HAIR?
I'D RATHER NOT EXPLAIN, BUT VERY WELL...
I KNOW THAT GROWING YOUR HAIR OUT MAKES YOU LOOK SEXIER...
...BUT IT OCCURRED TO ME THAT I'D NEVER BE A FUJIKO MINE...
AFTER CAREFUL CONSIDER-ATION.
SO THEN I...
... SO I COULD AT LEAST BE A RYOKO HIRO-SUE!
"AT LEAST" ?
FEEL FREE TO YELL AT HER, CHIYO-CHAN.

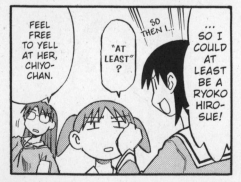

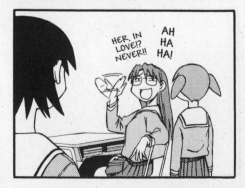

IT'S HARD TO BE AN ADULT

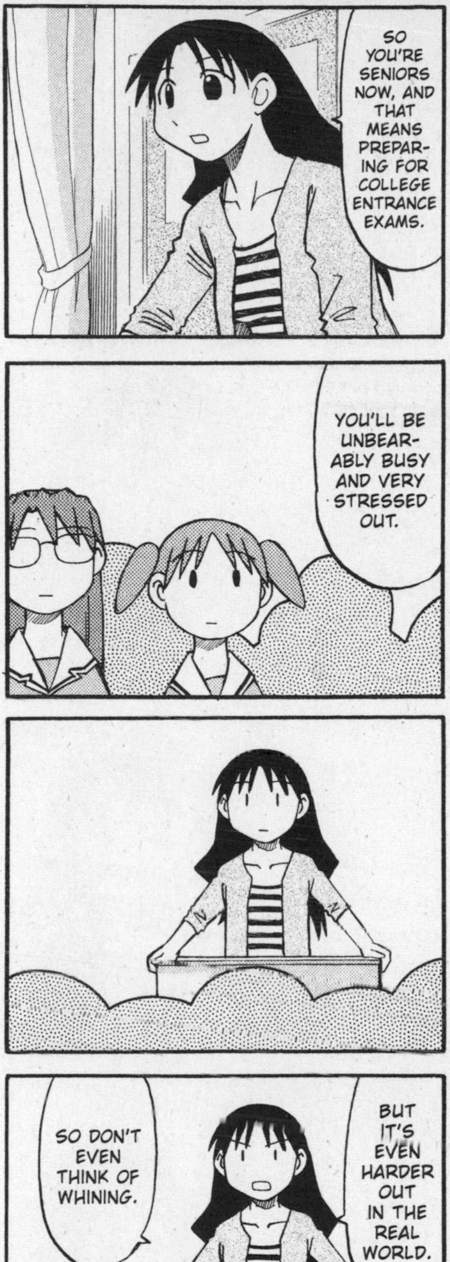
SO YOU'RE SENIORS NOW, AND THAT MEANS PREPARING FOR COLLEGE ENTRANCE EXAMS.
YOU'LL BE UNBEARABLY BUSY AND VERY STRESSED OUT.
BUT IT'S EVEN HARDER OUT IN THE REAL WORLD.
SO DON'T EVEN THINK OF WHINING.

DOES SHE HATE US?

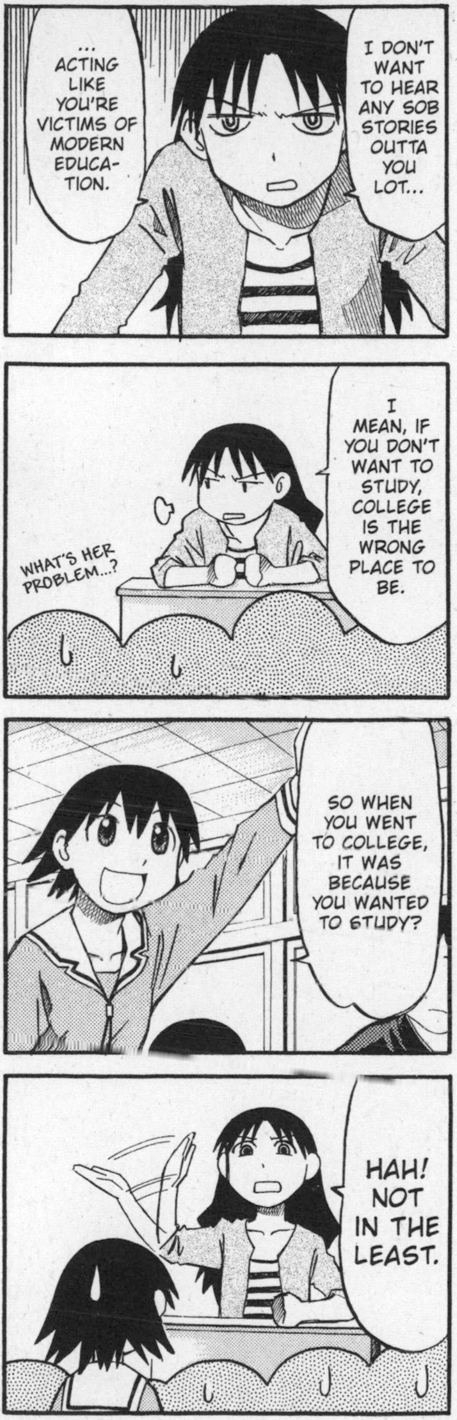
I DON'T WANT TO HEAR ANY SOB STORIES OUTTA YOU LOT...
... ACTING LIKE YOU'RE VICTIMS OF MODERN EDUCATION.
I MEAN, IF YOU DON'T WANT TO STUDY, COLLEGE IS THE WRONG PLACE TO BE.
WHAT'S HER PROBLEM...?
SO WHEN YOU WENT TO COLLEGE, IT WAS BECAUSE YOU WANTED TO STUDY?
HAH! NOT IN THE LEAST.

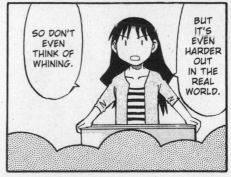

OTHER PEOPLE'S PROBLEMS

LOOK.
ALL YOU GUYS HAVE TO WORRY ABOUT ARE YOUR OWN EXAMS.
BUT I HAVE TO WORRY ABOUT DOZENS OF STUDENTS' EXAMS.
THAT'S TOUGH.
I SEE...
MAYBE I SHOULD JUST STOP THINKING ABOUT THEM.
EH...

DESPONDENCY

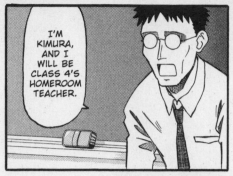

I'M KIMURA, AND I WILL BE CLASS 4'S HOMEROOM TEACHER.

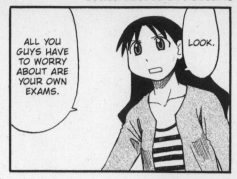

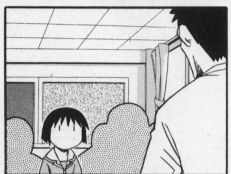

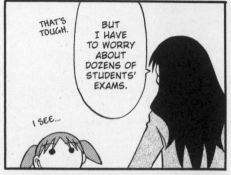

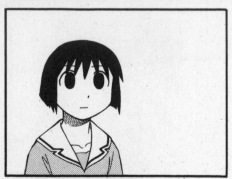

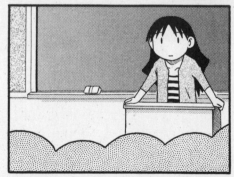

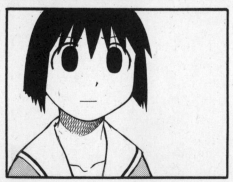

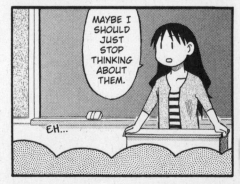

APPROVED

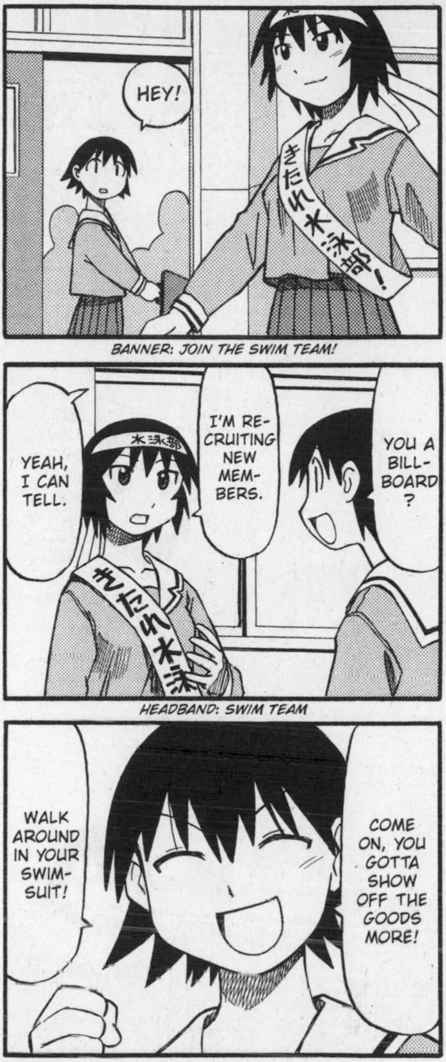
HEY!
きたれ水泳部!
BANNER: JOIN THE SWIM TEAM!
YOU A BILL-BOARD?
I'M RE-CRUITING NEW MEM-BERS.
YEAH, I CAN TELL.
水泳部
HEADBAND: SWIM TEAM
COME ON, YOU GOTTA SHOW OFF THE GOODS MORE!
WALK AROUND IN YOUR SWIM-SUIT!
!
A MOST EXCEL-LENT IDEA !!

THE UNHATCHED EGG

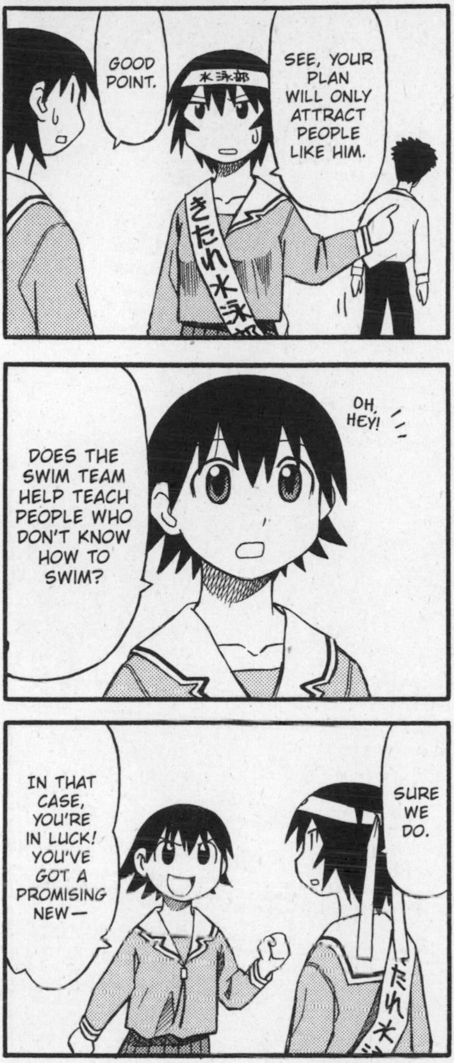
SEE, YOUR PLAN WILL ONLY ATTRACT PEOPLE LIKE HIM.
GOOD POINT.
OH, HEY!
DOES THE SWIM TEAM HELP TEACH PEOPLE WHO DON'T KNOW HOW TO SWIM?
SURE WE DO.
IN THAT CASE, YOU'RE IN LUCK! YOU'VE GOT A PROMISING NEW—
WE DON'T WANT YOU.
HUH!?

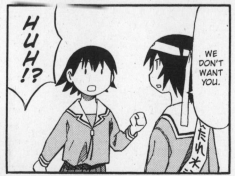

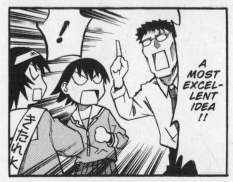

ELEMENTARY, MIDDLE, HIGH

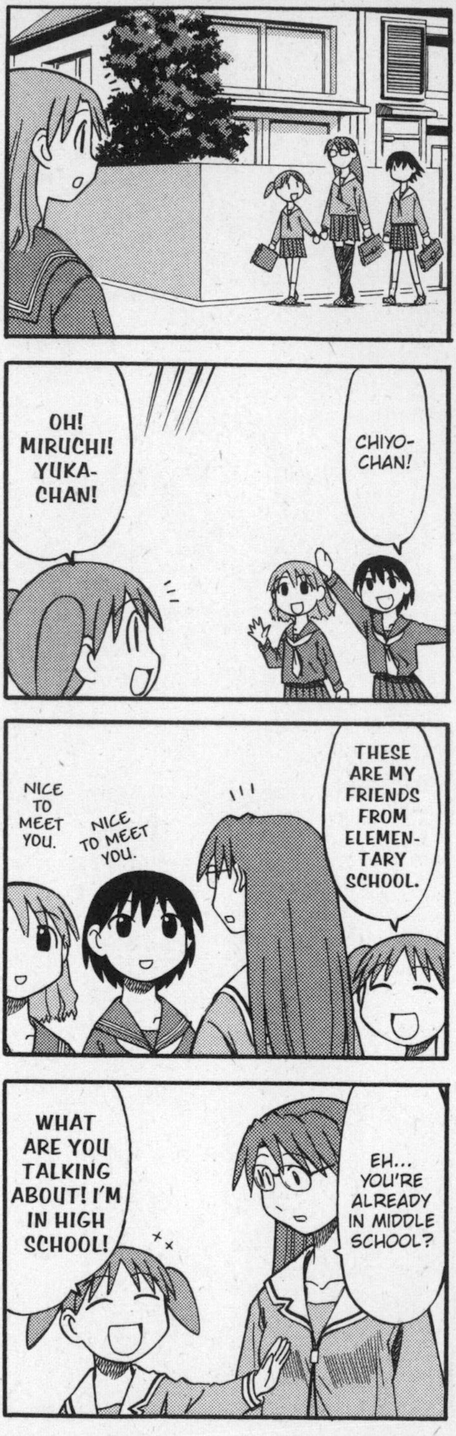

CHIYO-CHAN!
OH! MIRUCHI! YUKA-CHAN!
THESE ARE MY FRIENDS FROM ELEMEN-TARY SCHOOL.
NICE TO MEET YOU.
NICE TO MEET YOU.
EH... YOU'RE ALREADY IN MIDDLE SCHOOL?
WHAT ARE YOU TALKING ABOUT! I'M IN HIGH SCHOOL!

PERKS

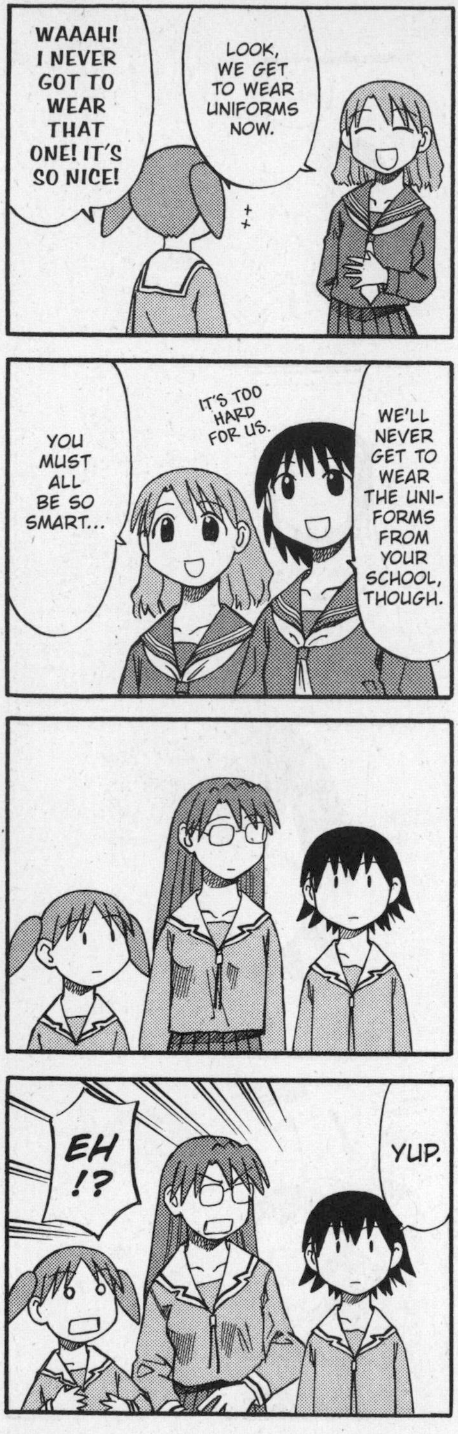

LOOK, WE GET TO WEAR UNIFORMS NOW.
WAAAH! I NEVER GOT TO WEAR THAT ONE! IT'S SO NICE!
WE'LL NEVER GET TO WEAR THE UNI-FORMS FROM YOUR SCHOOL, THOUGH.
IT'S TOO HARD FOR US.
YOU MUST ALL BE SO SMART...
YUP.
EH !?

FLIGHTLESS BIRD

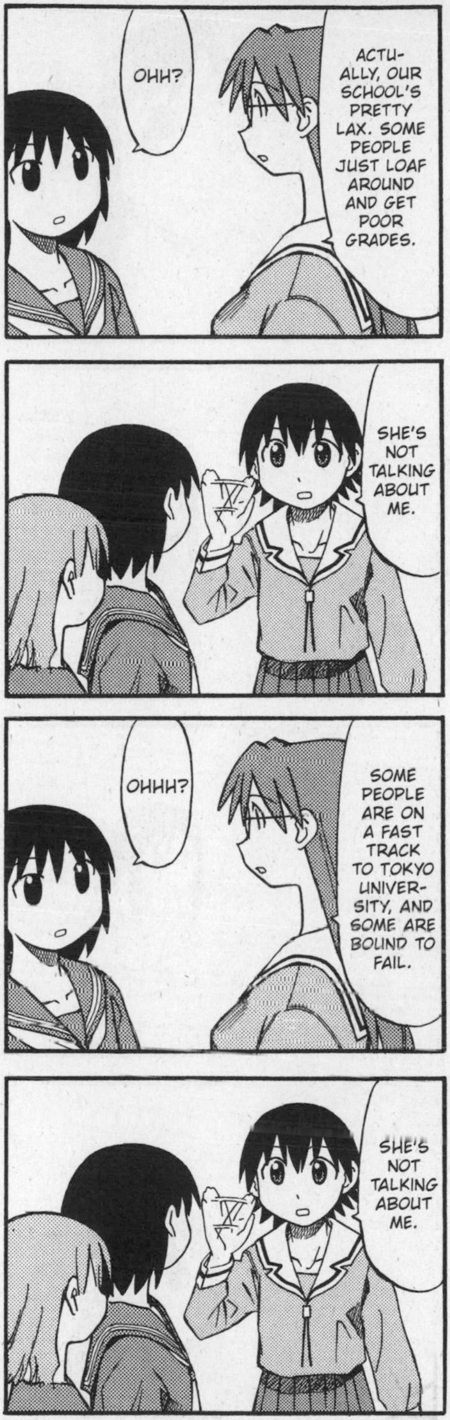
ACTU-ALLY, OUR SCHOOL'S PRETTY LAX. SOME PEOPLE JUST LOAF AROUND AND GET POOR GRADES.
OHH?
SHE'S NOT TALKING ABOUT ME.
SOME PEOPLE ARE ON A FAST TRACK TO TOKYO UNIVER-SITY, AND SOME ARE BOUND TO FAIL.
OHHH?
SHE'S NOT TALKING ABOUT ME.

HUH?

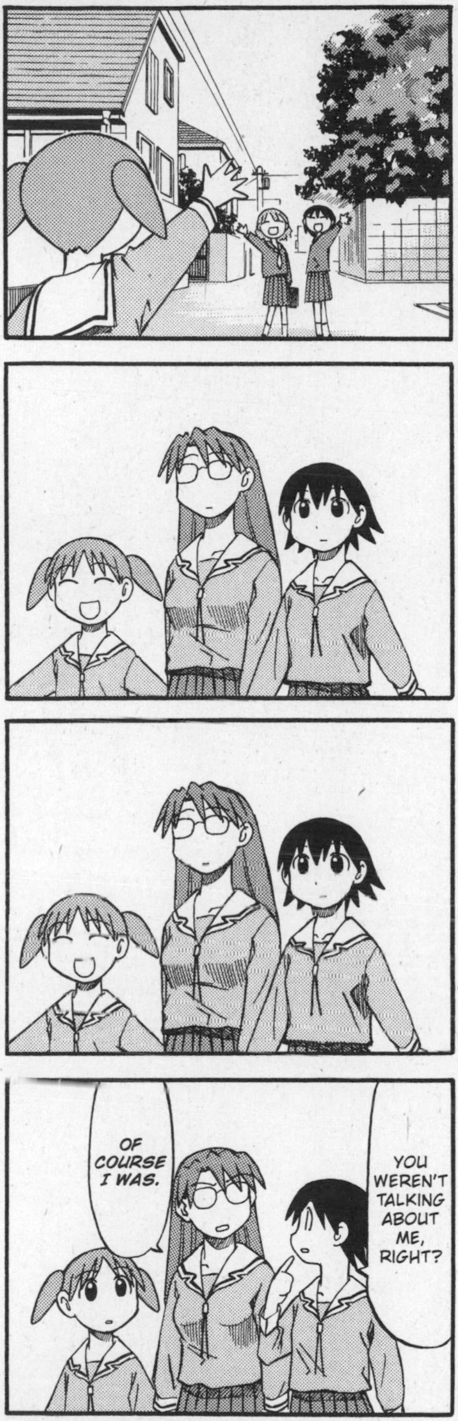
YOU WEREN'T TALKING ABOUT ME, RIGHT?
OF COURSE I WAS.

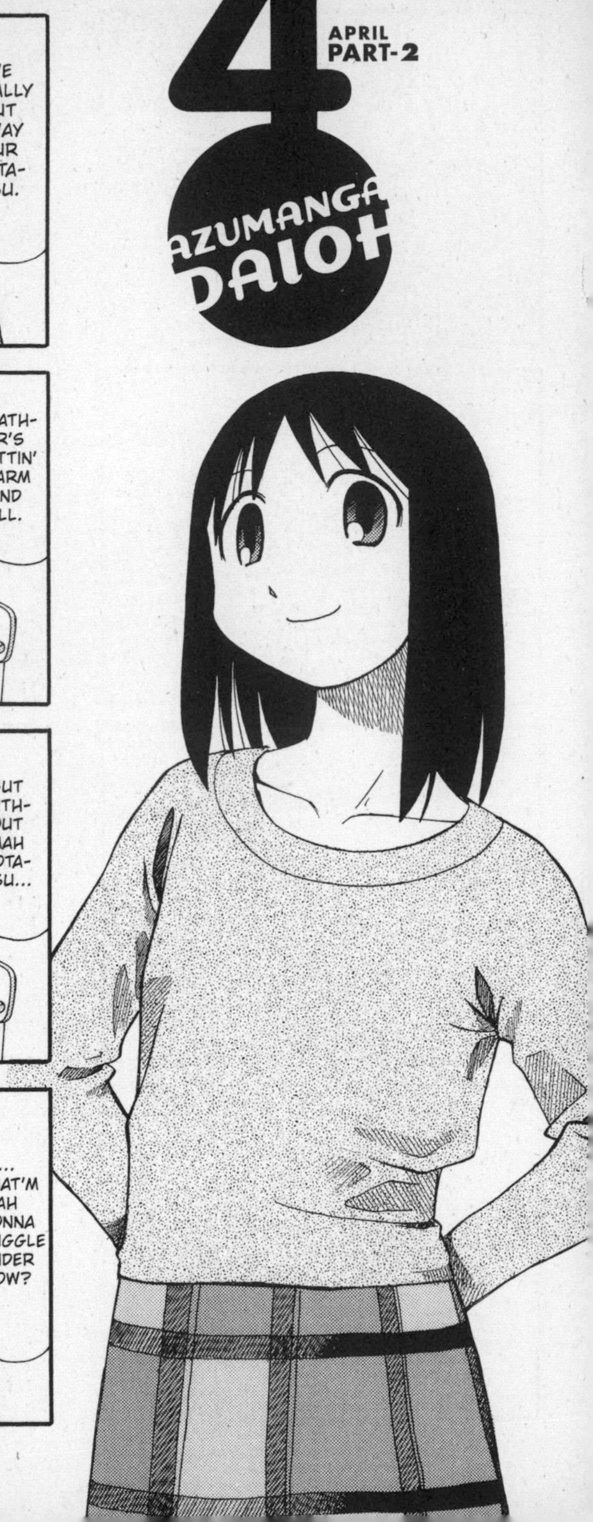
4
APRIL
PART-2
AZUMANGA DAIOH

CRAB WITHOUT A SHELL

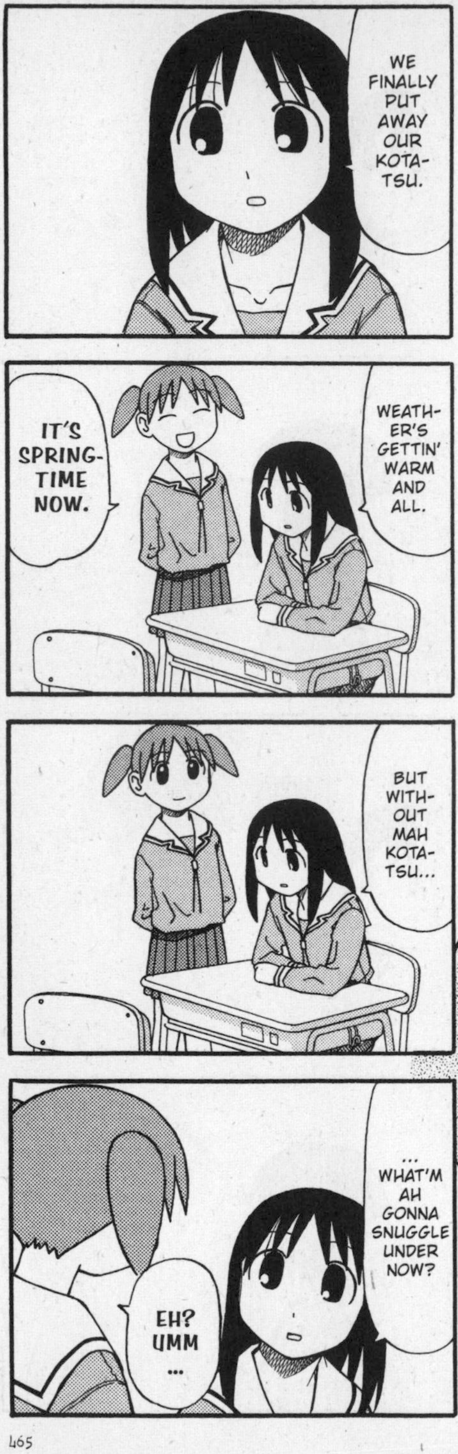
WE FINALLY PUT AWAY OUR KOTATSU.
WEATHER'S GETTIN' WARM AND ALL.
IT'S SPRINGTIME NOW.
BUT WITHOUT MAH KOTATSU...
... WHAT'M AH GONNA SNUGGLE UNDER NOW?
EH? UMM ...

DELICIOUS PORK BUNS

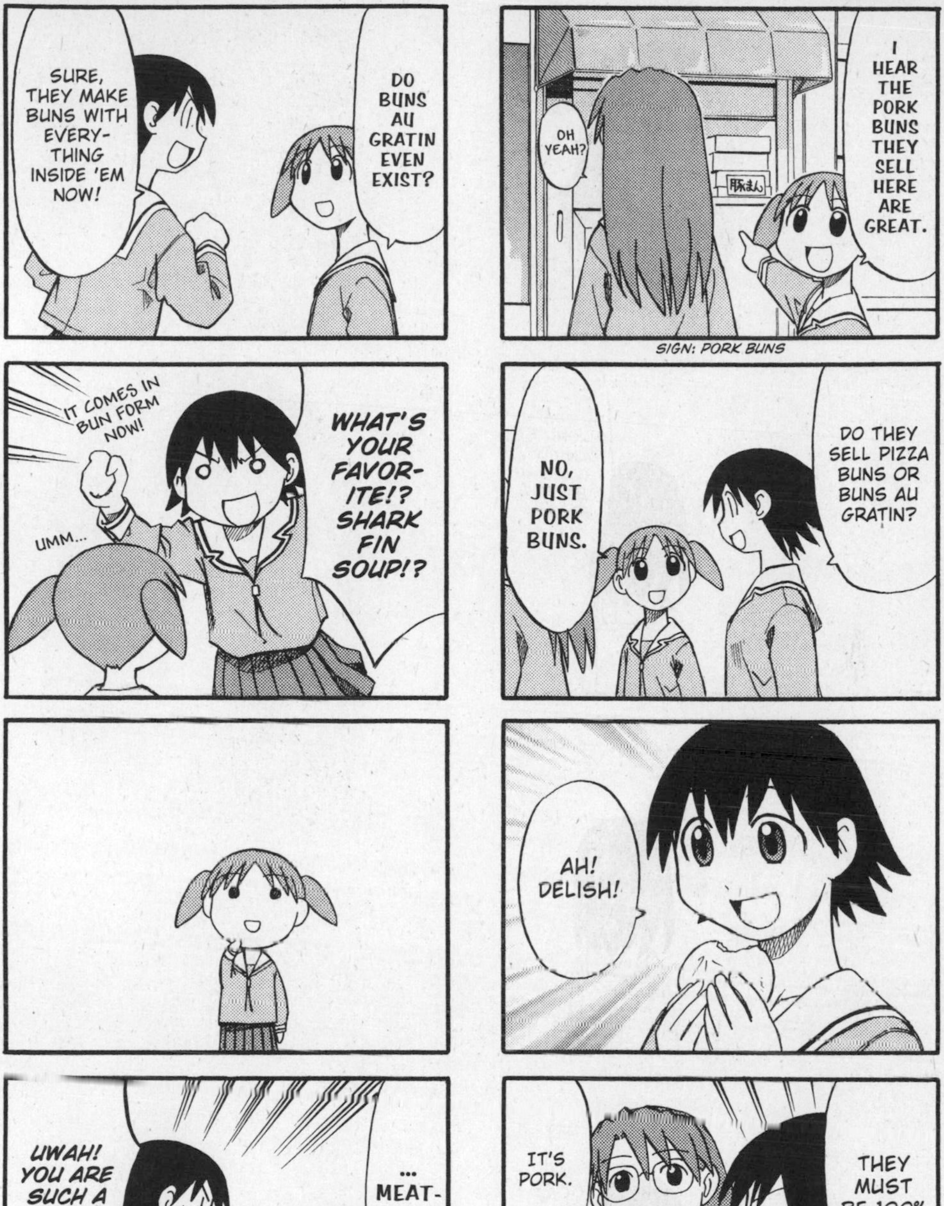
I HEAR THE PORK BUNS THEY SELL HERE ARE GREAT.
OH YEAH?
豚まん
SIGN: PORK BUNS
DO THEY SELL PIZZA BUNS OR BUNS AU GRATIN?
NO, JUST PORK BUNS.
AH! DELISH!
THEY MUST BE 100% BEEF TO BE THIS GOOD!!
IT'S PORK.
DO BUNS AU GRATIN EVEN EXIST?
SURE, THEY MAKE BUNS WITH EVERY-THING INSIDE 'EM NOW!
WHAT'S YOUR FAVOR-ITE!? SHARK FIN SOUP!?
IT COMES IN BUN FORM NOW!
UMM...
... MEAT-BALLS.
UWAH! YOU ARE SUCH A LITTLE KID!

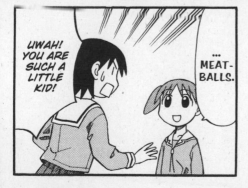

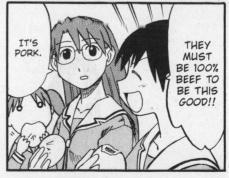

MONKEY

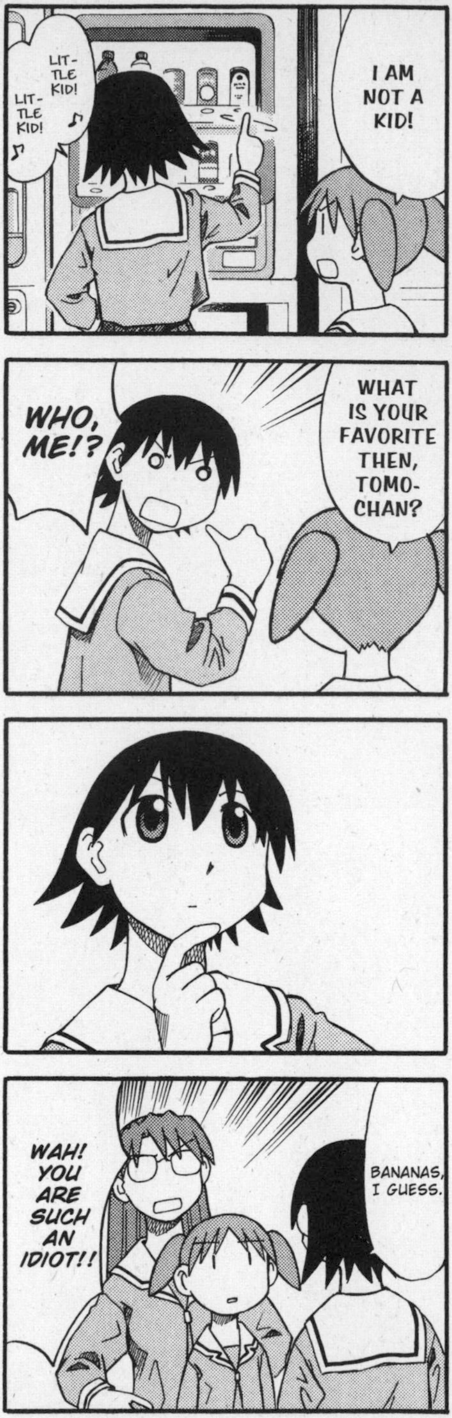
I AM NOT A KID!
LIT-TLE KID! ♪
LIT-TLE KID! ♪
WHAT IS YOUR FAVORITE THEN, TOMO-CHAN?
WHO, ME!?
BANANAS, I GUESS.
WAH! YOU ARE SUCH AN IDIOT!!

NEVER MIND, Y'ALL

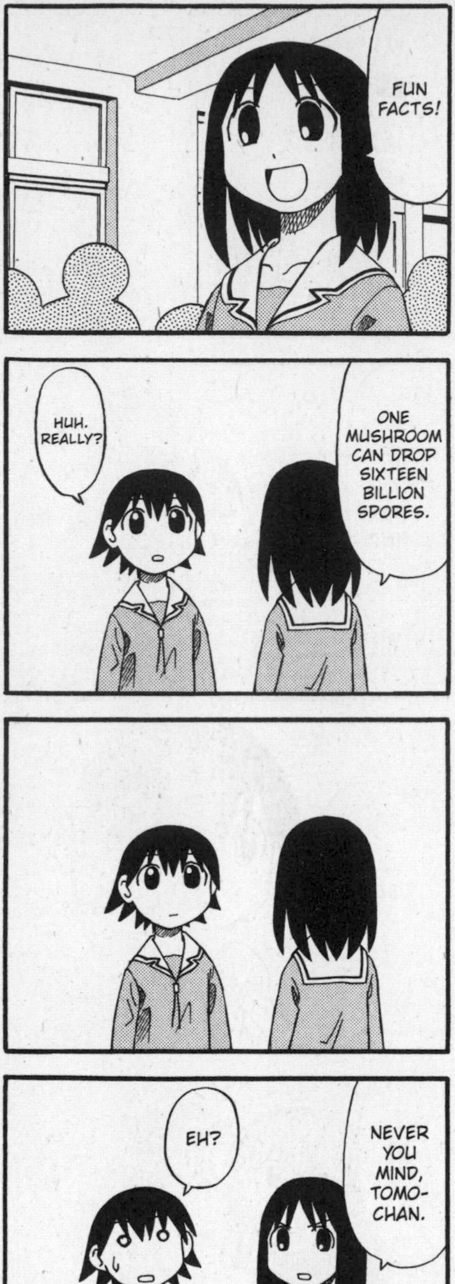
FUN FACTS!
ONE MUSHROOM CAN DROP SIXTEEN BILLION SPORES.
HUH. REALLY?
NEVER YOU MIND, TOMO-CHAN.
EH?

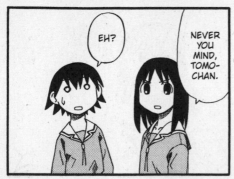

EXPECTATIONS

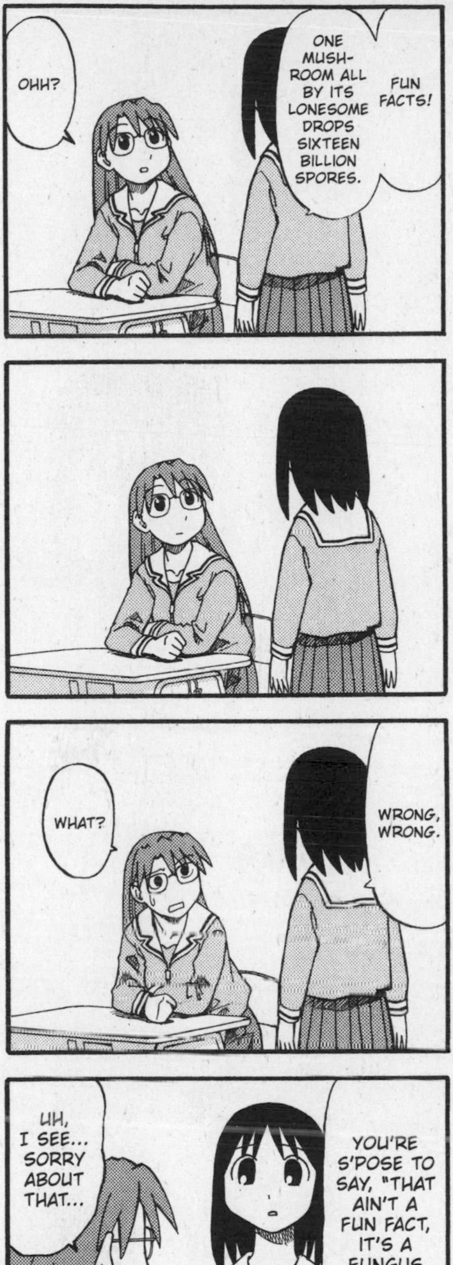
FUN FACTS!
ONE MUSH-ROOM ALL BY ITS LONESOME DROPS SIXTEEN BILLION SPORES.
OHH?
WRONG, WRONG.
WHAT?
YOU'RE S'POSE TO SAY, "THAT AIN'T A FUN FACT, IT'S A FUNGUS FACT."
UH, I SEE... SORRY ABOUT THAT...

OVERACTIVE IMAGINATION

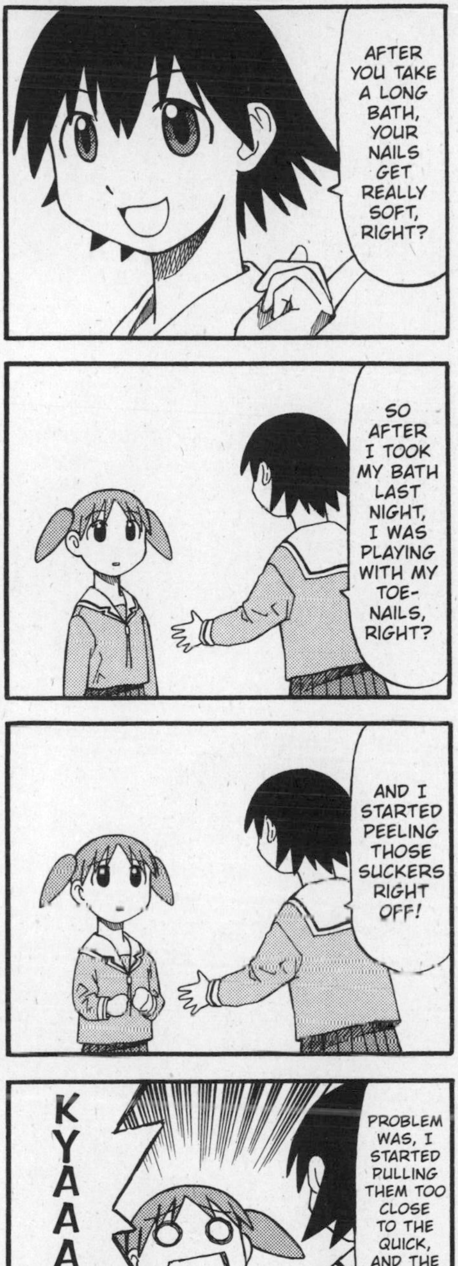
AFTER YOU TAKE A LONG BATH, YOUR NAILS GET REALLY SOFT, RIGHT?
SO AFTER I TOOK MY BATH LAST NIGHT, I WAS PLAYING WITH MY TOE-NAILS, RIGHT?
AND I STARTED PEELING THOSE SUCKERS RIGHT OFF!
PROBLEM WAS, I STARTED PULLING THEM TOO CLOSE TO THE QUICK, AND THE NEXT THING I KNEW...
KYAAAAH!!

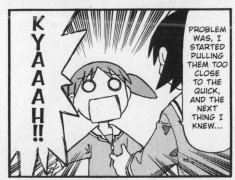

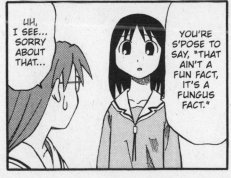

THE VIOLENCE OF LANGUAGE

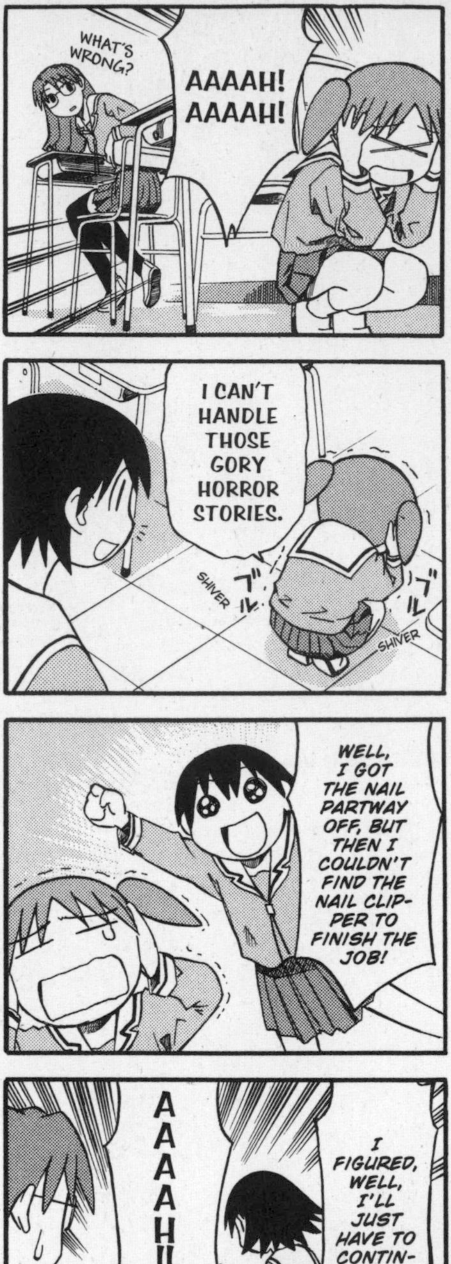
AAAAH! AAAAH!
WHAT'S WRONG?
I CAN'T HANDLE THOSE GORY HORROR STORIES.
ブル
SHIVER
ブル
SHIVER
WELL, I GOT THE NAIL PARTWAY OFF, BUT THEN I COULDN'T FIND THE NAIL CLIPPER TO FINISH THE JOB!
I FIGURED, WELL, I'LL JUST HAVE TO CONTINUE—
AAAAAH!!

BAD FEELING ABOUT THIS

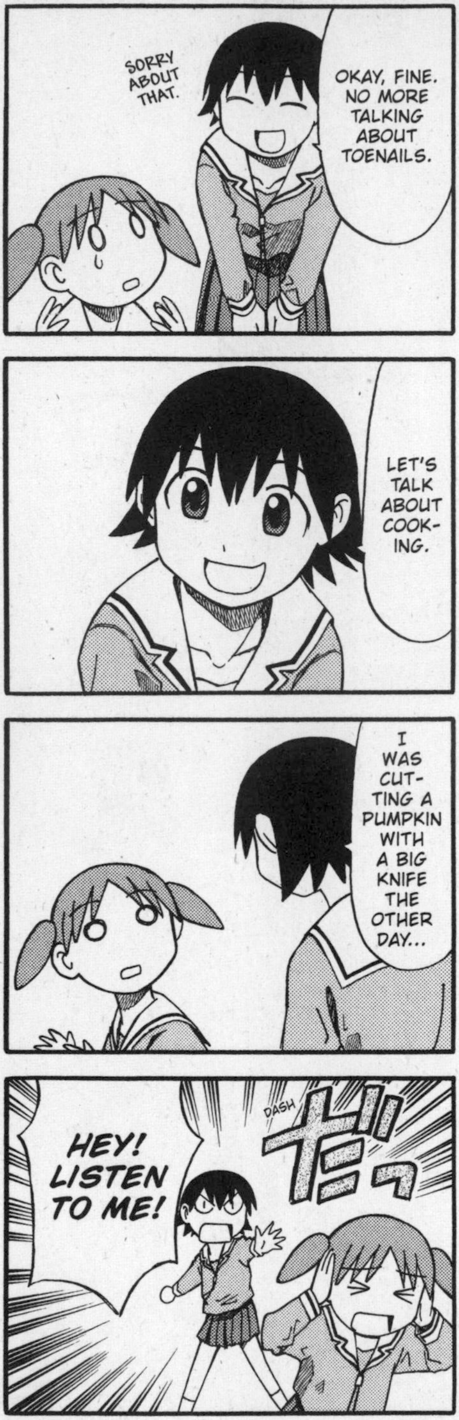
OKAY, FINE. NO MORE TALKING ABOUT TOENAILS.
SORRY ABOUT THAT.
LET'S TALK ABOUT COOKING.
I WAS CUTTING A PUMPKIN WITH A BIG KNIFE THE OTHER DAY...
ダッ
DASH
HEY! LISTEN TO ME!

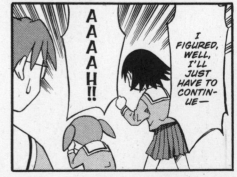

BRUISES ARE OKAY

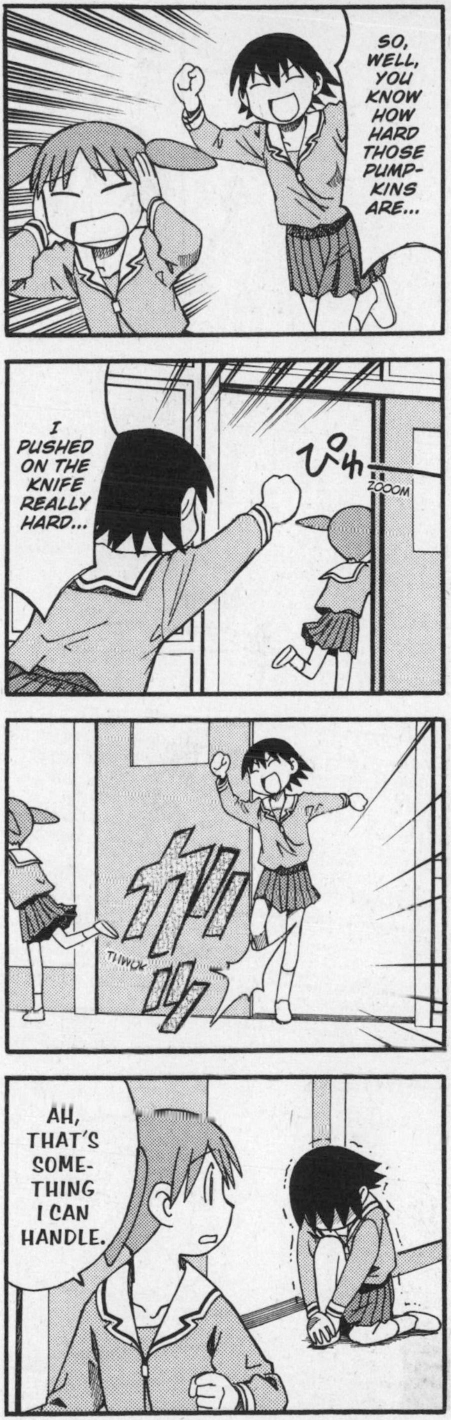
SO, WELL, YOU KNOW HOW HARD THOSE PUMPKINS ARE...
I PUSHED ON THE KNIFE REALLY HARD...
ZOOOM
THWOK
AH, THAT'S SOMETHING I CAN HANDLE.

I WAS SCARED TOO

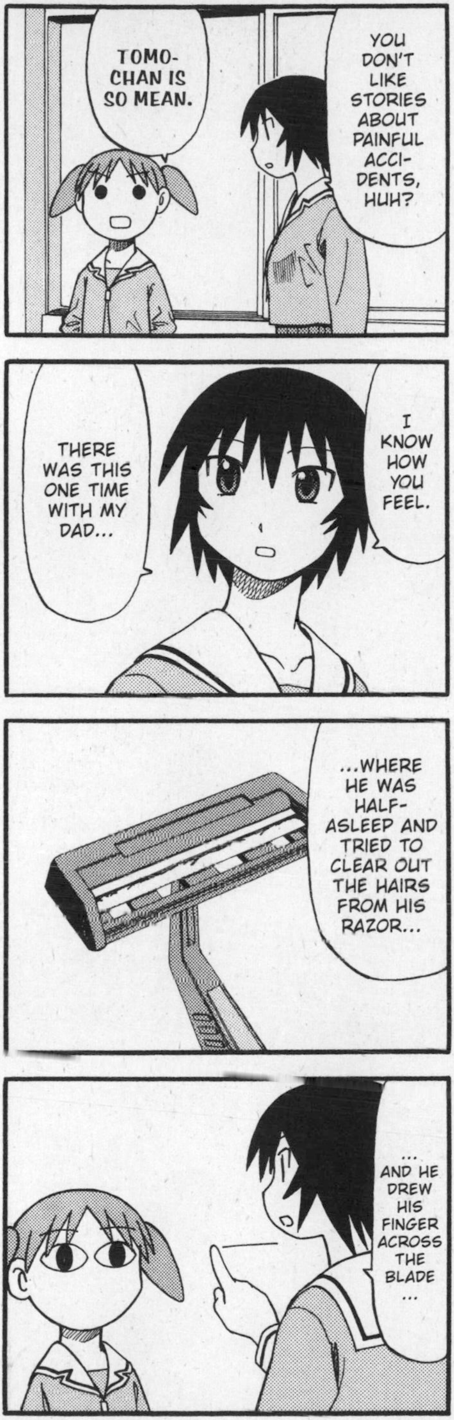
YOU DON'T LIKE STORIES ABOUT PAINFUL ACCIDENTS, HUH?
TOMO-CHAN IS SO MEAN.
I KNOW HOW YOU FEEL.
THERE WAS THIS ONE TIME WITH MY DAD...
...WHERE HE WAS HALF-ASLEEP AND TRIED TO CLEAR OUT THE HAIRS FROM HIS RAZOR...
...AND HE DREW HIS FINGER ACROSS THE BLADE...

INTERFERENCE

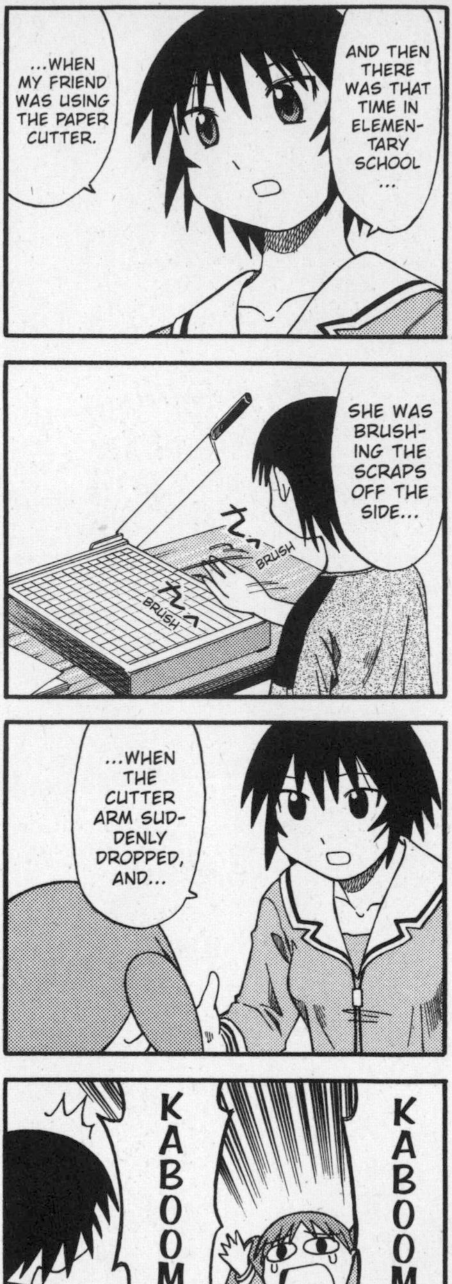
AND THEN THERE WAS THAT TIME IN ELEMENTARY SCHOOL...
...WHEN MY FRIEND WAS USING THE PAPER CUTTER.
SHE WAS BRUSHING THE SCRAPS OFF THE SIDE...
BRUSH
BRUSH
...WHEN THE CUTTER ARM SUDDENLY DROPPED, AND...
KABOOOM!!
KABOOOM!!

BEGONE

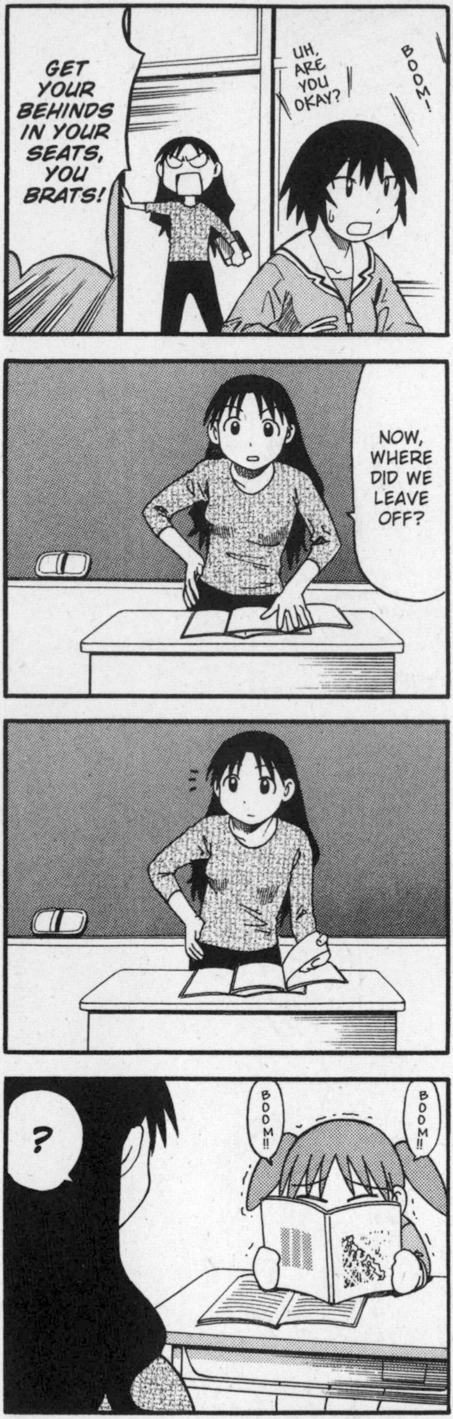
BOOM!
UH, ARE YOU OKAY?
GET YOUR BEHINDS IN YOUR SEATS, YOU BRATS!
NOW, WHERE DID WE LEAVE OFF?
BOOM!!
BOOM!!
?

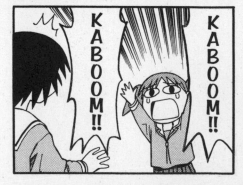

MEDITATION

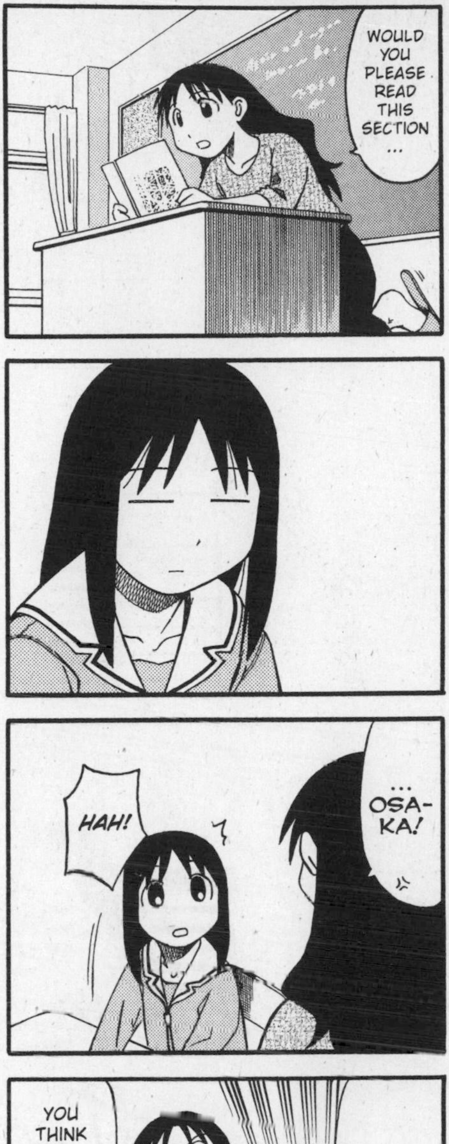
WOULD YOU PLEASE READ THIS SECTION ...
... OSA-KA!
HAH!
YOU THINK I'M GOING TO FALL FOR THAT CHILDISH EXCUSE ...?
NO! AH WAS ONLY CLOSIN' MAH EYES TO THINK!

TRUST

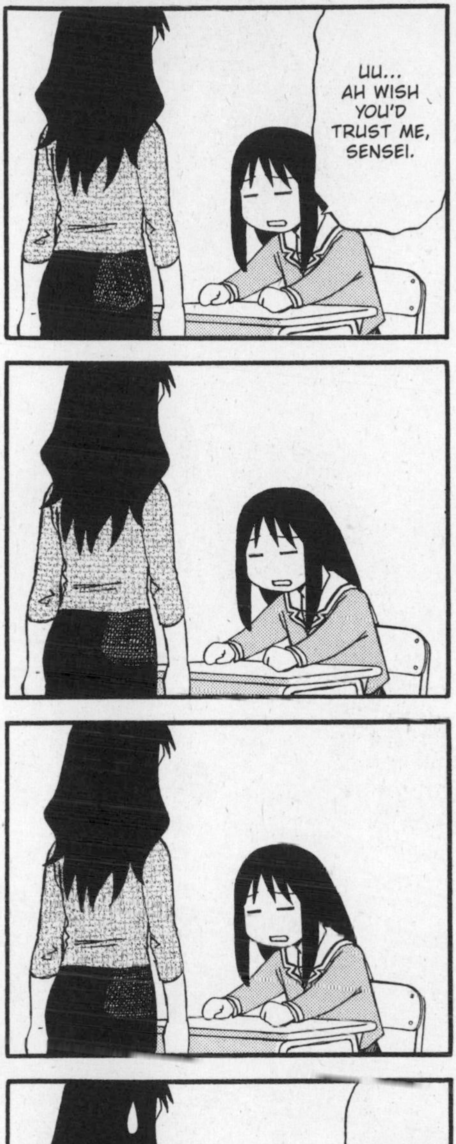
UU... AH WISH YOU'D TRUST ME, SENSEI.
AH'M SORRY... AH WAS SLEEP-ING.

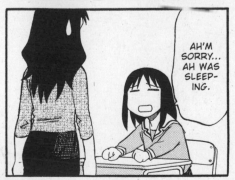

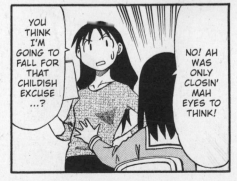

AZUMANGA DAIOH 5

MAY PART-1

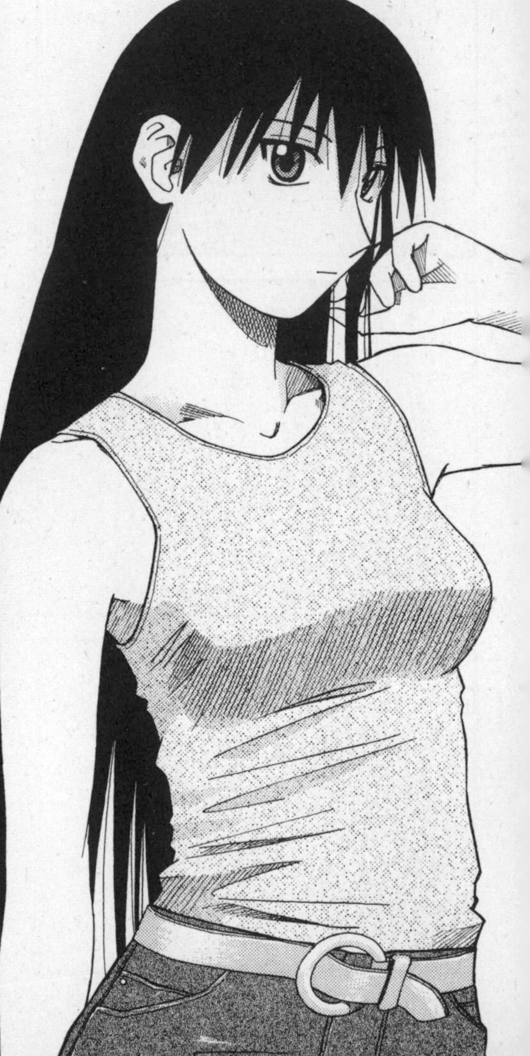

SPRING

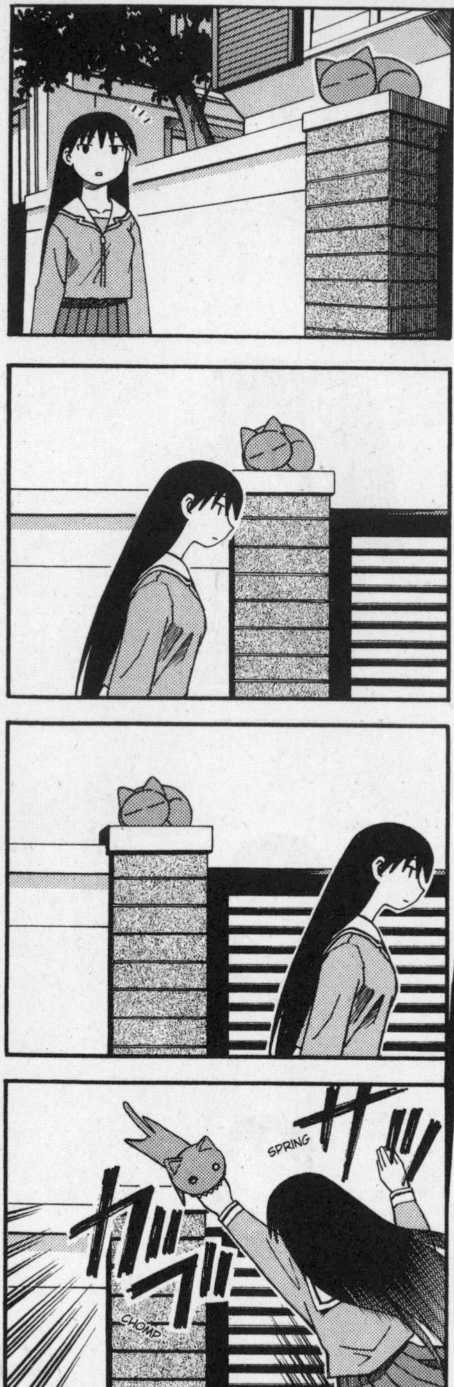
SPRING
CHOMP

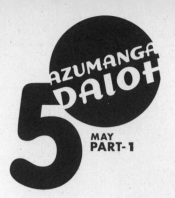

STOP

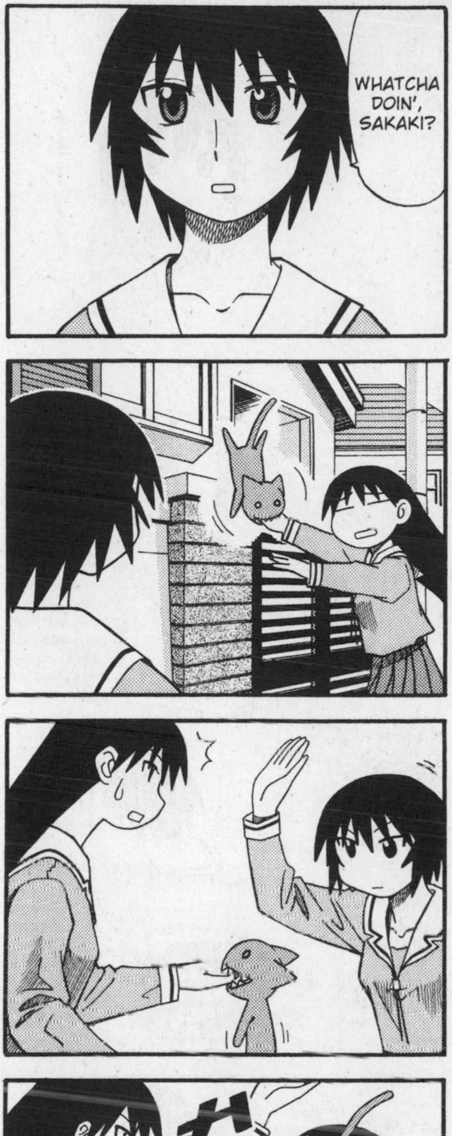
WHATCHA DOIN', SAKAKI?
むぎゅ
SPLAT

CATFACE KAGURA

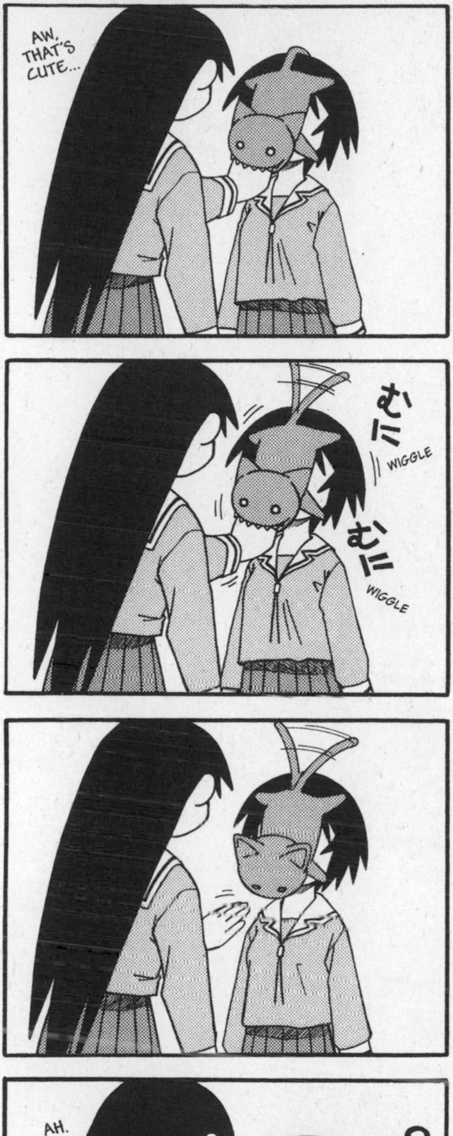
AW, THAT'S CUTE...
むに
WIGGLE
むに
WIGGLE
AH.
ぽい
TOSS

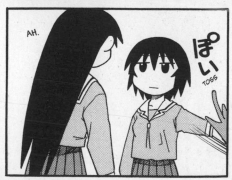

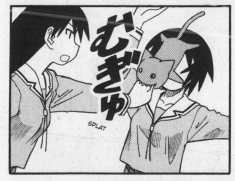

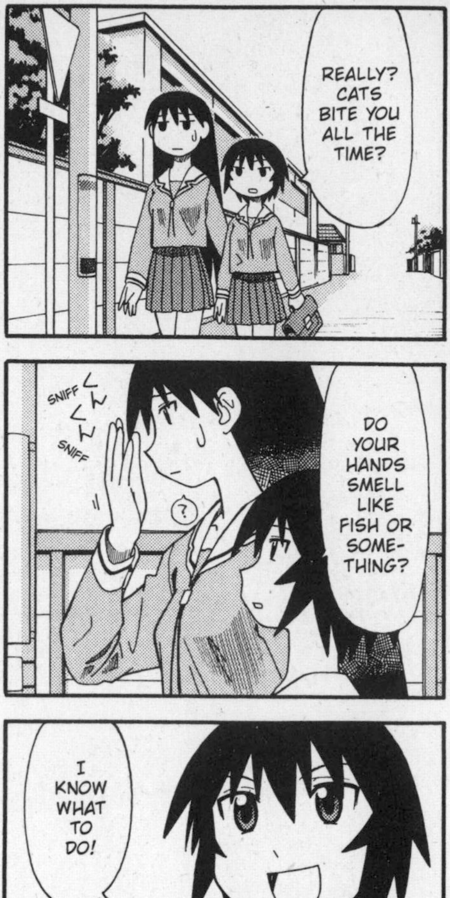
REALLY? CATS BITE YOU ALL THE TIME?
SNIFF くん くん SNIFF
DO YOUR HANDS SMELL LIKE FISH OR SOME-THING?
?
I KNOW WHAT TO DO!
I'LL GUARD YOU AND DRIVE OFF ALL THE CATS WHO TRY TO ATTACK!

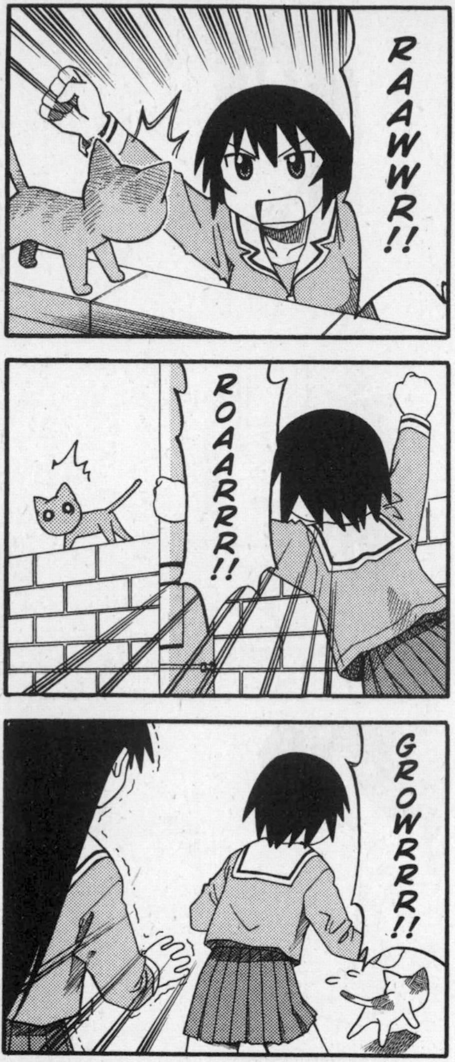
RAAAWWR!!
ROAAARRR!!
GROWRRRR!!
RAWWW!
S-STOP …

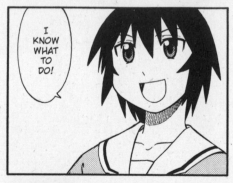

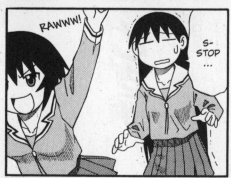

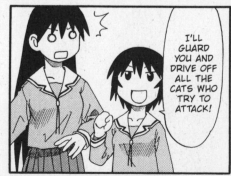

LEFT OUT?

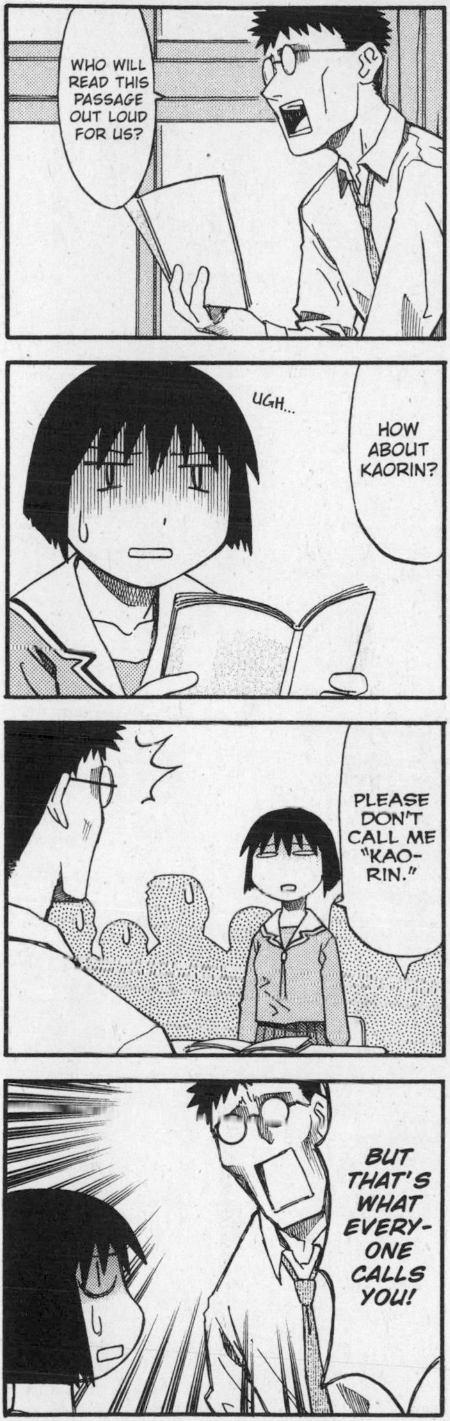
WHO WILL READ THIS PASSAGE OUT LOUD FOR US?
HOW ABOUT KAORIN?
UGH...
PLEASE DON'T CALL ME "KAO-RIN."
BUT THAT'S WHAT EVERY-ONE CALLS YOU!

PAIR

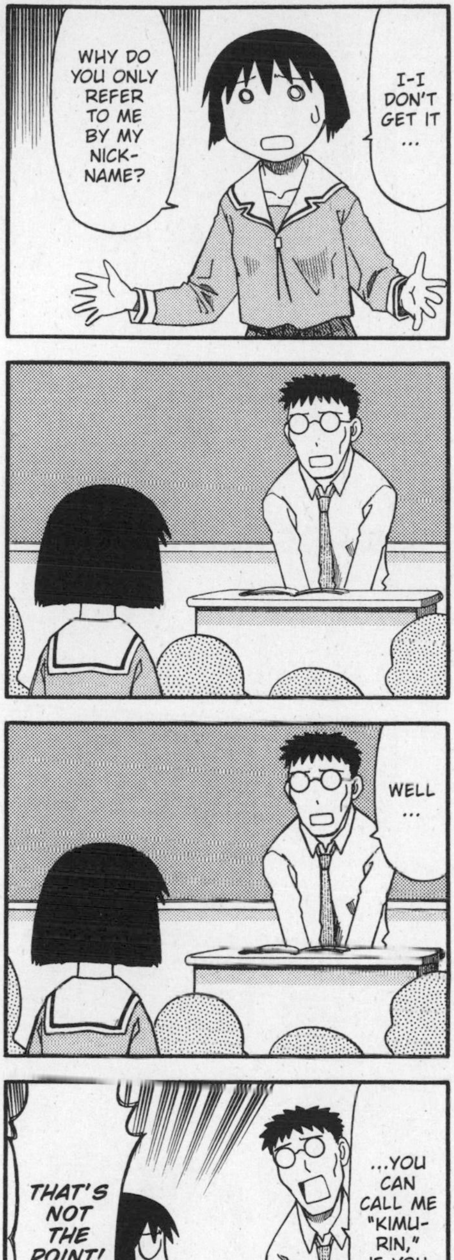
I-I DON'T GET IT ...
WHY DO YOU ONLY REFER TO ME BY MY NICK-NAME?
WELL ...
...YOU CAN CALL ME "KIMU-RIN," IF YOU WANT.
THAT'S NOT THE POINT!

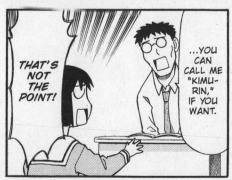

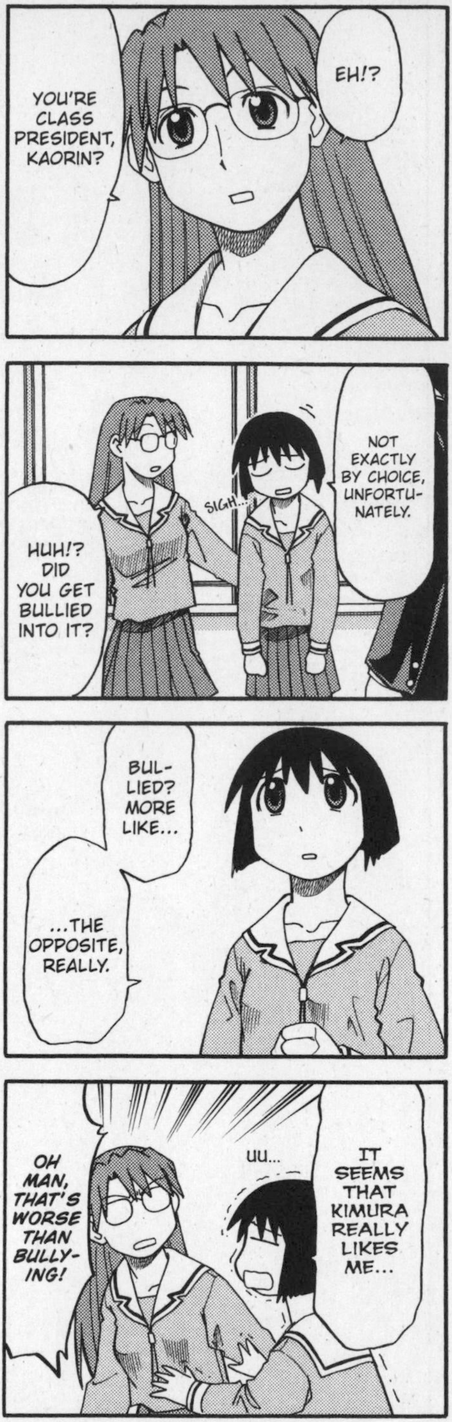
EH!?
YOU'RE CLASS PRESIDENT, KAORIN?
NOT EXACTLY BY CHOICE, UNFORTUNATELY.
SIGH...
HUH!? DID YOU GET BULLIED INTO IT?
BULLIED? MORE LIKE...
...THE OPPOSITE, REALLY.
IT SEEMS THAT KIMURA REALLY LIKES ME...
UU...
OH MAN, THAT'S WORSE THAN BULLYING!

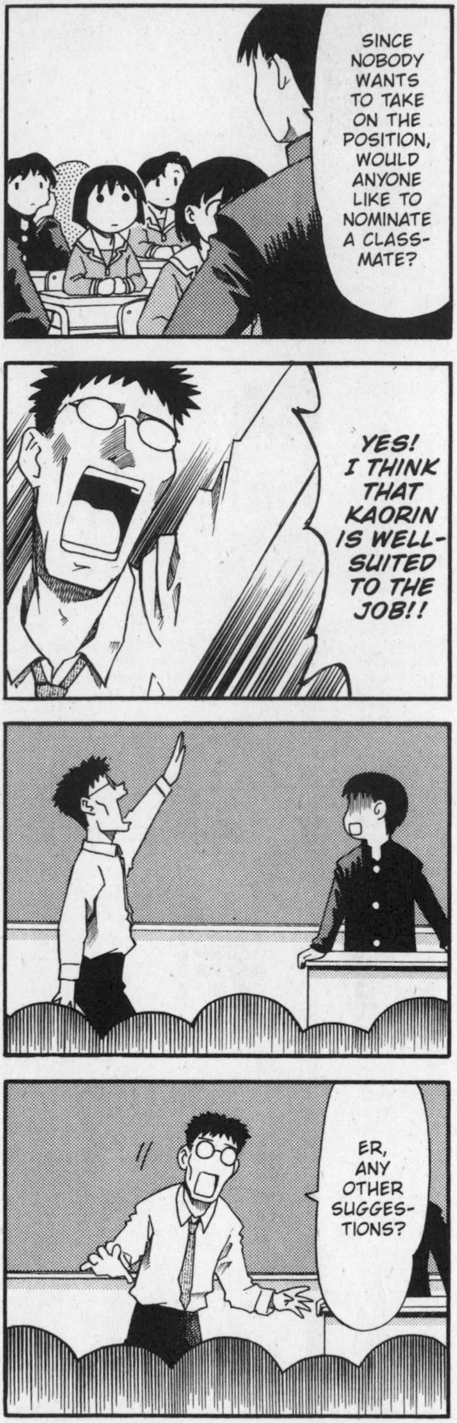
SINCE NOBODY WANTS TO TAKE ON THE POSITION, WOULD ANYONE LIKE TO NOMINATE A CLASSMATE?
YES! I THINK THAT KAORIN IS WELL-SUITED TO THE JOB!!
ER, ANY OTHER SUGGESTIONS?

WOULD IT HURT?

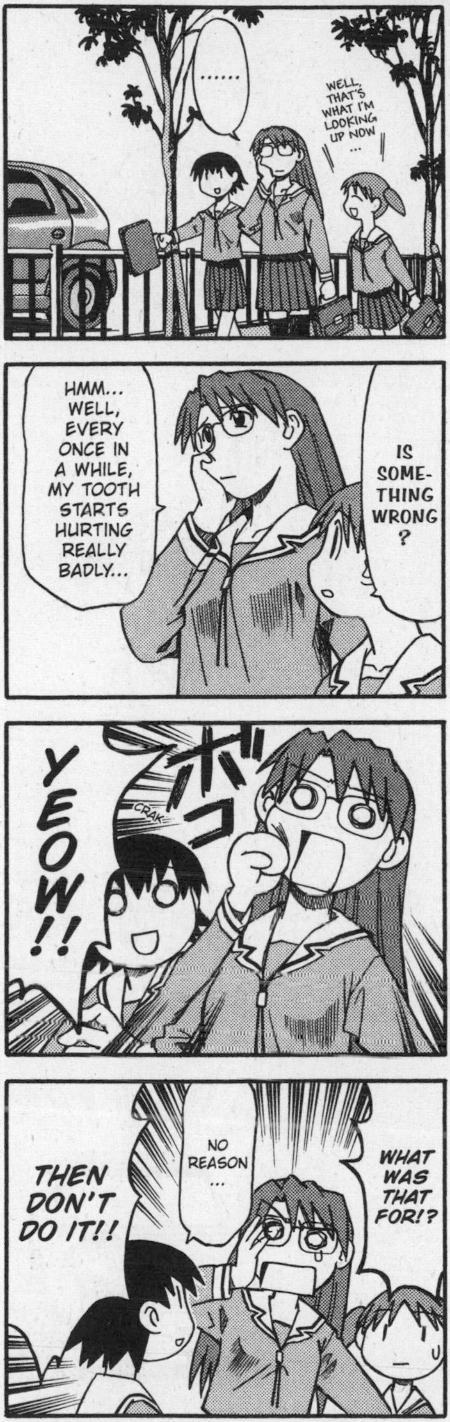
WELL, THAT'S WHAT I'M LOOKING UP NOW ...
......
IS SOMETHING WRONG?
HMM... WELL, EVERY ONCE IN A WHILE, MY TOOTH STARTS HURTING REALLY BADLY...
CRAK
YEOW!!
WHAT WAS THAT FOR!?
NO REASON ...
THEN DON'T DO IT!!

PAINFUL MISTAKE

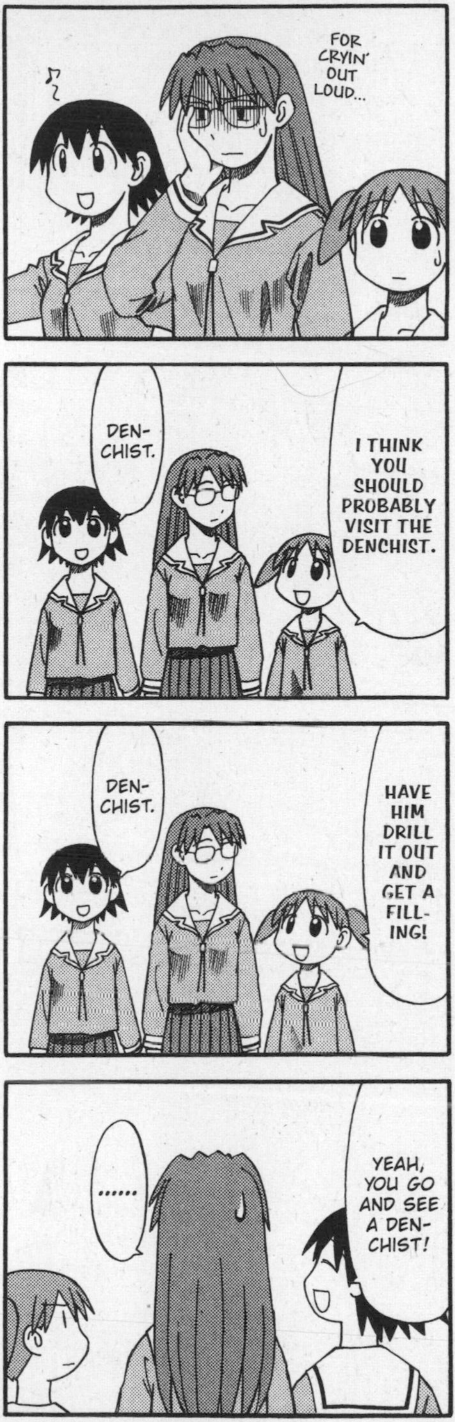
FOR CRYIN' OUT LOUD...
I THINK YOU SHOULD PROBABLY VISIT THE DENCHIST.
DEN-CHIST.
HAVE HIM DRILL IT OUT AND GET A FILL-ING!
DEN-CHIST.
YEAH, YOU GO AND SEE A DEN-CHIST!
......

SAFETY SPINNING

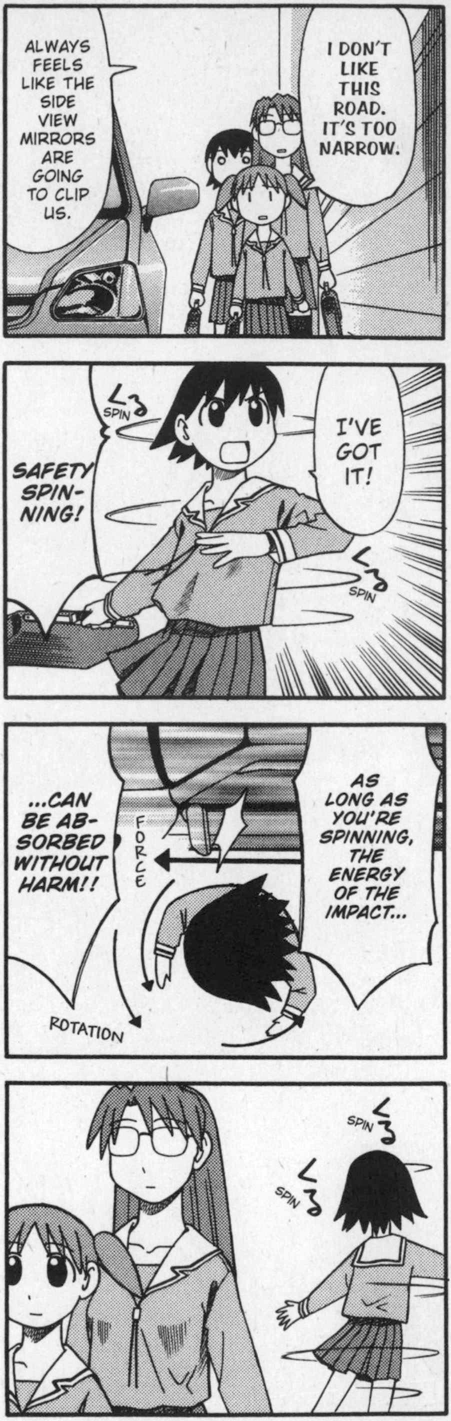
I DON'T LIKE THIS ROAD. IT'S TOO NARROW.
ALWAYS FEELS LIKE THE SIDE VIEW MIRRORS ARE GOING TO CLIP US.
I'VE GOT IT!
くる SPIN
SAFETY SPIN-NING!
くる SPIN
AS LONG AS YOU'RE SPINNING, THE ENERGY OF THE IMPACT...
FORCE
...CAN BE AB-SORBED WITHOUT HARM!!
ROTATION
くる SPIN
くる SPIN

SPIN

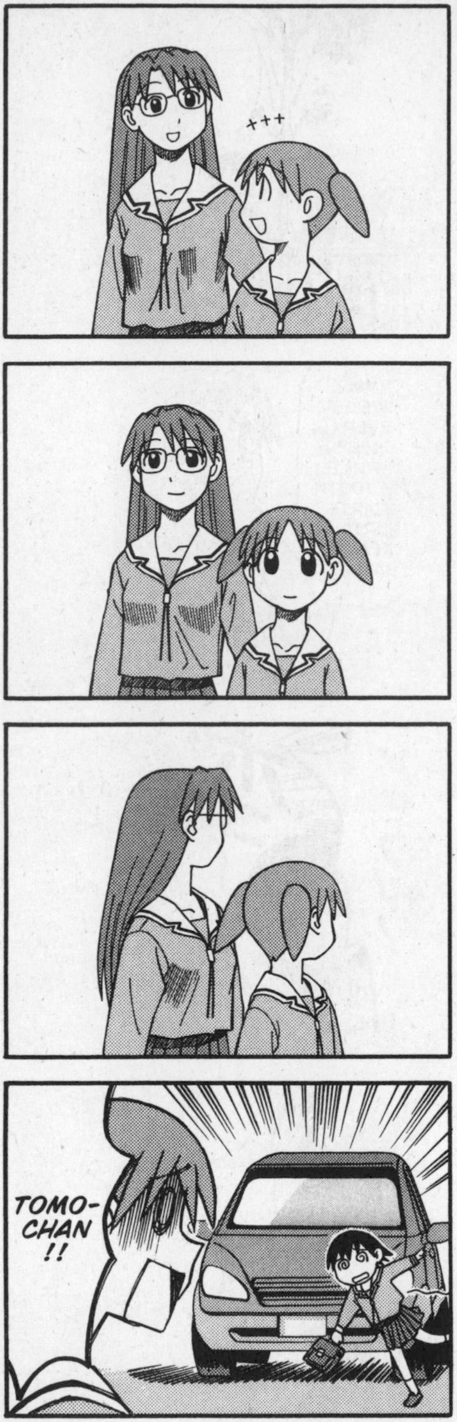
+++
TOMO-CHAN!!

TWENTY EACH WAY

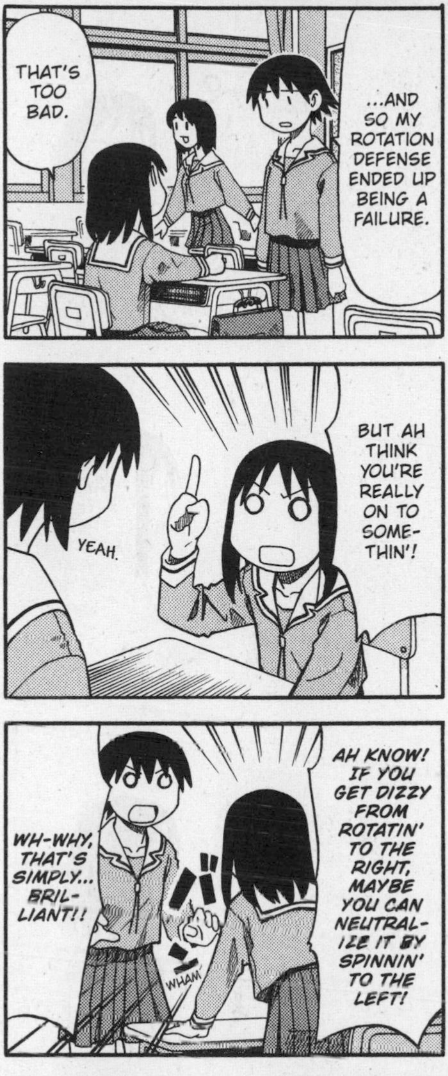

...AND SO MY ROTATION DEFENSE ENDED UP BEING A FAILURE.
THAT'S TOO BAD.
BUT AH THINK YOU'RE REALLY ON TO SOME-THIN'!
YEAH.
AH KNOW! IF YOU GET DIZZY FROM ROTATIN' TO THE RIGHT, MAYBE YOU CAN NEUTRAL-IZE IT BY SPINNIN' TO THE LEFT!
WHAM
WH-WHY, THAT'S SIMPLY... BRIL-LIANT!!
AH'LL TRY IT.
GO, OSAKA, GO!

THE RESULT

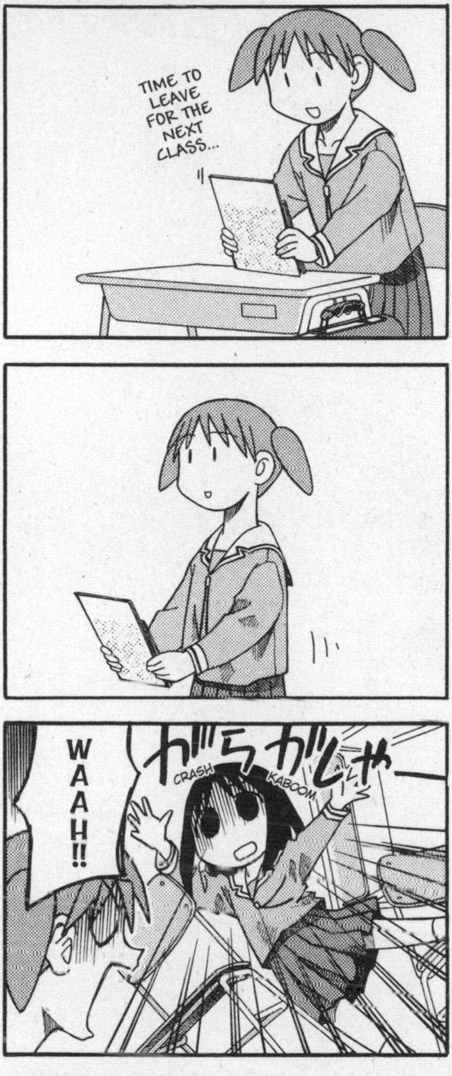

TIME TO LEAVE FOR THE NEXT CLASS...
KABOOM
CRASH
WAAAH!!
WHAT HAPPENED TO YOU, OSAKA-SAN!!?

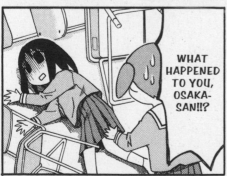

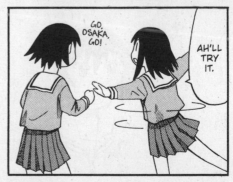

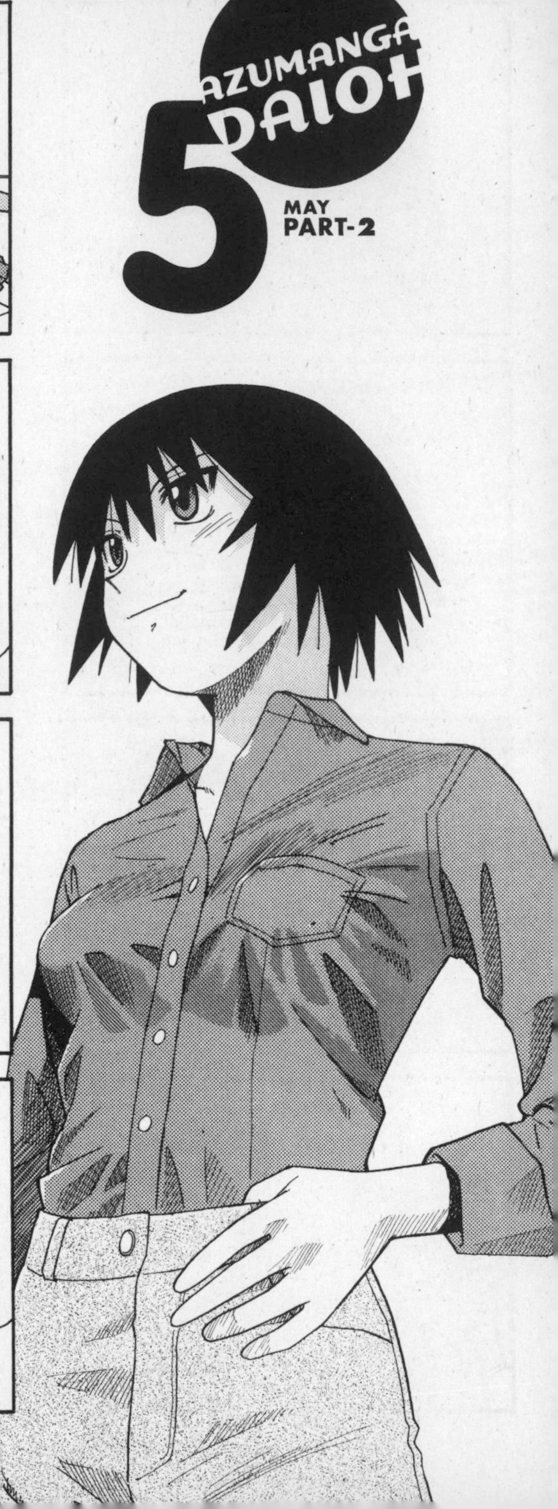
AZUMANGA DAIOH
5
MAY
PART-2

GOTCHA

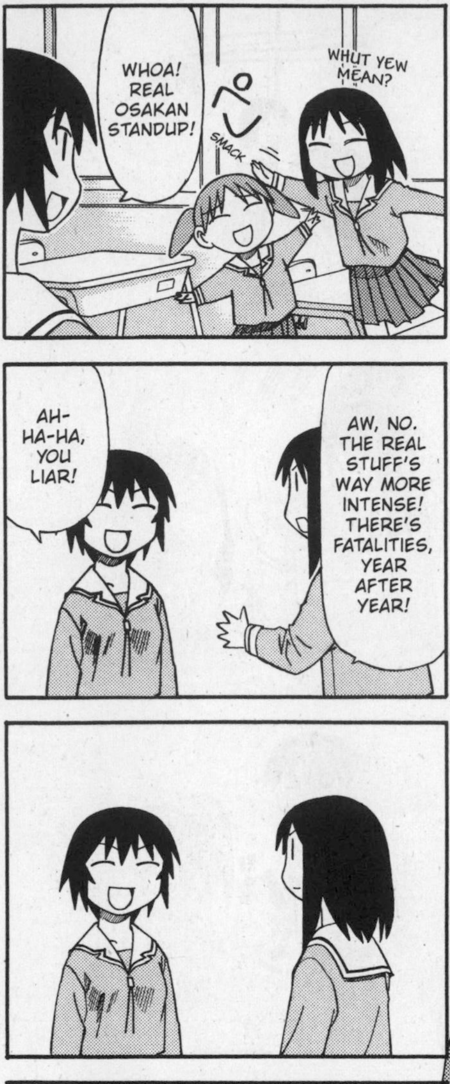
WHUT YEW MEAN?
ぺし
SMACK
WHOA! REAL OSAKAN STANDUP!
AW, NO. THE REAL STUFF'S WAY MORE INTENSE! THERE'S FATALITIES, YEAR AFTER YEAR!
SMACK
AH-HA-HA, YOU LIAR!
REALLY!?
NAW.

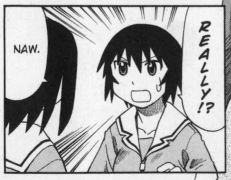

TODAY'S COMPETITION

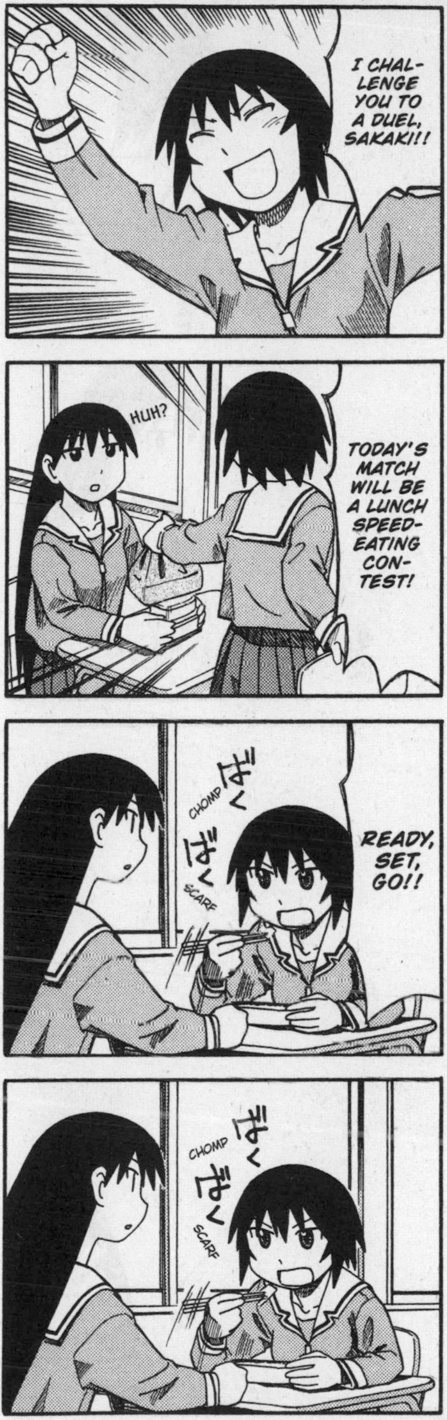
I CHAL-LENGE YOU TO A DUEL, SAKAKI!!
HUH?
TODAY'S MATCH WILL BE A LUNCH SPEED-EATING CON-TEST!
READY, SET, GO!!
ばく
CHOMP
ばく
SCARF
ばく
CHOMP
ばく
SCARF

APPRECIATION

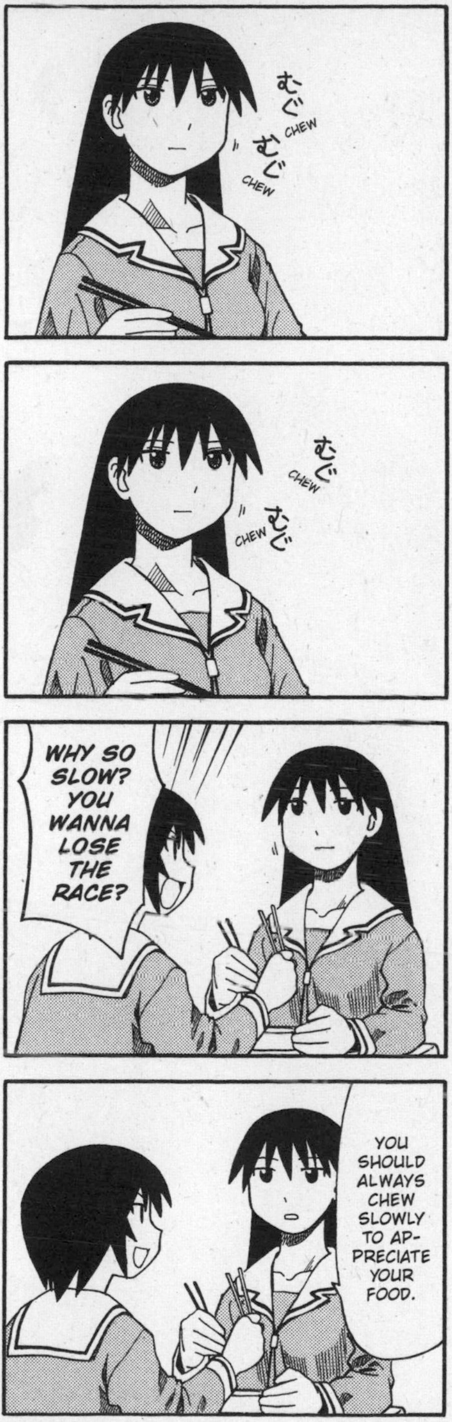
むぐ
CHEW
むぐ
CHEW
むぐ
CHEW
むぐ
CHEW
WHY SO SLOW? YOU WANNA LOSE THE RACE?
YOU SHOULD ALWAYS CHEW SLOWLY TO AP-PRECIATE YOUR FOOD.

NOTE

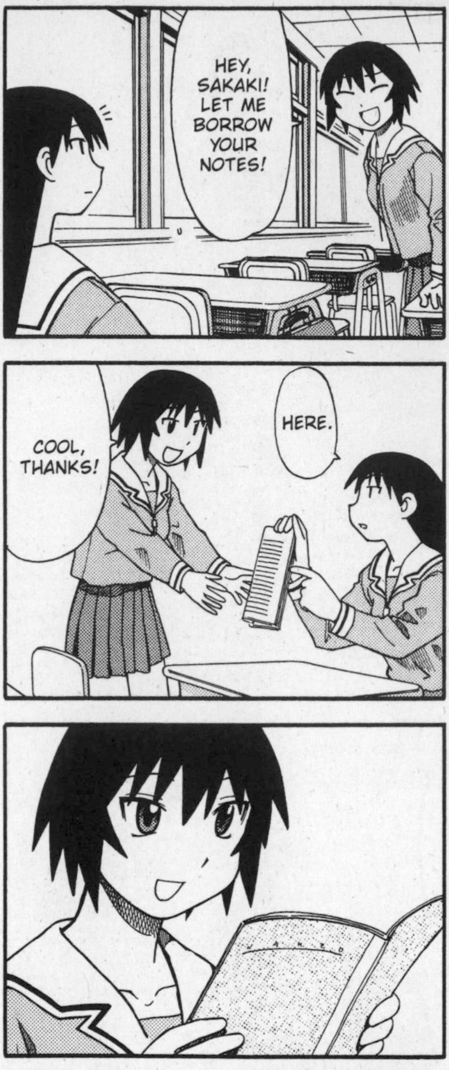
HEY, SAKAKI! LET ME BORROW YOUR NOTES!
HERE.
COOL, THANKS!
ポイント
チェック

CAT LABELS: POINT / CHECK

EVOLUTION

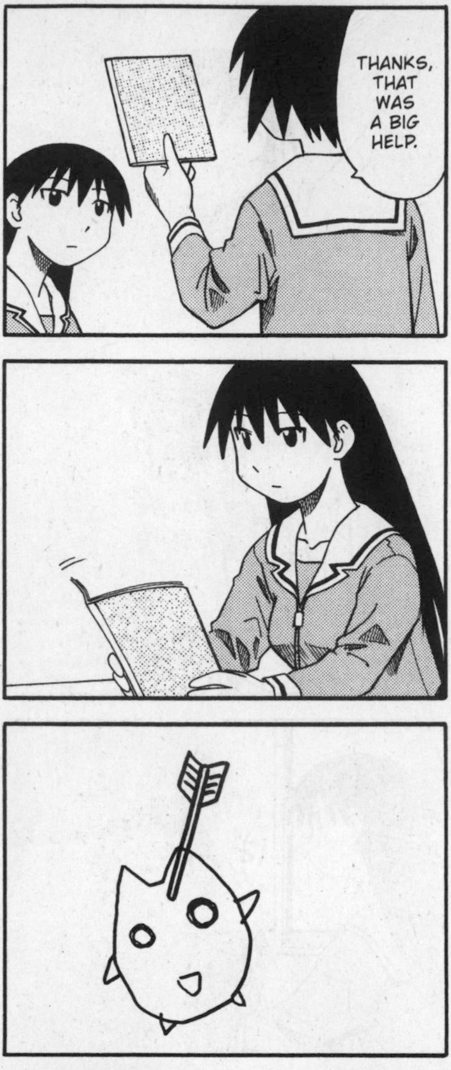
THANKS, THAT WAS A BIG HELP.
HEY, TOMO!

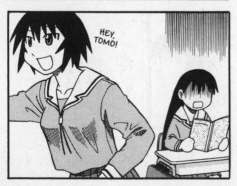

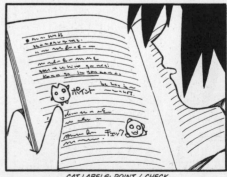

DON'T RUN

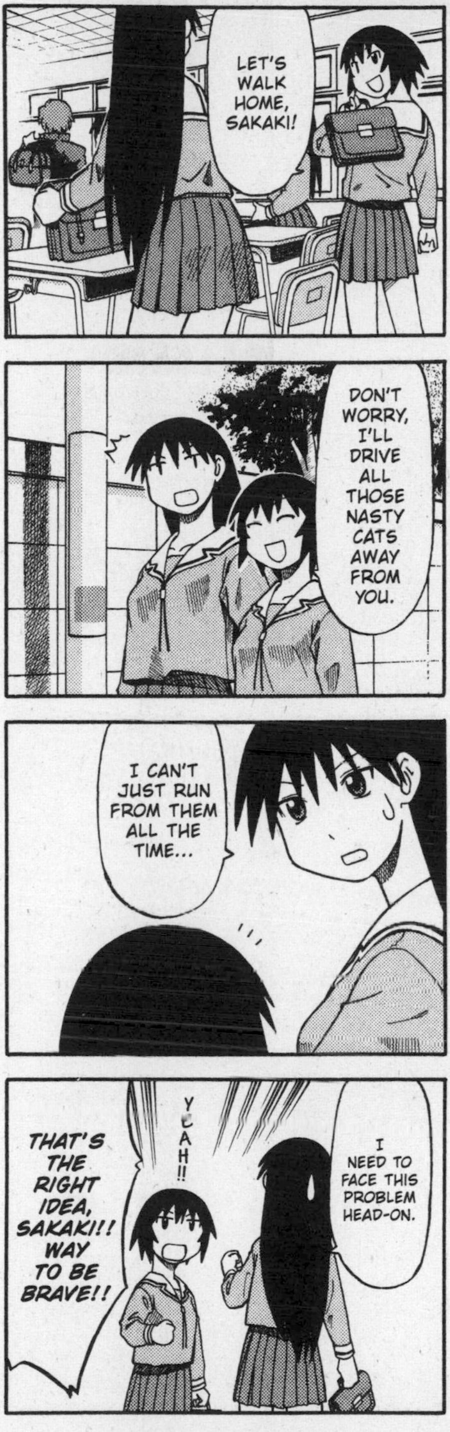
LET'S WALK HOME, SAKAKI!
DON'T WORRY, I'LL DRIVE ALL THOSE NASTY CATS AWAY FROM YOU.
I CAN'T JUST RUN FROM THEM ALL THE TIME...
I NEED TO FACE THIS PROBLEM HEAD-ON.
YEAH!!
THAT'S THE RIGHT IDEA, SAKAKI!! WAY TO BE BRAVE!!

KITTY

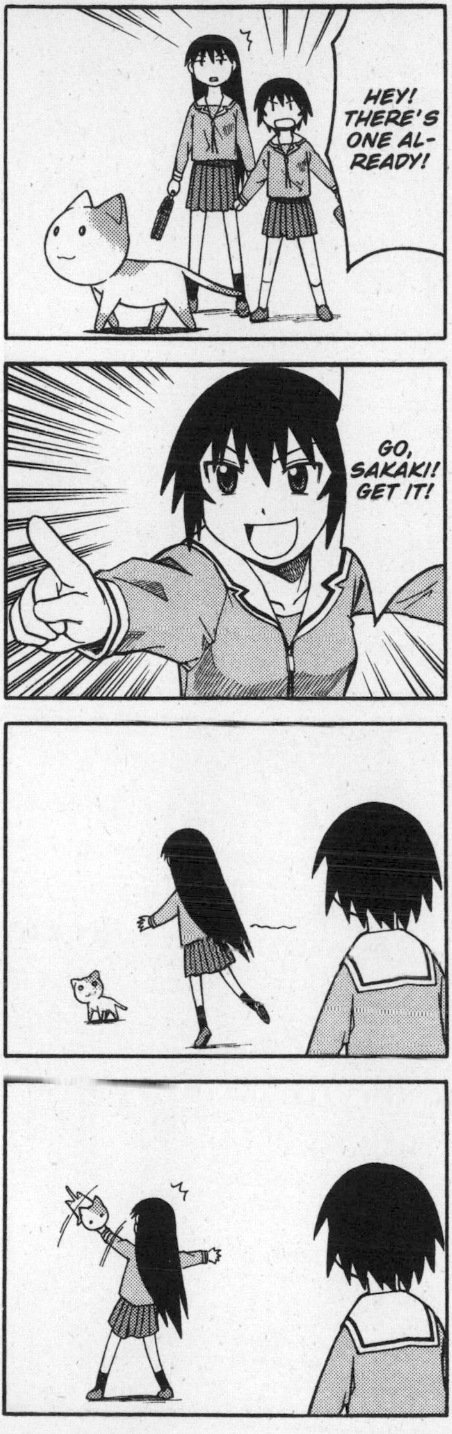
HEY! THERE'S ONE AL-READY!
GO, SAKAKI! GET IT!

HIGH SPEED

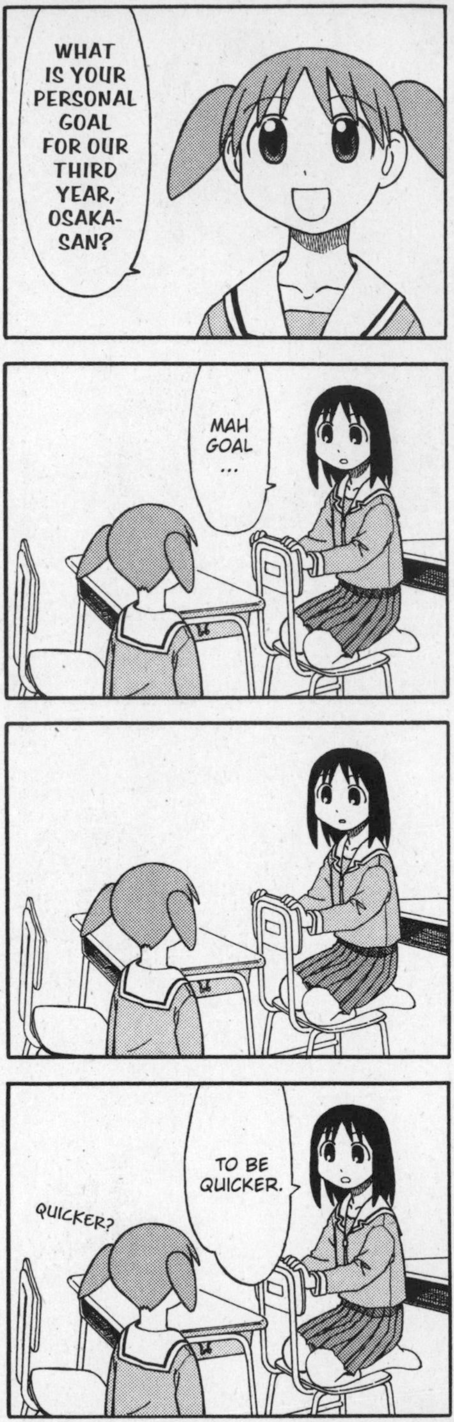
WHAT IS YOUR PERSONAL GOAL FOR OUR THIRD YEAR, OSAKA-SAN?
MAH GOAL ...
TO BE QUICKER.
QUICKER?

GOT LEFT OUT

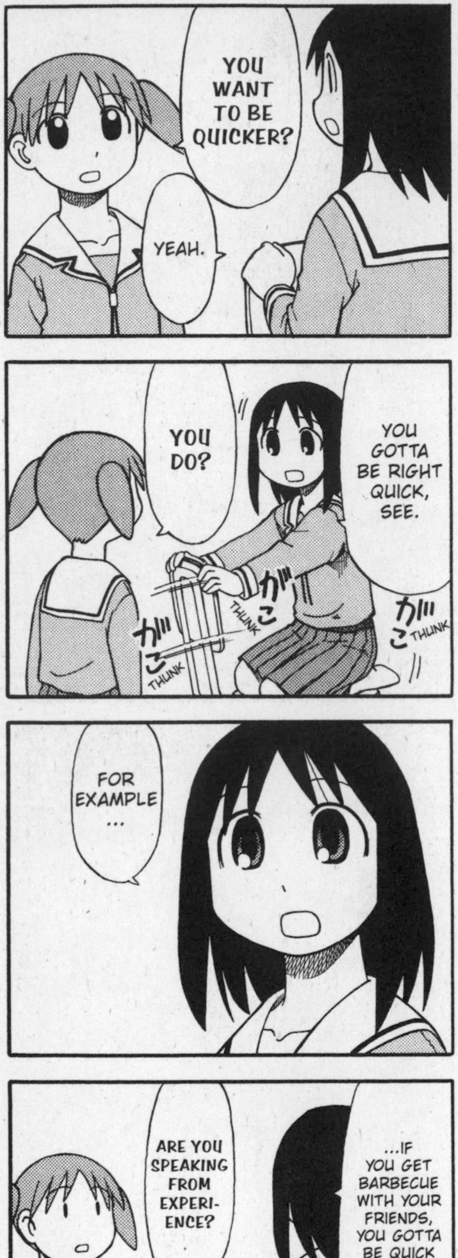
YOU WANT TO BE QUICKER?
YEAH.
YOU GOTTA BE RIGHT QUICK, SEE.
YOU DO?
ガこ THUNK
ガこ THUNK
ガこ THUNK
FOR EXAMPLE ...
...IF YOU GET BARBECUE WITH YOUR FRIENDS, YOU GOTTA BE QUICK SO THEY DON'T EAT EVERYTHIN' FIRST.
ARE YOU SPEAKING FROM EXPERIENCE?

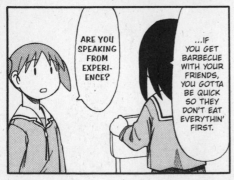

GET STARTED

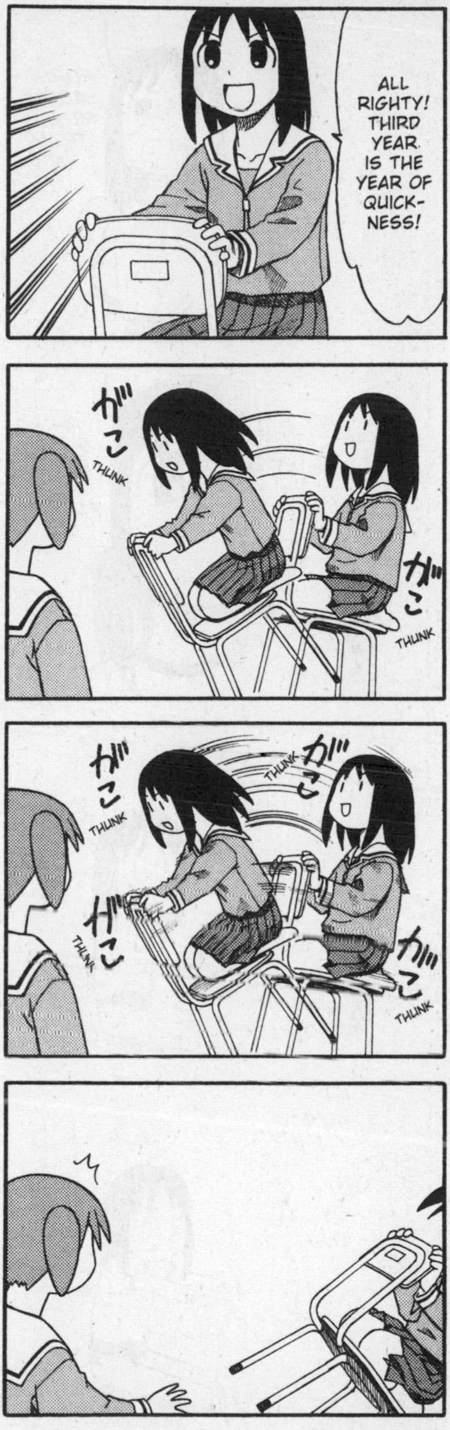
ALL RIGHTY! THIRD YEAR IS THE YEAR OF QUICK-NESS!
がこ
THUNK
がこ
THUNK
がこ
THUNK
がこ
THUNK
がこ
THUNK
がこ
THUNK

TOUGH

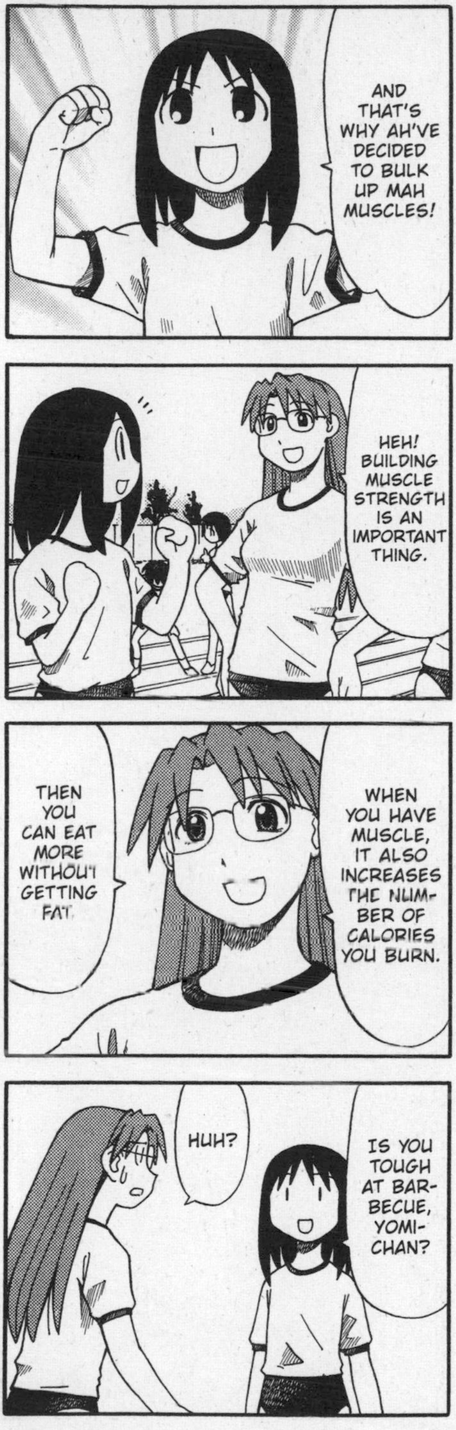
AND THAT'S WHY AH'VE DECIDED TO BULK UP MAH MUSCLES!
HEH! BUILDING MUSCLE STRENGTH IS AN IMPORTANT THING.
WHEN YOU HAVE MUSCLE, IT ALSO INCREASES THE NUM-BER OF CALORIES YOU BURN.
THEN YOU CAN EAT MORE WITHOUT GETTING FAT.
IS YOU TOUGH AT BAR-BECUE, YOMI-CHAN?
HUH?

TRICKY

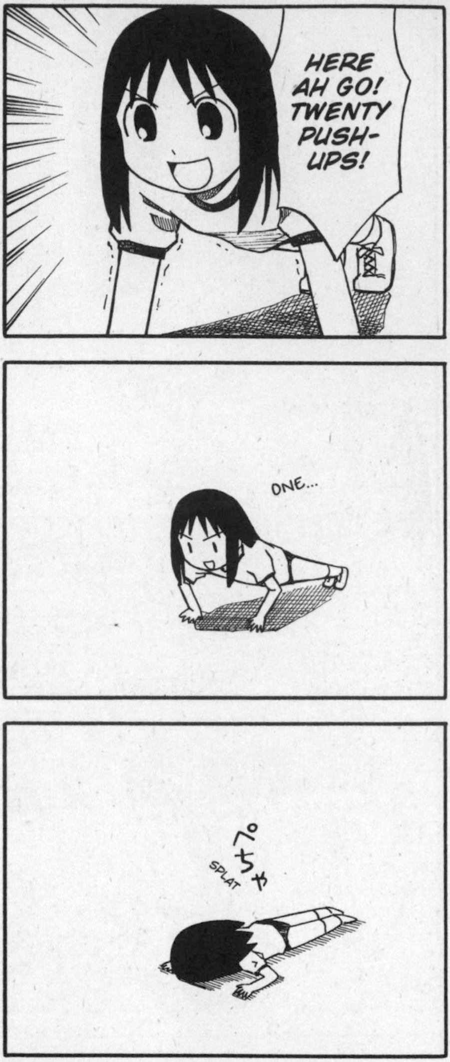
HERE AH GO! TWENTY PUSH-UPS!
ONE...
ぺちゃ
SPLAT
PLEASE TEACH ME THE TRICK TO PUSH-UPS.
THERE'S NO TRICK.

CHANGE OF PLANS

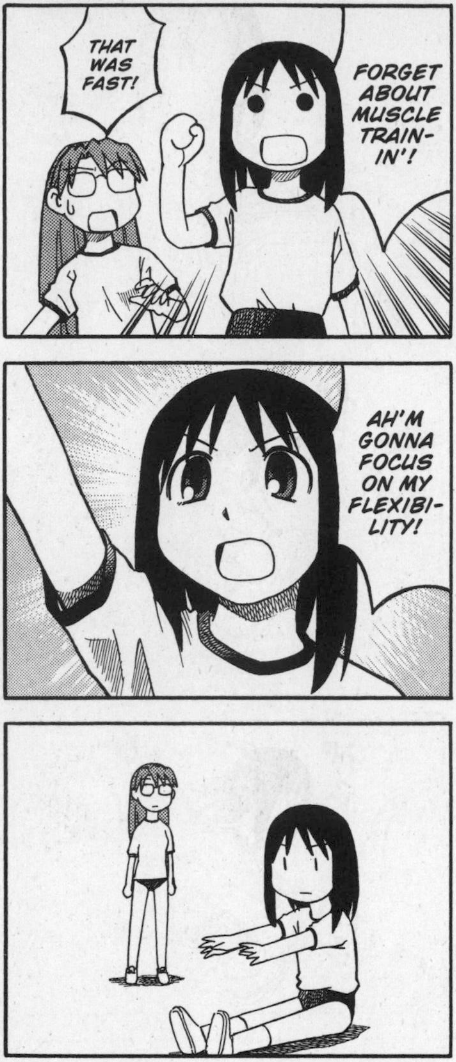
FORGET ABOUT MUSCLE TRAIN-IN'!
THAT WAS FAST!
AH'M GONNA FOCUS ON MY FLEXIBI-LITY!
NNNNG!!
EH!?

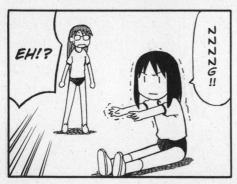

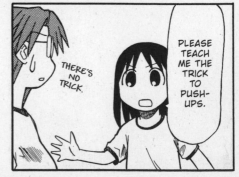

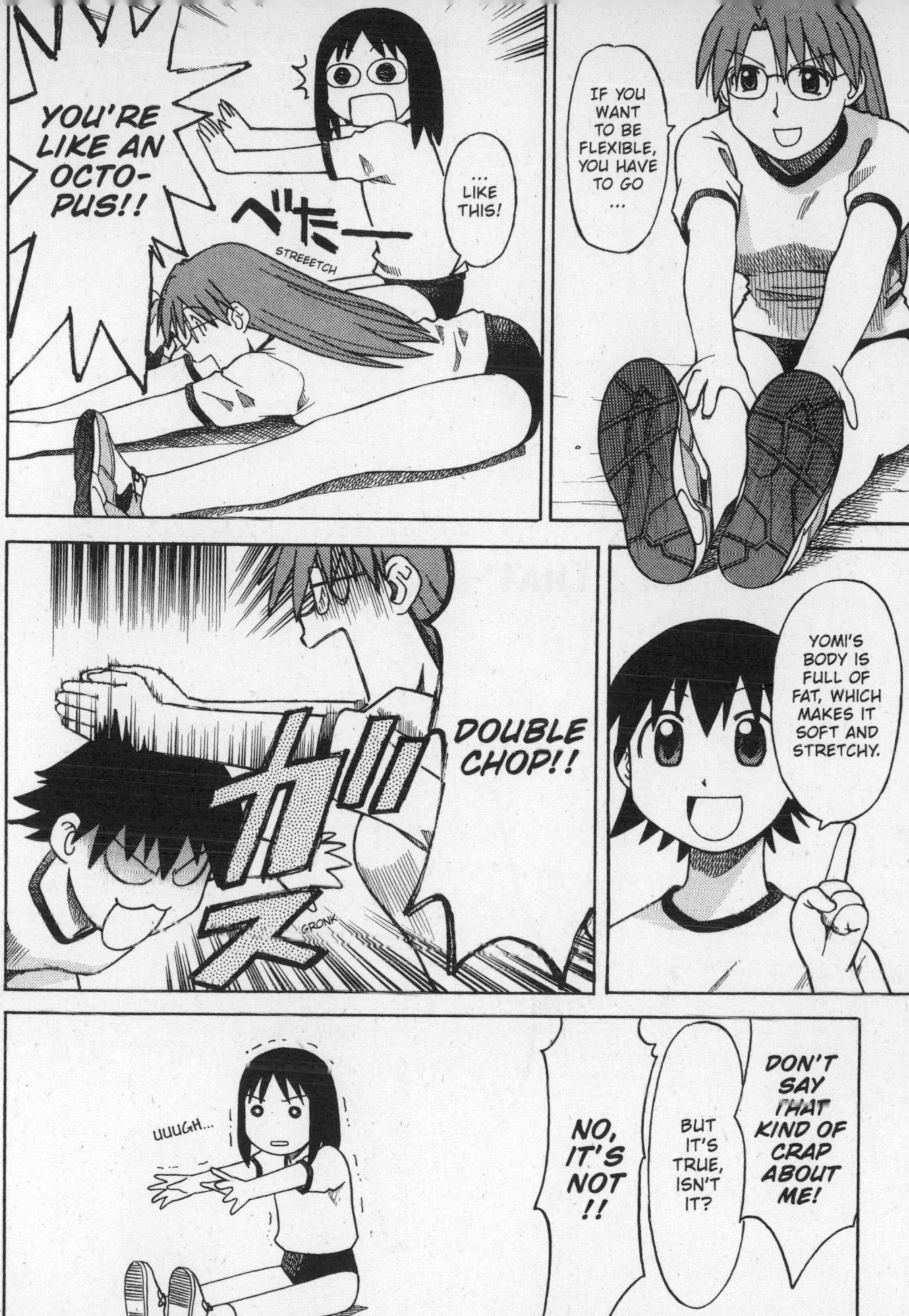
IF YOU WANT TO BE FLEXIBLE, YOU HAVE TO GO ...
... LIKE THIS!
べたー
STREEETCH
YOU'RE LIKE AN OCTO-PUS!!
YOMI'S BODY IS FULL OF FAT, WHICH MAKES IT SOFT AND STRETCHY.
DOUBLE CHOP!!
GRONK
DON'T SAY THAT KIND OF CRAP ABOUT ME!
BUT IT'S TRUE, ISN'T IT?
NO, IT'S NOT!!
UUUGH...

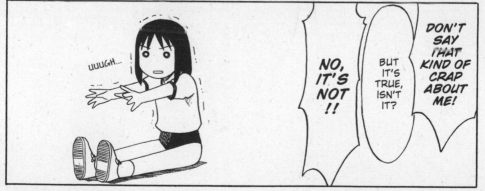

WELL, THAT'S ALL FOR NOW.

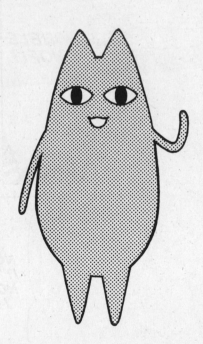

PAGE 465
Kotatsu: A special Japanese piece of furniture, consisting of a short table with a small heater stuck underneath. A heavy futon-style comforter is placed over the top, trapping the heat underneath. An indispensable part of winter in Japan!

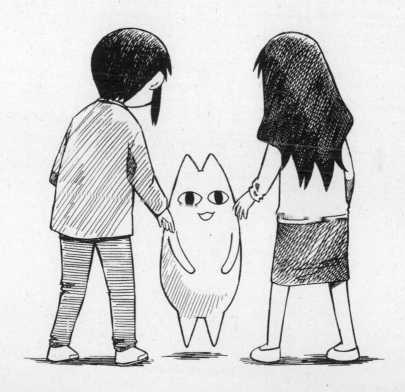

PAGE 335
Ultraman: The mask Osaka wears here is the recognizable face of the long-running live-action TV series hero, Ultraman. Including all the different series broadcast through time, Ultraman has been on TV for over four decades, using his powers to grow to enormous size to protect the town from attacking monsters.

PAGE 350
Mushrooms: Within Japanese cuisine, no mushroom is more prized than matsutake. Due to its rarity and demand, matsutake can be incredibly pricey. Shiitake mushrooms, while similarly important to Asian cuisines, are much easier to cultivate and therefore quite a bit cheaper.

Curry and *hayashi* rice: *Hayashi* rice is a thick beef sauce poured over rice that bears a strong resemblance to typical Japanese curry.

PAGE 367
Morning Musume: An ultra-famous pop supergroup consisting entirely of girls ("*musume*" meaning "girl" in this context) handpicked by the group's manager, Tsunku. One of the group's defining features is the practice of regularly "graduating" and scouting new members for replacement, so the lineup of members can be radically different from year to year.

PAGE 370
***Nurikabe* and *Karakasa*:** Two of the many spooks and goblins found in Japanese folklore. The *nurikabe* is said to be an invisible wall that extends endlessly to block the way of travelers. It is often depicted in art as a wall with a face and limbs. The *karakasa* is an umbrella that is said to come to life once it is one hundred years old. A *karakasa* is shown with one eye, a protuding tongue, and one foot.

PAGE 392
Chiyosuke: *-suke* is a common ending for Japanese boys' names. Yukari is teasing Chiyo by adding it to her name.

PAGE 413
Hokkaido: As the northernmost of the four main islands of Japan, Hokkaido is the coldest. In addition to its sizable agriculture, the island's relatively recent colonization and development leave it with extensive wilderness and wildlife. There's a lot of special regional seafood and exotic meat for the adventurous gourmet.

PAGE 418
Noboribetsu: A town in western Hokkaido famed for its many luxurious natural hot springs. The Karurusu Hot Spring—whose name is based on the Japanese reading of the Czech hot spring town, Karlovy Vary—is a particularly well-known location, due to the use of its name in a brand of bath softener.

PAGE 421
Futon: Rather than a cushion to sit on, the Japanese futon is a bed consisting of a heavy comforter to lie on with another heavy blanket on top. When Tomo mentions patterns, she is referring to a common school rule that no personal clothes in addition to the school uniform may have attention-drawing patterns or marks.

PAGE 432
***Ramen* and *soba*:** While most people may be familiar with instant ramen noodles, *soba* is a less common sight in the Western world. *Soba* is made with buckwheat flour and has a grayish-purple color. Rather than being served in a soup, *soba* typically comes on a plate and is dipped into small cups of strong broth before eating.

PAGE 433
Seto Inland Sea: This body of water, which is now officially known simply as "The Inland Sea," lies between three of the four main islands of Japan: Honshu, Kyushu, and Shikoku. It's a long and narrow sea that's also rather shallow.

PAGE 457
Floors: The typical Japanese high school building has three floors, with each floor corresponding to one of the school years: first-years on the bottom floor, second-years on the middle floor, and third-years on the top.

PAGE 459
Haircut: It's a common practice among Japanese girls to cut their hair short after they've suffered a broken heart.

Ryoko Hirosue: An actress who exploded into Japanese show business in the late 1990s. She's often sported a short-cut hairstyle, but needless to say, Tomo's got a long way to go to match her in looks. Hirosue was also the lead actress in *Departures*, the winner of the Academy Awards' Best Foreign Language Film in 2008.

6 AZUMANGA DAIOH

JUNE
PART-1

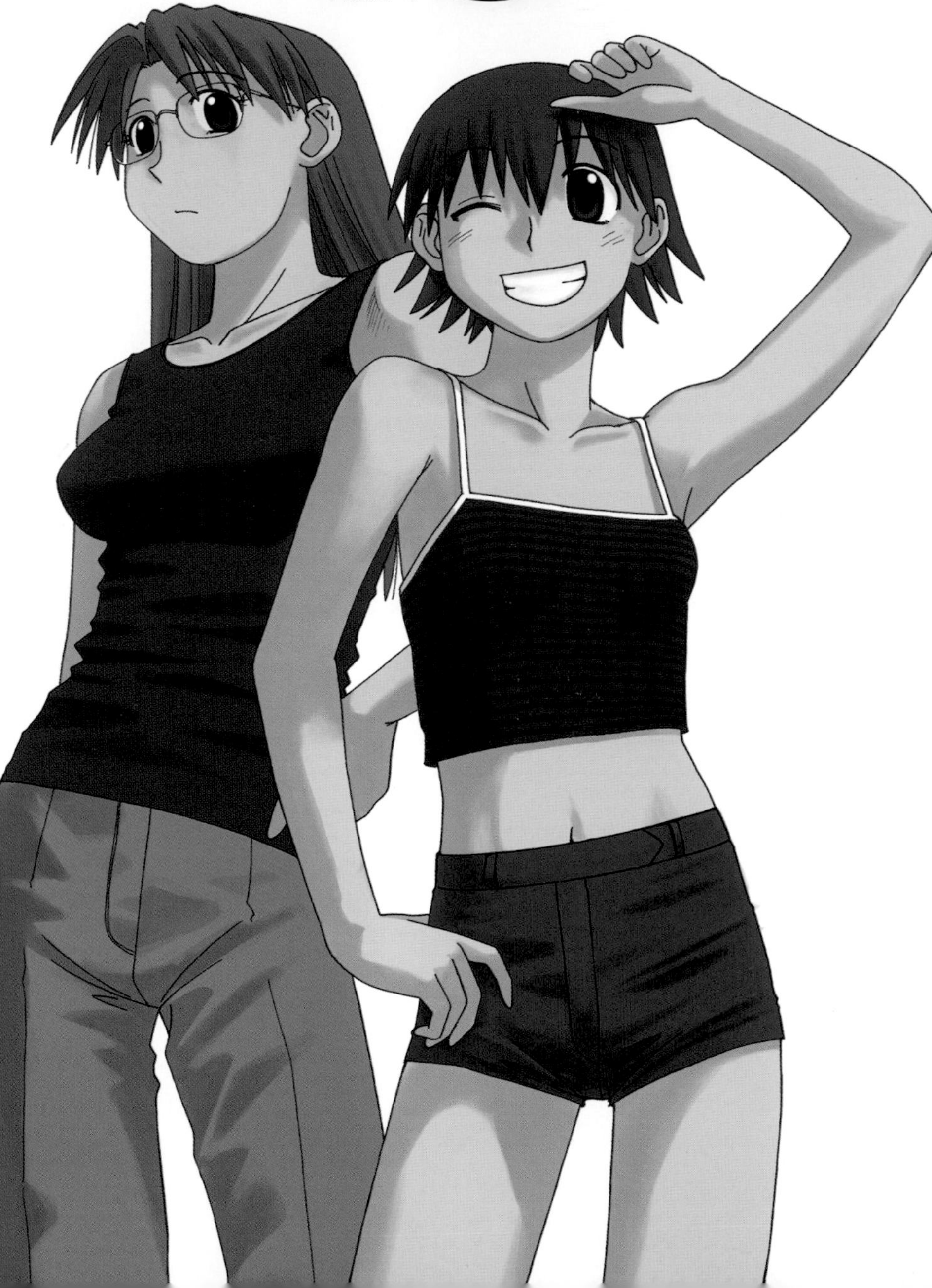

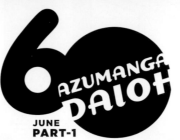

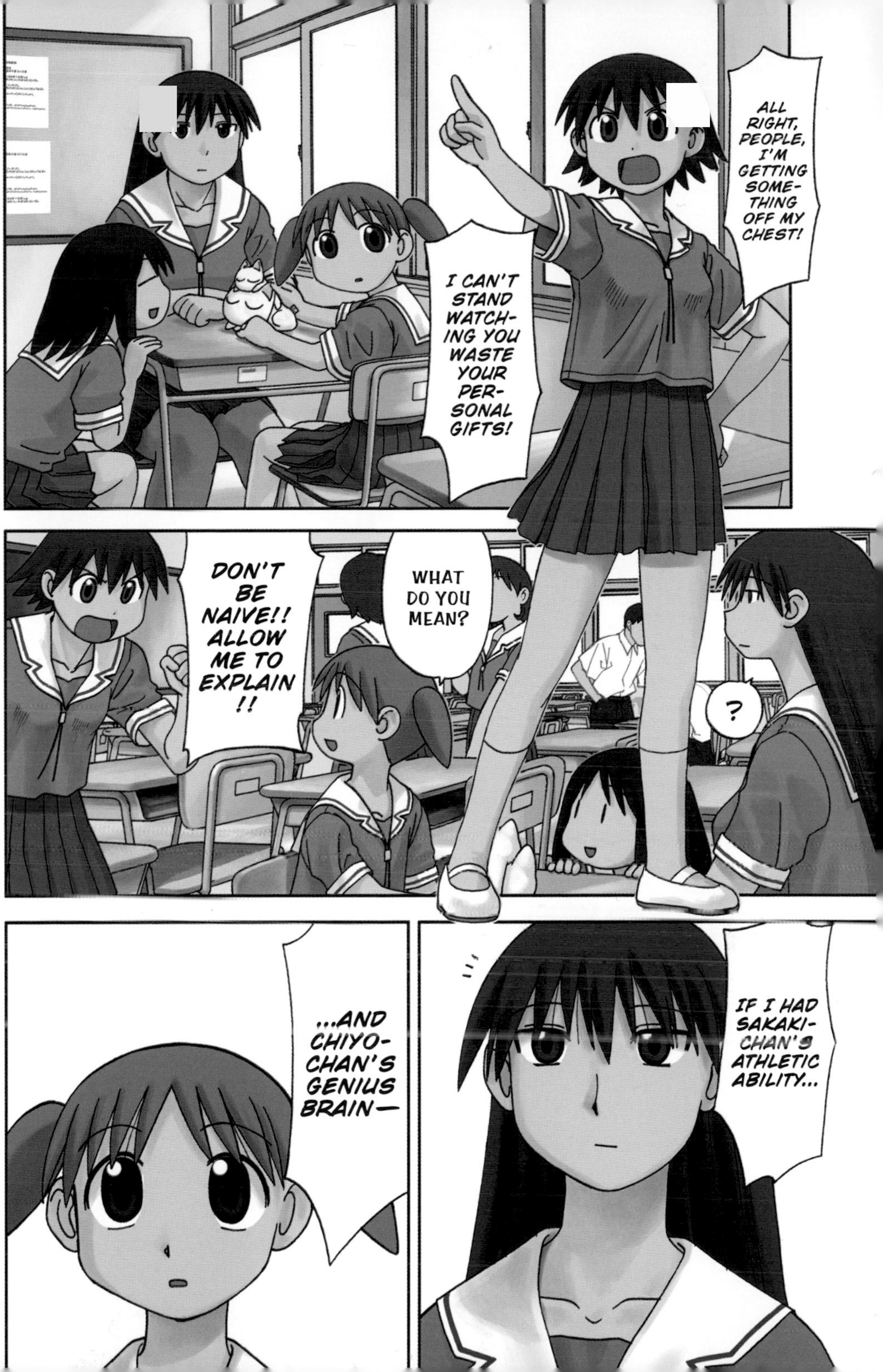
ALL RIGHT, PEOPLE, I'M GETTING SOMETHING OFF MY CHEST!
I CAN'T STAND WATCHING YOU WASTE YOUR PERSONAL GIFTS!
?
WHAT DO YOU MEAN?
DON'T BE NAIVE!! ALLOW ME TO EXPLAIN!!
IF I HAD SAKAKI-CHAN'S ATHLETIC ABILITY...
...AND CHIYO-CHAN'S GENIUS BRAIN—

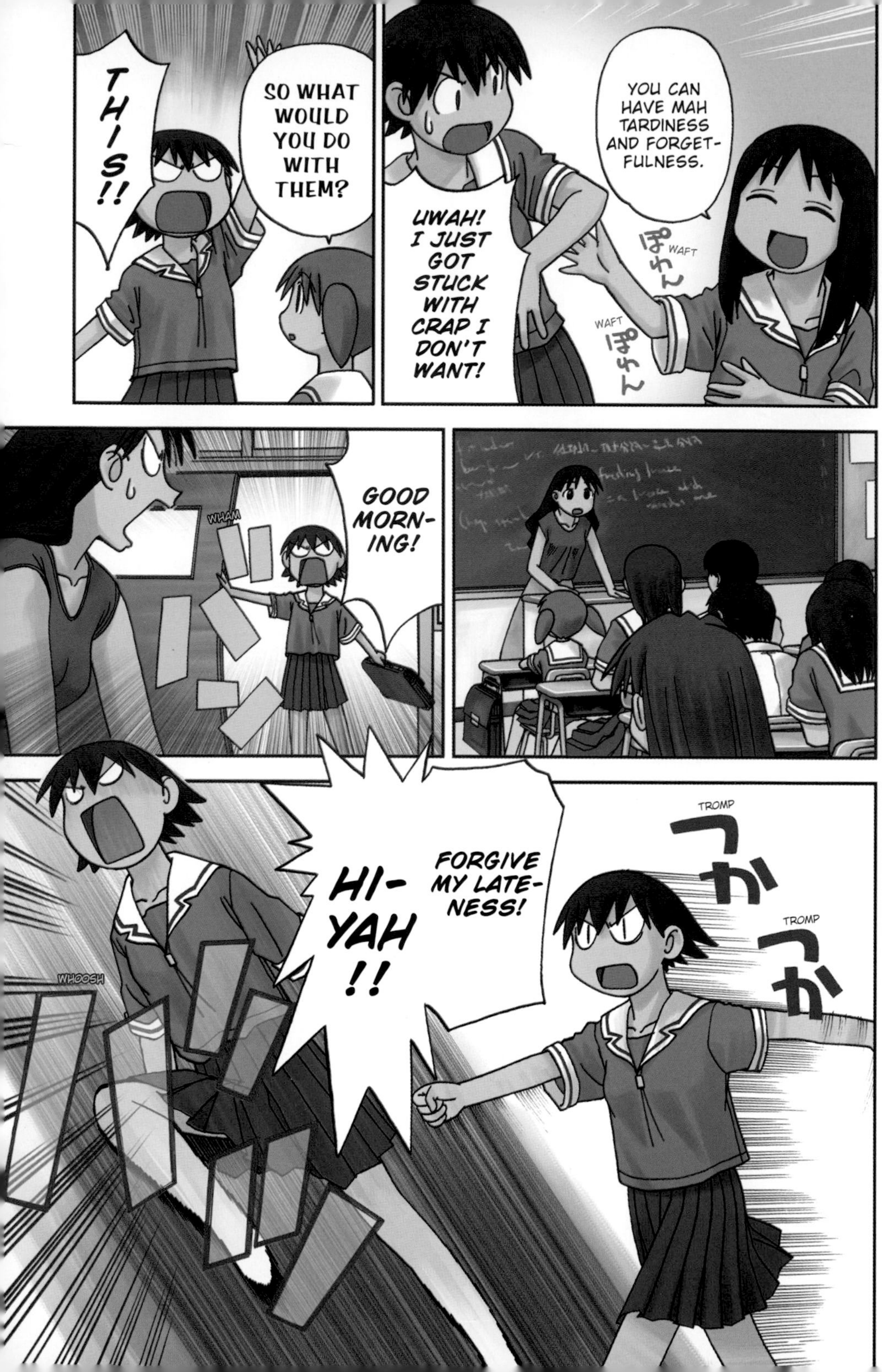
YOU CAN HAVE MAH TARDINESS AND FORGET-FULNESS.
ぽわん
WAFT
ぽわん
WAFT
UWAH! I JUST GOT STUCK WITH CRAP I DON'T WANT!
SO WHAT WOULD YOU DO WITH THEM?
THIS!!
GOOD MORN-ING!
WHAM
つか
TROMP
つか
TROMP
FORGIVE MY LATE-NESS!
HI-YAH!!
WHOOSH

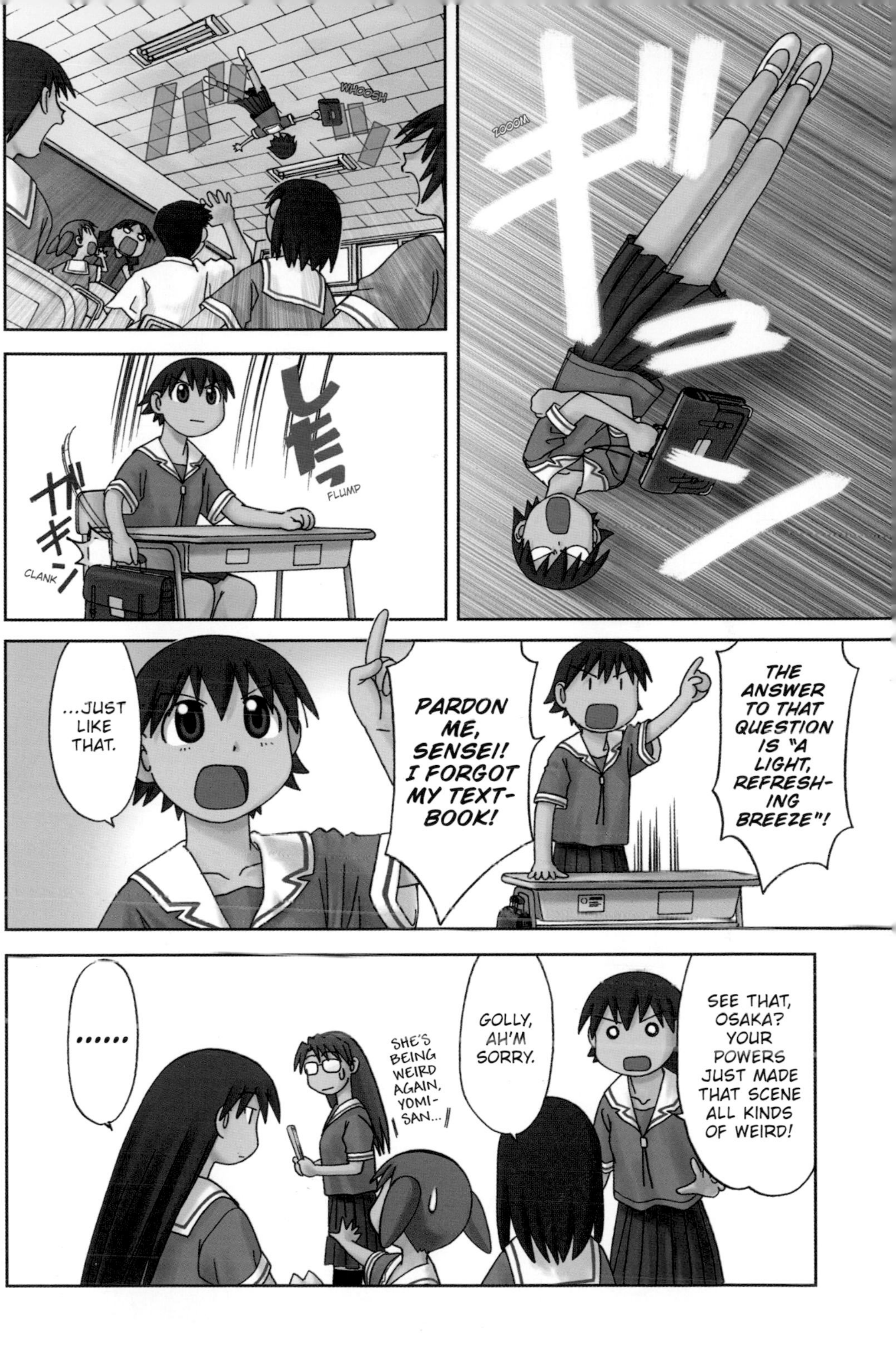
ZOOOM
WHOOSH
FLUMP
CLANK
THE ANSWER TO THAT QUESTION IS "A LIGHT, REFRESHING BREEZE"!
PARDON ME, SENSEI! I FORGOT MY TEXTBOOK!
...JUST LIKE THAT.
SEE THAT, OSAKA? YOUR POWERS JUST MADE THAT SCENE ALL KINDS OF WEIRD!
GOLLY, AH'M SORRY.
SHE'S BEING WEIRD AGAIN, YOMI-SAN...
......

UNNEEDED

HEY! WAIT, WAIT!
YOU HAVEN'T ASKED FOR MY ABILITIES YET!
YOU DON'T HAVE ANY.
WHAA!? YES, I DO! I'M GOOD AT SPORTS AND STUFF!
I ALREADY GOT THAT FROM SAKAKI-CHAN. I DON'T NEED IT FROM YOU.
ACK ...
YOU WANT A LITTLE BIT OF THE GENIUS BRAINS?
DON'T TRY TO FEEL SORRY FOR ME!!

GOOD DAUGHTER

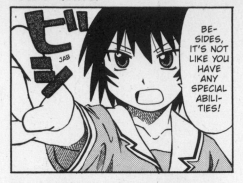

BE-SIDES, IT'S NOT LIKE YOU HAVE ANY SPECIAL ABILI-TIES!
JAB
YOU AREN'T GOOD ON THE FIELD OR IN THE CLASS-ROOM.
UGH ...
I-I DO TOO HAVE ABILI-TIES!
MY DAD SAYS THAT I'M REALLY GOOD AT GIVING SHOULDER MASSAGES!
REALLY? GOSH, THAT'S ... SWELL.
DON'T TRY TO FEEL SORRY FOR ME!!

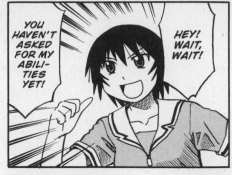

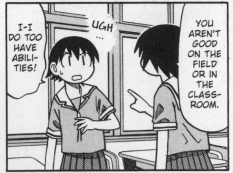

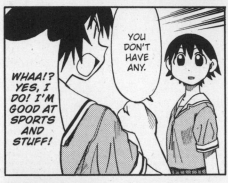

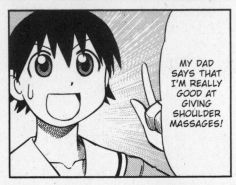

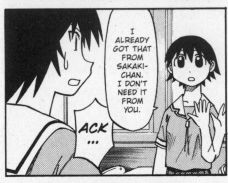

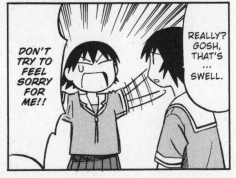

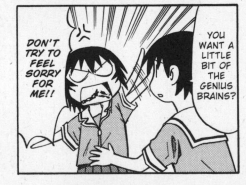

MISTAKE

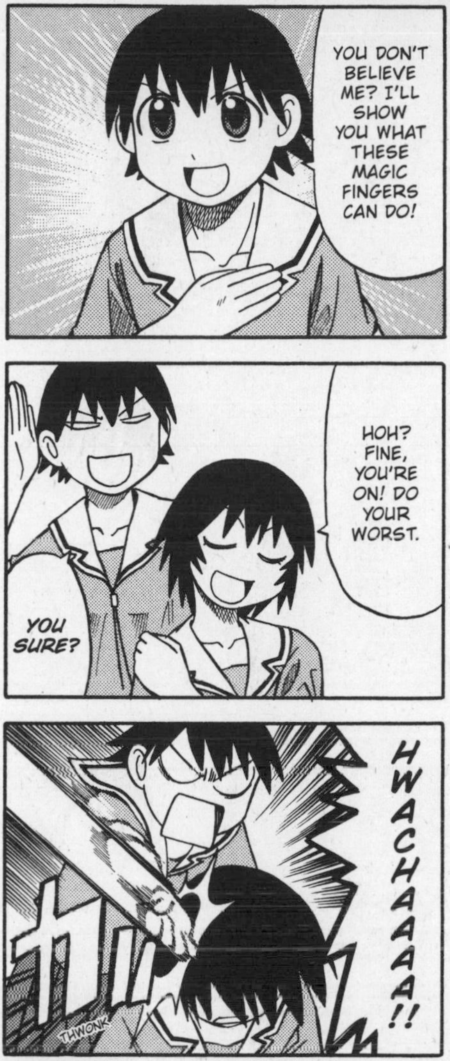
YOU DON'T BELIEVE ME? I'LL SHOW YOU WHAT THESE MAGIC FINGERS CAN DO!
HOH? FINE, YOU'RE ON! DO YOUR WORST.
YOU SURE?
HWACHAAAAAA!!
THWONK
AWW, MAN ... MY POOR HAND ...
OUCH... OWWW ...

NEKOSAKA

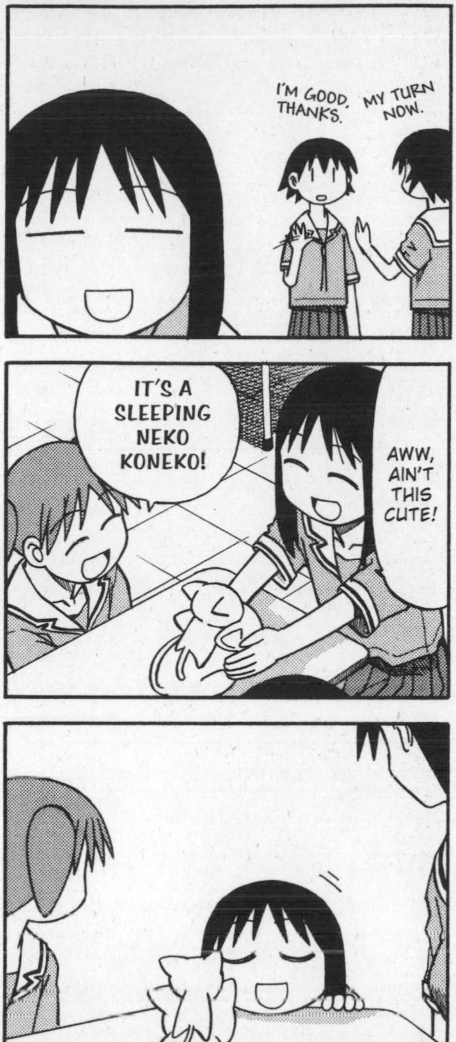
MY TURN NOW.
I'M GOOD, THANKS.
AWW, AIN'T THIS CUTE!
IT'S A SLEEPING NEKO KONEKO!

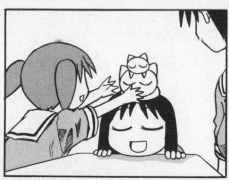

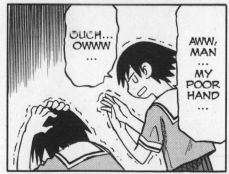

WHOOPSY

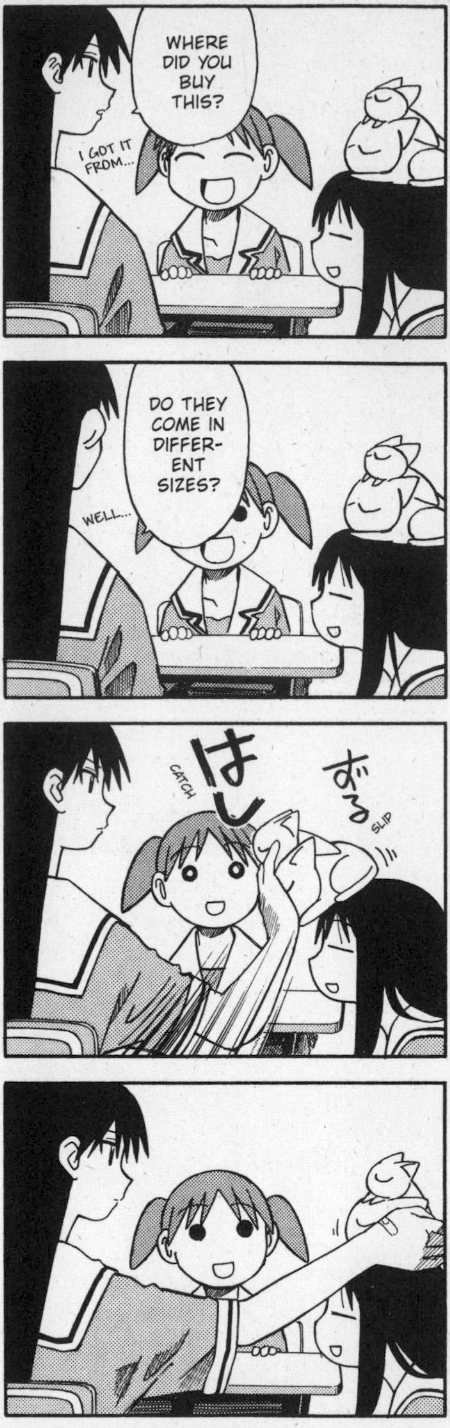
WHERE DID YOU BUY THIS?
I GOT IT FROM...
DO THEY COME IN DIFFER-ENT SIZES?
WELL...
はし
CATCH
ずる
SLIP

THAT'S NOT IT

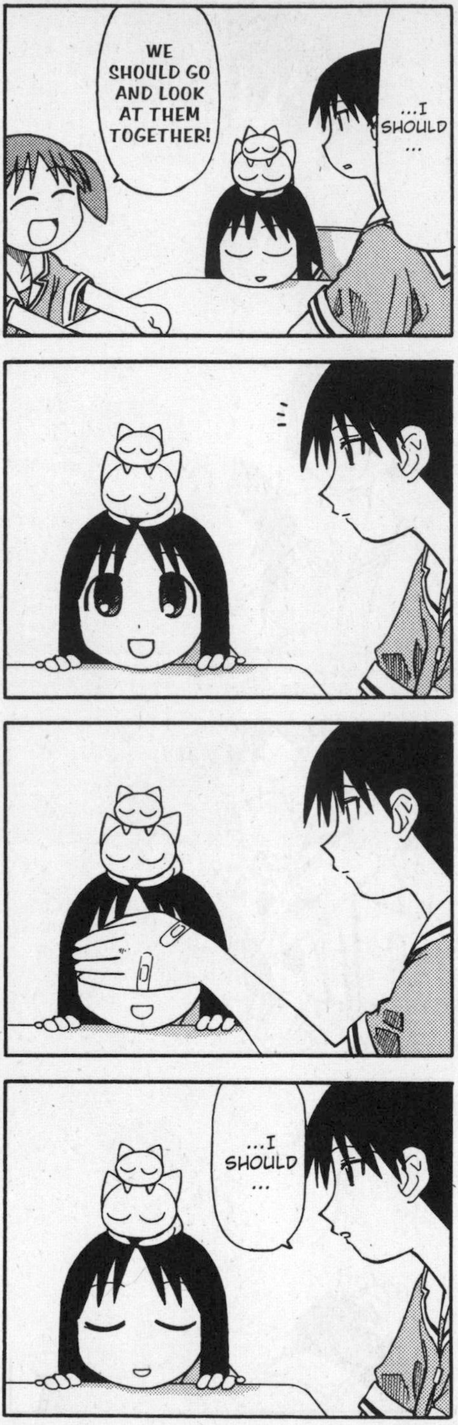
WE SHOULD GO AND LOOK AT THEM TOGETHER!
...I SHOULD ...
...I SHOULD ...

MAKE IT SO I CAN UNDERSTAND

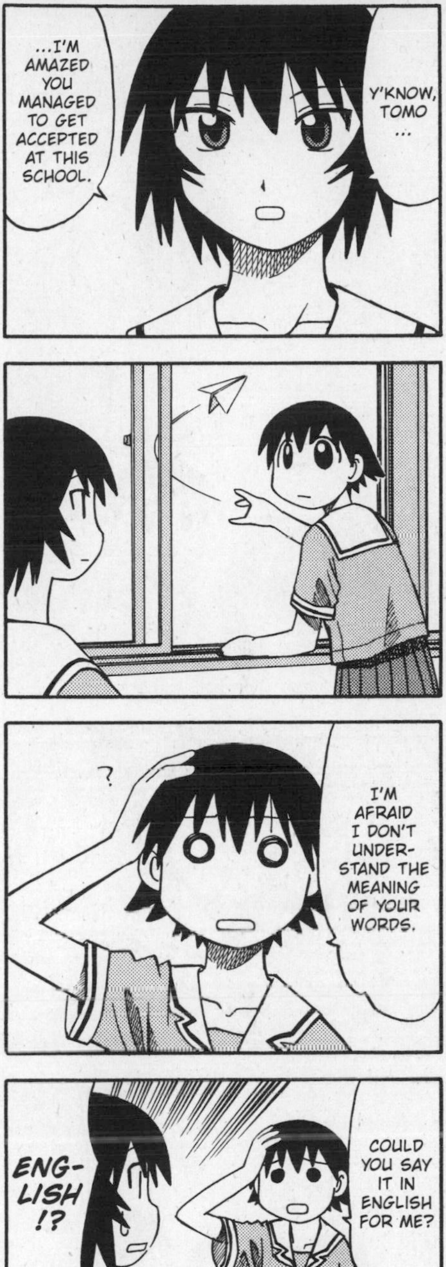
Y'KNOW, TOMO ...
...I'M AMAZED YOU MANAGED TO GET ACCEPTED AT THIS SCHOOL.
?
I'M AFRAID I DON'T UNDER-STAND THE MEANING OF YOUR WORDS.
COULD YOU SAY IT IN ENGLISH FOR ME?
ENG-LISH !?

ENGLISH TRANSLATION

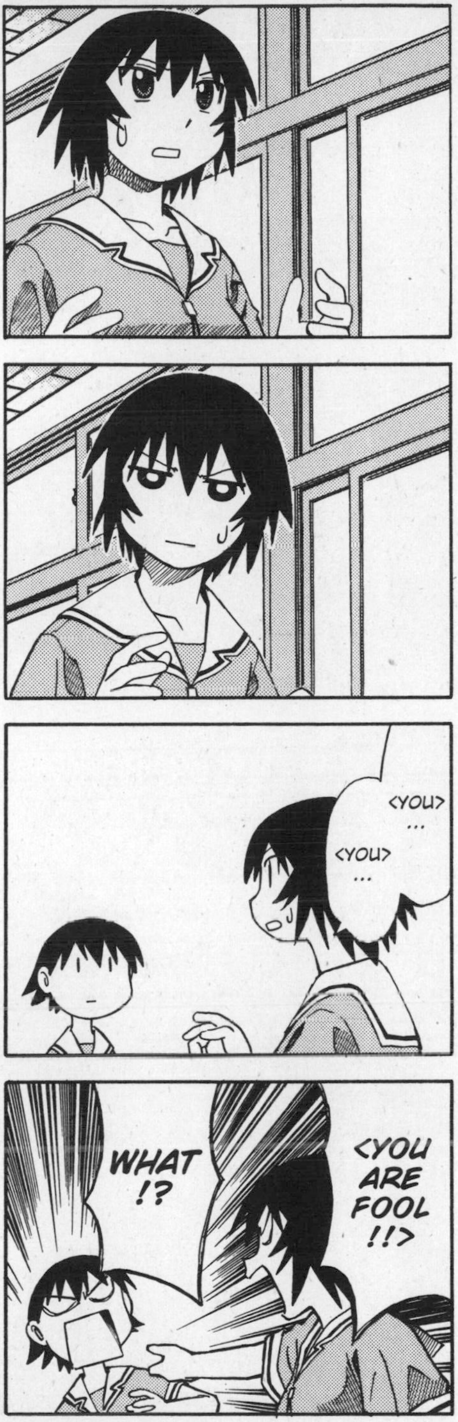
<YOU> ...
<YOU> ...
<YOU ARE FOOL !!>
WHAT !?

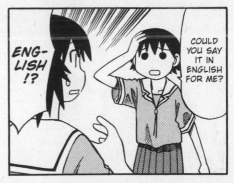

JAPANESE TRANSLATION

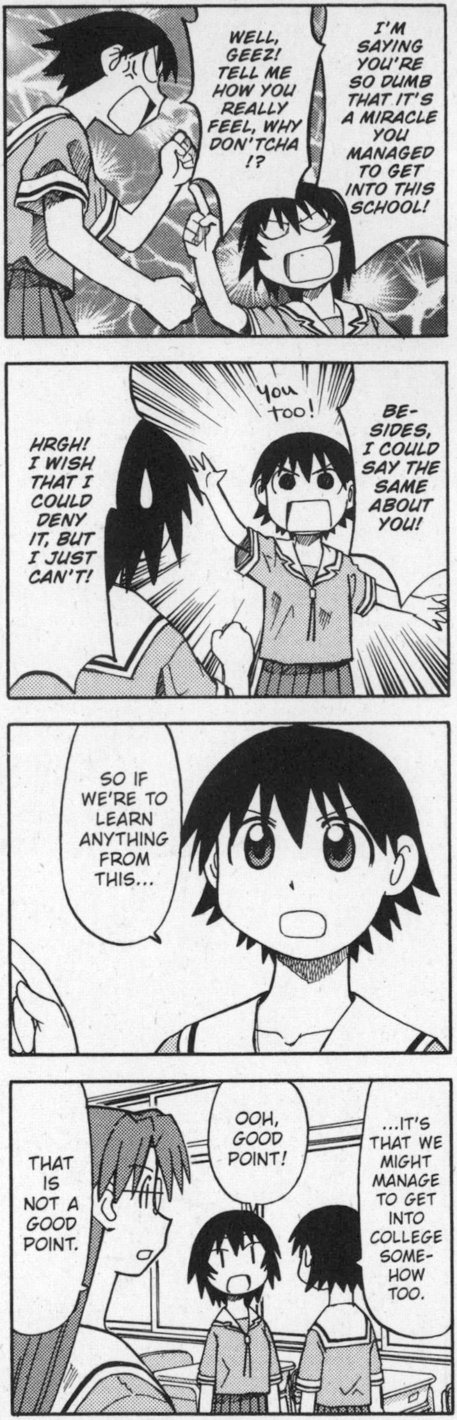
I'M SAYING YOU'RE SO DUMB THAT IT'S A MIRACLE YOU MANAGED TO GET INTO THIS SCHOOL!
WELL, GEEZ! TELL ME HOW YOU REALLY FEEL, WHY DON'TCHA !?
BE-SIDES, I COULD SAY THE SAME ABOUT YOU!
You too!
HRGH! I WISH THAT I COULD DENY IT, BUT I JUST CAN'T!
SO IF WE'RE TO LEARN ANYTHING FROM THIS...
...IT'S THAT WE MIGHT MANAGE TO GET INTO COLLEGE SOME-HOW TOO.
OOH, GOOD POINT!
THAT IS NOT A GOOD POINT.

TOMO'S MEMORY

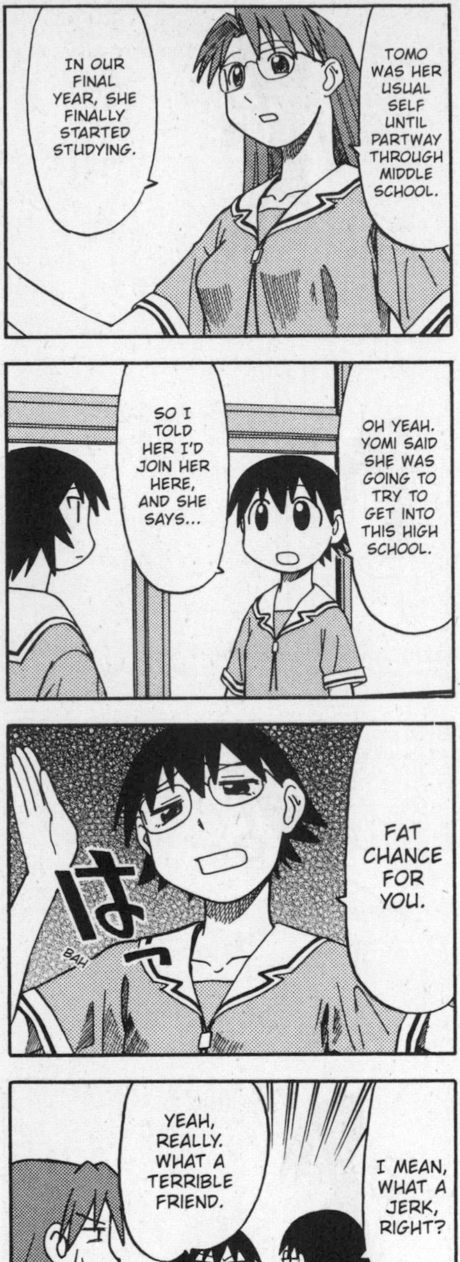
TOMO WAS HER USUAL SELF UNTIL PARTWAY THROUGH MIDDLE SCHOOL.
IN OUR FINAL YEAR, SHE FINALLY STARTED STUDYING.
OH YEAH. YOMI SAID SHE WAS GOING TO TRY TO GET INTO THIS HIGH SCHOOL.
SO I TOLD HER I'D JOIN HER HERE, AND SHE SAYS...
FAT CHANCE FOR YOU.
はっ
BAH
I MEAN, WHAT A JERK, RIGHT?
YEAH, REALLY. WHAT A TERRIBLE FRIEND.
GIVE BACK MY GLASSES...

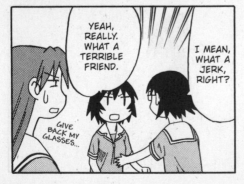

GREAT MEMORIES

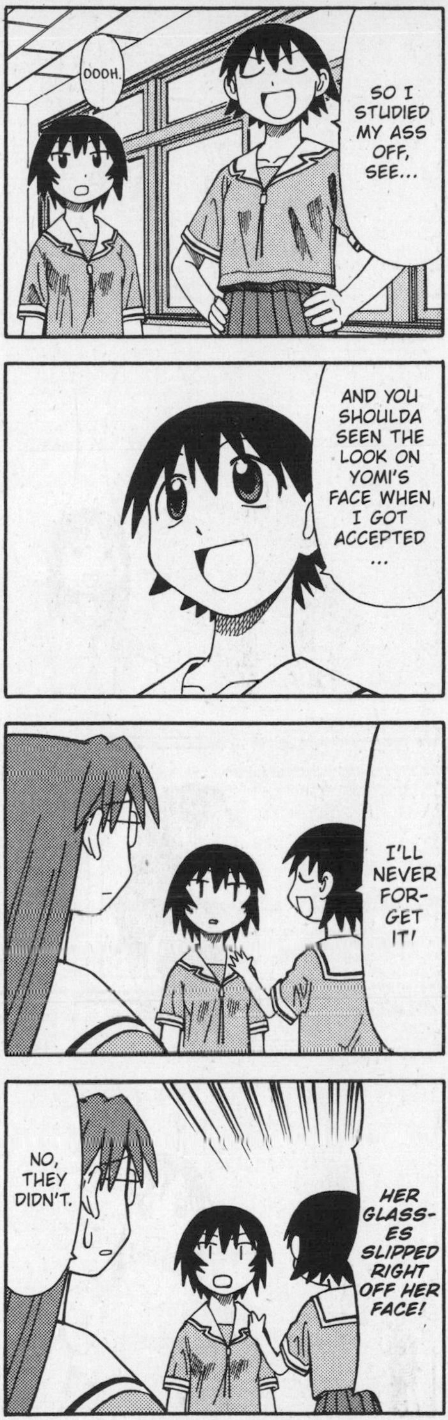
SO I STUDIED MY ASS OFF, SEE...
OOOH.
AND YOU SHOULDA SEEN THE LOOK ON YOMI'S FACE WHEN I GOT ACCEPTED ...
I'LL NEVER FOR-GET IT!
HER GLASS-ES SLIPPED RIGHT OFF HER FACE!
NO, THEY DIDN'T.

PRAISE ME

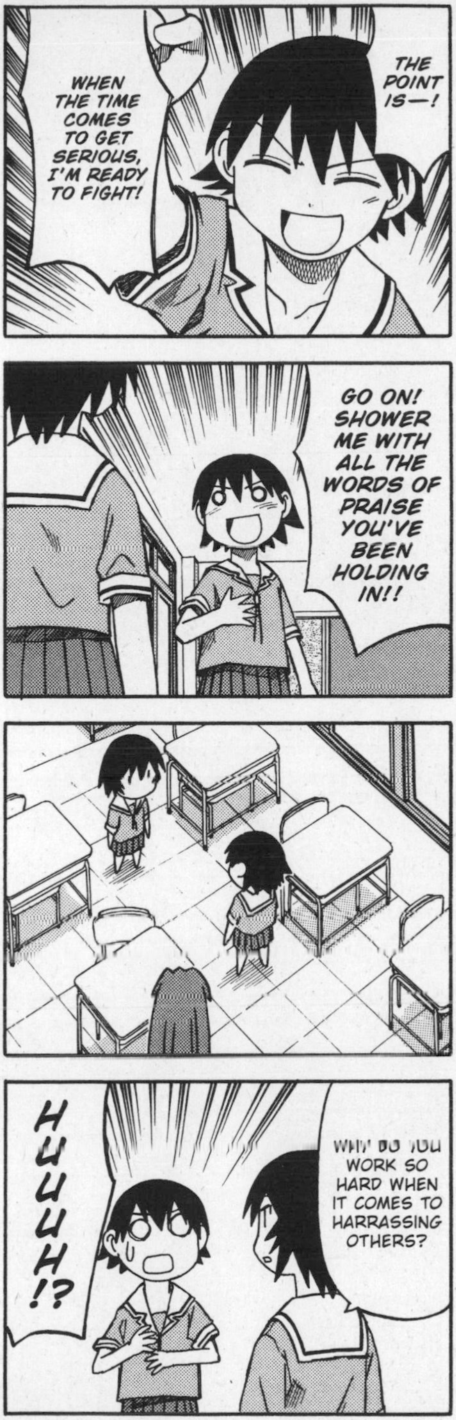
THE POINT IS—!
WHEN THE TIME COMES TO GET SERIOUS, I'M READY TO FIGHT!
GO ON! SHOWER ME WITH ALL THE WORDS OF PRAISE YOU'VE BEEN HOLDING IN!!
WHY DO YOU WORK SO HARD WHEN IT COMES TO HARRASSING OTHERS?
HUUUH!?

NAW

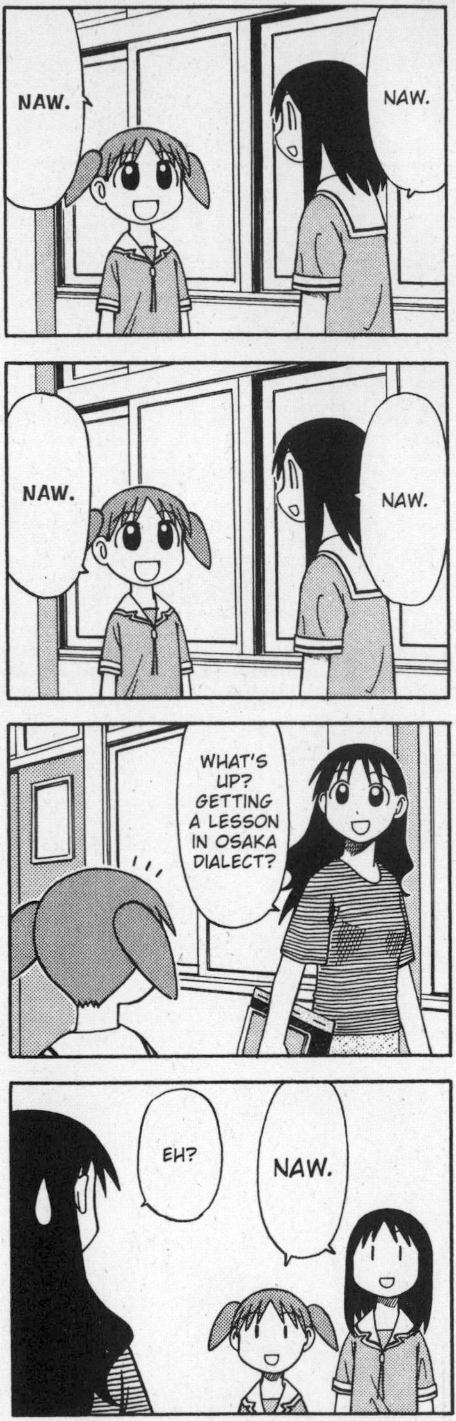
NAW.
NAW.
NAW.
NAW.
WHAT'S UP? GETTING A LESSON IN OSAKA DIALECT?
NAW.
EH?

INFECTION

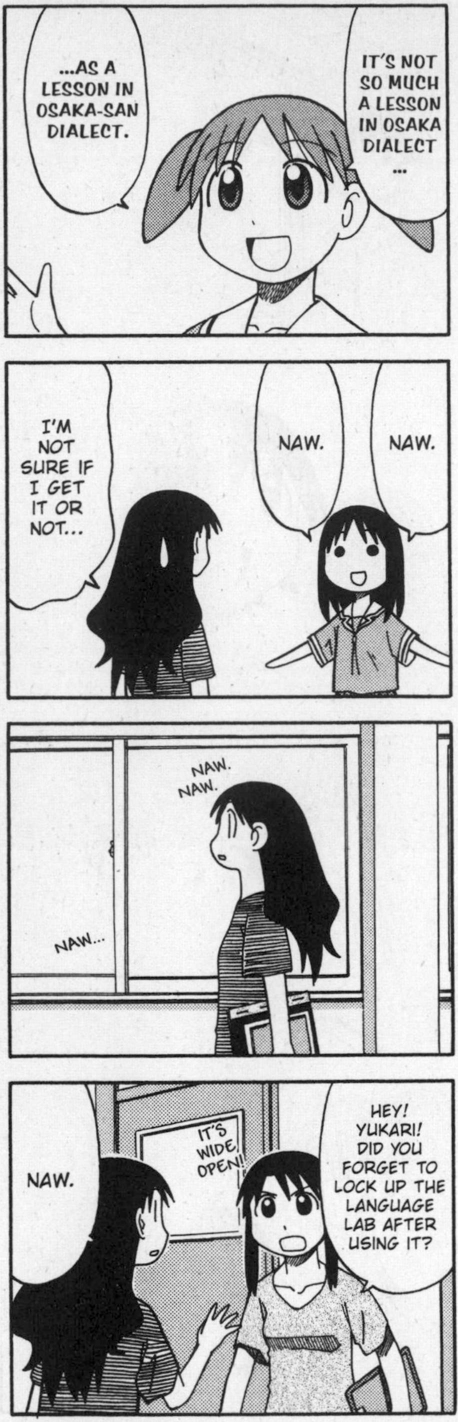
IT'S NOT SO MUCH A LESSON IN OSAKA DIALECT ...
...AS A LESSON IN OSAKA-SAN DIALECT.
NAW.
NAW.
I'M NOT SURE IF I GET IT OR NOT...
NAW. NAW.
NAW...
HEY! YUKARI! DID YOU FORGET TO LOCK UP THE LANGUAGE LAB AFTER USING IT?
IT'S WIDE OPEN!
NAW.

PLAYING CAT?

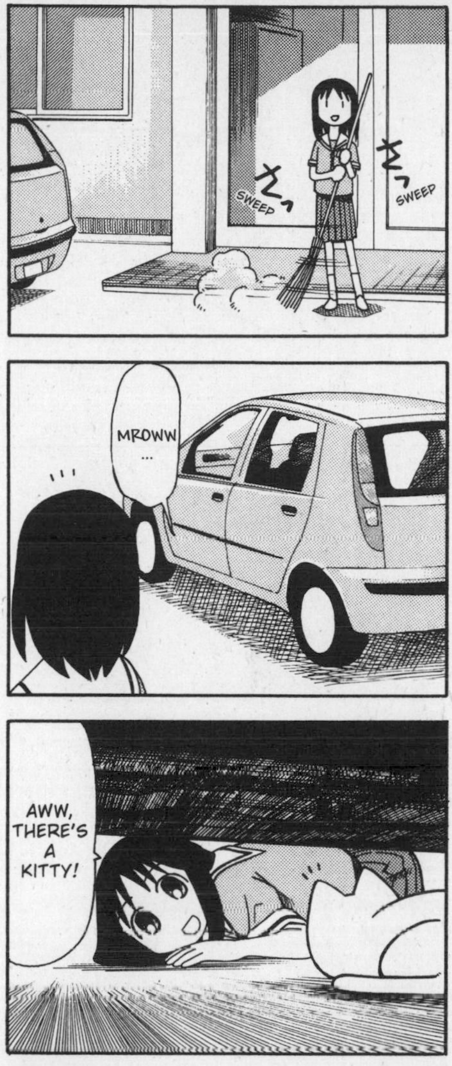
SWEEP
SWEEP
MROWW ...
AWW, THERE'S A KITTY!
MEOW MEOW!
WHAT ARE YOU DOING?

CATFISHING

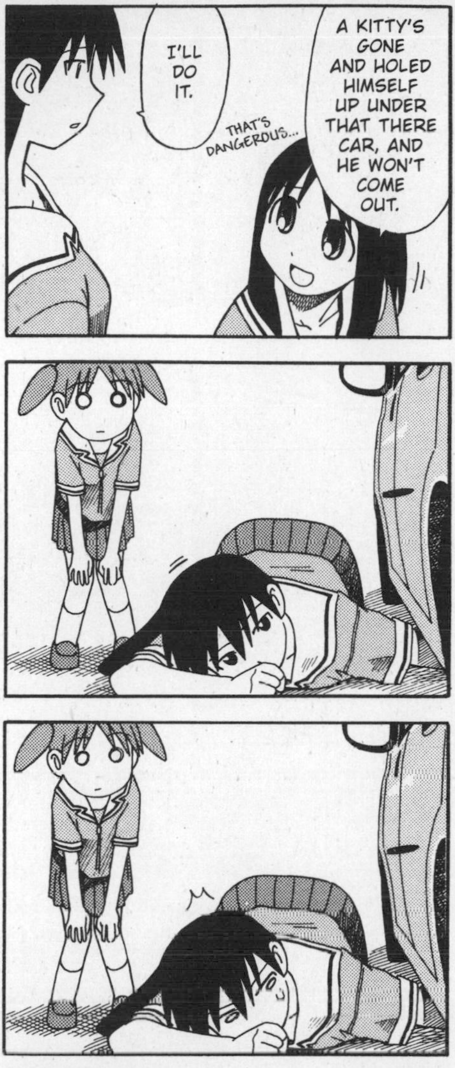
A KITTY'S GONE AND HOLED HIMSELF UP UNDER THAT THERE CAR, AND HE WON'T COME OUT.
THAT'S DANGEROUS...
I'LL DO IT.
... THERE GOT A BITE.
A BITE?

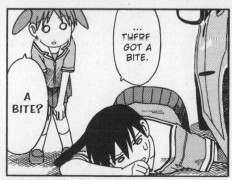

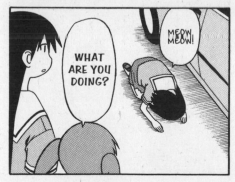

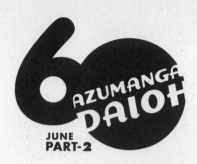

60 AZUMANGA DAIOH

JUNE PART-2

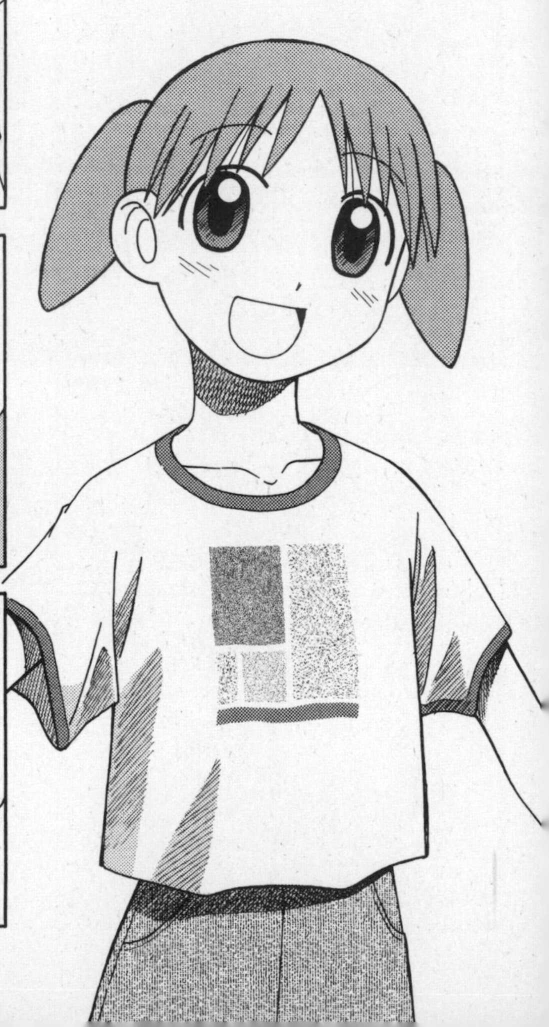

NEW CHIYO

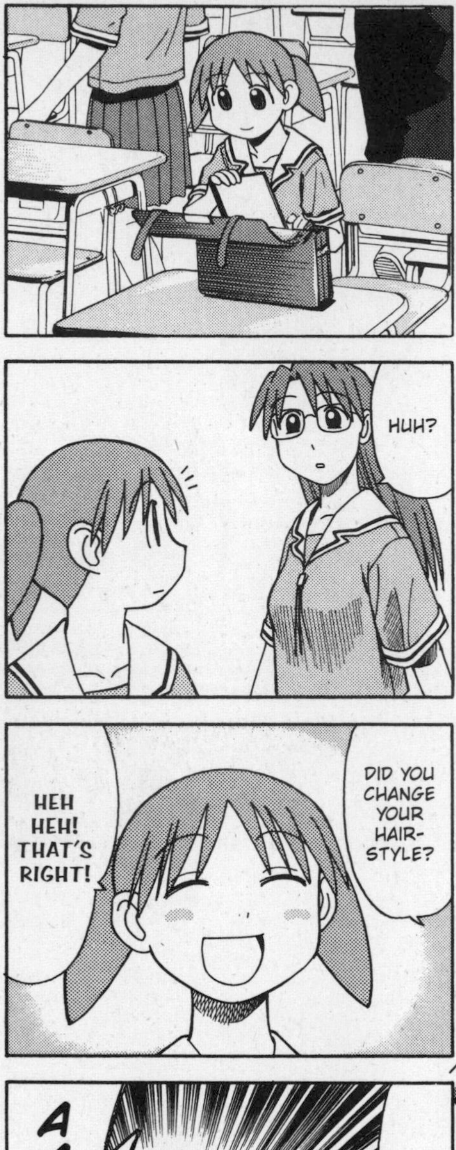
HUH?
DID YOU CHANGE YOUR HAIR-STYLE?
HEH HEH! THAT'S RIGHT!
JUST A BIT, THOUGH ...
AAAAAAH!!

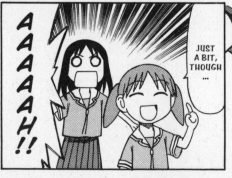

WHAT'S GOIN' ON?

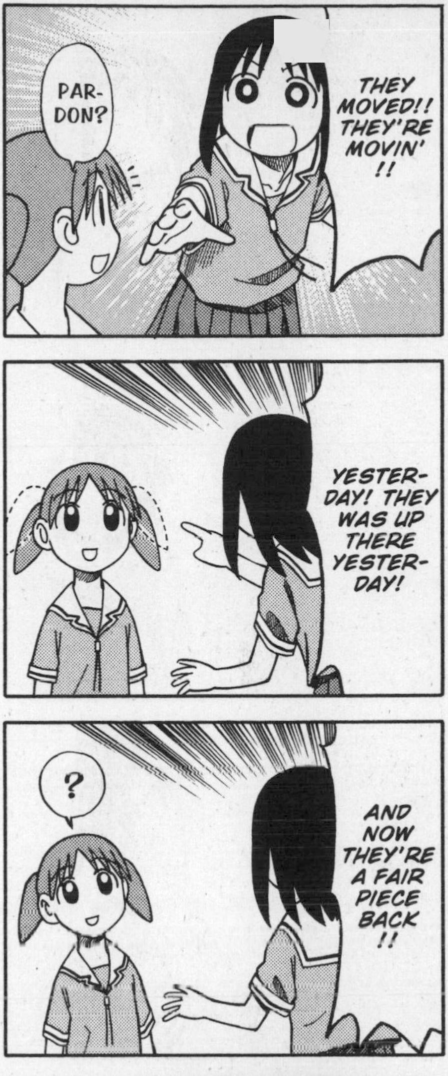
THEY MOVED!! THEY'RE MOVIN' !!
PAR-DON?
YESTER-DAY! THEY WAS UP THERE YESTER-DAY!
AND NOW THEY'RE A FAIR PIECE BACK !!
?
S-SCARY ...
EH?
EH?

WHAT IS SHE TALKING ABOUT?

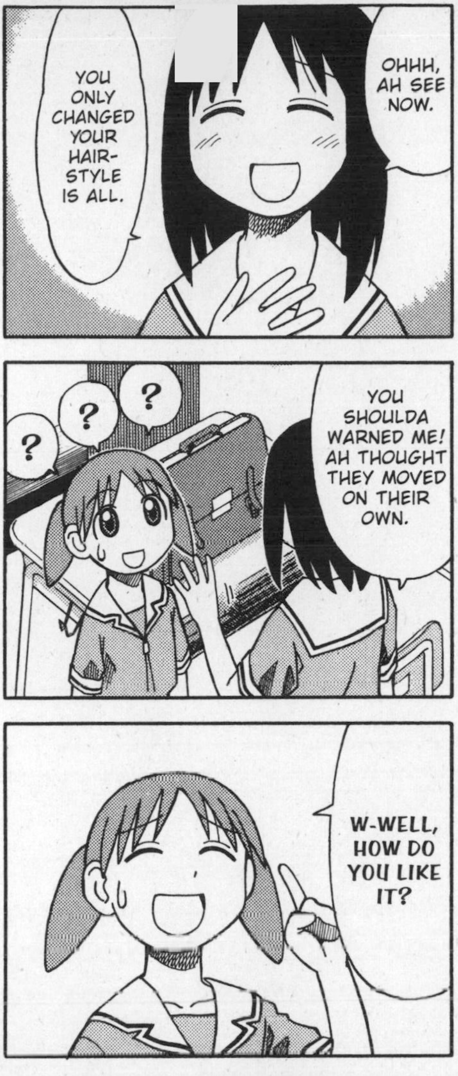
OHHH, AH SEE NOW.
YOU ONLY CHANGED YOUR HAIR-STYLE IS ALL.
YOU SHOULDA WARNED ME! AH THOUGHT THEY MOVED ON THEIR OWN.
?
?
?
W-WELL, HOW DO YOU LIKE IT?
UMM... LOOKS MORE AERO-DYNAMIC.
LESS RESIS-TANCE.
... HUH?

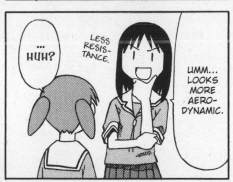

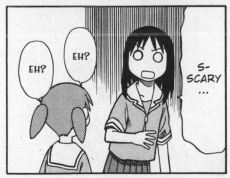

WHERE SHOULD I GO?

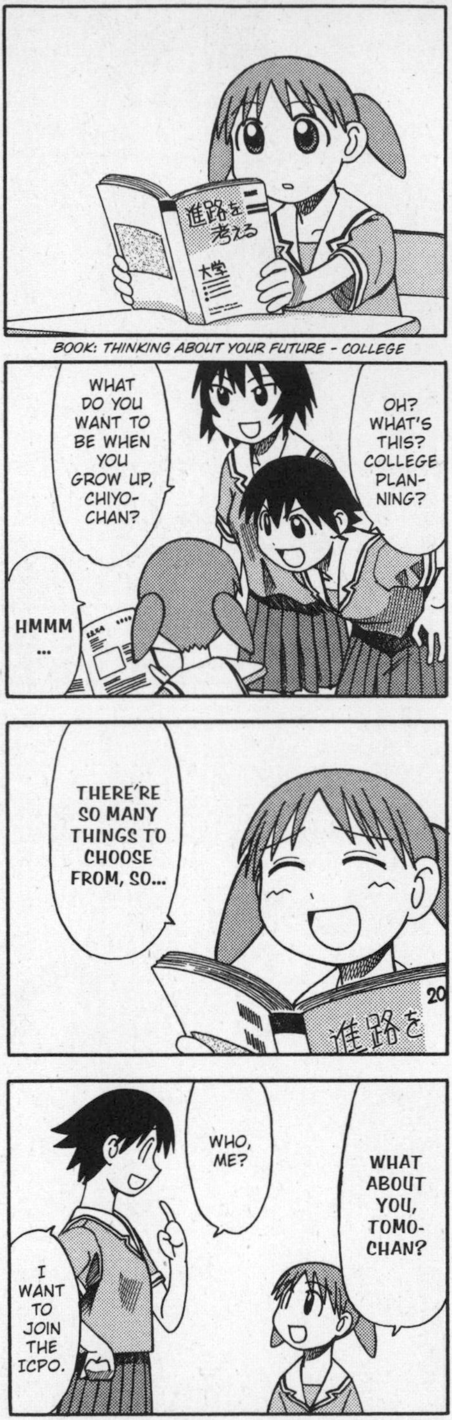
進路を考える
大学
BOOK: THINKING ABOUT YOUR FUTURE - COLLEGE
OH? WHAT'S THIS? COLLEGE PLANNING?
WHAT DO YOU WANT TO BE WHEN YOU GROW UP, CHIYO-CHAN?
HMMM ...
THERE'RE SO MANY THINGS TO CHOOSE FROM, SO...
WHAT ABOUT YOU, TOMO-CHAN?
WHO, ME?
I WANT TO JOIN THE ICPO.

DREAMS

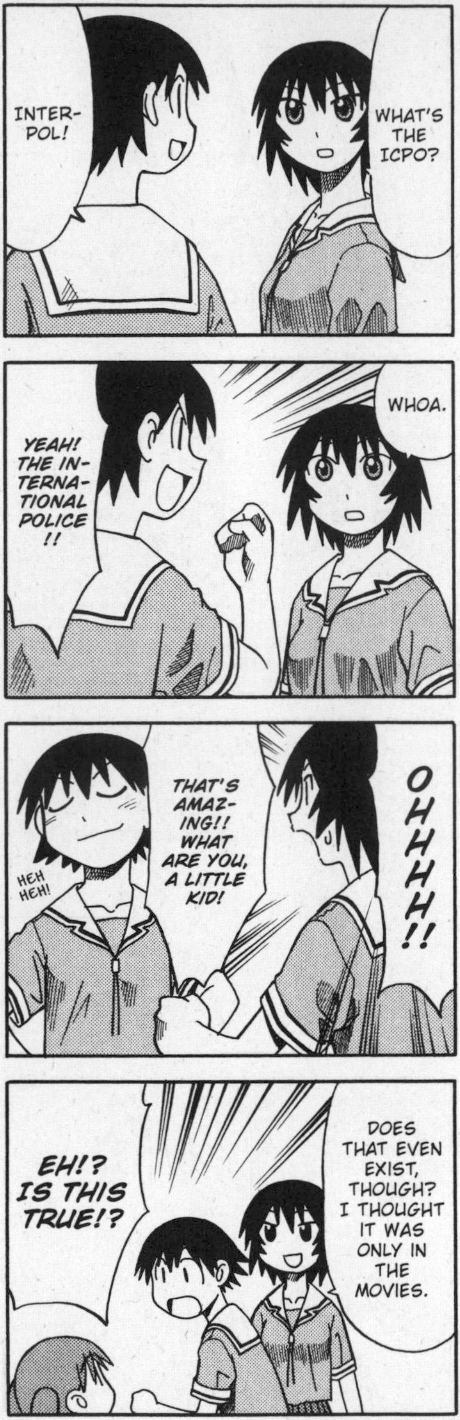
WHAT'S THE ICPO?
INTER-POL!
WHOA.
YEAH! THE IN-TERNA-TIONAL POLICE !!
OHHHHH!!
THAT'S AMAZ-ING!! WHAT ARE YOU, A LITTLE KID!
HEH HEH!
DOES THAT EVEN EXIST, THOUGH? I THOUGHT IT WAS ONLY IN THE MOVIES.
EH!? IS THIS TRUE!?

MYSTERY ORGANIZATION

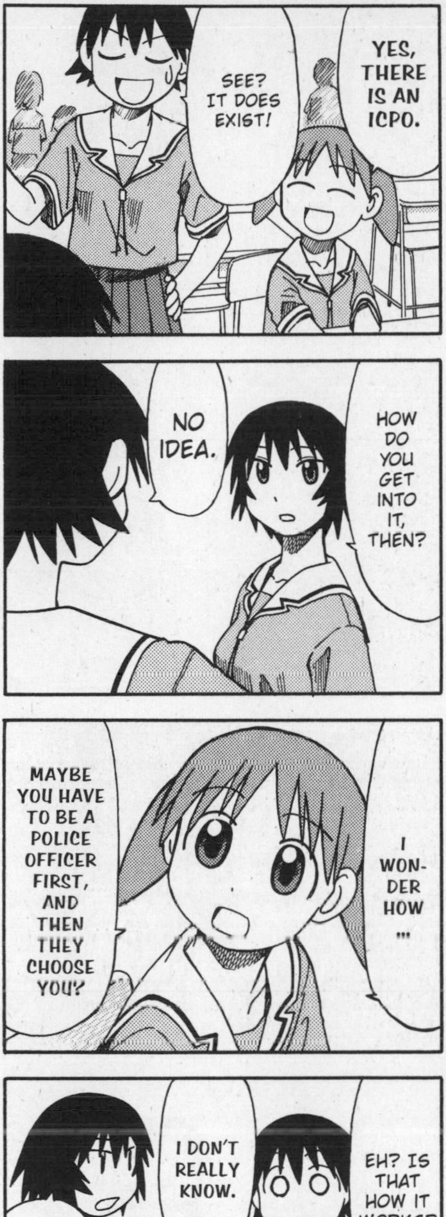
YES, THERE IS AN ICPO.
SEE? IT DOES EXIST!
HOW DO YOU GET INTO IT, THEN?
NO IDEA.
I WONDER HOW...
MAYBE YOU HAVE TO BE A POLICE OFFICER FIRST, AND THEN THEY CHOOSE YOU?
EH? IS THAT HOW IT WORKS?
I DON'T REALLY KNOW.
WELL, YOU STILL KNOW MORE THAN HER.

I'LL DO IT

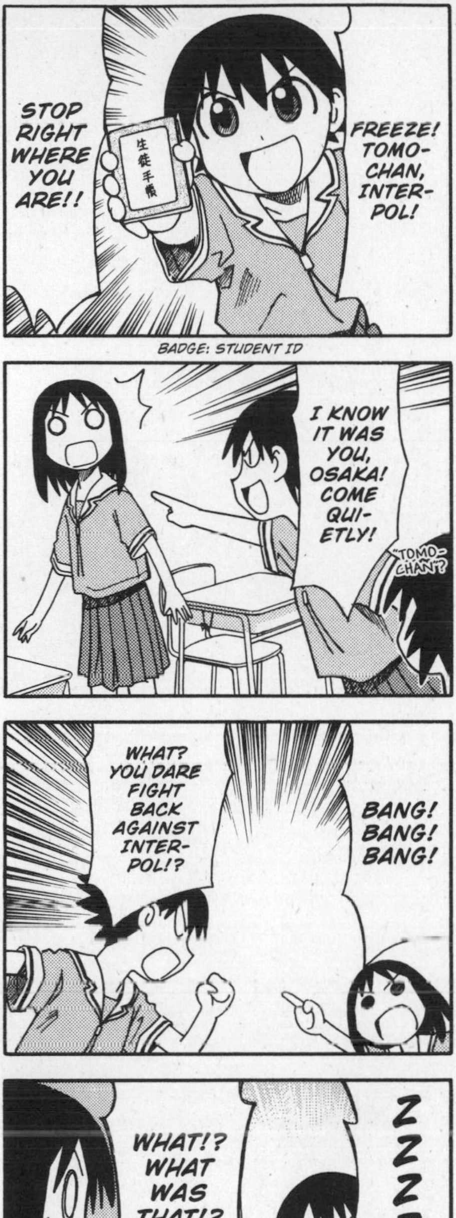
FREEZE! TOMO-CHAN, INTERPOL!
STOP RIGHT WHERE YOU ARE!!
生徒手帳
BADGE: STUDENT ID
I KNOW IT WAS YOU, OSAKA! COME QUIETLY!
"TOMO-CHAN"?
BANG! BANG! BANG!
WHAT? YOU DARE FIGHT BACK AGAINST INTERPOL!?
ZZZZAP!!
WHAT!? WHAT WAS THAT!?

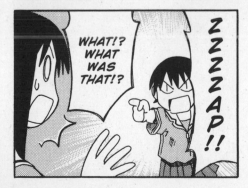

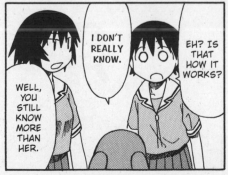

EXPECTATIONS

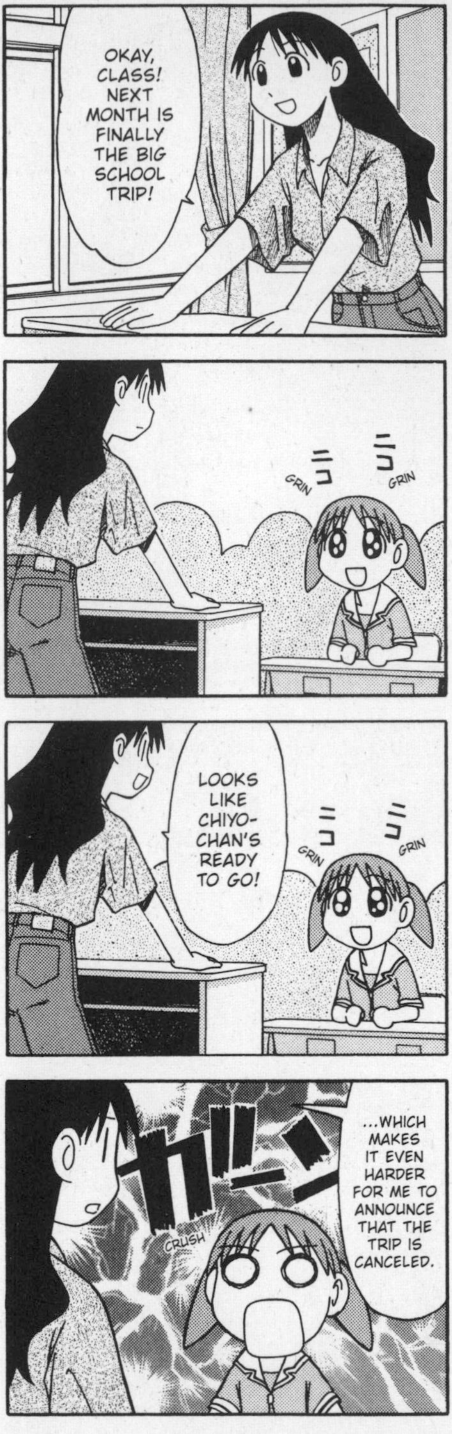
OKAY, CLASS! NEXT MONTH IS FINALLY THE BIG SCHOOL TRIP!
GRIN
GRIN
LOOKS LIKE CHIYO-CHAN'S READY TO GO!
GRIN
GRIN
...WHICH MAKES IT EVEN HARDER FOR ME TO ANNOUNCE THAT THE TRIP IS CANCELED.
CRUSH

DEFLATION

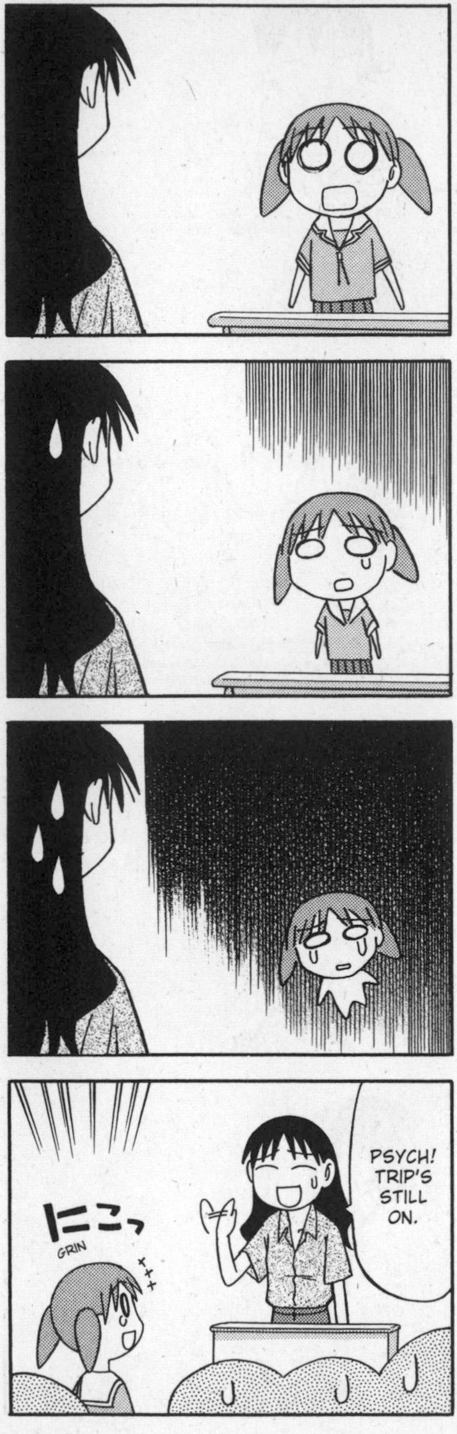
PSYCH! TRIP'S STILL ON.
にこっ
GRIN

JUST FELT LIKE IT

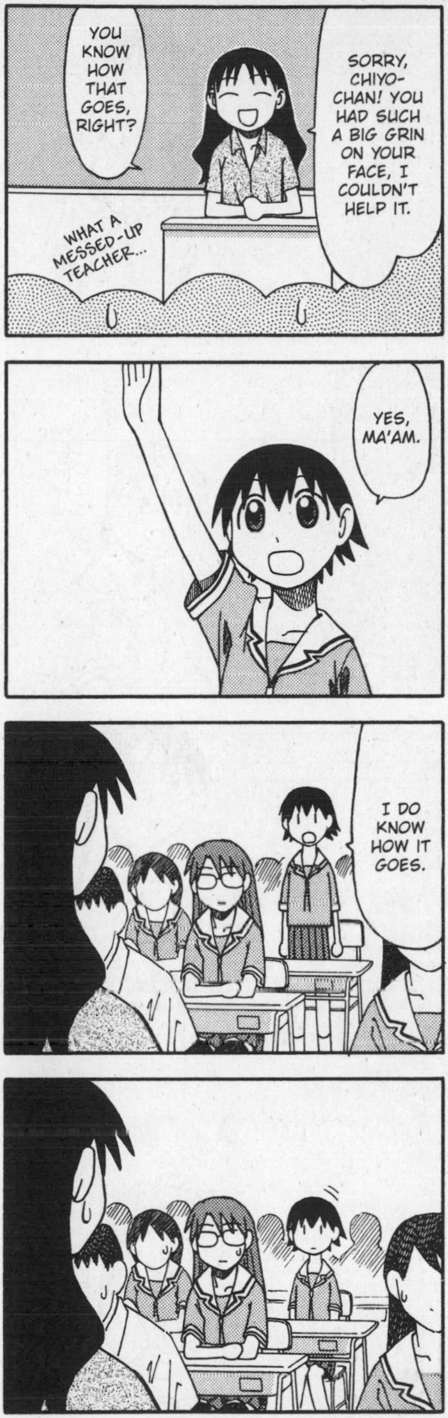
SORRY, CHIYO-CHAN! YOU HAD SUCH A BIG GRIN ON YOUR FACE, I COULDN'T HELP IT.
YOU KNOW HOW THAT GOES, RIGHT?
WHAT A MESSED-UP TEACHER...
YES, MA'AM.
I DO KNOW HOW IT GOES.

PROPHECY

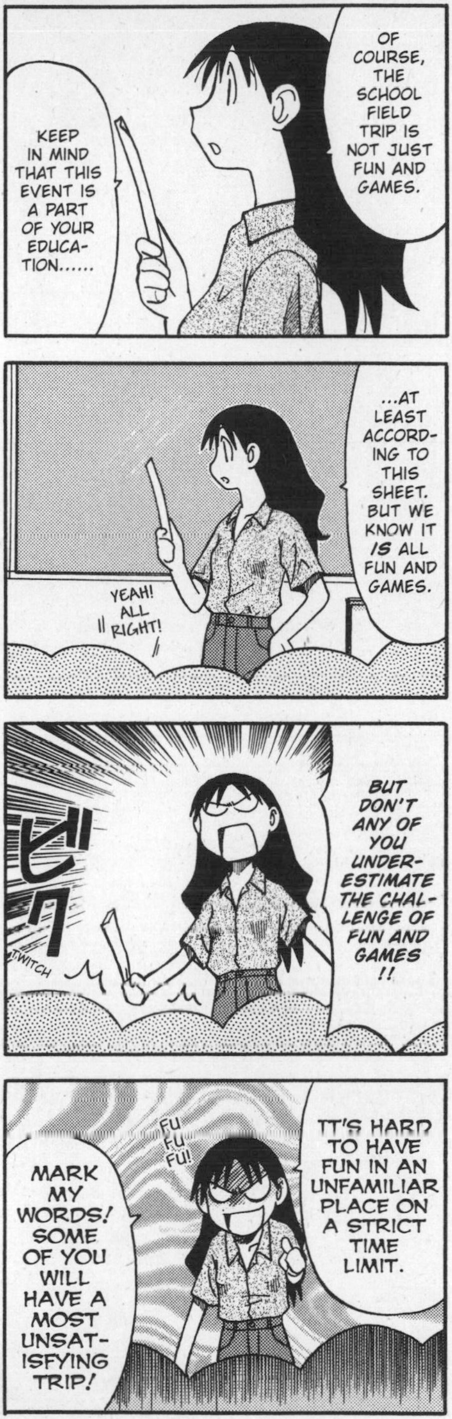
OF COURSE, THE SCHOOL FIELD TRIP IS NOT JUST FUN AND GAMES.
KEEP IN MIND THAT THIS EVENT IS A PART OF YOUR EDUCATION......
...AT LEAST ACCORDING TO THIS SHEET. BUT WE KNOW IT IS ALL FUN AND GAMES.
YEAH! ALL RIGHT!
BUT DON'T ANY OF YOU UNDERESTIMATE THE CHALLENGE OF FUN AND GAMES !!
ビク
TWITCH
IT'S HARD TO HAVE FUN IN AN UNFAMILIAR PLACE ON A STRICT TIME LIMIT.
FU FU FU!
MARK MY WORDS! SOME OF YOU WILL HAVE A MOST UNSATISFYING TRIP!

NUMBER ONE

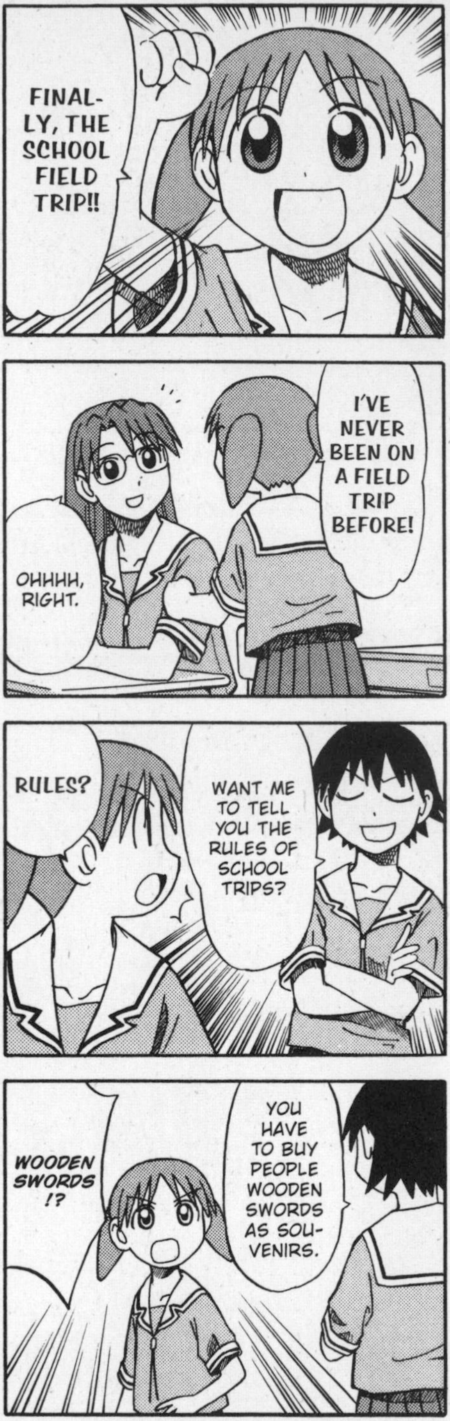
FINAL-LY, THE SCHOOL FIELD TRIP!!
I'VE NEVER BEEN ON A FIELD TRIP BEFORE!
OHHHH, RIGHT.
WANT ME TO TELL YOU THE RULES OF SCHOOL TRIPS?
RULES?
YOU HAVE TO BUY PEOPLE WOODEN SWORDS AS SOU-VENIRS.
WOODEN SWORDS !?

I SENSE FAILURE

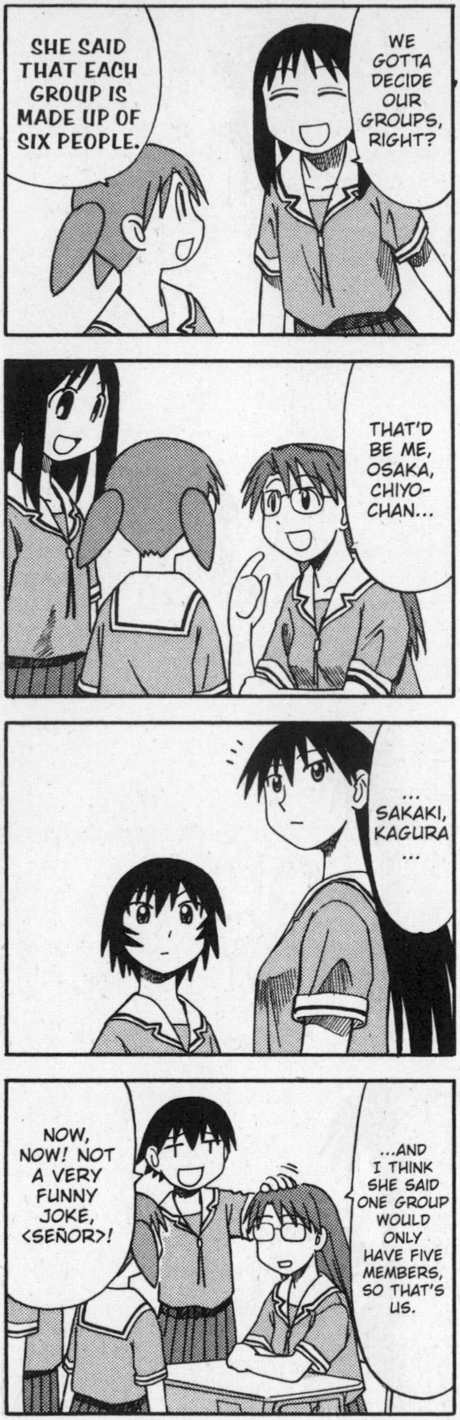
WE GOTTA DECIDE OUR GROUPS, RIGHT?
SHE SAID THAT EACH GROUP IS MADE UP OF SIX PEOPLE.
THAT'D BE ME, OSAKA, CHIYO-CHAN...
... SAKAKI, KAGURA ...
...AND I THINK SHE SAID ONE GROUP WOULD ONLY HAVE FIVE MEMBERS, SO THAT'S US.
NOW, NOW! NOT A VERY FUNNY JOKE, <SEÑOR>!

EXCITEMENT

WE'RE GOING TO HAVE PLENTY OF FREE TIME TO-GETHER, RIGHT!?
IN OUR GROUPS!
WHERE SHOULD WE GO?
DON'T GET TOO AHEAD OF YOURSELF, CHIYO-CHAN.
I'M GOING TO BE EXCITED FOR THE WHOLE MONTH UNTIL THE TRIP!
AH-HA-HA! UH-OH!
UMMM...
UMMM...
WOULD YOU LIKE TO SEE A GUIDE-BOOK?
HUH? YOU'RE SO PREPARED!

TO BE CONTINUED

OH, I CAN'T WAIT!
IT'S GONNA BE SO MUCH FUN!
I JUST KNOW IT WILL BE!!
BUT AT THE TIME, SHE HAD NO IDEA...
...OF THE TRAGEDY AND HORROR THAT WOULD UNFOLD...
STOP INSERTING THAT RIDI-CULOUS VOICE-OVER!!

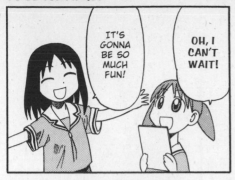

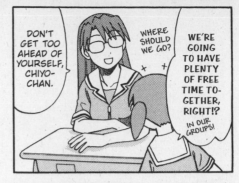

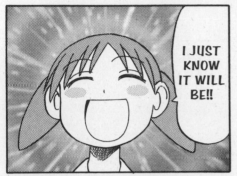

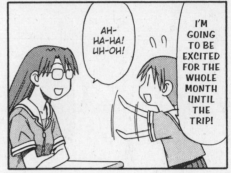

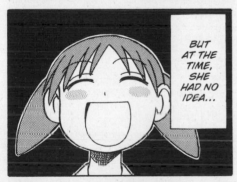

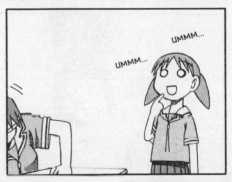

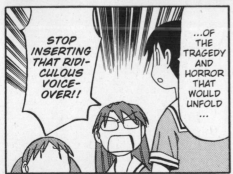

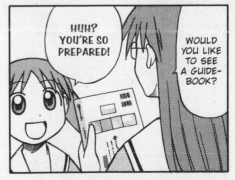

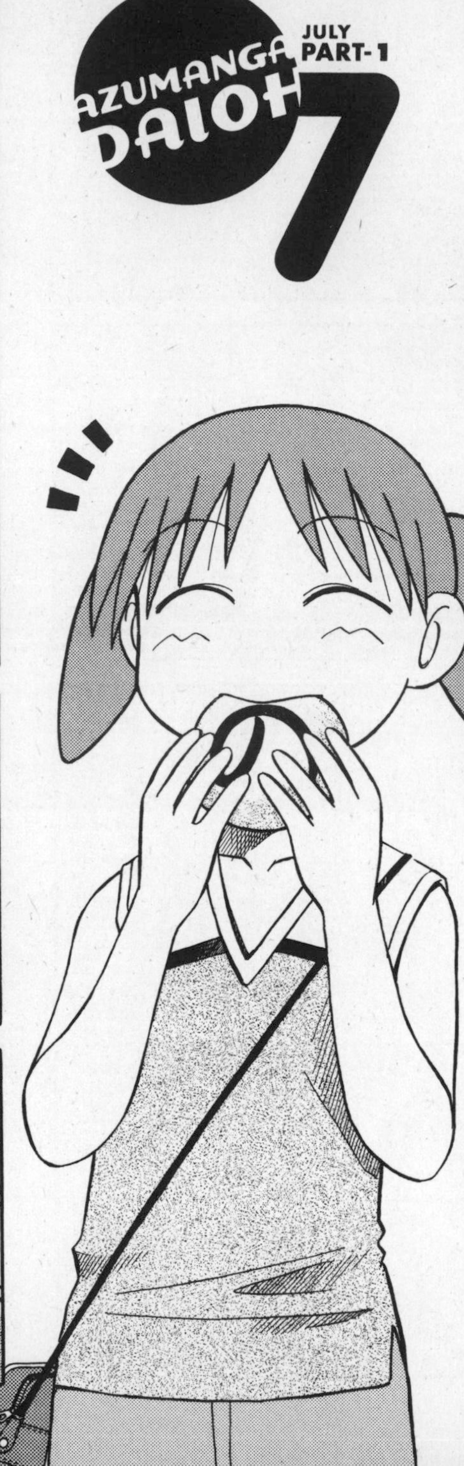
AZUMANGA DAIOH
7
JULY PART-1

WAKE-UP CALL

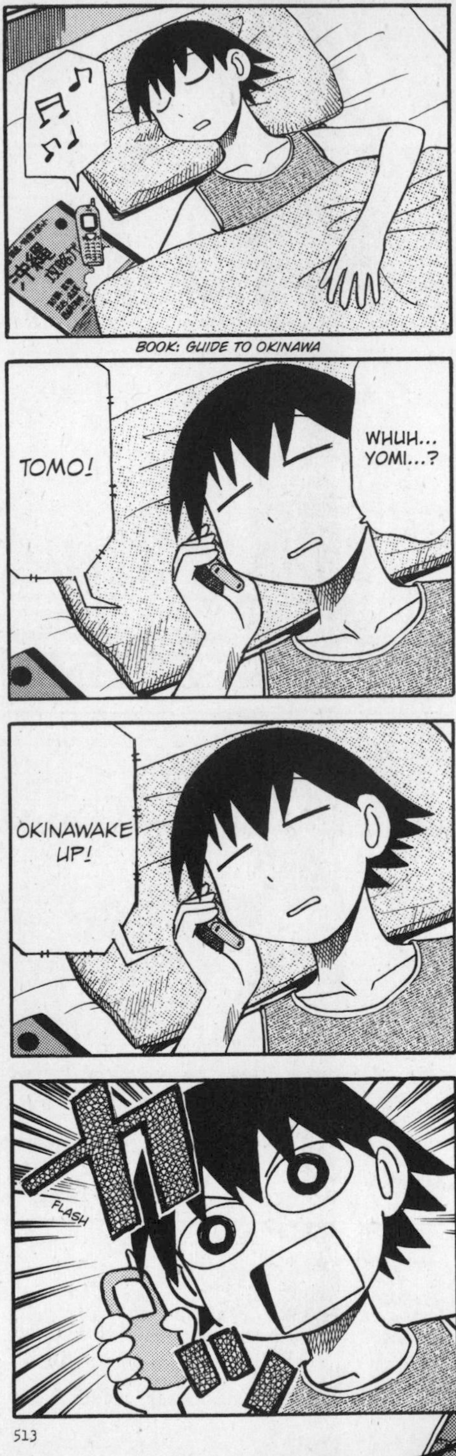
BOOK: GUIDE TO OKINAWA
WHUH... YOMI...?
TOMO!
OKINAWAKE UP!
FLASH

AIRPORT

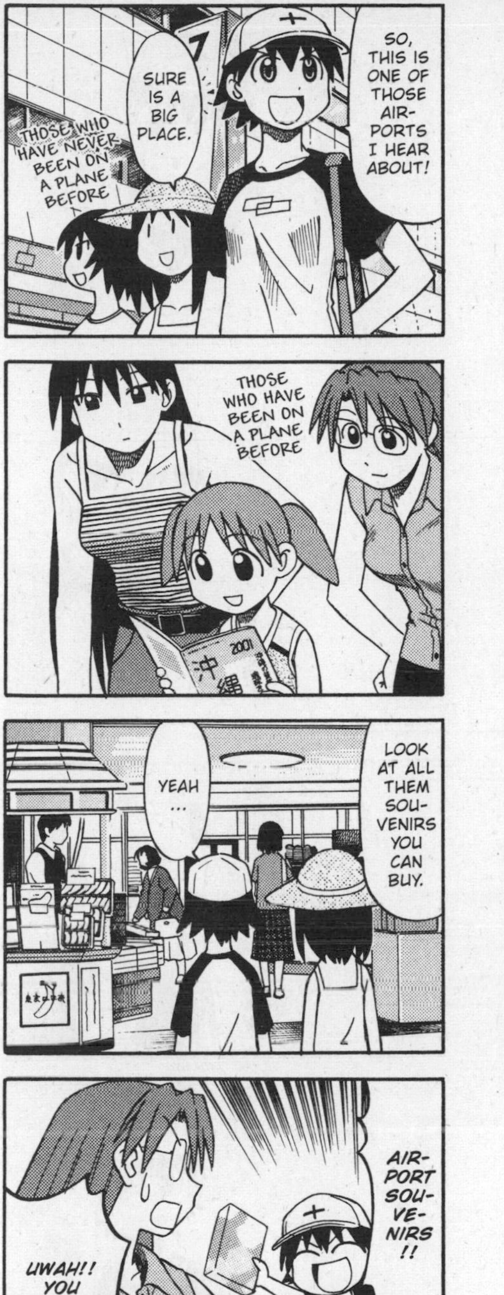
SO, THIS IS ONE OF THOSE AIRPORTS I HEAR ABOUT!
SURE IS A BIG PLACE.
THOSE WHO HAVE NEVER BEEN ON A PLANE BEFORE
THOSE WHO HAVE BEEN ON A PLANE BEFORE
2001 沖縄
LOOK AT ALL THEM SOUVENIRS YOU CAN BUY.
YEAH ...
AIRPORT SOUVENIRS!!
UWAH!! YOU ALREADY BOUGHT SOME!?

GO!

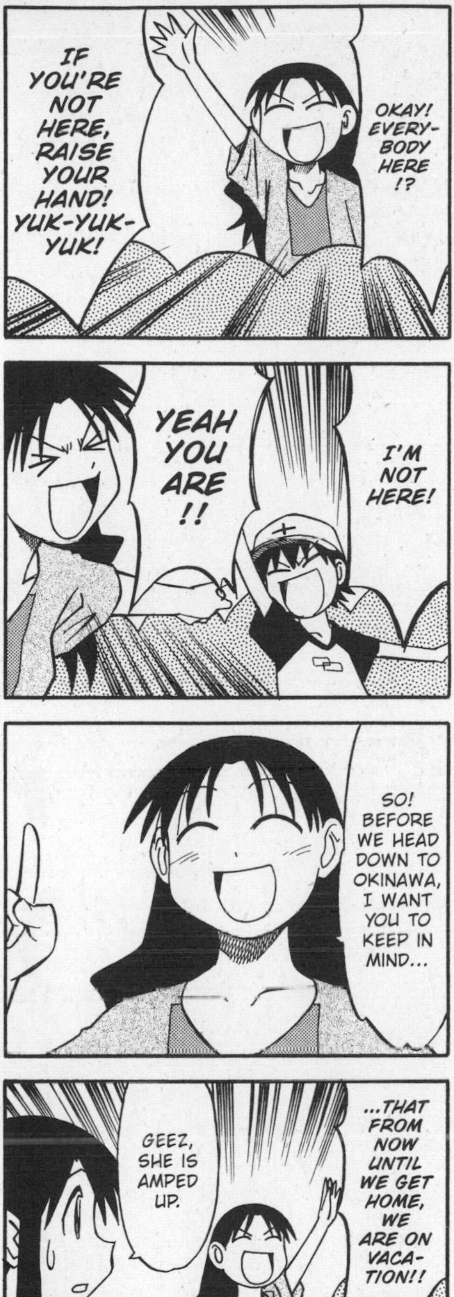
OKAY! EVERYBODY HERE !?
IF YOU'RE NOT HERE, RAISE YOUR HAND! YUK-YUK-YUK!
I'M NOT HERE!
YEAH YOU ARE !!
SO! BEFORE WE HEAD DOWN TO OKINAWA, I WANT YOU TO KEEP IN MIND...
...THAT FROM NOW UNTIL WE GET HOME, WE ARE ON VACATION!!
GEEZ, SHE IS AMPED UP.
ALREADY?

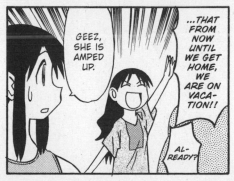

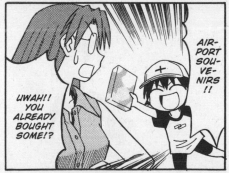

INTO THE AIR

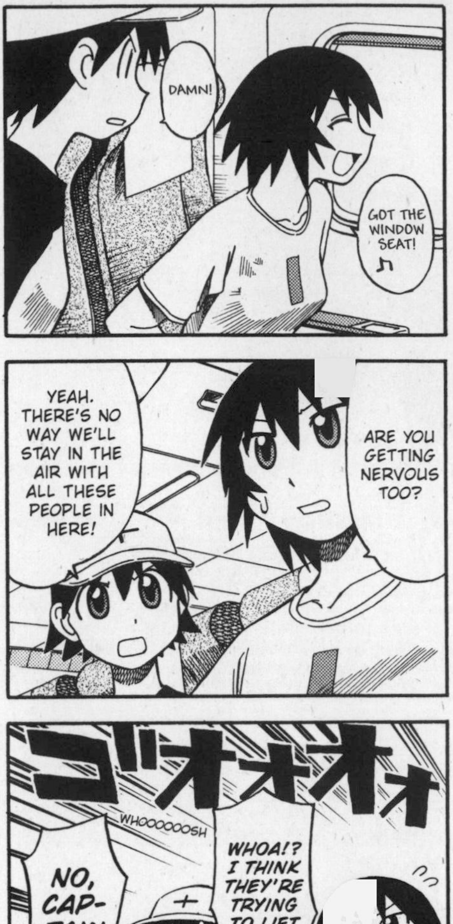
GOT THE WINDOW SEAT! ♪
DAMN!
ARE YOU GETTING NERVOUS TOO?
YEAH. THERE'S NO WAY WE'LL STAY IN THE AIR WITH ALL THESE PEOPLE IN HERE!
ゴオオオオォ
WHOOOOOOSH
WHOA!? I THINK THEY'RE TRYING TO LIFT OFF!!
NO, CAPTAIN!!
WOW!! CAN YOU FEEL THAT POWER!!?
ゴゴゴ
WHOOOSH
I THINK WE'VE GOT ENOUGH TO GET OFF THE GROUND AFTER ALL!!
WILL YOU SHUT UP?

AMAZING

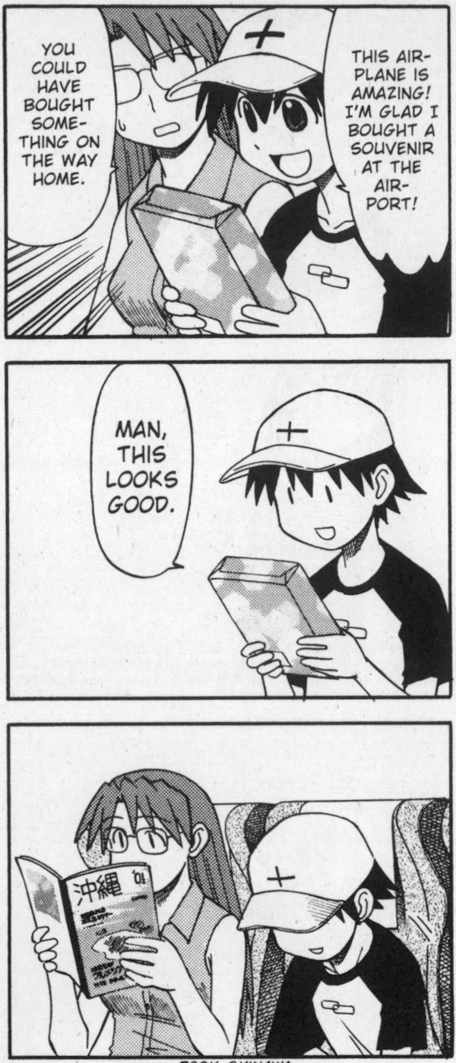
THIS AIRPLANE IS AMAZING! I'M GLAD I BOUGHT A SOUVENIR AT THE AIRPORT!
YOU COULD HAVE BOUGHT SOMETHING ON THE WAY HOME.
MAN, THIS LOOKS GOOD.
沖縄 '01
I COULDN'T HELP MYSELF...
YOU OPENED UP YOUR SOUVENIRS!?

BOOK: OKINAWA

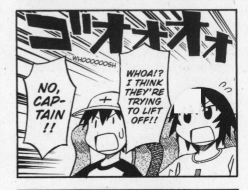

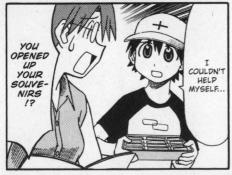

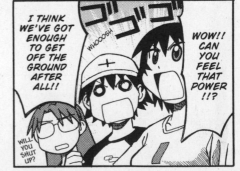

CAN'T STAND STILL

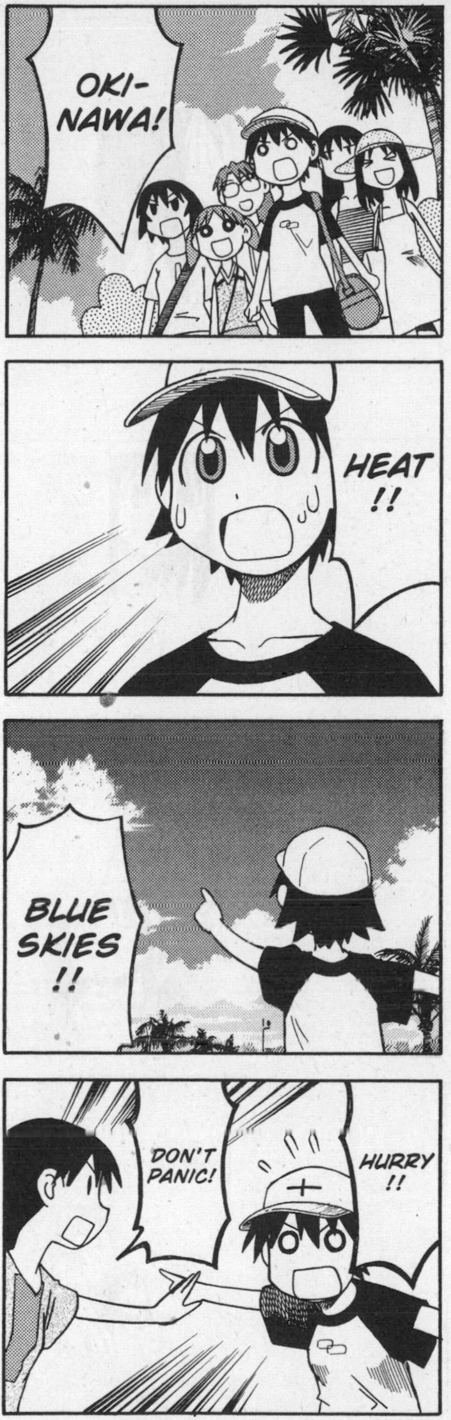
OKI-NAWA!
HEAT!!
BLUE SKIES!!
HURRY!!
DON'T PANIC!

SHE PRACTICED

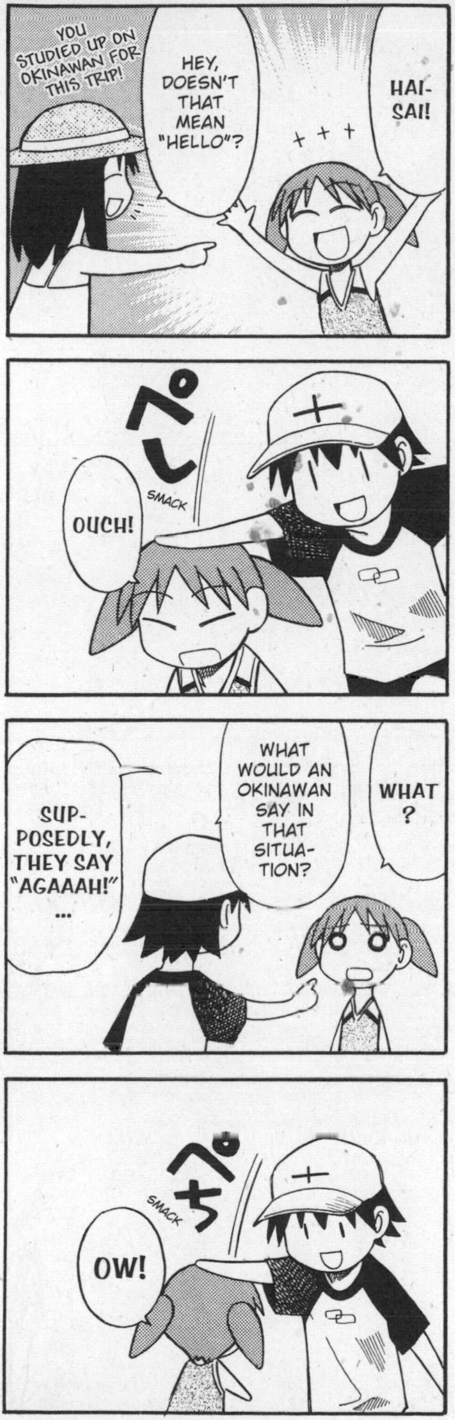
HAI-SAI!
HEY, DOESN'T THAT MEAN "HELLO"?
YOU STUDIED UP ON OKINAWAN FOR THIS TRIP!
ぺし
SMACK
OUCH!
WHAT?
WHAT WOULD AN OKINAWAN SAY IN THAT SITUATION?
SUP-POSEDLY, THEY SAY "AGAAAH!" ...
ぺち
SMACK
OW!

SHURI CASTLE

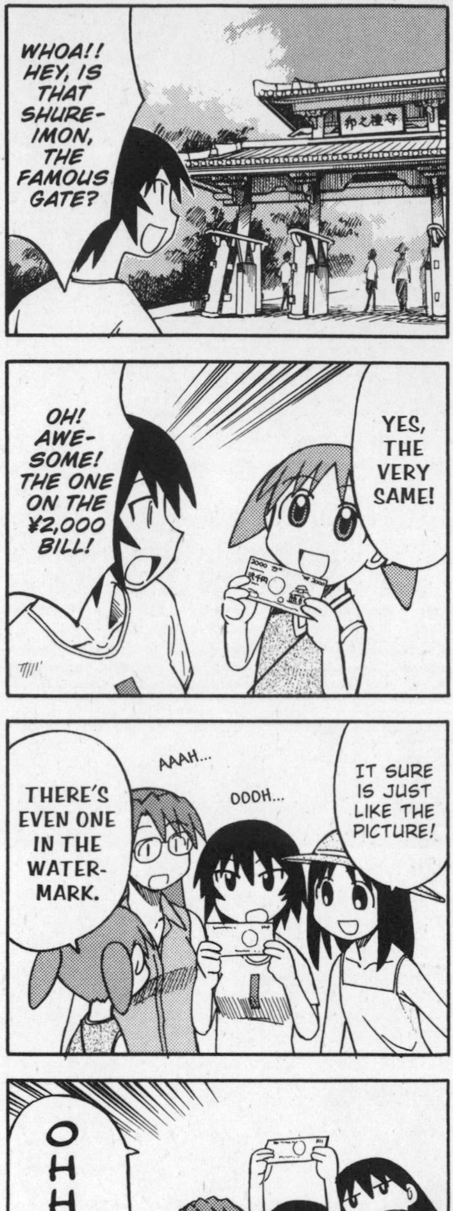
WHOA!! HEY, IS THAT SHURE-IMON, THE FAMOUS GATE?
YES, THE VERY SAME!
OH! AWE-SOME! THE ONE ON THE ¥2,000 BILL!
IT SURE IS JUST LIKE THE PICTURE!
OOOH...
AAAH...
THERE'S EVEN ONE IN THE WATER-MARK.
OHHHHH!!

IT'S A SHISA

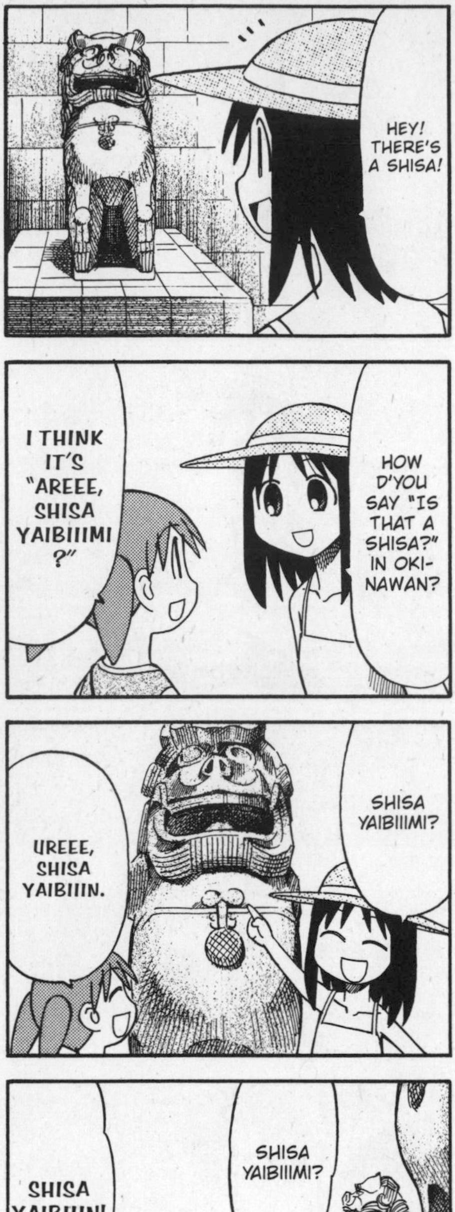
HEY! THERE'S A SHISA!
HOW D'YOU SAY "IS THAT A SHISA?" IN OKI-NAWAN?
I THINK IT'S "AREEE, SHISA YAIBIIIMI?"
SHISA YAIBIIIMI?
UREEE, SHISA YAIBIIIN.
SHISA YAIBIIIMI?
SHISA YAIBIIIN!

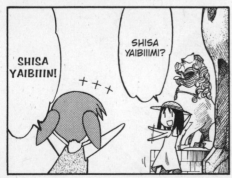

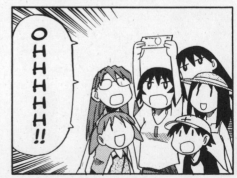

THAT'S NOT A SHISA

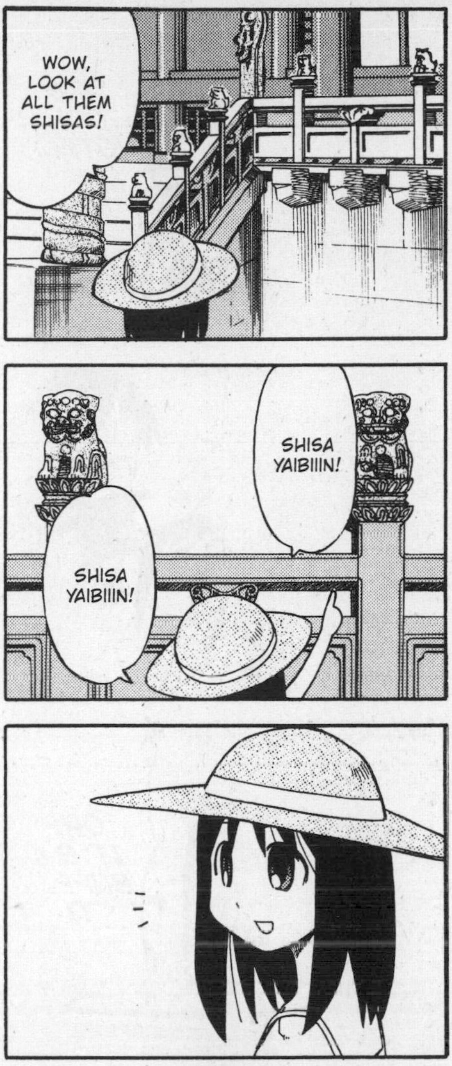
WOW, LOOK AT ALL THEM SHISAS!
SHISA YAIBIIIN!
SHISA YAIBIIIN!
SHISA YAIBIIIMI?
?
AREEE, SHISA AIBI-RAN!

CHAAA!

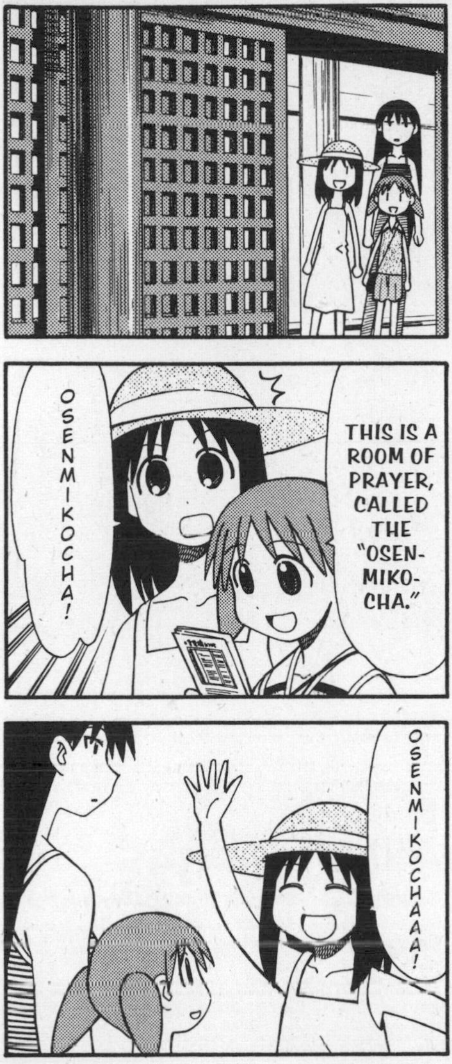
THIS IS A ROOM OF PRAYER, CALLED THE "OSEN-MIKO-CHA."
OSENMIKOCHA!
OSENMIKOCHAAA!
AH HA HA!
AH-HA-HA-HA-HA-HA-HA-HA!
?

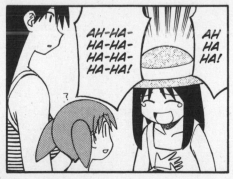

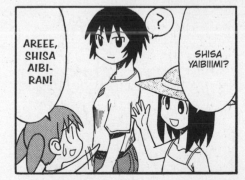

FUNNY BONE

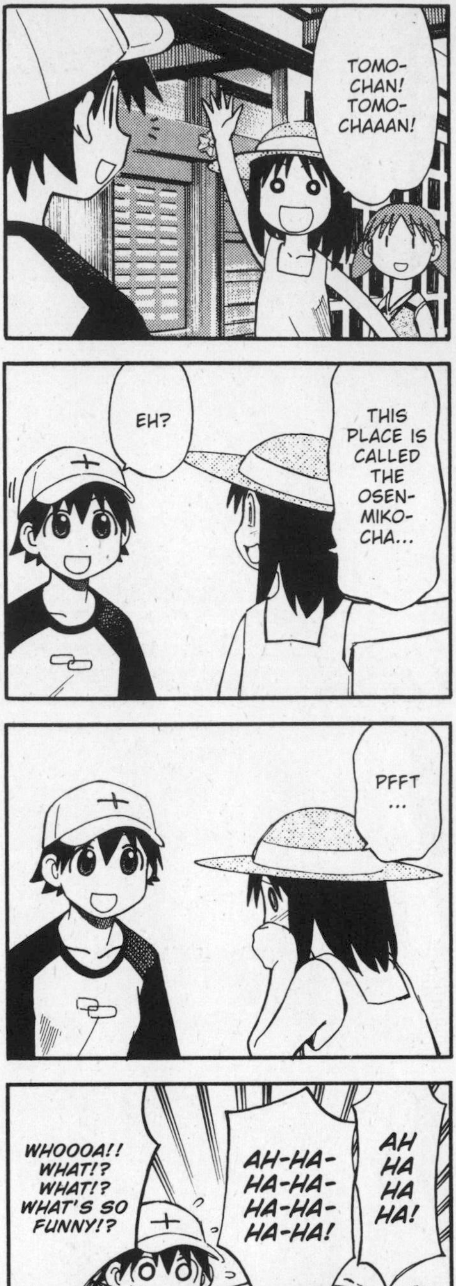
TOMO-CHAN! TOMO-CHAAAN!
THIS PLACE IS CALLED THE OSEN-MIKO-CHA...
EH?
PFFT ...
AH HA HA HA!
AH-HA-HA-HA-HA-HA-HA-HA-HA!
WHOOOA!! WHAT!? WHAT!? WHAT'S SO FUNNY!?

BUFFET

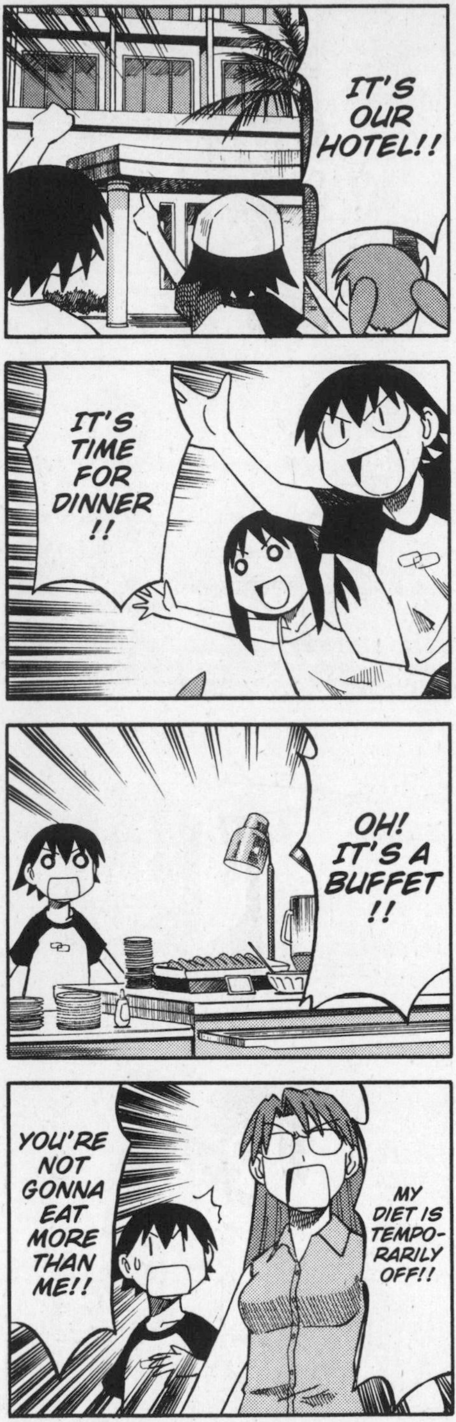
IT'S OUR HOTEL!!
IT'S TIME FOR DINNER !!
OH! IT'S A BUFFET !!
MY DIET IS TEMPORARILY OFF!!
YOU'RE NOT GONNA EAT MORE THAN ME!!

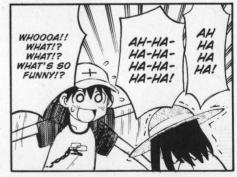

CHANPURU

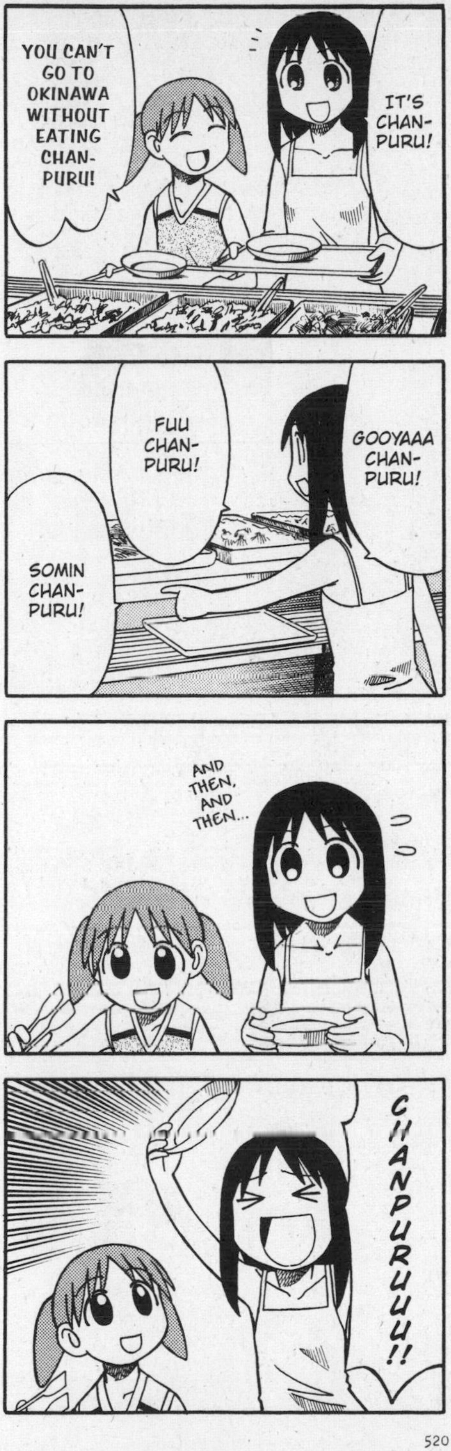
IT'S CHAN-PURU!
YOU CAN'T GO TO OKINAWA WITHOUT EATING CHAN-PURU!
GOOYAAA CHAN-PURU!
FUU CHAN-PURU!
SOMIN CHAN-PURU!
AND THEN, AND THEN...
CHANPURUUU!!

STUFFED

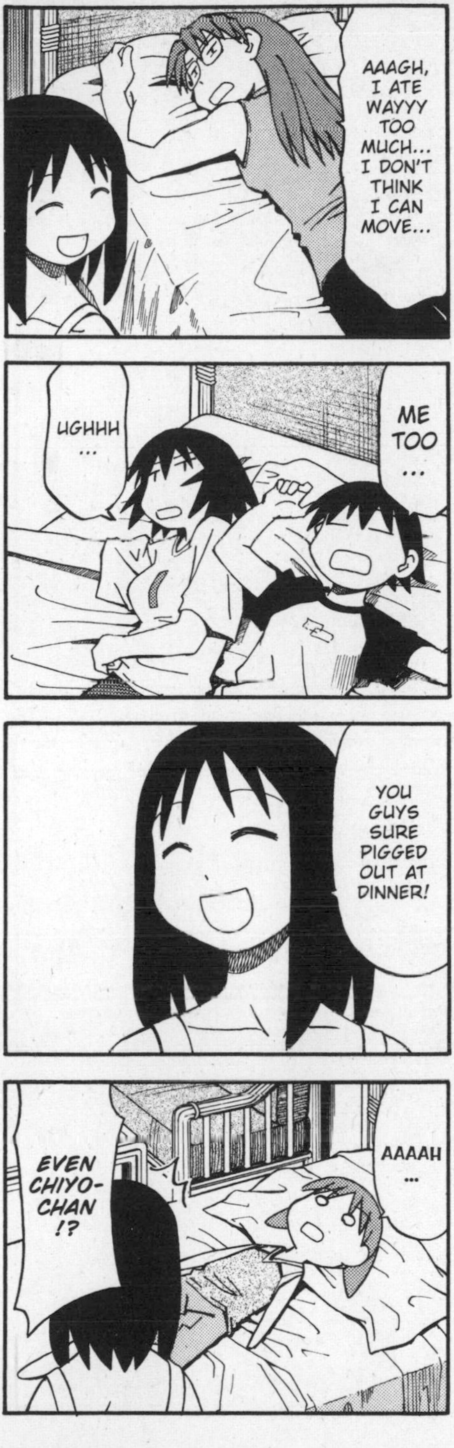
AAAGH, I ATE WAYYY TOO MUCH... I DON'T THINK I CAN MOVE...
ME TOO ...
UGHHH ...
YOU GUYS SURE PIGGED OUT AT DINNER!
AAAAH ...
EVEN CHIYO-CHAN !?

ELEPHANT

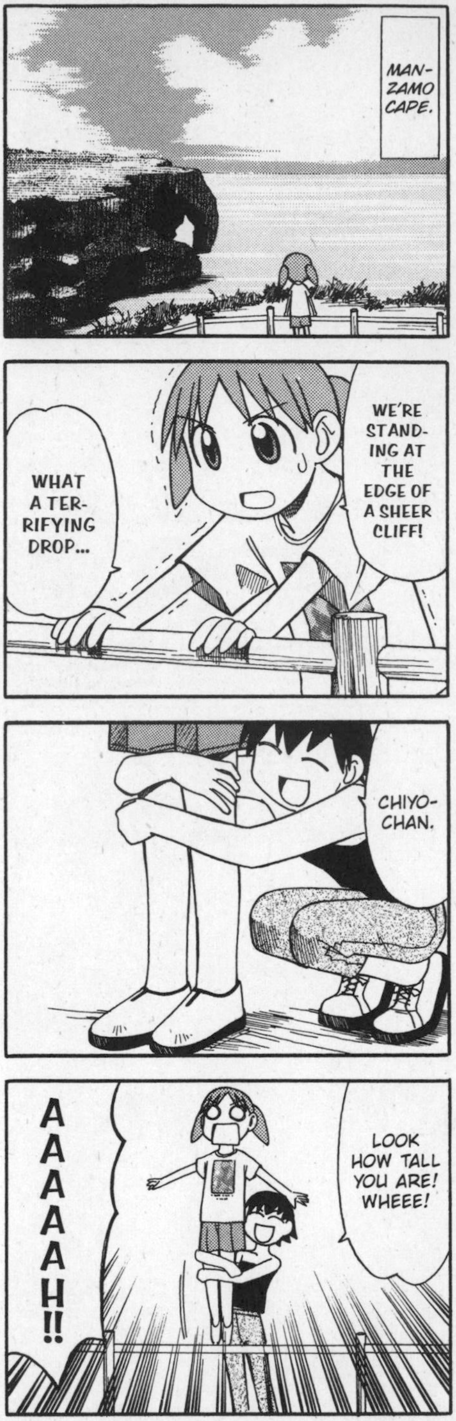
MAN-ZAMO CAPE.
WE'RE STANDING AT THE EDGE OF A SHEER CLIFF!
WHAT A TERRIFYING DROP...
CHIYO-CHAN.
LOOK HOW TALL YOU ARE! WHEEE!
AAAAAAH!!

SLEEPING WITH THE FISHES

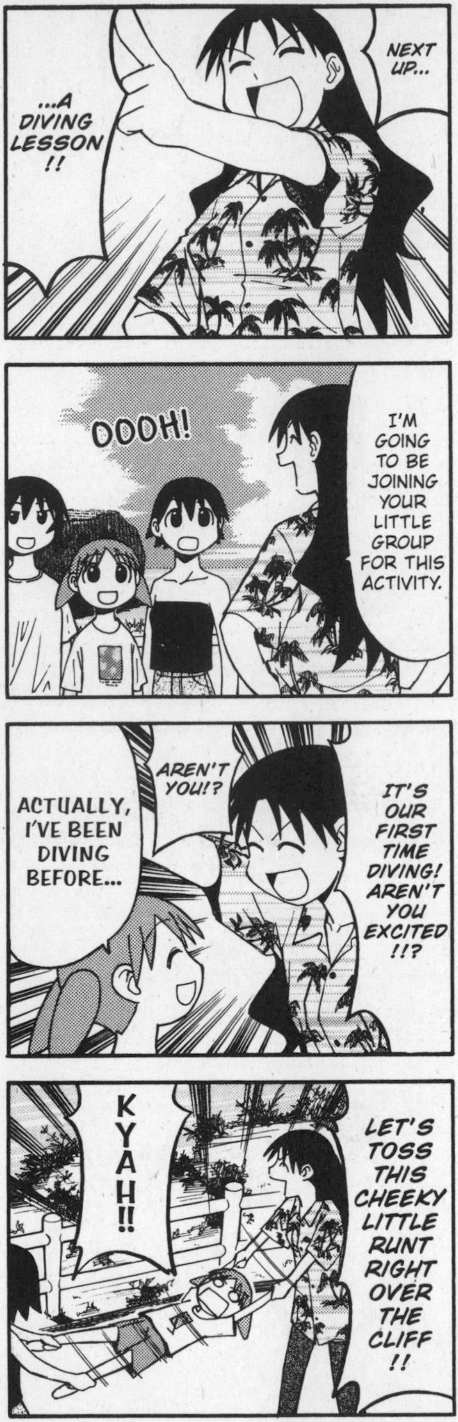
NEXT UP...
...A DIVING LESSON!!
I'M GOING TO BE JOINING YOUR LITTLE GROUP FOR THIS ACTIVITY.
OOOH!
IT'S OUR FIRST TIME DIVING! AREN'T YOU EXCITED!!?
AREN'T YOU!?
ACTUALLY, I'VE BEEN DIVING BEFORE...
LET'S TOSS THIS CHEEKY LITTLE RUNT RIGHT OVER THE CLIFF!!
KYAH!!

SEEFOOD

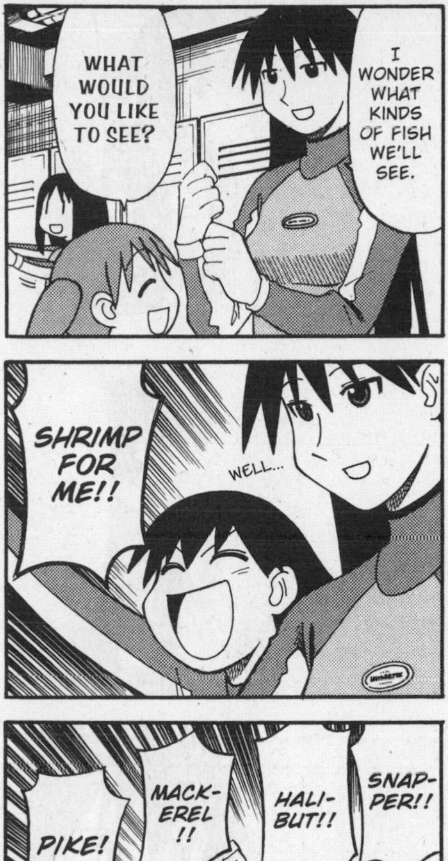
I WONDER WHAT KINDS OF FISH WE'LL SEE.
WHAT WOULD YOU LIKE TO SEE?
WELL...
SHRIMP FOR ME!!
SNAP-PER!!
HALI-BUT!!
MACK-EREL !!
PIKE!
SALMON ROE!
SALMON ROE!?

CAUGHT 'EM

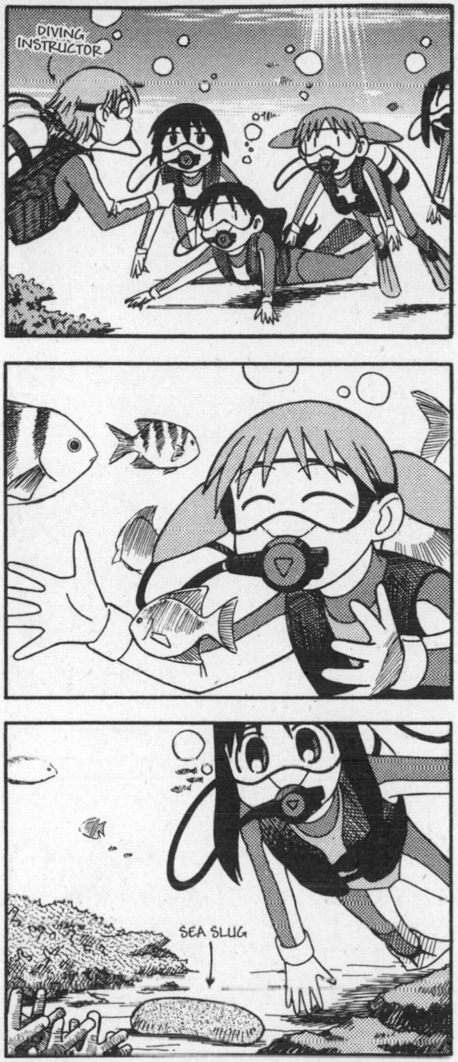
DIVING INSTRUCTOR
SEA SLUG

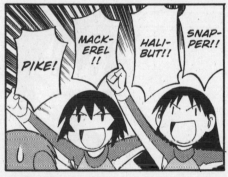

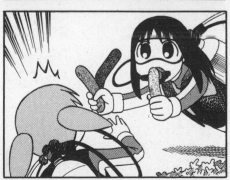

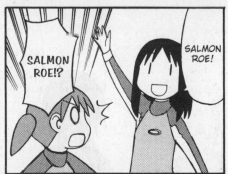

CHIYO-CHAN GETS EATEN

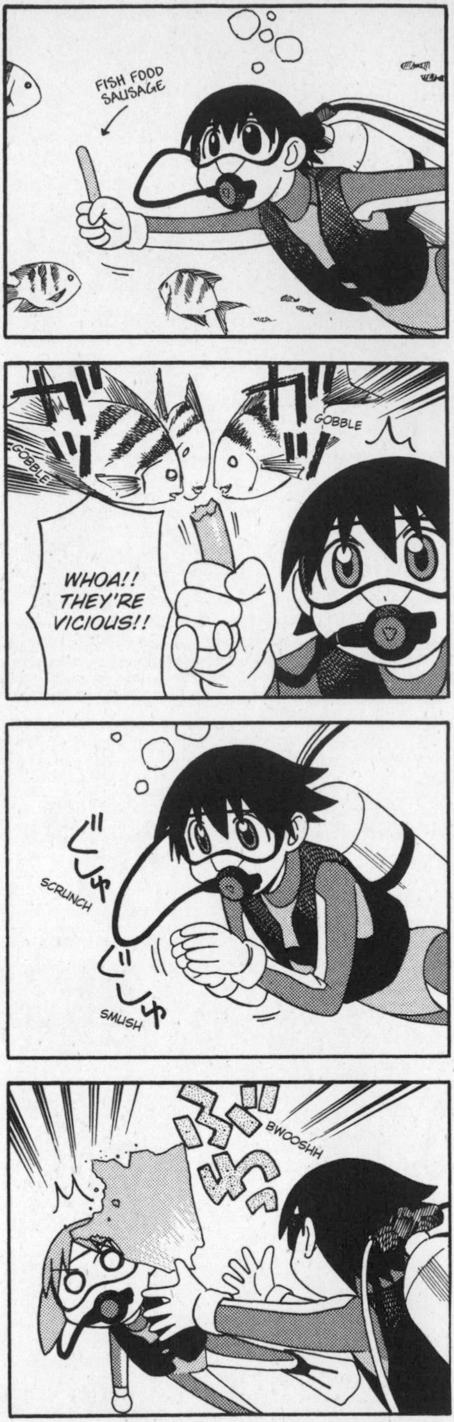
FISH FOOD SAUSAGE
GOBBLE
GOBBLE
WHOA!! THEY'RE VICIOUS!!
SCRUNCH
SMUSH
BWOOSHH

SUPER

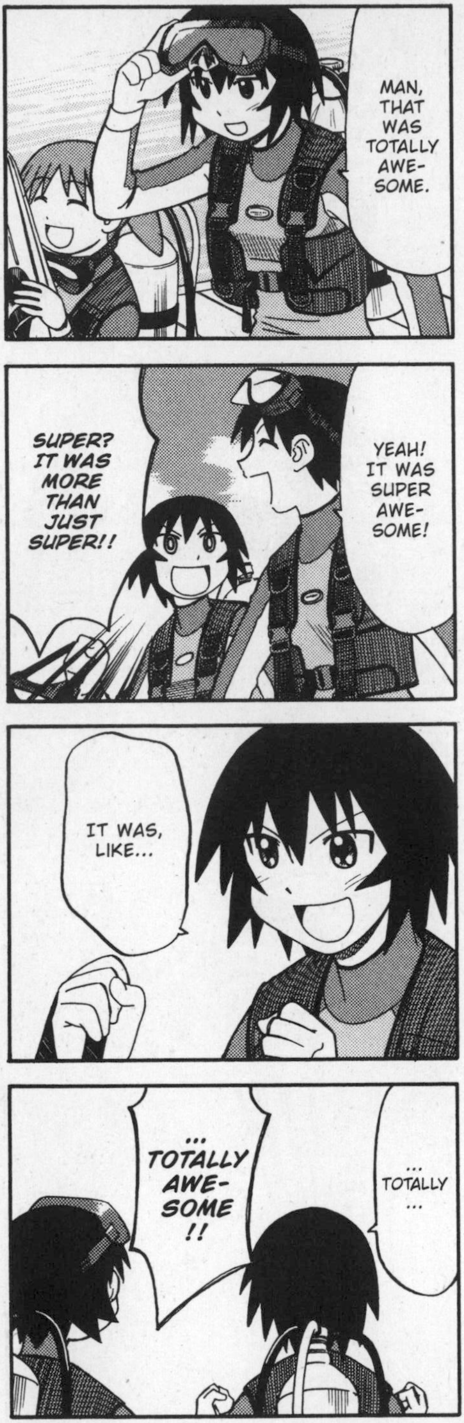
MAN, THAT WAS TOTALLY AWE-SOME.
YEAH! IT WAS SUPER AWE-SOME!
SUPER? IT WAS MORE THAN JUST SUPER!!
IT WAS, LIKE...
... TOTALLY ...
... TOTALLY AWE-SOME !!

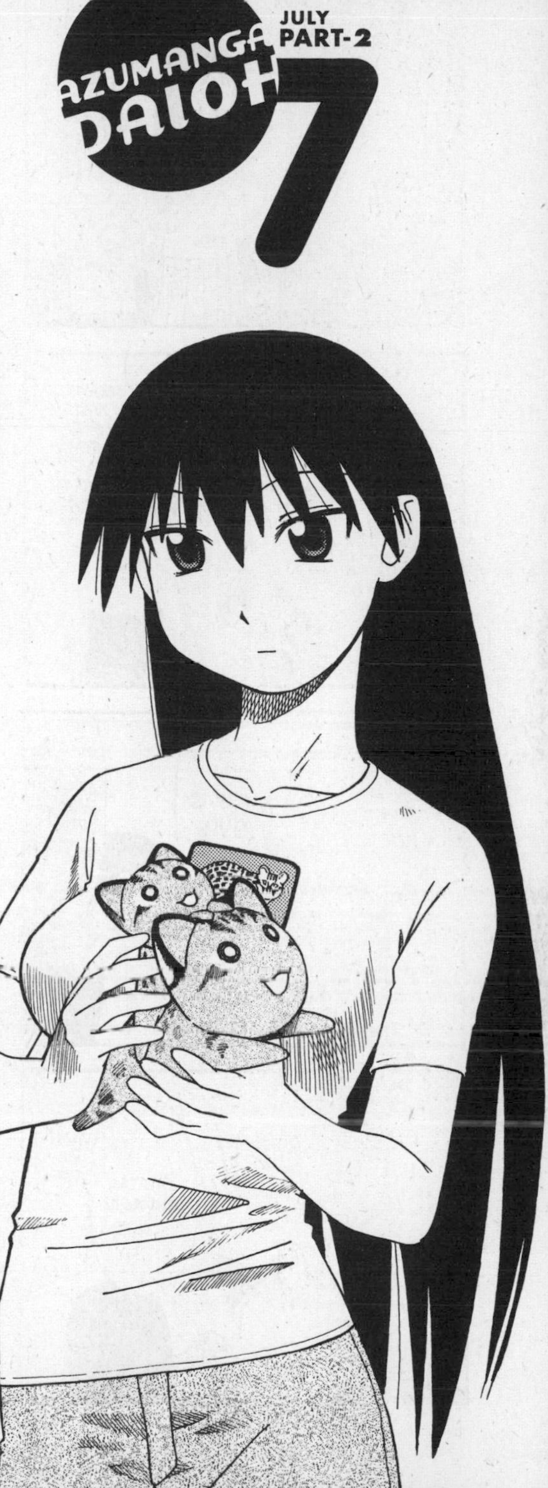
AZUMANGA DAIOH
JULY PART-2
7

BUY IT

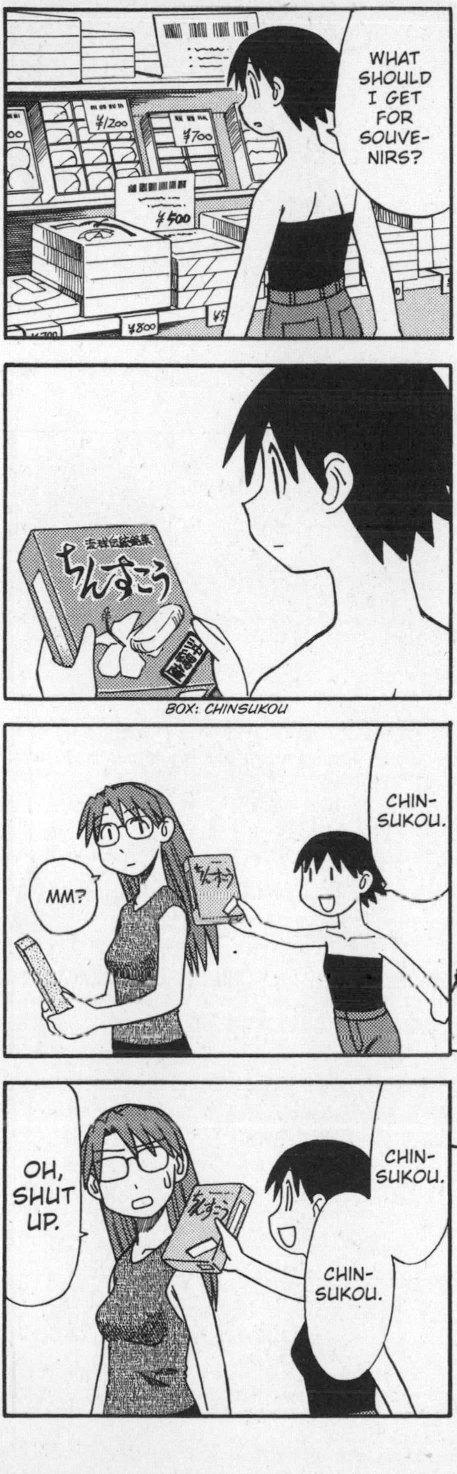
WHAT SHOULD I GET FOR SOUVE-NIRS?
¥1200
¥700
¥500
¥800
ちんすこう
CHIN-SUKOU.
MM?
CHIN-SUKOU.
OH, SHUT UP.
CHIN-SUKOU.
BOX: CHINSUKOU

THAT ONE'S THE BEST

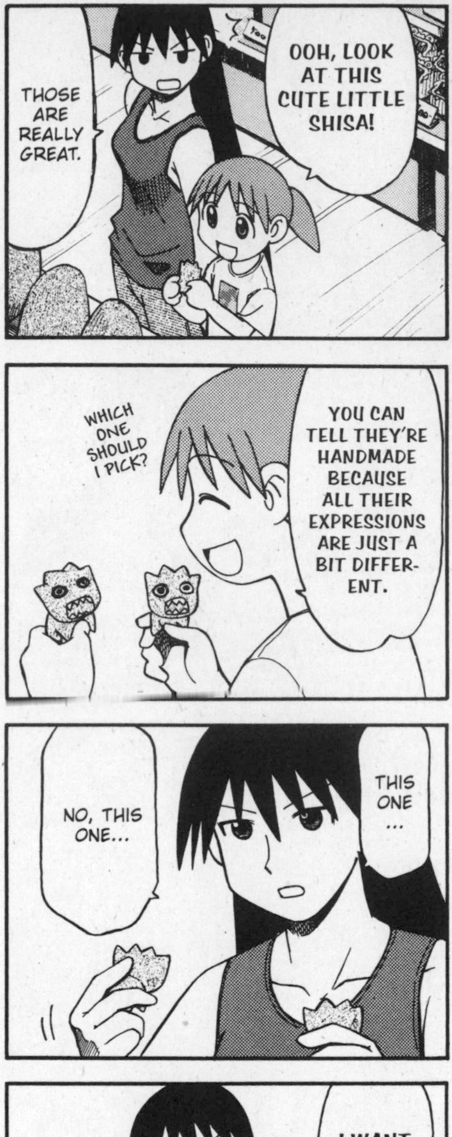
OOH, LOOK AT THIS CUTE LITTLE SHISA!
THOSE ARE REALLY GREAT.
YOU CAN TELL THEY'RE HANDMADE BECAUSE ALL THEIR EXPRESSIONS ARE JUST A BIT DIFFER-ENT.
WHICH ONE SHOULD I PICK?
THIS ONE ...
NO, THIS ONE...
I WANT THIS ONE!
AH!

SUGARY TEMPURA

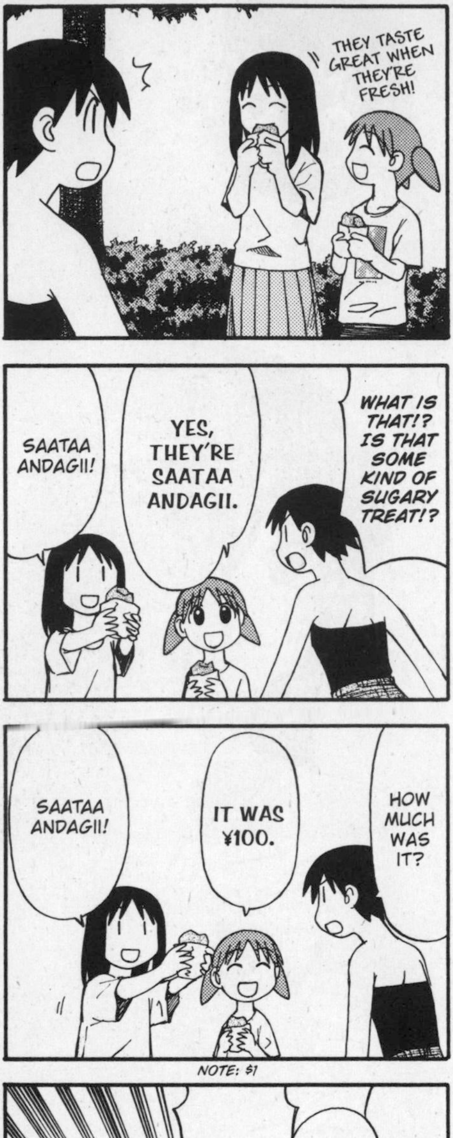
THEY TASTE GREAT WHEN THEY'RE FRESH!
WHAT IS THAT!? IS THAT SOME KIND OF SUGARY TREAT!?
YES, THEY'RE SAATAA ANDAGII.
SAATAA ANDAGII!
HOW MUCH WAS IT?
IT WAS ¥100.
SAATAA ANDAGII!
WHERE ARE THEY —
SAATAA ANDAGII!
SHUT UP AL-READY!!
SAATAA ANDAGII!

NOTE: $1

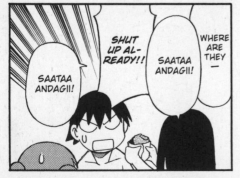

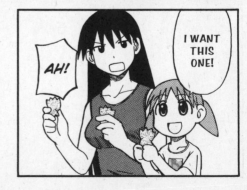

THE ISLAND OF DREAMS

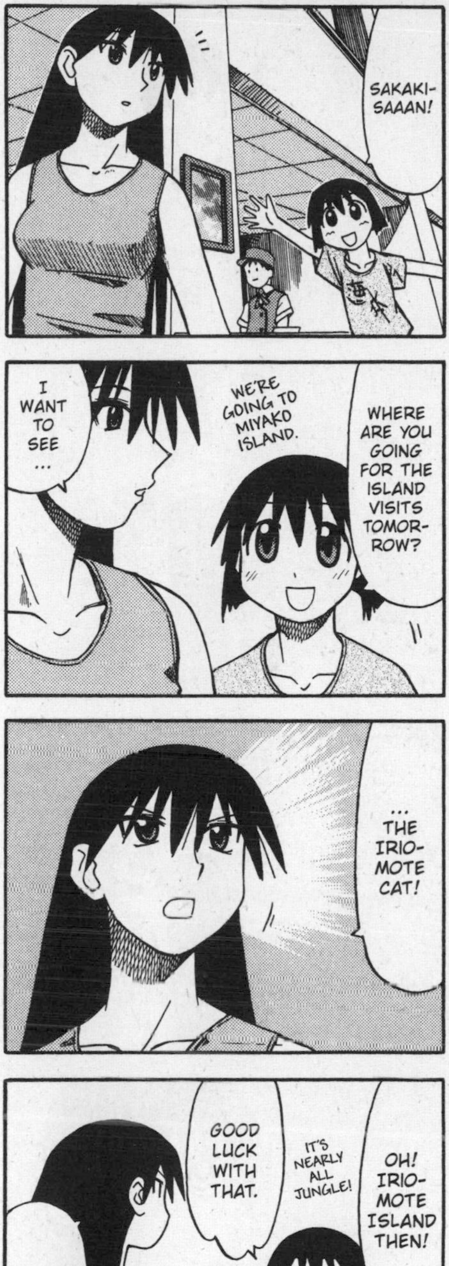
SAKAKI-SAAAN!
海人
WHERE ARE YOU GOING FOR THE ISLAND VISITS TOMORROW?
WE'RE GOING TO MIYAKO ISLAND.
I WANT TO SEE ...
... THE IRIOMOTE CAT!
OH! IRIOMOTE ISLAND THEN!
IT'S NEARLY ALL JUNGLE!
GOOD LUCK WITH THAT.
THANK YOU.

THEY MATCH

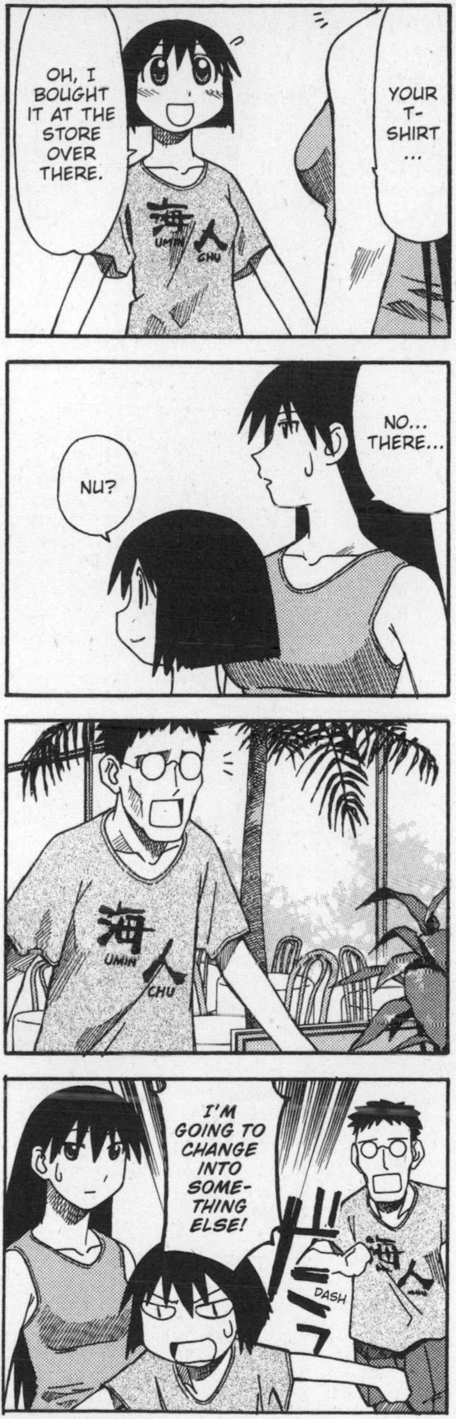
YOUR T-SHIRT ...
OH, I BOUGHT IT AT THE STORE OVER THERE.
海人
UMIN
CHU
NO... THERE...
NU?
海人
UMIN
CHU
I'M GOING TO CHANGE INTO SOMETHING ELSE!
DASH

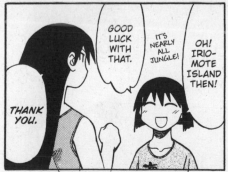

HIDDEN PARADISE

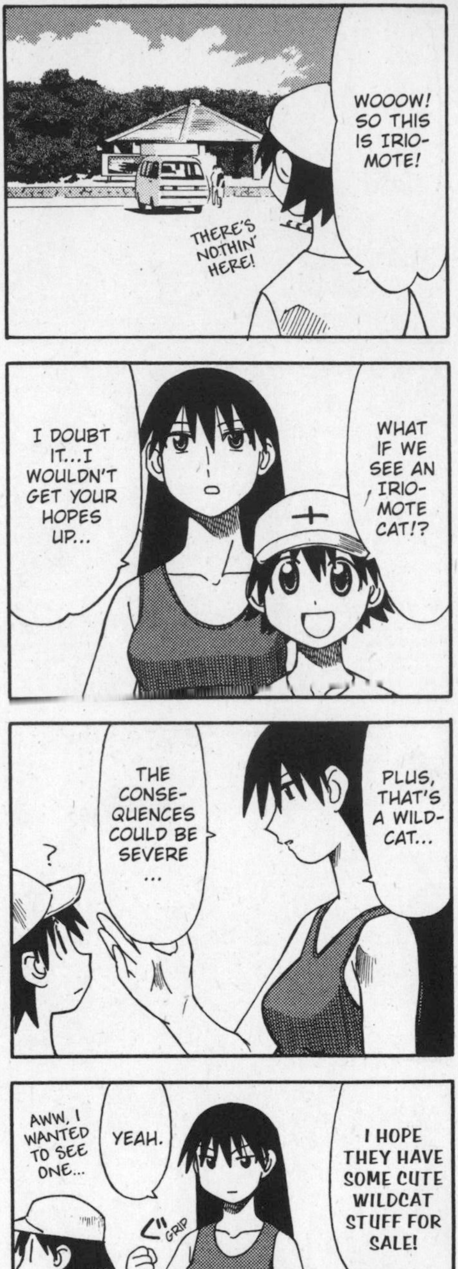
WOOOW! SO THIS IS IRIO-MOTE!
THERE'S NOTHIN' HERE!
WHAT IF WE SEE AN IRIO-MOTE CAT!?
I DOUBT IT...I WOULDN'T GET YOUR HOPES UP...
PLUS, THAT'S A WILD-CAT...
THE CONSE-QUENCES COULD BE SEVERE ...
?
I HOPE THEY HAVE SOME CUTE WILDCAT STUFF FOR SALE!
YEAH.
AWW, I WANTED TO SEE ONE...
GRIP

FATE

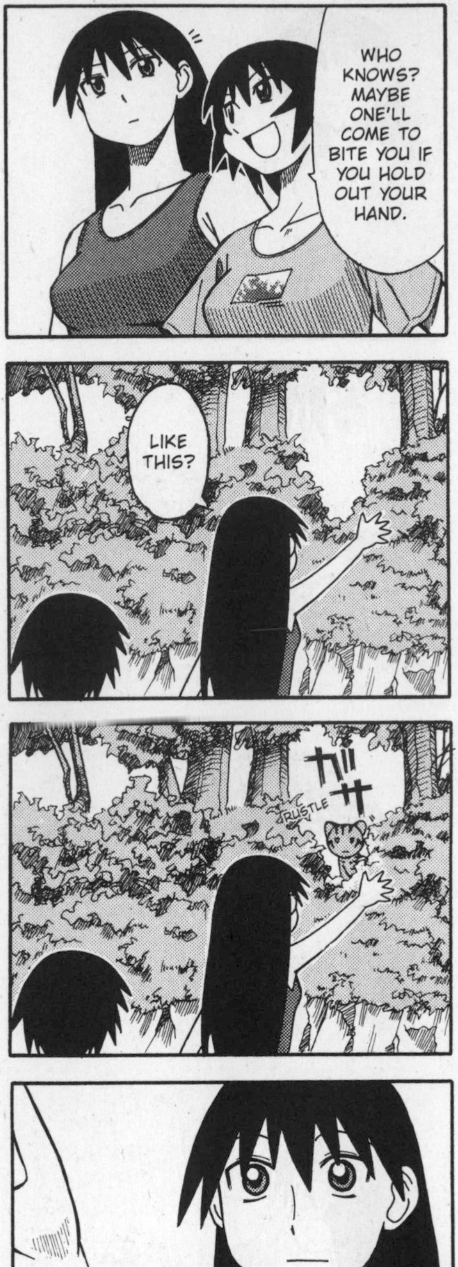
WHO KNOWS? MAYBE ONE'LL COME TO BITE YOU IF YOU HOLD OUT YOUR HAND.
LIKE THIS?
ガサ
RUSTLE

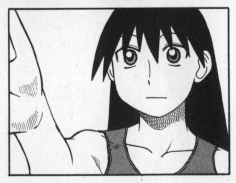

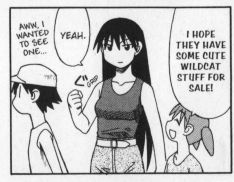

THAT WHICH SHINES IN THE MOUNTAINS

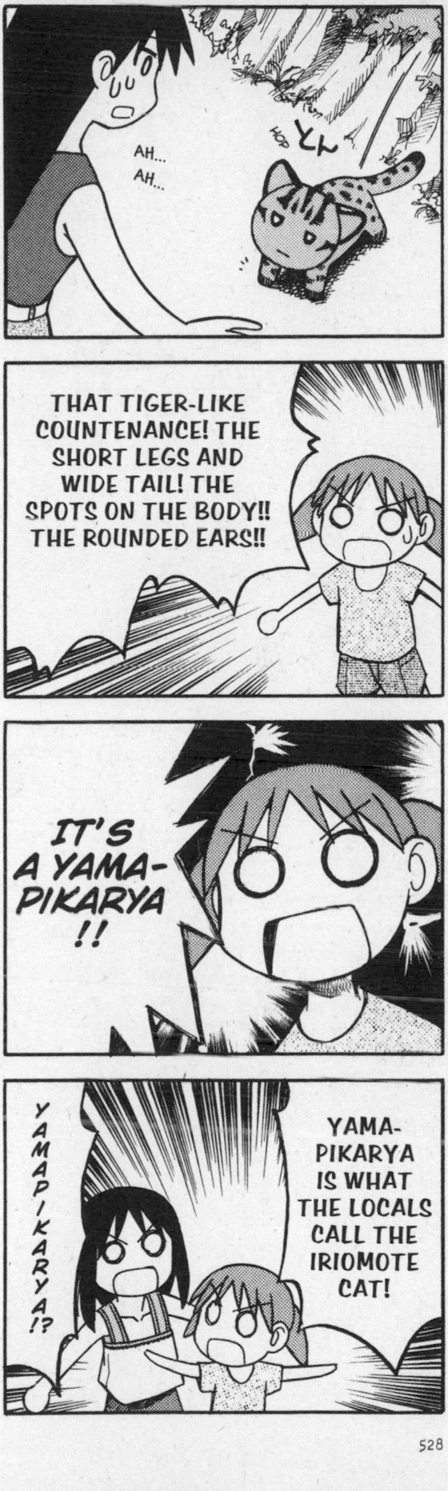
HOP とん
AH... AH...
THAT TIGER-LIKE COUNTENANCE! THE SHORT LEGS AND WIDE TAIL! THE SPOTS ON THE BODY!! THE ROUNDED EARS!!
IT'S A YAMA-PIKARYA!!
YAMA-PIKARYA IS WHAT THE LOCALS CALL THE IRIOMOTE CAT!
YAMAPIKARYA!?

PALS

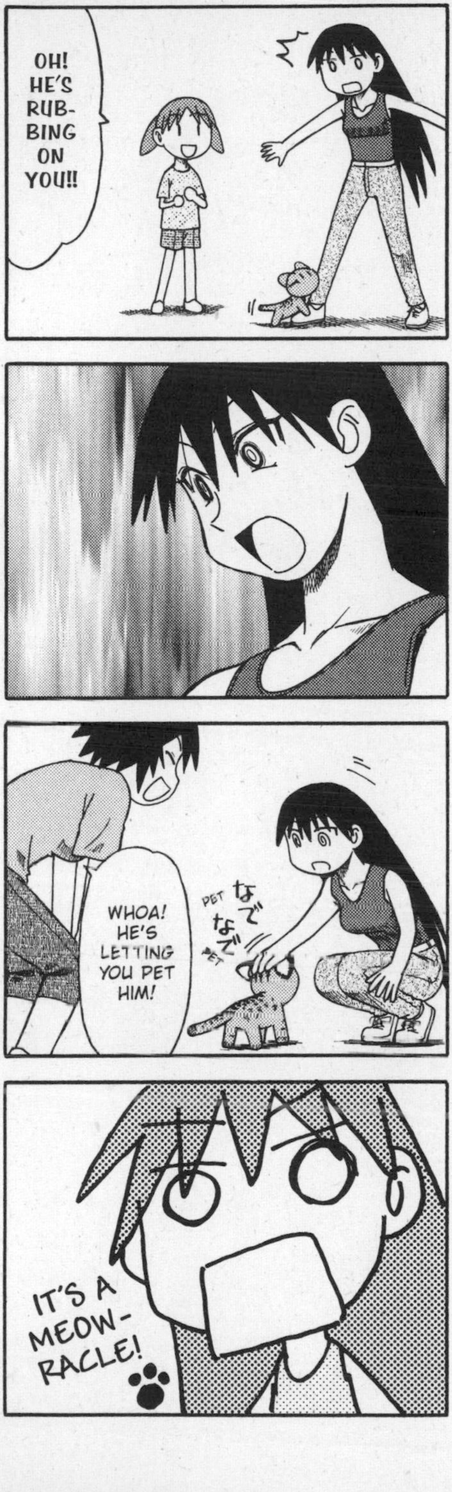
OH! HE'S RUB-BING ON YOU!!
WHOA! HE'S LETTING YOU PET HIM!
PET なで なで PET
IT'S A MEOW-RACLE!

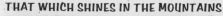

THE CAT THAT LIVES IN THE MOUNTAINS

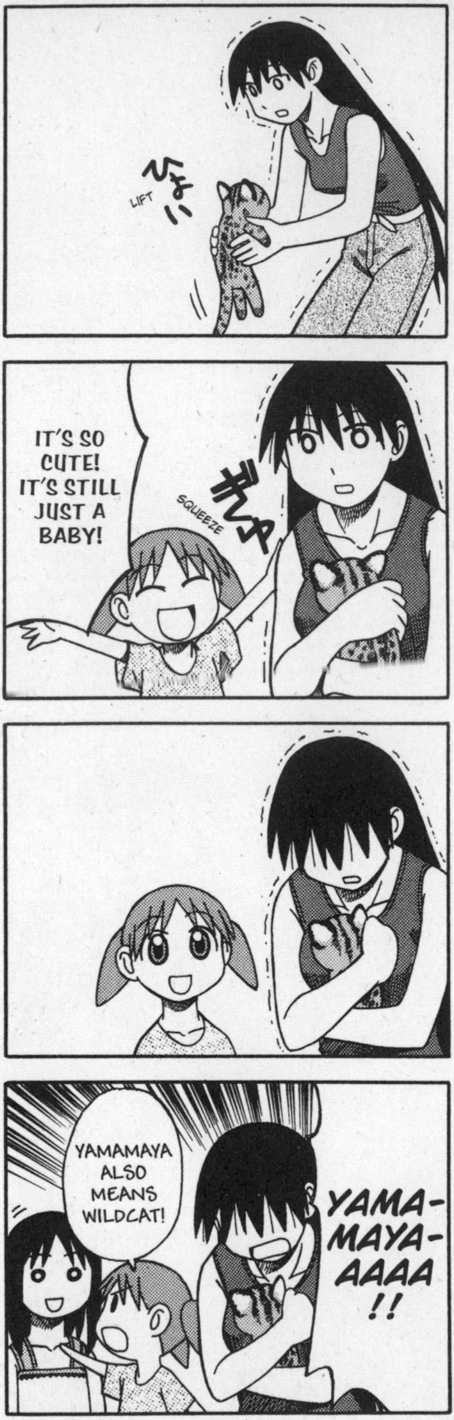
ひょい
LIFT
IT'S SO CUTE! IT'S STILL JUST A BABY!
ぎゅ
SQUEEZE
YAMAMAYA ALSO MEANS WILDCAT!
YAMA-MAYA-AAAA!!

THE THINGS WE SAW TOGETHER

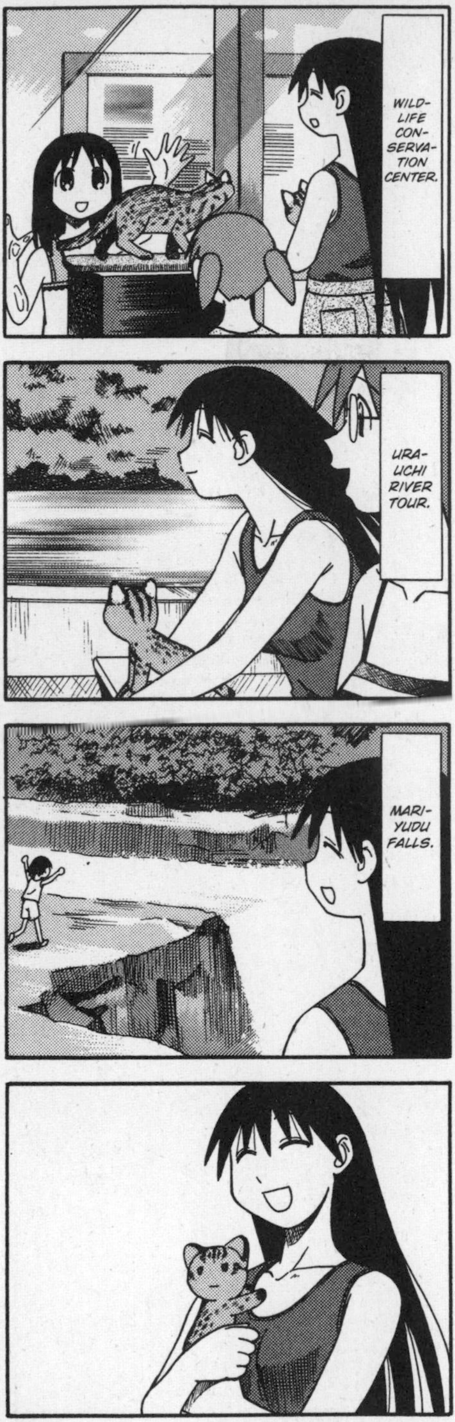
WILD-LIFE CON-SERVA-TION CENTER.
URA-UCHI RIVER TOUR.
MARI-YUDU FALLS.

LIVE WILD, LIVE FREE

WHOOOSH
ヒュウゥ
IT'S TIME TO SAY GOOD-BYE...
I SUP-POSE I SHOULDN'T TAKE HIM BACK WITH ME...
...I CAN'T HAVE A CAT AT MY HOUSE... AND YOU'RE AN ENDANGERED WILD ONE...
YOU CAN'T FOLLOW ME.
?
ガザッ
RUSTLE
IS THAT YOUR MOM?

GOOD-BYE

ドドドド
VRRRMMM

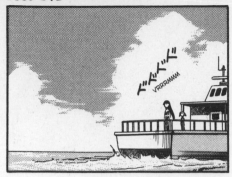

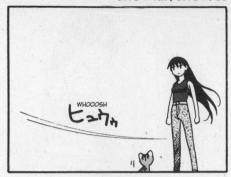

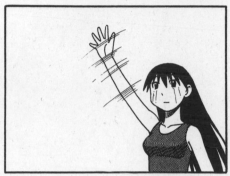

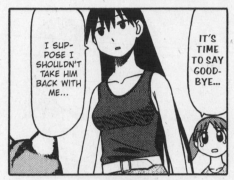

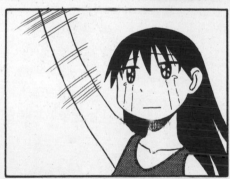

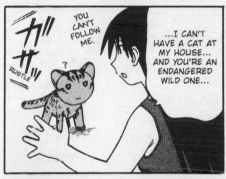

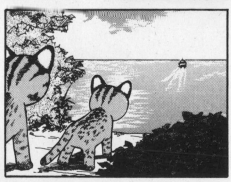

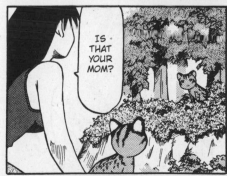

BEACH AND WATERMELON

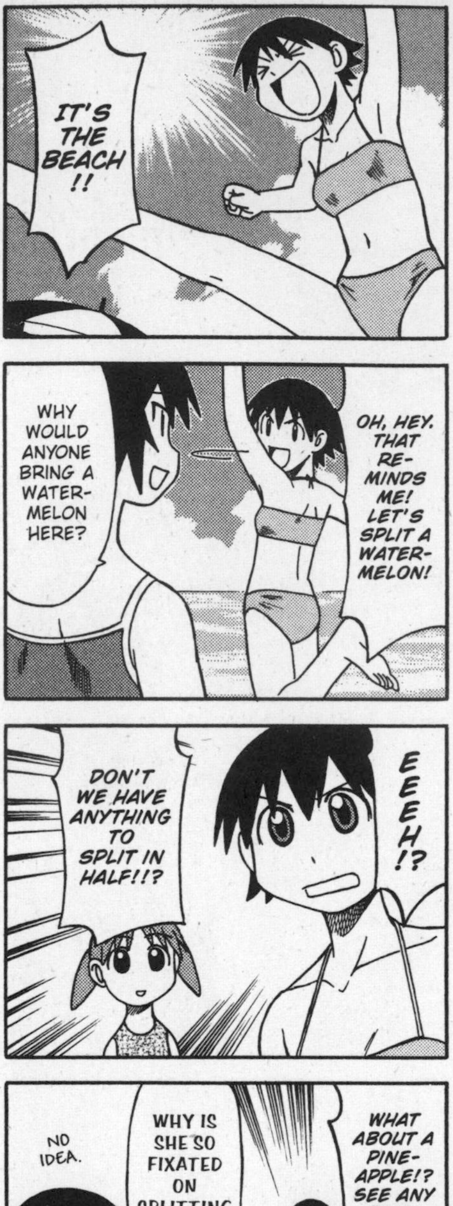
IT'S THE BEACH!!
OH, HEY. THAT RE-MINDS ME! LET'S SPLIT A WATER-MELON!
WHY WOULD ANYONE BRING A WATER-MELON HERE?
EEEH!?
DON'T WE HAVE ANYTHING TO SPLIT IN HALF!!?
WHAT ABOUT A PINE-APPLE!? SEE ANY PINE-APPLES LYING AROUND!?
WHY IS SHE SO FIXATED ON SPLITTING FRUIT?
NO IDEA.

TAKE THAT!

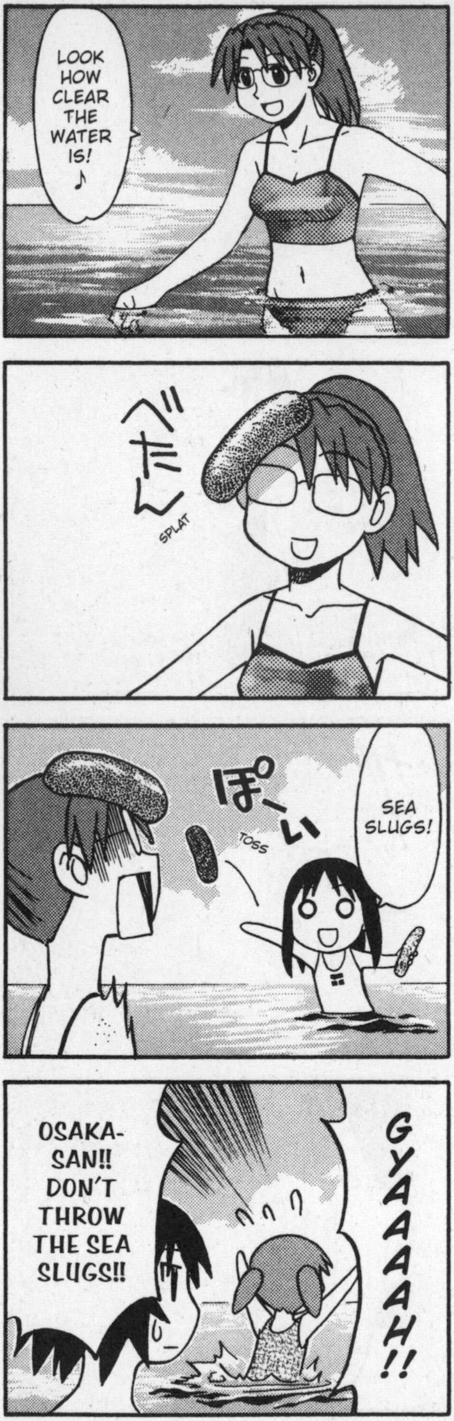
LOOK HOW CLEAR THE WATER IS! ♪
べたん
SPLAT
SEA SLUGS!
ぽーい
TOSS
GYAAAAAH!!
OSAKA-SAN!! DON'T THROW THE SEA SLUGS!!

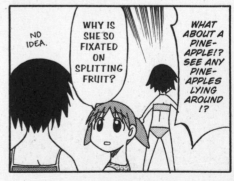

SOUVENIRS

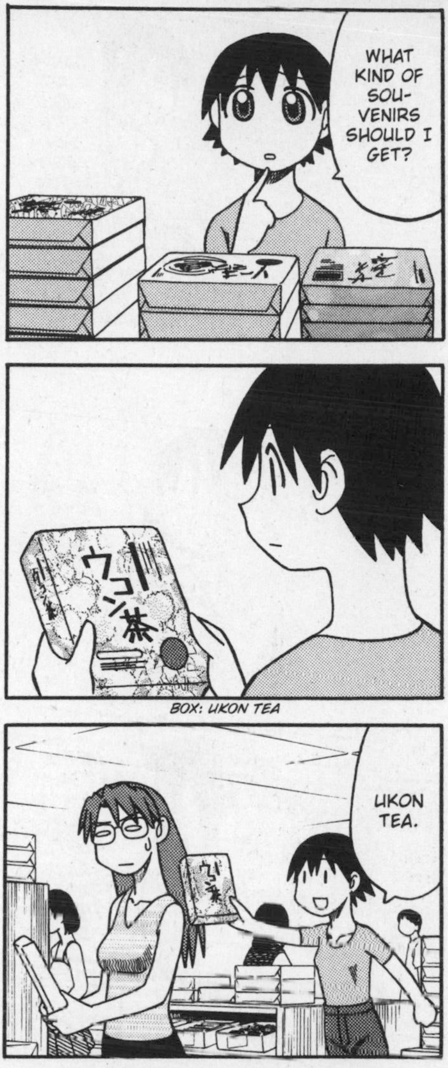
WHAT KIND OF SOU-VENIRS SHOULD I GET?
BOX: UKON TEA
UKON TEA.
UKON TEA.
UKON TEA.
SHUT UP!!

OKINAWA

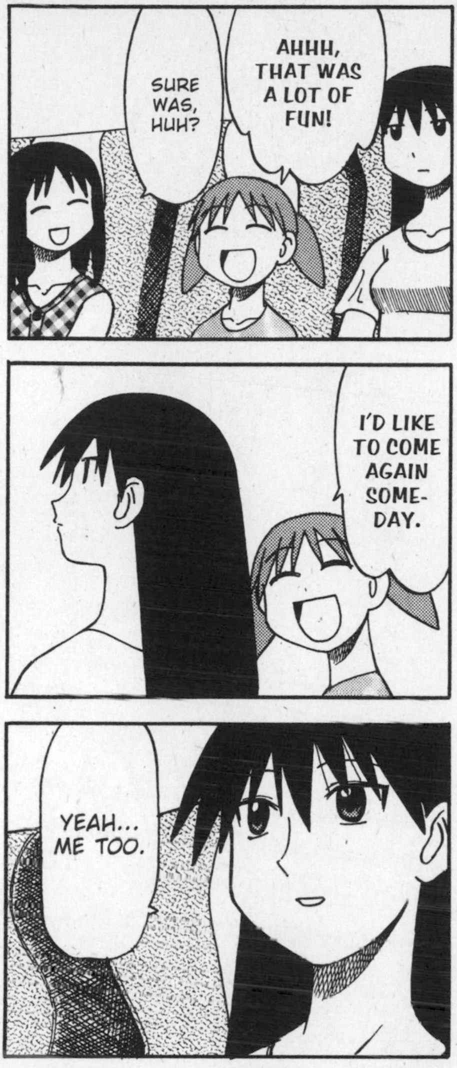
AHHH, THAT WAS A LOT OF FUN!
SURE WAS, HUH?
I'D LIKE TO COME AGAIN SOME-DAY.
YEAH... ME TOO.

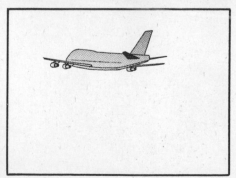

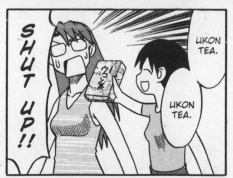

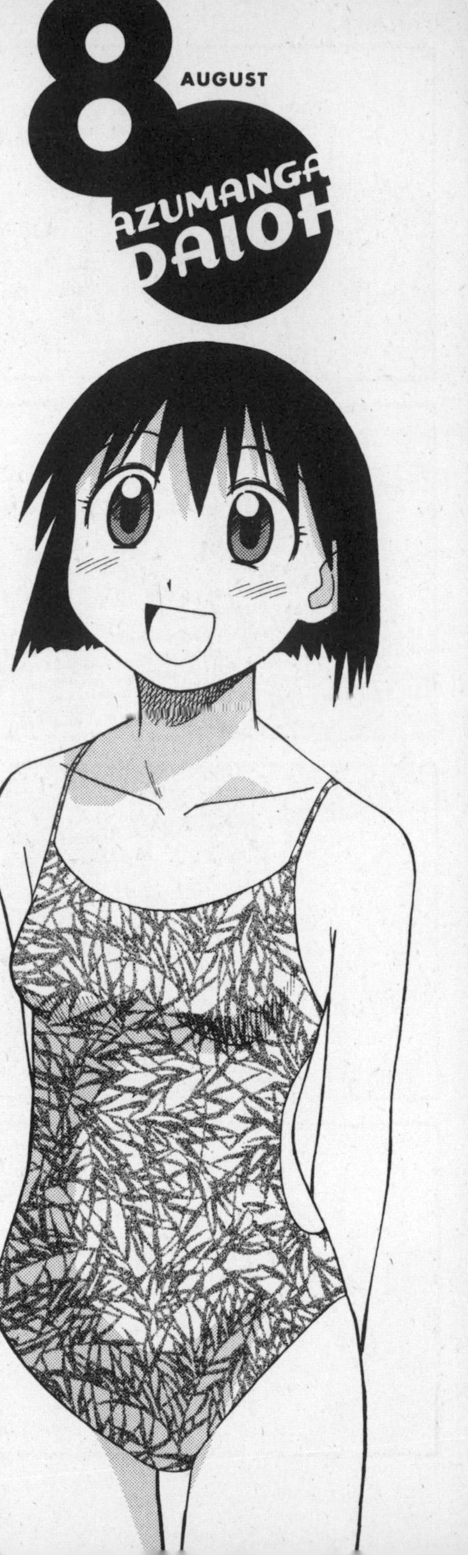
8
AUGUST
AZUMANGA DAIOH

NICE IDEA

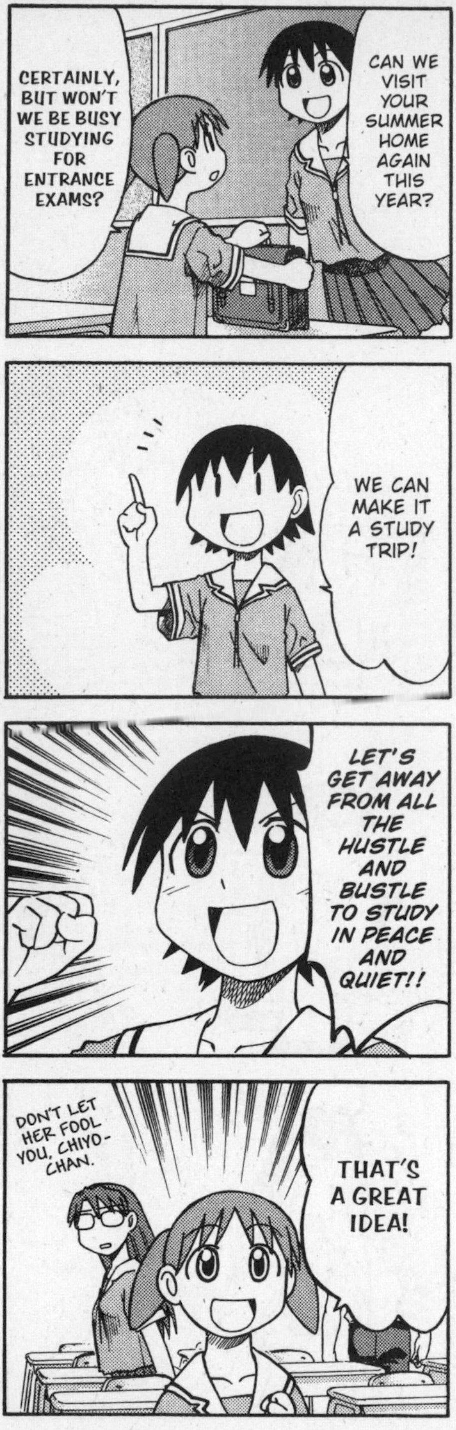
CAN WE VISIT YOUR SUMMER HOME AGAIN THIS YEAR?
CERTAINLY, BUT WON'T WE BE BUSY STUDYING FOR ENTRANCE EXAMS?
WE CAN MAKE IT A STUDY TRIP!
LET'S GET AWAY FROM ALL THE HUSTLE AND BUSTLE TO STUDY IN PEACE AND QUIET!!
THAT'S A GREAT IDEA!
DON'T LET HER FOOL YOU, CHIYO-CHAN.

IT'S A PLEASURE TO JOIN YOU

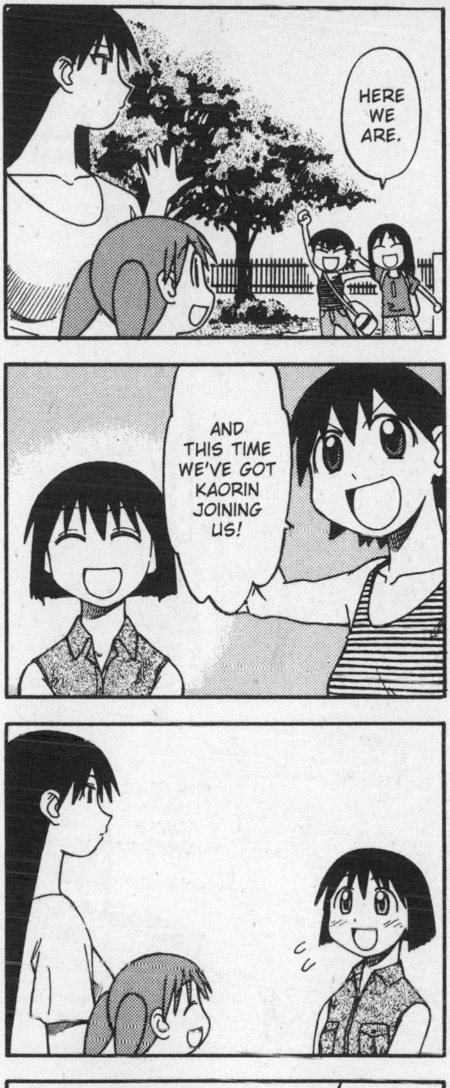
HERE WE ARE.
AND THIS TIME WE'VE GOT KAORIN JOINING US!
I DO HOPE YOU WILL ACCEPT ME INTO YOUR GROUP.

THIS ONE

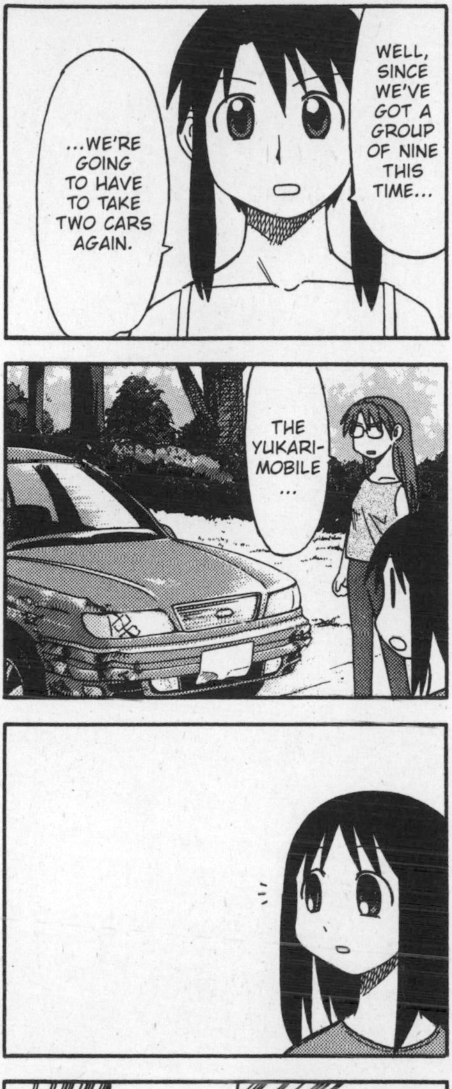
WELL, SINCE WE'VE GOT A GROUP OF NINE THIS TIME...
...WE'RE GOING TO HAVE TO TAKE TWO CARS AGAIN.
THE YUKARI-MOBILE ...
AAH! CHIYO-CHAN'S ALREADY IN NYAMO-SENSEI'S CAR!

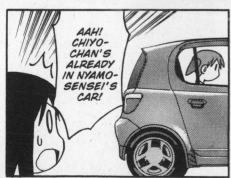

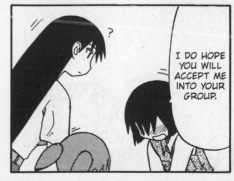

UNTIL THE END

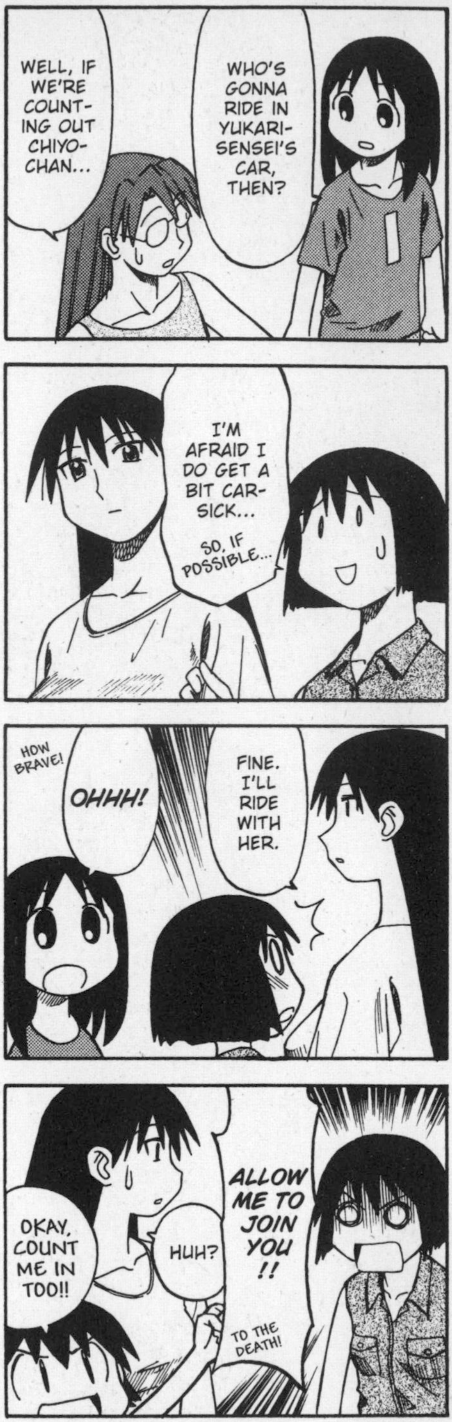
WHO'S GONNA RIDE IN YUKARI-SENSEI'S CAR, THEN?
WELL, IF WE'RE COUNTING OUT CHIYO-CHAN...
I'M AFRAID I DO GET A BIT CAR-SICK...
SO, IF POSSIBLE...
FINE. I'LL RIDE WITH HER.
OHHH!
HOW BRAVE!
ALLOW ME TO JOIN YOU!!
TO THE DEATH!
HUH?
OKAY, COUNT ME IN TOO!!

TAKEOVER

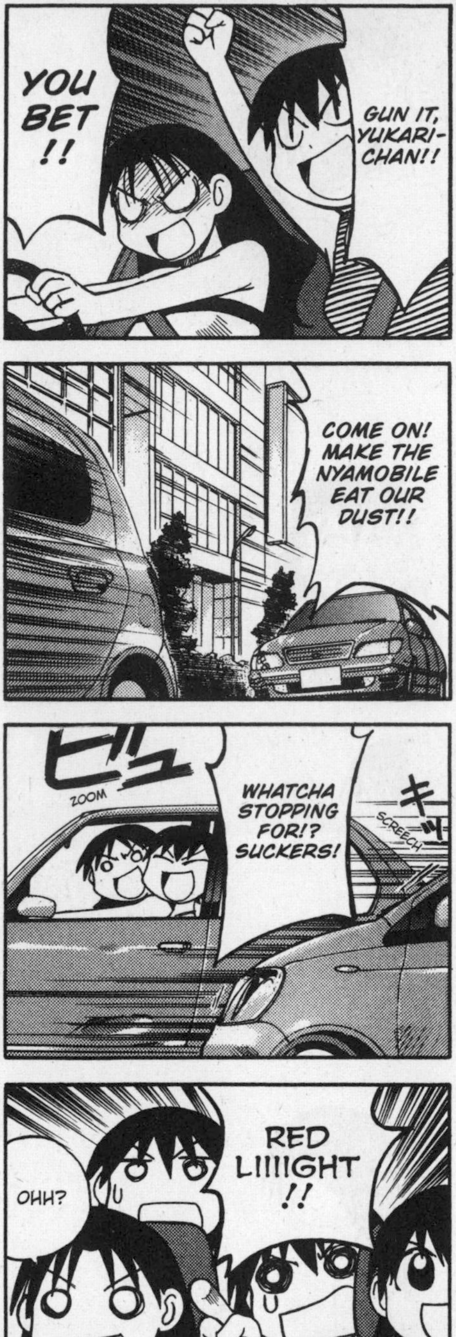
GUN IT, YUKARI-CHAN!!
YOU BET!!
COME ON! MAKE THE NYAMOBILE EAT OUR DUST!!
ZOOM
WHATCHA STOPPING FOR!? SUCKERS!
SCREECH
RED LIIIIGHT!!
OHH?

SILLY ME

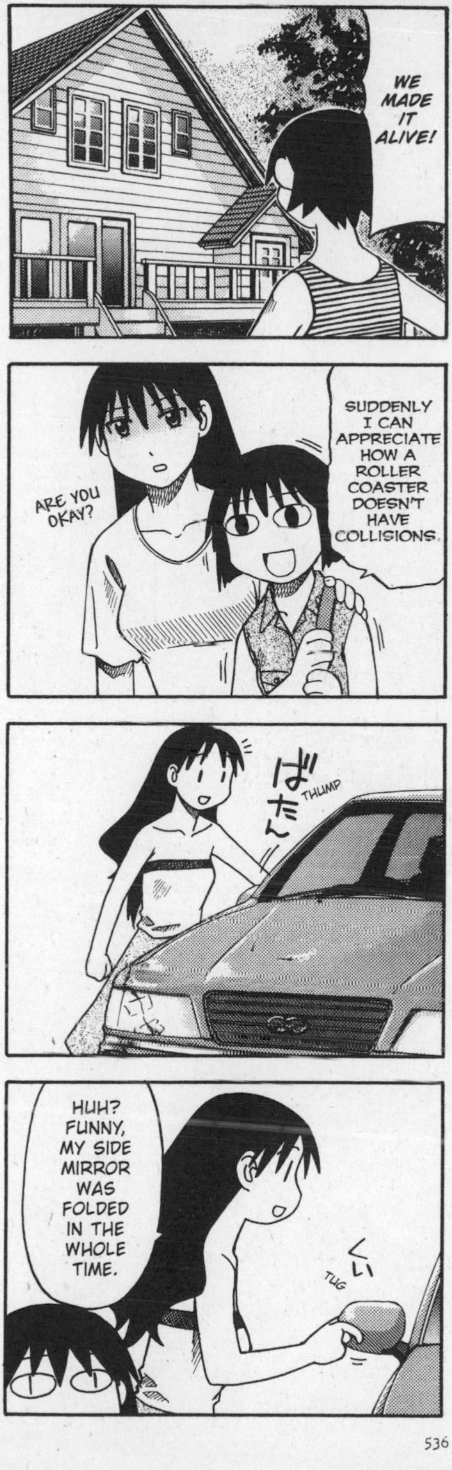
WE MADE IT ALIVE!
SUDDENLY I CAN APPRECIATE HOW A ROLLER COASTER DOESN'T HAVE COLLISIONS.
ARE YOU OKAY?
ばたん
THUMP
HUH? FUNNY, MY SIDE MIRROR WAS FOLDED IN THE WHOLE TIME.
くい
TUG

ROLL ROLL ROLL

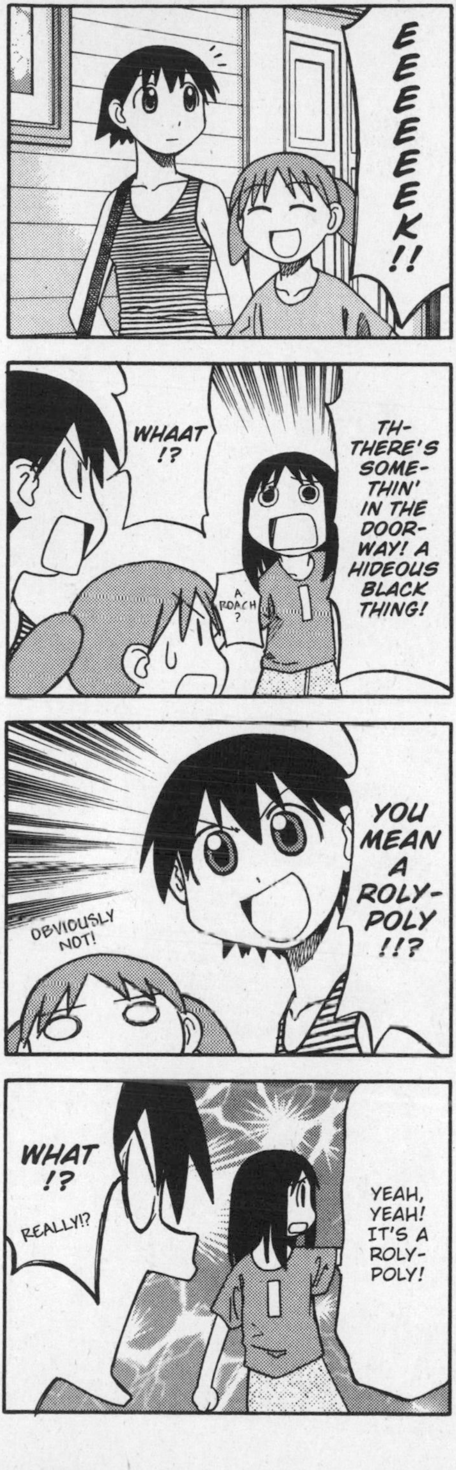
EEEEEEK!!
TH-THERE'S SOMETHIN' IN THE DOORWAY! A HIDEOUS BLACK THING!
WHAAT!?
A ROACH?
YOU MEAN A ROLY-POLY!!?
OBVIOUSLY NOT!
YEAH, YEAH! IT'S A ROLY-POLY!
WHAT!?
REALLY!?

YOU GOT FOOLED

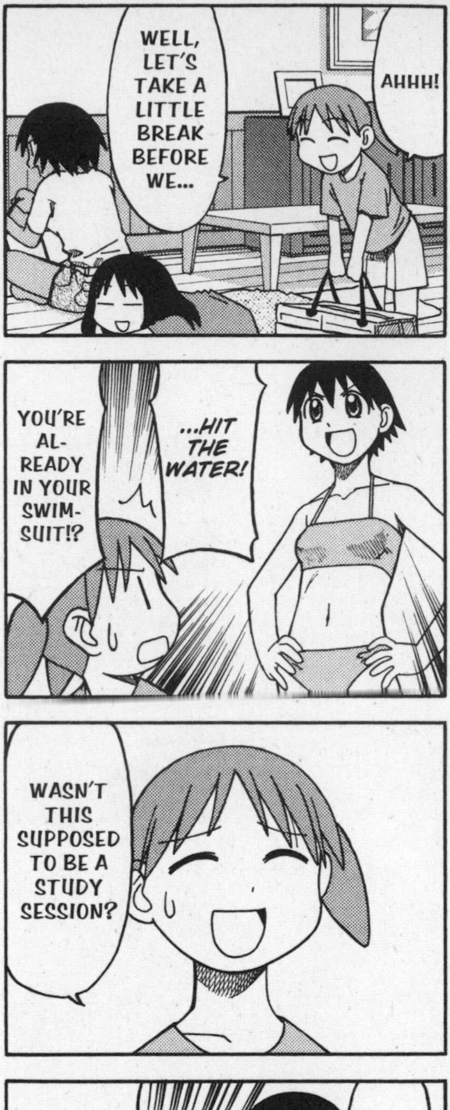
AHHH!
WELL, LET'S TAKE A LITTLE BREAK BEFORE WE...
...HIT THE WATER!
YOU'RE AL-READY IN YOUR SWIM-SUIT!?
WASN'T THIS SUPPOSED TO BE A STUDY SESSION?
THAT WAS A LIE.
YOU SAY THAT WIHOUT HESITA-TION!

EXAM STUDENTS

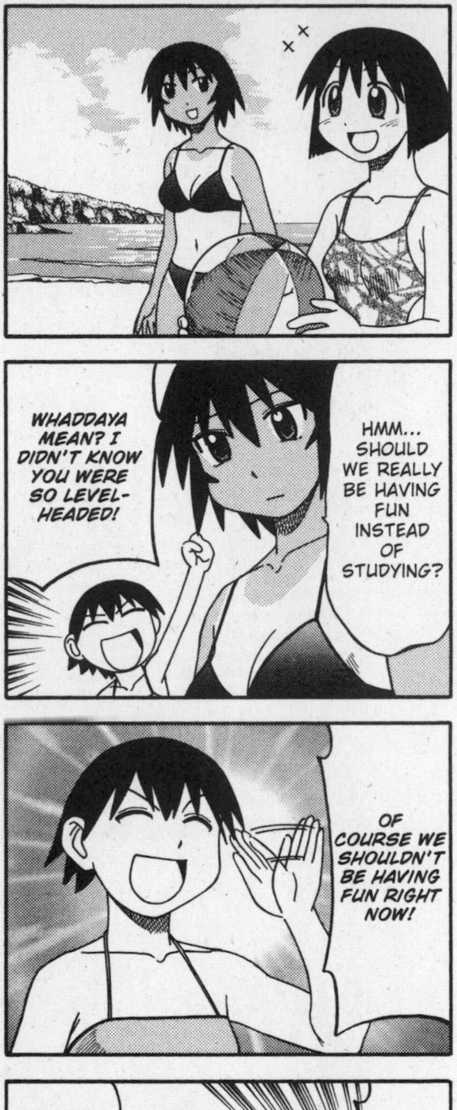
HMM... SHOULD WE REALLY BE HAVING FUN INSTEAD OF STUDYING?
WHADDAYA MEAN? I DIDN'T KNOW YOU WERE SO LEVEL-HEADED!
OF COURSE WE SHOULDN'T BE HAVING FUN RIGHT NOW!
ANY-WAY, LET'S HAVE SOME FUN!
YOU'RE REALLY SOME-THING, KNOW THAT?

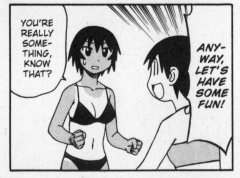

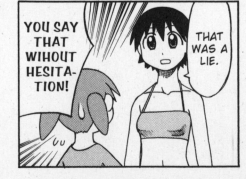

TOO LATE?

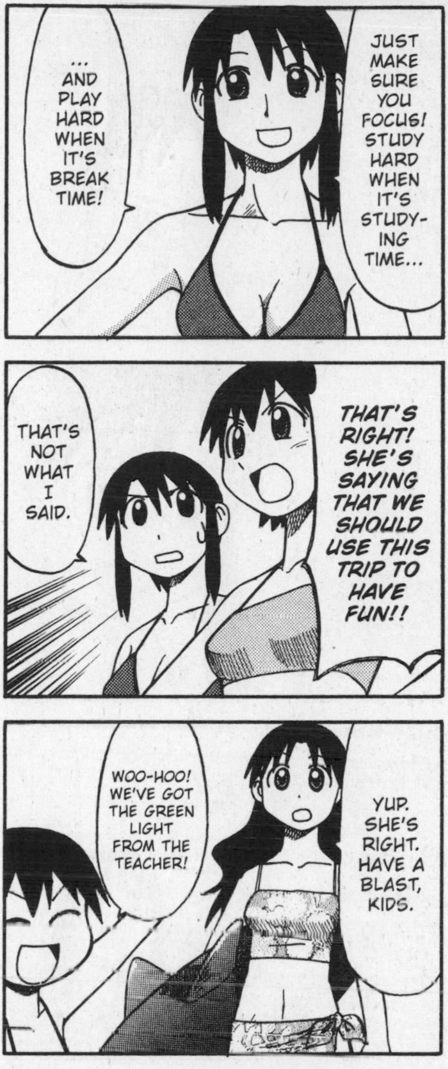
JUST MAKE SURE YOU FOCUS! STUDY HARD WHEN IT'S STUDYING TIME...
... AND PLAY HARD WHEN IT'S BREAK TIME!
THAT'S RIGHT! SHE'S SAYING THAT WE SHOULD USE THIS TRIP TO HAVE FUN!!
THAT'S NOT WHAT I SAID.
WOO-HOO! WE'VE GOT THE GREEN LIGHT FROM THE TEACHER!
YUP. SHE'S RIGHT. HAVE A BLAST, KIDS.
IT'S ALREADY WAY TOO LATE FOR YOU TO IMPROVE YOUR EXAM SCORES BY STUDYING.
SO WHY NOT HAVE FUN?
EH... REALLY?

I DON'T UNDERSTAND

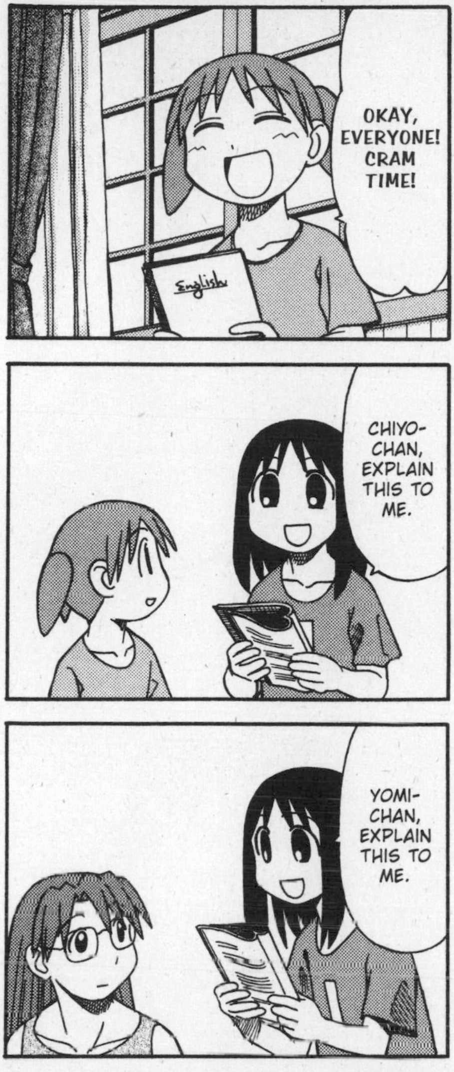
OKAY, EVERYONE! CRAM TIME!
English
CHIYO-CHAN, EXPLAIN THIS TO ME.
YOMI-CHAN, EXPLAIN THIS TO ME.
YUKARI-SENSEI, ABOUT THIS HERE PART...
HAVE YOU TRIED TO THINK THROUGH ANY OF THIS ON YOUR OWN?

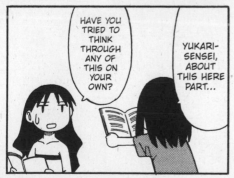

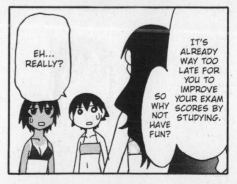

KUROSAWA-SENSEI

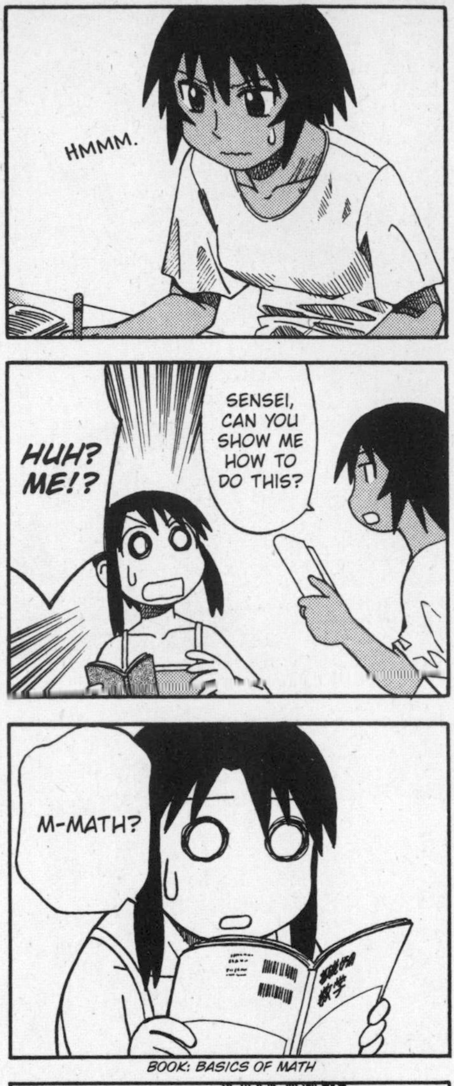
HMMM.
SENSEI, CAN YOU SHOW ME HOW TO DO THIS?
HUH? ME!?
M-MATH?
BOOK: BASICS OF MATH
じ———
STARE
ACK!

I DON'T KNOW

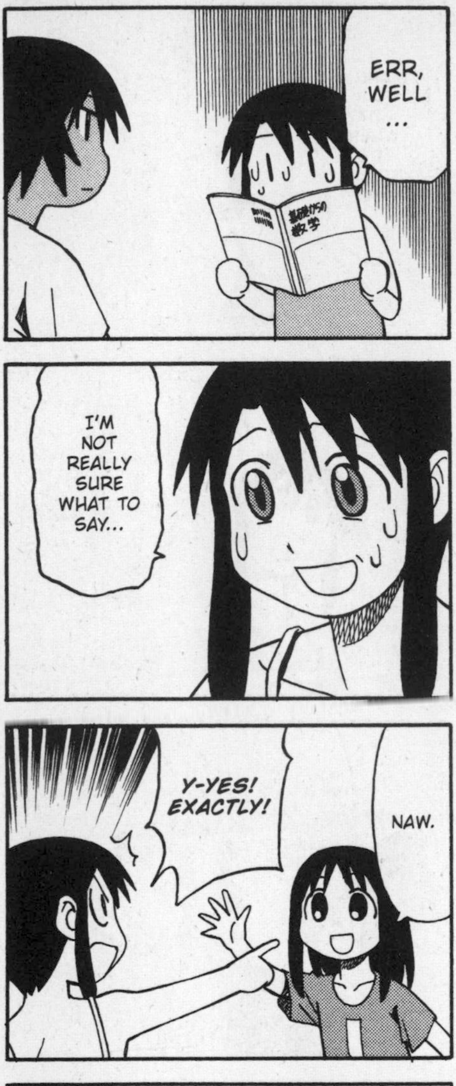
ERR, WELL ...
I'M NOT REALLY SURE WHAT TO SAY...
NAW.
Y-YES! EXACTLY!
NAW!

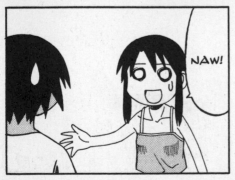

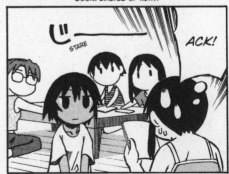

TEACHER

YUKARI'S STOCK RUNS HIGH

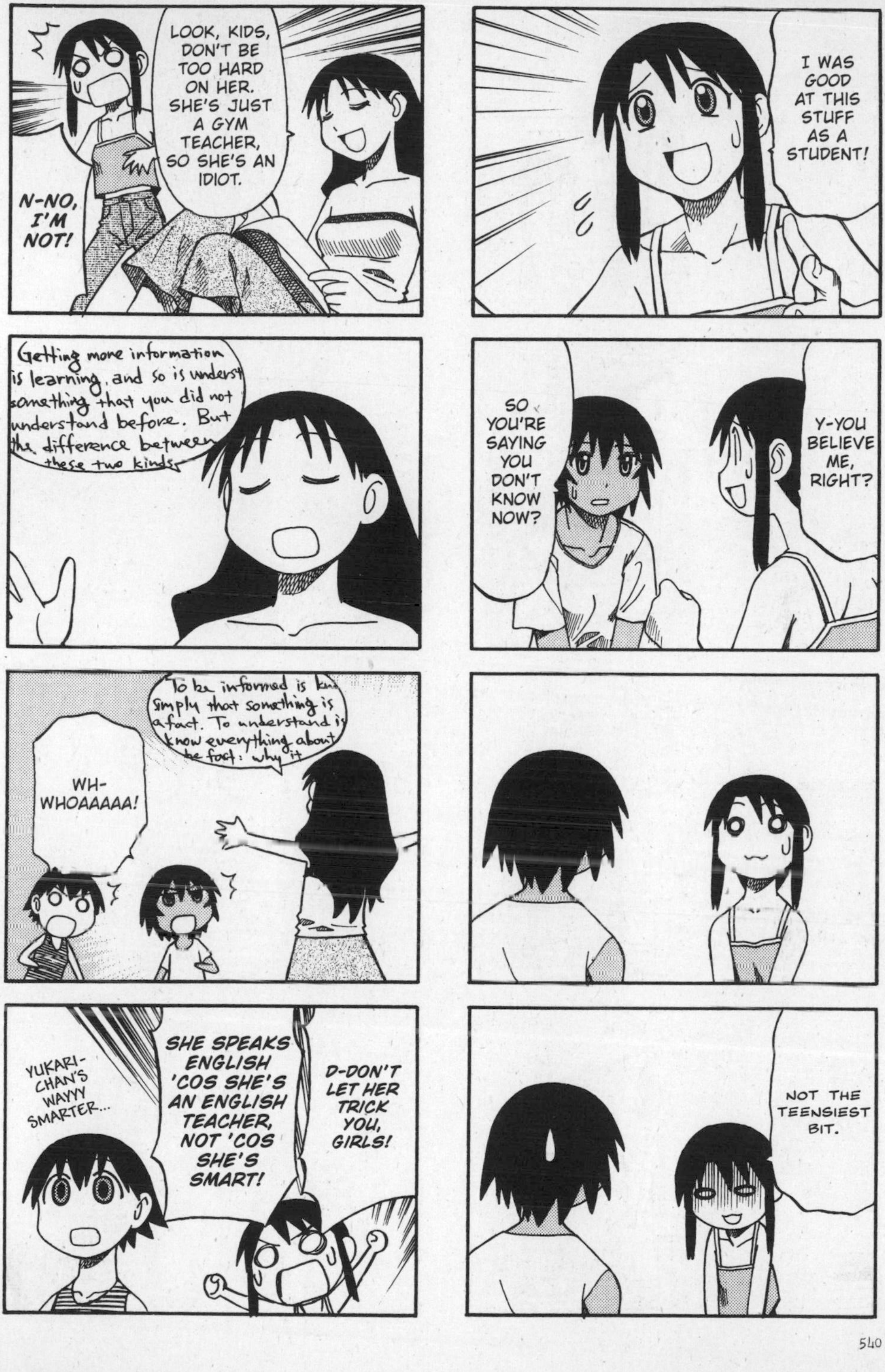
I WAS GOOD AT THIS STUFF AS A STUDENT!
SO YOU'RE SAYING YOU DON'T KNOW NOW?
Y-YOU BELIEVE ME, RIGHT?
NOT THE TEENSIEST BIT.
LOOK, KIDS, DON'T BE TOO HARD ON HER. SHE'S JUST A GYM TEACHER, SO SHE'S AN IDIOT.
N-NO, I'M NOT!
Getting more information is learning, and so is underst something that you did not understand before. But the difference between these two kinds
To be informed is kn simply that something is a fact. To understand is know everything about the fact: why it
WH-WHOAAAAA!
SHE SPEAKS ENGLISH 'COS SHE'S AN ENGLISH TEACHER, NOT 'COS SHE'S SMART!
D-DON'T LET HER TRICK YOU, GIRLS!
YUKARI-CHAN'S WAYYY SMARTER...

SAVING FACE

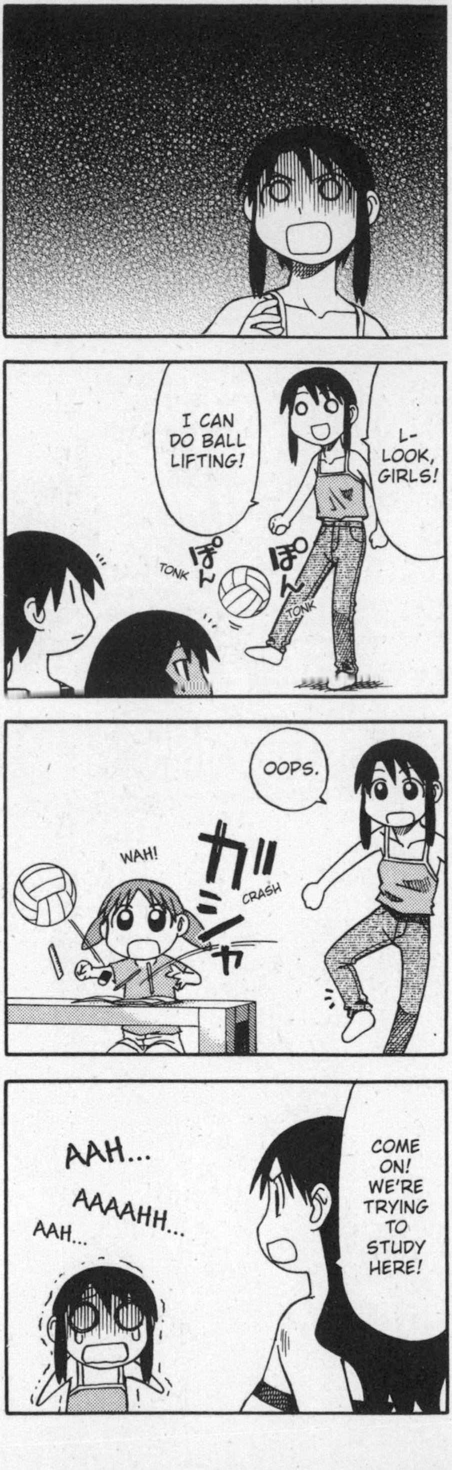
L-LOOK, GIRLS!
I CAN DO BALL LIFTING!
ぽん TONK
ぽん TONK
OOPS.
ガシャ CRASH
WAH!
COME ON! WE'RE TRYING TO STUDY HERE!
AAH...
AAAAHH...
AAH...

DEPRESSION

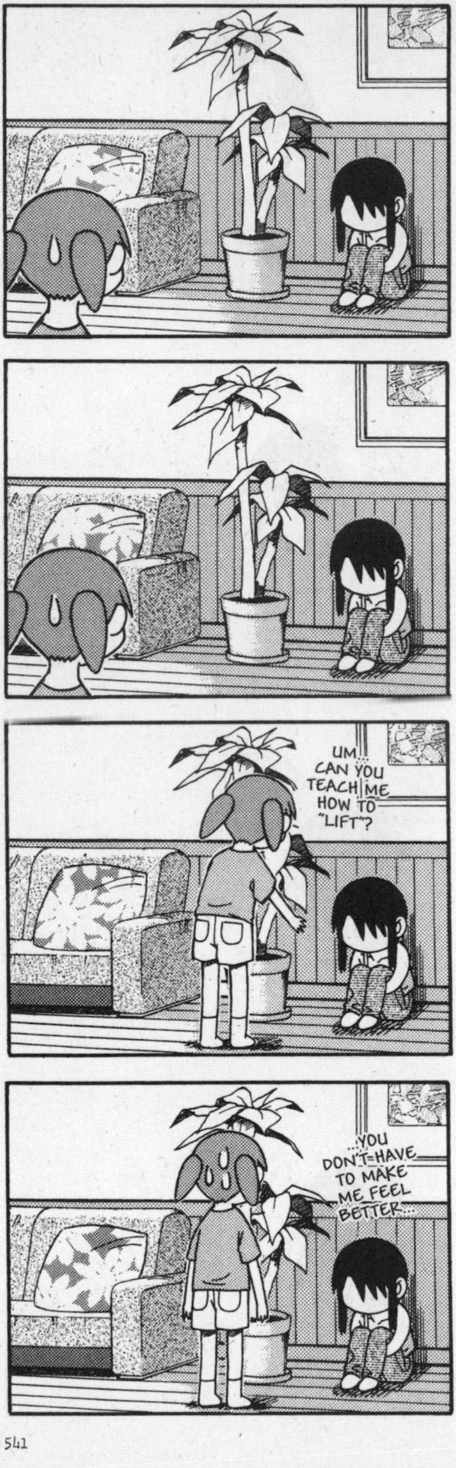
UM... CAN YOU TEACH ME HOW TO "LIFT"?
...YOU DON'T HAVE TO MAKE ME FEEL BETTER...

CANDIDS

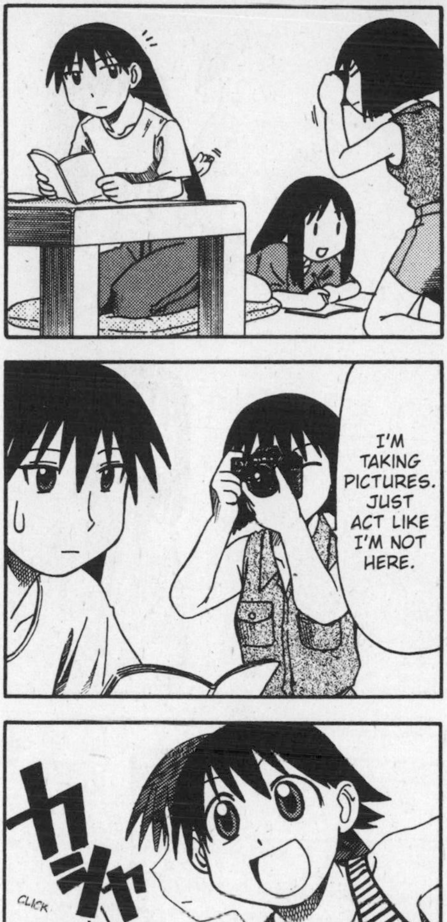
I'M TAKING PICTURES. JUST ACT LIKE I'M NOT HERE.
カシャ
CLICK
TCH!
カシャ
CLICK
WHOA !!
ばっ
LEAP

SUMMER VACATION HABITS

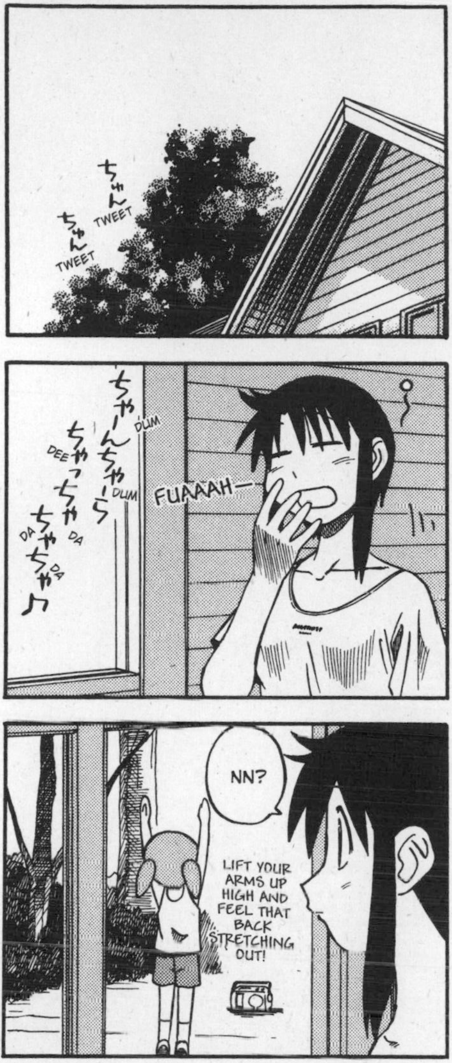
ちゅん
TWEET
ちゅん
TWEET
ちゃーんちゃーら
DUM DUM
ちゃっちゃ
DEE DA
ちゃちゃちゃ♪
DA DA
FUAAAH—
NN?
LIFT YOUR ARMS UP HIGH AND FEEL THAT BACK STRETCHING OUT!
RADIO EXERCISES, HUH?
I CAN'T TELL IF SHE'S ACTING LIKE A LITTLE KID OR AN OLD LADY...

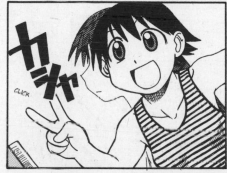

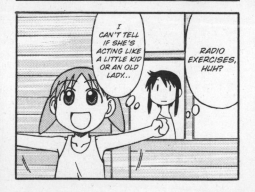

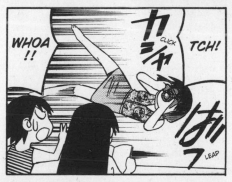

STAMP CARD

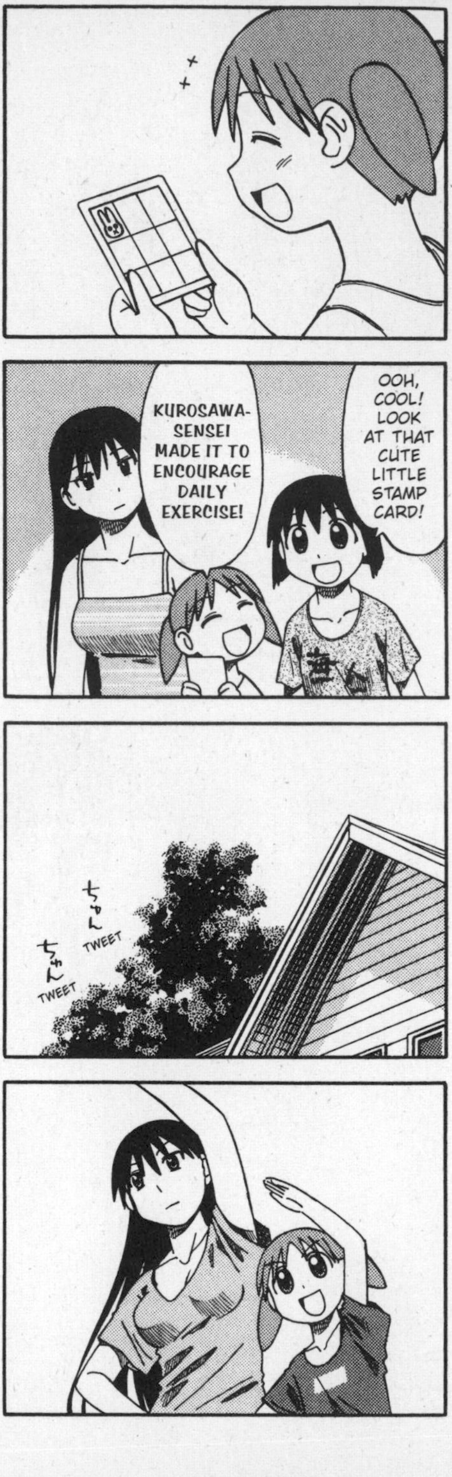
OOH, COOL! LOOK AT THAT CUTE LITTLE STAMP CARD!
KUROSAWA-SENSEI MADE IT TO ENCOURAGE DAILY EXERCISE!
ちゃん
TWEET
ちゃん
TWEET

HALF AWAKE

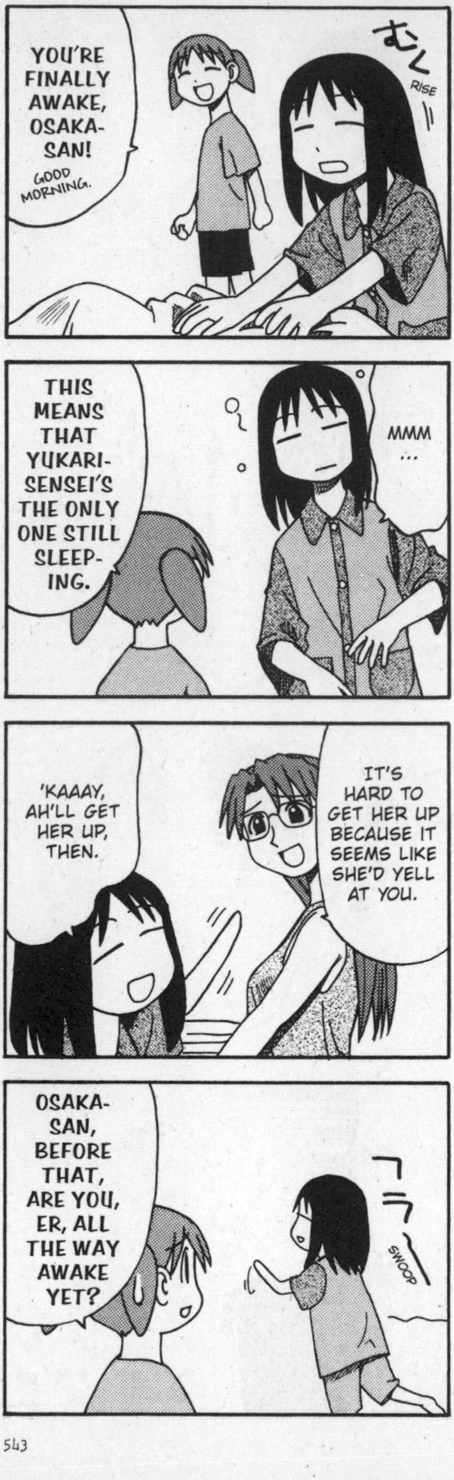
むく
RISE
YOU'RE FINALLY AWAKE, OSAKA-SAN!
GOOD MORNING.
MMM ...
THIS MEANS THAT YUKARI-SENSEI'S THE ONLY ONE STILL SLEEP-ING.
IT'S HARD TO GET HER UP BECAUSE IT SEEMS LIKE SHE'D YELL AT YOU.
'KAAAY, AH'LL GET HER UP, THEN.
フラ～
SWOOP
OSAKA-SAN, BEFORE THAT, ARE YOU, ER, ALL THE WAY AWAKE YET?

WAKE UP

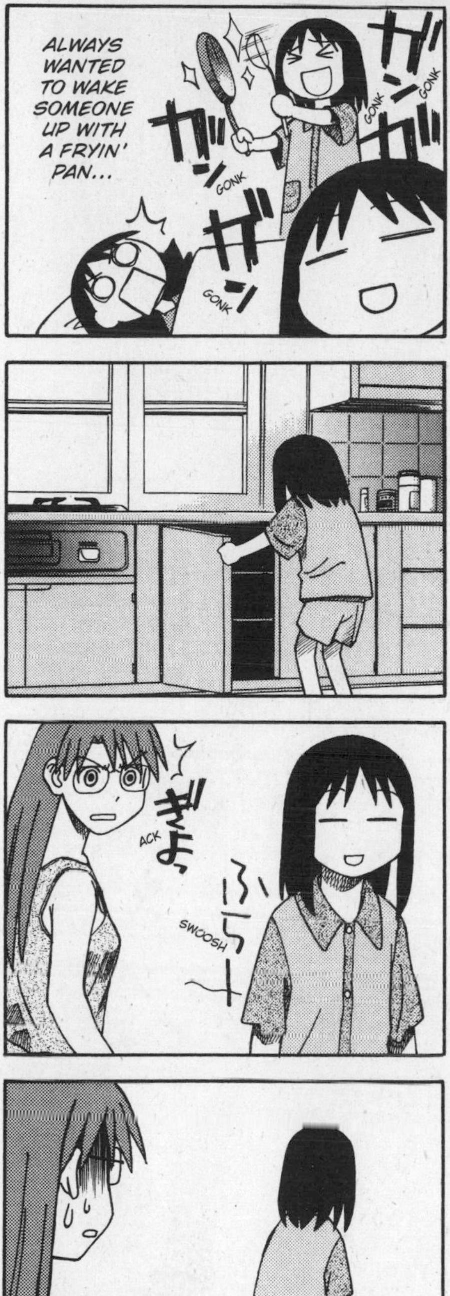
ALWAYS WANTED TO WAKE SOMEONE UP WITH A FRYIN' PAN...
ガン
GONK
GONK
ガン
GONK
ガン
GONK
ぎょっ
ACK
ふら〜
SWOOSH

FAILURE

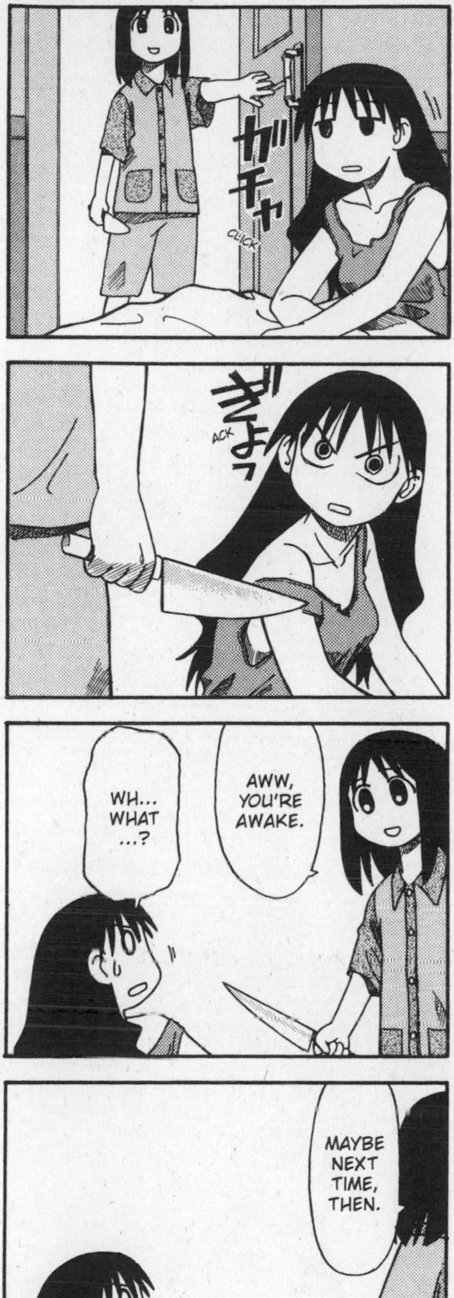
ガチャ
CLICK
ぎょっ
ACK
AWW, YOU'RE AWAKE.
WH... WHAT ...?
MAYBE NEXT TIME, THEN.

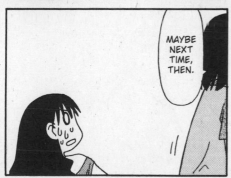

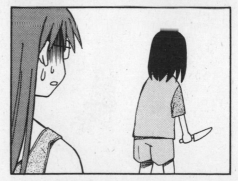

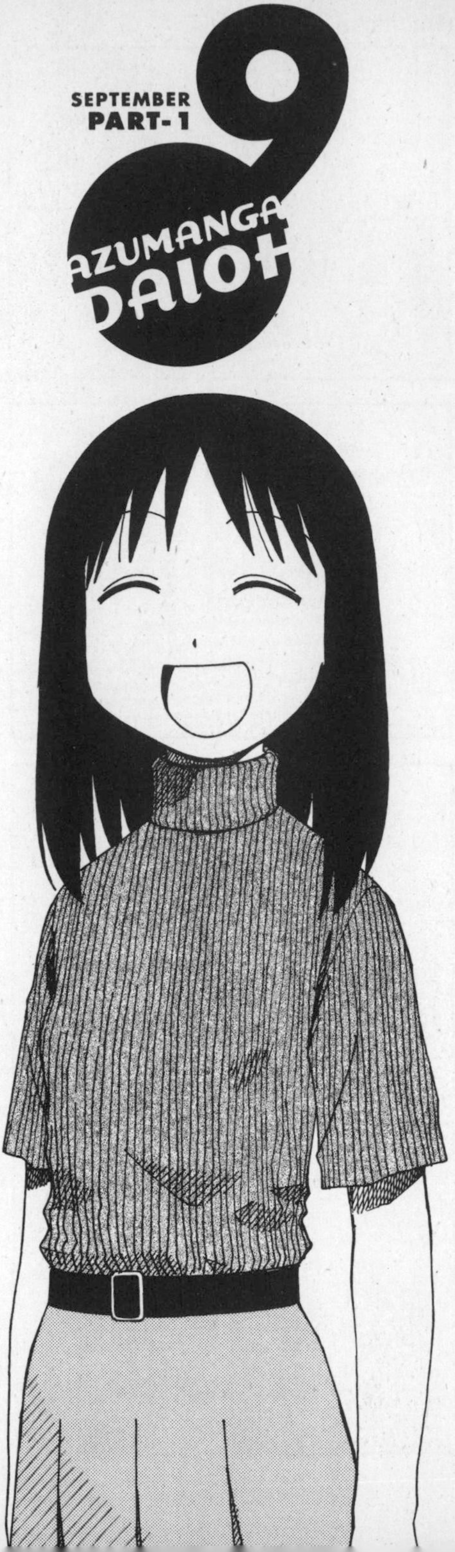
SEPTEMBER
PART-1
AZUMANGA DAIOH

IT'S NOT OVER YET

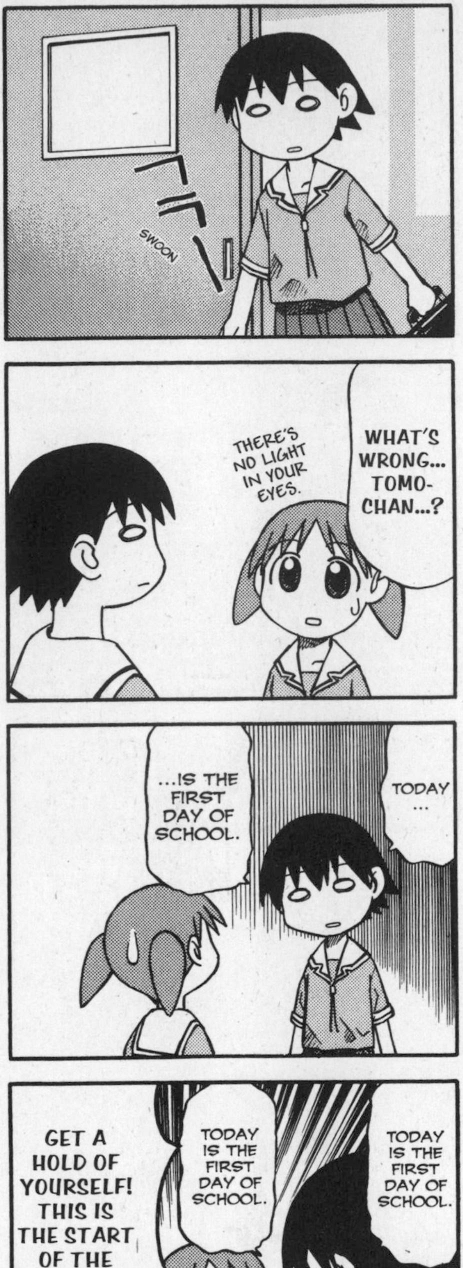
SWOON
WHAT'S WRONG... TOMO-CHAN...?
THERE'S NO LIGHT IN YOUR EYES.
TODAY ...
...IS THE FIRST DAY OF SCHOOL.
TODAY IS THE FIRST DAY OF SCHOOL.
TODAY IS THE FIRST DAY OF SCHOOL.
GET A HOLD OF YOURSELF! THIS IS THE START OF THE SECOND TERM AL-READY!!

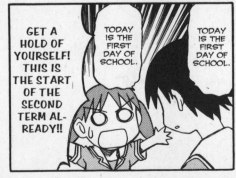

CONFUSION

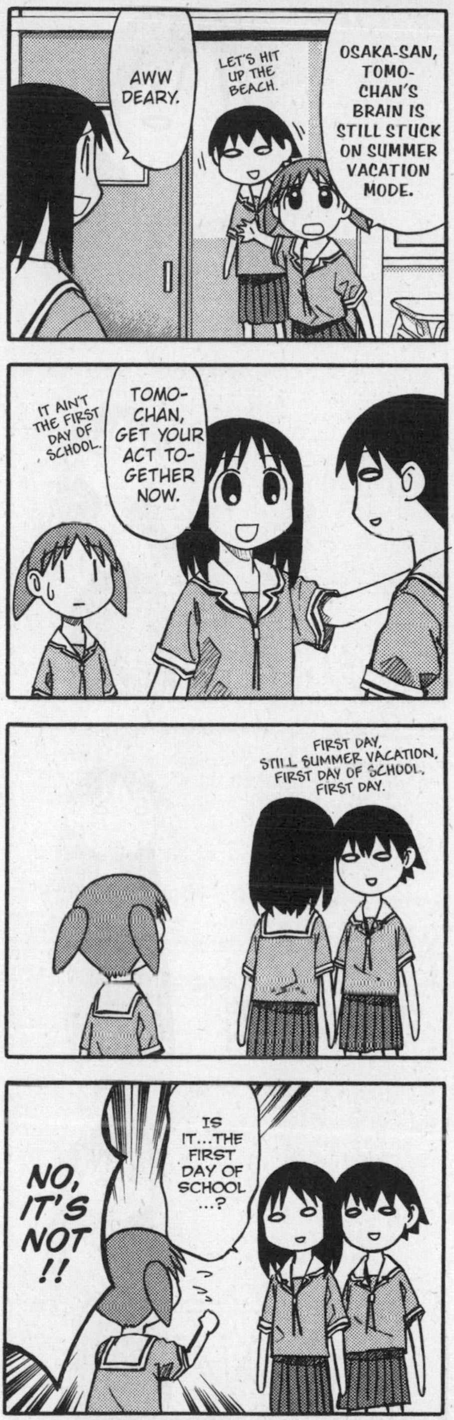
OSAKA-SAN, TOMO-CHAN'S BRAIN IS STILL STUCK ON SUMMER VACATION MODE.
LET'S HIT UP THE BEACH.
AWW DEARY.
TOMO-CHAN, GET YOUR ACT TO-GETHER NOW.
IT AIN'T THE FIRST DAY OF SCHOOL.
FIRST DAY, STILL SUMMER VACATION, FIRST DAY OF SCHOOL, FIRST DAY.
IS IT...THE FIRST DAY OF SCHOOL ...?
NO, IT'S NOT!!

MAGIC CHARM

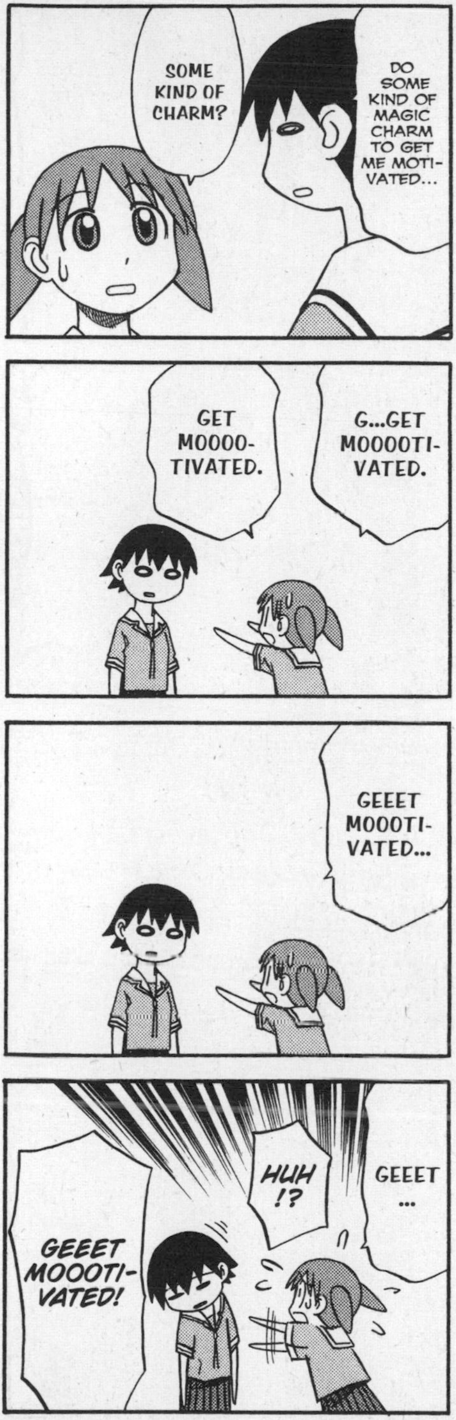
DO SOME KIND OF MAGIC CHARM TO GET ME MOTI-VATED...
SOME KIND OF CHARM?
G...GET MOOOOTI-VATED.
GET MOOOO-TIVATED.
GEEET MOOOTI-VATED...
GEEET ...
HUH !?
GEEET MOOOTI-VATED!

NO GOOD

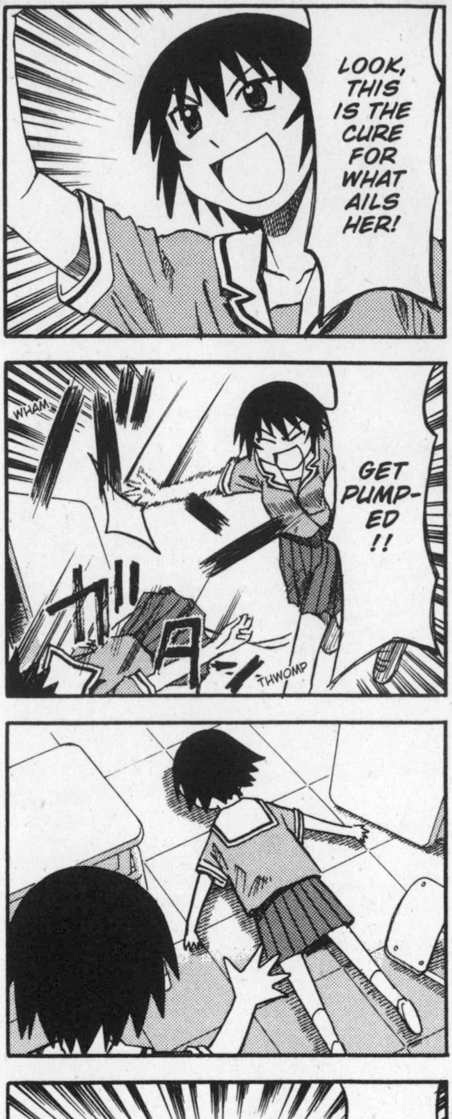
LOOK, THIS IS THE CURE FOR WHAT AILS HER!
WHAM
GET PUMP-ED !!
THWOMP
HEY, YOU OKAY !?

RETRY

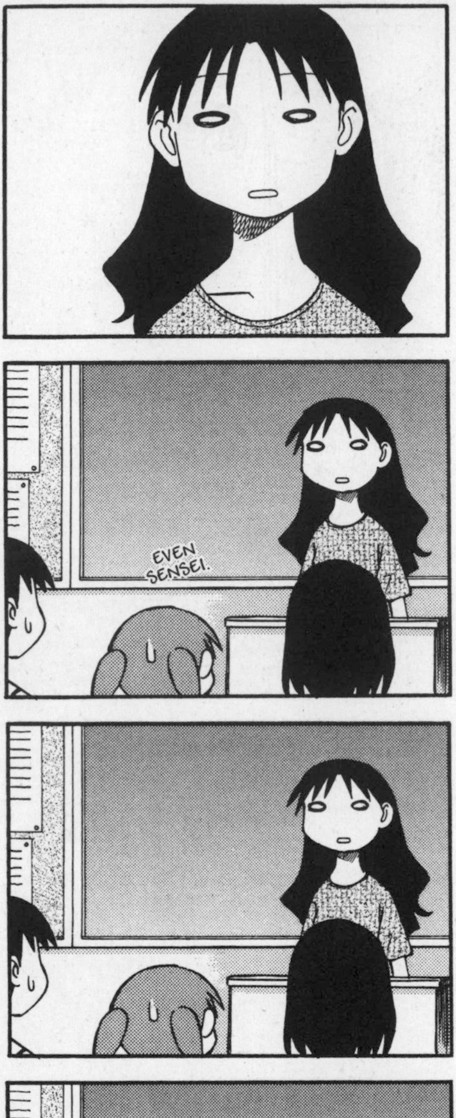
EVEN SENSEI.
GEEET MOOOTIVATED...

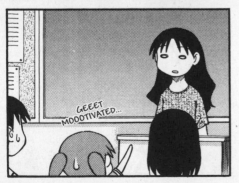

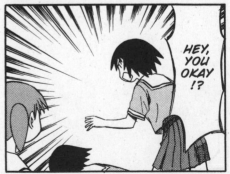

SHE'S BACK

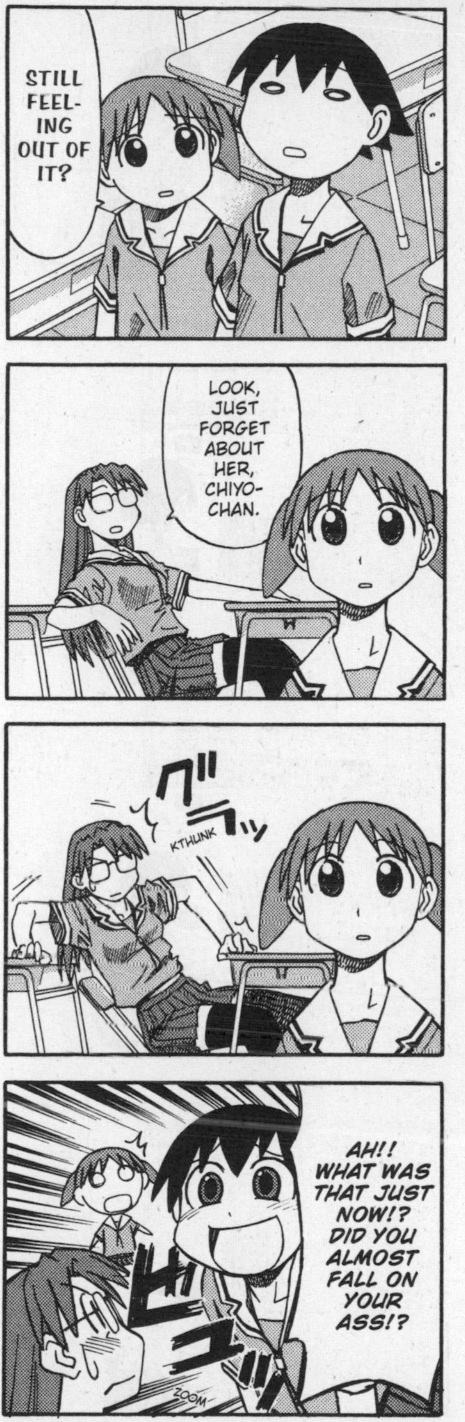
STILL FEELING OUT OF IT?
LOOK, JUST FORGET ABOUT HER, CHIYO-CHAN.
グラッ
KTHUNK
AH!! WHAT WAS THAT JUST NOW!? DID YOU ALMOST FALL ON YOUR ASS!?
ビュッ
ZOOM

MILK

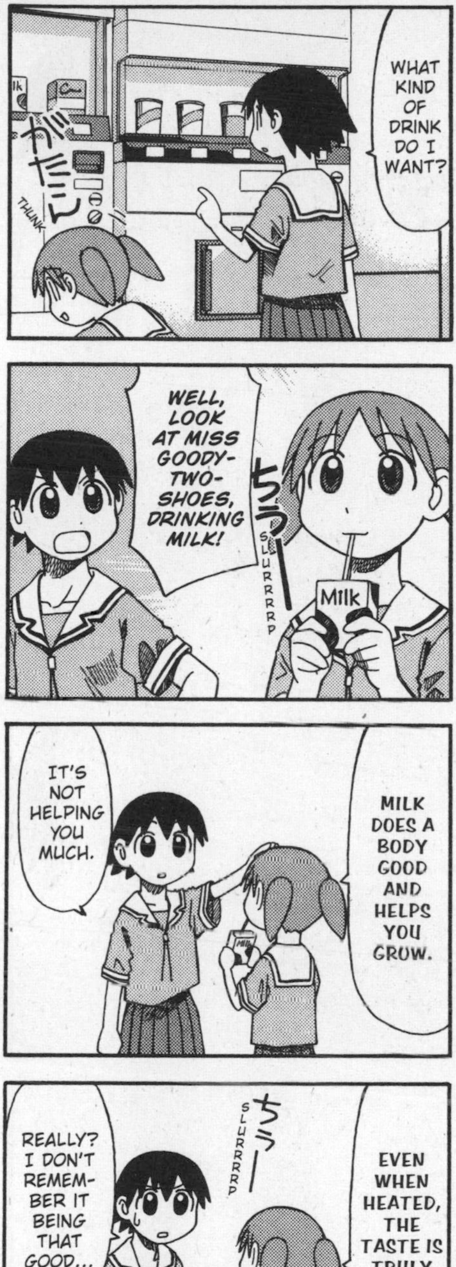
WHAT KIND OF DRINK DO I WANT?
がたん
THUNK
ちうー
SLURRRRP
Milk
WELL, LOOK AT MISS GOODY-TWO-SHOES, DRINKING MILK!
MILK DOES A BODY GOOD AND HELPS YOU GROW.
IT'S NOT HELPING YOU MUCH.
ちうー
SLURRRRP
EVEN WHEN HEATED, THE TASTE IS TRULY DELECTABLE.
REALLY? I DON'T REMEMBER IT BEING THAT GOOD...

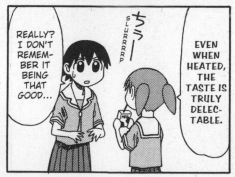

STOP!

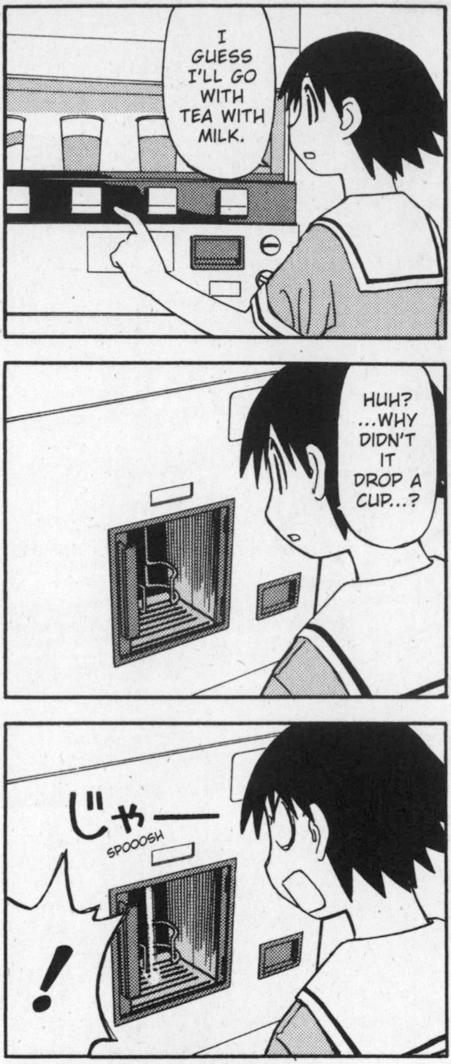
I GUESS I'LL GO WITH TEA WITH MILK.
HUH? ...WHY DIDN'T IT DROP A CUP...?
じゃー
SPOOOSH
!
NOOOO!! STOP, STOP!!
WHOA, THAT'S A RIGHT MESS!

BETRAYAL

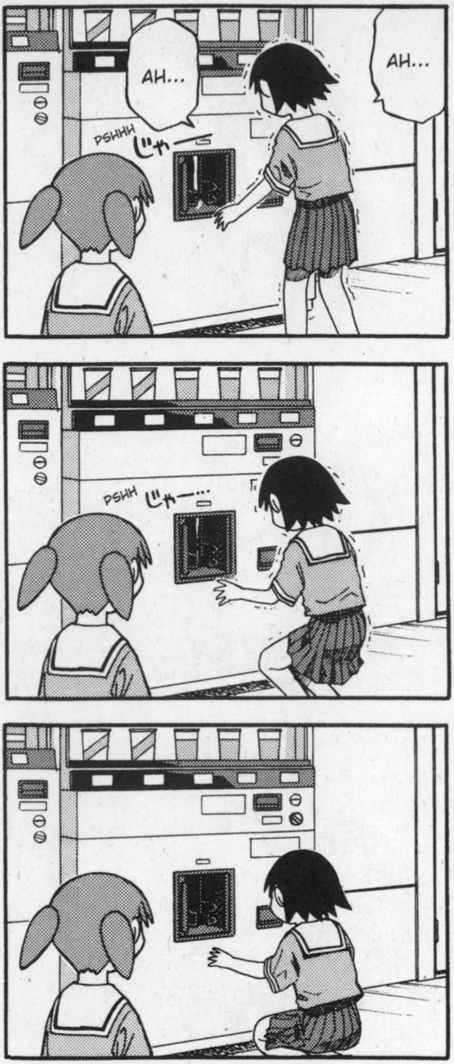
AH...
AH...
PSHHH
じゃー
PSHH
じゃー…
AND I BE-LIEVED IN YOU...
WOULD YOU LIKE SOME OF MY MILK?

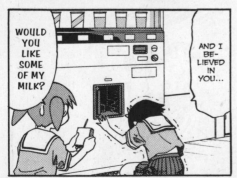

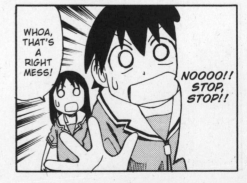

FEEL THE PAIN

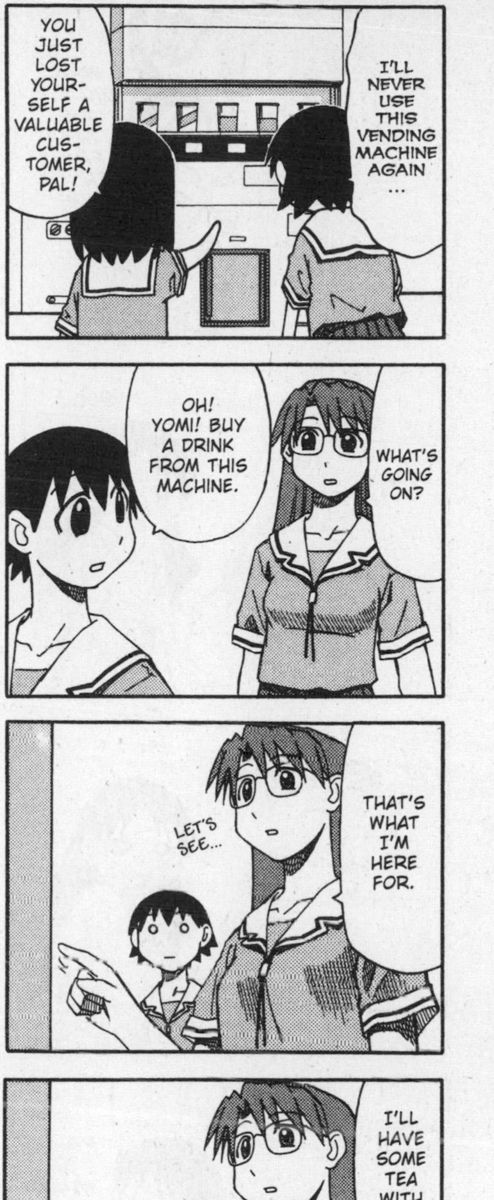
I'LL NEVER USE THIS VENDING MACHINE AGAIN ...
YOU JUST LOST YOUR-SELF A VALUABLE CUS-TOMER, PAL!
WHAT'S GOING ON?
OH! YOMI! BUY A DRINK FROM THIS MACHINE.
THAT'S WHAT I'M HERE FOR.
LET'S SEE...
I'LL HAVE SOME TEA WITH MILK.

THAT WAS MINE

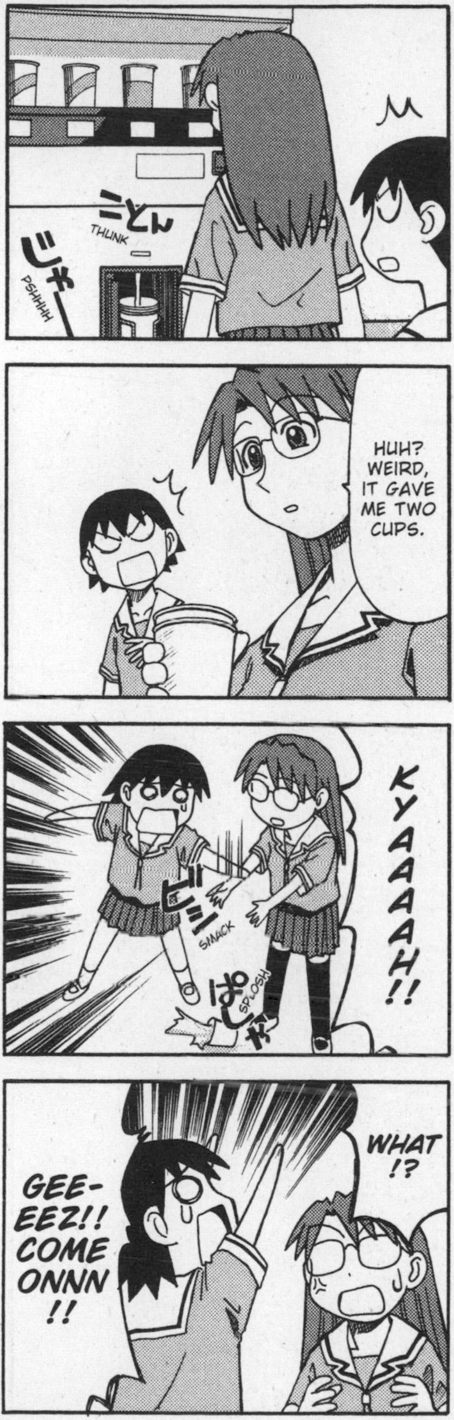
ごとん
THUNK
じゃー
PSHHHH
HUH? WEIRD, IT GAVE ME TWO CUPS.
KYAAAAAH!!
SMACK
SPLOSH
WHAT !?
GEE-EEZ!! COME ONNN !!

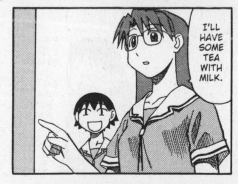

CAUGHT IN THE ACT

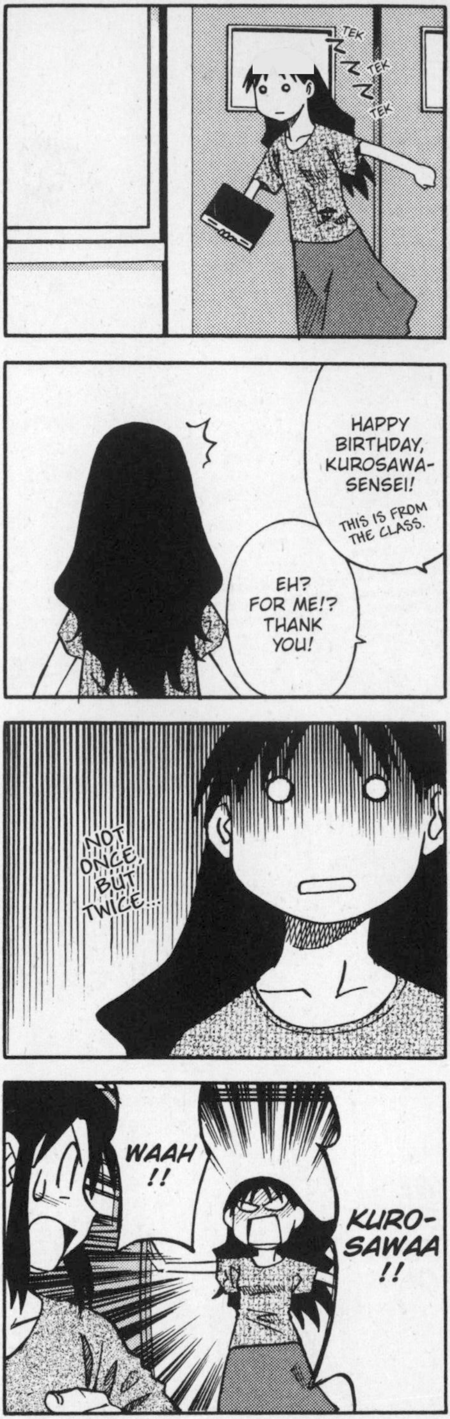
TEK
TEK
TEK
HAPPY BIRTHDAY, KUROSAWA-SENSEI!
THIS IS FROM THE CLASS.
EH? FOR ME!? THANK YOU!
NOT ONCE, BUT TWICE...
KURO-SAWAA !!
WAAH !!

NOT THAT I CARE

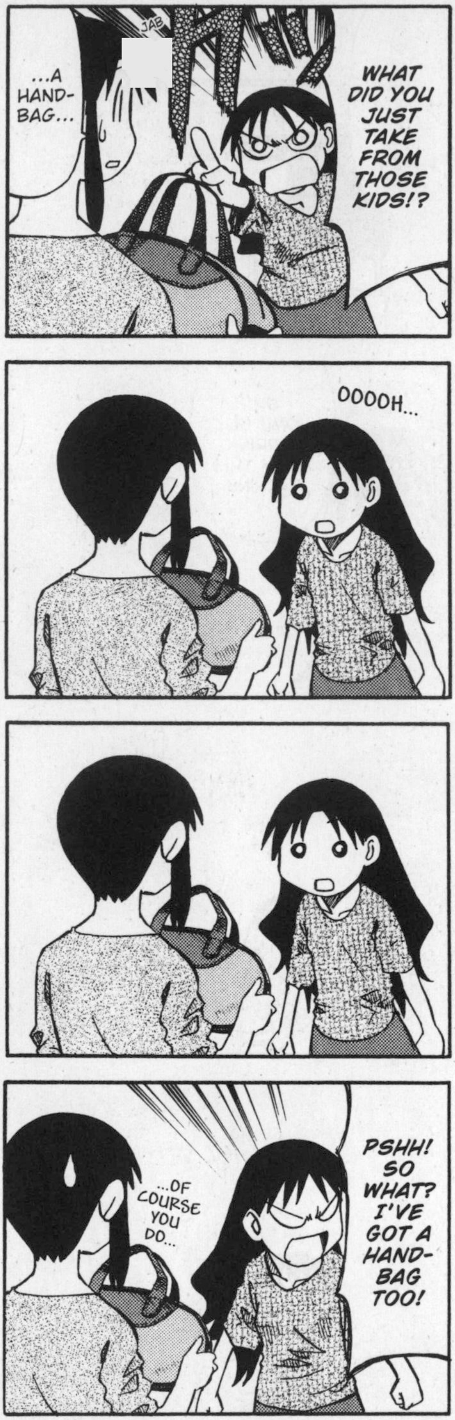
JAB
WHAT DID YOU JUST TAKE FROM THOSE KIDS!?
...A HAND-BAG...
OOOOH...
PSHH! SO WHAT? I'VE GOT A HAND-BAG TOO!
...OF COURSE YOU DO...

CHARGES

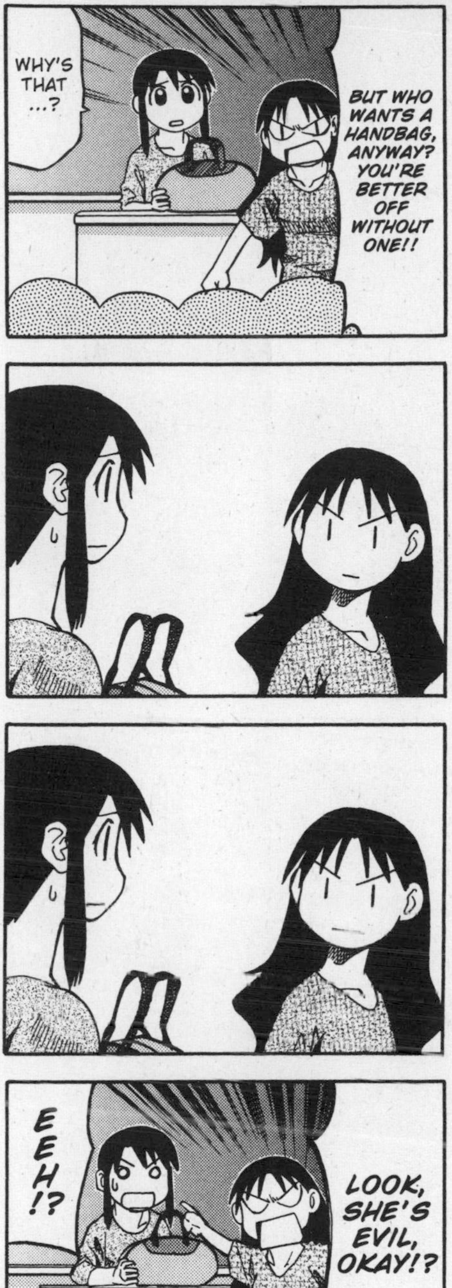
BUT WHO WANTS A HANDBAG, ANYWAY? YOU'RE BETTER OFF WITHOUT ONE!!
WHY'S THAT ...?
LOOK, SHE'S EVIL, OKAY!?
EEH!?

WE'RE SORRY, SENSEI

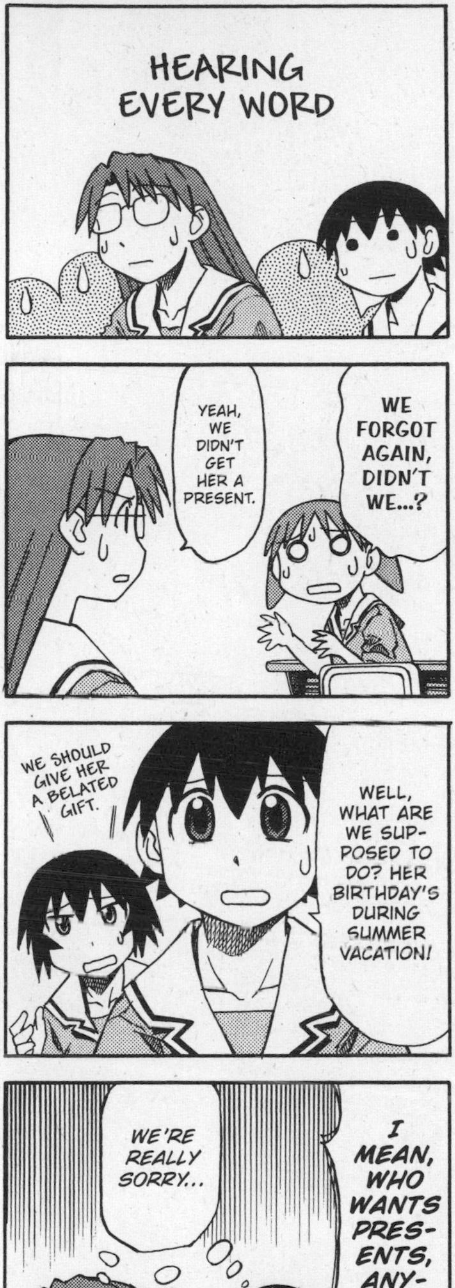
HEARING EVERY WORD
WE FORGOT AGAIN, DIDN'T WE...?
YEAH, WE DIDN'T GET HER A PRESENT.
WELL, WHAT ARE WE SUP-POSED TO DO? HER BIRTHDAY'S DURING SUMMER VACATION!
WE SHOULD GIVE HER A BELATED GIFT.
I MEAN, WHO WANTS PRES-ENTS, ANY-WAY!? NOT ME!!
WE'RE REALLY SORRY...

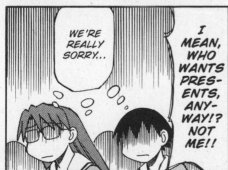

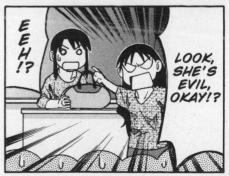

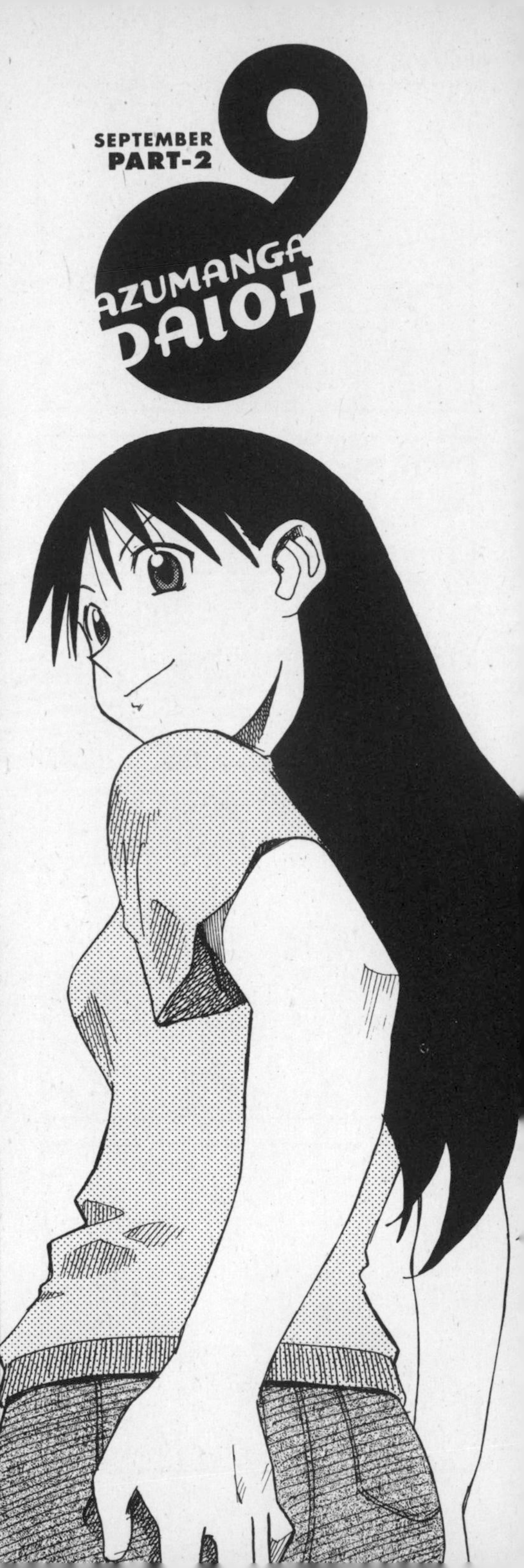
SEPTEMBER
PART-2
AZUMANGA DAIOH

MAKING UP FOR LOST TIME

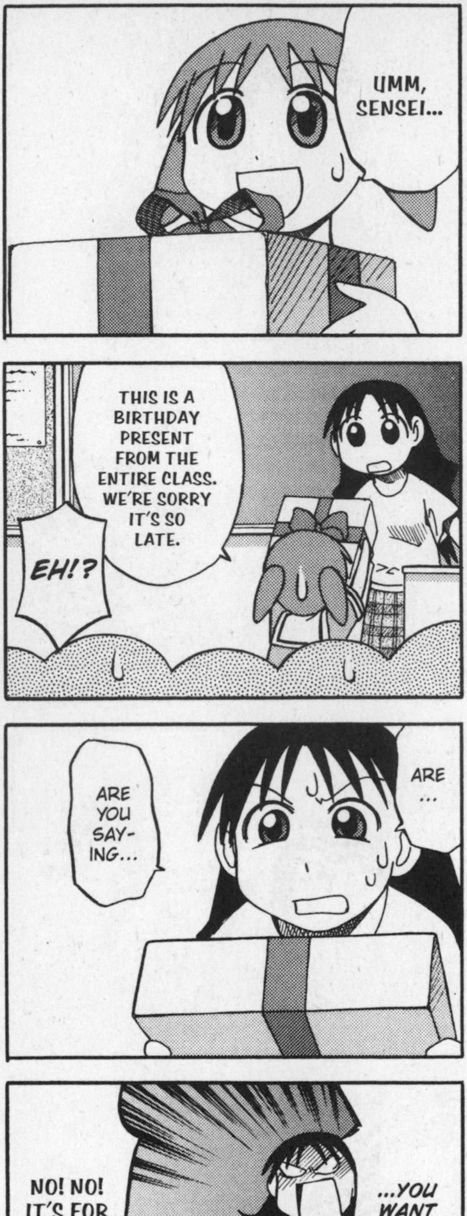
UMM, SENSEI...
THIS IS A BIRTHDAY PRESENT FROM THE ENTIRE CLASS. WE'RE SORRY IT'S SO LATE.
EH!?
ARE ...
ARE YOU SAY-ING...
...YOU WANT ME TO GO AND DELIVER THIS TO NYAMO!?
NO! NO! IT'S FOR YOU! REALLY!

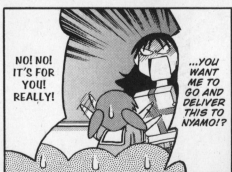

YUKARI'S BIRTHDAY

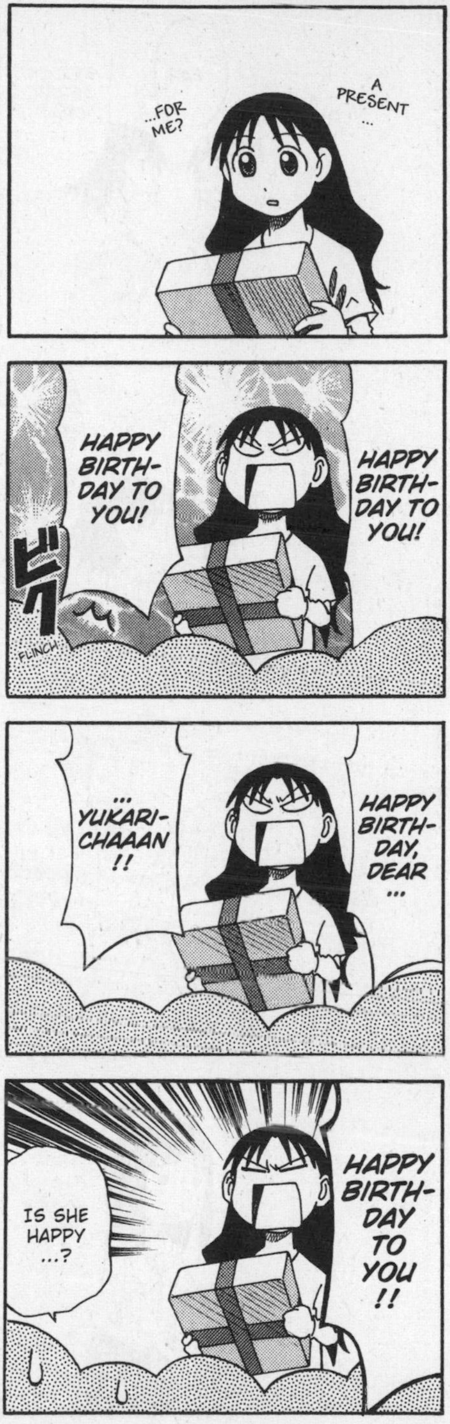
A PRESENT ...
...FOR ME?
HAPPY BIRTHDAY TO YOU!
HAPPY BIRTHDAY TO YOU!
FLINCH
HAPPY BIRTHDAY, DEAR ...
... YUKARI-CHAAAN !!
HAPPY BIRTHDAY TO YOU !!
IS SHE HAPPY ...?

CONSIDERATION

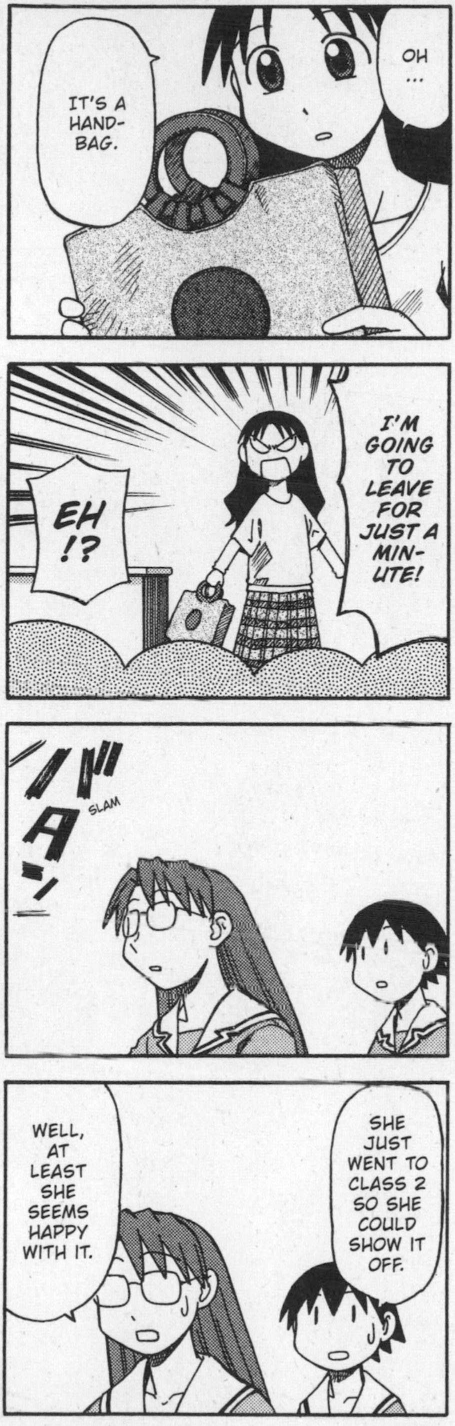
OH ...
IT'S A HANDBAG.
I'M GOING TO LEAVE FOR JUST A MINUTE!
EH !?
SLAM
SHE JUST WENT TO CLASS 2 SO SHE COULD SHOW IT OFF.
WELL, AT LEAST SHE SEEMS HAPPY WITH IT.

CHIYO GOES FOR THE GLORY

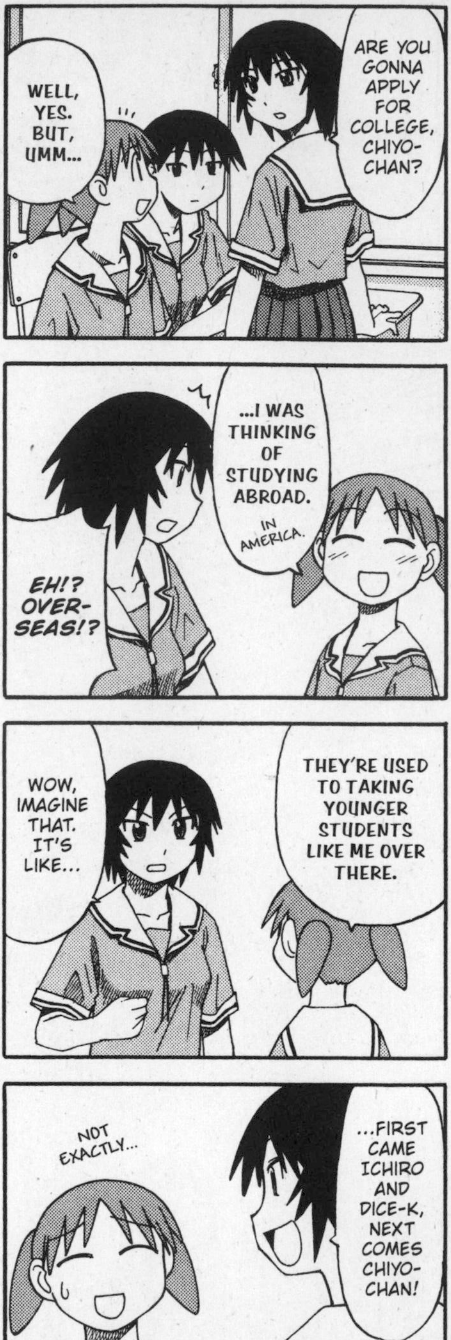
ARE YOU GONNA APPLY FOR COLLEGE, CHIYO-CHAN?
WELL, YES. BUT, UMM...
...I WAS THINKING OF STUDYING ABROAD.
IN AMERICA.
EH!? OVERSEAS!?
THEY'RE USED TO TAKING YOUNGER STUDENTS LIKE ME OVER THERE.
WOW, IMAGINE THAT. IT'S LIKE...
...FIRST CAME ICHIRO AND DICE-K, NEXT COMES CHIYO-CHAN!
NOT EXACTLY...

WORRIED

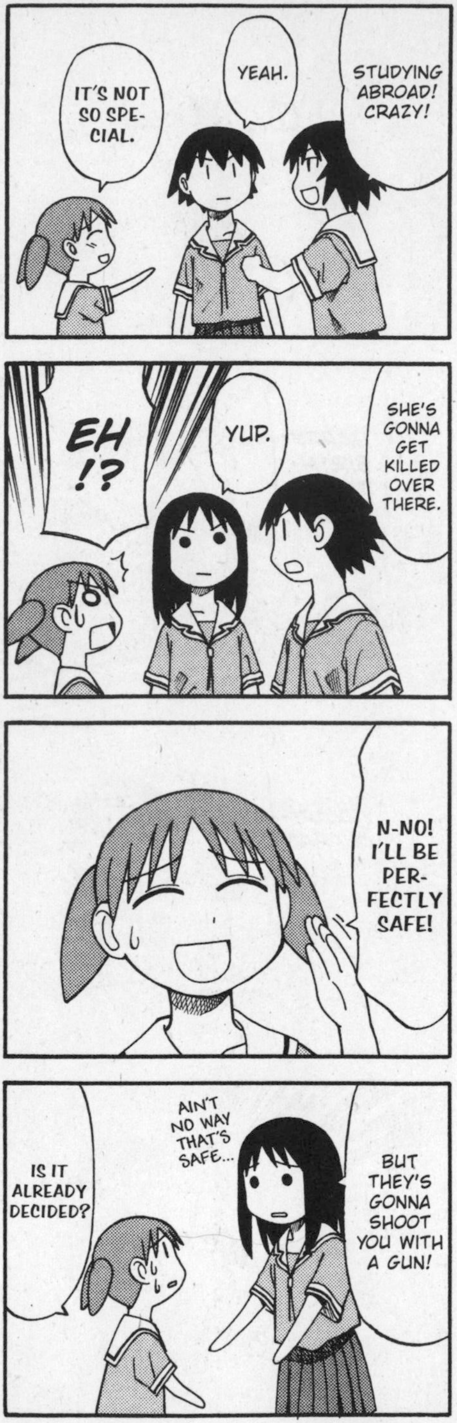
STUDYING ABROAD! CRAZY!
YEAH.
IT'S NOT SO SPE-CIAL.
SHE'S GONNA GET KILLED OVER THERE.
YUP.
EH !?
N-NO! I'LL BE PER-FECTLY SAFE!
BUT THEY'S GONNA SHOOT YOU WITH A GUN!
AIN'T NO WAY THAT'S SAFE...
IS IT ALREADY DECIDED?

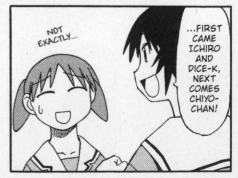

VERY WORRIED

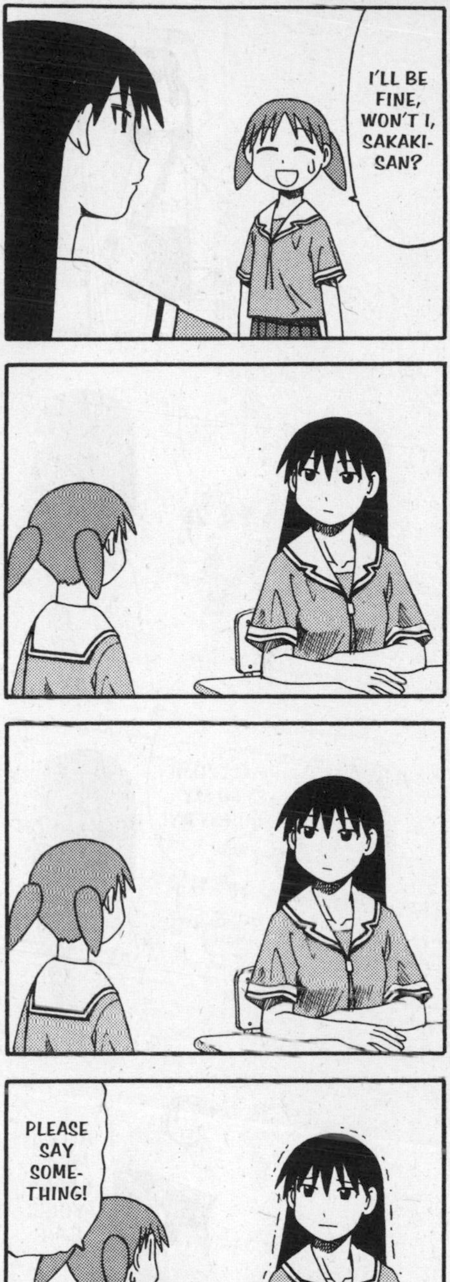
I'LL BE FINE, WON'T I, SAKAKI-SAN?
PLEASE SAY SOME-THING!

YOU PASS

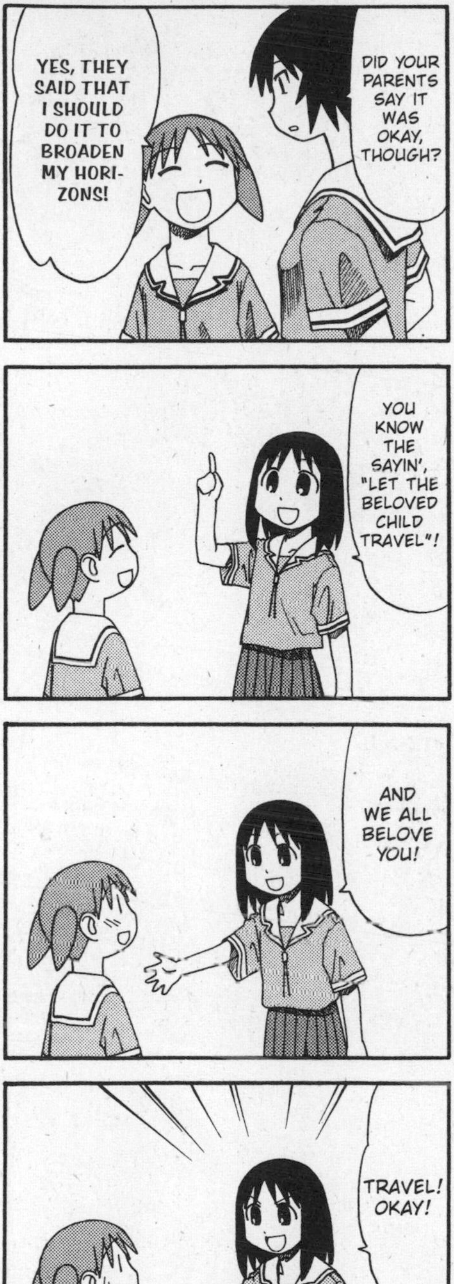
DID YOUR PARENTS SAY IT WAS OKAY, THOUGH?
YES, THEY SAID THAT I SHOULD DO IT TO BROADEN MY HORI-ZONS!
YOU KNOW THE SAYIN', "LET THE BELOVED CHILD TRAVEL"!
AND WE ALL BELOVE YOU!
TRAVEL! OKAY!

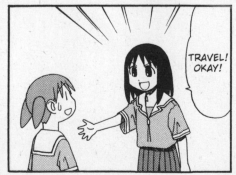

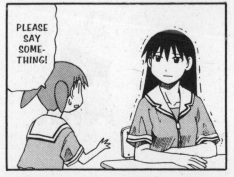

CHILD PRESIDENT

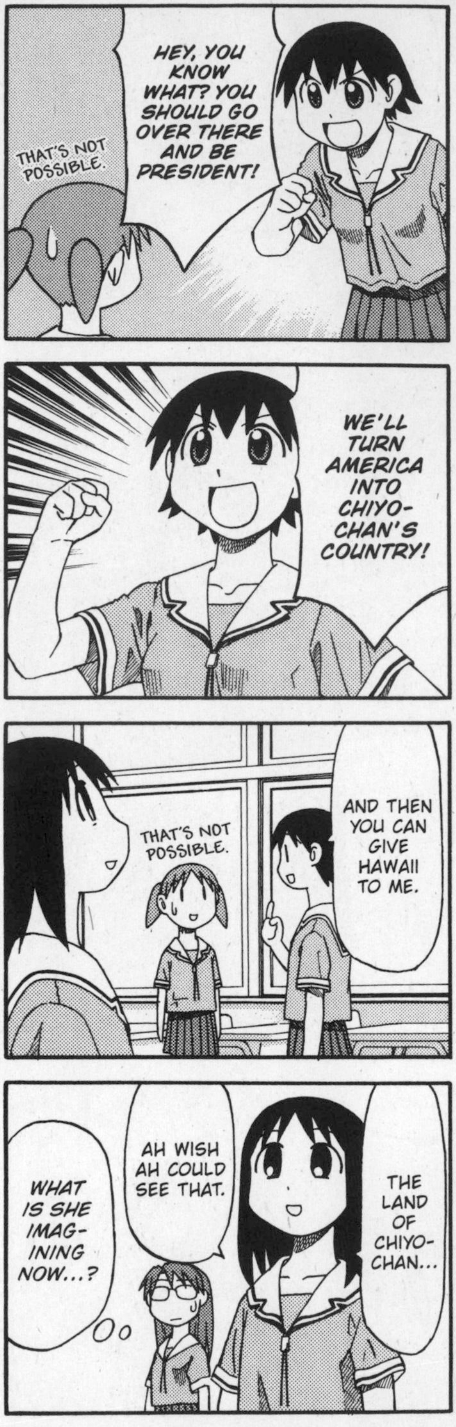
HEY, YOU KNOW WHAT? YOU SHOULD GO OVER THERE AND BE PRESIDENT!
THAT'S NOT POSSIBLE.
WE'LL TURN AMERICA INTO CHIYO-CHAN'S COUNTRY!
AND THEN YOU CAN GIVE HAWAII TO ME.
THAT'S NOT POSSIBLE.
THE LAND OF CHIYO-CHAN...
AH WISH AH COULD SEE THAT.
WHAT IS SHE IMAGINING NOW...?

THE LAND OF CHIYO-CHAN

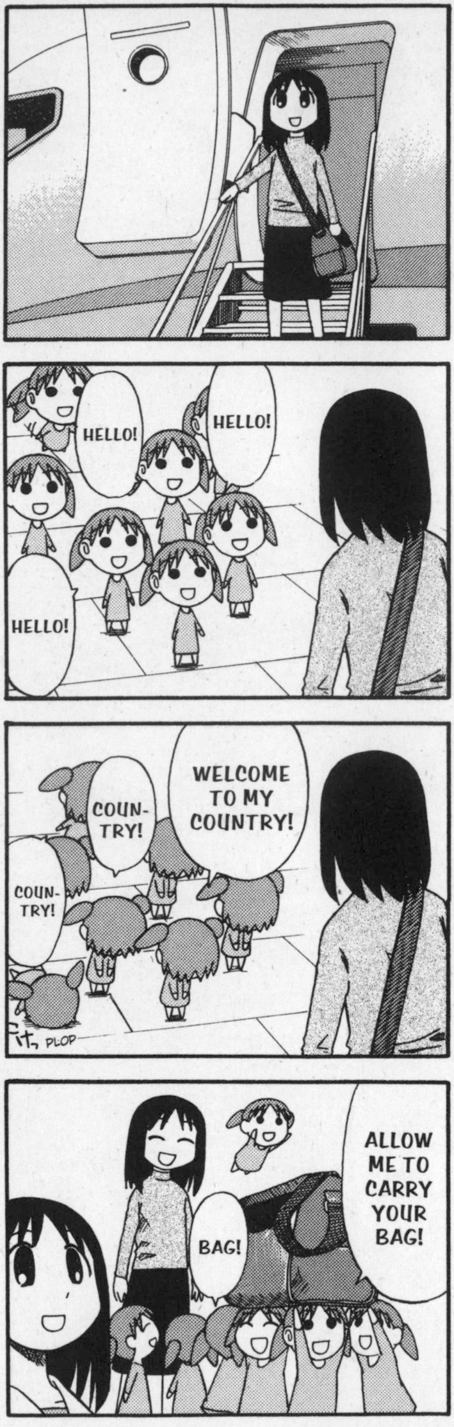
HELLO!
HELLO!
HELLO!
WELCOME TO MY COUNTRY!
COUN-TRY!
COUN-TRY!
PLOP
ALLOW ME TO CARRY YOUR BAG!
BAG!

CELEBRATING AMERICA

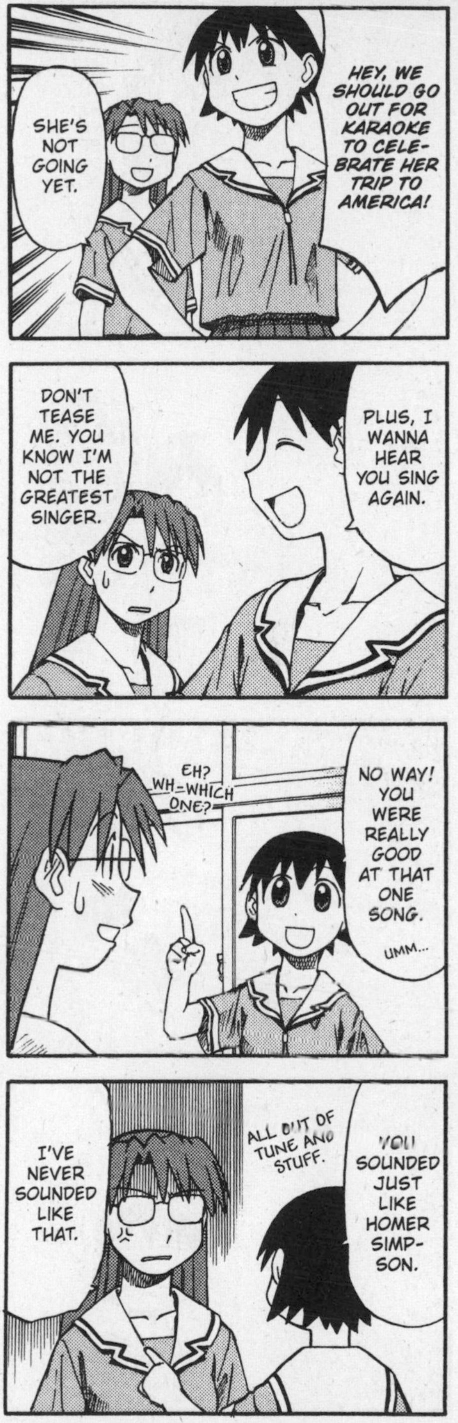
HEY, WE SHOULD GO OUT FOR KARAOKE TO CELE-BRATE HER TRIP TO AMERICA!
SHE'S NOT GOING YET.
PLUS, I WANNA HEAR YOU SING AGAIN.
DON'T TEASE ME. YOU KNOW I'M NOT THE GREATEST SINGER.
NO WAY! YOU WERE REALLY GOOD AT THAT ONE SONG.
UMM...
EH? WH-WHICH ONE?
YOU SOUNDED JUST LIKE HOMER SIMP-SON.
ALL OUT OF TUNE AND STUFF.
I'VE NEVER SOUNDED LIKE THAT.

TYPHOON SEASON

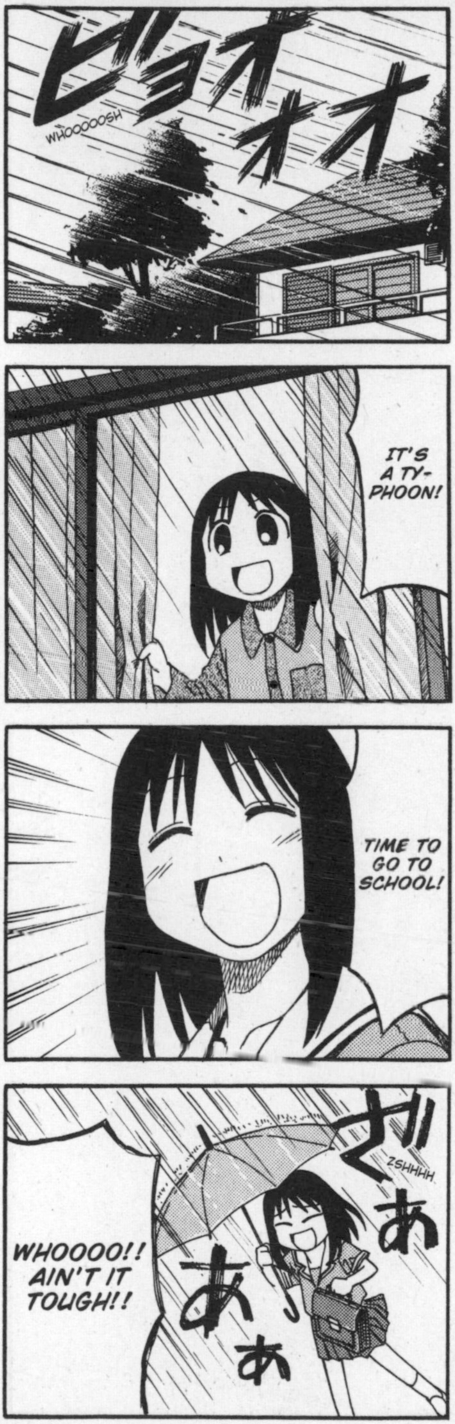
ビョオオオ
WHOOOOOSH
IT'S A TY-PHOON!
TIME TO GO TO SCHOOL!
ザ
ZSHHHH
あああ
WHOOOO!! AIN'T IT TOUGH!!

DISASTER MANAGEMENT

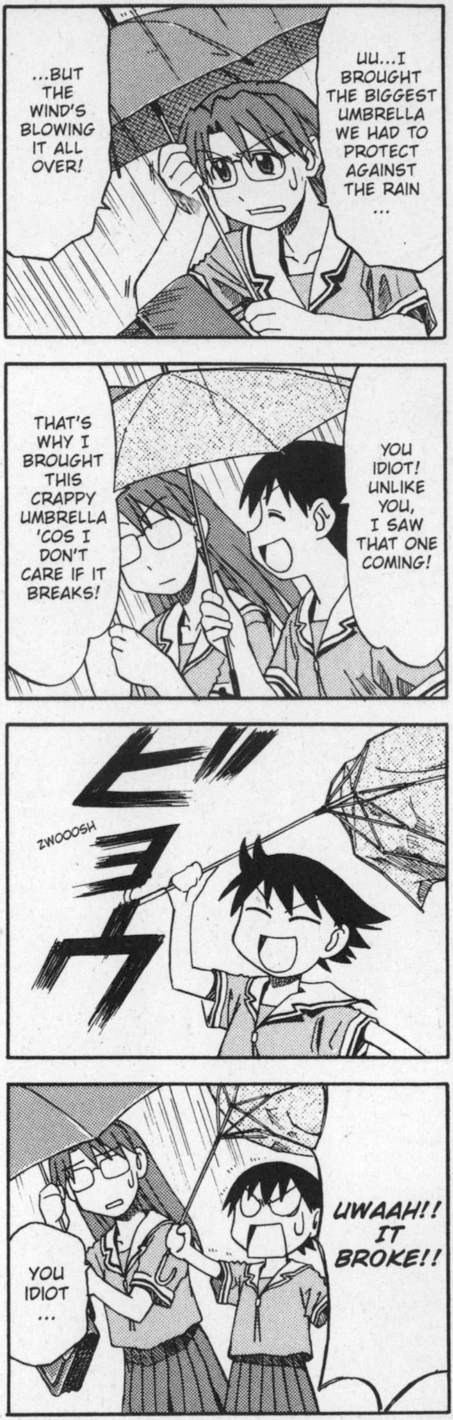
UU...I BROUGHT THE BIGGEST UMBRELLA WE HAD TO PROTECT AGAINST THE RAIN ...
...BUT THE WIND'S BLOWING IT ALL OVER!
YOU IDIOT! UNLIKE YOU, I SAW THAT ONE COMING!
THAT'S WHY I BROUGHT THIS CRAPPY UMBRELLA 'COS I DON'T CARE IF IT BREAKS!
ビュウ
ZWOOOSH
UWAAH!! IT BROKE!!
YOU IDIOT ...

SOAKING WET

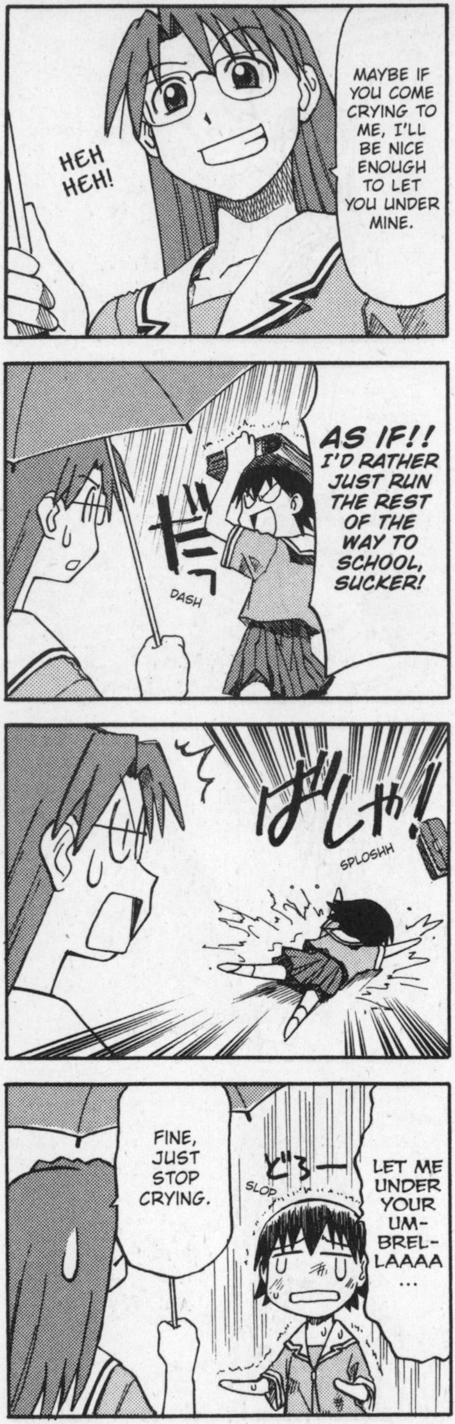
MAYBE IF YOU COME CRYING TO ME, I'LL BE NICE ENOUGH TO LET YOU UNDER MINE.
HEH HEH!
AS IF!! I'D RATHER JUST RUN THE REST OF THE WAY TO SCHOOL, SUCKER!
ダッ
DASH
ばしゃ!
SPLOSHH
LET ME UNDER YOUR UM-BREL-LAAAA ...
どろー
SLOP
FINE, JUST STOP CRYING.

SHARING

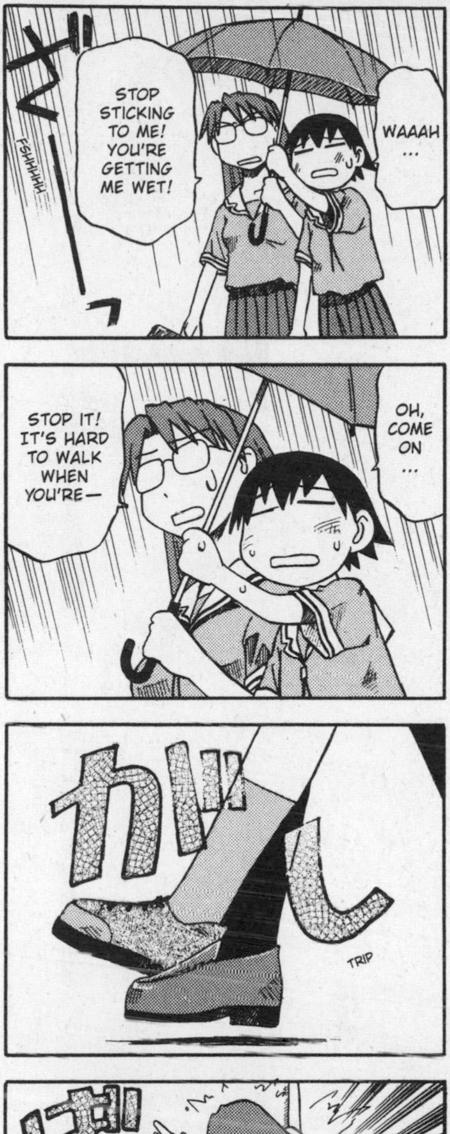
WAAAH ...
STOP STICKING TO ME! YOU'RE GETTING ME WET!
FSHHHHHH
OH, COME ON ...
STOP IT! IT'S HARD TO WALK WHEN YOU'RE—
TRIP
SPLAT

TYPHOON

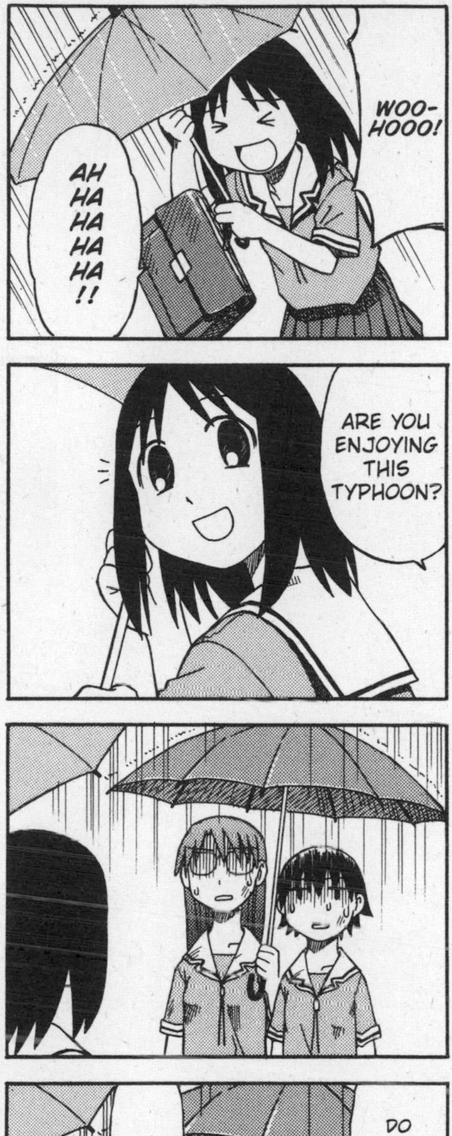
WOO-HOOO!
AH HA HA HA HA!!
ARE YOU ENJOYING THIS TYPHOON?
DO YOU FIND THIS EXPERIENCE TO BE FUN?
AH'M SORRY...

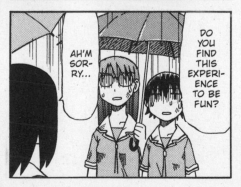

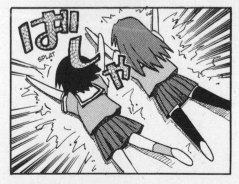

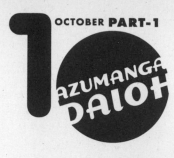

10 OCTOBER PART-1

AZUMANGA DAIOH

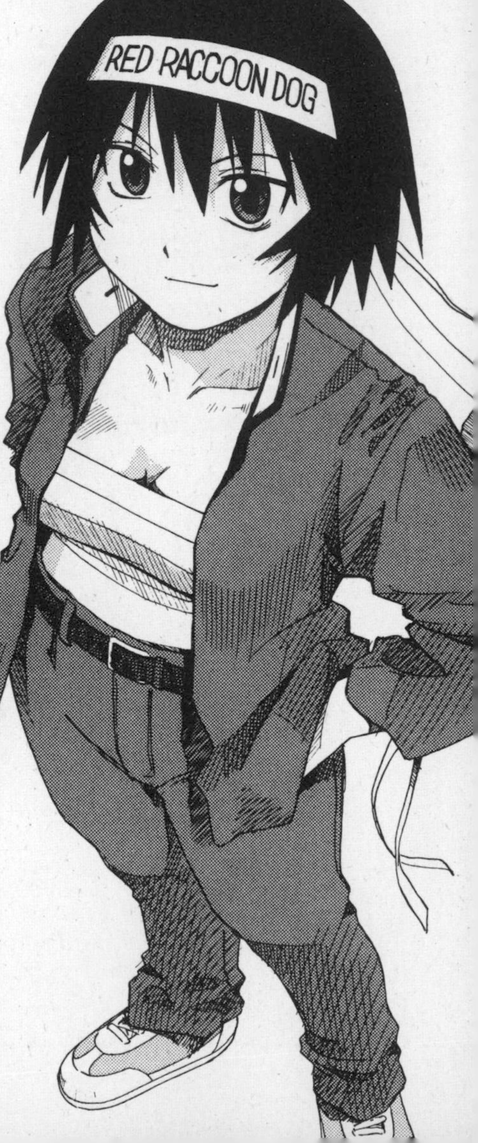
RED RACCOON DOG

TONGUE TRIPPED

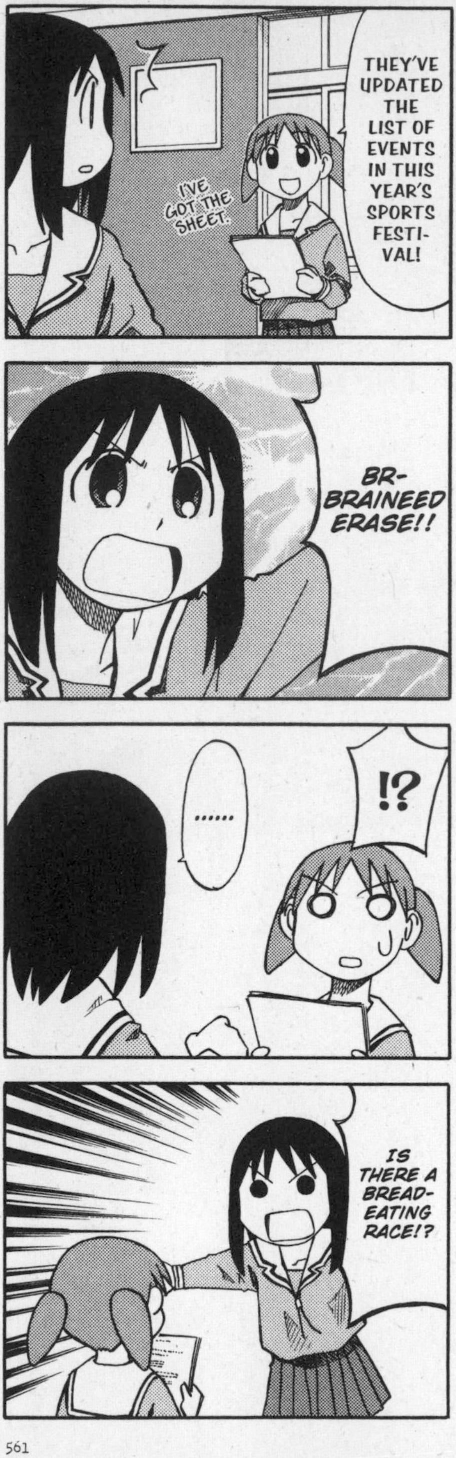
THEY'VE UPDATED THE LIST OF EVENTS IN THIS YEAR'S SPORTS FESTI-VAL!
I'VE GOT THE SHEET.
BR-BRAINEED ERASE!!
!?
......
IS THERE A BREAD-EATING RACE!?

I.Q. TEST

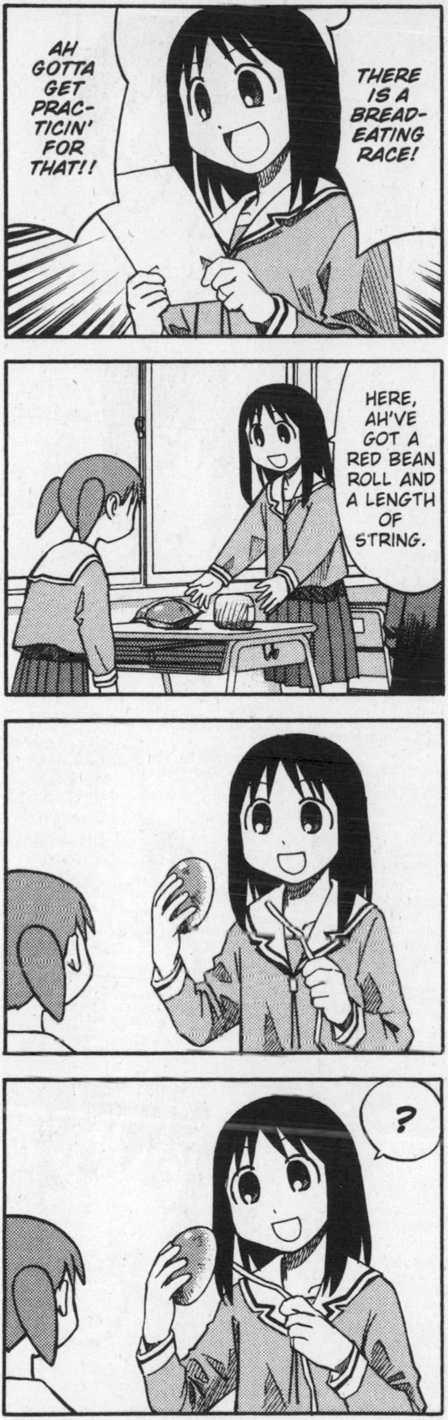
THERE IS A BREAD-EATING RACE!
AH GOTTA GET PRAC-TICIN' FOR THAT!!
HERE, AH'VE GOT A RED BEAN ROLL AND A LENGTH OF STRING.
?

OUCH, OUCH

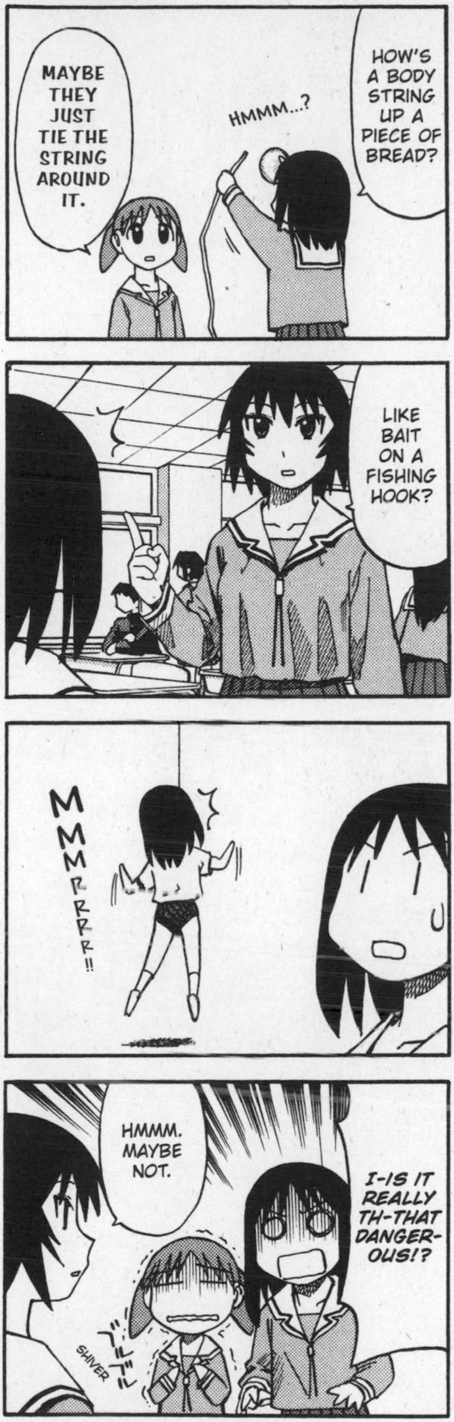
HOW'S A BODY STRING UP A PIECE OF BREAD?
HMMM...?
MAYBE THEY JUST TIE THE STRING AROUND IT.
LIKE BAIT ON A FISHING HOOK?
MMMRRRRR!!
I-IS IT REALLY TH-THAT DANGER-OUS!?
HMMM. MAYBE NOT.
SHIVER

PUSHOVER

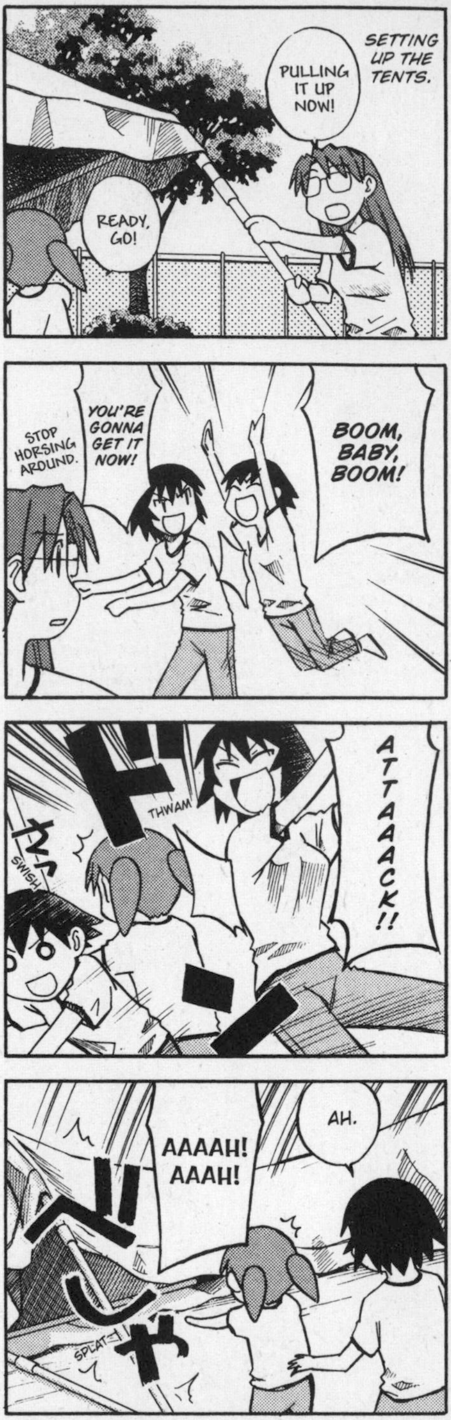
SETTING UP THE TENTS.
PULLING IT UP NOW!
READY, GO!
BOOM, BABY, BOOM!
YOU'RE GONNA GET IT NOW!
STOP HORSING AROUND.
ATTAAACK!!
THWAM
SWISH
AH.
AAAAH! AAAH!
SPLAT

WASTED EFFORT

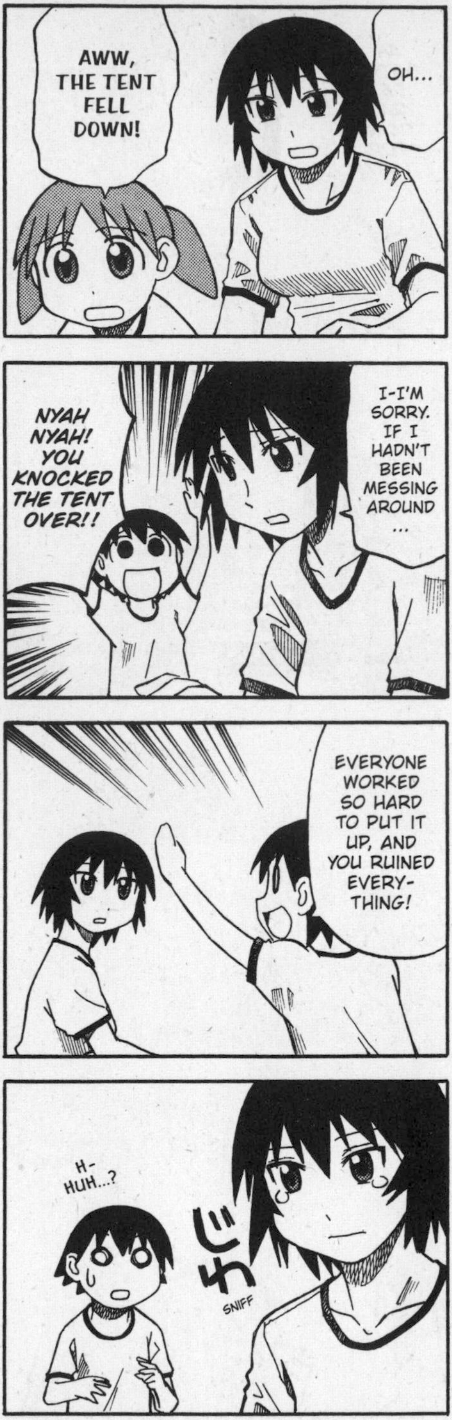
OH...
AWW, THE TENT FELL DOWN!
I-I'M SORRY. IF I HADN'T BEEN MESSING AROUND ...
NYAH NYAH! YOU KNOCKED THE TENT OVER!!
EVERYONE WORKED SO HARD TO PUT IT UP, AND YOU RUINED EVERYTHING!
じわ
SNIFF
H-HUH...?

RESPONSIBILITY

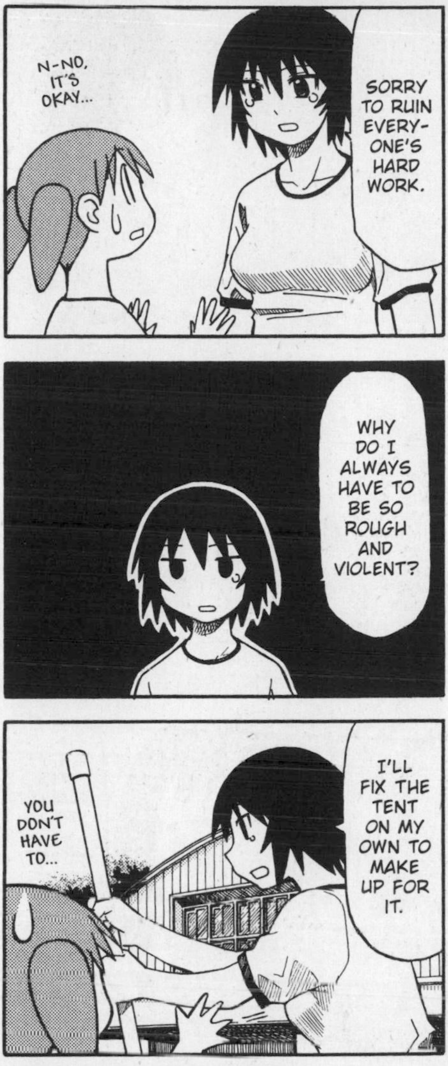
SORRY TO RUIN EVERY-ONE'S HARD WORK.
N-NO, IT'S OKAY...
WHY DO I ALWAYS HAVE TO BE SO ROUGH AND VIOLENT?
I'LL FIX THE TENT ON MY OWN TO MAKE UP FOR IT.
YOU DON'T HAVE TO...
WH-WHAT ARE YOU DOING!? YOU'RE SUPPOSED TO GO, "IT'S TOMO'S FAULT"!!
DON'T GET ALL RESPON-SIBLE! YOU'RE MAKING ME LOOK BAD!!

MOOD-MAKER

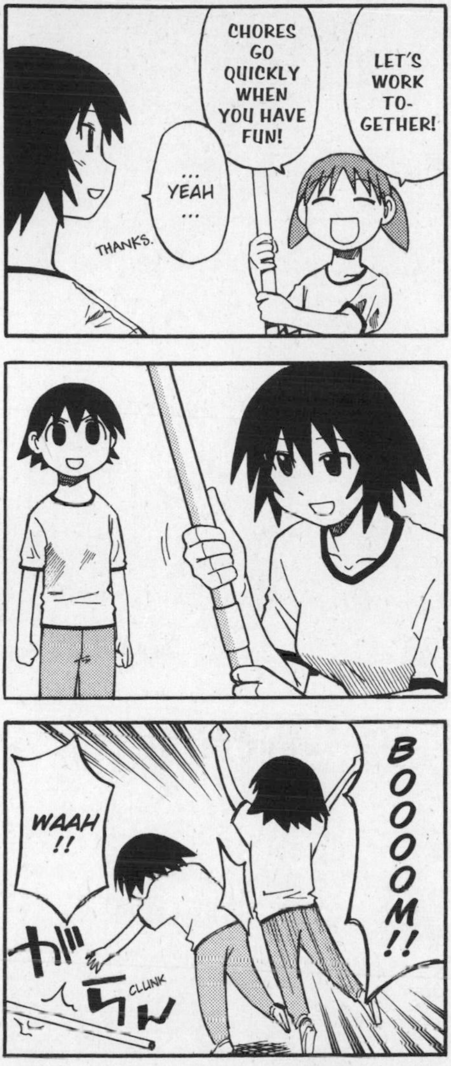
LET'S WORK TO-GETHER!
CHORES GO QUICKLY WHEN YOU HAVE FUN!
... YEAH ...
THANKS.
BOOOOOM!!
WAAH!!
がらん
CLUNK
WHAT THE HELL WAS THAT FOR!?
NOW THAT'S MORE LIKE IT!
NO, IT'S NOT...STOP BOTHERING US!

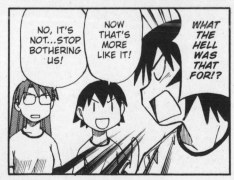

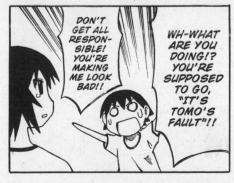

PACING YOURSELF

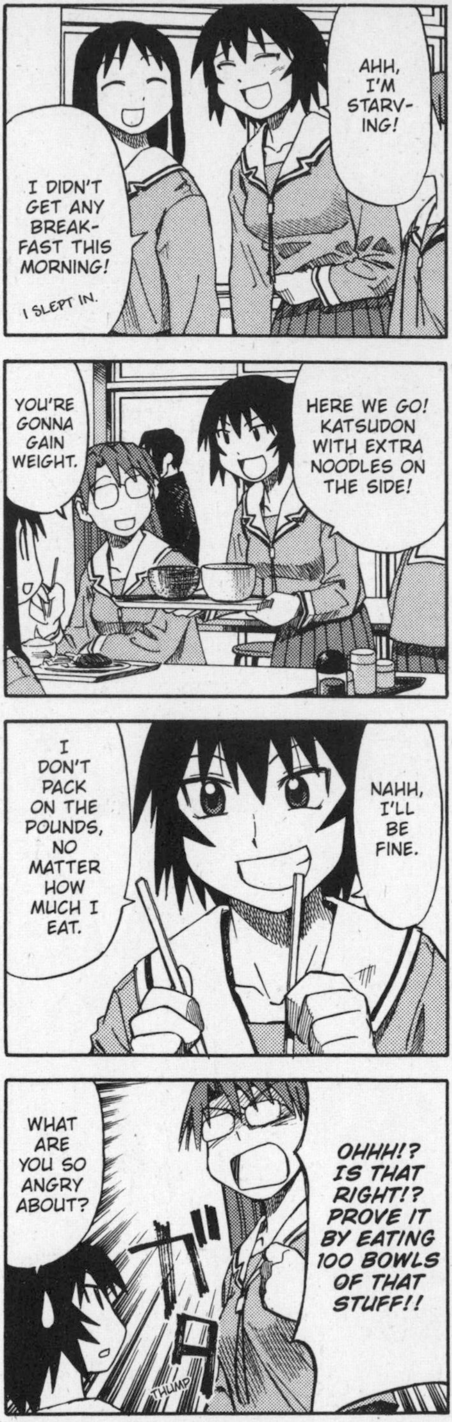
AHH, I'M STARVING!
I DIDN'T GET ANY BREAKFAST THIS MORNING!
I SLEPT IN.
HERE WE GO! KATSUDON WITH EXTRA NOODLES ON THE SIDE!
YOU'RE GONNA GAIN WEIGHT.
NAHH, I'LL BE FINE.
I DON'T PACK ON THE POUNDS, NO MATTER HOW MUCH I EAT.
OHHH!? IS THAT RIGHT!? PROVE IT BY EATING 100 BOWLS OF THAT STUFF!!
WHAT ARE YOU SO ANGRY ABOUT?
THUMP

LOW-CALORIE HAPPINESS

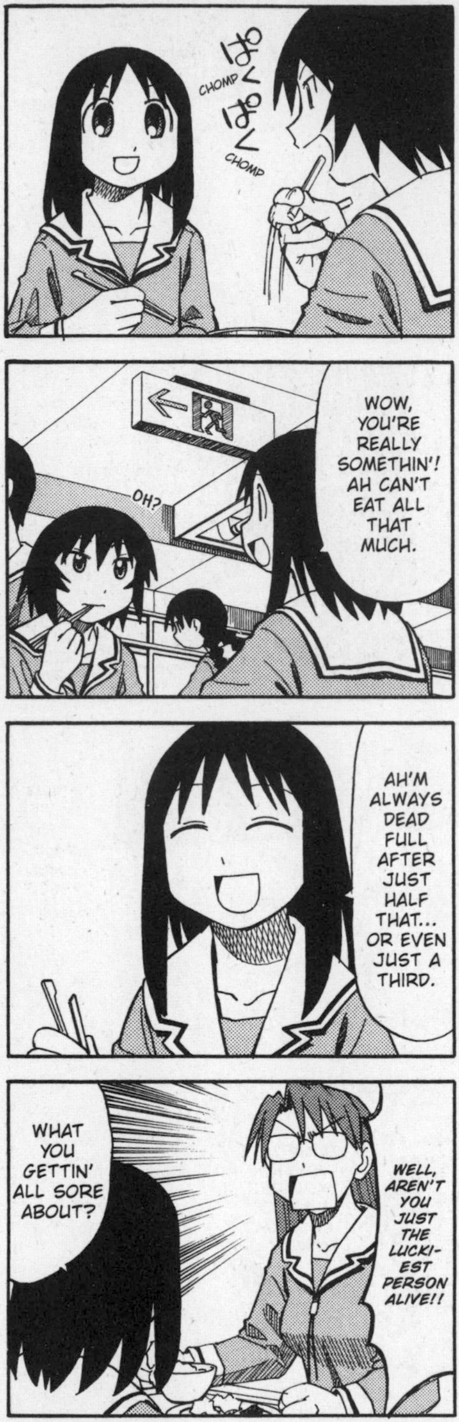
ぱくぱく
CHOMP
CHOMP
WOW, YOU'RE REALLY SOMETHIN'! AH CAN'T EAT ALL THAT MUCH.
OH?
AH'M ALWAYS DEAD FULL AFTER JUST HALF THAT... OR EVEN JUST A THIRD.
WELL, AREN'T YOU JUST THE LUCKIEST PERSON ALIVE!!
WHAT YOU GETTIN' ALL SORE ABOUT?

PRESIDENT OF THE GYM SHORTS COALITION

THE SPORTS FESTI-VAL.
LET'S DO THIS!
YEAAAH!
WHY ARE WE STILL WEARING THESE SKIMPY GYM SHORTS AT THIS AGE?
HMMM...
!
LONG LIVE GYM SHORTS !!
BAN-ZAI!! BAN-ZAI!!

CONFESSION

I LIKE ...
... THOSE SHORTS ...
...VERY MUCH.
<I...>
<...LIKE ...>
<... YOU.>
<YOU !?>

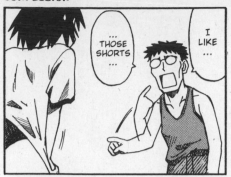

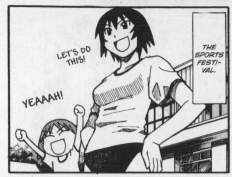

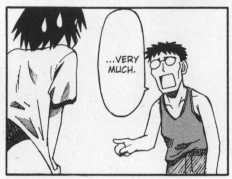

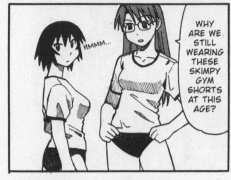

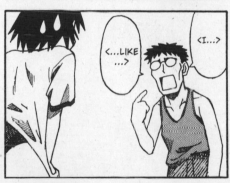

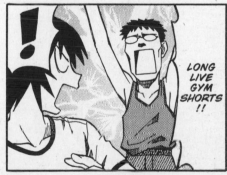

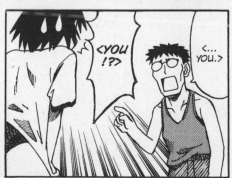

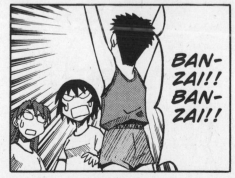

GOTCHA

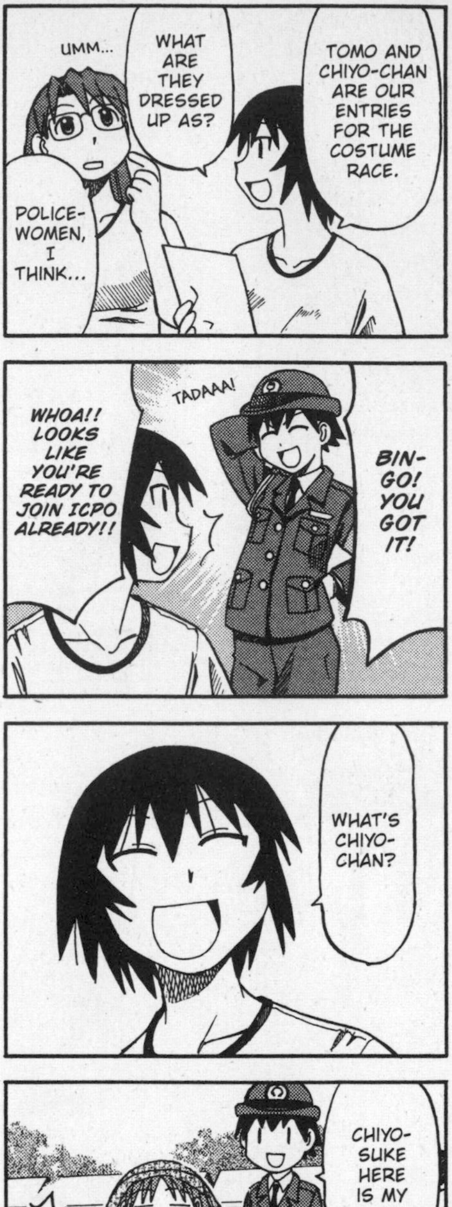
TOMO AND CHIYO-CHAN ARE OUR ENTRIES FOR THE COSTUME RACE.
WHAT ARE THEY DRESSED UP AS?
UMM...
POLICE-WOMEN, I THINK...
BIN-GO! YOU GOT IT!
TADAAA!
WHOA!! LOOKS LIKE YOU'RE READY TO JOIN ICPO ALREADY!!
WHAT'S CHIYO-CHAN?
CHIYO-SUKE HERE IS MY CULPRIT.

HAULED IN

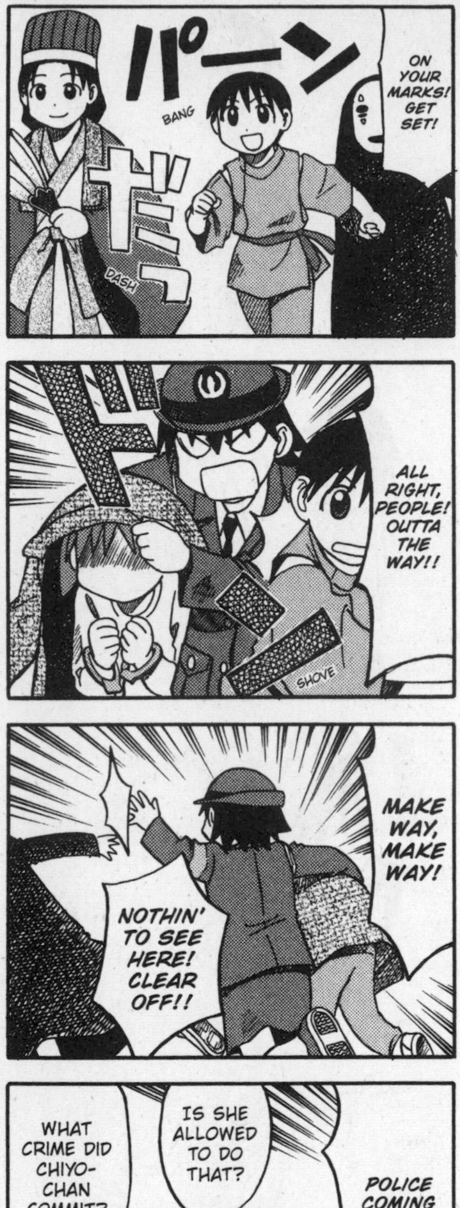
ON YOUR MARKS! GET SET!
パーン
BANG
ダッ
DASH
ALL RIGHT, PEOPLE! OUTTA THE WAY!!
SHOVE
MAKE WAY, MAKE WAY!
NOTHIN' TO SEE HERE! CLEAR OFF!!
POLICE COMING THROUGH! MOVE IT, BUSTER!!
IS SHE ALLOWED TO DO THAT?
WHAT CRIME DID CHIYO-CHAN COMMIT?

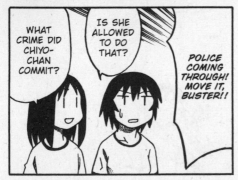

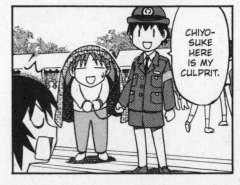

ADULT ENTERTAINMENT INDUSTRY

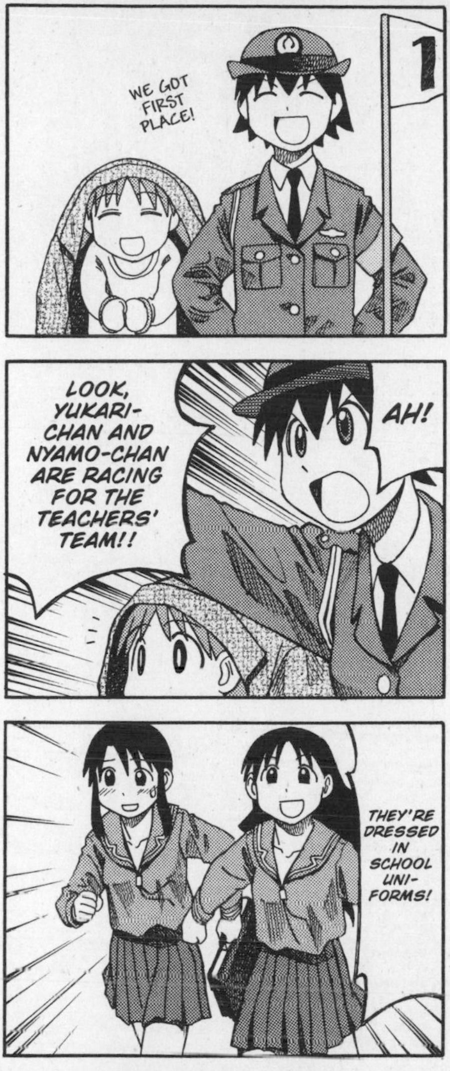
1
WE GOT FIRST PLACE!
AH!
LOOK, YUKARI-CHAN AND NYAMO-CHAN ARE RACING FOR THE TEACHERS' TEAM!!
THEY'RE DRESSED IN SCHOOL UNIFORMS!
YOU'RE UNDER ARREST FOR OPERATING WITHOUT A LICENSE!!
WHAT!?

STALKER

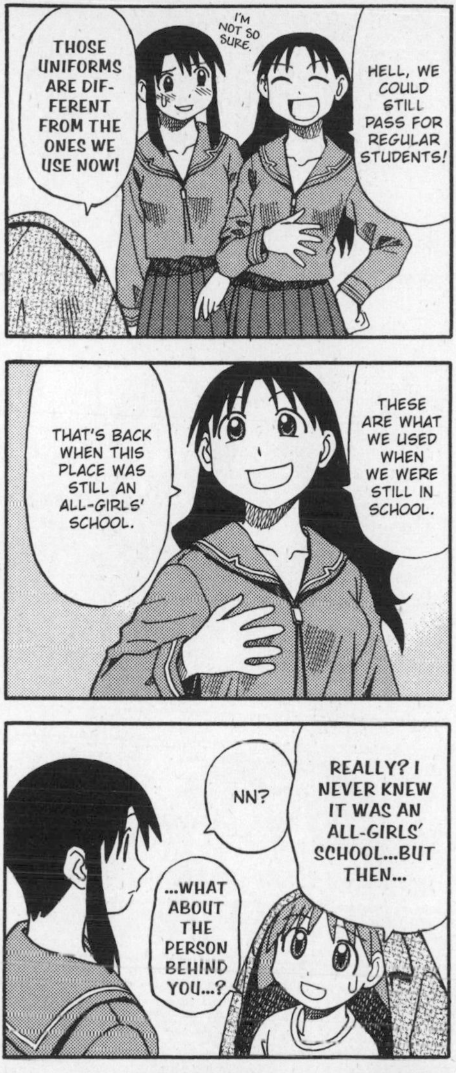
HELL, WE COULD STILL PASS FOR REGULAR STUDENTS!
I'M NOT SO SURE.
THOSE UNIFORMS ARE DIFFERENT FROM THE ONES WE USE NOW!
THESE ARE WHAT WE USED WHEN WE WERE STILL IN SCHOOL.
THAT'S BACK WHEN THIS PLACE WAS STILL AN ALL-GIRLS' SCHOOL.
REALLY? I NEVER KNEW IT WAS AN ALL-GIRLS' SCHOOL...BUT THEN...
NN?
...WHAT ABOUT THE PERSON BEHIND YOU...?
SENPAI...
READ THIS.
WAAH!! WHAT ARE YOU DOING, KIMURA-SENSEI!?
AND I'M NOT YOUR SENPAI!!

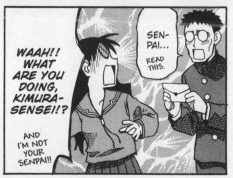

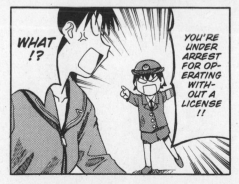

10 OCTOBER PART-2

AZUMANGA DAIOH

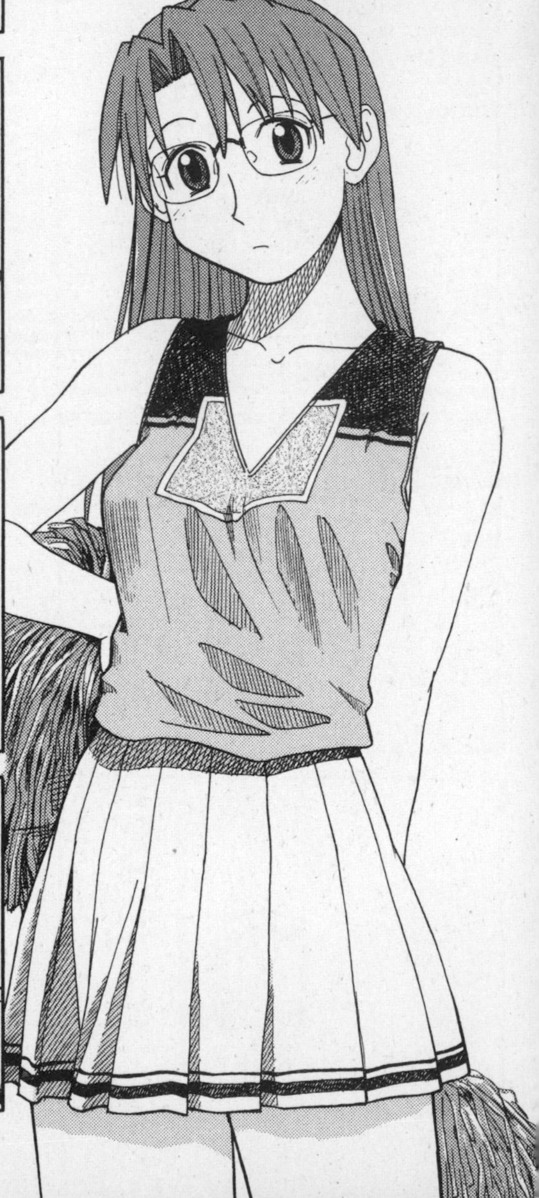

AH DIDN'T THINK OF THAT

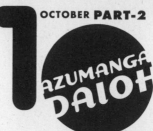

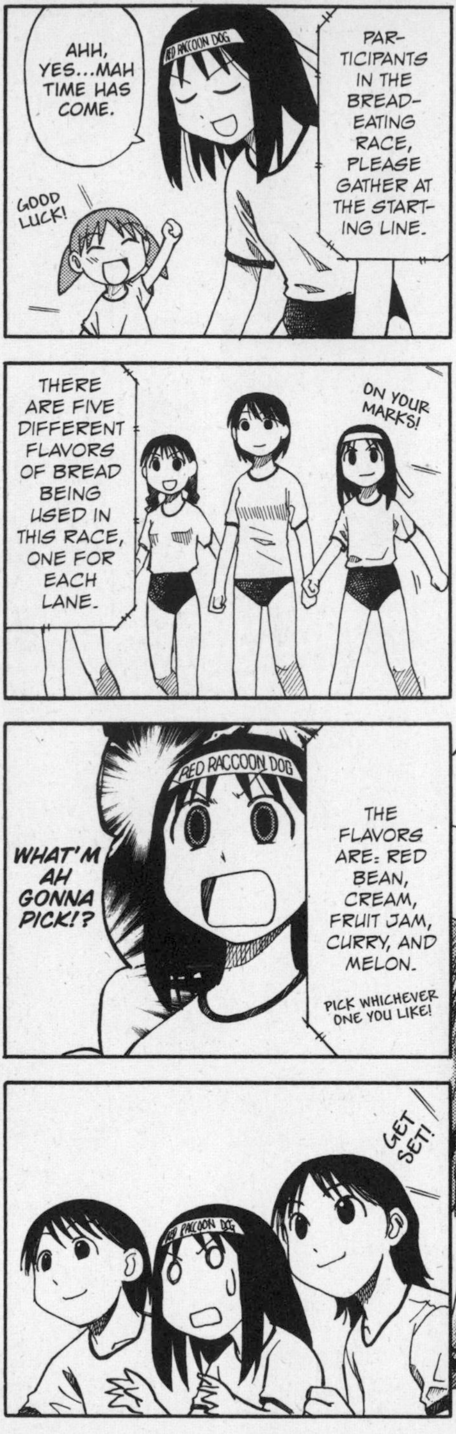
PARTICIPANTS IN THE BREAD-EATING RACE, PLEASE GATHER AT THE STARTING LINE.
RED RACCOON DOG
AHH, YES...MAH TIME HAS COME.
GOOD LUCK!
ON YOUR MARKS!
THERE ARE FIVE DIFFERENT FLAVORS OF BREAD BEING USED IN THIS RACE, ONE FOR EACH LANE.
THE FLAVORS ARE: RED BEAN, CREAM, FRUIT JAM, CURRY, AND MELON.
PICK WHICHEVER ONE YOU LIKE!
RED RACCOON DOG
WHAT'M AH GONNA PICK!?
GET SET!
RED RACCOON DOG

UMMM

DASH
BANG

MELON BREAD

I CAME IN LAST.

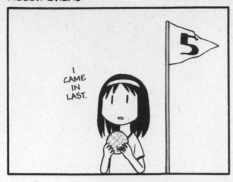

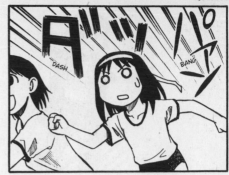

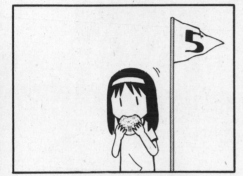

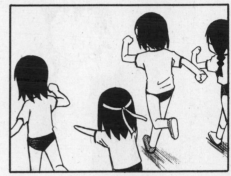

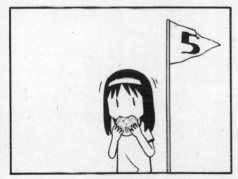

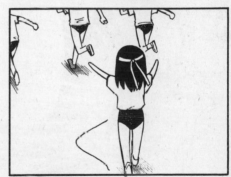

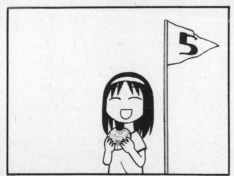

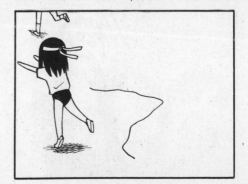

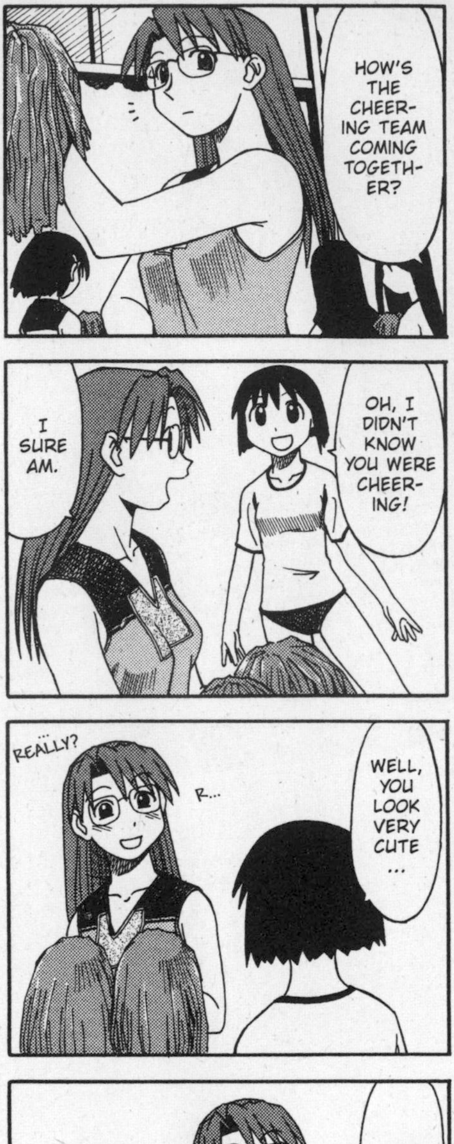
HOW'S THE CHEERING TEAM COMING TOGETHER?
OH, I DIDN'T KNOW YOU WERE CHEERING!
I SURE AM.
WELL, YOU LOOK VERY CUTE ...
R...
... REALLY?
... CHIYO-CHAN.
SHAKE
SHAKE

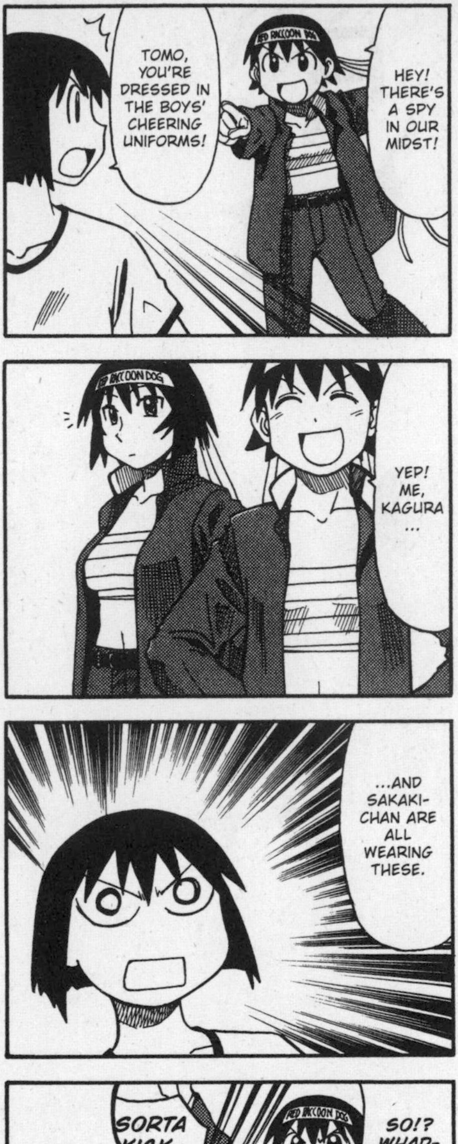
RED RACCOON DOG
HEY! THERE'S A SPY IN OUR MIDST!
TOMO, YOU'RE DRESSED IN THE BOYS' CHEERING UNIFORMS!
RED RACCOON DOG
YEP! ME, KAGURA ...
...AND SAKAKI-CHAN ARE ALL WEARING THESE.
RED RACCOON DOG
SO!? WHADDAYA THINK !?
SORTA KICK-ASS, HUH !?
WHERE IS SHE !?

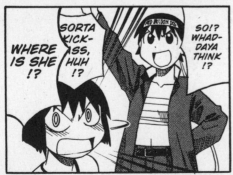

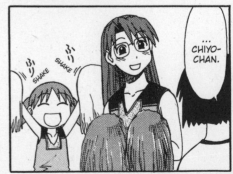

FLAG BEARER

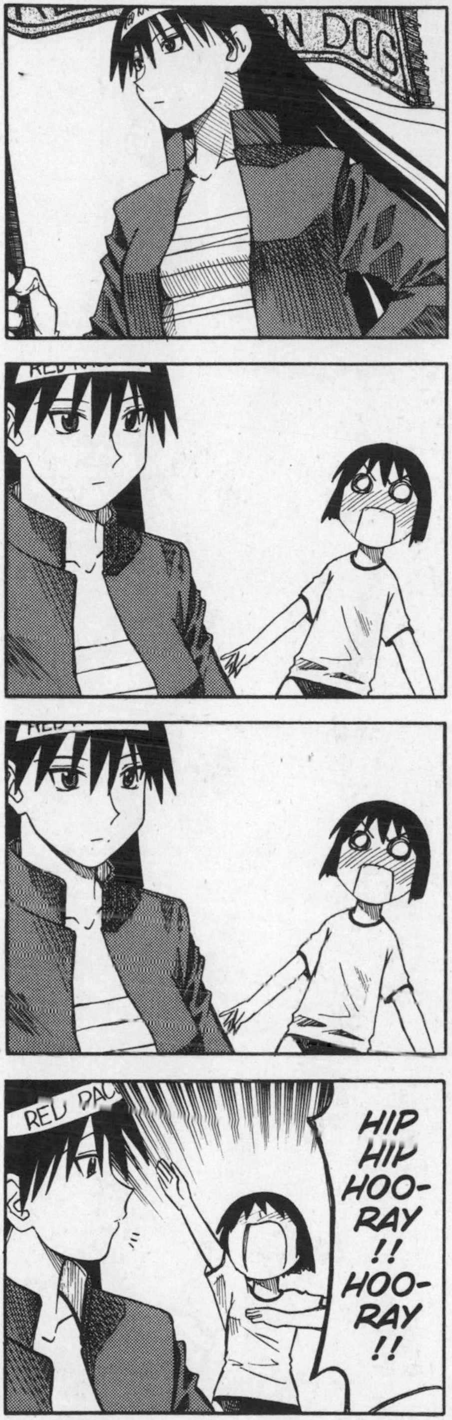
HIP HIP HOO-RAY!! HOO-RAY!!

WE ALL RUN TOGETHER

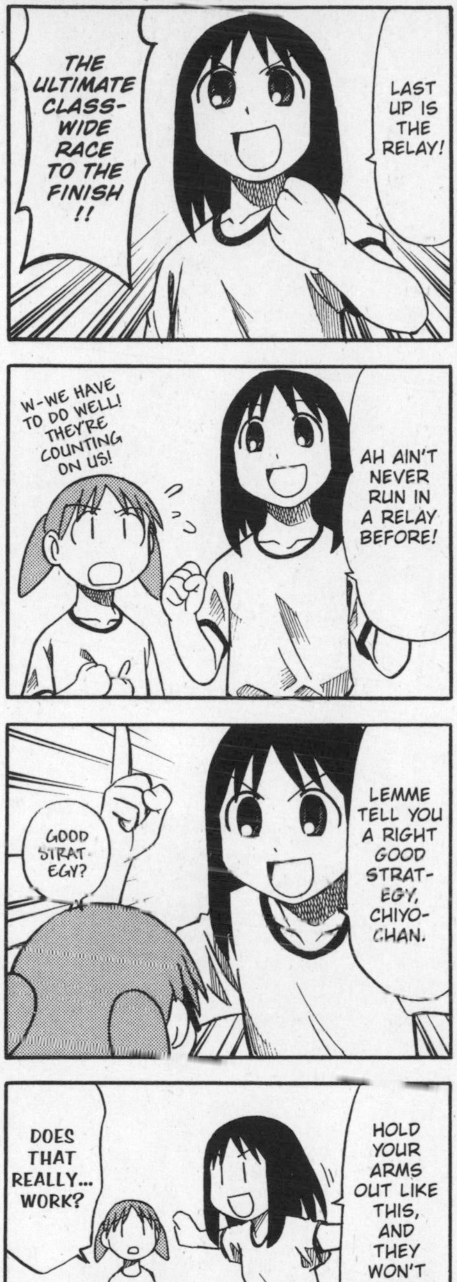
LAST UP IS THE RELAY!
THE ULTIMATE CLASS-WIDE RACE TO THE FINISH!!
AH AIN'T NEVER RUN IN A RELAY BEFORE!
W-WE HAVE TO DO WELL! THEY'RE COUNTING ON US!
LEMME TELL YOU A RIGHT GOOD STRAT-EGY, CHIYO-CHAN.
GOOD STRAT-EGY?
HOLD YOUR ARMS OUT LIKE THIS, AND THEY WON'T BE ABLE TO PASS YOU SO EASILY!
DOES THAT REALLY... WORK?
TEK
TEK
TEK

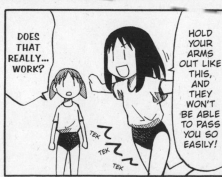

RUN SERIOUSLY

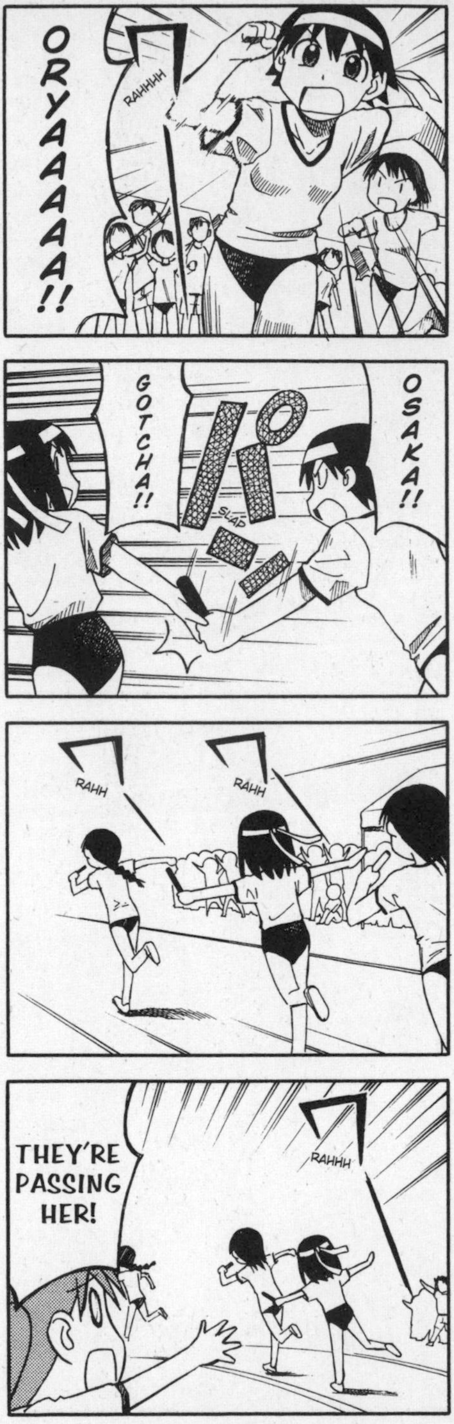
ORYAAAAAA!!
RAHHHH
OSAKA!!
GOTCHA!!
SLAP
RAHH
RAHH
RAHHH
THEY'RE PASSING HER!

GOTTA GO FASTER

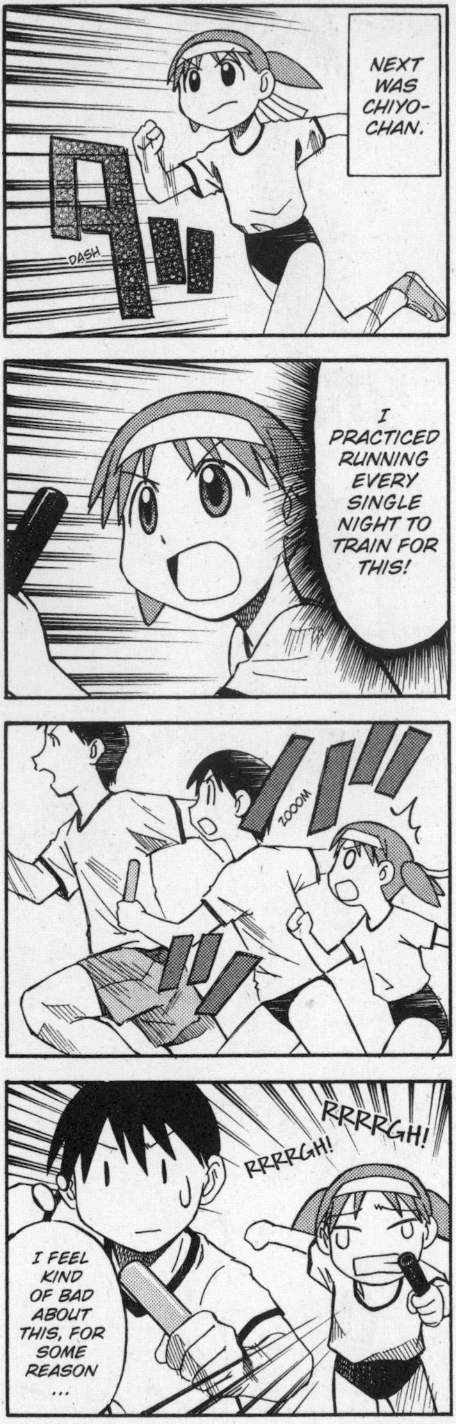
NEXT WAS CHIYO-CHAN.
DASH
I PRACTICED RUNNING EVERY SINGLE NIGHT TO TRAIN FOR THIS!
ZOOOM
RRRRGH!
RRRRGH!
I FEEL KIND OF BAD ABOUT THIS, FOR SOME REASON ...

JUST YOU WAIT

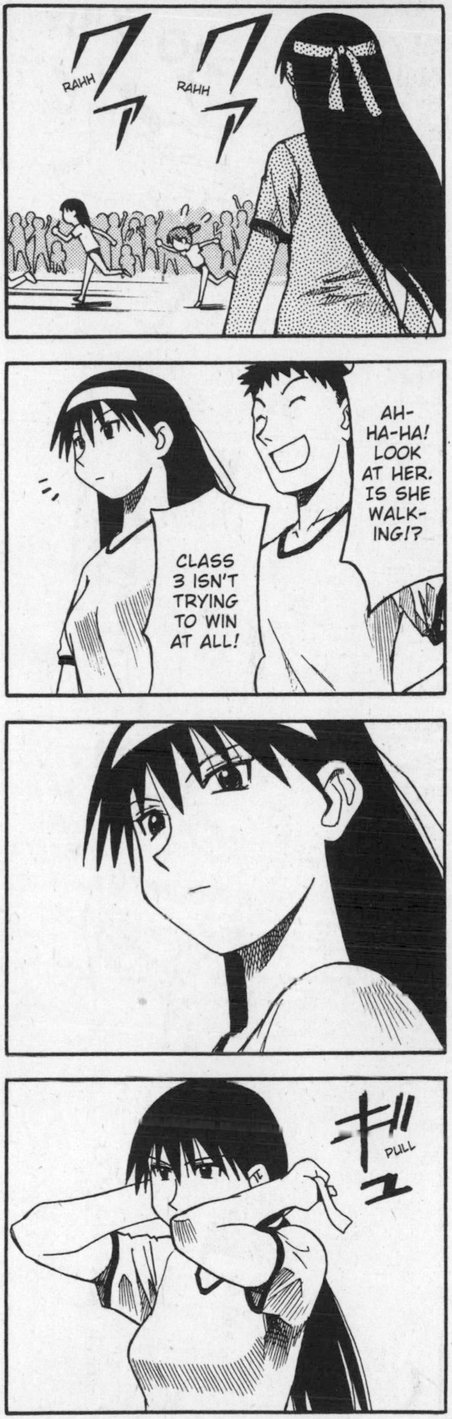
RAHH
RAHH
AH-HA-HA! LOOK AT HER. IS SHE WALKING!?
CLASS 3 ISN'T TRYING TO WIN AT ALL!
PULL

TRUST ME

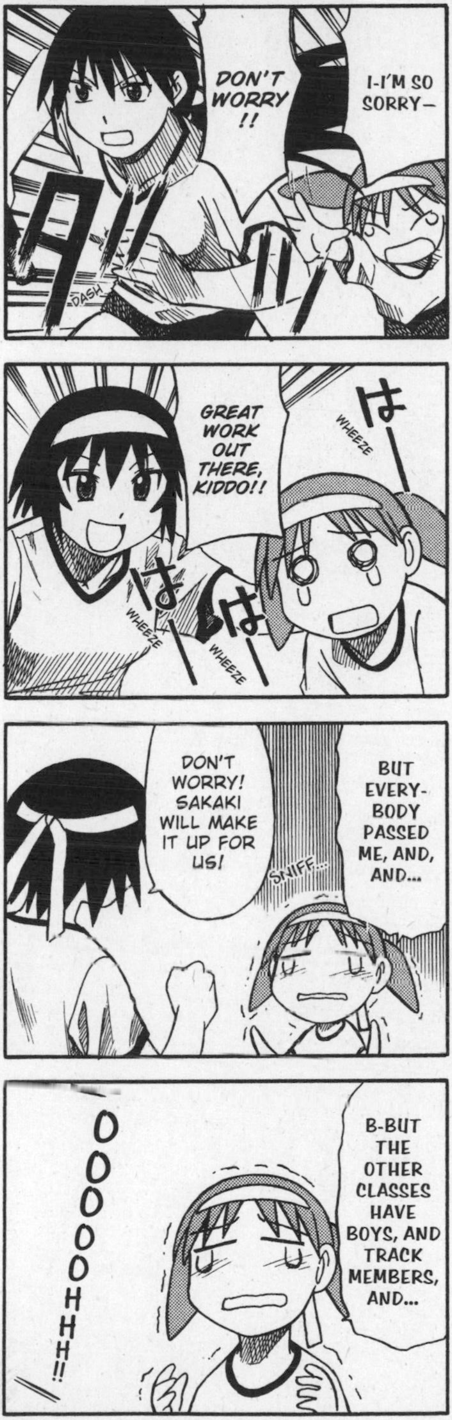
I-I'M SO SORRY—
DON'T WORRY!!
DASH
WHEEZE
GREAT WORK OUT THERE, KIDDO!!
WHEEZE
WHEEZE
BUT EVERY-BODY PASSED ME, AND, AND...
SNIFF...
DON'T WORRY! SAKAKI WILL MAKE IT UP FOR US!
B-BUT THE OTHER CLASSES HAVE BOYS, AND TRACK MEMBERS, AND...
OOOOOOHHH!!

TAKING CHARGE

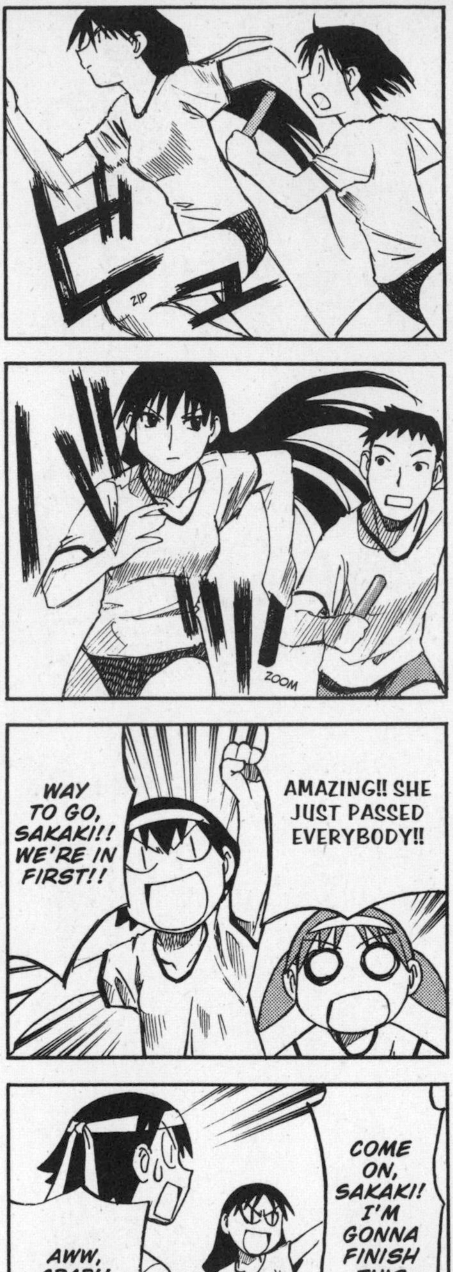
ZIP
ZOOM
AMAZING!! SHE JUST PASSED EVERYBODY!!
WAY TO GO, SAKAKI!! WE'RE IN FIRST!!
COME ON, SAKAKI! I'M GONNA FINISH THIS RACE!
AWW, CRAP!! OUR ANCHOR IS THE TEACHER!!

SHOWDOWN

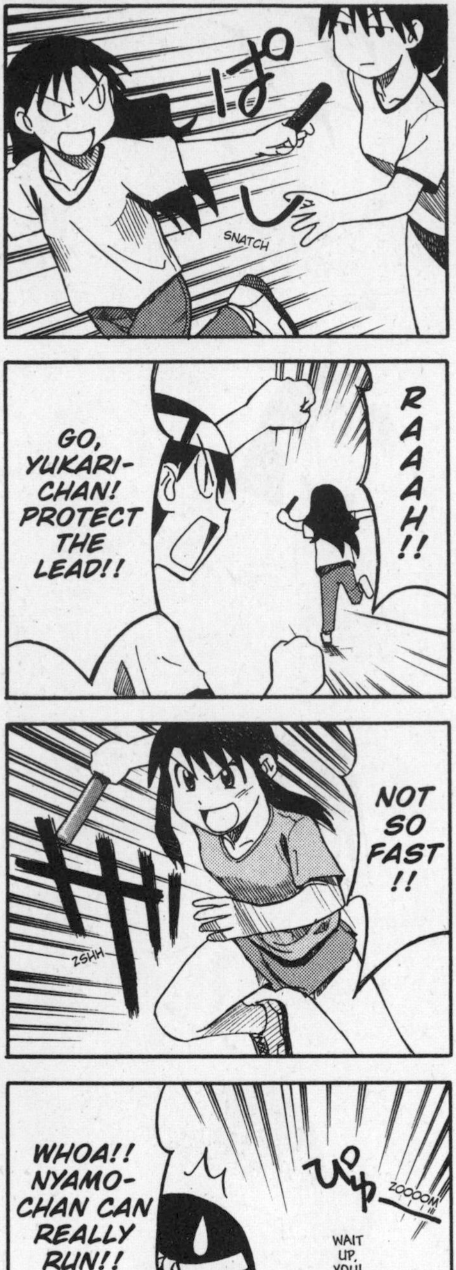
ぱし
SNATCH
RAAAAH!!
GO, YUKARI-CHAN! PROTECT THE LEAD!!
NOT SO FAST!!
ZSHH
ZOOOOM
WHOA!! NYAMO-CHAN CAN REALLY RUN!!
WAIT UP, YOU!

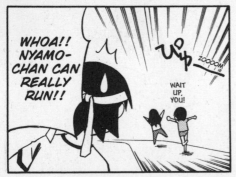

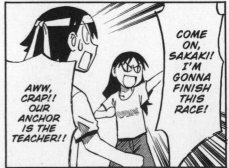

WIN OR DIE

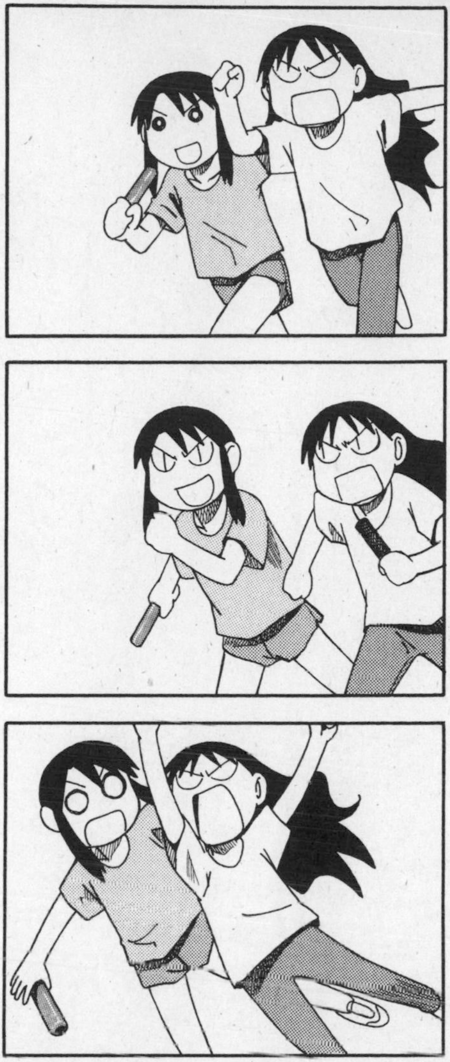

ALL TOGETHER

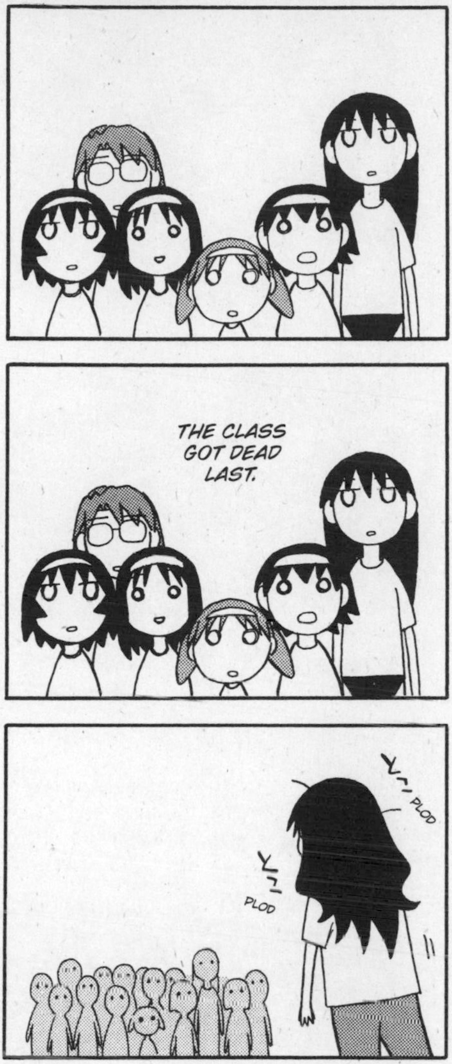
THE CLASS GOT DEAD LAST.
PLOD
PLOD
WELL, GANG...
...TOUGH LUCK OUT THERE!!

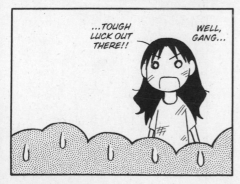

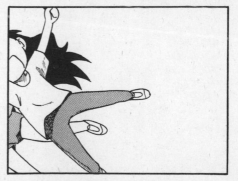

AZUMANGA-DAIOH

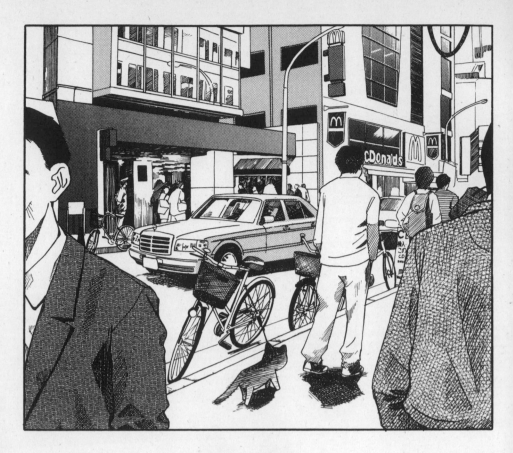

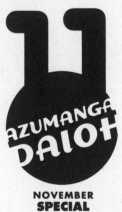

AZUMANGA DAIOH

NOVEMBER
SPECIAL

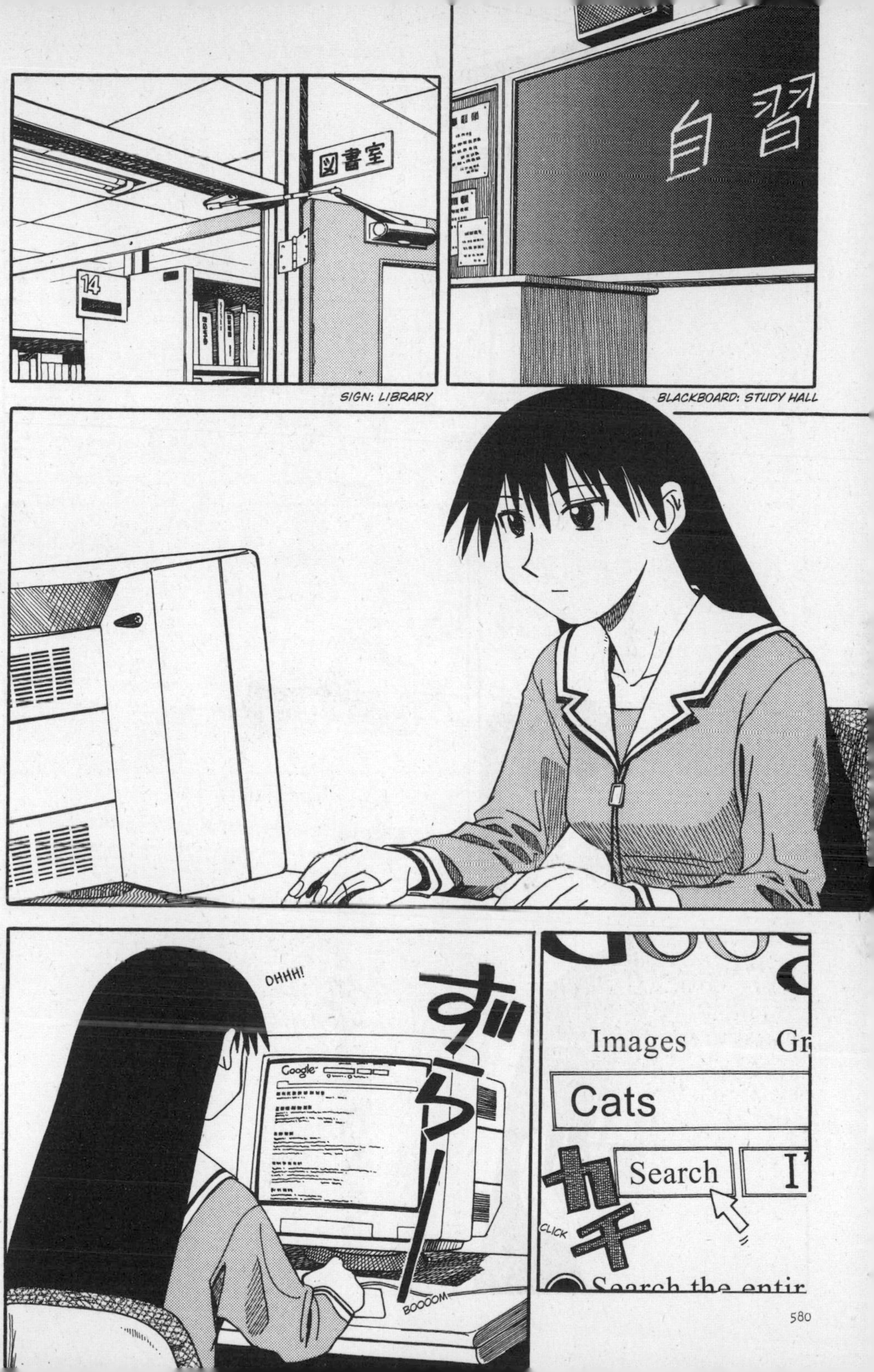
自習
BLACKBOARD: STUDY HALL
図書室
14
SIGN: LIBRARY
Images
Gr
Cats
Search
I'
カチ
CLICK
Search the entir
OHHH!
ずらー
BOOOOM
Google

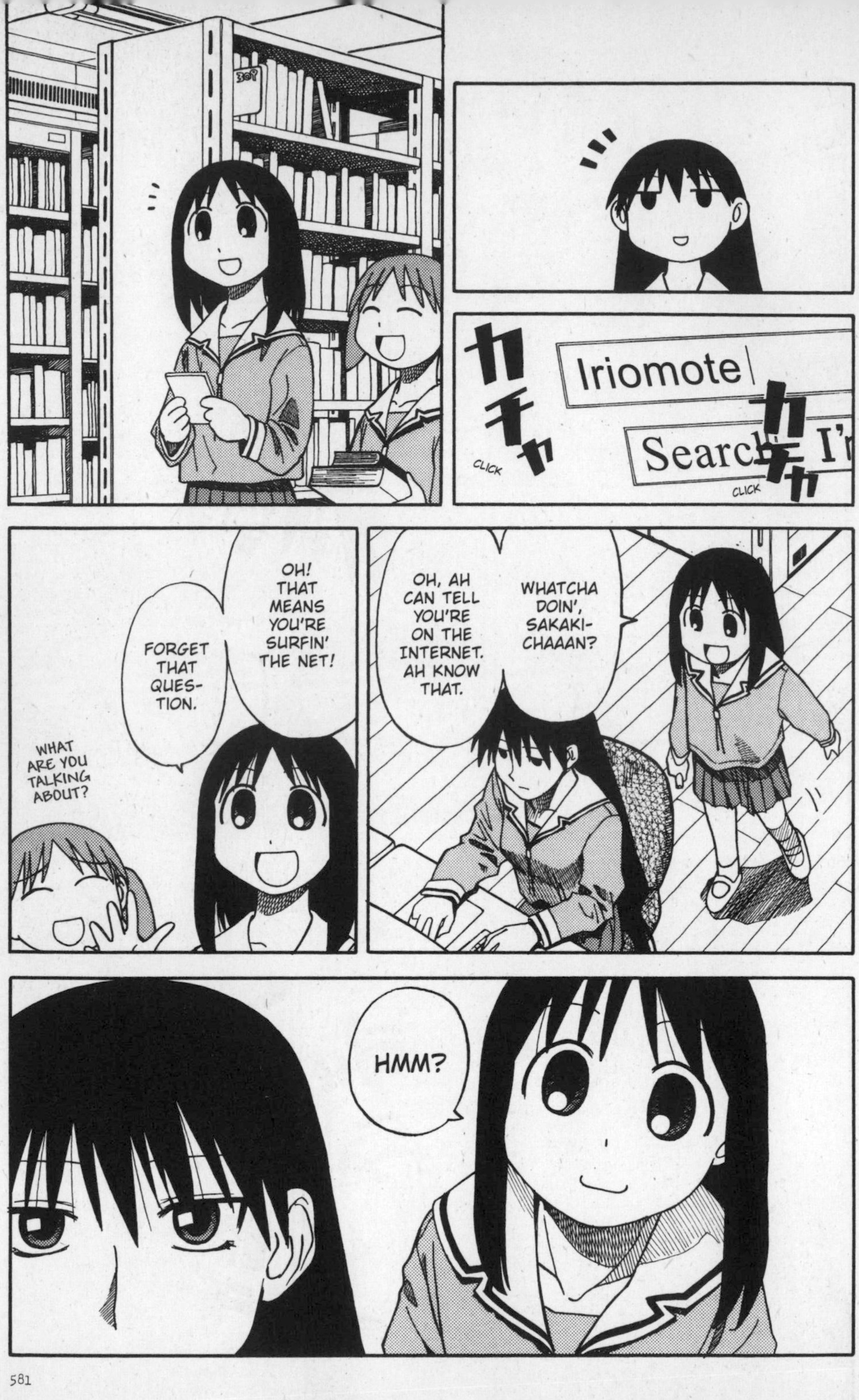

Iriomote
Searc
カチャ
CLICK
カチャ
CLICK
WHATCHA DOIN', SAKAKI-CHAAAN?
OH, AH CAN TELL YOU'RE ON THE INTERNET. AH KNOW THAT.
OH! THAT MEANS YOU'RE SURFIN' THE NET!
FORGET THAT QUES-TION.
WHAT ARE YOU TALKING ABOUT?
HMM?

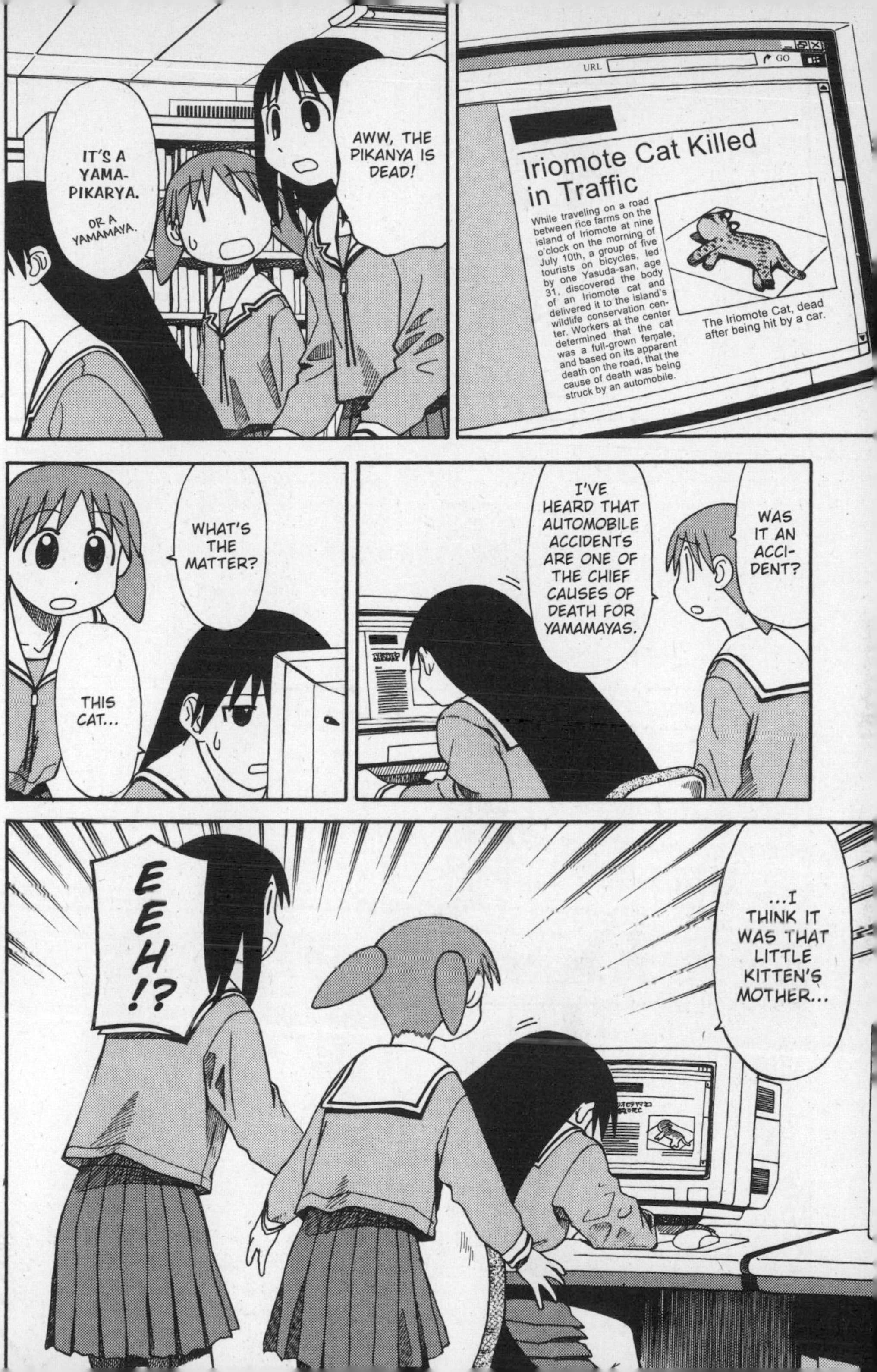
URL
GO
[redacted]
Iriomote Cat Killed in Traffic
While traveling on a road between rice farms on the island of Iriomote at nine o'clock on the morning of July 10th, a group of five tourists on bicycles, led by one Yasuda-san, age 31, discovered the body of an Iriomote cat and delivered it to the island's wildlife conservation center. Workers at the center determined that the cat was a full-grown female, and based on its apparent death on the road, that the cause of death was being struck by an automobile.
The Iriomote Cat, dead after being hit by a car.
AWW, THE PIKANYA IS DEAD!
IT'S A YAMA-PIKARYA.
OR A YAMAMAYA.
WAS IT AN ACCI-DENT?
I'VE HEARD THAT AUTOMOBILE ACCIDENTS ARE ONE OF THE CHIEF CAUSES OF DEATH FOR YAMAMAYAS.
WHAT'S THE MATTER?
THIS CAT...
...I THINK IT WAS THAT LITTLE KITTEN'S MOTHER...
EEEH!?

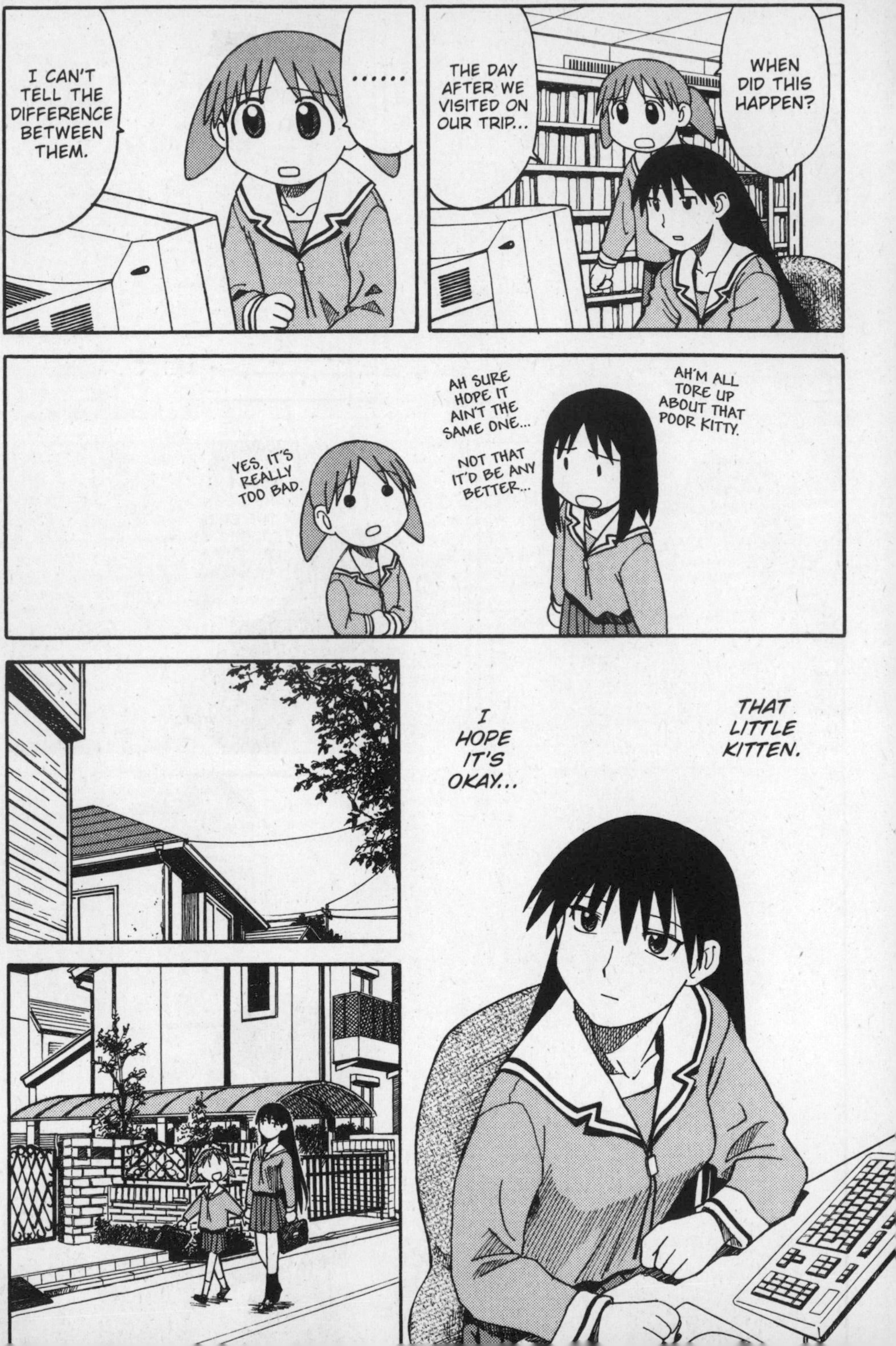
WHEN DID THIS HAPPEN?
THE DAY AFTER WE VISITED ON OUR TRIP...
......
I CAN'T TELL THE DIFFERENCE BETWEEN THEM.
AH'M ALL TORE UP ABOUT THAT POOR KITTY.
AH SURE HOPE IT AIN'T THE SAME ONE...
NOT THAT IT'D BE ANY BETTER...
YES, IT'S REALLY TOO BAD.
THAT LITTLE KITTEN.
I HOPE IT'S OKAY...

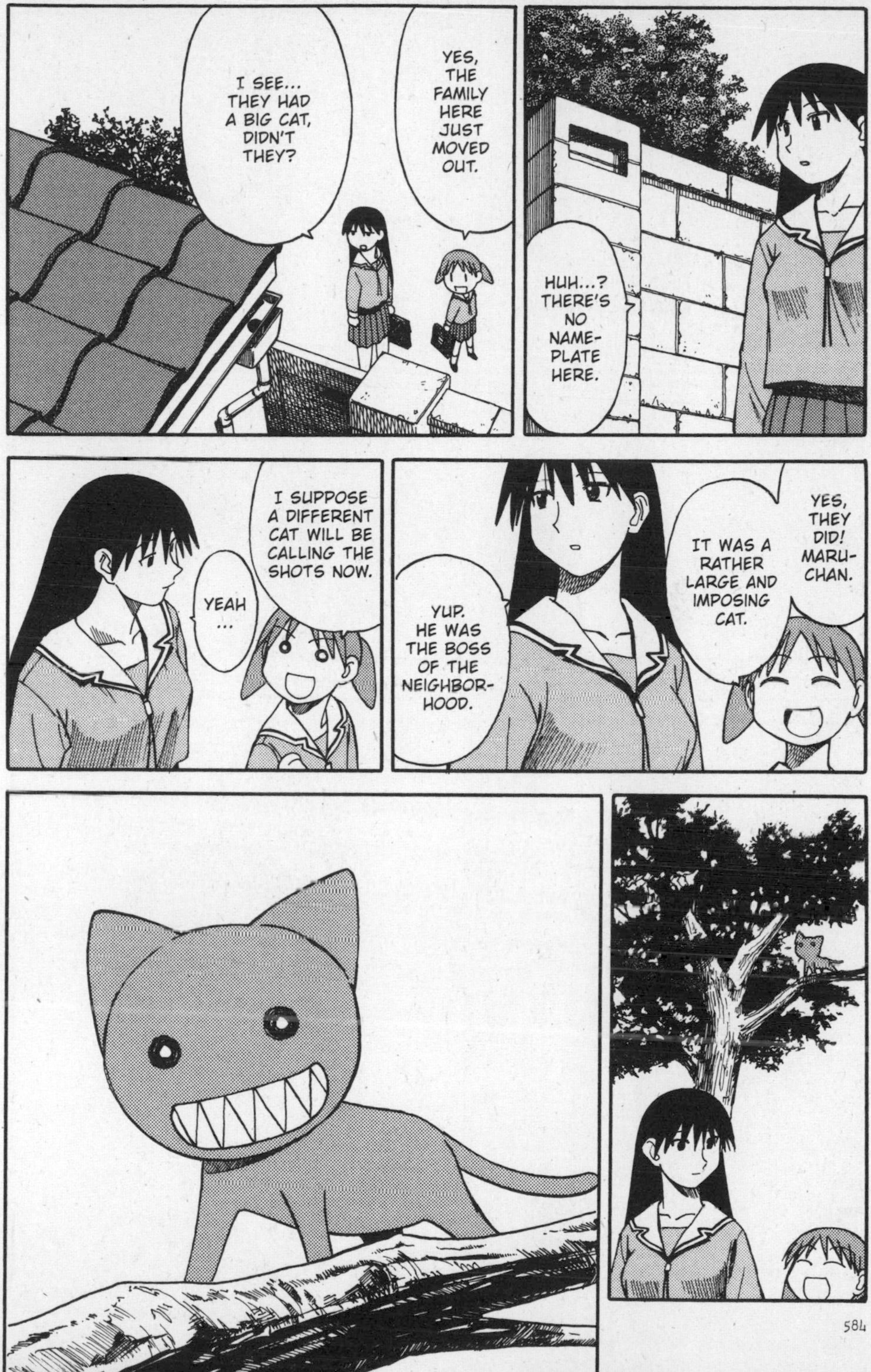
HUH...? THERE'S NO NAME-PLATE HERE.
YES, THE FAMILY HERE JUST MOVED OUT.
I SEE... THEY HAD A BIG CAT, DIDN'T THEY?
YES, THEY DID! MARU-CHAN.
IT WAS A RATHER LARGE AND IMPOSING CAT.
YUP. HE WAS THE BOSS OF THE NEIGHBOR-HOOD.
I SUPPOSE A DIFFERENT CAT WILL BE CALLING THE SHOTS NOW.
YEAH ...

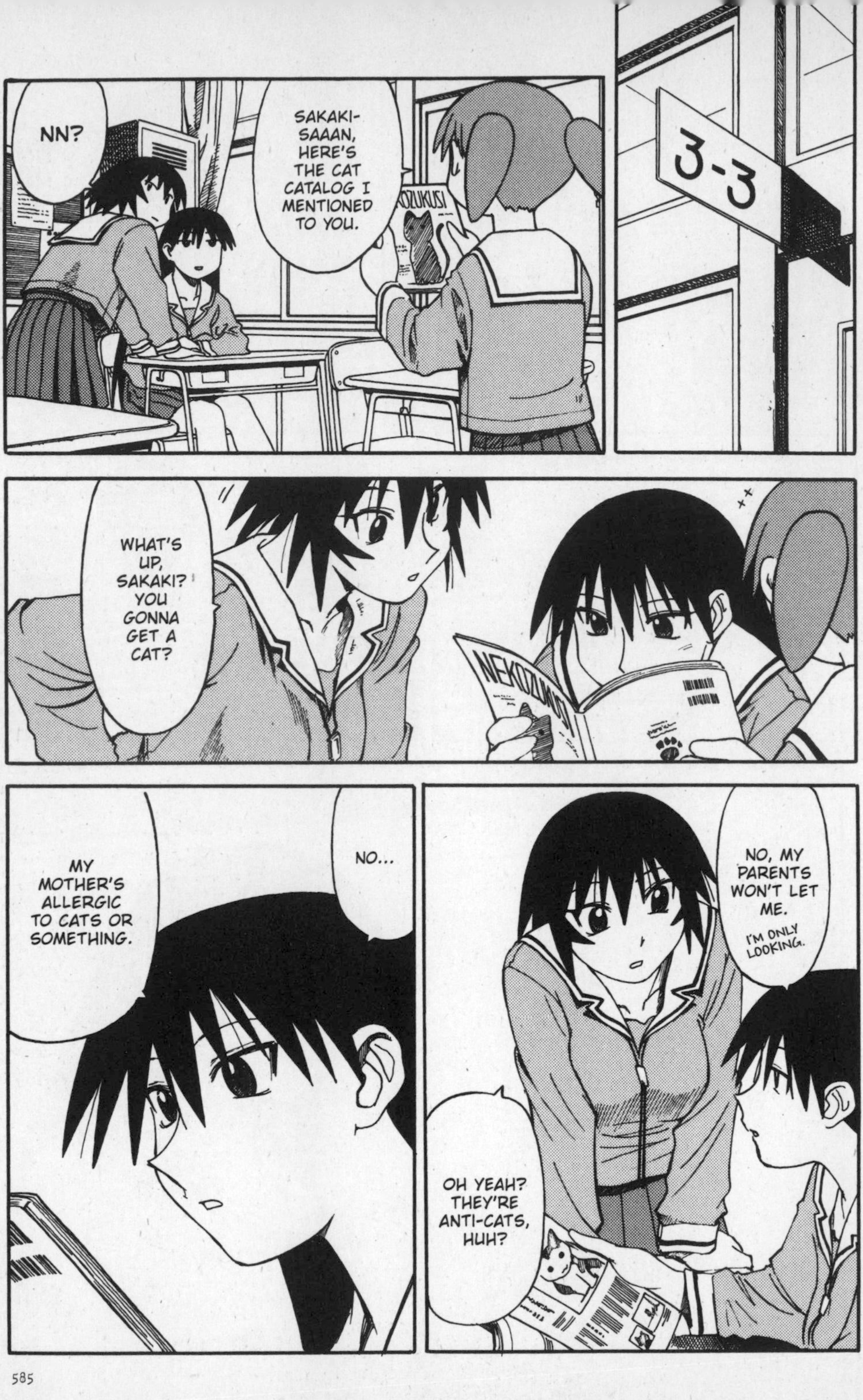
3-3
SAKAKI-SAAAN, HERE'S THE CAT CATALOG I MENTIONED TO YOU.
NN?
WHAT'S UP, SAKAKI? YOU GONNA GET A CAT?
NEKOZUKUSI
NO, MY PARENTS WON'T LET ME.
I'M ONLY LOOKING.
OH YEAH? THEY'RE ANTI-CATS, HUH?
NO...
MY MOTHER'S ALLERGIC TO CATS OR SOMETHING.

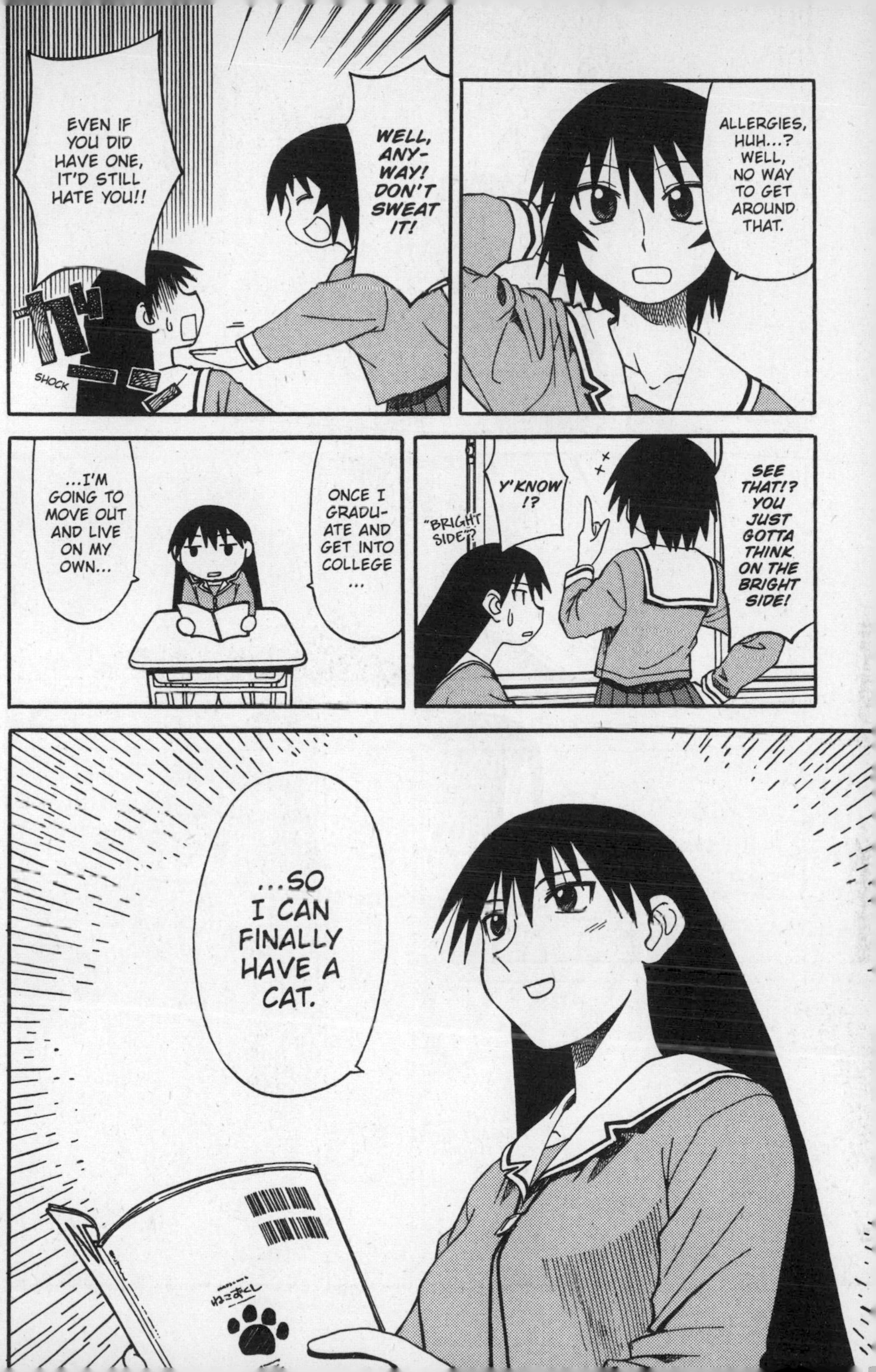
ALLERGIES, HUH...? WELL, NO WAY TO GET AROUND THAT.
WELL, ANYWAY! DON'T SWEAT IT!
EVEN IF YOU DID HAVE ONE, IT'D STILL HATE YOU!!
SHOCK
SEE THAT!? YOU JUST GOTTA THINK ON THE BRIGHT SIDE!
Y'KNOW!?
"BRIGHT SIDE"?
ONCE I GRADUATE AND GET INTO COLLEGE...
...I'M GOING TO MOVE OUT AND LIVE ON MY OWN...
...SO I CAN FINALLY HAVE A CAT.

CATALOG: NEKOZUKUSI

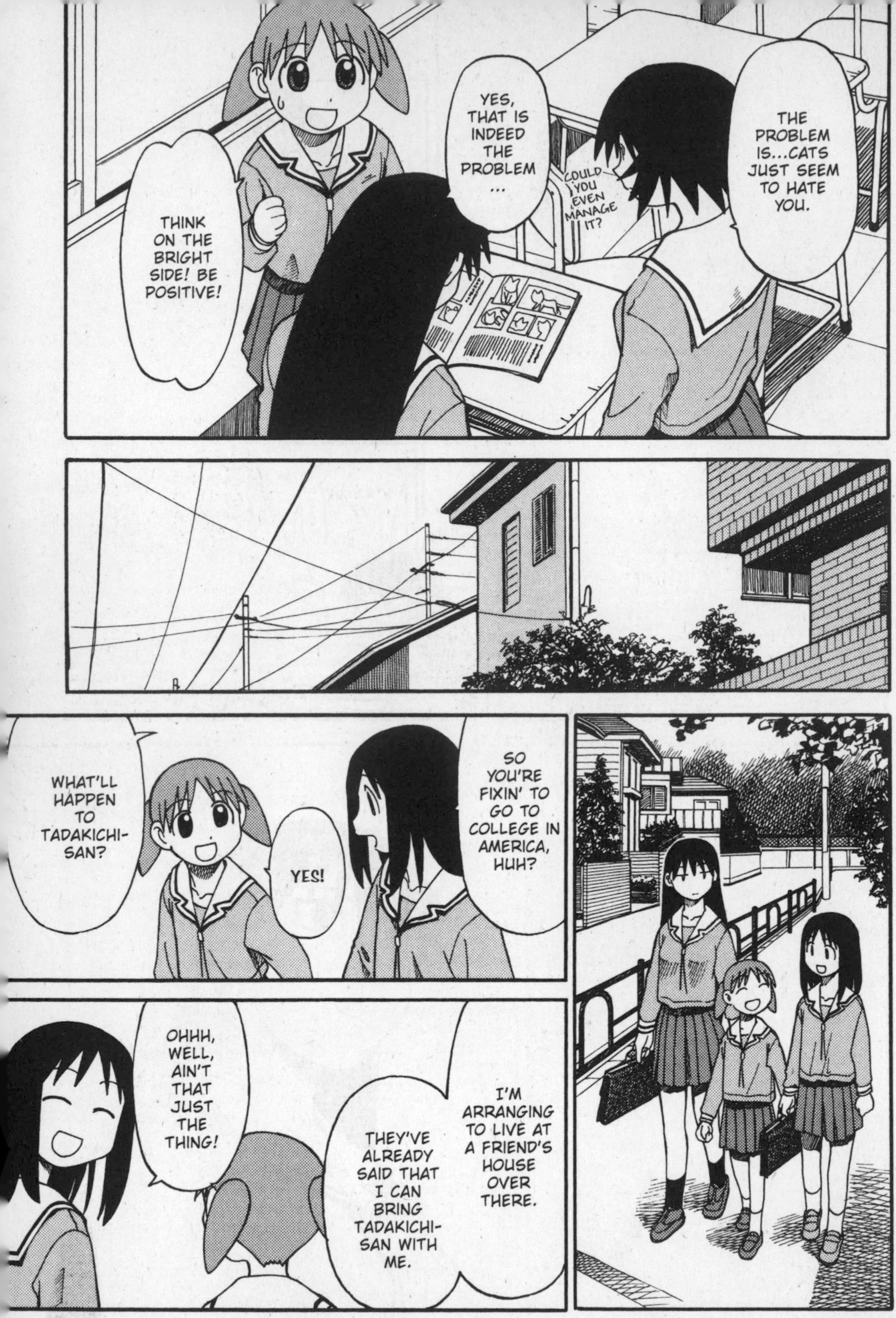
THE PROBLEM IS...CATS JUST SEEM TO HATE YOU.
COULD YOU EVEN MANAGE IT?
YES, THAT IS INDEED THE PROBLEM ...
THINK ON THE BRIGHT SIDE! BE POSITIVE!
SO YOU'RE FIXIN' TO GO TO COLLEGE IN AMERICA, HUH?
YES!
WHAT'LL HAPPEN TO TADAKICHI-SAN?
I'M ARRANGING TO LIVE AT A FRIEND'S HOUSE OVER THERE.
THEY'VE ALREADY SAID THAT I CAN BRING TADAKICHI-SAN WITH ME.
OHHH, WELL, AIN'T THAT JUST THE THING!

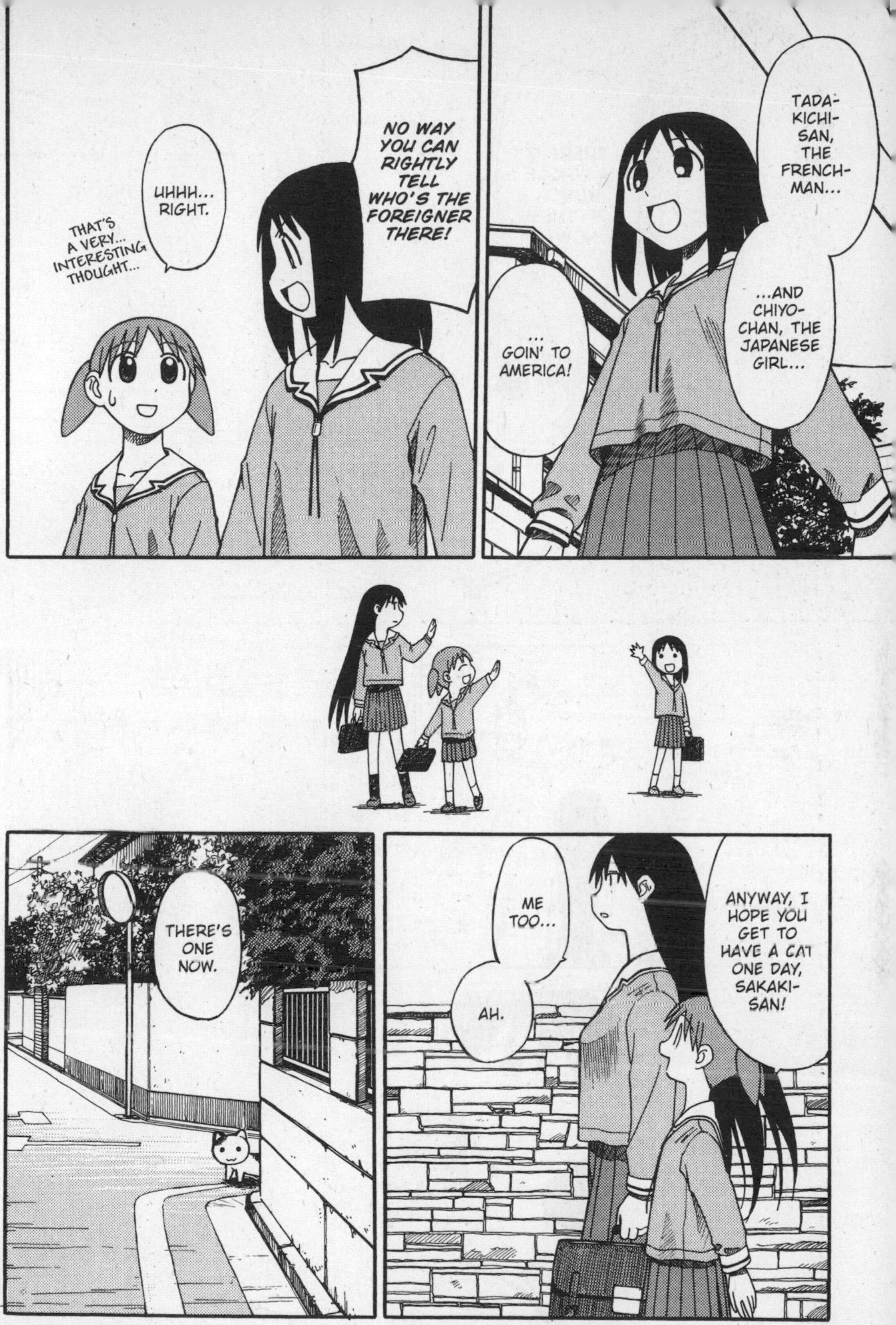
TADA-KICHI-SAN, THE FRENCH-MAN...
...AND CHIYO-CHAN, THE JAPANESE GIRL...
... GOIN' TO AMERICA!
NO WAY YOU CAN RIGHTLY TELL WHO'S THE FOREIGNER THERE!
UHHH... RIGHT.
THAT'S A VERY... INTERESTING THOUGHT...
ANYWAY, I HOPE YOU GET TO HAVE A CAT ONE DAY, SAKAKI-SAN!
ME TOO...
AH.
THERE'S ONE NOW.

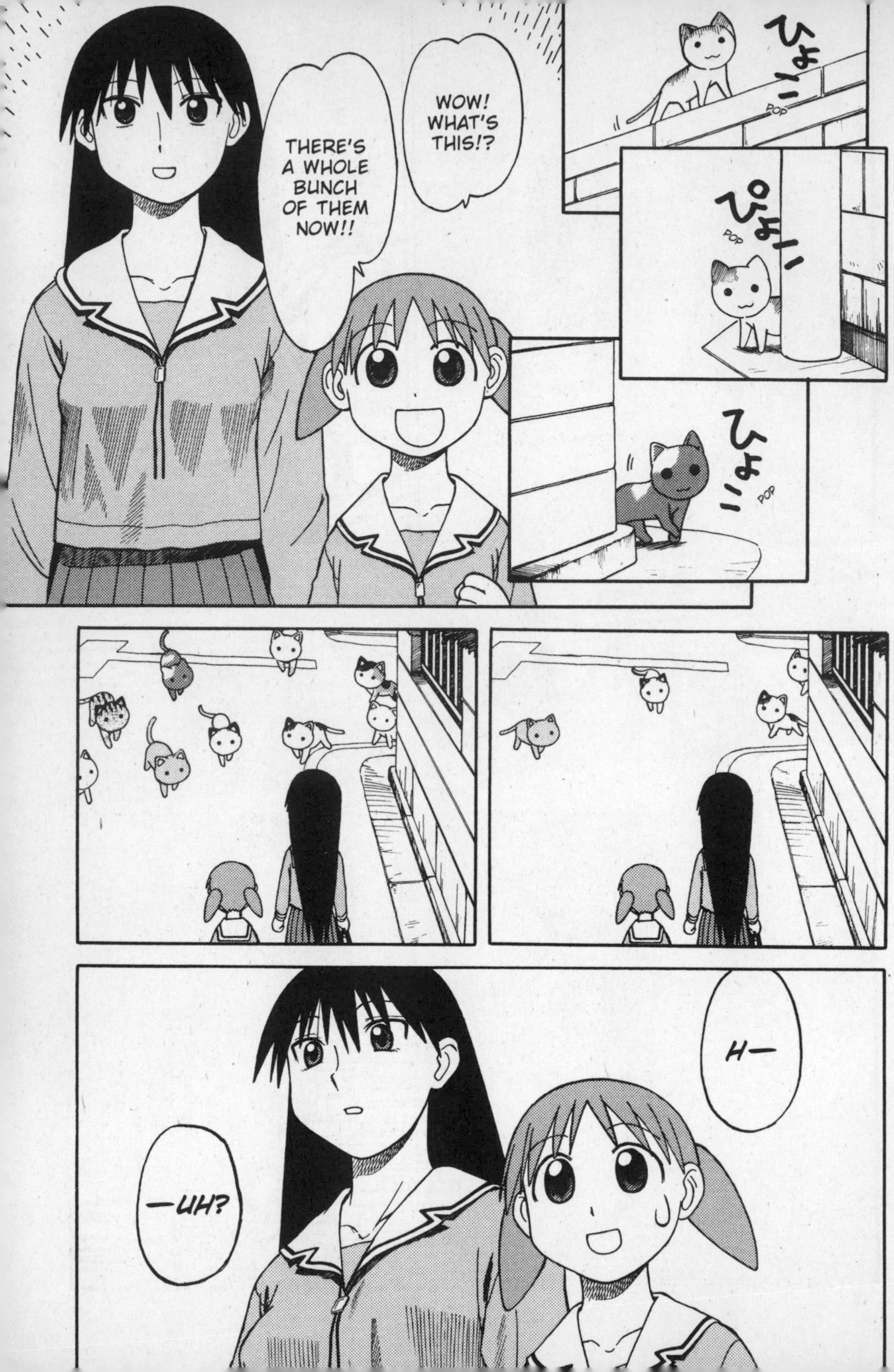
ひょこ
POP
ぴょこ
POP
ひょこ
POP
WOW! WHAT'S THIS!?
THERE'S A WHOLE BUNCH OF THEM NOW!!
H—
—UH?

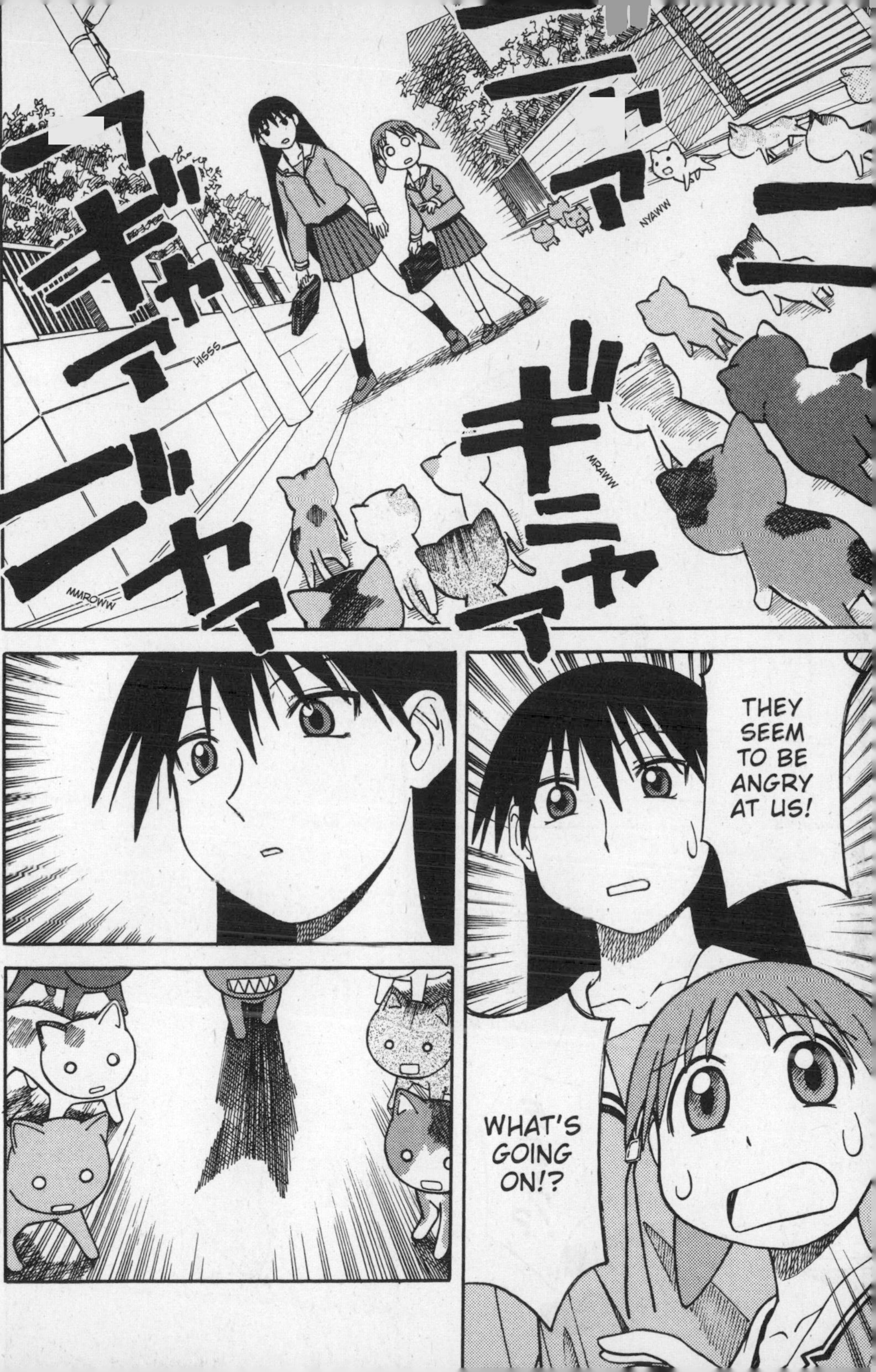
NYAWW
MRAWW
MRAWW
HISSS
MMROWW
THEY SEEM TO BE ANGRY AT US!
WHAT'S GOING ON!?

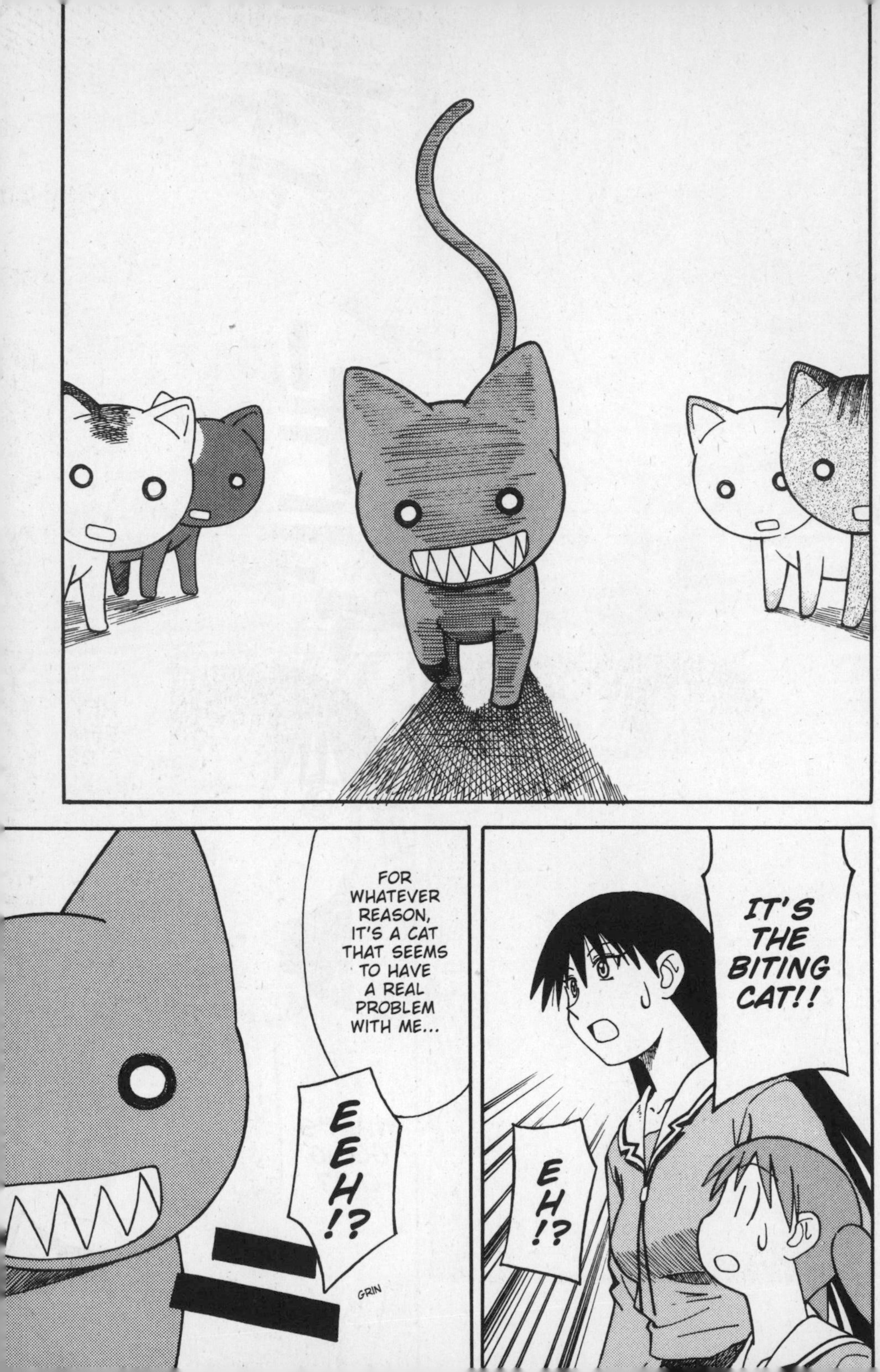
IT'S THE BITING CAT!!
EH!?
FOR WHATEVER REASON, IT'S A CAT THAT SEEMS TO HAVE A REAL PROBLEM WITH ME...
EEH!?
GRIN

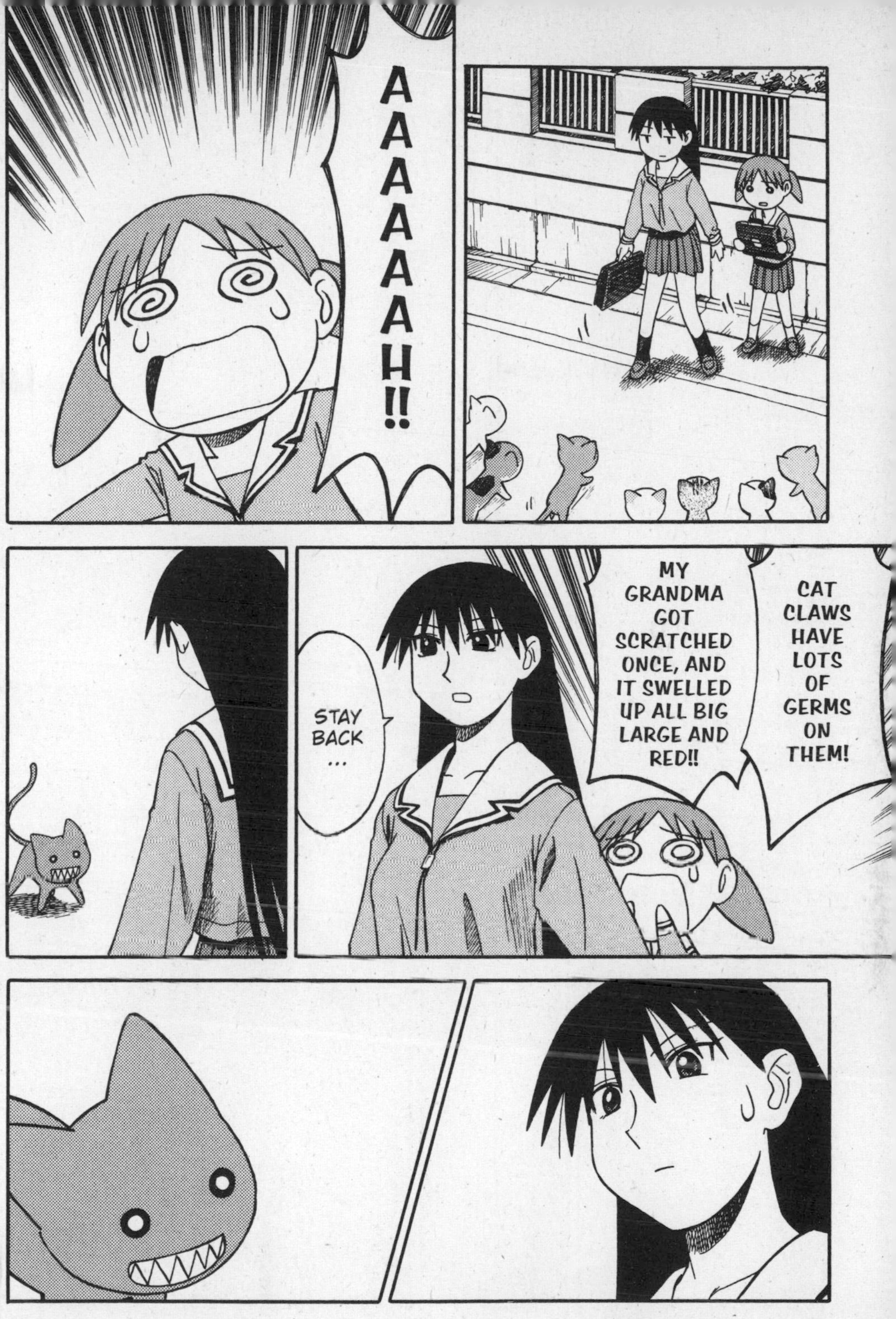
AAAAAAAH!!
CAT CLAWS HAVE LOTS OF GERMS ON THEM!
MY GRANDMA GOT SCRATCHED ONCE, AND IT SWELLED UP ALL BIG LARGE AND RED!!
STAY BACK ...

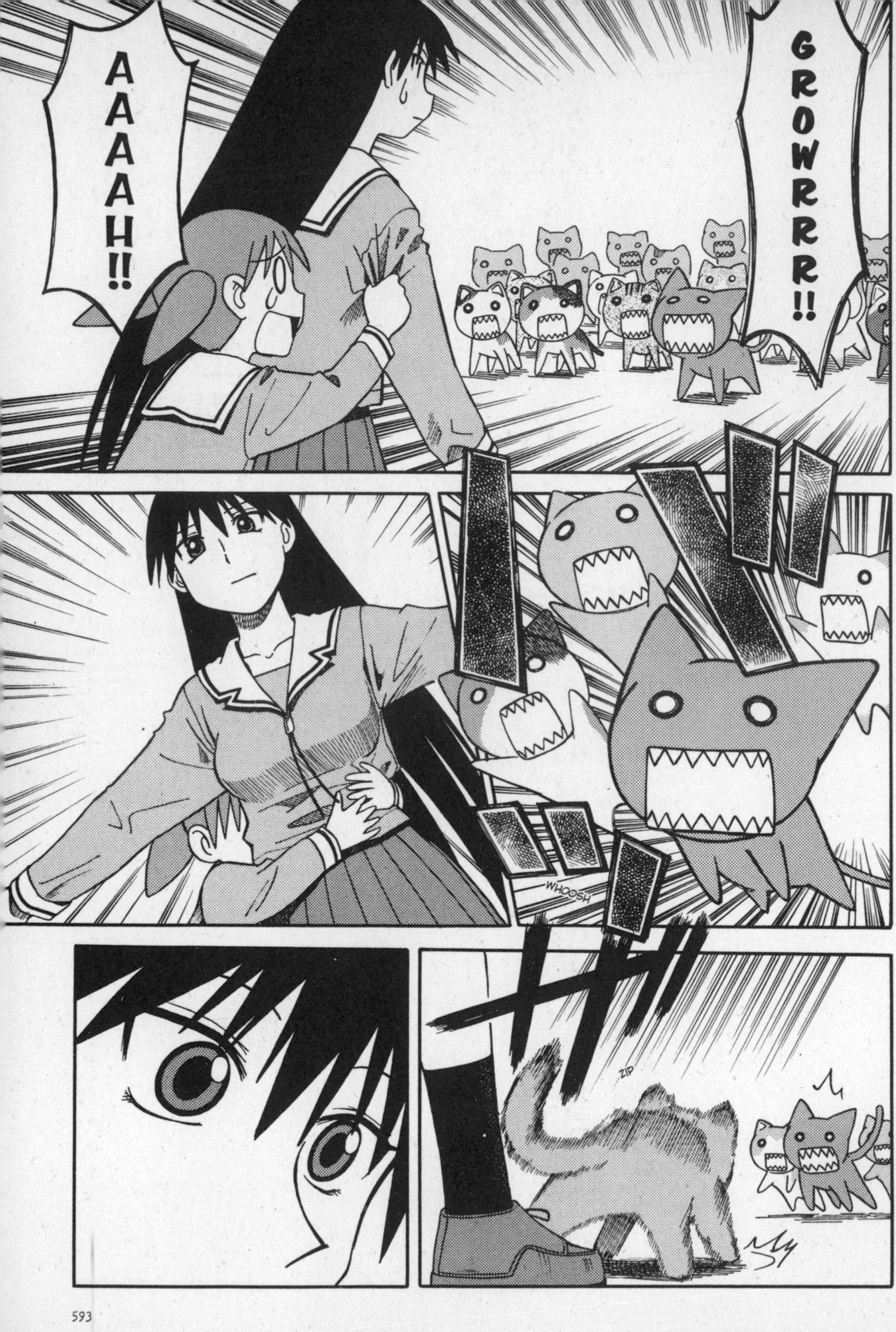
GROWRRRR!!
AAAAAH!!
WHOOSH
ZIP

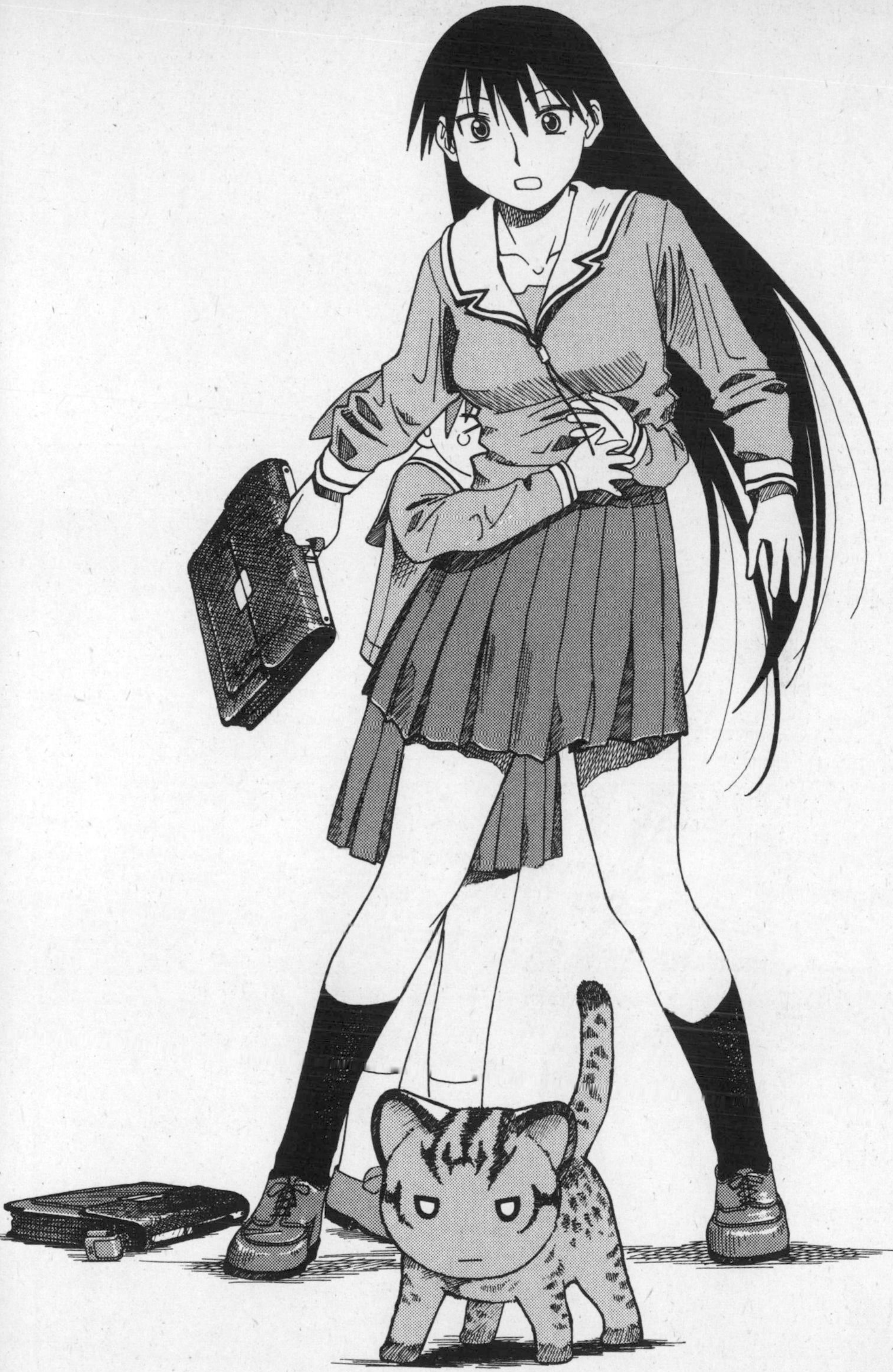

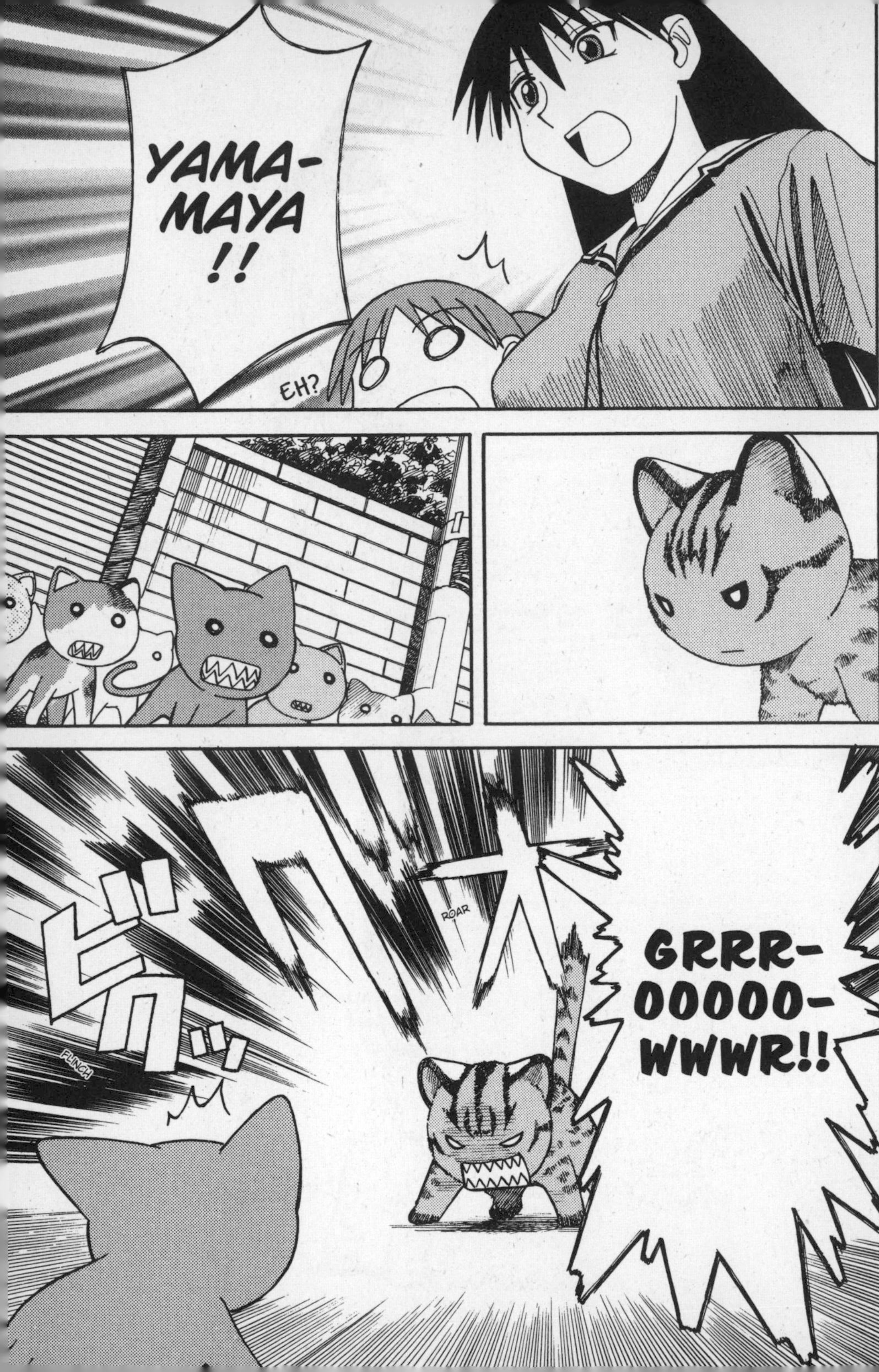
YAMA-MAYA!!
EH?
GRRR-OOOOO-WWWR!!
ROAR
ビクッ
FLINCH

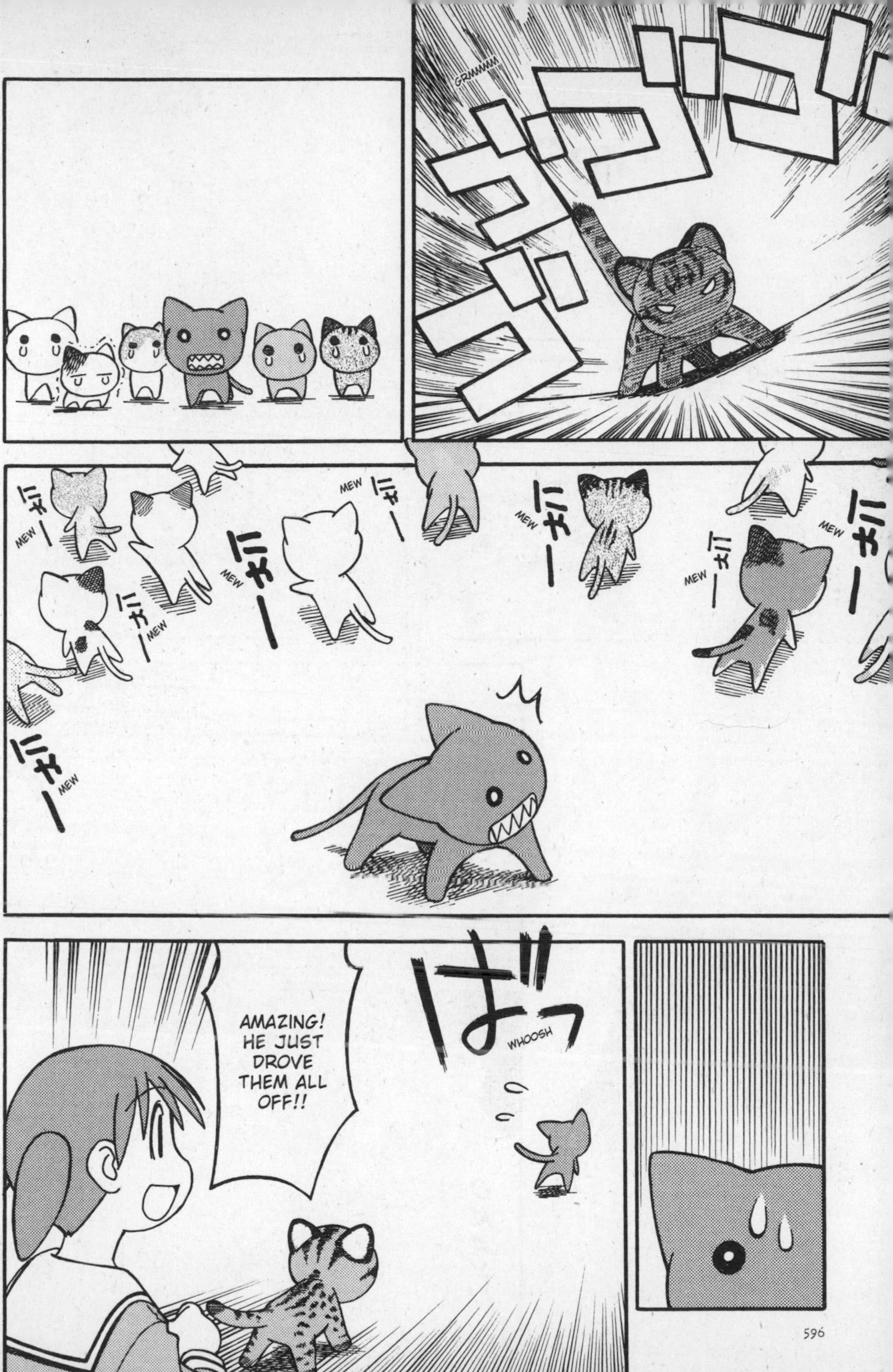
GRMMMM
MEW
MEW
MEW
MEW
MEW
MEW
MEW
MEW
WHOOSH
AMAZING! HE JUST DROVE THEM ALL OFF!!

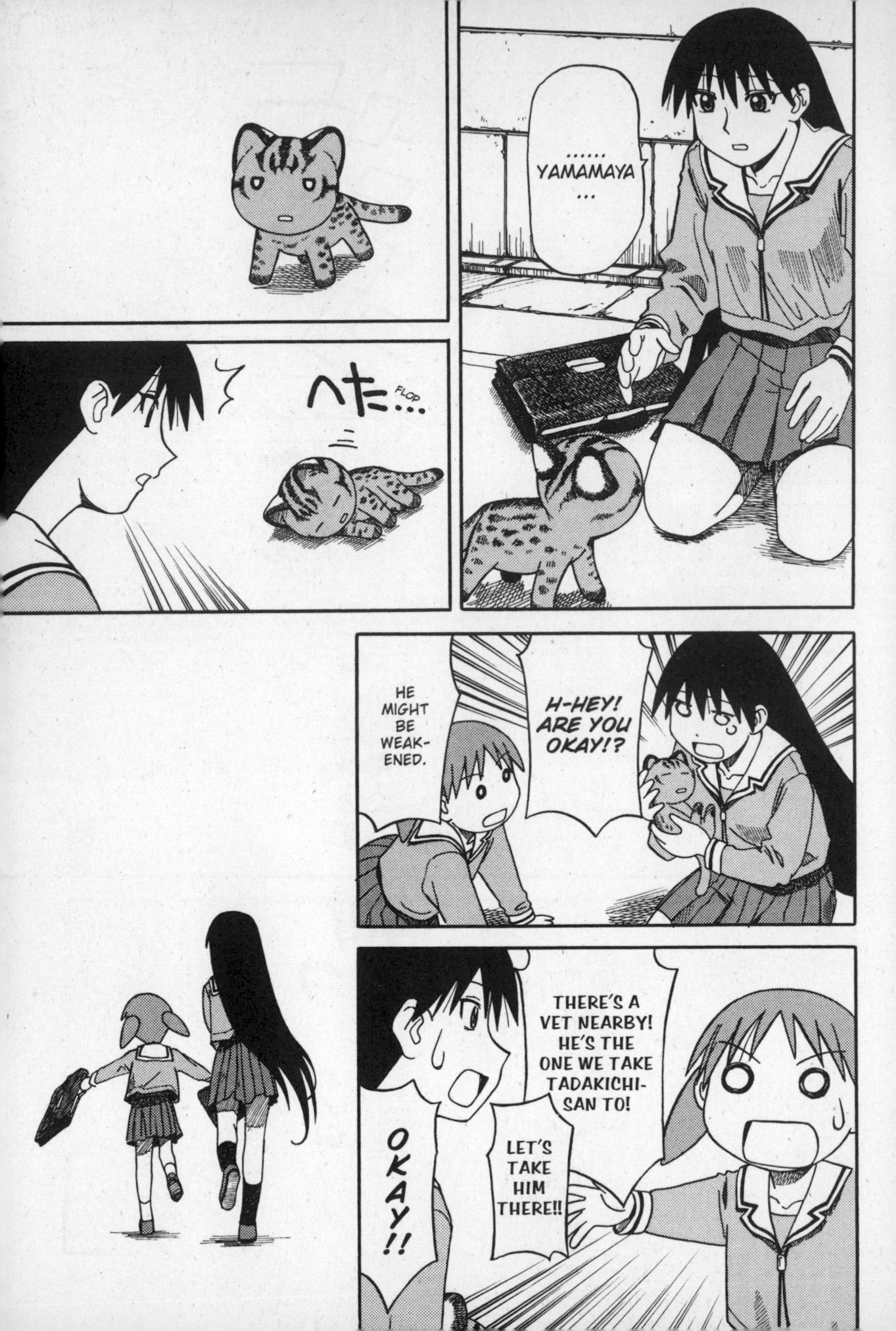
...... YAMAMAYA ...
へた... FLOP
H-HEY! ARE YOU OKAY!?
HE MIGHT BE WEAK-ENED.
THERE'S A VET NEARBY! HE'S THE ONE WE TAKE TADAKICHI-SAN TO!
LET'S TAKE HIM THERE!!
OKAY!!

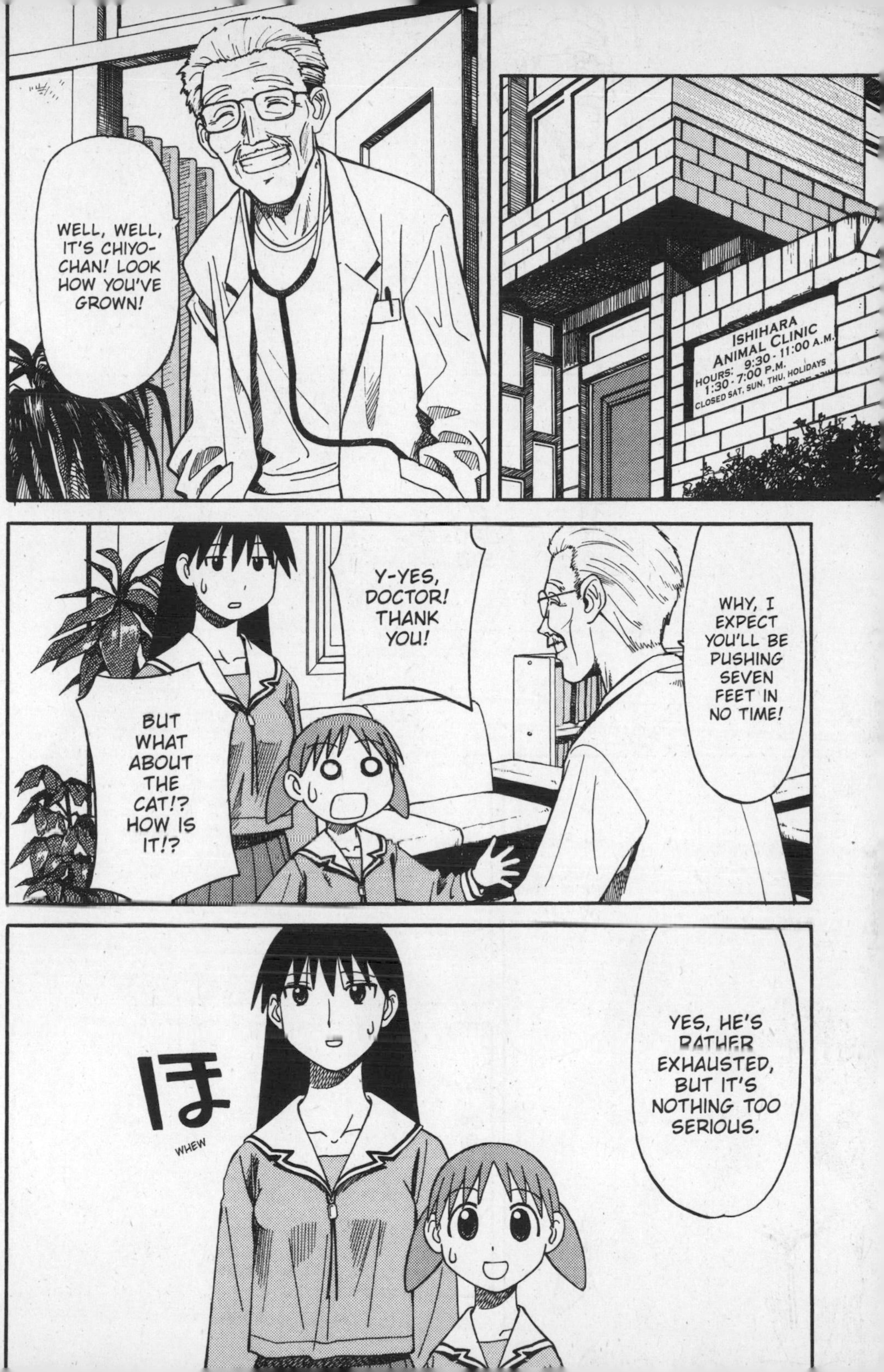
ISHIHARA
ANIMAL CLINIC
HOURS: 9:30 - 11:00 A.M.
1:30 - 7:00 P.M.
CLOSED SAT, SUN, THU, HOLIDAYS
WELL, WELL, IT'S CHIYO-CHAN! LOOK HOW YOU'VE GROWN!
WHY, I EXPECT YOU'LL BE PUSHING SEVEN FEET IN NO TIME!
Y-YES, DOCTOR! THANK YOU!
BUT WHAT ABOUT THE CAT!? HOW IS IT!?
YES, HE'S RATHER EXHAUSTED, BUT IT'S NOTHING TOO SERIOUS.
ほ
WHEW

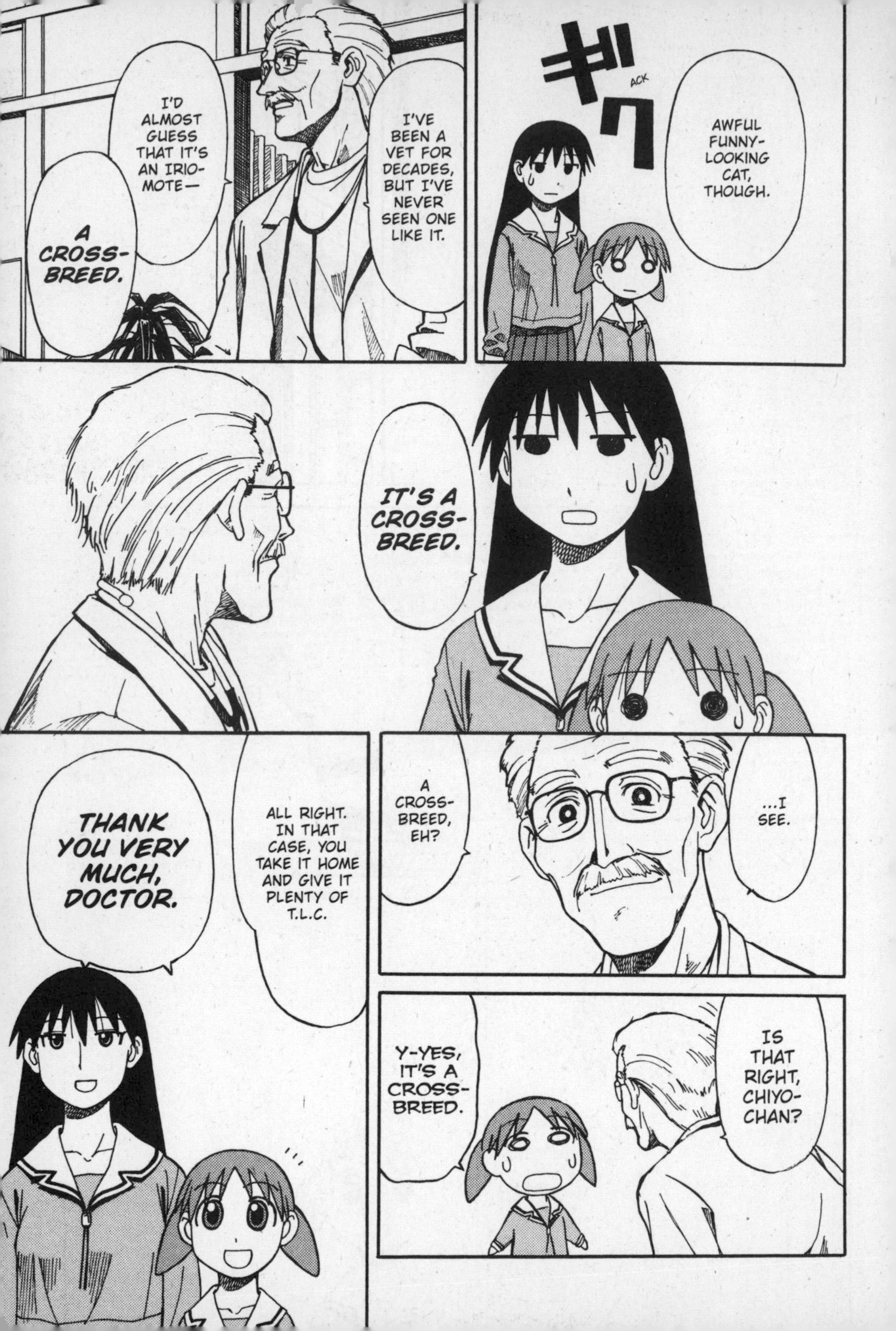
ギク
ACK
AWFUL FUNNY-LOOKING CAT, THOUGH.
I'VE BEEN A VET FOR DECADES, BUT I'VE NEVER SEEN ONE LIKE IT.
I'D ALMOST GUESS THAT IT'S AN IRIO-MOTE—
A CROSS-BREED.
IT'S A CROSS-BREED.
...I SEE.
A CROSS-BREED, EH?
IS THAT RIGHT, CHIYO-CHAN?
Y-YES, IT'S A CROSS-BREED.
ALL RIGHT. IN THAT CASE, YOU TAKE IT HOME AND GIVE IT PLENTY OF T.L.C.
THANK YOU VERY MUCH, DOCTOR.
...

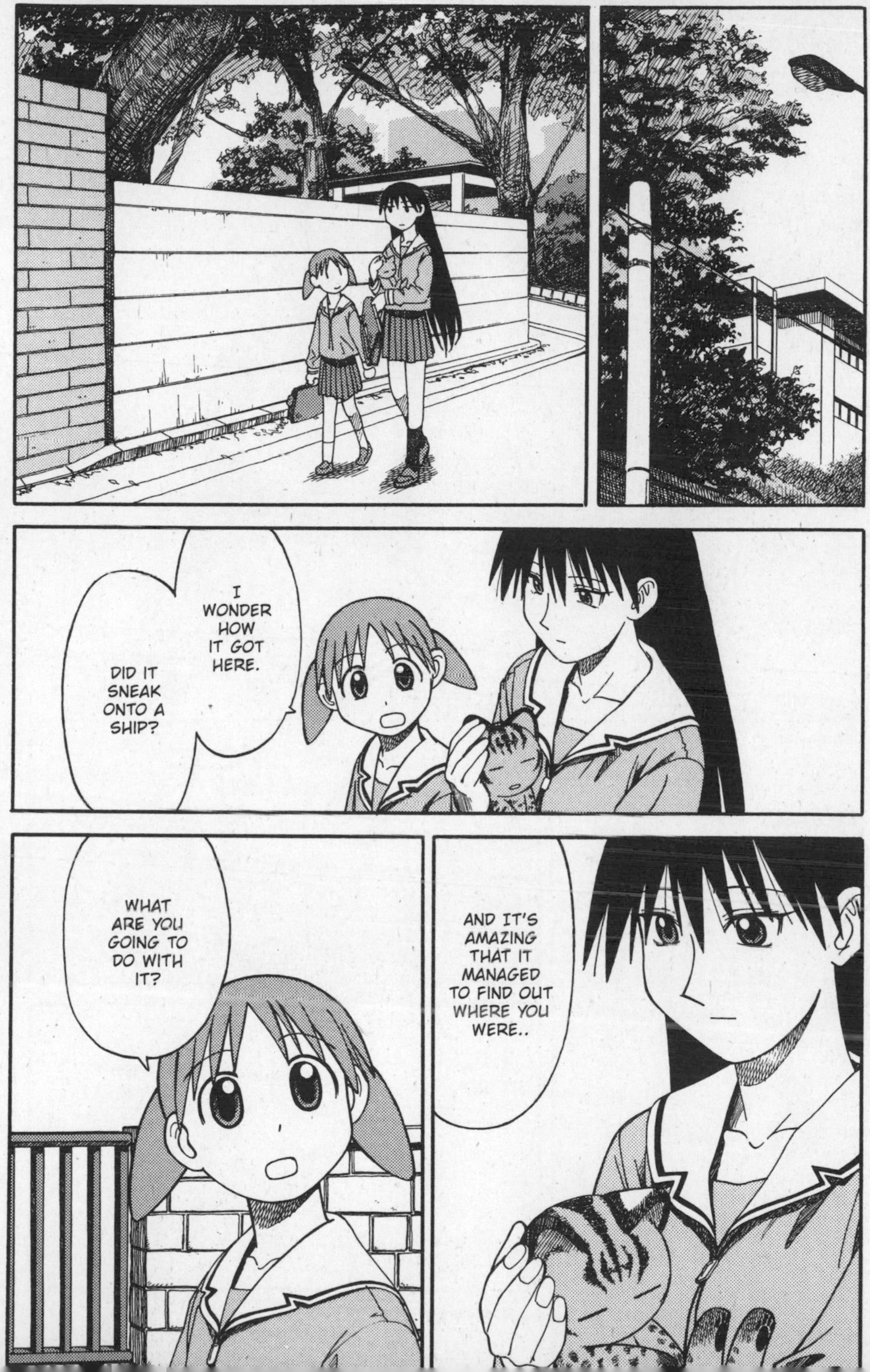
I WONDER HOW IT GOT HERE.
DID IT SNEAK ONTO A SHIP?
AND IT'S AMAZING THAT IT MANAGED TO FIND OUT WHERE YOU WERE..
WHAT ARE YOU GOING TO DO WITH IT?

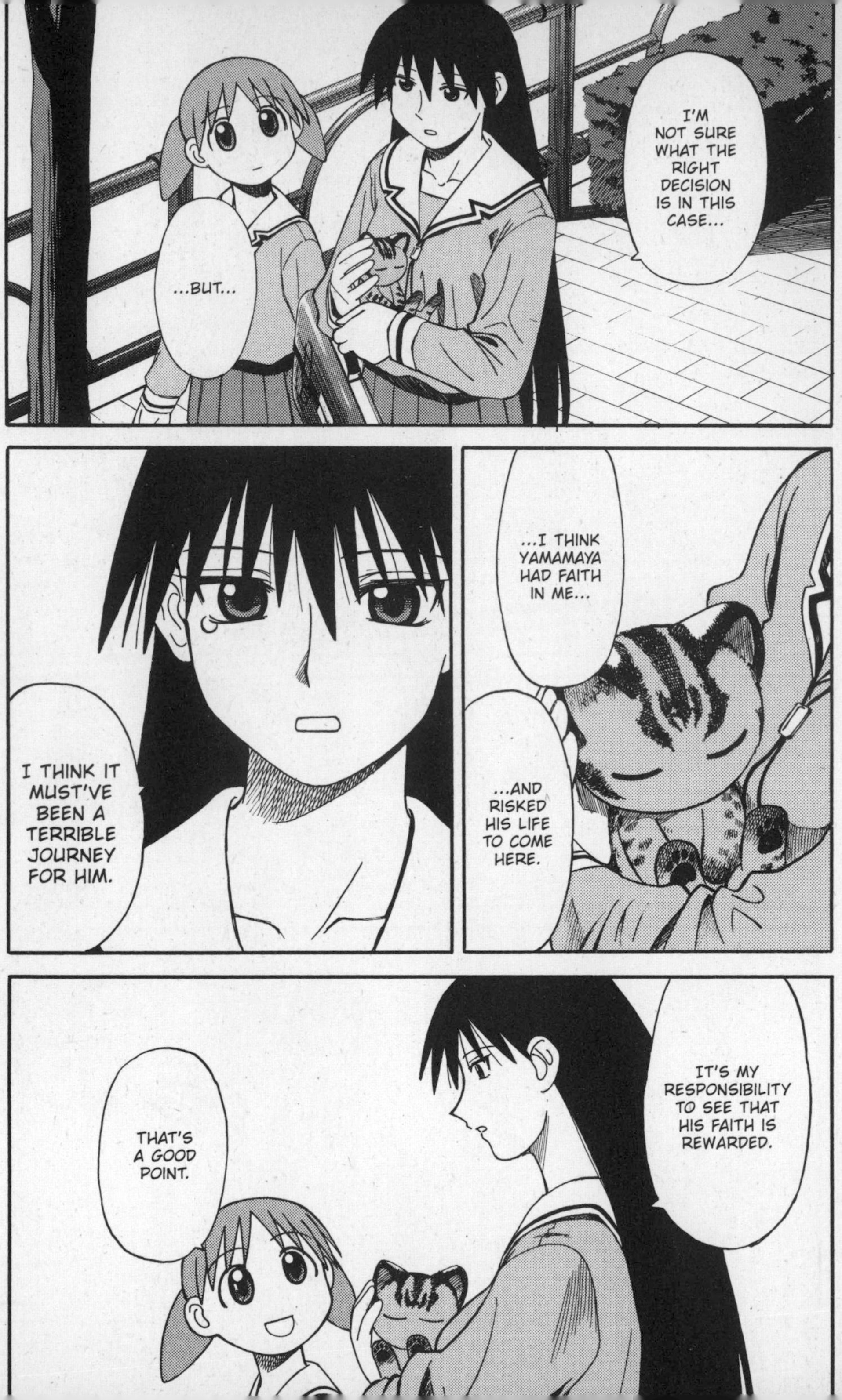
I'M NOT SURE WHAT THE RIGHT DECISION IS IN THIS CASE...
...BUT...
...I THINK YAMAMAYA HAD FAITH IN ME...
...AND RISKED HIS LIFE TO COME HERE.
I THINK IT MUST'VE BEEN A TERRIBLE JOURNEY FOR HIM.
IT'S MY RESPONSIBILITY TO SEE THAT HIS FAITH IS REWARDED.
THAT'S A GOOD POINT.

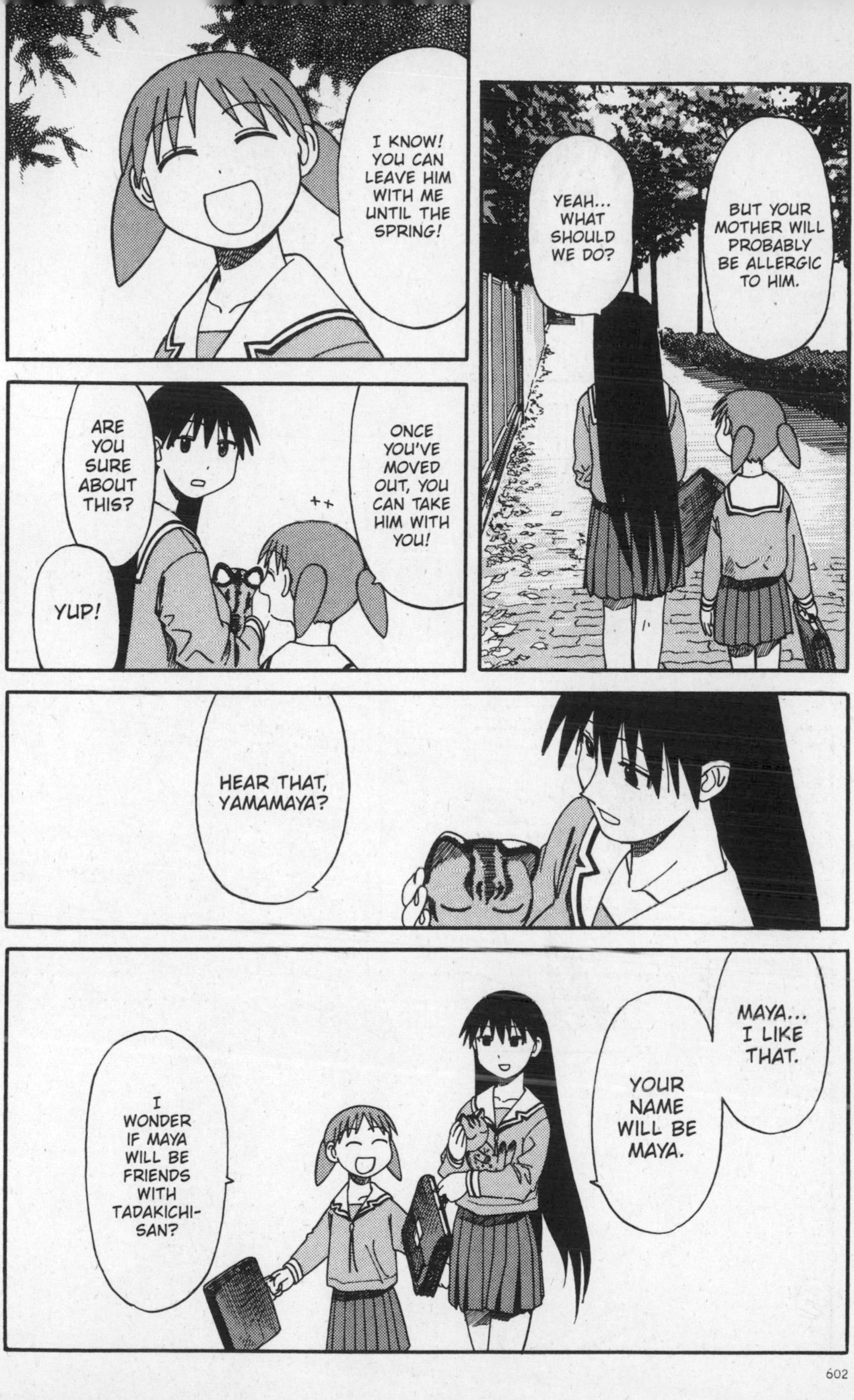
BUT YOUR MOTHER WILL PROBABLY BE ALLERGIC TO HIM.
YEAH... WHAT SHOULD WE DO?
I KNOW! YOU CAN LEAVE HIM WITH ME UNTIL THE SPRING!
ONCE YOU'VE MOVED OUT, YOU CAN TAKE HIM WITH YOU!
ARE YOU SURE ABOUT THIS?
YUP!
HEAR THAT, YAMAMAYA?
MAYA... I LIKE THAT.
YOUR NAME WILL BE MAYA.
I WONDER IF MAYA WILL BE FRIENDS WITH TADAKICHI-SAN?

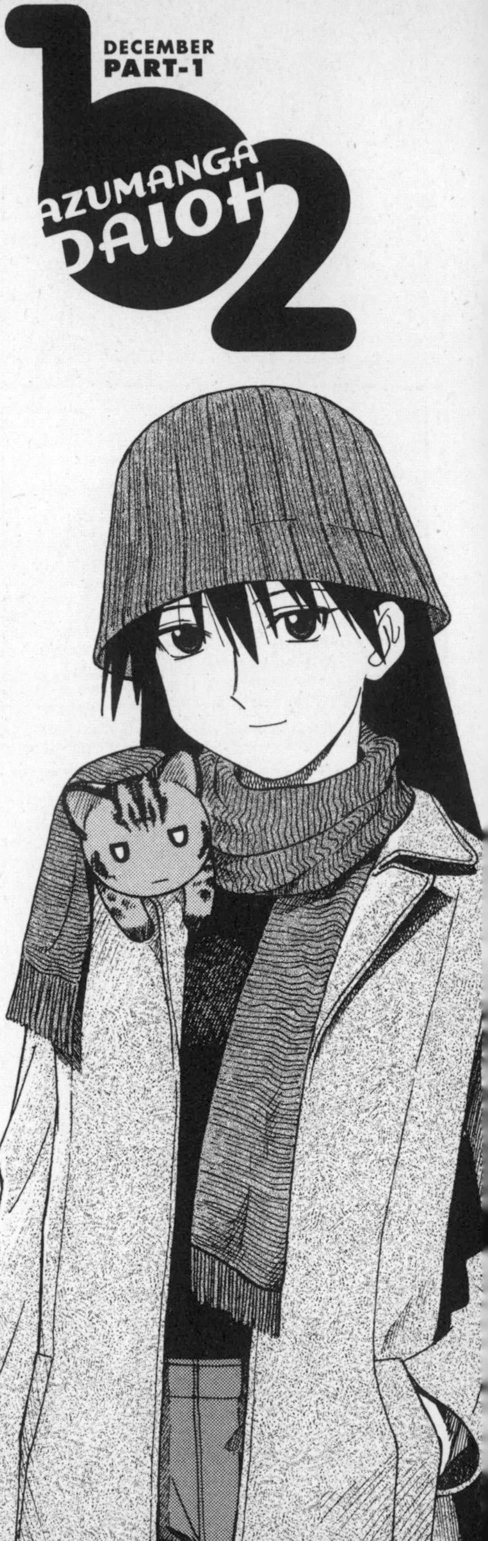
DECEMBER PART-1
AZUMANGA DAIOH 2

HURRY UP

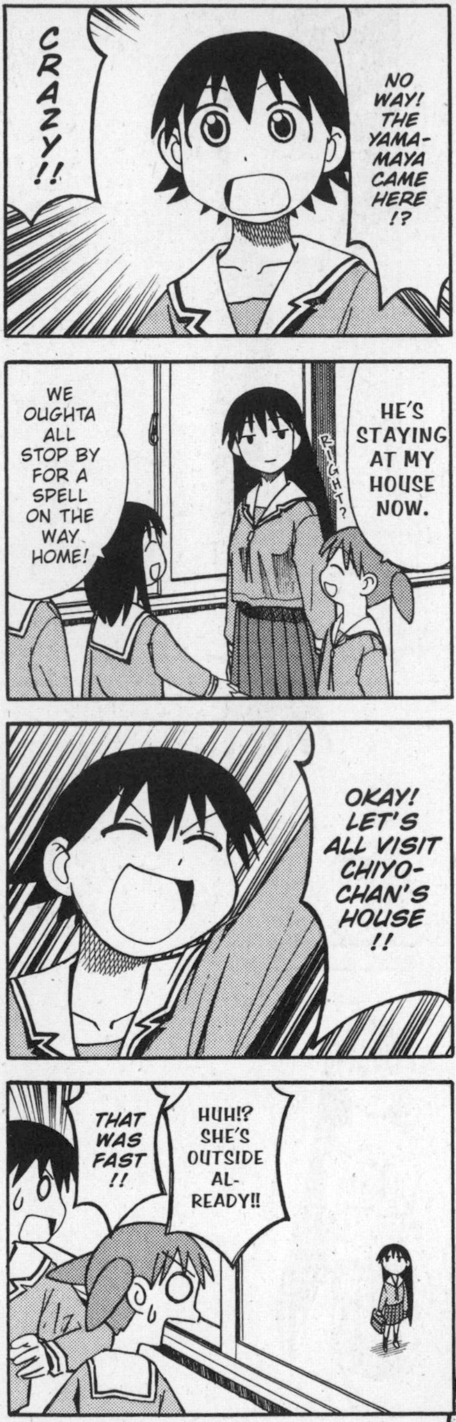
NO WAY! THE YAMA-MAYA CAME HERE !?
CRAZY!!
HE'S STAYING AT MY HOUSE NOW.
RIGHT?
WE OUGHTA ALL STOP BY FOR A SPELL ON THE WAY HOME!
OKAY! LET'S ALL VISIT CHIYO-CHAN'S HOUSE !!
HUH!? SHE'S OUTSIDE AL-READY!!
THAT WAS FAST !!

PIKA...

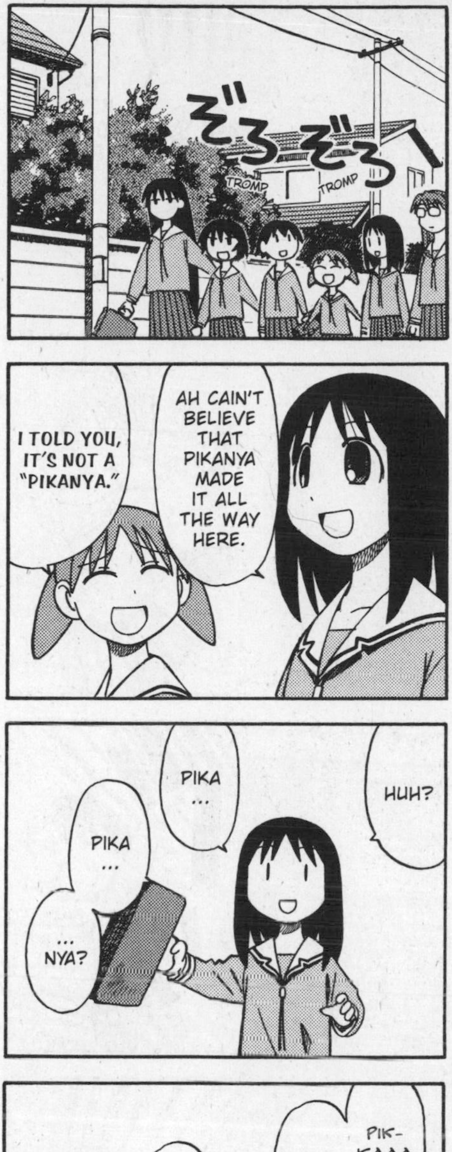
ぞろぞろ
TROMP
TROMP
AH CAIN'T BELIEVE THAT PIKANYA MADE IT ALL THE WAY HERE.
I TOLD YOU, IT'S NOT A "PIKANYA."
HUH?
PIKA ...
PIKA ...
... NYA?
PIK-KAAA ...
PIKA!?
?
PIII?
?

IRIOMOTE ISLAND

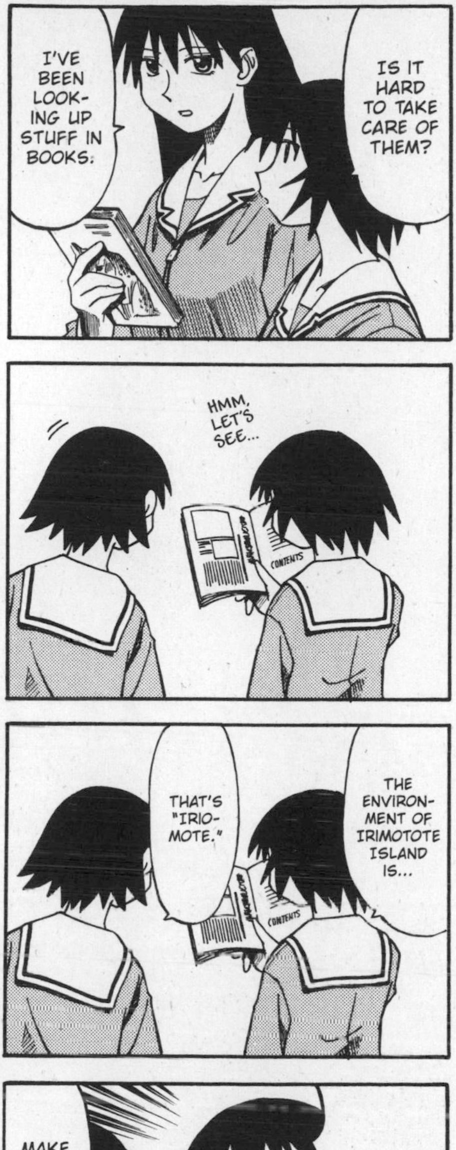
IS IT HARD TO TAKE CARE OF THEM?
I'VE BEEN LOOKING UP STUFF IN BOOKS.
HMM, LET'S SEE...
CONTENTS
THE ENVIRONMENT OF IRIMOTOTE ISLAND IS...
THAT'S "IRIOMOTE."
CONTENTS
I KNOW THAT! I SAID IT ON PURPOSE, OKAY!? IT WAS AN ACCIDENT!
MAKE UP YOUR MIND.
FLUSH

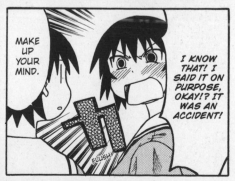

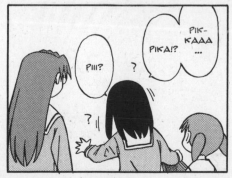

IT'S POWERFUL

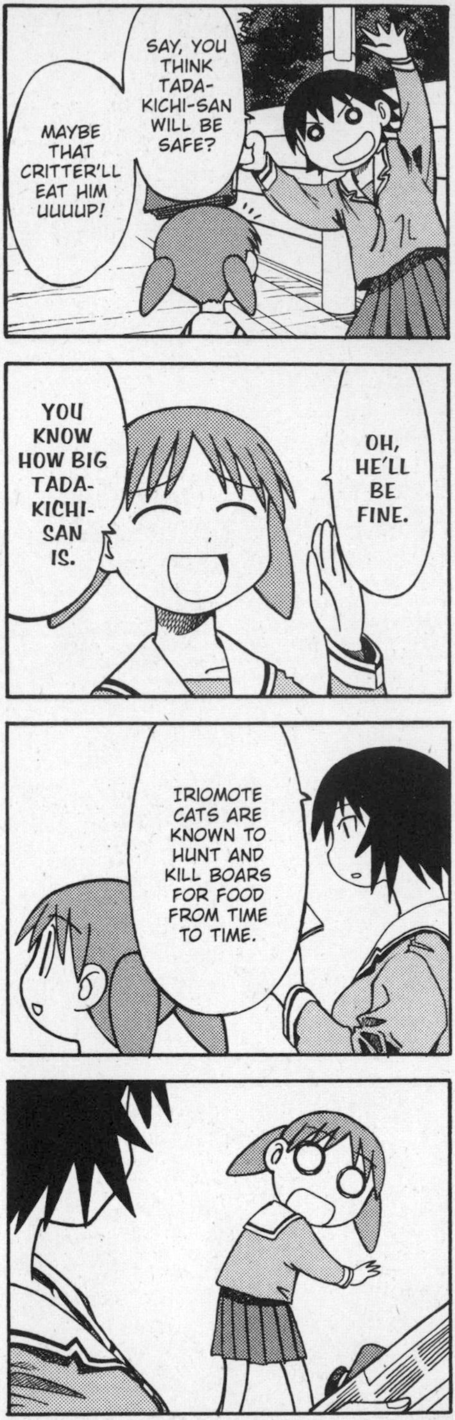
SAY, YOU THINK TADA-KICHI-SAN WILL BE SAFE?
MAYBE THAT CRITTER'LL EAT HIM UUUUP!
OH, HE'LL BE FINE.
YOU KNOW HOW BIG TADA-KICHI-SAN IS.
IRIOMOTE CATS ARE KNOWN TO HUNT AND KILL BOARS FOR FOOD FROM TIME TO TIME.

RESCUE REQUIRED

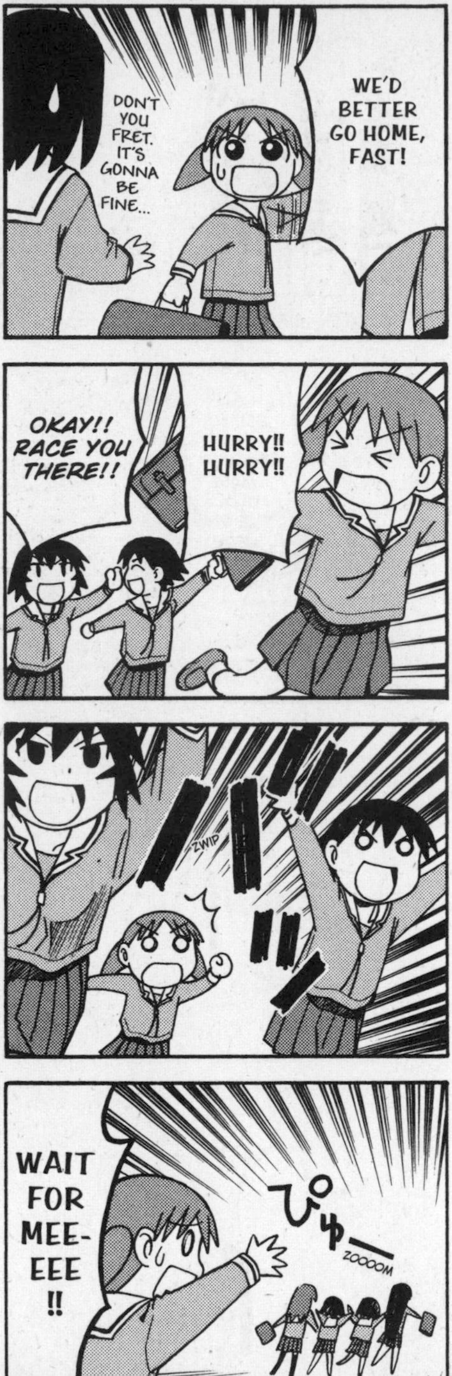
WE'D BETTER GO HOME, FAST!
DON'T YOU FRET. IT'S GONNA BE FINE...
HURRY!! HURRY!!
OKAY!! RACE YOU THERE!!
ZWIP
ぴゅー
ZOOOOM
WAIT FOR MEEE-EEE !!

TADAKICHI-SAN

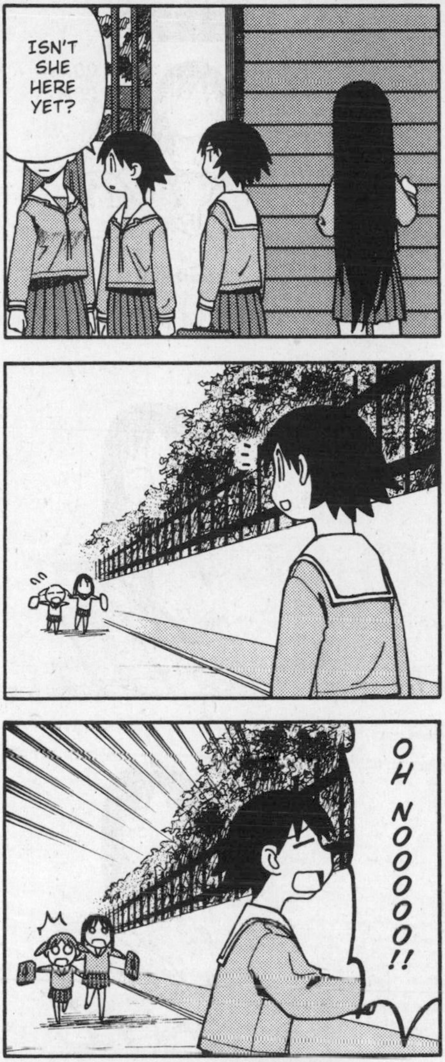
ISN'T SHE HERE YET?
OH NOOOOOO!!
WE DIDN'T MAKE IT IN TIME!
UWAAAAHN!!

IS IT OKAY?

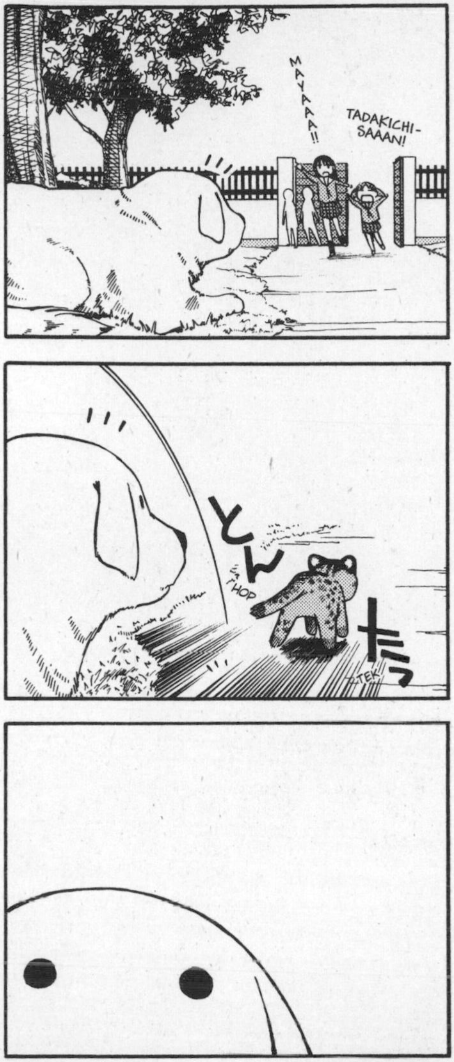
TADAKICHI-SAAAN!
MAYAAA!!
とん
HOP
たっ
TEK
GALUMPH
GALUMPH
ドドド
TEK
てててて
TEK
TEK

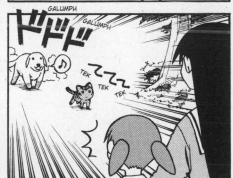

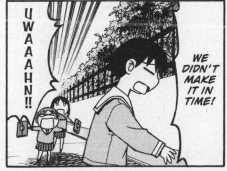

MY TURN

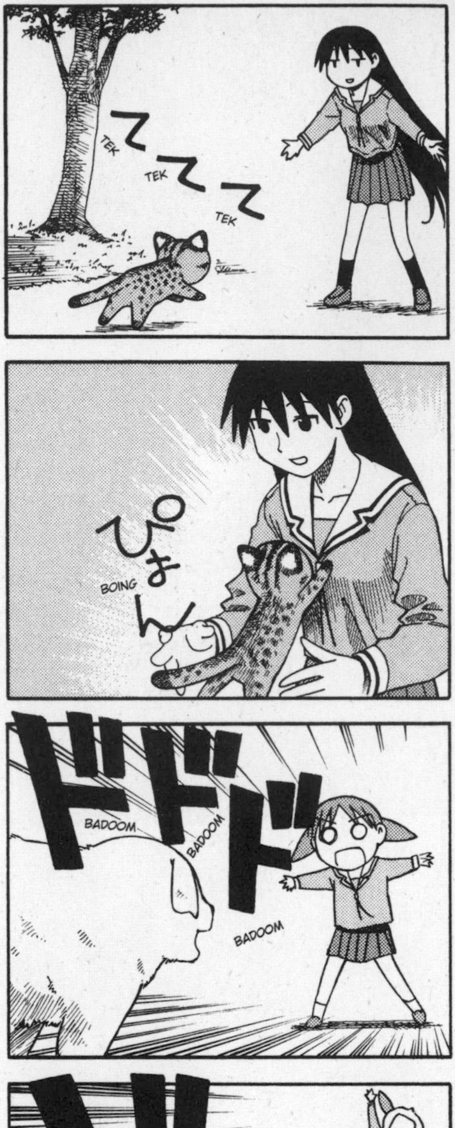
TEK
TEK
TEK
ぴょん
BOING
ドドド
BADOOM
BADOOM
BADOOM
ドド
BLAMMO

OVERWRITE IMPOSSIBLE

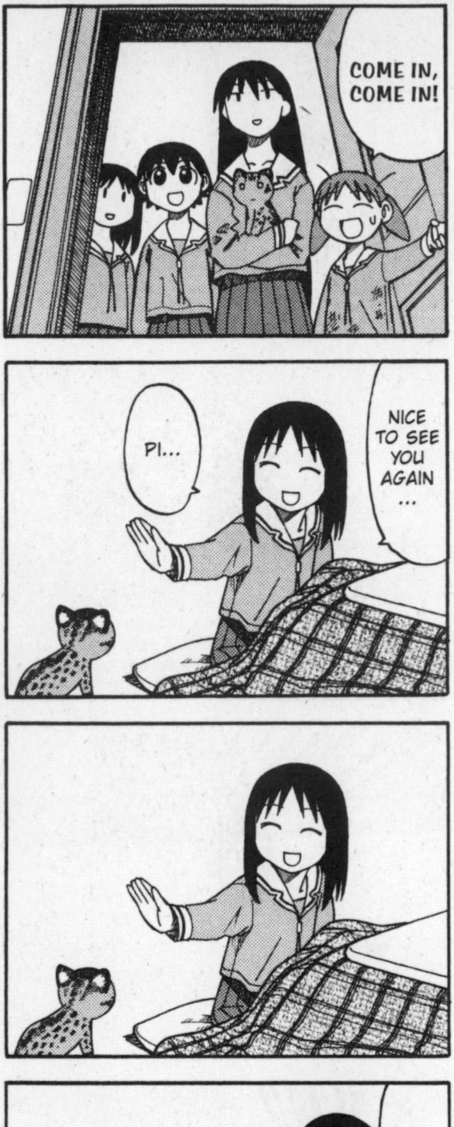
COME IN, COME IN!
NICE TO SEE YOU AGAIN ...
PI...
PIKA ...
... NYA ...
OH, FORGET IT. JUST CALL HIM "PIKANYA."

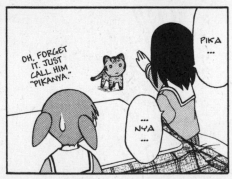

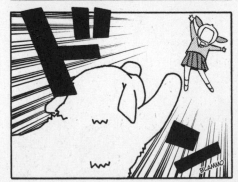

STOP IT

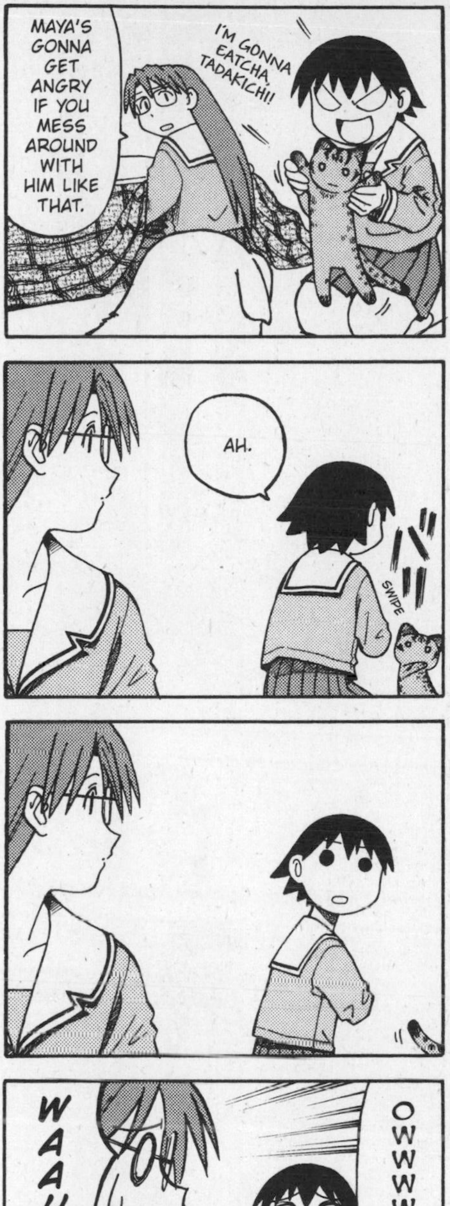
I'M GONNA EATCHA, TADAKICHI!!
MAYA'S GONNA GET ANGRY IF YOU MESS AROUND WITH HIM LIKE THAT.
AH.
SWIPE
OWWWWWW!!
SPLOSHH
だら~
WAAH!!

LESSON LEARNED

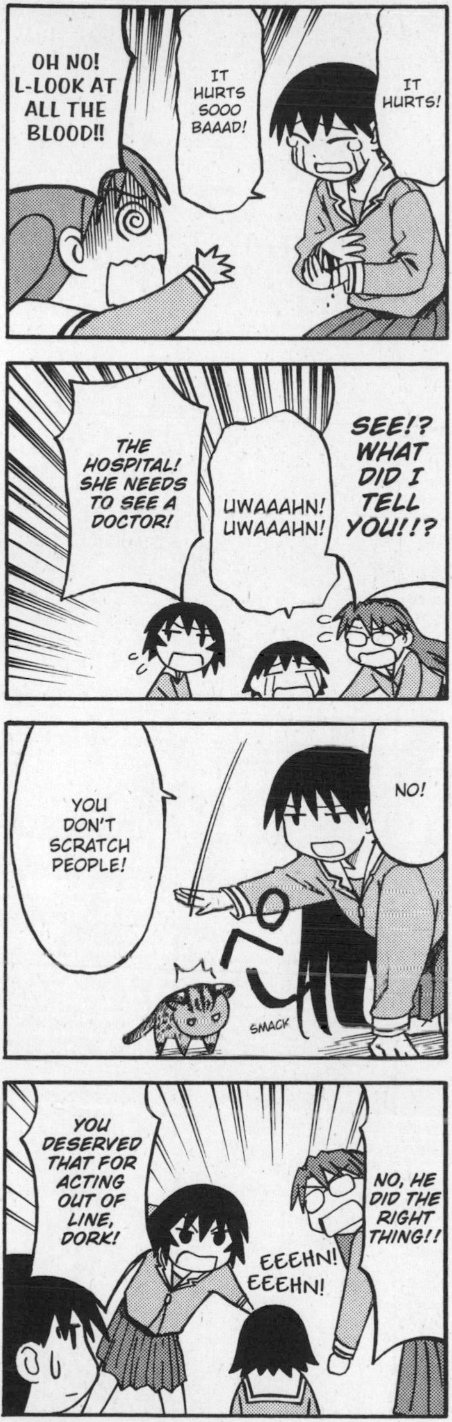
IT HURTS!
IT HURTS SOOO BAAAD!
OH NO! L-LOOK AT ALL THE BLOOD!!
SEE!? WHAT DID I TELL YOU!!?
UWAAAHN! UWAAAHN!
THE HOSPITAL! SHE NEEDS TO SEE A DOCTOR!
NO!
YOU DON'T SCRATCH PEOPLE!
SMACK
NO, HE DID THE RIGHT THING!!
EEEHN! EEEHN!
YOU DESERVED THAT FOR ACTING OUT OF LINE, DORK!

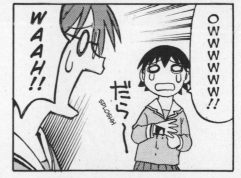

POPULAR

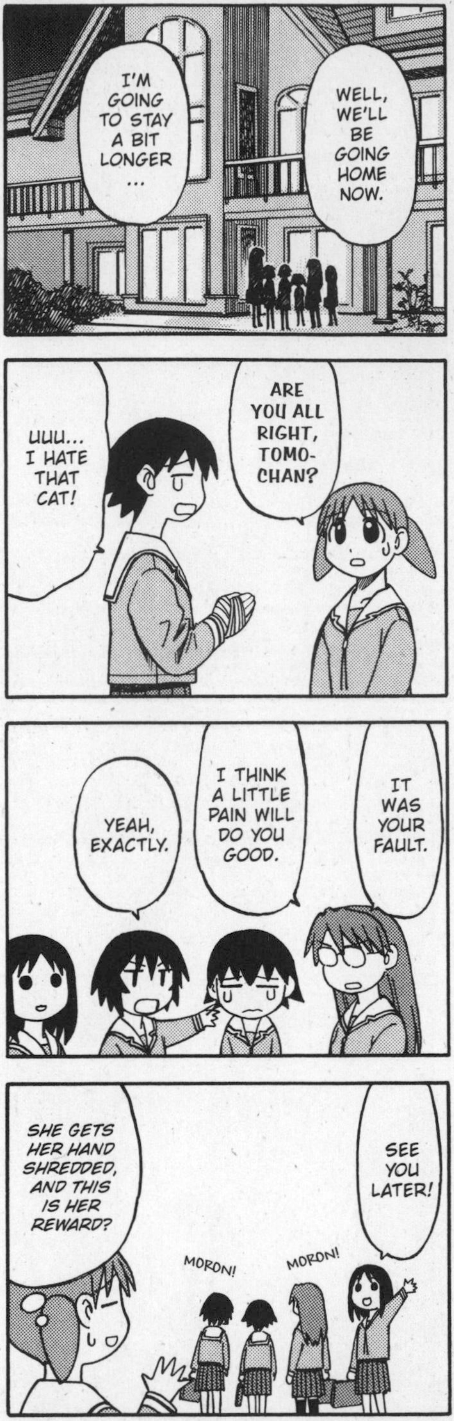
WELL, WE'LL BE GOING HOME NOW.
I'M GOING TO STAY A BIT LONGER ...
ARE YOU ALL RIGHT, TOMO-CHAN?
UUU... I HATE THAT CAT!
IT WAS YOUR FAULT.
I THINK A LITTLE PAIN WILL DO YOU GOOD.
YEAH, EXACTLY.
SEE YOU LATER!
SHE GETS HER HAND SHREDDED, AND THIS IS HER REWARD?
MORON!
MORON!

TOGETHER WITH MAYA

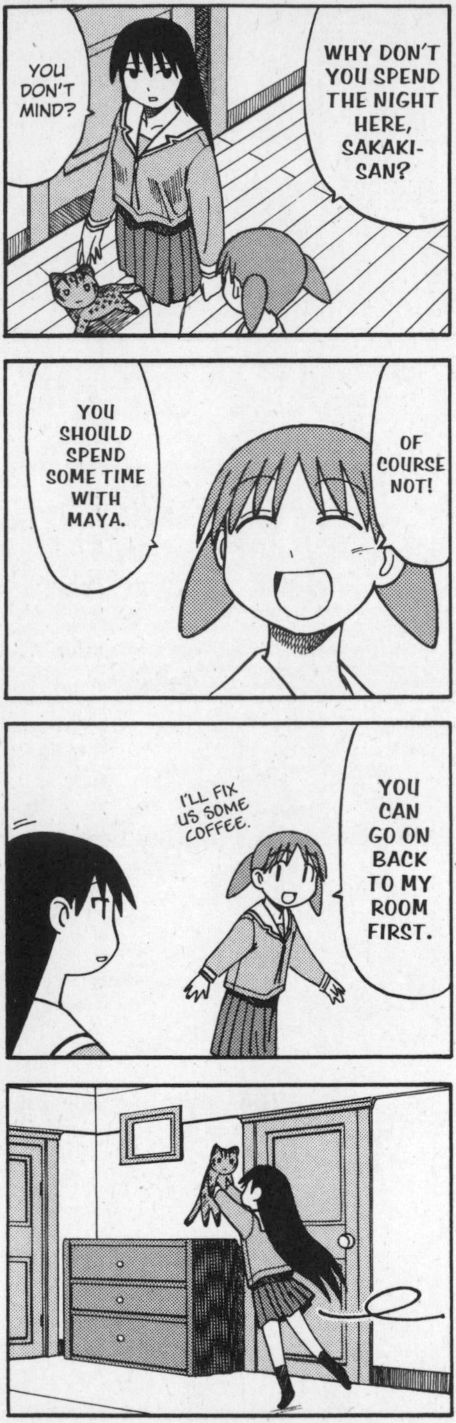
WHY DON'T YOU SPEND THE NIGHT HERE, SAKAKI-SAN?
YOU DON'T MIND?
OF COURSE NOT!
YOU SHOULD SPEND SOME TIME WITH MAYA.
YOU CAN GO ON BACK TO MY ROOM FIRST.
I'LL FIX US SOME COFFEE.

UNBEARABLE

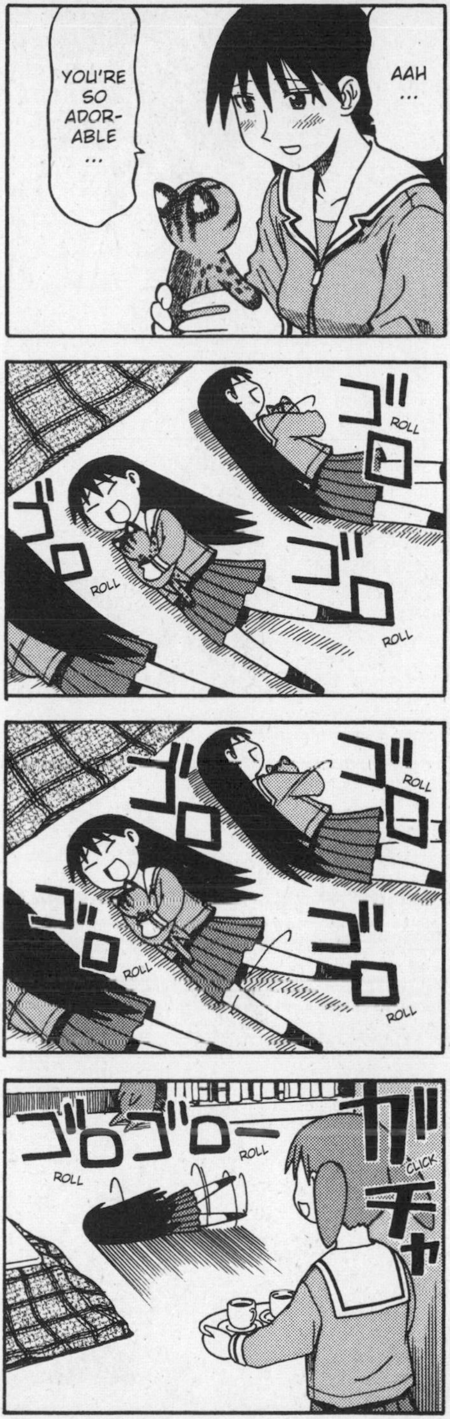
AAH ...
YOU'RE SO ADORABLE ...
ゴロ ROLL
ゴロ ROLL
ゴロ ROLL
ゴロ ROLL
ゴロ ROLL
ゴロ ROLL
ガチャ CLICK
ゴロゴロー ROLL ROLL

NOTHING

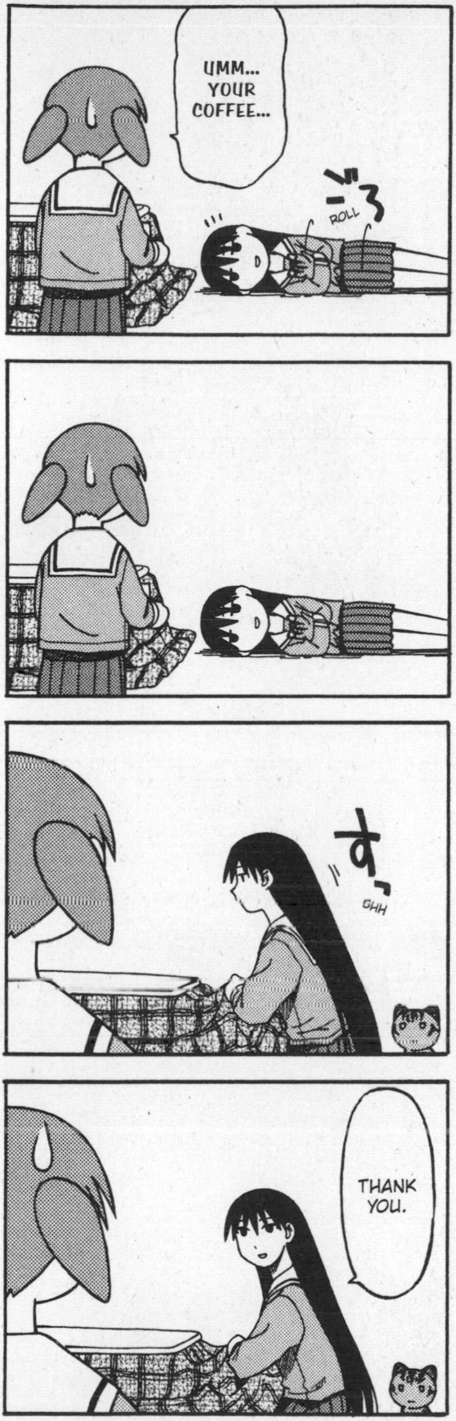
UMM... YOUR COFFEE...
ごろ ROLL
す SHH
THANK YOU.

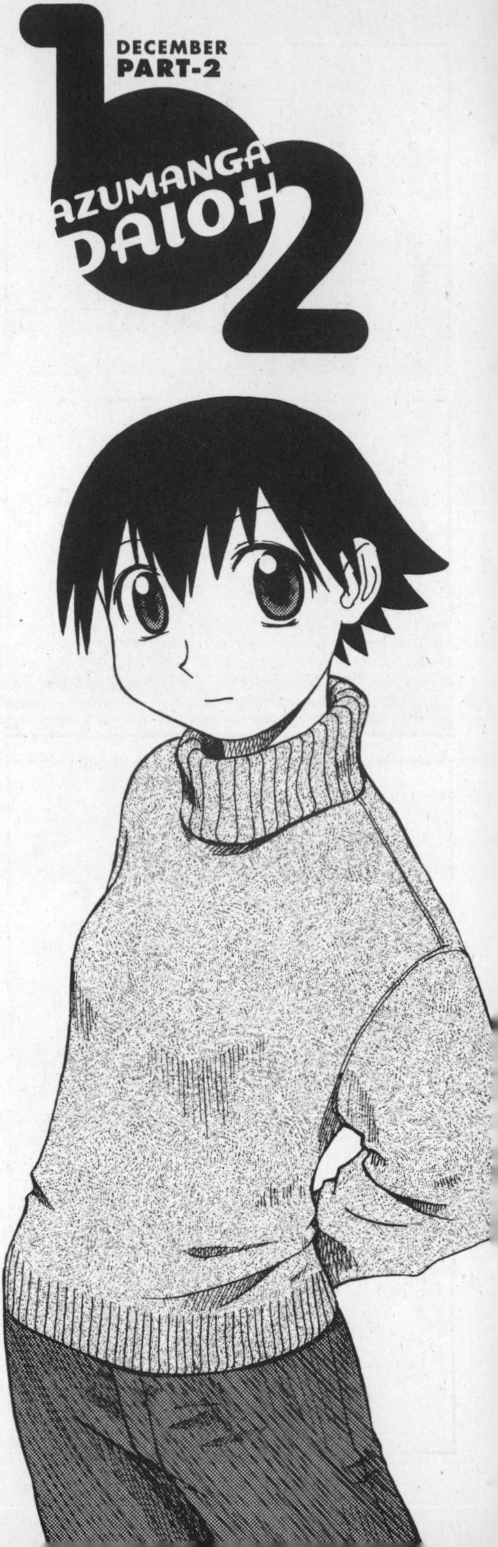
12
DECEMBER
PART-2
AZUMANGA DAIOH

WILD ANIMAL

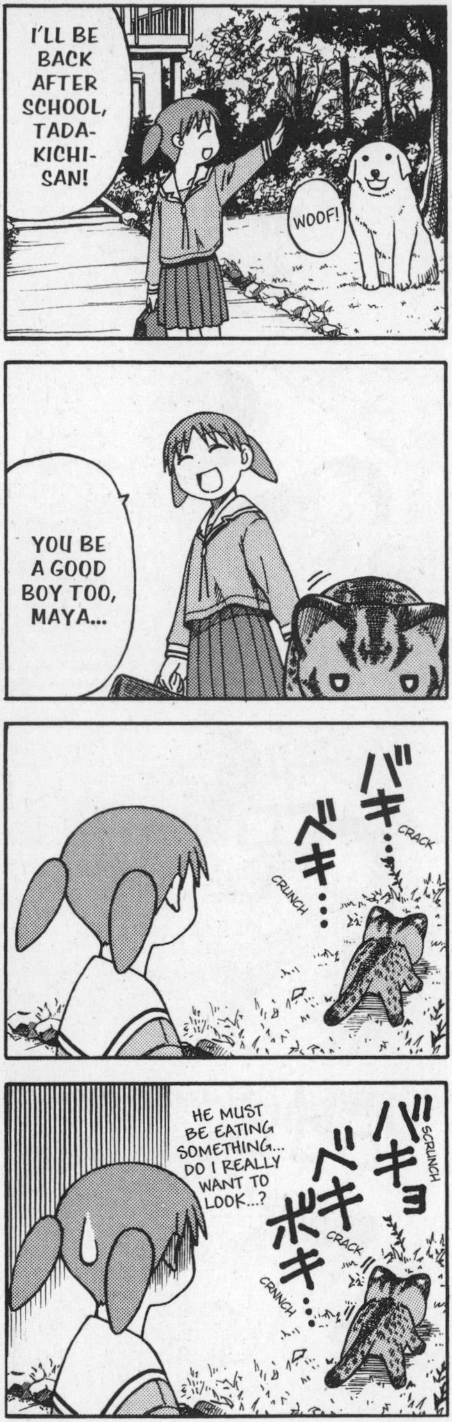
I'LL BE BACK AFTER SCHOOL, TADA-KICHI-SAN!
WOOF!
YOU BE A GOOD BOY TOO, MAYA...
バキ… CRACK
ベキ… CRUNCH
HE MUST BE EATING SOMETHING... DO I REALLY WANT TO LOOK...?
バキョ SCRUNCH
ベキ CRACK
ボキ… CRNNCH

EVASION

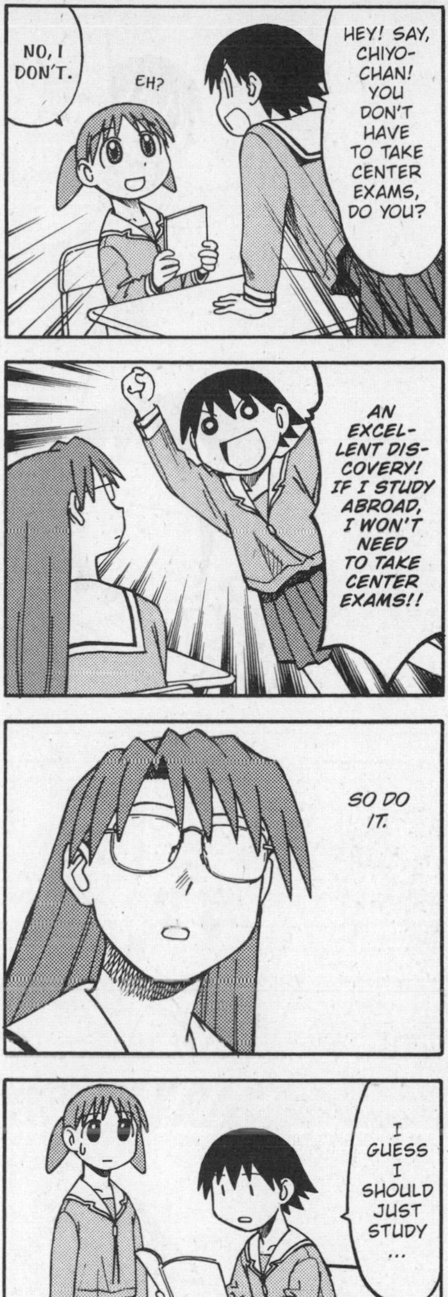
HEY! SAY, CHIYO-CHAN! YOU DON'T HAVE TO TAKE CENTER EXAMS, DO YOU?
EH?
NO, I DON'T.
AN EXCEL-LENT DIS-COVERY! IF I STUDY ABROAD, I WON'T NEED TO TAKE CENTER EXAMS!!
SO DO IT.
I GUESS I SHOULD JUST STUDY ...

QUESTION 1

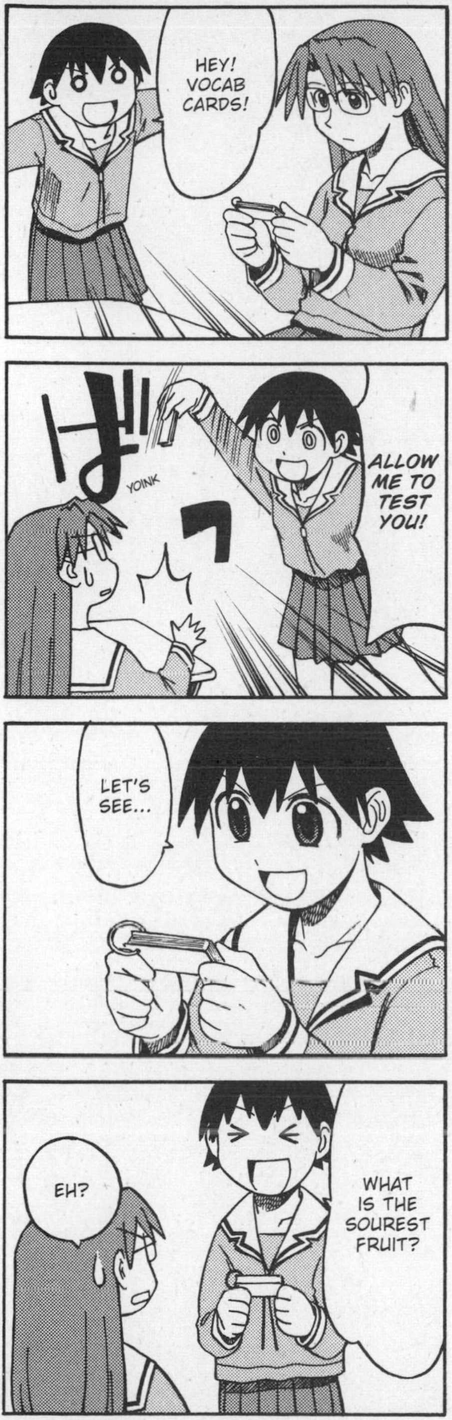
HEY! VOCAB CARDS!
ALLOW ME TO TEST YOU!
YOINK
LET'S SEE...
WHAT IS THE SOUREST FRUIT?
EH?

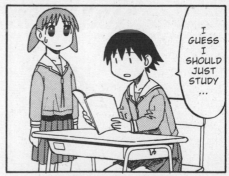

I GET IT!

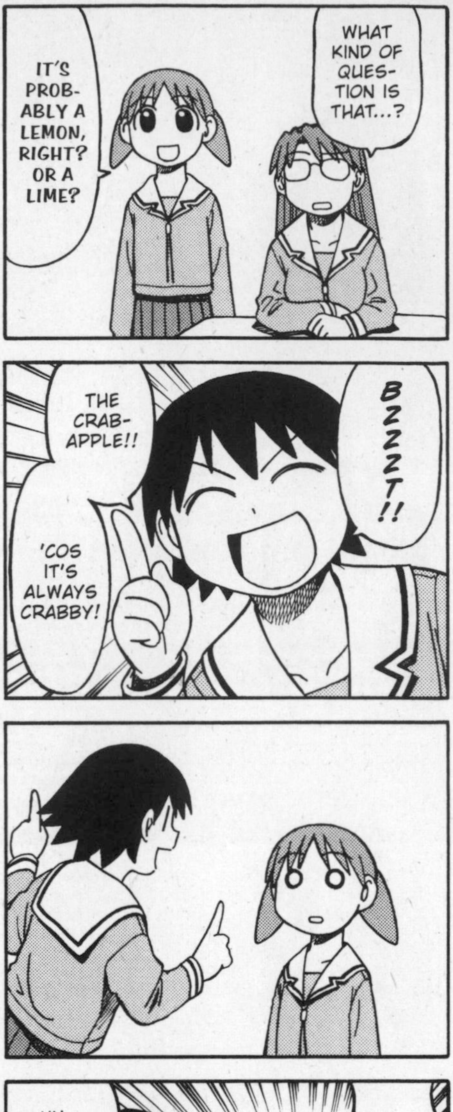

WHAT KIND OF QUES-TION IS THAT...?
IT'S PROB-ABLY A LEMON, RIGHT? OR A LIME?
BZZZT!!
THE CRAB-APPLE!!
'COS IT'S ALWAYS CRABBY!
!!
UH, DON'T TAKE IT TOO SERI-OUSLY NOW.
NOD
NOD

OF COURSE!!

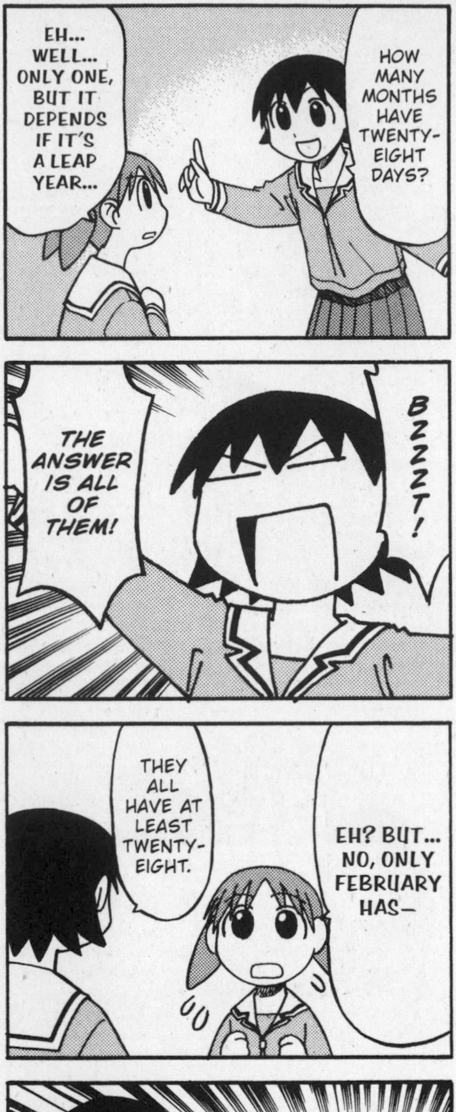

HOW MANY MONTHS HAVE TWENTY-EIGHT DAYS?
EH... WELL... ONLY ONE, BUT IT DEPENDS IF IT'S A LEAP YEAR...
BZZZT!
THE ANSWER IS ALL OF THEM!
EH? BUT... NO, ONLY FEBRUARY HAS—
THEY ALL HAVE AT LEAST TWENTY-EIGHT.
THIS IS KINDA FUN...

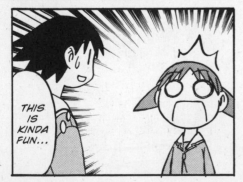

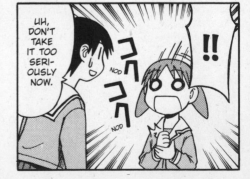

SPECIAL TALENT?

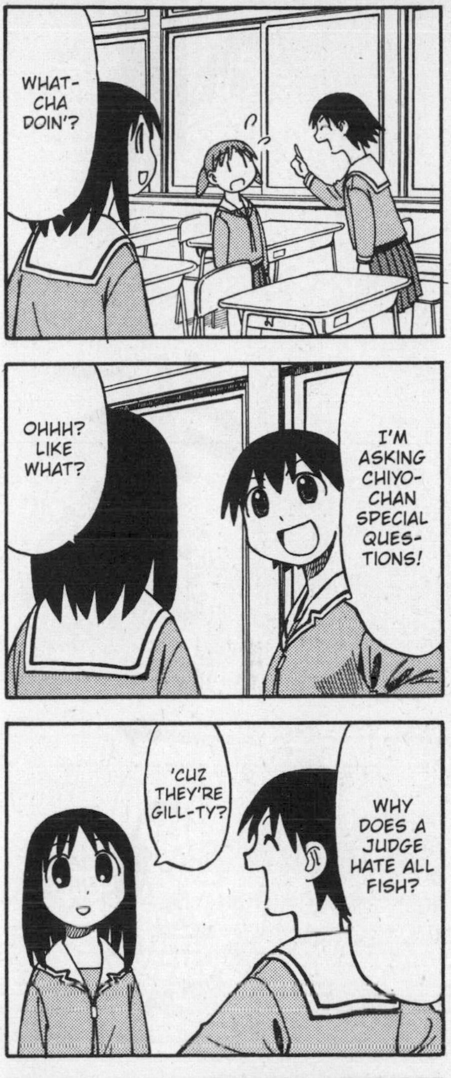
WHAT-CHA DOIN'?
I'M ASKING CHIYO-CHAN SPECIAL QUES-TIONS!
OHHH? LIKE WHAT?
WHY DOES A JUDGE HATE ALL FISH?
'CUZ THEY'RE GILL-TY?
SHE GOT IT RIGHT OFF!?
THAT WAS AMAZ-ING!!
HUH? IT WAS?

PIECE OF CAKE

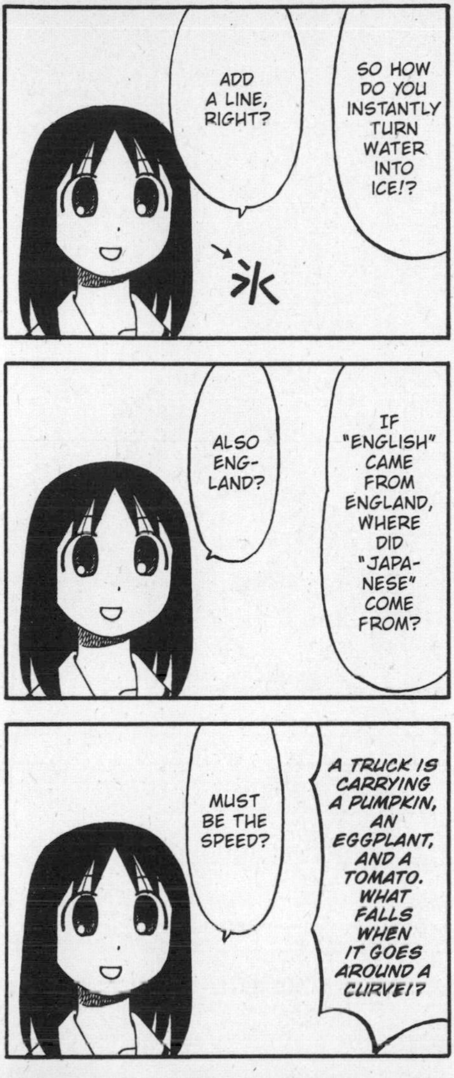
SO HOW DO YOU INSTANTLY TURN WATER INTO ICE!?
ADD A LINE, RIGHT?
氷
IF "ENGLISH" CAME FROM ENGLAND, WHERE DID "JAPANESE" COME FROM?
ALSO ENG-LAND?
A TRUCK IS CARRYING A PUMPKIN, AN EGGPLANT, AND A TOMATO. WHAT FALLS WHEN IT GOES AROUND A CURVE!?
MUST BE THE SPEED?
H-HOLY CRAP!
HOW DOES SHE DO IT!!?
ぱちぱち
CLAP CLAP
ぱちぱち
CLAP CLAP
WHAT? DID AH GET 'EM RIGHT?

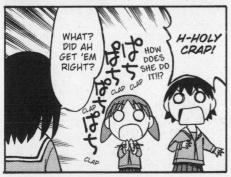

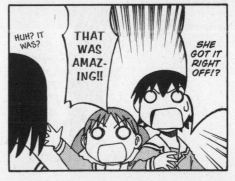

CAREER COUNSELING

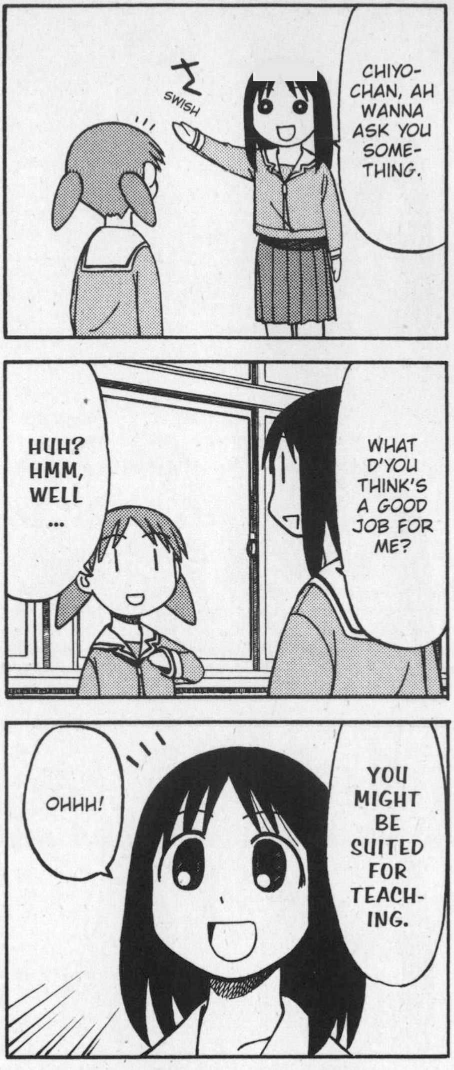
CHIYO-CHAN, AH WANNA ASK YOU SOME-THING.
SWISH
WHAT D'YOU THINK'S A GOOD JOB FOR ME?
HUH? HMM, WELL ...
YOU MIGHT BE SUITED FOR TEACH-ING.
OHHH!
I FEEL LIKE YOUR STUDENTS WOULD HAVE VERY CREATIVE MINDS!
COOL!
I DON'T KNOW ABOUT THAT ...

DON'T INSULT ME

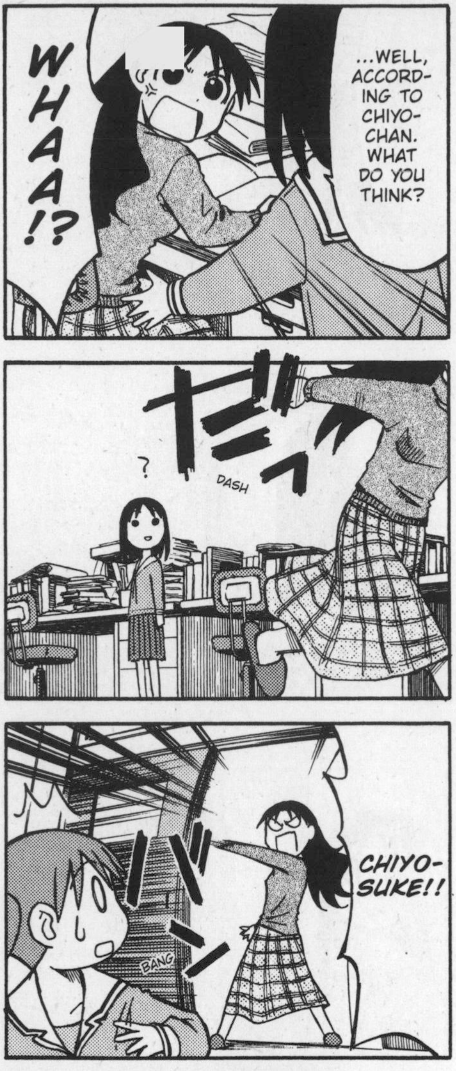
...WELL, ACCORD-ING TO CHIYO-CHAN. WHAT DO YOU THINK?
WHAAA!?
DASH
?
CHIYO-SUKE!!
BANG
SO I HEAR YOU THINK I'M AN IDIOT!
?
?

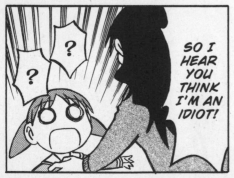

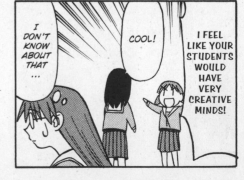

DREAMS

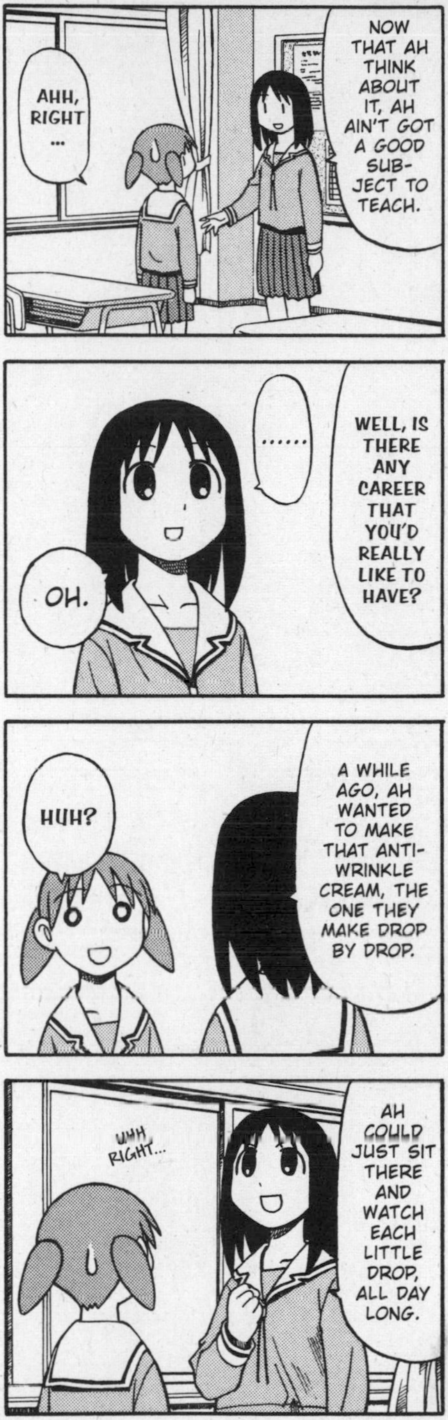
NOW THAT AH THINK ABOUT IT, AH AIN'T GOT A GOOD SUBJECT TO TEACH.
AHH, RIGHT ...
WELL, IS THERE ANY CAREER THAT YOU'D REALLY LIKE TO HAVE?
......
OH.
A WHILE AGO, AH WANTED TO MAKE THAT ANTI-WRINKLE CREAM, THE ONE THEY MAKE DROP BY DROP.
HUH?
AH COULD JUST SIT THERE AND WATCH EACH LITTLE DROP, ALL DAY LONG.
UHH RIGHT...

GUIDANCE

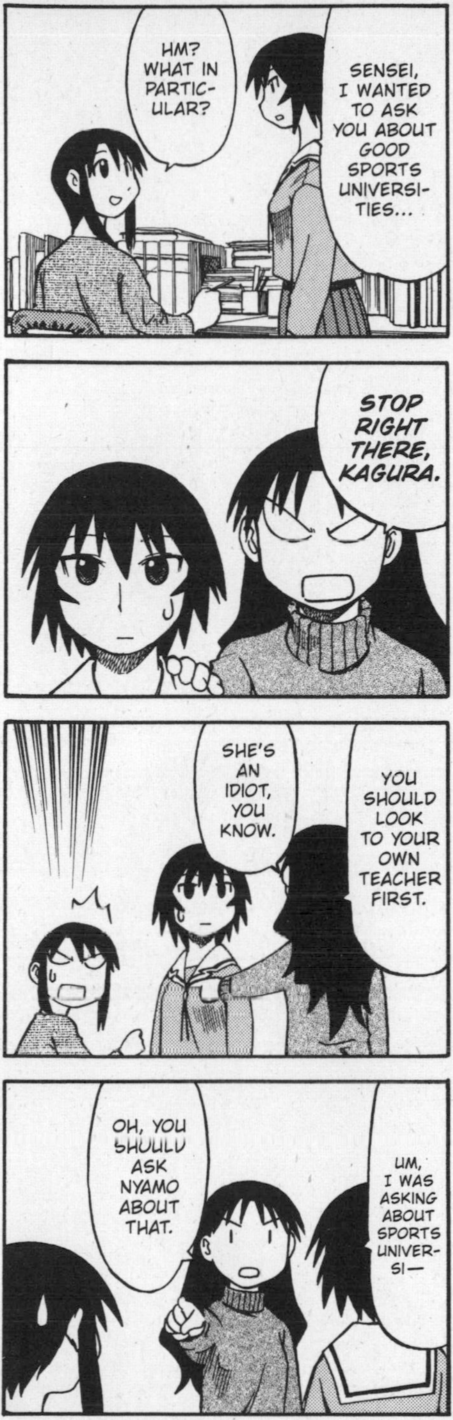
SENSEI, I WANTED TO ASK YOU ABOUT GOOD SPORTS UNIVERSITIES...
HM? WHAT IN PARTICULAR?
STOP RIGHT THERE, KAGURA.
YOU SHOULD LOOK TO YOUR OWN TEACHER FIRST.
SHE'S AN IDIOT, YOU KNOW.
UM, I WAS ASKING ABOUT SPORTS UNIVERSI—
OH, YOU SHOULD ASK NYAMO ABOUT THAT.

FORTUNE-TELLING

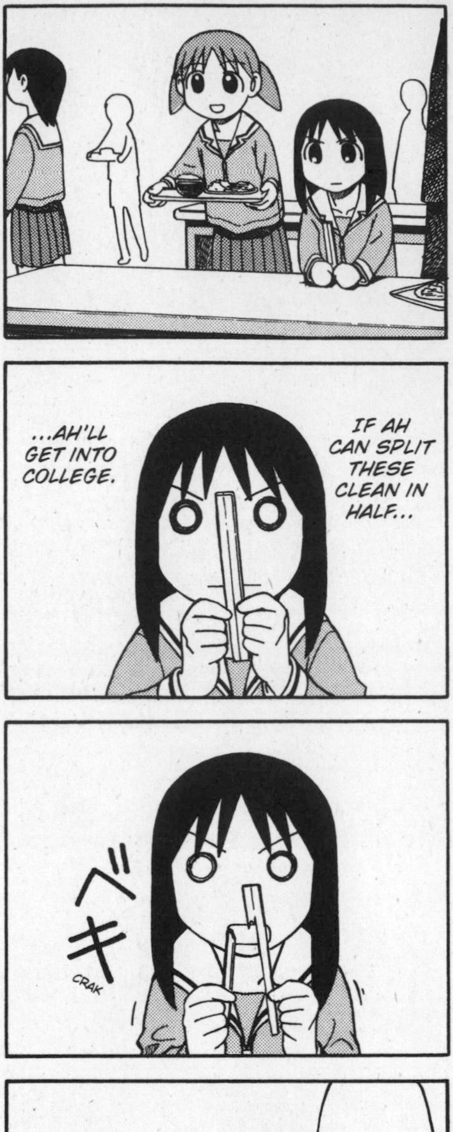
IF AH CAN SPLIT THESE CLEAN IN HALF...
...AH'LL GET INTO COLLEGE.
ベキ
CRAK
THAT ONE... DON'T COUNT.

TEACHING THE SECRET

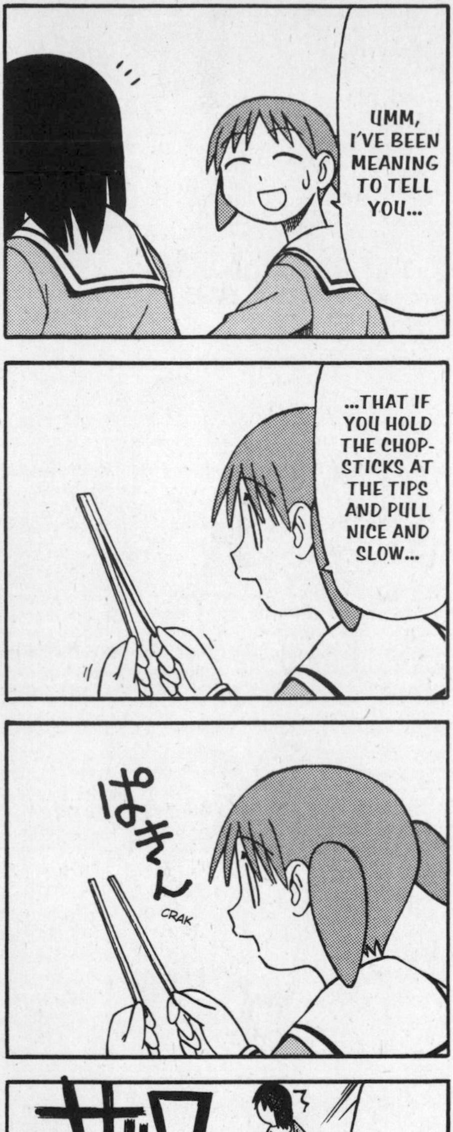
UMM, I'VE BEEN MEANING TO TELL YOU...
...THAT IF YOU HOLD THE CHOP-STICKS AT THE TIPS AND PULL NICE AND SLOW...
ぱきん
CRAK
ザワ
MURMUR
...THEY'LL BREAK CLEANLY...

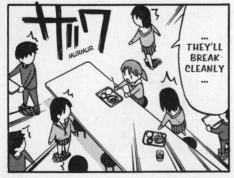

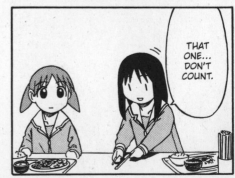

THE BACKDOOR WAY INTO COLLEGE

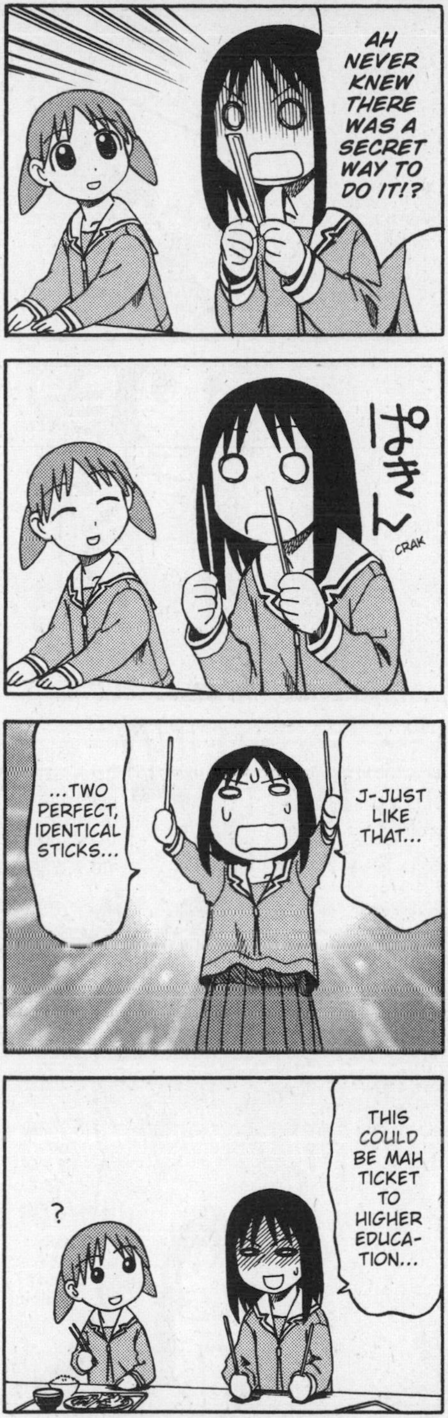
AH NEVER KNEW THERE WAS A SECRET WAY TO DO IT!?
ぱきん
CRAK
J-JUST LIKE THAT...
...TWO PERFECT, IDENTICAL STICKS...
THIS COULD BE MAH TICKET TO HIGHER EDUCATION...
?

FOR GOOD LUCK

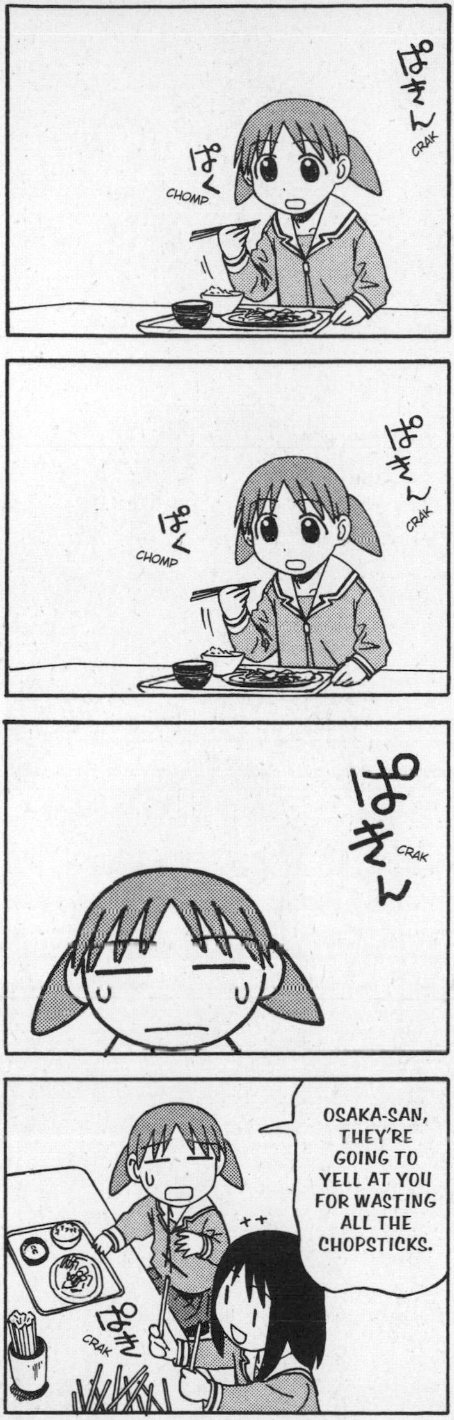
ぱきん
CRAK
ぱく
CHOMP
ぱきん
CRAK
ぱく
CHOMP
ぱきん
CRAK
OSAKA-SAN, THEY'RE GOING TO YELL AT YOU FOR WASTING ALL THE CHOPSTICKS.
ぱき
CRAK

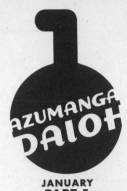

AZUMANGA DAIOH

JANUARY PART-1

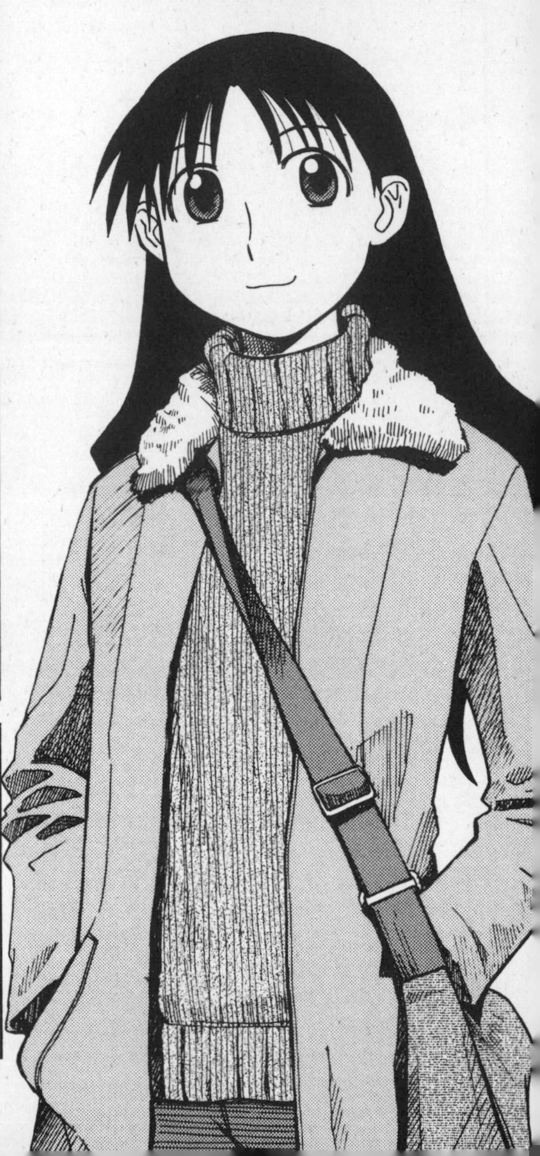

LANDMARK

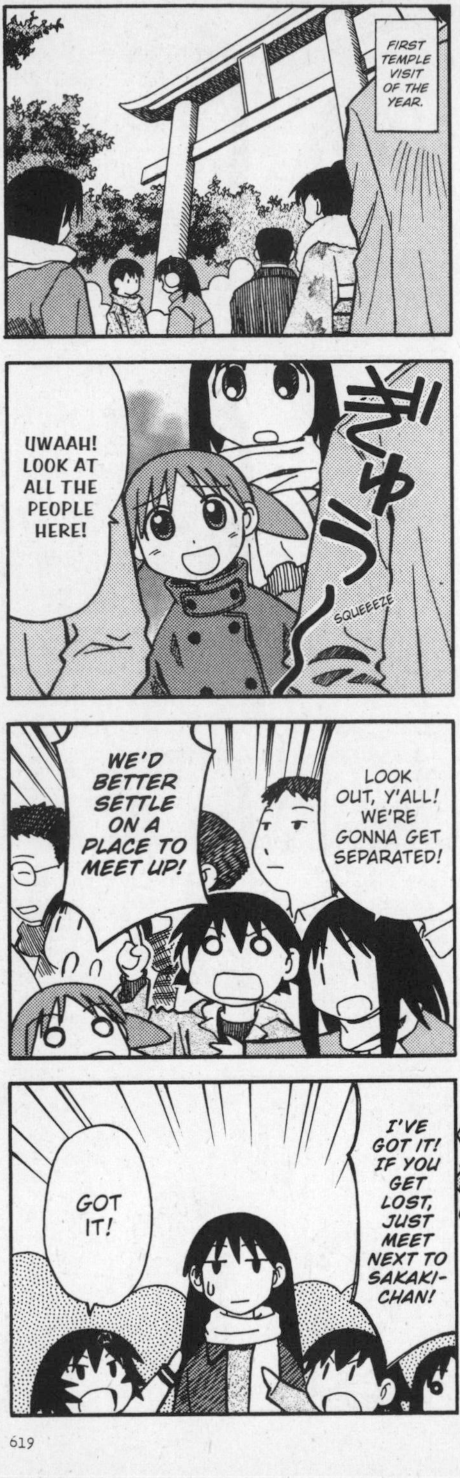
FIRST TEMPLE VISIT OF THE YEAR.
ぎゅう
SQUEEEZE
UWAAH! LOOK AT ALL THE PEOPLE HERE!
LOOK OUT, Y'ALL! WE'RE GONNA GET SEPARATED!
WE'D BETTER SETTLE ON A PLACE TO MEET UP!
I'VE GOT IT! IF YOU GET LOST, JUST MEET NEXT TO SAKAKI-CHAN!
GOT IT!

NO GOOD

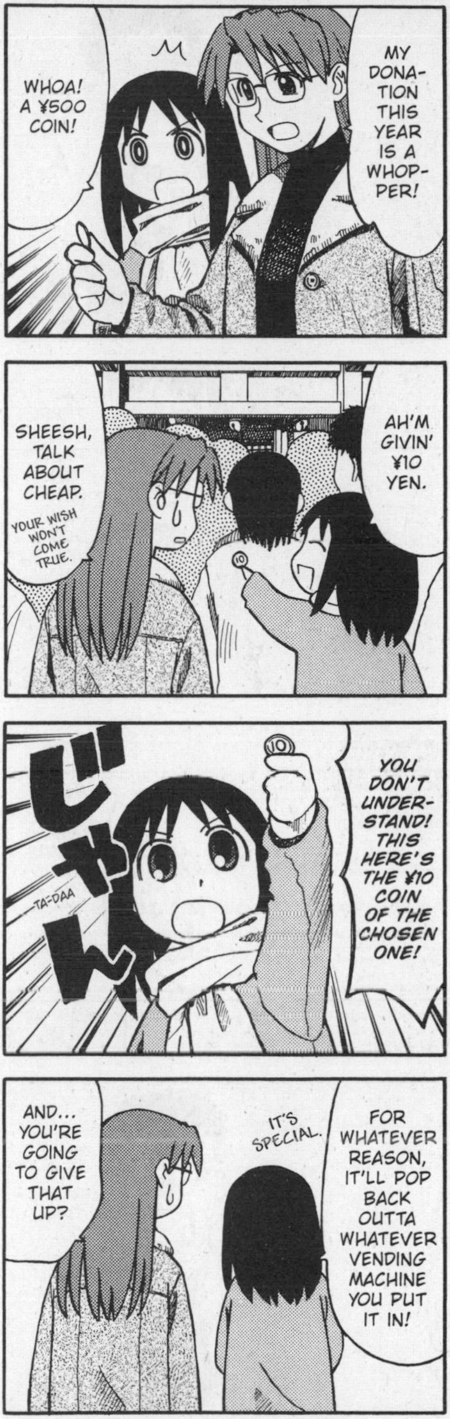
MY DONATION THIS YEAR IS A WHOPPER!
WHOA! A ¥500 COIN!
AH'M GIVIN' ¥10 YEN.
SHEESH, TALK ABOUT CHEAP.
YOUR WISH WON'T COME TRUE.
YOU DON'T UNDERSTAND! THIS HERE'S THE ¥10 COIN OF THE CHOSEN ONE!
じゃん
TA-DAA
FOR WHATEVER REASON, IT'LL POP BACK OUTTA WHATEVER VENDING MACHINE YOU PUT IT IN!
IT'S SPECIAL.
AND... YOU'RE GOING TO GIVE THAT UP?

THIS IS FUN

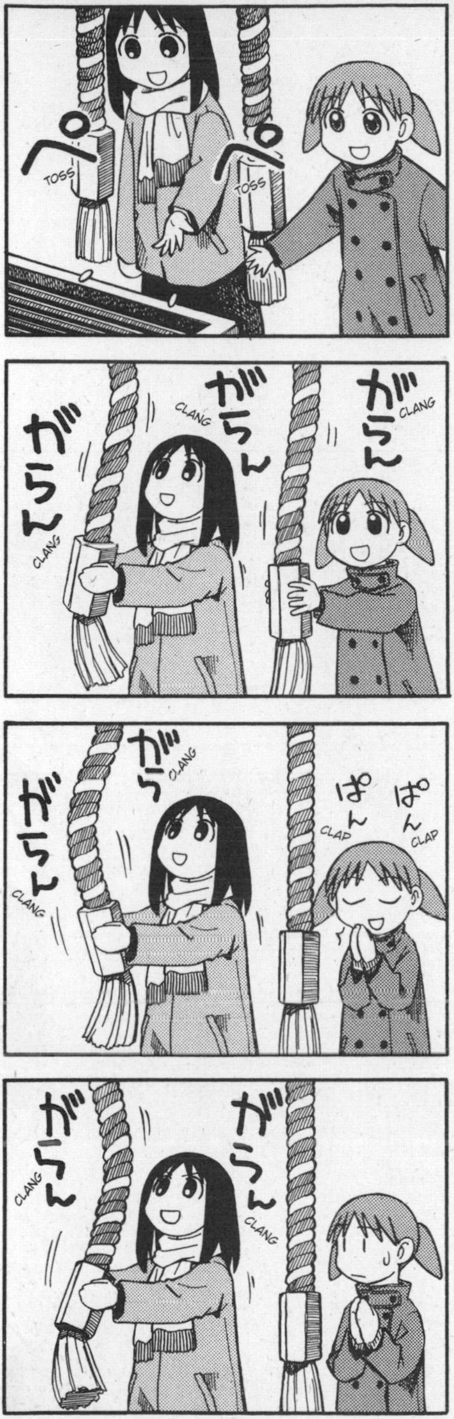
TOSS
TOSS
がらん
CLANG
がらん
CLANG
がらん
CLANG
ぱん
CLAP
ぱん
CLAP
がら
CLANG
がらん
CLANG
がらん
CLANG
がらん
CLANG

THE POWER OF WEALTH

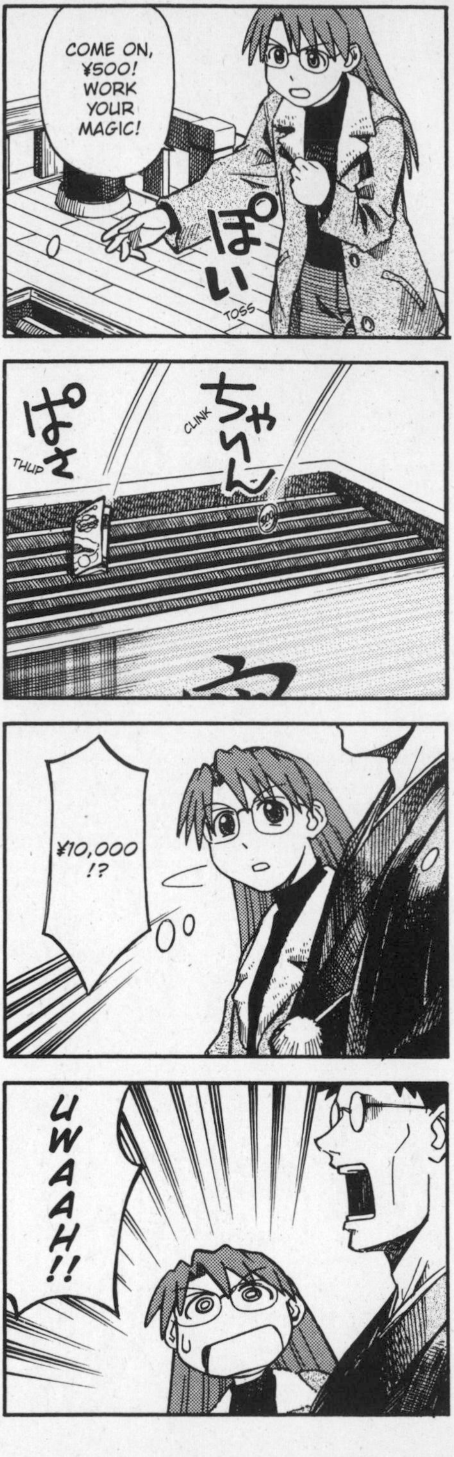
COME ON, ¥500! WORK YOUR MAGIC!
ぽい
TOSS
ちゃりん
CLINK
ぱさ
THUP
¥10,000!?
UWAAAH!!

WISH

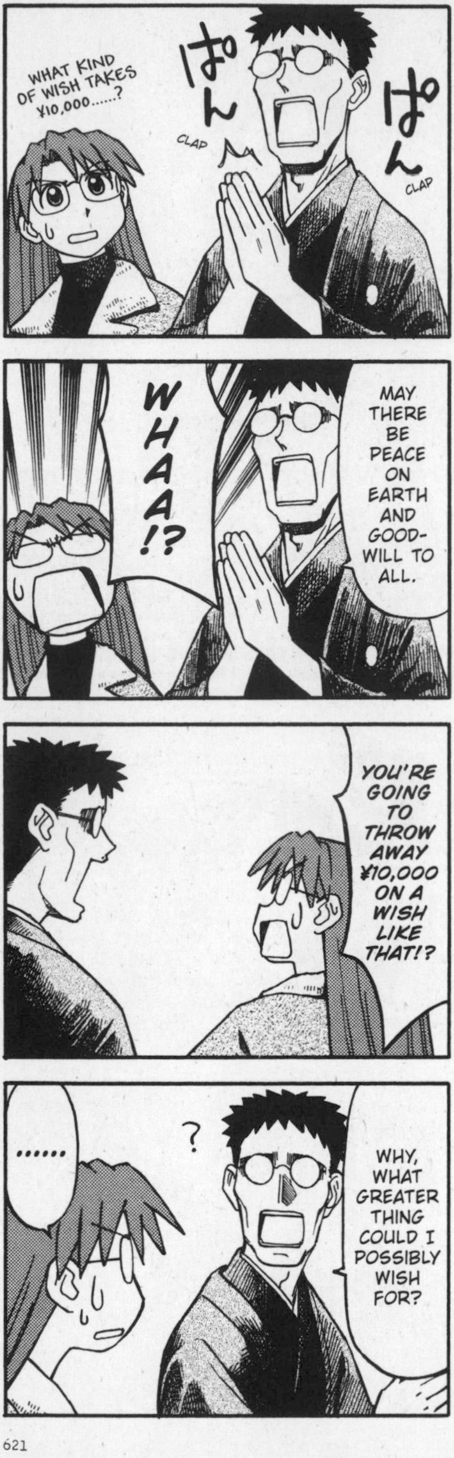
ぱん
CLAP
ぱん
CLAP
WHAT KIND OF WISH TAKES ¥10,000......?
MAY THERE BE PEACE ON EARTH AND GOOD-WILL TO ALL.
WHAAA!?
YOU'RE GOING TO THROW AWAY ¥10,000 ON A WISH LIKE THAT!?
WHY, WHAT GREATER THING COULD I POSSIBLY WISH FOR?
?
......

FOOD

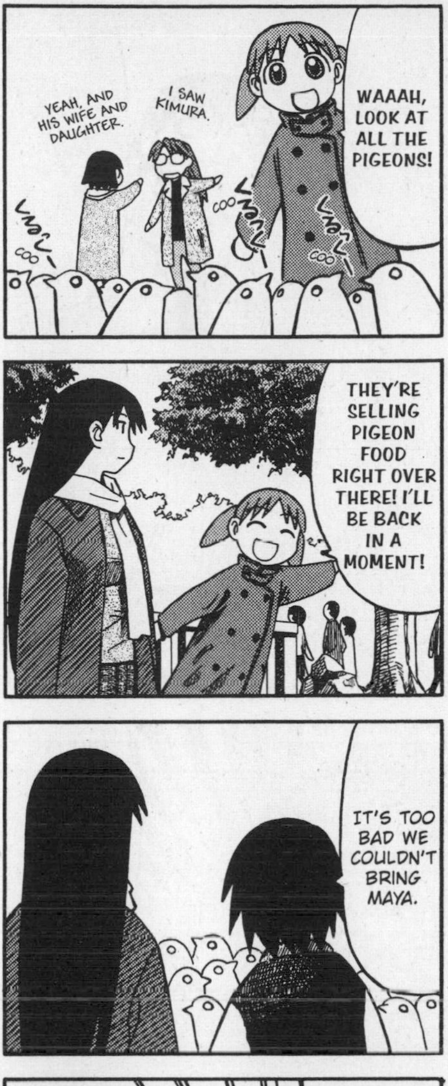
WAAAH, LOOK AT ALL THE PIGEONS!
I SAW KIMURA.
YEAH, AND HIS WIFE AND DAUGHTER.
くるっくー
COO
THEY'RE SELLING PIGEON FOOD RIGHT OVER THERE! I'LL BE BACK IN A MOMENT!
IT'S TOO BAD WE COULDN'T BRING MAYA.
HE COULDA WIPED OUT THIS WHOLE FLOCK OF PIGEONS IN TWO SECONDS. THE DOLTS WOULDA NEVER SEEN IT COMIN'!
COO
くるっくー

PIGEON POST

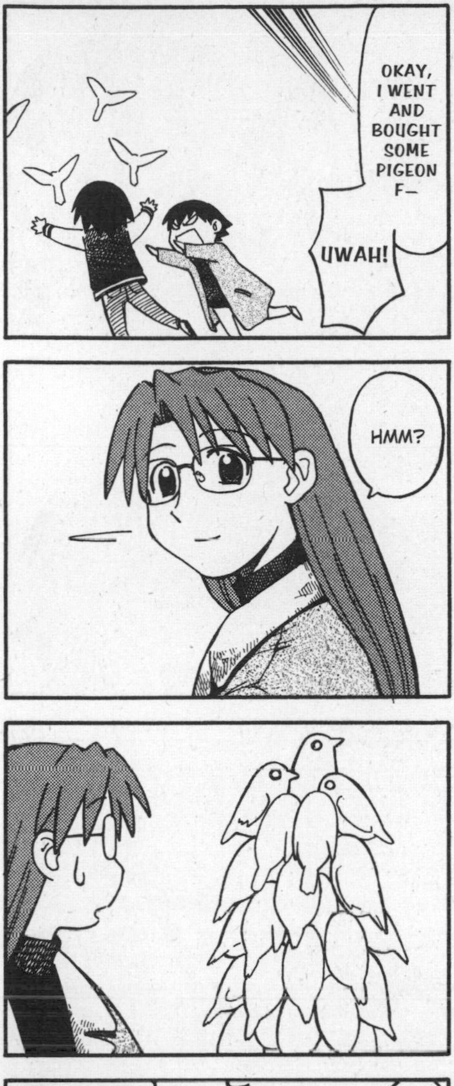
OKAY, I WENT AND BOUGHT SOME PIGEON F—
UWAH!
HMM?
CHIYO-CHAN !?
AAAH!!

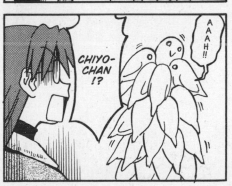

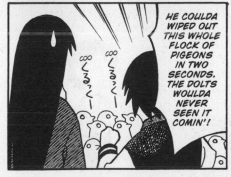

FORTUNE CONTEST

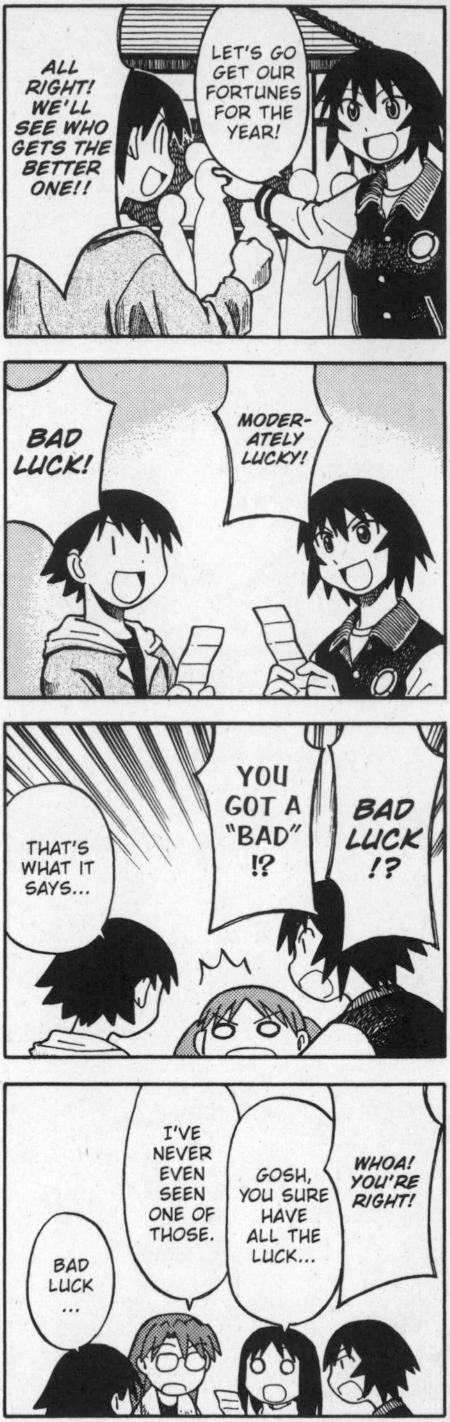
LET'S GO GET OUR FORTUNES FOR THE YEAR!
ALL RIGHT! WE'LL SEE WHO GETS THE BETTER ONE!!
MODERATELY LUCKY!
BAD LUCK!
BAD LUCK !?
YOU GOT A "BAD" !?
THAT'S WHAT IT SAYS...
WHOA! YOU'RE RIGHT!
GOSH, YOU SURE HAVE ALL THE LUCK...
I'VE NEVER EVEN SEEN ONE OF THOSE.
BAD LUCK ...

WHAT SHOULD I DO?

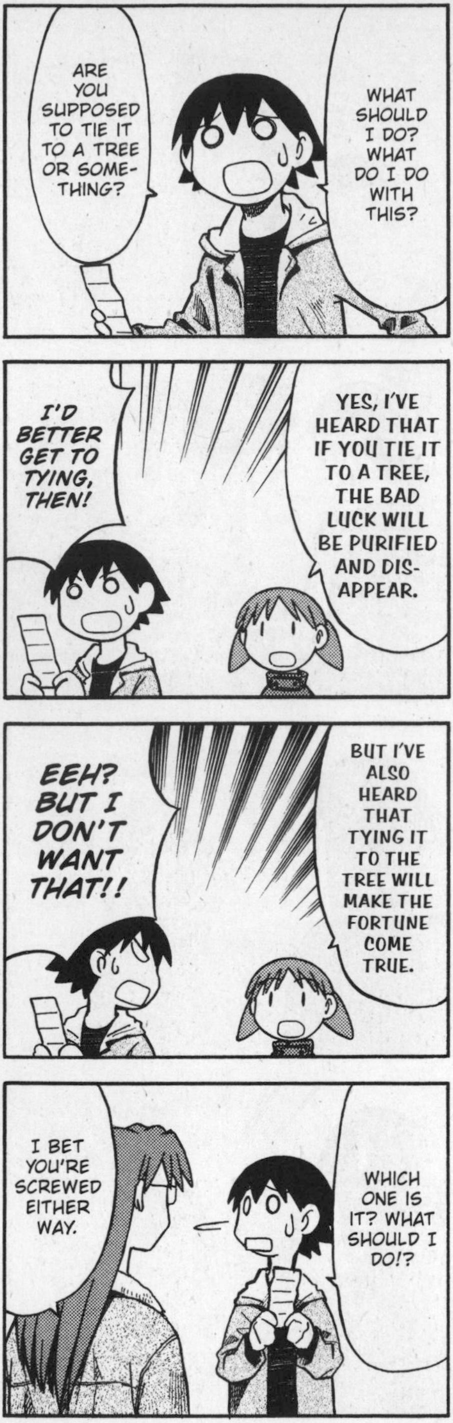
WHAT SHOULD I DO? WHAT DO I DO WITH THIS?
ARE YOU SUPPOSED TO TIE IT TO A TREE OR SOMETHING?
YES, I'VE HEARD THAT IF YOU TIE IT TO A TREE, THE BAD LUCK WILL BE PURIFIED AND DISAPPEAR.
I'D BETTER GET TO TYING, THEN!
BUT I'VE ALSO HEARD THAT TYING IT TO THE TREE WILL MAKE THE FORTUNE COME TRUE.
EEH? BUT I DON'T WANT THAT!!
WHICH ONE IS IT? WHAT SHOULD I DO!?
I BET YOU'RE SCREWED EITHER WAY.

VICTORY IS AT HAND

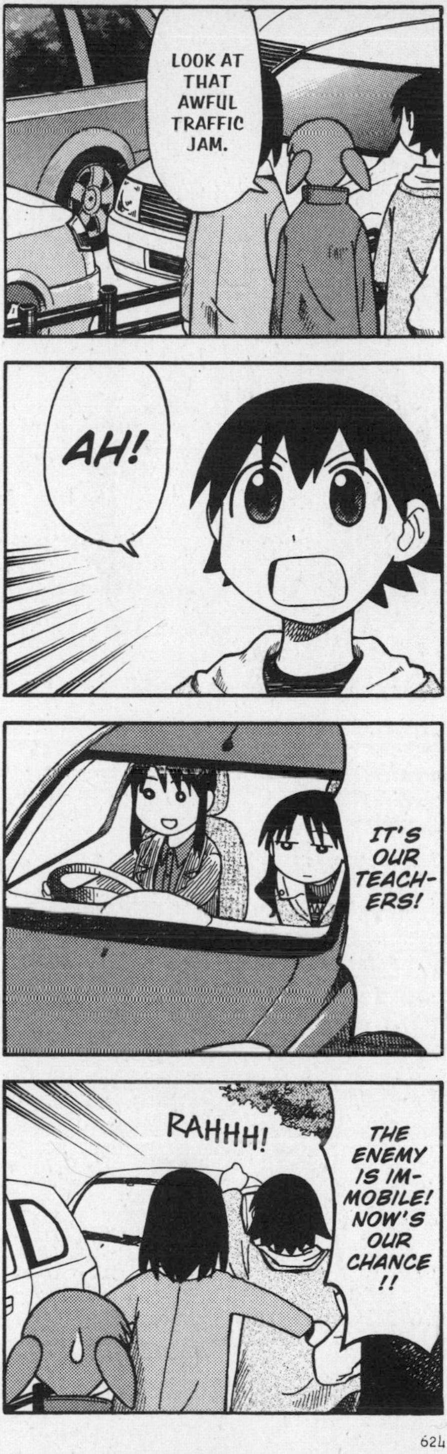
LOOK AT THAT AWFUL TRAFFIC JAM.
AH!
IT'S OUR TEACHERS!
THE ENEMY IS IMMOBILE! NOW'S OUR CHANCE!!
RAHHH!

BONEHEAD ATTACK

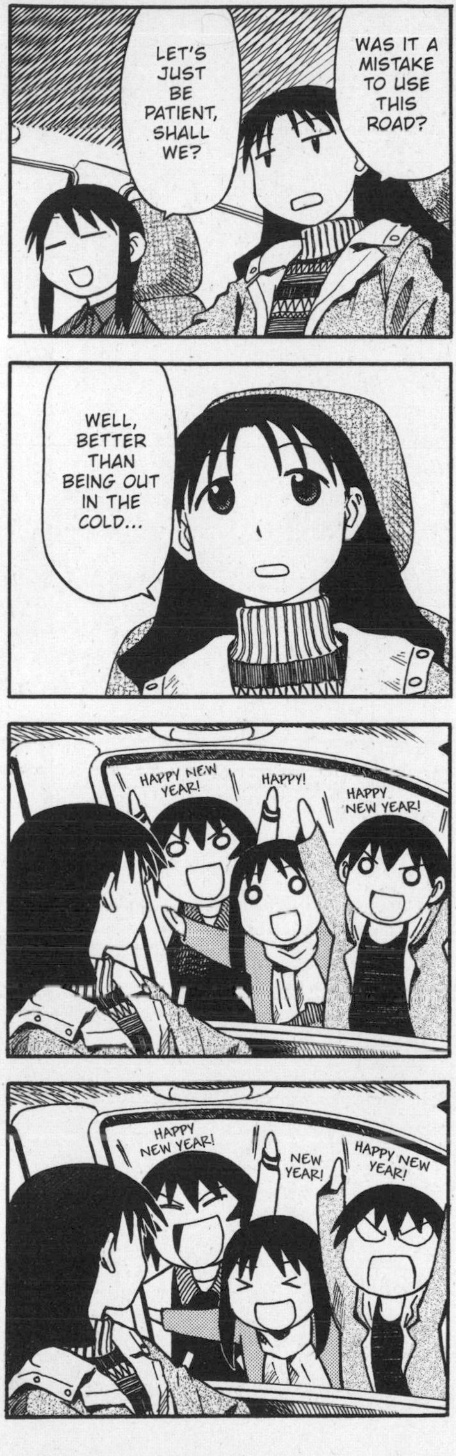
WAS IT A MISTAKE TO USE THIS ROAD?
LET'S JUST BE PATIENT, SHALL WE?
WELL, BETTER THAN BEING OUT IN THE COLD...
HAPPY NEW YEAR!
HAPPY!
HAPPY NEW YEAR!
HAPPY NEW YEAR!
NEW YEAR!
HAPPY NEW YEAR!

PRETTY PLEASE?

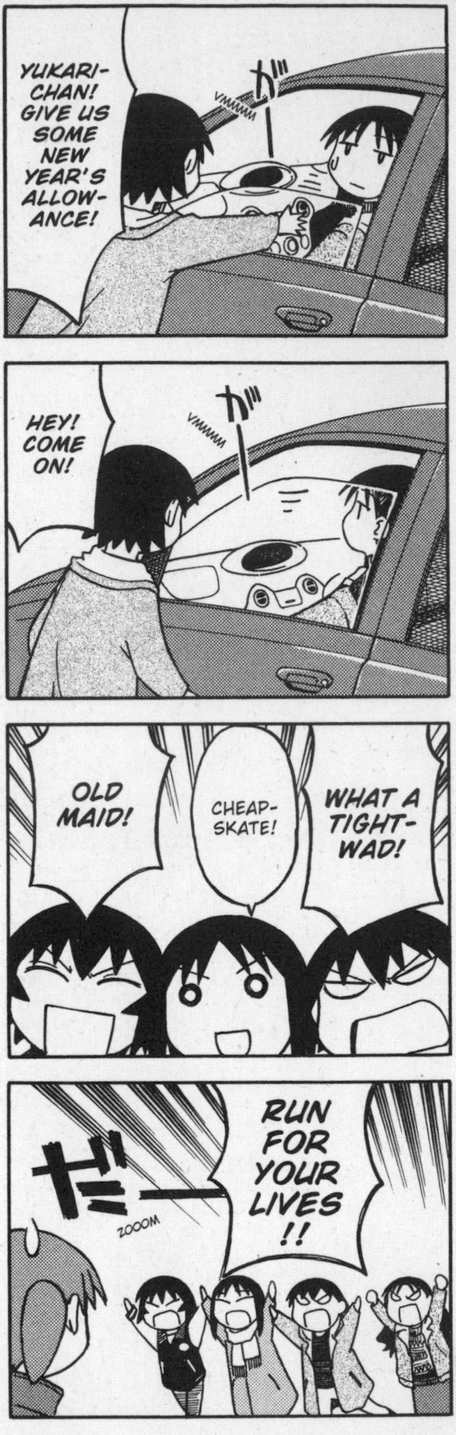
YUKARI-CHAN! GIVE US SOME NEW YEAR'S ALLOWANCE!
VMMMMM
HEY! COME ON!
VMMMMM
WHAT A TIGHT-WAD!
CHEAP-SKATE!
OLD MAID!
RUN FOR YOUR LIVES !!
ZOOOM

HAPPY NEW YEAR, INDEED

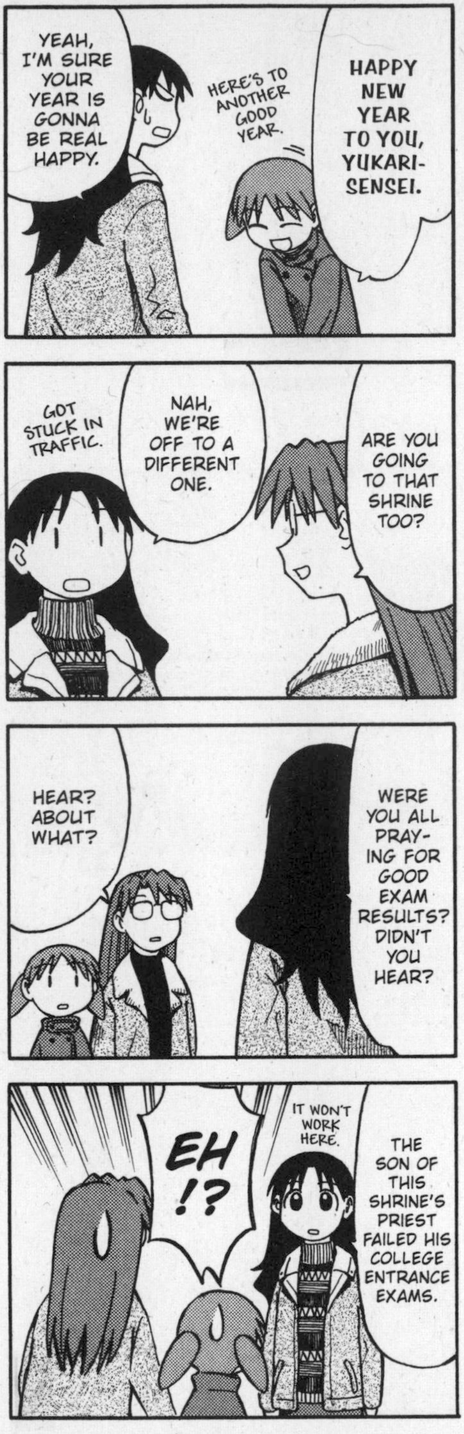
HAPPY NEW YEAR TO YOU, YUKARI-SENSEI.
HERE'S TO ANOTHER GOOD YEAR.
YEAH, I'M SURE YOUR YEAR IS GONNA BE REAL HAPPY.
ARE YOU GOING TO THAT SHRINE TOO?
NAH, WE'RE OFF TO A DIFFERENT ONE.
GOT STUCK IN TRAFFIC.
WERE YOU ALL PRAYING FOR GOOD EXAM RESULTS? DIDN'T YOU HEAR?
HEAR? ABOUT WHAT?
THE SON OF THIS SHRINE'S PRIEST FAILED HIS COLLEGE ENTRANCE EXAMS.
IT WON'T WORK HERE.
EH !?

PRAYING FOR SUCCESS

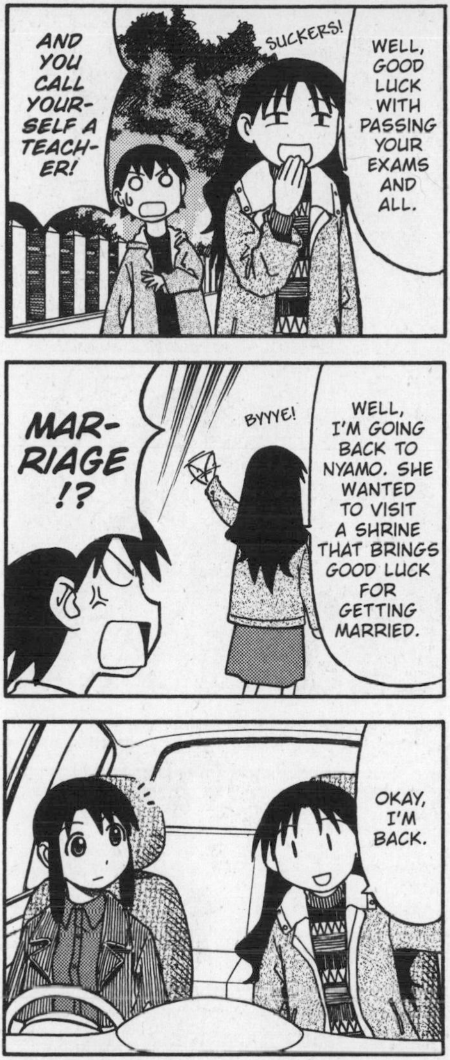
WELL, GOOD LUCK WITH PASSING YOUR EXAMS AND ALL.
SUCKERS!
AND YOU CALL YOUR-SELF A TEACH-ER!
WELL, I'M GOING BACK TO NYAMO. SHE WANTED TO VISIT A SHRINE THAT BRINGS GOOD LUCK FOR GETTING MARRIED.
BYYYE!
MAR-RIAGE !?
OKAY, I'M BACK.
NYAMO-CHAN, YOU HORN-DOG!
THAT'S COLD, NYAMO-SENSEI!
YOU SHOULD PRAY FOR US TO HAVE GOOD LUCK ON OUR EXAMS!
EH? EEH?

HERE YOU GO

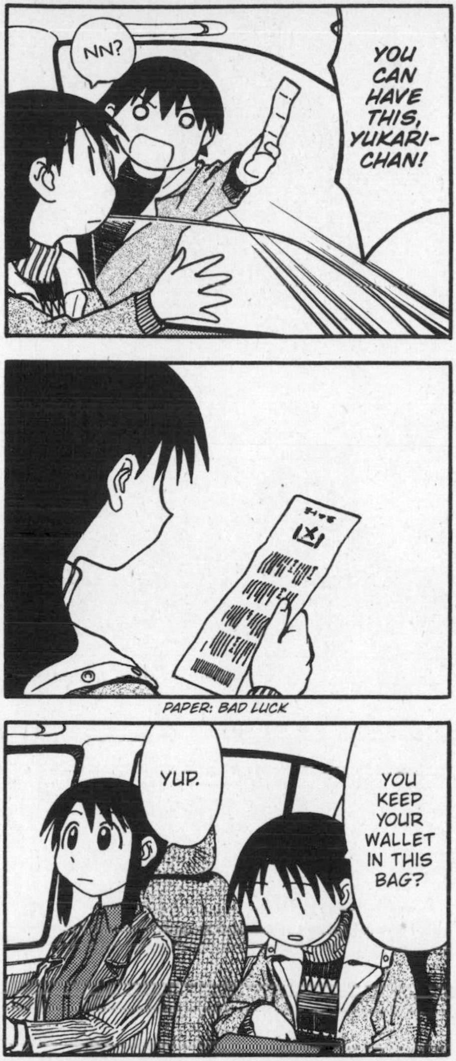
YOU CAN HAVE THIS, YUKARI-CHAN!
NN?
PAPER: BAD LUCK
YOU KEEP YOUR WALLET IN THIS BAG?
YUP.
WHAT ARE YOU DOING? DON'T TAKE ANY OF MY MONEY!
DON'T WORRY, I'M NOT TAKING ANYTHING.
JUST INSERT-ING.

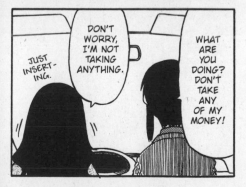

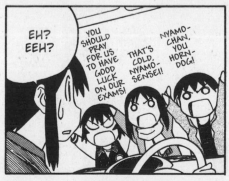

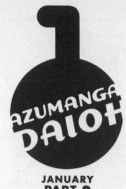

AZUMANGA DAIOH

JANUARY
PART-2

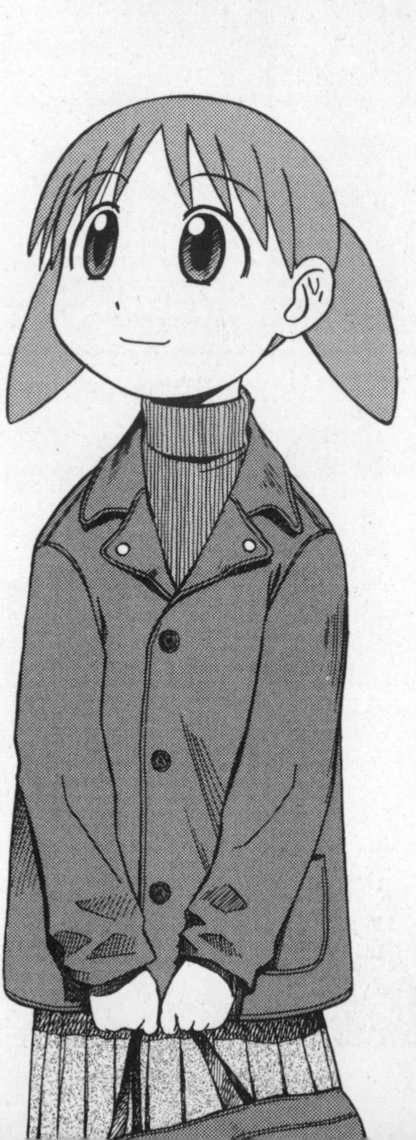

HERE WE GO

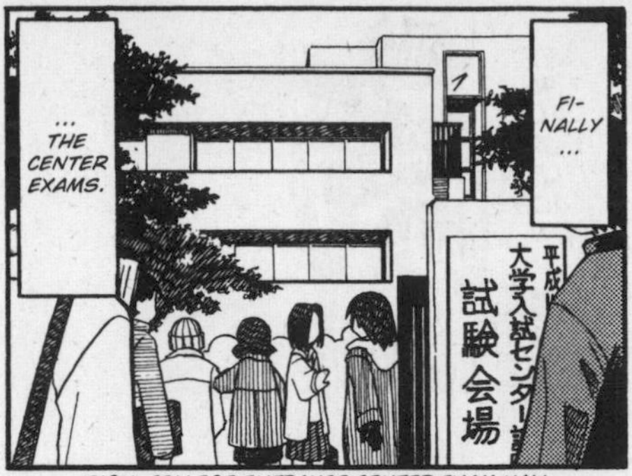
FI-
NALLY
...
...
THE
CENTER
EXAMS.
試験会場

SIGN: COLLEGE ENTRANCE CENTER EXAM HALL

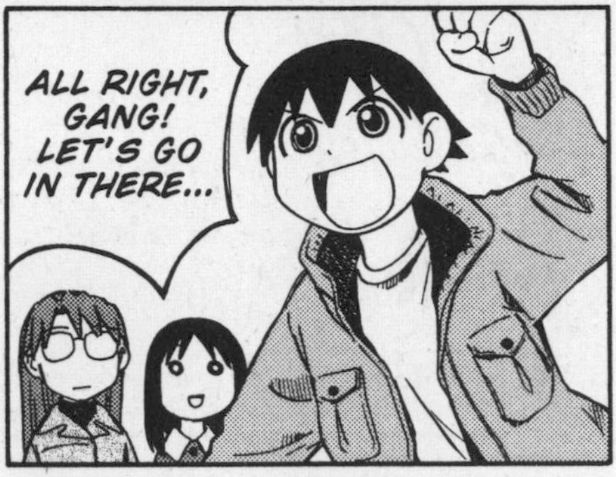
ALL RIGHT, GANG! LET'S GO IN THERE...

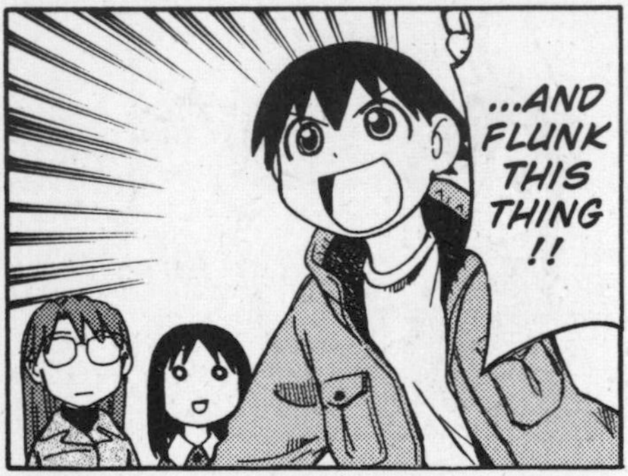
...AND FLUNK THIS THING !!

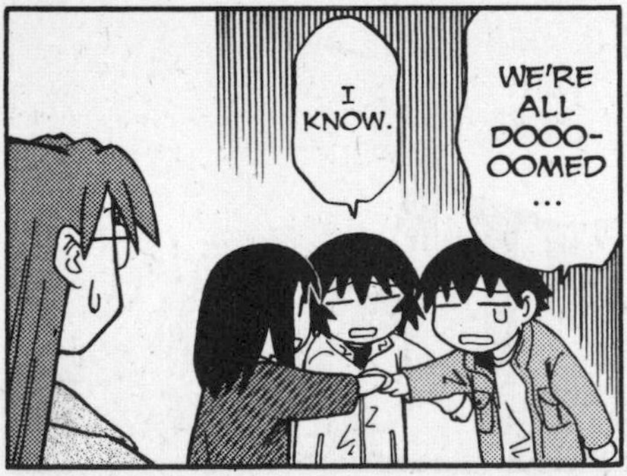
WE'RE ALL DOOOO-OOMED ...
I KNOW.

YOU WILL PASS

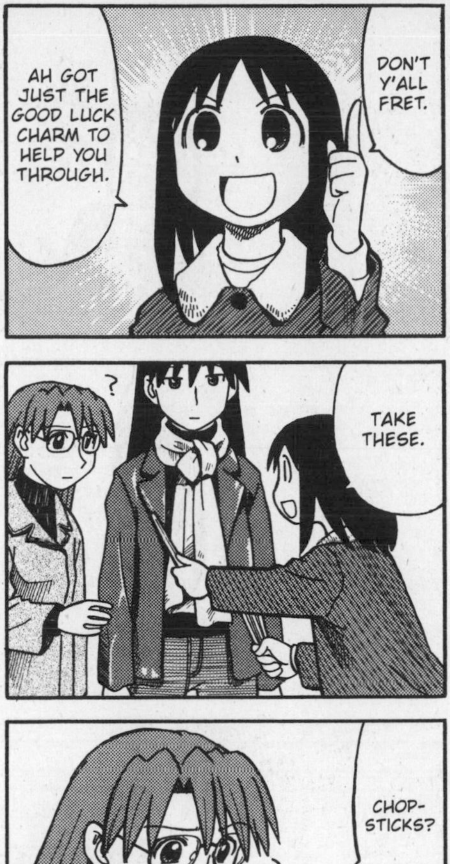
DON'T Y'ALL FRET.
AH GOT JUST THE GOOD LUCK CHARM TO HELP YOU THROUGH.
TAKE THESE.
CHOP-STICKS?
NOW LISTEN UP, Y'ALL.
WHAT'S ABOUT TO HAPPEN?

OSAKA CHARM

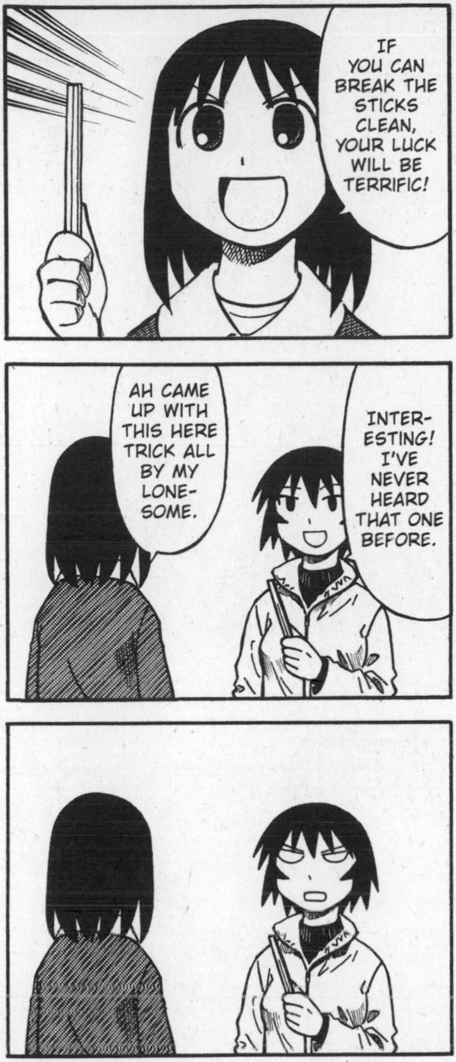
IF YOU CAN BREAK THE STICKS CLEAN, YOUR LUCK WILL BE TERRIFIC!
INTER-ESTING! I'VE NEVER HEARD THAT ONE BEFORE.
AH CAME UP WITH THIS HERE TRICK ALL BY MY LONE-SOME.
REALLY, IT WORKS LIKE A CHARM.
THAT'S NOT A GUARAN-TEE AT ALL.

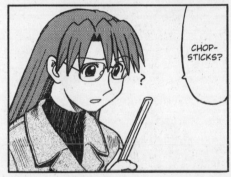

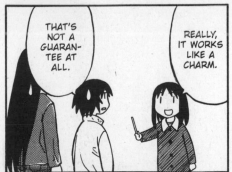

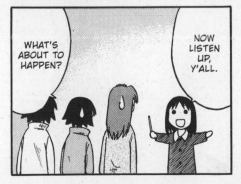

ONE, TWO, THREE, GO

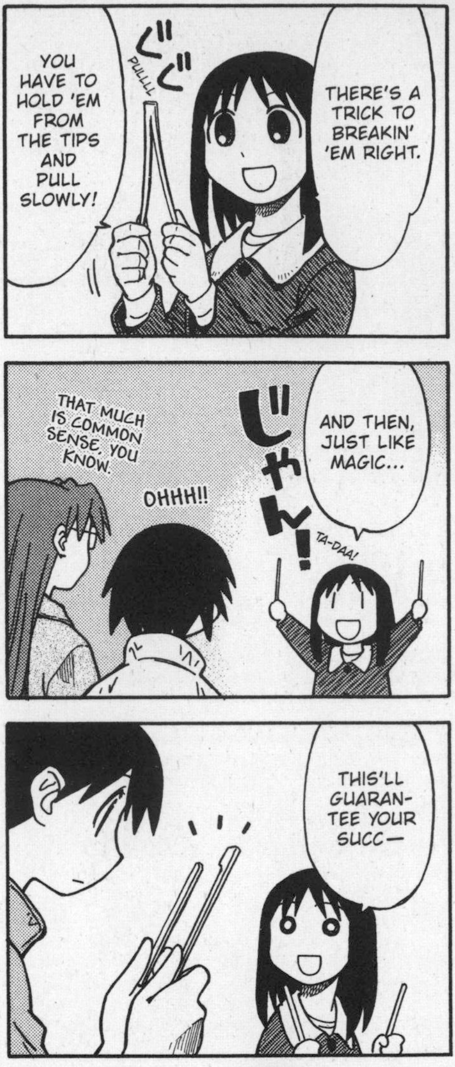
THERE'S A TRICK TO BREAKIN' 'EM RIGHT.
ぐぐ
PULLLL
YOU HAVE TO HOLD 'EM FROM THE TIPS AND PULL SLOWLY!
AND THEN, JUST LIKE MAGIC...
じゃん!
TA-DAA!
OHHH!!
THAT MUCH IS COMMON SENSE, YOU KNOW.
THIS'LL GUARANTEE YOUR SUCC—
HUH!? TOMO-CHAN!?
HUH?

HOW COULD YOU?

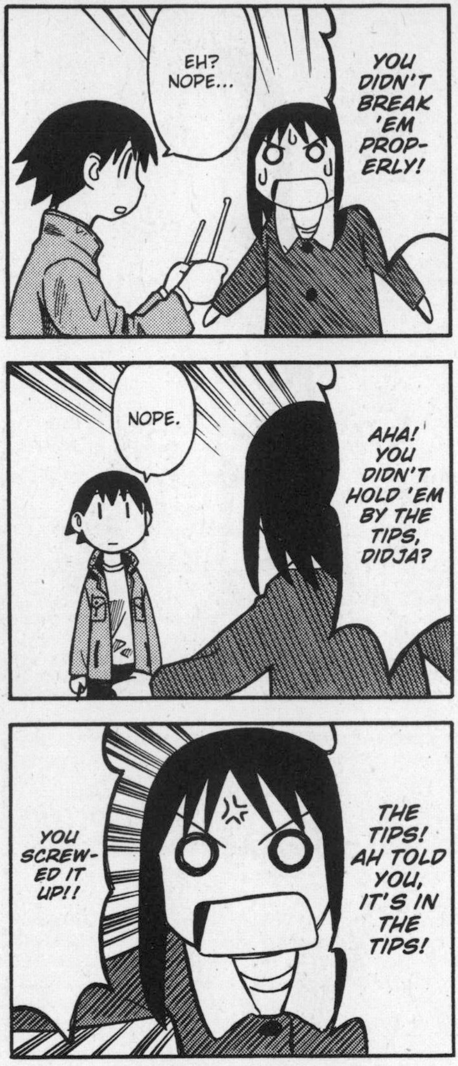
YOU DIDN'T BREAK 'EM PROPERLY!
EH? NOPE...
AHA! YOU DIDN'T HOLD 'EM BY THE TIPS, DIDJA?
NOPE.
THE TIPS! AH TOLD YOU, IT'S IN THE TIPS!
YOU SCREWED IT UP!!
WHY DIDN'T-CHA LISTEN TO ME!?
RAHHH
UH, S-SORRY. ......WHY ARE YOU SCREAMING AT ME?

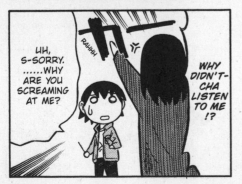

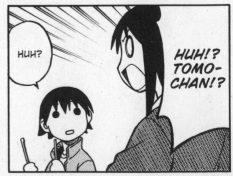

CHIYO'S CHARMS

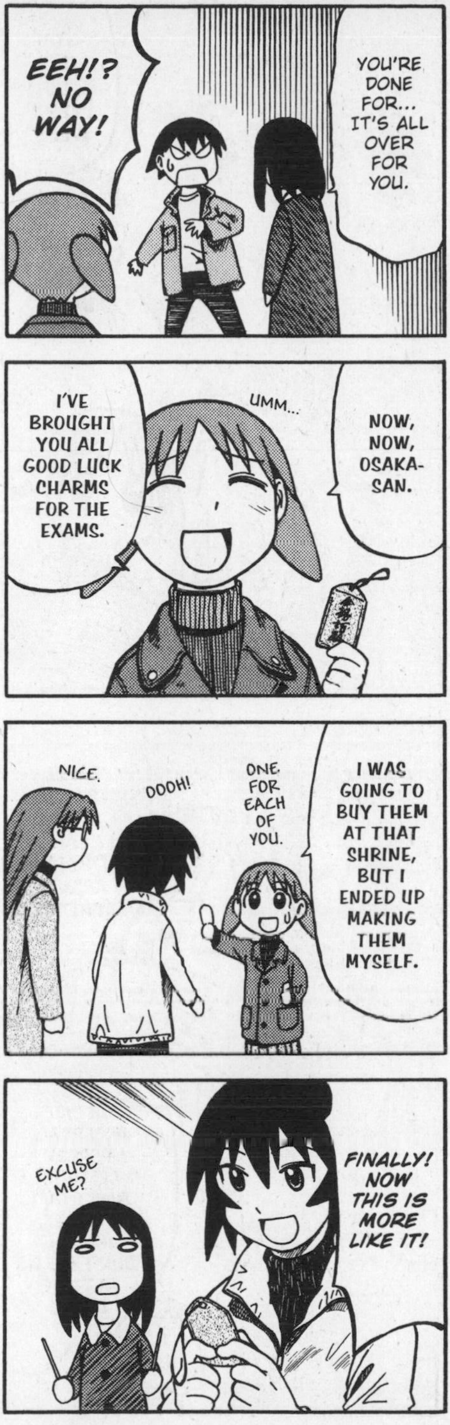
YOU'RE DONE FOR... IT'S ALL OVER FOR YOU.
EEH!? NO WAY!
NOW, NOW, OSAKA-SAN.
UMM...
I'VE BROUGHT YOU ALL GOOD LUCK CHARMS FOR THE EXAMS.
I WAS GOING TO BUY THEM AT THAT SHRINE, BUT I ENDED UP MAKING THEM MYSELF.
ONE FOR EACH OF YOU.
OOOH!
NICE.
FINALLY! NOW THIS IS MORE LIKE IT!
EXCUSE ME?

THE TIME HAS COME

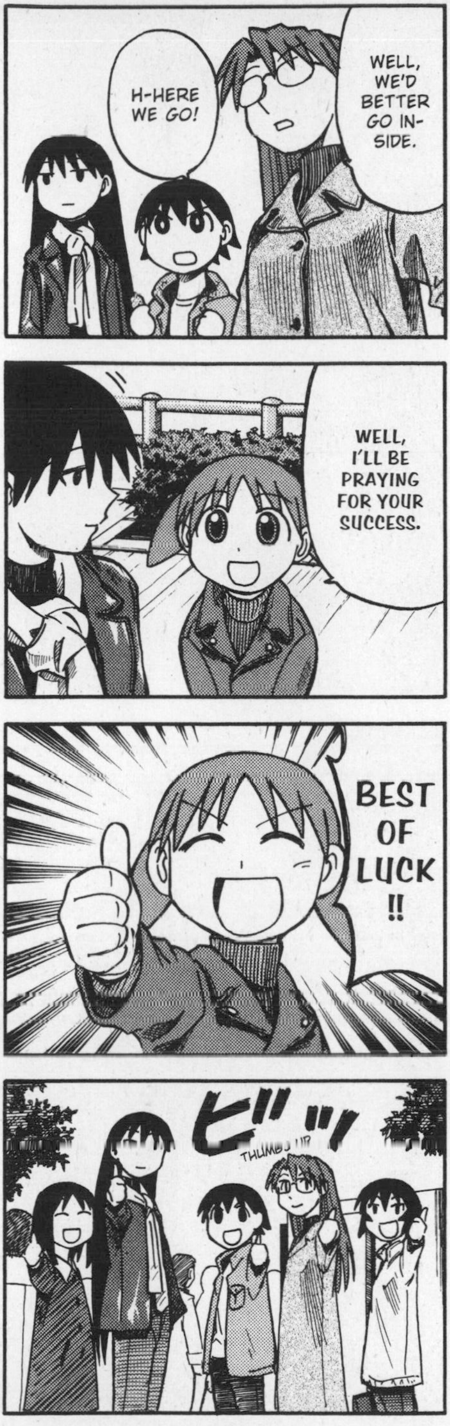
WELL, WE'D BETTER GO INSIDE.
H-HERE WE GO!
WELL, I'LL BE PRAYING FOR YOUR SUCCESS.
BEST OF LUCK!!
ビッ
THUMBS UP

ALL DONE

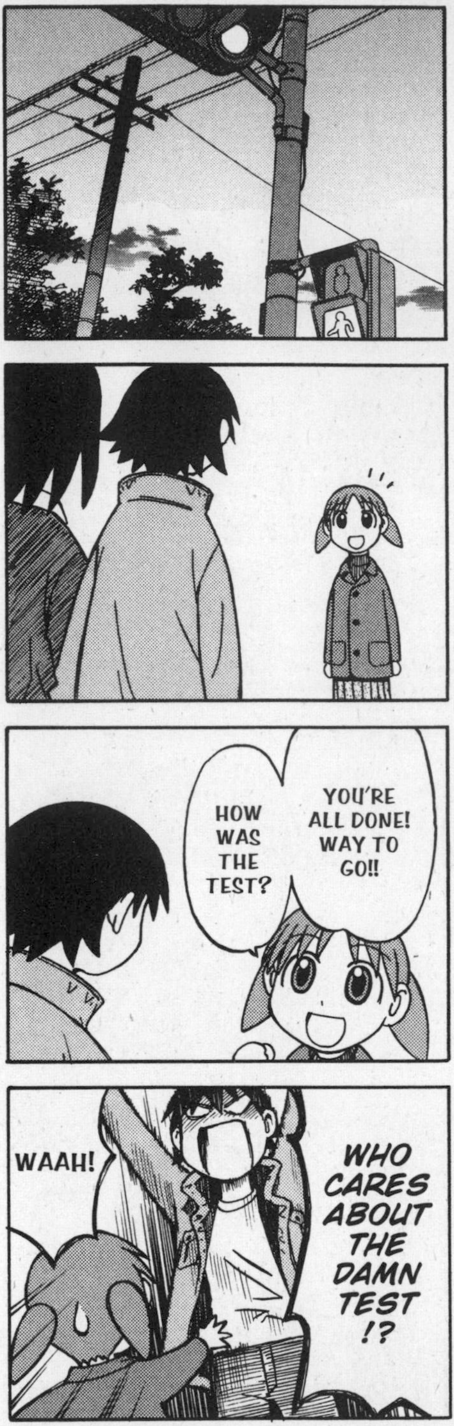

YOU'RE ALL DONE! WAY TO GO!!
HOW WAS THE TEST?
WHO CARES ABOUT THE DAMN TEST !?
WAAH!

ALL OVER THE PLACE

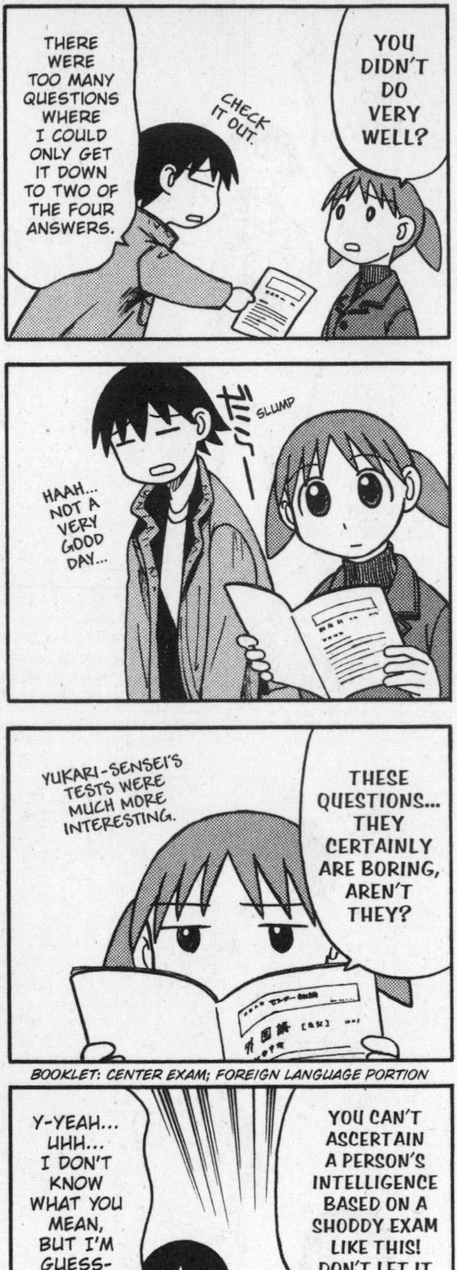

YOU DIDN'T DO VERY WELL?
CHECK IT OUT.
THERE WERE TOO MANY QUESTIONS WHERE I COULD ONLY GET IT DOWN TO TWO OF THE FOUR ANSWERS.
SLUMP
HAAH... NOT A VERY GOOD DAY...
THESE QUESTIONS... THEY CERTAINLY ARE BORING, AREN'T THEY?
YUKARI-SENSEI'S TESTS WERE MUCH MORE INTERESTING.
YOU CAN'T ASCERTAIN A PERSON'S INTELLIGENCE BASED ON A SHODDY EXAM LIKE THIS! DON'T LET IT GET YOU DOWN!
Y-YEAH... UHH... I DON'T KNOW WHAT YOU MEAN, BUT I'M GUESSING IT'S GOOD!?

BOOKLET: CENTER EXAM; FOREIGN LANGUAGE PORTION

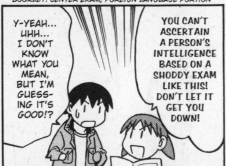

AH PLUMB DON'T GET IT

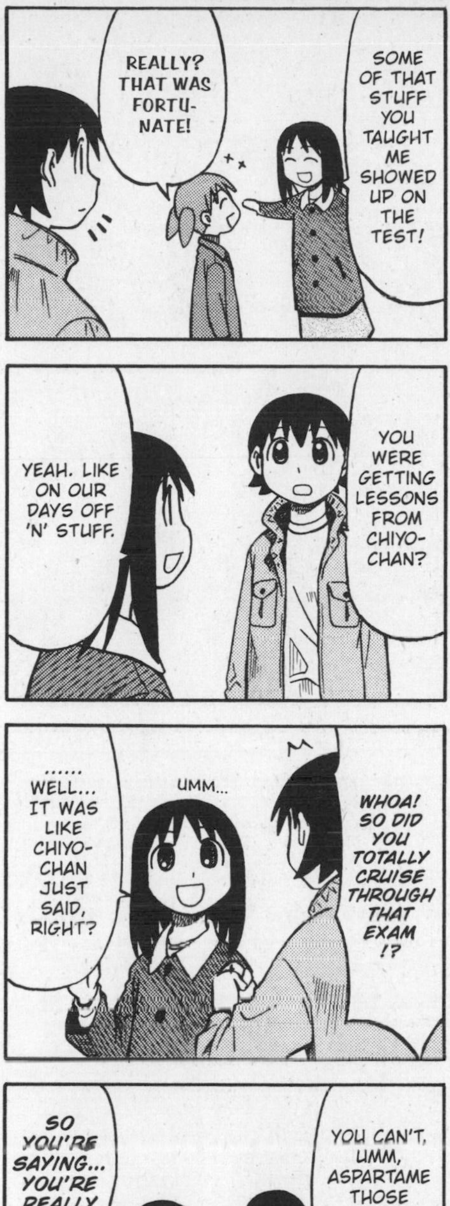
SOME OF THAT STUFF YOU TAUGHT ME SHOWED UP ON THE TEST!
REALLY? THAT WAS FORTUNATE!
YOU WERE GETTING LESSONS FROM CHIYO-CHAN?
YEAH. LIKE ON OUR DAYS OFF 'N' STUFF.
WHOA! SO DID YOU TOTALLY CRUISE THROUGH THAT EXAM!?
UMM...
...... WELL... IT WAS LIKE CHIYO-CHAN JUST SAID, RIGHT?
YOU CAN'T, UMM, ASPARTAME THOSE QUESTIONS WITH MAH INTELLIGENCE.
SO YOU'RE SAYING... YOU'RE REALLY DUMB?

TEACHER, DOG, CAT

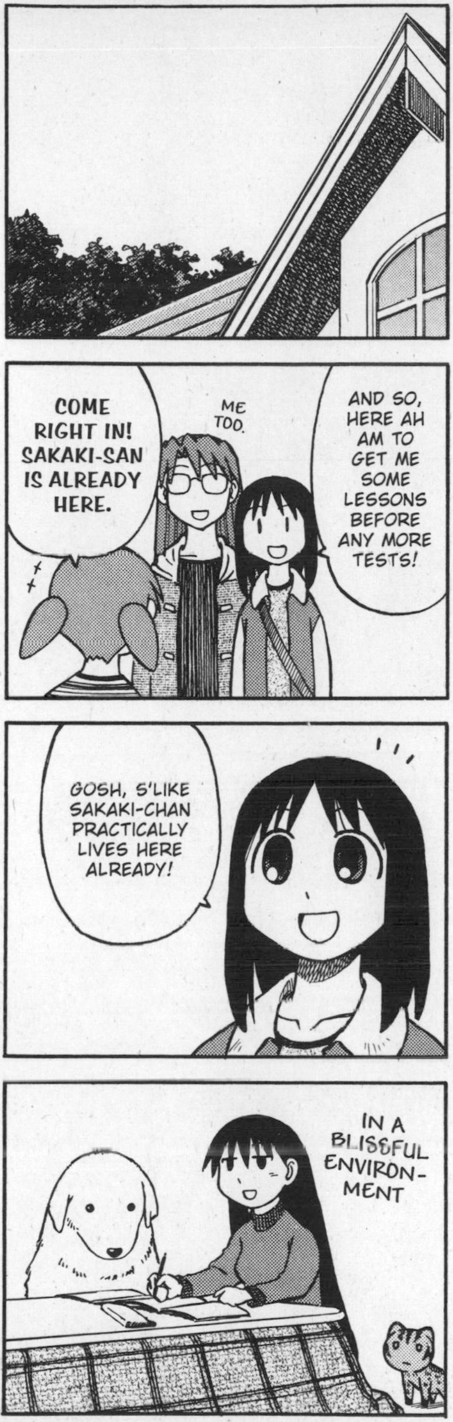
AND SO, HERE AH AM TO GET ME SOME LESSONS BEFORE ANY MORE TESTS!
ME TOO.
COME RIGHT IN! SAKAKI-SAN IS ALREADY HERE.
GOSH, S'LIKE SAKAKI-CHAN PRACTICALLY LIVES HERE ALREADY!
IN A BLISSFUL ENVIRONMENT

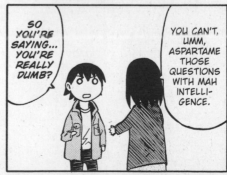

FOR A JUST CAUSE

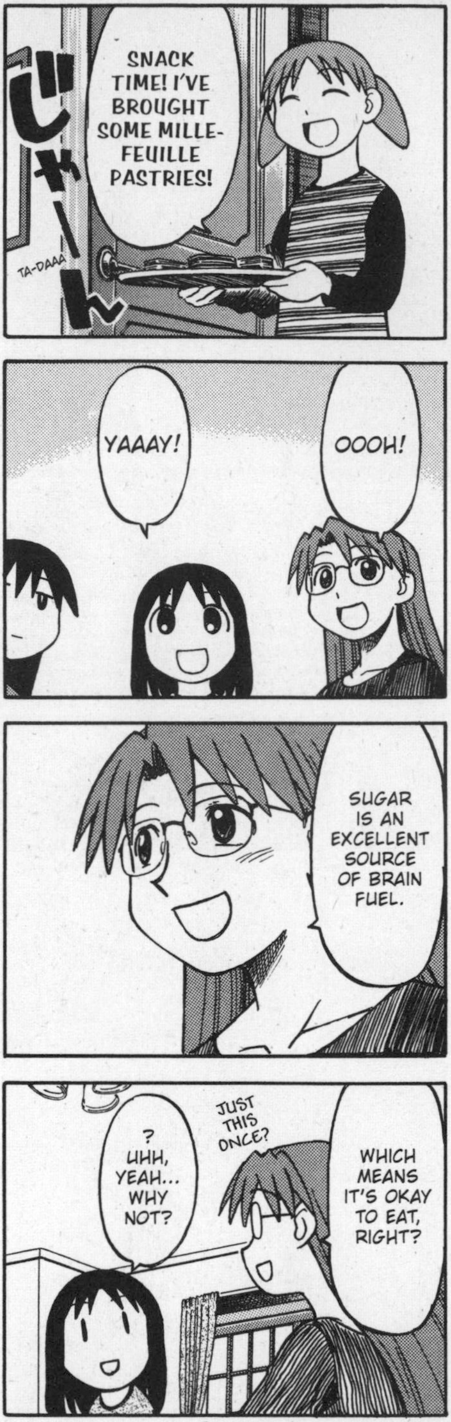

SNACK TIME! I'VE BROUGHT SOME MILLE-FEUILLE PASTRIES!
じゃーん
TA-DAAA
OOOH!
YAAAY!
SUGAR IS AN EXCELLENT SOURCE OF BRAIN FUEL.
WHICH MEANS IT'S OKAY TO EAT, RIGHT?
JUST THIS ONCE?
? UHH, YEAH... WHY NOT?

GIVE ME SOME, SAKAKI-SAN

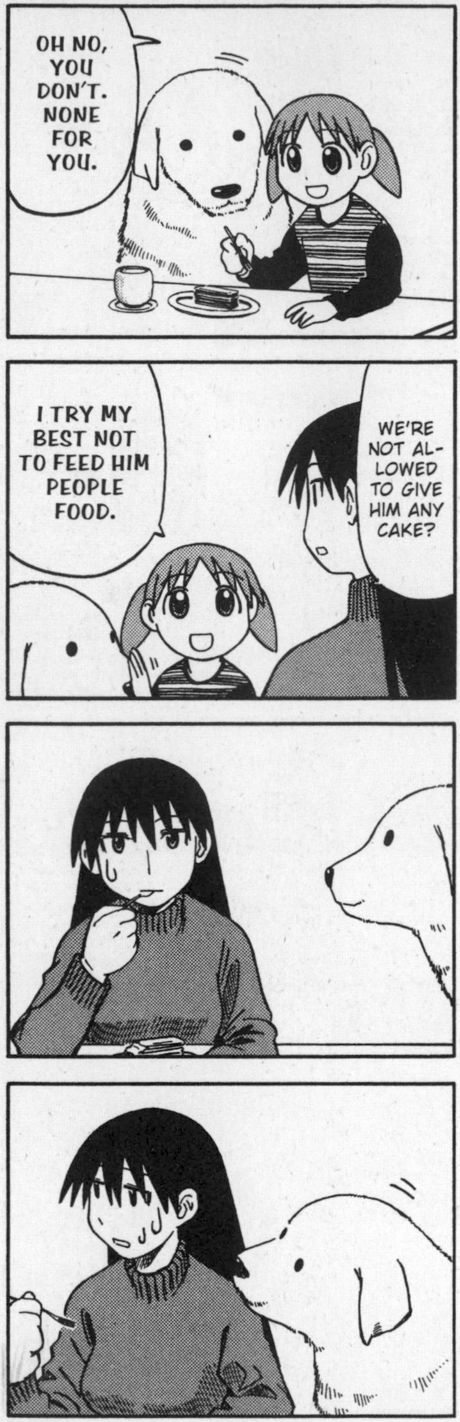

OH NO, YOU DON'T. NONE FOR YOU.
WE'RE NOT AL-LOWED TO GIVE HIM ANY CAKE?
I TRY MY BEST NOT TO FEED HIM PEOPLE FOOD.

GOOD NIGHT

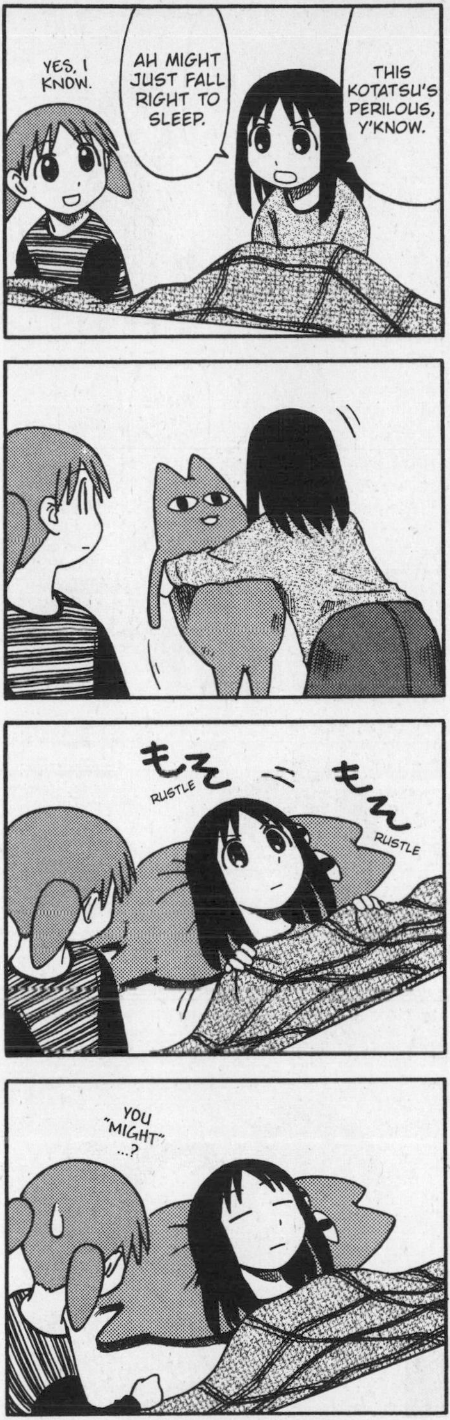
THIS KOTATSU'S PERILOUS, Y'KNOW.
AH MIGHT JUST FALL RIGHT TO SLEEP.
YES, I KNOW.
もそ
RUSTLE
もそ
RUSTLE
YOU "MIGHT" ...?

THE HUNT

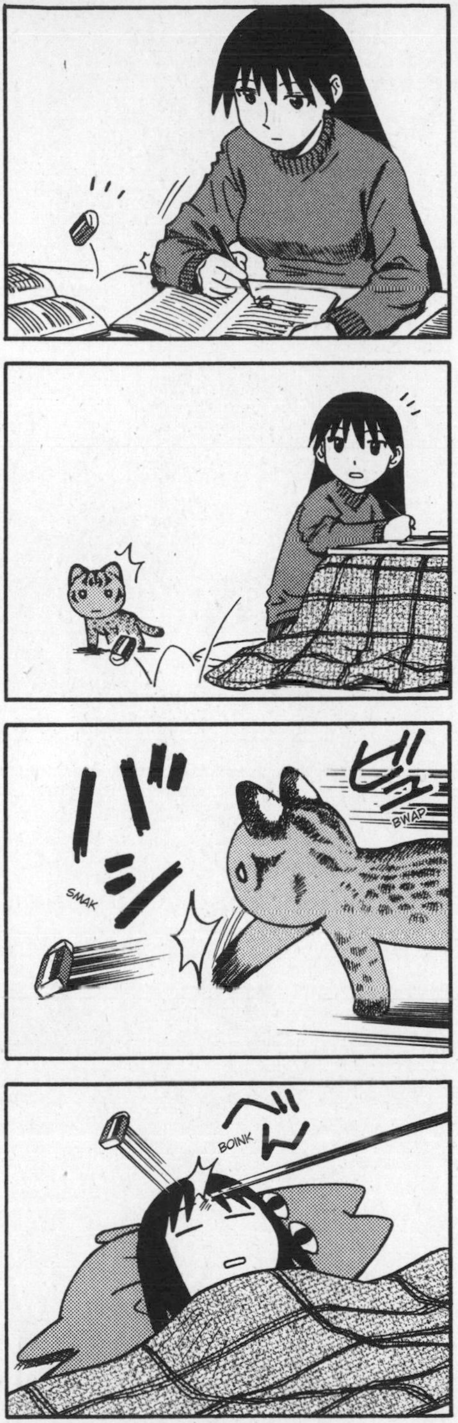
ビシ
BWAP
バシ
SMAK
べん
BOINK

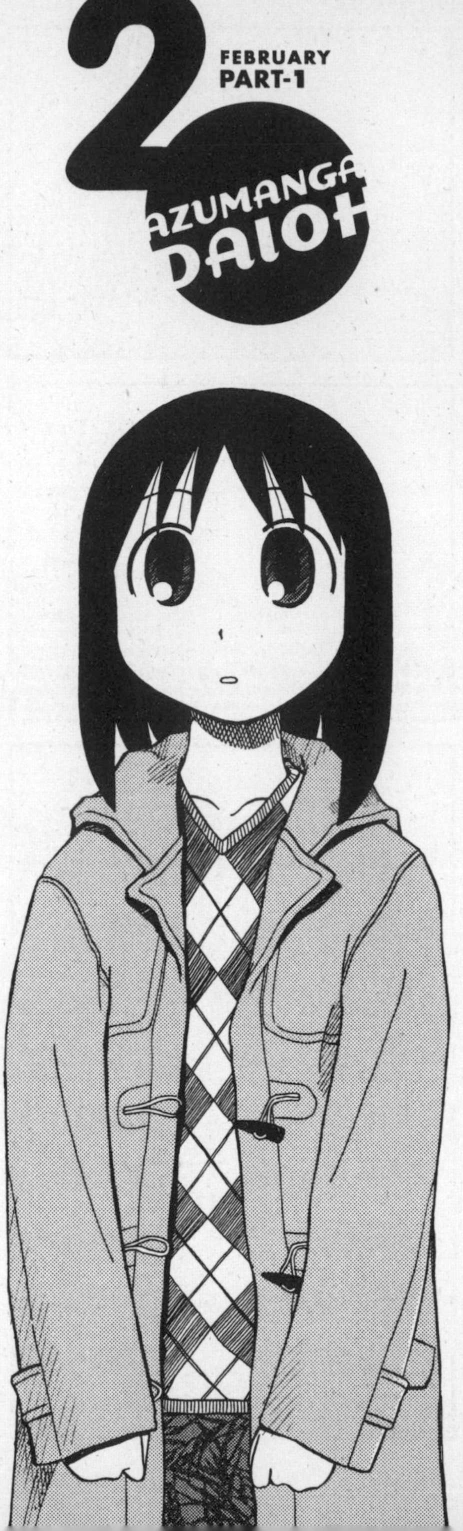
2
FEBRUARY
PART-1
AZUMANGA DAIOH

STUDY SESSION

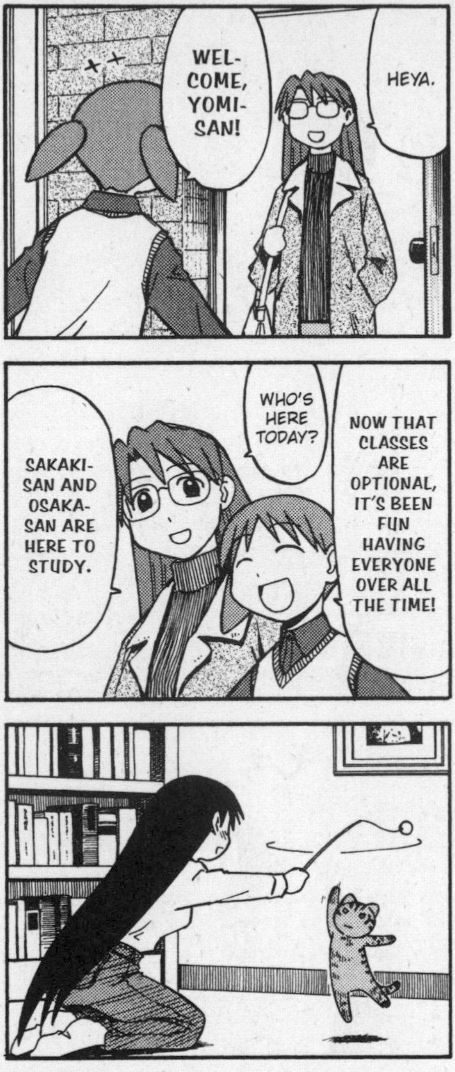
HEYA.
WEL-COME, YOMI-SAN!
NOW THAT CLASSES ARE OPTIONAL, IT'S BEEN FUN HAVING EVERYONE OVER ALL THE TIME!
WHO'S HERE TODAY?
SAKAKI-SAN AND OSAKA-SAN ARE HERE TO STUDY.
YOU CALL THIS STUDY-ING?

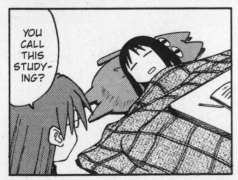

GRAND APPEARANCE

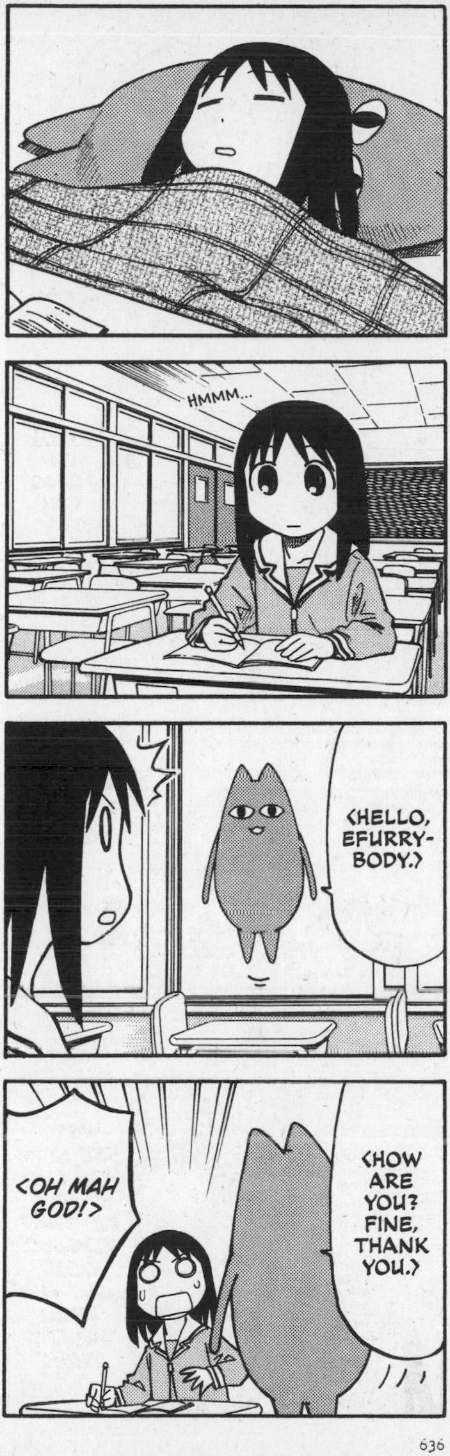
HMMM...
<HELLO, EFURRY-BODY.>
<HOW ARE YOU? FINE, THANK YOU.>
<OH MAH GOD!>

CHIYO'S DAD

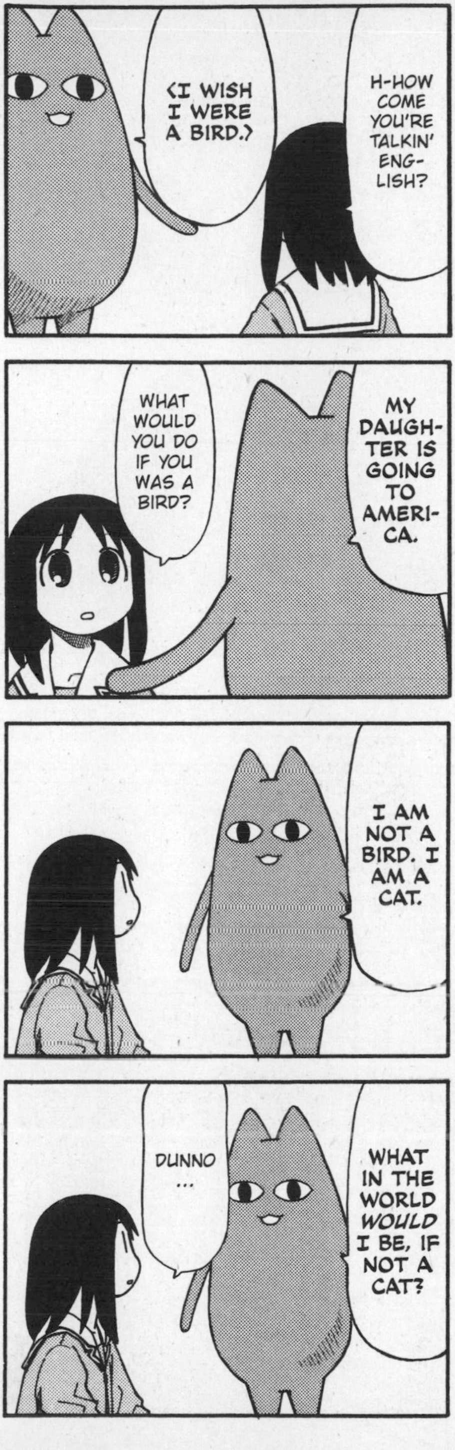
H-HOW COME YOU'RE TALKIN' ENG-LISH?
<I WISH I WERE A BIRD.>
MY DAUGHTER IS GOING TO AMERI-CA.
WHAT WOULD YOU DO IF YOU WAS A BIRD?
I AM NOT A BIRD. I AM A CAT.
WHAT IN THE WORLD *WOULD* I BE, IF NOT A CAT?
DUNNO ...

HOW RUDE

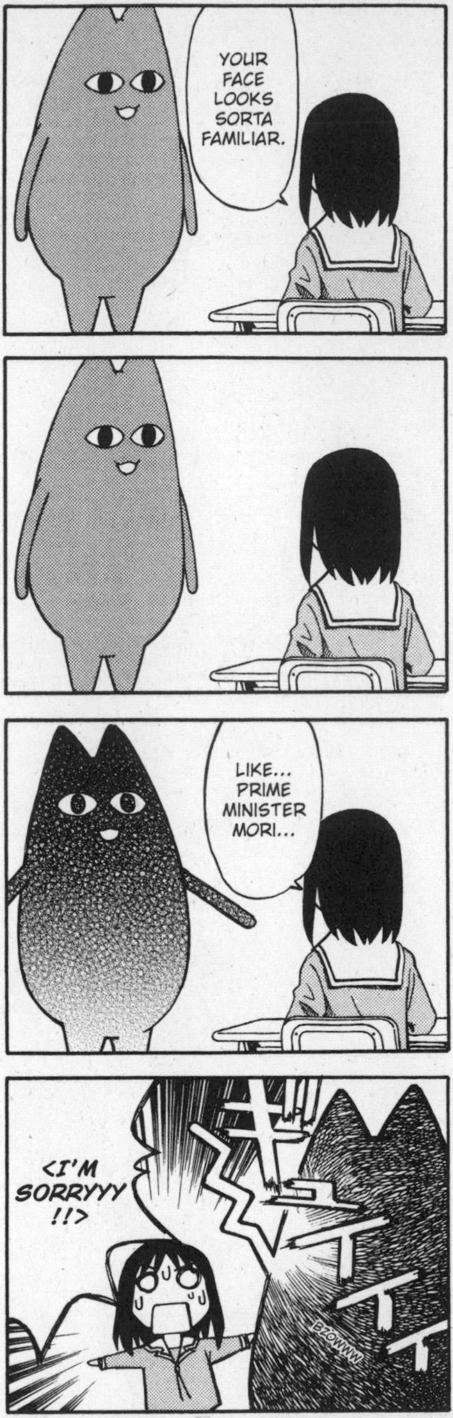
YOUR FACE LOOKS SORTA FAMILIAR.
LIKE... PRIME MINISTER MORI...
<I'M SORRYYY!!>
BZOWWW

CAT

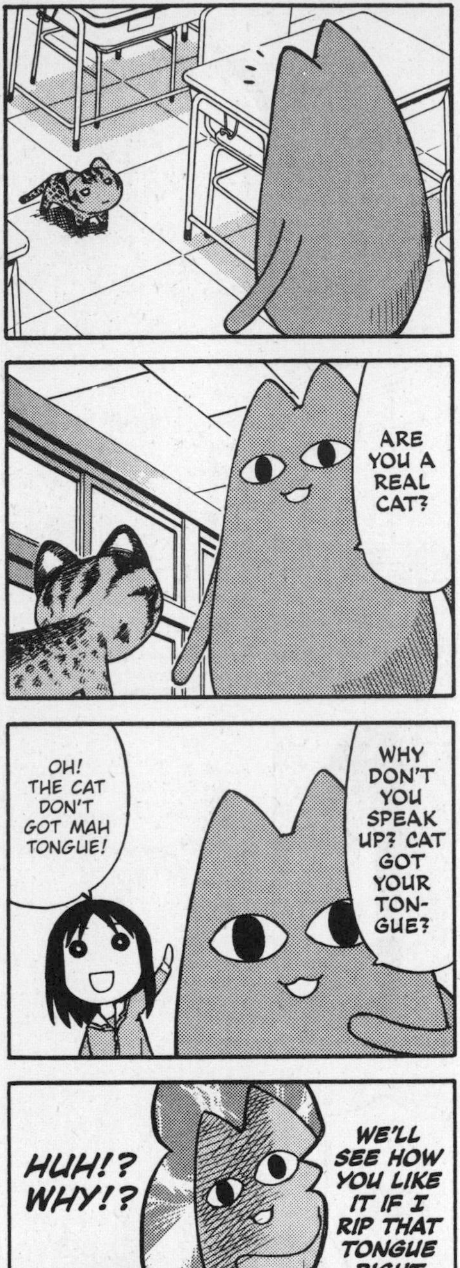
ARE YOU A REAL CAT?
WHY DON'T YOU SPEAK UP? CAT GOT YOUR TON-GUE?
OH! THE CAT DON'T GOT MAH TONGUE!
WE'LL SEE HOW YOU LIKE IT IF I RIP THAT TONGUE RIGHT OUT OF YOUR MOUTH, THEN!
HUH!? WHY!?

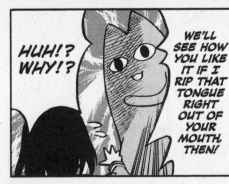

WAKE

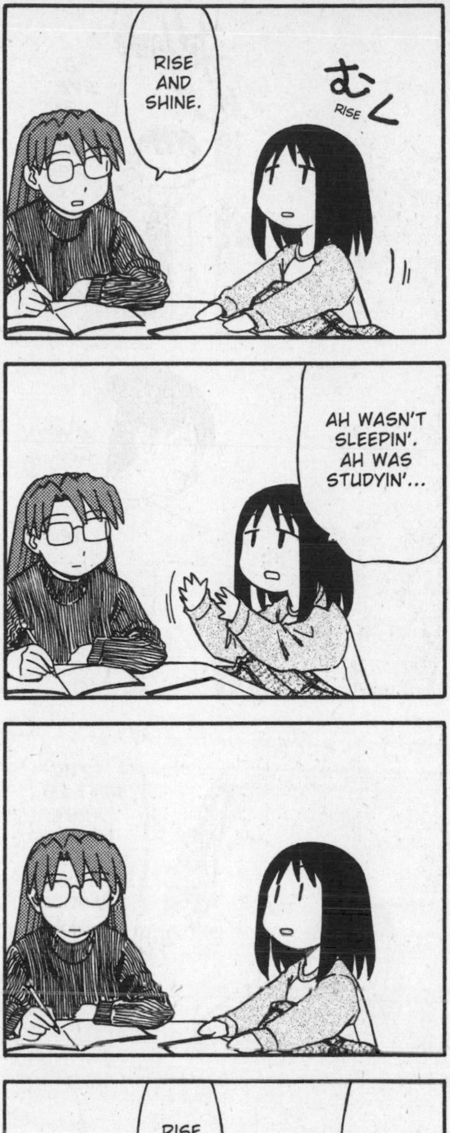
RISE AND SHINE.
むく
RISE
AH WASN'T SLEEPIN'. AH WAS STUDYIN'...
RISE AND SHINE.
HUH? WHY'M AH AT CHIYO-CHAN'S?

FREEZE!

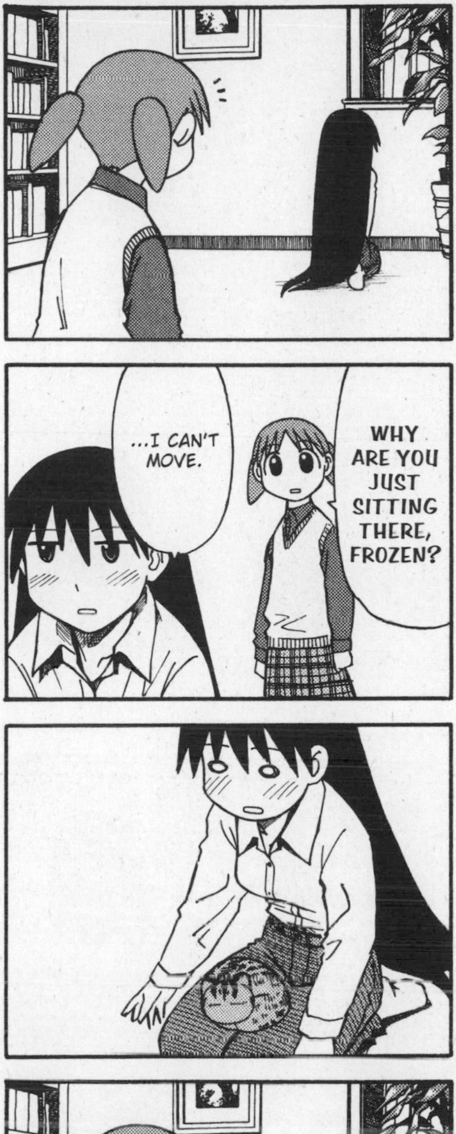
WHY ARE YOU JUST SITTING THERE, FROZEN?
...I CAN'T MOVE.

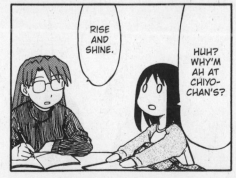

IDENTITY REVEALED

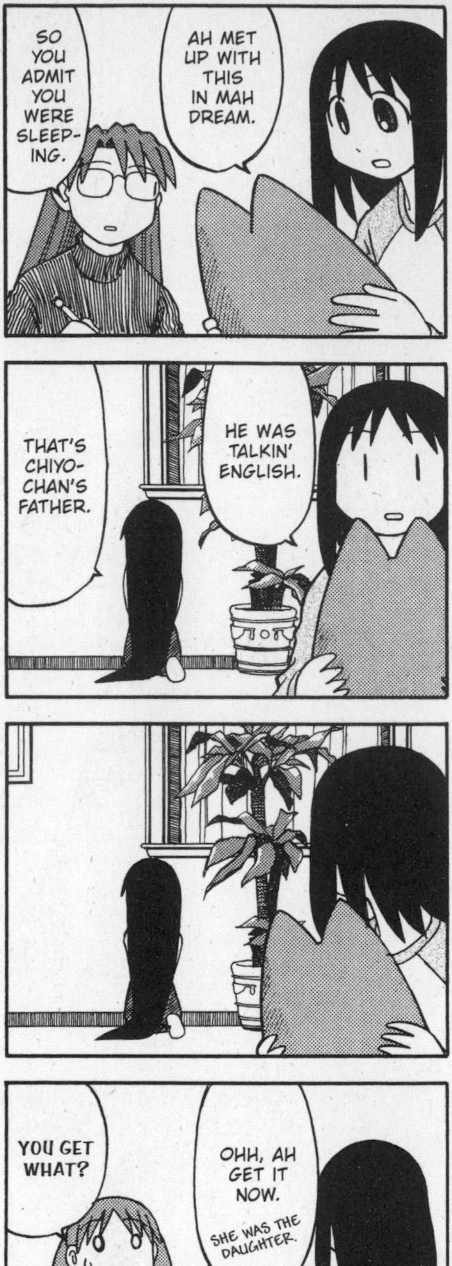

AH MET UP WITH THIS IN MAH DREAM.
SO YOU ADMIT YOU WERE SLEEPING.
HE WAS TALKIN' ENGLISH.
THAT'S CHIYO-CHAN'S FATHER.
OHH, AH GET IT NOW.
SHE WAS THE DAUGHTER.
YOU GET WHAT?

COMBINE FORCES

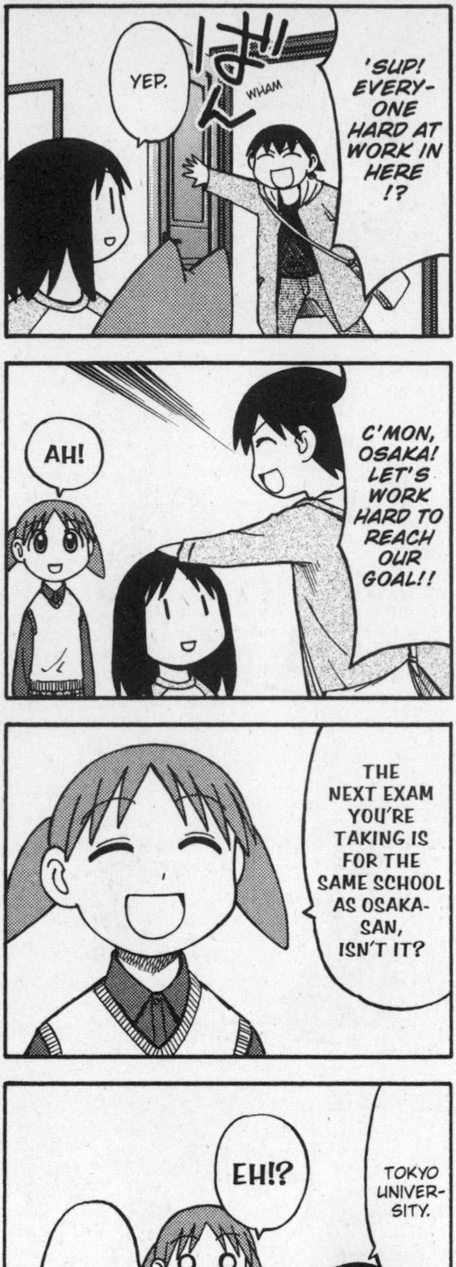

'SUP! EVERYONE HARD AT WORK IN HERE!?
WHAM
YEP.
C'MON, OSAKA! LET'S WORK HARD TO REACH OUR GOAL!!
AH!
THE NEXT EXAM YOU'RE TAKING IS FOR THE SAME SCHOOL AS OSAKA-SAN, ISN'T IT?
TOKYO UNIVERSITY.
EH!?
JUST KIDDIN'.

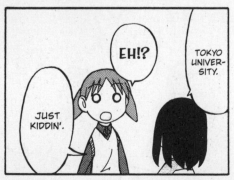

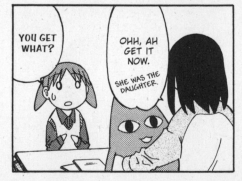

INSTANT REFLEXES

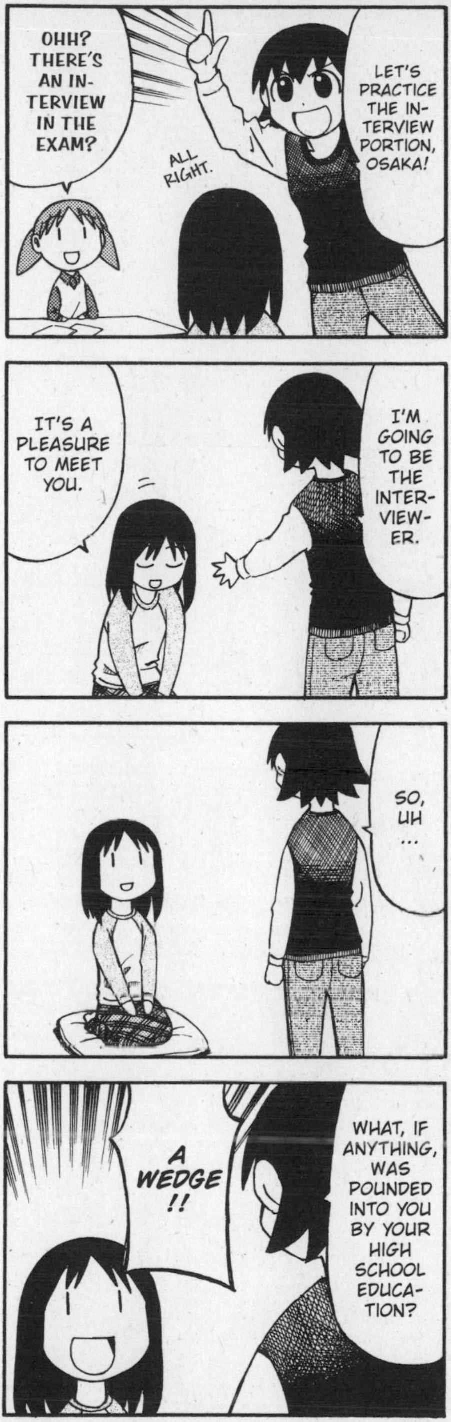
LET'S PRACTICE THE INTERVIEW PORTION, OSAKA!
OHH? THERE'S AN INTERVIEW IN THE EXAM?
ALL RIGHT.
I'M GOING TO BE THE INTERVIEWER.
IT'S A PLEASURE TO MEET YOU.
SO, UH ...
WHAT, IF ANYTHING, WAS POUNDED INTO YOU BY YOUR HIGH SCHOOL EDUCATION?
A WEDGE !!

OKAY, NOT REALLY

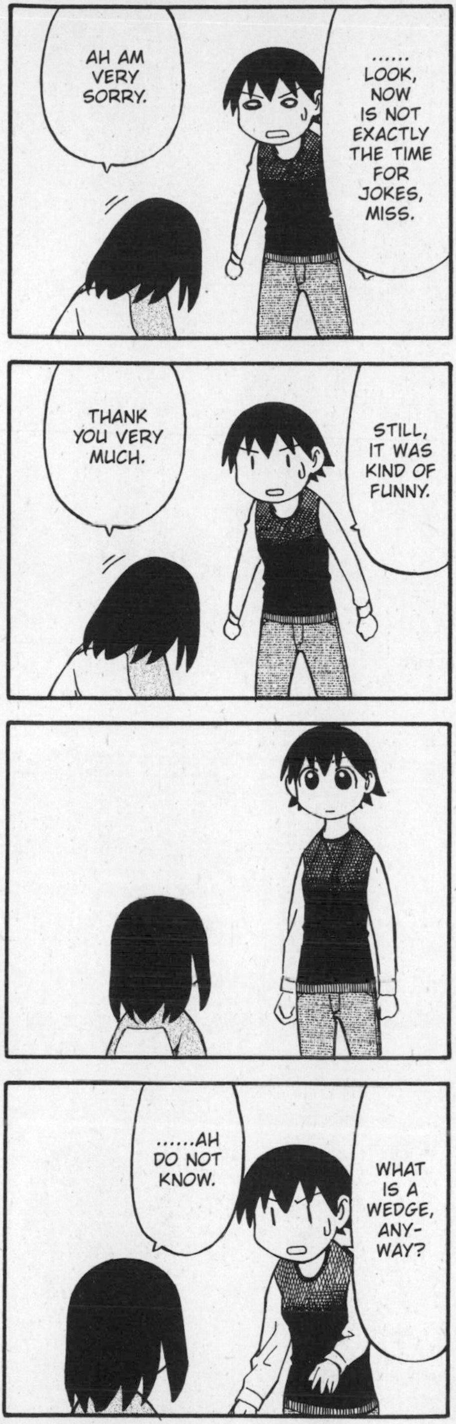
......LOOK, NOW IS NOT EXACTLY THE TIME FOR JOKES, MISS.
AH AM VERY SORRY.
STILL, IT WAS KIND OF FUNNY.
THANK YOU VERY MUCH.
WHAT IS A WEDGE, ANYWAY?
......AH DO NOT KNOW.

WEDGE (N.)

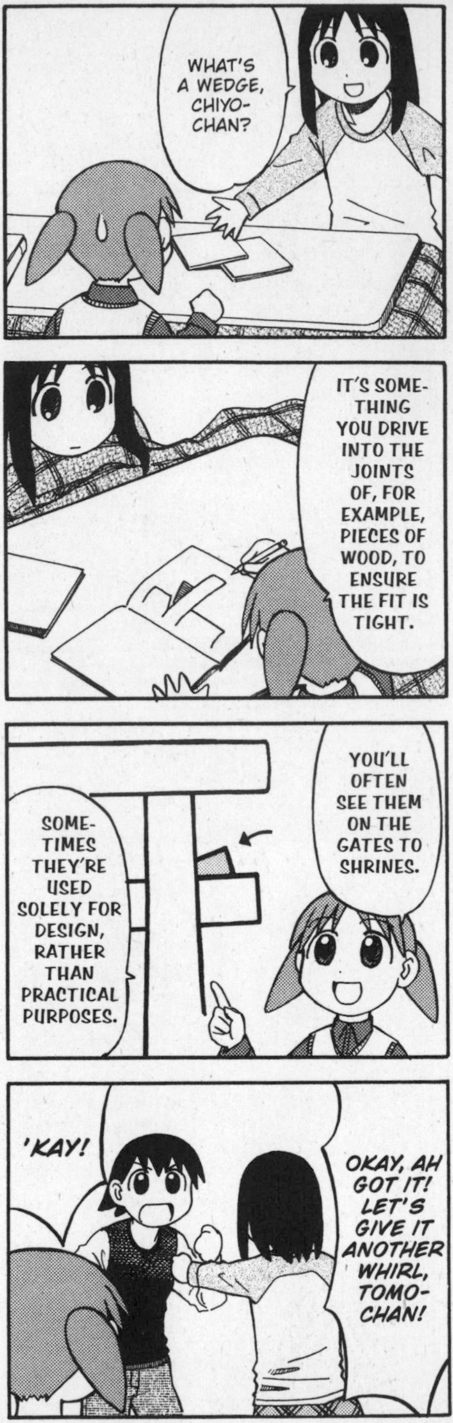
WHAT'S A WEDGE, CHIYO-CHAN?
IT'S SOMETHING YOU DRIVE INTO THE JOINTS OF, FOR EXAMPLE, PIECES OF WOOD, TO ENSURE THE FIT IS TIGHT.
YOU'LL OFTEN SEE THEM ON THE GATES TO SHRINES.
SOMETIMES THEY'RE USED SOLELY FOR DESIGN, RATHER THAN PRACTICAL PURPOSES.
OKAY, AH GOT IT! LET'S GIVE IT ANOTHER WHIRL, TOMO-CHAN!
'KAY!

PERFECT

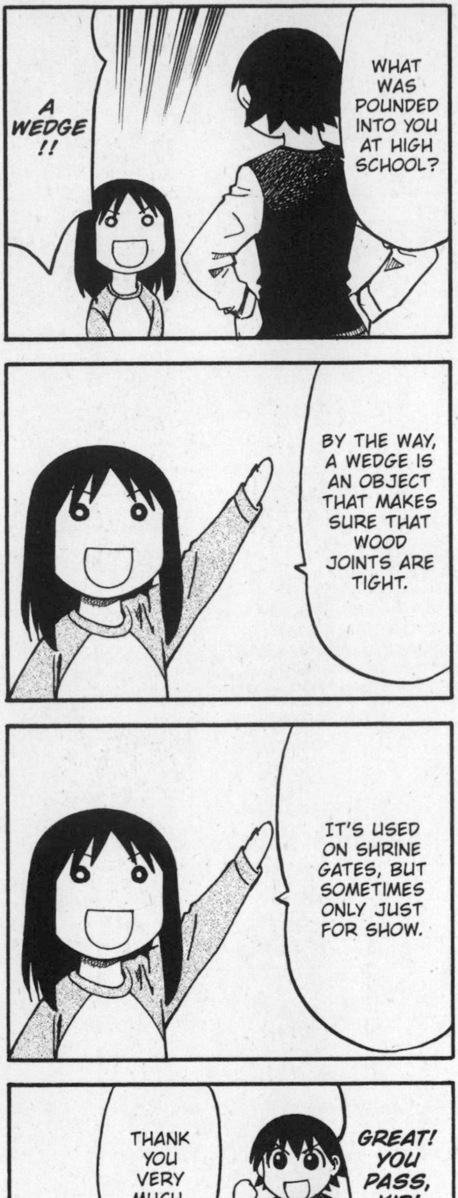
WHAT WAS POUNDED INTO YOU AT HIGH SCHOOL?
A WEDGE !!
BY THE WAY, A WEDGE IS AN OBJECT THAT MAKES SURE THAT WOOD JOINTS ARE TIGHT.
IT'S USED ON SHRINE GATES, BUT SOMETIMES ONLY JUST FOR SHOW.
GREAT! YOU PASS, KID!
THANK YOU VERY MUCH.

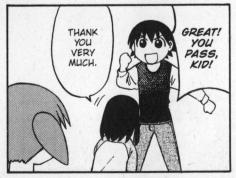

ALL I CAN DO

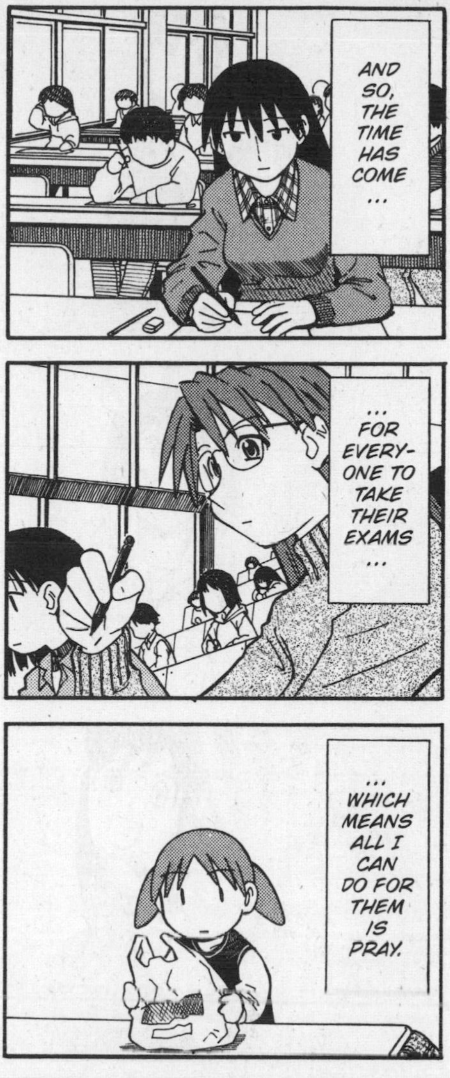
AND SO, THE TIME HAS COME ...
... FOR EVERYONE TO TAKE THEIR EXAMS ...
... WHICH MEANS ALL I CAN DO FOR THEM IS PRAY.

LABELS: DISPOSABLE CHOPSTICKS

A THOUSAND CHOPSTICKS

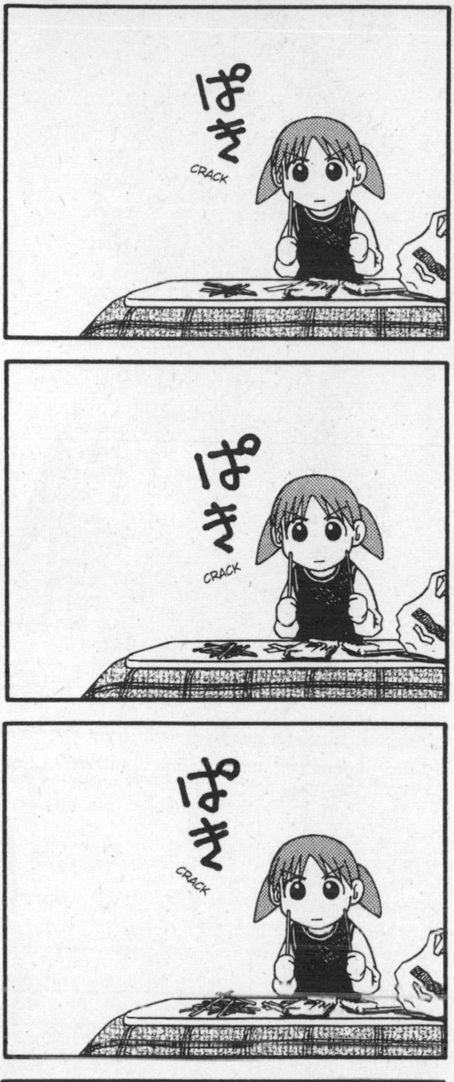
ぱき
CRACK
ぱき
CRACK
ぱき
CRACK
ぱき
CRACK

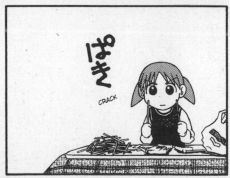

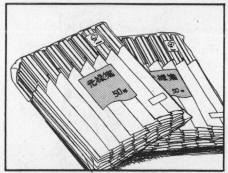

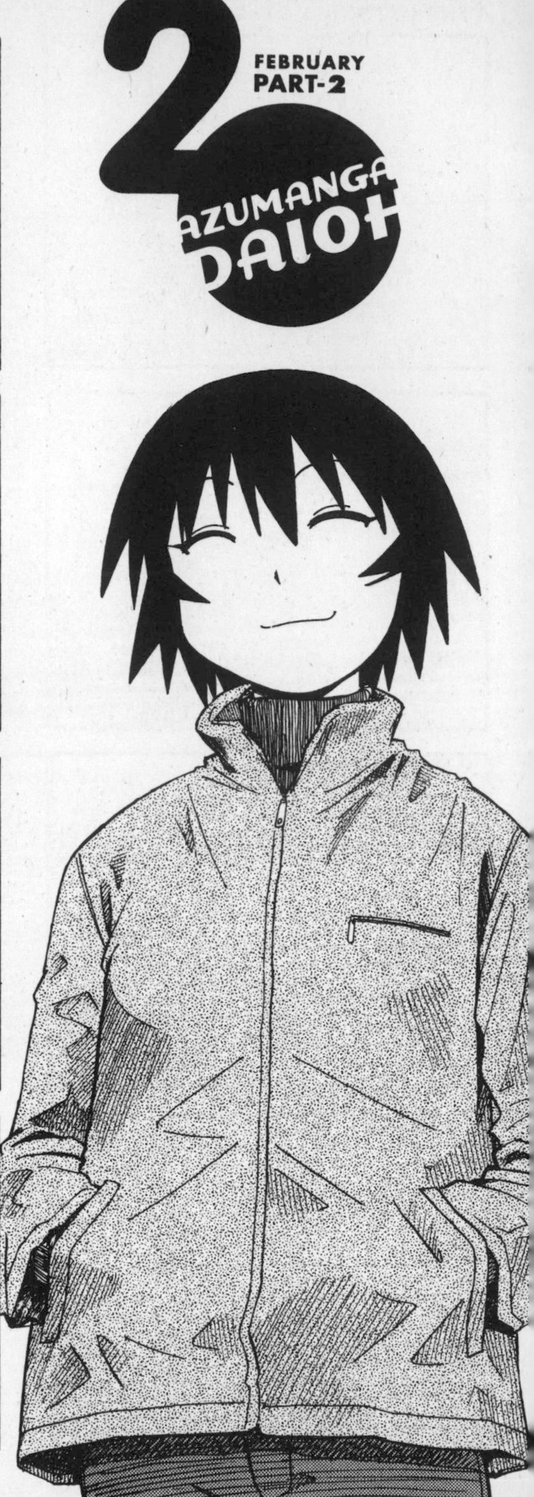
2
FEBRUARY
PART-2
AZUMANGA DAIOH

SPORTS UNIVERSITY

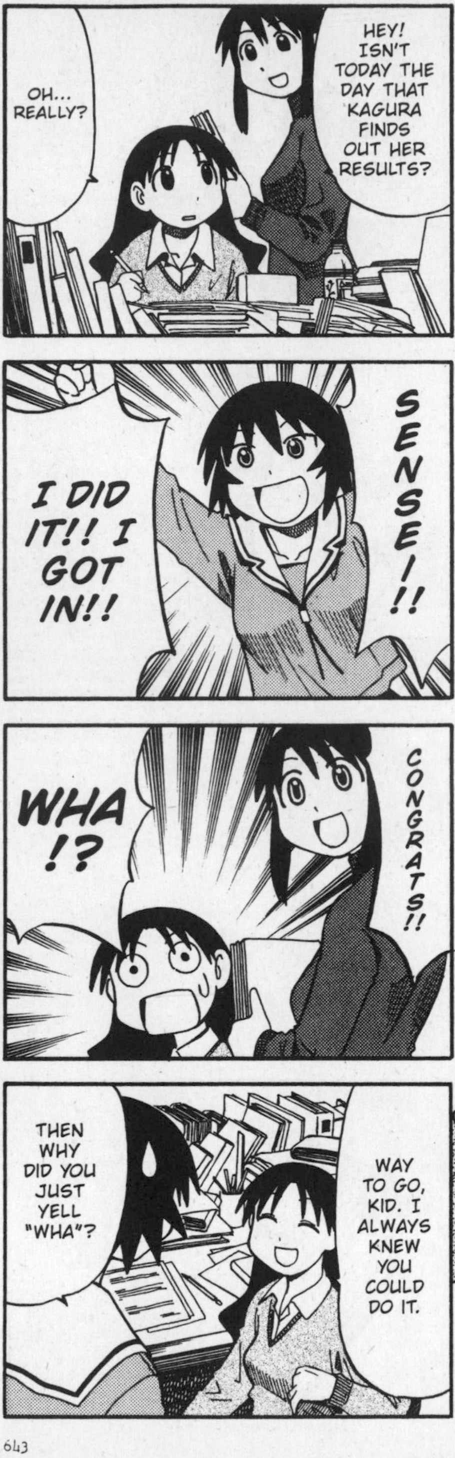
HEY! ISN'T TODAY THE DAY THAT KAGURA FINDS OUT HER RESULTS?
OH... REALLY?
SENSEI!!
I DID IT!! I GOT IN!!
CONGRATS!!
WHA!?
WAY TO GO, KID. I ALWAYS KNEW YOU COULD DO IT.
THEN WHY DID YOU JUST YELL "WHA"?

SHINING BRIGHT

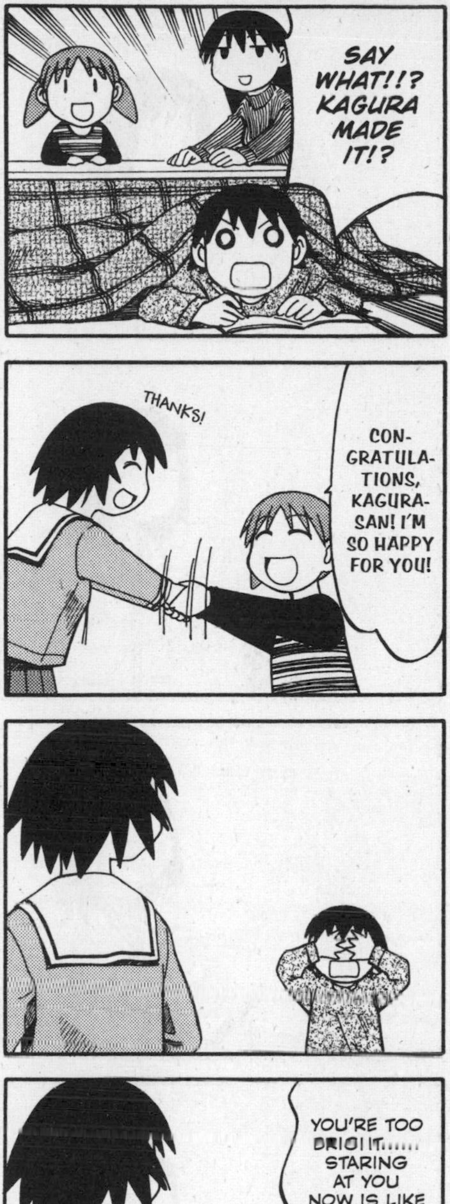
SAY WHAT!!? KAGURA MADE IT!?
CONGRATULATIONS, KAGURA-SAN! I'M SO HAPPY FOR YOU!
THANKS!
YOU'RE TOO BRIGHT...... STARING AT YOU NOW IS LIKE LOOKING INTO THE SUN...

NO GOOD

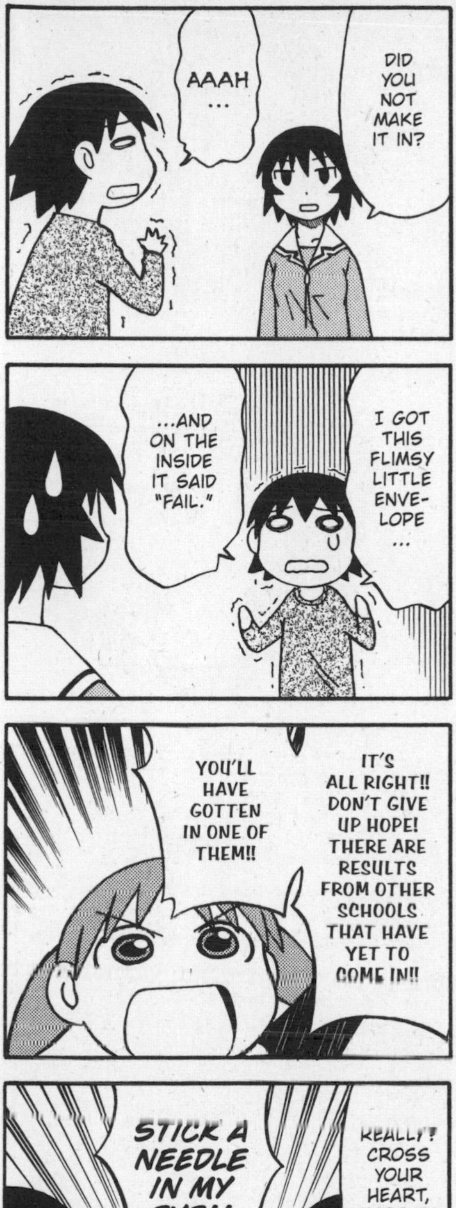
DID YOU NOT MAKE IT IN?
AAAH ...
I GOT THIS FLIMSY LITTLE ENVELOPE ...
...AND ON THE INSIDE IT SAID "FAIL."
IT'S ALL RIGHT!! DON'T GIVE UP HOPE! THERE ARE RESULTS FROM OTHER SCHOOLS THAT HAVE YET TO COME IN!!
YOU'LL HAVE GOTTEN IN ONE OF THEM!!
REALLY? CROSS YOUR HEART, HOPE TO DIE?
STICK A NEEDLE IN MY EYE!!

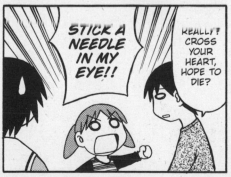

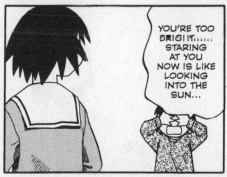

DON'T OPEN IT

HIYA!
THE WHOLE GANG'S HERE!!
AH, OSAKA-SAN...
GUESS WHAT? AH GOT ONE OF MY SCHOOL RESULTS BACK.
BUT AH AIN'T LOOKED INSIDE YET.
SINCE YOU HELPED ME SO MUCH WITH PREPARIN' FOR THE EXAMS 'N' ALL...
...AH WANT YOU TO OPEN THE RESULTS WITH ME.
WHAT'S IT GONNA BE?
UUU... IT'S ANOTHER FLIMSY ONE!

AWW

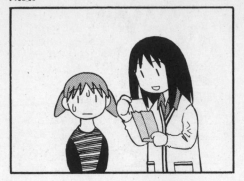

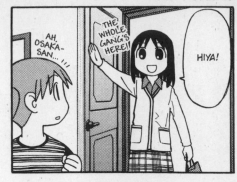

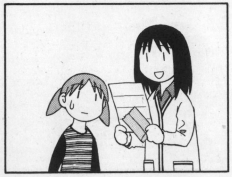

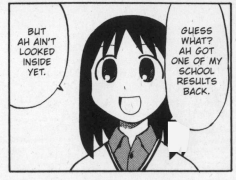

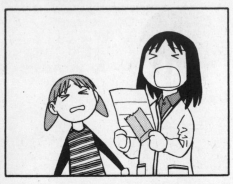

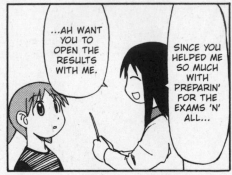

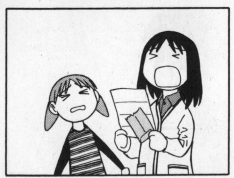

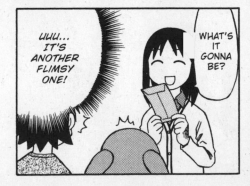

BACKUP FAILURE

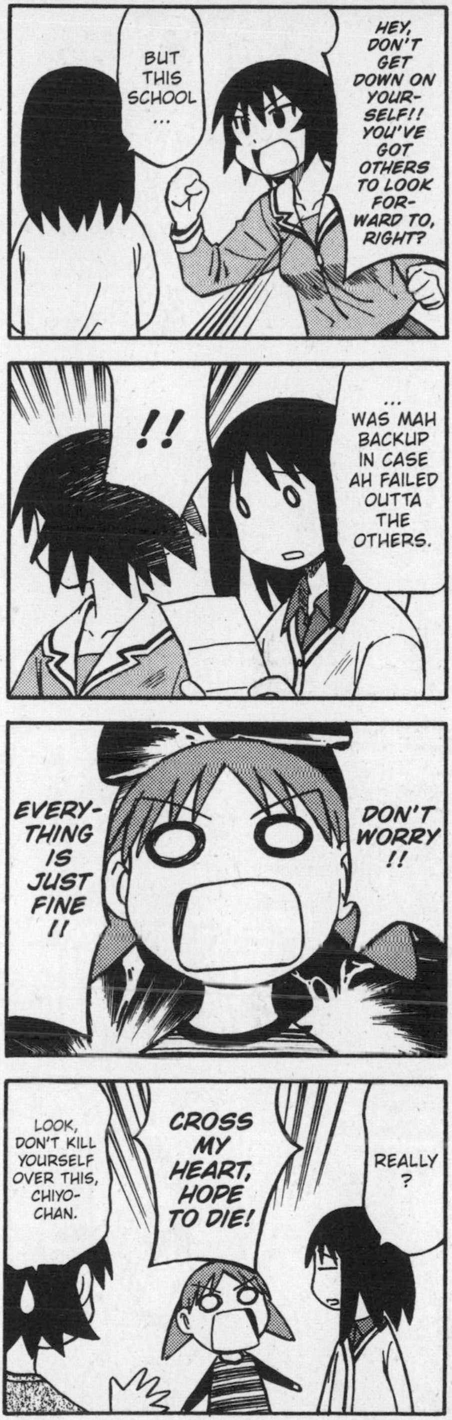
HEY, DON'T GET DOWN ON YOURSELF!! YOU'VE GOT OTHERS TO LOOK FORWARD TO, RIGHT?
BUT THIS SCHOOL ...
... WAS MAH BACKUP IN CASE AH FAILED OUTTA THE OTHERS.
!!
DON'T WORRY!!
EVERYTHING IS JUST FINE!!
REALLY?
CROSS MY HEART, HOPE TO DIE!
LOOK, DON'T KILL YOURSELF OVER THIS, CHIYO-CHAN.

IF IT GETS HURT

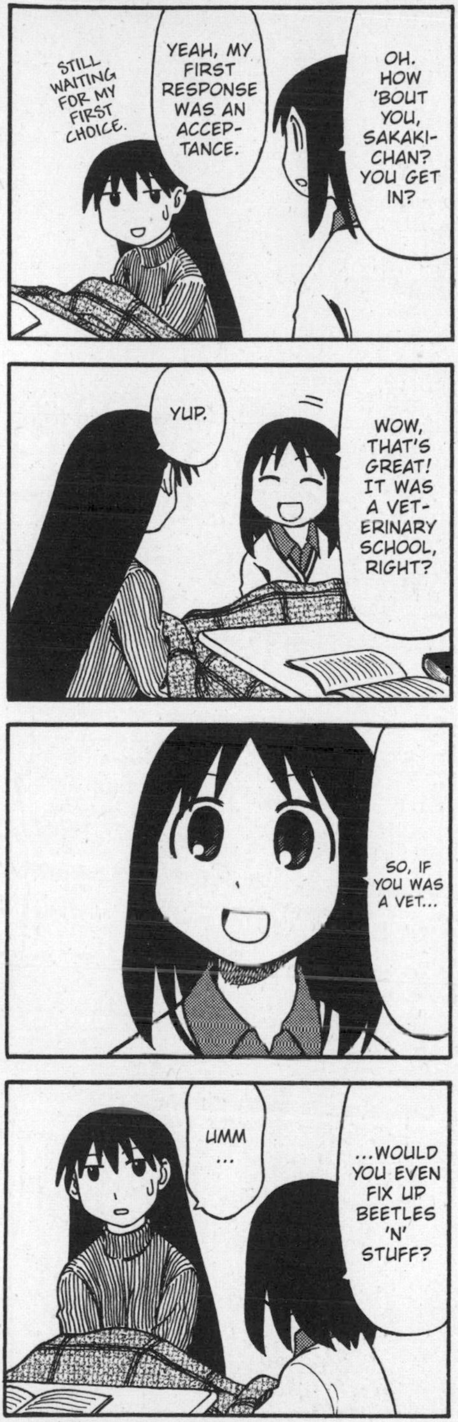
OH. HOW 'BOUT YOU, SAKAKI-CHAN? YOU GET IN?
YEAH, MY FIRST RESPONSE WAS AN ACCEPTANCE.
STILL WAITING FOR MY FIRST CHOICE.
WOW, THAT'S GREAT! IT WAS A VETERINARY SCHOOL, RIGHT?
YUP.
SO, IF YOU WAS A VET...
...WOULD YOU EVEN FIX UP BEETLES 'N' STUFF?
UMM ...

TOMO AND OSAKA'S BIG DAY

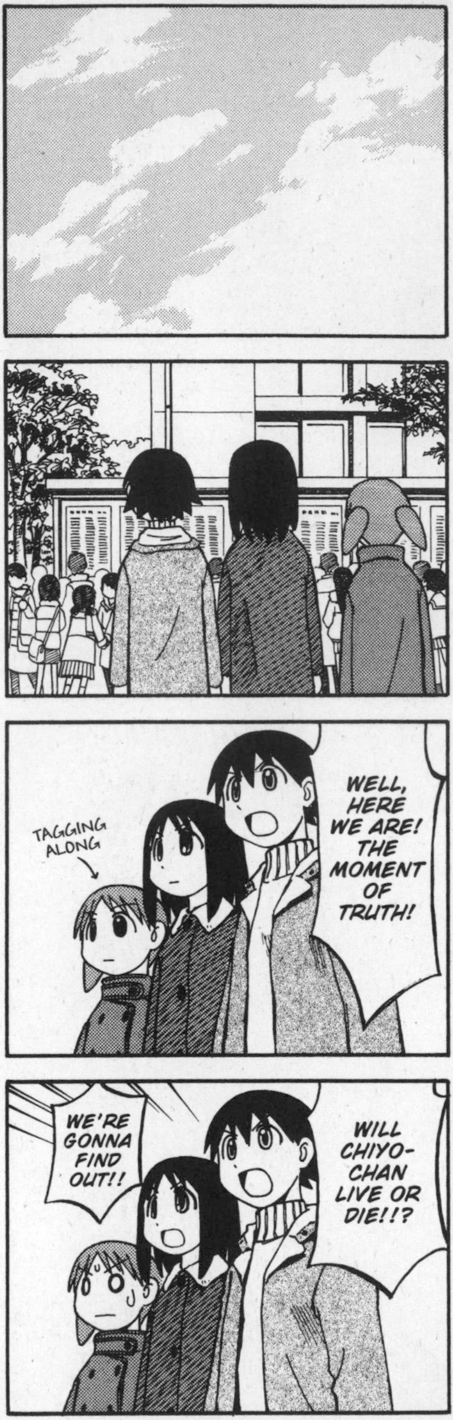
WELL, HERE WE ARE! THE MOMENT OF TRUTH!
TAGGING ALONG
WILL CHIYO-CHAN LIVE OR DIE!!?
WE'RE GONNA FIND OUT!!

GENIUS POWER

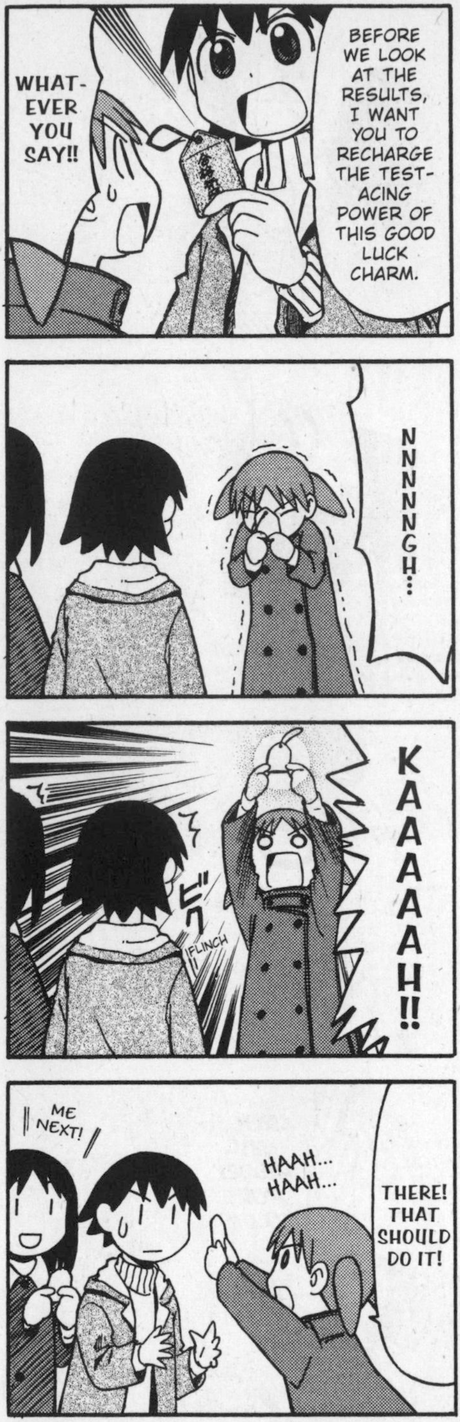
BEFORE WE LOOK AT THE RESULTS, I WANT YOU TO RECHARGE THE TEST-ACING POWER OF THIS GOOD LUCK CHARM.
WHAT-EVER YOU SAY!!
NNNNNNGH...
KAAAAAAAH!!
ビク
FLINCH
THERE! THAT SHOULD DO IT!
HAAH... HAAH...
ME NEXT!

AH

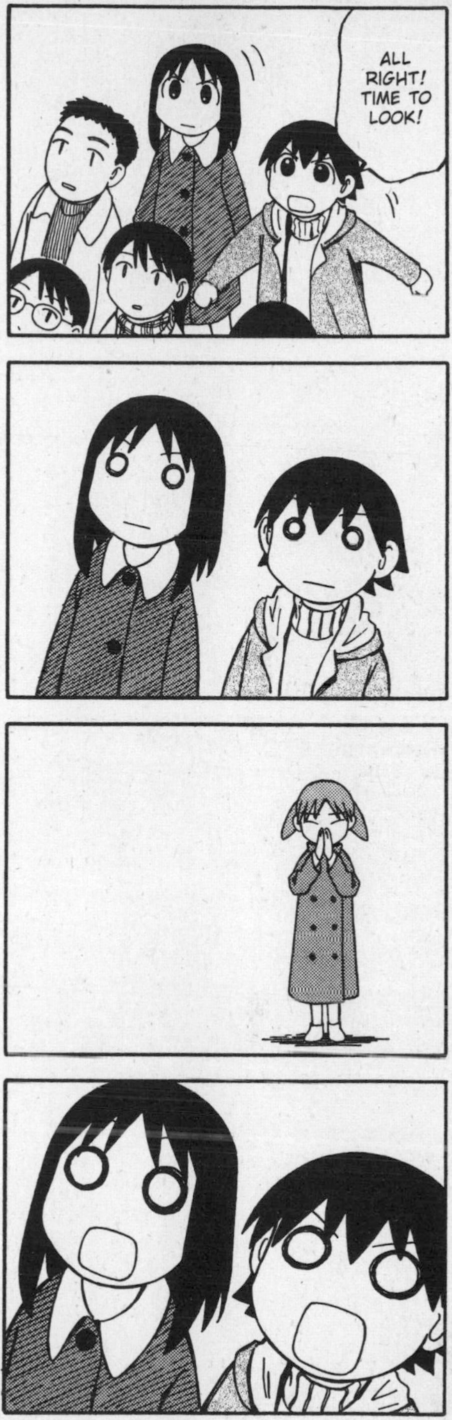
ALL RIGHT! TIME TO LOOK!

SHE LIVES

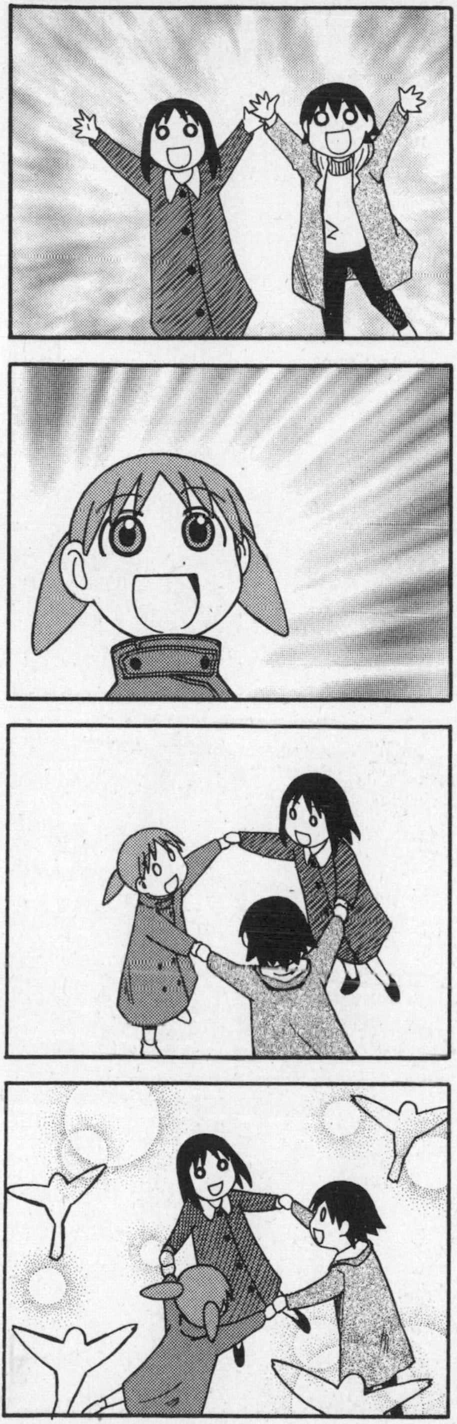

LOSING STREAK

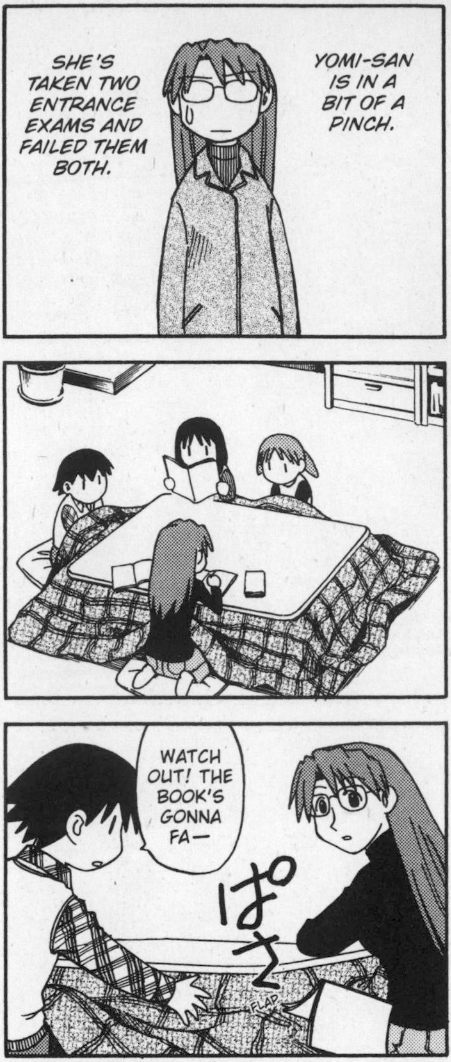
YOMI-SAN IS IN A BIT OF A PINCH.
SHE'S TAKEN TWO ENTRANCE EXAMS AND FAILED THEM BOTH.
WATCH OUT! THE BOOK'S GONNA FA—
ぱさ
FLAP
CRAP ...!
......

ENCOURAGEMENT

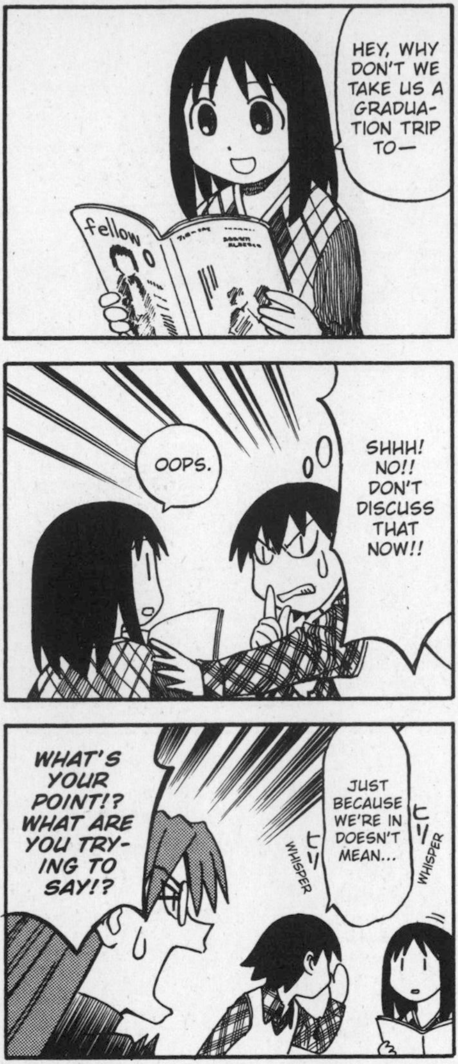
HEY, WHY DON'T WE TAKE US A GRADUATION TRIP TO—
fellow
SHHH! NO!! DON'T DISCUSS THAT NOW!!
OOPS.
ヒソ WHISPER
JUST BECAUSE WE'RE IN DOESN'T MEAN...
ヒソ WHISPER
WHAT'S YOUR POINT!? WHAT ARE YOU TRYING TO SAY!?
DON'T WORRY, YOMI! YOU'LL DEFINITELY PASS THE NEXT ONE... I THINK!
DON'T SAY THAT LIKE YOU'RE FEELING SORRY FOR ME!!

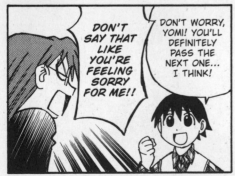

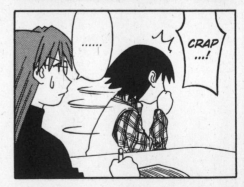

ALL TOGETHER

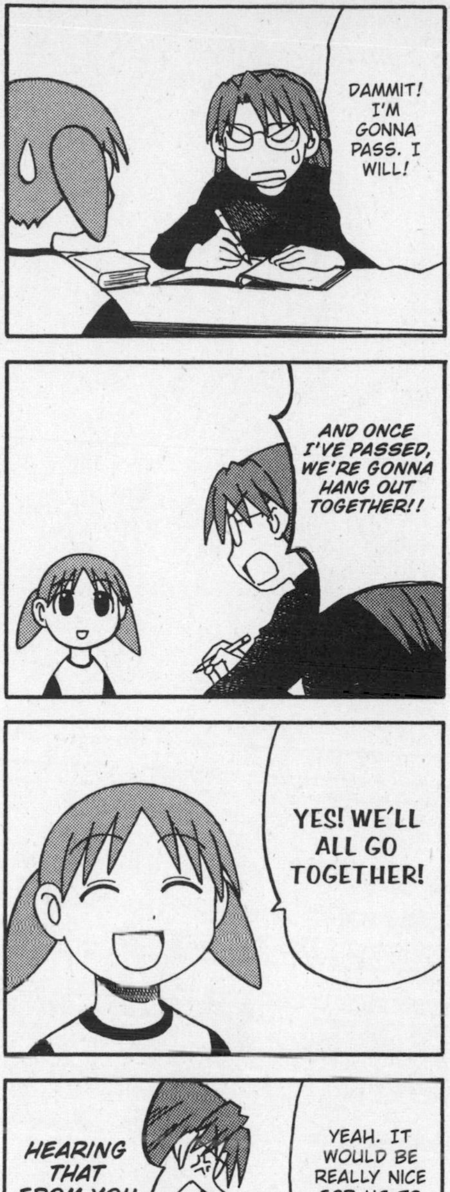
DAMMIT! I'M GONNA PASS. I WILL!
AND ONCE I'VE PASSED, WE'RE GONNA HANG OUT TOGETHER!!
YES! WE'LL ALL GO TOGETHER!
YEAH. IT WOULD BE REALLY NICE FOR US TO CELEBRATE TOGETHER.
HEARING THAT FROM YOU IS JUST PLAIN WRONG!!

EXAMS ARE HARD

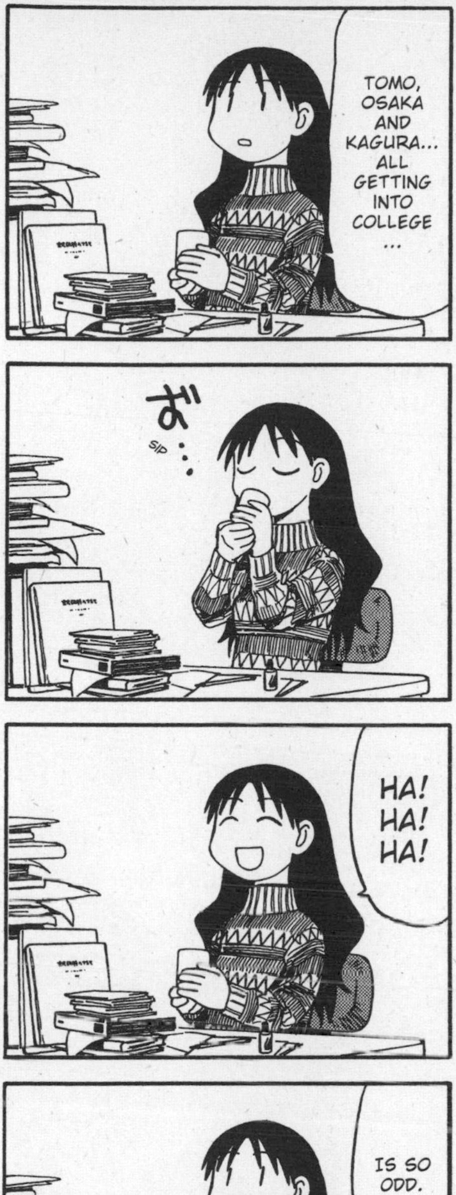
TOMO, OSAKA AND KAGURA... ALL GETTING INTO COLLEGE ...
ず
SIP
HA! HA! HA!
IS SO ODD.

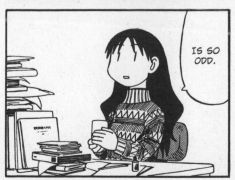

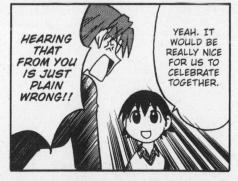

AZUMANGA-DAIOH

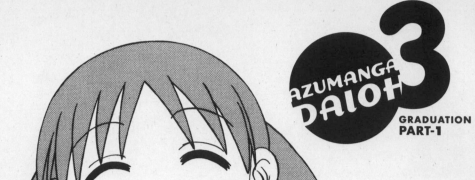

AZUMANGA DAIOH 3

GRADUATION PART-1

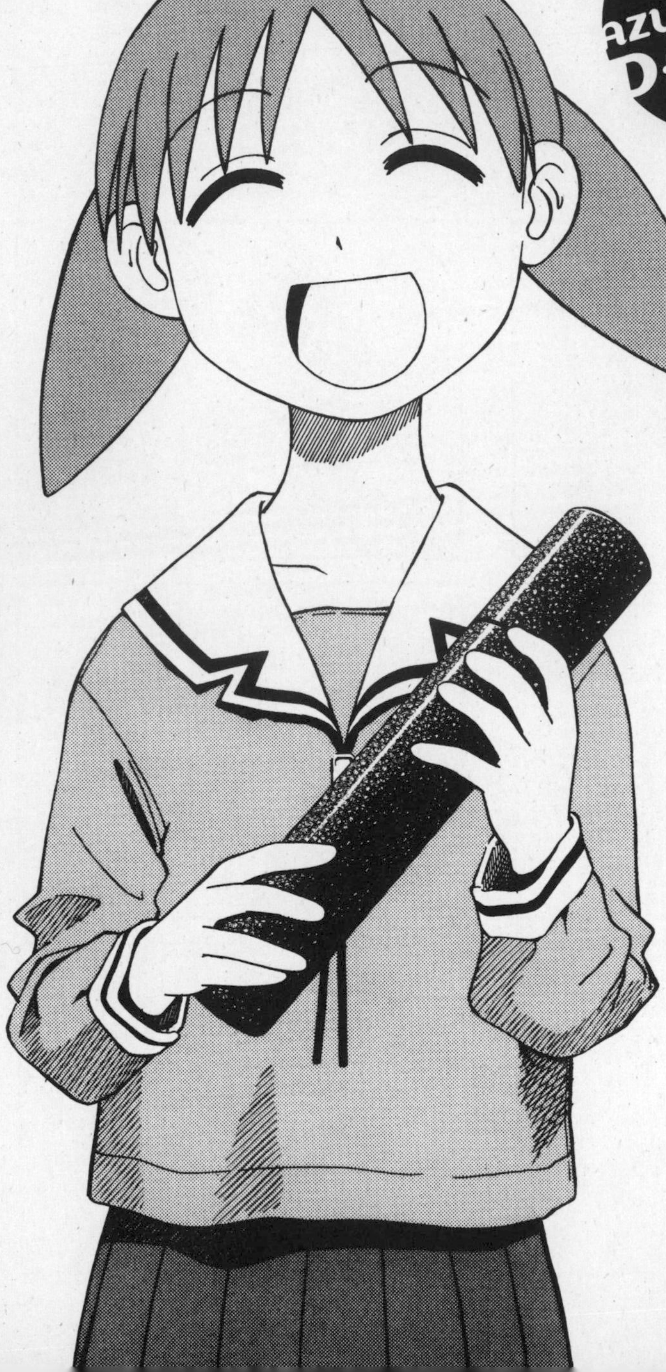

MALNUTRITION

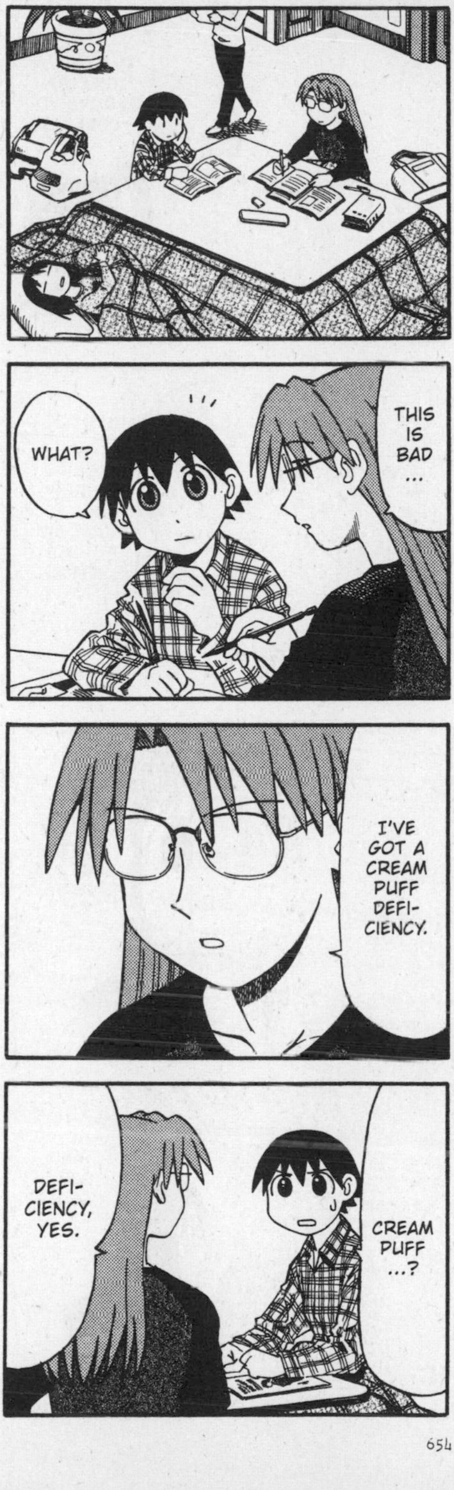
THIS IS BAD ...
WHAT?
I'VE GOT A CREAM PUFF DEFI- CIENCY.
CREAM PUFF ...?
DEFI- CIENCY, YES.

NEW THEORY

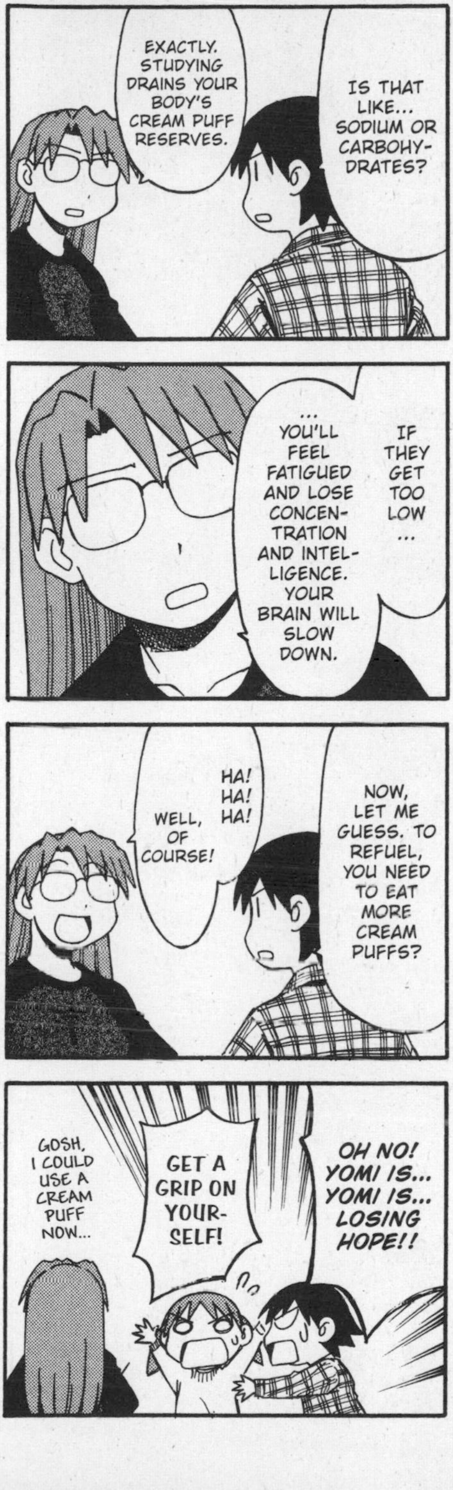
IS THAT LIKE... SODIUM OR CARBOHY- DRATES?
EXACTLY. STUDYING DRAINS YOUR BODY'S CREAM PUFF RESERVES.
IF THEY GET TOO LOW ...
... YOU'LL FEEL FATIGUED AND LOSE CONCEN- TRATION AND INTEL- LIGENCE. YOUR BRAIN WILL SLOW DOWN.
NOW, LET ME GUESS. TO REFUEL, YOU NEED TO EAT MORE CREAM PUFFS?
HA! HA! HA!
WELL, OF COURSE!
OH NO! YOMI IS... YOMI IS... LOSING HOPE!!
GET A GRIP ON YOUR- SELF!
GOSH, I COULD USE A CREAM PUFF NOW...

EEEHN, EEEHN

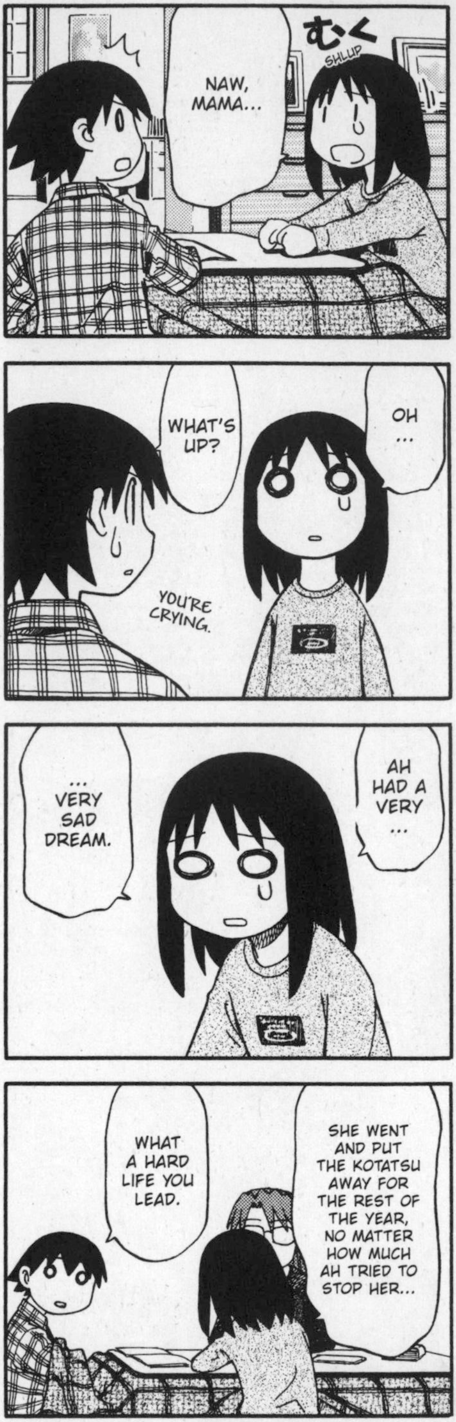
むく
SHLUP
NAW, MAMA...
OH ...
WHAT'S UP?
YOU'RE CRYING.
AH HAD A VERY ...
... VERY SAD DREAM.
SHE WENT AND PUT THE KOTATSU AWAY FOR THE REST OF THE YEAR, NO MATTER HOW MUCH AH TRIED TO STOP HER...
WHAT A HARD LIFE YOU LEAD.

SHE'S GROWN

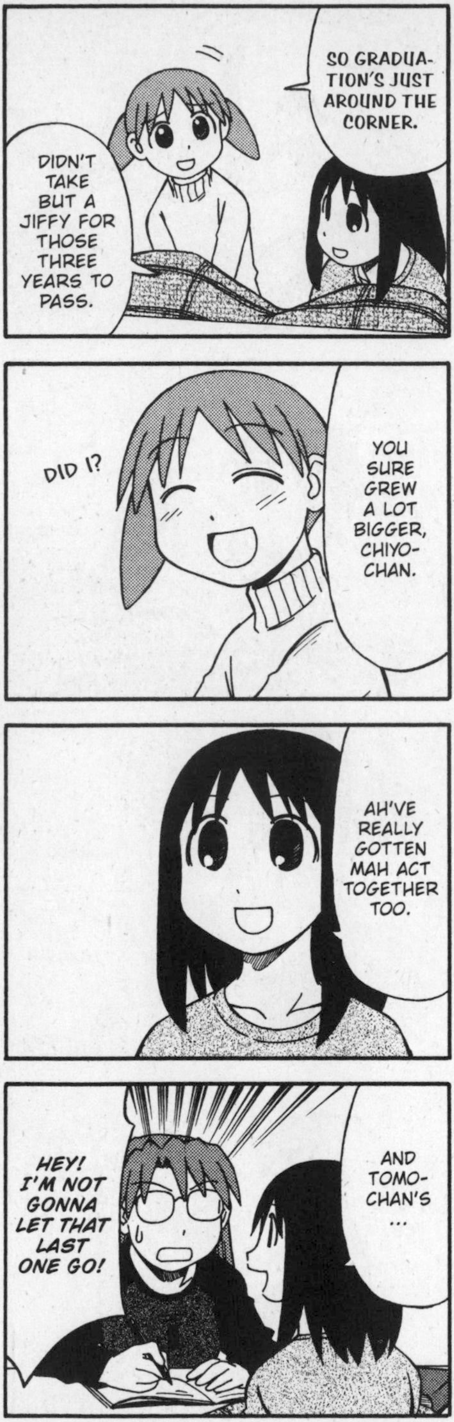
SO GRADUATION'S JUST AROUND THE CORNER.
DIDN'T TAKE BUT A JIFFY FOR THOSE THREE YEARS TO PASS.
YOU SURE GREW A LOT BIGGER, CHIYO-CHAN.
DID I?
AH'VE REALLY GOTTEN MAH ACT TOGETHER TOO.
AND TOMO-CHAN'S ...
HEY! I'M NOT GONNA LET THAT LAST ONE GO!

LET'S VISIT THE THEME PARK

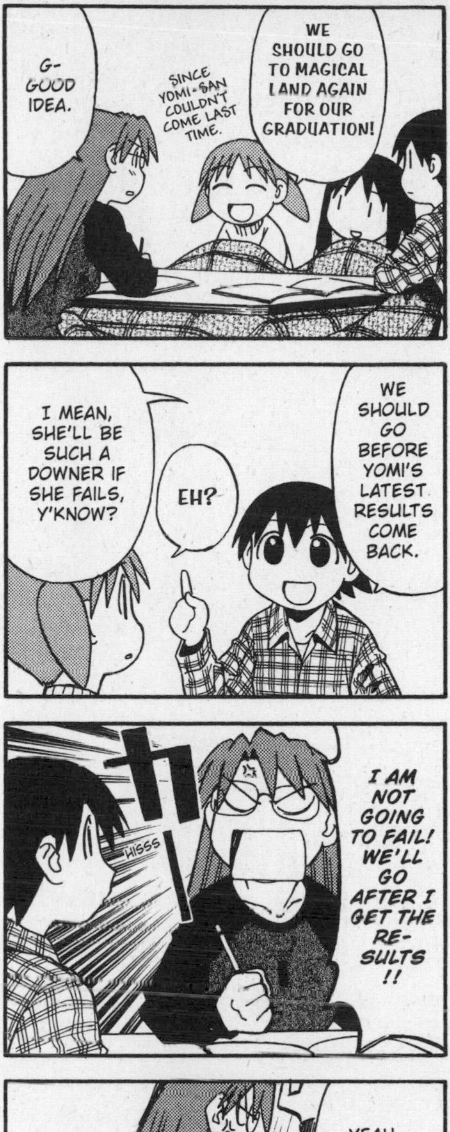
WE SHOULD GO TO MAGICAL LAND AGAIN FOR OUR GRADUATION!
SINCE YOMI-SAN COULDN'T COME LAST TIME.
G-GOOD IDEA.
WE SHOULD GO BEFORE YOMI'S LATEST RESULTS COME BACK.
EH?
I MEAN, SHE'LL BE SUCH A DOWNER IF SHE FAILS, Y'KNOW?
I AM NOT GOING TO FAIL! WE'LL GO AFTER I GET THE RE-SULTS!!
HISSS
YEAH... SURE! YOU'LL GET IN! HAVING FAITH IS IMPORTANT!
ARRRGH! I CAN'T STAND TO LISTEN TO THIS ANYMORE!!

RUNNING LOW ON CHIYO POWER

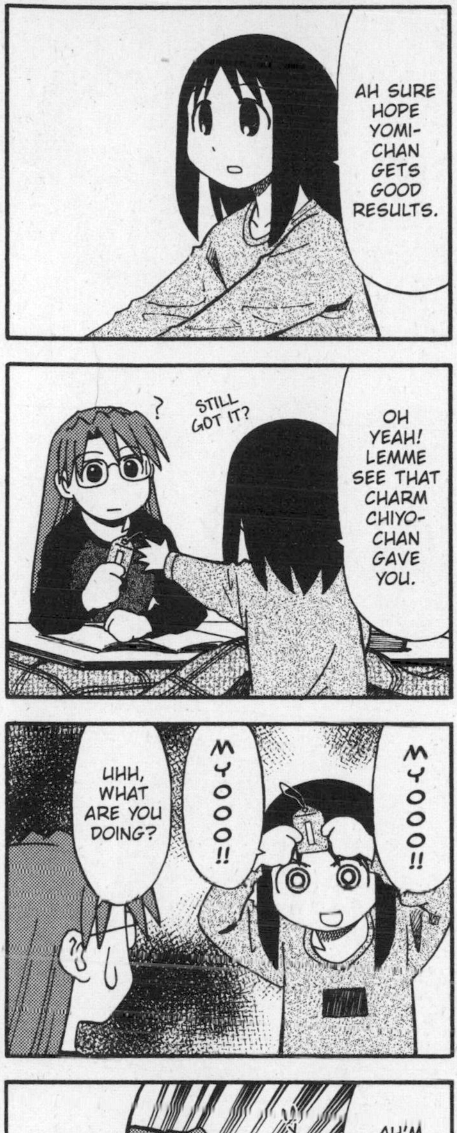
AH SURE HOPE YOMI-CHAN GETS GOOD RESULTS.
OH YEAH! LEMME SEE THAT CHARM CHIYO-CHAN GAVE YOU.
STILL GOT IT?
?
MYOOOO!!
MYOOOO!!
UHH, WHAT ARE YOU DOING?
AH'M FILLIN' IT WITH MAH BRAIN-POWER!
MYOOO!!
THIS IS NOT HELPING!!

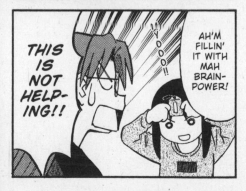

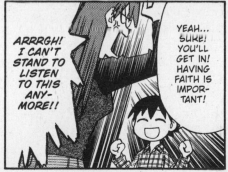

FIRST GRADUATION

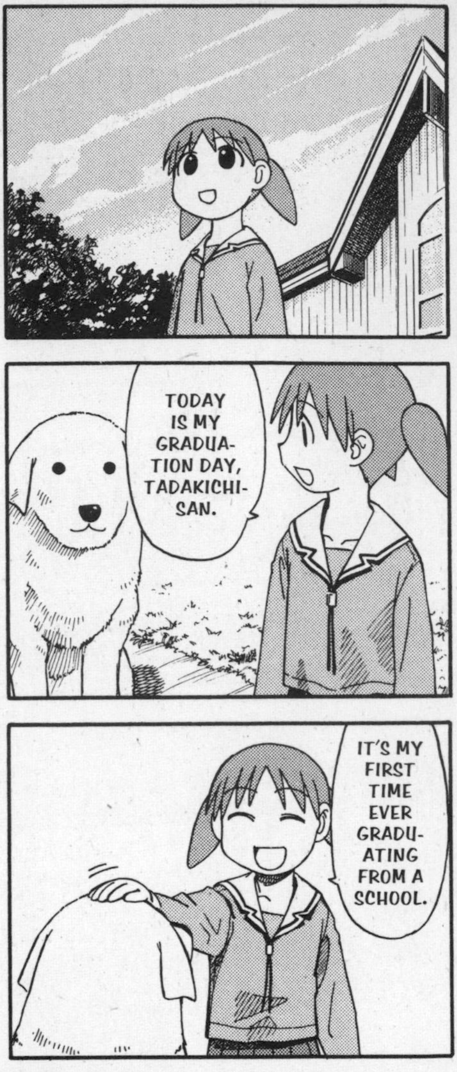
TODAY IS MY GRADUATION DAY, TADAKICHI-SAN.
IT'S MY FIRST TIME EVER GRADUATING FROM A SCHOOL.
I'M GOING NOW! BE BACK LATER!
WOOF!!

NO AGGRESSION?

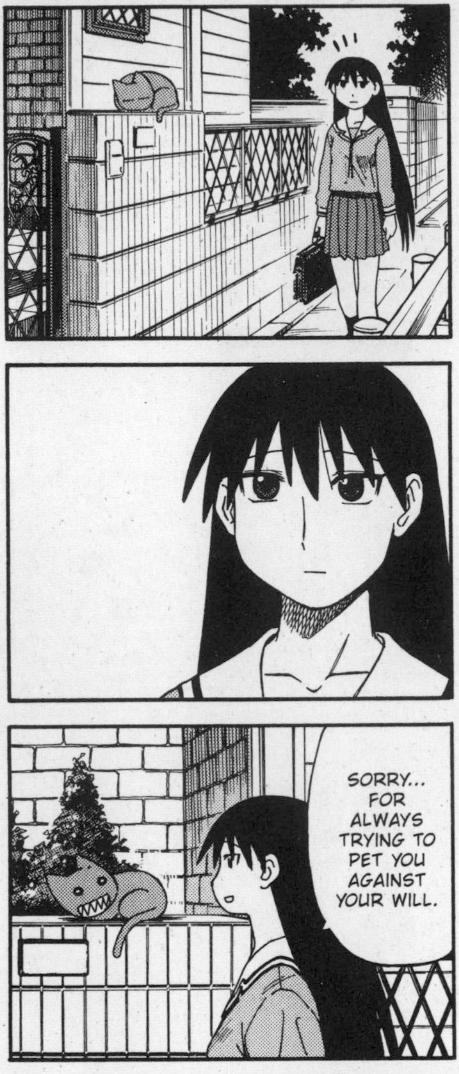
SORRY... FOR ALWAYS TRYING TO PET YOU AGAINST YOUR WILL.
?

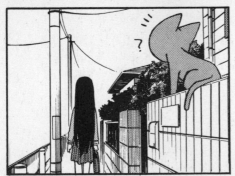

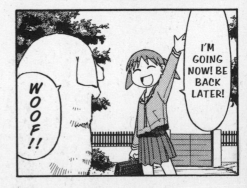

THE BITING CAT

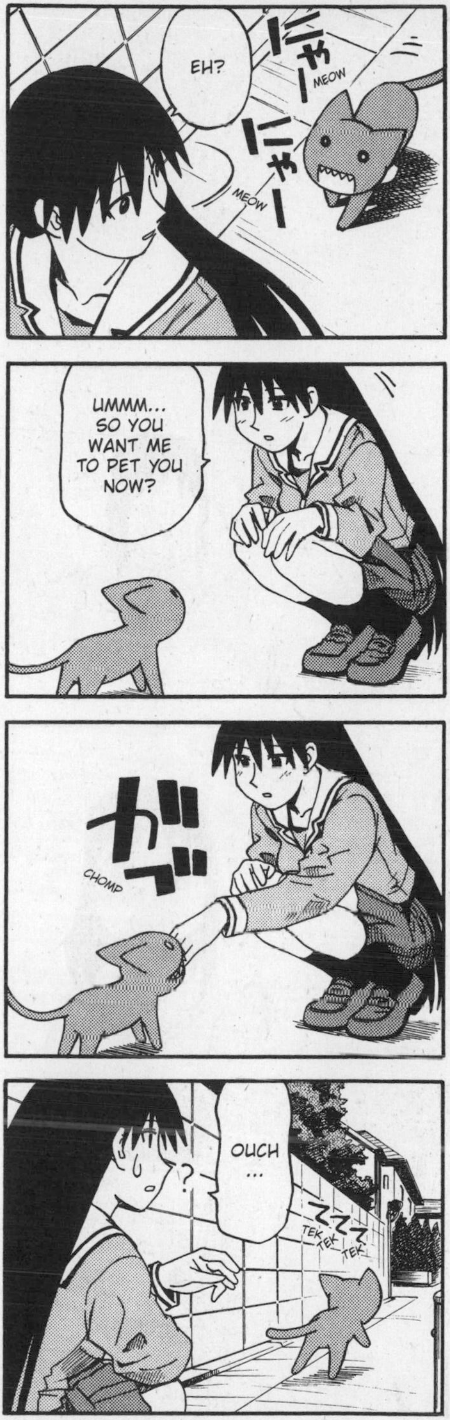
EH?
にゃー MEOW
にゃー MEOW
UMMM... SO YOU WANT ME TO PET YOU NOW?
がぶ
CHOMP
OUCH ...
?
ててて
TEK TEK TEK

BROUGHT SOMETHING

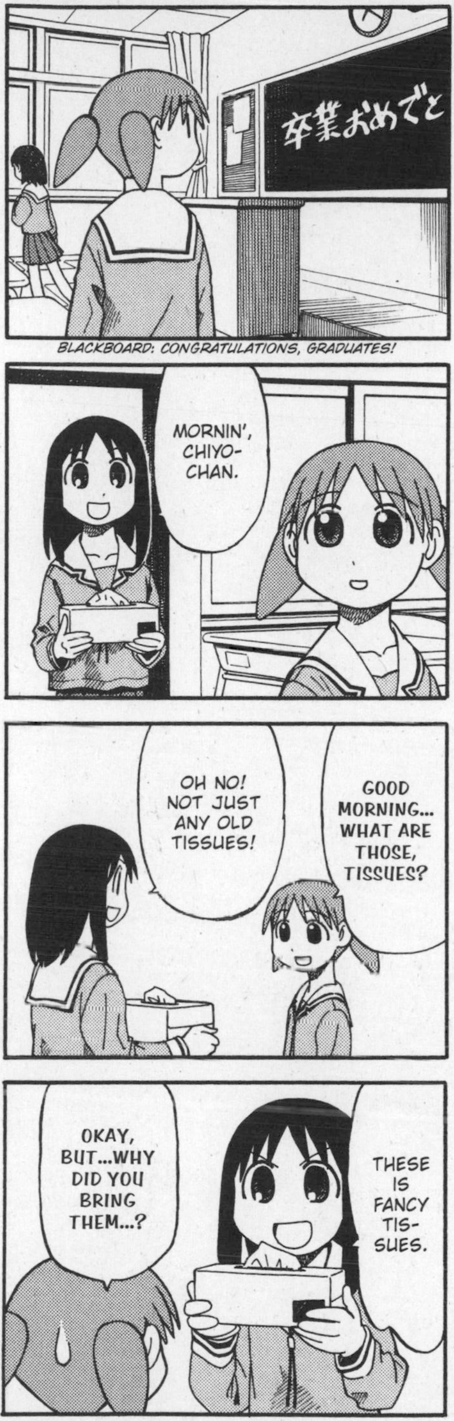
卒業おめでと
BLACKBOARD: CONGRATULATIONS, GRADUATES!
MORNIN', CHIYO-CHAN.
GOOD MORNING... WHAT ARE THOSE, TISSUES?
OH NO! NOT JUST ANY OLD TISSUES!
THESE IS FANCY TIS-SUES.
OKAY, BUT...WHY DID YOU BRING THEM...?

SECRETS DISCLOSED

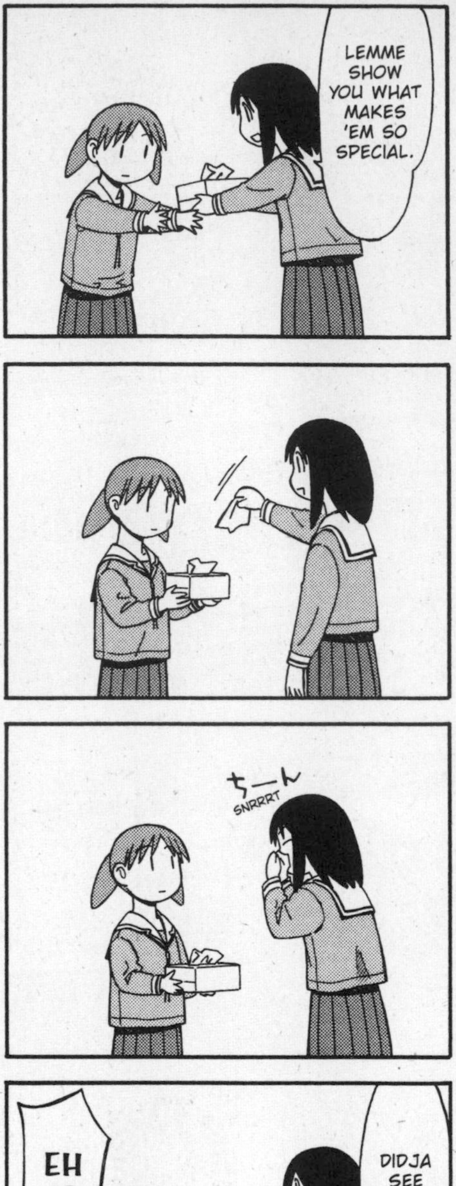
LEMME SHOW YOU WHAT MAKES 'EM SO SPECIAL.
ち—ん
SNRRRT
DIDJA SEE THAT?
EH !?

TRICKY

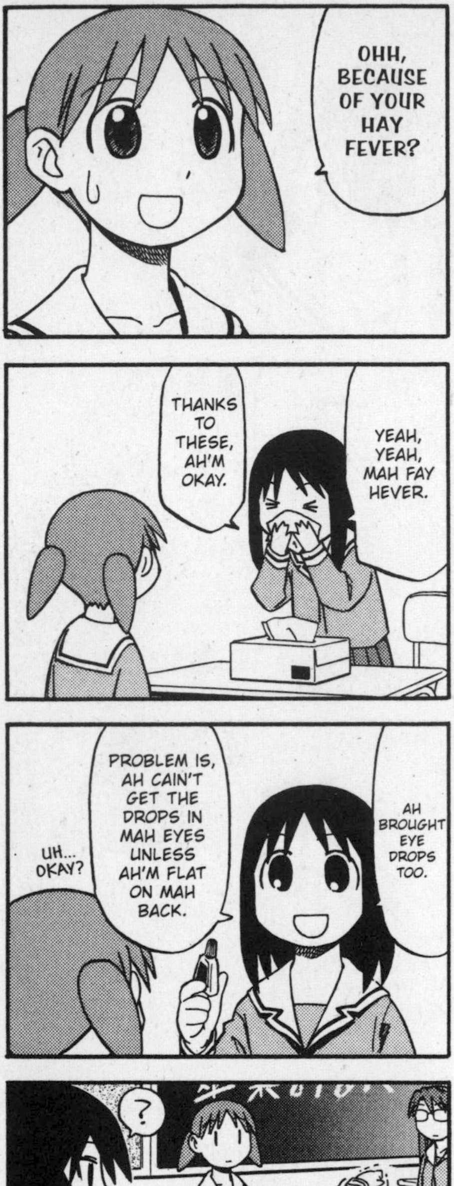
OHH, BECAUSE OF YOUR HAY FEVER?
YEAH, YEAH, MAH FAY HEVER.
THANKS TO THESE, AH'M OKAY.
AH BROUGHT EYE DROPS TOO.
PROBLEM IS, AH CAIN'T GET THE DROPS IN MAH EYES UNLESS AH'M FLAT ON MAH BACK.
UH... OKAY?
?

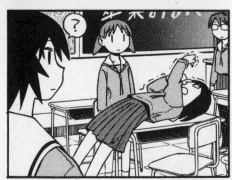

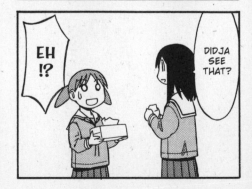

GRAND ENTRANCE

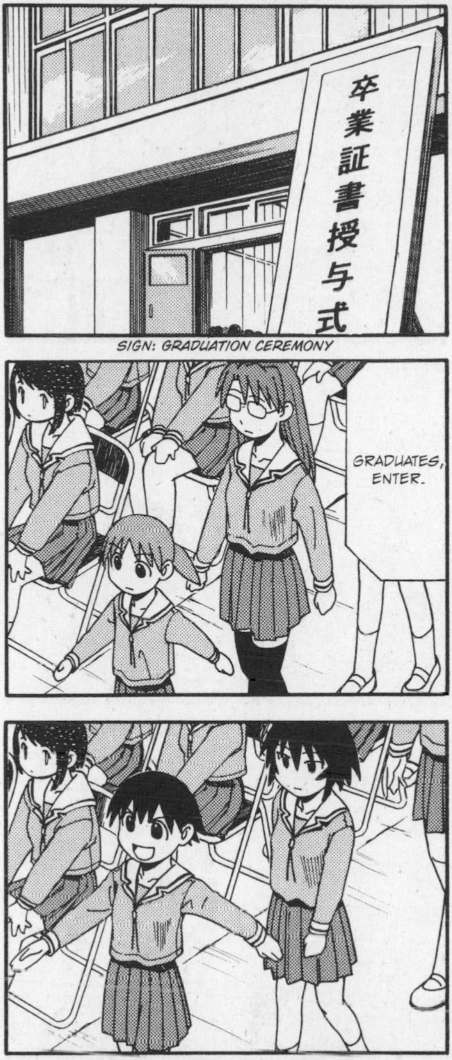
卒業証書授与式
GRADUATES, ENTER.
......

SIGN: GRADUATION CEREMONY

THE OSAKAN ADDRESS

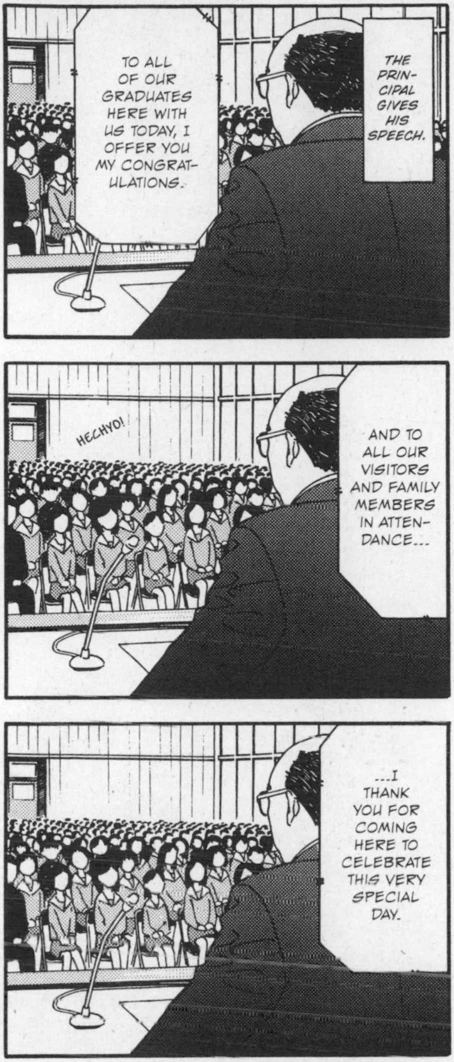
THE PRINCIPAL GIVES HIS SPEECH.
TO ALL OF OUR GRADUATES HERE WITH US TODAY, I OFFER YOU MY CONGRATULATIONS.
AND TO ALL OUR VISITORS AND FAMILY MEMBERS IN ATTENDANCE...
HECHYO!
...I THANK YOU FOR COMING HERE TO CELEBRATE THIS VERY SPECIAL DAY.
NOW, YOU GRADUATES WILL FIND THAT ALTHOUGH YOUR TIME HERE IS AT AN END, THIS IS JUST A...
WHAT WAS THAT?
NO IDEA.

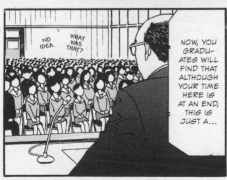

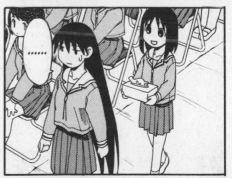

THE STRONGEST STUDENT

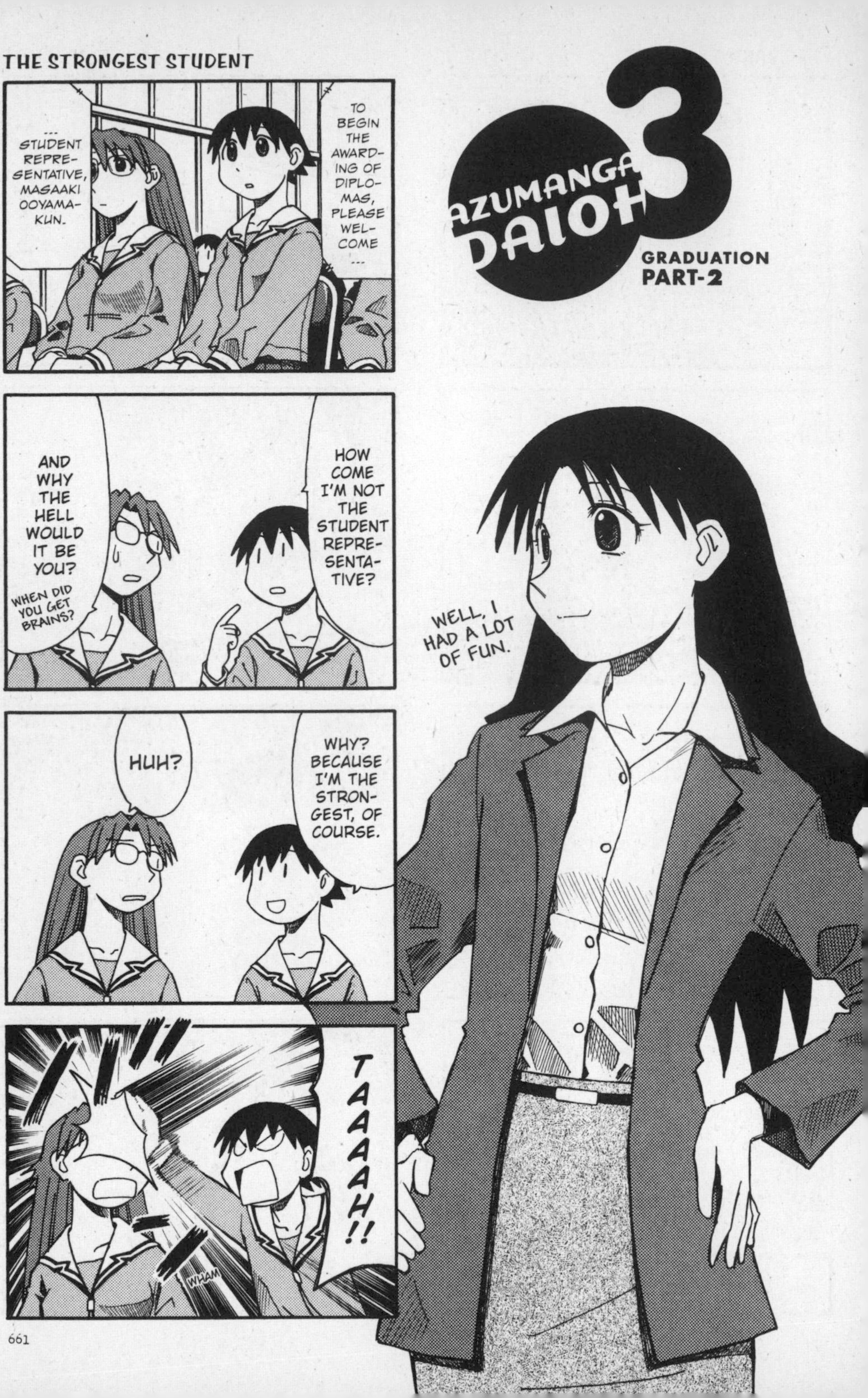
AZUMANGA DAIOH 3
GRADUATION PART-2
WELL, I HAD A LOT OF FUN.
TO BEGIN THE AWARDING OF DIPLOMAS, PLEASE WELCOME ...
... STUDENT REPRESENTATIVE, MASAAKI OOYAMA-KUN.
HOW COME I'M NOT THE STUDENT REPRESENTATIVE?
AND WHY THE HELL WOULD IT BE YOU?
WHEN DID YOU GET BRAINS?
WHY? BECAUSE I'M THE STRONGEST, OF COURSE.
HUH?
TAAAAAH!!
WHAM

CHOP, CHOP, CHOP

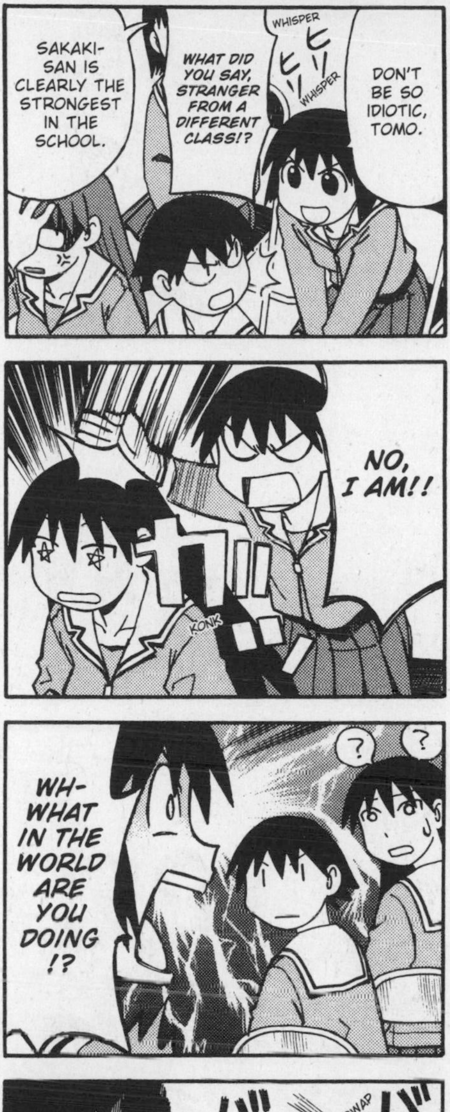
DON'T BE SO IDIOTIC, TOMO.
WHISPER
WHISPER
WHAT DID YOU SAY, STRANGER FROM A DIFFERENT CLASS!?
SAKAKI-SAN IS CLEARLY THE STRONGEST IN THE SCHOOL.
NO, I AM!!
KONK
WH- WHAT IN THE WORLD ARE YOU DOING!?
BWAP
BWAP

THAT'S ME

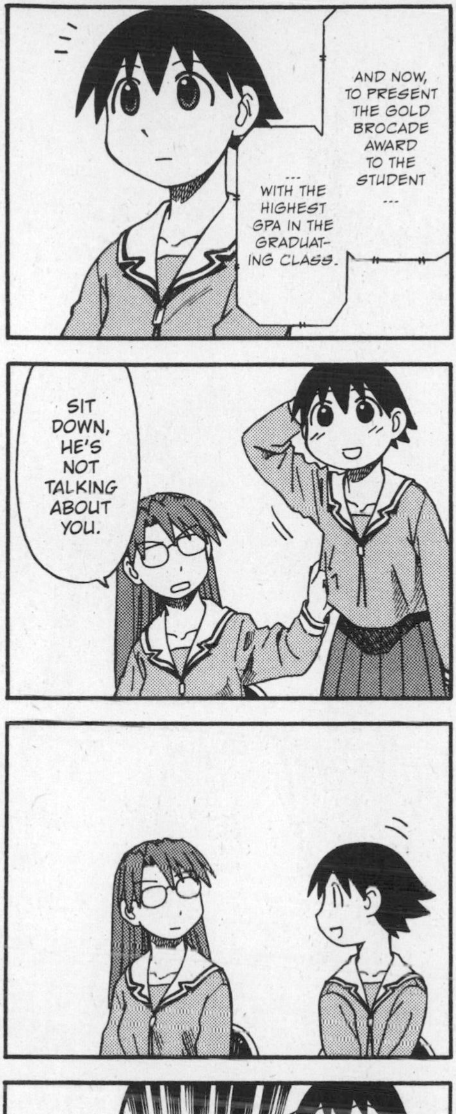
AND NOW, TO PRESENT THE GOLD BROCADE AWARD TO THE STUDENT ---
--- WITH THE HIGHEST GPA IN THE GRADUATING CLASS.
SIT DOWN, HE'S NOT TALKING ABOUT YOU.
I SAID, SIT YOUR ASS DOWN!!

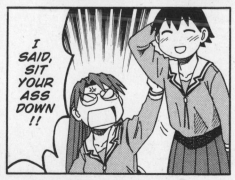

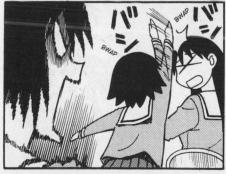

THE REAL STRONGEST STUDENT

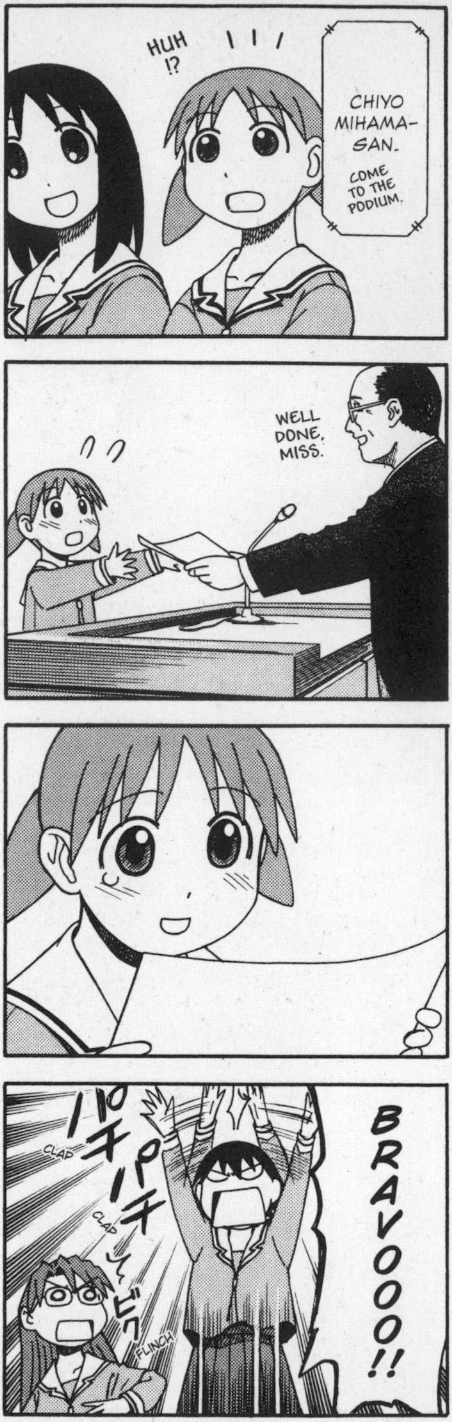
CHIYO MIHAMA-SAN.
COME TO THE PODIUM.
HUH !?
WELL DONE, MISS.
BRAVOOOO!!
パチ CLAP
パチ CLAP
ビク FLINCH

CONGRATULATIONS

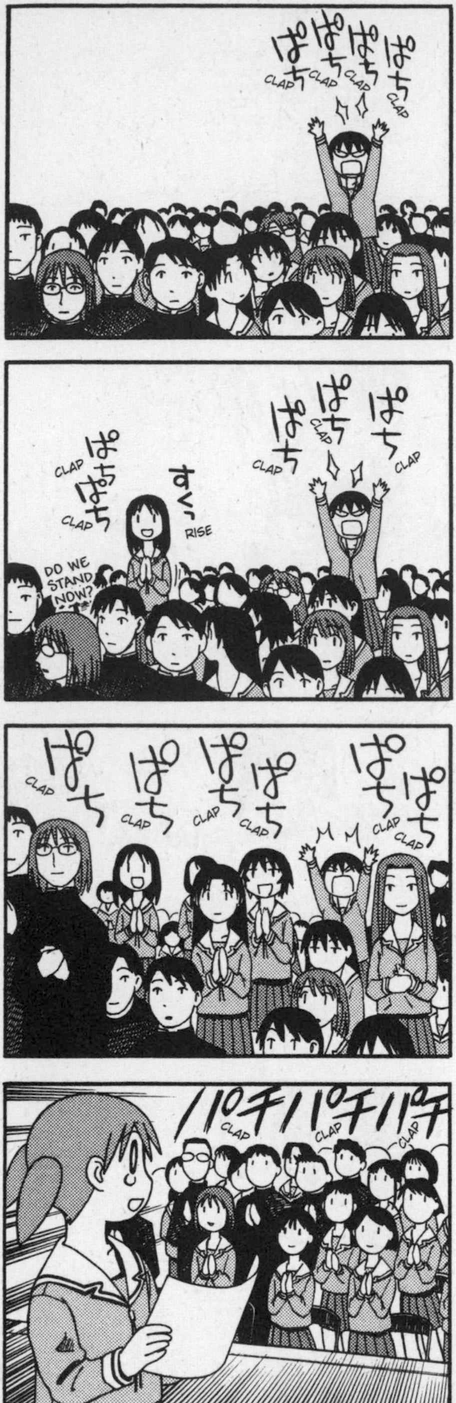
ぱち CLAP
ぱち CLAP
ぱち CLAP
ぱち CLAP
ぱち CLAP
ぱち CLAP
ぱち CLAP
すくっ RISE
ぱち CLAP
ぱち CLAP
DO WE STAND NOW?
ぱち CLAP
ぱち CLAP
ぱち CLAP
ぱち CLAP
ぱち CLAP
ぱち CLAP
パチ CLAP
パチ CLAP
パチ CLAP

FLOOD OF EMOTION

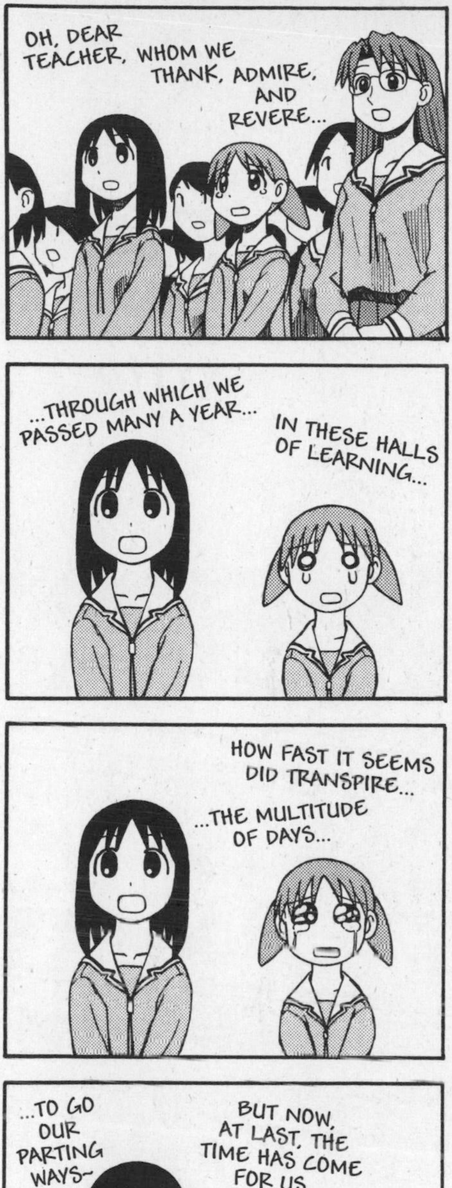
OH, DEAR TEACHER, WHOM WE THANK, ADMIRE, AND REVERE...
IN THESE HALLS OF LEARNING...
...THROUGH WHICH WE PASSED MANY A YEAR...
HOW FAST IT SEEMS DID TRANSPIRE...
...THE MULTITUDE OF DAYS...
BUT NOW, AT LAST, THE TIME HAS COME FOR US...
...TO GO OUR PARTING WAYS~

SADNESS

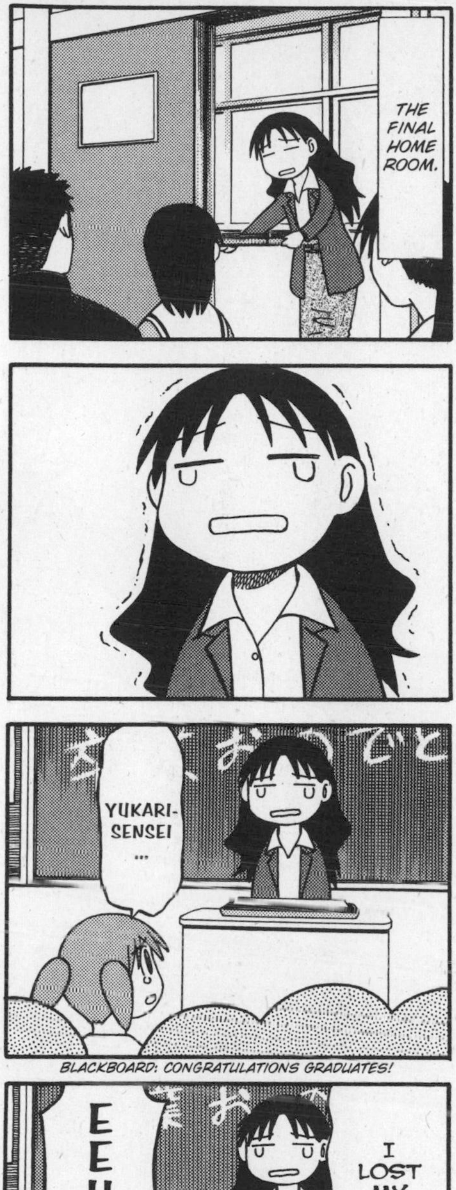
THE FINAL HOME ROOM.
YUKARI-SENSEI ...
I LOST MY WALLET ...
EEH!?

BLACKBOARD: CONGRATULATIONS GRADUATES!

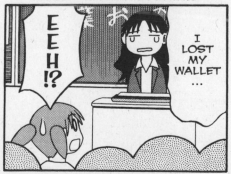

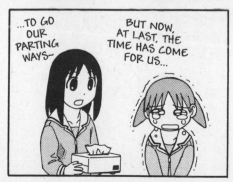

THERE YOU GO

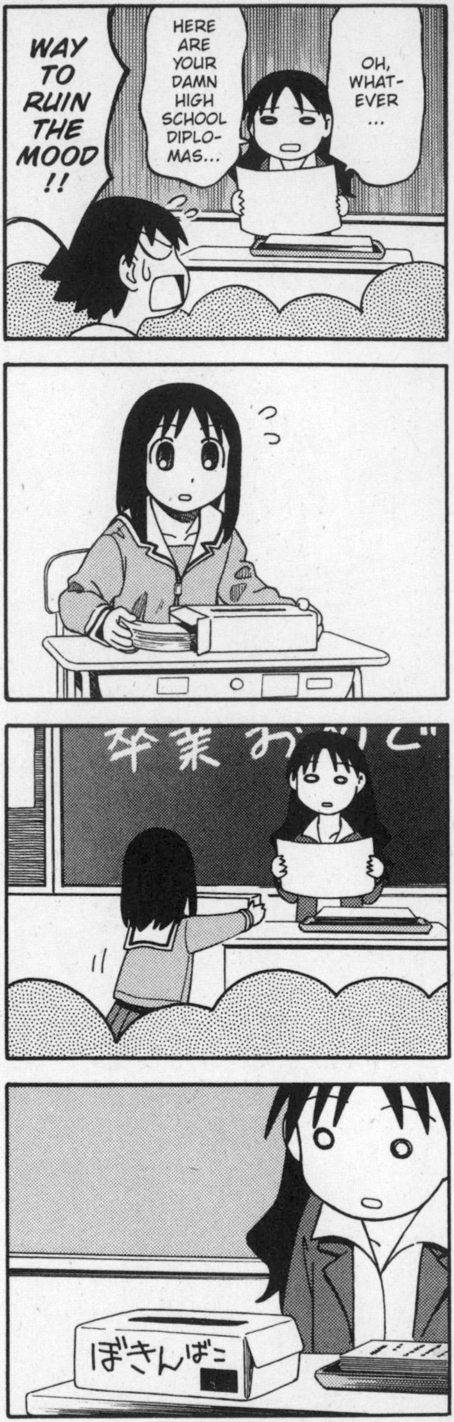
OH, WHAT-EVER ...
HERE ARE YOUR DAMN HIGH SCHOOL DIPLO-MAS...
WAY TO RUIN THE MOOD !!
ぼきんばこ

BOX: DONATION BOX

UNSATISFIED

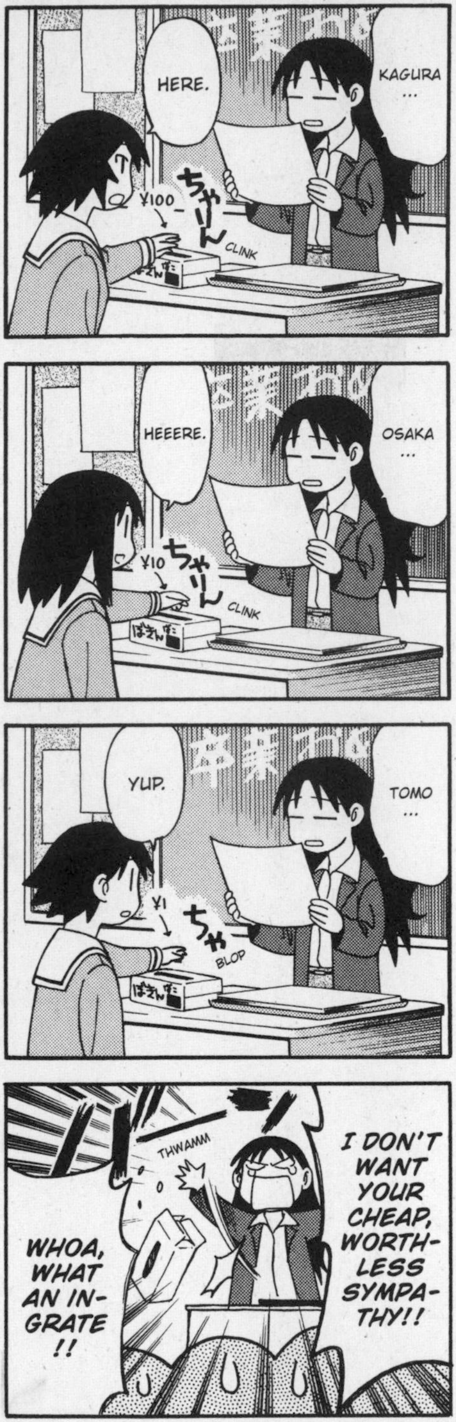
KAGURA ...
HERE.
ちゃりん
¥100
CLINK
OSAKA ...
HEEERE.
ちゃりん
¥10
CLINK
TOMO ...
YUP.
ちゃ
¥1
BLOP
I DON'T WANT YOUR CHEAP, WORTH-LESS SYMPA-THY!!
THWAMM
WHOA, WHAT AN IN-GRATE !!

CONGRATS

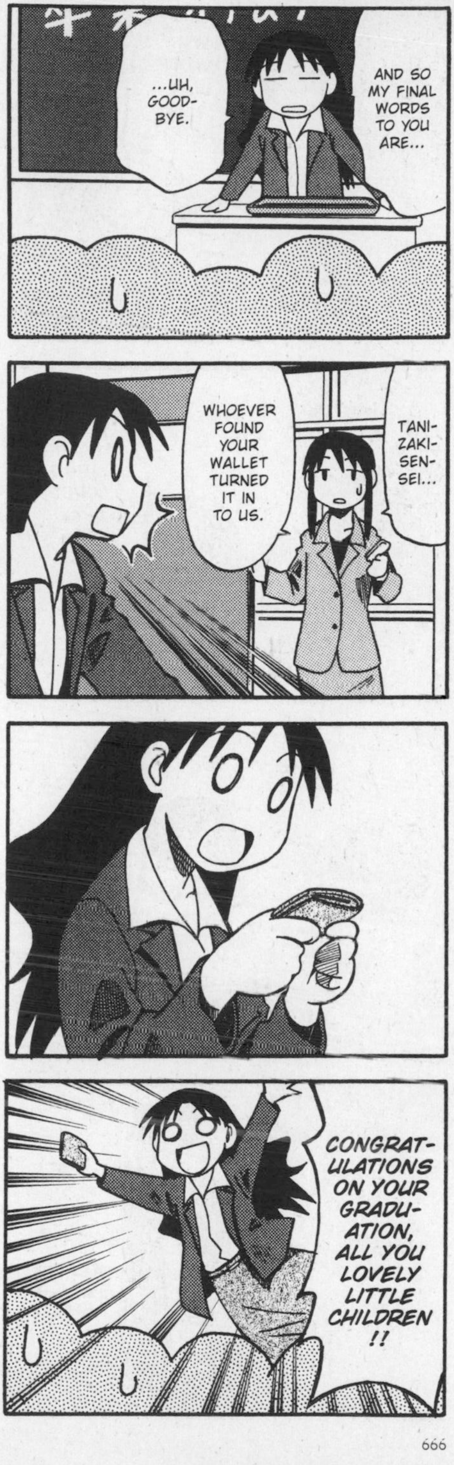
AND SO MY FINAL WORDS TO YOU ARE...
...UH, GOOD-BYE.
TANI-ZAKI-SEN-SEI...
WHOEVER FOUND YOUR WALLET TURNED IT IN TO US.
CONGRAT-ULATIONS ON YOUR GRADU-ATION, ALL YOU LOVELY LITTLE CHILDREN !!

FLOWERS

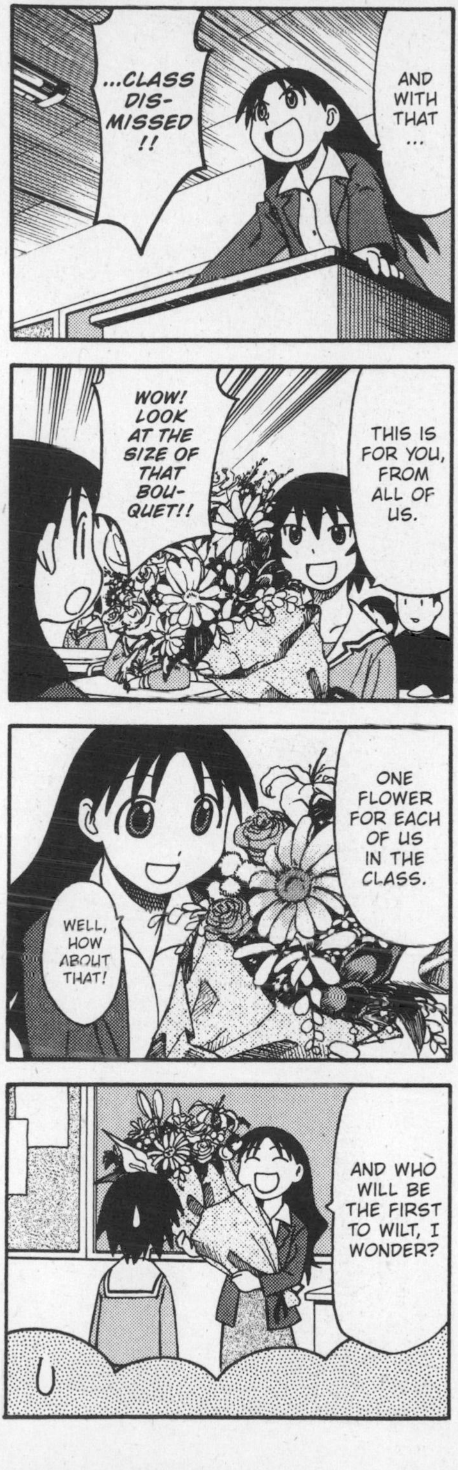
AND WITH THAT ...
...CLASS DIS-MISSED !!
THIS IS FOR YOU, FROM ALL OF US.
WOW! LOOK AT THE SIZE OF THAT BOU-QUET!!
ONE FLOWER FOR EACH OF US IN THE CLASS.
WELL, HOW ABOUT THAT!
AND WHO WILL BE THE FIRST TO WILT, I WONDER?

TOGETHER

JUST FELT LIKE IT

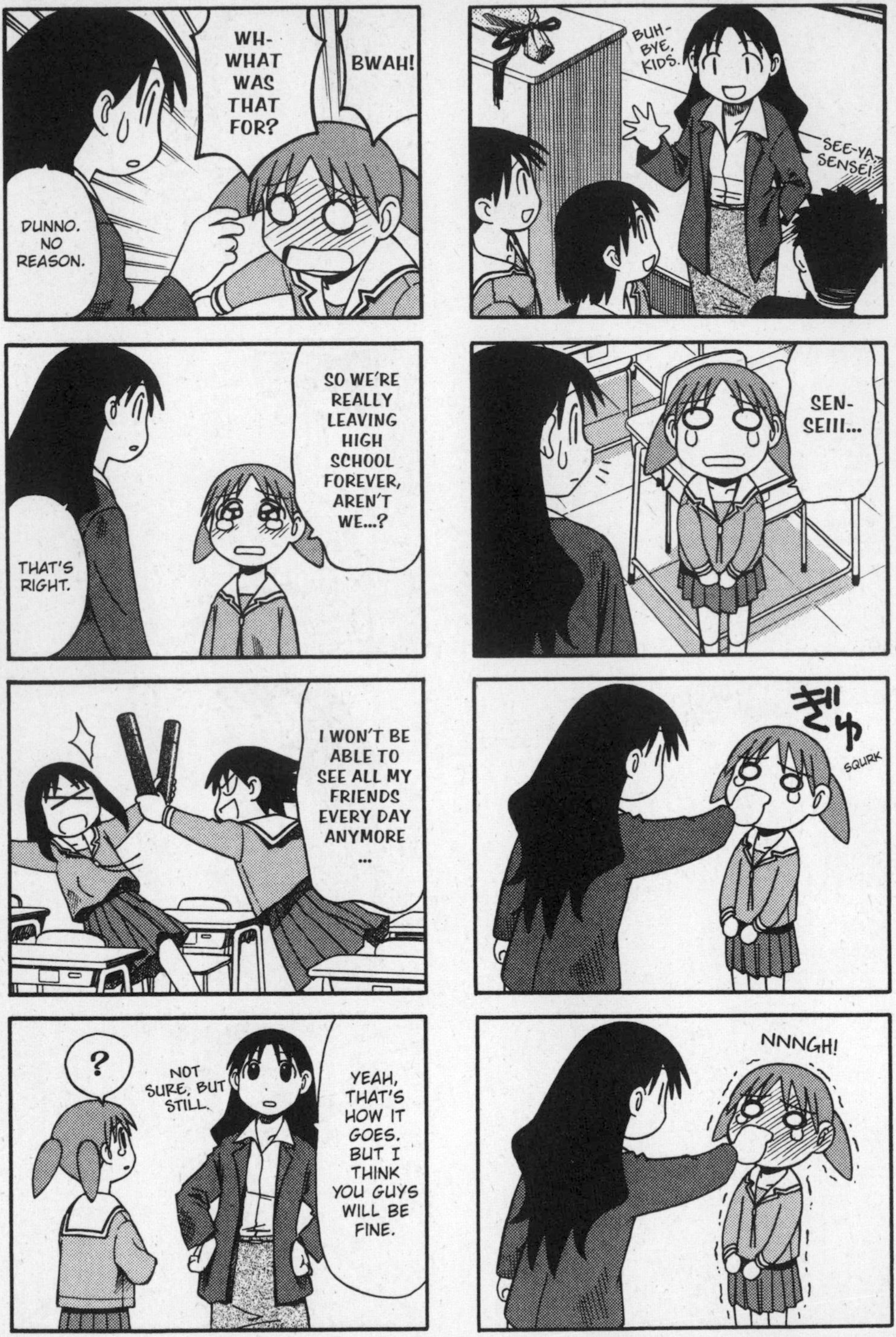

BUH-BYE, KIDS.
SEE-YA, SENSEI!
SEN-SEIII...
ぎゅ
SQURK
NNNGH!
BWAH!
WH-WHAT WAS THAT FOR?
DUNNO. NO REASON.
SO WE'RE REALLY LEAVING HIGH SCHOOL FOREVER, AREN'T WE...?
THAT'S RIGHT.
I WON'T BE ABLE TO SEE ALL MY FRIENDS EVERY DAY ANYMORE ...
YEAH, THAT'S HOW IT GOES. BUT I THINK YOU GUYS WILL BE FINE.
NOT SURE, BUT STILL.
?

DESPERATE TIMES, MEASURES

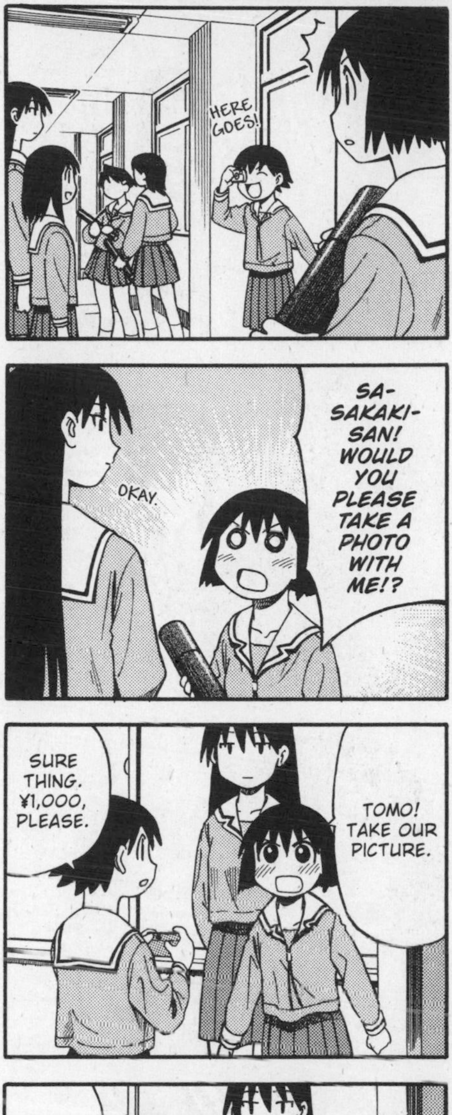
HERE GOES!
SA-SAKAKI-SAN! WOULD YOU PLEASE TAKE A PHOTO WITH ME!?
OKAY.
TOMO! TAKE OUR PICTURE.
SURE THING. ¥1,000, PLEASE.
ARGH...
UH, THAT WAS A JOKE.

BEHEADED

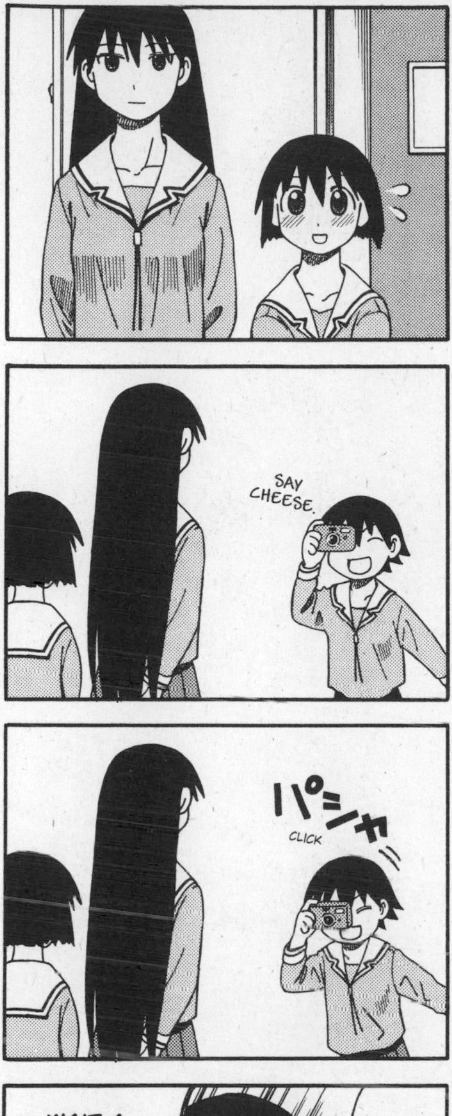
SAY CHEESE.
パシャ
CLICK
AND THERE YOU GO.
WAIT A MINUTE!! YOU JUST POINTED THE CAMERA TOWARD THE FLOOR, DIDN'T YOU!!?

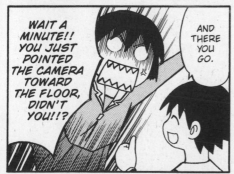

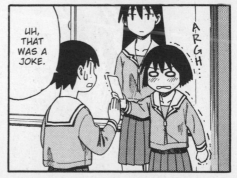

TREASURE

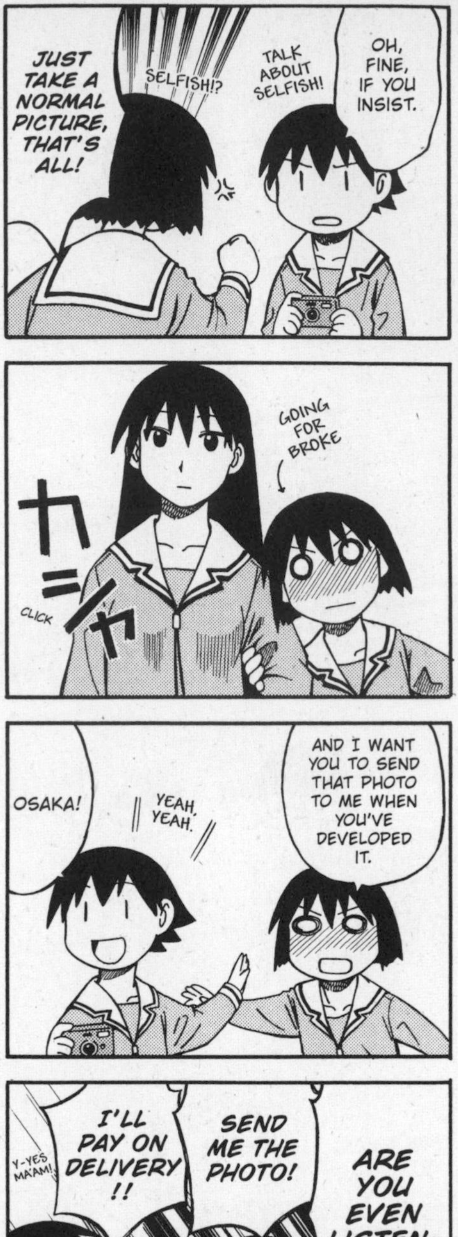
OH, FINE, IF YOU INSIST.
TALK ABOUT SELFISH!
SELFISH!?
JUST TAKE A NORMAL PICTURE, THAT'S ALL!
GOING FOR BROKE
カシャ
CLICK
AND I WANT YOU TO SEND THAT PHOTO TO ME WHEN YOU'VE DEVELOPED IT.
YEAH, YEAH.
OSAKA!
ARE YOU EVEN LISTENING TO ME!!?
SEND ME THE PHOTO!
I'LL PAY ON DELIVERY!!
Y-YES MA'AM!

SMILE

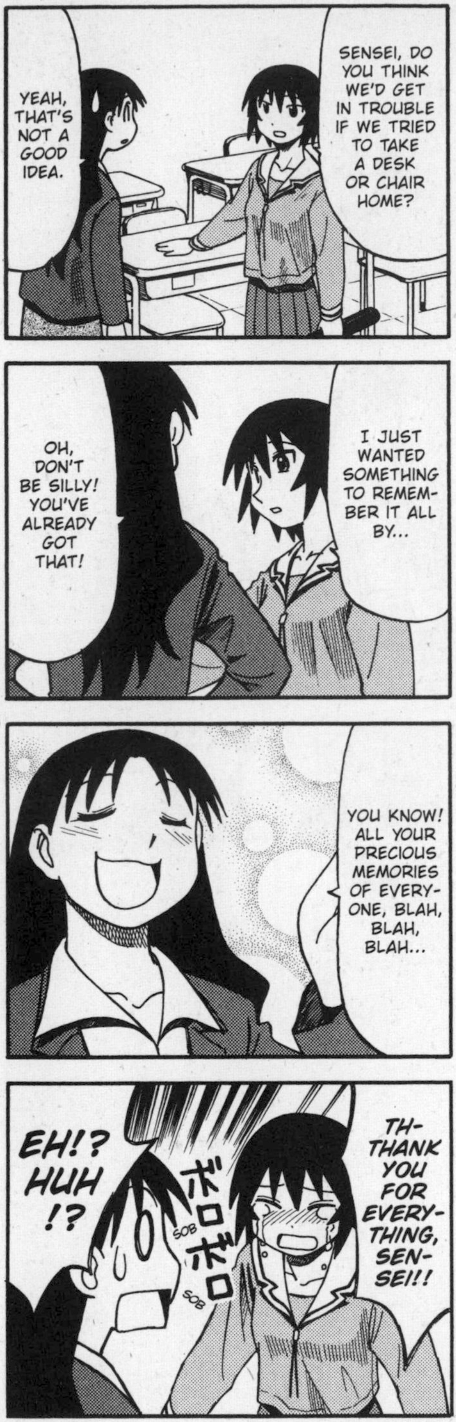
SENSEI, DO YOU THINK WE'D GET IN TROUBLE IF WE TRIED TO TAKE A DESK OR CHAIR HOME?
YEAH, THAT'S NOT A GOOD IDEA.
I JUST WANTED SOMETHING TO REMEMBER IT ALL BY...
OH, DON'T BE SILLY! YOU'VE ALREADY GOT THAT!
YOU KNOW! ALL YOUR PRECIOUS MEMORIES OF EVERYONE, BLAH, BLAH, BLAH...
TH-THANK YOU FOR EVERYTHING, SENSEI!!
ボロボロ
SOB
SOB
EH!? HUH!?

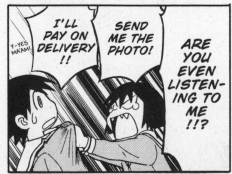

IT WAS A BLAST

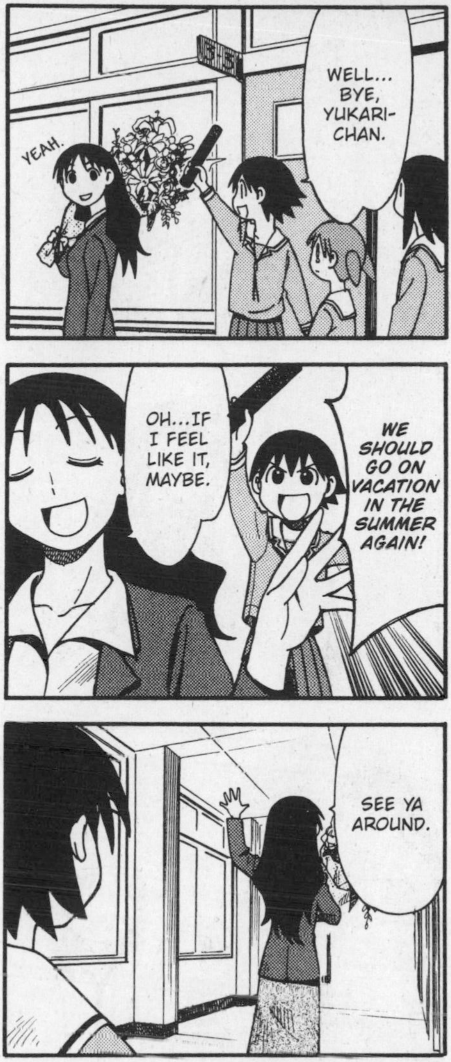
WELL... BYE, YUKARI-CHAN.
YEAH.
WE SHOULD GO ON VACATION IN THE SUMMER AGAIN!
OH...IF I FEEL LIKE IT, MAYBE.
SEE YA AROUND.
THANK YOU FOR EVERYTHING.

PREPARATIONS

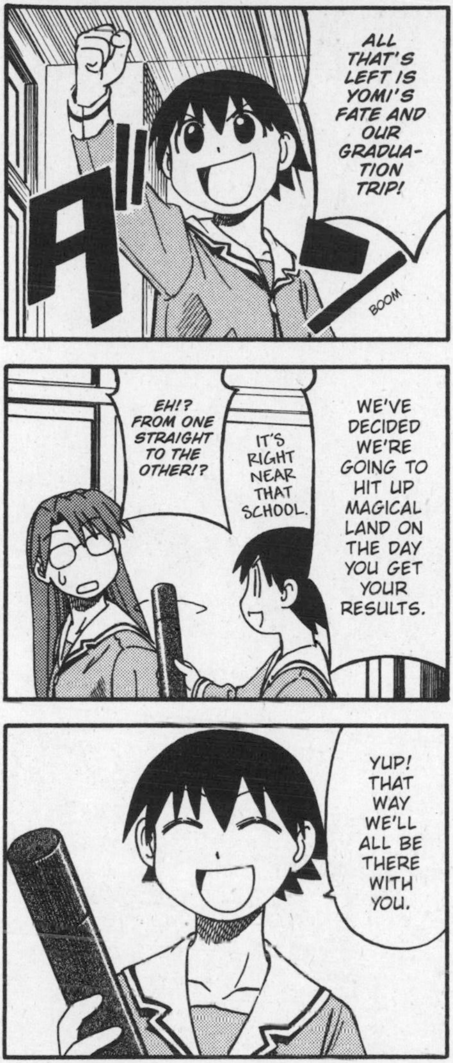
ALL THAT'S LEFT IS YOMI'S FATE AND OUR GRADUATION TRIP!
BOOM
WE'VE DECIDED WE'RE GOING TO HIT UP MAGICAL LAND ON THE DAY YOU GET YOUR RESULTS.
IT'S RIGHT NEAR THAT SCHOOL.
EH!? FROM ONE STRAIGHT TO THE OTHER!?
YUP! THAT WAY WE'LL ALL BE THERE WITH YOU.
SO START THINKING OF YOUR CONSOLATION SPEECHES NOW, GIRLS.

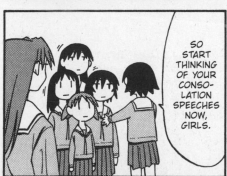

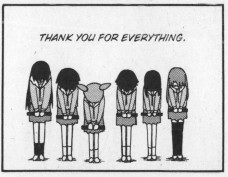

ALMA MATER

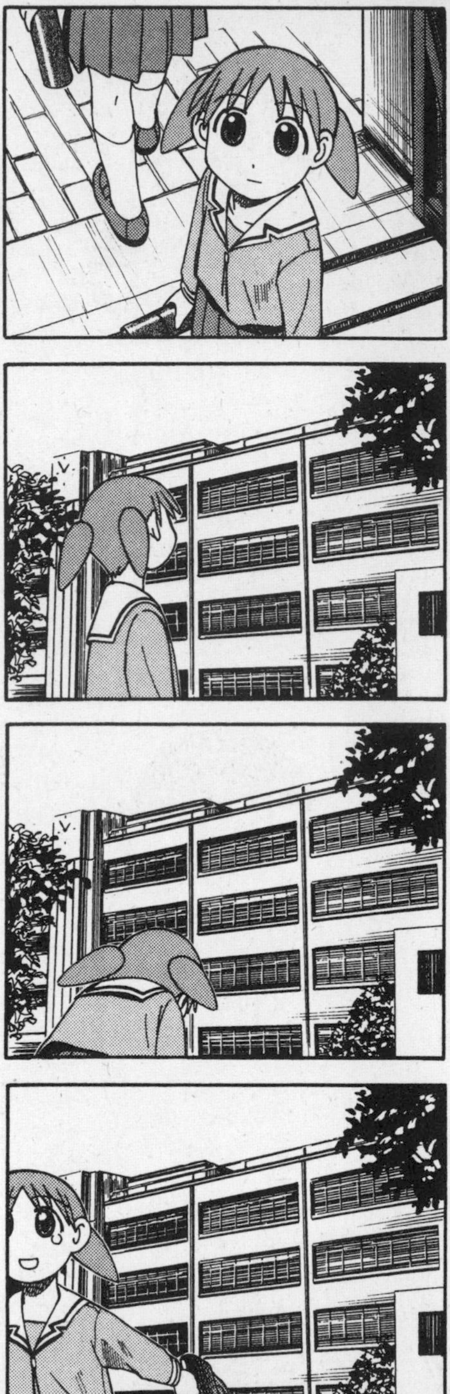

ON VACATION

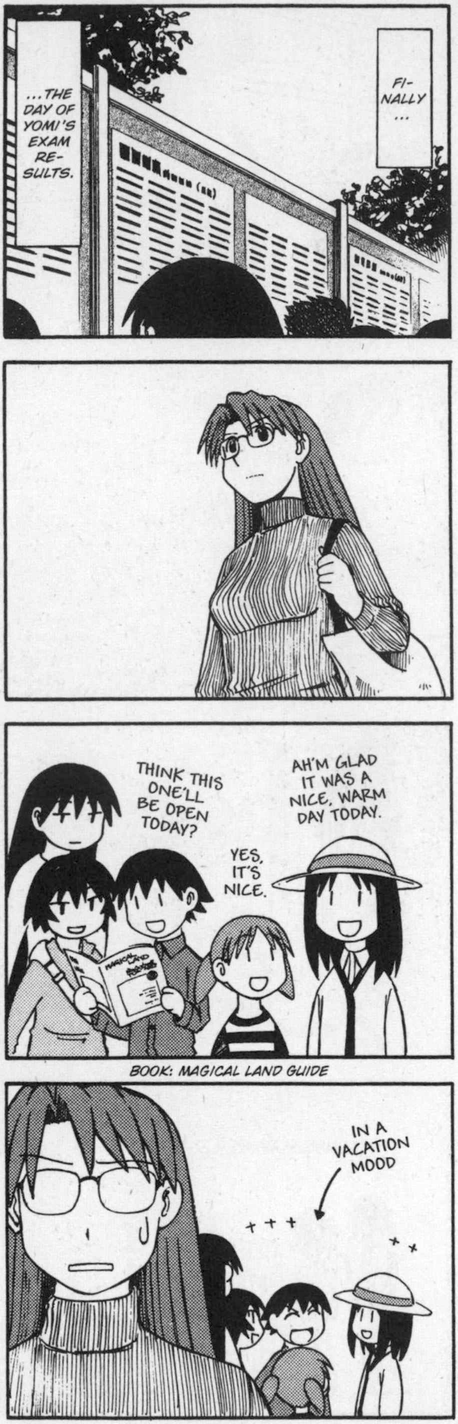
FI-NALLY...
...THE DAY OF YOMI'S EXAM RE-SULTS.
AH'M GLAD IT WAS A NICE, WARM DAY TODAY.
THINK THIS ONE'LL BE OPEN TODAY?
YES, IT'S NICE.
BOOK: MAGICAL LAND GUIDE
IN A VACATION MOOD

THE RESULTS

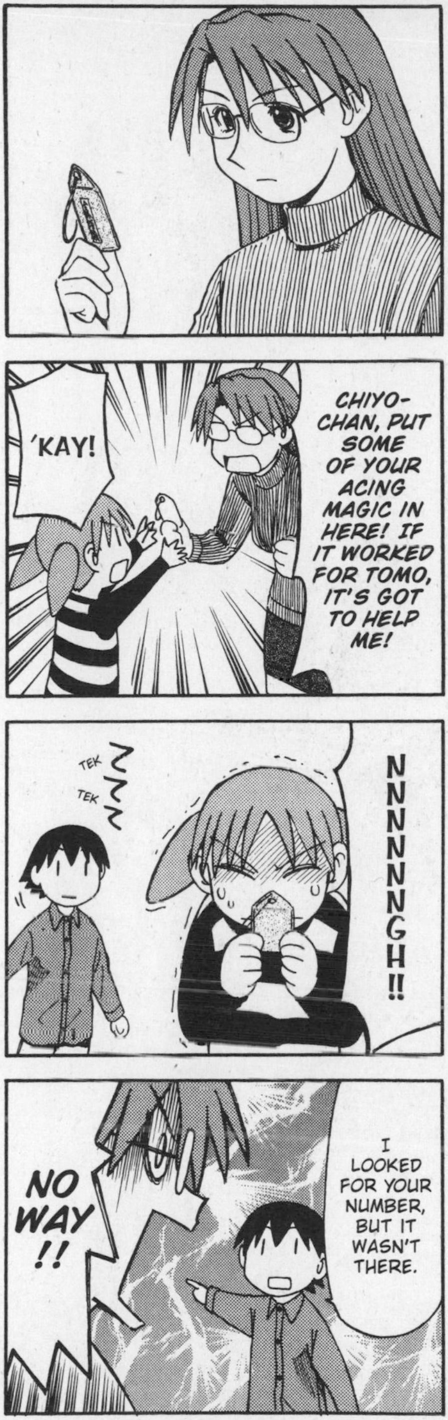
CHIYO-CHAN, PUT SOME OF YOUR ACING MAGIC IN HERE! IF IT WORKED FOR TOMO, IT'S GOT TO HELP ME!
'KAY!
NNNNNNNGH!!
TEK TEK
I LOOKED FOR YOUR NUMBER, BUT IT WASN'T THERE.
NO WAY!!

AH

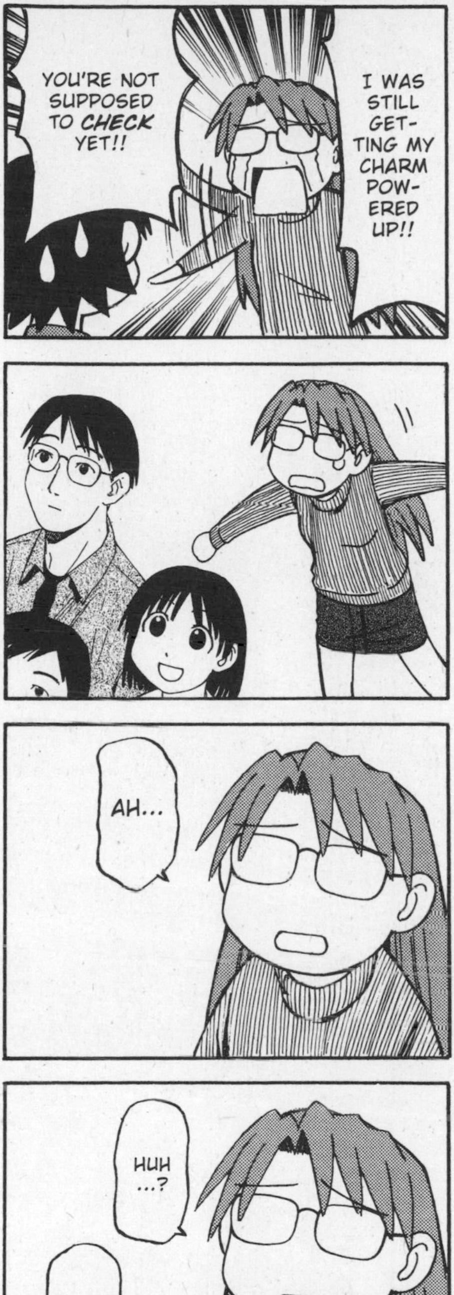
I WAS STILL GETTING MY CHARM POWERED UP!!
YOU'RE NOT SUPPOSED TO CHECK YET!!
AH...
HUH...?
I'M ON THERE...

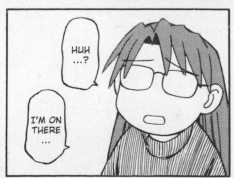

SHE PUT IT THERE

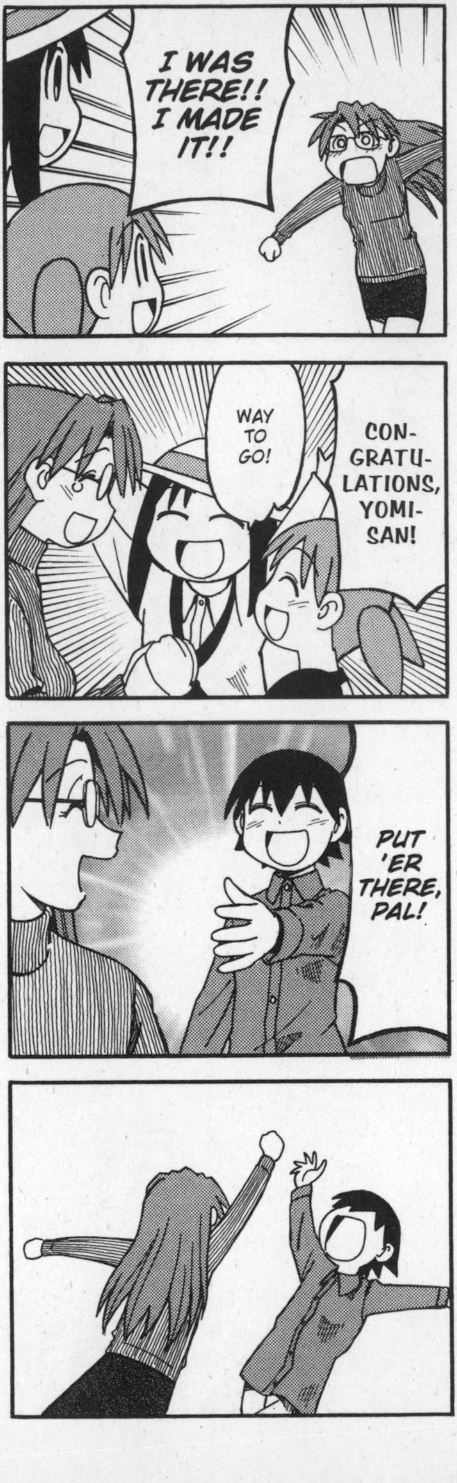
I WAS THERE!! I MADE IT!!
CON-GRATU-LATIONS, YOMI-SAN!
WAY TO GO!
PUT 'ER THERE, PAL!

HIGHER AND HIGHER

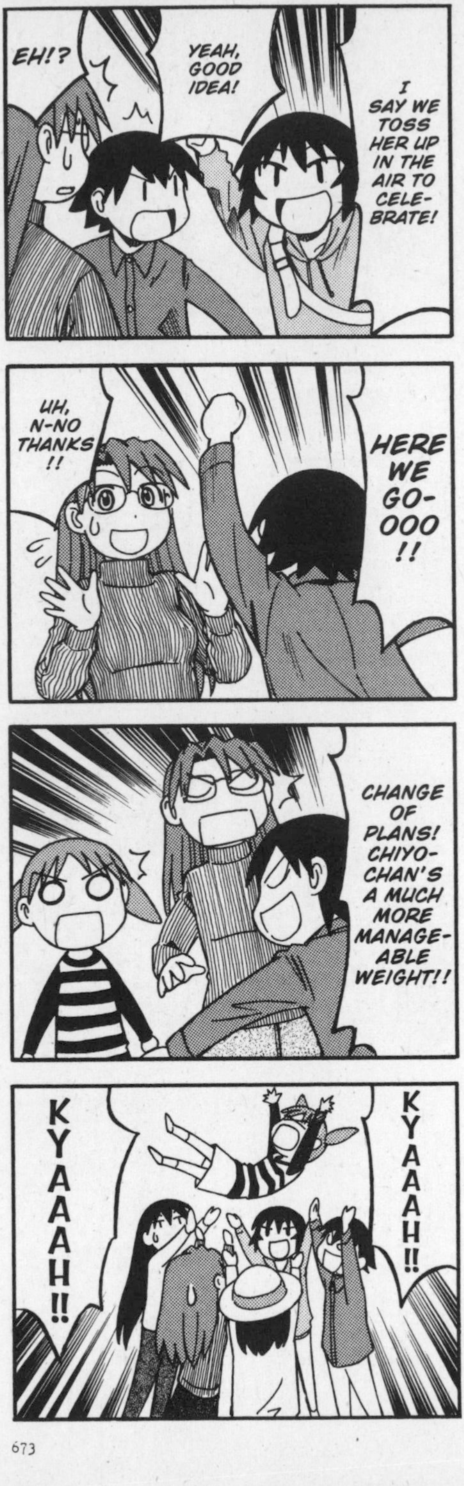
I SAY WE TOSS HER UP IN THE AIR TO CELE-BRATE!
YEAH, GOOD IDEA!
EH!?
HERE WE GO-OOO!!
UH, N-NO THANKS!!
CHANGE OF PLANS! CHIYO-CHAN'S A MUCH MORE MANAGE-ABLE WEIGHT!!
KYAAAH!!
KYAAAH!!

WE WILL BE FINE

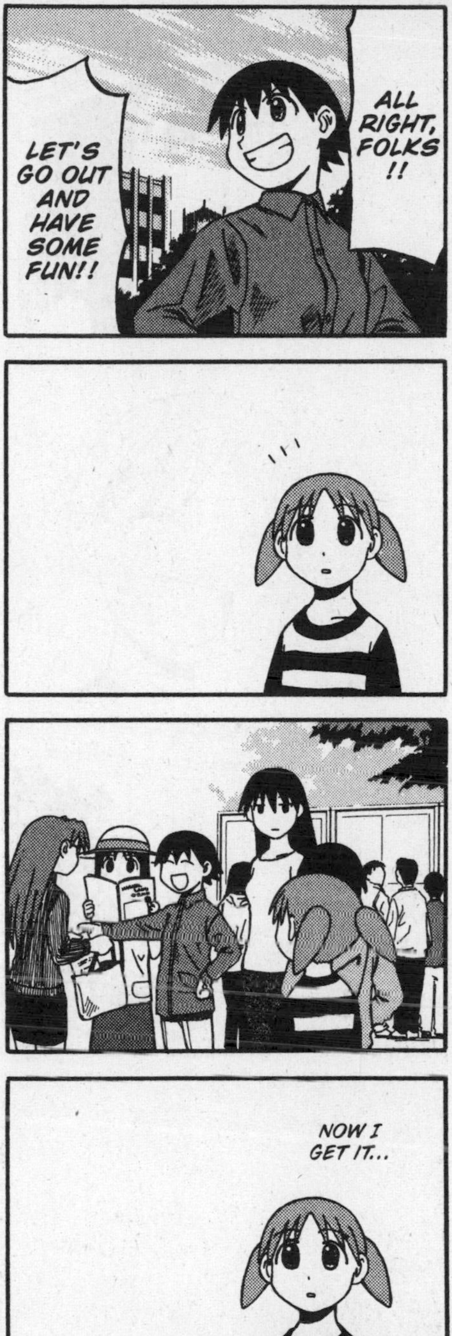
ALL RIGHT, FOLKS!!
LET'S GO OUT AND HAVE SOME FUN!!
NOW I GET IT...

TOGETHER

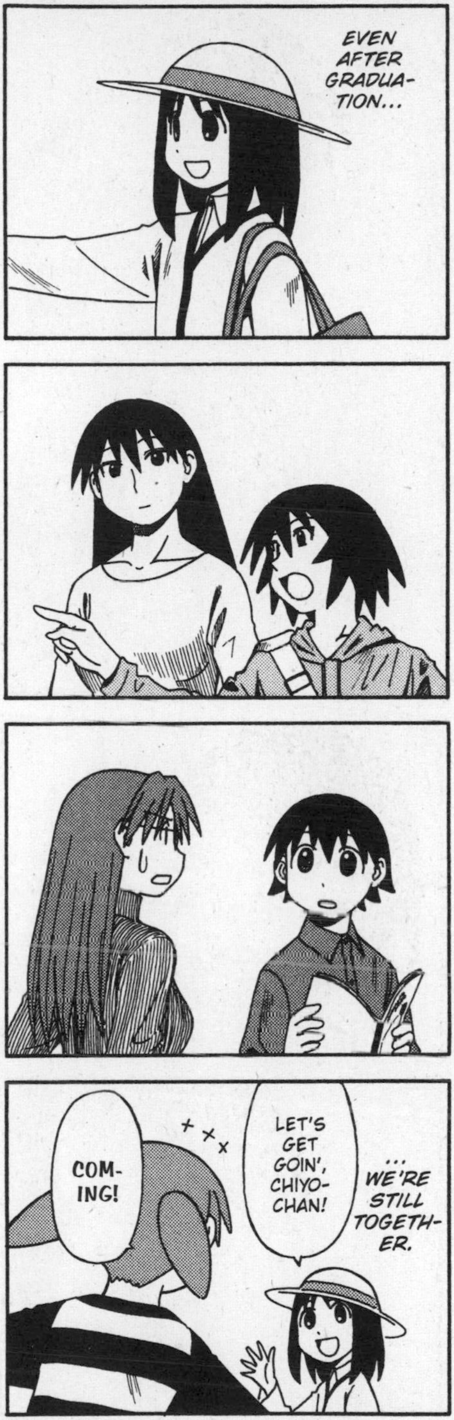
EVEN AFTER GRADUATION...
... WE'RE STILL TOGETHER.
LET'S GET GOIN', CHIYO-CHAN!
COMING!

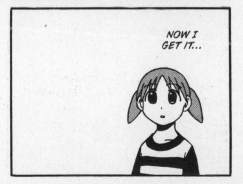

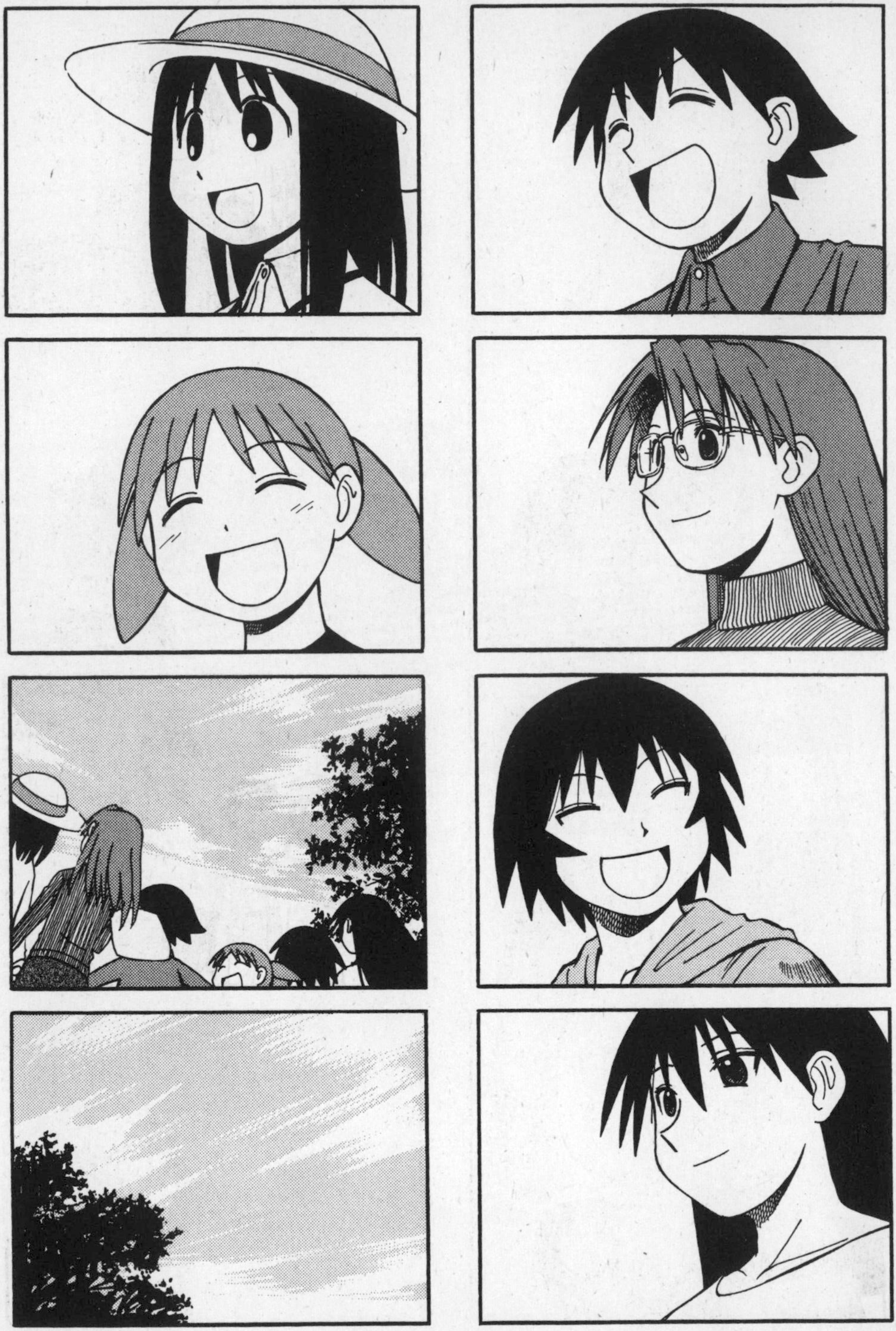

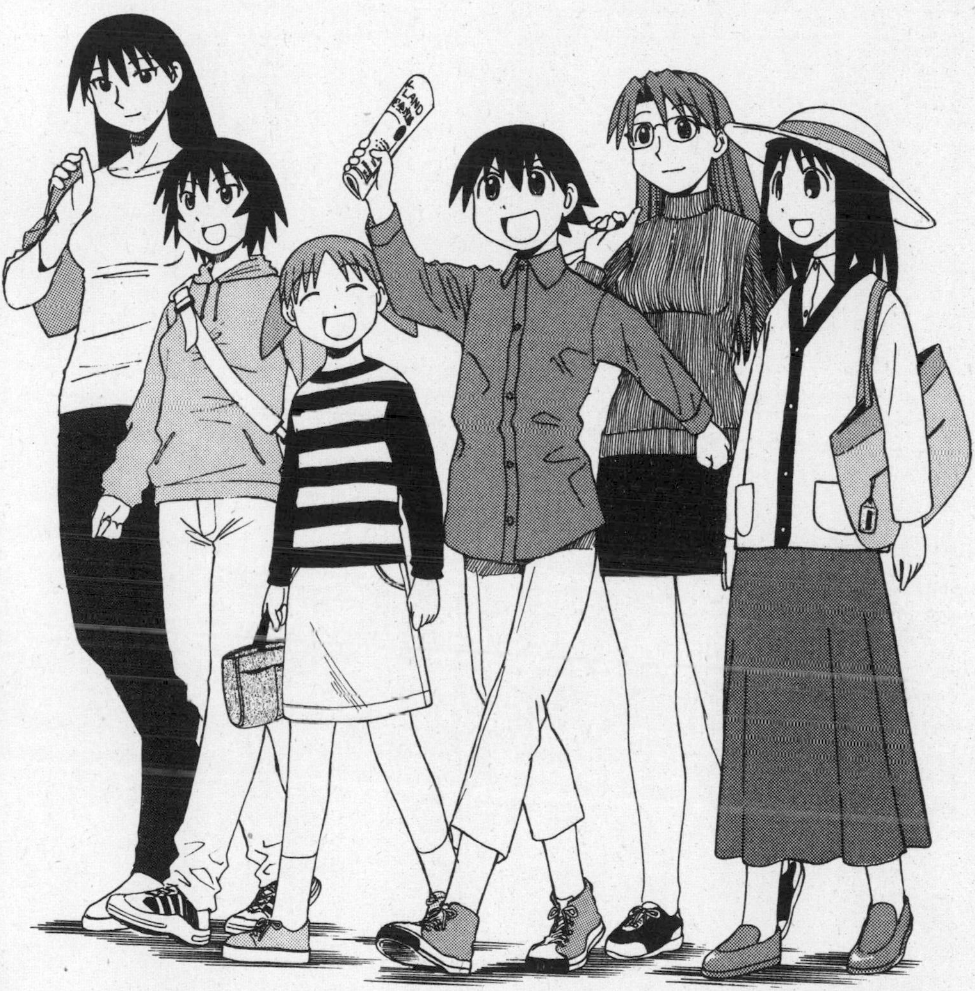
LAND

though to nowhere near the success found in its home country.

PAGE 568

School uniforms: Technically, sex trade businesses like brothels are illegal in Japan, but they are usually tolerated as long as they give the authorities sufficient notice of their activity. Tomo seems to be under the impression that the teachers are dressing up in their old school uniforms for the benefit of their "clients."

PAGE 571

Male cheerleaders: While most of the time, you might think of male cheerleaders as effeminate guys who catch the girls during acrobatic routines, Japanese cheering squads are vastly different. Utilizing old-fashioned long coats, headbands, and ornate flags, these male cheerleaders are almost militaristic in their rigid actions and codes. They're considered very manly and old-fashioned, and thanks to exaggerated depictions in manga, anime, and video games, they often exude a retro coolness in contemporary use.

PAGE 585

Nekozukusi: The title of this catalog (which would usually be romanized *"Nekozuku-shi"*) means "all about cats."

PAGE 604

Irimotote: In Japanese edition, Kagura is actually making a mispronunciation by reading the characters for "Iriomote" by their most common readings, *nishi* ("west") and *hyou* ("chart").

PAGE 612

Center exams: A Japanese standardized test designed to rank students intending to enter college, similar to the SATs.

PAGE 614

Where did "Japanese" come from: This joke might be a bit confusing at first glance. Hint: think about what language you're reading.

PAGE 623

Omikuji: These paper fortunes can be bought at a temple during the year's first visit on New Year's Day and are said to foretell one's luck for the entire year. The fortunes come in a range of quality, from "great fortune" to "terrible misfortune" (though actual "bad luck" fortunes are usually rare). The temple or shrine will typi-

cally have a pine tree on its premises, to which visitors can tie poor fortunes. This is because the word for "pine," *matsu*, is a homonym of the verb "to wait," signifying that the misfortune of the *omikuji* will wait by the tree rather than accompany its host back home.

PAGE 646

"I am a cat": This phrase, which in Japanese reads *Wagahai wa Neko de Aru*, is the title of legendary author Soseki Natsume's first novel, written in 1905. It's a satire of the Meiji period, as Western influences and industrialism crept into traditional Japanese society, all told from the perspective of a family cat. It's a classic book and there is a very clever and excellent English translation available now.

PAGE 147

Mori: Yoshiro Mori was the prime minister of Japan from 2001 to 2002, following a stroke that incapacitated his predecessor, Keizo Obuchi. Known for his many careless gaffes and public relations mistakes, he was an unpopular PM who was quickly replaced by the much more appealing and lively Junichiro Koizumi. Admittedly, he has a rather funny-looking face (run an image search online to see for yourself). There's also a hidden joke in this strip—when Osaka says "I'm sorry" in English, the Japanese pronunciation of "sorry" is the same as *souri*, the word for "prime minister." It's a goofy bit of wordplay that pops up every now and then in comedy material.

PAGE 639

Tokyo University: The premier university in Japan. It only takes the brightest and best, and a degree from Tokyo U virtually guarantees you a cushy corporate job in the real world.

PAGE 664

The song being sung here, under the title "Aogeba Totoshi," is a traditional graduation song expressing the gratitude of the students to the teachers who helped raise them.

PAGE 513

Okinawa: An island well to the south of the main Japanese islands, known for its tropical weather, similar to Hawaii's. A popular tourist destination with its own indigenous history and language, and a unique take on Japanese culture.

"Okinawake up!": In Japanese, one way of saying "wake up" is pronounced like Okinawa (the place), hence our decision to make a pun out of the homonym.

PAGE 517

Shuri Castle: An Okinawan castle located in the city of Naha, capital of Okinawa Prefecture. It was destroyed during the Battle of Okinawa in World War II and later rebuilt from photographs. Shureimon is a gate outside of the castle, also destroyed and reconstructed. And yes, it does indeed appear on the 2,000 yen note.

Shisa: A famous mythological creature, resembling a cross between a lion and a dog, that is used in Okinawan culture as a decoration to ward away evil. They are usually found perched on rooftops or beside gates.

PAGE 520

Chanpuru: An Okinawan stir fry dish, literally meaning "something mixed." The typical *chanpuru* is made with *goya* (bitter melon), but *fu chanpuru* (flatbread) and *somin chanpuru* (thin noodles) are also popular styles. In addition to the main ingredient of the *chanpuru*, it usually includes veggies, tofu, eggs, and meat or fish.

PAGE 524

Chinsuko: A simple and traditional Okinawan confection made of lard and flour. Perhaps Tomo finds this funny because the name is a bit similar to *chinko*, a word for penis.

PAGE 525

Saataa andagii: Another Okinawan treat, *saataa andagii* are balls of sweet, deep fried dough, similar to donuts. They're usually fried so that they're crispy on the outside while still fluffy and soft in the middle.

PAGE 526

Islands: While Okinawa Island is the main destination for people vacationing in Okinawa, the area actually encompasses many small islands, which are collectively known as the Ryukyu Islands. Iriomote Island is known for its very light human settlements,

as most of the island is still covered by a dense jungle. The Iriomote Cat is a species of wildcat only found on Iriomote, and is estimated to have only one hundred specimens left.

Uminchu: Kaorin and Kimura's shirt, which read "*Uminchu*," mean "man of the sea" (i.e. fisherman) in Okinawan Japanese.

PAGE 529

Urauchi River: A large river running from the center of Iriomote Island. Boating up the river is a common tourist activity, as it allows you to go inland without trekking through the thick jungle. Eventually you will reach the Mariyudu Falls, where the boat must turn around and go back.

PAGE 532

Ukon tea: An Okinawan tea made from turmeric roots. Tomo's probably repeating this because it's close to *unko*, the word for poop.

PAGE 542

Radio exercise: A series of light exercises set to music that is played early in the mornings. It's mostly popular among young children and the elderly, and oftentimes neighborhood groups will meet to exercise together at, for example, the local shrine or park. Sometimes children will be attracted to the activity over summer break by offering stamp cards with the promise of a prize for those who participate a certain number of days, as shown on the following page.

PAGE 555

Ichiro and Dice-K: Ichiro refers to Ichiro Suzuki, a world-famous, record-holding Japanese baseball player who plays as an outfielder in the American major leagues (MLB) for the Seattle Mariners. He is widely regarded as the first Japanese-born regular position player in the MLB. Dice-K refers to Daisuke Matsuzaka, a renowned starting pitcher for the Boston Red Sox in the MLB. Looks like Chiyo-chan might be next!

PAGE 558

Yomi's song: Originally Tomo was referring to the character of Gian (or Jaian) from the classic kid's cartoon *Doraemon*. Gian is a big spoiled bully whose closest equivalent in American TV is probably Cartman from *South Park*, but his deep and goofy voice (which Tomo mentions) is more similar to Homer Simpson's. For what it's worth, *The Simpsons* has been dubbed into Japanese and broadcast on Japanese TV for years,

INDEX azumanga daioh

#A

B

C

D

INDEX (cont.)

Y

the index tells no tales.

INDEX (yup, there's more.)

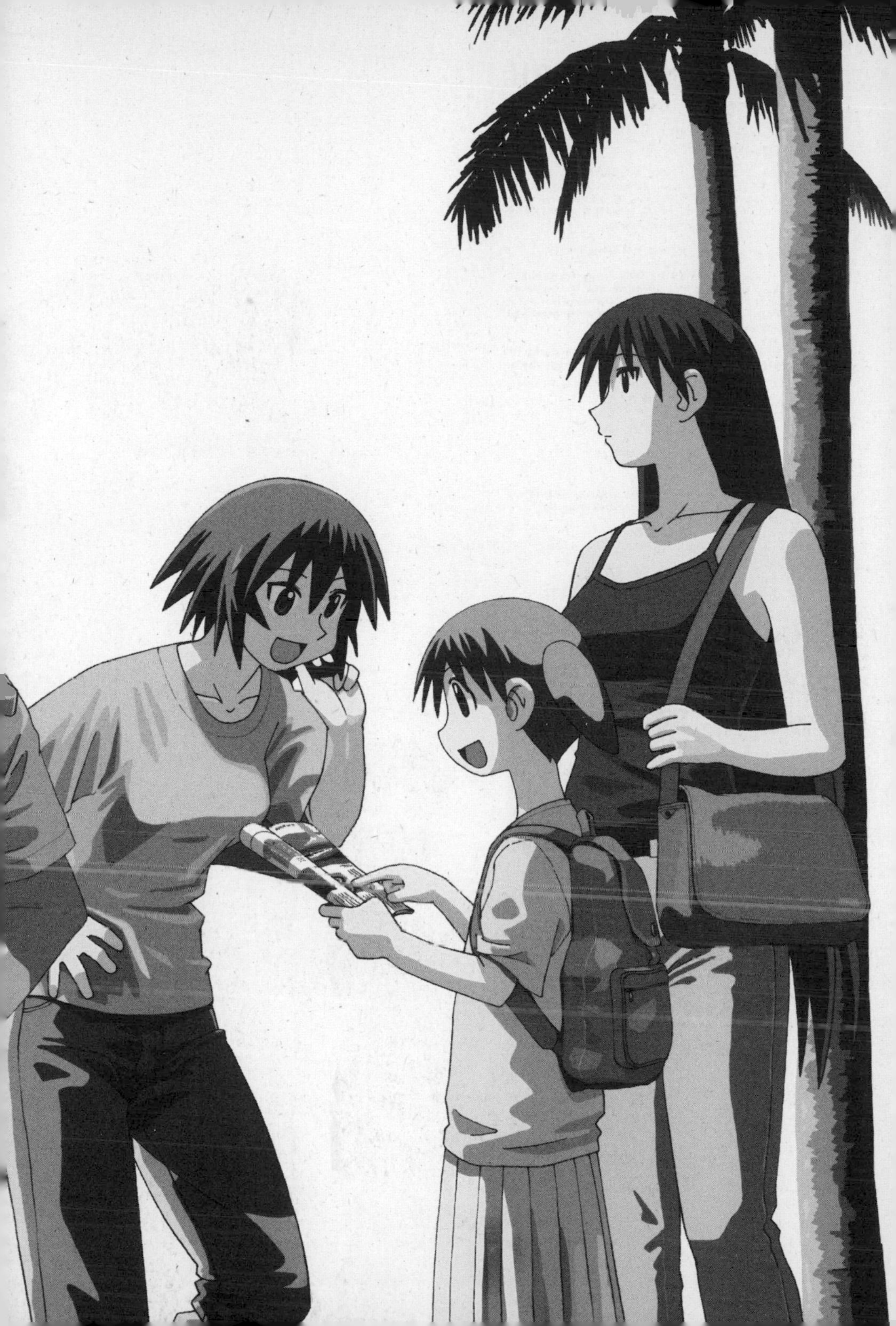

AZUMANGA DAIOH
KIYOHIKO AZUMA

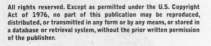

Translation: Stephen Paul
Lettering: Hope Donovan

AZUMANGA DAIOH © KIYOHIKO AZUMA/YOTUBA SUTAZIO
2000, 2001, 2002. All rights reserved. First published in Japan in
2000, 2001, 2002 by MEDIA WORKS INC., Tokyo. English translation
rights in USA, Canada, and UK arranged with ASCII MEDIA WORKS
INC. through Tuttle-Mori Agency, Inc., Tokyo.

English translation © 2009 Hachette Book Group, Inc.

Yen Press
Hachette Book Group
237 Park Avenue, New York, NY 10017

www.HachetteBookGroup.com
www.YenPress.com

Yen Press is an imprint of Hachette Book Group, Inc. The Yen Press
name and logo are trademarks of Hachette Book Group, Inc.

First Yen Press Edition: December 2009

ISBN: 978-0-316-07738-5

10 9 8 7 6 5

BVG
Printed in the
United States of America

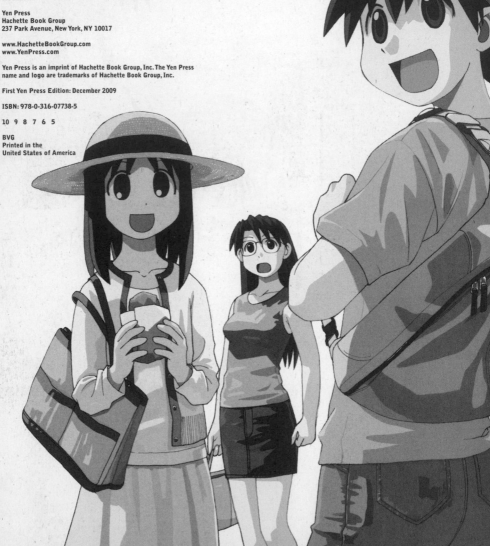

AZUMANGA DAIOH

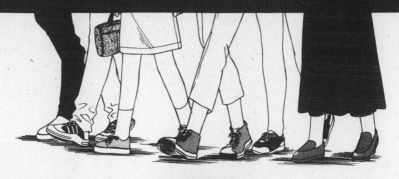

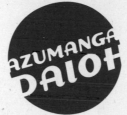

THE END.